Lecture Notes in Computer Science 11134

Commenced Publication in 1973
Founding and Former Series Editors:
Gerhard Goos, Juris Hartmanis, and Jan van Leeuwen

More information about this series at http://www.springer.com/series/7412

Laura Leal-Taixé · Stefan Roth (Eds.)

Computer Vision –
ECCV 2018 Workshops

Munich, Germany, September 8–14, 2018
Proceedings, Part VI

Springer

Editors
Laura Leal-Taixé
Technical University of Munich
Garching, Germany

Stefan Roth ⓘ
Technische Universität Darmstadt
Darmstadt, Germany

ISSN 0302-9743   ISSN 1611-3349 (electronic)
Lecture Notes in Computer Science
ISBN 978-3-030-11023-9   ISBN 978-3-030-11024-6 (eBook)
https://doi.org/10.1007/978-3-030-11024-6

Library of Congress Control Number: 2018966826

LNCS Sublibrary: SL6 – Image Processing, Computer Vision, Pattern Recognition, and Graphics

This Springer imprint is published by the registered company Springer Nature Switzerland AG
The registered company address is: Gewerbestrasse 11, 6330 Cham, Switzerland

Foreword

It was our great pleasure to host the European Conference on Computer Vision 2018 in Munich, Germany. This constituted by far the largest ECCV event ever. With close to 2,900 registered participants and another 600 on the waiting list one month before the conference, participation more than doubled since the last ECCV in Amsterdam. We believe that this is due to a dramatic growth of the computer vision community combined with the popularity of Munich as a major European hub of culture, science, and industry. The conference took place in the heart of Munich in the concert hall Gasteig with workshops and tutorials held on the downtown campus of the Technical University of Munich.

One of the major innovations for ECCV 2018 was the free perpetual availability of all conference and workshop papers, which is often referred to as open access. We note that this is not precisely the same use of the term as in the Budapest declaration. Since 2013, CVPR and ICCV have had their papers hosted by the Computer Vision Foundation (CVF), in parallel with the IEEE Xplore version. This has proved highly beneficial to the computer vision community.

We are delighted to announce that for ECCV 2018 a very similar arrangement was put in place with the cooperation of Springer. In particular, the author's final version will be freely available in perpetuity on a CVF page, while SpringerLink will continue to host a version with further improvements, such as activating reference links and including video. We believe that this will give readers the best of both worlds; researchers who are focused on the technical content will have a freely available version in an easily accessible place, while subscribers to SpringerLink will continue to have the additional benefits that this provides. We thank Alfred Hofmann from Springer for helping to negotiate this agreement, which we expect will continue for future versions of ECCV.

September 2018

Horst Bischof
Daniel Cremers
Bernt Schiele
Ramin Zabih

Preface

It is our great pleasure to present these workshop proceedings of the 15th European Conference on Computer Vision, which was held during September 8–14, 2018, in Munich, Germany. We are delighted that the main conference of ECCV 2018 was accompanied by 43 scientific workshops. The ECCV workshop proceedings contain contributions of 36 workshops.

We received 74 workshop proposals on a broad set of topics related to computer vision. The very high quality and the large number of proposals made the selection process rather challenging. Owing to space restrictions, only 46 proposals were accepted, among which six proposals were merged into three workshops because of overlapping themes.

The final set of 43 workshops complemented the main conference program well. The workshop topics presented a good orchestration of new trends and traditional issues, built bridges into neighboring fields, as well as discussed fundamental technologies and novel applications. We would like to thank all the workshop organizers for their unreserved efforts to make the workshop sessions a great success.

September 2018

Stefan Roth
Laura Leal-Taixé

Organization

General Chairs

Horst Bischof	Graz University of Technology, Austria
Daniel Cremers	Technical University of Munich, Germany
Bernt Schiele	Saarland University, Max Planck Institute for Informatics, Germany
Ramin Zabih	CornellNYCTech, USA

Program Chairs

Vittorio Ferrari	University of Edinburgh, UK
Martial Hebert	Carnegie Mellon University, USA
Cristian Sminchisescu	Lund University, Sweden
Yair Weiss	Hebrew University, Israel

Local Arrangement Chairs

Björn Menze	Technical University of Munich, Germany
Matthias Niessner	Technical University of Munich, Germany

Workshop Chairs

Stefan Roth	Technische Universität Darmstadt, Germany
Laura Leal-Taixé	Technical University of Munich, Germany

Tutorial Chairs

Michael Bronstein	Università della Svizzera Italiana, Switzerland
Laura Leal-Taixé	Technical University of Munich, Germany

Website Chair

Friedrich Fraundorfer	Graz University of Technology, Austria

Demo Chairs

Federico Tombari	Technical University of Munich, Germany
Joerg Stueckler	Technical University of Munich, Germany

Publicity Chair

Giovanni Maria   University of Catania, Italy
  Farinella

Industrial Liaison Chairs

Florent Perronnin   Naver Labs, France
Yunchao Gong   Snap, USA
Helmut Grabner   Logitech, Switzerland

Finance Chair

Gerard Medioni   Amazon, University of Southern California, USA

Publication Chairs

Albert Ali Salah   Boğaziçi University, Turkey
Hamdi Dibeklioğlu   Bilkent University, Turkey
Anton Milan   Amazon, Germany

Workshop Organizers

W01 – The Visual Object Tracking Challenge Workshop

Matej Kristan   University of Ljubljana, Slovenia
Aleš Leonardis   University of Birmingham, UK
Jiří Matas   Czech Technical University in Prague, Czechia
Michael Felsberg   Linköping University, Sweden
Roman Pflugfelder   Austrian Institute of Technology, Austria

W02 – 6th Workshop on Computer Vision for Road Scene Understanding and Autonomous Driving

Mathieu Salzmann   EPFL, Switzerland
José Alvarez   NVIDIA, USA
Lars Petersson   Data61 CSIRO, Australia
Fredrik Kahl   Chalmers University of Technology, Sweden
Bart Nabbe   Aurora, USA

W03 – 3D Reconstruction in the Wild

Akihiro Sugimoto   The National Institute of Informatics (NII), Japan
Tomas Pajdla   Czech Technical University in Prague, Czechia
Takeshi Masuda   The National Institute of Advanced Industrial Science
                           and Technology (AIST), Japan
Shohei Nobuhara   Kyoto University, Japan
Hiroshi Kawasaki   Kyushu University, Japan

W04 – Workshop on Visual Learning and Embodied Agents in Simulation Environments

Peter Anderson   Georgia Institute of Technology, USA
Manolis Savva   Facebook AI Research and Simon Fraser University, USA
Angel X. Chang   Eloquent Labs and Simon Fraser University, USA
Saurabh Gupta   University of California, Berkeley, USA
Amir R. Zamir   Stanford University and University of California, Berkeley,
                      USA
Stefan Lee   Georgia Institute of Technology, USA
Samyak Datta   Georgia Institute of Technology, USA
Li Yi   Stanford University, USA
Hao Su   University of California, San Diego, USA
Qixing Huang   The University of Texas at Austin, USA
Cewu Lu   Shanghai Jiao Tong University, China
Leonidas Guibas   Stanford University, USA

W05 – Bias Estimation in Face Analytics

Rama Chellappa   University of Maryland, USA
Nalini Ratha   IBM Watson Research Center, USA
Rogerio Feris   IBM Watson Research Center, USA
Michele Merler   IBM Watson Research Center, USA
Vishal Patel   Johns Hopkins University, USA

W06 – 4th International Workshop on Recovering 6D Object Pose

Tomas Hodan   Czech Technical University in Prague, Czechia
Rigas Kouskouridas   Scape Technologies, UK
Krzysztof Walas   Poznan University of Technology, Poland
Tae-Kyun Kim   Imperial College London, UK
Jiří Matas   Czech Technical University in Prague, Czechia
Carsten Rother   Heidelberg University, Germany
Frank Michel   Technical University Dresden, Germany
Vincent Lepetit   University of Bordeaux, France
Ales Leonardis   University of Birmingham, UK
Carsten Steger   Technical University of Munich, MVTec, Germany
Caner Sahin   Imperial College London, UK

W07 – Second International Workshop on Computer Vision for UAVs

Kristof Van Beeck   KU Leuven, Belgium
Tinne Tuytelaars   KU Leuven, Belgium
Davide Scaramuzza   ETH Zurich, Switzerland
Toon Goedemé   KU Leuven, Belgium

W08 – 5th Transferring and Adapting Source Knowledge in Computer Vision and Second VisDA Challenge

Tatiana Tommasi	Italian Institute of Technology, Italy
David Vázquez	Element AI, Canada
Kate Saenko	Boston University, USA
Ben Usman	Boston University, USA
Xingchao Peng	Boston University, USA
Judy Hoffman	Facebook AI Research, USA
Neela Kaushik	Boston University, USA
Antonio M. López	Universitat Autònoma de Barcelona and Computer Vision Center, Spain
Wen Li	ETH Zurich, Switzerland
Francesco Orabona	Boston University, USA

W09 – PoseTrack Challenge: Articulated People Tracking in the Wild

Mykhaylo Andriluka	Google Research, Switzerland
Umar Iqbal	University of Bonn, Germany
Anton Milan	Amazon, Germany
Leonid Pishchulin	Max Planck Institute for Informatics, Germany
Christoph Lassner	Amazon, Germany
Eldar Insafutdinov	Max Planck Institute for Informatics, Germany
Siyu Tang	Max Planck Institute for Intelligent Systems, Germany
Juergen Gall	University of Bonn, Germany
Bernt Schiele	Max Planck Institute for Informatics, Germany

W10 – Workshop on Objectionable Content and Misinformation

Cristian Canton Ferrer	Facebook, USA
Matthias Niessner	Technical University of Munich, Germany
Paul Natsev	Google, USA
Marius Vlad	Google, Switzerland

W11 – 9th International Workshop on Human Behavior Understanding

Xavier Alameda-Pineda	Inria Grenoble, France
Elisa Ricci	Fondazione Bruno Kessler and University of Trento, Italy
Albert Ali Salah	Boğaziçi University, Turkey
Nicu Sebe	University of Trento, Italy
Shuicheng Yan	National University of Singapore, Singapore

W12 – First Person in Context Workshop and Challenge

Si Liu	Beihang University, China
Jiashi Feng	National University of Singapore, Singapore
Jizhong Han	Institute of Information Engineering, China
Shuicheng Yan	National University of Singapore, Singapore
Yao Sun	Institute of Information Engineering, China

Yue Liao   Institute of Information Engineering, China
Lejian Ren   Institute of Information Engineering, China
Guanghui Ren   Institute of Information Engineering, China

W13 – 4th Workshop on Computer Vision for Art Analysis

Stuart James   Istituto Italiano di Tecnologia, Italy and University College
                         London, UK
Leonardo Impett   EPFL, Switzerland and Biblioteca Hertziana, Max Planck
                         Institute for Art History, Italy
Peter Hall   University of Bath, UK
João Paulo Costeira   Instituto Superior Tecnico, Portugal
Peter Bell   Friedrich-Alexander-University Nürnberg, Germany
Alessio Del Bue   Istituto Italiano di Tecnologia, Italy

W14 – First Workshop on Fashion, Art, and Design

Hui Wu   IBM Research AI, USA
Negar Rostamzadeh   Element AI, Canada
Leonidas Lefakis   Zalando Research, Germany
Joy Tang   Markable, USA
Rogerio Feris   IBM Research AI, USA
Tamara Berg   UNC Chapel Hill/Shopagon Inc., USA
Luba Elliott   Independent Curator/Researcher/Producer
Aaron Courville   MILA/University of Montreal, Canada
Chris Pal   MILA/PolyMTL, Canada
Sanja Fidler   University of Toronto, Canada
Xavier Snelgrove   Element AI, Canada
David Vazquez   Element AI, Canada
Julia Lasserre   Zalando Research, Germany
Thomas Boquet   Element AI, Canada
Nana Yamazaki   Zalando SE, Germany

W15 – Anticipating Human Behavior

Juergen Gall   University of Bonn, Germany
Jan van Gemert   Delft University of Technology, The Netherlands
Kris Kitani   Carnegie Mellon University, USA

W16 – Third Workshop on Geometry Meets Deep Learning

Xiaowei Zhou   Zhejiang University, China
Emanuele Rodolà   Sapienza University of Rome, Italy
Jonathan Masci   NNAISENSE, Switzerland
Kosta Derpanis   Ryerson University, Canada

W17 – First Workshop on Brain-Driven Computer Vision

Simone Palazzo	University of Catania, Italy
Isaak Kavasidis	University of Catania, Italy
Dimitris Kastaniotis	University of Patras, Greece
Stavros Dimitriadis	Cardiff University, UK

W18 – Second Workshop on 3D Reconstruction Meets Semantics

Radim Tylecek	University of Edinburgh, UK
Torsten Sattler	ETH Zurich, Switzerland
Thomas Brox	University of Freiburg, Germany
Marc Pollefeys	ETH Zurich/Microsoft, Switzerland
Robert B. Fisher	University of Edinburgh, UK
Theo Gevers	University of Amsterdam, Netherlands

W19 – Third International Workshop on Video Segmentation

Pablo Arbelaez	Universidad de los Andes, Columbia
Thomas Brox	University of Freiburg, Germany
Fabio Galasso	OSRAM GmbH, Germany
Iasonas Kokkinos	University College London, UK
Fuxin Li	Oregon State University, USA

W20 – PeopleCap 2018: Capturing and Modeling Human Bodies, Faces, and Hands

Gerard Pons-Moll	MPI for Informatics and Saarland Informatics Campus, Germany
Jonathan Taylor	Google, USA

W21 – Workshop on Shortcomings in Vision and Language

Dhruv Batra	Georgia Institute of Technology and Facebook AI Research, USA
Raffaella Bernardi	University of Trento, Italy
Raquel Fernández	University of Amsterdam, The Netherlands
Spandana Gella	University of Edinburgh, UK
Kushal Kafle	Rochester Institute of Technology, USA
Moin Nabi	SAP SE, Germany
Stefan Lee	Georgia Institute of Technology, USA

W22 – Second YouTube-8M Large-Scale Video Understanding Workshop

Apostol (Paul) Natsev	Google Research, USA
Rahul Sukthankar	Google Research, USA
Joonseok Lee	Google Research, USA
George Toderici	Google Research, USA

W23 – Second International Workshop on Compact and Efficient Feature Representation and Learning in Computer Vision

Jie Qin	ETH Zurich, Switzerland
Li Liu	National University of Defense Technology, China and University of Oulu, Finland
Li Liu	Inception Institute of Artificial Intelligence, UAE
Fan Zhu	Inception Institute of Artificial Intelligence, UAE
Matti Pietikäinen	University of Oulu, Finland
Luc Van Gool	ETH Zurich, Switzerland

W24 – 5th Women in Computer Vision Workshop

Zeynep Akata	University of Amsterdam, The Netherlands
Dena Bazazian	Computer Vision Center, Spain
Yana Hasson	Inria, France
Angjoo Kanazawa	UC Berkeley, USA
Hildegard Kuehne	University of Bonn, Germany
Gül Varol	Inria, France

W25 – Perceptual Image Restoration and Manipulation Workshop and Challenge

Yochai Blau	Technion – Israel Institute of Technology, Israel
Roey Mechrez	Technion – Israel Institute of Technology, Israel
Radu Timofte	ETH Zurich, Switzerland
Tomer Michaeli	Technion – Israel Institute of Technology, Israel
Lihi Zelnik-Manor	Technion – Israel Institute of Technology, Israel

W26 – Egocentric Perception, Interaction, and Computing

Dima Damen	University of Bristol, UK
Giuseppe Serra	University of Udine, Italy
David Crandall	Indiana University, USA
Giovanni Maria Farinella	University of Catania, Italy
Antonino Furnari	University of Catania, Italy

W27 – Vision Meets Drone: A Challenge

Pengfei Zhu	Tianjin University, China
Longyin Wen	JD Finance, USA
Xiao Bian	GE Global Research, USA
Haibin Ling	Temple University, USA

W28 – 11th Perceptual Organization in Computer Vision Workshop on Action, Perception, and Organization

Deepak Pathak	UC Berkeley, USA
Bharath Hariharan	Cornell University, USA

W29 – AutoNUE: Autonomous Navigation in Unconstrained Environments

Manmohan Chandraker   University of California San Diego, USA
C. V. Jawahar   IIIT Hyderabad, India
Anoop M. Namboodiri   IIIT Hyderabad, India
Srikumar Ramalingam   University of Utah, USA
Anbumani Subramanian   Intel, Bangalore, India

W30 – ApolloScape: Vision-Based Navigation for Autonomous Driving

Peng Wang   Baidu Research, USA
Ruigang Yang   Baidu Research, China
Andreas Geiger   ETH Zurich, Switzerland
Hongdong Li   Australian National University, Australia
Alan Yuille   The Johns Hopkins University, USA

W31 – 6th International Workshop on Assistive Computer Vision and Robotics

Giovanni Maria   University of Catania, Italy
    Farinella
Marco Leo   National Research Council of Italy, Italy
Gerard G. Medioni   University of Southern California, USA
Mohan Trivedi   University of California, USA

W32 – 4th International Workshop on Observing and Understanding Hands in Action

Iason Oikonomidis   Foundation for Research and Technology, Greece
Guillermo   Imperial College London, UK
    Garcia-Hernando
Angela Yao   National University of Singapore, Singapore
Antonis Argyros   University of Crete/Foundation for Research
    and Technology, Greece
Vincent Lepetit   University of Bordeaux, France
Tae-Kyun Kim   Imperial College London, UK

W33 – Bioimage Computing

Jens Rittscher   University of Oxford, UK
Anna Kreshuk   University of Heidelberg, Germany
Florian Jug   Max Planck Institute CBG, Germany

W34 – First Workshop on Interactive and Adaptive Learning in an Open World

Erik Rodner   Carl Zeiss AG, Germany
Alexander Freytag   Carl Zeiss AG, Germany
Vittorio Ferrari   Google, Switzerland/University of Edinburgh, UK
Mario Fritz   CISPA Helmholtz Center i.G., Germany
Uwe Franke   Daimler AG, Germany
Terrence Boult   University of Colorado, Colorado Springs, USA

Juergen Gall   University of Bonn, Germany
Walter Scheirer   University of Notre Dame, USA
Angela Yao   University of Bonn, Germany

W35 – First Multimodal Learning and Applications Workshop

Paolo Rota   University of Trento, Italy
Vittorio Murino   Istituto Italiano di Tecnologia, Italy
Michael Yang   University of Twente, The Netherlands
Bodo Rosenhahn   Leibniz-Universität Hannover, Germany

W36 – What Is Optical Flow for?

Fatma Güney   Oxford University, UK
Laura Sevilla-Lara   Facebook Research, USA
Deqing Sun   NVIDIA, USA
Jonas Wulff   Massachusetts Institute of Technology, USA

W37 – Vision for XR

Richard Newcombe   Facebook Reality Labs, USA
Chris Sweeney   Facebook Reality Labs, USA
Julian Straub   Facebook Reality Labs, USA
Jakob Engel   Facebook Reality Labs, USA
Michael Goesele   Technische Universität Darmstadt, Germany

W38 – Open Images Challenge Workshop

Vittorio Ferrari   Google AI, Switzerland
Alina Kuznetsova   Google AI, Switzerland
Jordi Pont-Tuset   Google AI, Switzerland
Matteo Malloci   Google AI, Switzerland
Jasper Uijlings   Google AI, Switzerland
Jake Walker   Google AI, Switzerland
Rodrigo Benenson   Google AI, Switzerland

W39 – VizWiz Grand Challenge: Answering Visual Questions from Blind People

Danna Gurari   University of Texas at Austin, USA
Kristen Grauman   University of Texas at Austin, USA
Jeffrey P. Bigham   Carnegie Mellon University, USA

W40 – 360° Perception and Interaction

Min Sun   National Tsing Hua University, Taiwan
Yu-Chuan Su   University of Texas at Austin, USA
Wei-Sheng Lai   University of California, Merced, USA
Liwei Chan   National Chiao Tung University, USA
Hou-Ning Hu   National Tsing Hua University, Taiwan
Silvio Savarese   Stanford University, USA

Kristen Grauman   University of Texas at Austin, USA
Ming-Hsuan Yang   University of California, Merced, USA

W41 – Joint COCO and Mapillary Recognition Challenge Workshop

Tsung-Yi Lin   Google Brain, USA
Genevieve Patterson   Microsoft Research, USA
Matteo R. Ronchi   Caltech, USA
Yin Cui   Cornell, USA
Piotr Dollár   Facebook AI Research, USA
Michael Maire   TTI-Chicago, USA
Serge Belongie   Cornell, USA
Lubomir Bourdev   WaveOne, Inc., USA
Ross Girshick   Facebook AI Research, USA
James Hays   Georgia Tech, USA
Pietro Perona   Caltech, USA
Deva Ramanan   CMU, USA
Larry Zitnick   Facebook AI Research, USA
Riza Alp Guler   Inria, France
Natalia Neverova   Facebook AI Research, France
Vasil Khalidov   Facebook AI Research, France
Iasonas Kokkinos   Facebook AI Research, France
Samuel Rota Bulò   Mapillary Research, Austria
Lorenzo Porzi   Mapillary Research, Austria
Peter Kontschieder   Mapillary Research, Austria
Alexander Kirillov   Heidelberg University, Germany
Holger Caesar   University of Edinburgh, UK
Jasper Uijlings   Google Research, UK
Vittorio Ferrari   University of Edinburgh and Google Research, UK

W42 – First Large-Scale Video Object Segmentation Challenge

Ning Xu   Adobe Research, USA
Linjie Yang   SNAP Research, USA
Yuchen Fan   University of Illinois at Urbana-Champaign, USA
Jianchao Yang   SNAP Research, USA
Weiyao Lin   Shanghai Jiao Tong University, China
Michael Ying Yang   University of Twente, The Netherlands
Brian Price   Adobe Research, USA
Jiebo Luo   University of Rochester, USA
Thomas Huang   University of Illinois at Urbana-Champaign, USA

W43 – WIDER Face and Pedestrian Challenge

Chen Change Loy	Nanyang Technological University, Singapore
Dahua Lin	The Chinese University of Hong Kong, SAR China
Wanli Ouyang	University of Sydney, Australia
Yuanjun Xiong	Amazon Rekognition, USA
Shuo Yang	Amazon Rekognition, USA
Qingqiu Huang	The Chinese University of Hong Kong, SAR China
Dongzhan Zhou	SenseTime, China
Wei Xia	Amazon Rekognition, USA
Quanquan Li	SenseTime, China
Ping Luo	The Chinese University of Hong Kong, SAR China
Junjie Yan	SenseTime, China

Contents – Part VI

W36 – What Is Optical Flow for?

W31 – 6th International Workshop on Assistive Computer Vision and Robotics

W31 – 6th International Workshop on Assistive Computer Vision and Robotics

This document introduces the contributed papers accepted for presentation during the Sixth International Workshop on Assistive Computer Vision and Robotics (ACVR2018) that was held in Munich on September 9, 2018 as a satellite event of the 15th European Conference on Computer Vision (ECCV2018). The interest of the research community to the workshop topics has been once again proved by the quality and the number of contributed submissions. In particular, this year the workshop received 25 submissions that were double-blind peer reviewed by at least 4 experts each. Reviewers' comments have leaded to accept 4 papers as oral and poster and 8 papers as only poster presentation.

In addition to contributed papers, the ACVR2018 proceeding is completed by a not peer-reviewed summary paper. This paper has been written by the workshop organizers who discuss about the new frontiers in assistive technologies. In particular, the paper starts from the recent advances in computer vision that are strongly pushing forward many application fields and then it concentrates on how assistive technologies are dragged by this revolution mainly pushed forward by new learning paradigms based on deep architectures but not just.

The workshop program was completed by two invited speeches by Tae-Kyun Kim (Imperial College of London, United Kingdom) who gave a really eye-opening talk about "3D Hand Pose Estimation for Novel Man-Machine Interface" and Fabio Galasso (OSRAM GmbH, Germany) who gave and enlightening talk about "Computer Vision and Smart Lighting relevant to Assistive Technologies". Organizers take this opportunity to to thanks all the members of the the technical program committee who carefully reviewed the contributed papers, the endorsers (TOSHIBA, ST, ORCAM and CVPL) and all the attendees whose observations helped to start a good discussion on how the world of assistive technologies is changing and on which are the open research areas of greatest scientific interest.

September 2018

Giovanni M. Farinella
Marco Leo
Gerard G. Medioni
Mohan Trivedi

Deep Learning for Assistive Computer Vision

Marco Leo[1]([✉]), Antonino Furnari[2], Gerard G. Medioni[3], Mohan Trivedi[4], and Giovanni M. Farinella[2]

[1] Institute of Applied Sciences and Intelligent Systems,
National Research Council of Italy, Lecce, Italy
marco.leo@cnr.it
[2] University of Catania, Catania, Italy
{furnari,gfarinella}@dmi.unict.it
[3] University of Southern California, Los Angeles, USA
medioni@usc.edu
[4] University of California, Oakland, USA
mtrivedi@soe.ucsd.edu

Abstract. This paper revises the main advances in assistive computer vision recently fostered by deep learning. To this aim, we first discuss how the application of deep learning in computer vision has contributed to the development of assistive techinologies, then analyze the recent advances in assistive technologies achieved in five main areas, namely, object classification and localization, scene understanding, human pose estimation and tracking, action/event recognition and anticipation. The paper is concluded with a discussion and insights for future directions.

Keywords: Assistive technologies · Computer vision · Deep learning

1 Introduction

Computer vision is attracting more and more people coming from academia and industry. In the context of Assistive Technologies (AT), researches have already proved how computer vision algorithms can be effectively exploited to address different user's needs pointed by the World Health Organization (e.g., Mental Function, Mobility, Sensory Substitution and Assisted Living) [20]. It is straightforward to figure out that the opportunities to address more challenging assistive tasks depend on the speed with which the fundamentals of knowledge evolve, as commonly happens when knowledge is transferred from theoretical to application fields.

After a decade in which visual intelligence performances remained quite stable, over the past 5 years or so, it has been pushed up by the impact of the application of the deep learning paradigm. This has gone from a somewhat niche field comprised of a strict group of researchers to being mainstream and enabling breakthrough applications of diverse areas such as image and video understanding, speech recognition, medical imaging and self driving vehicles. The idea of

© Springer Nature Switzerland AG 2019
L. Leal-Taixé and S. Roth (Eds.): ECCV 2018 Workshops, LNCS 11134, pp. 3–14, 2019.
https://doi.org/10.1007/978-3-030-11024-6_1

deep learning dates back to the end of 80's when Neural Networks (NN) began to be used for mapping inputs to outputs with the aim to automatically recognize handwritten characters.

In the mid of the 90's, the interest of the computer vision community in NN decreased since the architectures did not allow to be scaled to complex contexts where other methods, such as Kernel Machines based on linear classifiers (e.g., SVM), were more effective in most of the application domains involving visual recognition tasks. This scenario changed when large visual datasets and powerful computational resources became available at hand, making possible the increase of the complexity of architecture based on neural networks, as well as the learning capabilities, thus moving the focus from shallow machine learning to deep machine learning. Indeed, supervised deep learning methods thrive on big datasets, which before the ImageNet era were only available for some specific tasks (e.g., handwriting recognition). Nowadays, datasets for image understanding have become big enough to train deep learning systems, and modern GPUs allow researchers to implement effective algorithms which beat almost any record in computer vision. This fact has gained the attention not only of the computer vision community, but also the one of other scientific research fields.

One of the greatest advantage of deep learning is the possibility to learn effective representations of the data for a given task [14]. For this reason, deep learning is currently considered the primary candidate for any visual recognition task [38] and it is being extended to visual reasoning [17]. This is made evident by the availability of several books which introduce and discuss the different deep learning approaches, as well as by the number of papers describing its use in different application fields such us medical imaging [22], health informatics [31], feature learning [50], etc. Assistive technologies do not escape this trend since they have been already flooded by deep learning. An up-to-date overview on different types of deep neural networks and recent progresses is given in [23] where also applications of deep learning techniques on some selected areas (speech recognition, pattern recognition and computer vision) are highlighted. This paper tries to summarize instead how deep learning has been recently exploited to deal with assistive tasks. The rest of the paper is organized as follows. Section 2 introduces a taxonomy concerning the way in which deep learning influenced assistive technologies. Section 3 discusses recent works in the context of assistive computer vision. Finally, Sect. 4 gives some hints for possible future directions.

2 How Deep Learning in CV Is Being Strengthening and Improving AT

The task of automatically recognizing and locating objects is one of the primary tasks for humans in order to survive, work and communicate. As a consequence, the ability to automatically perform this task starting from images and videos is fundamental to build very powerful assistive devices able to understand and/or interact with their surroundings and, as a consequence, to help people with cognitive and/or physical limitations. On the other hand, deep architectures can learn more complex models than shallow ones, since they learn powerful representations of the objects without the need to perform hand design features. The deep learning frameworks for object recognition methods can mainly be categorized into two groups: one follows the traditional object detection pipeline, involving the generation of region proposals and the classification of each proposal into different object categories. The other regards object detection as a regression or classification problem, adopting a unified framework to achieve final results (categories and locations) directly. Recent advances in this area can be found in [52].

A strictly related task is the one so called scene understanding, i.e. the ability not only to identify the targets (as object recognition does), but also to understand the other properties of the observed scene. In other words, this task entails recognizing the semantic constituents of a scene and the complex interactions that occur between them. Humans have no difficulty with these tasks and can associate semantic information with the scene at different levels. This challenging task can be approached in different ways. At a very high level, the approaches can be divided into two main categories: using low-level features, and using object recognition. However, many other techniques are integrated into each of these approaches, including probabilistic, and/or fuzzy techniques, in order to deal with the uncertainty which often attends the result of image understanding. Convolutional Neural Networks (CNNs) can be really useful also to solve this task. A recent approach to address the aforementioned challenge consists in using the convolutional patch networks, which are CNNs trained to distinguish different image patches giving the possibility to perform pixel-wise labeling [5]. One of the bottlenecks in training for better representations is the amount of available per-pixel ground truth data that is required for core scene understanding tasks such as semantic segmentation, normal prediction, and object boundary detection. To address this problem, a number of works proposed using synthetic data and some of them also provide a systematic study of how such synthetic data is generated [51].

Many assistive technologies aim at assisting people in overcoming physical and cognitive barriers by tracking their body pose or by recognizing their activity and their actions. Different approaches using deep learning have been recently proposed and, among all, the one based on ensemble of models, each of which is optimized for a limited variety of poses, is capable of modeling a large variety of human body configurations [19]. Alternative approaches rely on inferring the dependencies between human joints that are modelled via a max-margin structured learning framework [18]. However tracking multiple people in realistic videos is still an open research area in which the introduction of new large-scale benchmarks is helping to build increasingly performing models [3]. A related research topic concerns the recognition of an event that is a conceptually higher semantic problem that could capture the complex behavior of a group of people, interacting with multiple objects, and taking place in a specific environment. Transferring deep object and scene representations for event recognition is a very smart solution recently proposed in [46]. The recognition and understanding of these tasks are fundamental in human-robot interactions, where there is also a need for the machine to make decisions based on the understanding of the near future, i.e to anticipate the next event [7] or object [12]. This ability comes naturally to us and we make use of it subconsciously. Almost all human interactions rely on this action-anticipation capability. The ability to anticipate the action of other individuals is essential for our social life and even survival. Therefore, it is critical to transfer these abilities to computers, and these challenging tasks have been strongly pushed forward in knowledge thanks to Deep Learning. By using CNNs it is possible to predict human actions only observing a few frames of a video containing an action [34]. Exploiting an encoder-decoder recurrent neural network to address the action prediction problem, it is possible to predict multiple and variable-length action sequences [36]. Of course there are many other areas of computer vision that are receiving a strong impact from the development of the deep learning paradigm. However, the tasks just mentioned are the foundations for many assistive frameworks, as we will see in the next section, and therefore in this paper we will limit the discussion to them.

3 Recent Advances in at Exploiting DL Strategies

In the following subsections we will analyze how the recent deep learning based advances in computer vision tasks, described in Sect. 2, have been exploited to improve AT frameworks. As already anticipated, the following tasks will be considered:

- Object localization and recognition;
- Scene understanding;
- Human pose estimation and tracking;
- Action and event recognition;
- Anticipation.

3.1 Object Localization and Recognition

Object Localization and Recognition is one of the areas of computer vision that is maturing very rapidly thanks to deep learning. Nowadays, there is a plethora of pre-trained deep learning models which can be used for this task, so it only takes a small amount of effort to build a system able to detect most of the objects in an image or video even in the presence of multiple overlapping objects and different backgrounds. In addition to detecting even multiple objects in a scene, recent deep learning based architectures are also able to precisely identify their boundaries and relations to one another. This is achieved by deep structured learning which, for example, can learn relationship by using both feature, geometry, label [53] and, even physics and inferences about the abstract properties of the whole system [4].

The recent advantages in object localization and recognition have been already employed in different AT applications. For instance CNNs are effectively exploited to improve the performance in the autonomous navigation [8].

In [25] the YOLOv2 engine [32], which is one of the fastest strategies for object detection, is used to improve interaction with other subjects within an indoor navigation system that guides a user from point A to point B with high accuracy. The Yolov2 engine was recently used also in [16] to build a multimodal computer vision framework for human assistive robotics with the purpose of giving accessibility to persons with disabilities. Recently, object detection and recognition has been exploited to build a marker-less model for motion-aware gait assessment by localizing feet in egocentric videos [26].

3.2 Scene Understanding

At low level, this concerns the detection of structures of the scene, such as the task of finding edges arising from the physical surfaces of a scene. The extraction of useful scene information can underpin many computer vision tasks such as sketch recognition and 3D scene reconstruction, and is important for conveying knowledge for assistive navigation systems. This is also a key task in retinal implants. Improving the recovery of structural edges using RGB-D input was addressed in [10] with an end-to-end fully convolutional neural network approach. At the higher level, scene understanding concerns the ability of vision systems to infer and describe the content of the scene. As example, in [48] it is proposed a visual question answering system based on DL designed around spoken questions asked by blind people about their surroundings using a mobile phone camera picture. Another example of high level scene understanding regards the ability of a vision system to recognize locations of interest for a user in order to perform temporal segmentation of videos for lifelogging applications [11]. Scene understanding also plays a key role in automatic story comprehension that trough CNN can provide effective solutions for the visually impaired or cognitive robotics [42].

3.3 Human Pose Estimation and Tracking

The estimation of the articulated motion of the human body is useful for a number of real world applications including medical rehabilitation, human-robot interaction and in general to create smart environments suitable to understand people behaviours.

Pose estimation is generally pursued by detecting and extracting the positions of the joints of the human body from different sources such as a single image, a sequence of images, and RGB-D data. The main goal is to reconstruct the skeletal structures of the people in the scene and hence provide information about their body posture, the motion of the body, and human gestures. Understanding human poses from images is considered one of the major challenges in the field of Computer Vision and has been intensively studied in the last few decades by the research community. A propulsion in this research field has been given by the work reported in [43], where the problem of pose estimation is formulated as a regression problem to infer the position of the joints of the body in a Deep Neural Network framework. In the context of assistive technologies, monitoring the pose of a child over time could reveal important information both during clinical trials [21] or natural behaviors [40]. Human pose estimation methods have been tested on a variety of challenging conditions, but few studies to highlight performance specifically on children's poses have been done. Infants, toddlers and children are not only smaller than adults, but also significantly different in anatomical proportions. In [37] is proposed a study in which different deep learning based approaches for human pose estimation are compared when subjects are children. Results reveal that accuracy of the state of art methods drops significantly, opening new challenges for the research community. The pose of humans can be also used to understand emergency situations, such as unintended falls of an elderly person which lives alone. Fall recognition can be treated as a binary classification problem to obtain frame-wise semantic labels, so that fall recognition and its localization in time can be addressed simultaneously. In the recent literature different methods based on convolutional neural networks using both, RGB and RGB-D data have been proposed to address the fall recognition problem [15].

3.4   Action and Event Recognition

The action recognition task is related to the identification of the different possible actions performed by a human from a sequence of frames, where the actions may or may not be performed throughout the entire duration of the video. Generally speaking an action can be regarded to as a temporal evolution of some visual features. Hence the task becomes to model this evolution to recognize the occurrence of actions.

Common examples of actions to be recognized are "answer phone", "shake hands" (Short actions), "make sandwich", "do homework" (Activities/events with one actor), "birthday party", "parade" (Activities/events involving several persons), but also facial actions such as "smile". Current state-of-the-art approaches for spatio-temporal action localization [45] rely on detections at the frame level and model the temporal context with 3D ConvNets. Advanced approaches model spatio-temporal relations to capture the interactions between human actors, relevant objects and key scene elements to discriminate among human actions [41].

Action recognition in first person vision (proprioceptive activity recognition) is a new frontier of research with a series of additional challenges with respect to classic action recognition.

First-person vision (FPV) activity recognition involves the use of wearable cameras and is greatly beneficial for assisted living, life-logging and summarization [27]. In this context, motion representations which use stacked spectrograms have been proposed in [1]. These spectrograms were generated over temporal windows from mean grid-optical-flow vectors and the displacement vectors of the intensity centroid. The stacked representation enables the system to use 2D convolutions to learn and extract global motion features. Moreover, a long short-term memory (LSTM) network was used to encode the temporal dependency among consecutive samples recursively.

In [30], a deep learning model useful to predict the next action task to be performed by a robot is proposed. The model exploits both, the recognition of objects and their relations. The preconditions and effects of the robot actions are modeled through symbolic language, and the next goal state learning is obtained with a multi-layered LSTM architecture fed by the predicates with terms verified by vision.

One of the main problems with the use of assistive visual monitoring systems in the wild is the requirement of a large amount of training data for each new environment, as models trained in one location tend not to generalize well to others. If improvements could be found by leveraging existing data to circumvent or at least speed the training process in new environments, the deployment of such systems could become faster and easier, enabling more widespread use and providing robust results. In [29], the issue of transfer learning for frame-based event classification using RNNs was tackled.

3.5 Anticipation

The ability to anticipate future events is a desirable capability for assistive technologies. Algorithms to anticipate future events in order to support automated decisions and assist the user have been recently investigated by the computer vision research community. Some efforts have focused on the use of egocentric cameras, which allow to acquire video from the point of view of the user, in order to infer their future actions. Among these works, in [39] it is proposed a method able to anticipate the next action likely to be performed by a user from egocentric video and infer whether that action is correct in the work-flow. The authors of [28] used CNNs to predict the future location of the camera wearer in an egocentric video. The study in [49] designed a method based on Generative Adversarial Networks (GAN) to infer the gaze of the user in future frames (e.g., to infer what the user will observe next). In [9] it is proposed a deep learning architecture to anticipate the position of specific objects and hands in future frames, whereas the study reported in [33] used inverse reinforcement learning to understand the user's goal and anticipate the next location and object they will be interested in. The authors of [7] proposed the task of anticipating future actions performed by the camera wearer on a newly proposed large dataset of videos of egocentric activities in kitchens.

Other works investigated anticipation tasks in the context of third person vision. For instance, in [44] it is proposed to use deep convolutional networks to anticipate multiple future representation from the current frame of a video. The anticipated representations were then used to forecast future actions and objects. In [13] it is proposed an encoder-decoder LSTM architecture capable of anticipating future representation and predict future actions. The study in [24] describes a systems to predict future actions and their starting time. The authors of [2] investigated two deep models to predict multiple future actions and their duration from video.

4   Future Directions

The possible topics most likely to be explored thanks to deep learning will be oriented towards the effective modeling of human behaviors and cognition. Indeed, these aspects are essential to build adaptation and personalization mechanisms for assistive systems. Since eye gaze has been frequently studied in interactive intelligent systems as a cue for inferring user's internal states and to have priors about the user intent, a significant body of works could investigate the relationships between eye movements and cognitive processes to provide an understanding into memory recall, cognitive load, interest, the level of domain knowledge, problem solving, desire to learn, and strategy use in reasoning. A contribution in this direction has already been proposed in [6], where a CNN-based method was trained to estimate user's gaze fixations on the tablet screen (while answering a question) to automatically gather a set of eye movement features useful to discriminate users knowing the correct answer with respect to the others.

Another very promising research line concerns the ability to automatically discover properties and affordances of regions of scenes (e.g., the affordance of objects), which indicate their relevance for a certain functional interaction with the user. Segmenting affordance regions, however, is more difficult than classical semantic image segmentation, where the focus in more on the objects present in the scene. This means that affordance segmentation requires to predict a set of labels per pixel since an object region might contain multiple affordance types. A weakly supervised semantic image segmentation approach based on deep learning was recently proposed in [35], where it is exploited an adaptive approach for binarizing the predictions of a convolutional neural network.

Anticipation methods will evolve to incorporate long term relationship between the observed events to perform better predictions of the future. This research area will allow to build proactive assistive systems and improve human-machine as well as help to anticipate the interactions between a human and the surrounding objects [12].

For some assistive tasks, the application of deep learning strategies has not yet happened, even if it would be highly required to standardize some critical procedures such as support to early diagnosis or assessment of neurodevelopmental disorders. This is manly due to the lack of publicly available datasets. For example in [47] a dataset containing RGB-D data related to real infant movements with varying realistic textures, shapes and backgrounds has been proposed in order to speed-up the medical infant motion analysis based on the training of deep learning approaches.

Acknowledgments. This research has been supported by Piano della Ricerca 2016–2018 linea di Intervento 2 of DMI, University of Catania.

References

1. Abebe, G., Cavallaro, A.: A long short-term memory convolutional neural network for first-person vision activity recognition. In: Proceedings of International Conference on Computer Vision Workshops (ICCVW) (2017)
2. Abu Farha, Y., Richard, A., Gall, J.: When will you do what?-anticipating temporal occurrences of activities. In: Proceedings of the IEEE Conference on Computer Vision and Pattern Recognition, pp. 5343–5352 (2018)
3. Andriluka, M., et al.: PoseTrack: a benchmark for human pose estimation and tracking. In: Proceedings of the IEEE Conference on Computer Vision and Pattern Recognition, pp. 5167–5176 (2018)
4. Battaglia, P., Pascanu, R., Lai, M., Rezende, D.J., et al.: Interaction networks for learning about objects, relations and physics. In: Advances in Neural Information Processing Systems, pp. 4502–4510 (2016)
5. Brust, C.A., Sickert, S., Simon, M., Rodner, E., Denzler, J.: Efficient convolutional patch networks for scene understanding. In: International Conference on Computer Vision Theory and Applications (VISAPP) (2015)
6. Celiktutan, O., Demiris, Y.: Inferring human knowledgeability from eye gaze in m-learning environments. In: Leal-Taixé, L., Roth, S. (eds.) ECCV 2018 Workshops, LNCS, vol. 11134, pp. 193–209. Springer, Cham (2019)
7. Damen, D., et al.: Scaling egocentric vision: the EPIC-KITCHENS dataset. arXiv preprint arXiv:1804.02748 (2018)
8. Erol, B.A., Majumdar, A., Lwowski, J., Benavidez, P., Rad, P., Jamshidi, M.: Improved deep neural network object tracking system for applications in home robotics. In: Pedrycz, W., Chen, S.-M. (eds.) Computational Intelligence for Pattern Recognition. SCI, vol. 777, pp. 369–395. Springer, Cham (2018). https://doi.org/10.1007/978-3-319-89629-8_14
9. Fan, C., Lee, J., Ryoo, M.S.: Forecasting hand and object locations in future frames. CoRR abs/1705.07328 (2017). http://arxiv.org/abs/1705.07328
10. Feng, D., Barnes, N., You, S.: DSD: depth structural descriptor for edge-based assistive navigation. In: 2017 IEEE International Conference on Computer Vision Workshop (ICCVW), pp. 1536–1544. IEEE (2017)
11. Furnari, A., Battiato, S., Farinella, G.M.: Personal-location-based temporal segmentation of egocentric videos for lifelogging applications. J. Vis. Commun. Image Represent. **52**, 1–12 (2018)
12. Furnari, A., Battiato, S., Grauman, K., Farinella, G.M.: Next-active-object prediction from egocentric videos. J. Vis. Commun. Image Represent. **49**, 401–411 (2017)
13. Gao, J., Yang, Z., Nevatia, R.: RED: reinforced encoder-decoder networks for action anticipation. In: British Machine Vision Conference (2017)
14. Goodfellow, I., Bengio, Y., Courville, A.: Deep Learning. MIT Press (2016). http://www.deeplearningbook.org
15. Hesse, N., Bodensteiner, C., Arens, M., Hofmann, U., Weinberger, R., Schroeder, S.: An empirical study towards understanding how deep convolutional nets recognize falls. In: Leal-Taixé, L., Roth, S. (eds.) ECCV 2018 Workshops. LNCS, vol. 11134, pp. 112–127. Springer, Cham (2019)
16. Ivorra, E., Ortega, M., Alcañiz, M., Garcia-Aracil, N.: Multimodal computer vision framework for human assistive robotics. In: 2018 Workshop on Metrology for Industry 4.0 and IoT, pp. 1–5. IEEE (2018)

17. Johnson, J., et al.: Inferring and executing programs for visual reasoning. In: 2017 IEEE International Conference on Computer Vision (ICCV), pp. 3008–3017, October 2017. https://doi.org/10.1109/ICCV.2017.325
18. Katircioglu, I., Tekin, B., Salzmann, M., Lepetit, V., Fua, P.: Learning latent representations of 3D human pose with deep neural networks. Int. J. Comput. Vis. (2018). https://doi.org/10.1007/s11263-018-1066-6
19. Kawana, Y., Ukita, N., Huang, J.B., Yang, M.H.: Ensemble convolutional neural networks for pose estimation. Comput. Vis. Image Underst. **169**, 62–74 (2018). https://doi.org/10.1016/j.cviu.2017.12.005
20. Leo, M., Medioni, G., Trivedi, M., Kanade, T., Farinella, G.: Computer vision for assistive technologies. Comput. Vis. Image Underst. **154**(Suppl. C), 1–15 (2017)
21. Leo, M., Del Coco, M., Carcagnì, P., Mazzeo, P.L., Spagnolo, P., Distante, C.: A technological framework to support standardized protocols for the diagnosis and assessment of ASD. In: Hua, G., Jégou, H. (eds.) ECCV 2016. LNCS, vol. 9914, pp. 269–284. Springer, Cham (2016). https://doi.org/10.1007/978-3-319-48881-3_19
22. Litjens, G., et al.: A survey on deep learning in medical image analysis. Med. Image Anal. **42**, 60–88 (2017)
23. Liu, W., Wang, Z., Liu, X., Zeng, N., Liu, Y., Alsaadi, F.E.: A survey of deep neural network architectures and their applications. Neurocomputing **234**, 11–26 (2017). https://doi.org/10.1016/j.neucom.2016.12.038. http://www.sciencedirect.com/science/article/pii/S0925231216315533
24. Mahmud, T., Hasan, M., Roy-Chowdhury, A.K.: Joint prediction of activity labels and starting times in untrimmed videos. In: 2017 IEEE International Conference on Computer Vision (ICCV), pp. 5784–5793 (2017)
25. Nair, V., Budhai, M., Olmschenk, G., Seiple, W.H., Zhu, Z.: ASSIST: personalized indoor navigation via multimodal sensors and high-level semantic information. In: Leal-Taixé, L., Roth, S. (eds.) ECCV 2018 Workshops. LNCS, vol. 11134, pp. 128–143. Springer, Cham (2019)
26. Nouredanesh, M., Li, A.W., Godfrey, A., Hoey, J., Tung, J.: Chasing feet in the wild: a proposed egocentric motion-aware gait assessment tool. In: Leal-Taixé, L., Roth, S. (eds.) ECCV 2018 Workshops. LNCS, vol. 11134, pp. 176–192. Springer, Cham (2019)
27. Ortis, A., Farinella, G.M., D'Amico, V., Addesso, L., Torrisi, G., Battiato, S.: Organizing egocentric videos of daily living activities. Pattern Recogn. **72**, 207–218 (2017)
28. Park, H.S., Hwang, J.J., Niu, Y., Shi, J.: Egocentric future localization. In: CVPR 2016, pp. 4697–4705 (2016)
29. Perrett, T., Damen, D.: Recurrent assistance: cross-dataset training of LSTMs on kitchen tasks. In: Proceedings of the IEEE Conference on Computer Vision and Pattern Recognition, pp. 1354–1362 (2017)
30. Pirri, F., Mauro, L., Alati, E., Sanzari, M., Ntouskos, V.: Deep execution monitor for robot assistive tasks. In: Leal-Taixé, L., Roth, S. (eds.) ECCV 2018 Workshops. LNCS, vol. 11134, pp. 158–175. Springer, Cham (2019)
31. Ravì, D., et al.: Deep learning for health informatics. IEEE J. Biomed. Health Inform. **21**, 4–21 (2017)
32. Redmon, J., Farhadi, A.: YOLO9000: better, faster, stronger. arXiv preprint (2017)
33. Rhinehart, N., Kitani, K.M.: First-person activity forecasting with online inverse reinforcement learning. In: ICCV (2017)
34. Rodriguez, C., Fernando, B., Li, H.: Action anticipation by predicting future dynamic images. arXiv preprint arXiv:1808.00141 (2018)

35. Sawatzky, J., Gall, J.: Adaptive binarization for weakly supervised affordance segmentation. arXiv preprint arXiv:1707.02850 (2017)
36. Schydlo, P., Rakovic, M., Jamone, L., Santos-Victor, J.: Anticipation in Human-Robot Cooperation: A Recurrent Neural Network Approach for Multiple Action Sequences Prediction. arXiv e-prints, February 2018
37. Sciortino, G., Farinella, G.M., Battiato, S., Leo, M., Distante, C.: On the estimation of children's poses. In: Battiato, S., Gallo, G., Schettini, R., Stanco, F. (eds.) ICIAP 2017. LNCS, vol. 10485, pp. 410–421. Springer, Cham (2017). https://doi.org/10.1007/978-3-319-68548-9_38
38. Sharif Razavian, A., Azizpour, H., Sullivan, J., Carlsson, S.: CNN features off-the-shelf: an astounding baseline for recognition. In: Proceedings of the IEEE Conference on Computer Vision and Pattern Recognition Workshops, pp. 806–813 (2014)
39. Soran, B., Farhadi, A., Shapiro, L.: Generating notifications for missing actions: don't forget to turn the lights off! In: Proceedings of the IEEE International Conference on Computer Vision, pp. 4669–4677 (2016)
40. Soran, B., Lowes, L., Steele, K.M.: Evaluation of infants with spinal muscular atrophy type-I using convolutional neural networks. In: Hua, G., Jégou, H. (eds.) ECCV 2016. LNCS, vol. 9914, pp. 495–507. Springer, Cham (2016). https://doi.org/10.1007/978-3-319-48881-3_34
41. Sun, C., Shrivastava, A., Vondrick, C., Murphy, K., Sukthankar, R., Schmid, C.: Actor-centric relation network. arXiv preprint arXiv:1807.10982 (2018)
42. Tapaswi, M., Zhu, Y., Stiefelhagen, R., Torralba, A., Urtasun, R., Fidler, S.: MovieQA: understanding stories in movies through question-answering. In: Proceedings of the IEEE Conference on Computer Vision and Pattern Recognition, pp. 4631–4640 (2016)
43. Toshev, A., Szegedy, C.: DeepPose: human pose estimation via deep neural networks. In: Proceedings of the IEEE Conference on Computer Vision and Pattern Recognition, pp. 1653–1660 (2014)
44. Vondrick, C., Pirsiavash, H., Torralba, A.: Anticipating visual representations from unlabeled video. In: IEEE Conference on Computer Vision and Pattern Recognition, pp. 98–106 (2016)
45. Wang, A., Dantcheva, A., Broutart, J.C., Robert, P., Bremond, F., Bilinski, P.: Comparing methods for assessment of facial dynamics in patients with major neurocognitive disorders. In: Leal-Taixé, L., Roth, S. (eds.) ECCV 2018 Workshops. LNCS, vol. 11134, pp. 144–157. Springer, Cham (2019)
46. Wang, L., Wang, Z., Qiao, Y., Van Gool, L.: Transferring deep object and scene representations for event recognition in still images. Int. J. Comput. Vis. **126**(2), 390–409 (2018). https://doi.org/10.1007/s11263-017-1043-5
47. Yan, Z.: Computer vision for medical infant motion analysis: state of the art and RGB-D data set. In: Leal-Taixé, L., Roth, S. (eds.) ECCV 2018 Workshops. LNCS, vol. 11134, pp. 32–49. Springer, Cham (2019)
48. Jiang, Y., Natarajan, V., Chen, X., Rohrbach, M., Batra, D., Parikh, D.: Pythia v0.1: the winning entry to the VQA challenge 2018. arXiv preprint arXiv:1807.09956 (2018)
49. Zhang, M., Ma, K.T., Lim, J.H., Zhao, Q., Feng, J.: Deep future gaze: gaze anticipation on egocentric videos using adversarial networks. In: Conference on Computer Vision and Pattern Recognition, pp. 4372–4381 (2017)
50. Zhang, Q., Yang, L.T., Chen, Z., Li, P.: A survey on deep learning for big data. Inf. Fusion **42**(Suppl. C), 146–157 (2018)

51. Zhang, Y., et al.: Physically-based rendering for indoor scene understanding using convolutional neural networks. In: 2017 IEEE Conference on Computer Vision and Pattern Recognition (CVPR), pp. 5057–5065. IEEE (2017)
52. Zhao, Z.Q., Zheng, P., Xu, S., Wu, X.: Object Detection with Deep Learning: A Review. arXiv e-prints, July 2018
53. Zhu, Y., Jiang, S.: Deep structured learning for visual relationship detection. In: The Thirty-Second AAAI Conference on Artificial Intelligence (AAAI-2018) (2018)

Recovering 6D Object Pose: A Review and Multi-modal Analysis

Caner Sahin[✉] and Tae-Kyun Kim

ICVL, Imperial College London, London, UK
c.sahin14@imperial.ac.uk

Abstract. A large number of studies analyse object detection and pose estimation at visual level in 2D, discussing the effects of challenges such as occlusion, clutter, texture, *etc.*, on the performances of the methods, which work in the context of RGB modality. Interpreting the depth data, the study in this paper presents thorough multi-modal analyses. It discusses the above-mentioned challenges for full 6D object pose estimation in RGB-D images comparing the performances of several 6D detectors in order to answer the following questions: What is the current position of the computer vision community for maintaining "automation" in robotic manipulation? What next steps should the community take for improving "autonomy" in robotics while handling objects? Our findings include: (i) reasonably accurate results are obtained on textured-objects at varying viewpoints with cluttered backgrounds. (ii) Heavy existence of occlusion and clutter severely affects the detectors, and similar-looking distractors is the biggest challenge in recovering instances' 6D. (iii) Template-based methods and random forest-based learning algorithms underlie object detection and 6D pose estimation. Recent paradigm is to learn deep discriminative feature representations and to adopt CNNs taking RGB images as input. (iv) Depending on the availability of large-scale 6D annotated depth datasets, feature representations can be learnt on these datasets, and then the learnt representations can be customized for the 6D problem.

1 Introduction

Object detection and pose estimation is an important problem in the realm of computer vision, for which a large number of solutions have been proposed. One line of the solutions is based on visual perception in RGB channel. Existing evaluation studies [1,2] addressing this line of the solutions discuss the effects of challenges, such as occlusion, clutter, texture, *etc.*, on the performances of the methods, which are mainly evaluated on large-scale datasets, *e.g.*, ImageNet [3], PASCAL [4]. These studies have made important inferences for generalized object detection, however, the discussions have been restricted to visual level in 2D, since the interested methods are designed to work in the context of RGB modality.

© Springer Nature Switzerland AG 2019
L. Leal-Taixé and S. Roth (Eds.): ECCV 2018 Workshops, LNCS 11134, pp. 15–31, 2019.
https://doi.org/10.1007/978-3-030-11024-6_2

Fig. 1. Benchmarks collected mainly differ from the point of challenges that they involve. Row-wise, the 1st benchmark concerns texture-less objects at varying viewpoint with cluttered background, the 2nd is interested in multi-instance, the 3rd has scenes with severely occluded objects, the 4th reflects the challenges found in bin-picking scenarios, and the 5th is related to similar-looking distractors.

Increasing ubiquity of Kinect-like RGB-D sensors has prompted an interest in full 6D object pose estimation. Interpreting the depth data, state-of-the-art approaches for object detection and 6D pose estimation [5–7] report improved results tackling the aforesaid challenges in 6D. This improvement is of great importance to many higher level tasks, *e.g.*, scene interpretation, augmented reality, and particularly, to robotic manipulation.

Robotic manipulators that pick and place the goods from conveyors, shelves, pallets, *etc.*, can facilitate several processes comprised within logistics systems, *e.g.*, warehousing, material handling, packaging. Amazon Picking Challenge (APC) [8] is an important example demonstrating the promising role of robotic manipulation for the facilitation of such processes. APC integrates many tasks, such as mapping, motion planning, grasping, object manipulation, *etc.*, with the goal of "*autonomously*" moving items by robotic systems from a warehouse shelf into a tote [9,10]. Regarding the *"automated"* handling of items by robots, accurate object detection and 6D pose estimation is an important task that when successfully performed improves the autonomy of the manipulation. Within this context, we ask the following questions. What is the current position of the computer vision community for maintaining automation in robotic manipulation, with respect to the accuracy of the 6D detectors introduced? What next steps should the community take for improving the autonomy in robotics while handling objects? We aim at answering these questions performing multi-modal analyses for object detection and 6D pose estimation where we compare state-of-the-art baselines regarding the challenges involved in the interested datasets.

Direct comparison of the baselines is difficult, since they are tested on samples which are collected at non-identical scenarios by using RGB-D sensors with different characteristics. Additionally, different evaluation criteria are utilized for performance measure. In order to address such difficulties, we follow a three-fold strategy: we firstly collect five representative object datasets [5–7,11,12] (see Fig. 1). Then, we investigate 10 state-of-the-art detectors [5–7,11,13–18] on the collected datasets under uniform scoring criteria of the Average Distance (AD) metric. We further extend our investigations comparing 2 of the detectors [5,6], which are our own implementations, using the Visible Surface Discrepancy (VSD) protocol. We offer a number of insights for the next steps to be taken, for improving the autonomy in robotics. To summarize, our main contributions are as follows:

- This is the first time, the current position of the field is analysed regarding object detection and 6D pose estimation.
- We collect five representative publicly available datasets. In total, there are approximately 50 different object classes. We investigate ten classes of the state-of-the-art 6D detectors on the collected datasets under uniform scoring criteria.
- We discuss baselines' strength and weakness with respect to the challenges involved in the interested RGB-D datasets. We identify the next steps for improving the robustness of the detectors, and for improving the autonomy in robotic applications, consequently.

2 Related Work

Methods producing 2D bounding box hypotheses in color images [19–28] form one line of the solutions for object detection and pose estimation. Evaluation studies interested in this line of the solutions mainly analyse the performances of the methods regarding the challenges involved within the datasets [3,4], on which the methods have been tested. In [29], the effect of different context sources, such as geographic context, object spatial support, *etc.*, on object detection is examined. Hoiem et al. [1] evaluate the performances of several baselines on PASCAL dataset particularly analysing the reasons why false positives are hypothesised. Since there are less number of object categories in PASCAL dataset, Russakovsky et al. [2] use ImageNet in order to do meta-analysis, and to examine the influences

Table 1. Datasets collected: each dataset shows different characteristics mainly from the challenge point of view (VP: viewpoint, O: occlusion, C: clutter, SO: severe occlusion, SC: severe clutter, MI: multiple instance, SLD: similar looking distractors, BP: bin picking).

Dataset	Challenge	# Obj. classes	Modality	# Total frame	Obj. Dist. [mm]
LINEMOD	VP + C + TL	15	RGB-D	15770	600–1200
MULT-I	VP + C + TL + O + MI	6	RGB-D	2067	600–1200
OCC	VP + C + TL + SO	8	RGB-D	9209	600–1200
BIN-P	VP + SC + SO + MI + BP	2	RGB-D	180	600–1200
T-LESS	VP + C + TL + O + MI + SLD	30	RGB-D	10080	600–1200

of color, texture, *etc.*, on the performances of object detectors. Torralba et al. [30] compares several datasets regarding the involved samples, cross-dataset generalization, and relative data bias, *etc.* Recently published retrospective evaluation [31] and benchmarking [32] studies perform the most comprehensive analyses on 2D object localization and category detection, by examining the PASCAL Visual Object Classes (VOC) Challenge, and the ImageNet Large Scale Visual Recognition Challenge, respectively. These studies introduce important implications for generalized object detection, however, the discussions are restricted to visual level in 2D, since the concerned methods are engineered for color images. In this study, we target to go beyond visual perception and extend the discussions on existing challenges to 6D, interpreting depth data.

3 Datasets

Every dataset used in this study is composed of several object classes, for each of which a set of RGB-D test images are provided with ground truth 6D object poses. The collected datasets mainly differ from the point of the challenges that they involve (see Table 1).

Viewpoint (VP) + Clutter (C). Every dataset involves the test scenes in which objects of interest are located at *varying viewpoints* and *cluttered backgrounds*.

VP + C + Texture-less (TL). Test scenes in the LINEMOD [5] dataset involve *texture-less* objects at varying viewpoints with cluttered backgrounds. There are 15 objects, for each of which more than 1100 real images are recorded. The sequences provide views from 0–360° around the object, 0–90° degree tilt rotation, $\mp45°$ in-plane rotation, and 650 mm–1150 mm object distance.

VP + C + TL + Occlusion (O) + Multiple Instance (MI). Occlusion is one of the main challenges that makes the datasets more difficult for the task of object detection and 6D pose estimation. In addition to close and far range 2D and 3D clutter, testing sequences of the Multiple-Instance (MULT-I) dataset [6] contain *foreground occlusions* and *multiple object instances*. In total, there are approximately 2000 real images of 6 different objects, which are located at the range of 600 mm–1200 mm. The testing images are sampled to produce sequences that are uniformly distributed in the pose space by [0° –360°], [−80° –80°], and [−70° –70°] in the yaw, roll, and pitch angles, respectively.

VP + C + TL + Severe Occlusion (SO). Occlusion, clutter, texture-less objects, and change in viewpoint are the most well-known challenges that could successfully be dealt with the state-of-the-art 6D object detectors. However, *heavy existence* of these challenges severely degrades the performance of 6D object detectors. Occlusion (OCC) dataset [7] is one of the most difficult datasets in which one can observe up to 70–80% occluded objects. OCC includes the extended ground truth annotations of LINEMOD: in each test scene of the LINEMOD [5] dataset, various objects are present, but only ground truth poses for one object are given. Brachmann et al. [7] form OCC considering the images of one scene (benchvise) and annotating the poses of 8 additional objects.

VP + SC + SO + MI + Bin Picking (BP). In *bin-picking* scenarios, multiple instances of the objects of interest are arbitrarily stocked in a bin, and hence, the objects are inherently subjected to severe occlusion and severe clutter. Bin-Picking (BIN-P) dataset [11] is created to reflect such challenges found in industrial settings. It includes 183 test images of 2 textured objects under varying viewpoints.

VP + C + TL + O + MI + Similar Looking Distractors (SLD). *Similar-looking distractor(s)* along with similar looking object classes involved in the datasets strongly confuse recognition systems causing a lack of discriminative selection of shape features. Unlike the above-mentioned datasets and their corresponding challenges, the T-LESS [12] dataset particularly focuses on this problem. The RGB-D images of the objects located on a table are captured at different viewpoints covering 360° rotation, and various object arrangements generate occlusion. Out-of-training objects, similar looking distractors (planar surfaces), and similar looking objects cause 6 DoF methods to produce many false positives, particularly affecting the depth modality features. T-LESS has 30 texture-less industry-relevant objects, and 20 different test scenes, each of which consists of 504 test images.

4   Baselines

State-of-the-art baselines for 6D object pose estimation address the challenges studied in Sect. 3, however, the architectures used differ between the baselines. In this section, we analyse 6D object pose estimators architecture-wise.

Template-Based. Template-based approaches, matching global descriptors of objects to the scene, are one of the most widely used approaches for object detection tasks, since they do not require time-consuming training effort. Linemod [5], being at the forefront of object detection research, estimates cluttered object's 6D pose using color gradients and surface normals. It is improved by discriminative learning in [33]. Fast directional chamfer matching (FDCM) [34] is used in robotics applications.

Point-to-Point. Point-to-point techniques build point-pair features for sparse representations of the test and the model point sets. Drost et al. [13] propose create a global model description based on oriented point pair features and match that model locally using a fast voting scheme. Its further improved in [14] making the method more robust across clutter and sensor noise.

Conventional Learning-Based. These methods are in need of training sessions where training samples along with the ground truth annotations are learnt. Latent-class Hough forests [6,35], employing one-class learning, utilize surface normals and color gradients features in a part-based approach in order to provide robustness across occlusion. The random forest based method in [7] encodes contextual information of the objects with simple depth and RGB pixels, and improves the confidence of a pose hypothesis using a Ransac-like algorithm. An analysis-by-synthesis approach [36] and an uncertainty-driven methodology [15] are build upon random forests, using the architecture provided in [7]. The method based on random forests presented in [37] formulates the recognition problem globally and derives occlusion aware features computing a set of principal curvature ratios for all pixels in depth images. The depth-based architectures in [38,39] present iterative Hough forests that initially estimate coarse 6D pose of an object, and then iteratively refine the confidence of the estimation due to the extraction of more discriminative control point descriptors [40].

Deep Learning. Current paradigm in the community is to learn deep discriminative feature representations. Wohlhart et al. [41] utilize a CNN structure to learn discriminative descriptors and then pass the learnt descriptors to a Nearest Neighbor classifier in order to find the closest object pose. Although promising, this method has one main limitation, which is the requirement of background images during training along with the ones holistic foreground, thus making its performance dataset-specific. The studies in [11,16] learn deep representation of parts in an unsupervised fashion only from foreground images using auto-encoder architectures. The features extracted in the course of the test are fed into a Hough forest in [11], and into a codebook of pre-computed synthetic local object patches in [16] in order to hypothesise object 6D pose. While [41] focuses on learning feature embeddings based on metric learning with triplet comparisons, Balntas et al. [42] further examine the effects of using object poses as guidance to learning robust features for 3D object pose estimation in order to handle symmetry issue.

More recent methods adopt CNNs for 6D pose estimation, taking RGB images as inputs [17]. BB8 [43] and Tekin et al. [44] perform corner-point regression followed by PnP for 6D pose estimation. Typically employed is a computationally expensive post processing step such as iterative closest point (ICP) or a verification network [18].

5   Evaluation Metrics

Several evaluation metrics are proposed for measuring the performance of a 6D detector. Average Distance (AD) [5] outputs the score ω that calculates the distance between ground truth and estimated poses of a test object using its model. Hypotheses ensuring the following inequality is considered as correct:

$$\omega \le z_\omega \Phi \tag{1}$$

where Φ is the diameter of the 3D model of the test object, and z_ω is a constant that determines the coarseness of an hypothesis which is assigned as correct. Translational and rotational error function [45], being independent from the models of objects, measures the correctness of an hypothesis according to the followings: (i) $\mathcal{L}_2$ norm between the ground truth and estimated translations, (ii) the angle computed from the axis-angle representation of ground truth and estimated rotation matrices.

Visible Surface Discrepancy (VSD) has recently been proposed to eliminate ambiguities arising from object symmetries and occlusions [46]. The model of an object of interest is rendered at both ground truth and estimated poses, and their depth maps are intersected with the test image itself in order to compute the visibility masks. Comparing the generated masks, the score normalized in [0–1] determines whether an estimation is correct, according to the pre-defined thresholds.

In this study, we employ a twofold evaluation strategy for the 6D detectors using both AD and VSD metrics: (i) Recall. The hypotheses on the test images of every object are ranked, and the hypothesis with the highest weight is selected as the estimated 6D pose. Recall value is calculated comparing the number of correctly estimated poses and the number of the test images of the interested object. (ii) F1 scores. Unlike recall, all hypotheses are taken into account, and F1 score, the harmonic mean of precision and recall values, is presented.

6   Multi-modal Analyses

We analyse ten baselines on the datasets with respect to both challenges and the architectures. Two of the baselines [5,6] are our own implementations. The color gradients and surface normal features, presented in [5], are computed using the built-in functions and classes provided by OpenCV. The features in Latent-Class Hough Forest (LCHF) [6] are the part-based version of the features introduced in [5]. Hence, we inherit the classes given by OpenCV in order to generate part-based features used in LCHF. We train each method for the objects of interest by ourselves, and using the learnt classifiers, we test those on all datasets. Note that, the methods use only foreground samples during training/template generation. In this section, "LINEMOD" refers to the dataset, whilst "Linemod" is used to indicate the baseline itself.

6.1   Analyses Based on Average Distance

Utilizing the AD metric, we compare the chosen baselines along with the challenges, (i) regarding the recall values that each baseline generates on every dataset, (ii) regarding the F1 scores. The coefficient z_ω is 0.10, and in case we use different thresholds, we will specifically indicate in the related parts.

Table 2. Methods' performance are depicted object-wise based on recall values computed using the Average Distance (AD) evaluation protocol.

Method	ch.	ape	bvise	cam	can	cat	dril	duck	box	glue	hpunch	iron	lamp	phone	AVER
Kehl et al [16]	RGB-D	96.9	94.1	97.7	95.2	97.4	96.2	97.3	99.9	78.6	96.8	98.7	96.2	92.8	95.2
LCHF [6]	RGB-D	84	95	72	74	91	92	91	48	55	89	72	90	69	78.6
Linemod [5]	RGB-D	95.8	98.7	97.5	95.4	99.3	93.6	95.9	99.8	91.8	95.9	97.5	97.7	93.3	96.3
Drost et al [13]	D	86.5	70.7	78.6	80.2	85.4	87.3	46	97	57.2	77.4	84.9	93.3	80.7	78.9
Kehl et al [18]	RGB	65	80	78	86	70	73	66	100	100	49	78	73	79	76.7

(a) LINEMOD dataset

Method	ch.	camera	cup	joystick	juice	milk	shampoo	AVER
LCHF [6]	RGB-D	52.5	99.8	98.3	99.3	92.7	97.2	90
Linemod [5]	RGB-D	18.3	99.2	85	51.6	72.2	53.1	63.2

(b) MULT-I dataset

Method	ch.	ape	can	cat	dril	duck	box	glue	hpunch	AVER
Xiang et al. [17]	RGB-D	76.2	87.4	52.2	90.3	77.7	72.2	76.7	91.4	78
LCHF [6]	RGB-D	48.0	79.0	38.0	83.0	64.0	11.0	32.0	69.0	53
Hinters et al. [14]	RGB-D	81.4	94.7	55.2	86.0	79.7	65.5	52.1	95.5	76.3
Linemod [5]	RGB-D	21.0	31.0	14.0	37.0	42.0	21.0	5.0	35.0	25.8
Xiang et al. [17]	RGB	9.6	45.2	0.93	41.4	19.6	22.0	38.5	22.1	25

(c) OCC dataset

Method	ch.	cup	juice	AVER
LCHF [6]	RGB-D	90.0	89.0	90
Brach et al. [7]	RGB-D	89.4	87.6	89
Linemod [5]	RGB-D	88.0	40.0	64

(d) BIN-P dataset

Recall-Only Discussions. Recall-only discussions are based on the numbers provided in Table 2, and Fig. 2.

Clutter, Viewpoint, Texture-Less Objects. Highest recall values are obtained on the LINEMOD dataset (see Fig. 2(a)), meaning that the state-of-the-art methods for 6D object pose estimation can successfully handle the challenges, clutter, varying viewpoint, and texture-less objects. LCHF, detecting more than half of the objects with over 80% accuracy, worst performs on "box" and "glue" (see Table 2a), since these objects have planar surfaces, which confuses the features extracted in depth channel (example images are given in Fig. 2(b)).

Occlusion. In addition to the challenges involved in LINEMOD, occlusion is introduced in MULT-I. Linemod's performance decreases, since occlusion affects holistic feature representations in color and depth channels. LCHF performs better on this dataset than Linemod. Since LCHF is trained using the parts coming from positive training images, it can easily handle occlusion, using the information acquired from occlusion-free parts of the target objects. However, LCHF degrades on "camera". In comparison with the other objects in the dataset,

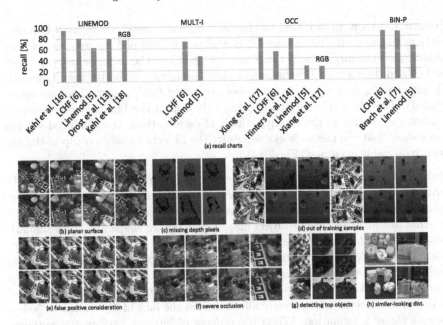

Fig. 2. (a) Success of each baseline on every dataset is shown, recall values are computed using the Average Distance (AD) metric. (b)–(h) challenges encountered during test are exemplified (green renderings are hypotheses, and the red ones are ground truths). (Color figure online)

"camera" has relatively smaller dimensions. In most of the test images, there are non-negligible amount of missing depth pixels (Fig. 2(c)) along the borders of this object, and thus confusing the features extracted in depth channel. In such cases, LCHF is liable to detect similar-looking out of training objects and generate many false positives (see Fig. 2(d)). The hypotheses produced by LCHF for "joystick" are all considered as false positive (Fig. 2(e)). When we re-evaluate the recall that LCHF produces on the "joystick" object setting z_w to the value of 0.15, we observe 89% accuracy.

Severe Occlusion. OCC involves challenging test images where the objects of interest are cluttered and severely occluded. The best performance on this dataset is caught by Xiang et al. [17], and there is still room for improvement in order to fully handle this challenge. Despite the fact that the distinctive feature of this benchmark is the existence of "severe occlusion", there are occlusion-free target objects in several test images. In case the test images of a target object include unoccluded and/or naively occluded samples (with the occlusion ratio up to 40%–50% of the object dimensions) in addition to severely occluded samples, methods produce relatively higher recall values (*e.g.* "can, driller, duck, holepuncher", Table 2c). On the other hand, when the target object has additionally other challenges such as planar surfaces, methods' performance (LCHF and Linemod) decreases (*e.g.* "box", Fig. 2(f)).

Severe Clutter. In addition to the challenges discussed above, BIN-P inherently involves severe clutter, since it is designed for bin-picking scenarios, where objects are arbitrarily stacked in a pile. According to the recall values presented in Table 2d, LCHF and Brachmann et al. [7] perform 25% better than Linemod. Despite having severely occluded target objects in this dataset, there are unoccluded/relatively less occluded objects at the top of the bin. Since our current analyses are based on the top hypothesis of each method, the produced success rates show that the methods can recognize the objects located on top of the bin with reasonable accuracy (Fig. 2(g)).

Similar-Looking Distractors. We test both Linemod and LCHF on the T-LESS dataset. Since most of the time the algorithms fail, we do not report quantitative analyses, instead we discuss our observations from the experiments. The dataset involves various object classes with strong shape and color similarities. When the background color is different than that of the objects of interest, color gradient features are successfully extracted. However, the scenes involve multiple instances, multiple objects similar in shape and color, and hence, the features queried exist in the scene at multiple locations. The features extracted in depth channel are also severely affected from the lack of discriminative selection of shape information. When the objects of interest have planar surfaces, the detectors cannot easily discriminate foreground and background in depth channel, since these objects in the dataset are relatively smaller in dimension (see Fig. 2(h)).

Part-Based vs. Holistic Approaches. Holistic methods [5,13,14,17,18] formulate the detection problem globally. Linemod [5] represents the windows extracted from RGB and depth images by the surface normals and color gradients features. Distortions along the object borders arising from occlusion and clutter, that is, the distortions of the color gradient and surface normal information in the test processes, mainly degrade the performance of this detector. Part-based methods [6,7,11,15,16] extract parts in the given image. Despite the fact that LCHF uses the same kinds of features as in Linemod, LCHF detects objects extracting parts, thus making the method more robust to occlusion and clutter.

Template-Based vs. Random Forest-Based. Template-based methods, *i.e.*, Linemod, match the features extracted during test to a set of templates, and hence, they cannot easily be generalized well to unseen ground truth annotations, that is, the translation and rotation parameters in object pose estimation. Methods based on random forests [6,7,11,15] efficiently benefit the randomisation embedded in this learning tool, consequently providing good generalisation performance on new unseen samples.

RGB-D vs. Depth. Methods utilizing both RGB and depth channels demonstrate higher recall values than methods that are of using only depth, since RGB provides extra clues to ease the detection. This is depicted in Table 2a where learning- and template-based methods of RGB-D perform much better than point-to-point technique [13] of depth channel.

Table 3. Methods' performance are depicted object-wise based on F1 scores computed using the Average Distance (AD) evaluation protocol.

Method	ch.	ape	bvise	cam	can	cat	dril	duck	box	glue	hpunch	iron	lamp	phone	AVER
Kehl et al. [16]	RGB-D	0.98	0.95	0.93	0.83	0.98	0.97	0.98	1	0.74	0.98	0.91	0.98	0.85	0.93
LCHF [6]	RGB-D	0.86	0.96	0.72	0.71	0.89	0.91	0.91	0.74	0.68	0.88	0.74	0.92	0.73	0.82
Linemod [5]	RGB-D	0.53	0.85	0.64	0.51	0.66	0.69	0.58	0.86	0.44	0.52	0.68	0.68	0.56	0.63
Kehl et al. [18]	RGB	0.76	0.97	0.92	0.93	0.89	0.97	0.80	0.94	0.76	0.72	0.98	0.93	0.92	0.88

(a) LINEMOD dataset

Method	ch.	camera	cup	joystick	juice	milk	shampoo	AVER
Kehl et al. [16]	RGB-D	0.38	0.97	0.89	0.87	0.46	0.91	0.75
LCHF [6]	RGB-D	0.39	0.89	0.55	0.88	0.40	0.79	0.65
Drost et al. [13]	D	0.41	0.87	0.28	0.60	0.26	0.65	0.51
Linemod [5]	RGB-D	0.37	0.58	0.15	0.44	0.49	0.55	0.43
Kehl et al. [18]	RGB	0.74	0.98	0.99	0.92	0.78	0.89	0.88

(b) MULT-I dataset

Method	ch.	ape	can	cat	dril	duck	box	glue	hpunch	AVER
LCHF [6]	RGB-D	0.51	0.77	0.44	0.82	0.66	0.13	0.25	0.64	0.53
Linemod [5]	RGB-D	0.23	0.31	0.17	0.37	0.43	0.19	0.05	0.30	0.26
Brach et al. [15]	RGB	-	-	-	-	-	-	-	-	0.51
Kehl et al. [18]	RGB	-	-	-	-	-	-	-	-	0.38

(c) OCC dataset

Method	ch.	cup	juice	AVER
LCHF [6]	RGB-D	0.48	0.29	0.39
Doumanoglou et al. [11]	RGB-D	0.36	0.29	0.33
Linemod [5]	RGB-D	0.48	0.20	0.34

(d) BIN-P dataset

RGB-D vs. RGB (CNN Structures). More recent paradigm is to adopt CNNs to solve 6D object pose estimation problem taking RGB images as inputs [17,18]. Methods working in the RGB channel in Table 2 are based on CNN structure. According to the numbers presented in Table 2, RGB-based SSD-6D [43] and RGB-D-based LCHF achieve similar performance. These recall values show the promising performance of CNN architectures across random forest-based learning methods.

Robotic manipulators that pick and place the items from conveyors, shelves, pallets, *etc.*, need to know the pose of one item per RGB-D image, even though there might be multiple items in its workspace. Hence our recall-only analyses mainly target to solve the problems that could be encountered in such cases. Based upon the analyses currently made, one can make important implications, particularly from the point of the performances of the detectors. On the other hand, recall-based analyses are not enough to illustrate which dataset is more challenging than the others. This is especially true in crowded scenarios where multiple instances of target objects are severely occluded and cluttered.

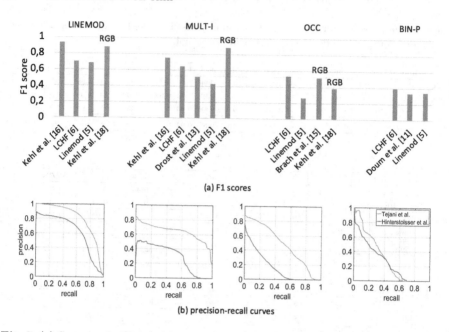

(a) F1 scores

(b) precision-recall curves

Fig. 3. (a) Success of each baseline on every dataset is shown, F1 scores are computed using the Average Distance (AD) metric. (b) Precision-recall curves of averaged F1 scores for Tejani et al. [6] and Hinterstoisser et al. [5] are shown: from left to right, LINEMOD, MULT-I, OCC, BIN-P.

Therefore, in the next part, we discuss the performances of the baselines from another aspect, regarding precision-recall curves and F1 scores, where the 6D detectors are investigated sorting all detection scores across all images.

Precision-Recall Discussions. Our precision-recall discussions are based on the F1 scores provided in Table 3, and Fig. 3(a).

We first analyse the performance of the methods [5,6,18,47] on the LINEMOD dataset. On the average, Kehl et al. [47] outperforms other methods proving the superiority of learning deep features. Despite estimating 6D in RGB images, SSD-6D [18] exhibits the advantages of using CNN structures for 6D object pose estimation. LCHF and Linemod demonstrate lower performance, since the features used by these methods are manually-crafted. The comparison between Figs. 2(a) and 3(a) reveals that the results produced by the methods have approximately the same characteristics on the LINEMOD dataset, with respect to recall and F1 scores.

The methods tested on the MULT-I dataset [5,6,13,47] utilize the geometry information inherently provided by depth images. Despite this fact, SSD-6D [18], estimating 6D pose only from RGB images, outperforms other methods clearly proving the superiority of using CNNs for the 6D problem over other structures.

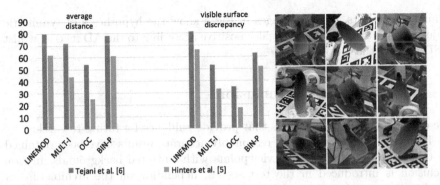

Fig. 4. Methods are evaluated based on Visible Surface Discrepancy. Samples on the right are considered as false positive with respect to Average Distance, whilst VSD deems correct.

LCHF [5] and Brachmann et al. [15] best perform on OCC with respect to F1 scores. As this dataset involves test images where highly occluded objects are located, the reported results depict the importance of designing part-based solutions.

The most important difference is observed on the BIN-P dataset. While the success rates of the detectors on this dataset are higher than 60% with respect to the recall values (see Fig. 2(a)), according to the presented F1 scores, their performance are less than 40%. When we take into account all hypotheses and the challenges particular to this dataset, which are severe occlusion and severe clutter, we observe strong degradation in the accuracy of the detectors.

In Fig. 3(b), we lastly report precision-recall curves of LCHF and Linemod. Regarding these curves, one can observe that as the datasets are getting more difficult, from the point of challenges involved, the methods produce less accurate results.

6.2 Analyses Based on Visible Surface Discrepancy

The analyses presented so far have been employed using the AD metric. We continue our discussions computing the recall values using the VSD metric, which is inherently proposed for tackling the pose-ambiguities arising from symmetry. We set δ, τ, and t, the thresholds defined in [46], to the values of 20 mm, 100 mm, and 0.5 respectively. Figure 4 shows the accuracy of each baseline on the LINEMOD, MULT-I, OCC, BIN-P datasets, respectively. Comparing the numbers in this chart, one can observe that the results from VSD are relatively lower than that are of the AD metric. This arises mainly from the chosen parameters. However, the characteristics of both charts are the same, that is, both methods, according to AD and VSD, perform best on the LINEMOD dataset, whilst worst on OCC. On the other hand, the main advantage of the proposed metric is that it features ambiguity-invariance: Since it is designed to evaluate the baselines over the visible parts of the objects, it gives more robust measurements across symmetric objects. Sample images in Fig. 4 show the hypotheses of symmetric objects which are considered as false positive according to the AD metric, whilst VSD accepts those as correct.

7 Discussions and Conclusions

We outline our key observations that provide guidance for future research.

From the challenges aspect, reasonably accurate results have been obtained on textured-objects at varying viewpoints with cluttered backgrounds. In case occlusion is introduced in the test scenes, depending on the architecture of the baseline, good performance demonstrated. Part-based solutions can handle the occlusion problem better than the ones global, using the information acquired from occlusion-free parts of the target objects. However, heavy existence of occlusion and clutter severely affects the detectors. It is possible that modelling occlusion during training can improve the performance of a detector across severe occlusion. But when occlusion is modelled, the baseline could be data-dependent. In order to maintain the generalization capability of the baseline contextual information can additionally be utilized during the modelling. Currently, similar looking distractors along with similar looking object classes seem the biggest challenge in recovering instances' 6D, since the lack of discriminative selection of shape features strongly confuse recognition systems. One possible solution could be considering the instances that have strong similarity in shape in a same category. In such a case, detectors trained using the data coming from the instances involved in the same category can report better detection results.

Architecture-wise, template-based methods, matching model features to the scene, and random forest based learning algorithms, along with their good generalization performance across unseen samples, underlie object detection and 6D pose estimation. Recent paradigm in the community is to learn deep discriminative feature representations. Despite the fact that several methods addressed 6D pose estimation utilizing deep features [11,16], end-to-end neural network-based solutions for 6D object pose recovery are still not widespread. Depending on the availability of large-scale 6D annotated depth datasets, feature representations can be learnt on these datasets, and then the learnt representations can be customized for the 6D problem.

These implications are related to automation in robotic systems. The implications can provide guidance for robotic manipulators that pick and place the items from conveyors, shelves, pallets, *etc.* Accurately detecting objects and estimating their fine pose under uncontrolled conditions improves the grasping capability of the manipulators. Beyond accuracy, the baselines are expected to show real-time performance. Although the detectors we have tested cannot perform real-time, their run-time can be improved by utilizing APIs like OpenMP.

References

1. Hoiem, D., Chodpathumwan, Y., Dai, Q.: Diagnosing error in object detectors. In: Fitzgibbon, A., Lazebnik, S., Perona, P., Sato, Y., Schmid, C. (eds.) ECCV 2012. LNCS, vol. 7574, pp. 340–353. Springer, Heidelberg (2012). https://doi.org/10.1007/978-3-642-33712-3_25
2. Russakovsky, O., Deng, J., Huang, Z., Berg, A.C., Fei-Fei, L.: Detecting avocados to zucchinis: what have we done, and where are we going? In: ICCV (2013)
3. Deng, J., Dong, W., Socher, R., Li, L.J., Li, K., Fei-Fei, L.: Imagenet: a large-scale hierarchical image database. In: CVPR (2009)
4. Everingham, M., Gool, L.V., Williams, C.K., Winn, J., Zisserman, A.: The pascal visual object classes (VOC) challenge. IJCV **88**, 303–338 (2010)
5. Hinterstoisser, S., et al.: Model based training, detection and pose estimation of texture-less 3D objects in heavily cluttered scenes. In: Lee, K.M., Matsushita, Y., Rehg, J.M., Hu, Z. (eds.) ACCV 2012. LNCS, vol. 7724, pp. 548–562. Springer, Heidelberg (2013). https://doi.org/10.1007/978-3-642-37331-2_42
6. Tejani, A., Tang, D., Kouskouridas, R., Kim, T.-K.: Latent-class hough forests for 3D object detection and pose estimation. In: Fleet, D., Pajdla, T., Schiele, B., Tuytelaars, T. (eds.) ECCV 2014. LNCS, vol. 8694, pp. 462–477. Springer, Cham (2014). https://doi.org/10.1007/978-3-319-10599-4_30
7. Brachmann, E., Krull, A., Michel, F., Gumhold, S., Shotton, J., Rother, C.: Learning 6D object pose estimation using 3D object coordinates. In: Fleet, D., Pajdla, T., Schiele, B., Tuytelaars, T. (eds.) ECCV 2014. LNCS, vol. 8690, pp. 536–551. Springer, Cham (2014). https://doi.org/10.1007/978-3-319-10605-2_35
8. Eppner, C., et al.: Lessons from the Amazon picking challenge: four aspects of building robotic systems. In: Proceedings of Robotics: Science and Systems (2016)
9. Jonschkowski, R., Eppner, C., Hofer, S., Martin-Martin, R., Brock, O.: Probabilistic multi-class segmentation for the Amazon picking challenge. In: IROS (2016)
10. Correll, N., et al.: Analysis and observations from the first Amazon picking challenge. IEEE Trans. Autom. Sci. Eng. **15**, 172–188 (2016)
11. Doumanoglou, A., Kouskouridas, R., Malassiotis, S., Kim, T.K.: Recovering 6D object pose and predicting next-best-view in the crowd. In: CVPR (2016)
12. Hodan, T., Haluza, P., Obdrzalek, S., Matas, J., Lourakis, M., Zabulis, X.: T-less: an RGB-D dataset for 6D pose estimation of texture-less objects. In: WACV (2017)
13. Drost, B., Ulrich, M., Navab, N., Ilic, S.: Model globally, match locally: efficient and robust 3D object recognition. In: CVPR (2010)
14. Hinterstoisser, S., Lepetit, V., Rajkumar, N., Konolige, K.: Going further with point pair features. In: Leibe, B., Matas, J., Sebe, N., Welling, M. (eds.) ECCV 2016. LNCS, vol. 9907, pp. 834–848. Springer, Cham (2016). https://doi.org/10.1007/978-3-319-46487-9_51
15. Brachmann, E., Michel, F., Krull, A., Yang, M., Gumhold, S., Rother, C.: Uncertainty-driven 6D pose estimation of objects and scenes from a single RGB image. In: CVPR (2016)
16. Kehl, W., Milletari, F., Tombari, F., Ilic, S., Navab, N.: Deep learning of local RGB-D patches for 3D object detection and 6D pose estimation. In: Leibe, B., Matas, J., Sebe, N., Welling, M. (eds.) ECCV 2016. LNCS, vol. 9907, pp. 205–220. Springer, Cham (2016). https://doi.org/10.1007/978-3-319-46487-9_13
17. Xiang, Y., Schmidt, T., Narayanan, V., Fox, D.: PoseCNN: a convolutional neural network for 6D object pose estimation in cluttered scenes. arxiv (2017)

18. Kehl, W., Manhardt, F., Tombari, F., Ilic, S., Navab, N.: SSD-6D: making RGB-based 3D detection and 6D pose estimation great again. In: CVPR (2017)
19. Felzenszwalb, P., Girshick, R., McAllester, D., Ramanan, D.: Object detection with discriminatively trained part-based models. In: TPAMI (2010)
20. Azizpour, H., Laptev, I.: Object detection using strongly-supervised deformable part models. In: Fitzgibbon, A., Lazebnik, S., Perona, P., Sato, Y., Schmid, C. (eds.) ECCV 2012. LNCS, vol. 7572, pp. 836–849. Springer, Heidelberg (2012). https://doi.org/10.1007/978-3-642-33718-5_60
21. Pepik, B., Stark, M., Gehler, P., Schiele, B.: Teaching 3D geometry to deformable part models. In: CVPR (2012)
22. Shrivastava, A., Gupta, A.: Building part-based object detectors via 3D geometry. In: ICCV (2013)
23. Donahue, J., et al.: DeCAF: a deep convolutional activation feature for generic visual recognition. ICML (2014)
24. Girshick, R., Donahue, J., Darrell, T., Malik, J.: Rich feature hierarchies for accurate object detection and semantic segmentation. In: CVPR (2014)
25. Sermanet, P., Eigen, D., Zhang, X., Mathieu, M., Fergus, R., LeCun, Y.: OverFeat: integrated recognition, localization and detection using convolutional networks. In: ICLR (2014)
26. He, K., Zhang, X., Ren, S., Sun, J.: Spatial pyramid pooling in deep convolutional networks for visual recognition. In: PAMI (2015)
27. Girshick, R.: Fast R-CNN. In: ICCV (2015)
28. Girshick, R., Iandola, F., Darrell, T., Malik, J.: Deformable part models are convolutional neural networks. In: CVPR (2015)
29. Divvala, S.K., Hoiem, D., Hays, J.H., Efros, A.A., Hebert, M.: An empirical study of context in object detection. In: CVPR (2009)
30. Torralba, A., Efros, A.A.: Unbiased look at dataset bias. In: CVPR (2011)
31. Everingham, M., Eslami, S.A., Gool, L.V., Williams, C.K., Winn, J., Zisserman, A.: The pascal visual object classes challenge: a retrospective. IJCV 111, 98–136 (2015)
32. Russakovsky, O., et al.: Imagenet large scale visual recognition challenge. IJCV 115, 211–252 (2015)
33. Rios-Cabrera, R., Tuytelaars, T.: Discriminatively trained templates for 3D object detection: a real time scalable approach. In: ICCV (2013)
34. Liu, M.Y., Tuzel, O., Veeraraghavan, A., Taguchi, Y., Marks, T.K., Chellappa, R.: Fast object localization and pose estimation in heavy clutter for robotic bin picking. IJRR 31, 951–973 (2012)
35. Sock, J., Kasaei, S.H., Lopes, L.S., Kim, T.K.: Multi-view 6D object pose estimation and camera motion planning using RGBD images. In: 3rd International Workshop on Recovering 6D Object Pose (2017)
36. Krull, A., Brachmann, E., Michel, F., Yang, M.Y., Gumhold, S., Rother, C.: Learning analysis-by-synthesis for 6D pose estimation in RGB-D images. In: ICCV (2015)
37. Bonde, U., Badrinarayanan, V., Cipolla, R.: Robust instance recognition in presence of occlusion and clutter. In: Fleet, D., Pajdla, T., Schiele, B., Tuytelaars, T. (eds.) ECCV 2014. LNCS, vol. 8690, pp. 520–535. Springer, Cham (2014). https://doi.org/10.1007/978-3-319-10605-2_34
38. Sahin, C., Kouskouridas, R., Kim, T.K.: Iterative hough forest with histogram of control points for 6 DoF object registration from depth images. In: IROS (2016)
39. Sahin, C., Kouskouridas, R., Kim, T.K.: A learning-based variable size part extraction architecture for 6D object pose recovery in depth images. Image Vis. Comput. (IVC) 63, 38–50 (2017)

40. Michel, F., et al.: Global hypothesis generation for 6D object pose estimation. In: CVPR (2017)
41. Wohlhart, P., Lepetit, V.: Learning descriptors for object recognition and 3D pose estimation. In: CVPR (2015)
42. Balntas, V., Doumanoglou, A., Sahin, C., Sock, J., Kouskouridas, R., Kim, T.K.: Pose guided RGBD feature learning for 3D object pose estimation. In: ICCV (2017)
43. Rad, M., Lepetit, V.: BB8: a scalable, accurate, robust to partial occlusion method for predicting the 3D poses of challenging objects without using depth. In: ICCV (2017)
44. Tekin, B., Sinha, S.N., Fua, P.: Real-time seamless single shot 6D object pose prediction. arxiv (2017)
45. Shotton, J., Glocker, B., Zach, C., Izadi, S., Criminisi, A., Fitzgibbon, A.: Scene coordinate regression forests for camera relocalization in RGB-D images. In: CVPR (2013)
46. Hodaň, T., Matas, J., Obdržálek, Š.: On evaluation of 6D object pose estimation. In: Hua, G., Jégou, H. (eds.) ECCV 2016. LNCS, vol. 9915, pp. 606–619. Springer, Cham (2016). https://doi.org/10.1007/978-3-319-49409-8_52
47. Kehl, W., Tombari, F., Navab, N., Ilic, S., Lepetit, V.: Hashmod: a hashing method for scalable 3D object detection. In: BMVC (2015)

Computer Vision for Medical Infant Motion Analysis: State of the Art and RGB-D Data Set

Nikolas Hesse[1]([✉]) [iD], Christoph Bodensteiner[1], Michael Arens[1] [iD],
Ulrich G. Hofmann[2] [iD], Raphael Weinberger[3], and A. Sebastian Schroeder[3]

[1] Fraunhofer Institute of Optronics, System Technologies and Image Exploitation
IOSB, Ettlingen, Germany
nikolas.hesse@iosb.fraunhofer.de
[2] University Medical Center Freiburg, Faculty of Medicine, University of Freiburg,
Freiburg im Breisgau, Germany
[3] Ludwig Maximilian University, Hauner Children's Hospital, Munich, Germany

Abstract. Assessment of spontaneous movements of infants lets trained experts predict neurodevelopmental disorders like cerebral palsy at a very young age, allowing early intervention for affected infants. An automated motion analysis system requires to accurately capture body movements, ideally without markers or attached sensors to not affect the movements of infants. A vast majority of recent approaches for human pose estimation focuses on adults, leading to a degradation of accuracy if applied to infants. Hence, multiple systems for *infant* pose estimation have been developed. Due to the lack of publicly available benchmark data sets, a standardized evaluation, let alone a comparison of different approaches is impossible. We fill this gap by releasing the Moving INfants In RGB-D (MINI-RGBD) (Data set available for research purposes at http://s.fhg. de/mini-rgbd) data set, created using the recently introduced *Skinned Multi-Infant Linear* body model (SMIL). We map real infant movements to the SMIL model with realistic shapes and textures, and generate RGB and depth images with precise ground truth 2D and 3D joint positions. We evaluate our data set with state-of-the-art methods for 2D pose estimation in RGB images and for 3D pose estimation in depth images. Evaluation of 2D pose estimation results in a PCKh rate of 88.1% and 94.5% (depending on correctness threshold), and PCKh rates of 64.2%, respectively 90.4% for 3D pose estimation. We hope to foster research in medical infant motion analysis to get closer to an automated system for early detection of neurodevelopmental disorders.

Keywords: Motion analysis · Infants · Pose estimation · RGB-D
Data set · Cerebral palsy

1 Introduction

Advances in computer vision and the widespread availability of low-cost RGB-D sensors have paved the way for novel applications in medicine [28], e.g.

© Springer Nature Switzerland AG 2019
L. Leal-Taixé and S. Roth (Eds.): ECCV 2018 Workshops, LNCS 11134, pp. 32–49, 2019.
https://doi.org/10.1007/978-3-030-11024-6_3

Alzheimer's disease assessment [17], quantification of multiple sclerosis progression [22], as well as gait [43] or motion analysis [8]. For the latter, accurately capturing human movements is the fundamental step. Human pose estimation from RGB or depth images, especially using convolutional neural networks (CNNs), currently receives a lot of attention from the research community [5, 12, 44, 45]. However, research is largely focused on adults. The ability to accurately capture *infant* movements is fundamental for an automated assessment of motor development.

In his pioneering work, Prechtl found that the quality of spontaneous movements of infants is a good marker for detecting impairments of the young nervous system [33]. This discovery led to the development of the General Movements Assessment (GMA) [11, 32, 33] which allows detection of neurodevelopmental disorders at a very young age. An automated system, relying on data captured by cheap RGB or RGB-D cameras could enable the widespread screening of all infants at risk of motion disorders. This would allow early intervention for affected children, which is assumed to improve outcome [41].

The application of state-of-the-art adult pose estimation systems to *children* was recently studied [36]. Authors found that children are underrepresented in most widely used benchmark data sets. Their analysis revealed that pose estimation accuracy decreases when approaches that were trained on adult data are applied to children. To mitigate this problem, they create a data set that was collected from internet videos, comprising 1176 images of 104 different children in unconstrained settings. For the evaluation of pose estimation approaches, they manually annotate 2D joint positions of 22 body keypoints.

Why does no *infant* data set exist? As mentioned above, computer vision research is primarily focused on adults. Reasons might include the higher number of potential applications for adults, with infant motion analysis being more of a niche application. Furthermore, it is not easy to generate reliable ground truth for infants. Manual annotation, especially in 3D, is error prone and cumbersome. Capturing ground truth with standard motion capture systems using markers may affect the infants' behavior, while suffering from problems with occlusions [27]. Researchers have used robotics to generate ground truth data [25, 37], but reproducing the complexity of real infant movements is not possible with justifiable efforts. Other than that, laws are more strict concerning the privacy of children, since infants can not decide whether or not they want their image to be published. This makes the creation of a data set containing real infant images more challenging.

We fill this gap by creating an RGB-D data set for the evaluation of motion capture systems for infant motion analysis using the recently introduced *Skinned Multi-Infant Linear* model (SMIL) [14]. Our *Moving INfants In RGB-D* (MINI-RGBD) data set contains realistic motion, realistic appearance, realistic shapes, and precise 2D and 3D ground truth, and covers a wide range of challenging motions. To preserve the privacy of infants, we generate new textures and shapes by averaging multiple textures and shapes of real infants. These are still highly realistic, yet do not show any existing infant. We map real infant movements to these new "synthetic infants" and render RGB and depth images to simulate standard commodity RGB-D sensors. Our data set (described in Sect. 3), differs from the data set of [36] in multiple ways: (i) it contains infants up to the age of 7 months, (ii) we consider constrained settings for medical motion analysis, i.e. infants lie in supine position, facing the camera, (iii) we provide sequences of continuous motions instead of single frames, (v) we render data from a realistic 3D infant body model instead of annotating real images, (iv) we generate RGB and depth images, and (vi) we provide accurate 2D and 3D ground truth joint positions that are directly regressed from the model.

In the following, we review the state of the art in infant motion analysis and analyze evaluation procedures (Sect. 2). We describe the creation of our data set in Sect. 3, and present pose estimation baseline evaluations for RGB and RGB-D data in Sect. 4.

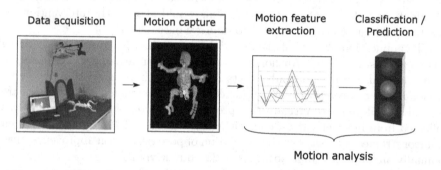

Fig. 1. Standard motion analysis pipeline. After data is acquired, motions are captured. Motion features are extracted and used to classify or predict the medical outcome. In this work, we focus on motion capture from RGB or depth images.

2   Medical Infant Motion Analysis - State of the Art

We review systems aiming at the automated prediction of cerebral palsy (CP) based on the assessment of motions. Although this problem is approached in different ways, the pipeline is similar for most systems, and can be divided into motion capture and motion analysis (Fig. 1). Motion features are extracted from captured movements, and used for training a classifier to predict the outcome. The reviewed systems report high sensitivity and specificity for CP prediction, mostly on study populations containing a small number of infants with confirmed CP diagnosis. Yet, the majority of approaches shows a considerable lack of evaluation of motion capture methods. The majority of approaches only scarcely evaluates the accuracy of motion capture methods. We believe that the second step should not be taken before the first one, i.e. each system should first demonstrate that it is capable of accurately capturing movements before predicting outcome based on these captured movements. Of course, the non-existence of a public benchmark data set makes it hard to conduct an extensive evaluation of motion capture accuracy.

In this section, we present an overview of methods used for infant motion capture and how these are evaluated. The reader is referred to [26] for an extensive overview of the motion analysis stage of different approaches.

2.1 Wearable Motion Sensors

Although a recent study shows that wearable sensors do not seem to affect the leg movement frequency [18], they supposedly have a negative influence on the infant's content. Karch et al. report that recordings for two thirds of participating infants had to be stopped after re-positioning the attached sensors due to crying (and technical difficulties) [20]. Furthermore, approaches relying on attached sensors generally suffer from practical limitations like time consuming human intervention for setup and calibration, and add the risk of affecting the movements of infants. Proposed systems using wearable sensors use wired [13] and wireless accelerometers [9,10,40], electromagnetical sensors [20,21], or a pressure mattress in combination with Inertial Measurement Units (IMU) [35]. In the following, we focus on vision-based approaches, and refer the reader to [7] for an overview of monitoring infant movements using wearable sensors.

2.2 Computer Vision for Capturing Movements

Cameras, opposed to motion sensors, are cheap, easy to use, require no setup or calibration, and can be easily integrated into standard examinations while not influencing infants' movements. This makes them more suitable for use in clinical environments, doctor's offices or even at home. Other than sensor-based approaches, vision-based approaches do not measure motions directly. More or less sophisticated methods are needed to extract motion information, e.g. by estimating the pose in every image of a video. We describe the methods used in the current state-of-the-art in infant motion analysis, as well as the evaluation protocols for these methods. Our findings further support the need for a standardized, realistic, and challenging benchmark data set.

Video-Based Approaches. We review approaches that process RGB (or infrared) images for the capture of infant motion. We include methods relying on attached markers, despite posing some of the same challenges as wearable sensors. They require human intervention for marker attachment, calibration procedures and most of all possibly affect the infants' behavior or content. Still, they use computer vision for tracking the pose of the infants.

One of the first approaches towards automated CP prediction was introduced in 2006 by Meinecke et al. [27]. A commercial Vicon system uses 7 infrared cameras to track 20 markers, distributed across the infant's body. After an initial calibration procedure, the known marker positions on a biomechanical model are used to calculate the rotation of head and trunk, as well as the 3D positions of upper arms, forearms, thighs, lower legs, and feet from the tracked markers on the infant. The system is highly accurate, authors report errors of

2 mm for a measurement volume of $2\,m^3$. However, the system suffers from certain limitations. Due to the unconstrained movements of the infants close to the underground, especially the markers of the upper extremities were occluded and therefore invisible to the cameras half of the measurement time. Attaching additional markers exceeded the system's capabilities and therefore, authors refrained from using motion features of upper extremities for CP prediction. The high cost of the system, the complex setup and calibration, and the occlusion problems stand against the highly accurate tracking of joints in 3D.

Kanemaru et al. use a commercial marker tracking system (Frame-DIAS) to record 2D positions of markers on arms, shoulders, hips and legs at 30 Hz using a single camera [19]. They normalize the marker displacement data using the body size of the infant and smooth the resulting 2D position data. The accuracy of the capture system is not reported.

Machireddy et al. [25] present a hybrid system that combines color-based marker tracking in video with IMU measurements. The different sensor types are intended to compensate for each others limitations. The IMU sensors are attached to the infant's hands, legs, and chest, together with colored patches. The 2D positions of patches are tracked based on color thresholds. From the known patch size and the camera calibration, an estimate for the 3D position of each patch is calculated. The IMUs are synchronized with the camera, and the output of all sensors is fused using an extended Kalman filter. Ground truth for evaluation is generated by rotating a plywood model of a human arm using a drill, equipped with one marker and one IMU. Authors present plots of ground truth positions and estimated positions for a circular and a spiral motion. Exact numbers on accuracy are not presented.

Adde et al. take a more holistic approach [1]. Instead of tracking individual limbs, they calculate the difference image between two consecutive frames to generate what they call a motion image. They calculate the centroid of motion, which is the center of the pixel positions forming the motion regions in the motion image. Furthermore, they construct a motiongram by compressing all motion images of a sequence either horizontally or vertically by summing over columns, respectively rows, and stacking them to give a compact impression on how much an infant moved, and where the movements happened. The accuracy of the system is not evaluated.

Stahl et al. use a motion tracking method based on optical flow between consecutive RGB frames [42]. They initialize points on a regular grid, distributed across the image, and track them over time. They evaluate the approach by manually selecting five points to be tracked from the grid as head, hands, and feet, and manually correct tracking errors. They display the result of their evaluation in one plot over 160 frames. Numbers on average accuracy are not given.

Rahmati et al. present an approach for motion segmentation using weak supervision [34]. Initialized by manual labeling, they track the body segmentation trajectories using optical flow fields. In case a trajectory ends due to fast motion or occlusion, they apply a particle matching algorithm for connecting a newly started trajectory for the same body segment. They evaluate the accuracy

Table 1. Summary of motion capture methods and corresponding evaluation of depth-based approaches for medical infant motion analysis. SD denotes standard deviation.

First author, year, reference	Method // tracked limbs	Ground truth (GT) generation // Reported avg. accuracy
Olsen 2014 [30]	Geodesic distances // 11 3D joint positions	Manual annotation (number of frames not specified) // 9 cm (extracted from plot)
Olsen 2014 [29]	Model-based tracking // 11 3D joint positions	Manual annotation (number of frames not specified) // 5 cm (SD: 3 cm) (extracted from plot)
Hesse 2015 [16]	Random ferns body part classifier // 21 3D joint positions	Manual annotation of 1082 frames // 4.1 cm
Hesse 2017 [15]	Random ferns (extension of [16]) // 21 3D joint positions	3D model fitting (+ visual verification), 5500 frames (3 seq.) // 1.2 cm (SD: 0.9 cm)
Hesse 2018 [14]	Model-based tracking // full body pose and shape	No GT, evaluation on 37 seq. (200K frames, $\sim$2 h), pose errors determined from visual examination // average scan to model distance 2.51 mm, 34 pose errors lasting 90 s ($\approx$1.2%)
Serrano 2016 [37]	Model based tracking // angles of hip, knee, and ankle	Robot leg kicking, angle comparison for knee and ankle, 250 frames // 2–2.5° error
Cenci 2017 [6]	Movement blobs // arms and legs	No evaluation
Shivakumar 2017 [38]	Optical flow + color-based segmentation // 3D positions of head, torso, hands, feet	Manual annotation of 60 frames // 8.21 cm, SD: 8.75 cm

on 20 manually annotated frames from 10 infant sequences, reporting an F-measure of 96% by calculating the overlap between ground truth and estimated segmentation. They compare their tracking method to different state-of-the-art trackers on the same data set, with their tracker showing superior results. Furthermore, they evaluate their segmentation method on the Freiburg-Berkeley data set containing moving objects (e.g. cats and ducks) and compare results to an optical flow method. Their method achieves best results, at an F-measure of 77%.

Depth-Based Approaches. With the introduction of low-cost RGB-D sensors, motion analysis approaches started taking advantage of depth information. The most well-known RGB-D camera is probably the Microsoft Kinect, which was introduced as a gesture control device for the gaming console XBox, but soon became widely used in research due to its affordable price. The motion tracking provided by the Kinect SDK has been used for motion analysis purposes, but does not work for infants as it was purposed for gaming scenarios of standing humans taller than one meter. We review approaches that aim at estimating infants' poses from RGB-D data and turn our attention to the respective evaluation procedures. An overview of examined approaches is given in Table 1.

Olsen et al. transfer an existing pose estimation approach to infants [30]. The underlying assumption is that extremities have maximum geodesic distance to the body center. The body center is localized by filtering the infant's clothing color, based on a fixed threshold. They locate five anatomical extremities by finding points on the body farthest from the body center. Assuming a known body orientation, each of these points is assigned to one of the classes head, left/right hand, left/right foot, based on the spatial location and the orientation of the path to body center. Intermediate body parts like elbows, knees and chest are calculated based on fractional distances on the shortest path from body center to extremities, resulting in 3D positions of eleven joints. For evaluation, they annotate 3D joint positions on an unspecified number of frames. Annotated joints lie in the interior of the body, while the estimated joints lie on the body surface. Results are presented in a plot, numbers given here are read off this plot. The average joint position error is roughly 9 cm. Highest errors occur for hands and elbows (15 cm), lowest for body center, chest, and head (3 cm).

In subsequent work, the same authors use a model-based approach for tracking eleven 3D joint positions [29]. They construct a human body model from simplistic shapes (cylinders, sphere, ellipsoid). After determining size parameters of the body parts, their previous method [30] is used for finding an initial pose. They fit the body model to the segmented infant point clouds that are computed from depth images. They optimize an objective function, defined by the difference of closest points from point cloud and model, with respect to the model pose parameters using the Levenberg-Marquardt algorithm. As in previous work, they evaluate the accuracy of their system on manually annotated 3D joint positions of an unspecified number of frames. The results are compared to their previous approach. Numbers are extracted from presented plots. The model-based system achieves an average joint position error of 5 cm (standard deviation (SD) 3 cm). Largest errors occur for right hand (7 cm) and stomach (6 cm).

Inspired by the approach used in the Kinect SDK, Hesse et al. propose a system for the estimation of 21 joint positions using a random ferns body part classifier [16]. A synthetic infant body model is used for rendering a large number of labeled depth images, from which a pixel-wise body part classifier based on binary depth comparison features is trained. 3D joint positions are calculated as the mean of all pixels belonging to each estimated body part. The system is trained on synthetic adult data and evaluated on the PDT benchmark data set containing adults. An average joint positions error of 13 cm is reported, compared to 9.6 cm for the Kinect SDK. The authors manually annotated 3D joint positions of an infant sequence consisting of 1082 frames. They report an average joint position error of 4.1 cm, with left hand (14.9 cm) and left shoulder (7.3 cm) showing the largest errors. They explain the errors with wrongly classified body parts for poses that were not included in the training set.

The approach is extended in [15] by including a feature selection step, generating more infant-like poses for training data, integrating kinematic chain constraints, and by applying PCA on torso pixels to correct for body rotations. Ground truth joint positions are generated for 5500 frames of 3 sequences by fitting a body model and visually verifying the accuracy of the results. The best average error of the proposed methods is reported as 1.2 cm (SD 0.9 cm), compared to 1.8 cm (SD 3.1 cm) of the initial approach [16]. Additionally, a more strict evaluation metric, the worst-case accuracy, is applied. It denotes the percentage of frames for which all joint errors are smaller than a given threshold. For a threshold of 5 cm, 90% of frames are correct for [15], and 55% for [16], a threshold of 3 cm decreases the accuracy to 50%, and less than 30%, respectively.

In recent work, Hesse et al. propose a model-based approach for estimating pose and shape of infants [14]. They learn an infant body model from RGB-D recordings and present an algorithm for fitting the model to the data. They optimize an objective function, consisting of scan to model distance, similar to [29], but add more terms, e.g. integrating prior probabilities of plausible shapes and poses. The average distance of scan points to model surface for 200K frames of 37 infant sequences (roughly 2 h) is 2.51 mm (SD 0.21 mm). From manual inspection of all sequences, they report 18 failure cases in 7 sequences and 16 unnatural foot rotations lasting altogether 90 s, which corresponds to 1.2% of overall duration.

Serrano et al. track lower extremities using a leg model [37]. The approach is semi-automatic and requires some manual intervention. The infant's belly is manually located from the point cloud and the tracker's view is restricted to one leg. After the length and width of each segment of the leg model are defined, the model parameters (angles) are optimized using robust point set registration. They generate ground truth for 250 frames using a robotic leg that simulates kicking movements of infants. The average angle error of the proposed method is reported with 2.5° for the knee and 2° for the ankle.

In [6], Cenci et al. use the difference image between two frames with a defined delay in between. After noise filtering, the difference image is segmented into motion blobs using a threshold. K-means clustering assigns each of the movement blobs to one of four different body parts (arms and legs). A state vector is generated for each frame, which contains information on which limb moves/does not move in this frame. There is no evaluation of the correctness of assigning blobs to limb classes.

Opposed to previous approaches, which rely on readily available depth sensors, Shivakumar et al. introduce a stereo camera system, providing higher depth resolution than existing sensors [38]. After initially locating the body center based on a color threshold, an ellipse is fitted to the colored region and tracked. In addition to the torso center, hands, legs and head regions are selected by the user, which are then tracked based on their color. The positions of limbs are defined as the pixel in the corresponding limb region that is farthest from the body center. In case of overlap of multiple limb regions, a recovery step distinguishes them. An optical flow method is used for estimating the motion of the limb positions in the successive frame. An evaluation is presented on 60 manually annotated frames from three sequences, showing an average error of 8.21 cm (SD: 8.75 cm) over all limbs.

To summarize the evaluation protocols of reviewed approaches, comparison to previous work was limited to works of the same authors. Ground truth was mostly, if at all, generated by manual annotation of a small number of frames or by relying on robotics. This emphasizes the need for an infant benchmark RGB-D data set.

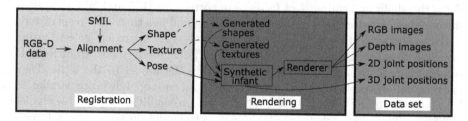

Fig. 2. Overview of data set creation pipeline. SMIL body model [14] is aligned to real infant RGB-D data. Subsets of shapes and textures are used for generating realistic, privacy preserving infant bodies. We animate the new "synthetic infants" with real movements (poses) from the registration stage. We render RGB and depth images, and create ground truth 2D and 3D joint positions to complete our new data set.

3   Moving INfants in RGB-D Data Set (MINI-RGBD)

An RGB-D data set for the evaluation of infant pose estimation approaches needs to fulfill several requirements. It has to cover (i) realistic infant movements, (ii) realistic texture, (iii) realistic shapes, and (iv) precise ground truth, while (v) not violating privacy. Our presented data set fulfills all of these requirements.

The data set creation procedure can be divided into two stages, registration and rendering (see Fig. 2). Two samples of rendered images and joint positions are displayed in Fig. 3.

3.1   Registration

The capturing of shape and pose is achieved by registering SMIL to 12 RGB-D sequences of moving infants that were recorded in a children's hospital. Written informed consent was given by parents and ethics approval was obtained from Ludwig Maximilian University Munich. SMIL is based on SMPL [23], and shares the same properties. The model can be regarded as a parametric mapping, with pose and shape parameters serving as input, and output being a triangulated mesh of the shaped and posed infant, consisting of 6890 vertices. The model contains 23 body joints, each of which has three degrees of freedom (DOF). Together with 3 DOF for the global orientation this gives 72 pose parameters.

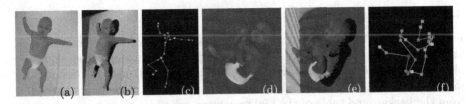

Fig. 3. Two samples from MINI-RGBD data set. (a) and (d): RGB image. (b) and (e): point cloud created from depth image. (c) and (f): ground truth skeleton. Viewpoint for (b), (c), (e), and (f) is slightly rotated to side. Best viewed in color. (Color figure online)

We follow the protocol of [14] to register the SMIL model to point clouds created from RGB-D sequences (which we will also call "scans"). We briefly recap the method and refer the reader to [14] for additional details.

To register the model to a scan, an objective function is optimized w.r.t. pose and shape parameters of SMIL. The function consists of the following terms: (i) distance between scan points and model mesh surface, (ii) a landmark error terms that penalizes distances between model landmarks projected to 2D and 2D body, face, and hand landmark estimates from RGB images using OpenPose library [5,31,39,44], (iii) a temporal pose smoothness term, (iv) a penalty for self intersections, (v) a term for keeping the back-facing model vertices close to, but not inside the background table, and (vi) prior probabilities on plausible shapes and poses. This results in a posed and shaped model mesh that describes the input point cloud data. The initialization frame is automatically selected based on 2D pose estimates. For the rest of the sequence, the resulting parameters of the last processed frame are used as initialization for the subsequent frame.

Going beyond the methods of [14], we generate one texture for each sequence, similar to [3,4]. We create a texture map by finding closest points from textured point cloud and registered model mesh, as well as a corresponding normal map for each frame. We merge 300 randomly selected texture maps from each sequence by averaging texture maps that are weighted according to their normal maps, with higher weights for points with normals directed towards the camera. Infants tend to lie on their backs without turning, which is why the merged texture maps have blank areas depending on the amount of movement in the sequence. We fill the missing areas by expanding the borders of existing body areas. To preserve the privacy of the infants we do not use textures from single sequences, but generate average textures from subsets of all textures. The resulting texture maps (sample displayed in Fig. 4(a)) are manually post-processed by smoothing borders and visually enhancing areas of the texture for which the filling did not create satisfying results. We create a variety of realistic body shapes by averaging different subsets of shapes from the registration stage (Fig. 4(b)).

3.2 Rendering

For each of the 12 sequences, we randomly select one of the average shapes and one of the average textures. We map the pose parameters of the sequence, obtained in the registration stage, to the new shape, and animate textured 3D meshes of realistic, yet artificial infants. Based on plane parameters extracted from the background table of the real sequences, we add a plane to simulate the background. We texture the plane with one of various background images (e.g. examination table, crib, changing table) to account for background variation. We use OpenDR [24] to render RGB and depth images from the meshes and backgrounds. We select 1000 consecutive frames from each sequence where the infant is the most active. The rendered depth image is overly smooth, which is why we add random noise of up to ±0.5 cm to simulate noise levels of depth sensors. We use camera parameters similar to Microsoft Kinect V1, which is the most frequently used sensor in approaches in Sect. 2, at a resolution of 640 * 480, at 30 frames per second. The distance of the table to the camera is roughly 90 cm for all sequences. The 3D joint positions are directly regressed from the model vertices (see Fig. 3(c) and (f)). To provide 2D ground truth, we project the 3D joints to 2D using the camera calibration. For completeness, we add depth values for each joint. To simplify data set usage, we provide a segmentation mask discriminating between foreground and background.

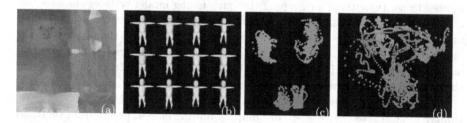

Fig. 4. (a) Sample of generated texture. (b) Generated shapes in T-pose. (c) Plotted joint positions from an "easy" sequence. Hand positions shown in light and dark green. Foot positions in red and blue. (d) Hand and foot positions for a "difficult" sequence. Color coding as in (c). Best viewed in color. (Color figure online)

3.3 MINI-RGBD Data Set Summary

We generate 12 sequences, each with different shape, texture, movements, and background, and provide 2D and 3D ground truth joint positions, as well as foreground segmentation masks. Movements are chosen to be representative of infants in the first half year of life, and we divide the sequences into different levels of difficulty (see Fig. 4(c) and (d) for examples): (i) easy: lying on back, moving arms and legs, mostly besides body, without crossing (sequences 1–4), (ii) medium: slight turning, limbs interact and are moved in front of the body, legs cross (sequences 5–9), and (iii) difficult: turning to sides, grabbing legs, touching face, directing all limbs towards camera simultaneously (sequences 10–12).

Different approaches utilize different skeletons. To properly compare these approaches, we add one frame in T-pose (extended arms and legs, cf. Fig. 4(b)) for each sequence to calculate initial offsets between estimation and ground truth that can be used to correct for skeleton offsets.

The limitations of the underlying SMIL model include finger motions, facial expressions and hair. These are not represented by the model, which is why the hand is fixed as a fist, and the face has a neutral expression.

4   Evaluation

We provide baseline evaluations using state-of-the-art approaches for the RGB, as well as the RGB-D part of our MINI-RGBD data set.

4.1   2D Pose Estimation in RGB Images

We use a state-of-the-art adult RGB pose estimation system from OpenPose library [5,31] as baseline for evaluation of the RGB part of the data set. To account for differences in skeletons between OpenPose and SMIL, we calculate joint offsets for neck, shoulders, hips, and knees from the T-pose frame (Sect. 3.3), and add these offsets to the estimated joint positions in every frame.

Error Metrics. We apply the PCKh error metric from [2], which is commonly used for the evaluation of pose estimation approaches [5,12,36,44]. It denotes the percentage of correct keypoints with the threshold for correctness being defined as 50% of the head segment length. The SMIL model has a very short head segment (head joint to neck joint, cf. Fig. 3(c) and (f)), which is why we present results using the full head segment length (PCKh 1.0), as well as two times the head segment length (PCKh 2.0) as thresholds. The head segment length for each sequence is calculated from the ground truth joint positions in the T-pose frame. Average 2D head segment length over all sequences is 11.6 pixels. We calculate the PCKh values for each joint for each sequence, and average numbers over all sequences, respectively over all joints.

OpenPose estimates 15 joint positions (nose, neck, shoulders, elbow, hands, hips, knees, feet) that we map to corresponding SMIL joints. Unlike SMIL, Open-Pose estimates the nose position instead of head position. We add the model vertex of the tip of the nose as additional joint instead of using SMIL head joint.

Results. We display average PCKh per joint in Fig. 5(a), and average PCKh per sequence in Fig. 5(b). The mean average precision, i.e. the average PCKh over all joints and sequences, for PCKh 1.0 is 88.1% and 94.5% for PCKh 2.0. PCKh rates are very consistent over most body parts, with a slight decrease of PCKh 1.0 for lower limb joints, especially knees. Results for some body joints (e.g. nose, neck, shoulders, Fig. 5(a)) as well as for some sequences (1, 2, 3, 6, 7, 11, Fig. 5(b)) are close to perfect (according to the error metric). We observe largest errors when the limbs are directed towards the camera.

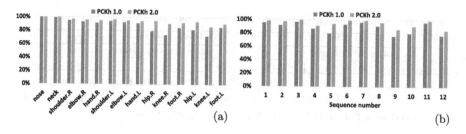

(a)   (b)

Fig. 5. RGB evaluation. Results for 2D pose estimation from OpenPose library. (a) Percentage of correct keypoints in relation to head segment length (PCKh) per joint. *PCKh 1.0* denotes a correctness threshold of one time head segment length, *PCKh 2.0* of twice the head segment length. (b) PCKh per sequence.

OpenPose has reportedly shown impressive results on unconstrained scenes containing adults [5], and confirms these on our synthetic infant data set. Being trained on real images of unconstrained scenes, the results further validate the high level of realism of our data set, but also show how challenging the data is, and that there is still room for improvement (e.g. sequences 9, 10, 12).

4.2   3D Pose Estimation in Depth Images

We evaluate the system with the lowest reported average joint position error for RGB-D data from our overview (Table 1), the extension of the pixelwise body part classifier based on random ferns [15,16]. For each pixel of an input depth image, the label is predicted as one of 21 body parts (spine, chest, neck, head, shoulders, elbows, hands, fingers, hips, knees, feet, and toes). The 3D joint positions are then calculated as the mean of each body part region. RGB is not used in this approach. Similar to Sect. 4.1, we calculate joint offsets in the T-pose frame and add them to the estimated joint positions throughout each sequence.

Error Metrics. We use the PCKh error metric as described above, here in 3D. Average 3D head segment length over all sequences is 2.64 cm. Additionally, we evaluate the average joint position error (AJPE), which denotes the euclidean distance from estimated joint position to corresponding ground truth.

Results. We present results in Fig. 6. Mean average precision, i.e. average PCKh over all joints and sequences, for PCKh 1.0 is 64.2%, and 90.4% for PCKh 2.0. Compared to the RGB evaluation, we experience a bigger difference between PCKh 1.0 and PCKh 2.0. Very high PCKh 2.0 rates are achieved for torso and head body parts, while lowest rates are obtained for joints related to extremities (Fig. 6(a)). PCKh 1.0 rates differ a lot from PCKh 2.0 for elbows, hands, and feet. We observe that the estimated hand and foot regions are too large, leading to the hand joints lying more in the direction of the elbow, respectively the foot joints in direction of the knees. With an expansion of the threshold for correctness (PCKh 2.0) these displacements are accepted as correct, leading to large jumps from around 30% (PCKh 1.0) to 70–80% (PCKh 2.0).

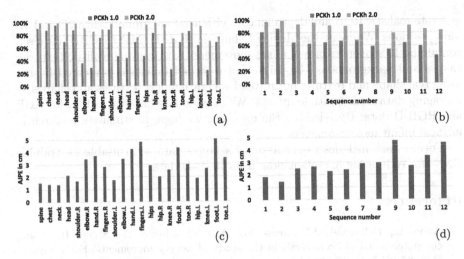

Fig. 6. RGB-D evaluation. Results for 3D pose estimation based on random ferns [15,16]. (a) Percentage of correct keypoints in relation to head segment length (PCKh) per joint. *PCKh 1.0* denotes a correctness threshold of one time head segment length, *PCKh 2.0* of twice the head segment length. (b) PCKh per sequence. (c) Average joint position error (AJPE) per joint. (d) AJPE per sequence.

The average joint position error (AJPE) over all sequences and joints is 2.86 cm. Joint position errors are largest for the extremities, at an average distance to ground truth of up to 5 cm (Fig. 6(c)). If the estimate for a joint was missing in a frame, we ignored this joint for the calculation of AJPE, i.e. we only divided the sum of joint errors by the number of actually estimated joints. The number of frames with missing estimates, denoted by joint (in 12K frames, average for left and right sides): neck 37, elbows 12, hands 62, fingers 156, feet 79, toes 607, all others 0. For the calculation of PCKh metric, missing joints were considered as lying outside the correctness threshold.

The evaluated approach shows high accuracy when arms and legs are moving beside the body, but the accuracy decreases, especially for hands and feet, when limbs move close to or in front of the body. This becomes extremely visible in sequence 9, where the infant moves the left arm to the right side of the body multiple times, leading to the highest overall AJPE of 4.7 cm (Fig. 6(d)). Best AJPE results are achieved for sequence 2, at 1.46 cm, which is close to results reported in [15]. The varying accuracy for different sequences shows the levels of difficulty and the variance of motion patterns included in the data set.

5 Conclusions

We presented an overview of the state-of-the-art in medical infant motion analysis, with a focus on vision-based approaches and their evaluation. We observed non-standardized evaluation procedures, which we trace back to the lack of publicly available infant data sets. The recently introduced SMIL model allows us to generate realistic RGB and depth images with accurate ground truth 2D and 3D joint positions. We create the Moving INfants In RGB-D (MINI-RGBD) data set, containing 12 sequences of real infant movements with varying realistic textures, shapes and backgrounds. The privacy of recorded infants is preserved by not using real shape and texture, but instead generating new textures and shapes by averaging data from multiple infants. We provide baseline evaluations for RGB and RGB-D data. By releasing the data set, we hope to stimulate research in medical infant motion analysis.

Future work includes the creation of a larger data set, suitable for training CNNs for estimating 3D infant pose from RGB-D data.

References

1. Adde, L., Helbostad, J.L., Jensenius, A.R., Taraldsen, G., Støen, R.: Using computer-based video analysis in the study of fidgety movements. Early Human Dev. **85**(9), 541–547 (2009)
2. Andriluka, M., Pishchulin, L., Gehler, P., Schiele, B.: 2D human pose estimation: new benchmark and state of the art analysis. In: IEEE Conference on Computer Vision and Pattern Recognition (CVPR), pp. 3686–3693 (2014)
3. Bogo, F., Black, M.J., Loper, M., Romero, J.: Detailed full-body reconstructions of moving people from monocular RGB-D sequences. In: 2015 IEEE International Conference on Computer Vision (ICCV) (2015)
4. Bogo, F., Romero, J., Loper, M., Black, M.J.: FAUST: dataset and evaluation for 3D mesh registration. In: 2014 IEEE Conference on Computer Vision and Pattern Recognition (CVPR) (2014)
5. Cao, Z., Simon, T., Wei, S.E., Sheikh, Y.: Realtime multi-person 2D pose estimation using part affinity fields. In: 2017 IEEE Conference on Computer Vision and Pattern Recognition (CVPR), pp. 1302–1310 (2017)
6. Cenci, A., Liciotti, D., Frontoni, E., Zingaretti, P., Carinelli, V.P.: Movements analysis of preterm infants by using depth sensor. In: International Conference on Internet of Things and Machine Learning (IML 2017) (2017)
7. Chen, H., Xue, M., Mei, Z., Bambang Oetomo, S., Chen, W.: A review of wearable sensor systems for monitoring body movements of neonates. Sensors **16**(12), 2134 (2016)
8. Chen, L., Wei, H., Ferryman, J.: A survey of human motion analysis using depth imagery. Pattern Recognit. Lett. **34**(15), 1995–2006 (2013)
9. Fan, M., Gravem, D., Cooper, D.M., Patterson, D.J.: Augmenting gesture recognition with erlang-cox models to identify neurological disorders in premature babies. In: Proceedings of the 2012 ACM Conference on Ubiquitous Computing, pp. 411–420. ACM (2012)
10. Gravem, D., et al.: Assessment of infant movement with a compact wireless accelerometer system. J. Med. Devices **6**(2), 021013 (2012)
11. Hadders-Algra, M., Nieuwendijk, A.W., Maitijn, A., Eykern, L.A.: Assessment of general movements: towards a better understanding of a sensitive method to evaluate brain function in young infants. Dev. Med. Child Neurol. **39**(2), 88–98 (1997)
12. Haque, A., Peng, B., Luo, Z., Alahi, A., Yeung, S., Fei-Fei, L.: Towards viewpoint invariant 3D human pose estimation. In: Leibe, B., Matas, J., Sebe, N., Welling, M. (eds.) ECCV 2016. LNCS, vol. 9905, pp. 160–177. Springer, Cham (2016). https://doi.org/10.1007/978-3-319-46448-0_10

13. Heinze, F., Hesels, K., Breitbach-Faller, N., Schmitz-Rode, T., Disselhorst-Klug, C.: Movement analysis by accelerometry of newborns and infants for the early detection of movement disorders due to infantile cerebral palsy. Med. Biol. Eng. Comput. **48**(8), 765–772 (2010)
14. Hesse, N., et al.: Learning an infant body model from RGB-D data for accurate full body motion analysis. In: Frangi, A.F., Schnabel, J.A., Davatzikos, C., Alberola-López, C., Fichtinger G. (eds.) Medical Image Computing and Computer Assisted Intervention - MICCAI 2018, pp. 792–800. Springer, Cham (2018)
15. Hesse, N., Schröder, A.S., Müller-Felber, W., Bodensteiner, C., Arens, M., Hofmann, U.G.: Body pose estimation in depth images for infant motion analysis. In: IEEE 39th Annual International Conference of the Engineering in Medicine and Biology Society (EMBC) (2017)
16. Hesse, N., Stachowiak, G., Breuer, T., Arens, M.: Estimating body pose of infants in depth images using random ferns. In: 2015 IEEE International Conference on Computer Vision Workshop (ICCVW) (2015)
17. Iarlori, S., Ferracuti, F., Giantomassi, A., Longhi, S.: RGBD camera monitoring system for Alzheimer's disease assessment using recurrent neural networks with parametric bias action recognition. IFAC Proc. Vol. **47**(3), 3863–3868 (2014)
18. Jiang, C., Lane, C.J., Perkins, E., Schiesel, D., Smith, B.A.: Determining if wearable sensors affect infant leg movement frequency. Dev. Neurorehabil. **21**, 1–4 (2017)
19. Kanemaru, N., et al.: Specific characteristics of spontaneous movements in preterm infants at term age are associated with developmental delays at age 3 years. Dev. Med. Child Neurol. **55**(8), 713–721 (2013)
20. Karch, D., et al.: Kinematic assessment of stereotypy in spontaneous movements in infants. Gait Posture **36**(2), 307–311 (2012)
21. Karch, D., Kim, K.S., Wochner, K., Pietz, J., Dickhaus, H., Philippi, H.: Quantification of the segmental kinematics of spontaneous infant movements. J. Biomech. **41**(13), 2860–2867 (2008)
22. Kontschieder, P., et al.: Quantifying progression of multiple sclerosis via classification of depth videos. In: Golland, P., Hata, N., Barillot, C., Hornegger, J., Howe, R. (eds.) MICCAI 2014. LNCS, vol. 8674, pp. 429–437. Springer, Cham (2014). https://doi.org/10.1007/978-3-319-10470-6_54
23. Loper, M., Mahmood, N., Romero, J., Pons-Moll, G., Black, M.J.: SMPL: a skinned multi-person linear model. ACM Trans. Graph. **34**(6), 248:1–248:16 (2015)
24. Loper, M.M., Black, M.J.: OpenDR: an approximate differentiable renderer. In: Fleet, D., Pajdla, T., Schiele, B., Tuytelaars, T. (eds.) ECCV 2014. LNCS, vol. 8695, pp. 154–169. Springer, Cham (2014). https://doi.org/10.1007/978-3-319-10584-0_11
25. Machireddy, A., van Santen, J., Wilson, J.L., Myers, J., Hadders-Algra, M., Song, X.: A video/IMU hybrid system for movement estimation in infants. In: 39th Annual International Conference of the IEEE Engineering in Medicine and Biology Society (EMBC), pp. 730–733. IEEE (2017)
26. Marcroft, C., Khan, A., Embleton, N.D., Trenell, M., Plötz, T.: Movement recognition technology as a method of assessing spontaneous general movements in high risk infants. Front. Neurol. **5**, 284 (2014). https://doi.org/10.3389/fneur.2014.00284
27. Meinecke, L., Breitbach-Faller, N., Bartz, C., Damen, R., Rau, G., Disselhorst-Klug, C.: Movement analysis in the early detection of newborns at risk for developing spasticity due to infantile cerebral palsy. Hum. Mov. Sci. **25**(2), 125–144 (2006)

28. Morrison, C., Culmer, P., Mentis, H., Pincus, T.: Vision-based body tracking: turning Kinect into a clinical tool. Disabil. Rehabil.: Assist. Technol. **11**(6), 516–520 (2016)
29. Olsen, M.D., Herskind, A., Nielsen, J.B., Paulsen, R.R.: Model-based motion tracking of infants. In: Agapito, L., Bronstein, M.M., Rother, C. (eds.) ECCV 2014. LNCS, vol. 8927, pp. 673–685. Springer, Cham (2015). https://doi.org/10.1007/978-3-319-16199-0_47
30. Olsen, M.D., Herskindt, A., Nielsen, J.B., Paulsen, R.R.: Body part tracking of infants. In: 22nd International Conference on Pattern Recognition (ICPR), pp. 2167–2172. IEEE (2014)
31. OpenPose   Library: https://github.com/CMU-Perceptual-Computing-Lab/openpose. Accessed June 2018
32. Prechtl, H.F., Einspieler, C., Cioni, G., Bos, A.F., Ferrari, F., Sontheimer, D.: An early marker for neurological deficits after perinatal brain lesions. Lancet **349**(9062), 1361–1363 (1997)
33. Prechtl, H.: Qualitative changes of spontaneous movements in fetus and preterm infant are a marker of neurological dysfunction. Early Human Dev. **23**(3), 151–158 (1990)
34. Rahmati, H., Dragon, R., Aamo, O.M., Adde, L., Stavdahl, Ø., Van Gool, L.: Weakly supervised motion segmentation with particle matching. Comput. Vis. Image Underst. **140**, 30–42 (2015)
35. Rihar, A., Mihelj, M., Pašič, J., Kolar, J., Munih, M.: Infant trunk posture and arm movement assessment using pressure mattress, inertial and magnetic measurement units (IMUs). J. Neuroeng. Rehabil. **11**(1), 133 (2014)
36. Sciortino, G., Farinella, G.M., Battiato, S., Leo, M., Distante, C.: On the estimation of children's poses. In: Battiato, S., Gallo, G., Schettini, R., Stanco, F. (eds.) ICIAP 2017. LNCS, vol. 10485, pp. 410–421. Springer, Cham (2017). https://doi.org/10.1007/978-3-319-68548-9_38
37. Serrano, M.M., Chen, Y.P., Howard, A., Vela, P.A.: Lower limb pose estimation for monitoring the kicking patterns of infants. In: 38th Annual International Conference of the IEEE Engineering in Medicine and Biology Society (EMBC), pp. 2157–2160. IEEE (2016)
38. Shivakumar, S.S., et al.: Stereo 3D tracking of infants in natural play conditions. In: International Conference on Rehabilitation Robotics (ICORR), pp. 841–846. IEEE (2017)
39. Simon, T., Joo, H., Matthews, I., Sheikh, Y.: Hand keypoint detection in single images using multiview bootstrapping. In: 2017 IEEE Conference on Computer Vision and Pattern Recognition (CVPR), pp. 4645–4653 (2017)
40. Singh, M., Patterson, D.J.: Involuntary gesture recognition for predicting cerebral palsy in high-risk infants. In: International Symposium on Wearable Computers (ISWC), pp. 1–8. IEEE (2010)
41. Spittle, A., Orton, J., Anderson, P.J., Boyd, R., Doyle, L.W.: Early developmental intervention programmes provided post hospital discharge to prevent motor and cognitive impairment in preterm infants. Cochrane Database Syst. Rev. 11 (2015). https://doi.org/10.1002/14651858.CD005495.pub4
42. Stahl, A., Schellewald, C., Stavdahl, Ø., Aamo, O.M., Adde, L., Kirkerød, H.: An optical flow-based method to predict infantile cerebral palsy. IEEE Trans. Neural Syst. Rehabil. Eng. **20**(4), 605–614 (2012)
43. Sun, B., Liu, X., Wu, X., Wang, H.: Human gait modeling and gait analysis based on Kinect. In: IEEE International Conference on Robotics and Automation (ICRA), pp. 3173–3178. IEEE (2014)

44. Wei, S.E., Ramakrishna, V., Kanade, T., Sheikh, Y.: Convolutional pose machines. In: 2016 IEEE Conference on Computer Vision and Pattern Recognition (CVPR), pp. 4724–4732 (2016)
45. Zimmermann, C., Welschehold, T., Dornhege, C., Burgard, W., Brox, T.: 3D human pose estimation in RGBD images for robotic task learning. In: IEEE International Conference on Robotics and Automation (ICRA) (2018)

Vision Augmented Robot Feeding

Alexandre Candeias[1](✉) [iD], Travers Rhodes[2] [iD], Manuel Marques[1] [iD],
João P. Costeira[1] [iD], and Manuela Veloso[2] [iD]

[1] ISR - IST Universidade de Lisboa, Lisbon, Portugal
alexandre.candeias@tecnico.ulisboa.pt,
{manuel,jpc}@isr.tecnico.ulisboa.pt
[2] Carnegie Mellon University, Pittsburgh, USA
traversr@andrew.cmu.edu, mmv@cs.cmu.edu

Abstract. Researchers have over time developed robotic feeding assistants to help at meals so that people with disabilities can live more autonomous lives. Current commercial feeding assistant robots acquire food without feedback on acquisition success and move to a preprogrammed location to deliver the food. In this work, we evaluate how vision can be used to improve both food acquisition and delivery. We show that using visual feedback on whether food was captured increases food acquisition efficiency. We also show how Discriminative Optimization (DO) can be used in tracking so that the food can be effectively brought all the way to the user's mouth, rather than to a preprogrammed feeding location.

Keywords: Assistive technologies · Manipulation aids
Computer vision · Feeding assistance

1 Introduction

Disabilities that can affect control of the arms, including paralysis, Parkinson's disease, and cerebral palsy, may prevent or hinder someone from feeding themselves. In that case, the person may require a human caretaker to assist in the feeding task. To help people with disabilities live more autonomous lives, researchers have over time developed and tested how robotic feeding assistants may help at the difficult task of having a meal [1]. A feeding robot is a way of achieving greater independence at meals and can make the mealtime a more social event. Also, compared to a human caretaker, a robotic feeding assistant can have more time and patience in soliciting user requests for what type of food to acquire and in following the user's desired pace of the meal [2].

A. Candeias and T. Rhodes—Contributed equally.

Electronic supplementary material The online version of this chapter (https:// doi.org/10.1007/978-3-030-11024-6_4) contains supplementary material, which is available to authorized users.

L. Leal-Taixé and S. Roth (Eds.): ECCV 2018 Workshops, LNCS 11134, pp. 50–65, 2019.
https://doi.org/10.1007/978-3-030-11024-6_4

There are several commercial assistive feeding robots, including the Obi [3], Bestic [4], and Meal Buddy [5]. All of these robots allow the user or a caretaker to program the desired feeding location to which the robot will bring the food. However, that feeding location remains constant throughout the meal. Current feeding systems are not equipped with a perception scheme and are not able to perceive the changes in the pose of the user or in the environment. People without sufficient head control to bring their mouth to the programmed feeding location might be better accommodated by a robot that can bring the spoon all the way to the current location of the user's mouth.

To solve this problem we propose in this paper to create a complete robotic feeding assistant system that incorporates a visual perception module to locate the user's face and mouth. Our system setup is shown in Fig. 1.

We propose a real-time system that uses depth images to track the user's mouth in 3D space and a separate vision system to provide useful feedback for how much food was acquired on the robotic spoon. Real experiments show that the visual feedback module significantly improves the feeding system's performance.

Fig. 1. Our feeding system includes a MICO robot arm, an RGB-D camera, and an RGB camera. The first image also labels the axis orientations of the robot coordinate system. (Color figure online)

2   Related Work

Several approaches have been used previously in detecting mouth location for robotic feeding tasks. In [6], an ARTag was affixed to the user's forehead. In [7], Park et al. extend their system to localize the user's mouth using a RGB-D camera, but do not specify or evaluate the algorithm used. Hawkins et al. [8] also focus on head pose estimation including user's feedback to help the head detection. Visual servoing was used to find the user's mouth in [9], but that system was unable to ascertain the distance to the user's mouth along the principal axis, as it did not use a depth camera. Their system takes roughly 10 s to identify the mouth location [9], whereas our system tracks mouth location in real time.

In [10], the user's face is tracked using three specific face points (one on the forehead, and one on each cheek), and those points are used to infer the mouth location. Like their system, the proposed approach is robust to occlusions of the mouth. However, unlike [10], our tracking algorithm is able to track faces even in profile.[1]

Discriminative Optimization (DO) [11] was applied in the work of Silva et al. [12] to track the user's face for robotic feeding, however they do not provide results about the performance of the tracking or the feeding system.

Research into anomaly detection during feeding tasks was performed in [7], which is used to detect errors during the feeding motion to the user's mouth. However, anomalies related to food acquisition were not analyzed in that work. The anomalies we investigate in our work are related to failures in acquiring a sufficient amount of food. Herlant [13] also uses feedback on the state of the fork in order to detect an anomalously low mass of food acquired. They use an expensive 6DOF force-torque sensor, while we use an inexpensive vision system as our feedback sensor, in the hope that a cheaper system will accessible to a broader range of people.

The work of Ragusa et al. [14] focuses on food/non-food detection on plate images. In that work, they benchmark different deep-learning based approaches. They used pre-trained convolution neural networks (CNNs) to capture features and trained a support vector machine (SVM) and Soft-Max classifier to classify food/non-food images. That work also analyses the impact of fine tuning the CNNs to capture more relevant features to the food/non-food detection. Although those approaches are successful, in this work we are interested in classification of specific spoon images. We also go beyond classification and compute a continuous measure of how much food is present in the image of the spoon.

3   Feeding System

The developed feeding system is composed of two parts: a vision system that is responsible for tracking the user and also for detecting if there is food on the spoon and a control system that is responsible for transforming visual perception into tasks executed by the robot arm. These tasks are food acquisition from the plate and delivering the food to the user's mouth.

In the next subsections, we describe each component in the system diagram presented in Fig. 2.

3.1   Vision System

Our vision system is composed of two parts. One is responsible for tracking the person's face using an RGB-D sensor, and the other is responsible for detecting what is on the spoon using a small RGB camera mounted on the robot's end-effector.

---

[1] A video of our system working is available at https://www.youtube.com/watch?v=X7McqWk1AK8.

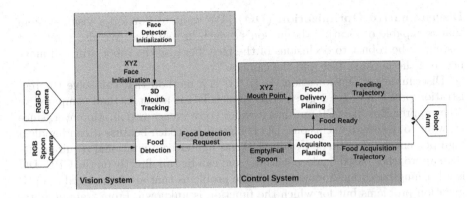

Fig. 2. Feeding system architecture diagram

Tracking a person's face is a challenging task because faces are non-rigid. However, since the face movements are constrained by the head movements, we can, in a first approximation, track the person's head and assume that the mouth is just a point in the rigid body shaped by the head.

Given a front view 3D model of the person's head (P_M) and a 3D point cloud of the scene given by the RGB-D sensor (P_S), we can formulate the problem of tracking the person's head as a 3D point registration problem. This can be formulated as the following optimization problem:

$$(R^*, t^*, C^*) = \operatorname*{argmin}_{R,t,C} \sum_{i=1}^{N_{P_S}} \sum_{j=1}^{N_{P_M}} C_{ij} \left\| p_S^i - R \cdot p_M^j - t \right\|^2 \tag{1}$$
$$\text{subject to } \det(R) = 1, \quad R^T R = I, \quad C_{ij} \in \{0,1\}$$

where we want to fit the rotation R^* and translation t^* that align the model point cloud with the scene point cloud. p_S^i and p_M^j are, respectively, points from the point clouds P_S and P_M. C_{ij}^* represents the optimal point correspondences between the two point clouds. C_{ij}^* is equal to 1 if p_S^i and p_M^j are corresponding points and the model point p_M^j is visible on the scene. Otherwise, C_{ij}^* will be 0. Since we do not know the correspondences C^* between the two point clouds, we have to include them in the optimization problem. This leads to a non-convex combinatorial problem.

When the correspondences between the model and scene point clouds are not known, it is a common practice to solve 3D registration problems using ICP [15]. Although ICP is a standard procedure to use, it tends to get trapped in local minima near the initialization provided and to have problems when dealing with a high percentage of outliers.

To overcome these problems we use Discriminative Optimization (DO) [11] to solve the model-based 3D registration tracking problem presented in Eq. 1. In [11] it is shown that DO is better than ICP in terms of computation time and more robust to outliers.

Discriminative Optimization (DO). We want to develop a vision system that is capable of locating the person's mouth in real time. We also want that system to be robust to occlusions of the face, because the robot arm will move between the person's face and the camera.

Discriminative Optimization (DO) [11] is a method that can solve the registration problem of Eq. 1 given a 3D model. DO is a fast method compared to other approaches like ICP and has a wider convergence region. Moreover, since we want to deal with occlusions, DO is a good approach because it can handle a high percentage of outliers. Finally, DO has lighter computational requirements than approaches based on deep learning and can be run directly on the CPU. DO is a learning-based methodology to tackle problems that are formulated as optimization problems but for which the function is unknown. From training data, DO learns a vector field, represented by a series of linear maps, that "emulate" the gradient of a function. During testing, given unseen data, DO follows this "gradient" leading to a stationary point that solves the optimization problem. Specifically in our case, the algorithm is given a 3D model of the rigid body that we want to track and generates a set of synthetic training data by applying random rotations and translations to the 3D model. This augmented training data is used to discover a sequence of linear maps that represent the descending directions. Those maps are used during inference, which is an iterative procedure that repeatedly updates the translation and rotation of the 3D model of the head to better align it with the point cloud of the scene.

Initialization. 3D registration algorithms, like ICP and DO, require an initialization step that places the model of the face close to the face in the scene. We use a face detector as our initial guess for where the face is in the RGB-D image of the scene.

A popular face detector is the Viola Jones face detector [16]. Though this face detector is fast, it is not invariant to different face poses. MTCNN [17] is more robust to different face poses and also provides landmarks of the mouth, nose, and eyes. Though MTCNN is based on deep learning, it can still run on a CPU at a lower speed. Since initialization does not happen frequently, the speed of the initialization step is not an important concern, and we remove the need for a GPU in our system by running initialization on a CPU.

We initialize our face tracker using the average 3D location of the facial landmarks given by MTCNN. The 3D locations of these landmark points can be computed because we are using an RGB-D camera. With these 3D points, we approximate the initial translation $\tilde{t}$ of the face model in the scene as:

$$\tilde{t} = \frac{1}{L}\sum_{i=1}^{L} p_S^i - \frac{1}{N}\sum_{j=1}^{N} p_M^j, \qquad (2)$$

where L is the number of landmarks and N is the number of points in the model. For the initial rotation of the model, we assume $R = I$, where I is the 3×3 identity. The MTCNN landmarks are also used to compute the mouth 3D location in the model's point cloud.

Food Detection. To see what is on the spoon, we place a tiny RGB camera on the end-effector of the robot arm. After a simple calibration step of holding a light-colored background behind the spoon, we compute a mask for the image that only contains the spoon. We use this masked image for two purposes, to detect if there is enough food to serve the user, and to detect if the user has eaten the food off the spoon. To detect if there is enough food on the spoon we use a detection algorithm that we can tune to specify the required amount of food. To detect if the user has eaten the food, we use a classifier with two classes: "food" and "no food."

Calibration is performed by acquiring an image with a white sheet of paper under the spoon. Otsu's method [18] is used to select a threshold and segment the image which provides a spoon mask. This method works well because the colored spoon contrasts sharply with the white sheet of paper. In the calibration step, we also record a histogram, H_s, of the H channel of the HSV image of the empty spoon after applying the calibration mask.

The recorded histogram, H_s, is compared with the histograms of subsequent images of the spoon, H_a. To compare the histograms, we used the normalized correlation between the two histograms,

$$d(H_s, H_a) = \frac{\sum_{i=1}^{N}(H_s(i) - \bar{H}_s)(H_a(i) - \bar{H}_a)}{\sqrt{\sum_{i=1}^{N}(H_s(i) - \bar{H}_s)^2 \sum_{i=1}^{N}(H_a(i) - \bar{H}_a)^2}}, \tag{3}$$

where $\bar{H} = \frac{1}{N}\sum_{i=1}^{N} H(i)$ is the histogram mean. If the value of the correlation is below a certain threshold, then the algorithm reports that there is enough food on the spoon.

To tune the correlation threshold, we gathered a dataset containing 387 data points of correlations and the corresponding weight of food present on the spoon. Example images collected are shown in Fig. 3. We use peanuts and fried rice as our test foods. We train a linear regression to discover the relationship between the histogram correlation value and the weight of the food on the spoon. This regression can be used to inform the choice of the threshold for "enough food" on the spoon.

We can detect if there is food on the spoon after the user's bite using a classifier. We tried two different classifiers: a logistic regression and a linear support vector machine (SVM). The input feature to the logistic regression is the value of the histogram correlation, and the input features to the SVM are the

Fig. 3. Example masked images of the plastic spoon, showing the spoon empty, with nuts, and with rice.

bins of the H color channel histogram of the spoon image. Both classifiers were trained using a dataset containing 119 empty spoon images and 118 non-empty spoon images.

3.2   Control System

Gradient-Based Planning. The goal of our planning algorithm is to move the tip of the spoon from its current location to the user's mouth. Because the mouth of the user may be moving, we need our planning algorithm to be able to quickly re-compute its plan based on updated mouth-target positions. For this reason, we choose a planning algorithm that iteratively moves the tip of the spoon one step in a straight line toward the current location of the mouth. We also want to ensure that the spoon does not dump its contents during transit, so we control the orientation of the spoon during transit.

A flexible approach to allow quick re-planning and to constrain orientation is a gradient-based approach. At each timestep, we compute an intermediate Cartesian end-effector target that is a certain distance, parameterized by a parameter "translationStepSize," from the current location. The intermediate Cartesian target is the mouth location itself if the mouth location is within "translationStepSize."

We similarly compute an intermediate orientation target by computing the rotation necessary to convert from the current orientation of the end-effector to the target orientation. We define the target orientation to along the y-axis direction shown in Fig. 1. We set our intermediate orientation target to be the orientation that is at most a certain angle rotation, parameterized by a parameter "rotationStepSize," away from the current orientation. During transit from the plate to the user's mouth, the orientation is never more than a very small angle away from the desired final feeding orientation, so the target orientation is always the desired final orientation.

We use OpenRave [19] to compute the Cartesian Jacobian, which is a $3 \times$ DOF matrix showing how changes in each joint angle locally moves the end-effector in Cartesian space. We also use OpenRave to compute the angular velocity Jacobian, which is a $3 \times$ DOF matrix showing how changes in each joint angle locally rotates the end-effector, where rotations are given in angle-axis representation.

We write our desired translation as a length three vector. We concatenate that vector with the angle-axis representation of our desired rotation to give us a length 6 vector representing our desired change in end-effector pose. Our "translationStepSize" and "rotationStepSize" parameters guarantee that our intermediate target pose is "close" to our current pose, so we can reasonably linearize our problem to be Eq. 4, where J_c and J_r are the Cartesian and rotation Jacobian defined above, and Δ_c and Δ_r are the desired translation and rotation to move the end-effector to the intermediate target. In our experiments, we use a 6DOF robot, so we can use ordinary least-squares regression to compute the required joint changes necessary to satisfy that equation. For a robot with more degrees of freedom, regularization could be used to prefer solutions with small joint angle changes.

$$\begin{bmatrix} J_c \\ J_r \end{bmatrix} \Theta = \begin{bmatrix} \Delta_c \\ \Delta_r \end{bmatrix} \tag{4}$$

We find that this simple architecture works for the majority of our feeding tests. Since this gradient-based algorithm is greedy, we do note that it is possible for the robot arm to follow trajectories into local minima where joint constraints prevent the robot arm from continuing all the way to the user's mouth. In our setup, we find that this would generally happen if the trajectory brings the robot end-effector too close to the robot base. Placing the user and plate so that the path between them stays more than a certain distance from the robot base circumvents this issue and leads to successful trajectories, though we also implement a more robust solution that modifies planned trajectories to keep away from the robot base while moving.

Learning from Demonstration. In addition to defining trajectories from the plate to the mouth and back, we also need to train the robot to acquire food from the plate. To do so, we use Learning from Demonstration to imitate human utensil trajectories. In this manner, we do not need to perform the complex task of modeling different food types in order to plan a food acquisition strategies. The ability of Learning from Demonstration to plan trajectories without an explicit model of the domain dynamics [20] is an attractive benefit for us in this context. "Learning from demonstration" in the robotics context usually means some mechanism of automatically acquiring knowledge from human demonstration, but for this work it was sufficient to pick and imitate a single trajectory from a collection of trajectories for assistive feeding. In [21], Bhattacharjee et al. collected detailed fork trajectories in a simulated assistive feeding environment. We visualize several of those trajectories in Rviz and select and truncate a single fork trajectory that follows a simple scooping motion in acquiring coleslaw. Our robot imitates that single fork trajectory to acquire food with a spoon. We find that single scooping trajectory to be sufficient for scooping up the different food types we tested, but we expect that there are food types and serving plate configurations for which more nuanced trajectory learning is required.

To have our robot spoon replicate the training trajectories, we want the robot to move its arm in such a way that the tip of the spoon follows the demonstrated tip of the fork in both position and orientation. In addition, we want the robot to be able to translate the demonstration trajectory target by various offsets so that the robot can scoop food from different parts of the serving plate. To accomplish this, we use the same gradient-based planner described above, where now the target position and orientation of our gradient-based controller are generated by playing back the recorded utensil tip poses, offset by the desired translation. We slow down the played-back demonstration to one fifth the demonstration speed due to speed constraints of the robot arm and to ensure safety.

4   Experimental Setup and Results

4.1   Hardware Setup

To test our feeding algorithm in a real robotic setting, we use a 6 degree-of-freedom Kinova MICO robot affixed rigidly to a dining table. We place a serving bowl of food in front of the robot and have the robot hold a spoon in its end-effector. We attach an iDS-xs RGB camera to the end-effector pointed toward the bowl of the spoon. Our user sits at the table, and across from the user we place a Kinect V1 RGB-D camera on a tripod so that it can see the robot arm and the user's face. The two cameras publish ROS topics which are used in our planning architecture.

4.2   Calibration of Camera to Robot

In order for the robot to use the information from the RGB-D camera in a meaningful way, we have to calibrate the robot base frame with the RGB-D camera frame. We want to do this calibration in an automatic way so that we can use the feeding system quickly after changing the position of the camera or the robot arm.

To automatically calibrate the robot frame with the camera frame, we attach an orange ball to the robot arm end-effector and then we move the robot arm to different positions. These positions are known in the robot base frame because we know the robot kinematics. For each of the positions, we acquire the corresponding RGB-D images from the camera. We use color segmentation to detect the ball in those images and get its corresponding 3D points. We fit a sphere to the 3D points of the ball using RANSAC to compute the 3D center of the ball in the camera frame. Finally, using these 3D correspondences between the camera frame and the robot base frame, we fit a rotation and a translation by solving an Orthogonal Procrustes Problem [22].

4.3   Mouth Tracking Accuracy Over Time

Setup. To test the performance of our tracking system, we acquired an RGB-D video of a person moving his head in front of the camera. In the first part of the video, we ask the user to look in different directions but to keep his torso still. In the second part, we ask the user to move his head to different places in addition to looking in different directions.

Since DO requires a 3D face model, we acquire the face model of the user using MTCNN to detect the face and DBSCAN [23] to filter the model point cloud.

The error of our tracking system was measured by annotating the mouth point in our dataset at a frame-rate of 2 FPS and then measuring the error between the output mouth point of our tracking and the annotated label in each frame.

Results. The error in each frame is presented in Fig. 4. The experiment was performed on a single thread on a Intel Core i7-6500U CPU 2.50 GHz with 8 GB of memory. Our tracking achieved speeds of 8–10 FPS.

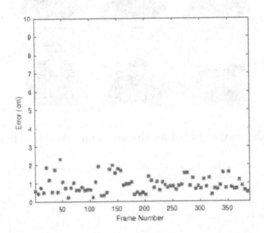

Fig. 4. Tracking error in each frame

Figure 4 shows that our tracking method can track the person's mouth with an error below 3 cm through the entire video. This is on the order of magnitude of the mouth's size, so the output of our system will not be far from the real location of the mouth.

To have a better visual insight about the output of our tracking method, we show in red on Fig. 5 the output mouth point of our algorithm.

As discussed previously, our tracking works well for rotations and translations of the user's head. With our method we can give an accurate position of the user's mouth.

4.4 Food Detection

Setup. We also analyze the performance of the food detector. In this section, we evaluate the performance of our two methods for food detection. To train the classifiers and the linear regression we split our dataset of spoon images into 70% train data and 30% test data.

Results. Figure 6 shows the linear regression fit modeling the weight of food in the spoon with the correlation of histograms between the current image of the spoon and the image of the empty spoon. The regression has a validation mean squared error of 1.37 g and a correlation coefficient (r^2) of 0.75 on the test set. There is a strong negative correlation between the weight of the food that is on the spoon and the correlation between the histograms. Even if the model is not

Fig. 5. Tracking output in red for the user's mouth. (Color figure online)

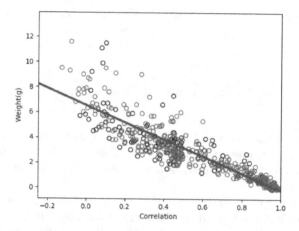

Fig. 6. Relationship between the correlation measure and the weight of food on the spoon. The correlation measure is computed as shown in Eq. 3 by taking the histogram of the image of the spoon with food on it and correlating that with the histogram of the baseline image of the spoon without food on it. The data points used for training are shown in red, the data used for test is shown in black, and the linear regression is shown in blue. (Color figure online)

perfect in measuring the amount of food that is on the spoon, we can use this model to calibrate our correlation threshold to require more or less food per bite.

In the classification task, we achieved an accuracy of 95.8% with the logistic regression and 98.6% with the linear SVM. The SVM was trained using the whole histogram and the logistic regression using only the correlation between each sample of the train data and an empty spoon histogram example. We present, in Figs. 7 and 8, the confusion matrix results for the two classification methods. These results validate our classification approach to discover if there is still food on the spoon.

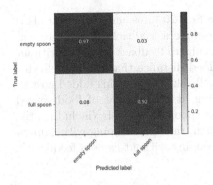
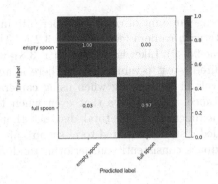

Fig. 7. Confusion matrix for logistic regression   **Fig. 8.** Confusion matrix for SVM

4.5 Ablation Study for Food Acquisition

Setup. To analyze the importance of various components of the food acquisition system, we perform an ablation study in the feeding task where we measure the efficiency of the feeding robot when it does and does not use certain food acquisition strategies. We define the efficiency to be the mass of food that is delivered to the feeding location as a function of the total distance that the tip of the spoon has traveled. We report the mass as a function of distance traveled rather than the time taken because we want to negate any effect that setting the robot to a faster or slower speed would have on the results.

The system components that we alter in our ablation study are (1) whether or not we re-scoop if the spoon-facing camera detects that not enough food was acquired and (2) whether the robot always scoops from the same position on the serving plate or whether it scoops from a uniformly random position within a 6 cm × 3 cm rectangle on the plate. We perform the ablation experiment on two different kinds of food: peanuts and fried rice. In this way, we can determine if the importance of system components depends on the type of food.

For consistency in results, we use the same random seed for all trials that randomize the scooping location on the plate. To speed up data collection, the robot dumps the food directly onto the scale after food acquisition. Then, in our data analysis we add in the distance to the user's mouth and back. Cutting out the travel time between the plate and the user's mouth cuts the data acquisition time by a factor of three. On average, the distance traveled by the spoon tip in a single scooping motion is 32 cm and the average distance to and from the user's mouth is 49 cm in each direction. We use these average distance values when representing the amount of food served as a function of distance.

Results. In our ablation study for food acquisition, we find that vision feedback significantly increases the amount of food brought to the user in each bite. For the spoon-facing vision feedback system, we use a histogram correlation cutoff of 0.5 for both rice and nuts. For rice, when randomizing the scooping location, the

average amount of rice served per bite in the first 20 bites across three trials is
4.8 g with camera feedback and 3.2 g without camera feedback (paired t-test p-
value 9e−6). Likewise for nuts it is 3.8 g with camera feedback and 2.7 g without
(paired t-test p-value 1e−5). There is an added distance that the end-effector
travels in re-scooping when using camera feedback. Despite this added cost in
distance, Fig. 9 shows that even when looking at the amount of food served
as a function of the total distance that the spoon tip travels (including the
added distance required to re-scoop), after 25 m, random scooping with camera
feedback consistently outperforms random scooping without camera feedback.

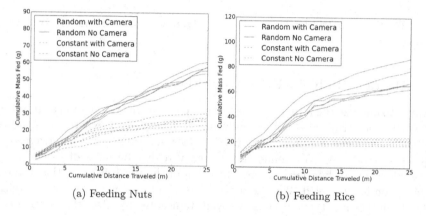

(a) Feeding Nuts   (b) Feeding Rice

Fig. 9. Charts showing the amount of food fed (in grams) as a function of the distance
the tip of the spoon has traveled, including the distance traveled in re-scooping. The
chart includes results for scooping location randomization (solid lines) compared to a
constant scooping location (dotted lines), and it includes results with (green lines) and
without (red lines) camera feedback on whether food was successfully acquired. We ran
three trials for each test type. (Color figure online)

For both rice and nuts we find that randomization of the scooping location
is a useful technique in food acquisition. Figure 9 also shows that randomization
coupled with visual feedback on the success of a scoop is the most effective. Most
interestingly, we find that the importance of our system components depends on
the type of food used. We find that randomizing the location of scoops is more
important when serving rice instead of nuts. This could be related to the fact
that nuts were observed to "settle" after each scoop, whereas fried rice will tend
not to fill in the hole left after scooping. Thus, scooping the same place for fried
rice will quickly result in very little (almost no) mass acquired by the spoon in
subsequent scoops.

5 Conclusion and Future Work

In this work, we explored how vision can be introduced in a robotic feeding
platform. By introducing a vision-based approach we can make the system more

intelligent and also more autonomous. The developed system is fully capable of feeding a user using a spoon with different types of food like rice or peanuts, and uses visual feedback to ensure spoons are full of food when presented to the user.

Our results show that DO approach can be used effectively for tracking a user's face. However, the method still needs improvements when generalizing to different users from the one for which we have the 3D face model. In future work, we are planning to test DO against other head-pose estimation approaches like OpenFace [24]. We also want to incorporate the user's facial expression information to detect the user's intention to be fed.

Using a camera that can see what is on the spoon, we are capable of ensuring there is an adequate amount of food per bite. We can also use the proposed classifiers to see if there is food on the spoon after the user's bite. Given the effectiveness in the spoon-facing vision feedback in identifying the mass of food on the spoon, we also plan to investigate using that vision feedback system to control the depth that the spoon digs into the food, so that the feeding system can alter its serving strategy to accommodate the gradually decreasing level of food in the serving bowl.

Using this vision framework, we hope in future work to personalize our system to different users and make our system learn with individual user experience. We plan to test our system in real-world situations with people living with disabilities and plan to use a broader range of food types, potentially needing to improve our food detection and acquisition algorithm. We hope to quantitatively and qualitatively analyze the efficacy of our entire system for several users. We will also compare our algorithm to the type of baseline algorithm found in current commercially-available robots.

Acknowledgements. We very specially thank Henny Admoni for generously making available the arm robots in her HARP lab for our work. We specially thank Jayakorn Vongkulbhisal for the help with the implementation of DO. We thank the CMU-Portugal program for their partial support of this work through an ERI grant, as well as for supporting the visit of Alexandre Candeias to CMU, which led to this exciting and successful joint collaboration and work. This work was also funded by FCT grant [UID/EEA/50009/2013] and FCT project IF/00879/2012 (Projecto Exploratório). Finally, the authors thank the anonymous reviewers for their comments. The views and conclusions of this document are those of the authors only.

References

1. Al-Halimi, R.K., Moussa, M.: Performing complex tasks by users with upper-extremity disabilities using a 6-DOF robotic arm: a study. IEEE Trans. Neural Syst. Rehabil. Eng. **25**(6), 686–693 (2017)
2. Topping, M.: Early experience in the use of the 'handy 1' robotic aid to eating. Robotica **11**(6), 525–527 (1993)
3. Obi: Obi, robotic feeding device designed for home care. https://meetobi.com. Accessed 19 May 2018

4. Camanio Care: Bestic. http://www.camanio.com/us/products/bestic/. Accessed 09 May 2018
5. Performance Health: Meal buddy. https://www.performancehealth.com/meal-buddy-systems. Accessed 18 Feb 2018
6. Park, D., Kim, Y.K., Erickson, Z.M., Kemp, C.C.: Towards assistive feeding with a general-purpose mobile manipulator. CoRR abs/1605.07996 (2016)
7. Park, D., Kim, H., Hoshi, Y., Erickson, Z., Kapusta, A., Kemp, C.C.: A multimodal execution monitor with anomaly classification for robot-assisted feeding. In: 2016 IEEE International Conference on Robots and Systems (IROS) (2017)
8. Hawkins, K.P., Grice, P.M., Chen, T.L., King, C.H., Kemp, C.C.: Assistive mobile manipulation for self-care tasks around the head. In: IEEE SSCI 2014–2014 IEEE Symposium Series on Computational Intelligence - CIR2AT 2014: 2014 IEEE Symposium on Computational Intelligence in Robotic Rehabilitation and Assistive Technologies, Proceedings, pp. 16–25 (2014)
9. Perera, C.J., Lalitharatne, T.D., Kiguchi, K.: EEG-controlled meal assistance robot with camera-based automatic mouth position tracking and mouth open detection. In: 2017 IEEE International Conference on Robotics and Automation (ICRA), pp. 1760–1765. IEEE (2017)
10. Schröer, S., et al.: An autonomous robotic assistant for drinking. In: 2015 IEEE International Conference on Robotics and Automation (ICRA), pp. 6482–6487. IEEE (2015)
11. Vongkulbhisal, J., De La Torre, F., Costeira, J.P.: Discriminative optimization: theory and applications to point cloud registration. In: Proceedings - 30th IEEE Conference on Computer Vision and Pattern Recognition, CVPR 2017, pp. 3975–3983, January 2017
12. Silva, C., Vongkulbhisal, J., Marques, M., Costeira, J.P., Veloso, M.: Feedbot - a robotic arm for autonomous assisted feeding. In: Oliveira, E., Gama, J., Vale, Z., Lopes Cardoso, H. (eds.) EPIA 2017. LNCS (LNAI), vol. 10423, pp. 486–497. Springer, Cham (2017). https://doi.org/10.1007/978-3-319-65340-2_40
13. Herlant, L.V.: Algorithms, implementation, and studies on eating with a shared control robot arm. Ph.D. dissertation, Carnegie Mellon University (2016)
14. Ragusa, F., Tomaselli, V., Furnari, A., Battiato, S., Farinella, G.M.: Food vs. non-food classification. In: Proceedings of the 2nd International Workshop on Multimedia Assisted Dietary Management - MADiMa 2016, pp. 77–81 (2016)
15. Besl, P.J., McKay, N.D.: A Method for Registration of 3-D Shapes (1992)
16. Viola, P., Jones, M.: Rapid object detection using a boosted cascade of simple features. In: Proceedings of the 2001 IEEE Computer Society Conference on Computer Vision and Pattern Recognition, CVPR 2001, vol. 1, pp. I-511–I-518 (2001)
17. Zhang, K., Zhang, Z., Li, Z., Qiao, Y.: Joint face detection and alignment using multitask cascaded convolutional networks. IEEE Sig. Process. Lett. 23(10), 1499–1503 (2016)
18. Otsu, N.: A threshold selection method from gray-level histograms. IEEE Trans. Syst. Man Cybern. 9(1), 62–66 (1979)
19. Diankov, R.: Automated construction of robotic manipulation programs. Ph.D. thesis, Carnegie Mellon University, Robotics Institute, August 2010
20. Argall, B.D., Chernova, S., Veloso, M., Browning, B.: A survey of robot learning from demonstration. Robot. Auton. Syst. 57(5), 469–483 (2009)
21. Bhattacharjee, T., Song, H., Lee, G., Srinivasa, S.S.: Food manipulation: a cadence of haptic signals. arXiv preprint arXiv:1804.08768 (2018)
22. Eggert, D.W., Lorusso, A., Fisher, R.B.: Estimating 3-D rigid body transformations: a comparison of four major algorithms. Mach. Vis. Appl. 9, 272–290 (1997)

23. Daszykowski, M., Walczak, B.: Density-based clustering methods. Compr. Chemom. **2**, 635–654 (2010)
24. Baltrusaitis, T., Robinson, P., Morency, L.P.: OpenFace: an open source facial behavior analysis toolkit. In: 2016 IEEE Winter Conference on Applications of Computer Vision, WACV 2016 (2016)

Human-Computer Interaction Approaches for the Assessment and the Practice of the Cognitive Capabilities of Elderly People

Manuela Chessa[(✉)] [iD], Chiara Bassano, Elisa Gusai, Alice E. Martis, and Fabio Solari [iD]

Department of Informatics, Bioengineering, Robotics, and Systems Engineering, University of Genoa, Genoa, Italy
manuela.chessa@unige.it

Abstract. The cognitive assessment of elderly people is usually performed by means of paper-pencil tests, which may not provide an exhaustive evaluation of the cognitive abilities of the subject. Here, we analyze two solutions based on interaction in virtual environments. In particular, we consider a non-immersive exergame based on a standard tablet, and an immersive VR environment based on a head-mounted display. We show the potential use of such tools, by comparing a set of computed metrics with the results of standard clinical tests, and we discuss the potential use of such tools to perform more complex evaluations. In particular, the use of immersive environments, which could be implemented both with head-mounted displays or with configurations of stereoscopic displays, allows us to track the patients' pose, and to analyze his/her movements and posture, when performing Activities of Daily Living, with the aim of having a further way to assess cognitive capabilities.

Keywords: Virtual reality · Exergames · Human pose tracking
Cognitive assessment · Immersive environments

1 Introduction

The increase of the population average age determines a greater incidence of neurodegenerative diseases that are specific of aging [1,2]. Such diseases compromise the ability of attention, concentration, memory, reasoning, calculation, logic and orientation, thus producing effects on the patients and his/her family [3]. Dementia is not a specific disease but a descriptive term for a set of symptoms that can be caused by various disorders that affect the brain. It is commonly preceded by a pre-dementia stage, named Mild Cognitive Impairment (MCI), where elderly people have a cognitive decline greater than expected for their age [4]. Such a cognitive decline might not interfere notably with Activities of Daily Living (ADL) [5], but see [6].

© Springer Nature Switzerland AG 2019
L. Leal-Taixé and S. Roth (Eds.): ECCV 2018 Workshops, LNCS 11134, pp. 66–81, 2019.
https://doi.org/10.1007/978-3-030-11024-6_5

Until a few decades ago, manifest dementia was considered a severe condition, however with the progress of research on the Central Nervous System and in the neuropsychological field, there was a greater knowledge of the characteristics of this pathology, a better differentiation of its forms and, as a consequence, a therapeutic approach. Though, clinical trials did not lead to important breakthroughs until now, thus rising a great interest for non-pharmacological treatments [7]. Among them, the use of the so-called exergames (video games for exercise), in general of Virtual Reality (VR) systems, i.e. enriched environments through which to assess and to stimulate cognitive functions [8], has gained popularity, as assistive technology [9].

In general, it is essential to use screening tools that can provide an early diagnosis. Currently, these tools include classical paper-pencil tasks, which try to evaluate the main cognitive functions that are compromised by the disease, through specific questions aimed at the patient. However, these tests have several limitations: they have a low specificity and sensitivity, especially in the early stages of the disease, and their scores are influenced by multiple factors, such as visual and auditory disturbances, patient education and psychological factors. For this reason, in the last few years researchers have been trying to develop further tools for the evaluation of cognitive functions that overcome these limits and are therefore able to actually measure what they are supposed to measure. This can be achieved by evaluating the symptoms, the impairments, the typical difficulties of the early stages of diseases through VR environments. Virtual Reality has several advantages with respect to traditional paper-pencil tests: ecological validity, i.e. similarity between the assessment environment and the real world; immediate performance feedback; personalization of the environment and task, thus producing engagement in participants [10–12].

1.1 Aim of This Paper

As we will describe in the next section, there are many approaches in the literature aiming to overcome the limits of the paper-pencil tests, usually considered in hospital and retirement homes to assess the cognitive status of elderly people.

Nevertheless, many of these approaches are still in the form of proofs-of-concept, and there is not an established use in the hospital practice.

This paper, starting from previous considerations about human-computer interaction (HCI) in immersive VR environments (see for example [13,14]), has the following aims.

- To propose two approaches that could be used to assess the following intellectual functions usually impaired by dementia: ability to concentrate and pay attention by using a non-immersive VR platform implementing a virtual supermarket; reasoning and visual perception difficulty in estimating distances and orientations by considering an immersive VR environment, where people play with a shape-sorter game.
- To evaluate the proposed approaches by comparing the obtained results with the scores of two standard clinical paper-pencil tests: the Pfeiffer an the GPCog.

- To put in evidence the limits and the potentialities of these two approaches, and to devise further steps in order to consider both the needs of overcoming the limitations of the standard tests, and the need of proposing non-invasive and natural HCI to patients.
- To consider other data that such kind of systems could provide to therapists and doctors, e.g. the possibility of measuring and tracking the 3D pose of patients, thus opening the way to the further clinical evaluations.

1.2   State of the Art

In the last twenty years, neuropsychology has been used as a tool for the diagnosis and management of cognitive decay. In fact, early diagnosis is one of the main objectives of the neuropsychological investigation, since it allows significant therapeutic and assistance interventions both by the medical and psychological staff and by the family [15]. The main objective of a neuropsychological evaluation is to provide data and evidence that contribute to the diagnostic framework of a specific patient [16].

One of the most common and significant symptoms of dementia is the loss of memory, however, taken individually does not necessarily imply the presence of the disease but must be accompanied by the impairment of at least one of the following intellectual functions so that we can actually talk about dementia [17]: (i) Communication and language: difficulty in following a conversation or finding the right words to express a concept; (ii) Ability to concentrate and pay attention: difficulty in making decisions or solving problems; (iii) Reasoning and judgment: difficulty in carrying out complex actions (for example cooking a meal); (iv) Visual perception: difficulty in assessing distances and orientations.

Paper-Pencil Tests for Assessing the Cognitive Decay. Here, we consider the classical paper-pencil tests that are relevant to our research, only. The Mini-Mental State Examination (MMSE) is composed of eleven items [18]. It presents some limitations: a low level of sensitivity for mild degrees of impairment and a dependence on cultural background [19]. The Short Portable Mental Status Questionnaire (SPMSQ) or Pfeiffer test [20] was developed with the aim of providing the clinician with a simple tool to assess the presence and degree of cognitive function impairment. Through a short interview, the clinician is able to establish whether the organic mental syndrome and the impairment of cognitive functions is the patient's main problem or whether it represents a complication of a medical or psychiatric disorder. The test consists of a list of ten questions that investigate some aspects of cognitive abilities: seven items are focused on orientation, two items evaluate long-term memory, and one item evaluates the concentration capacity. The patient's cognitive status is evaluated on the total number of errors: from 0–2 errors (intact intellectual functions) to 8–10 errors (severe deterioration of intellectual functions). The test is affected by the scholar degree of patients [21]. The General Practitioner Cognitive Assessment of Cognition (GPCog) is a cognitive impairment screening test consisting of two different sections: a cognitive section and an informative one [22]. The first section is the actual cognitive test to be administered to patients, the second consists of an informative interview with a family member and is useful to improve the efficiency of the test. The cognitive test includes nine items that investigate temporal orientation, visuospatial functionality and memory. The evaluation range is as follows: the maximum score obtainable is 9 (no cognitive impairment); a score of less than 5 highlights the presence of cognitive impairment; whereas a score between 5 and 8 is considered borderline.

New Approaches to Assess Cognitive Decay. In the last few years, researchers have tried to devise alternative methods to traditional paper-pencil tests to determine the cognitive state of older people. The main objective is to design tests that allow making an early diagnosis of dementia in order to study the symptoms and their course over time. Since people with MCI have difficulty performing normal ADL [6,23,24], the new approaches are focused on the simulation of this type of activity to evaluate the behavior of patients in different daily situations. This is possible thanks to the use of both non-immersive and immersive VR platforms, which allows reproducing complex situations of daily life in which the psychopathological reactions and cognitive functions of patients can be evaluated more immediately than the classic paper-pencil tests. In this way, screening instruments with a greater ecological validity can be obtained [25]. Moreover, through virtual reality, it is possible to reproduce environmental and social situations that can stimulate the subject in a similar way to the corresponding context [26], allowing to modulate the intensity and duration of the experience according to the needs of patients.

VR environments and, in general, serious games can provide useful tools for neuropsychological assessing and training of elderly people, by involving physical exercise, social engagement, and positive emotions [12,27,28].

Nevertheless, few works aim to understand how people interact within such kinds of immersive or non-immersive VR environments. A non natural interaction (see [29]) could negatively affect the validity of the developed approaches.

Non-immersive Virtual Reality Systems. By considering non-immersive VR systems, in [30] the authors proposed a music video game with the aim of increasing positive emotions in patients. A tablet-based cooking game was presented in [31], where the patient by following a recipe plans the steps to do the recipe. With the aim to combine physical stimulation and cognitive one an exergame for elderly people has been proposed in [32]. In [33] the authors proposed a virtual loft and tasks involving subjects in simulated daily activities. Each task has been designed to evaluate different cognitive functions: executive functions (reasoning and planning), attention (selective and divisive), memory (short term, long term and perspective) and visuospatial orientation. In this VR system, the subject interacts with the 3D environment through the touch screen of a computer. The serious game ECO-VR consists of a virtual apartment and interactions with the virtual environment and objects take place through the use of a joystick and a standard screen [34]. Each task requires the simultaneous involvement of two or more cognitive functions. The game was tested on healthy elderly, the scores obtained (total score, completion time, strategies) were compared with the score acquired with the MMSE and the comparison showed a moderate correlation. RehabCity simulates a district where four buildings can be visited (a supermarket, a post office, a bank and a pharmacy) [35]. By accessing each individual building, it is possible to perform tasks of different complexity. Each task requires the involvement of different cognitive domains, such as visuospatial orientation, attention and executive functions. RehabCity is a multiplatform environment in which interaction takes place via a computer screen and a joystick. It is used for the rehabilitation of people with cognitive deficits and also used as a cognitive assessment tool. The game presented in [36] simulates a supermarket, where the main objective is to buy the products in the shopping list and pay the amount due to the cash desk. The game has been implemented on a tablet so the subject interacts with the virtual environment by simply touching the screen. The execution of the tasks requires the simultaneous involvement of many cognitive processes, therefore the authors considered the game too challenging for patients with dementia and it was tested only on healthy elderly people and patients with MCI.

Immersive Virtual Reality Systems. By moving towards immersive VR, we can consider the use of stereo displays to add realism to the observed scene, as in [37], though for an ecological visual interactions the positions of user's eyes have to be considered [38]. In the immersive VR game presented in [39], the subject wears a headset that allows him to interface with the virtual world and interacts with it thanks to markers placed on the headset itself, and on a special glove. In this way, the system traces the position of the head and of the glove worn by the subject, so the latter can interact with the objects present in the scene through his/her hand. Furthermore, he/she can move in all directions within the supermarket through the use of a joystick. In this way, the patient is immersed in a virtual simulation that reflects different daily activities concerning shopping in a supermarket. Recently, a virtual shop was proposed to measure episodic memory for older adults [40]: the results show a negligible cybersickness symptoms and high levels of presence. Moreover, memory performances in the VR task are positively correlated with performance on a traditional memory task. The system proposed in [41] uses a treadmill to allow people to move in a scenario that simulates a fire evacuation drill consisting of six different scenarios of increasing difficulty, though the VR environments was displayed on a curved rear projection screen. The authors examined the relationships among the performances of three groups of participants in the VR setup and traditional neuropsychological tests employed to assess executive functions. A VR exergame for people with MCI is proposed in [42]: the results showed a new way of engaging older adults in physical activities that can tailored to their abilities. As a future work, the authors proposed an evaluation of the exergame against comparable human-guided movements.

2 Materials and Methods

2.1 Platforms and Virtual Environments

Both non-immersive and immersive virtual reality HCI platforms are considered in this experimental evaluation. Non-immersive platforms consist in PC and tablet applications, a comparison between two interaction modalities (i.e., interacting with a mouse and by using the touch screen) is considered in order to understand which is more suitable [13], especially targeting older people. Immersive platforms are based on head-mounted displays (HMD), where people can interact with both touchful or touchless devices [14].

The VR environments have been designed and implemented by using Unity3D platform, this allows a fast prototyping and an easy integration with the several interaction techniques we have considered. Also the deploy on different hardware platforms can be easily achieved.

As previously discussed, we implemented two scenarios for the assessment of the following cognitive capabilities: (i) attention and memory, with a "Supermarket Virtual Environment"; (ii) visual perception and reasoning, with a "Shape-sorter Immersive Virtual Environment".

Supermarket Virtual Environment. By taking inspiration from the existing works in the literature, and by considering an everyday life task, we implemented a virtual supermarket for PC and tablet devices. The environment is composed of three shelves, containing several common life items. The user receives a random generated item list and he/she should select and put them in a virtual basket, then go to the cash desk in order to pay the given amount of money. The procedure is identical to the corresponding real life task.

The layout of the scene, the dimension of the items and of the text, and all what concerns the user interface have been discussed with geriatrics medical staff and tested by a set of over-65 people before starting the experiments. It is also worth noting that 3D models of real objects (e.g. real objects brands) have been downloaded and modified with SketchUp, in order to increase the realism of the task.

Figure 1 shows a sketch of the "Supermarket" virtual environment, and of the cognitive assessment procedure by using the developed tool.

Shape-sorter Immersive Virtual Environment. To test the depth and shape perception, and the capability of planning simple re-ordering tasks, we devise an immersive virtual reality environment that consists of a large scale replica of the shape-sorter children game (see Fig. 2 for a sketch of the "Shape-sorter" immersive virtual environment and of the assessment procedure). The environment is composed of several solid shapes and of a structure with the corresponding holes. The user can interact with them, and he/she should place them in the correct location.

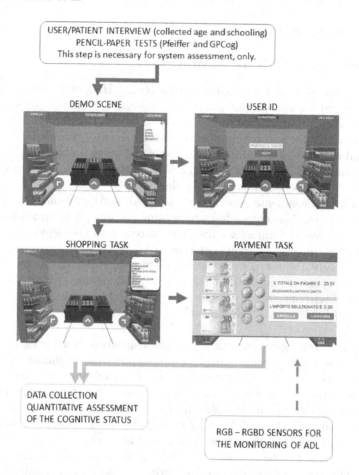

Fig. 1. A sketch of the "Supermarket" experimental setup, based on a standard tablet.

2.2 Participants

All the participants were informed about the aim of the experiment and the procedure, after that they signed a written consensus. No personal or sensitive data are stored.

Supermarket Virtual Environment. We have divided the experimental session in two phases: a preliminary assessment with 32 volunteer healthy people (ages between 21 and 78 years, average age 39.8 ± 18.8); and an experimental evaluation with 30 elderly volunteers[1] (ages between 60 and 94 years, mean age 74.6 ± 10.5), both healthy and affected by mild cognitive impairment.

---

[1] 13 people were from two retirement homes for the elderly people, 10 were recruited by the project Mo.Di.Pro., in collaboration with the hospital Galliera in Genova, 7 were volunteers recruited by the authors.

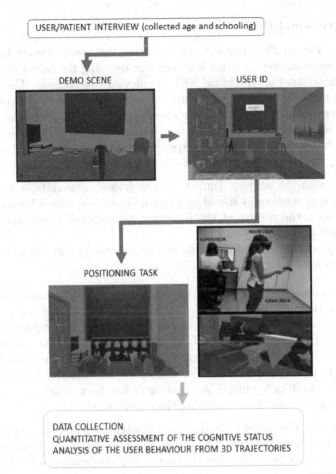

Fig. 2. A sketch of the "Shape-Sorter" experimental setup, based on an immersive VR technology.

Shape-sorter Immersive Virtual Environment. During this experimental session 35 volunteer subjects have been tested, including 30 adults (ages between 20 and 45 years (average age 26.0 ± 7.3) and 5 children and teenagers between 7 and 17 years old (average age 10.6 ± 4.6). It has been chosen to involve in the study a sample of children, although small, in accordance to two different motivations. First of all, for the purpose of determining whether the task is suitable even for people belonging to a low age range, both in terms of practical difficulties that the task itself requires and from a health point of view. Secondarily, in order to compare the technical and behavioral differences employed by the two categories of users to complete the task. It is worth noting that it is a preliminary analysis, prior to an effective use of such an immersive environment for the cognitive assessment of impaired people. For this reason, we have not included elderly people, since we are still evaluating the acceptance of the head-mounted displays.

2.3   Experimental Procedure

Supermarket Virtual Environment. By following the results shown in [13], we tested the "Supermarket" Virtual Environment by using the tablet device, thus inputs to the system are provided with the device touchscreen. The choice is given both by the fact that no significant differences between the use of a tablet with touchscreen and a PC with mouse are reported in [13], and by the fact that in an assistive context (i.e., a hospital or a retirement home) the use of portable device may be more practical. The experiment has been conducted as follows (see also Fig. 1 for a pipeline describing the experiment):

– Interview with the subject. During such interview some data (e.g., age and schooling that have been stored in an anonymous way) have been recorded, together with the results of the following paper-pencil questionnaires: the Pfeiffer test and the GPCog.
– Training phase, in order to allow the user to become familiar with the system.
– Test execution.

Shape-sorter Immersive Virtual Environment. In [14], the authors showed that interaction with touchful devices, e.g. the controllers provided with the HTC Vive headset, are more robust and stable with respect to interaction with a touchless technology, e.g. by using a Leap Motion. For this reason, since our aim is to interact with the VR environment in a reliable way, in this experiment we followed the touchful approach. The immersive VR environment has been tested in laboratory conditions, only. The experiment has been conducted as follows (see also Fig. 2 for a pipeline describing the experiment):

– Interview with the subject. During such interview some data (e.g., age and schooling that have been stored in an anonymous way) have been recorded.
– Training phase, in order to allow the user to become familiar with the system.
– Test execution.

2.4   Data Collection and Analysis

Supermarket Virtual Environment. Besides the possibility of a direct observation of the user performing the task by the doctors (or indirect by using RGB and RGBD sensors [43]), the developed system allows us to store the following data:

– Given and actual shopping list, i.e. the list randomly generated and provided to the user, and the shopping cart he/she effectively composes.
– List of errors in the "shopping task", i.e. number and typology of errors: wrong items put in the shopping cart, numbers of item deleted and/or re-inserted in the shopping cart.
– List of errors in the "payment task", i.e. whether the payed amount of money is wrong. It is worth noting that the system allows for the possibility of receiving back the change.
– List of errors in the "recall task", i.e. the number of items in the shopping list that are not correctly remembered after having completed the task.
– Partial time spent to complete the given tasks.

By defining as CI the number of bought items actually present in the shopping list, as WI the number of bought items that were not in the list, and DI the number of deleted items, we can define a score SS, empirically defined as follow:

$$SS = CI - \alpha WI - \beta DI, \tag{1}$$

where α and β are constant we defined in order to give different weights to errors of different importance.

In an analogous way, we can define:

$$PS = 10 - \gamma E, \tag{2}$$

if the payed amount is correct, where E counts the number of times the user reset the payment tasks and γ is an empirical constant, or $PS = 0$, if the payed amount is less than the required one.

Shape-sorter Immersive Virtual Environment. The immersive virtual environment and the tracking capabilities of the adopted system (in our prototype the HTC Vive lighthouse system), allows us to compute and store the following data:

- Number of errors and number of repositioned items, i.e. the total number of objects that have not been put in the corresponding holes, and the number of times the experiment supervisor resets an item position.
- Total completion time, i.e. the time to put in the right position all the elements.
- Partial times, i.e. the times to put in the right position each item.
- 3D positions of the user head, and of his/her hands (computed by using the HTC Vive sensors).

The availability of the 3D user's position allows us to better analyze the behavior of the subject acting in the immersive VR scenario, in particular the planning of actions (reaching and grasping tasks) and his/her posture.

3   Results

3.1   Supermarket Virtual Environment

Figure 3 shows the collected data and the metrics computed for the "Supermarket" experiment. Results are divided by considering separately healthy subjects (Healthy) and the one affected by mild cognitive impairment, i.e. MCI. By considering the shopping task, both the average score and the average time (Fig. 3(a)(b)) differ between the two groups ($p < 0.05$, t-test). By analyzing the data, it is worth to note that the lower score of MCI users is due to the fact that people bought less items, with respect the given list. This should be taken into consideration in a future work, since it could be an indication of fatigue or annoyance. Similar considerations can be done for the payment task

(Fig. 3(c)(d)): there is a significant difference between the two groups, MCI users obtained a lower payment score and needed more time to complete the task. In general, we can note that all the healthy users were able to complete the required tasks without any difficulty, whereas people affected by MCI found the task quite difficult. It is also worth noting that difficulties in using euro currency still remain among older people. Some could not understand how to play, e.g. where to click in order to add money. This is of great importance, since it put in evidence a lack of naturalness in the developed interface.

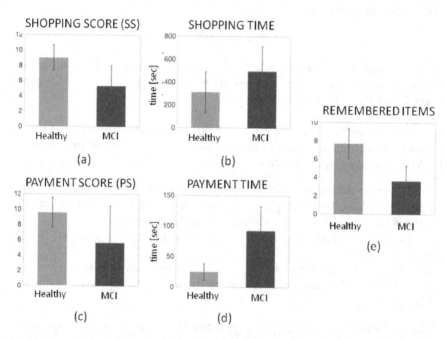

Fig. 3. The computed metrics for the "Supermarket" test for the "Healthy" group (light blue) and for the "MCI" group (dark blue). Average values and associated standard deviations are shown. (Color figure online)

Finally, it can be noticed that the number of remembered items is consistently different between Healthy and MCI subjects (see Fig. 3(e)). Healthy people can remember an average of 8 bought items (over 10), whereas for MCI users we have 3.60 ± 1.65. This is especially true for those who obtained a low rating in the session of the GPCog test, which assesses memory.

Since one of the aim of our approach is to evaluate, whether it could be possible to substitute the pencil-paper tests with more effective evaluation methods, it is interesting to understand if they can measure and evaluate similar aspects of the cognitive status. To this aim, we have computed the Pearson correlation coefficient among the results of the Pfeiffer and GPCog tests and the parameters computed by the "Supermarket" test. Results are reported in Table 1, from which it can be noticed how no correlation is present with respect the results of the Pfeiffer test, whereas there is moderate (Shopping Score, Shopping Time and Payment time) or strong (Payment Time and number of Remembered Items) correlation withe the results of the GPCog test. This result suggests that the proposed approach might be used to evaluate the cognitive status of elderly people. However, we should take into account that there is no correlation with the Pfeiffer test, for this reason a further study is necessary, though our aim is not to replicate the tests but to obtain a more complex evaluation.

Table 1. Pearson correlation coefficients among the parameters computed by the "Supermarket" test and the Pfeiffer and GPCog tests. $*p < 0.05$; $**p < 0.001$

	Pfeiffer	GPCog
Shopping Score	−0,06	0,57*
Shopping Time	0,04	0,62*
Payment Score	0,29	0,59*
Payment Time	0,42	0,84**
Remembered Items	0,16	0,78**

3.2 Shape-Sorter Immersive Virtual Environment

Results are divided by considering separately adult subjects (Adults) and younger ones (Children). Table 2 shows a comparison of the computed metrics for "Adults" and "Children" groups.

Table 2. Data collected for the "Shape-Sorter" test for "Adults" and "Children" groups.

	Adults	Children
Repositioned elements	0.5 ± 0.7	0.2 ± 0.5
Completion time [sec]	68.1 ± 13.5	112.4 ± 33.4
Positioning time for the single item [sec]	3.2 ± 4.5	2.8 ± 0.2

There are not statistically relevant differences, except for the "Completion time" metric, which is lower in the "Adults" group ($p < 0.05$, t-test). It is worth noting that "Completion time" takes into account both the time to put the single objects in the right position, and the time to plan the actions (i.e. to find the correspondence between a shape and a hole, to decide whether the hole is not occluded, and to decide which object grab first). This may be correlated with the cognitive capabilities of planning actions and distinguish shape and distance, thus it could be used as a further assessment of the cognitive status for older people. Nevertheless, a systematic analysis of such factors and a correlation with paper-pencil tests have been planned but not performed, yet.

A preliminary analysis of the trajectories shows that differences between children and adults are present, especially in the smoothness of the path. Figure 4 shows a comparison between the two groups, by looking at trajectories along the X-axis (the same is for the other axes). This suggests that a specific analysis of the 3D movements of the subject could be used in order to assess his/her cognitive capabilities. It is worth noting that the "Shape-Sorter" test can be implemented with configurations of stereoscopic displays, which allow the perception of depth, thus avoiding the use of HMDs [37,38]. The possibility of performing the test without wearing a HMD could be a factor to be considered for assessing elderly people.

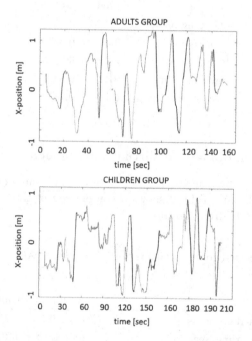

Fig. 4. Trajectories of the user dominant hand, along the X-axis for the "Adults" group (top) and for the "Children" group (bottom). Different colors represent the movements to place different objects in the corresponding holes. (Color figure online)

4   Discussion and Conclusion

In this paper, we propose human-computer interaction based tests to assess the cognitive status of elderly people. In particular, we have developed two VR applications that take into consideration some cognitive functionalities: memory and attention by using non-immersive VR (i.e. the "Supermarket" test), and reasoning and visual perception by employing immersive VR (i.e. the "Shape-Sorter" test). We designed the two approaches in order to allow a natural interaction in VR (also in collaboration with the medical staff), which is a fundamental aspect for using them with elderly people. The results show that subjects can accomplish the proposed tasks: this is a good starting point for further development of VR approaches, though some works is still necessary to simplify the interaction and to improve the engagement of MCI patients.

The comparison of the results of our proposed VR tests with two standard paper-pencil tests, i.e. the Pfeier and the GPCog, shows a good correlation with the latter, only. This deserves further investigations in order to understand the evidenced difference.

During the tests performed by using the immersive VR application, the 3D trajectories of the participants have been recorded: a preliminary analysis shows that there are differences between the two analyzed groups. This suggests that also the behavioral data could be used to assess the cognitive capabilities. However, there is the need of further studies to assess these preliminary results and to apply the proposed approach to the assessment of elderly people.

The obtained results suggest that the proposed approaches can help doctors to assess the cognitive status of elderly people in a objective and automatic way. Moreover, in perspective, these VR approaches could be used both for a more complete assessment and for the cognitive training of elderly people.

References

1. Giannakouris, K., et al.: Ageing characterises the demographic perspectives of the European societies. Stat. Focus **72**, 2008 (2008)
2. Prince, M., Comas-Herrera, A., Knapp, M., Guerchet, M., Karagiannidou, M.: World Alzheimer report 2016: improving healthcare for people living with dementia: coverage, quality and costs now and in the future (2016)
3. Aalten, P., et al.: Behavioral problems in dementia: a factor analysis of the neuropsychiatric inventory. Dement. Geriatr. Cogn. Disord. **15**(2), 99–105 (2003)
4. Winblad, B., et al.: Mild cognitive impairment-beyond controversies, towards a consensus: report of the international working group on mild cognitive impairment. J. Intern. Med. **256**(3), 240–246 (2004)
5. Gauthier, S., et al.: Mild cognitive impairment. Lancet **367**(9518), 1262–1270 (2006)
6. Farias, S.T., Mungas, D., Reed, B.R., Harvey, D., Cahn-Weiner, D., DeCarli, C.: MCI is associated with deficits in everyday functioning. Alzheimer Dis. Assoc. Disord. **20**(4), 217 (2006)
7. Hertzog, C., Kramer, A.F., Wilson, R.S., Lindenberger, U.: Enrichment effects on adult cognitive development: can the functional capacity of older adults be preserved and enhanced? Psychol. Sci. Public Interest **9**(1), 1–65 (2008)
8. Powers, K.L., Brooks, P.J., Aldrich, N.J., Palladino, M.A., Alfieri, L.: Effects of video-game play on information processing: a meta-analytic investigation. Psychon. Bull. Rev. **20**(6), 1055–1079 (2013)
9. Anderson-Hanley, C., et al.: Exergaming and older adult cognition: a cluster randomized clinical trial. Am. J. Prev. Med. **42**(2), 109–119 (2012)

10. Zakzanis, K.K., Quintin, G., Graham, S.J., Mraz, R.: Age and dementia related differences in spatial navigation within an immersive virtual environment. Med. Sci. Monitor **15**(4), CR140–CR150 (2009)
11. Yeh, S.C., Chen, Y.C., Tsai, C.F., Rizzo, A.: An innovative virtual reality system for mild cognitive impairment: diagnosis and evaluation. In: 2012 IEEE EMBS Conference on Biomedical Engineering and Sciences (IECBES), pp. 23–27. IEEE (2012)
12. McCallum, S., Boletsis, C.: Dementia games: a literature review of dementia-related serious games. In: Ma, M., Oliveira, M.F., Petersen, S., Hauge, J.B. (eds.) SGDA 2013. LNCS, vol. 8101, pp. 15–27. Springer, Heidelberg (2013). https://doi.org/10.1007/978-3-642-40790-1_2
13. Martis, A.E., Bassano, C., Solari, F., Chessa, M.: Going to a virtual supermarket: comparison of different techniques for interacting in a serious game for the assessment of the cognitive status. In: Battiato, S., Farinella, G.M., Leo, M., Gallo, G. (eds.) ICIAP 2017. LNCS, vol. 10590, pp. 281–289. Springer, Cham (2017). https://doi.org/10.1007/978-3-319-70742-6_26
14. Gusai, E., Bassano, C., Solari, F., Chessa, M.: Interaction in an immersive collaborative virtual reality environment: a comparison between leap motion and HTC controllers. In: Battiato, S., Farinella, G.M., Leo, M., Gallo, G. (eds.) ICIAP 2017. LNCS, vol. 10590, pp. 290–300. Springer, Cham (2017). https://doi.org/10.1007/978-3-319-70742-6_27
15. Ashford, J.W., et al.: Should older adults be screened for dementia? Alzheimer's Dement. J. Alzheimer's Assoc. **2**(2), 76–85 (2006)
16. Lezak, M.D., Howieson, D.B., Loring, D.W., Fischer, J.S.: Neuropsychological Assessment. Oxford University Press, USA (2004)
17. Alzheimer's Society: What is dementia? https://www.alzheimers.org.uk/get-support/publications-factsheets-full-list. Accessed 07 June 2018
18. Folstein, M.F., Folstein, S.E., McHugh, P.R.: "mini-mental state": a practical method for grading the cognitive state of patients for the clinician. J. Psychiatr. Res. **12**(3), 189–198 (1975)
19. Tombaugh, T.N., McIntyre, N.J.: The mini-mental state examination: a comprehensive review. J. Am. Geriatr. Soc. **40**(9), 922–935 (1992)
20. Pfeiffer, E.: A short portable mental status questionnaire for the assessment of organic brain deficit in elderly patients. J. Am. Geriatr. Soc. **23**(10), 433–441 (1975)
21. Malhotra, C., et al.: Diagnostic performance of short portable mental status questionnaire for screening dementia among patients attending cognitive assessment clinics in Singapore. Ann. Acad. Med. Singap. **42**(7), 315–319 (2013)
22. Brodaty, H., et al.: The GPCOG: a new screening test for dementia designed for general practice. J. Am. Geriatr. Soc. **50**(3), 530–534 (2002)
23. Ahn, I.S., et al.: Impairment of instrumental activities of daily living in patients with mild cognitive impairment. Psychiatry Investig. **6**(3), 180–184 (2009)
24. Aretouli, E., Brandt, J.: Everyday functioning in mild cognitive impairment and its relationship with executive cognition. Int. J. Geriatr. Psychiatry **25**(3), 224–233 (2010)
25. Spooner, D.M., Pachana, N.A.: Ecological validity in neuropsychological assessment: a case for greater consideration in research with neurologically intact populations. Arch. Clin. Neuropsychol. **21**(4), 327–337 (2006)
26. Rizzo, A.A., Schultheis, M., Kerns, K.A., Mateer, C.: Analysis of assets for virtual reality applications in neuropsychology. Neuropsychol. Rehabil. **14**(1–2), 207–239 (2004)

27. Maillot, P., Perrot, A., Hartley, A.: Effects of interactive physical-activity video-game training on physical and cognitive function in older adults. Psychol. Aging **27**(3), 589 (2012)

28. Laamarti, F., Eid, M., Saddik, A.E.: An overview of serious games. Int. J. Comput. Games Technol. **2014**, 11 (2014)

29. Chessa, M., Noceti, N.: Investigating natural interaction in augmented reality environments using motion qualities. In: VISIGRAPP (6: VISAPP), pp. 110–117 (2017)

30. Benveniste, S., Jouvelot, P., Pin, B., Péquignot, R.: The MINWii project: renarcissization of patients suffering from Alzheimer's disease through video game-based music therapy. Entertain. Comput. **3**(4), 111–120 (2012)

31. Manera, V., et al.: "Kitchen and cooking," a serious game for mild cognitive impairment and Alzheimer's disease: a pilot study. Front. Aging Neurosci. **7**, 24 (2015)

32. Ben-Sadoun, G., et al.: Physical and cognitive stimulation using an exergame in subjects with normal aging, mild and moderate cognitive impairment. J. Alzheimer's Dis. **53**(4), 1299–1314 (2016)

33. Zucchella, C., et al.: Serious games for screening pre-dementia conditions: from virtuality to reality? a pilot project. Funct. Neurol. **29**(3), 153 (2014)

34. Oliveira, C.R., et al.: Development and feasibility of a virtual reality task for the cognitive assessment of older adults: the ECO-VR. Span. J. Psychol. 19 (2016)

35. Vourvopoulos, A., Faria, A.L., Ponnam, K., Bermudez i Badia, S.: Rehabcity: design and validation of a cognitive assessment and rehabilitation tool through gamified simulations of activities of daily living. In: Proceedings of the 11th Conference on Advances in Computer Entertainment Technology, p. 26. ACM (2014)

36. Zygouris, S., et al.: A preliminary study on the feasibility of using a virtual reality cognitive training application for remote detection of mild cognitive impairment. J. Alzheimer's Dis. **56**(2), 619–627 (2017)

37. Manera, V., et al.: A feasibility study with image-based rendered virtual reality in patients with mild cognitive impairment and dementia. PloS one **11**(3), e0151487 (2016)

38. Solari, F., Chessa, M., Garibotti, M., Sabatini, S.P.: Natural perception in dynamic stereoscopic augmented reality environments. Displays **34**(2), 142–152 (2013)

39. Parsons, T.D., McPherson, S., Interrante, V.: Enhancing neurocognitive assessment using immersive virtual reality. In: 2013 1st Workshop on Virtual and Augmented Assistive Technology (VAAT), pp. 27–34. IEEE (2013)

40. Corriveau Lecavalier, N., Ouellet, É., Boller, B., Belleville, S.: Use of immersive virtual reality to assess episodic memory: A validation study in older adults. Neuropsychological rehabilitation, pp. 1–19 (2018)

41. Tarnanas, I., Schlee, W., Tsolaki, M., Müri, R., Mosimann, U., Nef, T.: Ecological validity of virtual reality daily living activities screening for early dementia: longitudinal study. JMIR Serious Games **1**(1), e1 (2013)

42. Eisapour, M., Cao, S., Domenicucci, L., Boger, J.: Participatory design of a virtual reality exercise for people with mild cognitive impairment. In: Extended Abstracts of the 2018 CHI Conference on Human Factors in Computing Systems. ACM (2018). CS15

43. Chessa, M., Noceti, N., Martini, C., Solari, F., Odone, F.: Designing assistive tools for the market. In: Computer Vision for Assistive Healthcare, pp. 337–362. Elsevier (2018)

Analysis of the Effect of Sensors for End-to-End Machine Learning Odometry

Carlos Marquez Rodriguez-Peral$^{(\boxtimes)}$ (ID) and Dexmont Peña$^{(\boxtimes)}$ (ID)

Intel Research and Development, Movidius Group, Kildare, Ireland
carlos.marquez.rp@gmail.com, dexmont.pena@intel.com

Abstract. Accurate position and orientation estimations are essential for navigation in autonomous robots. Although it is a well studied problem, existing solutions rely on statistical filters, which usually require good parameter initialization or calibration and are computationally expensive. This paper addresses that problem by using an end-to-end machine learning approach. This work explores the incorporation of multiple sources of data (monocular RGB images and inertial data) to overcome the weaknesses of each source independently. Three different odometry approaches are proposed using CNNs and LSTMs and evaluated against the KITTI dataset and compared with other existing approaches. The obtained results show that the performance of the proposed approaches is similar to the state-of-the-art ones, outperforming some of them at a lower computational cost allowing their execution on resource constrained devices.

Keywords: Navigation · Visual · Inertial · Odometry
Machine learning · CNN · LSTM

1 Introduction

Motion estimation is one of the main pillars of mobile robotics. It provides a robot with the capability to know its position and orientation in an unknown environment and it can be combined with mapping approaches to develop Simultaneous Localization and Mapping (SLAM), which is essential to perform human assistance and exploration tasks. A robot can use different sources of data to perform such motion estimation depending on the type of sensor: proprioceptive, when it offers the robot's internal information such as Inertial Measurement Units (IMU), or exteroceptive, when it offers information of the robot's surroundings such as cameras or LiDARs. Due to the autonomous nature of a robot, it should be able to perform such motion estimation on board in real time, often resource-limited. Thus, finding a solution that can run in an embedded device under such restrictions is desirable.

© Springer Nature Switzerland AG 2019
L. Leal-Taixé and S. Roth (Eds.): ECCV 2018 Workshops, LNCS 11134, pp. 82–95, 2019.
https://doi.org/10.1007/978-3-030-11024-6_6

This paper explores the performance of different end-to-end machine learning based systems depending on the type of sensor used. The contributions of this paper are:

- Three end-to-end trainable networks using different kind of sensor data are proposed.
- The proposed networks are tested on real world data and compared with other state-of-the-art approaches.

The rest of the paper is organized as follows: Sect. 2 shows existing visual and inertial odometry approaches based on both classical and machine learning techniques. Section 3 shows the architecture of the proposed approaches. In Sect. 4, the training parameters, optimizer and objective function used are explained. The results of the training as well as their performance comparison is done in Sect. 5. Section 6 presents the conclusions of this work and shows the future work that can be done.

2   Related Work

This section analyzes and highlights different works that have been done to solve the pose estimation problem with classic approaches and, more recently, with deep learning techniques.

Cameras capture the surroundings of the robot and can be used to track the robot's movement, this process is known as Visual Odometry (VO) [1]. Classic VO approaches estimate motion from geometry constraints, and can be divided into two groups: sparse feature based methods and direct methods. On one hand, sparse feature based methods extract and match feature points to estimate the motion between frames such as in LIBVISO2 [2]. In addition, some VO approaches such as ORB-SLAM [3] add and maintain a feature map in order to correct the drift suffered due to the presence of outliers and noisy images. On the other hand, direct [4] and semi-direct [5,6] methods use all the image pixels to estimate the pose by minimizing the photometric error between consecutive images.

However, classical VO approaches need external information (such as camera height or templates) to perceive the scale and recover distances in real world units. Castle et al. address this problem by combining a monocular SLAM system with object recognition [7]. Pillai et al. combine ORB-SLAM [3] with object recognition, introducing a multi-view object proposal and an efficient feature encoding method [8].

Nevertheless, VO systems are not reliable in the presence of rapid movements or when there are sudden changes in illumination. To solve this lack of reliability, the camera information can be combined with inertial sensors, which can provide acceleration and angular rate information. This sensors usually offer data at much higher frequencies (about 10 times faster) than a camera. Therefore, inertial information can be used to overcome VO systems' weaknesses in the case of rapid camera motion.

Visual-Inertial Odometry (VIO) systems take advantage of visual and inertial information to provide position and orientation estimations. In state-of-the-art methods, the visual-inertial data fusion is done by using probabilistic filter approaches such as Extended Kalman Filter (EKF) or Unscented Kalman Filter (UKF), which are compared in [9]. In [10], the visual-inertial data fusion is performed with an EKF based system, which they used to compare different fusion models using only gyroscope data, or gyroscope and accelerometer data. Other variations of the EKF have been used for this purpose, such as the Multi-state Constraint Kalman Filter (MSCKF). Mourikis et al. implemented a MSCKF system in which several past camera poses were used to detect static features and add a constraint to the state vector [11].

In recent years, deep learning approaches have overcome the weaknesses of classic VO approaches, such as lack of robustness to blurred or noisy images or when changes in illumination or occlusion occurs. Convolutional Neural Networks (CNN) have shown to perform well even with blurred and noisy images, providing a robust method for extracting image features [12]. CNNs have been also used to compute the Optical Flow between two consecutive images [13,14]. The Optical Flow represents the change in location of the objects on the camera view [15], therefore it is related to the motion that the camera has experienced between two consecutive frames. The image features extracted by the Optical Flow network in [13] have been used in [16] along with two Long Short Term Memory (LSTM) [17] layers to implement a monocular VO system in an end-to-end deep learning manner, clearly outperforming a classic monocular VO approach based on LIBVISO2 [2].

VIO approaches based on probabilistic filters for sensor fusion may require a hard and complex calibration process in order to bring camera and IMU measurements to the same reference coordinate system [18,19]. In [20] the calibration process is done in real time while a tracking system is running, adding complexity to the filtering process. Moreover, some IMU's parameters are difficult to model, such as the noise scaling over the measurements found in most commercial IMUs [21]. Deep Learning techniques have been used in order to solve the issues with the sensor fusion process. In [22], Rambach et al. use an LSTM to track past IMU raw measurements (accelerometer and gyroscope) to estimate the pose of a robot, which is then fused with a VO system. LSTMs have been also used in VINet [23] to extract encoded features from IMU's raw measurements. These encoded features are combined in a features vector with features extracted from a CNN, being this features vector tracked over time by a second LSTM, which provides a pose estimation of a robot. VINet approach outperforms OKVIS [24], which is an optimization-based sensor fusion approach.

3   Proposed Approaches

This work explores the performance of different end-to-end trainable neural network architectures, varying the amount and type of the input. Three different networks have been trained for this purpose. The first one takes as input RGB images, the second one takes as input IMU raw measurements and the last one is a combination of the previous networks, taking as input both RGB images and IMU raw measurements. All the networks are trainable in an end-to-end manner, eliminating any need of calibration or preprocessing.

The networks have been trained to produce at every frame a pose estimation relative to the previous frame. Each pose estimation represents a transformation, which is usually represented as elements of the Special Euclidean Group of transformations SE(3), which is described in [25]. All the transformations represented in SE(3) (Eq. 1) are composed of a rotation matrix and a translation vector, being that rotation matrix part of the Special Orthogonal group SO(3), described in [25].

$$SE(3) : (R|T), \ R \in SO(3), \ T \in \mathbb{R}^3 \tag{1}$$

Finding a transformation in the SE(3) is not straightforward for the network because R has to be orthogonally constrained. Thus, to make easier the learning process, the estimated transformations are represented in the Lie Algebra se(3) (Eq. 2) of SE(3).

$$se(3) : (\omega|t), \ \omega \in so(3), \ t \in \mathbb{R}^3 \tag{2}$$

The pose estimations in se(3) are 6-D vectors and are not orthogonally constrained. Once estimated, the poses in se(3) can be converted into transformations of the SE(3) by doing an exponential mapping: $se(3) \rightarrow SE(3)$ (Eq. 10) as described in [25].

$$\theta = \sqrt{\omega^T \omega} \tag{3}$$

$$A = \frac{sin\theta}{\theta} \tag{4}$$

$$B = \frac{1 - cos\theta}{\theta^2} \tag{5}$$

$$C = \frac{1 - A}{\theta^2} \tag{6}$$

$$\omega_x = \begin{pmatrix} 0 & -\omega_3 & \omega_2 \\ \omega_3 & 0 & -\omega_1 \\ -\omega_2 & \omega_1 & 0 \end{pmatrix} \tag{7}$$

$$R = I + A\omega_x + B\omega_x^2 \tag{8}$$

$$V = I + B\omega_x + C\omega_x^2 \tag{9}$$

$$se(3) \rightarrow SE(3) : exp(\omega|t) = (R|Vt) \tag{10}$$

Matrices R and V can be calculated using Eqs. 8 and 9, respectively. A, B, C and θ can be obtained through Eqs. 4, 5, 6 and 3. ω_x matrix is composed by ω values (Eq. 7).

3.1 Network 1: Visual Odometry

The first proposed network is illustrated in Fig. 1. It takes as input two consecutive RGB images, which are stacked composing an input tensor of size 512×384 with 6 channels. This image size has been used because it has shown to contain enough features while resulting in a light CNN. FlowNetS [13] has been used to extract images' features, as its good performance for motion estimation was shown in [16,23]. This network was trained on a synthetic dataset to learn how to estimate the Optical Flow between frames, which represents the motion undergone by the robot over time.

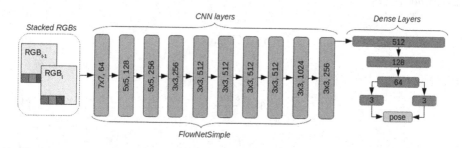

Fig. 1. Architecture of the proposed visual odometry network. All the layers are followed by a LeakyReLU activation layer except the last two FC layers.

FlowNetS is taken up to its 9th convolutional layer, followed by an additional convolutional layer to reduce the output size of the CNN to a $2 \times 3 \times 256$ tensor. After the CNN, a series of Fully Connected layers combine the extracted features to produce an output 6-D vector pose that represents the transformation of the current frame (t) relative to the previous frame ($t-1$), expressed in the Lie Algebra of SE(3).

3.2   Network 2: Inertial Odometry

The second proposed network is shown in Fig. 2. In this case, only inertial data is used as input to the network. Specifically, the input is a subsequence composed by 10 6-D vectors with the x-y-z raw data components from accelerometer and gyroscope. This subsequence of 10 measurements is ordered in time, being the last one the most up to date, encoding the motion that the sensor has experienced over time.

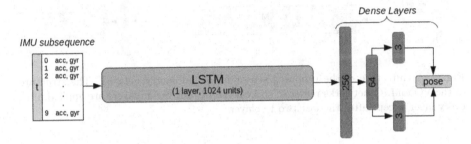

Fig. 2. Architecture of the proposed inertial odometry network. The first two FC layers are followed by a LeakyReLU activation layer.

An LSTM is used as a regression layer to track measurements over the subsequence and extract motion information as it is able to store in its hidden states short and long term dependencies produced by past inputs. Each input is combined with the hidden state as it passes through the LSTM, finding temporal correspondences between the current and past measurements. The LSTM used has 1 layer, 1024 units and is followed by 4 Fully Connected layers that output a 6-D vector representing the transformation undergone by the robot from the last to the first element of the subsequence. These architecture and parameters have been selected as a result of their performance in a montecarlo analysis, which was done to explore different combination of layers.

3.3   Network 3: Visual-Inertial Odometry

The third proposed network is shown in Fig. 3. It combines the networks 1 and 2, taking advantage of both visual and inertial sensors. The input is a pair of consecutive RGB images and a subsequence of 10 inertial measurements following the idea of the VIO networks, which combine inertial and visual data to overcome the weaknesses of each other, as stated in Sect. 1. The structure of the VO network remains up to its third Fully Connected layer. Similarly, the Inertial Odometry (IO) network is used up to its second FC layer. The idea behind this is to maintain both VO and IO networks until the last layer that provides useful features.

Then, vision and inertial feature vectors are concatenated into a 128-D vector and passed through three FC layers to output a pose estimation. As before, each

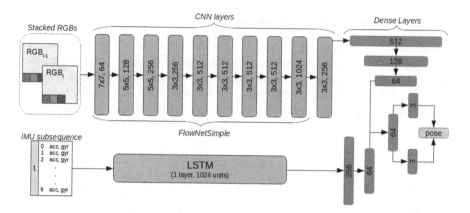

Fig. 3. Architecture of the proposed sensor fusion odometry network. The structure of the VO and IO networks remains, so LeakyReLU activation layers are applied after every layer except after the last two FC layers.

pose estimation represents the transformation undergone by the robot at the current frame with respect to the previous one.

4 Training Setup

This section describes the parameters used to train the networks as well as the dataset structure. All the networks described have been trained separately but maintaining the same parameters and training data in order to be able to do a fair comparison between them.

The data used for training is part of the raw data section of KITTI Vision Benchmark Suite [26], which involves a car based odometry problem suitable for the analysis carried out in this paper. The odometry dataset is composed by 22 sequences, being the first 11 of these provided with its groundtruth transformations. Sequences 11–22 are intended to be used as evaluation, so no groundtruth is provided. Sequences 00, 02, 08 and 09, which contain the highest number of frames, are used for training and sequences 05, 07 and 10 for evaluation. The training data is augmented by randomly applying gaussian noise, gaussian blur and changes in intensity to the images as follows:

– 2/3 of the data: gaussian noise (mean = 0, standard deviation = [0, 32]) and change in pixels intensity [−25%, 25%]
– 1/3 of the data: gaussian blur with kernels 3, 5 and 7.

After augmenting the data, the training dataset has a total of 22912 image frames. The images recorded in the dataset are sampled at 10 Hz as well as the groundtruth. The IMU data arrives at 100 Hz, meaning that there are 10 IMU measurements per image frame. However, there are frames where some IMU data are missing. In that case, the first IMU measurement of the frame is used to pad the missing measurements to fill the subsequence.

The loss function (Eq. 11) used represents the euclidean distance between every estimated relative pose and its respective groundtruth, expressed in se(3). This loss function was inspired by VINet paper [23].

$$\mathcal{L}_{se(3)} = \Sigma||\omega - \hat{\omega}|| + \beta||t - \hat{t}|| \tag{11}$$

ω, $\hat{\omega}$, t and $\hat{t}$ represent the estimated and groundtruth rotation and translation in *se(3)*, respectively. The parameter β is useful to balance the different magnitude order between ω and t, and it is fixed to 0.1 in all trainings. Nesterov Accelerated Gradient (NAG) [27] is used as optimizer (Eqs. 12 and 13). It speeds up the convergence with respect to the standard Gradient Descent, as stated in [28], measuring the gradient of the loss function not at the local position but slightly ahead in the direction of the momentum, m.

$$m = \beta m + \lambda \nabla(w^{se(3)} + \beta m) \tag{12}$$

$$w^{se(3)} = w^{se(3)} - m \tag{13}$$

β acts as a friction factor, preventing the momentum from growing too large and λ is the learning rate. The weights $w^{se(3)}$ are then updated according to m. For training, a friction factor $\beta = 0.9$ was used. Senior et al. performed an empirical study of different learning rate schedules [29], showing that implementing an exponential schedule (Eq. 14) leads to a faster convergence and it is easier to implement in comparison with other methods such as the performance schedule.

$$\lambda(t) = \lambda_0 2^{-t/r} \tag{14}$$

An initial learning rate (λ_0) of 10^{-5} and a step (r) of 50 were used. With these parameters, the learning rate is divided by 2 every 50 iterations. All the networks have been implemented on TensorFlow and trained using a NVIDIA GeForce GTX Titan X GPU. In order to reduce the training time, FlowNetS' [13] weights were frozen during training.

5   Results

This section shows the evaluation results of all the networks. Initially, the VO and VIO are compared separately with existing approaches that use the same type of data. Then, the evaluation performance of all the networks proposed in this paper are compared.

The proposed VO network has been evaluated using the metrics proposed in KITTI's odometry development kit. According to these metrics, the network is executed on sequences 05, 07 and 10, getting the absolute pose for every frame with respect to the first one. Then, the Root Mean Squared Error (RMSE) is calculated for different trajectory lengths (100 m, 200 m, 300 m, ...800 m) over the sequence. These results are shown in Table 1 along with VISO2_M and DeepVO for comparison.

Table 1. All the errors represent the average RMSE for all the possible sequence lengths. t_{rel} is translation error and r_{rel} is rotation error. DeepVO and VISO2_M results are taken from [16].

Seq	t_{rel} (%)			r_{rel} (deg/m)		
	Proposed VO	VISO2_M	DeepVO	Proposed VO	VISO2_M	DeepVO
05	14.03	19.22	2.62	0.10	0.17	0.03
07	28.6	23.61	3.91	0.21	0.29	0.04
10	11.83	41.56	8.11	0.08	0.32	0.08

The VO network proposed in this paper outperforms VISO2_M in terms of both translation and rotation errors for Sequences 05 and 10, being slightly worse in translation for Sequence 07.

The proposed VIO network has been compared with the method proposed by Hu and Chen in [30], which uses a MSCKF to perform monocular VIO. They evaluate their VIO method in the first section of sequence 00. Therefore, in order to do a fair comparison, the proposed VIO network has been trained again eliminating the first 1000 frames of sequence 00 from the training dataset. Then, the trained network has been evaluated in frames 0–800 of sequence 00, which involve a total translation distance of 556.1 m. The estimated trajectory is shown in Fig. 4 and the end point translation and rotation errors are shown in Table 2.

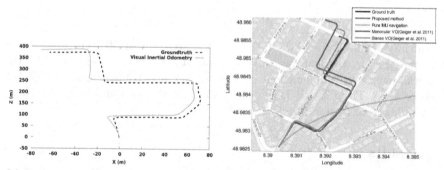

(a) Proposed VIO method estimated trajectory.   (b) Hu and Chen VIO method estimated trajectory.

Fig. 4. Estimated trajectory comparison between the proposed VIO and Hu and Chen VIO methods. The evaluation trajectories have been made over the first frames of sequence 00. Subfigure (b) has been taken from [30], in which *Proposed method* refers to the VIO method proposed by Hu and Chen.

Although the proposed VIO method translation error is considerably bigger than the one obtained by Hu and Chen, most of the contribution to that error comes from Y axis error, which represents the height of the robot. X, Y and

Table 2. Final point position and orientation error for the proposed VIO method and the method proposed by Hu and Chen [30]. The translation error is shown both in terms of absolute error of the final point and of percentage of that error with respect of the total distance covered in frames 0–800.

	Proposed VIO method	Hu and Chen VIO [30]
Translation (m)/(%)	37.20/6.68	6.44/1.15
Rotation (deg)	15.64	1.05

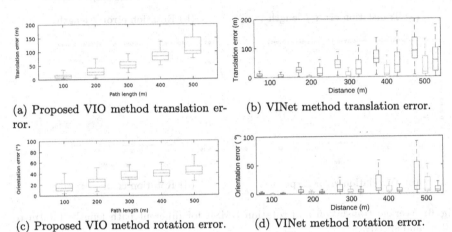

(a) Proposed VIO method translation error.

(b) VINet method translation error.

(c) Proposed VIO method rotation error.

(d) VINet method rotation error.

Fig. 5. The boxplot graphs show the translation and rotation errors distribution for the different path lengths. In VINet error graphs, three different approaches are shown for each path length . According to VINet paper [23], from left to right: VINet vision only, VINet and EKF+Viso2. Subfigures (b) and (d) have been taken from VINet paper.

Z errors for the end point are 6.90, 34.59 and 11.84 respectively. Moreover, the translation percentage errors show that the translation error of the proposed VIO method represents a 6.68% with respect to the total distance covered, meanwhile this percentage is 1.15% for the Hu and Chen VIO approach.

In addition, the VIO network has been compared with VINet [23]. For this purpose, the network has been executed over the whole sequence 10 and the evaluation results have been calculated with KITTI metrics for paths of length: 100 m, 200 m, 300 m, 400 m and 500 m. These results are shown in Fig. 5 along with VINet results.

In order to compare the performance of the networks proposed, all of them have been evaluated on sequences 05, 07 and 10. The results of this evaluation are presented in Figs. 6 and 7. The checkpoint size of the proposed IO, VO and VIO networks are 34 MB, 173 MB and 207 MB respectively. Figure 6 shows graph errors for translation and rotation depending on the path length and speed. On one hand, the IO network outperforms the VO network in terms of rotation and it gets similar results to the VIO network. The reason behind this result

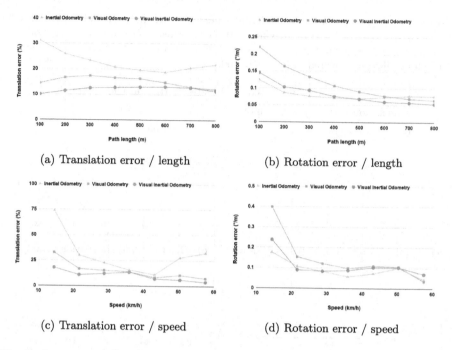

(a) Translation error / length

(b) Rotation error / length

(c) Translation error / speed

(d) Rotation error / speed

Fig. 6. Average translation and rotation RMSE for different path lengths (100 m to 800 m) and speeds.

might be that inertial information is better suited for movements that imply big changes in the frontal view of the robot. That is because when the robot is turning, the images captured by the camera suffer from temporary changes in illumination and blurring, causing the Optical Flow extracted by the CNN to become unreliable.

On the other hand, the VO network outperforms the IO network in terms of translation error. This result shows that pure IMU based odometry suffer from drift over time. This can be seen in Fig. 7, which shows the estimated trajectory for every network on Sequences 05, 07 and 10.

Analyzing Sequence 07, the IO network, while maintaining a good performance in rotation, gets drifted in translation. In contrary, the VO network performs better in terms of translation, but fails in estimating rotations. The best performance, in sequences 05 and 07, is achieved by the VIO network. The trajectories obtained with this network show that the combination of visual and inertial information allows the network to provide better estimations both in term of translation and rotation, maintaining a better transformation scale over time.

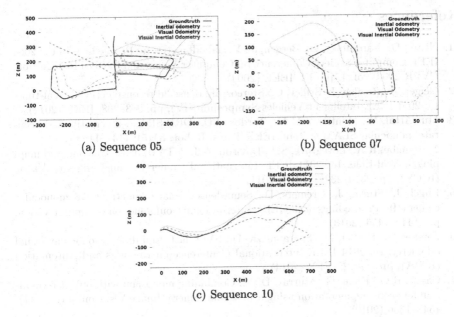

(a) Sequence 05   (b) Sequence 07

(c) Sequence 10

Fig. 7. Evaluation trajectories for the three network proposed run on Sequences 05, 07 and 10.

6 Conclusions and Future Work

This work proposed, trained and evaluated three end-to-end approaches for Odometry estimation. A performance comparison between them was carried out in order to show how different combinations of a camera and an IMU can lead to different results. The Inertial Odometry network has shown a large drift error over time. However, when it is combined with the Visual Odometry network, the drift is considerably reduced. Moreover, the Visual Inertial Odometry showed a better performance when the robot is turning, outperforming the Visual Odometry network. This showed how the IMU compensates the large displacement of the objects in the camera. These networks have been compared with existing approaches, showing promising results and outperforming (in the case of the Visual Odometry network) classical methods at a smaller memory footprint than existing approaches.

Nevertheless, the proposed networks performance may be improved by increasing the amount of data used for training to include indoor scenarios and drone flying as they present a bigger challenge for Visual Inertial Odometry systems due to the sudden and unstable movements. Further research is being performed on the introduction of sensor reading failures and approaches to overcome them.

References

1. Nistér, D., Naroditsky, O., Bergen, J.: Visual odometry. In: Proceedings of the 2004 IEEE Computer Society Conference on Computer Vision and Pattern Recognition, CVPR 2004, vol. 1, pp. I-I. IEEE (2004)
2. Geiger, A., Ziegler, J., Stiller, C.: Stereoscan: dense 3d reconstruction in real-time. In: 2011 IEEE Intelligent Vehicles Symposium (IV), pp. 963–968. IEEE (2011)
3. Mur-Artal, R., Montiel, J.M.M., Tardos, J.D.: ORB-SLAM: a versatile and accurate monocular SLAM system. IEEE Trans. Robot. **31**(5), 1147–1163 (2015)
4. Newcombe, R.A., Lovegrove, S.J., Davison, A.J.: DTAM: dense tracking and mapping in real-time. In: 2011 IEEE International Conference on Computer Vision (ICCV), pp. 2320–2327. IEEE (2011)
5. Engel, J., Sturm, J., Cremers, D.: Semi-dense visual odometry for a monocular camera. In: Proceedings of the IEEE International Conference on Computer Vision, pp. 1449–1456 (2013)
6. Forster, C., Pizzoli, M., Scaramuzza, D.: SVO: fast semi-direct monocular visual odometry. In: 2014 IEEE International Conference on Robotics and Automation (ICRA), pp. 15–22. IEEE (2014)
7. Castle, R.O., Klein, G., Murray, D.W.: Combining monoslam with object recognition for scene augmentation using a wearable camera. Image Vis. Comput. **28**(11), 1548–1556 (2010)
8. Pillai, S., Leonard, J.: Monocular slam supported object recognition. arXiv preprint arXiv:1506.01732 (2015)
9. D'Alfonso, L., Lucia, W., Muraca, P., Pugliese, P.: Mobile robot localization via EKF and UKF: a comparison based on real data. Robot. Auton. Syst. **74**, 122–127 (2015)
10. Bleser, G., Stricker, D.: Advanced tracking through efficient image processing and visual-inertial sensor fusion. Comput. Graph. **33**(1), 59–72 (2009)
11. Mourikis, A.I., Roumeliotis, S.I.: A multi-state constraint Kalman filter for vision-aided inertial navigation. In: 2007 IEEE International Conference on Robotics and Automation, pp. 3565–3572. IEEE (2007)
12. Mayer, N., et al.: A large dataset to train convolutional networks for disparity, optical flow, and scene flow estimation. In: Proceedings of the IEEE Conference on Computer Vision and Pattern Recognition, pp. 4040–4048 (2016)
13. Dosovitskiy, A., et al.: Flownet: learning optical flow with convolutional networks. In: Proceedings of the IEEE International Conference on Computer Vision, pp. 2758–2766 (2015)
14. Zhu, Y., Lan, Z., Newsam, S., Hauptmann, A.G.: Guided optical flow learning. arXiv preprint arXiv:1702.02295 (2017)
15. Raudies, F.: Optical flow. http://www.scholarpedia.org/article/Optic_flow. Accessed 26 June 2018
16. Wang, S., Clark, R., Wen, H., Trigoni, N.: Deepvo: towards end-to-end visual odometry with deep recurrent convolutional neural networks. In: 2017 IEEE International Conference on Robotics and Automation (ICRA), pp. 2043–2050. IEEE (2017)
17. Hochreiter, S., Schmidhuber, J.: Long short-term memory. Neural Comput. **9**(8), 1735–1780 (1997)
18. Lobo, J., Dias, J.: Relative pose calibration between visual and inertial sensors. Int. J. Robot. Res. **26**(6), 561–575 (2007)

19. Petersen, A., Koch, R.: Video-based realtime IMU-camera calibration for robot navigation. In: Real-Time Image and Video Processing 2012, vol. 8437, p. 843706. International Society for Optics and Photonics (2012)

20. Weiss, S., Achtelik, M.W., Lynen, S., Chli, M., Siegwart, R.: Real-time onboard visual-inertial state estimation and self-calibration of MAVs in unknown environments. In: 2012 IEEE International Conference on Robotics and Automation (ICRA), pp. 957–964. IEEE (2012)

21. Skog, I., Händel, P.: Calibration of a MEMS inertial measurement unit. In: XVII IMEKO World Congress, pp. 1–6 (2006)

22. Rambach, J.R., Tewari, A., Pagani, A., Stricker, D.: Learning to fuse: a deep learning approach to visual-inertial camera pose estimation. In: 2016 IEEE International Symposium on Mixed and Augmented Reality (ISMAR), pp. 71–76. IEEE (2016)

23. Clark, R., Wang, S., Wen, H., Markham, A., Trigoni, N.: VINet: visual-inertial odometry as a sequence-to-sequence learning problem. AAAI I, 3995–4001 (2017)

24. Leutenegger, S., Lynen, S., Bosse, M., Siegwart, R., Furgale, P.: Keyframe-based visual-inertial odometry using nonlinear optimization. Int. J. Robot. Res. **34**(3), 314–334 (2015)

25. Eade, E.: Lie groups for 2d and 3d transformations, revised December 2013. http://ethaneade.com/lie.pdf

26. Geiger, A., Lenz, P., Stiller, C., Urtasun, R.: Vision meets robotics: the kitti dataset. Int. J. Robot. Res. **32**(11), 1231–1237 (2013)

27. Nesterov, Y.: A method for unconstrained convex minimization problem with the rate of convergence o $1/k^2$. In: Doklady AN USSR, vol. 269, pp. 543–547 (1983)

28. Gron, A.: Hands-on machine learning with scikit-learn and tensorflow: concepts, tools, and techniques to build intelligent systems (2017)

29. Senior, A., Heigold, G., Yang, K., et al.: An empirical study of learning rates in deep neural networks for speech recognition. In: 2013 IEEE International Conference on Acoustics, Speech and Signal Processing (ICASSP), pp. 6724–6728. IEEE (2013)

30. Hu, J.S., Chen, M.Y.: A sliding-window visual-imu odometer based on tri-focal tensor geometry. In: 2014 IEEE international conference on Robotics and automation (ICRA), pp. 3963–3968. IEEE (2014)

RAMCIP Robot: A Personal Robotic Assistant; Demonstration of a Complete Framework

Ioannis Kostavelis[1]([✉]), Dimitrios Giakoumis[1], Georgia Peleka[1],
Andreas Kargakos[1], Evangelos Skartados[1], Manolis Vasileiadis[1,2],
and Dimitrios Tzovaras[1]

[1] Centre for Research and Technology, Hellas Information Technologies Institute
(CERTH/ITI), 6th Km Charilaou-Thermi Road, 57001 Thessaloniki, Greece
{gkostave,dgiakoum,gepe,akargakos,dimitrios.tzovaras}@iti.gr
[2] Department of Electrical and Electronic Engineering, Imperial College London,
London SW7 2AZ, UK
m.vasileiadis16@imperial.ac.uk

Abstract. At the last decades, personal domestic robots are considered
as the future for tackling the societal challenge inherent in the growing elderly population. Ageing is typically associated with physical and
cognitive decline, altering the way an older person moves around the
house, manipulates objects and senses the home environment. This paper
aims to demonstrate the RAMCIP robot, which is a Robotic Assistant
for patients with Mild Cognitive Impairments (MCI), suitable to provide its services in domestic environments. The use cases that the robot
addresses are described herein outlining the necessary requirements that
set the basis for the software and hardware architectural components. A
short description of the integrated cognitive, perception, manipulation
and navigation capabilities of the robot is provided. Robot's autonomy
is enabled through a specific decision making and task planning framework. The robot has been evaluated in ten real home environments of
real MCI users exhibiting remarkable performance.

Keywords: Robotic Assistant · Integrated framework · Manipulation
Navigation · Perception · Task planning · Decision making · MCI

1 Introduction

The paper at hand aims to provide a comprehensive demonstration of a personal
service robot, namely RAMCIP, which was researched and developed within the
scope of the European Project "Robotic Assistant for MCI Patients at Home".
This is a novel service robot able to proactively assist older persons at the early
stages of dementia (MCI), in a wide range of their daily activities (see Fig. 1).

The classification of a robot as service, personal service or professional service robot, strongly depends on the task that the respective agent is dedicated to

© Springer Nature Switzerland AG 2019
L. Leal-Taixé and S. Roth (Eds.): ECCV 2018 Workshops, LNCS 11134, pp. 96–111, 2019.
https://doi.org/10.1007/978-3-030-11024-6_7

perform [24]. In this scope, contemporary robots require task-specific capabilities to cope with their mission (e.g. robot serving people in a house), however, there are also common abilities, which are vital for the majority of robotic applications and are always considered during the design of a new service robot. These abilities are highly related to the way the robots understand, interpret and represent their environment and the way the robots apprehend the human occurrence and activities within it [9]. Considering personal service robots the majority of them target domestic applications and can be classified as mobile servant, people carrier, physical assistant, personal care and health care assistant robots [7,19].

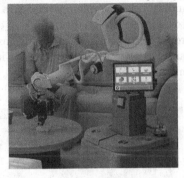

There are several types of health care robots, an indicative classification of which can distinguish them among those that provide physical assistance, those that provide companionship, and those that monitor health and safety. However, they all share the same primary objective which is to improve or protect the health and lifestyle of the human user [4]. The demand for health care robots is more intensive for the aged population, where "aging in place" is present, in accordance to which older are living independently in their own homes and want to stay there as long as possible [21]. Contemporary paradigm of such robot can be the Kompaii 2 robot which aims to assist

Fig. 1. The RAMCIP robot engaged on a medication assistive task.

seniors and dependent persons at home. However, the situation is even more challenging for elderly being at early stages of dementia, in accordance to which they are not fully aware of their cognitive impairments and in this respect, their participation in everyday activities inherently involves significant risks. Towards this direction, the last years important research has been conducted for the development of artificial agents that will significantly assist elderly and support their independence. These efforts realized robots with significant capabilities related to autonomous motion and manipulations, entertainment provision, telepresence functions, objects fetching, detection of falls, mobility assistance to older persons, all necessary skills for addressing challenging tasks during human-robot cohabitation. Representative examples of such robots are referred herein. Notable assisting robots for the elderly have been derived from several research projects in the past. Specifically the HOBBIT project [8] combined research from robotics, gerontology, and human'robot interaction to develop a care robot which is capable to prevent falls, detect emergencies, bringing of objects and offering reminder to the users. The Hobbit robot was equipped with a mobile robot platform and 5 DoF manipulator accompanied with a gripper and was evaluated with real users in domestic environments. The ACCOMPANY project was build upon the Care-O-Bot®3 integrated in smart-home environment aiming empathic and social human-robot interaction, robot learning and memory visualisation as well as persons' monitoring at home [3].

A series of research projects are currently working towards the development of service robots, which could be used to support older adults at home. The RADIO robot objectives are focused on using the integrated smart home/assistant robot system as the sensing equipment for health monitoring with sensors that do not need to be discreet and distant or masked and cumbersome to install. Instead, sensors are realized as a natural component of the smart home/assistant robot functionalities, attempting to increase the levels of acceptance and unobtrusiveness. In addition ENRICHME robot [1] aims to enrich the day-to-day experiences of elderly people at home by means of technologies that enable health monitoring, complementary care and social support. ENRICHME's objective is to improve the quality of life of elderly people suffering of MCI, using a service robot within an assisted living environment. Opposed to RAMCIP, both RADIO and ENRICHME robots do not have a dexterous robotic hand and arm and act mainly as observers.

No	Use Case Category	SubUc	SubUc Description
UC1	Emergency	1.1	Fall Detection
UC2	Assistance in maintaining the home and keeping it safe	2.1	Assist in turning off electric appliances
		2.2	Turning on the light
		2.3	Detection of improperly place objects
UC3	Support in Daily Activities (Medication)	3.1	Medication intake, bringing and monitoring
UC4	Support in Daily Activities (Food Preparation)	4.1	Assistance upon detection of abnormalities related to electric appliance during cooking
		4.2	Assistance for fallen objects
UC5	Support in Daily Activities (Eating)	5.1	Proactive bringing of bottle of water to the user
		5.2	On demand bringing of food (snac)
UC6	Support in socialization and mental stimulation	6.1	Provision of cognitive training programs
		6.2	Communication with relatives and friends

Fig. 2. A summary of the target use cases for the RAMCIP robot.

Albeit the fact that significant steps forward have been achieved in the respective domain, major challenges still need to be addressed towards service robots of the future. Of such can be assumed the capability of assisting older persons in a wide variety of activities, discreetly and transparently, yet proactively and in tight cooperation with the human, acting at the same time as effective promoters of the patients mental health. The challenges that have been addressed in order to allow RACMIP robot to successfully realize its mission are summarized as follows:

- Development of a perception system suitable for continuous monitoring of the user and the environment.
- Establishment of multimodal human-robot communication interfaces.
- Endorsement of robust robotic skills, related to safe manipulation, grasping and navigation that enable safe robot interaction with the human and the environment.
- Provision of cognitive skills to the robot, suitable to enable it to optimally decide for its assistive interventions, while at the same time ensuring sequential skill applications for each scenario denouement, through a task planner that allows fail safe mechanisms.

Towards addressing the above challenges, a series of S/W and H/W modules were developed in the course of the RAMCIP project, carefully designed on the basis of detailed end user requirements and target use cases. The paper at hand aims to describe the overall framework of these components integration, starting from the target use cases and moving along to outlines of their key capabilities and how these were integrated, so as to lead into the RAMCIP robot, a robot that is currently being evaluated in a series of different real home environments (ten so far), of real end users, i.e. older persons with MCI. In this context, the paper underlines the importance of how robot cognition and task planning have been fused so as to orchestrate the subordinate S/W modules of the integrated robot and eventually, provides insight on the level to which this has led to effective robot operation on the target use cases, within the real domestic environments of the RAMCIP project pilot trials.

2   The RAMCIP Use Cases

In order to realize a robotic assistant useful for the target population group, i.e. MCI patients in our case, the user needs and requirements have been firstly identified. To achieve this a specific methodology has been followed [12]. In accordance to it, firstly, research questions were established towards analysing user needs and expectations. Then, a mapping among the posed research questions and the existing investigation approaches has been performed. In that stage, a literature survey along with moderated group discussions was established and surveys with questionnaires were performed. The outcome of this procedure was the user requirements elicitation and their prioritization considering the material obtained from the conducted surveys. The next step comprised the definition of the RAMCIP robot use cases, i.e. user-centred scenarios, which demonstrated interactions between the robotic system, the user and the environment. The main aim for each use case is to accomplish the task and achieve a planned goal. Due to the multitask nature of the RAMCIP robot, all potential activities stemming from the prioritized user requirements analysis, were classified into high level use cases (UC) and each one consisted of sub-use cases (SubUc), which are specific goal-orientated interactions between the robot, the user and the environment. The identified RAMCIP UC and SubUc are summarized in Fig. 2. Each SubUc is analysed as follows:

SubUc-1.1: The robot is capable of detecting a fallen user, approach him/her and establish communication about the user's current status. If needed the robot is capable of establishing communication with an external person/caregiver.

SubUc-2.1: The robot detects the state of a cooker appliance after a cooking session of the user. If a knob has been forgotten turned on, the robot firstly stimulates the user with communication to turn it off and, then, if needed it turns off the knob by engaging with a robotic manipulation.

SubUc-2.2: The robot can detect the user while walking around under low-illumination conditions and if necessary turns on a light switch with robotic manipulation.

SubUc-2.3: The robot can detect improperly placed objects after the user has interacted with them. Specifically, after the medication intake activity, the robot prompts the user to take the pill box back to its storage position. If the user does not perform the task, the robot is engaged in the scenario to fulfill the task with robotic manipulations.

SubUc-3.1: The robot is able to provide the user with reminders considering the daily medication schedule. The robot can also bring the medication to the user and monitor the medication intake activity.

SubUc-4.1: The robot detects the state of a fridge appliance after the finishing of a cooking session. If the fridge-door has been forgotten open, the robot firstly stimulates the user with communication and, then, if needed, closes the fridge-door by engaging with a robotic manipulation.

SubUc-4.2: The robot monitors the user and the environment during the cooking activity and upon detection of a fallen object, the robot notifies the user about the situation. If the object is graspable, the robot is engaged into a manipulation task to pick it up from the floor.

SubUc-5.1: The robot monitors the user during the eating activity. In case the user doesn't drink any water, the robot proactively brings a bottle of water to the user.

SubUc-5.2: The user communicates with the robot and asks for a snack or a bottle of water. The robot is capable of executing the fetching task.

SubUc-6.1: The robot prompts the user to participate in a cognitive training game which is integrated into the robot's communication interfaces.

SubUc-6.2: The robot monitors the user's emotions and in case of negative affective state detection, it prompts the user to engage in a telco-call with a relative.

3   The Robot Hardware Components

After the identification of the RAMCIP requirements, the target use cases and the available technology base, the robot hardware architecture was established. During planning the component list, a series of factors were considered in order to justify the necessity of each component and map its functionality to a user requirement, ensuring this way that the designed robot can be fully justified and can meet the posed specifications. The robot has been developed in an iterative fashion distinguished in two phases. Firstly, the V1 robot has been developed based on the preliminary posed requirements and use cases. The developed robot has been evaluated with real users and the feedback obtained was utilized for the construction of the V2 robot. Figure 3 exhibits the two versions of the robot. The basic hardware components are summarized as follows:

Mobile Platform: The mobile platform provides the locomotion functionality and is based on the 2DoF differential kinematics model. It hosts the entire computational system of the robot, offering lower center of gravity and at the same time ensuring lightweight construction of the rest of the robot body.

Elevation Mechanism: The elevation mechanism allows the robot to reach both higher (around 1,75 m) and lower (floor) locations with the same robotic arm.

Body: In the front of the RAMCIP body, interaction components are included such as microphone, tablet PC and speakers, allowing communication with the user.

Arm manipulator: The RAMCIP robot arm manipulator is relied in a 5 DoF kinematic model including also the prismatic joint of the elevation mechanism.

Hand and Wrist: The robot is equipped with a 2DoF wrist that maximizes the robot's workspace and holds a dexterous manipulation hand. The latter is a three-fingered robotic hand with nine degrees-of-freedom, suitable to perform grasping of different objects with various grasping strategies.

Head and AR-Module: The robot has a 2DoF head equipped with a display for facial expressions that enables robot-user interaction and augments it with affective cues. It also has a projector to interact with the user through augmented reality, since part of the multimodal communication is the ability of the robot to display pointers and information on a chosen surface/object. Both components are merged into a commonly motorized part.

Fig. 3. The RAMCIP robot; on the left the first and on the right the second version of the robot, after the iterative development procedure.

Perception System: The robot perception system consists of one RGB-D sensor mounted on the robot's head and two laser scanners mounted on the platform. The RGB-D sensor is utilized for the mapping, the environment monitoring and the human tracking. The laser scanners are utilized mainly for the robot localization and navigation and for leg human tracking.

4   The Software Components of the Robot

4.1   Perception Modules

Environment Hierarchical Semantic Mapping. The metric mapping solution adopted, is the RGBD-SLAM presented in [6], yet enhanced in terms of memory and speed management in order to be operable for large scale mapping requirements of real houses. The 3D metric map is constructed once during the installation of the robot to a new house. In that phase the robot is teleoperated and acquires color and depth images in order to progressively build the map, utilizing feature tracking and graph optimization techniques. The 3D map is utilized for the extraction of the dominant supporting surfaces (e.g. table, kitchen bench) of the house and the definition of the robot's parking positions for human and environment monitoring (e.g. robot parking position for the cooking monitoring) according the use cases. The semantic information is stored in an XML schema and comprises the following structure: the house environment is organised in rooms, the room types consist of large objects and frequently visited standing positions, the large objects are related with the robot parking positions and with small objects. The small objects are organized in terms of their attributes, their grasping strategy and their relations to other objects [13]. Then the 3D map is top down projected and converted into a 2D costmap to be utilized for robot navigation (see Fig. 4).

Large and Small Object Detection and State Tracking. Tha RAMCIP robot is capable of detecting and tracking the state of small and large objects, a functionality that allows it to successfully monitor the human activities and grasp objects from various places. Considering the small object detection and tracking, a dedicated custom tailored solution has been developed based on RGB-D data. Specifically, a model based 6Dof object detection algorithm has been developed as described in [5], which has been utilized for object grasping purposes. A lighter version of this algorithm has been also utilized for performing initial detection of small objects on a supporting surface and then a connected component based solution has been applied for the tracking of such objects while manipulated from the user. The app-

Fig. 4. The first row illustrates examples of metric maps in different houses, the second and third rows exhibit examples from the large object state tracking and the small object detection and tracking components respectively.

roach is applied when the robot is at a human activity monitoring state and the human actions and manipulated objects should be tracked.

The large object (fridge, cooker) state tracking component is essential for the detection of the state of the electric appliances in the house environment. Due to the great unevenness of the appliances that can be met in different houses, a holistic solution has been developed. The latter comprises the a priori rough modelling of the home appliances during the robot's installation in the environment and the anchoring of their pose to the hierarchical semantic map. Given that the robot is parked in a specific pose, a search is performed in the hierarchical semantic map, to acquire a list of the large scale objects that are in the current field of view. The retrieved object IDs are used to recall the corresponding 3D models from the respective collection of models in the hierarchical semantic model. The retrieved object models undergo multiple registration (ICP) steps in order to be aligned with the point cloud in the observed scene. Then, depending on the context of the robotic task, a large object state tracking based on articulated ICP is performed to detect the state of the parts of the observed object (e.g. fridge door), or vision based processing techniques are applied to detect the state of the respective appliance (e.g knob state detection). Illustrative examples of these approaches are exhibited in Fig. 4.

Human Monitoring. The human monitoring module involves first of all the continuous detection and tracking of the human in the environment and the inference upon the performed daily activities. A hybrid methodology for the human detection has been developed, comprising of RGB-D skeleton and leg tracking components. The first one relies on a model based 3D skeleton joint tracking algorithm presented in [22] and is appropriate for full and partial human observability in the scene. The second one, is a laser based human tracking relied on the methodology introduced in [17] and is capable of human tracking while the robot is moving or the user is outside the camera's field of view. The seamless integration of the two approaches ensures continuous robot awareness regarding the human presence and location in the house.

Fig. 5. Characteristic examples of human tracking used for action recognition in occluded scenes.

The human action recognition module is the one developed in [20], which is specifically designed to operate in realistic conditions, with robotic platforms. It employs the tracked human's skeleton joints and by extending the classic EigenJoints [23] method, it improves recognition robustness for a series of actions involved in common daily activities. In addition, it associates specific actions with information related to the user's manipulated objects, taking into account that several actions may be similar, yet performed with different objects e.g. "eating" can be analysed as a "hand to mouth" atomic action with object "spoon" and drinking can be analysed also as a "hand to mouth" action with object "cup". Figure 5 illustrates some characteristic examples of human tracking used for action recognition in cluttered environment. Last but not least, the human monitoring includes also a user affect recognition module. This is based on multimodal data, derived from facial expressions recognition and biosignals monitoring. Emphasis is put on the detection of the user's negative emotions, such as sadness or stress. During the robot's installation at a user's house, baseline recordings are taken from the specific user, to help the respective machine learning system counteract common issues of affect-related between-subjects variability.

4.2   Action Modules

Navigation. The RAMCIP navigation framework has been designed based on the existing architecture of ROS, known as the navigation stack. This is a framework that orchestrates the robot odometry information, the sensor's stream, the constructed maps of the environment and the velocity commands send to the platform. The reason for the selection of the navigation stack is that it already implements a communication architecture among the modalities that need to work together in order for the robot to navigate successfully. The overall navigation approach is structured in a global (GPP) and local path planning (LPP) framework. For the GPP of navigation, a socially-aware path planning method was developed which explicitly takes the human into account in terms of human motion prediction, extensively described in [15]. The predicted path is extended by a human comfort zone which is derived from proxemics theory on human-human interaction. By including the result in the cost-map structure for global path planning, trajectories that avoid unnecessary proximity to the human are derived. This enhances the acceptance of the robot by the human and helps to avoid hazardous situations already in the early stage of off-line planning. For the execution of planned trajectories a dynamic window approach has been integrated as a local planner [16]. It allows the system to find locally optimal solutions in velocity space that are collision free and explicitly consider the dynamic capabilities of the robotic platform, thus guaranteeing safe solutions. The approach works on a local map obtained from online laser range scanners and RGB-D sensors. In many cases, the robot can find its way around a priori undetected obstacles without having to re-plan, bringing increased robustness to the navigation system.

Manipulation. The manipulation system of RAMCIP robot is endorsed with safety features. An adaptive compliance controller has been implemented [11] as a nominal controller that adapts arm stiffness and damping parameters dynamically to the task, the risk of collision and uncertainties stemming from the perception system of the robot. The adaptive compliance allows the robot to efficiently reduce the collision impact in the event of unintended contacts while being stiffer and executing motion accurately when the environment is collision-free with a higher level of confidence. For the arm motion, biologically inspired motion profiles are used, aiming at a more predictable behaviour. To avoid unintended collisions whenever possible, an invariance control scheme is implemented that supervises the nominal control with respect to safety boundaries that are defined as hard constraints to the system. This model-based method takes the dynamics of the robot explicitly into account which allows for a mathematically proven adherence to boundaries. An augmented version of this approach was developed in course of this task to enable the adherence to smoothness requirements for system states and control inputs.

Grasping. The RAMCIP robot targeted interaction with various objects that retain different geometrical attributes. For example in the medication intake activity, the robot has to grasp very small and flat objects (pillbox), which may be at ashelf of increased height, while for the assistance on eating and drinking the robot should be able to grasp a bottle of water. It is apparent that for each object and context in terms of supporting surface and surrounding environment, a specific grasping strategy should be developed. Thus the grasping affordances are associated with the small object and stored in the hieratical semantic map. To this end, and in order to compensate with various geometry constraints and errors from the vision component to the object

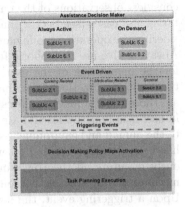

Fig. 6. The architecture of the RAMCIP cognitive functionalities

pose estimation, novel grasping strategies that exploit environmental contacts have been developed. Emphasis has been given in the development of grasping strategies suitable, for flat, directly graspable, and top reachable objects [10]. By exploiting force sensors mounted on the robot's fingertips, a method for grasp stability during transfer has been developed in order to enable gentle degradation of the system upon a failure (e.g. object fall due to a loosen grasp) [2].

4.3 Cognitive Functionalities

The RAMCIP robot aims to address multiple use cases yet in an autonomous manner. Considering that on-board robot computational resources are limited and that the addressing of target SubUcs with diverse context is related to various human activities during the day, a *hierarchical architecture* has been embodied within the cognitive functionalities by developing an "Assistance Decision Maker (ADM)" cognitive module that decides *when* and *how* the robot should intervene to offer a coherent and relevant, proactive and discreet care solution. The hierarchical architecture of the RAMCIP robot cognitive functions is illustrated in Fig. 6. The developed architecture consists of two levels i.e. the high-level component which is responsible for the continuous monitoring of human end environment semantics through specific parameters in order to decide in which SubUc the RAMCIP robot should be engaged. The high level component also regulates the prioritization framework according to which, specific robot functionalities are always active and render RAMCIP ready to provide the respective type of intervention even if the robot is already engaged in another SubUc. In order to provide a prioritized and autonomous care solution, the RAMCIP robot continuously monitors specific parameters that sign the initiation of a target use case. This functionality comprises a deterministic part of the RAMCIP ADM which orchestrates the initiation of a necessitated SubUc, the denouement of which is undertaken by a probabilistic POMDP policy map (see Sect. 4.3) that considers observations of the environment, the human and the robot state. The target use cases (see Sect. 2) have been analysed in terms of their priority considering the operation mode namely, *always active, on demand* and *event driven*. Always active are the robotic functionalities that address use cases responsible for the monitoring of the user's safety and health condition. On demand, are those robotic functionalities that are emerged after user request. Event driven, are those robotic functionalities that are related to SubUcs responsible to assist in user's daily activities and are organized in three different groups with respect to the human and environment semantics. A deterministic regulatory framework has been developed, based on which a dedicated software component continuously monitors all the triggering events gathered from the robot's perception mechanism and upon activation of an event, the respective SubUc is triggered. Upon a triggering event, the low-level decision making undertakes the denouement of the scenario.

Decision Making Policy. The first component of the low-level ADM architecture is responsible to provide a suitable intervention policy, which the robot should follow in order to resolve the assistance scenario imposed by the respective SubUc. To achieve this, a dedicated mechanism has been developed based on the Partially Observable Markov Decision Process (POMDP), which is able to model the uncertainties stemming from realistic situations. The justification of such selection relies on the fact that complete situation awareness from the robot is not feasible, since the environment should be constantly monitored with limited robot sensors and the acquired sensor observations are noisy. Therefore, the robot belief uncertainty about the current state of the human, the environment and the robot itself should be broadened. For each SubUc, a handcrafted POMDP model has been designed which produces a specific policy map as described in [14]. Each state of the POMDP model corresponds to a robotic action or the activation of a perception module. Upon execution of the selected action, the RAMCIP perception mechanism observes the alterations in the environment, associates them with the policy map and the next best robotic action is selected until the finalization of the scenario. To create a comprehensive POMDP model, an exhaustive finite state machine (FSM) has been developed for each SubuUc. Each FSM was then modeled as POMDP model and by exploiting a dedicated solver [18], a policy map was created for each SubUc. An example of such FSM is illustrated in Fig. 7, where each state corresponds to a state in the policy map and is associated with a specific robotic action.

Task Planning. The robot task planner is responsible to implement the developed robotic skills, in accordance to which each selected action from the POMDP corresponds to a software component that realizes the respective functionality. Thus, the developed task planner comprises a skills library that directly interfaces with the policy map of the POMDP. The skills library has been developed with the ROS framework exploiting the intra-node communication functionalities, (service calls, actions, topics,

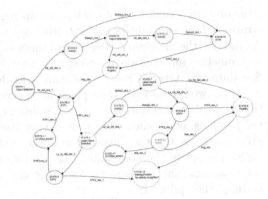

Fig. 7. An example of an FSM that is utilized for the construction of a POMDP model. (Color figure online)

etc.) to allow continuous operation and repeatability of each skill and scenario. Considering again the state diagram of Fig. 7, it is exhibited that each state is associated with a specific robot action. The states marked in blue color correspond to drastic robotic intervention including navigation, manipulation and grasping. The states in green color indicate perception functionalities of the robot, required for the monitoring of the environment and the user. States in magenta color are related to the communication modalities, while red colored states are control points in the scenario that allow fail safe mechanisms and re-initialization of a problematic robotic action due failures.

5 RAMCIP Robot Installation in Pilot Trials

The RAMCIP robot has being evaluated in real house environments with MCI patients. Two robots have been prepared to operate in parallel. The first one is deployed at a simulated room of Medical University of Lublin Poland, where the robot capabilities are assessed with 20 participants and each user interacts with the RAMCIP robot for at least 3 days. The second robot, has been moved to Barcelona, Spain to be evaluated with 12 participants. Each participant interacted with the robot at her/his own house for at least 7 days. Preliminary results of Barcelona pilot site are reported herein. The robot installation at each participant's house involves one day of transportation and deployment. The deployment procedure concerns both robot preparation to operate in the specific environment as well as familiarization of the user with the robot. The robot preparation requires the environment mapping and the construction of the hand-crafted hierarchical semantic model, to denote supporting surfaces, robot parking positions for the large object manipulation, and relations of small and large objects. Familiarization of user regarding the robot concerns short demonstration of its capabilities and introduction to the communication framework. Alongside, the necessary user measurements are taken by the robot, related to biometric information necessary for user identification, affect-related baseline data etc. Overall robot's software was designed in a way that minimum invasions would have to take place at the participants' houses. In situations that the robot was not to execute a scenario due to environment restrictions, i.e. grasping of a fallen object in a very narrow kitchen area, this skill was excluded from the task planner and the ADM steered the scenario flow by exploiting solely the communication modalities; i.e. notifying the user of the event, stimulating her/him to resolve it and monitoring the user accordingly.

During the pilot trials, the robot has been exposed to all the SubUcs described in Fig. 2, more than one times. In order to keep track of the evolution of the scenarios, two peripheral tools have been utilized. An external camera with video recording has been employed to capture the entire interaction among robot and human during to the exposure of the robot at each scenario. These video recordings were

Table 1. Preliminary evaluation results of the RAMCIP robot during pilot installation in Spain.

SubUc	Total executions	Erroneous executions	% Correct execution rate
SubUc 1.1	15	1	93.33
SubUc 2.1	31	7	77.41
SubUc 2.2	16	2	87.5
SubUc 2.3	31	4	87.09
SubUc 3.1	17	3	82.35
SubUc 4.1	20	3	85.00
SubUc 4.2	26	3	88.46
SubUc 5.1	18	1	94.44
SubUc 5.2	16	2	85.71
SubUc 6.1	26	3	88,46

kept as ground truth for the evaluation of the examined scenarios. The second tool is a logging framework that kept track of the ADM's executed policy file that registers the robotic executed actions, utilized perception modules along with the exchanged communication messages, in order to be compared with the ground-truth data (video recordings). Table 1 summarizes the total number of repetitions of each SubUc and outlines the correct executions, where the scenario was successfully completed. The majority of the erroneous executions are referred to the situations where the scenarios ended-up to a "System-Reset" state of the ADM, as part of failure of a subordinate component, i.e. the robot was not able to reach its target location after N attempts due to localization errors. Figure 8 exhibits the RAMCIP robot interaction with the user or the environment in different apartments, for each one of the target SubUcs.

Fig. 8. Examples of RAMCIP interacting with users and the environment during the preliminary trials. Top row: SU1.1 (emergency), SU2.1 (turning off electric appliances), SU2.2 (turning on the light), SU2.3 (detection of improperly place objects), SU3.1 (medication bringing). Bottom row: SU4.1 (assistance upon detection of abnormalities during cooking), SU4.2 (assistance for fallen objects), SU5.1 (proactive bringing bottle of water), SU5.2 (on demand bringing a snack), SU6.1 (provision of cognitive training).

6 Discussion

In this paper we presented the multidimensional approach needed for the development of a domestic assistance robot for patients with MCI. The process varies from the establishment of users requirements, to integrating social and empathic aspects into the basic components of the robotic platform. Human, environment, and activity monitoring have been employed so that RAMCIP can combine information about its environment, its user and her/his tasks, enabling it with the ability to provide proactive assistance by integrating these technologies under one single robotic platform. The preliminary results from the pilot trials in Barcelona indicate that the RAMCIP prototype can successfully accomplish its core tasks and provide assistance for the target group within the rather challenging environments of real end-users homes. Even if, in some limited cases, users may have initially approached the robot with uncertainty and doubt on its ability to be helpful and assistive, RAMCIP was able to interact with all participants and their house environments, by performing all of its target tasks, leading to a final positive assessment in terms of its usability and acceptance.

Acknowledgment. This work has been supported by the EU Horizon 2020 funded project namely: Robotic Assistant for MCI Patients at home (RAMCIP) under the grant agreement with no: 643433. The robotic platform with the arm manipulator has been developed by ACCREA Engineering and the robotic hand has been developed by Shadow Robot Company. Pilot trials have organized by ACE and LUM.

References

1. Agrigoroaie, R., Ferland, F., Tapus, A.: The ENRICHME project: lessons learnt from a first interaction with the elderly. In: Agah, A., Cabibihan, J.-J., Howard, A.M., Salichs, M.A., He, H. (eds.) ICSR 2016. LNCS (LNAI), vol. 9979, pp. 735–745. Springer, Cham (2016). https://doi.org/10.1007/978-3-319-47437-3_72
2. Agriomallos, I., Doltsinis, S., Mitsioni, I., Doulgeri, Z.: Slippage detection generalizing to grasping of unknown objects using machine learning with novel features. IEEE Robot. Autom. Lett. **3**(2), 942–948 (2018)

3. Amirabdollahian, F., et al.: Accompany: acceptable robotics companions for ageing years multidimensional aspects of human-system interactions. In: The 6th International Conference on Human System Interaction, pp. 570–577. IEEE (2013)

4. Broadbent, E., Stafford, R., MacDonald, B.: Acceptance of healthcare robots for the older population: review and future directions. Int. J. Soc. Robot. **1**(4), 319 (2009)

5. Doumanoglou, A., Kouskouridas, R., Malassiotis, S., Kim, T.K.: Recovering 6D object pose and predicting next-best-view in the crowd. In: IEEE Conference on Computer Vision and Pattern Recognition, pp. 3583–3592 (2016)

6. Endres, F., Hess, J., Engelhard, N., Sturm, J., Cremers, D., Burgard, W.: An evaluation of the RGB-D slam system. In: IEEE International Conference on Robotics and Automation, pp. 1691–1696. IEEE (2012)

7. Engelhardt, K.G.: An overview of health and human service robotics. Robot. Auton. Syst. **5**(3), 205–226 (1989)

8. Fischinger, D., et al.: Hobbit, a care robot supporting independent living at home: first prototype and lessons learned. Robot. Auton. Syst. **75**, 60–78 (2016)

9. Garcia, E., Jimenez, M.A., De Santos, P.G., Armada, M.: The evolution of robotics research. IEEE Robot. Autom. Mag. **14**(1), 90–103 (2007)

10. Sarantopoulos, I., Koveos, Y., Doulgeri, Z.: Grasping flat objects by exploiting non-convexity of the object and support surface. IEEE (2018, Accepted)

11. Jähne, C., Hirche, S.: Augmented invariance control for impedance-controlled robots with safety margins. IFAC PapersOnLine **50**(1), 12053–12058 (2017)

12. Korchut, A., et al.: Challenges for service robots requirements of elderly adults with cognitive impairments (2017)

13. Kostavelis, I., Giakoumis, D., Malassiotis, S., Tzovaras, D.: Human aware robot navigation in semantically annotated domestic environments. In: Antona, M., Stephanidis, C. (eds.) UAHCI 2016. LNCS, vol. 9738, pp. 414–423. Springer, Cham (2016). https://doi.org/10.1007/978-3-319-40244-4_40

14. Kostavelis, I., Giakoumis, D., Malassiotis, S., Tzovaras, D.: A POMDP design framework for decision making in assistive robots. In: Kurosu, M. (ed.) HCI 2017. LNCS, vol. 10271, pp. 467–479. Springer, Cham (2017). https://doi.org/10.1007/978-3-319-58071-5_35

15. Kostavelis, I., Kargakos, A., Giakoumis, D., Tzovaras, D.: Robot's workspace enhancement with dynamic human presence for socially-aware navigation. In: Liu, M., Chen, H., Vincze, M. (eds.) ICVS 2017. LNCS, vol. 10528, pp. 279–288. Springer, Cham (2017). https://doi.org/10.1007/978-3-319-68345-4_25

16. Lawitzky, A., Althoff, D., Wollherr, D., Buss, M.: Dynamic window approach for omni-directional robots with polygonal shape. In: ICRA, pp. 2962–2963 (2011)

17. Leigh, A., Pineau, J.: Laser-based person tracking for clinical locomotion analysis. In: IROS Workshop on Rehabilitation and Assistive Robotics (2014)

18. Meuleau, N., Kim, K.E., Kaelbling, L.P., Cassandra, A.R.: Solving POMDPs by searching the space of finite policies. In: Proceedings of the Fifteenth Conference on Uncertainty in Artificial Intelligence, pp. 417–426. Morgan Kaufmann Publishers Inc. (1999)

19. Spyridon, M.G., Eleftheria, M.: Classification of domestic robots. In: ARSA-Advanced Research in Scientific Areas, vol. 1, no. 7, p. 1693 (2012)

20. Stavropoulos, G., Giakoumis, D., Moustakas, K., Tzovaras, D.: Automatic action recognition for assistive robots to support MCI patients at home. In: 10th International Conference on PErvasive Technologies Related to Assistive Environments, pp. 366–371. ACM (2017)

21. Tinker, A., Lansley, P.: Introducing assistive technology into the existing homes of older people: feasibility, acceptability, costs and outcomes. J. Telemed. Telecare **11**(1_suppl), 1–3 (2005)

22. Vasileiadis, M., Malassiotis, S., Giakoumis, D., Bouganis, C.S., Tzovaras, D.: Robust human pose tracking for realistic service robot applications. In: IEEE Conference on Computer Vision and Pattern Recognition, pp. 1363–1372 (2017)

23. Yang, X., Tian, Y.: Effective 3D action recognition using eigenjoints. J. Vis. Commun. Image Represent. **25**(1), 2–11 (2014)

24. Zielinska, T.: Professional and personal service robots. Int. J. Robot. Appl. Technol. **4**(1), 63–82 (2016)

An Empirical Study Towards Understanding How Deep Convolutional Nets Recognize Falls

Yan Zhang[(✉)] and Heiko Neumann

Institute of Neural Information Processing, Ulm University, Ulm, Germany
{yan.zhang,heiko.neumann}@uni-ulm.de

Abstract. Detecting unintended falls is essential for ambient intelligence and healthcare of elderly people living alone. In recent years, deep convolutional nets are widely used in human action analysis, based on which a number of fall detection methods have been proposed. Despite their highly effective performances, the behaviors of how the convolutional nets recognize falls are still not clear. In this paper, instead of proposing a novel approach, we perform a systematical empirical study, attempting to investigate the underlying fall recognition process. We propose four tasks to investigate, which involve five types of input modalities, seven net instances and different training samples. The obtained quantitative and qualitative results reveal the patterns that the nets tend to learn, and several factors that can heavily influence the performances on fall recognition. We expect that our conclusions are favorable to proposing better deep learning solutions to fall detection systems.

Keywords: Deep convolutional nets · Fall recognition
Empirical study

1 Introduction

Due to cognitive impairment or deficiencies of motor functionalities, unintended falls occur frequently in the group of elderly people, and can lead to severe or even fatal injuries [8,9]. Therefore, to build up fall detection systems for elderly people healthcare, it is essential to recognize falls in an automatic and effective manner.

Fall recognition has been intensively studied in the past. If the human body dynamics has been precisely measured, identifying an unintended fall is straightforward. For example, one can recognize falls via measuring the vertical velocity of the human body towards the ground. If the velocity is above a threshold, then a fall occurs. Consequently, researchers tend to propose novel solutions to capture the body configurations and motions. For example, the work of [44] uses a wearable triaxial accelerometer to measure the body motion and recognizes falls via one-class support vector machine. The work of [41] develops a wearable

© Springer Nature Switzerland AG 2019
L. Leal-Taixé and S. Roth (Eds.): ECCV 2018 Workshops, LNCS 11134, pp. 112–127, 2019.
https://doi.org/10.1007/978-3-030-11024-6_8

system (mainly based on the accelerometer and GPS) to detect and localize falls in the wild. Wearable sensors enable measuring physical attributes of the human body in a precise and real-time manner. However, the sensors have to be physically attached to people, causing obstructive interventions to their daily living activities.

Computer vision technologies realize non-obstructive measurement of human body motions and conduct behavior recognition only based on imagery data. The effectiveness is highly improved when deep convolutional networks trained on large-scale image datasets are employed. To recognize a fall, two families of methods can be considered: The first family attempts to capture precise body configurations over time, such as [4] and [14] for 2D pose estimation and [12] for 3D pose estimation. Such pose estimation methods can replace the functionality of wearable sensors but perform human body measurement in a non-contacting manner. The second family, which is usually based on deep convolutional nets, aims at inferring the semantic content of the input data via creating a mapping from the input data to the action labels in an end-to-end fashion. For example, [31] yields an action label for an input sequence, [23] yields both action labels and temporal durations, and [17] produces frame-wise labels for temporal action segmentation. In this paper, we focus on the second family of methods, since the end-to-end inference behavior does not need any intermediate step, e.g., training a classifier based on the captured body poses. In addition, the data annotation procedure only requires to assign action labels to frames/videos, instead of annotating the key joints on the human bodies in each frame as the first family of methods.

Although several relevant methods like [24] have been proposed, the underlying reasons of the effectiveness are still not clear. In this paper, rather than proposing a novel method for fall recognition, we aim at attaining insights of how the deep convolutional net recognizes falls via a series of empirical investigations. Our study is based on a family of convolutional encoder-decoder nets, different types of input modalities and recordings from different environments. According to our investigations, we discover: (1) Human body motion represented by the optical flow is highly informative for the net to recognize falls. (2) The net tends to learn human body-centered context, namely the appearance surrounding the human body, if the training samples have RGB frames. However, the net cannot get rid of the influence of the background context irrelevant to falling, and lacks generalizability across different environments. (3) The human-centered context and human body motion are complementary. (4) Inaccurate body pose information can degrade the performances.

Organization. This paper is organized as follows. Section 2 introduces related work on vision-based methods for fall recognition and work on model explanation. Section 3 introduces the employed convolutional net, as well as different sorts of attribute maps for model explanation. In Sect. 4, we present our empirical investigations, results and discussions. In the end, we conclude our work and propose future studies in Sect. 5.

2 Related Work

Systematic reviews of fall recognition and detection systems can be found in [13] and [22], which cover solutions based on diverse types of sensors. For vision-based methods, a typical processing pipeline consists of background subtraction, feature extraction and classification, as presented in [27,39] and others. Each step in this pipeline is normally hand-crafted, separately considered and implemented based on certain heuristic rules. A frequently considered rule is that the background information is redundant for fall detection. Thus, background subtraction is performed by algorithms like training Gaussian mixture models, subspace clustering or other sophisticated approaches [25]. Another heuristic rule is that the body shape is a pronounced feature of falling. Consequently, the silhouette of the human body [2,27], or the shape of the foreground bounding box [38,39], is extracted and analyzed. Nevertheless, heuristics are not always precise and comprehensive. The studies of [35] and [34] present effective fall detection solutions when considering the ground plane, indicating that the background information can be very useful.

Comparing with traditional vision-based approaches, deep learning methods enable end-to-end inference with minimal pre-processing on the input data, and the deep nets can learn representative features from the data automatically. Therefore, the algorithm is not necessary to rely on non-guaranteed heuristics. Several studies report that deep learning methods lead to better performances in terms of action recognition [5,31], action detection [10,28,43], action parsing [17,19] and other tasks of human behavior analysis. Their success encourages many studies of fall recognition based on deep neural networks. For example, the work of [24] employs a convolutional net with a similar architecture to the VGG-16 net [32] and uses optical flow as the input modality. The work of [40] uses a PCANet to recognize falls from image sequences with the assistance of foreground detection.

To understand the behaviors of deep convolutional nets, several types of attribute maps have been proposed [1,3]. For a specific input and a target class, the attribute map has the same spatial resolution with the input, and reveals the influence of each input pixel to the probability of the target class. The work of [30] proposes a saliency map, which is computed as the derivative of the output with respect to the input. [36] proposes the integrated gradients, in which the values show the difference between the net output of a reference input (normally zero) and the net output of a sample. [29] proposes the DeepLIFT attribute measure, which can be regarded as an approximated version of integrated gradients according to [1].

3 The Convolutional Net

We formulate fall recognition as a binary classification problem, and expect to obtain frame-wise semantic labels, so that recognition and temporal localization can be solved simultaneously. Therefore, we use a convolutional encoder-decoder

(CED) architecture, which is modified from the non-causal ED-TCN model [17]. Comparing with [17], our CED net combines the spatial net and the temporal net into a coherent structure. The architecture is illustrated in Fig. 1 and the specifications are presented in Fig. 2.

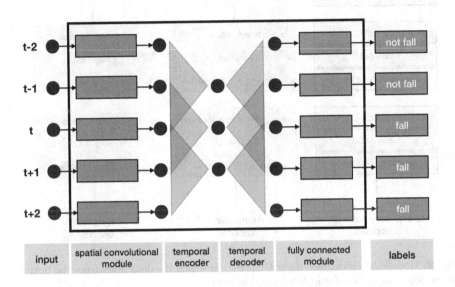

Fig. 1. The architecture of the convolutional encoder-decoder (CED) net. In the input layer, each frame (the gray node) is a 3D tensor with [height, width, channels].

The CED architecture has several advantages besides generating frame-wise labels: (1) The CED net can capture long-range temporal dependencies, and outperforms recurrent nets, e.g. bidirectional LSTMs [11,33], w.r.t. temporal action segmentation [17] and motion prediction [20]. (2) The CED net can generate piece-wise constant label sequences directly, without post-processing steps like median filtering. (3) Comparing with recurrent neural nets, in our trials we find that CED is much easier to train and converges much faster. (4) Once CED is trained, the model can process sequences of arbitrary lengths. Because of such merits, we only consider the convolutional net in our study, and investigating recurrent neural nets is beyond our scope.

The CED model consists of several modules as shown in Fig. 1. In the following content, we introduce each of them.

3.1 The Spatial Convolutional Module

Our convolutional module aims at extracting the feature of each individual frame in the video. It consists of three convolutional blocks, and each block contains a 2D convolutional layer, an activation function layer and a 2D max-pooling

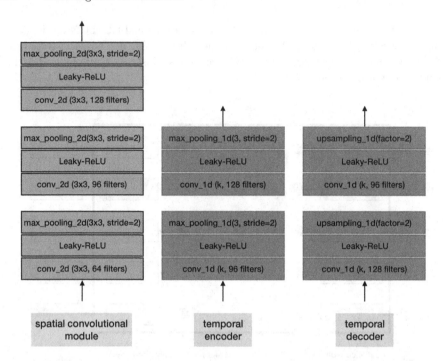

Fig. 2. Module specifications of our CED net, in which the data flows from the bottom to the top. The value of k is determined in Sect. 4.

layer, following the architecture of the VGG net [17,32]. After each block, the spatial resolution is downsampled by the factor of 2. At the end of the module, the input 3D tensor is flattened to a 1D vector. The specifications of the spatial convolutional module are shown in Fig. 2. The number of convolution filters are suggested by [18]. In our work, we use the leaky-ReLU [21] activation function, due to the superior performances to standard to the ReLU function, as indicated in [42]. Moreover, the spatial convolution module is applied on each individual frame of the input tensor sequence, and has shared parameters across all frames.

3.2 The Temporal Encoder and Decoder

After the spatial convolutional module, the 3D tensor of each frame converts to a 1D vector, and then all the vectors are stacked along the temporal dimension to compose a 2D tensor with the shape of [time, dimension] (or a 3D tensor with the shape of [batch, time, dimension]).

Similar to the 2D convolution operation, which can effectively capture spatial local features, the 1D temporal convolution computes temporal correlations between frames, in which the value of the kernel size k specifies the size of the receptive field. The 1D max pooling operation downsamples the data along the time dimension to yield a compressed data representation. On the other and, the upsampling operation increases the temporal resolution to recover the original time length. The encoder and decoder have symmetric architectures, and hence the temporal encoder input and the temporal decoder output has the same temporal length.

3.3 The Fully Connected Module

The fully connected module consists of a fully connected layer, a dropout layer and a softmax layer, and is applied on individual frames in the output of temporal decoder with shared parameters. Due to our binary classification setting, the output dimension of the fully connected layer can be 1 or 2. Here we use the two-dimensional output, since we expect that the insights derived from our work can be extended to multi-class classification problems straightforwardly. The dropout layer (with a keep ratio of 0.5) is used to avoid overfitting, and the softmax layer converts the scores to probabilities.

3.4 Training the Network

In our work, all the modules are trained jointly, in contrast to [17] that only trains the temporal encoder-decoder using the outputs from a pre-trained spatial net. For each frame, we compute the *cross-entropy* between the one-hot encoded ground truth label and the softmax output. Then the loss of the sequence is the sum of the cross-entropy values of all frames. After specifying the loss, the model parameters are learned via the Adam algorithm [16]. Comparing with the stochastic gradient descent method, Adam can lead to superior results as reported in [16]. In addition, the adaptive momentum nature is suitable for our problems, since our input modality can cause sparse gradients, like optical flows with motion information only on the foreground. Implementation details refer to Sect. 4.

4 Experiments

In this section, we present our empirical experiments to investigate how the deep convolutional net CED recognize falls. We propose 4 tasks, and for each task the quantitative results are shown by cross-validated frame-wise accuracies and the qualitative results are shown by attribute maps.

4.1 Dataset

We use the **Le2i** Fall detection dataset presented in [7], which is built using a single camera in realistic surveillance setting containing illumination variations, occlusions by furnitures, different appearances of the subjects, different types of falls (e.g. falling forward, falling while sitting, etc.), and other factors that simulate falls in daily lives. The video has spatial resolution of 320×240 of pixels and is captured with 25 fps. Each video is annotated in a frame-wise fashion, which fits the CED architecture.

The original dataset contains 4 environments, i.e. *home, lecture room, coffee room* and *office*. Due to loss of annotation files, we only use the recordings from *home* and *coffee room* in our study. For each of the two environments, there exist two groups of recordings.

 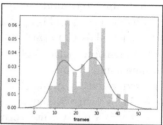

Fig. 3. From left to right: (1) Sample frames of falls in *home* and *coffee room*. (2) The statistics of time durations of falls across all videos, in which the x-axis denotes the fall duration, the y-axis and the bins show the normalized occurrence frequencies and the curve shows the fitted distribution.

Data Preparation. Since we focus on frame-wise fall recognition, in order to balance the number of fall and not-fall frames, from each video containing falling we extract a video snippet consisting of frames before, during and after the fall. Video trimming is based on the statistics of time durations of falls, which is shown in Fig. 3. Specifically, the extracted snippet has 60 frames (2.4 s), starting from $T - 49$ to $T + 10$, where T is the timestamp of the last frame of fall in the video.

Depending on the recording environment, we perform a *high-level* splitting to divide the dataset into 2 folds, each of which contains recordings from either *home* or *coffee room*. Since there are two groups for each environment, we perform a *low-level* splitting to divide the dataset into 4 folds. Therefore, the *high-level* splitting can be used for cross-environment validation, and the *low-level* splitting can be used for cross-validation under small environment variations.

After such preparation step, we obtain a new dataset incorporating 99 video snippets with 2 *high-level* splits and 4 *mid-level* splits.

4.2   Input Modalities to the Net

Besides the RGB frames, we also compute time differences, TV-L1 optical flows [6], and score maps of human body poses[1] [14,15] as the net input modalities. For computational purposes, we downsample the spatial resolution to 56 × 56.

---

[1] The MPII body model has 14 keypoints and hence the method generates 14 pose score maps for each image. In our experiment, we average these 14 score maps to one map.

Similar to [17], each frame of the net input contains a stack of frames from the original data sequence. Denoting the *standardized* RGB image sequence as $\{I_t\}$, the optical flow sequence as $\{w_t\}$ (values within $[-20, 20]$) and the sequence of score maps as $\{s_t\}$ (values within $[0, 1]$), the modalities used in our experiments are shown in Table 1.

Table 1. The input modalities used in our experiments, in which the **Pose+Optical Flow** modality uses the normalized optical flow $\tilde{w}_t$.

Modalities	Format of each frame
RGB+TimeDifference	$\{I_{t-1}, I_t, I_{t+1}, I_t - I_{t-1}, I_{t+1} - I_t\}$
TimeDifference	$\{I_t - I_{t-1}, I_{t+1} - I_t\}$
Optical Flow	$\{w_{t-1}, w_t, w_{t+1}\}$
Pose	$\{s_{t-1}, s_t, s_{t+1}\}$
Pose+Optical Flow	$\{s_{t-1}, \tilde{w}_{t-1}, s_t, \tilde{w}_t, s_{t+1}, \tilde{w}_{t+1}\}$

The **RGB+TimeDifference** modality is suggested by [17], in which the RGB frames encode the appearances of the visual scene and the time differences have the functionality of attention. Image standardization is performed frame-wisely, in order to eliminate the influence of illumination changes. Since the background is static, **TimeDifference** and **Optical Flow** focus on the human body, while **TimeDifference** does not incorporate directional human body motions. The pose information is represented by the score map produced by the pre-trained model of [14,15], which is beneficial for person re-identification and tracking [37]. When combining optical flow and pose, we expect that the pose score map works as an attention mechanism, encouraging the net to learn motion features around the body key points.

One can note that the **Pose+Optical Flow** modality uses the normalized optical flow $\tilde{w}_t$, which is computed by $w_t/20$ and hence ranges within $[-1, 1]$. In this case, the ranges of the pose score map and the optical flow are similar. We find that such flow normalization process is beneficial in our trials. A probable reason is that the normalization leads to similar ranges of convolution parameters for the flow and the pose map in **Pose+Optical Flow**.

4.3 Implementation

The implementation is based on Tensorflow. The batch size is fixed to 8, meaning 8 tensor sequences are fed to the net for one iteration. The Adam algorithm is used to train the model [16], where the initial learning rate is 0.001 and other parameters are set to the Tensorflow default values. The learning rate is decayed every 10 epochs, namely $0.001 \times 0.9^{\lfloor \frac{epoch}{10} \rfloor}$, and training terminates after 100 epochs. In our trials, more iterations lead to comparable or worse results.

In addition, attribute map extraction is implemented based on the DeepExplain library introduced in [1].

4.4 Evaluation Methods

Rather than performing model selection as in [17], we use a family of net instances to verify whether some conditions can consistently influence the performances. We vary two influential factors in the net architecture, i.e., the temporal convolution kernel size k determining the temporal receptive field, and the temporal length of the input sequence l determining the up-limit range of the temporal structure that the net can learn. In our experiments, we use the net instances with $(k, l) \in \{(3, 8), (3, 16), (3, 32), (5, 16), (5, 32), (7, 16), (7, 32)\}$.

For the *high-level* splitting, 2-fold cross-validation is performed, in which each net instance is trained on the first fold and validated on the second, and vice versa. Then, for each net instance, the two validated accuracies are averaged to derive the cross-validated accuracy. For the *low-level* splitting, 4-fold cross-validation is performed in an identical manner. Since each net instance associates with an accuracy value, the quantitative performance of the CED model is presented in terms of a box plot.

The qualitative results are shown by attribute maps, i.e. DeepLIFT [29], integrated gradients [1] and saliency maps [30]. In addition, each attribute map is stacked to the map of edges of the input for visualization purposes.

4.5 Tasks, Results and Discussions

Task 1: Investigating the Cross-Environment Generalizability. In this task, we aim at investigating the generalizability across environments, namely, how the CED performs if training samples and testing samples are collected from totally different environments. Therefore, we conduct a 2-fold cross-validation procedure based on the *high-level* splitting, and use **RGB+TimeDifference**, **TimeDifference** and **Optical Flow** as the input modalities. The results are shown in Fig. 4.

From the box plots, one can see that **RGB+TimeDifference** performs inferior to **TimeDifference** and **Optical Flow**, and **Optical Flow** outperforms **TimeDifference**. In addition, the attribute maps from four testing recordings consistently show that many pixels on the background can heavily affect the net inference process.

Discussion. The net with **RGB+TimeDifference** performs just slightly better than random guess, due to the binary classification setting. The attribute maps show that irrelevant background information has strong influence on fall recognition, and hence we consider that the net cannot discard irrelevant background information automatically during training, and leads to degraded generalizability across environments. Excluding the background information, as in **TimeDifference** and **Optical Flow**, can improve the performances dramatically. This fact can indicate that real influential and environment-invariant features of falls are human body-centered. In addition, the superior performances of **Optical Flow** to **TimeDifference** can indicate that the directional body motion contains more representative information of falls.

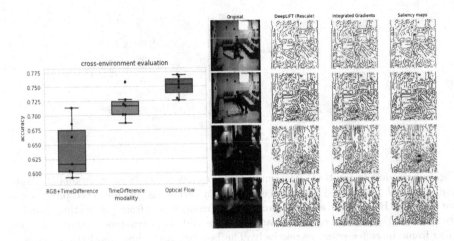

Fig. 4. From left to right: (1) The quantitative results of the 2-fold cross-validation, where the results from each net instance are shown as black dots in parallel to the box plots. In each box plot, the bar inside the box denotes the median, and the box shows the interquartile range (IQR) and the samples between whiskers with 1.5×IQR are inliers. (2) The attribute maps of frames from four testing recordings are shown, where the red color and the blue color denote contribution and suppression effects on the probability of falling. (Color figure online)

Task 2: Investigating the Influence of Training Samples.

In this task, we aim at investigating the influence of training samples recorded from similar environments to the testing samples. Thus, we perform 4-fold cross-validation based on the *low-level* dataset splitting, and compare the performances with the 2-fold cross-validation setting (see Task 1). The employed input modality is **RGB+TimeDifference** and the results are shown in Fig. 5. The reason of only using **RGB+TimeDifference** is that other modalities used in Task 1, namely, **TimeDifference** and **Optical Flow**, are environment-independent and cannot reveal the influence of environment variations.

The box plots show that the training recordings from similar environments to testing can largely improve the performances. Indicated by all attribute maps on the right, we can find that the influential pixels noticeably become more human body-centered.

Discussion. Quantitatively, training recordings similar to the testing recordings are highly favorable. The reason can be revealed from the attribute maps. Specifically, the fact that influential pixels are more concentrated around the human body can also indicate that the fall features are human body-centered. In addition, one can notice that the body-centered influential pixels tend to locate around the contour of the body, instead of directly on the body. This fact may indicate that the body-centered context, or the interaction between the human body and the environment, is a representative feature of fall.

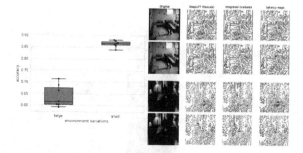

Fig. 5. From left to right: (1) The quantitative results under large environment variations (the *high-level* splits) and small environment variations (the *low-level* splits), with
the modality **RGB+TimeDifference**. (2) Attribute maps from two testing samples
are shown. The first two rows compare the large and small evaluation settings on the
same frame in *coffee room*, respectively. The last two rows show another comparison
on the same frame in *home*.

Task 3: Investigating the Human Body-Centered Pattern. Based on
the results in Task 1 and Task 2, we believe that the convolutional net tends to
learn body-centered patterns for fall recognition. Here we perform further investigations based on the *low-level* data splitting and the **RGB+TimeDifference**
and **Optical Flow** modalities, which represent body-centered context and body
motion, respectively. Afterwards, we fuse the two modalities following the work
of [31]. Specifically, we average the softmax outputs from two streams of CED
nets with the same (k, l) values. Figure 6 shows the results.

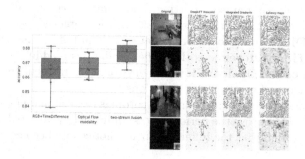

Fig. 6. From left to right: (1) The quantitative results of different modalities under
small environment variations (the *low-level* splits). (2) Examples of attribute maps of
the two modalities are presented. In particular, the optical flow is visualized using the
color coding scheme attached at the bottom-right corner. (Color figure online)

One can see that **Optical Flow** and **RGB+TimeDifference** lead to comparable performances according to the box plots, yet the net with the **Optical
Flow** modality behaves more stable than the other case. The fusion results outperform individual modalities. Additionally, from the attribute maps of optical

flows we can see that the influential pixels are within the contour of the human body, in contrast to the attribute maps of **RGB+TimeDifference**. One can note that the saliency map is not reliable for **Optical Flow**, since the saliency values are computed as the derivatives of the output w.r.t. the input and zero-value input can cause numerical problems.

Discussion. A probable reason of the stable performance with **Optical Flow** is that human body motion can represent falls more robustly than the body-centered context, which can be easily influenced by the background information. The superior performance of modality fusion can indicate that body-centered context and body motion are complementary. The complementary property can also be viewed from the attribute maps, since the influential pixels are at different locations.

Task 4: Investigating the Influence of Body Pose Information. Here we aim at investigating the influence of the 2D pose information. Since motion capture devices are not used in the dataset and no body pose annotations are available, the pose maps are extracted using the pre-trained model associated with [14,15]. The evaluation is based on the *low-level* splitting, as well as the modalities of **Pose, Optical Flow** and **Pose+Optical Flow**. The results are shown in Fig. 7.

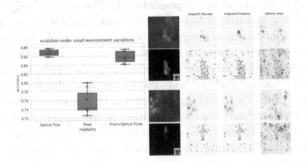

Fig. 7. From left to right: (1) The quantitative results presented by box plots. (2) The attribute maps of pose and optical flow modalities. The selected frames are the same with previous figures. The pose score map, in which the value increases from blue to yellow, is overlaid with the RGB image only for visualization. The RGB image is not input to the net. (Color figure online)

One can see that the pose information leads to inferior performances, and also deteriorates the performances of **Optical Flow** when combing flow and pose information. On the right hand, one can find that the influential pixels on the pose score maps mainly locate at the positions the non-zero pose scores. Similar to the optical flow case, the saliency maps of **Pose** are deteriorated by numerical problems. Moreover, from the third row on the right, one can see that the pose estimation is not always reliable.

Discussion. Pose estimation from images is a challenging problem. Although the state-of-the-art algorithms perform quite well on standard benchmarks, the estimation result is not guaranteed. In case of fall recognition, we can see that incorrect pose estimation can dramatically degrade the performances.

5   Conclusion and Future Work

In this paper, we aim at investigating the behaviors of the convolutional neural net when conducting fall recognition. To enable frame-wise recognition, we use the convolutional encoder-decoder (CED) architecture and employ a set of net instances. Based on different types of input modalities and dataset splits, our empirical studies show several influential factors of the model performances. In particular, we find that: (1) The net tends to learn body-centered patterns, but cannot eliminate the influence of background information, leading to poor cross-environment generalizability. Therefore, for cross-environment uses in practice, it is better to perform person detection as a pre-processing step, or incorporate a region-of-interest proposing module into an end-to-end model, like the Faster R-CNN model [26]. (2) Training samples captured from the testing environment can considerably improve the performance and encourage the net to encode body-centered context, for which the most influential pixels are located around the body contour. Thus, in practice, we suggest to collect training samples from the deployment environment when possible. (3) The human body motion contains representative features of falls robust to environment changes, and influences on fall recognition in a complementary manner with the body-centered context. In this case, we suggest to use the two-stream (the appearance stream and the motion stream) architecture [31] when detecting falls. In addition, since the body-centered context and the body motion are from different image regions, their correlation could be trivial and we probably can effectively fuse the two types of feature vectors only by concatenation or averaging. (4) Incorrect pose information can degrade the performances heavily. At the current stage, body pose estimation is a challaging task by itself, and the performances are not guaranted. We hence recommend not to incorporate pose information for fall recognition without additional checking.

Herein we focus on trimmed videos for investigating the net behaviors. Based on the obtained insights, we consider to develop an effective fall detection system based on the CED architecture for untrimmed videos or even streaming data in future.

Acknowledgements. This work is supported by a grant of the Federal Ministry of Education and Research of Germany (BMBF) for the project of SenseEmotion.

References

1. Ancona, M., Ceolini, E., Öztireli, C., Gross, M.: A unified view of gradient-based attribution methods for deep neural networks. arXiv preprint arXiv:1711.06104 (2017)
2. Anderson, D., Keller, J.M., Skubic, M., Chen, X., He, Z.: Recognizing falls from silhouettes. In: Proceedings of the 28th IEEE EMBS Annual International Conference, pp. 6388–6391. IEEE (2006)
3. Babiker, H.K.B., Goebel, R.: An introduction to deep visual explanation. arXiv preprint arXiv:1711.09482 (2017)
4. Cao, Z., Simon, T., Wei, S.E., Sheikh, Y.: Realtime multi-person 2D pose estimation using part affinity fields. In: IEEE Conference on Computer Vision and Pattern Recognition (CVPR) (2017)
5. Carreira, J., Zisserman, A.: Quo Vadis, action recognition? A new model and the kinetics dataset. In: IEEE Conference on Computer Vision and Pattern Recognition (CVPR), July 2017
6. Chambolle, A.: An algorithm for total variation minimization and applications. J. Math. Imag. Vis. **20**(1–2), 89–97 (2004)
7. Charfi, I., Miteran, J., Dubois, J., Atri, M., Tourki, R.: Optimized spatio-temporal descriptors for real-time fall detection: comparison of support vector machine and adaboost-based classification. J. Electron. Imag. **22**(4), 041106 (2013)
8. Dykes, P.C., et al.: Fall prevention in acute care hospitals: a randomized trial. Jama **304**(17), 1912–1918 (2010)
9. Gillain, S., Elbouz, L., Beaudart, C., Bruyère, O., Reginster, J., Petermans, J.: Falls in the elderly. Revue medicale de Liege **69**(5–6), 258–264 (2014)
10. Gkioxari, G., Malik, J.: Finding action tubes. In: IEEE Conference on Computer Vision and Pattern Recognition (CVPR), pp. 759–768. IEEE (2015)
11. Graves, A., Fernández, S., Schmidhuber, J.: Bidirectional LSTM networks for improved phoneme classification and recognition. In: Duch, W., Kacprzyk, J., Oja, E., Zadrożny, S. (eds.) ICANN 2005. LNCS, vol. 3697, pp. 799–804. Springer, Heidelberg (2005). https://doi.org/10.1007/11550907_126
12. Güler, R.A., Neverova, N., Kokkinos, I.: Densepose: dense human pose estimation in the wild. arXiv preprint arXiv:1802.00434 (2018)
13. Igual, R., Medrano, C., Plaza, I.: Challenges, issues and trends in fall detection systems. Biomed. Eng. Online **12**(1), 66 (2013)
14. Insafutdinov, E., et al.: Arttrack: articulated multi-person tracking in the wild. In: IEEE Conference on Computer Vision and Pattern Recognition (CVPR), pp. 1293–1301 (2017)
15. Insafutdinov, E., Pishchulin, L., Andres, B., Andriluka, M., Schiele, B.: DeeperCut: a deeper, stronger, and faster multi-person pose estimation model. In: Leibe, B., Matas, J., Sebe, N., Welling, M. (eds.) ECCV 2016. LNCS, vol. 9910, pp. 34–50. Springer, Cham (2016). https://doi.org/10.1007/978-3-319-46466-4_3
16. Kingma, D.P., Ba, J.: Adam: a method for stochastic optimization. arXiv preprint arXiv:1412.6980 (2014)
17. Lea, C., Flynn, M.D., Vidal, R., Reiter, A., Hager, G.D.: Temporal convolutional networks for action segmentation and detection. In: IEEE Conference on Computer Vision and Pattern Recognition (CVPR), pp. 1003–1012, July 2017
18. Lea, C., Reiter, A., Vidal, R., Hager, G.D.: Segmental spatiotemporal CNNs for fine-grained action segmentation. In: Leibe, B., Matas, J., Sebe, N., Welling, M. (eds.) ECCV 2016. LNCS, vol. 9907, pp. 36–52. Springer, Cham (2016). https://doi.org/10.1007/978-3-319-46487-9_3

19. Lea, C., Vidal, R., Reiter, A., Hager, G.D.: Temporal convolutional networks: a unified approach to action segmentation. In: Hua, G., Jégou, H. (eds.) ECCV 2016. LNCS, vol. 9915, pp. 47–54. Springer, Cham (2016). https://doi.org/10.1007/978-3-319-49409-8_7

20. Li, C., Zhang, Z., Lee, W.S., Lee, G.H.: Convolutional sequence to sequence model for human dynamics. In: IEEE Conference on Computer Vision and Pattern Recognition (CVPR), pp. 5226–5234 (2018)

21. Maas, A.L., Hannun, A.Y., Ng, A.Y.: Rectifier nonlinearities improve neural network acoustic models. In: Proceedings of ICML, vol. 30, p. 3 (2013)

22. Mubashir, M., Shao, L., Seed, L.: A survey on fall detection: principles and approaches. Neurocomputing 100, 144–152 (2013)

23. Neverova, N., Wolf, C., Taylor, G.W., Nebout, F.: Multi-scale deep learning for gesture detection and localization. In: Agapito, L., Bronstein, M.M., Rother, C. (eds.) ECCV 2014. LNCS, vol. 8925, pp. 474–490. Springer, Cham (2015). https://doi.org/10.1007/978-3-319-16178-5_33

24. Núñez-Marcos, A., Azkune, G., Arganda-Carreras, I.: Vision-based fall detection with convolutional neural networks. Wirel. Commun. Mob. Comput. 2017 (2017)

25. Piccardi, M.: Background subtraction techniques: a review. In: IEEE International Conference on Systems, Man and Cybernetics, vol. 4, pp. 3099–3104. IEEE (2004)

26. Ren, S., He, K., Girshick, R., Sun, J.: Faster R-CNN: towards real-time object detection with region proposal networks. In: Advances in Neural Information Processing Systems, pp. 91–99 (2015)

27. Rougier, C., Meunier, J., St-Arnaud, A., Rousseau, J.: Robust video surveillance for fall detection based on human shape deformation. IEEE Trans. Circ. Syst. Video Technol. 21(5), 611–622 (2011)

28. Shou, Z., Chan, J., Zareian, A., Miyazawa, K., Chang, S.F.: CDC: convolutional-de-convolutional networks for precise temporal action localization in untrimmed videos. In: IEEE Conference on Computer Vision and Pattern Recognition (CVPR), pp. 1417–1426 (2017)

29. Shrikumar, A., Greenside, P., Kundaje, A.: Learning important features through propagating activation differences. arXiv preprint arXiv:1704.02685 (2017)

30. Simonyan, K., Vedaldi, A., Zisserman, A.: Deep inside convolutional networks: visualising image classification models and saliency maps. arXiv preprint arXiv:1312.6034 (2013)

31. Simonyan, K., Zisserman, A.: Two-stream convolutional networks for action recognition in videos. In: Advances in Neural Information Processing Systems, pp. 568–576 (2014)

32. Simonyan, K., Zisserman, A.: Very deep convolutional networks for large-scale image recognition. arXiv preprint arXiv:1409.1556 (2014)

33. Singh, B., Marks, T.K., Jones, M., Tuzel, O., Shao, M.: A multi-stream bi-directional recurrent neural network for fine-grained action detection. In: IEEE Conference on Computer Vision and Pattern Recognition (CVPR), pp. 1961–1970. IEEE (2016)

34. Solbach, M.D., Tsotsos, J.K.: Vision-based fallen person detection for the elderly. arXiv preprint arXiv:1707.07608 (2017)

35. Stone, E.E., Skubic, M.: Fall detection in homes of older adults using the microsoft kinect. IEEE J. Biomed. Health Inf. 19(1), 290–301 (2015)

36. Sundararajan, M., Taly, A., Yan, Q.: Axiomatic attribution for deep networks. arXiv preprint arXiv:1703.01365 (2017)

37. Tang, S., Andriluka, M., Andres, B., Schiele, B.: Multiple people tracking by lifted multicut and person re-identification. In: IEEE Conference on Computer Vision and Pattern Recognition (CVPR), pp. 3539–3548 (2017)
38. Töreyin, B.U., Dedeoğlu, Y., Çetin, A.E.: HMM based falling person detection using both audio and video. In: Sebe, N., Lew, M., Huang, T.S. (eds.) HCI 2005. LNCS, vol. 3766, pp. 211–220. Springer, Heidelberg (2005). https://doi.org/10.1007/11573425_21
39. Vishwakarma, V., Mandal, C., Sural, S.: Automatic detection of human fall in video. In: Ghosh, A., De, R.K., Pal, S.K. (eds.) PReMI 2007. LNCS, vol. 4815, pp. 616–623. Springer, Heidelberg (2007). https://doi.org/10.1007/978-3-540-77046-6_76
40. Wang, S., Chen, L., Zhou, Z., Sun, X., Dong, J.: Human fall detection in surveillance video based on pcanet. Multimed. Tools Appl. 75(19), 11603–11613 (2016)
41. Wu, F., Zhao, H., Zhao, Y., Zhong, H.: Development of a wearable-sensor-based fall detection system. Int. J. Telemedicine Appl. 2015, 2 (2015)
42. Xu, B., Wang, N., Chen, T., Li, M.: Empirical evaluation of rectified activations in convolutional network. arXiv preprint arXiv:1505.00853 (2015)
43. Yeung, S., Russakovsky, O., Mori, G., Fei-Fei, L.: End-to-end learning of action detection from frame glimpses in videos. In: IEEE Conference on Computer Vision and Pattern Recognition (CVPR), pp. 2678–2687 (2016)
44. Zhang, T., Wang, J., Xu, L., Liu, P.: Fall detection by wearable sensor and one-class SVM algorithm. In: Huang, D.S., Li, K., Irwin, G.W. (eds.) Intelligent Computing in Signal Processing and Pattern Recognition. Lecture Notes in Control and Information Sciences, vol. 345, pp. 858–863. Springer, Heidelberg (2006). https://doi.org/10.1007/978-3-540-37258-5_104

ASSIST: Personalized Indoor Navigation via Multimodal Sensors and High-Level Semantic Information

Vishnu Nair[1]([✉]), Manjekar Budhai[1], Greg Olmschenk[1,2], William H. Seiple[3], and Zhigang Zhu[1,2]

[1] Department of Computer Science, The City College of New York,
New York, NY, USA
{vnair000,mbudhai000}@citymail.cuny.edu
[2] Department of Computer Science, CUNY Graduate Center,
New York, NY, USA
golmschenk@gradcenter.cuny.edu, zhu@cs.ccny.cuny.edu
[3] Lighthouse Guild, New York, NY, USA
WSeiple@lighthouseguild.org

Abstract. Blind & visually impaired (BVI) individuals and those with Autism Spectrum Disorder (ASD) each face unique challenges in navigating unfamiliar indoor environments. In this paper, we propose an indoor positioning and navigation system that guides a user from point A to point B indoors with high accuracy while augmenting their situational awareness. This system has three major components: *location recognition* (a hybrid indoor localization app that uses Bluetooth Low Energy beacons and Google Tango to provide high accuracy), *object recognition* (a body-mounted camera to provide the user momentary situational awareness of objects and people), and *semantic recognition* (map-based annotations to alert the user of static environmental characteristics). This system also features personalized interfaces built upon the unique experiences that both BVI and ASD individuals have in indoor wayfinding and tailors its multimodal feedback to their needs. Here, the technical approach and implementation of this system are discussed, and the results of human subject tests with both BVI and ASD individuals are presented. In addition, we discuss and show the system's user-centric interface and present points for future work and expansion.

Keywords: Indoor positioning
Environmental & situational awareness · Bluetooth beacons
Google Tango

1 Introduction

Assistive technologies aim to open access to skills and opportunities that are often inaccessible to those with disabilities. Considering that there are 285 million blind & visually impaired (BVI) individuals worldwide [22] and that people

© Springer Nature Switzerland AG 2019
L. Leal-Taixé and S. Roth (Eds.): ECCV 2018 Workshops, LNCS 11134, pp. 128–143, 2019.
https://doi.org/10.1007/978-3-030-11024-6_9

with Autism Spectrum Disorder (ASD) often lack the ability to develop cognitive maps of places they have been to [8], a need was identified for an assistive technology that can aid these individuals in indoor navigation. In light of this, we propose a specialized, full-fledged, multisensor system called ASSIST ("Assistive Sensor Solutions for Independent and Safe Travel") with the goal of promoting independent and safe travel within complex indoor environments for BVI and ASD individuals. ASSIST is centered around an Android mobile application that relies on the use of Bluetooth Low Energy (BLE) beacons alongside the area learning, motion tracking, and localization capabilities provided by Google Tango. In addition to providing turn-by-turn indoor navigation, we introduce provisions for situational and environmental awareness, including people detection/recognition and static environment information. These capabilities are combined and presented in a flexible and user-friendly application ("app") which can be operated using either touch or voice inputs and can be configured as needed by varying the type and level of feedback, allowing for a unique experience for each user. Our main goal with this system is to improve the quality of life of our users by promoting confidence and independence when it comes to daily indoor navigation. To this end, our work has the following four unique features:

1. **A multi-level recognition mechanism for robust navigation**: (a) Location recognition by improving our previously-created hybrid BLE-Tango system [10] to ensure robustness; (b) object recognition by utilizing a wearable camera to provide reliable alerting of dynamic situational elements (such as people in the user's surroundings); and (c) semantic recognition by using map annotations to provide alerting of static environmental characteristics.
2. **User-centric multimodal interfaces**: The ASSIST app provides a user-centric interface that features multimodal feedback, including a visual interface, voice input and feedback, and vibration reminders. Users can also customize the interfaces for various metrics (steps, meters, feet) and modalities (visual, audio, tactile) based on their challenges (i.e., BVI or ASD).
3. **Near real-time response and zero training**: The ASSIST system is optimized such that information is provided to the user in near real-time. Next to no training is needed for a user to use the app and system. We have also performed user-centric, real-world tests with the overall system to determine its usability to people with disabilities, including BVI and ASD individuals (the results for which are presented).
4. **Modular hardware/software design**: We formulate a hardware/software workflow to produce a working system and open avenues for future work. A modular implementation is targeted to allow for easy adding/upgrading of features.

2   Related Work

2.1   Indoor Map Learning and Localization

Research into accurate indoor positioning and navigation has proposed the use of various technologies, including but not limited to the use of cameras on smartphones [9], RFID tags [3], NFC signals [13] and inertial measurement unit (IMU) sensors [16]. Bluetooth Low Energy (BLE) beacons have been a popular technology of interest; perhaps the most relevant project is NavCog, a smartphone-based "mobility aid" which solely uses BLE beacons to provide turn-by-turn navigation and information about nearby points-of-interest and accessibility issues [1]. Another BLE-based system proposed the use of beacons as part of a system to provide the visually impaired with information about the topology of an approaching urban intersection [2]. However, these BLE-based systems have relatively low localization accuracy (up to meters) and, thus, cannot work well in crowded or cramped indoor environments. Google Tango has also been of interest with the most relevant project being ISANA, a context-aware indoor navigation system implemented using Tango, which parses CAD files to create indoor semantic maps which are then used in path planning alongside other assistive features such as sign reading and obstacle alerting using the onboard camera [7]. However, limited real-world tests have been performed.

Our own previous work proposed a method of indoor localization that involves combining both BLE beacon localization and Google Tango map learning to create a highly accurate indoor positioning and navigation system [10]. The work we present here extends the work in [10] by providing a multi-layer recognition mechanism and generalizing coverage of the modeling and navigation across multiple floors of a building. In addition, new interfaces are created, and human subject tests are also performed for both BVI and ASD users; whereas, our previous work only tested the system with BVI users.

2.2 Object Detection and Recognition

Object detection is an integral part of providing situational awareness. Detecting and classifying local persons or objects, within real-time speeds, is a key point of research that can improve safety for users. YOLOv2 is a convolutional neural network (CNN) that was built with the goal of being able to detect a large number of classes and having fast detection speeds by applying the network to an entire image, as opposed to localized areas [15]. Using a smartphone as the main mode for detecting objects and alerting users is another main point of research. [20] use the Lucas-Kanade algorithm, in addition to other optical flow methods, to identify and track potential obstacles. Attempting to improve the detection performance, as well as providing vibrotactile and audio alerts for their users, [14] limit the total number of pixels needed for performing detection, and only analyze the floor-area immediately in front of the phone's camera.

2.3 Methods of Environmental Understanding

Much research has been done on giving those with cognitive and visual disabilities a greater understanding of their surrounding environment. Visually impaired individuals usually use a cane to detect obstacles in their immediate vicinity. Some studies have attempted to put sensors on canes to preemptively warn the user about upcoming obstacles [18]. Other projects have taken a more vision-based approach. A project called "SoundView" uses a mini-CCD camera to detect objects tagged with barcodes and relay information about the presence of these objects to a visually impaired user via an earpiece [11]. Another project developed a sensor module that acted like a barcode scanner that a user could use to obtain information about the characteristics of an object of interest [5].

The system we propose is targeted toward users who have difficulties in developing cognitive maps of complex (and often unfamiliar) environments. To this end, several works have been published that use a wearable camera to recognize locations and localize within an environment. Furnari et al. propose a method to segment egocentric (first-person view) videos based on the locations visited by the holder of the camera [4]. Ortis et al. then extend this work to automatically connect the habitual actions of users with their locations [12]. Finally, Spera et al. extend this automatic recognition of locations in egocentric videos to localize shopping carts within a large retail store [17]. Our work utilizes a hybrid sensor approach so that the system may continue to work even if one sensor modality (such as the camera) fails to work properly.

3   System Sensory Components

ASSIST consists of three primary components: location recognition via hybrid sensors, real-world person and object detection via a body-mounted camera, and map-based semantic recognition of the user's environment. These three components interact with each other to provide a user with sufficient information to move them successfully to their destination while augmenting their understanding of the environment around them. With regards to the initial setup of a location, it is worth noting that, other than the initial installation of BLE beacons at strategic positions hidden from view, no manipulation of the visible environment is required for the system (including the camera portion) to work correctly.

3.1   Location Recognition via Hybrid Sensors

Two methods of indoor positioning were of particular interest to us: Bluetooth Low Energy (BLE) beacons and Google Tango. (Note that, although we have continued to use it for our tests and development, Tango was deprecated by Google in the first half of 2018. Future work will focus on integrating Tango's successor, ARCore, into the system, once development of ARCore adds features to the platform such that it can act as a replacement for Tango, specifically, after the implementation of a substitute for Tango's "area learning" feature.)

A main consideration with using BLE beacons for localization is that received signal strength (RSS) values are often volatile. We found that BLE signals are extremely noisy, because they are easily attenuated by materials commonly found in a building [6]. Thus, without the use of complex probabilistic algorithms, fine localization using BLE is difficult. In [10], we found that, even with a relatively dense placement of one beacon every 3–5 m placed out of sight just above ceiling tiles, beacons were only accurate enough by themselves to *approximate* a user's position (i.e., determine a coarse location). Yet, some users, especially BVI, require highly accurate (fine) positioning to avoid collisions with obstacles.

Thus, we looked into using Google Tango, which utilizes an Android-integrated RGB-D camera with capabilities of 6-degrees-of-freedom VIO (visual-inertial odometry) and feature-based indoor localization to allow for device pose (orientation and position) estimation in a 3D environment [7]. Tango makes use of Area Description Files (ADFs), which are feature maps of an indoor environment, and its onboard sensors to determine a device's position within an ADF down to a few centimeters [10]. However, due to limitations in the Tango SDK, it is a known issue that the loading of larger ADFs (usually with a size above 60 MB) can often trigger an internal timeout/crash within the Tango SDK. The areas mapped in our testbed ranged in size from 600 to 1000 sq. ft. and produced ADFs that ranged in size from 15 to 40 MB (depending on the features in the environment). Although suitable for our specific testbed, this is not practical for an area such as a large public transportation hub, where a single "floor" could be much larger and have many features. Thus, we require multiple ADFs to cover an expansive area. However, this requires that the appropriate ADF be selected automatically based on the user's current position. (ADFs are aligned with the area's floor plan/map as described in our previous work, via an affine transformation of the Tango-returned coordinates from the ADF's coordinate space to the map's coordinate space [10].)

To account for these respective strengths and weaknesses, we utilize a hybrid system that uses BLE beacons to figure out the approximate area that the user/device is located in. The area selected by BLE beacons is represented by a specific ADF that Google Tango uses to get the user/device's exact position.

Hybrid Localization. For the coarse localization component, the phone searches for all beacons it can detect in a one second interval. Of the beacons it detects in this interval, the three strongest beacons are taken and run against a pre-built database of "fingerprints" for all of the areas in question. Each fingerprint represents a specific (x, y) position in the map coordinate space and consists of (1) the three strongest beacons (in terms of their RSS) that can be detected at that position and (2) the (general/coarse) area in which that (x, y) position lies. A simple matching algorithm then matches each real-time capture with the database entries and selects the general region associated with the matched fingerprint. Each coarse region is associated with a specific Tango ADF. When the BLE component successfully selects a new general region, Tango is restarted with the ADF of this region and locks onto this new region within a few seconds.

An important consideration is the switching of ADFs when navigating on the same floor. Since scans for BLE beacons are done at intervals of several seconds, the system may not respond fast enough when trying to switch between areas on the same floor. It is thus necessary to work around this delay and find a faster method for switching in these situations. We introduce an additional mechanism to compensate for this.

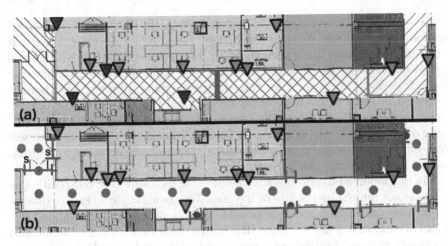

Fig. 1. Visualization of map annotations on the floor plan of a long corridor. *Top (a)*: ADF and beacon annotations. Diagonal lines represent coverages of respective ADFs (one blue and one green). Area where diagonal lines overlap represents overlap between both ADFs. Thick red line in center represents "primary" ADF border, where respective BLE/coarse localization areas meet each other. Thin orange lines to either side represent "secondary" ADF borders where overlaps between both ADFs end. Triangles represent installed beacons. Dark blue triangles are beacons representing area of blue-lined ADF; green triangles/beacons represent area of green-lined ADF. Lighter-blue triangles/beacons are irrelevant to this example (i.e., they represent another area above). Since these beacons are located on the other side of the wall from the hallway and Bluetooth signals are known to be attenuated by materials commonly found in a building [6], it is highly unlikely that area will be selected. *Bottom (b)*: Environment and navigation annotations. Triangles represent all beacons. Green dots represent navigational nodes. Smaller, dark blue dots represent checkpoints (i.e., points of interest). Red "H"-like symbols represent all doorways annotated. Letter "S" next to each of both doors on far left represents annotation for a "security" door (i.e., one that requires a key card to open) (Color figure online)

Boundary-Based ADF Switching for Hybrid Localization. We can rely on map-based labeling of borders between ADFs. When the device approaches the border between two ADFs (i.e., a "primary" border), the system can preemptively restart Tango with the approaching ADF so that when we do reach it, Tango will have already localized into the new ADF and can continue. We also make use of "secondary" borders that act as fallbacks in situations where primary border switching fails (e.g., when the device is close to the border with another ADF and BLE localization locks the device into the other ADF). Secondary borders make use of overlaps between adjacent ADFS such that Tango localization will still be successful even if we have selected the wrong ADF. Figure 1a visualizes an example of beacon placement and ADF switching logic.

ADFs are mapped strategically in the offline phase to optimize this mechanism. During an ADF switch, Tango is restarted; however, it may take up to several seconds to lock onto a position in the new ADF. During this "deadlock," positioning capabilities are suspended; thus, the interface does not update. It is of paramount importance then that this deadlock not interfere with normal navigation activities (for example, a turn cannot come up during the possible deadlock period). To account for this, during mapping, primary ADF borders are placed in areas where little or no navigational turns are available (e.g., in a long corridor). Via this strategic border placement, the system is provided a buffer during which it can lock on to its position while ensuring that the user will not need its guidance during this period (i.e., the user simply needs to continue walking forward during this period).

Via this modified hybrid method, we are able to ensure that our positioning system is not limited by the size of the area. We are also able to ensure that we can provide the highest accuracy possible (especially for BVI individuals who require it) and that a failure of the BLE/coarse location system can be handled in a timely manner. Furthermore, map-based ADF border marking can ensure that the system responds as quickly as possible to general location changes. In the end, this approach combines the coarse yet expansive location recognition of beacons with the fine yet limited-scale location recognition of Tango.

3.2   Body Camera-Based Recognition and Alerting of Variable Situational Elements

As part of the modular implementation of ASSIST, people within the locality of the user can be detected via an on-person body camera. Currently, the system utilizes a YOLOv2 CNN model that is trained to detect people's heads. It was trained utilizing the Hollywood Heads dataset, consisting of 224,740 annotated movie frames including actors' heads [21]. This model, when running on a server (in our case, an Amazon EC2 p2.xlarge instance running an Nvidia K80 GPU) as opposed to a phone, has detection speeds of approximately 30 ms.

CNN-Based Head Detection on the Mobile Device. Our work originally attempted to perform both head detection and tracking on the Tango device. This was done by modifying a sample Tensorflow Android application which allowed for a Tiny YOLO model to be loaded and utilized to perform detection. The Tiny YOLO model, which aims to run very quickly at the cost of accuracy, consists of only 16 layers and utilizes a 416×416 input image size [15]. As such, the application read RGB images sized at 640×480 pixels, minimizing the need for image resizing. Our model was trained using a subset of 50,000 images from the Hollywood Heads dataset. When running on the Lenovo Phab 2 Pro, we achieved detection speeds of approximately 800 ms. The advantages to performing detection on the mobile device include having access to tracking capabilities and the availability of depth/point cloud information provided by Tango. The sample application implemented tracking by executing the Lucas-Kanade algorithm. The points utilized for tracking were identified via a Harris filter, used both inside and outside of detected bounding boxes. The resulting application

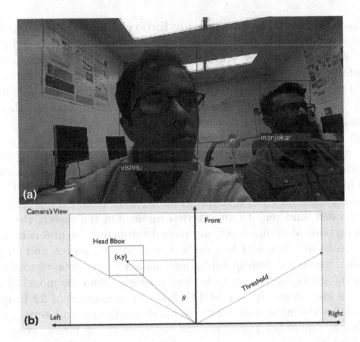

Fig. 2. *Top (a):* Detection server-annotated image showing detected heads (from YOLOv2 CNN) and facial recognition outputs (from facial recognition model used). Image was taken using our test body camera (a GoPro Hero5 Session). *Bottom (b):* Mobile camera view utilized for determining orientation of detected person with respect to the user's point of view

is capable of tracking up to 6 persons, while maintaining the detection speed of 800 ms mentioned previously. (These values were attained by setting an internal class confidence level of 0.01, an ultimate detection confidence of 0.25, and keeping a record of 200 frames of optical flow deltas.)

Utilizing Tango's point cloud generator, we can expand our 2D RGB detections to include specific 3D information. Via a series of frame transformations, we were able to evaluate a depth value for the centers of generated detection bounding boxes. By transforming a point in the 640 × 480 frame (in which the detected bounding boxes are placed) into a point in the 1920 × 1080 frame (used for the point cloud buffer), we can then grab relative depth information via a Tango method (which utilizes bilateral filtering on the most recently-saved point cloud). Furthermore, by dividing the RGB frame as shown in Fig. 2b, we can relay a relative orientation of the detected person with respect to the user.

This application, though successful as a standalone implementation, proved to be a challenge when it came to merge it with the remainder of the system. Because the detection and tracking requires a great deal of computing power, finding an approach for scheduling these functionalities within the full application proved to be difficult and was subsequently abandoned.

CNN-Based Head Detection on an External Server. For our current implementation, we run a YOLOv2 model on an external server dedicated to detection. An external server was chosen because of (1) the relative ease with which modular vision-based functionality could be implemented or removed and (2) the fact that the mobile application does not need to be continuously updated with every such server change provided that the interface between the mobile application/camera and the server remains the same.

As part of a proof-of-concept, we used a GoPro Hero5 Session as our camera. (This extra camera was selected, in part, to offload computations from the mobile device. Future work will focus on an optimized onboard implementation using the mobile device's camera.) The GoPro is connected via a WiFi dongle and accessed through a Python script. From here, the recorded images are compressed, encoded, and sent to an external server. On the server, the received package is decoded, decompressed, and passed through the neural network. The detection results are then sent to a dedicated navigation server, and ultimately to the phone, where the corresponding information can be relayed to the user.

The model sitting on the server is more extensive than the model that originally ran on the phone. It is a YOLOv2 model, consisting of 32 layers, also utilizing a 416×416 input image size. By running detection on a server, we have access to more processing resources, and can thus utilize larger images which can be resized. In order to maximize speed, however, the GoPro was set to read in images sized at 864×480 pixels. The model was trained for 15,000 iterations, utilizing the entire Hollywood Heads dataset. The increase in processing power will allow for more than 6 people to be both detected and tracked, while maintaining real-time speeds. Currently, we do not have tracking implemented on the server, but it can be done via a similar process to the mobile implementation.

The modular nature of the server-based detection system ensures that we can add or remove functionality. For example, we have tested the addition of a pre-trained facial recognition model[1] with which we can relay the identity of known, detected persons to the user. Figure 2a shows an example of face detection and recognition using a body camera.

3.3 Map-Based Semantic Recognition and Alerting of Static Environmental Characteristics

Our system is heavily dependent on having pre-existing floor plans/maps of the area in question. Map-based pixel coordinates are used to mark the map on the interface and perform related calculations, such as distance measurements. We also label the map with navigational nodes and checkpoints. However, we can use these floor plans further to our advantage by explicitly annotating the map with various static characteristics of the environments represented on the map (e.g., the locations of doorways and elevators, as shown in Fig. 1b). We can then use these annotations to alert the user of these static elements and incorporate them into navigation. This concept is further prominently used in our system in

---

[1] https://github.com/ageitgey/face_recognition.

the recognition of elevators, including the identification of the specific elevator that the user has entered and subsequent start of navigation from the front of this same elevator door on the destination floor.

Through this map-based semantic recognition and alerting via a heavily annotated graph, our system can update a user in real-time about any pre-established environment characteristics. The operation is a simple and lightweight one that involves recognizing the environment (via the user's current position), searching for the appropriate information in the database, and communicating it to the user. The amount of information that will be communicated will depend on the preferences of the user. It should be noted that such an annotated map can be generated automatically as shown in our previous work [19].

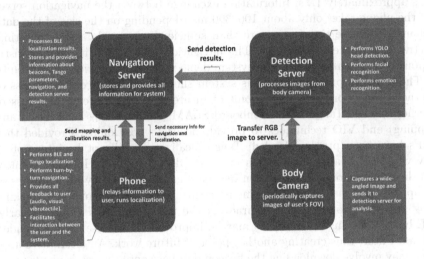

Fig. 3. System implementation pipeline

4   Architecture and Interfaces

4.1   System Architecture

The full system has been implemented using a client-server architecture (Fig. 3) due to size, speed, and scaling concerns. Although many of these operations could theoretically be performed on a phone, doing so would not be ideal for a large facility, because the size and scale of these operations would consume processing power, battery life, and storage space if done on the phone itself. Thus, the total system contains two servers in addition to the phone and body camera. One server (called the "detection server") receives images from the body camera and processes them, detecting and recognizing faces, emotions, and other objects it has been trained to detect. This particular server is equipped with a graphics processing unit (GPU) and can thus perform these detections in mere milliseconds. The results of this processing of the images are sent to another server. This second server (called the "navigation server") forms the system's "brain" and contains all information about all aspects of the system, including but not limited to information about the map, Tango ADFs, coordinate transformations, installed BLE beacon characteristics, and visual processing results from body camera images. Because of this, the phone is in constant contact with the server and exchanges the necessary information with it as needed.

4.2   Real-Time Response and Fallback Plans

This information exchange occurs very quickly. A full trip of the body camera data (from the moment the photo is taken to the announcing of the results) takes approximately 1.1 s. Information exchange between the navigation server and the phone takes only about 100–300 ms (depending on the size of the data exchanged). These times are more than sufficient to provide a near real-time reactive experience for the user. The navigation system and its characteristic responsiveness can be seen in the system demo video (link provided at the end).

The recovery procedure for this system should a failure occur (e.g., loss of Internet connection) is a main point of future work. In the case of a loss of Internet, Google Tango utilizes onboard SLAM (simultaneous localization and mapping) and VIO techniques to provide accurate positioning. Provided that ADFs have been pre-downloaded, Tango localization will not be interrupted. However, BLE beacon localization currently does require an Internet connection, because a cloud-based beacon database can be shared by all instances of the app. In this case, it may become necessary to fall back to onboard tracking using an IMU. However, the accuracy of the use of the IMU (and, similarly, BLE beacon readings themselves) may be improved via the use of an Extended Kalman Filter, thus creating another point of future work. An alternative approach may involve downloading the beacon database onto the user's phone when an Internet connection is readily available and thus locally performing BLE-based localization.

4.3   User-Centric Navigation Experience

Our system employs a user-centric navigation interface by promoting configurability. Both the type (audio, visual, and vibrotactile) and level (information density and vibration intensity) of feedback can be adjusted to suit varying levels of disabilities. The system also utilizes a conversation-style voice engine, implemented using Google's DialogFlow, to enable voice input. This voice engine can be currently used to initiate navigation and will be expanded to allow for changing application settings and asking for additional route and situational information during navigation. In addition, the system also provides modular integration for smartwatches for additional forms of feedback. The design of the system is such that next to no real "training" is required for a user to safely use the application. Figure 4 shows some interface screens for the mobile application. The system demo video (link provided at the end) shows a BVI individual using

Fig. 4. Interface screens for mobile application. *From left to right*: (a) home screen, (b) navigation interface, and (c) voice engine interface

the voice engine to start feedback, the audio feedback during navigation, and specialized visual and vibrotactile feedback for individuals with ASD.

5   User Testing

Our previous work compared navigation using solely BLE beacons with navigation using a hybrid BLE-Tango system [10]. Human subjects tests involved numerical evaluations of runs to record statistics such as total interventions, trip duration, and total bumps. In that study, we found that when subjects used hybrid navigation, they required significantly fewer interventions and less assistance when compared to their runs with BLE navigation. For comparison purposes, each path covered a single area, such as a corridor or a group of cubicles.

In this study, our goal was to evaluate the high-level usability of the entire system and to allow users to travel across areas and floors during a single test, thus requiring them to peruse doors and/or elevators. To this end, we performed human subjects tests on both BVI individuals and those with ASD. For these experiments, we used the Lenovo Phab 2 Pro, a Tango device. These tests were performed at Lighthouse Guild, a vision rehabilitation center in New York City, and evaluated the experiences of users when using the app and assessing subjects' impressions of the app in guiding them between points safely and accurately. The system demo video (link provided at the end) shows some runs.

5.1   Procedures

We conducted two separate tests (one each for BVI and ASD) of the system and mobile application, where we asked subjects to traverse pre-selected paths using the guidance provided by the system. To evaluate our subjects' experiences, we administered both a pre-experiment survey (which asked for demographics) and a post-experiment survey (which assessed subjects' impressions of the application and its various components). The BVI test had a convenience sample of 11 individuals (ranging from low vision to totally blind) use the application to navigate themselves on three separate paths that brought them across floors. There were **8** participants 55 years old or older, **1** participant 45–54 years old, **1** participant 35–44 years old, and **1** participant 18–24 years old; there were **7** males and **4** females. The ASD test had a small convenience sample of five **male** individuals with medium-low- to high-functioning forms of ASD try two to three separate paths on a single floor (depending on the focus of the subject). There were **2** participants aged 25–34 years and **3** participants aged 18–24 years.

5.2   Results

According to the surveys, subjects generally had a very favorable impression of the system. (Results are reported as **means**.) For the ASD tests, all five subjects agreed to strongly agreed that using the app was easy (**4.6/5**), that they felt safe while using the app (**4.6/5**), and that they could easily reach a destination with the app (**4.4/5**). The subjects also found the app helpful to extremely helpful (**4.6/5**) and were moderately to very satisfied (**3.4/5**) with it. Those individuals who used the smartwatch to receive supplementary vibrotactile cues found them moderately helpful (**3.75/5**).

Similar results were recorded for our tests with BVI individuals. The subjects agreed to strongly agreed (**4.5/5**) that using the app was easy, agreed (**4.2/5**) that they felt safe while using it, agreed (**4.3/5**) that they could easily reach a destination using it, and generally found the app helpful (**4.3/5**). The subjects almost universally agreed that the voice feedback provided by the app was extremely helpful (**4.8/5**). We also tested other features with our BVI subjects. With regards to the voice assistant which allowed them to initiate navigation, almost all of our subjects who used it found it extremely helpful (**4.9/5**). The app would also issue guidance on corrective turns if the user was not facing the correct direction; users found them moderately to extremely helpful (**4.6/5**).

5.3   Discussion of Results

The app was generally very well-received by all subjects. BVI subjects approved of the voice feedback provided by the app as well as the simplicity of the voice assistant. ASD subjects expressed favorable opinions on the visual and vibro-tactile cues provided by the app and also liked the addition of a smartwatch to keep their attention. However, we noted that BVI and ASD subjects each gave very different feedback in what they would like to see in such a system.

Feedback gathered from our ASD tests centered mostly on optimizing the interface and feedback provided by the app for ASD individuals (e.g., simpler instructions for medium-low functioning ASD individuals). In contrast, feedback gathered from our BVI tests mostly centered around fine-tuning and then augmenting the experience provided by the app (e.g., expansion of the voice assistant and possible use of smart glasses with built-in cameras). This difference in feedback highlights the importance of personalizing the navigation experience to each disability. Thus, offering users the choice to turn on or off certain features and pre-establishing some of the assistance to be given based on the user's disability can make the navigation experience much more comfortable for the user.

6 Conclusion

Through our work, we have created and tested a system that would not only guide a person indoors with high accuracy but would also augment that same user's understanding of his/her environment. This system consists of highly accurate, BLE-Tango hybrid navigation coupled with a body camera for the alerting of high-priority situational elements and a pre-built database of map annotations for the alerting of high-priority environmental characteristics. Our system provides a complete picture of the user's surroundings in a user-centric way by incorporating varying modes of feedback for different disabilities.

Evaluations have shown that such a system is welcomed by both BVI and ASD individuals. These tests have also opened many avenues for future work with which we could further improve and optimize this system. Additional evaluations are also required for the testing of the visual body camera-based alerting system which would play a pivotal role, especially for BVI users. However, in the end, our work has established a solid base from which we can expand our current system into a more full-fledged assistive application that can both effectively navigate a person and augment their understanding and awareness of their environment.

System Demo

A system demo can be viewed here: https://youtu.be/Hq1EYS9Jncg.

Acknowledgments. This research was supported by the U.S. Department of Homeland Security (DHS) Science & Technology (S&T) Directorate, Office of University Programs, Summer Research Team Program for Minority Serving Institutions, administered by the Oak Ridge Institute for Science and Education (ORISE) under DOE contract #DE-AC05-06OR23100 and #DE-SC0014664. This work is also supported by the U.S. National Science Foundation (NSF) through Awards #EFRI-1137172, #CBET-1160046, and #CNS-1737533; the VentureWell (formerly NCIIA) Course and Development Program (Award #10087-12); a Bentley-CUNY Collaborative Research Agreement 2017–2020; and NYSID via the CREATE (Cultivating Resources for Employment with Assistive Technology) Program. We would like to thank the staff at Goodwill NY/NJ for their invaluable feedback and for recruiting subjects for our tests with autistic individuals. We would especially like to thank all of our subjects for their participation and cooperation as well as for providing extremely helpful feedback in improving our system.

References

1. Ahmetovic, D., Gleason, C., Ruan, C., Kitani, K., Takagi, H., Asakawa, C.: NavCog: a navigational cognitive assistant for the blind. In: Proceedings of the 18th International Conference on Human-Computer Interaction with Mobile Devices and Services - MobileHCI 2016 (2016)
2. Bohonos, S., Lee, A., Malik, A., Thai, C., Manduchi, R.: Universal real-time navigational assistance (URNA): an urban bluetooth beacon for the blind. In: Proceedings of the 1st ACM SIGMOBILE International Workshop on Systems and Networking Support for Healthcare and Assisted Living Environments - HealthNet 2007 (2007)
3. Chumkamon, S., Tuvaphanthaphiphat, P., Keeratiwintakorn, P.: A blind navigation system using RFID for indoor environments. In: 5th International Conference on Electrical Engineering/Electronics, Computer, Telecommunications and Information Technology (2008)
4. Furnari, A., Battiato, S., Farinella, G.M.: Personal-location-based temporal segmentation of egocentric videos for lifelogging applications. J. Vis. Commun. Image Represent. **52**, 1–12 (2018)
5. Hub, A., Diepstraten, J., Ertl, T.: Design and development of an indoor navigation and object identification system for the blind. In: Proceedings of the 6th International ACM SIGACCESS Conference on Computers and Accessibility, Assets 2004 (2004)
6. Kara, A., Bertoni, H.: Blockage/shadowing and polarization measurements at 2.45 GHz for interference evaluation between bluetooth and IEEE 802.11 WLAN. In: IEEE Antennas and Propagation Society International Symposium (2001). https://doi.org/10.1109/aps.2001.960112
7. Li, B., Muñoz, J.P., Rong, X., Xiao, J., Tian, Y., Arditi, A.: ISANA: wearable context-aware indoor assistive navigation with obstacle avoidance for the blind. In: Hua, G., Jégou, H. (eds.) ECCV 2016. LNCS, vol. 9914, pp. 448–462. Springer, Cham (2016). https://doi.org/10.1007/978-3-319-48881-3_31
8. Lind, S., Williams, D., Raber, J., Peel, A., Bowler, D.: Spatial navigation impairments among intellectually high-functioning adults with autism spectrum disorder: exploring relations with theory of mind, episodic memory, and episodic future thinking. J. Abnorm. Psychol. **122**(4), 1189–1199 (2013)
9. Mulloni, A., Wagner, D., Barakonyi, I., Schmalstieg, D.: Indoor positioning and navigation with camera phones. IEEE Pervasive Comput. **8**(2), 22–31 (2009)
10. Nair, V., Tsangouri, C., Xiao, B., Olmschenk, G., Seiple, W.H., Zhu, Z.: A hybrid indoor positioning system for the blind and visually impaired using bluetooth and Google Tango. J. Technol. Persons Disabil. **6**, 61–81 (2018)
11. Nie, M., et al.: SoundView: an auditory guidance system based on environment understanding for the visually impaired people. In: Annual International Conference of the IEEE Engineering in Medicine and Biology Society (2009)
12. Ortis, A., Farinella, G.M., D'Amico, V., Addesso, L., Torrisi, G., Battiato, S.: Organizing egocentric videos of daily living activities. Pattern Recognit. **72**, 207–218 (2017)
13. Ozdenizci, B., Ok, K., Coskun, V., Aydin, M.N.: Development of an indoor navigation system using NFC technology. In: Fourth International Conference on Information and Computing (2011)

14. Peng, E., Peursum, P., Li, L., Venkatesh, S.: A smartphone-based obstacle sensor for the visually impaired. In: Yu, Z., Liscano, R., Chen, G., Zhang, D., Zhou, X. (eds.) UIC 2010. LNCS, vol. 6406, pp. 590–604. Springer, Heidelberg (2010). https://doi.org/10.1007/978-3-642-16355-5_45
15. Redmon, J., Farhadi, A.: YOLO9000: better, faster, stronger. arXiv preprint arXiv:1612.08242 (2016)
16. Ruiz, A.R.J., Granja, F.S., Honorato, J.C.P., Rosas, J.I.G.: Accurate pedestrian indoor navigation by tightly coupling foot-mounted imu and RFID measurements. IEEE Trans. Instr. Meas. 61(1), 178–189 (2012)
17. Spera, E., Furnari, A., Battiato, S., Farinella, G.M.: Egocentric shopping cart localization. In: International Conference on Pattern Recognition (ICPR) (2018)
18. Strumillo, P.: Electronic interfaces aiding the visually impaired in environmental access, mobility and navigation. In: 3rd International Conference on Human System Interaction (2010)
19. Tang, H., Tsering, N., Hu, F., Zhu, Z.: Automatic pre-journey indoor map generation using autocad floor plan. J. Technol. Persons Disabil. 4, 179–191 (2016)
20. Tapu, R., Mocanu, B., Bursuc, A., Zaharia, T.: A smartphone-based obstacle detection and classification system for assisting visually impaired people. In: The IEEE International Conference on Computer Vision (ICCV) Workshops, pp. 444–451 (2013)
21. Vu, T., Osokin, A., Laptev, I.: Context-aware CNNs for person head detection. In: The IEEE International Conference on Computer Vision (2015)
22. World Health Organization: Vision impairment and blindness (2017). http://www.who.int/mediacentre/factsheets/fs282/en/

Comparing Methods for Assessment of Facial Dynamics in Patients with Major Neurocognitive Disorders

Yaohui Wang[1]($\boxtimes$), Antitza Dantcheva[1,3], Jean-Claude Broutart[2],
Philippe Robert[3], Francois Bremond[1,3], and Piotr Bilinski[4]

[1] INRIA Sophia-Antipolis, STARS, Sophia Antipolis, France
{yaohui.wang,antitza.dantcheva,francois.bremond}@inria.fr
[2] GSF Noisiez, Biot, France
jc.broutart@free.fr
[3] EA CoBTeK-University Cote d'Azur, Nice, France
probert@unice.fr
[4] University of Oxford, Oxford, UK
piotr.bilinski@eng.ox.ac.uk

Abstract. Assessing facial dynamics in patients with major neurocognitive disorders and specifically with Alzheimer's disease (AD) has shown to be highly challenging. Classically such assessment is performed by clinical staff, evaluating verbal and non-verbal language of AD-patients, since they have lost a substantial amount of their cognitive capacity, and hence communication ability. In addition, patients need to communicate important messages, such as discomfort or pain. Automated methods would support the current healthcare system by allowing for telemedicine, *i.e.*, lesser costly and logistically inconvenient examination. In this work we compare methods for assessing facial dynamics such as talking, singing, neutral and smiling in AD-patients, captured during music mnemotherapy sessions. Specifically, we compare 3D ConvNets, Very Deep Neural Network based Two-Stream ConvNets, as well as Improved Dense Trajectories. We have adapted these methods from prominent action recognition methods and our promising results suggest that the methods generalize well to the context of facial dynamics. The Two-Stream ConvNets in combination with ResNet-152 obtains the best performance on our dataset, capturing well even minor facial dynamics and has thus sparked high interest in the medical community.

Keywords: Facial dynamics · Facial expressions
Neurocognitive disorders · Alzheimer's disease

1 Introduction

Major neurocognitive disorder (NCD), as introduced by the American Psychiatric Association (APA), known previously as dementia, is a decline in mental

© Springer Nature Switzerland AG 2019
L. Leal-Taixé and S. Roth (Eds.): ECCV 2018 Workshops, LNCS 11134, pp. 144–157, 2019.
https://doi.org/10.1007/978-3-030-11024-6_10

ability, threatening the independence of a large fraction of the elderly population. Alzheimer's disease (AD) is the most common form of major NCD, associated with loss of short-term-memory, problems with language, disorientation and other intellectual abilities, severely affecting daily life[1]. Worldwide, currently 35 Million people have been diagnosed with major neurocognitive disorder, which has been associated with 530 billion Euros in 2010[2]), tendency increasing[3]. While there is no palliative care, musical therapies have been proposed as efficient therapeutic means, acting as a powerful catalyst for precipitating memories, shown in a number of studies [22,33,36]. Specifically *mnemotherapy* can help elicit autobiographical memories by promoting positive emotional memories [2]. This and other therapies can improve the quality of life in AD patients [1,23]. However, the assessment of such therapies requires comprehensive manual observation by experienced clinicians [10,32]. Towards overcoming this limitation, computer vision based methods can offer objective assessment by *analyzing affect and expression behaviors, directly related to the effectiveness of therapies.*

While *expression recognition* has attracted significant research attention [19, 28,38], facial behavior analysis from naturalistic videos, associated to illumination changes, partial occlusions, pose variation, as well as low-intensity expressions pose challenges for current existing methods. In addition, while many areas of computer vision have experienced significant advancements with deep neural networks, analysis of facial dynamics has only recently benefited from deep convolutional networks [14,26,34,43].

Naturally, the accuracy of facial dynamics classification depends on features, as well as architecture used for assessment. Given the plethora of existing algorithms, exploring different types of features and architectures is necessary to devise a robust solution.

Motivated by the above, in this work we explore and compare computer vision methods, introduced in the context of *action recognition* in our challenging setting, namely in the context of *assessing naturalistic facial dynamics.* Specifically we have (a) 3D Convolutional Neural Network (C3D) [35], (b) Very Deep Two-Stream Convolutional Network (with VGG-16 and ResNet-152 [30,42]) and (c) Improved Dense Trajectories (iDT) [39], as well as combinations and variations thereof. Given a video sequence, we firstly detect the face and proceed to extract features pertaining to the respective method. The obtained feature set is then classified in one of four facial dynamics categories, namely *neutral, smiling, talking* and *singing.* The automatic detection of named facial dynamics indicates the involvement of the patients during mnemotherapy and hence can support the assessment of a therapy session. Specifically, given that AD-patients in later stages of the disease often suffer from apathy, the (frequent) occurrence of smiling, talking and singing indicates that the therapy is effective. Experiments are conducted on a challenging medical unconstrained dataset containing 322 video sequences of 16 AD-patients including continuous pose-changes,

---

[1] www.alz.org/alzheimers_disease_what_is_alzheimers.asp.

[2] http://www.alz.org/news_and_events_20608.asp.

[3] http://www.alz.org/.

occlusions, camera-movements and artifacts, as well as illumination changes. In addition, the dataset depicts naturalistic facial dynamics of predominantly elderly subjects, which vary in (generally less profound) intensity and occur jointly (*e.g.*, simultaneous talking and smiling). Moreover, we observe a high level of inter- and intra person variability (*e.g.*, expressive and apathetic AD-patients). We note that, despite that, it is imperative to work with such data, as it is representative for current (vast amount of) video-documentation of medical doctors, requiring automated analysis.

We note that we tested existing methods in expression recognition, such as smile detectors[4], [4] on the ADP - dataset, as well as facial-landmark based expression recognition algorithms without success, since already the first incorporated step of face detection failed throughout.

2   Related Work

Existing approaches for the *analysis of facial dynamics* are inspired by cognitive, psychological and neuroscientific findings. The most frequent way to describe facial dynamics is based on the Facial Action Coding System (FACS) proposed by Ekman *et al.* [7], representing movements of facial muscles in different terms of action units (AUs). Hence, classical methods analyze sequences of images containing the neutral face and the expression apex [19]. More recent methods involve linear deterministic and probabilistic methodologies including general or special Linear Dynamical Systems (LDS), as well as various extensions of deterministic Slow Feature Analysis (SFA) [43]. In addition, HMMs [27] have been used to capture the temporal segments of facial behaviour.

More recently, learning facial features in supervised and unsupervised manner using deep neural networks has attracted considerable attention. We proceed to provide such notable work, analyzing both, images and video sequences.

Recognizing Facial Dynamics in Images. Liu *et al.* [18] propose a Boosted Deep Belief Network, integrating three separate training stages for expression recognition in images. Han and Meng [11] present the incremental boosting of CNN for AUs recognition. Zhao *et al.* [44] combine region learning, as well as multiple label learning to detect AUs.

Recognizing Facial Dynamics in Video Sequences. When analyzing facial behavior in videos, many works usually focus on spatial-temporal feature extraction. Jung *et al.* [14] use two neural networks separately to extract temporal appearance features, as well as temporal geometric features for expression recognition. Zafeiriou *et al.* [43] propose a slow-feature-auto-encoder for both supervised and semi-supervised learning of facial behavioural dynamics analysis. Hasani and Mahoor [12] combine a 3D Inception-ResNet with a Long short-term memory (LSTM) network in order to extract both, spatial and temporal features from videos. Li *et al.* [17] combine VGG with ROI and LSTM together towards detection of AUs. Most recently, combining Variational Autoencoder (VAEs)

---

[4] https://ibug.doc.ic.ac.uk/resources/smile-detectors/.

and Generative Adversarial Networks (GANs) has allowed for learning a powerful latent representation utilized for facial behavior analysis in audience [26].

Previous and recent **computer vision work related to healthcare** have focused on, among others the assessment of: cognitive health in smart home environment [5], daily activities [15], AD symptoms [25], depression [6,45], assistive technologies [16], as well as pain [24].

The rest of the paper is organized as follows. Section 3 describes the methods we compare. Section 4 introduces our dataset, assembled for the purpose of medical patient recording. Section 5 presents experiments, validating the effectiveness of the evaluated methods in assessing facial dynamics. Finally, Sect. 5.3 discusses and Sect. 6 concludes the paper.

3   Evaluated Methods

Firstly, we utilize face detection, based on which we crop the faces and proceed to extract facial features using Improved Dense Trajectories, as well as two deep neural network models. The latter have been pre-trained on a *large-scale* human action dataset UCF101 [31]. We inherit the weights in the neural network models and proceed to extract features of our dataset. Finally, we employ Support Vector Machine (SVM) to classify video sequences into four facial dynamics: *smiling*, *talking*, *neutral* and *singing*.

3.1   Face Detection

There exist a large number of face detection algorithms, based on a large number of features and implementations. We compared a number of pre-trained algorithms including VGG [9], OpenCV [37], and Doppia [20] with our *ADP-dataset* (see Sect. 4). The latter performed the best and was hence included in the pre-processing step.

3.2   3D ConvNets

3D ConvNets (C3D) has a simple architecture (see Fig. 1) and has shown a performance of 85.2% accuracy on the UCF101 dataset. We adapt the C3D architecture and extract spatial-temporal features towards categorization of AD patients' facial dynamics.

The original C3D network has 8 convolutional layers, 5 max-pooling layers, 2 fully connected layers and a softmax loss layer. For 5 convolutional layers from 1 to 5, the number of convolutional kernels are 64, 128, 256, 256, 256 respectively. Because all kernels have 3 dimensions, the additional parameter d indicates the kernel temporal depth. Tran *et al.* [35], report for $d = 3$ the best among all experiments, which we also use in the present work. In C3D network, all convolutional kernels are $3 \times 3 \times 3$ with stride 1 in both, spatial and temporal directions, in order to ensure a 3 dimensional output. Such an architecture allows

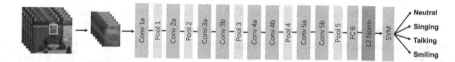

Fig. 1. C3D based facial dynamics detection: For each video sequence, faces are detected and the face sequences are passed into a pre-trained C3D network to extract a 4096-dim feature vector for each video. Finally a SVM classifier is trained to predict the final classification result. We have blurred the faces of the subject in this figure, in order to preserve the patient's privacy.

for preserving the temporal information between neighboring frames in a video-clip. With the exception of the first pooling layer, all pooling layers are max-pooling layers, with kernel size $2 \times 2 \times 2$ with stride 1, attaining that the size of the feature map of each layer is reduced by a factor of 8 as opposed to the input (see Fig. 2). The kernel size of the first pooling layer is $1 \times 2 \times 2$, which ensures that early merging of the temporal signals is avoided. Since we only need features from the FC6 activation layer in our context, we remove the FC7 and last soft max layers from the original model.

We note that the C3D network was pre-trained on the UCF101 dataset, which contains 13320 videos from 101 action categories including single and multiple person actions. Specifically, each video has been divided into video clips of 16-frames-length, with an 8-frame overlap between two video clips by a sliding window method. All these video clips serve as training-input for the C3D network. The computed C3D-feature of a single video sequence is the average of all these clip FC6 activations followed by an $L2$-normalization.

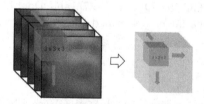

Fig. 2. 3D Convolutional kernel and 3D Max-pooling kernel: In each convolutional layer except the first one, the kernel size is $3 \times 3 \times 3$ and in each max-pooling layer the kernel size is $2 \times 2 \times 2$. This 3 dimensional design can preserve both spatial and temporal information. We have blurred the faces of the subject in this figure, in order to preserve the patient's privacy.

3.3 Very Deep Two-Stream ConvNets

The second method, which we explore is Two-Stream ConvNets [30] (see Fig. 3a), which has reportedly achieved 88% accuracy on the UCF101 action recognition dataset. It extracts features based on RGB frames, as well as based on optical flow from a video sequence. As reported by Wang *et al.* [42] and Feichtenhofer *et al.* [8], one successor network, namely the Very Deep Two-Stream ConvNets outperformed the original Two-Stream ConvNets (by 3% on UCF101).

Two-Stream ConvNets incorporates a *spatial ConvNet*, accepting as input single frame with dimension $224 \times 224 \times 3$, as well as a separate stream - a *temporal ConvNet*, accepting as input stacked optical flow fields, with dimension $224 \times 224 \times 20$. Specifically the optical flow field is composed of horizontal and vertical components D_x and D_y. A stack of D_x and D_y of 10 frames together are fed into the following ConvNet. Hence, while the first stream is based on RGB based features, the second stream is based on complementary motion between video frames, resulting to an increased accuracy over each of the streams.

We test two variations of Very Deep Two-Stream ConvNets, the first one including VGG-16 in both streams, the second one ResNet-152 in both streams. We note that for both, VGG-16 and ResNet-152, we remove the last fully connected layer and follow a $L2$-normalization step after the activations.

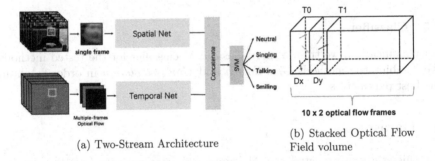

(a) Two-Stream Architecture

(b) Stacked Optical Flow Field volume

Fig. 3. (a) While the *spatial ConvNet* accepts a single *RGB* frame as input, the *temporal ConvNet*'s input is the D_x and D_y of 10 consecutive frames, namely 20 input channels. Both described inputs are fed into the Two-stream ConvNets, respectively. We use in this work two variations of Very Deep Two Stream ConvNets, incorporating VGG-16 [29] ResNet-152 [13] for both streams respectively. (b) The optical flow of each frame has two components, namely D_x and D_y. We stack 10 times D_y after D_x for each frame to form a 20 frames length input volume.

Input Configuration: Given a video sequence of T frames, we extract N *RGB* frames (*spatial ConvNet*) and N optical flow fields (*temporal ConvNet*). The step of sampling in *spatial ConvNet* is $\left\lfloor \frac{T-1}{N-1} \right\rfloor$. If we stack dense optical flow of 10 sequential frames to form a 20 input volume (see Fig. 3b, both horizontal and vertical components times 10), the sampling step for *temporal ConvNet* is $\left\lfloor \frac{T-10+1}{N} \right\rfloor$. For each optical flow field volume I, we have $I_{2t} = D_x, I_{2t+1} = D_y, t \in 10$.

The pre-trained *spatial* and *temporal* ConvNets extract two respective feature vectors, which concatenated serve as input for our classifier that we describe below.

3.4   Improved Dense Trajectories

Despite the prevalence of DNN, iDT as introduced by Wang *et al.* [40] constitute one of the best hand-crafted feature-based approaches. We employ iDT for their good coverage of foreground motion and high performance in action recognition (competitive to DNN). In addition, it is complementary to DNN and hence a fusion of iDT and DNN has shown to provide improved accuracy. iDT extracts local spatio-temporal video trajectories by applying dense sampling of feature points on multiple spatial scales with subsequent tracking of detected feature points using dense optical flow. We extract dense trajectories and proceed to extract local spatio-temporal video volumes around the detected trajectories. We extract 5 types of features aligned with the trajectories to characterize shape (point shifts), appearance (Histogram of Oriented Gradients (HOG) and motion (Histogram of Optical Flow (HOF) and Motion Boundary Histogram (MBHx, MBHy)). We encode the iDT features with bag-of-features (BOF) in order to represent video sequence using the extracted motion trajectories and their corresponding descriptors.

3.5   Classifier

For classification, we train a multi-class SVM classifier for the tested methods. We combine the methods *Grid-Search* and *Cross-validation* in order to obtain the best parameters.

4   Dataset

For this study, we created the Alzheimer's disease patients (ADP) - dataset, comprising of 322 video sequences including 16 female patients, with 5 or more takes of each facial dynamics class. The length of the video sequences ranged from 1.44 s to 33.08 s. All videos have been recorded on 25 fps, with resolution of 576 × 720. Two patients with aphasia endued only video sequences of *neutral, smiling* and *singing*. Interestingly, while these two patients were not able to speak, they performed singing-like facial movements, which we labeled as *singing*. For this study we manually segmented and annotated the data, which was challenging, due to high intra- and inter-class variability of patients, as well as facial dynamics. In terms of annotation, two researchers annotated the data (one working in the area of computer vision, the other one in clinical experiments), overlapping in >85%. We note that facial dynamics appeared jointly (*e.g.*, singing and smiling), due to the unintrusive nature of the setting. Currently, such overlaps were not considered in the annotation, classes were annotated mutually exclusively.

The patients participated in individual mnemotherapy sessions, located in a small auditorium. Videos of these sessions were acquired with a camescope Sony Handycam DCR-SR 32, placed sideways of patient and clinician, capturing predominantly non-frontal and highly unconstrained videos of the patient.

We identified the most frequent occurring facial dynamics as *neutral, smiling, talking* and *singing/singing-like movements*. We note that even "neutral" there are still facial movements (*e.g.* blinking), hand or head movements.

5 Experimental Results

5.1 Implementation Details

We conduct our experiments on a single GTX Titan X GPU for both face detection and feature extraction, with emphasis on the use of C3D Network and Two-Stream ConvNets.

Face detection is performed by Doppia [20]. Due to the challenging dataset including among others variations of illumination, patient pose, as well as camera-movements, some faces are not detected in single video frames (constituting to false negatives). In such cases, we remove the concerning frames. In case of prevalence of undetected faces, we exclude the concerning video sequences from the analysis.

To compute optical flow, we follow the work of Wang *et al.* [41] and use the TVL1 algorithm implemented in OpenCV. In our experiments, we set $N = 25$, for both, RGB and optical flow, following the works [41,42]. Each detected face (*RGB*-frame) is rescaled to $224 \times 224 \times 3$ and optical flow is rescaled to $224 \times 224 \times 20$ in Two-Stream Networks. For C3D we rescale each detected face to $112 \times 112 \times 3$.

For classification we use the scikit-learn library [21]. We employ a Stratified 10-Folds cross-validation scheme, which preserves the ratio of samples for each category for train and test set (see Table 2). The dataset is divided into 10-folds, 9 folds are used for training and the remaining fold is used for testing. This is repeated 10 times and reported results are the average thereof. We note that video sequences in the test set are not present in the training set. Per split, we compute mean accuracy (MA) (mean accuracy of 10 splits) and we report the MA over all splits.

We test SVM classifier with linear and radial basis function (RBF) kernels. Our experiments show that *e.g.*, for Two-Stream (ResNet-152) the RBF kernel performs best (with C = 25, gamma = 2).

5.2 Results

In Table 1 the performance of the facial dynamics-classification is presented as mean accuracy (MA) pertained to C3D, Two-Stream ConvNets (based on VGG-16 and ResNet-152), as well as separately to each spatial and temporal net. We observe that while the spatial and temporal net of Two-Stream ConvNets (ResNet-152) substantially outperform the VGG-16 counterparts, the overall Two-Stream ConvNets (VGG-16) and Two-Stream ConvNets (ResNet-152) perform comparably well. The best performance was obtained by the ResNet-152 based Two-Stream ConvNets, namely $MA = 76.40\%$, marginally outperforming VGG-16 based Two-Stream ConvNets (by 0.4%), and substantially outperforming C3D network (by 9%). In addition, we show performance of C3D and Two-Stream ConvNets fused with iDT. When fusing iDT with the other algorithms, the classification rate consistently increases, up to 79.5% for Two-Stream (ResNet-152).

Table 1. Classification accuracies of C3D, Very Deep Two-Stream ConvNets, iDT, as well as fusion thereof on the presented ADP-dataset. We report the Mean Accuracy (MA) associated to the compared methods. Abbreviations used: SN...Spatial Net, TN...Temporal Net.

Method	MA (%)
C3D	67.4
SN of Two-Stream ConvNets (VGG-16)	65.2
TN of Two-Stream ConvNets (VGG-16)	69.9
Two-Stream ConvNets (VGG-16)	76.1
SN of Two-Stream ConvNets (ResNet-152)	69.6
TN of Two-Stream ConvNets (ResNet-152)	75.8
Two-Stream ConvNets (ResNet-152)	76.4
iDT	61.2
C3D + iDT	71.1
Two-Stream ConvNets (VGG-16) + iDT	78.9
Two-Stream ConvNets (ResNet-152) + iDT	**79.5**

The classification rates for each split of the 10-fold cross-validation are reported in Table 2.

In Fig. 4 we present the overall confusion matrix, associated to the best performing algorithm – Two-Stream ConvNets (ResNet-152). The related results indicate that the highest confusion rates are observed between the dynamics *smiling*, *singing* and *talking*. This may be explainable by the co-occurrence of facial dynamics, as well as with the general low-intensity facial dynamics exhibited by the elderly patients. In some cases, the categories *neutral* and *smiling* have been confused. In Table 2 we show accuracy for each facial dynamics-category associated to Fig. 4. We see that the facial dynamic with highest classification rate is *neutral*, which is intuitive due to the discriminative low-motion. *Smiling* on the other hand is classified with the biggest error, which might be due to the low-intensity expressions exhibited by the elderly patients (see Fig. 5). We here note that annotation was performed utilizing audio and video.

In a similar healthcare setting, an algorithm distinguishing between similar facial expressions and activities, based on spatio-temporal Dense Trajectories and improved Fisher Vectors has been proposed [3], which we outperform by 16.1% utmost (Table 3).

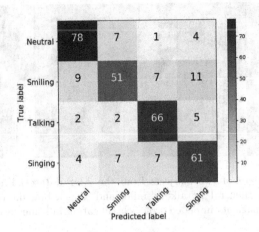

Fig. 4. Confusion matrix for categorized facial dynamics of Two-Stream ResNet-152 + iDT (best performing method) on the ADP-Dataset.

Table 2. Classification accuracy of Two-Stream ConvNets (ResNet-152) + iDT on the ADP dataset. The numbers in parentheses indicate the number of "neutral", "smiling", "talking" and "singing" samples in each split.

Split	Train	Test	Accuracy (%)
1	289 (81, 70, 67, 71)	33 (9, 8, 8, 8)	78.8
2	289 (81, 70, 67, 71)	33 (9, 8, 8, 8)	75.8
3	289 (81, 70, 67, 71)	33 (9, 8, 8, 8)	78.8
4	289 (81, 70, 67, 71)	33 (9, 8, 8, 8)	87.9
5	289 (81, 70, 67, 71)	33 (9, 8, 8, 8)	78.8
6	290 (81, 70, 68, 71)	32 (9, 8, 7, 8)	78.1
7	290 (81, 70, 68, 71)	32 (9, 8, 7, 8)	84.4
8	290 (81, 70, 68, 71)	32 (9, 8, 7, 8)	71.9
9	291 (81, 71, 68, 71)	31 (9, 7, 7, 8)	83.9
10	292 (81, 71, 68, 72)	30 (9, 7, 7, 7)	76.7
Average			79.5

Table 3. Mean Accuracy (%) of Two-Stream ConvNets (ResNet-152) + iDT on the ADP dataset. Assessment by category.

Method	Neutral	Smiling	Talking	Singing
iDT	75.6	39.8	68.0	59.5
C3D + iDT	75.6	53.8	81.3	64.4
Two-Stream (ResNet-152)+iDT	86.7	65.4	88.0	77.2

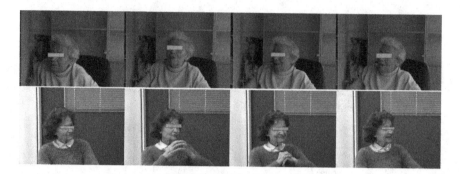

Fig. 5. Example images of two subjects from the ADP-dataset. From left to right we depict the classes "neutral", "talk", "smile" and "sing". Low-intensity expressions exhibited by elderly patients impede correct classification in some cases.

5.3   Observations and Future Work

In this section we summarize the main findings of this research.

- Based on our experiments with iDT and the DNN-architectures, we observe that DNNs contribute highly in obtaining very promising classification rates, despite the small size of our dataset. We note that while the presented results significantly outperform previous methods based on handcrafted features (*i.e.*, [3]), when fusing handcrafted features (*e.g.*, iDT) with DNN-based approaches, accuracy increases consistently.
- The methods adapted from action recognition generalize well to classification of facial dynamics. We observe this by the good classification rates, as well as by the facts that (a) *temporal ConvNets* performs better than *spatial ConvNets* (cf. [8,30]), (b) fusion with iDT consistently improves the performance of DNNs (cf. [8,42]), (c) Two-Stream ConvNets outperforms C3D (cf. [8]).
- Due to the limited size of our dataset, an end-to-end training from scratch of a DNN architecture is not feasible. Large action recognition datasets such as the UCF101 human action dataset offer suitable training alternatives for DNN-architectures.
- The accuracy of facial dynamics classification depends on the features, as well as architecture used for assessment. Given the myriad of existing algorithms, exploring different types of features and architectures will be necessary to devise a robust solution.
- High inter- and intra-variance of subjects and facial dynamics contribute to the remaining error rates. Further challenges include the low-intensity of facial dynamics exhibited by elderly patients, the unconstrained setting, allowing for facial dynamics to occur jointly, as well as ambiguous human annotation.

However, more work is necessary in this regard. Future work will involve fine-tuning of the involved methods. In addition, we intend to explore personalized facial dynamics assessment, where we will train algorithms on video sequences related to each patient, individually. Finally, we will design specific neural network models for facial dynamics assessment, placing emphasis on a single end-to-end model, incorporating face detection, facial feature extraction, as well as classification.

6   Conclusions

In this work we have compared three methods for assessment of facial dynamics exhibited by AD-patients in mnemotherapy. The three tested methods include Improved Dense Trajectories, 3D ConvNets and Two-Stream ConvNets, which we have adapted from action recognition. Despite the pre-training of mentioned methods on an action recognition dataset, the methods have generalized very well to facial dynamics. Experiments conducted on an assembled dataset of Alzheimer's disease patients have resulted in a true classification rate of up to 79.5% for the fusion of Two-Stream ConvNets (ResNet-152) and iDT.

References

1. Ashida, S.: The effect of reminiscence music therapy sessions on changes in depressive symptoms in elderly persons with dementia. J. Music Ther. **37**(3), 170–182 (2000)
2. Broutart, J.C., Robert, P., Balas, D., Broutart, N., Cahors, J.: Démence et perte cognitive: Prise en charge du patient et de sa famille, chap. Mnémothérapie, reviviscence et maladie d'Alzheimer. De Boeck Superieur, March 2017
3. Dantcheva, A., Bilinski, P., Nguyen, H.T., Broutart, J.C., Bremond, F.: Expression recognition for severely demented patients in music reminiscence-therapy. In: EUSIPCO (2017)
4. Dantcheva, A., Bremond, F.: Gender estimation based on smile-dynamics. IEEE Trans. Inf. Forensics Secur. (TIFS) **12**(3), 719–729 (2017)
5. Dawadi, P.N., Cook, D.J., Schmitter-Edgecombe, M., Parsey, C.: Automated assessment of cognitive health using smart home technologies. Technol. Health Care **21**(4), 323–343 (2013)
6. Dibeklioglu, H., Hammal, Z., Cohn, J.F.: Dynamic multimodal measurement of depression severity using deep autoencoding. IEEE J. Biomed. Health Inform. **PP**(99), 1 (2017)
7. Ekman, P., Friesen, W.: Facial Action Coding System: A Technique for the Measurement of Facial Movement. Consulting Psychologists, Palo Alto (1978)
8. Feichtenhofer, C., Pinz, A., Zisserman, A.: Convolutional two-stream network fusion for video action recognition. In: IEEE Conference on Computer Vision and Pattern Recognition (2016)
9. Felzenszwalb, P.F., Girshick, R.B., McAllester, D., Ramanan, D.: Object detection with discriminatively trained part-based models. IEEE Trans. Pattern Anal. Mach. Intell. **32**(9), 1627–1645 (2010)
10. Folstein, M.F., Folstein, S.E., McHugh, P.R.: "Mini-mental state": a practical method for grading the cognitive state of patients for the clinician. J. Psychiatr. Res. **12**(3), 189–198 (1975)

11. Han, S., Meng, Z., Khan, A.S., Tong, Y.: Incremental boosting convolutional neural network for facial action unit recognition. In: Lee, D.D., Sugiyama, M., Luxburg, U.V., Guyon, I., Garnett, R. (eds.) Advances in Neural Information Processing Systems, vol. 29, pp. 109–117 (2016)
12. Hasani, B., Mahoor, M.H.: Facial expression recognition using enhanced deep 3D convolutional neural networks. In: IEEE Conference on Computer Vision and Pattern Recognition Workshops (CVPRW), pp. 2278–2288. IEEE (2017)
13. He, K., Zhang, X., Ren, S., Sun, J.: Deep residual learning for image recognition. arXiv preprint arXiv:1512.03385 (2015)
14. Jung, H., Lee, S., Yim, J., Park, S., Kim, J.: Joint fine-tuning in deep neural networks for facial expression recognition. In: IEEE International Conference on Computer Vision (ICCV), pp. 2983–2991. IEEE (2015)
15. König, A., Crispim Junior, C.F., Derreumaux, A., Bensadoun, G., Petit, P.D., Bremond, F., David, R., Verhey, F., Aalten, P., Robert, P.: Validation of an automatic video monitoring system for the detection of instrumental activities of daily living in dementia patients. J. Alzheimer's Dis. **44**(2), 675–685 (2015)
16. Leo, M., Medioni, G., Trivedi, M., Kanade, T., Farinella, G.M.: Computer vision for assistive technologies. Comput. Vis. Image Underst. **154**, 1–15 (2017)
17. Li, W., Abtahi, F., Zhu, Z.: Action unit detection with region adaptation, multi-labeling learning and optimal temporal fusing. In: IEEE Conference on Computer Vision and Pattern Recognition (CVPR), pp. 6766–6775. IEEE (2017)
18. Liu, P., Han, S., Meng, Z., Tong, Y.: Facial expression recognition via a boosted deep belief network. In: Proceedings of the IEEE Conference on Computer Vision and Pattern Recognition (CVPR), pp. 1805–1812 (2014)
19. Martinez, B., Valstar, M.F., Jiang, B., Pantic, M.: Automatic analysis of facial actions: a survey. IEEE Trans. Affect. Comput. (2017)
20. Mathias, M., Benenson, R., Pedersoli, M., Van Gool, L.: Face detection without bells and whistles. In: Fleet, D., Pajdla, T., Schiele, B., Tuytelaars, T. (eds.) ECCV 2014. LNCS, vol. 8692, pp. 720–735. Springer, Cham (2014). https://doi.org/10.1007/978-3-319-10593-2_47
21. Pedregosa, F., Varoquaux, G., Gramfort, A., Michel, V., Thirion, B., Grisel, O., Blondel, M., Prettenhofer, P., Weiss, R., Dubourg, V., Vanderplas, J., Passos, A., Cournapeau, D., Brucher, M., Perrot, M., Duchesnay, E.: Scikit-learn: machine learning in Python. J. Mach. Learn. Res. **12**, 2825–2830 (2011)
22. Raglio, A., et al.: Music, music therapy and dementia: a review of literature and the recommendations of the Italian psychogeriatric association. Maturitas **72**(4), 305–310 (2012)
23. Ridder, H.M., Gummesen, E., et al.: The use of extemporizing in music therapy to facilitate communication in a person with dementia: an explorative case study. Aust. J. Music Ther. **26**, 6 (2015)
24. Rodriguez, P., et al.: Deep pain: exploiting long short-term memory networks for facial expression classification. IEEE Trans. Cybern. (2017)
25. Romdhane, R., et al.: Automatic video monitoring system for assessment of Alzheimer's disease symptoms. J. Nutr. Health Aging **16**(3), 213–218 (2012)
26. Saha, S., Navarathna, R., Helminger, L., Weber, R.M.: Unsupervised deep representations for learning audience facial behaviors. arXiv preprint arXiv:1805.04136 (2018)
27. Sandbach, G., Zafeiriou, S., Pantic, M., Rueckert, D.: Recognition of 3D facial expression dynamics. Image Vis. Comput. **30**(10), 762–773 (2012)

28. Sariyanidi, E., Gunes, H., Cavallaro, A.: Automatic analysis of facial affect: a survey of registration, representation, and recognition. IEEE Trans. Pattern Anal. Mach. Intell. **37**(6), 1113–1133 (2015)

29. Simonyan, K., Zisserman, A.: Very deep convolutional networks for large-scale image recognition. CoRR abs/1409.1556 (2014)

30. Simonyan, K., Zisserman, A.: Two-stream convolutional networks for action recognition in videos. In: Ghahramani, Z., Welling, M., Cortes, C., Lawrence, N.D., Weinberger, K.Q. (eds.) Advances in Neural Information Processing Systems, vol. 27, pp. 568–576 (2014)

31. Soomro, K., Roshan Zamir, A., Shah, M.: UCF101: a dataset of 101 human actions classes from videos in the wild. In: CRCV-TR-12-01 (2012)

32. Suzuki, M., et al.: Behavioral and endocrinological evaluation of music therapy for elderly patients with dementia. Nurs. Health Sci. **6**(1), 11–18 (2004)

33. Svansdottir, H., Snaedal, J.: Music therapy in moderate and severe dementia of Alzheimer's type: a case-control study. Int. Psychogeriatr. **18**(04), 613–621 (2006)

34. Tran, D.L., Walecki, R., Rudovic, O., Eleftheriadis, S., Schuller, B.W., Pantic, M.: DeepCoder: semi-parametric variational autoencoders for facial action unit intensity estimation. CoRR abs/1704.02206 (2017)

35. Tran, D., Bourdev, L., Fergus, R., Torresani, L., Paluri, M.: Learning spatiotemporal features with 3D convolutional networks. In: Proceedings of the IEEE International Conference on Computer Vision, pp. 4489–4497 (2015)

36. Vink, A.C., Bruinsma, M.S., Scholten, R.J.: Music therapy for people with dementia. The Cochrane Library (2003)

37. Viola, P., Jones, M.J.: Robust real-time face detection. Int. J. Comput. Vis. **57**(2), 137–154 (2004)

38. Walecki, R., Rudovic, O., Pavlovic, V., Pantic, M.: Variable-state latent conditional random field models for facial expression analysis. Image Vis. Comput. **58**, 25–37 (2017)

39. Wang, H., Kläser, A., Schmid, C., Liu, C.L.: Dense trajectories and motion boundary descriptors for action recognition. Research Report RR-8050, INRIA, August 2012

40. Wang, H., Schmid, C.: Action recognition with improved trajectories. In: Proceedings of the IEEE International Conference on Computer Vision, pp. 3551–3558 (2013)

41. Wang, L., Qiao, Y., Tang, X.: Action recognition with trajectory-pooled deep-convolutional descriptors. In: The IEEE Conference on Computer Vision and Pattern Recognition (CVPR), June 2015

42. Wang, L., Xiong, Y., Wang, Z., Qiao, Y.: Towards good practices for very deep two-stream convnets. CoRR abs/1507.02159 (2015)

43. Zafeiriou, L., Nikitidis, S., Zafeiriou, S., Pantic, M.: Slow features nonnegative matrix factorization for temporal data decomposition. In: IEEE International Conference on Image Processing (ICIP), pp. 1430–1434. IEEE (2014)

44. Zhao, K., Chu, W.S., Zhang, H.: Deep region and multi-label learning for facial action unit detection. In: Proceedings of the IEEE Conference on Computer Vision and Pattern Recognition, pp. 3391–3399 (2016)

45. Zhu, Y., Shang, Y., Shao, Z., Guo, G.: Automated depression diagnosis based on deep networks to encode facial appearance and dynamics. IEEE Trans. Affect. Comput. **PP**(99), 1 (2017). https://doi.org/10.1109/TAFFC.2017.2650899

Deep Execution Monitor for Robot Assistive Tasks

Lorenzo Mauro⬤, Edoardo Alati⬤, Marta Sanzari, Valsamis Ntouskos⬤,
Gianluca Massimiani, and Fiora Pirri$^{(\boxtimes)}$⬤

Alcor Lab, Diag, University of Rome La Sapienza, Rome, Italy
pirri@dis.uniroma1.it

Abstract. We consider a novel approach to high-level robot task execution for a robot assistive task. In this work we explore the problem of learning to predict the next subtask by introducing a deep model for both sequencing goals and for visually evaluating the state of a task. We show that deep learning for monitoring robot tasks execution very well supports the interconnection between task-level planning and robot operations. These solutions can also cope with the natural non-determinism of the execution monitor. We show that a deep execution monitor leverages robot performance. We measure the improvement taking into account some robot helping tasks performed at a warehouse.

1 Introduction

In this paper, we present a novel approach to model high-level robot task execution. An execution monitor is a real-time decision process, which amounts to choosing at each step of the execution the next subtask and deciding whether the current task succeeded or failed [12,34]. A real-time execution monitor involves plan inference, verification of the current robot state, and choice of next goal state.

Several authors, in the planning community, have explored hierarchical task networks (HTN) (see for instance [10]) and hierarchical goal networks (HGN) (see for example [44]) to provide a way of sequencing a suitable decision process [2] at the correct level. However, both HTN and HGN require that these decisions are stacked a priory in the network, putting on the designer the burden to provide a task decomposition, for each task.

In this paper we overcome these difficulties by integrate two deep models to predict next state choice. The first model is a DCNN, identifying the objects in the scene and supporting recognition of relations holding at the current execution time. The second is a sequence to sequence model (*seq2seq*) [46] with attention [3,30,31] inferring a plausible next robot world-state given the current world-state. The interplay between the two models and classical planning grounds the specification of a world-state. The execution monitor manages the interaction amid the models at execution time. This is a very preliminary contribution, considering only the high-level robot decisions. Direct robot control is managed by state charts [48].

© Springer Nature Switzerland AG 2019
L. Leal-Taixé and S. Roth (Eds.): ECCV 2018 Workshops, LNCS 11134, pp. 158–175, 2019.
https://doi.org/10.1007/978-3-030-11024-6_11

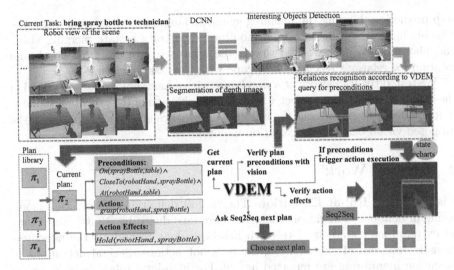

Fig. 1. The schema above presents the flow of information managed by the deep execution monitor (VDEM) for the task *bring the spray bottle to the technician*. While the robot observes the scene, the state is built by the detected relations, restricted according to what is required by the current planner. The VDEM queries the vision system to both verify the preconditions for action to be executed, and the realization of the action effects. A plan library (see e.g. [22] for a reference) provides background knowledge in a symbolic language. The seq2seq model learns to predict goal-states, according to the specific task and current state, and it is invoked by the VDEM whenever a new goal state is required.

Main Idea and Contribution. In this paper we address a *vision-based deep execution monitor* (VDEM) for robot tasks. The main idea is the introduction of a robot learning model to predict the next goal from the current one, verifying the preconditions and effects of the currently executed action. Preconditions and effects are specified in a symbolic language. Whether they hold or not at a state can be determined by the robot vision. The robot monitors the states of its execution by linking the symbolic language with the vision interpretation, such that the objects in the scene are the terms of the symbolic language, and the relations are the predicates. The next goal state is inferred by associating to each goal described by some plan in the plan library, the goal which is the most plausible successor state. Therefore, given that X is a goal descriptions, and Y is the next goal description, the seq2seq model infers $P(Y|X)$. A description is formed by the predicates and terms verified by vision, which form the current robot world-state. The seq2seq model is formed by an encoder fed by token of the symbolic language, an attention mechanism that pairs each description with the task, which is a sort of memory of the goals concerned with such a task, and a decoder, which infers the most likely successor state.

Though recent approaches [1,27,33,53,54] have considered vision based execution, our approach is novel in combining vision based execution with next step prediction, binding the planning symbolic languages with visual instances. The binding allows the execution monitor to generate a state merging vision and planning feedbacks. Furthermore, the approach provides both depth and location for relations recognition to cope with the task dynamics.

We tested the framework at a warehouse with a humanoid robot, described in the experiment section, see Sect. 6. We provide ablation of the execution monitor functionalities to experiment the robotic performance and the advantages of the proposed vision based deep execution monitor.

2   Related Work

Vision Based Robot Execution. The earliest definitions of execution monitoring in nondeterministic environments were introduced by [12,34]. Since then an extraordinary amount of research has been done to address the nondeterministic response of the environment to robot actions. Several definitions of execution monitoring are reported in [38]. For high-level robot tasks, a review of these efforts is given in [24]. The role of perception in execution monitoring was already foreseen in the work of [9]. Likewise, recovery from errors that could occur at execution time was already faced by [50]. Despite this foresight, the difficulties in dealing with scene recognition have directed the effort toward models managing the effects of actions such as [4,47], allowing to execute actions in partially observable environments, similarly as in [5,13,15]. On the other hand, different approaches have studied learning policies for planning as in [28] and also for decision making, in partially observable domains [18]. Vision based planning has been studied in [54]. These approaches did not consider execution monitor and the duality between perception and learning. Likewise despite facing the integration of observations in high-level monitor [23,32] did not use perception for verifying the current state, which is crucial for both monitoring and further decision learning.

Relations Recognition in Videos. Relations in videos dynamically change, in the sense that the configuration of the involved objects is altered according to the robot vantage points. Recently a number of approaches have studied spatial relations and their grounding, such as [8,16,29,42]. Among them, only [16] faces the problem from the point of view of robot task execution. There are also recent contributions concerned with human activity recognition and human-objects interaction studying the problem regarding human dynamics such as [36,43,49,51,53], here in particular for container and containee relations. Although these latter approaches consider both videos and 3D objects they do not face general relations amid objects. The main difficulty seems that of recognizing relations in a complex scenario without overloading the perceptual scene, namely what the robot has to infer from the scene. To this end, and also to maintain real time execution, we rely on the execution monitor querying the visual interpretation at each current state about the existence of specific relations. Relations computation exploits approximate depth estimation within the object bounding box. To obtain this good performance we use DCNN trained on different classes of models, which are retrieved by the execution monitor, and the active features of the recognized objects, involved in the relation, to estimate the object depth.

Sequence to Sequence Models and Next Step Prediction. Sequence to sequence models (seq2seq) [46] are made of two networks, one for processing the input and a second network generating the output, in an encoder-decoder configuration. They have shown an excellent performance in several sequence prediction problems especially in machine translation, image captioning and even in high-level decision processing. In planning problems, [25] have proposed recently QMDP-Net combining POMDP and LSTM to obtain a neural network architecture under partial observability. They applied their model to 2D grids to cope with 2D path planning. While we do not know of other approaches to execution monitor and high-level planning with seq2seq architecture, LSTM have been used for path planning, while [17] show that their CMP approach to navigation outperforms LSTM. The introduction of an attention mechanism [3,30,31] has improved sequence to sequence models essentially for neural translation and also for image captioning. Attention mechanisms for robot execution have been studied in [35], and here in particular we base our approach on the attention mechanism to exploit the task context.

The problem of predicting next step has not yet faced with seq2seq models. An approach to driving the focus of attention to the next useful object has been introduced by [14]. On the other hand [7] have designed a new public database including annotations also for the next action, which is relevant for execution monitor, where prediction of next state can take advantage of surrounding people actions.

3   Deep Execution Monitoring

In this section we give an overview of the execution monitor (VDEM) altogether, providing at the end of the section the main algorithms.

Preliminaries on the Environment and the Tasks. We consider robot assistive tasks related to maintenance activities at a warehouse. The robot language $\mathcal{L}$ is defined by atoms, which are formed by predicates taking terms as arguments. Terms, can be either variables or constants, and they are instantiated by the objects that the robot identify in the environment. Likewise, predicates are the relations the robot is able to identify in the environment. Predicates take also indexed terms denoting the frame as arguments. The robot language $\mathcal{L}$ is extended with meta terms denoting tasks, hence $\mathcal{L} \cup \{T\}_{i=1}^{K}$. Where T_i is a sentence specifying a task. Tasks sentences are, for example, *pass the brush and the cloth to the technician, help the technician to hold the guard*. Therefore a task sentence is expressed in natural language, and the execution of a task requires a number of actions to be performed, for both controlling the robot visual process and the robot motion. These actions are specified by plans collected into the plan library.

$VisionOn(robot, t_0) \wedge Free(robot\_hand, t_0),$
$Detected(brush, t_1) \wedge Detected(ladder, t_1) \wedge On(brush, ladder, t_1),$
$At(robot, ladder, t_2) \wedge Holding(robot\_hand, brush, t_3),$
$Detected(technician, t_3) \wedge CloseTo(robot, technician, t_3),$ $\qquad$ (1)
$Detected(technician\_hand, t_4) \wedge Holding(technician\_hand, brush, t_4) \wedge$
$Free(robot\_hand, t_4)$

Plans and Plan Library. Let us assume that the execution of a task requires the execution of n plans, where each plan specifies a number of actions.

A *plan library is a collection of plans.* In a plan library, each plan defines all the actions needed to achieve a goal of a part of a task, by a suitable axiomatization. For example, to grasp an object the robot needs to be close to the object, which is a partial task.

A plan is formed by a *problem* specifying the initial state and a goal, defined in the propositional Planning Domain Definition Language (*pddl*), and by a *domain* providing an axiomatization of actions, which is first-order *pddl* with types and equality. Plans, therefore, form the background knowledge of the robot about what is needed for an action to be performed.

A state s, with respect to an action a, is formed by either the preconditions for executing a or by the effects of a execution. When s is a goal state this is the goal of the *problem*. To simplify the presentation here we assume that the preconditions and effects are conjunctions of binary or unary atoms, and a state can be reduced to $s = \bigwedge_i R_i(\nu_{i1}, \ldots, \nu_{ik}, t)$, where $(\nu_{i1}, \ldots, \nu_{ik})$, $k >= 1$, are ground terms. Plan inference amounts to deduce the goal of the problem, given the starting state. A goal of a problem is, for example, $At(robotHand, table)$, requiring to search where the table is, and reaching it.

To facilitate inference, the set of actions axiomatized in a plan domain are partitioned into actions that affect the state of the world (like moving objects around) and ecological actions, which affect only the state of the robot. Ecological actions are for example *search, verify_vision, turn_head, look_up, look_down*. A plan is formed by at most a single action that can affect the world and by a number of ecological actions. This allows to partition the terms of the plan into terms denoting the world, with their types hierarchy, and terms related to the robot representation, requiring appropriate measures, for vision and motion control.

The plan library is the collection of all plans needed for the assistive tasks and it is generated together with the maintenance experts to cope with the foreseen assistive tasks, hence the hypothesis is that: *for all foreseen tasks there exists a sequence of goals factoring them.*

Task Factorization. Given a task, factorization amounts to decompose the task into plans, which are supposed to belong to the plan library. Task factorization is crucial for a number of issues. It avoids useless combinations of unrelated groups of objects, it limits the inference of a goal just to the involved objects, it ensures a high flexibility in robot execution, and allows to easily recover from failures. A top down factorization, such as HTN [10] or HGN [44], might be too costly to be achieved in real-time, and also might not be able to take care of the state resulting after the execution of the n-th plan. An incongruence would require, in fact, to search backward for a previous reliable state.

The solution we propose here is to learn to predict the next goal, given the current goal state. In this way, given a task and its initial state goal, a successor state goal can be predicted after the success of the current goal state is confirmed.

Execution. The execution monitor loops over the following operations: (1) get the next goal; (2) identify the plan for the given goal; (3) forward the inferred actions to the *state charts* [48], as soon as the preconditions are satisfied, according to the vision process; (4) verify the effect of the inferred actions; (5) if the current plan goal is obtained ask the seq2seq model to infer next goal and go to (2) else continue with the current plan. The execution, illustrated in Fig. 1, is resumed in Algorithms 1, 2 and 3.

Algorithm 1. Vision based deep execution monitor

Input: Current task T, plan Π, current state s, plan library Lib_Π
Output: end-task T

1 **while** *not end-task* **do**
2   **if** $\Pi \neq \emptyset$ *and* $s = \bigwedge_i^N R_i(\nu, a)$ **then**
3        $(\alpha, bounding\_box, depth):=query\_vision(s)$
4   **if** $\alpha = True$ **then**
5   **if** s *goal of* Π **then**
6              $\Pi:=query\_seq2seq(T, s, Lib_\Pi)$
7   **else**
8   Continue Π
9   **else**
10   Return end-task T
11   **if** $\Pi = \emptyset$ *and* $s = start(T, s_0)$ **then**
12        $\Pi:=query\_seq2seq(T, s, Lib_\Pi)$
13   **if** $\Pi \neq \emptyset$ *and* $s = goal(T)$ **then**
14   Return *end-task* T

Algorithm 2. Query seq2seq

Input: seq2seq model, plan library Lib_Π, current task T, current state s
Output: subplan Π

1 Compute seq2seq output with input (T, s) and choose the goal state s_g maximizing: $p(s_g|s, T)$
2 Search in Lib_Π best match Π with $\nu, \{R\}_i^M$, mentioned in s_g, goal of Π
3 Return Π

Algorithm 3. Query Vision

Input: video-stream at current time lapse $t_i{:}t_{i+n}$, DCNN models $\mathcal{M}_1, \ldots, \mathcal{M}_k$,
      current state s, thresholds μ, τ
Output: Boolean
1 $s = \bigwedge_i^N R_i(\boldsymbol{\nu}, a)$
2 Compute bounding boxes in video-stream using models $\mathcal{M}_1, \ldots, \mathcal{M}_k$
3 Segment objects in depth images in video-stream for each $\nu \in \boldsymbol{\nu}$ (Sect. 4)
4 **if** $confidence(\boldsymbol{\nu}) > \mu$ **then**
5 $\quad \lfloor$ Compute $R_i, i = 1, \ldots N$

6 **else**
7 $\quad$ **while** *time lapse* $T < \tau$ **do**
8 $\quad\quad \lfloor$ Search for missed $\nu \in \boldsymbol{\nu}$

9 **if** $T \leq \tau$ **then**
10 $\quad \lfloor$ Return $True$, bounding box for $\boldsymbol{\nu}$, depth
11 **else**
12 $\quad \lfloor$ Return $(False, \{\}, -1)$

Terms in robot language for detected objects

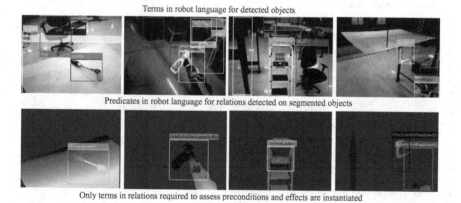

Predicates in robot language for relations detected on segmented objects

Only terms in relations required to assess preconditions and effects are instantiated

Fig. 2. Objects detected in the scene observed by the robot, while it is executing its task, are terms of the robot language. Only relations needed by the planner and queried by the VDEM to vision are considered and instantiated with detected terms.

Note, therefore, that according to the algorithms the seq2seq model is called only if the current state is either a goal of the current plan, just concluded, or the start state of a task. Note that in case of failure a new task $\mathcal{T}'$ can be recovered from last successful state.

4   Vision Interpretation

As highlighted in the previous section, the execution monitor gets from the current plan the state to be verified in the form of a conjunction of atoms, and query the *vision interpretation* to assess if the current state holds. An example is shown in Fig. 2.

To detect both objects and relations we have trained Faster R-CNN [40] on ImageNet [26], Pascal-VOC [11] dataset, and with images taken on site. We have trained 5 models to increase accuracy, obtaining a detection accuracy above 0.8. The good accuracy is also due to a confidence value measured on a batch of 10 images, taken at 30 *fps*, simply computing the most common value in the batch and returning the sampling mean accuracy for that object.

The model is called according to the state request. For example, if $On(brush, ladder)$ is requested from the plan state, the execution monitor asks the vision interpretation to call the models for *brush* and *ladder* first and for On relation for all the found terms, after. Though the main difficult part is searching the objects and the relations, we shall not discuss this here.

To infer spatial-relations we have introduced a look-up table for the definition of each relation of interest for the assistive task. The relations require the depth within the bounding boxes of each object denoted by the queried terms. Depth is crucial in the warehouse environment, because objects at different distances appear within the bounding box of an object, as shown in the first image of Fig. 2. There is, indeed a tradeoff between using MaskRCNN [19] and Faster. With Mask we have the depth segmentation immediately, by projecting the mask on the RGBD image, but objects of the warehouse need to be manually segmented. On the other hand Faster using Imagenet offers a huge amount of data, but depth needs to be obtained. In this version of our work we considered Faster R-CNN [40] and did a local segmentation by clustering.

We have first trained a non-parametric Bayes model to determine for each object of interest the number of feature classes. To this end, we estimate a statistics of the active features with dimension $38 \times 50 \times 512$, taken before the last pooling layer, at each pixel inside the recognized object bounding box (here we are referring to VGG, though we have considered also ZF, see [45,52]). Once the number of classes for each object is established we have trained a normal mixture model on the selected feature classes for each object, resulting in a probability map that a pixel belongs to the specific class of the object.

During execution, as the object is known, we choose the learned parameters for the model to estimate a probability that the pixel in the bounding box belongs to the object. The distribution on the bounding box is projected onto the depth map and a ball-tree is built using only the pixels with a probability greater than a threshold (we used 0.7). Using unsupervised nearest neighbor, checking the distance, a resulting segmentation is sufficiently accurate for the task at hand. Depth is considered relative to the robot-camera. See Fig. 2.

Having the depth, the relations are established, a reference are the spatial relations based on the connection calculus [6], though here distance and depth play a primary role, which are not considered in [6]. To establish the relation amid $n \leq 3$ objects we consider the distance first (within a moving visual cone with vertex the center of projection) and further the other properties consistently with the connection calculus and its 3D extensions (see [41]). See Sect. 6 for an overview of the relations and the accuracy on the recognition.

5   The seq2seq Architecture for Deep Monitoring

As gathered in previous sections the robot is given a *high level task* specified by a sentence, such as *help the technician to support the guard*. The objective, here, is to find the sequence of plans, in the plan library, ensuring the task to succeed. We have seen that relevant steps to this end are the definition of states, which are conjunctions of literals, inferred by the plans and verified by the vision interpretation to hold before or after the robot executes an action.

We have also introduced the notion of *goal state* as the state of a plan problem in which the goal holds. When a goal state is achieved, task execution requires to predict the next goal, in so ensuring to progress in the accomplishment of the assigned task.

We show that a sequence to sequence architecture is effective for mapping a current goal state, expressed as a conjunction of literals into a new goal state, where it is intended (see Sect. 3) that the predicted goal is a goal of some plan in the plan library.

A sequence to sequence system mapping a state of the robot into a new state is a network modeling the conditional probability $p(Y|X)$ of mapping a source state $x_1, \ldots, x_n$ into a target state $y_1, \ldots, y_m$. The encoder-decoder is made of two elements: an encoder which transform the source into a representation S and a decoder generating one target item at a time, so that the conditional probability is [30]:

$$\log p(y|x) = \sum_{j=1}^{m} \log p(y_j|y_1, \ldots y_{j-1}, S) \tag{2}$$

We define an input state as a set of tokens belonging to the extended robot language $\mathcal{L} \cup \{T\}_{i=1}^{K}$ with $\mathcal{L}$ the language including terms (denoting objects in the scene) and predicates, denoting relations in the scene, and with T_i a task sentence. Given an input state $\mathbf{s} = (u_1, \ldots, u_n)$, this is initially mapped into a low dimensional vector $\mathbf{x}$. With $\mathbf{x} = W\mathbf{s}$, where W is the embedding matrix, which is fine-tuned during the training of the seq2seq model.

Given the encoded sequence $\mathbf{x}$ and the true output sequence $\mathbf{y}$, encoded as well, the goal is to learn how they match in order to predict, at inference time, the correct $\mathbf{y}'$ given the input $\mathbf{s}'$.

Attention [3,39] has become, recently a hot topic for measuring similarities and dissimilarities between input and output sequences, according to the specific objective of the mapping. For example, while in neural machine translation (NMT) alignment can be quite relevant, in the case of a new state prediction alignment is not really relevant while the task at hand it is, since a new goal is looked for while a specific task is executed. In general attention computes the relevance of each token in the encoded sequence with respect to the true encoded sequence $\mathbf{y}$ via a function $\varphi(x_i, \mathbf{y})$, which returns a score whose distribution, via a softmax function, determines the relevance of each token in $\mathbf{x}$ with respect to the encoded output **y**. This can be expressed as the expectation of a token given the distribution induced by the score:

$$\sum p(z = i|\mathbf{x}, \mathbf{y})x_i \tag{3}$$

Where $p(z = i|\mathbf{x}, \mathbf{y})$ is the distribution induced by the softmax applied to the score given to each token x_i, with z the indicator of the encoded input tokens. In the literature different score function have been proposed, e.g. additive or multiplicative [3,31]:

$$\begin{aligned} \varphi(x_i, \mathbf{y}) &= w^\top \sigma(W^{(1)}x_i + W^{(2)}\mathbf{y}) \text{ (additive)} \\ \varphi(x_i, \mathbf{y}) &= \langle W^{(1)}x_i + W^{(2)}\mathbf{y} \rangle \quad \text{(multiplicative)} \end{aligned} \tag{4}$$

Where $W^{(i)}$ are learned weights. In our case we have two basic structures, the task sentence and the sequence of atoms. We have also specific separators: for the atoms $\langle eoa \rangle$, for the end of task sequence $\langle ets \rangle$ and for the end of the state description $\langle eos \rangle$. The attention mechanism required here needs to score the compatibility of each atom, namely a subsequence of the output sequence **y**, with the task and with each input token. For example we expect that in the context of the task *pass the brush to technician* the output subsequence *Hold, technician, brush* has an encoding similar to *Hold, robot, brush* while this is not true in the context of the task *help the technician to hold the guard*, in which the correct subsequence would be *On, table, brush*.

To this end we formulate the input and output embedded sequences in terms of subsequences $\boldsymbol{\tau}^{\mathbf{x}} = (\tau_1^{\mathbf{x}}, \dots \tau_K^{\mathbf{x}})$ and $\boldsymbol{\tau}^{\mathbf{y}} = (\tau_1^{\mathbf{y}}, \dots, \tau_m^{\mathbf{y}})$, using both the $\langle eoa \rangle$ and $\langle ets \rangle$, in order to compute the weights of the attention mechanism. Weights are learned by a dense layer taking as input the concatenation of the previous predicted $\tau_{t-1}^{\mathbf{y}}$, from the decoder, the embedded task, which is always $\tau_1^{\mathbf{y}}$, and the previous hidden state of the decoder. The weights for each τ form a matrix, hence we obtain:

$$\varphi(\tau_i^{\mathbf{x}}, \boldsymbol{\tau}^{\mathbf{y}}) = W^\top \sigma(W^{(1)}\tau_i^{\mathbf{x}} + W^{(2)}\boldsymbol{\tau}^{\mathbf{y}}) \tag{5}$$

Finally, following the softmax application, we have a prediction of the importance of each token of the encoder according to the 'context' atom and according to the task. Thus we have $p(\mathbf{z} = i|\tau_i^{\mathbf{x}}, x_i, \boldsymbol{\tau}^{\mathbf{y}})$, which is a vector of the dimension of $\tau_i^{\mathbf{x}}$. This is the probability that a subsequence, namely an atom, is relevant for the current task and the predicted sequence. Then the output is obtained as the expectation over all the atoms:

$$s = \sum p(\mathbf{z} = i|\tau_i^{\mathbf{x}}, x_i, \boldsymbol{\tau}^{\mathbf{y}})\tau_i^{\mathbf{x}} \tag{6}$$

We can note that in (6) also words are made pivotal, since the probability is a vector. For example, in case the task is *bring the brush to the technician*, the *brush* is a pivotal word, and the context will most probably imply that the mapping of the predicate *Hold* is from $Hold(robotHand, brush)$ to

Hold(technician, brush) and the task sentence triggers attention to both the term *brush* and the relation *Hold*.

Data Collection for the seq2seq Model. The robot vocabulary is formed by 18 unary predicates, 13 binary predicates and 42 terms. We build the Herbrand Universe from predicates and terms, obtaining a language of more than 35k atoms. Elements of the language are illustrated in Fig. 3.

A number of the atoms does not respect the type hierarchy, which is defined in *pddl*, therefore are deleted from the language. Finally we have grown all the goal states provided in the plan library up to 20k states.

Some of the predicates from the whole set are listed in Table 1, detailing the recognition ability of the vision interpretation. We should note that a number of predicates concerns the robot inner state, such as for example *VisionOn* or the head and body positions, which are not listed in Table 1.

6   Experiments and Results

Experiments Setup. Experiments have been done at a customer fulfillment center warehouse, under different conditions in order to test different aspects of the model. To begin with, all experiments have been performed with a humanoid robot, created at the High Performance Humanoid Technologies Lab (H^{2}T). The robot has two 8-DoF torque-controlled arms, two 6-DoF wrists, two underactuated 5-finger hands, a holonomic mobile base and 2-DoF head with two stereo camera systems and an RGB-D sensor. The Asus Xtion PRO live RGB-D camera has been mounted on the robot head to provide the video stream to the visual system and ran the *VDEM* on two of the computers mounted on the robot. We dedicated one to the planning and management of the execution and another one, equipped with an Nvidia Titan GPU, to ran the *visual stream*. Robot control is interfaced with the VDEM via the state charts [48].

Results for the Visual Stream. We trained the visual stream system using images taken from the ImageNet dataset, Pascal VOC, as well as images collected inside the warehouse by the RGB-D camera of the robot. Most of the objects, indeed, are specific of the warehouse and cannot be found in public databases. The relations considered were essentially those relevant to the maintenance tasks (see Table 1). To train the DCNN models we split the set of images in training and validation sets with a proportion of 80%–20%. We trained a number of different models for the different types of objects, and we performed 70000 training iterations for each model on a PC equipped with 2 GPUs. The visual stream has been tested under different conditions, in a standalone tests and during the execution of different tasks. The accuracy has been computed considering the batch of 10 images, accuracy of objects recognition and relations recognition is shown in Table 1, evaluating accuracy and ablation study specifically for relations.

Mean average precision mAP for object detection is 0.87 and localization in depth is 0.98 accurate up to 3 m.

Table 1. Accuracy and ablation study of predicate grounding. **Legend:** *BB*: bounding boxes only, *masks*: segmentations masks only, *no prior*: without use of distance *no shape*: without use of shape properties *no depth*: without use of depth.

Predicate	Full	BB	Masks	No prior	No shape	No depth
CloseTo	89%	79%	82%	79%	72%	49%
Found	95%	85%	81%	85%	80%	61%
Free	91%	86%	91%	86%	83%	68%
Hold	88%	72%	82%	75%	74%	56%
Inside	87%	64%	78%	71%	65%	57%
On	96%	77%	85%	79%	78%	65%
InFront	95%	81%	85%	84%	83%	63%
Left	95%	81%	88%	85%	86%	72%
Right	91%	79%	88%	79%	80%	61%
Under	88%	76%	69%	79%	76%	59%
Behind	81%	78%	78%	76%	79%	61%
Clear	82%	75%	80%	73%	73%	60%
Empty	83%	72%	78%	79%	68%	61%
Average	**89%**	**77%**	**83%**	**79%**	**77%**	**62%**

Results of the seq2seq. We used for the seq2seq network the encoder decoder structure with LSTM [21], in particular a multilayer bidirectional LSTM for the encoder. The maximum input sentence length is set to 17 predicates and a task, which is equivalent to 72 words among relations and terms. The embedding layer transforms the index encoding of every word in the input into a vector of size 20, the encoder then uses a bidirectional LSTM and an LSTM to transform the input question in a vector of size 10. This vector is repeated 3 times, as the length of output sentence and then it is fed to the decoder network. A fully connected layer is then applied to every time sequence returned and then it is passed to a softmax activation layer. The attention function is modeled by a fully connected two layers network.

The seq2seq training uses the Categorical Cross Entropy loss and Adam as an optimizer using batches of 5 sequences for a total of 100 epochs. The total size of the dataset is of 20 thousand sequence pairs.

The accuracy, calculated as the percentage of correct prediction made on a test set extracted from the dataset is used to evaluate the training results. The measurement is done under three different hypotheses. First we considered only the best combination, then we considered the first three combinations, randomly changing the length of the input sequences, finally we considered the accuracy under the local attention model. As shown in Fig. 3 we vary the number of predicates from one to nineteen, which is equivalent to a sequence length varying from 4 to 72 considering both relations and terms. It is possible to see

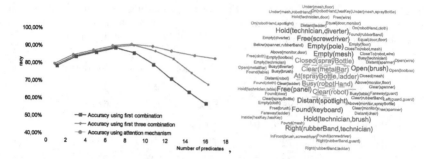

Fig. 3. Accuracy plot at variable number of predicates in the input sequence, considering the first combination, the first three and, finally with attention. On the right a cloud representation of the robot language expressed in the form of an Herbrand Universe, namely, all predicates are instantiated with all terms.

that initially the accuracy increases as the amount of atoms increases, this is caused by the fact that with more than one atom the sequence is more specific and characteristic. The maximum accuracy is reached at seven atoms with 94,2% of accuracy for the first combination and 97,9% using the first three. After this point the accuracy starts to decrease with the increase of the atoms in the input sequence. On the other hand we can note that by adding the attention mechanism the accuracy keeps high also with a large number of atoms.

Experiments of the VDEM Framework at Warehouse. In this section, we report the results of the experiments carried out with the VDEM deployed on the humanoid robot inside the warehouse. In the absence of other frameworks to make a comparison with, we perform a comprehensive ablation study. Table 2 shows the results. We identify the components of our framework with: PL = Planning, Ex = Execution, M = Monitoring (Visual Stream), GPr = Goals Prediction (LSTM). Furthermore, we indicate with Kn the complete knowledge of the world.

The experiments were performed on 5 tasks: *remove panel, support panel, clean diverter, bring object, find object*. Snapshots taken from two of these tasks are shown in Fig. 4. Each task was executed 50 times for assessing the accuracy, excluding failures caused by the robot controllistic part (grasping failure, platform movement error, etc.). The tasks have been tested for each framework configuration, making 750 total experiments. Note that for Task 5, there are no values related to the first configuration. This is because this task intrinsically requires perceptive and search skills, which can not be tested in the first configuration.

Starting from the $PL + Ex + Kn$ case, the framework is tested with the FastDownward (FD) [20] based planning system and the execution component. FD was adopted as it proved to be the fastest among the other planners that were considered, i.e. POMDP and PKS [37]. In this configuration a complete knowledge of the world was provided. We note that the system in this case

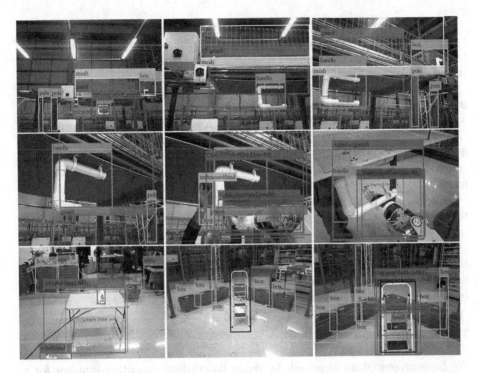

Fig. 4. Recognition during tasks execution. The sequence shows the detection of *guard* (panel), *handle* and its manipulation to lower it helping the technician to hold the guard for inspecting the rollers. The involved relations are *At, Hold, InFront, On,* and *CloseTo.*

Table 2. Accuracy and average execution time according to task and configuration.

		$PL + Ex + Kn$	$PL + Ex + M$	$PL + Ex + M + GPr$
a. ex. time	Task 1	540 s	135 s	135 s
	Task 2	260 s	70 s	70 s
	Task 3	596 s	147 s	147 s
	Task 4	477 s	121 s	121 s
	Task 5	x	52 s	52 s
accuracy (%)	Task 1	23	72	81
	Task 2	52	78	80
	Task 3	24	68	79
	Task 4	26	75	86
	Task 5	x	85	93

suffers from long planning times caused by considering knowledge of the entire scene. Furthermore, this setting excludes dynamic and non-deterministic tasks.

Considering the $PL + Ex + M$ setting, the robot is able to complete all the tasks correctly, as it is possible to manage the non-deterministic nature of the tasks in this case. An example of the detection and monitoring capacity is shown in the first row of Fig. 4.

A limitation of this setting concerns the management of failures due to the inability to predict the correct sequence of the goals.

Finally, the complete configuration of the framework is taken into consideration, $PL + Ex + M + GPr$. In this setting tasks are decomposed and executed dynamically, identifying in real time different ways to complete a task. A direct consequence of this greater flexibility, as can be seen in Table 2, is the improvement of the accuracy on the successful execution of the tasks.

An example is shown at the bottom row of Fig. 4. In this case the task is to find, grab and bring the brush to the technician. Based on experience, the seq2seq system first suggests *on(brush, table)*.

The goal fails, as another object is found (*on(spraybottle, table)* detected). At this point the possibility of recovery using seq2seq comes into play. The execution monitor takes the second proposal (regarding the first goal to be achieved) made by the seq2seq-based proposal system, namely *on(brush, ladder)*.

7   Conclusions

We have presented an approach to vision based deep execution monitor for a robot assistive task. Both the idea and the realization are novel and promising. The experiment with the humanoid robot created at the High Performance Humanoid Technologies Lab (H2T) have proved that the framework proposed works as far as the specific tasks are considered and as far as the high level actions are taken into account. Weak elements of the approach are the ability of the robot to search the environment, which should cope with the limitation of vision at distances greater than 2.5 m. We are currently facing this problem by modeling search with deep reinforcement learning, so that the robot can optimize its search of objects and relations.

Acknowledgments. The research has been granted by the H2020 Project Second Hands under grant agreement No. 643950. We thanks in particular our partners: the team at Ocado, Graham Deacon, Duncan Russel, Giuseppe Cotugno and Dario Turchi, the team of KIT led by Tamim Asfour, the team at UCL with Lourdes Agapito, Martin Runz and Denis Tome, and the group at EPFL led by Aude Billiard.

References

1. Al-Omari, M., Chinellato, E., Gatsoulis, Y., Hogg, D.C., Cohn, A.G.: Unsupervised grounding of textual descriptions of object features and actions in video. In: KR 2016, pp. 505–508 (2016)
2. Alford, R., Shivashankar, V., Roberts, M., Frank, J., Aha, D.W.: Hierarchical planning: relating task and goal decomposition with task sharing. In: IJCAI 2016, pp. 3022–3029 (2016)

3. Bahdanau, D., Cho, K., Bengio, Y.: Neural machine translation by jointly learning to align and translate. arXiv preprint arXiv:1409.0473 (2014)
4. Bertsekas, D.P., Tsitsiklis, J.N.: Neuro-dynamic programming: an overview. Decis. Control 1, 560–564 (1995)
5. Boutilier, C., Reiter, R., Soutchanski, M., Thrun, S., et al.: Decision-theoretic, high-level agent programming in the situation calculus. In: AAAI/IAAI 2000, pp. 355–362 (2000)
6. Cohn, A.G., Hazarika, S.M.: Qualitative spatial representation and reasoning: an overview. Fun. Inf. 46(1–2), 1–29 (2001)
7. Damen, D., et al.: Scaling egocentric vision: the epic-kitchens dataset. In: ECCV 2018 (2018)
8. Das, A., Agrawal, H., Zitnick, C.L., Parikh, D., Batra, D.: Human attention in visual question answering: do humans and deep networks look at the same regions? arXiv preprint arXiv:1606.03556 (2016)
9. Doyle, R.J., Atkinson, D.J., Doshi, R.S.: Generating perception requests and expectations to verify the execution of plans. In: AAAI 1986, pp. 81–88 (1986)
10. Erol, K., Hendler, J.A., Nau, D.S.: UMCP: a sound and complete procedure for hierarchical task-network planning. In: AIPS, vol. 94, pp. 249–254 (1994)
11. Everingham, M., Eslami, S.M.A., Van Gool, L., Williams, C.K.I., Winn, J., Zisserman, A.: The Pascal visual object classes challenge: a retrospective. IJCV 111(1), 98–136 (2015)
12. Fikes, R.E.: Monitored execution of robot plans produced by strips, SRI, Technical report (1971)
13. Finzi, A., Pirri, F.: Combining probabilities, failures and safety in robot control. In: International Joint Conference on Artificial Intelligence, vol. 17, no. 1. Lawrence Erlbaum Associates Ltd., pp. 1331–1336 (2001)
14. Furnari, A., Battiato, S., Grauman, K., Farinella, G.M.: Next-active-object prediction from egocentric videos. J. Vis. Commun. Image Represent. 49, 401–411 (2017)
15. Gianni, M., Kruijff, G.-J.M., Pirri, F.: A stimulus-response framework for robot control. ACM Trans. Interact. Intell. Syst. (TIIS) 4(4), 21 (2015)
16. Guadarrama, S., et al.: Grounding spatial relations for human-robot interaction. In: IROS 2013, pp. 1640–1647 (2013)
17. Gupta, S., Davidson, J., Levine, S., Sukthankar, R., Malik, J.: Cognitive mapping and planning for visual navigation. arXiv preprint arXiv:1702.03920, vol. 3 (2017)
18. Haarnoja, T., Ajay, A., Levine, S., Abbeel, P.: Backprop KF: learning discriminative deterministic state estimators. In: Advances in Neural Information Processing Systems, pp. 4376–4384 (2016)
19. He, K., Gkioxari, G., Dollár, P., Girshick, R.: Mask R-CNN. In: IEEE International Conference on Computer Vision (ICCV), pp. 2980–2988. IEEE (2017)
20. Helmert, M.: The fast downward planning system. JAIR 26, 191–246 (2006)
21. Hochreiter, S., Schmidhuber, J.: Long short-term memory. Neural Comput. 9(8), 1735–1780 (1997)
22. Hofmann, T., Niemueller, T., Lakemeyer, G.: Initial results on generating macro actions from a plan database for planning on autonomous mobile robots (2017)
23. Hornung, A., Böttcher, S., Schlagenhauf, J., Dornhege, C., Hertle, A., Bennewitz, M.: Mobile manipulation in cluttered environments with humanoids: integrated perception, task planning, and action execution. In: Humanoids 2014, pp. 773–778 (2014)
24. Ingrand, F., Ghallab, M.: Deliberation for autonomous robots: a survey. Artif. Intell. 247, 10–44 (2017)

25. Karkus, P., Hsu, D., Lee, W.S.: QMDP-Net: deep learning for planning under partial observability. In: Advances in Neural Information Processing Systems, pp. 4697–4707 (2017)
26. Krizhevsky, A., Sutskever, I., Hinton, G.E.: Imagenet classification with deep convolutional neural networks. In: NIPS 2012, pp. 1097–1105 (2012)
27. Lenz, I., Lee, H., Saxena, A.: Deep learning for detecting robotic grasps. Int. J. Robot. Res. **34**(4–5), 705–724 (2015)
28. Littman, M.L., Sutton, R.S.: Predictive representations of state. In: Advances in Neural Information Processing Systems, pp. 1555–1561 (2002)
29. Lu, C., Krishna, R., Bernstein, M., Fei-Fei, L.: Visual relationship detection with language priors. In: Leibe, B., Matas, J., Sebe, N., Welling, M. (eds.) ECCV 2016. LNCS, vol. 9905, pp. 852–869. Springer, Cham (2016). https://doi.org/10.1007/978-3-319-46448-0_51
30. Luong, M.-T., Pham, H., Manning, C.D.: Effective approaches to attention-based neural machine translation. arXiv preprint arXiv:1508.04025 (2015)
31. Luong, M.-T., Sutskever, I., Le, Q.V., Vinyals, O., Zaremba, W.: Addressing the rare word problem in neural machine translation. arXiv preprint arXiv:1410.8206 (2014)
32. Mendoza, J.P., Veloso, M., Simmons, R.: Plan execution monitoring through detection of unmet expectations about action outcomes. In: ICRA 2015, pp. 3247–3252 (2015)
33. Mirowski, P., et al.: Learning to navigate in complex environments. arXiv:1611.03673 (2016)
34. Nilsson, N.J.: A hierarchical robot planning and execution system. SRI (1973)
35. Ntouskos, V., Pirri, F., Pizzoli, M., Sinha, A., Cafaro, B.: Saliency prediction in the coherence theory of attention. In: Biologically Inspired Cognitive Architectures, vol. 5, pp. 10–28 (2013)
36. Ntouskos, V., et al.: Component-wise modeling of articulated objects. In: Proceedings of the IEEE International Conference on Computer Vision, pp. 2327–2335 (2015)
37. Petrick, R.P., Bacchus, F.: PKS: knowledge-based planning with incomplete information and sensing. In: Proceedings of the System Demonstration session at ICAPS (2004)
38. Pettersson, O.: Execution monitoring in robotics: a survey. Robot. Auton. Syst. **53**(2), 73–88 (2005)
39. Raffel, C., Luong, M.-T., Liu, P.J., Weiss, R.J., Eck, D.: Online and linear-time attention by enforcing monotonic alignments. arXiv preprint arXiv:1704.00784 (2017)
40. Ren, S., He, K., Girshick, R., Sun, J.: Faster R-CNN: towards real-time object detection with region proposal networks. In: NIPS 2015, pp. 91–99 (2015)
41. Sabharwal, C.L., Leopold, J.L., Eloe, N.: A more expressive 3D region connection calculus. In: DMS, pp. 307–311. Citeseer (2011)
42. Santoro, A., et al.: A simple neural network module for relational reasoning. In: Advances in Neural Information Processing Systems, pp. 4974–4983 (2017)
43. Sanzari, M., Ntouskos, V., Pirri, F.: Bayesian image based 3D pose estimation. In: Leibe, B., Matas, J., Sebe, N., Welling, M. (eds.) ECCV 2016. LNCS, vol. 9912, pp. 566–582. Springer, Cham (2016). https://doi.org/10.1007/978-3-319-46484-8_34
44. Shivashankar, V.: Hierarchical goal networks: formalisms and algorithms for planning and acting, Ph.D. dissertation, University of Maryland, College Park (2015)
45. Simonyan, K., Zisserman, A.: Very deep convolutional networks for large-scale image recognition. arXiv:1409.1556 (2014)

46. Sutskever, I., Vinyals, O., Le, Q.V.: Sequence to sequence learning with neural networks. In: Advances in Neural Information Processing Systems, pp. 3104–3112 (2014)

47. Sutton, R.S., Barto, A.G.: Reinforcement Learning: An Introduction, 2nd edn. MIT Press, Cambridge (2017)

48. Wächter, M., Ottenhaus, S., Kröhnert, M., Vahrenkamp, N., Asfour, T.: The ArmarX statechart concept: graphical programing of robot behavior. Front. Robot. AI **3**, 33 (2016)

49. Wang, H., Liang, W., Yu, L.-F.: Transferring objects: joint inference of container and human pose. In: CVPR 2017, pp. 2933–2941 (2017)

50. Wilkins, D.E.: Recovering from execution errors in SIPE. Comput. Intell. **1**(1), 33–45 (1985)

51. Wu, C., Zhang, J., Sener, O., Selman, B., Savarese, S., Saxena, A.: Watch-n-patch: unsupervised learning of actions and relations. In: TPAMI 2017 (2017)

52. Zeiler, M.D., Fergus, R.: Visualizing and understanding convolutional networks. In: Fleet, D., Pajdla, T., Schiele, B., Tuytelaars, T. (eds.) ECCV 2014. LNCS, vol. 8689, pp. 818–833. Springer, Cham (2014). https://doi.org/10.1007/978-3-319-10590-1_53

53. Zhu, L., Xu, Z., Yang, Y., Hauptmann, A.G.: Uncovering the temporal context for video question answering. IJCV **124**(3), 409–421 (2017)

54. Zhu, Y., et al.: Visual semantic planning using deep successor representations. CoRR abs/1712.05474 (2017)

Chasing Feet in the Wild: A Proposed Egocentric Motion-Aware Gait Assessment Tool

Mina Nouredanesh[1] (ID), Aaron W. Li[2], Alan Godfrey[3] (ID), Jesse Hoey[2] (ID), and James Tung[1](✉) (ID)

[1] Department of Mechanical and Mechatronics Engineering,
University of Waterloo, Waterloo, Canada
{m2noured,james.tung}@uwaterloo.ca
[2] David R. Cheriton School of Computer Science, University of Waterloo,
Waterloo, Canada
w89li@edu.uwaterloo.ca, jhoey@cs.uwaterloo.ca
[3] Department of Computer and Information Science, Northumbria University,
Newcastle upon Tyne, UK
alan.godfrey@northumbria.ac.uk

Abstract. Despite advances in gait analysis tools, including optical motion capture and wireless electrophysiology, our understanding of human mobility is largely limited to controlled conditions in a clinic and/or laboratory. In order to examine human mobility under natural conditions, or the 'wild', this paper presents a novel markerless model to obtain gait patterns by localizing feet in the egocentric video data. Based on a belt-mounted camera feed, the proposed hybrid FootChaser model consists of: (1) the FootRegionProposer, a ConvNet that proposes regions with high probability of containing feet in RGB frames (global appearance of feet), and (2) LocomoNet, which is sensitive to the periodic gait patterns, and further examines the temporal content in the stacks of optical flow corresponding to the proposed region. The LocomoNet significantly boosted the overall model's result by filtering out the false positives proposed by the FootRegionProposer. This work advances our long-term objective to develop novel markerless models to extract spatiotemporal gait parameters, particularly step width, to complement existing inertial measurement unit (IMU) based methods.

Keywords: Ambulatory gait analysis · Wearable sensors
Deep convolutional neural networks · Egocentric vision · Optical flow

1 Introduction

The lack of clinical information on a day-to-day basis hinders our understanding of disease trajectories on multiple time scales, including diseases affecting gait and balance (e.g., neurological conditions). Free-living (habitual) ambulatory gait analysis has demonstrated unique insight into disease progression, with

© Springer Nature Switzerland AG 2019
L. Leal-Taixé and S. Roth (Eds.): ECCV 2018 Workshops, LNCS 11134, pp. 176–192, 2019.
https://doi.org/10.1007/978-3-030-11024-6_12

implications for diagnosis and evaluating treatment efficacy. For example, spatial metrics (e.g., step length), temporal metrics (e.g., step time), and gait irregularities (e.g., compensatory balance reactions or near-falls) of free-living mobility behaviour have demonstrated promising capabilities to predict the risk of falling in older adult populations.

The recent explosion of ambient sensors (e.g., motion capture sensors, force mats), smart phones, and wearable sensor systems (e.g., inertial measurement units, IMUs) have facilitated the emergence of new techniques to monitor gait and balance control in natural environments and during everyday activities [8,22,29]. Embedded into living environments, ambient third-person video (TPV) and depth cameras (e.g., Microsoft Kinect) have been investigated as means to extract gait parameters [10,14], detect episodes of freezing of gait in Parkinson's disease [5], detect falls, and longitudinal changes in the patient's mobility patterns [3,4,36]. While TPV systems have demonstrated potential to detect small changes over long periods (i.e., months to years), these approaches suffer from visual occlusions (e.g., furniture), difficulty handling multiple residents, and extraction of spatiotemporal parameters when the full-body view is unavailable. Moreover, they are restricted to fixed areas. Considering mobility is characterized by moving the body from one location (i.e., environment) to another, significant daily-life mobility data may go uncaptured without multiple camera coverage using ambient sensors.

An alternative approach is to use wearables sensors affixed to the user's body. There have been many successful research programs using IMUs to monitor physical (and sedentary) activity, identify activity types, estimate full body pose, and measure gait parameters [8,17,21,22,29]. Body-worn IMUs have demonstrated excellent capabilities to measure temporal gait parameters. However, a critical drawback associated with the use of IMUs is inaccurate estimation of key spatial parameters. In particular, step width is linked to gait stability and possesses a strong association to fall risk [6,27]. This measurement limitation is largely attributed to a relative lack of motion in the frontal plane during gait, resulting in small IMU excitation and low signal-to-noise ratio.

Egocentric first-person video (FPV), acquired via body-worn cameras, may outperform IMUs for the purpose of estimating spatial parameters of gait. Bearing in mind a waist-worn camera pointed down and ahead of the user, FPV offers a potentially stronger signal for spatial estimation, especially in the frontal plane. For instance, a smartphone-based camera was mounted on the waist to quantify gait characteristics in [25]. However, the system requires additional markers on the feet. There are also secondary reasons for investigating FPV as a sensing modality for gait assessment. Vision captures rich information on the properties of the environment that influence mobility behaviour, including slope changes (e.g., stairs, curbs, ramps) and surfaces (e.g., gravel, grass, concrete) [32,33]. Furthermore, FPV offers the potential to reconstruct events by capturing the immediate environmental context more readily than IMU-based data alone. Without detailed information of the mobility context, such as the presence of other pedestrians, terrain characteristics, and obstacles, the ability to interpret ambulatory gait data is constrained. For example, FPV recordings have been used for the purpose of validation of other IMU-based algorithms [17, 46] by manually viewing video frames and identifying specific events.

To address the problem of ambulatory measurement of spatial gait parameters, this paper tackles the initial problem of localizing feet in FPV frames in 2D coordinates of video captured from a belt-mounted camera. In comparison to head- and chest-mounted camera views, we hypothesized that a waist-level view would offer the best view for 3 reasons. First, waist-level FPV offers a consistent view of the legs and feet even when turning. In contrast, head- or chest-mounted views tend to rotate in anticipation of turns or changes in attention, which reduces the available views of the feet. Second, a waist-level view affords greater resolution of the feet than views higher on the body. Finally, camera egomotion is hypothesized to provide a rich source of temporal information to segment body parts [28]. We propose a method to generate pixel-wise foot placement outputs towards the eventual goal of estimating spatial parameters (e.g., step width). The transformation between pixel outputs to distances, likely using 2D metrology approaches, is beyond the scope of the current study and will be examined in subsequent works. To achieve the foot localization solution, we propose a FPV-based deep hybrid architecture called the FootChaser model (see Fig. 3). The models comprise of (a) the FootRegionProposer model, which uses a ConvNet to propose high confidence feet regions (or bounding boxes), and (b) the LocomoNet, which examines the temporal dynamics of the proposed regions to refine the FootRegionProposer output by filtering the false positives to locate feet. An evaluation of the proposed method to accurately localize feet is reported and discussed.

1.1   Related Work

While there have been TPV-based research efforts utilizing smartphone or ambient camera video to assess gait (e.g., [10,14,36]) and estimate pose (e.g., [9,12,15,20,50]), the challenges and signals associated with FPV are distinct. There are several factors that challenge the proposed concept: (1) occlusion or extreme illumination conditions, (2) similar objects/terrain patterns to the feet (e.g., other people's feet), and (3) motion blur from fast movements. In this section, we focus on reviewing previous efforts using FPV to address these challenges and to inform our chosen camera type and location.

There are relatively few previous works aiming to extract spatial gait parameters using FPV. An interesting and novel approach was using a walker-mounted depth and/or color camera to estimate 3D pose of lower limbs, mainly in frontal plane [18,31,35]. To achieve this, Ng et al. [31] used general appearance model (texture and colour cues) within a Bayesian probabilistic framework. In [18], a Kinect (depth) sensor along with two RGB cameras were placed on a moving walker, and the 3D pose was formulated as a particle filtering problem with a hidden Markov model. The key limitation of these works is the dependency on a stable platform (i.e., walker) to afford consistent views of the lower limbs and monitor pose over time, which is not generalizable to individuals that do not require a walking aid for ambulation.

The possibility of using one or several body-mounted cameras is investigated for 3D full body [24,43,51] and upper limb (arms and hands) [30,40] pose estimation. In [24,43], outward-looking body-mounted cameras along with optimization approaches were used to estimate 3D body pose. In [43] more than ten cameras were attached to the person's joints, and structure from motion approach was used to localize the cameras, estimate the joint angles and reconstruct human motion. The main limitation of the proposed method is the obtrusive multi-camera setup and intensive computational load required to infer pose in a video sequence. To alleviate the main weaknesses of [43], Jiang et al. [24] developed a model based on synchronized egocentric videos captured by a chest-mounted camera and a Kinect sensor. The 3D body pose model employs camera ego-motion and contextual cues to infer body pose, without direct views of the key body parts (i.e., legs, feet) desired for gait assessment. Moreover, the videos were restricted to relatively static activities (i.e., sitting, standing). Such restrictions and the failure to examine more complex (i.e., dynamic) scenarios limits the applicability of their approach to the gait assessment problem.

In contrast to the previous studies, [39,51] utilized body-related visual cues (outside-in/top-down view) provided by fisheye cameras attached to a bike helmet and baseball cap, respectively. In [51], a ConvNet for 3D body pose estimation was developed to address limitations in its former version [39], including dependency on 3D actor model initialization and inability to run in real-time. Although the authors compensated for the distortion imposed by the fisheye lens, estimation of the lower body 2D heatmaps (ankles, knees, hip, and toes) was less accurate due to the strong perspective distortion (i.e., a large upper body and small lower body).

The closest approach in spirit to the proposed approach is a hybrid method which combines both global object appearance (spatial network) and motion patterns (temporal network) in a two-stream ConvNets structure. This approach was inspired by Simonyan and Zisserman [44], in which a ConvNet was trained by stacks of optical flow for the task of TPV-based activity recognition. Similar architecture is also employed in FPV-based methods to recognize different activities [28,45]. To capture long-term sequential information from FPV data, recurrent neural network/long-short term memory (LSTM) was used by Abebe et al. [1,2] where stacked spectrograms generated over temporal windows from mean grid-optical-flow vectors were used to represent motion [45].

Modeling temporal information in a specific regions enclosed by bounding boxes in consecutive frames is investigated in some TPV-based studies [7,47]. In [23] an object-centric motion compensation scheme was implemented by training CNNs as regressors to estimate the shift of the person from the center of the bounding box. These shifts were further applied to the image stack (a rectified spatiotemporal volume) so that the subject remains centered. More related to our LocomoNet approach is the work by Brattoli et al. [7], in which a fully connected network was trained to analyze the grasping behavior of rats over time. Based on optical flow data of both initial positives (paw regions) and random negatives cropped from other regions, temporal representation was learned to detect paws.

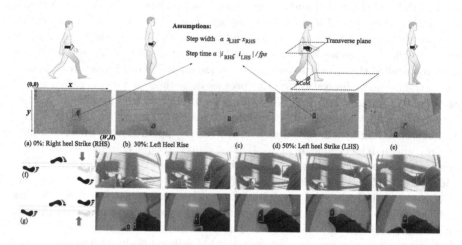

Fig. 1. Egocentric camera-based gait assessment overview. Panels a, b, c, d, e represent different phases of gait captured by a belt-mounted camera. The x and y location of the right foot (red bounding boxes) and left foot (green boxes) over consecutive frames (XCoM: extrapolated center of mass). Rows f and g depict lateral sidestep and lateral crossover compensatory balance reactions, respectively. These reactions are important behaviours related to fall risk. Note the transformation between pixel-wise box coordinates to distances is not covered in the current study. (Color figure online)

2   The FootChaser Framework

In this section, we describe the framework for proposing high confidence regions by incorporating both temporal and spatial data, for the task of gait assessment. As an alternative to inferring gait parameters from 3D pose estimates, we hypothesized that tracking the centers of the person's feet in 2D plane of walking over time could provide accurate spatial estimates. The scope of this paper is to first detect the feet, and examine the transformation between camera coordinates to spatial locations in subsequent efforts.

Let I_i be the ith frame in a video sequence with the length N, captured by a belt-mounted camera with an outside-in top-down view ($i = \{1, 2 \cdots N\}$). The manually annotated ground truth (GT) data is in the form of bounding boxes $GT_{f,i} = [x_{f,i}^{GT}, y_{f,i}^{GT}, w_{f,i}^{GT}, h_{f,i}^{GT}]$ indicating the camera wearer's feet ($f = \{left, right\}$) in 2D 1080 × 1920 coordinate system of each frame (see Fig. 1). x and y denote the center ($C_{f,i}^{GT}$), and w and h represent the width and height of the bounding box(es) respectively (see Fig. 2). The goal of the *FootChaser* framework is to detect and localize the centers of each foot (if present in the frame) in the form $P_{f,i} = [x_{f,i}^{P}, y_{f,i}^{P}, w_{f,i}^{P}, h_{f,i}^{P}]$ during the gait. In an ideal case, the error measure (E) will be minimized for x ($E(x_{f,i}^{GT}, x_{f,i}^{P})$) and y ($E(y_{f,i}^{GT}, y_{f,i}^{P})$) trajectories and the underlying area should be the same for the Ps and GTs, i.e, the intersection over union (IoU) measure will be maximized ($IoU = 1$). The predicted x ($\approx$ frontal axis) and y ($\approx$ sagittal axis) trajectories can be used to estimate pixel-wise step width and step length gait parameters, respectively.

To investigate the feasibility of pixel-wise step-by-step gait parameter extraction, the x_{left}^{GT}, x_{right}^{GT} data are plotted in Fig. 2. While y_{left}^{GT} and y_{right}^{GT} were examined for measurement of step length, we focus on step width estimation in the current study. We observed that (a) the trajectories roughly resemble the center of pressure (CoP) data captured by forceplates, (b) the local maxima and minimuma seem to be correlated with right heel strike (RHSs) and left heel strike (LHSs), respectively (further investigation is required using gold-standard gait analysis methods, e.g., Vicon), and (c) GT data can be divided into frames with one foot ($GT - One$), and both feet ($GT - Two$).

In most of the $GT - Two$ frames, a small portion of the trailing foot is observable (see Fig. 1), and is irrelevant for extraction of gait parameters. Considering shape distortions affect detection results, we hypothesized that the ConvNet is more likely to detect the other foot rather than the less-visible one similar to the findings of Huang et al. [19] and Rozamtsev et al. [41]. In other words, in the frames with two GT, the network often locates the center of the foot that is required for the extraction of gait parameters.

Considering these cues, we surmised that tracking each foot separately is unnecessary and frames with only one predicted foot center can be used to extract step width. Specifically, (C_i^{P-one}) obtained from the FootChaser ($P - One = [x_i^{P-one}, y_i^{P-one}, w_i^{P-one}, h_i^{P-one}]$), regardless of the foot type f. As the key signals for the calculation of spatiotemporal gait parameters (e.g., LHS and RHS points), these can be observed from the x^{P-one} and y^{P-one} trajectories.

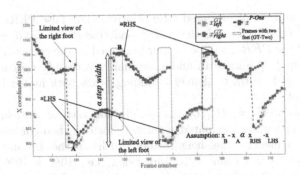

Fig. 2. Sample bounding box X-coordinate time series data from dataset 2. Ground Truth (GT) data for left (green) and right (red) feet, and FootChaser predictions with 1 identified region (blue). The expected x location of left heel strike (LHS) and right heel strike (RHS) are marked (further investigation is required using gold-standard gait analysis methods, e.g., Vicon). Periods with 2 identified feet (GT-Two) are indicated by dotted boxes. (Color figure online)

To achieve feet localization, we propose a two-stage *FootChaser* framework comprised of two ConvNets: (1) *FootRegionProposer* and (2) *LocomoNet*. The FootRegionProposer proposes $n \in \mathbb{N}$ bounding boxes as 'proposed foot regions', or $PFR_{j,i}$, $j = \{1,...,n\}$ in the ith frame. As there may be several false positives in the proposed regions, we hypothesized that the FootRegionProposer results may be boosted by applying another ConvNet, called LocomoNet, trained to be sensitive to the periodic/specific movement patterns embedded in the user's feet regions during gait. In other words, the LocomoNet is expected to filter out false positives by selecting the most confident regions. After applying the LocomoNet on $PFR_{j,i}$, only the frames with a single PFR are used for step width estimation (see Fig. 2).

2.1   FootRegionProposer

The FootRegionProposer is a ConvNet fine-tuned to propose $PFRs$ in a frame. The jth proposed region is in the form of a bounding box $PFR_{j,i} = [x_{j,i}, y_{j,i}, w_{j,i}, h_{j,i}]$, where $x_{j,i}$, $y_{j,i}$, $w_{j,i}$, and $h_{j,i}$ denote the center coordinates, and width and height of the box, respectively (see sample $PFRs$ marked by red rectangles in Fig. 3). The training procedure for the LocomoNet is discussed in Subsect. 3.2. As noted above, there are several factors that may challenge the performance of the FootRegionProposer: (1) occlusion or extreme illumination conditions can increase the number of false negatives, (2) objects or terrain similar to the feet (i.e., noise, see Fig. 4-c), and (3) motion blur from fast movements. In addition to incorporating a fast and precise object localization/detection ConvNet (e.g., faster R-CNN [38], or YOLO [37]), a second ConvNet was applied to the FootRegionProposer output to filter false $PFRs$ (Subsect. 2.2).

2.2   LocomoNet: Learning from Gait Patterns

To reduce the number of proposed false positives (i.e., false PFRs) by FootRegionProposer Network (towards the goal of 'one' true PFR), the dynamic temporal structure of the $PFR_{j,i}$ will be further examined by the proposed LocomoNet ConvNet. Inspired by Simonyan and Zisserman's work [44], we consider examining optical flow features to deliver bounding boxes with higher confidence of representing feet.

The horizontal $U = \{U_1, U_2, ..., U_{N-1}\}$ and vertical optical flow $V = \{V_1, V_2, ..., V_{N-1}\}$ can be calculated separately for each two consecutive frames in the video sequence (the height and width of the U and V components are equal to the frame's 2D dimension, i.e., 1080×1920). Considering a fixed length of L consecutive frames, the optical flow volume $OFV_i = \{U_{i-L/2}, V_{i-L/2}, ..., U_{i+L/2-1}, V_{i+L/2-1}\}$ is obtained for the ith frame. In order to represent the temporal information of $PFR_{j,i}$, a fixed $(W_c \times H_c)$ region centered at $(x_{j,i}, y_{j,i})$ is cropped from OFV_i, which ends up to a $(2L \times W_c \times H_c)$ volume of interest $(OFV - PFR_{j,i})$ corresponding to that proposal (see Fig. 3). Each of these volumes are fed into the LocomoNet for filtering. The training procedure for LocomoNet is discussed in Subsect. 3.3. After applying the LocomoNet, if the

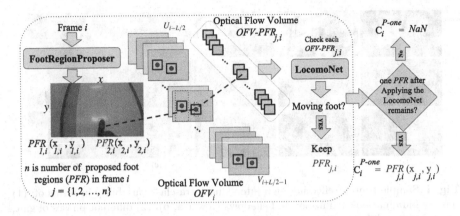

Fig. 3. The FootChaser framework. First, the FootRegionProposer proposes $n \in \mathbb{N}$ $PFR_{j,i}$ bounding boxes (red boxes), $j = \{1,2,...,n\}$ in the ith frame. Multiple regions proposed are examined by LocomoNet to filter out false positives. After obtaining the stacks of optical flow volume OFV_i (V and U are vertical and horizontal 2D flow components) from the $[i - L/2, i + L/2 - 1]$ frames (L denotes the depth/length of stack), LocomoNet inputs are obtained by cropping fixed size regions centered at the center of each $PFR_{j,i}$, i.e., $(x_{j,i}, y_{j,i})$, which creates the optical flow volumes from PFRs ($OFV-PFR_{j,i}$). Final FootChaser outputs reflect frames with a single proposed region ((C_i^{P-one}). (Color figure online)

output frame has only one remaining FPR, the center of that $PFR_{j,i}$ will be saved in the center vector (C_i^{P-One}). Otherwise, the corresponding component will be replaced by NaN and will not be considered in the evaluation.

3 Experiments

3.1 Dataset

Sufficiently large datasets are challenging to collect, often the primary bottleneck for deep learning. However, there are no publicly available datasets specific to our needs, i.e., large dataset captured by a belt-mounted camera including the images/videos of feet from different people with a considerable diversity in appearance (e.g., shoes with different colors, shape, barefoot, socks) and movement (i.e., gait). To facilitate training, we decided to fine-tune [34] the ConvNet based on real images with normal optics from large scale datasets, which also boosts the generalizability of the network. We fine-tuned the ConvNet on Footwear (footgear) subcategory images ($\approx$ 1300 images with bounding boxes, and 446 images of shoes from top-down view with and without bounding boxes, and we added the bounding boxes manually) from the ImageNet 2011 [42] dataset. Such images resemble more realistic appearance of one's footwear from different views (compared to alternatives such as UT-Zap50K [52]).

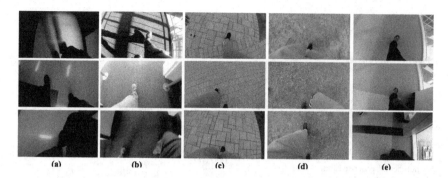

(a)   (b)   (c)   (d)   (e)

Fig. 4. Sample frames reflecting high inter- and intra-class variability in terms of: (1) intense illuminations conditions and shadows (row 1-a, b), (2) different phases of gait, (3) different walking surfaces, e.g., color, texture (each column corresponds to a specific environment and walking surface), and (4) motion blur during crossover and side-step compensatory reactions (row 3-a, b).

In our dataset, 3 healthy young participants (researchers affiliated with the Neural and Rehabilitation Engineering and Computational Health Informatics Labs, at the University of Waterloo) participated in our data collection procedure. The FPV data was collected, using a GoPro Hero 5 Session camera centered on participants' belt (30 fps, 1080×1920), with no specific calibration and setup. A wearable IMU was attached as closely as possible to the camera to collect movement signals (for future experiments). Overall, 5 datasets (including 2 separate datasets from 2 participants in different environments) were captured in five different indoor (tiles, carpet) and outdoor environments (bricks, grass/muddy) around the University of Waterloo campus, resulting in 4505 ($= 5 \times N, N = 901$) total frames (Fig. 4 shows samples from the dataset). Frames were annotated by drawing bounding boxes around the right and left shoes (in PASCAL VOC format), using the LabelImg tool [48].

In addition to the normal walking sequences, in two datasets, simulated compensatory balance reactions (CBRs: lateral sidestep, crossover stepping) during gait were also collected (see Fig. 4-row 3 columns a, b for sets 1 and 2, and the GT plot for dataset 2 in Fig. 6). CBRs (near falls) are reactions to recover stability following a loss of balance (see Fig. 1-panels f and g), characterized by rapid step movements (or reaching) to widen the base of support. CBRs also introduce more challenge to our dataset as the corresponding FPV data is usually blurry (i.e., fast foot displacement) (see Fig. 4) and the field of view may be occluded.

3.2 FootRegionProposer Training

There are several models that can be taken into account for FootRegionProposer, including SSD (Single Shot MultiBox Detector) [26], faster R-CNN [38], R-FCN [11]. In [19], it is shown that SSD models typically have (very) poor performance on small objects, e.g. the relatively small feet regions in our experiments. Among related approaches, YOLO [37] shows state-of-the-art results in terms of speed and accuracy.

To implement the FootRegionProposer, the original YOLO version 2 from the Darknet deep learning framework was used [37]. The pre-trained weights on the large-scale ImageNet dataset were used for network initialization, which was then fine-tuned on ImageNet shoe sub-category. The ConvNet was further fine-tuned on images of shoes that are captured in realistic scenes from a top-down view. All of the network inputs were resized to $K \times 3 \times 832 \times 832$, where $K = 64$ was the batch size (mini-batch size: 32). Moreover, the stochastic gradient descent with momentum was used as optimization method, with an initial learning rate of $\gamma = 0.001$, momentum: 0.9, and decay rate of 0.0005 (at steps 100 and 25000) selected using a Nvidia Titan X GPU. To further address the problem of limited data, the data was augmented (i.e., random crops and rotation) to improve the generalization of the network.

3.3   LocomoNet Training

Although YOLO is very fast, it often suffers from a high number of false positives. The goal of the LocomoNet is to improve FootChaser performance by reducing the number of false proposals. The LocomoNet output maps each OFV to one of the two possible classes. Similar to [28,45,49], the TVL1 optical flow algorithm [53] is chosen, here with OpenCV GPU implementation. Moreover, similar to [28,44,49], the stack length of $L = 10$ (i.e., 20 input modality channels for LocomoNet) is selected, and crop size is set to $W_c = H_c = 224$.

Based on our experiments, a 224×224 region and the stack length of $L = 10$ provided sufficient temporal information for foot regions during gait. Moreover, we handled off-the-frame crops by shifting the 224×224 box in the opposite direction in place of resizing to retain the aspect ratio. To train the LocomoNet, 300 positive (shoe/foot regions) volumes were extracted for left and right feet in each of the 5 datasets, resulting in a total of 3000 ($= 2 \times 300 \times 5$) true positive volumes. An equal number of negative volumes (i.e. 3000) were also randomly cropped from the non-shoe regions from the consecutive frames, with a constraint of $IoU \approx 0$ with the shoe regions at the ith frame, the past and next frames in the volume were not constrained to allow for a more realistic evaluation.

The approach proposed in [49], where the authors demonstrated the possibility of pre-training temporal nets with ImageNet model, was applied in the current study. After extracting optical flow fields and discretizing the fields into [0, 255], the authors averaged the ImageNet model filters of first layer across the channel to account for the difference in input channel number for temporal and spatial nets (20 vs. 3), then copied the average results 20 times as the initialization of temporal nets. Considering such an approach, a motion stream ConvNet (ResNet-101 [16] architecture) pre-trained on video information in UCF101 dataset was used, with stochastic gradient descent and cross entropy loss. Batch size, initial learning rate, and momentum were set to $K = 64$, 0.01, and 0.9, respectively.

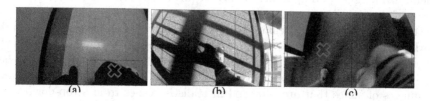

Fig. 5. Example FootRegionProposer results (PFRs) for three frames marked by red boxes. Correct foot regions were identified by the FootRegionProposer; however, false positives were also proposed. After applying the LocomoNet, some false positives were filtered out (marked with ($\times$)). In (a) and (c) false positive(s) are successfully removed, (b) shows a case of intense illumination and shadows challenging LocomoNet, resulting two false positives that were not filtered out.

3.4 Evaluation

(1) **Model generalizability.** To evaluate the extent to which *subject-related movement patterns* in *different environments* can be handled by LocomoNet, a leave-one-dataset-out (LODO) cross-validation was performed. To achieve this, a $LocomoNet_{N_D}$ ($N_D = \{1, 2, ...5\}$) model was trained using the whole dataset except N_D dataset (i.e., 4800 volumes for training) and tested on the dataset N_D (i.e., 1200 volumes for testing), and repeated 5 times. The following LODO accuracies were obtained for our 5 datasets: 1: 92.41%, 2: 91.16%, 3: 98.33%, 4: 83.83%, and 5: 96.25%. The high accuracies indicate the generalizability of LocomoNet to discriminate foot-related $OFV - PFR$ in unseen datasets. The following average IoU scores were obtained for each set: 1: 0.7626, 2: 0.7304, 3: 0.3794, 4: 0.7155, and 5: 0.5235. Considering an IoU threshold of 0.5 is typically used in object detection evaluation to determine whether detection is positive (IoU of true positive > 0.5) [13], we interpret that the generalizability of the model except for $N_D = 3$, is satisfactory. We attributed the lower performance of the network on dataset 3 to the patterns of walking surface (tiles with different sizes, see Fig. 4-c).

(2) **The number of proposed regions with $IoU < 0.2$ (false positives) dramatically reduced after applying the LocomoNet on FPRs.** To assess the false positive removal performance of the $LocomoNet_{N_D}$, we define a elimination rate metric as $ER_{N_D} = \frac{\text{Number of filtered PFRs in a specific IoU interval}}{\text{Total number of PFRs in a specific IoU interval}} \times 100$, ($IoU = Area(GT \cap P)/Area(GT \cup P)$). As shown in Table 1, the PFRs in a low IoU score range ($\in [0, 0.2)$), representing false positives, were removed with a high rate (e.g., in $IoU_{[0,0.1)}$ with 83.25% reduction). The relatively low true positive removal score (i.e., in $IoU_{[0.9,1)}$ with 8.09% reduction) reflects satisfactory performance of LocomoNet in retaining the true positives (refer to Fig. 5 for some failure and success cases).

(3) **FootChaser prediction trajectories closely match ground truth trajectories.** The performance of the FootChaser in tracing the GT data can be assessed by measuring (1) the individual IoU scores, and (2) the pixel-wise

Table 1. Number of proposed foot regions (N_{PFR,N_D}) and elimination rate (ER) in different intersection-over-union (IoU) intervals indicating LocomoNet ability to remove false positives by dataset. N_{PFR,N_D} dramatically reduced after applying the LocomoNet. ER_T is the weighted average of elimination rate, $IoU > 0.5$ and < 0.5, representing the true and false positives, respectively [13].)

	IoU									
	0.1	0.2	0.3	0.4	0.5	0.6	0.7	0.8	0.9	1
$N_{PFR,1}$	1219	36	7	4	11	22	114	218	312	110
$N_{PFR,2}$	654	10	2	3	10	26	122	282	277	76
$N_{PFR,3}$	781	0	4	12	13	35	89	156	116	15
$N_{PFR,4}$	1225	2	2	1	6	31	119	293	294	36
$N_{PFR,5}$	229	18	17	27	55	106	188	195	83	10
$N_{PFR,T-}$	4108	66	32	47	95	220	632	1144	1082	247
ER1	73.83	55.55	42.85	0.00	0.00	4.54	4.38	8.25	7.05	1.81
ER2	92.20	100.00	0.00	0.00	10	11.53	13.11	17.37	13.35	10.52
ER3	97.18	100.00	0.00	8.33	7.69	5.71	0.00	1.28	3.44	6.66
ER4	83.91	50.00	100	100.00	16.66	35.48	31.93	27.30	26.87	19.44
ER5	83.40	77.77	0.00	0.00	0.00	0.00	3.72	4.61	8.43	20.00
ER_T	83.25	68.18	15.62	2.14	3.15	7.72	9.82	13.81	13.77	8.09

Table 2. Mean absolute error (MAE) results for the $GT - One$ region in absolute pixels and as a fraction of image resolution. $MAE = 1/N \sum |GT - One_{a,f,i} - P - One_{a,i}|$, where $a = \{x, y\}$, $f = \{left, right\}$, $N = length(GT - One)$. MAE/R as a fraction of image resolution, where (R): $R_x = 1920$, $R_y = 1080$.

	MAE (pixel)				MAE/R			
Dataset	x_{Left}	x_{Right}	y_{Left}	y_{Right}	x_{Left}	x_{Right}	y_{Left}	y_{Right}
D_1	41.68	87.50	55.66	54.81	0.021	0.045	0.051	0.050
D_2	32.90	44.00	54.29	55.94	0.017	0.022	0.050	0.051
D_3	125.74	194.85	75.19	154.46	0.065	0.101	0.069	0.143
D_4	64.40	62.57	76.11	74.11	0.059	0.070	0.057	0.068
D_5	99.31	37.68	101.52	92.04	0.051	0.019	0.094	0.085

distance (error, E) between the predicted foot center and its corresponding point in GT data, i.e. as discussed in Sect. 2, by comparing the predicted $P - One$ bounding boxes with $GT - one$ ($E(a^{P-One}, a^{GT-One})$, $a = \{x, y\}$), where mean absolute error (MAE) is taken into account as the error metric E (see Table 2). For $GT - Two$ (e.g., the black dotted parts in Fig. 2), the performance was evaluated by comparing the a_i^{P-One} with the nearest GT point regardless of the foot type (Table 3 displays the results). At first glance, this may appear to be a weak metric. However, as discussed in Sect. 2 and depicted in Figs. 6 and 2, in $GT - Two$ data the FootChaser is biased toward proposing regions corresponding to the nearly-full-view feet (rather than partially-observable ones). In this application, the observed bias to larger objects is

Table 3. Mean absolute error (MAE) for $GT - Two$ regions in absolute pixels and as a fraction of resolution (MAE/R), where (R:) $R_x = 1920$, $R_y = 1080$.

Dataset	MAE (pixel)		MAE/R	
	x	y	x	y
D_1	58.11	84.00	0.030	0.077
D_2	36.12	80.44	0.018	0.074
D_3	121.47	117.78	0.063	0.109
D_4	103.55	94.90	0.053	0.087
D_5	25.28	101.52	0.013	0.094

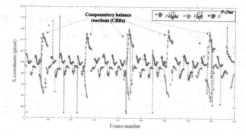

Fig. 6. Time series plot of X coordinate center of the most confident proposed foot regions (PFR, blue) predicted by the FootChaser framework for dataset 2. Ground truth (GT) for the left and right feet are plotted in green and red, respectively. Spikes represent compensatory balance reactions (CBRs) performed by the participant. (Color figure online)

a strength as it predicts the center of the foot required for the extraction of spatiotemporal gait parameters. This can be attributed to the fact that the $FootRegionProposer$ is trained on ImageNet dataset that mainly includes the full-view images of feet. Moreover, this is in line with the findings of [19,41], where a higher performance was reported for the detection of bigger objects in videos. Considering these points, the error criteria for $GT - Two$ regions seem to be a satisfactory representation of performance.

In addition to the relatively low error rates ($< 10\%$ for the x trajectories), as presented in Fig. 6, the framework also predicted many of the points at the timings of CBRs (spikes). Therefore, these trajectories can be a promising avenue for the detection of CBRs. High E values for D_3 (Tables 2 and 3) also support the low IoU rate achieved for that dataset (due to the patterns of the walking surface).

4   Conclusion and Future Work

As the main contribution, this study addressed the potential of incorporating a body-mounted camera to develop automated markerless algorithms to assess gait in natural environments. This advances our long-term objective to develop novel markerless models to extract spatiotemporal gait parameters, particularly step width, to complement existing IMU-based methods.

As the next steps, we aim to: (1) collect synchronized criterion (gold) standard human movement data using motion capture (e.g., Vicon) or gait analysis tools (e.g., pressure-sensitive mat, GaitRite) synchronized to FPV data and develop a model to directly extract spatiotemporal gait parameters from FPV data, convert the pixel-wise results of the FootChaser into the commonly-used distance units (e.g., m or cm) and directly extract spatiotemporal gait parameters, and (2) develop a more robust version of FootChaser framework by collecting a large free-living FPV+IMU dataset from older adults with different frailty levels, annotate the data, and make the dataset publicly available.

This paper contributes an advance in the field of ambulatory gait assessment to localize feet in a waist-mounted FPV feed towards a fully automatic system to detect abnormalities (e.g., compensatory balance reactions, or near-falls), identify environmental hazards (e.g., slope changes, stairs, curbs, ramps) and surfaces (e.g., gravel, grass, concrete) that influence mobility and potential risk to falls. As described earlier, FPV data also provides objective evidence on cause and circumstances of perturbed balance during activities of daily living, Our future studies will examine the potential for automatic detection of these environmental fall risk hazards [32,33].

Given massive amounts of unlabeled FPV data collected during longer-term study, we aim to develop approaches that can robustly handle significant diversity in movement patterns (e.g., rhythm, speed), different populations (e.g., older fallers, Alzheimer's disease), and varying clothing and footwear appearance. To address these aspects, similar to [9], we aim to *personalize* both of the FootRegionProposer and LocomoNet ConvNets to introduce an adaptive pipeline "*AdaFootChaser*" in our future work.

Acknowledgments. Research supported by National Sciences and Engineering Research Council of Canada (NSERC), and by AGE-WELL NCE Inc. M. Nouredanesh was funded by an AGE-WELL Inc. (Canada's technology and aging network) Graduate Scholarship.

References

1. Abebe, G., Cavallaro, A.: Inertial-vision: cross-domain knowledge transfer for wearable sensors. In: Proceedings of International Conference on Computer Vision Workshops (ICCVW), Venice, Italy, vol. 7 (2017)
2. Abebe, G., Cavallaro, A.: A long short-term memory convolutional neural network for first-person vision activity recognition. In: Proceedings of International Conference on Computer Vision Workshops (ICCVW) (2017)
3. Auvinet, E., Multon, F., Manning, V., Meunier, J., Cobb, J.: Validity and sensitivity of the longitudinal asymmetry index to detect gait asymmetry using microsoft kinect data. Gait Posture **51**, 162–168 (2017)

4. Taati, B., Mihailidis, A.: Vision-based approach for long-term mobility monitoring: single case study following total hip replacement. J. Rehabil. Res. Dev. **51**(7), 1165 (2014)
5. Bigy, A.A.M., Banitsas, K., Badii, A., Cosmas, J.: Recognition of postures and freezing of gait in Parkinson's disease patients using microsoft kinect sensor. In: 2015 7th International IEEE/EMBS Conference on Neural Engineering (NER), pp. 731–734. IEEE (2015)
6. Brach, J.S., Berlin, J.E., VanSwearingen, J.M., Newman, A.B., Studenski, S.A.: Too much or too little step width variability is associated with a fall history in older persons who walk at or near normal gait speed. J. Neuroeng. Rehabil. **2**(1), 21 (2005)
7. Brattoli, B., Büchler, U., Wahl, A.S., Schwab, M.E., Ommer, B.: LSTM self-supervision for detailed behavior analysis. In: Proceedings of the IEEE Conference on Computer Vision and Pattern Recognition (CVPR), vol. 2 (2017)
8. Brodie, M.A., Lord, S.R., Coppens, M.J., Annegarn, J., Delbaere, K.: Eight-week remote monitoring using a freely worn device reveals unstable gait patterns in older fallers. IEEE Trans. Biomed. Eng. **62**(11), 2588–2594 (2015)
9. Charles, J., Pfister, T., Magee, D., Hogg, D., Zisserman, A.: Personalizing human video pose estimation. In: Proceedings of the IEEE Conference on Computer Vision and Pattern Recognition, pp. 3063–3072 (2016)
10. Cippitelli, E., Gasparrini, S., Spinsante, S., Gambi, E.: Kinect as a tool for gait analysis: validation of a real-time joint extraction algorithm working in side view. Sensors **15**(1), 1417–1434 (2015)
11. Dai, J., Li, Y., He, K., Sun, J.: R-FCN: object detection via region-based fully convolutional networks. In: Advances in Neural Information Processing Systems, pp. 379–387 (2016)
12. Elhayek, A., et al.: Marconi-convnet-based marker-less motion capture in outdoor and indoor scenes. IEEE Trans. Pattern Anal. Mach. Intell. **39**(3), 501–514 (2017)
13. Everingham, M., Van Gool, L., Williams, C.K., Winn, J., Zisserman, A.: The pascal visual object classes (VOC) challenge. Int. J. Comput. Vis. **88**(2), 303–338 (2010)
14. Gabel, M., Gilad-Bachrach, R., Renshaw, E., Schuster, A.: Full body gait analysis with kinect. In: 2012 Annual International Conference of the IEEE Engineering in Medicine and Biology Society (EMBC), pp. 1964–1967. IEEE (2012)
15. Güler, R.A., Neverova, N., Kokkinos, I.: DensePose: dense human pose estimation in the wild. arXiv preprint arXiv:1802.00434 (2018)
16. He, K., Zhang, X., Ren, S., Sun, J.: Deep residual learning for image recognition. In: Proceedings of the IEEE Conference on Computer Vision and Pattern Recognition, pp. 770–778 (2016)
17. Hickey, A., Del Din, S., Rochester, L., Godfrey, A.: Detecting free-living steps and walking bouts: validating an algorithm for macro gait analysis. Physiol. Meas. **38**(1), N1 (2016)
18. Hu, R.Z.L., Hartfiel, A., Tung, J., Fakih, A., Hoey, J., Poupart, P.: 3D pose tracking of walker users' lower limb with a structured-light camera on a moving platform. In: 2011 IEEE Computer Society Conference on Computer Vision and Pattern Recognition Workshops (CVPRW), pp. 29–36. IEEE (2011)
19. Huang, J., et al.: Speed/accuracy trade-offs for modern convolutional object detectors. In: IEEE CVPR, vol. 4 (2017)
20. Huang, Y.: Towards accurate marker-less human shape and pose estimation over time. In: 2017 International Conference on 3D Vision (3DV), pp. 421–430. IEEE (2017)

21. Ihlen, E.A., Weiss, A., Bourke, A., Helbostad, J.L., Hausdorff, J.M.: The complexity of daily life walking in older adult community-dwelling fallers and non-fallers. J. Biomech. **49**(9), 1420–1428 (2016)

22. Iluz, T., et al.: Automated detection of missteps during community ambulation in patients with Parkinson's disease: a new approach for quantifying fall risk in the community setting. J. Neuroeng. Rehabil. **11**(1), 48 (2014)

23. Jain, A., Tompson, J., LeCun, Y., Bregler, C.: MoDeep: a deep learning framework using motion features for human pose estimation. In: Cremers, D., Reid, I., Saito, H., Yang, M.-H. (eds.) ACCV 2014. LNCS, vol. 9004, pp. 302–315. Springer, Cham (2015). https://doi.org/10.1007/978-3-319-16808-1_21

24. Jiang, H., Grauman, K.: Seeing invisible poses: estimating 3D body pose from egocentric video. In: 2017 IEEE Conference on Computer Vision and Pattern Recognition (CVPR), pp. 3501–3509. IEEE (2017)

25. Kim, A., Kim, J., Rietdyk, S., Ziaie, B.: A wearable smartphone-enabled camera-based system for gait assessment. Gait Posture **42**(2), 138–144 (2015)

26. Liu, W., et al.: SSD: single shot MultiBox detector. In: Leibe, B., Matas, J., Sebe, N., Welling, M. (eds.) ECCV 2016. LNCS, vol. 9905, pp. 21–37. Springer, Cham (2016). https://doi.org/10.1007/978-3-319-46448-0_2

27. Lord, S., Galna, B., Verghese, J., Coleman, S., Burn, D., Rochester, L.: Independent domains of gait in older adults and associated motor and nonmotor attributes: validation of a factor analysis approach. J. Gerontol. Series A Biomed. Sci. Med. Sci. **68**(7), 820–827 (2012)

28. Ma, M., Fan, H., Kitani, K.M.: Going deeper into first-person activity recognition. In: Proceedings of the IEEE Conference on Computer Vision and Pattern Recognition, pp. 1894–1903 (2016)

29. von Marcard, T., Rosenhahn, B., Black, M.J., Pons-Moll, G.: Sparse inertial poser: automatic 3D human pose estimation from sparse IMUS. In: Computer Graphics Forum, vol. 36, pp. 349–360. Wiley Online Library (2017)

30. Mueller, F., Mehta, D., Sotnychenko, O., Sridhar, S., Casas, D., Theobalt, C.: Real-time hand tracking under occlusion from an egocentric RGB-D sensor. In: Proceedings of International Conference on Computer Vision (ICCV), vol. 10 (2017)

31. Ng, S., Fakih, A., Fourney, A., Poupart, P., Zelek, J.: Towards a mobility diagnostic tool: tracking rollator users' leg pose with a monocular vision system. In: International Conference of IEEE Engineering in Medicine and Biology Society (EMBC), vol. 1, pp. 662–666 (2009)

32. Nouredanesh, M., McCormick, A., Kukreja, S.L., Tung, J.: Wearable vision detection of environmental fall risk using Gabor Barcodes. In: 2016 6th IEEE International Conference on Biomedical Robotics and Biomechatronics (BioRob), pp. 956–956. IEEE (2016)

33. Nouredanesh, M., McCormick, A., Kukreja, S.L., Tung, J.: Wearable vision detection of environmental fall risks using convolutional neural networks. arXiv preprint arXiv:1611.00684 (2016)

34. Oquab, M., Bottou, L., Laptev, I., Sivic, J.: Learning and transferring mid-level image representations using convolutional neural networks. In: Proceedings of the IEEE Conference on Computer Vision and Pattern Recognition, pp. 1717–1724 (2014)

35. Page, S., Martins, M.M., Saint-Bauzel, L., Santos, C.P., Pasqui, V.: Fast embedded feet pose estimation based on a depth camera for smart walker. In: 2015 IEEE International Conference on Robotics and Automation (ICRA), pp. 4224–4229. IEEE (2015)

36. Phillips, L.J., et al.: Using embedded sensors in independent living to predict gait changes and falls. West. J. Nurs. Res. **39**(1), 78–94 (2017)
37. Redmon, J., Farhadi, A.: Yolo9000: better, faster, stronger. arXiv preprint arXiv:1612.08242 (2017)
38. Ren, S., He, K., Girshick, R., Sun, J.: Faster R-CNN: towards real-time object detection with region proposal networks. In: Advances in Neural Information Processing Systems, pp. 91–99 (2015)
39. Rhodin, H., et al.: EgoCap: egocentric marker-less motion capture with two fisheye cameras. ACM Trans. Graph. (TOG) **35**(6), 162 (2016)
40. Rogez, G., Supancic, J.S., Ramanan, D.: First-person pose recognition using egocentric workspaces. In: Proceedings of the IEEE Conference on Computer Vision and Pattern Recognition, pp. 4325–4333 (2015)
41. Rozantsev, A., Lepetit, V., Fua, P.: Flying objects detection from a single moving camera. In: Proceedings of the IEEE Conference on Computer Vision and Pattern Recognition, pp. 4128–4136 (2015)
42. Russakovsky, O., et al.: Imagenet large scale visual recognition challenge. Int. J. Comput. Vis. **115**(3), 211–252 (2015)
43. Shiratori, T., Park, H.S., Sheikh, Y., Hodgins, J.K., et al.: Motion capture from body mounted cameras. US Patent 8,786,680, 22 July 2014
44. Simonyan, K., Zisserman, A.: Two-stream convolutional networks for action recognition in videos. In: Advances in Neural Information Processing Systems, pp. 568–576 (2014)
45. Song, S., et al.: Multimodal multi-stream deep learning for egocentric activity recognition. In: Proceedings of the IEEE Conference on Computer Vision and Pattern Recognition Workshops, pp. 24–31 (2016)
46. Taylor, K., et al.: Context focused older adult mobility and gait assessment. In: 2015 37th Annual International Conference of the IEEE Engineering in Medicine and Biology Society (EMBC), pp. 6943–6946. IEEE (2015)
47. Tekin, B., Rozantsev, A., Lepetit, V., Fua, P.: Direct prediction of 3D body poses from motion compensated sequences. In: Proceedings of the IEEE Conference on Computer Vision and Pattern Recognition, pp. 991–1000 (2016)
48. Tzutalin: Labelimg. Git code (2015). https://github.com/tzutalin/labelImg
49. Wang, L., et al.: Temporal segment networks: towards good practices for deep action recognition. In: Leibe, B., Matas, J., Sebe, N., Welling, M. (eds.) ECCV 2016. LNCS, vol. 9912, pp. 20–36. Springer, Cham (2016). https://doi.org/10.1007/978-3-319-46484-8_2
50. Wang, Y., Liu, Y., Tong, X., Dai, Q., Tan, P.: Outdoor markerless motion capture with sparse handheld video cameras. IEEE Trans. Vis. Comput. Graph. **24**(5), 1856–1866 (2018)
51. Xu, W., et al.: Mo2cap2: real-time mobile 3d motion capture with a cap-mounted fisheye camera. arXiv preprint arXiv:1803.05959 (2018)
52. Yu, A., Grauman, K.: Fine-grained visual comparisons with local learning. In: Proceedings of the IEEE Conference on Computer Vision and Pattern Recognition, pp. 192–199 (2014)
53. Zach, C., Pock, T., Bischof, H.: A duality based approach for realtime TV-L^1 optical flow. In: Hamprecht, F.A., Schnörr, C., Jähne, B. (eds.) DAGM 2007. LNCS, vol. 4713, pp. 214–223. Springer, Heidelberg (2007). https://doi.org/10.1007/978-3-540-74936-3_22

Inferring Human Knowledgeability from Eye Gaze in Mobile Learning Environments

Oya Celiktutan$^{(\boxtimes)}$ and Yiannis Demiris

Personal Robotics Laboratory, Department of Electrical and Electronic Engineering,
Imperial College London, London, UK
{o.celiktutan-dikici,y.demiris}@imperial.ac.uk

Abstract. What people look at during a visual task reflects an interplay between ocular motor functions and cognitive processes. In this paper, we study the links between eye gaze and cognitive states to investigate whether eye gaze reveal information about an individual's knowledgeability. We focus on a mobile learning scenario where a user and a virtual agent play a quiz game using a hand-held mobile device. To the best of our knowledge, this is the first attempt to predict user's knowledgeability from eye gaze using a noninvasive eye tracking method on mobile devices: we perform gaze estimation using front-facing camera of mobile devices in contrast to using specialised eye tracking devices. First, we define a set of eye movement features that are discriminative for inferring user's knowledgeability. Next, we train a model to predict users' knowledgeability in the course of responding to a question. We obtain a classification performance of 59.1% achieving human performance, using eye movement features only, which has implications for (1) adapting behaviours of the virtual agent to user's needs (e.g., virtual agent can give hints); (2) personalising quiz questions to the user's perceived knowledgeability.

Keywords: Assistive mobile applications · Noninvasive gaze tracking
Analysis of eye movements · Human knowledgeability prediction

1 Introduction

Interactive intelligent systems are becoming a ubiquitous part of everyday life, motivated by numerous practical applications in web services, healthcare, education, and much more. In such applications, effective modelling of human behaviours and cognition is essential to build adaptation and personalisation mechanisms. Interaction logs are generally not adequate for genuinely interpreting human behaviours; tasks such as problem solving and reading are hard to be assessed based on verbal protocols [5,17]. In addition, the more information exchanged between the user and the system through multiple modalities, the more versatile, efficient and natural the interaction becomes [17].

© Springer Nature Switzerland AG 2019
L. Leal-Taixé and S. Roth (Eds.): ECCV 2018 Workshops, LNCS 11134, pp. 193–209, 2019.
https://doi.org/10.1007/978-3-030-11024-6_13

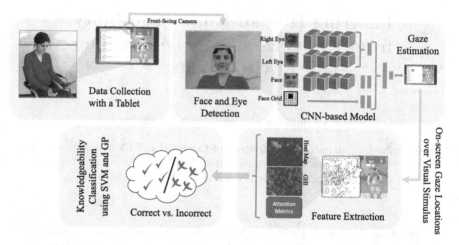

Fig. 1. Automatic inference of user's knowledgeability from eye gaze in mobile learning settings: We focus on a quiz game where we record interactions between a user and a virtual agent using the front facing camera of the tablet. We train a CNN-based system to estimate user's gaze fixations on the tablet screen. From estimated gaze fixations, we define a set of eye movement features to discriminate between users knowing the correct answer and users not knowing the correct answer. We train binary classifiers to predict users' knowledgeability from eye movement features.

Eye gaze has been frequently studied in interactive intelligent systems as a cue for inferring user's internal states. Eye movements directly reflects what is at the centre of an individual's visual attention, and are linked to cognitive processes in the mind [19]. A significant body of work has investigated the relationships between eye movements and cognitive processes to provide an understanding into memory recall [8], cognitive load [18], interest [13], level of domain knowledge [9], problem solving [5,11], desire to learn [4], and strategy use in reasoning [20]. However, so far relatively little research [13] has focused on the interpretation of eye behaviours from the perspective of a camera enabled mobile device. This is due to its long list of challenges including randomness in the camera view, camera motion, drastic illumination changes and partially visible faces.

Accurate eye tracking, namely measuring eye gaze precisely to estimate where the participant is looking at on the screen, requires the use of invasive devices that are not practical to use in everyday life. Although not as precise as the eye tracking devices, recent convolutional neural network (CNN) based approaches such as iTracker [12] provide us with a positive outlook for reliably predicting user's gaze fixations from a mobile device's front-facing camera in a non-obstructive manner. Building upon the deep-learning based approaches, this paper sets out to explore the inference of user's knowledgeability from noisy and temporally sparse gaze estimations in a mobile learning setting. Intelligent tutoring systems can significantly benefit from incorporating such reasoning mechanisms to improve system adaptation and enhance learning.

As illustrated in Fig. 1, we focus on an interaction setting where a user plays a quiz game with a virtual agent while being recorded by front-facing camera of the tablet. Once we estimate on-screen gaze locations based on a deep-learning method, we make a simplifying assumption that the user's knowledgeability is binary, i.e. either the user knows correct answer of a question or not. There is a strong correlation between the correctness of a person's answer and their Feeling of Knowing (FoK) [6]. FoK is a meta-cognitive state where people assess their knowledge of a subject when being posed a question. During this state, people exhibit certain nonverbal cues through face and voice such as smiles, gaze acts, which are indicator of their knowledgeability [6]. In addition, humans can predict the performance of others solving a multiple choice reasoning task by looking at their eye movements only [21]. Humans make use of high distinctive patterns and gaze dynamics to judge whether a person knows the correct answer or not. Motivated from [6,21], we extract a multitude of features from eye movements such that gaze behaviours of a person knowing the answer and a person not knowing the answer appear dissimilar by classification schemes.

Overall, the key contributions of this paper are: (1) introducing a novel yet very challenging computer vision problem, predicting human knowledgeability from eye gaze only, and introducing the first automatic vision-based method to detect knowledgeability from eye gaze on tablets without using any additional sensor; (2) introducing the first audio-visual dataset for predicting human knowledgeability in an interactive mobile learning setting; and (3) providing baseline results for knowledgeability classification from eye movement features. Proposed features based on eye gaze only improves the performance by 7% as compared to facial features (i.e. action units).

2   Related Work

This paper focuses on the problem of inferring user's cognitive states from eye movements in mobile learning settings, which lies at the crossroad of various research areas.

Gaze Estimation. The first challenge of building an eye movement analysis framework is to develop a gaze estimation method that can reliably work during unconstrained interactions with a mobile device. There are a few prominent works that perform gaze estimation without using specialised sensors or devices. These methods can be divided into two groups: (i) methods learning a mapping from input space to 3D gaze direction (3D gaze estimation) [22–24]; and (ii) methods learning a mapping from input space to on-screen gaze location (2D gaze estimation) [10,12].

Two recent works [10,12] focused on 2D gaze estimation using hand-held mobile devices such as smart phones, tablets. Huang *et al.* [10] collected a gaze estimation dataset using a tablet in a systematic way, which is called TabletGaze dataset. They asked 51 subjects to gaze at a dot being displayed on the tablet screen while holding the tablet in four different body postures, namely, standing, sitting, slouching and lying. They showed that recordings from hand-held mobile devices are more characterised by partially visible faces, random camera motion and random camera angles (e.g., centred view vs. low-angle view), as compared to recordings from a laptop placed on a desk [24]. For 2D gaze estimation, they compared four generic regression approaches including Random Forests (RF), Support Vector Regression (SVR) in conjunction with commonly used appearance features (e.g., Histogram of Gradient - HoG, Local Binary Patterns - LBP) extracted from eye regions. Following the TabletGaze dataset [10], Krafka *et al.* [12] introduced the largest 2D gaze estimation dataset, called the Gaze-Capture dataset. The GazeCapture Dataset was collected via a crowd-sourcing service, which enabled gathering data from a large number of subjects (1474 in total) and 15 different mobile devices (iPhones and iPads only) at four different orientations, resulting in a large variability in illumination, appearance and pose. In addition, the GazeCapture dataset enabled training a CNN model from scratch for gaze estimation. Cross-dataset evaluations showed that the iTracker outperforms the 2D gaze estimation methods in [10] by a large margin.

Eye Movement Analysis. There is a long list of prominent works focusing on eye movement analysis to provide an insight into human cognitive processing [4, 5,7–9,11,13,18,20,21]. Among these works, [4,7,9,21] collected eye movement data using a specialised eye tracking device, and investigated internal states relevant to knowledgeability and learning. In [7], Broekens *et al.* focused on a scenario where 31 users played a card game against a desktop computer. The card game involved matching numbers, shapes and colours of objects displayed on a total of 12 cards, and selecting out of 3 cards, called Set, based on a set of rules (e.g., all 3 cards have the same shape). If user claimed a Set among 12 cards, the decision made by the user was annotated as *correct* or *incorrect* based on whether the Set identified by the user satisfied all of the rules or not. For automatically classifying user's decisions, Broekens *et al.* first extracted a set of eye movement features such as duration of fixation, attention spread, saccade length, etc., which are widely used in the literature, and then used various traditional classification methods. Using eye movement features only, Bagging resulted in the best performance of 77.9% for predicting whether the user identified a set or not, and MLP resulted in the best performance of 75.1% for classifying the Set identified by the user into *correct* or *incorrect*.

We are aware of only one work that performed gaze estimation from the front facing camera of a mobile device with the goal of inferring user's internal states. Li *et al.* [13] focused on predicting user's interest in an online store setting. They designed a task where they asked 36 users to interact with the Google Play Store and mentally pick up the items that they found interesting. They estimated the on-screen gaze locations from eye regions using a CNN-based method similar to [12,24]. They recorded calibration data consisting of 13 points from each user prior to the task and during the task, which was further used to fine-tune the gaze estimation method, and collected users' explicit responses after the task was performed. From the estimated on-screen gaze locations, they computed two types of attention metrics: (i) gaze metrics including gaze well time, gaze dwell fraction and gaze time to first visit; and (ii) viewport metrics including viewport time, viewport dwell fraction and viewport time to first visit. They formalised the problem of inferring user's interest as a binary classification task, i.e., predicting whether a user was interested in an item or not, and used the calculated metrics both singly and jointly to compare three traditional classification methods. They obtained the best classification performance of 90.32% with nonlinear Support Vector Machine (SVM) by fusing all of the attention metrics.

Intelligent Tutoring Systems. Personalising system's actions to individual differences is compulsory for achieving good learning outcomes. To this effect, there have been some works (e.g., [2]) that focused on automatically detecting student's mental states such as satisfied, confused or bored. Alyuz *et al.* [2] collected data from 20 students (14–15 years) over the course of several months as part of a math course. Each student worked independently in the class using a laptop, and was recorded using a 3D camera. From the recordings, they extracted two types of features, namely, appearance features and contextual features. While appearance features were composed of face location, head pose, facial gestures and seven basic facial emotions (e.g., happiness, sadness, etc.), contextual features were extracted from (i) user profiles including age, gender; (ii) session information including video duration, time within a session; and (iii) performance features including number of trials until success, number of hints used, grade. For inferring mental states, they trained Random Forest classifiers for each feature type, where the contextual features yielded better performance in overall (90.89% for assessment sessions).

The work most relevant to ours was proposed by Bourai *et al.* [6]: they developed an automatic method for predicting human knowledgeability from facial features such as head pose, gaze direction, facial action units and audio features such as speaking rate, voice pitch. They collated a dataset of 198 clips from the British Broadcasting Service's University Challenge trivia show. Each clip contained a participant answering a question posed by the moderator, and was further annotated either with *correct* or *incorrect*. Classification results with SVM showed that facial features alone can be informative enough, yielding a performance above chance (56.1%), while combining facial features with audio features significantly improved the performance (67.5%), and outperformed the human performance by a margin of 4%.

Our Work. Similarly to [10,12], this paper is concerned with 2D gaze estimation. We propose an automatic method for predicting human knowledgeability from estimated on-screen gaze locations. We design a study where we use a tablet-based quiz game. We record users on video while they are playing the quiz game with a virtual agent to answer a set of general knowledge questions. Following [6], we formalise the problem of human knowledgeability prediction as a binary problem, and use a multitude of eye movement features in conjunction with a classification scheme to predict whether a user gives the *correct* answer to a question or not.

Taken together, to the best of our knowledge, we introduce the first dataset for predicting human knowledgeability in mobile learning settings, which we name the PAL M-Learning corpus, and we introduce the first automatic method to detect human knowledgeability from eye movements on tablets without using any additional sensor. Considering the widespread use of mobile devices and the potential of technology-enhanced learning and e-health applications, our work has significant implications for adapting system behaviours to user's individual profiles and needs beyond just clicks.

3   The PAL M-Learning Corpus

We are not aware of an existing dataset that supports research in predicting user's internal states from eye gaze in a mobile learning setting. This section therefore introduces a novel corpus, called PAL Mobile Learning (M-Learning) Corpus. The PAL M-Learning Corpus comprises two datasets: (i) PAL M-Learning Interaction dataset; and (ii) PAL M-Learning Gaze dataset. The PAL M-Learning Interaction dataset consists of audio-visual recordings of 31 users using a tablet to play Quiz Game with a virtual agent, which is further used to develop automatic models for predicting knowledgeability. The PAL M-Learning Gaze dataset is built by following a similar approach as in [10, 12], namely, it is collected by showing users a sequence of dots one at a time on the screen and recording their gaze using the front-facing camera. We use the PAL M-Learning Gaze dataset to fine-tune gaze estimation models trained using larger datasets [10, 12].

3.1   Data Collection

For collecting data, we used the mobile interactive platform of our PAL (Personal Assistant for healthy Lifestyle) EU H2020 Project[1], which is based on an Android app. This Android app offers a wide range of tools including a virtual diary and several games, from which we focused on a quiz game as an educational tool. The quiz game is played with a virtual agent, and involves user and the virtual agent asking each other multiple choice questions about a topic. As illustrated in Fig. 1, quiz game interface consists three components, namely, a virtual agent, a question box and an information box.

We designed a study using the quiz game with the goal of developing an automatic method for inferring user's internal states. For the quiz game, we generated a question database by randomly selecting questions at different levels of difficulty (i.e., easy, medium, hard) from a trivia question database, called Open Trivia Database [14]. There is a total of 24 question categories in the Open Trivia Database. Since our goal was to observe different internal states from our target users (e.g., confident vs. uncertain), we conducted a preliminary study where we asked a total of 16 participants to assess whether they found each question category easy or hard, and whether they found them boring or interesting. Using the results of the preliminary study, we hand-picked 9 question categories ranging from boring (e.g., Celebrities) to interesting (e.g., Books, Science & Nature)

---

[1] http://www.pal4u.eu/index.php/project/about/.

and from easy (e.g., Computers, Mathematics) to hard (e.g., Mythology, Art), and generated a question database for the quiz game by randomly selecting 5 questions from each category, resulting in 45 questions in total.

We used a Lenovo TB2-X30F tablet during the data collection procedure. 31 users (10 of which were females; age ranging from 18 to 37 with a mean of 27) were recorded, and gave written informed consent for their participation. Each user were guided into the experimental room that had natural lighting. The users were asked to sit on a chair, and hold the tablet in the landscape orientation as they felt comfortable. Apart from these, no further instructions were given to the users. We collected interaction videos by asking each user to play the quiz game with the virtual agent for a duration of 12 mins. Each interaction video contained alternately user and the virtual agent asking questions (20 questions in total, half of which were asked by the virtual agent). These questions were randomly selected from the question database generated as explained before. Before we started to record the interaction, we allowed users to play the quiz game for a couple of questions to familiarise themselves with the Android app. This is a common practice widely used to reduce the novelty effect of a new technology. In both sessions, we recorded users on video from the front-facing camera of the tablet at a rate of 30 fps with an image resolution of 1280 × 800 pixels. Prior to collecting interaction videos, we collected gaze estimation data by asking each user to look at a sequence of red circles - one at a time - shown on the tablet screen. The red circles were appeared at 35 fixed locations and 25 random locations on the tablet screen, each for a duration of 3 s. Following [10], the fixed locations were equally distributed on the tablet screen, arranged in 5 rows and 7 columns and spaced 2.71 cm vertically and 3.10 cm horizontally. This procedure resulted in gaze estimation data for a duration of 3 mins and a total of 60 on-screen locations per user.

Fig. 2. Example snapshots from the PAL M-Learning Interaction dataset, which are taken from the perspective of the front-facing camera while users were answering a question posed by the virtual agent using the tablet.

From the conducted study, we built two datasets, namely, the PAL M-Learning Interaction dataset and the PAL M-Learning Gaze dataset. The interaction dataset was created by segmenting each interaction video into a set of short clips. Each clip contained either the user or the virtual agent asking a question and the other one responding. More explicitly, a short clip started when a new quiz question together with four choices appeared on the tablet screen, and finished when a response was given by the user/the virtual agent. For further automatic analysis, in this paper, we only focused on the clips where the virtual agent was asking a question and the user was answering. Example snapshots from these clips are shown in Fig. 2. The gaze dataset was generated by segmenting gaze estimation data into a set of short clips, where each clip contained user gazing at an on-screen location for 2 s (i.e., we removed the first 0.5 s and the last 0.5 s to obtain a clean dataset).

3.2 Summary of the Datasets and Statistics

PAL M-Learning Interaction Dataset. We removed 5 users and some of the clips from the interaction dataset as they were not usable, for example, users' eyes were not visible. The resulting dataset consists of 27 participants and a total of 242 clips. On average there are 9 short clips per participant, and each clip has a duration ranging from 10.67 s to 39.43 s with a mean duration of 22.6 s.

After the study took place, we conducted a post-study where we collected assessments from a subset of users (9 in total) for each quiz question with respect to three difficulty levels, namely, easy, medium and hard. We labelled each quiz question as easy, medium or hard by taking average of the collected assessments over all the users, where medium appears in the largest number - 106 of the 242 clips contain questions at the medium level of difficulty. For predicting user's knowledgeability, we used interaction logs to annotate each clip based on the user's response. If the user's response to a question is correct, we annotated the corresponding clip with "correct". Otherwise, we annotated the clip with "incorrect". This resulted in 136 incorrect clips and 106 correct clips, which were used for automatically predicting knowledgeability (see Sect. 6).

In addition to users' responses, we used a crowdsourcing service to collect perceived knowledgeability annotations from external observers. Each clip was viewed and annotated by a total of 5 external observers, according to whether the user in the clip knows the correct answer to the question being asked or not. Observers provided their responses on a 6-point scale ranging from strongly disagree to strongly agree (we did not include neutral as a response). We also included two trapping questions about the question's topic and the person in the clip to filter spam responses, also known as Honeypot technique [15]. We approved responses submitted by each external observer based on their responses to trapping questions before reimbursing them for their time. We computed the inter-observer reliability in terms of Intra-Class Correlation (ICC) [16], where we used ICC(1,k) as in our experiments each target user was rated by a different set of k observers (k = 5), randomly sampled from a larger population of observers (K = 80). We obtained a significant correlation ($ICC(1, k) = 0.69$, $p < 0.0001$), indicating a high-level agreement among observers. Motivated from this, we evaluated human performance for knowledgeability prediction task. We aggregated the responses from multiple external observers by computing the mean, and assigned the aggregated annotations to either "correct" or "incorrect" class. For this challenging task, humans achieved a classification accuracy of 59.2%. However, we observed a bias towards the incorrect class, namely, the respective F-scores ($\times 100$) were 45.2% and 73.2% for the correct and incorrect classes. We further compared these results with machine performance in Sect. 6.

PAL M-Learning Gaze Dataset. The gaze dataset is composed of 103, 911 images captured from 31 users, 6 of which were wearing eye glasses, with corresponding gaze fixation locations. In our experiments, we benefit from the GazeCapture dataset to build a gaze estimation model, and use the PAL M-Learning Gaze dataset to fine-tune the trained model to the Lenovo tablet in landscape mode (see Sect. 4). As demonstrated in [12], different mobile device brands have different screen sizes and camera-screen configurations, and therefore fine-tuning the generic gaze estimation model to the target device (Lenovo in our case) is compulsory to obtain reliable results.

4   Gaze Estimation

Deep learning has proven to be successful in many end-to-end learning tasks, yielding previously unattainable performances in various challenging computer vision problems. Its performance has been validated for gaze estimation in [12, 24]. For example, the iTracker outperformed the best method using multilevel HoG and RF in [10], reducing the estimation error by 0.59 cm on the TabletGaze dataset. We therefore adopted the iTracker for gaze estimation in this work.

The architecture of the iTracker [12] is illustrated in Fig. 1. The iTracker has four networks in parallel, and takes as an input (1) the image of the eyes; (2) the image of the face; and (3) a binary mask indicating the location of the face in the image (namely, face grid), and outputs the estimated x and y positions of a gaze fixation on the device screen. The eyes are included as individual inputs into the network to allow the network to identify subtle changes, and the weights are shared between the eye networks. In addition to eye images, face image and face grid are given as inputs into the network to incorporate head pose variations without explicitly estimating the head pose relative to the camera in contrast to [24]. In [12], it was also demonstrated that training the CNN model with sufficient and variable training examples (>1M) can remedy appearance changes due to head pose. The iTracker maps the input data onto a unified prediction space that enables training a single joint model using all the data from 15 different devices, and the model is trained using a Euclidean loss on the x and y gaze positions in the unified prediction space.

In our experiments, as in [12], we used 1,251,983 images (1271 subjects) for training, 59,480 images (50 subjects) for validation and 179,496 images (150 subjects) for testing. Firstly, we followed the implementation described in [12], and trained the model for 150,000 iterations with an initial learning rate of 0.001 and a reduced learning rate of 0.0001 after 75,000 iterations, with a batch size of 256. Similar to [12], we used stochastic gradient descent optimisation method with a momentum of 0.9. However, the trained model yielded worse results as compared to the results presented in [12]. Secondly, we repeated a similar training procedure by (1) applying batch normalisation and (2) using ADAM optimizer with an initial learning rate of 0.001 for 50,000 iterations and a reduced learning rate of 0.0001 for another 50,000 iterations. We called our first and second implementations as iTrackerTF and iTrackerTF*, respectively. We evaluated the estimation error in terms of Euclidean distance (in centimeters) between the estimated location and the location of the true gaze fixation. We also computed dot error, where we took average of gaze estimations of the model for all the consecutive images corresponding to the same gaze fixation at a certain location. As it was done in the original paper [12], we compared our gaze estimation results with a baseline method that applies support vector regression on features extracted from a pre-trained ImageNet network (called baseline, hereafter). Our gaze estimation results are presented in Table 1: our both implementations of iTracker outperforms baseline, and using batch normalisation and ADAM optimizer further improves the accuracy by a margin of 0.62 cm in mobile phones and 0.54 cm in tablets, respectively (see iTrackerTF vs. iTrackerTF*).

Table 1. Gaze estimation error in cm as Euclidean distance between the true fixation and the estimated position on the Gaze Capture dataset and the PAL M-Learning Gaze dataset.

Model	Gaze capture dataset				PAL M-learning gaze		
	Mobile phone		Tablet		Model	Tablet	
	Error	Dot error	Error	Dot error		Error	Dot error
Baseline	2.99	2.40	5.13	4.54	iTrackerTF*	5.31	5.23
iTrackerTF	2.91	2.33	4.40	3.95	fc1 features + SVR	6.63	6.56
iTrackerTF*	**2.37**	**1.97**	**3.86**	**3.55**	fc1 + fc2 finetuning	**3.66**	**3.40**

Since our goal was to apply gaze estimation on the PAL M-Learning Interaction dataset in which the full face was not always available, we experimented with different network architectures. We obtained an average error of 4.21 cm using eye images only and 3.45 cm using eye images together with face grid (without face) on the GazeCapture dataset. We obtained the minimum error when we took into account the face as well (3.11 cm). When the full face was not available, we filled the face by repeating the last row of the face image.

Finetuning iTrackerTF* with the PAL M-Learning Gaze Dataset. The Gaze-Capture dataset was captured using iPhones and iPads only. On the other hand, in the PAL M-Learning experiments we used a Lenovo tablet that has different camera-screen configuration from an iPad. In addition, out of 1249 subjects, only 225 subjects used iPads during the data collection, resulting in unbalanced data distribution between mobile phones and tablets. In order to obtain on-screen gaze estimations on the PAL M-Learning Gaze and Interaction datasets, we followed [12], and extracted features from the penultimate fully connected layer of the iTrackerTF*. We used these features to train Support Vector Regression (SVR) models using 6-fold cross validation in a subject-independent manner. More explicitly, we divided the dataset into 3 sets: train (20 subjects), validation

(5 subjects) and test (6 subjects), and each time we selected the optimum parameters (C and γ) on the validation set, and tested the best model on the unseen subset of test subjects. Using fc1 features in conjunction with SVR resulted in a decrease in the accuracy as compared to the jointly trained network, namely, the error increased from 5.31 cm to 6.59 cm (see fc1 features + SVR results in Table 1). In [12], this approach reduced the error on the TabletGaze dataset [10]. However, only 35 fixed on screen gaze locations were considered in [10], whereas the PAL M-Learning Gaze dataset comprises 25 random locations in addition to 35 fixed locations. We conjecture that the SVR models were not able to generalise due to the randomness in the locations of dots.

We therefore finetuned the iTrackerTF* network using the PAL M-Learning Tablet Gaze Dataset. Using the cropped faces and eyes from OpenFace [3] as inputs, we only updated the weights in the original-dataset-specific layers, namely, in the last two fully-connected layers (fc1 and fc2). As explained above, we followed the same 6-fold cross validation strategy, where we used the validation set to select a learning rate and a stopping criteria, and tested the fine-tuned model using a non-overlapping set of unseen test subjects each time. This resulted in 6 networks finetuned with a learning rate of 0.0001 for 10,000 iterations, and reduced the error from 5.31 cm to 3.66 cm on the PAL M-Learning Gaze dataset. We further used these networks for gaze estimation on the PAL M-Learning Interaction dataset (see Sect. 5).

In summary, our implementation has three necessary differences from [12]: (i) we applied batch normalisation; (2) we used ADAM optimizer; and (3) we mirrored right eye images before feeding into the network as it resulted in smaller estimation error. We also showed that fine-tuning the last two layers is a better approach for cross-dataset generalization in our case. Finally, we optimised the trained model for deployment on mobile devices using Tensorflow Mobile. Without face and eye detection, inference using the trained model on a GPU enabled mobile device (namely, Google Pixel C) takes approximately 400–450 ms per frame. As proposed in [12], we then trained a smaller version of the network, namely, reduced the size of the input images from 224 × 224 to 80 × 80. The smaller version of the network achieved 80–100 ms per frame, with a slight increase in the mean error on the GazeCapture dataset (i.e., 0.15 cm).

5   Feature Extraction

Once we finetuned the iTracker to the Lenovo tablet using the PAL M-Learning Gaze dataset, we applied it onto the PAL M-Learning Interaction dataset to obtain estimated on-screen gaze locations, and defined a set of eye movement features to model gaze behaviour for knowledgeability classification. Prior to feature extraction, we used OpenFace [3] to detect faces and eyes. In addition, similarly to [6], we used OpenFace [3] to detect and estimate the intensity of facial Action Units (AUs), which are codes that describe certain facial muscle movements (e.g. AU12 is lip corner puller, AU43 is eye blinking, etc.). Since we do not have ground-truth for the true locations of the gaze fixations in the

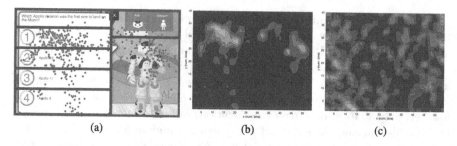

(a)   (b)   (c)

Fig. 3. (a) Visual stimulus divided into seven region of interests (ROIs) overlaid with sample estimated on-screen locations that are shown with circles in red and green; (b) A heat map computed from the estimated on-screen locations in (a); (c) A gaze history image (GHI) computed from the estimated on-screen locations in (a). (Color figure online)

PAL M-Learning Interaction dataset, we manually inspected the results. Our manual inspection showed that eye blinking results in spurious gaze estimations. As a post-processing step, we therefore removed the corresponding gaze estimations where an eye blink occurred. Given gaze fixations estimated in a clip, we extracted three types of eye movement features: (1) attention metrics; (2) heat map; and (3) gaze history images. We also compared eye movement features with the features extracted from AUs.

For computing the attention metrics, we divided the visual stimulus into seven regions of interest (ROIs) including the region enclosing the virtual agent, the region showing whose turn to ask a question, the regions enclosing the quiz question and the four options as shown in Fig. 3-(a). We computed two attention metrics [13], namely, gaze dwell fraction and gaze dwell time. Let T be the total time spent on the stimulus, given a total of N on-screen gaze estimations along vertical and horizontal directions with corresponding time instants, $\{x_i, y_i, t_i\}$, gaze dwell time is defined the amount of time a user spends viewing a ROI: $GDT(ROI) = \sum_{\{x_i, y_i\} \in ROI} (t_{i+1} - t_i)$. For computing gaze dwell fraction, we took into account the percentage of time a user gazes at a ROI: $GDF(ROI) = \frac{\sum_{\{x_i, y_i\} \in ROI} (t_{i+1} - t_i)}{T}$.

Heat map is one of the most widely used representations to analyse eye movements, which shows how looking is distributed over the stimulus. For each clip, we generated a 54×40 heat map as illustrated in Fig. 3-(b). We first vectorised the resulting heat map and then applied Principal Component Analysis (PCA) to reduce its dimension from 2160 to 50.

Although heat map is a powerful representation to model gaze behaviours, it does not incorporate the temporal information. On the other hand, as reported in [21], people use gaze dynamics to judge whether a person knows the correct answer or not. Inspired by motion history images [1], we transformed gaze estimations into an image representation while encoding temporal information. We first divided the gaze estimations over time into temporal slices ($\{\Delta t_i\}_{i=1:S}$) of a duration of 1 s, and then for each temporal slice

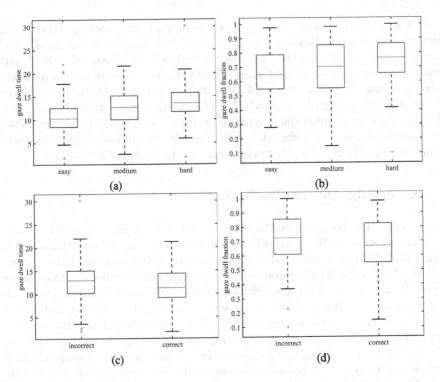

Fig. 4. (a–b) The effect of question's difficulty level on the gaze dwell time and gaze dwell fraction; (c–d) The effect of user's response (incorrect vs. correct) on the gaze dwell time and gaze dwell fraction.

we built a heat map. From time-dependent heat maps, we computed a gaze history image (GHI) per clip as follows. If a user gazes at a certain location within a certain temporal slice Δt_i, we set $GHI_\tau(x, y, \Delta t_i) = \tau$. Otherwise, $GHI_\tau(x, y, \Delta t_i) = \max(0, GHI_\tau(x, y, \Delta t_{i-1}) - 1)$, where τ is set to total number of temporal slices in a clip, namely S. More explicitly, intensity at a certain location is a function of recency of gaze fixation, where higher intensity values are associated with a more recent gaze fixation. A GHI is illustrated in Fig. 3-(c), where more recent gaze fixations are highlighted in yellow, and dark blue regions correspond to areas that were never visited throughout the clip. As we did for the heat map, we vectorised the resulting gaze history image and applied PCA to reduce its dimension to 50.

Taken together, we extracted a total of 114 eye movement features, consisting of 7 gaze dwell time features, 7 gaze dwell fraction features, 50 heat map features and 50 gaze history image (GHI) features. In Fig. 4, we presented the impact of question difficulty level (i.e., easy, medium, hard) on the gaze dwell time and gaze dwell fraction (we only considered the 5 ROIs associated with the question box). One can clearly observe that (i) gaze dwell fraction increases as the question's difficulty level increases; and (ii) people knowing the correct answer tend to spend less time on the question box.

In addition to eye movement features, for comparison purposes, we extracted features from detected facial action units (AUs). We considered that an AU was successfully detected when the confidence score was higher than a threshold, and took into account a total of 7 AUs associated with upper face muscle movements only, including inner brow raiser (AU1), outer brow raiser (AU2), brow lowerer (AU4), upper lid raiser (AU5), cheek raiser (AU6), lid tightener (AU7), and blink (AU45). Then we counted the number of occurrences of each AU and converted these numbers into a histogram for each clip. We also took average of intensity values of each AU over the whole clip, resulting in a total of 14 features.

6   Knowledgeability Prediction

We provided the baseline results with Support Vector Machines (SVM) and Gaussian Processes (GP) as classification schemes. We trained a nonlinear SVM with a Radial Basis Function (RBF) kernel to discriminate correct and incorrect samples. We optimized the parameters in a subject-independent fashion. More explicitly, we evaluated the classification performance using a double cross validation approach. This is a common practice to ensure better generalizablity of the trained models to the unseen subjects. In the outer loop, each time we used all the data from one participant for testing, and all the data from the remaining 26 participants for training and validation. In the inner loop, we selected the best parameters (C and γ) on the training and validation sets using a leave-one subject out validation approach. For GP, we adopted single leave-one-subject-out cross validation approach, and used RBF kernel variety. We randomly subsampled from the class having larger number of samples in order to balance the data prior to training both of the classifiers, and reported classification results as average F-Score/accuracy over multiple runs.

In Table 2, we presented our classification results for each feature type. As mentioned before, this is the first attempt to predict human knowledgeability from eye movements without using any specialised device. We are aware of only one work that proposed an automatic method for predicting human knowledgeability from observable visual cues [6]. However, their work differs from our work along three aspects: (1) they focused on a different setting; (2) they used clips recorded from a static, third person vision perspective; and (3) they extracted visual features from facial action units, head pose and 3D gaze direction. Nevertheless, we compared our classification accuracy with the proposed method in [6]. Looking at Table 2, using heat map only in conjunction with SVM yielded the best classification accuracy of 59.1%, and outperformed the method based on visual features in [6] (56.1%) in a more challenging scenario.

We observed three trends from Table 2. Firstly, SVM worked slightly better as compared to GP. Secondly, gaze dwell time and heat map features yielded better results with both classifiers as compared to gaze dwell fraction and gaze history image features. Finally, in our setting, action unit features performed just above chance, namely, yielding a classification accuracy of 51.8%.

Table 2. Knowledgeability classification in terms of F-Score ($\times 100$) and average accuracy (ACC%) on the PAL M-Learning Interaction dataset. The best results are highlighted in bold. (DwellTime: gaze dwell time; DwellFrac.: gaze dwell fraction; HeatMap: heat map; HistoryImage: gaze history image; ActionUnit: facial action units)

Feature type	Support vector machines (SVM)			Gaussian processes (GP)		
	F-score		ACC	F-score		ACC
	Incorrect	Correct	Ave.	Incorrect	Correct	Ave.
Human	73.2	45.2	59.2	73.2	45.2	59.2
DwellTime	58.9	**57.4**	58.2	58.0	**56.4**	**57.2**
DwellFrac.	57.9	50.5	54.5	57.2	51.4	54.5
HeatMap	**65.3**	50.0	**59.1**	62.6	50.0	**57.2**
HistoryImage	47.3	45.3	46.3	46.8	45.8	46.3
ActionUnit	52.7	45.8	49.5	53.1	50.4	51.8
VisualFeatures [6]	-	-	56.1	-	-	-

7   Conclusion and Future Work

In this paper, we introduced a novel computational approach to the problem of predicting human knowledgeability from eye movements without using any additional sensor, in mobile learning settings. We designed a study using a mobile interactive platform, where we recorded users on video while they were playing quiz game with a virtual agent to answer a set of general knowledge questions. We then formalised the problem of human knowledgeability prediction as a binary problem, and used a multitude of eye movement features in conjunction with SVM and GP to predict whether a user gave the *correct* answer to a question or not. Our results showed that heat map in conjunction with SVM was able to discriminate users clicking the correct response and users clicking the incorrect response with an accuracy of 59.1%. We believe that combining eye movements together with action units will help to improve the accuracy. From our manual inspection of the recorded data, we also observed that people tend to divert their attention from the tablet when thinking or bored. Eye contact [25] might be an important cue to detect in these situations. Our research reported in this paper has demonstrated results that warrant further investigation of non-obstructive eye movement analysis to adapt system behaviours to users' individual profiles.

Acknowledgements. This work was funded by the Horizon 2020 Framework Programme of the European Union under grant agreement no. 643783 (project PAL).

References

1. Ahad, M.A.R., Tan, J.K., Kim, H., Ishikawa, S.: Motion history image: its variants and applications. Mach. Vis. Appl. **23**, 255–281 (2010)
2. Alyuz, N., et al.: Towards an emotional engagement model: can affective states of a learner be automatically detected in a 1:1 learning scenario. In: Proceedings of the 6th Workshop on Personalization Approaches in Learning Environments (PALE 2016). 24th Conference on User Modeling, Adaptation, and Personalization (UMAP 2016), CEUR Workshop Proceedings (2016)
3. Baltrušaitis, T., Robinson, P., Morency, L.P.: OpenFace: an open source facial behavior analysis toolkit. In: IEEE Winter Conference on Applications of Computer Vision (2016)
4. Baranes, A., Oudeyer, P.Y., Gottlieb, J.: Eye movements reveal epistemic curiosity in human observers. Vis. Res. **117**(Suppl. C), 81–90 (2015)
5. Bednarik, R., Eivazi, S., Vrzakova, H.: A computational approach for prediction of problem-solving behavior using support vector machines and eye-tracking data. In: Nakano, Y., Conati, C., Bader, T. (eds.) Eye Gaze in Intelligent User Interfaces, pp. 111–134. Springer, London (2013). https://doi.org/10.1007/978-1-4471-4784-8_7
6. Bourai, A., Baltrušaitis, T., Morency, L.P.: Automatically predicting human knowledgeability through non-verbal cues. In: International Conference on Multimodal Interaction, ICMI 2017, pp. 60–67. ACM, New York (2017)
7. Broekens, J., Kosters, W.A. De Vries, T.: Eye movements disclosure decisions in set. In: Benelux Conference on Artificial Intelligence, pp. 29–30 (2009)
8. Bulling, A., Roggen, D.: Recognition of visual memory recall processes using eye movement analysis. In: Proceedings of the 13th International Conference on Ubiquitous Computing, UbiComp 2011, pp. 455–464. ACM, New York (2011)
9. Cole, M.J., Gwizdka, J., Liu, C., Belkin, N.J., Zhang, X.: Inferring user knowledge level from eye movement patterns. Inf. Process. Manage. **49**(5), 1075–1091 (2013)
10. Huang, Q., Veeraraghavan, A., Sabharwal, A.: TabletGaze: dataset and analysis for unconstrained appearance-based gaze estimation in mobile tablets. Mach. Vis. Appl. **28**(5), 445–461 (2017)
11. Knoblich, G., Öllinger, M., Spivey, M.: Tracking the eyes to obtain insight into insight problem solving, July 2005
12. Krafka, K., et al.: Eye tracking for everyone. In: The IEEE Conference on Computer Vision and Pattern Recognition (CVPR), June 2016
13. Li, Y., Xu, P., Lagun, D., Navalpakkam, V.: Towards measuring and inferring user interest from gaze. In: International Conference on World Wide Web Companion, WWW 2017 Companion, International World Wide Web Conferences Steering Committee, Republic and Canton of Geneva, Switzerland, pp. 525–533 (2017)
14. Open Trivia DB: Free to use, user-contributed trivia question database. opentdb.com. Accessed 21 Feb 2018
15. Quoc Viet Hung, N., Tam, N.T., Tran, L.N., Aberer, K.: An evaluation of aggregation techniques in crowdsourcing. In: Lin, X., Manolopoulos, Y., Srivastava, D., Huang, G. (eds.) WISE 2013. LNCS, vol. 8181, pp. 1–15. Springer, Heidelberg (2013). https://doi.org/10.1007/978-3-642-41154-0_1
16. Shrout, P., Fleiss, J.: Intraclass correlations: uses in assessing rater reliability. Psychology Bull. (1979)
17. Surakka, V., Illi, M., Isokoski, P.: Voluntary eye movements in human-computer interaction. In: The Mind's Eye, pp. 473–491. North-Holland, Amsterdam (2003)

18. Tessendorf, B., et al.: Recognition of hearing needs from body and eye movements to improve hearing instruments. In: Lyons, K., Hightower, J., Huang, E.M. (eds.) Pervasive 2011. LNCS, vol. 6696, pp. 314–331. Springer, Heidelberg (2011). https://doi.org/10.1007/978-3-642-21726-5_20

19. Underwood, G.: Cognitive Processes in Eye Guidance. Oxford University Press, Oxford (2005)

20. Vendetti, M.S., Starr, A., Johnson, E.L., Modavi, K., Bunge, S.A.: Eye movements reveal optimal strategies for analogical reasoning. Frontiers Psychol. **8**, 932 (2017)

21. van Wermeskerken, M., Litchfield, D., van Gog, T.: Eye see what you are doing: inferring task performance from eye movement data. In: European Conference on Eye Movements (2017)

22. Wood, E., Bulling, A.: EyeTab: model-based gaze estimation on unmodified tablet computers. In: Proceedings of the Symposium on Eye Tracking Research and Applications, ETRA 2014, pp. 207–210. ACM, New York (2014)

23. Zhang, X., Sugano, Y., Fritz, M., Bulling, A.: It's written all over your face: full-face appearance-based gaze estimation. In: 2017 IEEE Conference on Computer Vision and Pattern Recognition Workshops (CVPRW), pp. 2299–2308, July 2017

24. Zhang, X., Sugano, Y., Fritz, M., Bulling, A.: MPIIGaze: real-world dataset and deep appearance-based gaze estimation. IEEE Trans. Pattern Anal. Mach. Intell. **PP**(99), 1 (2018)

25. Zhang, X., Sugano, Y., Bulling, A.: Everyday eye contact detection using unsupervised gaze target discovery. In: Proceedings of the 30th Annual ACM Symposium on User Interface Software and Technology, UIST 2017, pp. 193–203. ACM, New York (2017)

W32 – 4th International Workshop on Observing and Understanding Hands in Action

W32 – 4th International Workshop on Observing and Understanding Hands in Action

The Fourth International Workshop on Observing and Understanding Hands in Action (HANDS 2018) was held in conjunction with the European Conference on Computer Vision 2018 (ECCV'18) on the 9th of September 2018 in Munich, Germany. It was held in the main building of the Technical University of Munich (TUM) in Arcisstraße 21, and specifically in the lecture hall Theresianum 606. The program of the workshop included five invited talks, six full papers, three extended abstracts, six invited posters, and a short award ceremony.

There were five invited talks in the workshop. The speakers were: Christian Theobalt (Max Planck Institute for Informatics), Tamim Asfour (Karlsruhe Institute of Technology), Andrew Fitzgibbon (Microsoft), Robert Wang (Facebook Reality Labs), and Andrea Tagliasacchi (Google).

The regular program of the workshop invited high quality original papers on the relevant areas. In total, there were seven submissions that were peer-reviewed by seventeen invited reviewers. Each paper was assigned three reviewers, aiming for at least two reviews per work. Through this review process, six of the seven submitted papers were accepted for publication in the workshop proceedings.

Apart from the regular papers, the workshop also had original contributions in the form of extended abstracts, with the goal of including high-potential but preliminary works. These works were presented as posters in the poster session but are not published as part of the workshop proceedings. Of the four submissions, three were chosen for acceptance by the program chairs.

Finally, the organizers invited six works from the main ECCV'18 conference related in aim to the workshop to be presented in the poster session.

Two works were given awards sponsored by Facebook Reality Labs. The best paper award was decided by the program chairs, while the best poster award was decided in a vote from selected workshop attendants including organizers, invited speakers and topic experts. The best paper award was given to the work "Hand-tremor Frequency Estimation in Videos" by Silvia L Pintea, Jian Zheng, Xilin Li, Paulina J. M. Bank, Jacobus J. van Hilten, and Jan van Gemert. The best poster award was given to the work "Hand Pose Estimation via Latent 2.5D Heatmap Regression", by Umar Iqbal, Pavlo Molchanov, Thomas Breuel, Juergen Gall, and Jan Kautz.

Detailed information and scientific contents of the workshop can be found in the discussion paper that follows this preface.

September 2018

Iason Oikonomidis
Guillermo Garcia-Hernando
Angela Yao
Antonis Argyros
Vincent Lepetit
Tae-Kyun Kim

Hand-Tremor Frequency Estimation in Videos

Silvia L. Pintea[1(✉)], Jian Zheng[1], Xilin Li[1], Paulina J. M. Bank[2], Jacobus J. van Hilten[2], and Jan C. van Gemert[1]

[1] Vision Lab, Delft University of Technology, Delft, Netherlands
Silvia.Laura.Pintea@gmail.com
[2] Department of Neurology, Leiden University Medical Center, Leiden, Netherlands

Abstract. We focus on the problem of estimating human hand-tremor frequency from input RGB video data. Estimating tremors from video is important for non-invasive monitoring, analyzing and diagnosing patients suffering from motor-disorders such as Parkinson's disease. We consider two approaches for hand-tremor frequency estimation: (a) a Lagrangian approach where we detect the hand at every frame in the video, and estimate the tremor frequency along the trajectory; and (b) an Eulerian approach where we first localize the hand, we subsequently remove the large motion along the movement trajectory of the hand, and we use the video information over time encoded as intensity values or phase information to estimate the tremor frequency. We estimate hand tremors on a new human tremor dataset, *TIM-Tremor*, containing static tasks as well as a multitude of more dynamic tasks, involving larger motion of the hands. The dataset has 55 tremor patient recordings together with: associated ground truth accelerometer data from the most affected hand, RGB video data, and aligned depth data.

Keywords: Video hand-tremor analysis
Phase-based tremor frequency detection · Human tremor dataset
Eulerian hand tremors

1 Introduction

We focus on human hand-tremor frequency estimation from videos captured with common consumer RGB cameras. The problem has a considerable importance in medical applications for aiding the medical personnel in the task of motor-disorder patient monitoring and tremor diagnosing [2,13,25,34]. Traditionally the clinical practice uses body-worn accelerometers which offer excellent measurements, yet is intrusive, slow to setup, and allows only measuring a single location per accelerometer. Replacing accelerometers with a common RGB camera brings forth a non-intrusive method of measuring full-body tremors, offering a strong advantage in the clinical practice.

© Springer Nature Switzerland AG 2019
L. Leal-Taixé and S. Roth (Eds.): ECCV 2018 Workshops, LNCS 11134, pp. 213–228, 2019.
https://doi.org/10.1007/978-3-030-11024-6_14

In the context of tremor analysis, existing approaches require the use of specialized sensors [6,8,14,15], which makes it difficult to apply these methods in practice. Moreover, the targeted application of these approaches are the more high-level tremor diagnosing problem [14,26] or tremor/no-tremor classification [28]. We propose to estimate human hand-tremor frequency from RGB videos, and compare against ground truth accelerometer data.

The main challenge, when performing human tremor frequency estimation, is the current lack of openly available realistic datasets. Existing work on human tremor analysis either evaluates using in-house data that is not publicly available [6,14,37], or on simulated tremor data where no ground truth tremor statistics are provided [28]. This limits the assessment of human tremor analysis methods and, thus, its progress. An open evaluation dataset is needed.

In this work: (i) we evaluate the frequency of human hand-tremors from RGB videos and we analyze two possible approaches: (i.a) a Lagrangian approach that focuses on the motion of the hand in the image plane, and estimates tremors over the hand positions; (i.b) an Eulerian approach that aligns the hand position over a temporal window, by tracking it, and subsequently uses the image information over time as extracted from intensity values and phase-images, to perform a windowed Fourier analysis at every hand pixel; (ii) we bring forth the *TIM-Tremor* dataset, containing: 55 RGB patient videos, together with associated ground-truth accelerometer recordings on the most affected hand, as well as aligned depth-data; (iii) we analyze two variants of the Lagrangian approach and two variants of the Eulerian approach and evaluate them numerically on our proposed *TIM-Tremor* human tremor dataset.

2   Related Work

2.1   Motion Analysis

Periodic Motion. The work in [22] performs action recognition by using space-time repetitive motion templates. Similar to using templates, in [5] a self-similarity relying on time-frequency analysis is used for action recognition. The work in [12] performs a spectral decomposition of moving objects to encode periodic motions for object recognition, while [30] performs eigen decomposition and describes periodic motion by the circularity or toroidality of an associated geometric space. Following a similar trend, in [19] complex motion is decomposed into a sequence of simple linear dynamic models for motion categorization. The work in [24] focuses on pedestrian detection through periodic movement analysis. Similar to us, the work in [28] performs tremor analysis, however in [28] videos are classified into tremor/no-tremor using optical flow features and SVM. In the recent work in [29] a CNN is used for discriminating between Parkinson patients and non-Parkinson patients, using wrist-worn senors. In this work we also focus on periodic motion analysis, however our end goal is tremor frequency estimation rather than action recognition, object tracking or recognition.

Differently, in [18,27,33] deep network architectures are trained for counting action repetitions. These actions must be clearly visible and recognizable in the camera view for the deep network architectures to work, while we focus on tremors which are subtle motions.

The most similar work to our work is the work performed in [31,32] where tremor frequency is measure from pixel intensities in the video. However these methods assumes the location of the body part at which the tremor is measured to be known in advance and moreover, the frequency is estimated over intensity values rather than detected hand location over time, or image phase-information over time, as we propose here. The authors do not publicly provide either code or data, which makes it impossible for us to compare with their approach.

Subtle Motion. Small motion, difficult to see with the bare eyes, can be magnified [17,35] through a complex steerable pyramid. In the more realistic case, when the subtle motion is combined with a large motion, follow up work can magnify subtle motions such as tremors in the presence of large object motion such as walking [9,39]. Video frequency analysis has been also employed for estimating the properties of physical materials [7]. We also employ signal analysis in the Fourier domain, however rather than magnifying the subtle motion or estimating material properties, we estimate the frequency of the subtle tremor motion. The works in [14,15] use specialized sensors or a digital light-processing projector, and a high frame-rate camera to detect small vibrations. Unlike [14,15], we do not employ specific cameras or expensive sensors, we estimate the tremor frequency from common RGB videos.

2.2   Human Body Pose Estimation

Works such as [3,21] perform body pose estimation over multiple people, in deep networks. In [3,4,23,36] cascaded prediction or iterative optimizations are used for body pose estimation. We use the method in [36] for estimating where to measure the tremors. We opt for [36] due to its ease of usage and robustness. In this work we use the MPII Human Body Pose dataset [1] for training the human body pose estimation models.

3   Hand-Tremor Frequency Estimation

We start by localizing the affected hand. Subsequently, we consider two methods for hand-tremor frequency estimation: (a) Lagrangian hand-tremor frequency estimation, and (b) Eulerian hand-tremor frequency estimation.

3.1   Hand Location Estimation

A first step in estimating human hand-tremors, is localizing the affected hand. For this, we use the robust human body pose estimation proposed in [36]. This method provides us a hand location per frame (x_i, y_i). We perform the tremor analysis on shorter temporal windows of the video, $w(t)$.

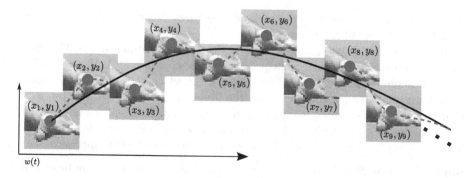

Fig. 1. Lagrangian hand-tremor estimation is based on frequency estimation of (x, y) coordinates. We detect the hand position $(x_i, y_i)_{i \in w(t)}$ at every frame i over a temporal window $w(t)$. The hand motion is characterized by a large motion, depicted by the black line, and a small motion, depicted by the red dotted line. We smooth this information over time, using a Kalman tracker to obtain the smooth coordinates of the hand. (Color figure online)

3.2   (a) Lagrangian Hand-Tremor Frequency Estimation

Figure 1 depicts the idea behind the Lagrangian hand-tremor frequency estimation. We start by detecting the hand locations $(x_i, y_i)_{i \in w(t)}$ over the temporal window $w(t)$. The hand motion is typically characterized by a combination of two motions: a large hand trajectory motion, depicted through the continuous black line, and a small motion corresponding to the tremor, depicted in Fig. 1 by the dotted red line. We first apply a Kalman-filter tracker [38] to the initial hand locations, detected by the pose estimation algorithm [36]. This step is used for smoothing the hand trajectory, to obtain the large hand motion. We subsequently subtract this smooth trajectory from the original hand locations to retain only the *x and y locations* of the small hand motion, corresponding to the tremor. Thereafter, we apply the windowed Fourier transform over these corrected locations. This provides us a PSD (Power Spectrum Density) function. We use the maximum frequency as the estimated hand-tremor frequency.

3.3   (b) Eulerian Hand-Tremor Frequency Estimation

Figure 2 illustrates the Eulerian frequency estimation. The first step is the same as in Fig. 1, where the hand locations are detected using the pose estimation method in [36], and subsequently, we smooth the trajectory given by these hand detections using a Kalman tracker. This gives us the smooth trajectory of the hand over time, in the video. We crop image windows around the temporally smoothed locations of the hand in the video—along the black line depicted in Fig. 2.(1). For each such image crop, we extract local motion information encoded as phase over different scales and orientations. Thereafter, we compute the frequency of the hand-tremor by using the most informative phase-image. Figure 2 depicts these individual steps.

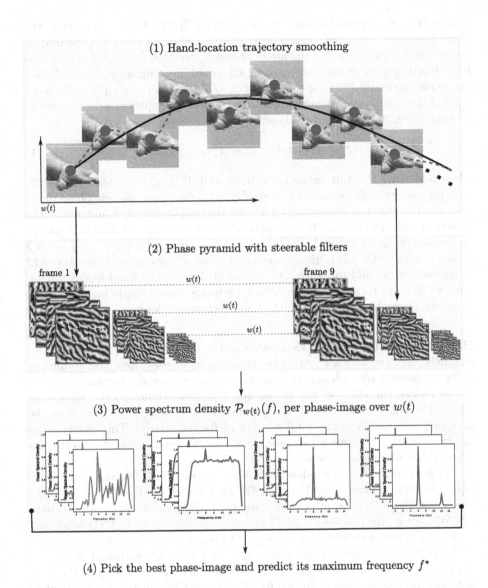

(1) Hand-location trajectory smoothing

$w(t)$

(2) Phase pyramid with steerable filters

frame 1   frame 9
$w(t)$
$w(t)$
$w(t)$

(3) Power spectrum density $\mathcal{P}_{w(t)}(f)$, per phase-image over $w(t)$

(4) Pick the best phase-image and predict its maximum frequency f^*

Fig. 2. Eulerian hand-tremor estimation is based on frequency estimation in images. (1) The fist step is the same as in the Lagrangian illustrated in Fig. 1: detecting a Kalman-filtered smoothed hand position at every frame over a temporal window $w(t)$. (2) We crop image windows around the smoothed hand locations. Each such cropped image is transformed into a phase-pyramid with 4 orientations and 3 scales using a steerable filter bank. (3) For every pixel, in every phase-image over the temporal window $w(t)$ we estimate a PSD (Power Spectrum Density). We accumulate these over the pixels in one phase-image, to obtain one PSD per phase-image. (4) We select the most informative phase-image PSD and use it to estimate the tremor-frequency.

Phase-Image Computation. Works such as [10,20,35,39] claim that the phase responses over time contain descriptive information regarding the motion present in the image. In [35] the use of complex steerable filters [11] is proposed for extracting local motion information. Given an input image $I(x,y)$ and a set of complex steerable filters of the form: $G_\sigma^\theta + iH_\sigma^\theta$, where $i = \sqrt{-1}$, σ defines the scale of the filter, and θ the orientation, we obtain a complex steerable pyramid by convolving the image with this set of filters

$$(G_\sigma^\theta + iH_\sigma^\theta) \circledast I(x,y) = A_\sigma^\theta(x,y)e^{i\phi_\sigma^\theta(x,y)}, \tag{1}$$

where $\circledast$ denotes the convolution operations, and $A_\sigma^\theta(x,y)$ is the resulting amplitude for scale σ and orientation θ, and $\phi_\sigma^\theta(x,y)$ is the corresponding phase information. To obtain a phase-image, we set the amplitude to 1 and apply the inverse transformation [11] to reconstruct back the image. Examples of phase-images are depicted in Fig. 1.(2). We use 4 orientations: $\theta \in \{0, \frac{\pi}{4}, \frac{\pi}{2}, \frac{3\pi}{4}\}$ and 3 scales: $\sigma \in \{1.0, 0.5, 0.25\}$, giving rise to 12 phase-images. In addition to the 12 phase-images, we add the grayscale version of the cropped hand-image. Therefore, we have in total 13 images, which we merge into a single image with 13 channels, over which we estimate the hand-tremor frequency.

Hand-Tremor Frequency Estimation. We filter each one of the 13 input channels over time with a 4th-order Butterworth band-pass filter. This eliminates noisy frequencies that cannot correspond to a natural human tremor.

To reduce the effect of the considered temporal window, $w(t)$, we use an adjustable Tukey window with the parameter α set to $\frac{f_s}{N-1}$, where f_s is the sampling rate and N is the total number of frames in $w(t)$. This ensures that the video signal over time is processed in a consistent manner while allowing for adjustable temporal window sizes, $w(t)$.

Within each temporal window, $w(t)$, we estimate a PSD function, over every input channel, at every pixel location. For an input channel, c, we estimate the final PSD, $\mathcal{P}_{w(t)}^c(f)$, by averaging spatially the PSDs over the pixels in that channel. We repeat this process for all 13 channels, giving rise to 13 PSD functions.

In [5] the power spectrum is considered to be periodic at a certain frequency, f, if the PSD response at that frequency is at least a few standard deviations away from the mean PSD response. This is indicative of how noisy is the PSD function. We use this same criterion to pick the most informative image channel; this is the channel over which we estimate the final hand-tremor frequency. We define for each channel a score, $\mathcal{S}^c(f)$:

$$\mathcal{S}^c(f) = \frac{1}{|w(t)|} \sum_{w(t)} \left(\mathcal{P}_{w(t)}^c(f) - \mu_{\mathcal{P}_{w(t)}^c} - k\sigma_{\mathcal{P}_{w(t)}^c} \right), \tag{2}$$

where $|w(t)|$ is the number of temporal windows per video, $\mu_{\mathcal{P}_{w(t)}^c}$ represents the mean of the PSD response, and $\sigma_{\mathcal{P}_{w(t)}}$ denotes the standard deviation, while k is an adjustable parameter. We set $k = 3$ in our experiments.

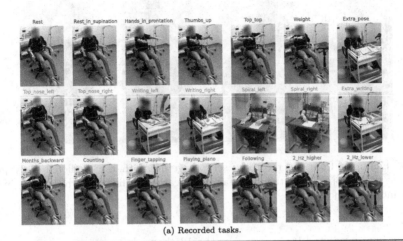

(a) Recorded tasks.

Task	Description
Rest	
Rest	Resting the arms on the chair handles.
Rest_in_supination	Resting the arms on the chair handles, hands in supination position.
Postures	
Hands_in_pronation	Both arms outstretched forward, hands in pronation position.
Thumbs_up	Both arms outstretched forward, thumbs up.
Top_top	Both hands in front of the chest with tips of the index fingers almost touching each other, elbows lifted sideways at approx. 90 degrees angle.
Weight	Affected arm outstretched forward, with a weight (1 kg) attached to the wrist.
Extra_pose	Holding a pose proposed by the medical expert to better visualize the tremor.
Actions	
Top_nose_left	Touching the top of the nose with the left index finger.
Top_nose_right	Touching the top of the nose with the right index finger.
Writing_left	Writing a given sentence with the left hand.
Writing_right	Writing a given sentence with the right hand.
Spiral_left	Drawing a spiral with the left hand.
Spiral_right	Drawing a spiral with the right hand.
Extra_writing	Extra writing task with a special pen, or diverging from the standard writing task with the affected hand.
Distraction	
Months_backward*	Naming the months backwards.
Counting*	Counting backwards (100 minus 7).
Finger_tapping*	Tapping with the index finger and thumb of the contralateral hand.
Playing_piano*	Moving the thumb of the contralateral hand across all fingers, from the index to the pinky finger and back.
Following*	Following a moving pointer with the index finger of the contralateral hand.
Entrainment	
2_Hz_higher*	Tapping with the contralateral hand in the rhythm of a flashing light, 2 Hz higher than the estimated tremor frequency of the affected hand.
2_Hz_lower*	Tapping with the contralateral hand in the rhythm of a flashing light, 2 Hz lower than the estimated tremor frequency of the affected hand.

*During these tasks, the affected hand was kept in the posture in which the tremor was most pronounced (i.e. arm on chair handle, arm outstretched with hand in pronation or thumbs up, or in front of the chest).

(b) Explanation.

Fig. 3. (a) We record motor-disorder patients in 21 tasks. Each task may elicit a tremor. (b) Short explanation of what each task involves.

Fig. 4. Examples from the recording setup together with the predicted body joint locations using [36]. We use this to obtain the location of the hand where we estimate the tremor frequency.

The final predicted frequency over the 13 channels becomes:

$$f^* = \arg \max_f (\max_c \mathcal{S}^c(f)). \tag{3}$$

4   Experiments

We test the considered frequency estimation approaches on our tremor patient dataset, *TIM-Tremor*, containing a multitude of tasks. The anonymized *TIM-Tremor* patient data can be found at https://doi.org/10.4121/uuid:522d14ed-3019-4206-b49e-a4e674b6440a.

4.1   Patient Data Evaluation

Data Description. We recorded the *TIM-Tremor* dataset, in which 55 patients are videotaped sitting in a chair and performing a multitude of tasks. The data is recorded with a Kinect^{TM} v2 device, and it consists of short RGB videos of resolution 1920×1080 px, and associated depth video recordings of 512×424 px using a 16-bit encoding, as well as depth videos aligned with the RGB videos following the method in [16]. To reduce the storage requirements, we rescale the video resolution to 960×540 px. The ground truth tremor frequency is measured on the wrist of the most affected hand: left/right. On this hand, during the recording, we position an accelerometer. The accelerometer recordings are included in the dataset. The hand on which the accelerometer is positioned, is annotated in the dataset for each patient. Thus, for each patient and each performed task, we provide a set of recorded videos of approximately 1 min each, together with a corresponding aligned depth map video, and the ground truth accelerometer recording from the most affected hand.

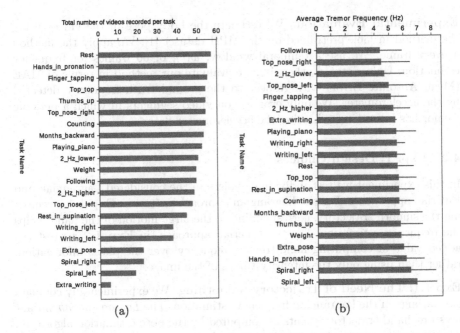

Fig. 5. (a) Total number of videos recorded per task. (b) Average frequency and standard deviation for all tasks across all 55 patient recordings.

Data collection occurred in parallel to the standard tremor clinical evaluation. The standard tremor evaluation consists of a set of 21 tasks, which are illustrated in Fig. 3.(a) and described in Fig. 3.(b). The tasks vary with respect to the adopted posture: e.g. arm supported by the arm rest, or held outstretched in front of the patient, the amount of motion involved: e.g. rest – no motion, or touching the top of the nose – intention-oriented motion, as well as the focus of attention: e.g. distraction by mental task. Changes in tremor frequency between these tasks are analyzed by the medical expert to classify the tremor. For example, certain types of tremor are present across most or all tasks (e.g. "Parkinsonian tremor"), while other types of tremor may only occur when performing a specific task (e.g. "postural tremor" occurs only when a patient maintains a specific posture such as *Thumbs_up*), while other tremors may show considerable variation in tremor frequency between tasks (e.g. "functional tremor").

Figure 4 displays a few examples of the recording setup together with the estimated joint locations using [36]. In Fig. 5 we show the total number of videos recorded for each task, and the average hand tremor frequency, as estimated by the accelerometer, together with the standard deviation, computed across all 55 patients. The average tremor frequency is around 5 Hz, which is a common in tremor affections such as Parkinson and Dystonia.

Experimental Evaluation. We estimate the body pose in the videos using the method in [36], pretrained on the MPII dataset [1]. We apply the method a every frame. We use a temporal window, $w(t)$, of 60 frames for frequency estimation. Unless stated otherwise, we evaluate our method in terms of MAE (Mean Absolute Error) with respect to the ground truth frequency detected by the accelerometer. We only evaluate on video segments in which a periodic tremor has been detected, using the accelerometer data.

4.2   Exp. 1: Design Choices

In this experiment we test individual choices in the considered Lagrangian and Eulerian approaches. For the Lagrangian approach we test in **Exp 1.1** if removing the smooth trajectory, corresponding to the large motion of the hand, helps the frequency estimation. For the Eulerian approach, in **Exp 1.2** we test the added value of computing hand-tremor frequency over the phase information, rather than using only the intensity values of the image.

Exp 1.1: The Need of Trajectory Smoothing. We experimentally compare two variants of the Lagrangian frequency estimation. The *Lag_no_smooth* variant uses raw hand trajectory points as computed by the pose estimation algorithm. The *Lag_with_smooth* variant removes the large motion of the hand obtained by subtracting the output of a Kalman tracker, which in effect retains only the small motions. The MAE numbers in Table 1 show that removing the large motion by using the Kalman tracker is beneficial to the overall performance. This is explained by the fact that subtracting the trajectory returned by the Kalman tracker from the original hand trajectory works as a data detrending step. This allows for the frequency to be estimated only over the small tremor motion.

Exp 1.2: The Added Value of Using Phase-Images. For both considered Eulerian approaches we stabilize the trajectory along which we measure the tremor by using the Kalman tracker, and subsequently perform the frequency estimation over the complete hand window. In Table 2 we test the added value of using phase information for frequency estimation. We compare two variants. The *Euler_gray* variant estimates the frequency over gray-scale pixels over gray-scale hand-images, obtained by cropping the hand location along the smoothed trajectory of the hand. The *Euler_phase* variant adds the 12 phase channels as detailed in Sect. 3.3. The phase channels allow the *Euler_phase* to more precisely capture the small motion corresponding to the tremor, because the phase is effective for describing motion. The MAE numbers in Table 2 validate that adding the phase information is beneficial for the hand-tremor frequency estimation.

Table 1. Exp 1.1: MAE when comparing the Lagrangian method with trajectory smoothing by using the Kalman tracker—*Lag_with_smooth*, versus not using trajectory smoothing, *Lag_no_smooth*. *Lag_with_smooth* performs slightly better than the default Lagrangian method, *Lag_no_smooth*. We highlight in bold the better performing method (lower is better).

Task	Lag_no_smooth (Hz)	Lag_with_smooth (Hz)
2_Hz_higher	1.917 (± 2.395)	**1.879** (± 2.127)
2_Hz_lower	2.248 (± 2.770)	**1.721** (± 2.266)
Counting	1.731 (± 2.336)	**1.377** (± 2.246)
Extra_pose	3.590 (± 2.369)	**1.918** (± 1.328)
Extra_writing	**1.968** (± 0.000)	**1.968** (± 0.000)
Finger_tapping	1.989 (± 2.783)	**1.326** (± 1.974)
Following	1.607 (± 1.745)	**1.312** (± 1.728)
Hands_in_pronation	2.582 (± 2.154)	**2.398** (± 2.024)
Months_backward	2.544 (± 2.703)	**2.031** (± 2.500)
Playing_piano	2.443 (± 2.826)	**2.033** (± 2.516)
Rest	**3.300** (± 3.271)	3.395 (± 3.226)
Rest_in_supination	2.889 (± 3.228)	**2.059** (± 2.248)
Spiral_left	**6.721** (± 1.896)	**6.721** (± 1.896)
Spiral_right	3.246 (± 1.762)	**3.148** (± 1.803)
Top_nose_left	3.743 (± 3.262)	**3.688** (± 3.242)
Top_nose_right	1.928 (± 2.323)	**1.771** (± 2.204)
Top_top	**1.388** (± 1.797)	1.669 (± 1.888)
Thumbs_up	**1.694** (± 1.807)	1.694 (± 1.836)
Weight	**2.660** (± 2.667)	2.795 (± 2.569)
Writing_left	**2.557** (± 1.139)	**2.557** (± 1.139)
Writing_right	**2.557** (± 1.139)	**2.557** (± 1.139)
Average MAE	2.633 (± 2.208)	**2.382** (± 1.995)

4.3 Exp 2: Eulerian Versus Lagrangian Tremor Frequency Estimation

In Fig. 6 we display the accuracy of our proposed frequency estimation methods over the complete set of 55 patient recordings, for all tasks. We show in dotted green line the number of videos per task where a periodic tremor was detected, according to the accelerometer data. In corresponding color, we show the number of videos in which we have correctly estimated the hand-tremor frequency, for each frequency estimation method: *Euler_phase* is the Eulerian method using 12 phase-channels and 1 grayscale channel; *Euler_gray* is the Eulerian method on image intensity information only; *Lag_no_smooth* is the Lagrangian method without Kalman trajectory smoothing; *Lag_with_smooth* is the Lagrangian method

Table 2. Exp 1.2: MAE showing the added value of the phase information. We compare the *Euler_gray*—Eulerian frequency estimation over grayscale hand-images, with *Euler_phase* – Eulerian frequency estimation over 12 phase-images and 1 grayscale image. Adding the 12 extra phase-images is beneficial for the frequency estimation. We highlight in bold the better performing method (lower is better).

Task	Euler_gray (Hz)	Euler_phase (Hz)
2_Hz_higher	0.882 (± 1.142)	**0.857** (± 1.533)
2_Hz_lower	1.335 (± 2.022)	**0.984** (± 1.333)
Counting	0.767 (± 1.252)	**0.472** (± 0.780)
Extra_pose	**1.180** (± 2.006)	1.623 (± 1.185)
Extra_writing	**0.984** (± 0.000)	**0.984** (± 0.000)
Finger_tapping	0.492 (± 0.893)	**0.385** (± 0.647)
Following	0.820 (± 1.327)	**0.557** (± 0.503)
Hands_in_pronation	1.271 (± 1.755)	**1.066** (± 1.506)
Months_backward	1.133 (± 1.848)	**1.219** (± 1.933)
Playing_piano	1.148 (± 1.832)	**1.148** (± 1.714)
Rest	1.459 (± 1.759)	**1.253** (± 1.770)
Rest_in_supination	**1.475** (± 1.919)	1.537 (± 1.728)
Spiral_left	3.278 (± 1.671)	**2.951** (± 1.391)
Spiral_right	3.246 (± 2.936)	**2.509** (± 2.021)
Top_nose_left	2.595 (± 2.216)	**1.776** (± 2.008)
Top_nose_right	3.108 (± 2.739)	**2.164** (± 2.015)
Top_top	0.860 (± 1.311)	**0.720** (± 1.200)
Thumbs_up	1.002 (± 1.419)	**1.002** (± 1.273)
Weight	1.207 (± 1.695)	**0.961** (± 1.226)
Writing_left	**0.394** (± 0.573)	0.492 (± 0.538)
Writing_right	**0.394** (± 0.573)	0.492 (± 0.538)
Average MAE	1.382 (± 1.566)	**1.198** (± 1.278)

with Kalman trajectory smoothing. We consider an estimated tremor frequency to be correct if the MAE between the accelerometer frequency and the one estimated by the method is lower than 1 Hz.

Figure 6 shows that on average the Eulerian frequency estimation methods are more precise than the Lagrangian methods. The gain of using the Eulerian approaches is especially clear for the *Weight* task and the *Hands_in_pronation* task. Figure 7 displays the MAE scores per patient for these two tasks. To avoid over-cluttering the image, we only show the best Lagrangian method: *Lag_with_smooth*, Lagrangian with Kalman trajectory smoothing, and the best Eulerian method: *Euler_phase*, Eulerian over 12 phase channels and 1 grayscale channel. The Eulerian method gives more precise frequency estimates for some

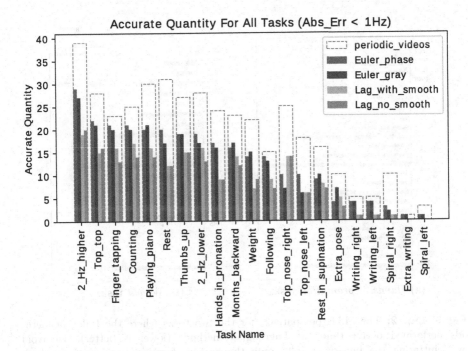

Fig. 6. Exp 2: We report accuracy on all recorded tasks, over the 55 patient recordings (higher is better). We consider the hand-tremor frequency to be correctly estimated for a task if the MAE (Mean Absolute Error) for that task is lower than 1 Hz. We plot in dotted green line the total number of videos recorded for each task, on which we have detected a periodic tremor. For each of our considered methods we show the number of videos for which the frequency was correctly estimated. On average the Eulerian methods perform better than the Lagrangian methods. (Color figure online)

of the patient recordings, while for others it performs similar to the Lagrangian method. The tasks are not characterized by large hand motion. The gain of the Eulerian method over the Lagrangian is explained by the Eulerian method better describing the subtle changes in image information over time at the hand location. Therefore, the Eulerian method more accurately captures the tremor in tasks that do not involve large hand motion, but exhibit small motion.

226   S. L. Pintea et al.

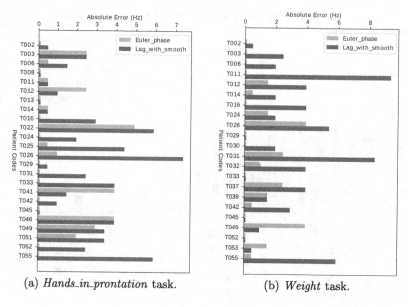

(a) *Hands_in_prontation* task.   (b) *Weight* task.

Fig. 7. Exp 2: The MAE per patient, for the two tasks where the Eulerian methods performed better than the Lagrangian methods (lower is better). To avoid over-cluttering the image, we plot only the best performing Lagrangian method: *Lag_with_smooth*—Lagrangian method with Kalman trajectory smoothing, and the best performing Eulerian method: *Euler_phase*—Eulerian method using 12 phase channels and 1 grayscale channel. The Lagrangian method makes large frequency estimation mistakes on a few patient videos, while the Eulerian method is more precise on some of the patient videos. (Note: for certain patients the task has not been recorded or no stable frequency, according to the accelerometer, has been found.)

5   Conclusions

We consider the task of hand-tremor frequency estimation from RGB videos. We propose two different approaches for measuring human hand-tremor frequencies: (a) Lagrangian hand-tremor frequency estimation, using the trajectory of the hand motion in the image plane throughout the video, to assess the hand-tremor frequency; and (b) Eulerian hand-tremor frequency estimation, which measures the change in the image information over time, at the location of hand in the image plane. We experimentally evaluate two variants of each approach on our proposed *TIM-Tremor* dataset containing 55 patient recordings performing a multitude of tasks. From our experimental analysis we learned that the Eulerian approaches are more accurate on average than the Lagrangian methods, with the difference being substantial on tasks on which there is a limited amount of large hand motion, but where there is a small hand-tremor motion present.

Acknowledgements. This work is part of the research program Technology in Motion (TIM) (628.004.001), which is financed by the Netherlands Organisation for Scientific Research (NWO). Many thanks for the help with data collection to Elma Ouwehand, MSc.

References

1. Andriluka, M., Pishchulin, L., Gehler, P., Schiele, B.: 2D human pose estimation: new benchmark and state of the art analysis. In: CVPR, pp. 3686–3693 (2014)
2. di Biase, L., et al.: Tremor stability index: a new tool for differential diagnosis in tremor syndromes. Brain (2017). awx104
3. Bulat, A., Tzimiropoulos, G.: Human pose estimation via convolutional part heatmap regression. In: Leibe, B., Matas, J., Sebe, N., Welling, M. (eds.) ECCV 2016. LNCS, vol. 9911, pp. 717–732. Springer, Cham (2016). https://doi.org/10.1007/978-3-319-46478-7_44
4. Carreira, J., Agrawal, P., Fragkiadaki, K., Malik, J.: Human pose estimation with iterative error feedback. In: CVPR, pp. 4733–4742 (2016)
5. Cutler, R., Davis, L.S.: Robust real-time periodic motion detection, analysis, and applications. PAMI 22(8), 781–796 (2000)
6. Dai, H., Zhang, P., Lueth, T.C.: Quantitative assessment of parkinsonian tremor based on an inertial measurement unit. Sensors 15(10), 25055–25071 (2015)
7. Davis, A., Bouman, K.L., Chen, J.G., Rubinstein, M., Durand, F., Freeman, W.T.: Visual vibrometry: estimating material properties from small motion in video. In: CVPR, pp. 5335–5343 (2015)
8. Elble, R.J., McNames, J.: Using portable transducers to measure tremor severity. Tremor Other Hyperkinetic Movements 6 (2016)
9. Elgharib, M., Hefeeda, M., Durand, F., Freeman, W.T.: Video magnification in presence of large motions. In: CVPR, pp. 4119–4127 (2015)
10. Fleet, D.J., Jepson, A.D.: Computation of component image velocity from local phase information. IJCV 5(1), 77–104 (1990)
11. Freeman, W.T., Adelson, E.H., et al.: The design and use of steerable filters. TPAMI 13(9), 891–906 (1991)
12. Goldenberg, R., Kimmel, R., Rivlin, E., Rudzsky, M.: Behavior classification by eigendecomposition of periodic motions. Pattern Recogn. 38(7), 1033–1043 (2005)
13. Hssayeni, M.D., Burack, M.A., Ghoraani, B.: Automatic assessment of medication states of patients with Parkinson's disease using wearable sensors. In: EMBC, pp. 6082–6085. IEEE (2016)
14. Jeon, H., et al.: Automatic classification of tremor severity in Parkinson's disease using a wearable device. Sensors 17(9), 2067 (2017)
15. Kayaba, H., Kokumai, Y.: Non-contact full field vibration measurement based on phase-shifting. In: CVPR, pp. 3655–3663 (2017)
16. Kooij, J.: SenseCap: synchronized data collection with Microsoft Kinect2 and Leap-Motion. In: ACMMM, pp. 1218–1221. ACM (2016)
17. Kooij, J.F.P., van Gemert, J.C.: Depth-aware motion magnification. In: Leibe, B., Matas, J., Sebe, N., Welling, M. (eds.) ECCV 2016. LNCS, vol. 9912, pp. 467–482. Springer, Cham (2016). https://doi.org/10.1007/978-3-319-46484-8_28
18. Levy, O., Wolf, L.: Live repetition counting. In: CVPR, pp. 3020–3028 (2015)
19. Lu, C., Ferrier, N.J.: Repetitive motion analysis: segmentation and event classification. PAMI 26(2), 258–263 (2004)

20. Pintea, S.L., van Gemert, J.C.: Making a case for learning motion representations with phase. In: Hua, G., Jégou, H. (eds.) ECCV 2016. LNCS, vol. 9915, pp. 55–64. Springer, Cham (2016). https://doi.org/10.1007/978-3-319-49409-8_8

21. Pishchulin, L., et al.: DeepCut: joint subset partition and labeling for multi person pose estimation. In: CVPR, pp. 4929–4937 (2016)

22. Polana, R., Nelson, R.C.: Detection and recognition of periodic, nonrigid motion. IJCV 23(3), 261–282 (1997)

23. Ramakrishna, V., Munoz, D., Hebert, M., Andrew Bagnell, J., Sheikh, Y.: Pose machines: articulated pose estimation via inference machines. In: Fleet, D., Pajdla, T., Schiele, B., Tuytelaars, T. (eds.) ECCV 2014. LNCS, vol. 8690, pp. 33–47. Springer, Cham (2014). https://doi.org/10.1007/978-3-319-10605-2_3

24. Ran, Y., Weiss, I., Zheng, Q., Davis, L.S.: Pedestrian detection via periodic motion analysis. IJCV 71(2), 143–160 (2007)

25. Ripin, Z.M., Chan, P.Y.: Pathological hand tremor measurement—challenges and advances. In: Ibrahim, F., Usman, J., Ahmad, M.Y., Hamzah, N., Teh, S.J. (eds.) ICIBEL 2017. IP, vol. 67, pp. 3–8. Springer, Singapore (2018). https://doi.org/10.1007/978-981-10-7554-4_1

26. Roy, K., Rao, G.S., Anouncia, S.M.: A learning based approach for tremor detection from videos. In: ICOS, pp. 71–76. IEEE (2013)

27. Runia, T.F., Snoek, C.G., Smeulders, A.W.: Real-world repetition estimation by Div, Grad and Curl. In: CVPR, pp. 9009–9017 (2018)

28. Soran, B., Hwang, J., Lee, S., Shapiro, L.: Tremor detection using motion filtering and SVM. In: ICPR, pp. 178–181 (2012)

29. Taewoong Um, T., et al.: Parkinson's Disease Assessment from a Wrist-Worn Wearable Sensor in Free-Living Conditions: Deep Ensemble Learning and Visualization. CoRR (2018)

30. Tralie, C.J., Perea, J.A.: (Quasi) periodicity quantification in video data, using topology. CoRR (2017)

31. Uhríková, Z., Růžička, E., Hlaváč, V., Nugent, C.D.: TremAn: a tool for measuring tremor frequency from video sequences. Mov. Disord. 25(4), 504–506 (2010)

32. Uhríková, Z., et al.: Validation of a new tool for automatic assessment of tremor frequency from video recordings. J. Neurosci. Methods 198(1), 110–113 (2011)

33. Victor, B., He, Z., Morgan, S., Miniutti, D.: Continuous video to simple signals for swimming stroke detection with convolutional neural networks. In: CVPR (2017)

34. Vidailhet, M., Roze, E., Jinnah, H.A.: A simple way to distinguish essential tremor from tremulous Parkinson's disease. Brain 140(7), 1820–1822 (2017)

35. Wadhwa, N., Rubinstein, M., Durand, F., Freeman, W.T.: Phase-based video motion processing. SIGRAPH 32(4), 80 (2013)

36. Wei, S., Ramakrishna, V., Kanade, T., Sheikh, Y.: Convolutional pose machines. In: CVPR, pp. 4724–4732 (2016)

37. Xia, L., Zou, B., Liu, H., Su, H., Qianghui, H.: A new method for evaluating postural hand tremor based on cmos camera. Optik-Int. J. Light Electron Optics 126(5), 507–512 (2015)

38. Zarchan, P., Musoff, H.: Fundamentals of Kalman Filtering: A Practical Approach (2013)

39. Zhang, Y., Pintea, S.L., van Gemert, J.C.: Video acceleration magnification. In: CVPR (2017)

DrawInAir: A Lightweight Gestural Interface Based on Fingertip Regression

Gaurav Garg$^{(\boxtimes)}$, Srinidhi Hegde, Ramakrishna Perla, Varun Jain,
Lovekesh Vig, and Ramya Hebbalaguppe

TCS Research, Gurgaon, India
{ga.gaurav,sri.hegde,r.perla,varun.in,lovekesh.vig,
ramya.hebbalaguppe}@tcs.com

Abstract. Hand gestures form a natural way of interaction on Head-Mounted Devices (HMDs) and smartphones. HMDs such as the Microsoft HoloLens and ARCore/ARKit platform enabled smartphones are expensive and are equipped with powerful processors and sensors such as multiple cameras, depth and IR sensors to process hand gestures. To enable mass market reach via inexpensive Augmented Reality (AR) headsets without built-in depth or IR sensors, we propose a real-time, in-air gestural framework that works on monocular RGB input, termed, *DrawInAir*. *DrawInAir* uses fingertip for writing in air analogous to a pen on paper. The major challenge in training egocentric gesture recognition models is in obtaining sufficient labeled data for end-to-end learning. Thus, we design a cascade of networks, consisting of a CNN with *differentiable spatial to numerical transform* (DSNT) layer, for fingertip regression, followed by a *Bidirectional Long Short-Term Memory* (Bi-LSTM), for a real-time pointing hand gesture classification. We highlight how a model, that is separately trained to regress fingertip in conjunction with a classifier trained on limited classification data, would perform better over *end-to-end* models. We also propose a dataset of 10 egocentric pointing gestures designed for AR applications for testing our model. We show that the framework takes 1.73 s to run end-to-end and has a low memory footprint of 14 MB while achieving an accuracy of 88.0% on egocentric video dataset.

Keywords: Egocentric gestures · Coordinate regression
Augmented reality

1 Introduction

Most popular interfaces in HMDs/Smartphones are speech and gestures. However, the accuracy of speech recognition tends to suffer in an industrial or an outdoor setting due to ambient noise [1]. To this end, gestural interfaces are

---

G. Garg, S. Hegde, R. Perla and V. Jain—Contributed equally.

© Springer Nature Switzerland AG 2019
L. Leal-Taixé and S. Roth (Eds.): ECCV 2018 Workshops, LNCS 11134, pp. 229–240, 2019.
https://doi.org/10.1007/978-3-030-11024-6_15

preferred in the areas of human-computer interaction and human-robot inter-action [1–3] as one does not require sophisticated skills to communicate, and they enable wider accessibility without bias on speech accents. However, real-time gesture tracking and recognition in First Person View (FPV) for wearable devices is still a challenging task (refer Fig. 1). Expensive AR devices such as the Microsoft *HoloLens*, *Daqri* and *Meta* Glasses are equipped with gestural interface powered by a variety of on-board sensors including a depth sensor and customized processors making the product expensive and unaffordable for mass adoption.

Fig. 1. Users performing egocentric *in-air* gestures in complex backgrounds such as outdoor environments, reflective backgrounds and different lighting conditions. Note: Variations in the speed of gestures and gesture trajectories between individuals are some of the issues that affect *in-air* hand gesture recognition [4].

In this paper we propose a novel gestural framework without the need of specialized hardware that would provide mass accessibility of gestural interfaces to the most affordable *video-see-through* HMDs such as *Wearality Sky* (50 USD) and *Google Cardboard*[1] (15 USD). These devices provide immersive AR experiences with the help of stereo rendering of the smartphone camera feed. The immediate applications are industrial inspection and repair, tele-presence, and FPV photography. *Google Cardboard* still employs primitive modes of user interaction, that is magnetic trigger and conductive lever, and any development is restricted to the hardware and sensors available on a smartphone. Hence, we aim to design pointing gesture based user interaction for frugal HMDs/smartphones.

3D CNNs and RNNs are found to be effective in analysis of egocentric gestures. However, these networks are highly reliant on the large scale video dataset and pixel-level depth information while training, often hindering real-time performance. In this work, we present a neural network architecture comprising of a base CNN and a *differentiable spatial to numerical transform* (DSNT) [18] layer followed by a Bidirectional Long Short-Term Memory (Bi-LSTM). The layer transforms the heatmap from CNN, that is rich in spatial information, to output spatial location of fingertip. The Bi-LSTM effectively captures the dynamic motion of user gesture that aids in classification. Feeding the fingertip keypoints to the Bi-LSTM, as opposed to traditional approaches of inputting

---

[1] https://vr.google.com/cardboard/.

featuremaps or images, reduces the computational cost in classification. Our key contributions are:

1. We propose *DrawInAir*, a neural network architecture, consisting of a base CNN and a DSNT network followed by a Bi-LSTM, for efficient classification of user gestures. It works in real-time, uses only RGB image sequence with no depth information, and can be ported on mobile devices due to low memory footprint.
2. *EgoGestAR*: a dataset of spatio-temporal sequences representing 10 gestures suitable for AR applications. We have published the dataset online at: https://github.com/varunj/EgoGestAR.

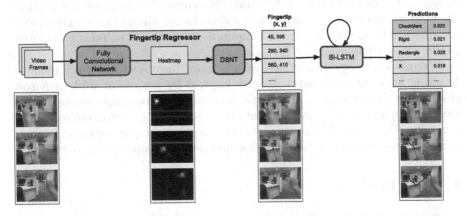

Fig. 2. *DrawInAir* framework. *DrawInAir* comprises a *Fingertip Regressor* module which accurately localizes the fingertip (the fingertip is analogous to a pen-tip in HCI) and a Bi-LSTM network is used for classification of fingertip detections on subsequent frames into different gestures (Images at the bottom show input/output at different stages).

2   Related Work

Despite being intuitive and natural, gestures are prone to inherent ambiguity which makes them a topic of interest to the research community [5]. Most of the early gesture recognition frameworks involve either (i) low-level image analysis such as detection of contours, texture, segmentation, histograms [6] or (ii) vision approaches such as feature extraction, object detection followed by tracking, and classification [7].

Recently using CNNs for object classification and detection has shown to give promising results. Huang *et al.* [8] proposed bi-level cascade CNNs approach for hand and key point detection in egocentric view using *HSV* color space information. Tompson *et al.* [9] proposed a pipeline for real-time pose recovery of human hands from a single depth image using a CNN. Coming to the gesture classification methods, in [10], Liu *et al.* presented two real-time third-person hand gesture recognition systems - (i) utilizing the stereo camera hardware setup with

DTW classifier and (ii) using dual-modality sensor fusion system with HMM classifier. Dardas *et al.* [11] presented a system for hand gesture recognition via bag-of-features and multi class Support Vector Machines (SVM). The Randomized Decision Forest classifier has also been explored for hand segmentation [9] and hand pose estimation [12]. Jain *et al.* [?] have shown the efficacy of using LSTM networks for the classification of 3-dimensional gestures.

In a recent work, Hegde *et al.* [1] discussed simple hand swipe gestures for Google Cardboard in egocentric view using GMM based modeling of skin pixel data. Further, this work was extended in [13] for accurate hand swipe classification. Implementing such ad-hoc recognizers is very challenging when the number and type of gestures increase. This is due to high inter class similarity among the gesture classes [14]. Unlike the works [15–17], which use RGB-D inputs to recognize multi pose gestures and occluding fingers in egocentric view, our proposed framework focuses on computationally efficient pointing pose-based gesture recognition using just RGB data.

In our work, we specifically deal with pointing finger gestures which requires detecting fingertip coordinates. We are inspired by the recent work of Nibali *et al.* [18] which proposed DSNT layer for numerical coordinate regression for estimating human body joints position. But they use a fully convolutional networks (FCN), a stacked hourglass network and other complex networks for generating heatmaps which makes their method slow in comparison to ours.

3   DrawInAir

A recent trend in the deep learning community has been to develop *end-to-end* models that learn several intermediate tasks simultaneously. While this has obvious benefits for learning joint tasks like object detection, regression and classification, it is reliant on the presence of sufficient labelled data to learn all the tasks in a pipeline.

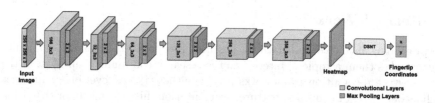

Fig. 3. Overview of our proposed *fingertip regressor* architecture for fingertip localization. The input to the network is $3 \times 256 \times 256$ sized RGB images. The network consists of 6 convolutional blocks, each with different convolutional layers followed by a max-pooling layer. Then we have a convolutional layer to output a heatmap which is input to DSNT. Finally, we get 2 coordinates denoting fingertip spatial location.

We, hence, propose a pointing hand gestural framework in egocentric view with limited labelled classification data. We focus on classifying the *point gesture* motion patterns into different gestures. Figure 2 shows the blocks which are: (a) *the Fingertip Regressor* that takes an RGB input image and accurately localizes the fingertip, (b) a Bi-LSTM network for classification of the fingertip detection on subsequent frames into different gestures.

We assume that the subjects are stationary while performing gestures to interact with the device. Slight errors introduced due to the head movement can be rectified by post-processing the *Fingertip Regressor* output and by the Bi-LSTM network used in classification. Bi-LSTM also has the ability to handle unexpected impulses/peaks arising in gesture pattern due to false detections or fingertip localizations for short duration.

3.1   Fingertip Regression

Estimating human pose by localizing human joints has been an important study in computer vision. Toshev *et al.* [19] propose *DeepPose*, which formulates the human pose estimation problem as a CNN based regression over body joints. In a similar context, we employ a CNN architecture followed by DSNT layer [18] (refer Fig. 3) for localizing fingertip by regressing over the coordinates, (x, y), of the fingertip.

Differentiable Spatial to Numerical Transform (DSNT): The proposed architecture consists of a CNN that produces a heatmap, Z, containing the spatial information of fingertip location. The heatmap is passed on to a *differentiable spatial to numerical transform* (DSNT) layer which transforms the heatmap to numerical coordinates of the fingertip location. The DSNT layer has no trainable parameters, preserves the differentiability and generalizes spatially, hence allowing the entire network to learn by back-propagation. DSNT normalizes the heatmap Z to $\hat{Z}$ such that all the elements of normalized heatmap are non-negative and sum to one. After normalization, the heatmap coordinates are scaled such that the top-left corner of the heatmap is at $(-1, -1)$ and bottom-right is at $(1, 1)$. This is followed by outputting the expected coordinates in the scaled coordinate system with normalized heatmap, $\hat{Z}$, as probability distribution map.

For training the network we use Euclidean loss as follows:

$$\mathcal{L}(\hat{Z}, p) = \|p - DSNT(\hat{Z})\|_2 + \lambda \mathcal{L}_{reg}(\hat{Z}) \tag{1}$$

where p is the ground truth coordinates and λ is a regularization constant. $DSNT(\hat{Z})$ is the expected scaled coordinates that is produced by the DSNT layer. Nibali *et al.* [18], suggest different regularizers, $\mathcal{L}_{reg}$, for training the network. We find that using Kullback-Leibler divergence (KLD) as regularizer gave us the best results. Thus, we have $\mathcal{L}_{reg}$ as follows:

$$\mathcal{L}_{reg}(\hat{Z}, p) = KLD(\hat{Z} \| \mathcal{N}(p, \sigma_t^2)) \tag{2}$$

where σ_t^2 is a variance hyper-parameter of a target normal distribution, $\mathcal{N}$. This regularizer encourages the heatmap to resemble a isotropic target Gaussian distribution.

3.2   Gesture Classification

The localization network discussed in the previous section outputs the spatial location of the fingertip (x, y), which is then fed as an input to our gesture classification network. Since we use the gestures that have only pointing fingers, the classification task reduces to analyzing the motion of the fingertip. Thus, we input (x, y) coordinate instead of the entire frame to the network. Motivated by the effectiveness of LSTMs [20] in learning long-term dependencies of sequential data [21], we employ a Bi-LSTM [22] network for the classification of gestures. We found that Bi-LSTM performs better than LSTM for classification as it processes the sequence in both forward and reverse direction.

We found the raw fingertip coordinates from the *fingertip regressor* to be noisy. This is due to the relative motion of head and hand of the user in an egocentric setting. Thus, we applied smoothing operation on the sequence of fingertip points as an egocentric correction measure (refer Fig. 4). We used Savitzky-Golay filter [23] on the fingertip sequence with window size of 15 and polynomial order 1 yielding the best classification accuracies on applying this filter. This filter operates by increasing the signal-to-noise ratio without greatly distorting the signal. The entire framework is also adaptable to videos/live feeds with variable length frame sequences. This is particularly important as the length of gestures depends on the user performing it.

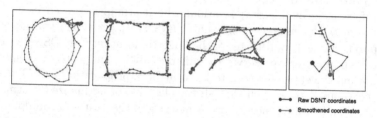

●—● Raw DSNT coordinates
●—● Smoothened coordinates

Fig. 4. Effect of smoothing for egocentric correction. (Left to right) Output of Savitzky-Golay filter [23] for samples of classes – Circle, Square, Star and Up respectively. The highlighted point in each gesture indicates the starting position of the gesture.

4   Datasets

4.1   Hand Dataset

We use the SCUT-Ego-Finger benchmark Dataset [8] for training the base CNN followed by DSNT layer model. Twenty four subjects in different environments (such as basketball field, canteen, teaching building, library, lake) contributed to the dataset to gather variations in illumination conditions, background and to address challenges such as variation in hand shape, hand color diversity, and motion blur. The dataset includes 93,729 frames with corresponding labels including hand candidate bounding boxes and index finger key point coordinates.

4.2   EgoGestAR Dataset

To train and evaluate the proposed Bi-LSTM architecture, we present *EgoGes-tAR*: a spatio-temporal sequence dataset for AR wearables. The dataset includes spatial patterns representing 10 gestures and inspired by industrial applications, we divided the gestures patterns primarily into 3 categories. (a) 4 swipe gesture patterns (*Up, Down, Left, and Right*) for navigating/selecting user preferences in AR HMDs. (b) 2 gesture patterns (*Rectangle and Circle*) for RoI highlighting in user's FoV for tele-support applications. (c) 4 gesture patterns (*Checkmark: Yes, Caret: No, X: Delete, Star: Bookmark*) for evidence capture in inspection, maintenance and repair applications.

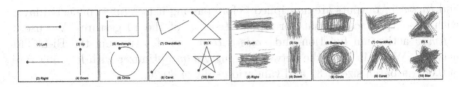

Fig. 5. EgoGestAR dataset: The first 3 columns show standard sequences shown to the users before the data collection and the last 3 columns (captured at a resolution of 640 × 480) depict the variations in the data samples. The highlighted point in each sequence indicates the starting position of the gesture.

We collected the data from 50 subjects in our research lab with ages in the range 21 to 50 with average age 27.8 years. The dataset consists of 2500 gesture patterns where each subject recorded 5 samples of each gesture. The gestures were recorded by mounting a 10.1 in. display HP Pro Tablet to a wall. The gesture pattern drawn by a user's index finger on a touch interface application with position sensing region was stored. The data was captured at a resolution of 640 × 480. Figure 5 describes the standard input sequences shown to the users before data collection and a sample subset of gestures from the dataset showing the variability introduced by the subjects. Detailed statistics of the EgoGestAR dataset is available at https://github.com/varunj/EgoGestAR.

5   Experiments and Results

Since the framework comprises of a cascade of two networks, we evaluate each network performance individually and then present the results of the entire pipeline. We use an 8 core Intel(R) Core(TM) i7-6820HQ CPU, 32 GB memory and an Nvidia Quadro M5000M GPU machine for experiments. The models are trained using Tensorflow v1.6.0.

5.1 Training

Fingertip Localization: We first train the *fingertip regressor* using the SCUT Ego-finger dataset (refer Sect. 4.1). Out of the 24 subjects in the dataset, we choose 17 subjects' data for training with a validation split of 70:30, and 7 subjects' data (24,155 images) for testing the networks. We use *Adam* optimizer with a learning rate of 6×10^{-5}. We set the hyper-parameters λ and σ_t to 1 and 4 respectively.

Classification: We then use *EgoGestAR* dataset (discussed in Sect. 3.2) for training and testing of the Bi-LSTM and also an LSTM network for classification. During training, we use 2000 gesture patterns in the training set. These patterns are fed as input to the *Bi-LSTM* layer consisting of 30 hidden units. The *forward* and *backward* outputs are multiplied before passing it to a fully connected layer with 10 output scores that correspond to each of the 10 gestures. We use a *softmax* activation function and *cross-entropy* loss for training the Bi-LSTM network. We train both the networks using *Adam* optimizer with learning rate of 0.001, a batch size of 32 and validation split of 80:20.

5.2 Performance Evaluation

Framework Evaluation: The average Euclidean loss in predicting the fingertip coordinates by the *fingertip regressor* is 1.147 on an input image of resolution 256×256. The mean absolute regression error is found to be 23.73 pixels for our approach. Table 1 presents comparison of the proposed LSTM and Bi-LSTM approach with DTW [10] and SVM [24]. We see that Bi-LSTM outperforms the

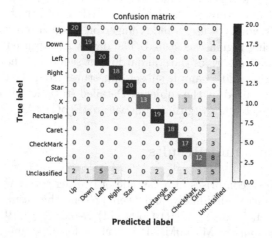

Fig. 6. The overall performance of our proposed framework on 240 egocentric videos (22 per class) captured using a smartphone based *Google Cardboard* head-mount. The gesture is detected when the predicted probability is more than 0.75. Accuracy of the model is 88%, ignoring unclassified class and 82.27% otherwise.

traditional approaches that are being used for similar classification tasks. Since the proposed approach is a series of different networks, the overall classification accuracy in real-time will vary depending on the performance of the earlier network used in the pipeline. Therefore, we evaluate the entire framework using 240 egocentric videos captured with a smartphone based Google Cardboard head-mount. Dataset and demos are available at https://ilab-ar.github.io/DrawInAir/. The overall framework achieved an accuracy of 88% on this dataset (as shown in Fig. 6).

Runtime and Memory Analysis: Table 2 shows the time profile of the proposed framework. The entire model has a very small memory footprint of 14 MB without compression and could be easily ported to mobile devices for testing.

Table 1. Performance of different classification methods on our proposed fingertip sequence dataset, EgoGestAR. Note that these results are observed on sequence data and not on hand gesture videos.

Method	Precision	Recall (Accuracy)	F_1 score
DTW [10]	0.763	0.749	0.756
SVM [24]	0.938	0.922	0.929
LSTM [20]	0.808	0.788	0.798
Bi-LSTM [22]	**0.967**	**0.966**	**0.966**

Table 2. Run-time analysis of different modules (with different inputs) of the framework. The input image resolution is 256×256 for the entire analysis. Note: the entire pipeline time is calculated starting from the first frame into the regressor to the prediction at the end of the entire video.

Module	Fingertip regressor (per frame)	Gesture classifier (per sequence)	Entire pipeline (per video)
Time (in s for unit input)	0.0096	0.0314	1.73

6 Discussion and Comparison

On deeper analysis, we observe that the *X (Del)* gesture is slightly correlated with the *CheckMark* since the difference in them is due to a triangle in the bottom of *X (Del)* gesture. Hence, due to variations in how users perform gestures and occlusion in users' hand, we observe a drop in their classification accuracies. Our framework is limited to a single finger in the user FoV and the accuracy drops if multiple fingers are present at roughly the same distance or on using any gesture different from pointing gesture. Figure 7 shows some cases, such as presence of multiple fingers (in case of reflection), where *DrawInAir* gives low accuracies. But our framework robustly detects and classifies fingertip of any of the fingers (even

238 G. Garg et al.

if the user is wearing nail paint or has minor finger injuries) provided it is the only finger in the user FoV. Our framework is also robust to variations in starting position of the gestures in frame, hand sizes and skin colors. The framework can accommodate a number of pointing gestures as per the requirements of FPV application, making it generic for all touch-less interaction systems.

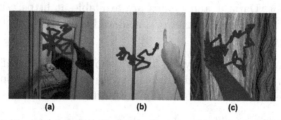

Fig. 7. Misclassified cases. Our framework fails to detect fingertip accurately in the cases of (a) reflective surfaces in the background, (b) near skin pixel background, and (c) very low illumination conditions.

Table 3. Analysis of gesture recognition accuracy and latency of various models against the proposed DrawInAir. We compared and evaluated all the end-to-end methods against ours on the 240 egocentric videos.

Method	Accuracy (%)	Time taken (in s)
Tsironi *et al.* [21]	32.14	0.76
VGG16 + LSTM [25]	58.37	**0.69**
C3D [26]	66.71	1.19
DrawInAir	**88.00**	1.73

We compared our framework against a few *end-to-end* baseline architectures used for video classification to highlight the importance of modular architectures, such as ours (see Table 3). We train these methods on our egocentric video dataset with a train, validation and test data split of 50:25:25. In [25], 2D CNNs are used to extract features of individual frames and then these frame-level features are encoded as video descriptors followed by training a classifier to predict the labels. Donahue *et al.* [26] use 3D CNNs to extract features of video clips. Then, clip features are aggregated into video descriptors for classifier training. As we can see, methods proposed by Tran *et al.* [25] and Donahue *et al.* [26] do not perform well as the data has high inter class similarity.

Tsironi *et al.* [21] propose *end-to-end* gesture classification method that works with differential image input to convolutional LSTMs. They use LSTMs to capture body parts motion involved in the gestures performed in second-person perspective. This method gave us a very low accuracy, even after fine-tuning the model on our egocentric video dataset. The possible reason for this behaviour could be that our data involved varying background and no static reference to the camera. Sharma *et al.* [27] propose attention based video classification that performed poorly owing to the high inter-class similarity which posed challenges in classification with the limited data available for *end-to-end* training. For such fine-grained classification tasks, we require features from a very small portion of the entire frame, that is, the fingertip location. In our scenario, since the fingertip location is known, training an attention model appears redundant.

7 Conclusion

We present an in-air gestural interface, *DrawInAir* to enable researchers to incorporate hand gestures in frugal HMDs. *DrawInAir* achieves an average accuracy of 88.0% when tested on EgoGestAR dataset. We have tested the two networks in the pipeline on an egocentric hand gesture video dataset to ensure robust fingertip detection and accurate gesture classification. The entire framework works just with monocular RGB data at real-time and can be used with frugal AR devices without any sensor fusion. Gestural interface with RGB data alone helps to facilitate mass market reach in frugal HMDs. Given that the model size is 14 MB, our framework is small enough to be ported on a resource constrained smartphone/HMD.

References

1. Hegde, S., Perla, R., Hebbalaguppe, R., Hassan, E.: Gestar: real time gesture interaction for AR with egocentric view. In: International Symposium on Mixed and Augmented Reality. IEEE (2016)
2. Hürst, W., Van Wezel, C.: Gesture-based interaction via finger tracking for mobile augmented reality. Multimed. Tools Appl. **62**(1), 233–258 (2013)
3. Waldherr, S., Romero, R., Thrun, S.: A gesture based interface for human-robot interaction. Auton. Robots **9**(2), 151–173 (2000)
4. Yang, C., Han, D.K., Ko, H.: Continuous hand gesture recognition based on trajectory shape information. Pattern Recogn. Lett. **99**(1), 39–47 (2017)
5. Wobbrock, J.O., Wilson, A.D., Li, Y.: Gestures without libraries, toolkits or training: a \$1 recognizer for user interface prototypes. In: Proceedings of the 20th Annual ACM Symposium on User Interface Software and Technology, pp. 159–168. ACM (2007)
6. Freeman, W.T.: Dynamic and static hand gesture recognition through low-level image analysis. US Patent 5,454,043, 26 Sept 1995
7. Liu, K., Kehtarnavaz, N.: Real-time robust vision-based hand gesture recognition using stereo images. J. Real-Time Image Process. **11**(1), 201–209 (2016)
8. Huang, Y., Liu, X., Jin, L., Zhang, X.: Deepfinger: a cascade convolutional neuron network approach to finger key point detection in egocentric vision with mobile camera. In: IEEE International Conference on Systems, Man, and Cybernetics (SMC), pp. 2944–2949. IEEE (2015)
9. Tompson, J., Stein, M., Lecun, Y., Perlin, K.: Real-time continuous pose recovery of human hands using convolutional networks. ACM Trans. Graph. (ToG) **33**(5), 169 (2014)
10. Liu, K., Kehtarnavaz, N., Carlsohn, M.: Comparison of two real-time hand gesture recognition systems involving stereo cameras, depth camera, and inertial sensor. In: SPIE Photonics Europe, International Society for Optics and Photonics, paper no. 91390C (2014)

11. Dardas, N.H., Georganas, N.D.: Real-time hand gesture detection and recognition using bag-of-features and support vector machine techniques. IEEE Trans. Instrum. Meas. **60**(11), 3592–3607 (2011)
12. Keskin, C., Kıraç, F., Kara, Y.E., Akarun, L.: Hand pose estimation and hand shape classification using multi-layered randomized decision forests. In: Fitzgibbon, A., Lazebnik, S., Perona, P., Sato, Y., Schmid, C. (eds.) ECCV 2012. LNCS, vol. 7577, pp. 852–863. Springer, Heidelberg (2012). https://doi.org/10.1007/978-3-642-33783-3_61
13. Mohatta, S., Perla, R., Gupta, G., Hassan, E., Hebbalaguppe, R.: Robust hand gestural interaction for smartphone based AR/VR applications. In: IEEE Winter Conference on Applications of Computer Vision (WACV), pp. 330–335. IEEE (2017)
14. Long Jr, A.C., Landay, J.A., Rowe, L.A.: Implications for a gesture design tool. In: Proceedings of the SIGCHI Conference on Human Factors in Computing Systems, pp. 40–47. ACM (1999)
15. Cao, C., Zhang, Y., Wu, Y., Lu, H., Cheng, J.: Egocentric gesture recognition using recurrent 3D convolutional neural networks with spatiotemporal transformer modules. In: The IEEE International Conference on Computer Vision (ICCV) (2017)
16. Sridhar, S., Oulasvirta, A., Theobalt, C.: Interactive markerless articulated hand motion tracking using RGB and depth data. In: Proceedings of the IEEE International Conference on Computer Vision, pp. 2456–2463 (2013)
17. Jang, Y., Noh, S.T., Chang, H.J., Kim, T.K., Woo, W.: 3D finger cape: clicking action and position estimation under self-occlusions in egocentric viewpoint. IEEE Trans. Visual. Comput. Graphics **21**(4), 501–510 (2015)
18. Nibali, A., He, Z., Morgan, S., Prendergast, L.: Numerical coordinate regression with convolutional neural networks. arXiv preprint arXiv:1801.07372 (2018)
19. Toshev, A., Szegedy, C.: DeepPose: human pose estimation via deep neural networks. In: Proceedings of the IEEE Conference on Computer Vision and Pattern Recognition, pp. 1653–1660 (2014)
20. Hochreiter, S., Schmidhuber, J.: Long short-term memory. Neural Comput. **9**(8), 1735–1780 (1997)
21. Tsironi, E., Barros, P., Wermter, S.: Gesture recognition with a convolutional long short-term memory recurrent neural network. In: Proceedings of the European Symposium on Artificial Neural Networks Computational Intelligence and Machine Learning (ESANN), pp. 213–218 (2016)
22. Graves, A., Schmidhuber, J.: Framewise phoneme classification with bidirectional LSTM and other neural network architectures. Neural Netw. **18**(5), 602–610 (2005)
23. Savitzky, A., Golay, M.J.: Smoothing and differentiation of data by simplified least squares procedures. Anal. Chem. **36**(8), 1627–1639 (1964)
24. Fan, R.E., Chang, K.W., Hsieh, C.J., Wang, X.R., Lin, C.J.: Liblinear: a library for large linear classification. J. Mach. Learn. Res. **9**(8), 1871–1874 (2008)
25. Donahue, J., et al.: Long-term recurrent convolutional networks for visual recognition and description. ArXiv e-prints arXiv:1411.4389, November 2014
26. Tran, D., Bourdev, L., Fergus, R., Torresani, L., Paluri, M.: Learning spatiotemporal features with 3D convolutional networks. ArXiv e-prints arXiv:1412.0767, December 2014
27. Sharma, S., Kiros, R., Salakhutdinov, R.: Action recognition using visual attention. ArXiv e-prints arXiv:1511.04119 (2015)

Adapting Egocentric Visual Hand Pose Estimation Towards a Robot-Controlled Exoskeleton

Gerald Baulig$^{(\boxtimes)}$, Thomas Gulde$^{(\boxtimes)}$, and Cristóbal Curio$^{(\boxtimes)}$

Computer Science, Reutlingen University, Reutlingen, Germany
{thomas.gulde,cristobal.curio}@reutlingen-university.de,
gerald.baulig@t-online.de
http://cogsys.reutlingen-university.de

Abstract. The basic idea behind a wearable robotic grasp assistance system is to support people that suffer from severe motor impairments in daily activities. Such a system needs to act mostly autonomously and according to the user's intent. Vision-based hand pose estimation could be an integral part of a larger control and assistance framework. In this paper we evaluate the performance of egocentric monocular hand pose estimation for a robot-controlled hand exoskeleton in a simulation. For hand pose estimation we adopt a Convolutional Neural Network (CNN). We train and evaluate this network with computer graphics, created by our own data generator. In order to guide further design decisions we focus in our experiments on two egocentric camera viewpoints tested on synthetic data with the help of a 3D-scanned hand model, with and without an exoskeleton attached to it. We observe that hand pose estimation with a wrist-mounted camera performs more accurate than with a head-mounted camera in the context of our simulation. Further, a grasp assistance system attached to the hand alters visual appearance and can improve hand pose estimation. Our experiment provides useful insights for the integration of sensors into a context sensitive analysis framework for intelligent assistance.

Keywords: Hand pose estimation · Egocentric view
Grasp assistance · Simulation

1 Introduction

Neurorobotics is a promising field to potentially support patients suffering from debilitating conditions, e.g. stroke, and allow them to regain motoric functions. (Fig. 1). Soekadar *et al.* [23] present an exoskeleton-based robotic system to support and treat patients suffering from motor impairments based on electroencephalography (EEG) and electrooculography (EOG) input. The concept is extendable to integrate intelligent sensors that perceive and understand the scene and can potentially increase the usability of such or similar systems for

© Springer Nature Switzerland AG 2019
L. Leal-Taixé and S. Roth (Eds.): ECCV 2018 Workshops, LNCS 11134, pp. 241–256, 2019.
https://doi.org/10.1007/978-3-030-11024-6_16

daily life usage. Such an approach would understand the context of the grasp interaction and the user's intention for a more autonomous assistance, since the interpretation of user input, solely based on EEG or EOG, might be prone to error. A computer vision based control instance could provide valuable input to support the decision whether the hand is or should be in a certain state. Therefore an autonomous grasp assistance could profit from hand pose estimation to control the grasping process and intervene, if necessary, to reach a certain goal. Parts of a grasp interaction are the exoskeleton, graspable objects as well as the bare hand. The development of a perception system would need to consider challenges like the estimation of the pose of the exoskeleton, the pose of the bare hand, the shape and pose of the graspable object as well as the classification of the interaction as input for a higher-level micro-controller.

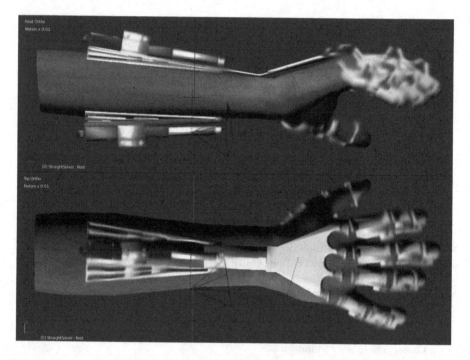

Fig. 1. Design of an exoskeleton prototype for grasp assistance simulated on our 3D hand scan model.

In this paper we focus on comparing hand pose estimation with and without an exoskeleton covering the hand and take a closer look at appropriate camera setups for further design decisions of the overall exoskeleton system. Thus our guiding questions are how does a computer vision based hand pose estimation perform on our exoskeleton and what are appropriate egocentric viewpoints for the camera sensors? Since the prototype is not available yet, we run a closed test scenario with our 3D test framework. Here we demonstrate our test framework

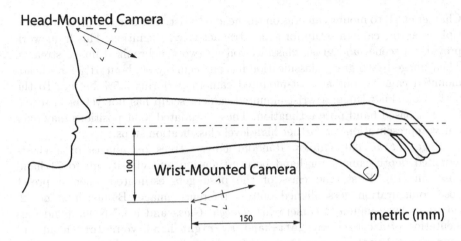

Fig. 2. The two camera setups we demonstrate and evaluate in a closed test scenario.

with the evaluation of two egocentric sensor viewpoint positions, on the forehead and on the wrist (Fig. 2). We present a closed test framework to compare several setups and scenarios to aid further design decisions for the exoskeleton. Although explicit knowledge about the actuator state of an exoskeleton may support the estimation accuracy, this closed test framework is focusing on a solution with computer vision based on deep learning only. We want to point out that our test framework is based on an established method for hand pose estimation. The system can support studying generalization from synthetic data to real scenarios in the wild.

The paper is structured as follows. In Sect. 3.1 we illustrate our own synthetic data generator to create data for monocular hand pose estimation especially in the context of a wearable exoskeleton allowing for flexible egocentric sensor viewpoint selection. For the hand pose estimation we employ an approach based on Convolutional Neural Networks (CNN) as described in Sect. 3.2. In Sect. 4 we train and evaluate our network with the produced simulated data. Further, in Sect. 5, we compare the accuracy of pose estimation between a head- versus wrist-mounted camera with the two conditions of a bare hand versus a hand covered by an exoskeleton. Based on a quantitative evaluation and the illustration of qualitative examples of our own and others' datasets we discuss our camera setups in Sect. 6. We conclude in Sect. 7 and outline potential next steps.

2   Related Work

Hand pose estimation is a very active field of research, documented in reviews like [3,8,17]. Primarily, recent research has focused on joint-based hand pose estimation, as listed in Chen *et al.* project [5]. Only few works pursue an approach based on egocentric perception viewpoint. We adopt the idea of

Chan *et al.* [4] to mount cameras on the head or wrist. The authors present a multiple wearable camera setup for egocentric activity recognition. This framework provides a scene- and grasp classification on two synchronized image streams. Their image-based grasp classification has an accuracy of about 51% for a head-mounted camera, but a wrist-mounted camera performs 5.5% better. To the best of our knowledge, a wrist-mounted camera setup has not yet been tested for joint-based hand pose estimation. These estimated joint positions may offer a new representation for further high-level classification steps.

Rogez *et al.* [20] employ Random Forest Trees on images of a chest-mounted depth-camera for hand pose estimation and classify up to 71 hand poses in [19]. First, the class of the pose gets estimated, then a preset pose configuration gets aligned onto a reference image. Bambach *et al.* [2] employ a head-mounted camera like *Google Glass* and a CNN for hand segmentation of 4 classes (my-left-hand, my-right-hand, your-left-hand and your-right-hand). Their dataset *EgoHands* provides scenes of two persons sitting in front of each other and playing cards or other games. Mueller *et al.* [16] employ chest- or rather shoulder-mounted depth-cameras and two derivations of *ResNet50* [10] to first detect the hand and then estimate the joint positions. After the joints are estimated, a kinematic model is aligned to these points. Their dataset *EgoDexter* provides annotations for visible fingertips only.

Maekawa *et al.* [14] employ sensor fusion of a wrist-mounted camera, microphone, accelerometer, illuminometer and magnetometer to classify with a hidden Markov model the activity of the hand, but do not focus on estimation of its pose. A wrist-mounted setup with pose-estimation is presented by Kim *et al.* [13]. They employ an infrared (IR)-camera combined with IR-laser. The IR-laser generates a kind of structured light as a line crossing the proximal bones of the hand. Those handcrafted features and the depth estimation of the fingertips are used to estimate the pose of the forward kinematic chain of each finger relative to the calibrated camera.

In this paper we want to evaluate the performance of a state-of-the-art CNN-based hand pose estimation method for wrist-mounted RGB-camera images compared to head-mounted RGB-camera images.

3   Methods

Even though a wearable data glove, potentially integrated into an exoskeleton and its actuator system, might provide a valuable hand pose estimation [6,24,27], the information would not be context sensitive. A thorough computer vision approach may offer a rich overall scene analysis that includes the state of graspable objects, bare hands and of an exoskeleton. Further, the available space to mount sensors on an exoskeleton is rather limited.

For our computer vision based hand pose estimation we investigate a staged CNN approach [25]. This kind of 2D joint estimation has already been used in several other approaches of pose estimation [12,22]. We train this CNN with synthetic data, similar to datasets like *SynthHands* [16] or *Rendered Handpose*

Dataset (RHD) [28]. However, since no data generator is available that enables to integrate an exoskeleton or to test different camera angles, we created our own data generator.

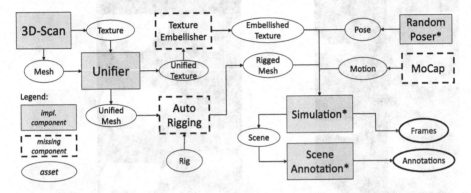

Fig. 3. Composition diagram of synthetic data generator. Components signified by * are implemented in *Blender*.

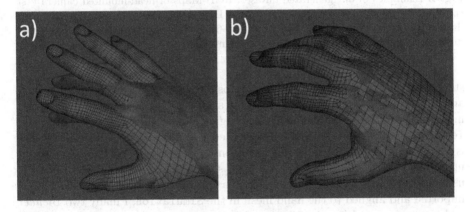

Fig. 4. Generalization of scanned meshes. (a) Base mesh (*blue*) aligned to the scanned mesh. (b) Base mesh wrapped around the scanned mesh. (Color figure online)

3.1 Synthetic Data Generator

Figure 3 shows the composition of our data generator. First a 3D scan of a real hand is made with the *Artec 3D Eva*[1], a hand-held 3D scanner based on structured light. The scanner produces mesh and texture at the same time. Then *Wrap3.3*[2] is used as a `Unifier` to generalize the scanned mesh to a well

---

[1] https://www.artec3d.com/de/portable-3D-scanners/artec-eva.

[2] http://www.russian3dscanner.com/.

Fig. 5. Examples of our generated dataset. RGB-Maps of head-mounted camera (1st column), Segmentation-Map (column 2) and Depth-Map (column 3). Corresponding data for the wrist-mounted camera (columns 4–6). Details of the exoskeleton are blurred due to proprietary reasons at the time of submission.

structured and rigged mesh. *Wrap3.3* wraps a well-structured base mesh around an unstructured scanned mesh (Fig. 4), as such the output is a new generalized mesh, easier to use for further steps, i.e. rigging and texturing. `AutoRigging` and `TextureEmbelishment` are not implemented yet. Editing textures and meshes is a laborious manual process. Therefore only one mesh and texture set is used up to now. For the `Simulation`, the open source 3D creation suite *Blender*[3] is used similar to [18,28]. An early version of a CAD prototype of the exoskeleton is imported and aligned to the hand mesh in the `Simulation`. Finally two *Blender* add-ons are scripted (`RandomPoser` and `SceneAnnotation`). A main script loads and triggers these add-ons. It also manages the render process and randomizes the background, camera positions and light conditions.

The add-on `RandomPoser` performs pseudo random poses by applying random transformations along the kinematic chain. Our hand model has 17 bones (Fig. 6). The Degrees of Freedom (DoF) of the hand model have been put under virtual constraints to simulate articulated hand configurations by considering natural constraints and limits of collisions and rotations, as suggested by *Dhaiba-Hand* and inspired by Jorg *et al.*

The add-on `SceneAnnotation` stores all relevant information about the rendered scene in an XML-file. With our data generator we are able to produce

---

[3] https://www.blender.org/.

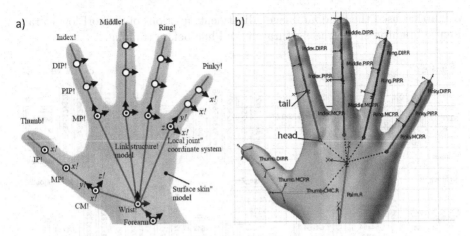

Fig. 6. Hand model of the simulation. (a) The DoF of *DhaibaHand* [7]. (b) Our hand model in *Blender*, each bone with head and tail vertex.

vast amounts of data automatically. Up to this point the following data has been extracted from a head- and wrist-mounted camera setup:

- **RGB-Map:** The reference image of visible light, with a resolution of $512 * 512$ and 24-bit PNG encoding. For background the indoor images of NYU Depth V1 dataset are used [21].
- **Depth-Map:** An 8-bit PNG gray scaled image of depth information. For the head camera viewpoint the first 100 cm are linearly quantized and for the wrist viewpoint the first 50 cm are quantized.
- **Segmentation-Map:** A 24-bit PNG encoded image where each part has its own color code.
- **Annotation:** An XML-file with coordinates of each component in world space (as $4 * 4$ *matrix*), in camera space and relative to the image plane (as *vertex*).

Each bone of our hand model is defined via two *vertices* (head and tail), 21 of them are used as keypoints. A *vertex* is a tuple represented as

$$vertex : (name, x, y, z, r, c, u, v, d), \tag{1}$$

which is parameterized as follows:

- *name* denotes if the *vertex* is head or tail of the bone.
- x, y, z are the relative coordinates in camera space with origin at the center of the camera.
- r, c are the pixel-based 2D coordinates on the image plane ($row, column$) with the origin being the upper-left corner.
- u, v are the normalized 2D coordinates on the image plane with the origin being the lower-left corner.
- d is the depth value relative to the image plane.

We further used the random image adjustment functions of TensorFlow to randomize brightness, contrast, saturation and hue before training.

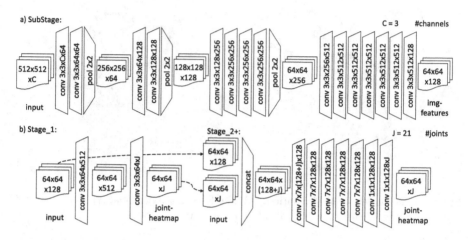

Fig. 7. Hand Pose Estimation with staged approach. (a) Shows the layers of SubStage for image feature extraction. (b) Shows the staged approach of [25], whereby img-features and joint-heatmap get concatenated for the subsequent stage.

3.2 Pose Estimation Model

For the pose estimation a *TensorFlow* [1] version of Wei's *et al.* [25] CNN approach is used, adapted by Ho *et al.* [11]. The input layer is increased to $512 * 512 * 3$, since we used a GeForce GTX 1080 Ti with enough storage. Our hand model has 21 joints (including 5 fingertips), therefore the output is a heatmap of 21 channels of size $64 * 64$. Our model has one SubStage for extracting image features and six stages for pose estimation as recommended by Wei *et al.* [25]. Except for the first stage, each stage uses the concatenated image features and the heatmap of the previous stage as input (Fig. 7). As such, the output of each heatmap gets refined in a feed-forward approach. This enables the machine to learn filters to verify the spatial context between the estimated keypoints provided in the heatmap of the previous stage.

4 Experiment

The data generator is used to create 4,000 samples with bare hands and 4,000 samples with an exoskeleton. Both contain images of head- and wrist-mounted cameras (Fig. 5). For each of the $i : (1 \ldots 21)$ joints a Gaussian map is created pixel-wise (m, n) with a radius of $r = 3$ at the joint position (x, y) stacked to a ground truth heatmap G of 21 $64 * 64$ channels and stored into a TensorFlow-Record together with the RGB reference image:

$$G_{mni} = exp\left(- \left((m - x_i)^2 + (n - y_i)^2\right) \frac{1}{2r^2} \right) \qquad (2)$$

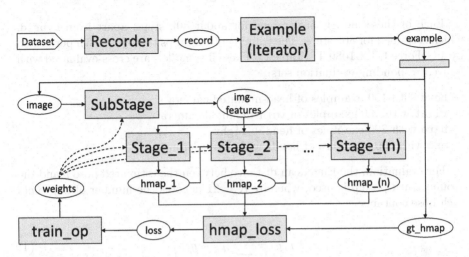

Fig. 8. Composite diagram of our CNN for hand pose estimation, inspired by Wei et al. [25], adapted by Ho *et al.* [11].

Table 1. Training 5 different models to compare head vs. wrist mounted cameras and bare hand vs. exoskeleton.

Model	Domain	Examples	Epochs	Steps	Time
Head	HeadCam	2,000	20	40,000	3.3 h
Right	RightCam	2,000	20	40,000	3.3 h
Bare	HeadCam + RightCam	4,000	10	40,000	3.3 h
Exo	Exoskeleton (Head + Right)	4,000	10	40,000	3.3 h
Hybrid	Bare + exo	8,000	10	80,000	6.6 h

For training (Fig. 8) the total difference between the estimated heatmaps H of all $K = 6$ stages and the ground truth heatmap G is used as a cost function:

$$hmap\_loss(H, G) = \sum_{k=1}^{K} |H_k - G| \tag{3}$$

For evaluating the two camera setups and the domain of the hand with and without the exoskeleton, five models have been trained:

- **head:** Trained on images of bare hands observed from head-mounted camera
- **right:** Trained on images of bare hands observed from right wrist-mounted camera
- **bare:** Trained on images of **head + right**
- **exo:** Trained on images of hands with exoskeleton from head- and wrist-mounted camera
- **hybrid:** Trained on images of bare hands and hands with exoskeleton (**bare + exo**).

Each of these models are trained for about 40k steps, apart from hybrid, which is trained for 80k steps. The training of 40k steps takes just 3.3 h performed by a GeForce GTX 1080 Ti (Table 1). These five models are cross-evaluated with four corresponding evaluation sets:

- head with 100 examples of head-mounted camera
- right with 100 examples of wrist-mounted camera
- bare with 200 examples of head + right
- exo with 200 examples of hands with exoskeleton.

For evaluation, the Euclidean distance between the estimated pose p and the ground truth pose g is used, whereby $K = 21$ denotes the number of keypoints each pose contains:

$$D(p, g) = \sum_{k=1}^{K} \|p_k - g_k\|_2 \tag{4}$$

Based on this error measure we test the performance of pose estimation on images of a head- versus a wrist-mounted camera and bare hand versus hands with exoskeleton. For comparison, the Percentage Correct Keypoints (PCK) [26] metric is used as in [12, 22, 25]. Though we do not normalize the PCK to the hand size, we normalize to the image aspect instead. So we do not give an extra penalty on small hands with lower resolution, just because they are more far from the image plane. Otherwise the evaluation set head would not be competitive with the evaluation set right. Since the image plane always has an aspect of $512 * 512$ pixels, an inaccuracy of 0.1 represents an error of 51.2 pixels.

5   Results

The y-axis of the PCK graphs (Figs. 9 and 10) show the percentage of examples that get estimated to an accepted accuracy, given as an increasing threshold on the x-axis. The accuracy is the total Euclidean distance of all keypoints normalized to the image aspect. Each line represents a model applied on an evaluation set. The earlier the line rises up to 100% the better the model performs on the evaluation set.

In Fig. 9, the PCK graphs of head- versus wrist-mounted cameras are shown. For qualitative examples, compare Fig. 11(a) with (b). The evaluations head-on-right and right-on-head have low accuracy, because the model head has never seen examples of the domain right before and vice versa. Both these evaluations act as control groups to prove that head and right are actually in a separate domain. A noteworthy observation is that right-on-right perform much better than head-on-head. This leads us to the point that hand pose estimation with our CNN performs better on wrist-mounted cameras than on head-mounted cameras. The model bare shows a clear tradeoff between both domains.

In Fig. 10, the PCK graphs of bare hands versus hands with exoskeleton are shown. For qualitative examples, compare Fig. 11 (a,b) with (c,d). The control

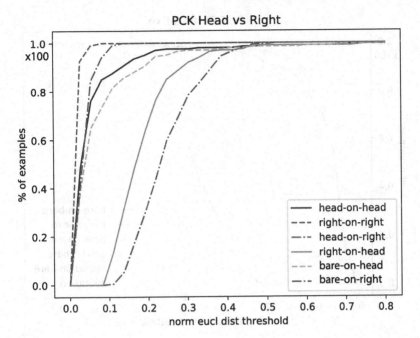

Fig. 9. Evaluation of Head versus Right. Each line describes a trained model applied on an evaluation set. *head-on-head*: A model trained and applied on head-mounted camera images. *right-on-right*: A model trained and applied on wrist-mounted camera images of the right hand. *head-on-right*: A model trained on head but applied on right wrist. *right-on-head*: Vice versa of *head-on-right*. *bare-on-head*: A model trained on both setups, but applied to head only. *bare-on-right*: A model trained on both setups, but applied to the right wrist.

groups `exo-on-bare` and `bare-on-exo` perform relatively poorly. Therefore the appearance of the exoskeleton dominates the bare hand domain. The observation in `exo-on-exo` is that the appearance of the exoskeleton condition leads to a slightly better pose estimation than bare hands do. We assume that the visual features of the exoskeleton are more significant, easier to detect and thus enhance the recognizability of the hand. Furthermore, the model `hybrid` also performs well on `exo`, with just a small reduction on `bare`. With this we conclude that a `hybrid` model with an extended training session may work well in the overall project application. In summary, we are able to estimate poses of the exoskeleton and of bare hands from head-mounted and wrist-mounted cameras within the context of our simulation, whereas the wrist-mounted camera performs better with respect to the metric presented above.

6 Discussion

Although the occlusion of the fingers on wrist-mounted camera images might be more severe, it does not seem to drastically affect the pose estimation. Interestingly, Chan et al. [4] have already shown that for the task of grasp classification

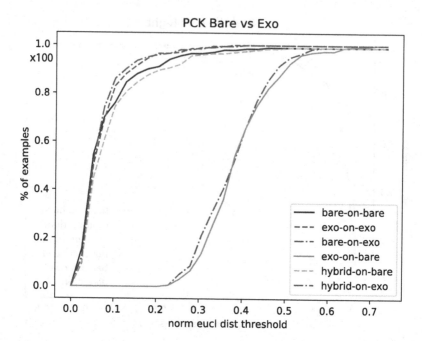

Fig. 10. Evaluation of Bare versus Exo. Each line describes a trained model applied on an evaluation set. *bare-on-bare*: A model trained and applied on images of bare hands. *exo-on-exo*: A model trained and applied on images of hands with exoskeleton. *bare-on-exo*: A model trained on bare hands, but applied to exoskeleton images. *exo-on-bare* vice versa of *bare-on-exo*. *hybrid-on-bare*: A model trained on both domains, but applied on bare hands only. *hybrid-on-exo*: A model trained on both domains, but applied to exoskeleton images only.

from a wrist-mounted camera, the performance is slightly better than from a head-mounted camera. In our evaluation we observed that the hand pose estimation performs significantly better on wrist-mounted cameras.

In addition to the technical challenges of hand pose estimation from an egocentric viewpoint we discuss some subjective issues of the camera setups. During lab testing and on qualitative examples from other datasets we developed an impression of the usability and some of its attributes. We extend the discussion here with insights from chest-mounted camera setups. Chest-mounted cameras are used in *EgoDexter* [16], *UCI-EGO* [20] and *GUN71* [19]. Head- or chest-mounted cameras have an aesthetic issue, because the user could feel uncomfortable with the camera at these positions. To wear a camera on the head might be more uncomfortable than on the chest. If miniaturized, chest cameras could be integrated into textiles. The dataset *EgoHands* [2] qualitatively demonstrates the shortcoming of head-mounted cameras. Obviously the user has to put the hands into the Field of View (FoV) towards a grasp goal during a potential application, such that all relevant scene elements can be observed from the camera. However, we recognize in datasets like *EgoHands* and in a self test that the

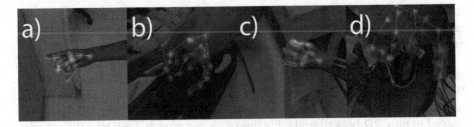

Fig. 11. Qualitative examples of pose estimation. The dots are from the heatmap as estimated, the lines connect the maxima of the heatmap by given topology: (a) Head-mounted camera on bare hand, (b) wrist-mounted camera on bare hand, (c) head-mounted camera on exoskeleton and (d) wrist-mounted camera on exoskeleton. Details of the exoskeleton are blurred due to proprietary reasons at the time of submission.

hand often disappears beyond the bottom image edge. Usually the user mainly fixates with his eyes and avoids to move his whole head. We assume that this behavior might be intensified by wearing a sensor on the head. Thus a user would need to get used to the setup and needs to learn to look straight and actively keep track of his interaction zone. Nevertheless, it might be more intuitive than a wrist- or chest-mounted camera. Yet, in such setups the user has less control of the camera's FoV. As long as a display of the camera is not present, the user will not be able to relate to what the camera might see or not. In the case of the wrist-mounted camera setup it is ensured that it will fixate the wearing hand, but the graspable object and the other hand might not always be in the FoV. The dataset *EgoDexter* [16] contains many examples in which the hand is beyond the FoV of the camera. Nevertheless, the workspace of the chest-mounted camera is much easier to analyze because the observation space is relatively stationary in front of the user, whereas the head- or wrist-mounted camera could move quite freely.

Before we can make further design decisions the different camera setups should be evaluated with subjects. Especially the user acceptance of aesthetic and comfort should be investigated. As a result of this paper the wrist-mounted camera setup has promising properties and should be tested in further scenarios of the wearable robotic grasp assistance application.

7   Conclusions

In this paper we presented a customizable data generator with *Blender* and used the approach of a staged CNN to evaluate the performance of hand pose estimation for egocentric viewpoints. The data generator is able to include a wearable exoskeleton making it unique in the field of hand simulation frameworks. We observed in our simulation that hand pose estimation on wrist-mounted camera images performs significantly better than on head-mounted camera images in terms of PCK scores. Furthermore we observe that our exoskeleton defines a new domain of appearance by covering large portions of the assisted hand.

Remarkably, the selected CNN approach seems to be powerful enough to learn and handle all domains captured from head- and wrist-mounted cameras with exoskeleton and bare hands in one hybrid model.

In the future we plan to classify all joints with fully-connected layers to a set of grasp poses and compare this approach with other grasp pose classifiers. We plan to extend our data generator in several aspects based on further assets, i.e. including more meshes, more textures, improved shaders and full 3D scenes instead of only 2D backgrounds. Furthermore, we want to look into the transfer of synthetic simulations to real data, e.g. with a Generative Adversarial Network (GAN) [9] as pursued for example in [15]. Instead of enhancing synthetic data to a natural look, it might be easier to downgrade real data to a synthetic look, or rather a generalization in between these conditions could be feasible.

However, we will also generate real data. We currently develop a setup for tracking hands in a motion capture laboratory with a marker-based system and synchronized sensors. In further studies, the influence of a real exoskeleton prototype will be investigated in comparison to simulated prototypes.

Acknowledgements. We gratefully acknowledge the Baden-Württemberg Foundation for supporting KONSENS-NHE (NEU007/3) in the program neurorobotics as well as the Federal Ministry of Education and Research (BMBF) for funding the projects MoCap 4.0 (03FH015IN6) and KollRo 4.0 (13FH049PX5). The exoskeleton CAD model prototype was kindly provided by Jonathan Eckstein from the University of Stuttgart.

References

1. Abadi, M., et al.: TensorFlow: a system for large-scale machine learning. CoRR abs/1605.08695 (2016). http://arxiv.org/abs/1605.08695
2. Bambach, S., Lee, S., Crandall, D.J., Yu, C.: Lending a hand: detecting hands and recognizing activities in complex egocentric interactions. In: The IEEE International Conference on Computer Vision (ICCV), December 2015
3. Barsoum, E.: Articulated hand pose estimation review. CoRR abs/1604.06195 (2016). http://arxiv.org/abs/1604.06195
4. Chan, C., Chen, S., Xie, P., Chang, C., Sun, M.: Recognition from hand cameras. CoRR abs/1512.01881 (2015). http://arxiv.org/abs/1512.01881
5. Chen, X.: Awesome work on hand pose estimation. GitHub (2018). https://github.com/xinghaochen/awesome-hand-pose-estimation
6. Dipietro, L., Sabatini, A.M., Dario, P.: A survey of glove-based systems and their applications. IEEE Trans. Syst. Man, Cybern. Part C Appl. Rev. **38**(4), 461–482 (2008). https://doi.org/10.1109/TSMCC.2008.923862
7. Endo, Y., Tada, M., Mochimaru, M.: Reconstructing individual hand models from motion capture data. J. Comput. Des. Eng. **1**(1), 1–12 (2014). https://doi.org/10.7315/JCDE.2014.001. http://www.sciencedirect.com/science/article/pii/S2288430014500012
8. Erol, A., Bebis, G., Nicolescu, M., Boyle, R.D., Twombly, X.: Vision-based hand pose estimation: a review. Comput. Vis. Image Underst. **108**(1), 52–73 (2007). https://doi.org/10.1016/j.cviu.2006.10.012. http://www.sciencedirect.com/science/article/pii/S1077314206002281, special Issue on Vision for Human-Computer Interaction

9. Goodfellow, I., et al.: Generative adversarial nets. In: Ghahramani, Z., Welling, M., Cortes, C., Lawrence, N.D., Weinberger, K.Q. (eds.) Advances in Neural Information Processing Systems, vol. 27, pp. 2672–2680. Curran Associates, Inc. (2014). http://papers.nips.cc/paper/5423-generative-adversarial-nets.pdf

10. He, K., Zhang, X., Ren, S., Sun, J.: Deep residual learning for image recognition. CoRR abs/1512.03385 (2015). http://arxiv.org/abs/1512.03385

11. Ho, T.: Convolutional pose machines - tensorflow. GitHub (2018). https://github.com/timctho/convolutional-pose-machines-tensorflow

12. Iqbal, U., Molchanov, P., Breuel, T., Gall, J., Kautz, J.: Hand pose estimation via latent 2.5d heatmap regression. CoRR abs/1804.09534 (2018). http://arxiv.org/abs/1804.09534

13. Kim, D., et al.: Digits: freehand 3D interactions anywhere using a wrist-worn gloveless sensor. In: Proceedings of the 25th Annual ACM Symposium on User Interface Software and Technology, UIST 2012, pp. 167–176. ACM, New York (2012). https://doi.org/10.1145/2380116.2380139

14. Maekawa, T., et al.: Object-based activity recognition with heterogeneous sensors on wrist. In: Floréen, P., Krüger, A., Spasojevic, M. (eds.) Pervasive 2010. LNCS, vol. 6030, pp. 246–264. Springer, Heidelberg (2010). https://doi.org/10.1007/978-3-642-12654-3_15

15. Mueller, F., et al.: Ganerated hands for real-time 3D hand tracking from monocular RGB. CoRR abs/1712.01057 (2017). http://arxiv.org/abs/1712.01057

16. Mueller, F., Mehta, D., Sotnychenko, O., Sridhar, S., Casas, D., Theobalt, C.: Real-time hand tracking under occlusion from an egocentric RGB-D sensor. In: Proceedings of International Conference on Computer Vision (ICCV), October 2017. http://handtracker.mpi-inf.mpg.de/projects/OccludedHands/

17. Pisharady, P., Saerbeck, M.: Recent methods and databases in vision-based hand gesture recognition: a review. Comput. Vis. Image Underst. 141, 152–165 (2015)

18. Rajpura, P.S., Hegde, R.S., Bojinov, H.: Object detection using deep CNNs trained on synthetic images. CoRR abs/1706.06782 (2017). http://arxiv.org/abs/1706.06782

19. Rogez, G., Supancic, J.S., Ramanan, D.: Understanding everyday hands in action from RGB-D images. In: 2015 IEEE International Conference on Computer Vision (ICCV), pp. 3889–3897, December 2015. https://doi.org/10.1109/ICCV.2015.443

20. Rogez, G., Supancic III, J.S., Khademi, M., Montiel, J.M.M., Ramanan, D.: 3D hand pose detection in egocentric RGB-D images. CoRR abs/1412.0065 (2014). http://arxiv.org/abs/1412.0065

21. Silberman, N., Fergus, R.: Indoor scene segmentation using a structured light sensor. In: Proceedings of the International Conference on Computer Vision - Workshop on 3D Representation and Recognition (2011)

22. Simon, T., Joo, H., Matthews, I.A., Sheikh, Y.: Hand keypoint detection in single images using multiview bootstrapping. CoRR abs/1704.07809 (2017). http://arxiv.org/abs/1704.07809

23. Soekadar, S.R., et al.: Hybrid EEG/EOG-based brain/neural hand exoskeleton restores fully independent daily living activities after quadriplegia. Sci. Robot. 1(1), eaag3296 (2016). https://doi.org/10.1126/scirobotics.aag3296, http://robotics.sciencemag.org/content/1/1/eaag3296

24. Sturman, D.J., Zeltzer, D.: A survey of glove-based input. IEEE Comput. Graph. Appl. 14(1), 30–39 (1994). https://doi.org/10.1109/38.250916

25. Wei, S., Ramakrishna, V., Kanade, T., Sheikh, Y.: Convolutional pose machines. CoRR abs/1602.00134 (2016). http://arxiv.org/abs/1602.00134

26. Yang, Y., Ramanan, D.: Articulated human detection with flexible mixtures of parts. IEEE Trans. Pattern Anal. Mach. Intell. **35**(12), 2878–2890 (2013). https://doi.org/10.1109/TPAMI.2012.261
27. Zhang, X., Chen, X., Li, Y., Lantz, V., Wang, K., Yang, J.: A framework for hand gesture recognition based on accelerometer and EMG sensors. IEEE Trans. Syst. Man Cybern. Part A Syst. Humans **41**(6), 1064–1076 (2011). https://doi.org/10.1109/TSMCA.2011.2116004
28. Zimmermann, C., Brox, T.: Learning to estimate 3D hand pose from single RGB images. CoRR abs/1705.01389 (2017). http://arxiv.org/abs/1705.01389

Estimating 2D Multi-hand Poses
from Single Depth Images

Le Duan[1]([✉]), Minmin Shen[1,3P], Song Cui[2,4P], Zhexiao Guo[1],
and Oliver Deussen[1]

[1] INCIDE Center, University of Konstanz, Konstanz, Germany
{duan.le,zhexiao.guo,oliver.deussen}@uni-konstanz.de,
mmshenntu@gmail.com
[2] Institute of High Performance Computing, Singapore, Singapore
songcui@acm.org
[3] Amazon Alexa, San Jose, USA
[4] Cisco Systems, San Jose, USA

Abstract. We present a novel framework based on Pictorial Structure
(PS) models to estimate 2D multi-hand poses from depth images. Most
existing single-hand pose estimation algorithms are either subject to
strong assumptions or depend on a weak detector to detect the human
hand. We utilize Mask R-CNN to avoid both aforementioned constraints.
The proposed framework allows detection of multi-hand instances and
localization of hand joints simultaneously. Our experiments show that
our method is superior to existing methods.

Keywords: Multi-hand pose estimation · Pictorial Structure
Mask R-CNN

1 Introduction

Accurate hand pose estimation from depth images or videos plays an essential role in human-computer interaction, as well as virtual and augmented
reality. However, challenges with estimating hand pose can arise from self-
similarity, self-occlusion, and large view-point variation. Although much progress
has been made in this area [8,18,23–27], multi-hand pose estimation is still
mostly unsolved. A good solution, however, would provide more flexibilities and
possibilities in many HCI applications.

Compared to single-hand pose estimation, estimating poses of multiple hands
from a single depth image is more difficult because it requires the correct detection of all hand instances while also precisely localizing the corresponding hand
joints. A straightforward way to solve this problem is to follow the common

Electronic supplementary material The online version of this chapter (https://
doi.org/10.1007/978-3-030-11024-6_17) contains supplementary material, which is
available to authorized users.

two-stage strategy [25] that first uses a traditional method (e.g., a random forest [2]) to extract regions of an image that contains a hand object. Having these regions, single-hand pose estimation methods are applied to each of them. However, a general framework with more powerful detectors that can fulfill multi-hand instance detection and hand joint localization simultaneously could be more reliable and convenient in real-world applications.

Recently, convolutional Neural Networks (CNN) have become a mainstream technique in computer vision tasks such as image classification [14], pose estimation [4,9] and object detection [22]. In [11], a multi-task learning framework named Mask R-CNN [11] was proposed for simultaneous object detection and instance segmentation. Mask R-CNN is a generic multi-task learning pipeline that can be generalized to multi-human pose estimation. Because minimal domain knowledge for human pose estimation is exploited, Mask R-CNN is not applicable to model joint relationships explicitly. Moreover, as pointed out in [3], key points might not be localized accurately in complex situations.

In this paper, we propose a Pictorial Structure (PS) [1] model-based framework to address limitations of methods based on Mask R-CNN by refining the output from these networks with a learned global structure of the current hand pose during the test stage. The overall structure of our proposed method is shown in Fig. 1. Our framework is composed of two stages: first, Mask R-CNN is adopted to predict possible key point locations (Fig. 1c) and segments each hand from the given images (Fig. 1d). Then, we utilize the instance segmentation output of Mask R-CNN to approximate the pose prior of each hand (Fig. 1d–g) and add this constraint in pose space. Finally, key point locations are estimated via combining local information and global constraints (Fig. 1f).

The main contributions of our work are:

- a new method for 2D multi-hand pose estimation from a single depth image.
- a PS model-based method to find global structure constraints of a hand pose online and two ways to implement the method.
- two multi-hand datasets, dexter2Hands and NYU2Hands, that are based on the popular single-hand datasets dexter1 [23] and NYU hand pose dataset [25].

2   Related Work

In this section, we first briefly review some relevant hand pose estimation algorithms with CNN. Because estimating body and hand pose share some similarities, algorithms for one object can be extended to serve the other. Further, related multi-human pose estimation methods are also reviewed. Finally, we introduce the Mask R-CNN framework, which serves as the baseline for our research.

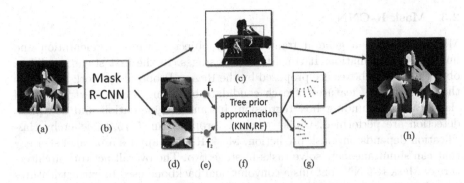

Fig. 1. Example of how our method localizes joints of left thumb finger and right index finger. Given an input image (a), we first use Mask R-CNN (b) to detect bounding boxes, possible joint positions (c), and hand segmentations (d). Then, we extract global features (e) of each hand from Mask R-CNN and find hand poses similar to input hands from training data (f). Afterwards, we compute global constraints of input hands (g). Final hands joint positions are localized by combining the local information and global constraints (h).

2.1 Hand Pose Estimation

More recently, CNN has been widely used in hand pose estimation. Authors in [25] first used CNN for predicting heat maps of joint positions, and this method was improved in [8] by predicting heat maps on three orthogonal views to better utilize the depth information. In [18], a multi-stage CNN that enforces priors to hand poses was presented to directly regress hand joints. Authors in [9] presented a 3D CNN that regresses 3D hand joint positions directly. In [27], a three-stage approach that can estimate 3D hand poses from regular RGB images was proposed. In that approach, the hand is first located by a segmentation network and serves as input to another network for 2D hand pose estimation. The final 3D hand joint positions are localized via combining the estimated 2D positions and the 3D pose prior information.

2.2 Multi-human Pose Estimation

In [7], a PS model-based framework was proposed for estimating poses of multiple humans, but it relies on an additional human detector and simple geometric body part relationships. Similarly, the model proposed in [15] also requires a human detector for initial human hypotheses generation, and the estimation of key points positions and instances are divided into two stages. Unlike previous strategies that need to first detect people and subsequently estimate their poses, the method proposed in [21] utilizes CNN for body part hypotheses generation and is able to jointly solve the task of detection and pose estimation. This work was extended in [13] with stronger part detectors and more constraints in the problem formulation.

2.3   Mask R-CNN

Mask R-CNN is a general framework for object instance segmentation and human pose estimation. It consists of two stages. In the first stage, candidate object bounding boxes are proposed by the Region Proposal Network (RPN). In the second stage, features of each candidate bounding box are extracted and classification, bounding box regression, instance segmentation and key point detection are performed. Unlike methods proposed in [5,16,20] whereby classification depends on mask prediction, Mask R-CNN applies a parallel strategy that can simultaneously solve tasks in stage two. The overall network architecture of Mask R-CNN contains a convolutional backbone used to extract features over the whole image and three parallel network heads: one for classification and bounding box regression, and two for the remaining tasks.

3   Problem Formulation

Mathematically, our objective is to estimate hand poses $\mathbf{P} = \{\mathbf{X}_1, \mathbf{X}_2, ..., \mathbf{X}_M\}$ from a single image I, where $\mathbf{X}_i$ denotes the pose of an instance and M is the number of instances in I. Following [1], we assume that a hand can be decomposed into a set of parts, the pose of a hand is defined as $\mathbf{X}_i = \{\mathbf{x}_i^n | 1 \leq n \leq N, \forall \mathbf{x}_i^n \in \Re^3\}$, where the state of part n is formulated as $\mathbf{x}_i^n = \{\mathbf{y}_i^n, t_i^n\}$. $\mathbf{y}_i^n = \{x_i^n, y_i^n\}$ is the position of the key point in image coordinate system and $t_i^n = \{0, 1\}$ denotes the state indicating the presence of part n.

We formulate the multi-hand poses estimation problem as finding the maximum posteriori of poses given an image I, i.e., $p(\mathbf{P}|I)$, which can be approximated as

$$p(\mathbf{P}|I) \propto p(I|\mathbf{P})p(\mathbf{P}), \tag{1}$$

where $p(I|\mathbf{P})$ is the likelihood of the image evidence given particular poses, and the $p(\mathbf{P})$ corresponds to poses prior. We assume that all hands are independent for simplicity, Eq. 1 can be factorized as

$$p(\mathbf{P}|I) \propto \prod_{i=1}^{M} p(I|\mathbf{X}_i)p(\mathbf{X}_i), \tag{2}$$

where $p(I|\mathbf{X}_i)$ is the likelihood of the image evidence given a particular pose, and the $p(\mathbf{X}_i)$ corresponds to a kinematic tree prior according to the Pictorial Structure [1] (PS) model, though this may not always hold when fingers of different hands are crossed. We propose a general framework based on PS model and utilize Mask R-CNN [11] to solve Eq. 2.

4   Mask R-CNN for Hand Pose Estimation

In this work, we use ResNet-50 [12] with Feature Pyramid Network (FPN) [17] as the backbone to extract features of the entire image. For details of ResNet

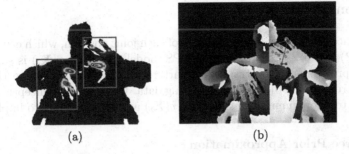

(a)   (b)

Fig. 2. (a) Confidence maps of left thumb finger joints and right index finger joints. (b) Mask R-CNN detection result.

and FPN, we refer readers to [12,17]. For the network head, we follow the three-parallel-branches architecture presented in [11] whereby one branch is for bounding box classification and regression, one for instance mask prediction and one for key point detection. In general, given a training image, features of the entire image are first extracted by the ResNet-FPN backbone. Based on the features, RPN generates a set of ROIs. Each positive ROI is fed into three parallel branches of the network head: one branch for bounding box classification and the other two for remaining tasks. The loss function is defined as $L = L_{cls} + L_{box} + L_{mask} + L_{kpt}$, where the classification loss L_{cls} is log loss over two classes (hand vs. background). The bounding box regression loss L_{box} is identical as that defined in [10]. The mask loss L_{mask} is the binary cross-entropy loss over predicted hand mask and groundtruth and the key point mask loss L_{kpt} is the average cross-entropy loss over the predicted N joints and N groundtruth points.

At test time, Mask R-CNN key point head branch outputs confidence maps of all joints. Figure 2(a) shows an example of confidence maps of left thumb finger joints and right index finger joints. Because relationships among hand joints are only implicitly learned during the training process, localizing key point positions via finding locations with maximum probabilities could lead to large pixel error. As shown in Fig. 2(b), two joints of the left thumb finger are estimated incorrectly on the left index finger. Similarly, joints of the right index finger are incorrectly predicted as the ring and little finger. Moreover, if we cannot guarantee the correctness of confidence maps, they cannot be used alone to infer the presence or visibility of joints. Inspired by PS models by which the poses of objects can be estimated by combing global structure constraints (which encode part relationships) and part confidence maps, we utilize the output of Mask R-CNN mask head to learn kinematic structures of hands explicitly. Learned kinematic structures are used to refine confidence maps of corresponding hands and infer presences of joints.

5   Confidence Refinement

Confidence maps provide probabilities of each joint position, which can be viewed as $p(I|\mathbf{P})$ in Eq. 2. According to the PS model, the prior $p(\mathbf{X}_i)$ is supposed to encode probabilistic constraints on part relationships and capture the unified global structure of objects in the training data. We present a conceptually simple method to approximate the tree prior $p(\mathbf{X}_i)$ and two methods to implement it.

5.1   Tree Prior Approximation

As illustrated in Fig. 1(d), masks predicted by Mask R-CNN mask head capture global structures of hand instances, but they lack information on part relationships (e.g., neighbouring joints of the same finger should lie close to each other). Our idea is to find a training subset $\mathbf{S}_i$ that has a similar mask as the i_{th} test hand mask, then the kinematic tree prior that encodes part relationships of the test hand can be learned from $\mathbf{S}_i$.

Before we introduce how we find out $\mathbf{S}_i$, there is one critical question: can we make masks comparable when they may have different scale and size? In Mask R-CNN, the mask head branch would first predict a fixed size mask for each instance and the predicted mask is further resized to have the true size of the corresponding instance. We reshape the fixed size mask into a feature vector so that every hand instance can be represented in a comparable form. This feature representation projects the instances to the feature space that visually similar instances are close to each other. Feature vectors of all hand instances in training data are extracted by the same procedure and stored on disk for future use.

Unsupervised Learned Tree Prior Approximation. Given that the i_{th} hand instance can be represented by a feature vector $\mathbf{f}_i$, we use K nearest neighbours (KNN) search to find features of training images that lie close to $\mathbf{f}_i$ in the feature space, $\mathbf{S}_i$ is composed of those corresponding training images. In order to learn $p(\mathbf{X}_i)$ from $\mathbf{S}_i$, for simplicity, we assume that all hand parts are independent, the prior $p(\mathbf{X}_i)$ is approximated as

$$p(\mathbf{X}_i) \approx p(\mathbf{x}_i^1, \mathbf{x}_i^2, ..., \mathbf{x}_i^N | \mathbf{f}_i) = \prod_{j=1}^{N} p(\mathbf{x}_i^j | \mathbf{f}_i) \qquad (3)$$

where $p(\mathbf{x}_i^j|\mathbf{f}_i)$ is the j_{th} part prior of i_{th} hand instance based on the feature vector $\mathbf{f}_i$. Let $coord = (x, y)$ denote the coordinate of a pixel in image, $p(\mathbf{x}_i^j|\mathbf{f}_i)$ is computed as

$$p(\mathbf{x}_i^j | \mathbf{f}_i) = \begin{cases} 1 & ||coord - mean_{\mathbf{S}_i}^j||_p \leq d \\ 0.5 & \text{otherwise} \end{cases} \qquad (4)$$

where $|| \bullet ||_p$ is the Minkowski distance between two points and $mean_{\mathbf{S}}^j$ is the mean coordinate of the j_{th} part in $\mathbf{S}_i$. d is a hyper-parameter that adjusts the

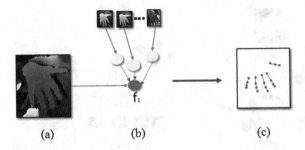

Fig. 3. KNN for hand instance kinematic prior approximation. A hand instance (a) is expressed by a feature vector $\mathbf{f}_1$, training data with similar features are found out by KNN search (b). The kinematic structure of the hand instance are learned from those training data (c).

influence of $p(\mathbf{X}_i)$. We adopt this formulation because it allows faster computation than other common probabilistic distributions and it is mainly defined to refine joint confidence maps. Though in our formulation we assume that all joints are independent, joint relationships are implicitly preserved by the subset of training data in $\mathbf{S}_i$. Figure 3 shows an example of this process. The absence of joint(s) is inferred by the absent joints in $\mathbf{S}_i$, e.g., if the number of absent tips of the ring finger from $\mathbf{S}_i$ result is greater than a threshold τ, the ring finger tip is deemed as invisible for the i_{th} hand instance.

Because the whole process needs to be repeated for every hand instance, KNN-based tree prior approximation method is computationally heavy. Moreover, features of training data need to be stored, which may require a large amount of space. These limitations motivate us to find $\mathbf{S}_i$ via other methods that require less computation and storage.

Supervised Learned Tree Prior Approximation. It is possible to use a supervised learning method to find out $\mathbf{S}_i$, which should be faster than KNN, provided that a labelling method could be found that is able to distinguish different hand poses. In our framework, a hand instance is assigned a label $L = \{j_1, j_2, ..., j_N\}$, where the index of j_i in the label vector indicates the joint name and N is the number of joints. We first compute distances between each hand joint and the origin. Those computed distances are stored in a vector $\mathbf{v}$, then we sort $\mathbf{v}$ in decent order. The value of j_i is determined by the index of the corresponding joint plus one in sorted $\mathbf{v}$. For example, if a sorted $\mathbf{v}$ is of the form $\mathbf{v} = \{dist(joint_2, org), ..., dist(joint_1, org)\}$, where $dist$ is the function computes the distance between two points, $joint_i$ is the coordinate of a joint and org is the coordinate of the origin, the values of j_1 and j_2 are N and 1 in the label vector L. If a joint is not visible, the corresponding entry in L is set to 0. In most cases, the presented labelling method is able to distinguish different hand poses and preserve joint spatial relationships, especially when we need to localize all joints and tips of a hand.

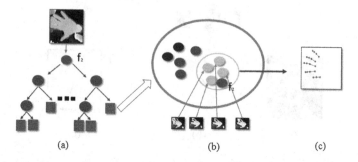

(a)   (b)   (c)

Fig. 4. Random forest for hand instance kinematic prior approximation. The feature vector $\mathbf{f}_2$ of hand instance is classified into a class by RF (a). Training data of the same label in nodes that $\mathbf{f}_2$ falls into are selected (b) and used to compute the kinematic prior (c).

The next step is to choose a proper classifier. We select Random Forest [2] (RF) because it is naturally designed for multi-class classification and it provides soft decision boundaries. Moreover, RF is able to handle high dimensional input data efficiently, which allows fast computation at test time. Figure 4 shows an example of how we use RF to predict the kinematic tree prior of a test hand. Feature vector $\mathbf{f}_2$ of the test hand goes through all trees and falls into some leaf nodes (Fig. 4a). It is assigned a label l by RF and we select training data with the same label l (Fig. 4b), which is actually the training subset $\mathbf{S}_i$. The kinematic tree prior (Fig. 4c) is estimated by Eq. 3. In practice, kinematic tree priors learned from each leaf node can be computed offline and it is only necessary to store joint coordinates, bounding box width and height, i.e., totally $N \times 2 + 2$ numbers, which requires much less storage space compared to our KNN method. Absences of joints or tips can be directly predicted by RF (entry in the label vector is 0).

5.2   Final Localization

Given $p(I|\mathbf{P})$ and $p(\mathbf{X}_i)$, the posterior probability $p(\mathbf{P}|I)$ can be computed by Eq. 2. Joints locations are estimated by finding image positions with highest probabilities. Note that both our tree prior approximation methods are able to detect presences of joints; if Mask R-CNN failed to detect the j_{th} joint of the i_{th} hand, the position of the j_{th} joint is estimated by $mean_{\mathbf{S}_i}^j$.

6   Data Preparation

We generated two 2-hands datasets, dexter2Hands and NYU2Hands, based on depth images of the popular single hand datasets dexter1 [23] and NYU hand pose dataset [25]. For the dexter2Hands dataset, we randomly selected 2504 images from 3154 images in the dexter1 dataset as a training set, and the remaining 600 images were equally split into a validation set and test set.

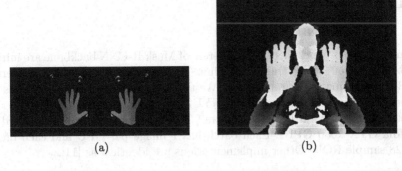

Fig. 5. (a) Sample image of Dexter2Hands dataset. (b) Sample image of NYU2Hands dataset.

Because images of dexter1 only contained hands and the image size was relatively small (320 × 240), images in the final training data of dexter2Hands are of size 640 × 240, and are generated by the concatenation of randomly selected left and right hand images from (mirrored-)training set. Same processes are applied to generate validation data and test data of dexter2Hands dataset. In our experiments, dexter2Hands training data contained 57404 images, validation data contained 14025 images and test data contained 9925 images. The key point number of a hand instance is 5, which are thumb finger tip, index finger tip, middle finger tip, ring finger tip and little finger tip, respectively. Figure 5(a) shows an example of images in dexter2Hands. Hand masks of the dexter2Hands dataset are generated by setting pixel values of hand object in each image to 1 and background to 0.

Processes used to generate the NYU2Hands dataset are similar, and we use only depth images from the view-point 1. However, the image size of NYU2Hands is the same as NYU, which is 640 × 480. Training data and validation data of NYU2Hands are generated by copying the mirrored left side hand (in image coordinate) to be the corresponding right side hand. The key point number of a hand instance is 19, which are little finger tip (LT), little finger joint 1 (L1), little finger joint 2 (L2), little finger joint 3 (L3), ring finger tip (RT), ring finger joint 1 (R1), ring finger joint 2 (R2), ring finger joint 3 (R3), middle finger tip (MT), middle finger joint 1 (M1), middle finger joint 2 (M2), middle finger joint 3 (M3), index finger tip (IT), index finger joint 1 (I1), index finger joint 2 (I2), index finger joint 3 (I3), thumb finger tip (TT), thumb finger joint 1 (T1) and thumb finger joint 2 (T2), respectively. Figure 5(b) shows a sample image of NYU2Hands. Because there are 75157 images in the NYU hand pose dataset with the same background, we randomly selected 62727 images to generate training data and 10000 images to generate validation data. We applied the same strategy of generating dexter2Hands training data to generate test data of NYU2Hands, which contained 6038 images. Synthetic depth images provided by the NYU dataset are used to generate training hand masks of the NYU2Hands dataset.

7   Implementation Details

7.1   Mask R-CNN

Training: In our experiments, parameters of Mask R-CNN backbone are initialized by Imagenet [6] pre-trained weights. Training depth images are converted into 3-channel images by replication. We train the model on 50K iterations for dexter2Hands and 60K iterations for NYU2Hands, starting from a learning rate of 0.002 and reducing it by 10 at 15K and 35K iterations. Models are trained on 4 Nvidia GTX 1080 GPUs. Each batch has 1 image per GPU and each image has 128 sample ROIs. Other implementations are identical as [11].

Inference: At test time, the bounding box branch directly predicts bounding boxes of hand instances. The instance segmentation branch predicts a mask of size 28×28 and the key point mask branch outputs a $56 \times 56 \times N$ joint mask for each hand instance. N is 5 for dexter2Hands and 19 for NYU2Hands. Those masks are further resized to the size of the bounding box, and binarized at a threshold t to obtain the final detection result. t is 0.1 for instance masks and 0.5 for key point masks. Instance threshold is chosen at a low value because we hope the estimated mask could cover hand finger tips. The feature vector of a hand instance is generated by reshaping the 28×28 mask into a vector of 1×784.

7.2   Tree Prior Approximation

For KNN search, we set $K = 10$ and threshold $\tau = 4$ for both datasets. For our RF approach, we use the RF implementation provided by [19] to construct a 10-tree RF and do not change other parameters. Each tree has a depth of around 30 and around 6000 leaf nodes. We choose Manhattan distance to compute part prior $p(\mathbf{x}_i^j | \mathbf{f}_i)$ in Eq. 4 since it is relatively fast and d is set to 30 for dexter2Hands dataset and 40 for NYU2Hands dataset.

8   Experiments

8.1   Evaluation

We evaluate our methods on test data of Dexter2Hands and NYU2Hands. Results of our methods are compared with two versions of Mask R-CNN, i.e., keypoint only and keypoint & mask, as well as groundtruth joint positions. Mask R-CNN keypoint only indicates that joint positions are localized via finding positions of joint confidence maps with maximum probabilities. Mask R-CNN keypoint & mask restricts keypoints lying on estimated masks. We employ two metrics to evaluate the performance of our proposed method. The first metric is the average Euclidean distance in pixels between the results and the groundtruth. The second metric is the percentage of success frames in which all joint errors are below a certain threshold. In addition, we compute the false positives (FP) rate and false negatives (FN) rate to infer the presence of each joint to validate the adequacy of our methods. In our experiments, we found that Mask R-CNN is able to correctly detect almost all hand instances, with fewer than 5 frames being wrongly detected.

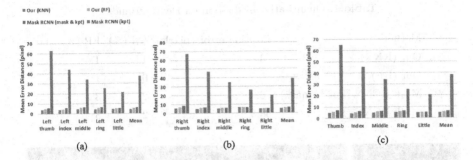

Fig. 6. Per-joint mean error distance in pixels on dexter2Hands. (a) Left hand. (b) Right hand. (c) Both hands.

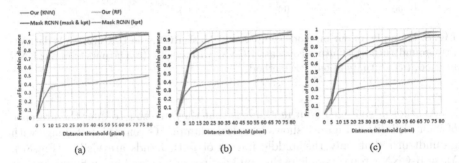

Fig. 7. Fraction of frames within distance on dexter2Hands. (a) Left hand. (b) Right hand. (c) Both hands.

8.2 Results and Discussion

Figure 6 shows the comparison results of our methods and Mask R-CNN on Dexter2Hands dataset. In all cases, we can see that our methods produce fewer pixel errors of each tip on each individual hand and both hands. Because the image background of this dataset is relatively clean, estimating joint locations via finding positions with maximum probabilities without constraint is noise sensitive. This is the reason for the large pixel errors in the method of Mask R-CNN keypoint only. As shown in Table 1, the average joint pixel error over all frames of our KNN method is 4.8, which is better than our RF method (5.7) and Mask R-CNN keypoint & mask method (6.2). The fraction of good frames over a different threshold for each individual hand and both hands is shown in Fig. 7. For the left hand, our KNN method achieves the best good frame rate (82%) when the threshold is 10 pixels, while the good frame rate is 78% for our RF method and 77% for mask R-CNN keypoint & mask. Similarly, the performance of our KNN and RF methods outperform other methods on the right hand (Fig. 7b) and both hands (Fig. 7c).

Table 1. Quantitative evaluation on Dexter2Hands.

Method	Position error (pixels)	FN (%)	FP (%)
Our (KNN)	4.8	1	1
Our (RF)	5.7	0	1
Mask RCNN (kpt & mask)	6.2	2	3
Mask RCNN (kpt)	38.5	2	3

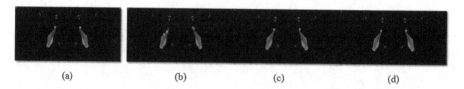

(a)   (b)   (c)   (d)

Fig. 8. Examples of our methods compared to Mask-RCNN on Dexter2Hands dataset. (a) Groundtruth. (b) Outputs of Mask RCNN (with mask). (c) Outputs of of our KNN method. (d) Outputs of our RF method.

Another advantage of our methods is that they are able to infer the presence of joint visibilities. Figure 8 shows a typical example. Given an input image with groundtruth that only the middle fingers of both hands are visible (Fig. 8a), Mask R-CNN wrongly predicts that pinky, ring, middle and index finger tips are visible on the left hand. Similarly, all finger tips are estimated to be overlapping on the right hand (Fig. 8b). Our methods successfully detect the presence of joints and correctly predict visible joint position (Fig. 8c, d). Both versions of Mask R-CNN produce FN rates of 2% and FP rates of 3%, while FN rate of our KNN and RF methods are 1% and 0%. The FP rate of our methods are 1%.

We also compare our methods with Mask R-CNN on the NYU2Hands dataset, which is more challenging since there are 19 joints on each hand. As shown in Fig. 9, our methods achieve fewer pixel errors than Mask R-CNN in all cases. Mean pixel errors of the left middle finger tip (MT in Fig. 9) of Mask R-CNN are 27.3 (keypoint only) and 22.4 (keypoint & mask), while mean pixel errors of our methods for that joint are 11.2 (KNN) and 12.2 (RF). For the right hand, though on some joints (e.g., Fig. 9b: L1, RT, MT, etc.) Mask R-CNN keypoint & mask has fewer pixel errors than our RF method, the largest margin is on the right middle finger tip, which is 1.4 (11.1 vs 12.5). Table 2 shows the averaged position errors in pixel for different methods. Mean joint pixel errors over all frames of our methods are 9.3 (KNN) and 10.1 (RF), which is better than Mask R-CNN keypoint & mask (12.4) and keypoint only (16.2). The proportion of good frames over different error thresholds is shown in Fig. 10, and we can see a clear order of performance of the four methods: our KNN method is better than our RF method and the proposed methods outperform Mask R-CNN. The FN and FP rates of our methods are all 0%, while FN rates of both versions of Mask R-CNN are 2% and FP rates are 0%. Some qualitative results for the

NYU2Hands dataset are shown in Fig. 11. As can be seen, our proposed methods can better preserve hand joint relationships and provide a more accurate estimation.

Table 2. Quantitative evaluation on NYU2Hands.

Method	Position error (pixels)	FN (%)	FP (%)
Our (KNN)	9.3	0	0
Our (RF)	10.1	0	0
Mask RCNN (kpt & mask)	12.4	1	0
Mask RCNN (kpt)	16.2	1	0

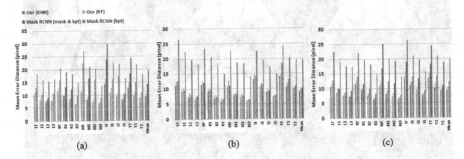

Fig. 9. Per-joint mean error distance in pixels on NYU2Hands. (a) Left hand. (b) Right hand. (c) Both hands.

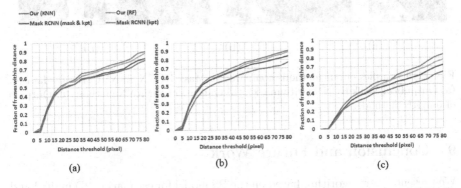

Fig. 10. Fraction of frames within distance on NYU2Hands. (a) Left hand. (b) Right hand. (c) Both hands.

Runtime: The runtime of both versions of Mask R-CNN to process a test image of dexter2hands dataset is 0.45 s on average, and it takes 0.5 s for our KNN method and 0.46 s for our RF method. For the test image of NYU2Hands dataset, the averaged process time of both versions of Mask R-CNN is 0.5 s because the image size is two times larger than test images of dexter2Hand and needs to locate more joints. The process time of our KNN method for the NYU2Hands dataset is around 0.85 s per image, including 0.25 s for the calculation of mean joint positions for each joint in KNN search result. Compared to our KNN method, our RF method is much faster because mean joint positions are already stored after training, which requires 0.55 s to process a NYU2Hands test image.

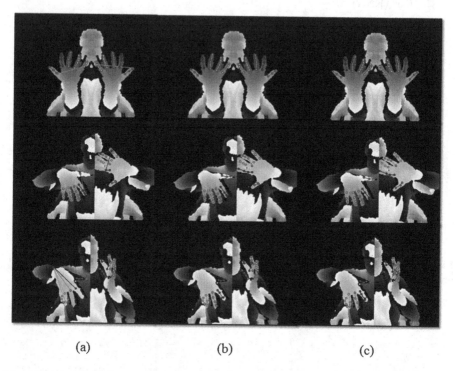

(a)   (b)   (c)

Fig. 11. Examples of our methods compared to Mask-RCNN on NYU2Hands dataset. (a) Outputs of Mask RCNN (with mask). (b) Outputs of our KNN method. (c) Outputs of our RF method.

9   Conclusion and Future Work

We present a new algorithm based on the PS model for estimating 2D multi-hand poses from single depth images. The proposed framework utilizes Mask R-CNN to learn the mapping from local informations of joints and global structures of hands to their corresponding poses. We formulate a new utilization of the segmentation output of Mask R-CNN and propose two ways to approximate pose priors of test instances. The estimated pose priors could be used to infer the presences of joints. Our method addresses issues of interchangeable estimations by solely using Mask R-CNN for the detection of hand key points. We also present interplays between Mask R-CNN and the PS model, as well as Mask R-CNN and random forests. The performance of our algorithm has been validated on two self-generated datasets with two hands that can also serve as a baseline for future research.

Future work will encompass generating a real multi-hand dataset with accurate labelling that not only labels the joint position but also provides visibility information of occluded joints. Our system could be extended to 3D multi-hand pose estimation and an improved method could be designed to model the relationships of joints, both in network structure design and the tree prior approximation step.

References

1. Andriluka, M., Roth, S., Schiele, B.: Pictorial structures revisited: people detection and articulated pose estimation. In: IEEE Conference on Computer Vision and Pattern Recognition, CVPR 2009, pp. 1014–1021. IEEE (2009)
2. Breiman, L.: Random forests. Mach. Learn. 45(1), 5–32 (2001)
3. Chen, Y., Wang, Z., Peng, Y., Zhang, Z., Yu, G., Sun, J.: Cascaded pyramids network for multi-person pose estimation. In: IEEE Conference on Computer Vision and Pattern Recognition (CVPR), pp. 7103–7112. IEEE (2018)
4. Chu, X., Ouyang, W., Li, H., Wang, X.: Structured feature learning for pose estimation. In: Proceedings of the IEEE Conference on Computer Vision and Pattern Recognition, pp. 4715–4723 (2016)
5. Dai, J., He, K., Sun, J.: Instance-aware semantic segmentation via multi-task network cascades. In: Proceedings of the IEEE Conference on Computer Vision and Pattern Recognition, pp. 3150–3158 (2016)
6. Deng, J., Dong, W., Socher, R., Li, L.J., Li, K., Fei-Fei, L.: Imagenet: a large-scale hierarchical image database. In: CVPR (2009)
7. Eichner, M., Ferrari, V.: We are family: joint pose estimation of multiple persons. In: Daniilidis, K., Maragos, P., Paragios, N. (eds.) ECCV 2010. LNCS, vol. 6311, pp. 228–242. Springer, Heidelberg (2010). https://doi.org/10.1007/978-3-642-15549-9_17
8. Ge, L., Liang, H., Yuan, J., Thalmann, D.: Robust 3D hand pose estimation in single depth images: from single-view CNN to multi-view CNNs. In: Proceedings of the IEEE Conference on Computer Vision and Pattern Recognition, pp. 3593–3601 (2016)
9. Ge, L., Liang, H., Yuan, J., Thalmann, D.: 3D convolutional neural networks for efficient and robust hand pose estimation from single depth images. In: Proceedings of the IEEE Conference on Computer Vision and Pattern Recognition, vol. 1, p. 5 (2017)
10. Girshick, R.: Fast R-CNN. In: 2015 IEEE International Conference on Computer Vision (ICCV), pp. 1440–1448. IEEE (2015)
11. He, K., Gkioxari, G., Dollár, P., Girshick, R.: Mask R-CNN. In: Proceedings of the International Conference on Computer Vision (ICCV) (2017)
12. He, K., Zhang, X., Ren, S., Sun, J.: Deep residual learning for image recognition. In: Proceedings of the IEEE Conference on Computer Vision and Pattern Recognition, pp. 770–778 (2016)

13. Insafutdinov, E., Pishchulin, L., Andres, B., Andriluka, M., Schiele, B.: DeeperCut: a deeper, stronger, and faster multi-person pose estimation model. In: Leibe, B., Matas, J., Sebe, N., Welling, M. (eds.) ECCV 2016. LNCS, vol. 9910, pp. 34–50. Springer, Cham (2016). https://doi.org/10.1007/978-3-319-46466-4_3
14. Krizhevsky, A., Sutskever, I., Hinton, G.E.: Imagenet classification with deep convolutional neural networks. In: Advances in Neural Information Processing Systems, pp. 1097–1105 (2012)
15. Ladicky, L., Torr, P.H., Zisserman, A.: Human pose estimation using a joint pixelwise and part-wise formulation. In: Proceedings of the IEEE Conference on Computer Vision and Pattern Recognition, pp. 3578–3585 (2013)
16. Li, Y., Qi, H., Dai, J., Ji, X., Wei, Y.: Fully convolutional instance-aware semantic segmentation. In: IEEE Conference on Computer Vision and Pattern Recognition (CVPR), pp. 2359–2367 (2017)
17. Lin, T.Y., Dollár, P., Girshick, R., He, K., Hariharan, B., Belongie, S.: Feature pyramid networks for object detection. In: CVPR, vol. 1, p. 4 (2017)
18. Oberweger, M., Wohlhart, P., Lepetit, V.: Hands deep in deep learning for hand pose estimation. arXiv preprint arXiv:1502.06807 (2015)
19. Pedregosa, F., et al.: Scikit-learn: machine learning in Python. J. Mach. Learn. Res. 12, 2825–2830 (2011)
20. Pinheiro, P.O., Collobert, R., Dollár, P.: Learning to segment object candidates. In: Advances in Neural Information Processing Systems, pp. 1990–1998 (2015)
21. Pishchulin, L., et al.: Deepcut: joint subset partition and labeling for multi person pose estimation. In: Proceedings of the IEEE Conference on Computer Vision and Pattern Recognition, pp. 4929–4937 (2016)
22. Ren, S., He, K., Girshick, R., Sun, J.: Faster R-CNN: towards real-time object detection with region proposal networks. In: Advances in Neural Information Processing Systems, pp. 91–99 (2015)
23. Sridhar, S., Oulasvirta, A., Theobalt, C.: Interactive markerless articulated hand motion tracking using RGB and depth data. In: Proceedings of the IEEE International Conference on Computer Vision (ICCV), December 2013
24. Tang, D., Jin Chang, H., Tejani, A., Kim, T.K.: Latent regression forest: structured estimation of 3D articulated hand posture. In: Proceedings of the IEEE Conference on Computer Vision and Pattern Recognition, pp. 3786–3793 (2014)
25. Tompson, J., Stein, M., Lecun, Y., Perlin, K.: Real-time continuous pose recovery of human hands using convolutional networks. ACM Trans. Graph. 33, 169 (2014)
26. Yuan, S., et al.: Depth-based 3D hand pose estimation: From current achievements to future goals. In: IEEE CVPR (2018)
27. Zimmermann, C., Brox, T.: Learning to estimate 3D hand pose from single RGB images. In: International Conference on Computer Vision (2017)

Spatial-Temporal Attention Res-TCN for Skeleton-Based Dynamic Hand Gesture Recognition

Jingxuan Hou[1], Guijin Wang[1]([✉]), Xinghao Chen[1], Jing-Hao Xue[2], Rui Zhu[3], and Huazhong Yang[1]

[1] Tsinghua University, Beijing, China
{houjx14,chen-xh13}@mails.tsinghua.edu.cn,
{wangguijin,yanghz}@tsinghua.edu.cn
[2] University College London, London, UK
jinghao.xue@ucl.ac.uk
[3] University of Kent, Kent, UK
R.Zhu@kent.ac.uk

Abstract. Dynamic hand gesture recognition is a crucial yet challenging task in computer vision. The key of this task lies in an effective extraction of discriminative spatial and temporal features to model the evolutions of different gestures. In this paper, we propose an end-to-end Spatial-Temporal Attention Residual Temporal Convolutional Network (STA-Res-TCN) for skeleton-based dynamic hand gesture recognition, which learns different levels of attention and assigns them to each spatial-temporal feature extracted by the convolution filters at each time step. The proposed attention branch assists the networks to adaptively focus on the informative time frames and features while exclude the irrelevant ones that often bring in unnecessary noise. Moreover, our proposed STA-Res-TCN is a lightweight model that can be trained and tested in an extremely short time. Experiments on DHG-14/28 Dataset and SHREC'17 Track Dataset show that STA-Res-TCN outperforms state-of-the-art methods on both the 14 gestures setting and the more complicated 28 gestures setting.

Keywords: Dynamic hand gesture recognition
Spatial-Temporal Attention · Temporal Convolutional Networks

1 Introduction

Dynamic hand gesture recognition has attracted increasing interests due to its potential relevance to a wide range of applications, such as touchless automotive user interfaces, gaming, robotics, etc [3,21,28]. However, it is still challenging to develop a highly precise hand gesture recognition system, owing to high intra-class variance derived from the various possibilities to perform the same gesture [3,5,30].

© Springer Nature Switzerland AG 2019
L. Leal-Taixé and S. Roth (Eds.): ECCV 2018 Workshops, LNCS 11134, pp. 273–286, 2019.
https://doi.org/10.1007/978-3-030-11024-6_18

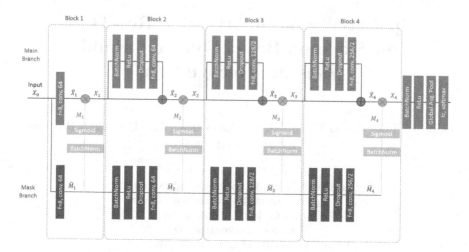

Fig. 1. Overall architecture of the proposed STA-Res-TCN, which consists of a main branch for feature processing, a mask branch for attention and an element-wise multiplication for the final generation of attention-aware features.

Early studies on dynamic hand gesture recognition mainly take 2D videos captured by RGB cameras as input, which inevitably causes the loss of valuable 3D spatial information and brings in extra challenges of occlusions and light variation [5,9,16,28,29]. In recent years, thanks to the drastic advances of cost-effective depth sensors, like Microsoft Kinect or Intel RealSense [10,15,27,33], reliable joint coordinates can be easily obtained using hand pose estimation algorithms [6,22,34], and thus skeleton-based dynamic hand gesture recognition has become an active research field.

Traditionally, spatial-temporal hand gesture descriptors are first extracted from the input skeleton sequences, and then a classifier is employed for the final predictions [3,5,9,24,25,28–30]. In recent years, computer vision has witnessed a great success of the introduction of deep learning methods [11,13,18,26]. However, there is significantly little work in the literature using Deep Neural Networks (DNNs) to deal with skeleton-based dynamic hand gesture recognition. To the best of our knowledge, the only literature [23], which does employ DNNs, sticks to a two-stage training strategy with a Convolution Neural Network (CNN) followed by a Long Short-Term Memory (LSTM) recurrent network, instead of an end-to-end framework. The CNN focuses on the extraction of spatial features related to the position of the skeleton joints in 3D space, and the LSTM recurrent network is then used to explore time evolutions and drawing predictions.

Recently a novel set of networks, Temporal Convolutional Networks (TCNs), is proved to be an effective approach to capture spatial-temporal patterns in the context of action segmentation and human action recognition task [16,18]. However, given the high intra-class variance nature of hand gestures, not all features extracted by TCN are necessarily informative for every specific input video at every time step. Attention mechanism needs to be introduced to assist the model to adaptively focus on the informative time frames and features.

Inspired by the work of TCN [16,18], we propose an end-to-end Spatial-Temporal Attention Res-TCN (STA-Res-TCN). The proposed STA-Res-TCN adaptively learns different levels of attention through a mask branch, and assigns them to each spatial-temporal feature extracted by a main branch through an element-wise multiplication. Experimental results demonstrate that the STA-Res-TCN has achieved state-of-the-art performance on DHG-14/28 Dataset [29] and SHREC'17 Track Dataset [30] on both the 14 gestures setting and the more complicated 28 gestures setting.

2   Related Work

In this section, we first provide a literature review on skeleton-based dynamic hand gesture recognition. We then extend our review to works focusing on attention mechanism.

2.1   Skeleton-Based Dynamic Hand Gesture Recognition

Skeleton-based dynamic hand gesture recognition has become a heated research field thanks to the advances of cost-effective depth sensors and hand pose estimation algorithms. In this section, we briefly review the existing literature on skeleton-based dynamic hand gesture recognition, which can be gathered into two main categories: approaches with **traditional feature extraction** and approaches with **DNNs**.

Approaches with Traditional Feature Extraction. Smedt et al. [29,30] propose a new descriptor named Shape of Connected Joints (SoCJ), from which a Fisher Vector (FV) representation is computed. The FV representation is then concatenated with two other descriptors, Histogram of Hand Directions (HoHD) and Histogram of Wrist Rotations (HoWR). The temporal information is encoded using a temporal pyramid and the classification process is performed by a linear Support Vector Machine (SVM) classifier. Smedt et al. [30] also evaluate the performances of the other two depth-based descriptors, HOG^2 [24] and HON4D [25], and a skeleton-based method proposed by Devanne et al. [9] originally presented for human action recognition. Chen et al. [5] first extract finger motion features and global motion features from the input dynamic hand gesture skeleton sequence, and then feed these motion features, along with the skeleton sequence, into a recurrent neural network (RNN) to get the final predictions. Boulahia et al. [3] introduce the HIF3D feature-set [2], which is initially conceived for modeling whole body actions, to the domain of dynamic hand gesture recognition. For final classification, they also employ the SVM classifier.

Approaches with DNNs. Nunez et al. [23] propose an architecture consists of a combination of a Convolution Neural Network (CNN) followed by a Long

Short-Term Memory (LSTM) recurrent network. The CNN focuses on the extraction of the spatial features, and the LSTM recurrent network is then used to capture the patterns related to the time evolution. The CNN is first pre-trained independently by connecting to a Fully-connected Multilayer Perceptron (MLP). Later, the output of the CNN is connected to the LSTM for the second stage training.

All the works above fail to develop an end-to-end framework to explore spatial features and temporal features at the same time, and to include the process of final classification in the same network.

2.2   Attention Mechanism

Studies in neural science show that attention mechanism plays an important role in human visual system [8,35]. Recently, the exploration of attention mechanism applied in deep learning has attracted increasing interests in various fields, including skeleton-based human action recognition [20,31]. However, to the best of our knowledges, there is no work in the literature applying attention mechanism to skeleton-based dynamic hand gesture recognition. Even for the works on human action recognition, the attention modules in the existing literatures are mostly built on top of the Long Short-Term Memory (LSTM) recurrent networks. There is a lack of investigation of TCNs, which exhibit totally different characteristics from LSTM-based models.

3   Spatial-Temporal Attention Res-TCN

Our proposed STA-Res-TCN consists of a main branch for feature processing and a mask branch for attention. The overall architecture is shown in Fig. 1. In this work, we employ TCN with residual units (Res-TCN) to construct the main branch.

In order to put our proposed model into context, we first provide a brief overview of TCN and its variant Res-TCN as in the original paper [16,18]. Then we describe our proposed Spatial-Temporal Attention Res-TCN for skeleton-based dynamic hand gesture recognition. Finally, the employed data augmentation techniques are introduced.

3.1   Overview of Temporal Convolution Networks

The Temporal Convolution Network (TCN) [18] is built from stacked units of 1-dimensional convolution across the temporal domain followed by a non-linear activation function and max pooling. The input to a TCN is a temporal sequence of D-dimensional feature vectors extracted per video frame. Specifically, for a video of T frames, the input X_0 is a concatenation of all frame-wise D-dimensional feature vector across time such that $X_0 \in \mathbb{R}^{T \times D}$. Note that T is the length of the input and D is the number of channels of the input. In a TCN, the l-th temporal convolution layer consists of N_l filters, each with a temporal window of f_l frames, denoted as $\{W_l^{(i)}\}_{i=1}^{N_l}$ where each filter is $W_l^{(i)} \in \mathbb{R}^{f_l \times N_{l-1}}$. Given the output from the previous layer $X_{l-1} \in \mathbb{R}^{T \times N_{l-1}}$, the activations $X_l \in \mathbb{R}^{T \times N_l}$ can be computed with

$$X_l = f(W_l \otimes X_{l-1}), \qquad (1)$$

where $f(\cdot)$ is non-linear activation function ReLU, and $\otimes$ denotes 1-dimensional temporal convolution.

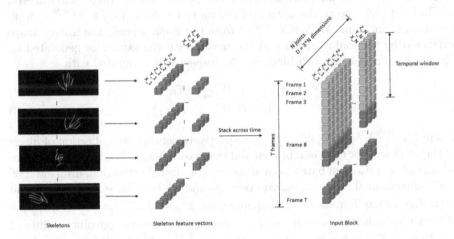

Fig. 2. The input data structure for the network. **Left:** The hand skeleton for each frame. **Middle:** The D-dimensional skeleton feature vector for each frame, constructed by concatenating the 3D coordinates of each hand joints. **Right:** The input block, constructed by stacking the skeleton feature vectors across time. The yellow-highlighted block demonstrates the first application of the $f_1 * N_0 = f_1 * D = 8 * 66$ 1-dimensional temporal convolution kernel.

Since the original TCN is designed for action segmentation task in RGB video, the encoder reviewed above is followed by a decoder with similar architecture, except that upsampling is used instead of pooling. Kim et al. [16] extend the original TCN to human action recognition task by adopting only the encoder portion and applying global average pooling and a softmax layer [19] for prediction. They also employ the residual connections as introduced in [11,12].

3.2   Spatial-Temporal Attention Res-TCN

We propose an end-to-end Spatial-Temporal Attention Res-TCN (STA-Res-TCN) for skeleton-based dynamic hand gesture recognition. The overall architecture is shown in Fig. 1.

For each video frame, a D-dimensional skeleton feature vector is constructed by concatenating the 3D coordinates of each hand joints. The frame-wise skeleton feature vectors are then stacked temporally across the entire video sequence to form the input block $X_0 \in \mathbb{R}^{T \times D}$, as shown in Fig. 2, which is later fed into the STA-Res-TCN.

Given the high-intra variance nature of hand gestures, we notice that not all video frames and not all features extracted by TCN contain the most discriminative information. Irrelevant time frames and features often bring in unnecessary noises. Given this observation, along with the main branch, we introduce an extra attention branch to generate same size masks at each layer which softly weight the feature maps extracted by the main branch. Such soft attention mechanism assists the model to adaptively focus more on the informative frames and features.

To be specific, given the output of the previous block $X_{l-1} \in \mathbb{R}^{T \times N_{l-1}}$ from the main branch and $\tilde{M}_{l-1} \in \mathbb{R}^{T \times N_{l-1}}$ from the mask branch, the feature maps extracted by the main branch and the masks with the same size generated by the mask branch at the l-th block can be respectively computed with:

$$\tilde{X}_l = X_{l-1} + F(W_{l_{main}}, X_{l-1}), \tag{2}$$

$$\tilde{M}_l = G(W_{l_{mask}}, \tilde{M}_{l-1}), \tag{3}$$

where $\{W_{l_{main}}^{(i)}\}_{i=1}^{N_l}$ and $\{W_{l_{mask}}^{(i)}\}_{i=1}^{N_l}$ respectively denotes the collection of filters of the l-th block for the main branch and the mask branch; $F(\cdot)$ and $G(\cdot)$ denotes a series of operations of batch normalization [14], ReLU activation, drop out [32] and 1-dimensional temporal convolution. $\tilde{X}_l$ and $\tilde{M}_l$ both have N_l channels, and each channel has T frames. For channel $i \in \{1, 2, ..., N_l\}$, $\tilde{X}_l^{(i)} = \{\tilde{x}_{l,1}^{(i)}, ..., \tilde{x}_{l,T}^{(i)}\} \in \mathbb{R}^T$ calculates the time evolution of the response to the i-th convolution filter of the l-block. The i-th channel mask $\tilde{M}_l^{(i)} = \{\tilde{m}_{l,1}^{(i)}, ..., \tilde{m}_{l,T}^{(i)}\} \in \mathbb{R}^T$ are the scores indicating the importance of each time frame. We softly weight $\tilde{X}_l^{(i)}$ with the scores $\tilde{M}_l^{(i)}$ to achieve temporal attention for the i-th channel. Similarly, for time step $t \in \{1, 2, ..., T\}$, $\tilde{M}_{l,t} = \{\tilde{m}_{l,t}^{(1)}, ..., \tilde{m}_{l,t}^{(N_l)}\} \in \mathbb{R}^{N_l}$ are the scores indicating the importance of each channel (i.e. each feature extracted by convolution filters). We softly weight $\tilde{X}_{l,t} \in \mathbb{R}^{N_l}$ with the scores $\tilde{M}_{l,t}$ to achieve spatial attention (i.e. attention upon features). Thus, by performing an element-wise multiplication between the main branch feature maps $\tilde{X}_l$ and the masks $\tilde{M}_l$, we gain the spatial-temporal attention-aware feature maps:

$$X_l = \tilde{X}_l * M_l, \tag{4}$$

$$M_l = Sigmoid(\tilde{M}_l). \tag{5}$$

A sigmoid layer is employed to restrict the output range of the masks to $[0, 1]$.

Note that the first block of STA-Res-TCN does not involve a residual unit or any normalization and activation layer, the computation can be formulated as follows:

$$\tilde{X}_1 = W_{1_{main}} \otimes X_0, \tag{6}$$

$$\tilde{M}_1 = W_{1_{mask}} \otimes X_0, \tag{7}$$

$$M_1 = Sigmoid(\tilde{M}_1), \tag{8}$$

$$X_1 = \tilde{X}_1 * M_1. \tag{9}$$

where $\otimes$ denotes 1-dimensional temporal convolution.

For classification, we employ global average pooling after the last block across the entire temporal sequence and followed by a softmax layer to draw final predictions.

3.3   Data Augmentation

Overfitting is a severe problem in deep neural networks. It leads to an adequate performance on the training set, but a poor performance on the test set [23,32]. Either the DHG-14/28 Dataset or the SHREC'17 Track Dataset contains no more than 2700 hand gesture sequences for training, which are not enough to prevent overfitting. We employ the same data augmentation techniques with Nunez et al. [23] for fair comparison, including **scaling, shifting, time interpolation** and **adding noise**. We expand the original training set by 4 times.

4   Experiments

We have evaluated our proposal on two challenging datasets, DHG-14/28 Dataset [29] and SHREC'17 Track Dataset [30]. Experimental results show that STA-Res-TCN outperforms the state-of-the-art methods.

4.1   Datasets and Settings

DHG-14/28 Dataset. DHG-14/28 dataset [29] is a public dynamic hand gesture dataset, which contains sequences of 14 hand gestures performed 5 times by 20 participants in 2 finger configurations, resulting in 2800 video sequences. The coordinates of 22 hand joints in the 3D world space are provided per frame, forming a full hand skeleton. The Intel RealSense short range depth camera is used to collect the dataset.

SHREC'17 Track Dataset. SHREC'17 Track Dataset [30] is a public dynamic hand gesture dataset presented for the SHREC'17 Track. It contains sequences of 14 gestures performed between 1 and 10 times by 28 participants in 2 finger configurations, resulting in 2800 sequences. The coordinates of 22 hand joints in the 3D world space are provided per frame. The dataset is captured by Intel Realsense camera.

Implementation Details. We perform all our experiments on a Nvidia GeForce GTX 1080 GPU with Keras 2.0 [7] using TensorFlow [1] backend. The learning rate is initially set to be 0.01 and then is gradually reduced by a factor 10 at 0.2, 0.5, 0.6 of the total epochs for the DHG-14/28 Dataset, and at 0.3, 0.6, 0.9 for the SHREC'17 Track Dataset. We employ the Adam algorithm [17] with parameters $\beta_1 = 0.9$, $\beta_2 = 0.999$ and $\epsilon = 1e^{-8}$. The batch size is set to 256, and the network is trained for up to 200 epochs. L-1 regularizer with a weight of $1e^{-4}$ is applied to all convolution layers. The dropout [32] rate is set to be 0.5 to prevent overfitting. The length of temporal window f_l is set to be 8 frames. Every skeleton sequence is subtracted by the palm position of the first frame.

4.2   Comparisons with State-of-the-Arts

In the experiment on DHG-14/28 Dataset, we follow a leave-one-subject-out cross-validation strategy, i.e., we perform 20 experiments, each one using data from 19 subjects for training and data from the rest 1 subject for testing. The reported results are computed as the average over these 20 cross-validation folds.

We show performance comparisons of STA-Res-TCN with state-of-the-art methods in Table 1. The recognition rate of our proposed model achieves 89.2% for the 14 gestures setting and 85.0% for the more complicated 28 gestures setting. The experimental results in Table 1 demonstrate a significant enhancement of recognition rates in comparison with state-of-the-art methods with both settings. Note that for fair comparison, we employ the same data augmentation techniques with Nunez et al. [23], the current state-of-the-art method, to both the baseline model Res-TCN and the attention model STA-Res-TCN. By comparing the performance of the baseline model and STA-Res-TCN, we can observe that our proposed attention mechanism brings 2.3% and 1.4% accuracy raise for the 14 gestures setting and 28 gestures setting respectively.

Table 1. Comparisons of accuracy (%) on DHG-14/28 Dataset.

Method	14 gestures	28 gestures
SoCJ+HoHD+HoWR [29]	83.1	80.0
Chen et al. [5]	84.7	80.3
CNN+LSTM [23]	85.6	81.1
Res-TCN (Baseline)	86.9	83.6
STA-Res-TCN (Ours)	**89.2**	**85.0**

The confusion matrices with 14 gestures setting and 28 gestures setting are shown in Figs. 3 and 4. It can be observed that our proposed STA-Res-TCN achieves recognition rate higher than 90.0% in 11 of the 14 gestures. The accuracy comparison for each individual gesture is favorable to our proposal in 10 of the 14 gestures compared to the work of [23]. It can also be observed from the confusion matrix that the gestures *Grab* and *Pinch* are usually misclassified due to the low inter-class variance.

In the experiment on SHREC'17 Track Dataset, we follow the division of the training set and the test set of the SHREC'17 Track [30], resulting in 1960 training sequences and 840 test sequences. We still employ the same data augmentation technique to both the baseline model and the attention model STA-Res-TCN.

As demonstrated in Table 2, the STA-Res-TCN achieves the accuracy of 93.6% for the 14 gestures setting and 90.7% for the more complicated 28 gestures setting. Our proposed model outperforms the state-of-the-art models, especially showing greater accuracy improvement with the more complicated 28 gestures

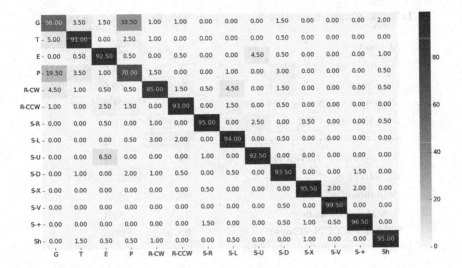

Fig. 3. Confusion matrix on DHG-14/28 Dataset with 14 gestures setting.

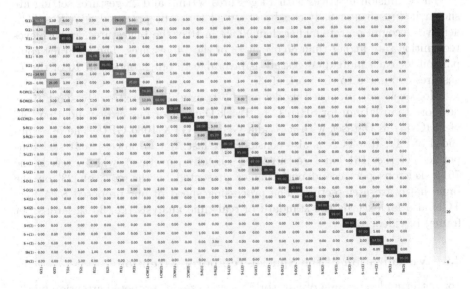

Fig. 4. Confusion matrix on DHG-14/28 Dataset with 28 gestures setting.

setting, which further validates the effectiveness of our proposed model. By comparing the performance of the baseline model Res-TCN and the attention model STA-Res-TCN, we can observe that our proposed attention mechanism brings 2.5% and 3.4% accuracy raise respectively for the 14 gestures setting and 28 gestures setting.

Table 2. Comparisons of accuracy (%) on SHREC'17 Track Dataset.

Method	14 gestures	28 gestures
Oreifej et al.[a] [25]	78.5	74.0
Devanne et al.[a] [9]	79.6	62.0
Classify Sequence by Key Frames [30]	82.9	71.9
Ohn-Bar et al.[a] [24]	83.9	76.5
SoCJ+Direction+Rotation [28]	86.9	84.2
SoCJ+HoHD+HoWR [29]	88.2	81.9
Caputo et al. [4]	89.5	-
Boulahia et al.[a] [3]	90.5	80.5
Res-TCN (Baseline)	91.1	87.3
STA-Res-TCN (Ours)	**93.6**	**90.7**

[a]Implement and evaluate by Smedt et al. [30]

The confusion matrices with 14 gestures setting and 28 gestures setting are shown in Figs. 5 and 6. It can be observed that our proposed STA-Res-TCN achieves recognition rate higher than 90.0% in 10 of the 14 gestures, and achieves recognition rate higher than 85.0% in 13 of the 14 gestures. The accuracy comparison for each individual gesture is favorable to our proposal in 10 of the 14 gestures compared to the work of [3].

Moreover, our proposed model can be trained in an extremely short time, no more than 30 min for SHREC'17 Track Dataset or one cross-validation fold of DHG-14/28 Dataset with a Nvidia GeForce GTX 1080 GPU. The inference speed of STA-Res-TCN is also considerably fast. It can process 9691 skeletons per second (i.e. 161 hand gestures per second on average), which exceeds the 7615 skeletons per second performance presented by the work of [23] on the same hardware architecture. The processing speed of our proposed STA-Res-TCN also far exceeds the standard of real time analysis (i.e. 30 skeletons per frame) in video.

4.3 Visualization of the Spatial-Temporal Attention

For better understanding of our work, we analyze our proposed attention mechanism by visualizing and comparing the feature maps before/after soft attention masks.

For a skeleton sequence of hand gesture "tap", as shown in Fig. 7(a), the key movements mainly relate to the tip joint of index finger, and the key frames that contain the most discriminative information range approximately from the 21st frame to the 34th frame. Figure 7(b) shows the two temporal convolution filters which our proposed attention mechanism has the greatest impact on. These two filters mainly learn a downward translation movement of the tip joint of index finger along the y axis, which is in accord with which human considers as key movement. Figure 7(c) shows a comparison between the feature maps

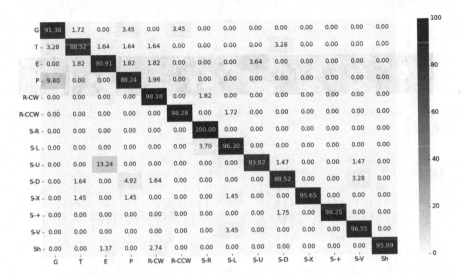

Fig. 5. Confusion matrix on SHREC-14/28 Dataset with 14 gestures setting.

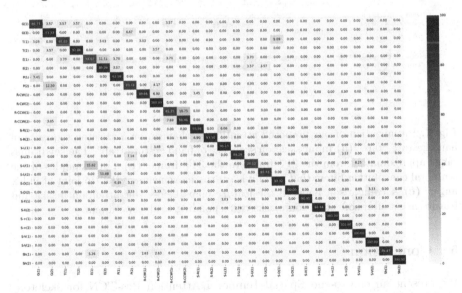

Fig. 6. Confusion matrix on SHREC-14/28 Dataset with 28 gestures setting.

before/after soft attention masks corresponding to the two convolution filters mentioned above. It can be observed that the time frames which our proposed attention mechanism stressed more attention on are consistent with which human perceives as discriminative.

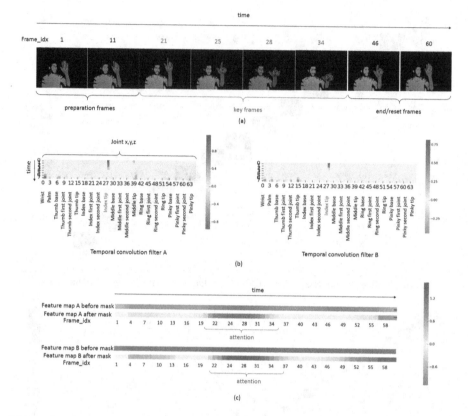

Fig. 7. Visualization of our proposed attention mechanism on a skeleton sequence of hand gesture "tap". **(a)** Input skeleton sequence of hand gesture "tap". The key frames range approximately from the 21st frame to the 34th frame. **(b)** Two examples of the temporal convolution filters that mainly learn the movements of the tip joint of index finger. **(c)** A comparison between the feature maps before soft attention masks and feature maps after soft attention masks corresponding to the two filters.

5   Conclusion

We present an end-to-end Spatial-Temporal Attention Res-TCN for skeleton-based dynamic hand gesture recognition, which learns to adaptively assign different levels of attention to each spatial-temporal features at each time step as layers going deeper. Experimental results demonstrate the effectiveness of the proposed STA-Res-TCN, which achieves significant accuracy enhancement in comparison with other state-of-the-art methods. Moreover, our proposed STA-Res-TCN is a lightweight model, which can be trained and tested in an extremely short time.

References

1. Abadi, M., et al.: TensorFlow: large-scale machine learning on heterogeneous systems (2015). https://www.tensorflow.org/, software available from tensorflow.org
2. Boulahia, S., Anquetil, E., Kulpa, R., Multon, F.: HIF3D: handwriting-inspired features for 3D skeleton-based action recognition. In: ICPR (2017)
3. Boulahia, S.Y., Anquetil, E., Multon, F., Kulpa, R.: Dynamic hand gesture recognition based on 3D pattern assembled trajectories. In: IPTA (2017)
4. Caputo, F., Prebianca, P., Carcangiu, A., Spano, L.D., Giachetti, A.: Comparing 3D trajectories for simple mid-air gesture recognition. Comput. Graph. **73**, 17–25 (2018)
5. Chen, X., Guo, H., Wang, G., Zhang, L.: Motion feature augmented recurrent neural network for skeleton-based dynamic hand gesture recognition. In: ICIP (2017)
6. Chen, X., Wang, G., Guo, H., Zhang, C.: Pose guided structured region ensemble network for cascaded hand pose estimation. In: Neurocomputing (2018)
7. Chollet, F., et al.: Keras (2015). https://github.com/fchollet/keras
8. Corbetta, M., Shulman, G.L.: Control of goal-directed and stimulus-driven attention in the brain. Nat. Rev. Neurosci. **3**, 201–215 (2002)
9. Devanne, M., Wannous, H., Berretti, S., Pala, P., Daoudi, M., Bimbo, A.D.: 3-D human action recognition by shape analysis of motion trajectories on riemannian manifold. IEEE Trans. Cybern. **45**(7), 1340–1352 (2015)
10. Han, J., Shao, L., Xu, D., Shotton, J.: Enhanced computer vision with microsoft kinect sensor: a review. IEEE Trans. Cybern. **43**(5), 1318–1334 (2013)
11. He, K., Zhang, X., Ren, S., Sun, J.: Deep residual learning for image recognition. In: CVPR (2016)
12. He, K., Zhang, X., Ren, S., Sun, J.: Identity mappings in deep residual networks. In: Leibe, B., Matas, J., Sebe, N., Welling, M. (eds.) ECCV 2016. LNCS, vol. 9908, pp. 630–645. Springer, Cham (2016). https://doi.org/10.1007/978-3-319-46493-0_38
13. Huang, G., Liu, Z., Maaten, L., Weinberger, K.Q.: Densely connected convolutional networks. In: CVPR (2017)
14. Ioffe, S., Szegedy, C.: Batch normalization: accelerating deep network training by reducing internal covariate shift. In: ICML (2015)
15. Keselman, L., Woodfill, J.I., Grunnet-Jepsen, A., Bhowmik, A.: Intel realsense stereoscopic depth cameras. In: CVPRW (2017)
16. Kim, T., Reiter, A.: Interpretable 3D human action analysis with temporal convolutional networks. In: CVPR BNMW Workshop (2017)
17. Kingma, D.P., Ba, J.L.: Adam: a method for stochastic optimization. arXiv preprint arXiv:1412.6980 (2014)
18. Lea, C., Flynn, M.D., Vidal, R., Reiter, A., Hager, G.D.: Temporal convolutional networks for action segmentation and detection. In: CVPR (2017)
19. Lin, M., Chen, Q., Yan, S.: Network in network. arXiv preprint arXiv:1312.4400 (2013)
20. Liu, J., Wang, G., Hu, P., Duan, L.Y., Kot, A.C.: Global context-aware attention LSTM networks for 3D action recognition. In: CVPR (2017)
21. Molchanov, P., Gupta, S., Kim, K., Kautz, J.: Hand gesture recognition with 3D convolutional neural networks. In: CVPRW (2015)
22. Moon, G., Chang, J.Y., Lee, K.M.: V2V-posenet: Voxel-to-Voxel prediction network for accurate 3D hand and human pose estimation from a single depth map. arXiv preprint arXiv:1711.07399 (2018)

23. Nunez, J.C., Cabido, R., Pantrigo, J.J., Montemayor, A.S., Velez, J.F.: Convolutional neural networks and long short-term memory for skeleton-based human activity and hand gesture recognition. Pattern Recognit. **76**, 80–94 (2018)
24. Ohn-Bar, E., Trivedi, M.: Joint angles similarities and HOG2 for action recognition. In: CVPRW (2013)
25. Oreifej, O., Liu, Z.: HON4D: histogram of oriented 4D normals for activity recognition from depth sequences. In: CVPR (2013)
26. Girshick, R., Donahue, J., Darrell, T., Malik, J.: Rich feature hierarchies for accurate object detection and semantic segmentation. In: CVPR (2014)
27. Shi, C., Wang, G., Yin, X., Pei, X., He, B., Lin, X.: High-accuracy stereo matching based on adaptive ground control points. IEEE Trans. Image Process. **24**(4), 1412–1423 (2015)
28. Smedt, Q.D.: Dynamic hand gesture recognition - from traditional handcrafted to recent deep learning approaches. In: Computer Vision and Pattern Recognition [cs.CV]. Universite de Lille 1, Sciences et Technologies; CRIStAL UMR 9189, English (2017)
29. Smedt, Q.D., Wannous, H., Vandeborre, J.P.: Skeleton-based dynamic hand gesture recognition. In: CVPRW (2016)
30. Smedt, Q.D., Wannous, H., Vandeborre, J.P., Guerry, J., Saux, B.L., Filliat, D.: SHREC'17 track: 3D hand gesture recognition using a depth and skeletal dataset. In: Eurographics Workshop on 3D Object Retrieval (2017)
31. Song, S., Lan, C., Xing, J., Zeng, W., Liu, J.: An end-to-end spatio-temporal attention model for human action recognition from skeleton data. In: AAAI (2017)
32. Srivastava, N., Hinton, G., Krizhevsky, A., Sutskever, I., Salakhutdinov, R.: Dropout: a simple way to prevent neural networks from overfitting. J. Mach. Learn. Res. **15**, 1929–1958 (2014)
33. Wang, G., Yin, X., Pei, X., Shi, C.: Depth estimation for speckle projection system using progressive reliable points growing matching. Appl. Opt. **52**, 516–524 (2013)
34. Wang, G., Chen, X., Guo, H., Zhang, C.: Region ensemble network: towards good practices for deep 3D hand pose estimation. J. Vis. Commun. Image Represent. **55**, 404–414 (2018)
35. Xu, K., et al.: Show, attend and tell: Neural image caption generation with visual attention. In: ICML (2015)

Task-Oriented Hand Motion Retargeting
for Dexterous Manipulation Imitation

Dafni Antotsiou$^{(\boxtimes)}$, Guillermo Garcia-Hernando, and Tae-Kyun Kim

Imperial College London, London, UK
{d.antotsiou17,g.garcia-hernando,tk.kim}@imperial.ac.uk

Abstract. Human hand actions are quite complex, especially when they involve object manipulation, mainly due to the high dimensionality of the hand and the vast action space that entails. Imitating those actions with dexterous hand models involves different important and challenging steps: acquiring human hand information, retargeting it to a hand model, and learning a policy from acquired data. In this work, we capture the hand information by using a state-of-the-art hand pose estimator. We tackle the retargeting problem from the hand pose to a 29 DoF hand model by combining inverse kinematics and PSO with a task objective optimisation. This objective encourages the virtual hand to accomplish the manipulation task, relieving the effect of the estimator's noise and the domain gap. Our approach leads to a better success rate in the grasping task compared to our inverse kinematics baseline, allowing us to record successful human demonstrations. Furthermore, we used these demonstrations to learn a policy network using generative adversarial imitation learning (GAIL) that is able to autonomously grasp an object in the virtual space.

Keywords: Hand pose estimation · Motion retargeting
PSO · Anthropomorphic hand model · Imitation learning · GAIL

1 Introduction

Learning to perform human-like tasks is an important goal of artificial intelligence. Achieving this goal though presents many challenges, predominantly adjusting the tasks to the agent's (i.e. robots) architecture and inferring intention about the task's desired outcome. This work is interested in the imitation of tasks performed by the human hand - such as grasping - using a dexterous anthropomorphic hand model.

There are two main difficulties when tackling this problem. First is the interpretation of the human motion to the agent's environment, which is called retargeting. Second is the inference of the tasks' objective and the ability to perform them in the agent's environment. One way of achieving this goal is through

Project webpage: https://daphneantotsiou.github.io/task-oriented-retargeting.html

L. Leal-Taixé and S. Roth (Eds.): ECCV 2018 Workshops, LNCS 11134, pp. 287–301, 2019.
https://doi.org/10.1007/978-3-030-11024-6_19

imitation learning, which involves using human demonstrations that the agent attempts to imitate [12]. That can become difficult, though, when the agent is a physical robot. That is why more and more studies use synthetic data to train imitation learning methods in a virtual environment [6,16,34,41].

The purpose of this work is to aid retargeting in the imitation learning pipeline to achieve dexterous tasks using a five-fingered anthropomorphic hand model. In contrast to previous work that used specialised mocap hardware to capture expert demonstrations [16], we use a state-of-the-art hand pose estimator (HPE) that aims to extract the skeleton of the hand in every frame captured by a depth camera. These demonstrations are then retargeted to the hand model's space, since that is the environment in which the imitation will take place. Final goal is for the agent to learn to perform the same tasks in its own environment using its own architecture.

The major problem in this pipeline that this work aims to address is the difficulties in successfully retargeting human motion, especially in real-time. These arise from the discrepancies between the human hand and the hand model, the different constraints of the environments and the noise coming from the camera and the hand pose estimator, whose output is less accurate when unseen views and articulations are captured. This leads to an output that is often not kinematically plausible. Hand pose estimators are also vulnerable to occlusions [37], be it self-occlusions [13,35] or occlusions from object manipulation [7,27]. All these discrepancies become especially important when the task involves delicate interaction with other objects, like grasping. In these cases, even the smallest error in the position of the end effectors can result in failure of the task.

This work addresses this difficulty by introducing task objective optimisation through the use of the particle swarm optimisation (PSO) algorithm [14]. The aim of this is to improve interaction with objects in the agent's environment, which allows easier acquisition of expert demonstrations for imitation learning. In order to achieve more robust results, we developed a Hybrid PSO method that uses inverse kinematics (IK) retargeting for pose initialisation and then refined that pose by driving it to touch the objects with as many fingers as possible. Recorded trajectories are then used to teach an agent how to grasp

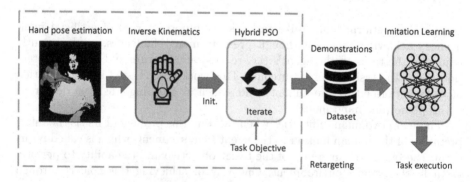

Fig. 1. Flow chart of our proposed framework.

in a simulated environment by using a generative adversarial imitation learning (GAIL) [10]. An overview of our framework is depicted in Fig. 1.

2   Related Work

Hand motion retargeting to anthropomorphic robot grippers is challenging to control due to their high dimensionality and kinematics discrepancy. Similar to our inverse kinematics baseline, [19] proposed to use relative transformations of positions, velocities and forces for grasping. As a result of advances in processing capacity, an interest for simulation environments for robotic learning and for virtual/augmented reality (VR/AR) has emerged. In robotic learning, simulation is usually combined with imitation learning [6,39], reinforcement learning [3], or a combination of the two [24,41]. In all those cases however, the used grippers are of low dimensionality (i.e. two or three moving joints) with the exception of a few works that we review in the next section. Regarding manipulation in a VR/AR, [1,2] used a bespoke hand glove and haptic sensors to capture hand information and mapped this information to either a realistic spring hand model or a simplistic two fingertips model. Physics-based approaches modelling hand meshes and forces for object interaction include [11,15,40]. [11] chose to use a spring hand model to infer contact forces, whereas [15] optimised hand deformation using a particle based approach. Similar to our work but requiring a large prerecorded motion dataset, [40] aimed to minimise the distance between contact points and the object in a data-driven fashion through the use of PSO.

In the hand pose estimation field, the interaction with (real) objects has also been studied [7,9,23,25,27,28,32]. Similar to our work but with a different objective, [32] used physics simulation and salient points to accurately estimate the hand pose in an object manipulation scenario. In our work, we circumvent the object occlusion by working in a mixed reality scenario similar to [23].

To conclude, we include related work on human body motion retargeting. [22,33] used deep learning techniques in a cyclic manner to minimise the error between angles and different models respectively. More related to our work, given their aim to accomplish a task, [26] combined IL and reinforcement learning to both perform tasks and achieve retargeting of motion to different models. Similarly to us, their reward function aims to minimise the distance in position and rotation between the expert demonstrations and the generated sequences.

Imitation learning (IL), or learning from demonstrations [29] is the process through which, given a set of demonstrations, an agent learns to map observations to actions [12]. The field has not been a exception of the success of deep learning approaches [5,6,10,12]. A recent successful approach is generative adversarial imitation learning [10] (GAIL). In their work, [10] designed a generative adversarial system inspired by the success of generative adversarial networks (GAN) [8]. [10] adapted the GANs concept of adversarial behaviour to IL as a policy search problem, where the generator aims to produce the ideal policy that will produce results similar to the demonstrations. Related to our framework, [16] use a mocap system consisting of a glove to record demonstrations in a virtual space that are late fed to an IL system. The key difference between their work and ours is that our input data is noisy due to the hand pose estimation stage and thus we propose a system that can help to alleviate the challenge of recording successful demonstrations.

3   Framework Overview

In our framework (Fig. 1), we use the hand skeleton, provided by the HPE, as input and retarget it to a hand model in a virtual scene. Retargeting is performed, first by approximating the pose with inverse kinematics (IK), and then optimising that pose for a number of iterations. The aim of the optimisation is to grasp an object, thus making lifting easier. Finally, this retargeting method is used to record multiple demonstrations of object lifting, which are then used to train an imitation learning network using the GAIL methodology. Final outcome is an agent that can imitate grasping and lifting objects with a dexterous hand model.

The hand pose estimator (HPE) used provides the 3D locations of 21 skeleton points of the hand. In order to perform dexterous actions, the hand model needs to be five-fingered and similar to the human hand. The hand model selected is a modified version of the MPL model presented in [17], which in turn is a virtual model of the Modular Prosthetic Limb developed by Johns Hopkins University [21]. The hand pose can be controlled through 23 actuators, each of which can rotate a joint by a given axis. Therefore, each actuator has 1 degree of freedom. Aside from the hand pose actuators, the hand model also has 6 degrees of freedom for its global position and rotation. Therefore, the model has a total of 29 degrees of freedom (Fig. 2).

Since the objective of this work is to retarget the hand pose to perform a task, the fitness function of the PSO is selected to minimise the difference between the input observation x, which is the skeleton produced by the HPE, and the observation y produced by the virtual environment after a particle had been applied to the simulation. Observations x and y can be seen in Fig. 2.

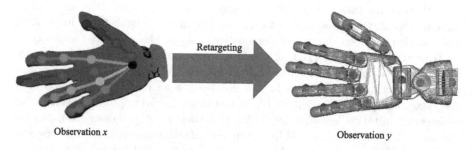

Fig. 2. Left: the input skeleton points from the hand pose estimator. Right: the hand model that performs imitation and its 23 internal actuators that control joint rotations.

4   Retargeting Through Stochastic Optimisation

In our framework, the mapping process of the hand pose in the real world to the corresponding action space in the virtual environment is achieved through the use of the particle swarm optimisation method [14], which is a type of stochastic optimisation. In PSO, a number of particles try to find an optimal solution by moving in the search space. Their position is evaluated by a fitness function and their new position depends on their personal and global best. As presented in [30], for each particle i, its position p and velocity v for iteration t are given by:

$$v_{i,t} = v_{i,t-1} + c_1 * (p_{i,t-1}^{best} - p_{i,t-1}) + c_2 * (g_{t-1}^{best} - p_{i,t-1}), \tag{1}$$

$$p_{i,t} = p_{i,t-1} * v_{i,t}, \tag{2}$$

where $p_{i,t-1}^{best}$ is the current personal best position of the particle, g_{t-1}^{best} is the current global best position for all particles and c_1 and c_2 are learning rates.

4.1   PSO Fitness Function

A key component in PSO is accurately defining its fitness function. In our work, we define the particles and the fitness function in different domains and involve a simulation integration between them. Whereas the particles are the actions that control the hand model, the fitness function evaluates the resulting hand pose of those actions. Therefore, the fitness function does not interact with the positions of the particles themselves, but rather with the outcome of those positions when they are applied to the environment. That way the fitness function aims to infer not only the effect the actions have on the hand pose, but also characteristics of the environment itself (i.e. external forces like gravity, impediment from other objects like walls, collisions).

Aside from matching the reference pose of the HPE skeleton, the PSO can also be used to aid in task execution. Hence, the final form of the fitness function is the following:

$$E(x, y, object) = \omega_{pose}E_{pose}(x, y) + \omega_{task}E_{task}(y, object), \tag{3}$$

where E_{pose} and E_{task} represent the hand pose approximation and the task objective respectively, and ω_{pose} and ω_{task} are their respective weights.

Hand Pose Energy Function E_{pose}

The E_{pose} energy function minimises the pose difference between input x and output y. Similarly to us, [20,31] used PSO to minimise the distance between the joints. In our work, though, we are also interested in the relative joint angles. [26] also minimised position and rotation of joints in their reward function, but they were only interested in the end effectors, whereas we want to optimise all the controls. Therefore, the hand pose energy function is:

$$E_{pose} = \omega_p E_p + \omega_a E_a. \tag{4}$$

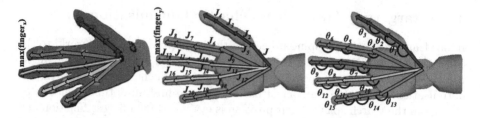

Fig. 3. Left: joint vectors J in observation x. Middle: joint vectors J in observation y. Right: angles θ in observation y

Position Energy Function E_p: it aims to minimise the euclidean distance between the corresponding points of observations x and y, and it is set as the normalised weighted mean squared error between them:

$$E_p = \frac{1}{\sum_{i=1}^{N_{joints}} \omega_{joint}^{(i)}} \sum_{i=1}^{N_{joints}} \omega_{joint}^{(i)} \| \frac{x\prime(i) - y(i)}{\| \max(finger_{x\prime}) \| + \| \max(finger_y) \|} \|^2, \tag{5}$$

where $x\prime$ is the representation of x in the y domain. The weights ω_{joint} represent the individual weights of each joint allowing prioritisation of some joints, such as the end effectors, above others. N_{joints} is the number of joints, being 21 in our model.

Since the two observations exist in different domains, observation x needs to be scaled to the environment and the hand model of observation y. The scaling factor used is the global ratio between the joint lengths of the two hand models. Therefore, if the joint vectors of domains x and y are $J_1(x) \ldots J_{N_{joints}}(x)$ and $J_1(y) \ldots J_{N_{joints}}(y)$ respectively (Fig. 3), then the normalised observation x is:

$$x\prime = sx \text{ where } s = \frac{1}{N_{joints} - 1} \sum_{i=1}^{N_{joints}-1} \frac{\| J_i(y) \|}{\| J_i(x) \|}. \tag{6}$$

Angle Energy Function E_a: While the position energy function minimises the distance between the points, thus preserving the position of the end effectors as well as the general structure and orientation of the hand pose, it is not guaranteed it can accurately preserve the local angles of all 21 points. Therefore, a second energy function E_a is introduced, that aims to minimise the difference between all the relative angles of the joints, N_{angles}, 15 in our model. For $\theta_i(x)$ and $\theta_i(y)$ as the 3D joint angles of observation x and y respectively (Fig. 3), the angle energy function is the normalised mean squared error between the two observations:

$$E_a = \frac{1}{N_{angles}} \sum_{i=1}^{N_{angles}} \| \frac{\theta_i(x) - \theta_i(y)}{\pi} \|^2. \tag{7}$$

Task Energy Function E_{task}

The second term of the fitness function E_{task} aims to assist in achieving the task's objective. Since the current task is grasping, the intention of this energy function is to minimise the distance between specific points of the hand model and the object in question. The points selected were the middle of the palm and the end effectors, which are the five fingertips (Fig. 4). With ω_{palm} and ω_{ee} as the individual weights of the palm and the end effectors respectively, the task energy function is the following:

$$E_{task} = \frac{1}{5\omega_{ee} + \omega_{palm}}(\sum_{i=2}^{6} \omega_{ee}\|\frac{d_i}{\omega_{cost}d_{max}}\|^2 + \omega_{palm}\|\frac{d_1}{\omega_{cost}d_{max}}\|^2), \quad (8)$$

where d_i is the minimum distance between point i and the various meshes of the object. To limit the distance search space, when a point's distance to the object is over a certain threshold d_{max}, then it is presumed it cannot interact with the object and is flagged as missing. Therefore, each point's distance to the object is:

$$d_i = \begin{cases} min(d_{ij}) & \text{if } d_{ij} < d_{max} \\ \omega_{cost}d_{max} & \text{otherwise} \end{cases}, \quad (9)$$

where i are the six points, j are all the meshes of the object and d_{ij} is the minimum planar distance between the two (Fig. 4). The points flagged as missing are punished by assigning them the maximum detectable distance multiplied by ω_{cost}. The purpose of the weight is to act as an incentive to have as many points close to the object as possible.

Fig. 4. Representation of the 6 points of the task energy function. When a point is close to the object, the minimum distance between the point and the object surface is used. When a point is too far from the object to achieve contact, the point is flagged as missing

4.2 Hybrid PSO - Task Optimisation

Due to the stochastic nature of PSO, it is not certain that the algorithm can manage to converge to an acceptable degree, especially when it needs to perform in real-time. For that reason, a Hybrid PSO method was developed, which uses an inverse kinematics approximation as a priori knowledge and applies localised PSO around that pose for task optimisation. This is achieved mainly thanks to the task objective energy function E_{task} that encourages contact.

The final Hybrid PSO method with all the refinements starts by initialising all the particles in a position similar to the one provided by the inverse kinematics approximation. Then, through a limited number of iterations, it updates the position of the particles, but only up to a certain amount. Finally, the algorithm terminates when a particle converges to an adequate degree. Even if the particles do not have enough time to reach that point due to execution time constraints, the result is still guaranteed to be close to the initial inverse kinematics pose and, therefore, stochasticity from the PSO is constrained.

An additional main advantage of our method is that Hybrid PSO can overcome the HPE's limited response time. Whereas retargeting with the pose energy function E_{pose} solely depends on observation x that comes from the HPE, the task energy function E_{task} only depends on the current state of the environment (observation y of the hand model and the object). That means that it can be applied at a higher frame rate than the HPE, providing continuous micro-corrections while the new hand pose is estimated. It can, therefore, lift the interaction limitations that stem from HPE's bottleneck. Algorithm 1 shows in detail the integration of our Hybrid method in the PSO pipeline, presented in [30].

5 Imitation Learning

To complete the framework's pipeline, we recorded a dataset of 161 grasping successful demonstrations using our Hybrid PSO retargeting method and fed them to a GAIL framework. The network aims to learn a policy between states and actions. The state space used in this framework comprises the relative distance and velocity between the hand model and the object, the local rotations and velocities of the internal hand joints, as well as the minimum contact distance between the hand end-effectors (five fingertips) and the object.

$$s_t = [pos_{hand} - pos_{object}, vel_{hand} - vel_{object}, angle_{joints}, vel_{joints}, d_{contact}]. \quad (10)$$

The action space consists of the 29 actuators of the hand model, which denote its 29 degrees of freedom.

6 Experiments

This section describes the experiments conducted to evaluate the effectiveness of the retargeting optimisation. First, the optimisation was tested under retargeting generalisation, where retargeting was performed solely using the PSO

Algorithm 1. Proposed Hybrid PSO Algorithm

    Input: x observation from HPE, swarmsize, iterations
    Output: $particle_{global}^{best}$
1 actions = IK(x)
    // initialise position of particles around the IK position
2 **for** *particle in swarmsize* **do**
3 | *particle* = *actions* + *rand()*
4 | $particle_{personal}^{best}$ = *particle*
5 **end**
6 $particle_{global}^{best}$ = *particle* which has the minimum $E(x, y, contact)$

    // optimise particles by minimising their fitness function
7 **for** *t* in *iterations* **do**
8 | **for** *particle* in *swarmsize* **do**
9 | | Update *particle* position and velocity according to PSO algorithm
10 | | $y_{particle}, contact = simulation(particle)$
11 | | $E_{t,particle}(x, y, object) = \omega_{pose} E_{pose}(x, y) + \omega_{task} E_{task}(y, object)$
12 | | **if** $E_{t,particle}(x, y, object) < E_{personal}^{best}$ **then**
13 | | | $E_{personal}^{best} = E_{t,particle}(x, y, contact)$
14 | | **end**
15 | **end**
16 | **if** $min(E_t) < E_{global}^{best}$ **then**
17 | | $E_{global}^{best} = min(E_t)$
18 | **end**
19 **end**

---

approach, without any prior information. Second, the hybrid method was tested in its ability to grasp compared to the inverse kinematics baseline. Third, the GAIL network trained with Hybrid PSO demonstrations was tested in its ability to imitate grasping.

The simulation environment used in this work was Mujoco Pro [17] and the hand pose estimator was the one presented in [36] and trained with BigHand2.2M dataset [38]. All the experiments were performed using an Intel Core i5-7600K 3.8 GHz CPU, an NVIDIA GeForce GTX 1080 Ti GPU and 32 GB of RAM.

All the results presented used $\omega_{joint} = 10$ for the thumb fingertip, $\omega_{joint} = 3$ for the remaining fingertips, $\omega_{joint} = 1$ for the rest of the joints, $\omega_{palm} = 3$, $\omega_{ee} = 1$, $\omega_{cost} = 2$, $d_{max} = 0.04$ and PSO minimum fitness step $= 10^{-4}$.

6.1 Retargeting Generalisation

The pose energy function E_{pose} was evaluated through the application of PSO, excluding the task energy function and comparing the results with the input hand pose observation x. Figure 5 shows the retargeting results using various combinations of the position and angle terms. The position energy function is the most important one since that is the one responsible for the position of the end effectors as well as the global rotation of the hand. The angle energy function on the other hand aims to preserve the relative angles between the joints, so that the final pose is similar to that extracted from the HPE. Using a greater weight for the angle term w_a compared to the position term weight w_p can lead to erroneous rotation directions, as evident in Fig. 5. For accurate retargeting results, the position term needs to be the most significant, with the angle energy function acting as auxiliary. That is because the angles do not hold the 3D direction (i.e. the rightmost images of Fig. 5, where global hand rotation is not represented and the finger angles are correct in magnitude but can be wrong in direction). That error can be alleviated with the position energy function E_p, which minimises the position error of the points. On the other hand, using only E_p does not guarantee the overall pose will be preserved as it is susceptible to accumulating errors, as seen in the leftmost simulation images of Fig. 5. Therefore, finding a balance between the two terms is not trivial. This indicates that the definition of the pose energy function E_{pose} for hand pose retargeting can be improved, but that is not the focus of our research, which mainly targets object manipulation.

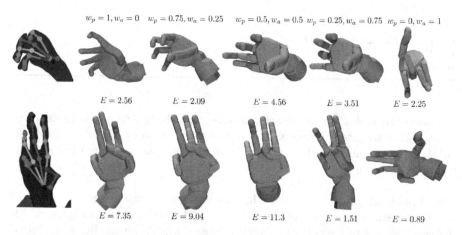

Fig. 5. Generalised PSO with different weights between position and angle terms (for illustration purposes energy values are scaled by a factor of 10^3).

6.2 Hybrid PSO

Our Hybrid PSO method aims to refine the inverse kinematics hand pose in order to achieve grasping. Therefore, the main coefficient of its fitness function is the objective coefficient E_{task}, the goal of which is to minimise the distance between the end effectors and a particular object.

In order to evaluate the Hybrid PSO retargeting method, we used our inverse kinematics baseline to record 10 trajectories where the grasping motion mostly failed, and then applied our method on the same actions. The demonstrations were recorded with a steady frame rate of 60 frames per second, and Hybrid PSO was applied to all of them off-line. The fitness function weights for all the experiments were: $\omega_{task} = 0.8$, $\omega_{pose} = 0.2$ and $\omega_p = 0.5$, $\omega_a = 0.5$. Figure 6 shows individual frames of a grasping motion with and without Hybrid PSO. This qualitative example indicates that the contact micro-corrections, applied at a high, steady rate, are capable of assisting in the grasping process (full videos at the project webpage).

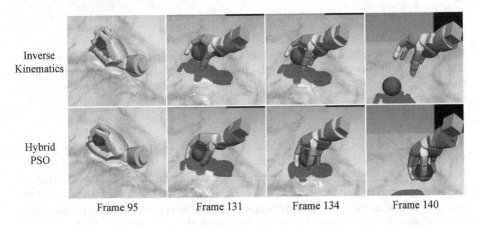

| | Frame 95 | Frame 131 | Frame 134 | Frame 140 |

Fig. 6. Top: individual frames of trajectory with our inverse kinematics baseline. Bottom: application of Hybrid PSO on the corresponding frames. The PSO parameters used were: $iterations = 100$, $swarm\ size = 100$

To quantitatively evaluate the method, we measured the percentage of frames the object is being lifted in each sequence. Since the trajectories also include the motion approaching the object, we denote the start of the "sequence of interest" as soon as at least two of the six points of E_{task} touch the object. From that moment onward, the hand model is in a position that could potentially lift the object. A frame is labelled as successfully lifting only when (a) the object is above the table, (b) the distance between the object and the palm is less than 0.2 and (c) at least one of the six contact points is close to the object. The final lifting ratio is the number of lifting frames divided by the number of frames in the "sequence of interest". Figure 7 shows the percentages for different iterations and swarm sizes. It can be seen that a relatively small number of iterations and particles (i.e. 25) can greatly boost the results, compared to our inverse kinematics baseline. It is worth noting that the optimisation quickly saturates, since there is not much improvement between 25 and 100 in swarm size and iterations.

Regarding the importance of the task energy function E_{task}, the bar graph on the right of Fig. 7 shows the percentage of successful trajectories for different ω_{task}. A trajectory is classified as successful if the object is being held in the

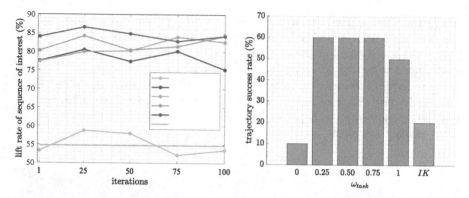

Fig. 7. Left: percentage of lifting frames in the "sequence of interest" part of the trajectories, which is the part where the hand model is capable of lifting the object. Right: percentage of successful trajectories for different ω_{task}, with *iterations* = 50 and *swarm size* = 25. ω_{pose} is normalised so that $\omega_{task} + \omega_{pose} = 1$

air in the last frame, or if the object is lifted over 17 cm during the sequence. From the graph, it becomes apparent that using only the pose energy function ($\omega_{pose} = 1$, $\omega_{task} = 0$) produces worse results than the baseline, mainly due to the non-optimal definition of the pose term E_{pose}. But the use of greater values of ω_{task} result in significant improvement of the success ratio, which indicates E_{task} does affect grasping. It should be noted that using $\omega_{task} = 1$ produces worse results than other values, which indicates that E_{pose} is also important, since it forces the hand pose to not deviate too far from the x observation and greatly alter the sequence of actions.

6.3 Imitation Learning

The imitation network was evaluated in its ability to successfully grasp from unseen initial conditions. To assist in quicker divergence and more natural motion, the network's generator was pretrained using behavioural cloning (BC). In the GAIL network, the trajectories were initialised using a method similar to [41], where initial conditions were either extracted from the demonstrations or random, based on a probability ϵ. The generator and discriminator architectures were identical, with two hidden layers of size 1024 and 512 respectively and *tanh* activation functions. Similarly to [10], the generator step function was further optimised using TRPO in order to ensure trajectories would not deviate too much from the demonstrations. The GAIL model was trained for 300 iterations, while its generator was also trained with BC for 100k iterations. We used the implementation of [4]. The unseen initial conditions were extracted from the demonstrations and then injected with uniform random noise with a standard deviation σ. Figure 8 shows the success rate of 100 trajectories compared to different σ. It can be seen that, while the policy is accurate when it is initialised at a condition it has previously seen, its success quickly drops when it tries to generalise to similar but unseen initial conditions. That behaviour though is expected, since GAIL offers limited generalisation and multi-modality [18], which is made even more difficult due to the high dimensionality of this framework's model.

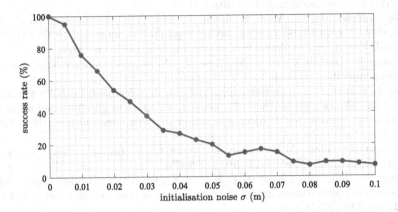

Fig. 8. Imitation success rate compared to different noise values in the initial state

7 Conclusion

In this work, we presented a Hybrid PSO method, which aims to assist in object grasping, using a hand pose estimator as input. Due to high input noise from hand pose estimators and absence of haptic feedback from virtual objects, the motivation behind this work was to allow easier and more robust grasping using a dexterous, human-like hand model. This method can then be used to record expert demonstrations by directly recording and retargeting human hand motion. Those demonstrations can then be used in a task learning environment, such as imitation or reinforcement learning, and model hand manipulation in a human-like manner. The presented work has the potential to be extended in several ways, such as: (i) exploring new tasks and objects via transfer learning; (ii) exploiting the hierarchical nature of the hand topology; (iii) end-to-end task-oriented retargeting (e.g. reinforcement learning) and (iv) enforcing natural hand motion using ground-truth hand pose data of manipulation actions [7].

Acknowledgement. This work is part of Imperial College London-Samsung Research project, supported by Samsung Electronics.

References

1. Borst, C.W., Indugula, A.P.: Realistic virtual grasping. In: VR (2005)
2. Buchmann, V., Violich, S., Billinghurst, M., Cockburn, A.: FingARtips: gesture based direct manipulation in augmented reality. In: GRAPHITE (2004)

3. Devin, C., Gupta, A., Darrell, T., Abbeel, P., Levine, S.: Learning modular neural network policies for multi-task and multi-robot transfer. In: ICRA (2017)
4. Dhariwal, P., et al.: Openai baselines (2017). https://github.com/openai/baselines
5. Duan, Y., et al.: One-shot imitation learning. In: ICRA (2018)
6. Finn, C., Yu, T., Zhang, T., Abbeel, P., Levine, S.: One-shot visual imitation learning via meta-learning. In: CoRL (2017)
7. Garcia-Hernando, G., Yuan, S., Baek, S., Kim, T.K.: First-person hand action benchmark with RGB-D videos and 3D hand pose annotations. In: CVPR (2018)
8. Goodfellow, I., et al.: Generative adversarial nets. In: NIPS (2014)
9. Hamer, H., Gall, J., Weise, T., Van Gool, L.: An object-dependent hand pose prior from sparse training data. In: CVPR (2010)
10. Ho, J., Ermon, S.: Generative adversarial imitation learning. In: NIPS (2016)
11. Höll, M., Oberweger, M., Arth, C., Lepetit, V.: Efficient physics-based implementation for realistic hand-object interaction in virtual reality. In: 2018 IEEEVR (2018)
12. Hussein, A., Gaber, M.M., Elyan, E., Jayne, C.: Imitation learning: a survey of learning methods. ACM CSUR 50, 21 (2017)
13. Jang, Y., Noh, S.T., Chang, H.J., Kim, T.K., Woo, W.: 3D finger cape: clicking action and position estimation under self-occlusions in egocentric viewpoint. TVCG 21, 501–510 (2015)
14. Kennedy, J., Eberhart, R.: Particle swarm optimization. In: ICANN (1995)
15. Kim, J.S., Park, J.M.: Physics-based hand interaction with virtual objects. In: ICRA (2015)
16. Kumar, V., Gupta, A., Todorov, E., Levine, S.: Learning dexterous manipulation policies from experience and imitation. IJRR (2018)
17. Kumar, V., Todorov, E.: MuJoCo HAPTIX: a virtual reality system for hand manipulation. In: IEEE-RAS (2015)
18. Li, Y., Song, J., Ermon, S.: Infogail: interpretable imitation learning from visual demonstrations. In: NIPS (2017)
19. Li, Z., Hsu, P., Sastry, S.: Grasping and coordinated manipulation by a multifingered robot hand. IJRR 8, 33–50 (1989)
20. Makris, A., Argyros, A.A.: Model-based 3D hand tracking with on-line shape adaptation. In: BMVC (2015)
21. McGee, T.G., Para, M.P., Katyal, K.D., Johannes, M.S.: Demonstration of force feedback control on the modular prosthetic limb. In: SMC (2014)
22. Mehta, D., et al.: VNect: real-time 3D human pose estimation with a single RGB camera. TOG 36, 44 (2017)
23. Mueller, F., Mehta, D., Sotnychenko, O., Sridhar, S., Casas, D., Theobalt, C.: Real-time hand tracking under occlusion from an egocentric RGB-D sensor. In: ICCV (2017)
24. Nair, A., McGrew, B., Andrychowicz, M., Zaremba, W., Abbeel, P.: Overcoming exploration in reinforcement learning with demonstrations. In: ICRA (2018)
25. Oikonomidis, I., Kyriazis, N., Argyros, A.A.: Full DOF tracking of a hand interacting with an object by modeling occlusions and physical constraints. In: ICCV (2011)
26. Peng, X.B., Abbeel, P., Levine, S., van de Panne, M.: DeepMimic: example-guided deep reinforcement learning of physics-based character skills. In: SIGGRAPH (2018)

27. Rogez, G., Khademi, M., Supančič III, J.S., Montiel, J.M.M., Ramanan, D.: 3D hand pose detection in egocentric RGB-D images. In: Agapito, L., Bronstein, M.M., Rother, C. (eds.) ECCV 2014. LNCS, vol. 8925, pp. 356–371. Springer, Cham (2015). https://doi.org/10.1007/978-3-319-16178-5_25

28. Romero, J., Kjellström, H., Kragic, D.: Hands in action: real-time 3D reconstruction of hands in interaction with objects. In: ICRA (2010)

29. Schaal, S.: Learning from demonstration. In: NIPS (1997)

30. Shi, Y., Eberhart, R.: A modified particle swarm optimizer. In: WCCI (1998)

31. Tompson, J., Stein, M., Lecun, Y., Perlin, K.: Real-time continuous pose recovery of human hands using convolutional networks. ToG 33, 169 (2014)

32. Tzionas, D., Ballan, L., Srikantha, A., Aponte, P., Pollefeys, M., Gall, J.: Capturing hands in action using discriminative salient points and physics simulation. IJCV 118, 172–193 (2016)

33. Villegas, R., Yang, J., Ceylan, D., Lee, H.: Neural kinematic networks for unsupervised motion retargetting. In: CVPR (2018)

34. Yang, Y., Hospedales, T.M.: A unified perspective on multi-domain and multi-task learning. In: ICLR (2014)

35. Ye, Q., Kim, T.-K.: Occlusion-aware hand pose estimation using hierarchical mixture density network. In: Ferrari, V., Hebert, M., Sminchisescu, C., Weiss, Y. (eds.) ECCV 2018. LNCS, vol. 11214, pp. 817–834. Springer, Cham (2018). https://doi.org/10.1007/978-3-030-01249-6_49

36. Ye, Q., Yuan, S., Kim, T.-K.: Spatial attention deep net with partial PSO for hierarchical hybrid hand pose estimation. In: Leibe, B., Matas, J., Sebe, N., Welling, M. (eds.) ECCV 2016. LNCS, vol. 9912, pp. 346–361. Springer, Cham (2016). https://doi.org/10.1007/978-3-319-46484-8_21

37. Yuan, S., et al.: Depth-based 3D hand pose estimation: from current achievements to future goals. In: CVPR (2018)

38. Yuan, S., Ye, Q., Stenger, B., Jain, S., Kim, T.K.: Bighand2. 2m benchmark: hand pose dataset and state of the art analysis. In: CVPR (2017)

39. Zhang, T., McCarthy, Z., Jow, O., Lee, D., Goldberg, K., Abbeel, P.: Deep imitation learning for complex manipulation tasks from virtual reality teleoperation. In: ICRA (2018)

40. Zhao, W., Zhang, J., Min, J., Chai, J.: Robust realtime physics-based motion control for human grasping. TOG 36, 207 (2013)

41. Zhu, Y., et al.: Reinforcement and imitation learning for diverse visuomotor skills. In: RSS (2018)

HANDS18: Methods, Techniques and Applications for Hand Observation

Iason Oikonomidis[3] , Guillermo Garcia-Hernando[1(✉)] , Angela Yao[5] ,
Antonis Argyros[2,3] , Vincent Lepetit[4] , and Tae-Kyun Kim[1]

[1] Imperial College London, London, UK
g.garcia-hernando@imperial.ac.uk
[2] University of Crete, Heraklion, Greece
[3] Foundation for Research and Technology, Heraklion, Greece
[4] University of Bordeaux, Bordeaux, France
[5] National University of Singapore, Singapore, Singapore

Abstract. This report outlines the proceedings of the Fourth International Workshop on Observing and Understanding Hands in Action (HANDS 2018). The fourth instantiation of this workshop attracted significant interest from both academia and the industry. The program of the workshop included regular papers that are published as the workshop's proceedings, extended abstracts, invited posters, and invited talks. Topics of the submitted works and invited talks and posters included novel methods for hand pose estimation from RGB, depth, or skeletal data, datasets for special cases and real-world applications, and techniques for hand motion re-targeting and hand gesture recognition. The invited speakers are leaders in their respective areas of specialization, coming from both industry and academia. The main conclusions that can be drawn are the turn of the community towards RGB data and the maturation of some methods and techniques, which in turn has led to increasing interest for real-world applications.

Keywords: Hand detection · Hand pose estimation · Hand tracking
Gesture recognition · Hand-object interaction · Hand pose dataset

1 Introduction

The Fourth International Workshop on Observing and Understanding Hands in Action was held in conjunction with the European Conference on Computer Vision 2018 (ECCV'18) on the 9th of September, 2018. It was held in the main building of the Technical University of Munich (TUM) in Arcisstraße 21, and specifically in the lecture hall Theresianum 606. The program of the workshop included five invited talks, six full papers, three extended abstracts, six invited posters, and a short award ceremony. This report presents in detail the proceedings of the workshop, and was not peer-reviewed (Fig. 1).

The workshop website can be found at https://sites.google.com/view/hands2018.

© Springer Nature Switzerland AG 2019
L. Leal-Taixé and S. Roth (Eds.): ECCV 2018 Workshops, LNCS 11134, pp. 302–312, 2019.
https://doi.org/10.1007/978-3-030-11024-6_20

Fig. 1. Left: attending the talk of Professor Tamim Asfour. Right: awards photo. From left to right: Guillermo Garcia-Hernando, Angela Yao, Pavlo Molchanov, Umar Iqbal, Jan van Gemert, and Iason Oikonomidis.

2 Invited Talks

There were five invited talks in the workshop, the slides of which can be found on the workshop website.

- Christian Theobalt (Max Planck Institute for Informatics) presented an overview of his recent works on hand pose estimation. He presented several different scenarios: varying input modalities including depth and regular RGB, egocentric viewpoints, and hand-object interactions [21,22,26,28].
- Tamim Asfour (Karlsruhe Institute of Technology) spoke about the connection between stable grasps and humanoid locomotion states. After presenting an overview of his work on humanoid robotics, he presented the KIT whole-body human motion database [20] that can be used to efficiently solve humanoid locomotion problems.
- Andrew Fitzgibbon (Microsoft) talked about various optimizations over his line of work to achieve accurate real-time hand tracking performance. Among them, he focused on the Iterative Closest Point (ICP) algorithm and how it can be improved by, counter-intuitively, formulating a much larger optimization problem that includes both the model parameters and the correspondences in the same level of optimization [30]. The key insight is that each optimization iteration of the larger problem can take a bigger and more accurate step towards the optimum compared to standard ICP.
- Robert Wang (Facebook Reality Labs) talked about the process of acquiring ground truth data for hand pose estimation with markerless motion capture. After a discussion on the limitations of current approaches, he gave an overview of recent work at Facebook Reality Labs that aims to extract very accurate ground truth annotations using off-the-shelf equipment [13].
- Andrea Tagliasacchi (Google) gave an overview of his recent hand pose estimation works, including an approach for real-time hand tracking [29], a method to better model the shape of the hand [31], and a method to quickly and robustly personalized the hand model to the observed user [32].

3   Presented Works

There were three types of contributions accepted for presentation in the workshop. Specifically, there were regular contributions in the form of full papers (Accepted Papers, AP), extended abstracts (EA), and invited posters (IP). Regular papers were accepted based on a peer review process. Extended abstracts were evaluated and accepted by the organizers, and had a limit of three pages. Finally, works from the main ECCV'18 conference related to the aims and scope of the workshop were invited to be presented in the poster session of the workshop.

3.1   Accepted Papers

The regular program of the workshop invited high quality original papers on the relevant areas. In total, there were seven submissions that were peer-reviewed by seventeen invited reviewers. Each paper was assigned three reviewers, aiming for at least two reviews per work. Through this review process, six of the seven submitted papers were accepted for publication in the workshop proceedings. In order of sumission, the six Accepted Papers (AP) are:

AP1: Hand-Tremor Frequency Estimation in Videos [25]. This paper deals with the problem of estimating the frequency of hand tremors in patients suffering from sensorimotor disorders such as Parkinson's disease. The authors used the highly successful 2D human keypoint estimation Pose Machine method by Wei et al. [35] to estimate 2D wrist positions over a sequence of frames. Using these positions, two alternative approaches are proposed for the estimation of the tremor frequency. The first was named the Lagrangian approach, in which a smooth trajectory was estimated from the sequence of 2D locations. Deviations of the hand from this smooth trajectory was then used to estimate the tremor frequency. For the second Eulerian method, again the same smoothed trajectory was used, but for this approach new image features are computed around the trajectory. An analysis of these new features yields the final frequency estimation. The two proposed methods were assessed on a new collected hand tremor dataset, TIM-Tremor, containing both static and dynamic tasks. The dataset contains data from 55 tremor patient recordings including accelerometer measurements that serve as ground truth, RGB images, and aligned depth data.

AP2: DrawInAir: A Lightweight Gestural Interface Based on Fingertip Regression [10]. "DrawInAir" proposes an in-air gestural recognition framework for Augmented Reality applications. The aim of this work is to enable real-time gesture recognition on lightweight devices such as a smartphones or other computationally constrained devices. The two main components of the framework are a fingertip localization module and a classification module that uses as input fingertip detection on subsequent frames and detects gestures. The first module is built using a fully convolutional network that outputs a heatmap of the fingertip. In contrast to common practice, an extra layer is used after the heatmap generation, applying a differentiable spatial-to-numerical transform (DSNT) [24] to convert the heatmap to numerical coordinates using a soft-argmax operation. For gesture clasiffication, a Bi-LSTM [12] approach is adopted; experimental evaluation shows that this performs better than standard LSTMs [15]. To experimentally evaluate the proposed method, the authors collect a new dataset called "EgoGestAR".

AP3: Adapting Egocentric Visual Hand Pose Estimation Towards a Robot-Controlled Exoskeleton [4]. This paper also deals with patients suffering from motor impairments – here, the patient is assumed to have lost most of their motor abilities, and use an exoskeleton as a robotic grasp assistant. The aim of the system is to autonomously help the patient by estimating the hand pose and acting appropriately. Given that hand keypoint estimation methods usually assume that the hand is mostly free, with observed occlusions occurring from interaction with handled objects, the target scenario needs special treatment since the hand wears an exoskeleton. Towards this end, the authors propose a synthetic dataset that takes this fact into account, modeling the device and rendering hand poses with it. They adopt and adapt the approach of Wei et al. [35] comparing networks that are trained on data with and without the modeled device.

AP4: Estimating 2D Multi-hand Poses From Single Depth Images [9]. This paper treats the problem of 2D hand keypoint detection of two hands in a single depth image. The authors use the Mask R-CNN object detector [14] to detect and segment the hands in the input image. Since Mask R-CNN can be generalized to multiple human bodies, or multiple hands pose estimation, a direct approach would be to train this pipeline on the target keypoints. However, as the authors state in the manuscript, minimal domain knowledge for human pose estimation is exploited so Mask R-CNN does not adequately model joint relationships. Moreover, another recent work [6] points out that, using this strategy, key points might not be localized accurately in complex situations. To address this limitations, the authors propose a Pictorial Structure [1] model-based framework. The authors evaluate the resulting system in two datasets that are generated from the single-hand datasets Dexter1 [27] and NYU hand pose dataset [33] by concatenating randomly selected left and right hand images.

AP5: Spatial-Temporal Attention Res-TCN for Skeleton-Based Dynamic Hand Gesture Recognition [16]. This paper presents the Spatial-Temporal Attention Residual Temporal Convolutional Network (STA-Res-TCN) is to recognize dynamic hand gestures using skeleton-based input. The framework consists of an end-to-end trainable network that exploits both spatial and temporal information on the input data and applies an attention mechanism on both input modalities. This results in a lightweight but accurate gesture recognition system and is evaluated on two publicly available datasets [7,8].

AP6: Task-Oriented Hand Motion Retargeting for Dexterous Manipulation Imitation [2]. This paper treats the problem of retargeting already captured motion of a human hand on another hand embodiment, such as a dexterous anthropomorphic robotic hand. The formulation follows a task-oriented approach, namely the successful grasp of the manipulated object and formulates an objective taking the task goal into account. They proceed to learn a policy network using generative adversarial imitation learning. Experiments show that this approach achieves a higher success rate on the grasping task compared to a baseline that only retargets the motion using inverse kinematics.

3.2   Extended Abstracts

Apart from the regular papers, the workshop also had original contributions in the form of extended abstracts, with the goal of including high-potential but preliminary works. These works were presented as posters in the poster session but are not published as part of the workshop proceedings. Of the four submissions, three were chosen for acceptance by the program chairs. In order of submission, the three extended abstracts (EA) are:

EA1: Model-Based Hand Pose Estimation for Generalized Hand Shape with Spatial Transformer Network. Recent work [39] has proposed using a hand kinematics model as a layer of a deep learning architecture, with the goal of making integrating differentiable coordinate transformations to enable end-to-end training. A limitation of that approach is the fact that the kinematics model has fixed parameters, making the resulting network specific for a single hand and not generalizing well to other hands. The authors of this work [19] extend the previous approach by adapting the kinematics parameters to the observed hand. A Spatial Transformer Network is also applied to the input image, which is shown by the experimental evaluation to be beneficial.

EA2: A New Dataset and Human Benchmark for Partially-Occluded Hand-Pose Recognition During Hand-Object Interactions from Monocular RGB Images. This work [3] proposes a dataset for pose estimation of partially occluded hands when handling an object. The authors collect a dataset that consists of a variety of images of hands grasping objects in natural settings. A simple strategy enables the recording of both occluded and un-occluded images of the same grasps. The error of human annotation is evaluated using this dataset.

EA3: 3D Hand Pose Estimation from Monocular RGB Images Using Advanced Conditional GAN. This work [23] presents a method to estimate the 3D position of hand keypoints using as input a monocular RGB image. The authors propose to decompose the problem in two stages: the first estimates a depth map from the input RGB image using a cycle-consistent GAN architecture [40]. The second stage employs a network based on Dense nets [17] to regress the joint positions using as input the estimated depth map.

3.3 Invited Posters

The organizers invited the following works from the main ECCV'18 conference related in aim to the workshop to be presented in the poster session:

IP1: "HandMap: Robust Hand Pose Estimation via Intermediate Dense Guidance Map Supervision" [36].

IP2: "Point-to-Point Regression PointNet for 3D Hand Pose Estimation" [11].

IP3: "Joint 3D tracking of a deformable object in interaction with a hand" [34].

IP4: "Occlusion-aware Hand Pose Estimation Using Hierarchical Mixture Density Network" [37].

IP5: "Hand Pose Estimation via Latent 2.5D Heatmap Regression" [18].

IP6: "Weakly-supervised 3D Hand Pose Estimation from Monocular RGB Images" [5].

4 Awards

Two works were given awards sponsored by Facebook Reality Labs. The best paper award was decided by the program chairs, while the best poster award was decided in a vote from selected workshop attendants including organizers, invited speakers and topic experts.

The best paper award was given to the work "Hand-tremor Frequency Estimation in Videos" by Silvia L Pintea, Jian Zheng, Xilin Li, Paulina J.M. Bank, Jacobus J. van Hilten and Jan van Gemert. Apart from a solid technical contribution, the work shows the applicability of the methods and techniques related to the scope of this workshop in the aid of real-world problems. The best poster award was given to the work "Hand Pose Estimation via Latent 2.5D Heatmap Regression", by Umar Iqbal, Pavlo Molchanov, Thomas Breuel, Juergen Gall and Jan Kautz. New works on hand pose estimation are increasingly turning again to regular RGB input. This work proposes a novel approach towards this end, and achieves state-of-the-art results.

5 Discussion

Table 1 provides an overview of the presented works: rows correspond to individual works (AP for Accepted Paper, EA for Extended Abstract, and IP for Invited Poster) and columns to work traits. Specifically, "RGB" is marked in works that use regular RGB images a input, "Depth" for ones that use depth data, and "Skeletal Data" for works that use as input an existing estimation of the keypoints of interest. The trait "Application" is marked for works that solve

Table 1. Overview of the presented works. AP stands for Accepted Paper, EA for Extended Abstract, and IP for Invited Poster. Works are listed in the order they were presented in the respective sections.

	RGB	Depth	Skeletal Data	Application	Dataset	Egocentric	Gesture
AP1			x	x	x		
AP2	x			x	x	x	
AP3				x		x	
AP4		x					
AP5			x				x
AP6			x	x			
EA1		x					
EA2					x		
EA3	x						
IP1		x					
IP2		x					
IP3		x		x	x		
IP4		x					
IP5	x						
IP6	x						
Total	4	6	3	5	4	2	1

real-world problems, "Dataset" for works that propose a new dataset, "Egocentric" for works that assume an egocentric observation of the hand, and "Gesture" for works that tackle the problem of recognizing hand gestures.

One conclusion that can be drawn is that the technical level of the related systems is reaching production-grade performance, with five of the fifteen works being applications. While depth-based works are still the norm, monocular RGB input is increasingly common. Furthermore, new datasets are being proposed for increasingly complex, real-world scenarios, and including stand-alone RGB input. Towards this end, relevant scenarios involve occlusions due to hand-object interactions, other environmental factors, haptics, and robotic learning methods such as imitation and reinforcement learning. All of these scenarios should be oriented towards applications that require high precision estimates. Some of these points were mentioned in the invited talks of the workshop, and current trends on datasets point in these directions.

Two main categories of hand pose estimation approaches have been identified in the relevant literature. Discriminative approaches, based on learning, directly map observations to output hand poses. On the other hand, generative approaches, often based on computer graphics techniques, synthesize observations that are then compared to inputs. Then, through optimization, the hand pose that most accurately matches the observation is identified. These two classes of approaches have had small overlap over the last years. There is still much to be done towards the integration of these approaches, despite the long line of research on both categories, and also towards their integration. The resulting, third category should combine the advantages of both categories in so called hybrid approaches. Some of the invited talks (Andrew Fitzgibbon, Andrea Tagliasacchi) focused on generative approaches while others (Christian Theobalt, Robert Wang) focused more on discriminative or hybrid approaches. Towards this integration, Andrea Tagliasacchi suggested the use of hand segmentation in a generative approach as a potential approach.

Generative approaches are focusing on more efficient methods for adaptive hand models, efficient model representations, and optimization strategies. A potentially useful observation is the fact that all modern generative approaches formulate and optimize differentiable objective functions. It is conceivable then that some of them could be used directly as loss functions in training neural networks. On the learning front, approaches that use semi-supervised learning or weak supervision [5] can potentially play a big role in the immediate future. Also, techniques that enable end-to-end network training such as Spatial Transformer Networks [19], Differentiable Spatial to Numerical Transform modules [10,18] and kinematic layers [39] are evidently useful.

Developed methods and techniques are already being applied to solve real-world problems in healthcare, robotics, and AR/VR [2,10,25]. Other candidate application domains include: automotive environments, both regular and autonomous, for gesture-based interactions with the car. The surgery room for training, monitoring and aiding operations. Laboratory monitoring to record the interactions of hands and objects, and therefore, the experimental procedure. Overall, all aspects of human activity involving the manipulation of physical or virtual objects are potential candidates.

In connection to the integration of different approaches, challenging new datasets will prove useful towards the assessment of hybrid approaches. Furthermore, they can help highlight the strengths and weaknesses of discriminative and generative approaches. Following previous cases [38], a goal for the next editions of this workshop is to organize a challenge towards this end.

References

1. Andriluka, M., Roth, S., Schiele, B.: Pictorial structures revisited: people detection and articulated pose estimation. In: Proceedings of the IEEE International Conference on Computer Vision (2017)
2. Antotsiou, D., Garcia-Hernando, G., Kim, T.K.: Task-oriented hand motion retargeting for dexterous manipulation imitation. In: Proceedings of the Fourth International Workshop on Observing and Understanding Hands in Action (2018)
3. Barbu, A., Myanganbayar, B., Mata, C., Dekel, G., Ben-Yosef, G., Katz, B.: A new dataset and human benchmark for partially-occluded hand-pose recognition during hand-object interactions from monocular RGB images. In: Extended Abstract Presentation at the Fourth International Workshop on Observing and Understanding Hands in Action (2018)
4. Baulig, G., Gulde, T., Curio, C.: Adapting egocentric visual hand pose estimation towards a robot-controlled exoskeleton. In: Proceedings of the Fourth International Workshop on Observing and Understanding Hands in Action (2018)

5. Cai, Y., Ge, L., Cai, J., Yuan, J.: Weakly-supervised 3D hand pose estimation from monocular RGB images. In: Ferrari, V., Hebert, M., Sminchisescu, C., Weiss, Y. (eds.) ECCV 2018. LNCS, vol. 11210, pp. 678–694. Springer, Cham (2018). https://doi.org/10.1007/978-3-030-01231-1_41

6. Chen, Y., Wang, Z., Peng, Y., Zhang, Z., Yu, G., Sun, J.: Cascaded pyramid network for multi-person pose estimation (2017). https://doi.org/10.1109/CVPR.2018.00742

7. De Smedt, Q., Wannous, H., Vandeborre, J.P., Guerry, J., Le Saux, B., Filliat, D.: SHREC'17 track: 3D hand gesture recognition using a depth and skeletal dataset (2017). https://doi.org/10.2312/3dor.20171049

8. De Smedt, Q., Wannous, H., Vandeborre, J.P.: Skeleton-based dynamic hand gesture recognition. In: IEEE Computer Society Conference on Computer Vision and Pattern Recognition Workshops, pp. 1206–1214 (2016). https://doi.org/10.1109/CVPRW.2016.153

9. Duan, L., Shen, M., Cui, S., Guo, Z., Oliver, D.: Estimating 2D multi-hand poses from single depth images. In: Proceedings of the Fourth International Workshop on Observing and Understanding Hands in Action (2018)

10. Garg, G., Hegde, S., Perla, R., Jain, V., Vig, L., Hebbalaguppe, R.: DrawInAir: a lightweight gestural interface based on fingertip regression. In: Proceedings of the Fourth International Workshop on Observing and Understanding Hands in Action (2018)

11. Ge, L., Ren, Z., Yuan, J.: Point-to-point regression PointNet for 3D hand pose estimation. In: Ferrari, V., Hebert, M., Sminchisescu, C., Weiss, Y. (eds.) ECCV 2018. LNCS, vol. 11217, pp. 489–505. Springer, Cham (2018). https://doi.org/10.1007/978-3-030-01261-8_29

12. Graves, A., Schmidhuber, J.: Framewise phoneme classification with bidirectional LSTM networks. In: Proceedings of the International Joint Conference on Neural Networks, vol. 5, pp. 2047–2052 (2005). https://doi.org/10.1109/IJCNN.2005.1556215

13. Han, S., Liu, B., Wang, R., Ye, Y., Twigg, C.D., Kin, K.: Online optical marker-based hand tracking with deep labels. ACM Trans. Graph. **37**(4), 1–10 (2018). https://doi.org/10.1145/3197517.3201399

14. He, K., Gkioxari, G., Dollár, P., Girshick, R.: Mask R-CNN. In: ICCV 2017 (2017)

15. Hochreiter, S., Urgen Schmidhuber, J.: Long short-term memory. Neural Comput. **8**, 1735–1780 (1997). https://doi.org/10.1162/neco.1997.9.8.1735

16. Hou, J., Wang, G., Chen, X., Xue, J.H., Zhu, R., Yang, H.: Spatial-temporal attention res-TCN for skeleton-based dynamic hand gesture recognition. In: Proceedings of the Fourth International Workshop on Observing and Understanding Hands in Action (2018)

17. Huang, G., Liu, Z., Van Der Maaten, L., Weinberger, K.Q.: Densely connected convolutional networks. In: Proceedings - 30th IEEE Conference on Computer Vision and Pattern Recognition, CVPR 2017, pp. 2261–2269 (2017). https://doi.org/10.1109/CVPR.2017.243

18. Iqbal, U., Molchanov, P., Breuel, T., Gall, J., Kautz, J.: Hand pose estimation via latent 2.5D heatmap regression. In: Ferrari, V., Hebert, M., Sminchisescu, C., Weiss, Y. (eds.) ECCV 2018. LNCS, vol. 11215, pp. 125–143. Springer, Cham (2018). https://doi.org/10.1007/978-3-030-01252-6_8

19. Li, S., Wöhlke, J., Lee, D.: Model-based hand pose estimation for generalized hand shape with spatial transformer network. In: Extended Abstract Presentation at the Fourth International Workshop on Observing and Understanding Hands in Action (2018)

20. Mandery, C., Terlemez, Ö., Do, M., Vahrenkamp, N., Asfour, T.: The KIT whole-body human motion database. In: International Conference on Advanced Robotics, ICAR, pp. 329–336 (2015). https://doi.org/10.1109/ICAR.2015.7251476

21. Mueller, F., et al.: GANerated hands for real-time 3D hand tracking from monocular RGB. In: CVPR 2018 (2018)

22. Mueller, F., Mehta, D., Sotnychenko, O., Sridhar, S., Casas, D., Theobalt, C.: Real-time hand tracking under occlusion from an egocentric RGB-D sensor. arXiv preprint arXiv:1704.02201 (2017). https://doi.org/10.1109/ICCV.2017.131

23. Nguyen, L.H., Quan, L.M., Kim, Y.G.: 3D hand pose estimation from monocular RGB images using advanced conditional GAN. In: Extended Abstract Presentation at the Fourth International Workshop on Observing and Understanding Hands in Action (2018)

24. Nibali, A., He, Z., Morgan, S., Prendergast, L.: Numerical coordinate regression with convolutional neural networks (2018)

25. Pintea, S.L., Zheng, J., Li, X., Bank, P.J.M., van Hilten, J.J., van Gemert, J.: Hand-tremor frequency estimation in videos. In: Proceedings of the Fourth International Workshop on Observing and Understanding Hands in Action (2018)

26. Sridhar, S., Mueller, F., Zollhöfer, M., Casas, D., Oulasvirta, A., Theobalt, C.: Real-time joint tracking of a hand manipulating an object from RGB-D input. In: Leibe, B., Matas, J., Sebe, N., Welling, M. (eds.) ECCV 2016. LNCS, vol. 9906, pp. 294–310. Springer, Cham (2016). https://doi.org/10.1007/978-3-319-46475-6_19

27. Sridhar, S., Oulasvirta, A., Theobalt, C.: Interactive markerless articulated hand motion tracking using RGB and depth data. In: Proceedings of the IEEE International Conference on Computer Vision, pp. 2456–2463 (2013). https://doi.org/10.1109/ICCV.2013.305

28. Sridhar, S., Rhodin, H., Seidel, H.P., Oulasvirta, A., Theobalt, C.: Real-time hand tracking using a sum of anisotropic gaussians model. In: Proceedings - 2014 International Conference on 3D Vision, 3DV 2014, pp. 319–326 (2015). https://doi.org/10.1109/3DV.2014.37

29. Tagliasacchi, A., Schröder, M., Tkach, A., Bouaziz, S., Botsch, M., Pauly, M.: Robust articulated-ICP for real-time hand tracking. In: Computer Graphics Forum (2015)

30. Taylor, J., et al.: Efficient and precise interactive hand tracking through joint, continuous optimization of pose and correspondences. ACM Trans. Graph. 35(4), 1–12 (2016). https://doi.org/10.1145/2897824.2925965

31. Tkach, A., Pauly, M., Tagliasacchi, A.: Sphere-meshes for real-time hand modeling and tracking. ACM Trans. Graph. 35(6), 1–11 (2016). https://doi.org/10.1145/2980179.2980226

32. Tkach, A., Tagliasacchi, A., Remelli, E., Pauly, M., Fitzgibbon, A.: Online generative model personalization for hand tracking. ACM Trans. Graph. 36(6), 1–11 (2017). https://doi.org/10.1145/3130800.3130830

33. Tompson, J., Stein, M., Lecun, Y., Perlin, K.: Real-time continuous pose recovery of human hands using convolutional networks. ACM Trans. Graph. (SIGGRAPH 2014) 33(5), 1–10 (2014). https://doi.org/10.1145/2629500

34. Tsoli, A., Argyros, A.A.: Joint 3D tracking of a deformable object in interaction with a hand. In: Ferrari, V., Hebert, M., Sminchisescu, C., Weiss, Y. (eds.) Computer Vision – ECCV 2018. LNCS, vol. 11218, pp. 504–520. Springer, Cham (2018). https://doi.org/10.1007/978-3-030-01264-9_30

35. Wei, S.E., Ramakrishna, V., Kanade, T., Sheikh, Y.: Convolutional pose machines. In: Proceedings of the IEEE Computer Society Conference on Computer Vision and Pattern Recognition, pp. 4724–4732 (2016). https://doi.org/10.1109/CVPR.2016.511
36. Wu, X., Finnegan, D., O'Neill, E., Yang, Y.-L.: HandMap: robust hand pose estimation via intermediate dense guidance map supervision. In: Ferrari, V., Hebert, M., Sminchisescu, C., Weiss, Y. (eds.) ECCV 2018. LNCS, vol. 11220, pp. 246–262. Springer, Cham (2018). https://doi.org/10.1007/978-3-030-01270-0_15
37. Ye, Q., Kim, T.-K.: Occlusion-aware hand pose estimation using hierarchical mixture density network. In: Ferrari, V., Hebert, M., Sminchisescu, C., Weiss, Y. (eds.) ECCV 2018. LNCS, vol. 11214, pp. 817–834. Springer, Cham (2018). https://doi.org/10.1007/978-3-030-01249-6_49
38. Yuan, S., et al.: Depth-based 3D hand pose estimation: from current achievements to future goals. In: CVPR 2018 (2018)
39. Zhou, X., Wan, Q., Wei, Z., Xue, X., Wei, Y.: Model-based deep hand pose estimation. In: IJCAI International Joint Conference on Artificial Intelligence, pp. 2421–2427 (2016)
40. Zhu, J.Y., Park, T., Isola, P., Efros, A.A.: Unpaired image-to-image translation using cycle-consistent adversarial networks. In: Proceedings of the IEEE International Conference on Computer Vision, pp. 2242–2251 (2017). https://doi.org/10.1109/ICCV.2017.244

W33 – Bioimage Computing

W33 – Bioimage Computing

Bioimage Computing is a series of workshops that focuses on the on the interface between engineering, biology and computer science. State-of-the-art light microscopy (LM) can deliver 2D and 3D image sequences of living cells with unprecedented image quality and ever growing resolution in space and time. The emergence of novel and quite diverse LM modalities has provided biologists with formidable means to explore cell mechanisms, embryogenesis, or neural development, to quote just a few fundamental biological issues. Electron microscopy (EM) supplies information on the cell structure down to the nanometer resolution.

Computer vision techniques play a key part in addressing some of these challenges. This motivates why this workshop has been held in conjunction the the European Conference for Computer Vision in Munich 2018. As organisers we are very grateful that the proposal to host this workshop at ECCV had been accepted. It provided the community with an opportunity to learn about the recent challenges in biological image computing.

In particular we would like to thank our invited speakers for their contributions to the conference. Although these talks are not captured in these proceedings we would like to list these in this preface:

- **Rene Vidal** - Blood Cell Reconstruction, Detection, Classification and Counting in Holographic Images
- **Virginie Uhlmann** - Mathematical models for bioimage analysis
- **Julia Mahamid** - Interpreting Molecular Landscapes by In-Cell Cryo-Electron Tomography
- **Florian Jug** - Content-aware Image Restoration

From all research papers submitted, the organisers nominated six papers as oral presentations. All papers were presented in a dedicated poster session. Given the high level of attendance we are keen to continue with this workshop series and aim to hold a workshop at one of the major computer vision conferences in 2019.

We would like to express our gratitude to all our colleagues for submitting papers to the Bioimage Computing 2018, as well as to the members of the Program Committee for providing valuable reviews. In addition we would like to thank Mariia Dmitrieva, Sharib Ali, Felix Zhou, Avelino Javer and Korsuk Sirinukunwattana for providing additional reviews.

September 2018

Anna Kreshuk
Florian Jug
Uens Rittscher

Automatic Classification
of Low-Resolution Chromosomal Images

Swati Swati, Monika Sharma$^{(\boxtimes)}$, and Lovekesh Vig

TCS Research, New Delhi, India
{j.swati,monika.sharma1,lovekesh.vig}@tcs.com

Abstract. Chromosome karyotyping is a two-staged process consisting of segmentation followed by pairing and ordering of 23 pairs of human chromosomes obtained from cell spread images during metaphase stage of cell division. It is carried out by cytogeneticists in clinical labs on the basis of length, centromere position, and banding pattern of chromosomes for the diagnosis of various health and genetic disorders. The entire process demands high domain expertise and considerable amount of manual effort. This motivates us to automate or partially automate karyotyping process which would benefit and aid doctors in the analysis of chromosome images. However, the non-availability of high resolution chromosome images required for classification purpose creates a hindrance in achieving high classification accuracy. To address this issue, we propose a Super-Xception network which takes the low-resolution chromosome images as input and classifies them to one of the 24 chromosome class labels after conversion into high resolution images. In this network, we integrate super-resolution deep models with standard classification networks e.g., Xception network in our case. The network is trained in an end-to-end manner in which the super-resolution layers help in conversion of low-resolution images to high-resolution images which are subsequently passed through deep classification layers for label assigning. We evaluate our proposed network's efficacy on a publicly available online Bioimage chromosome classification dataset of healthy chromosomes and benchmark it against the baseline models created using traditional deep convolutional neural network, ResNet-50 and Xception network.

Keywords: Low resolution chromosomes · Karyotyping
Chromosome classification · Super-Xception · Super-ResNet

1 Introduction

Chromosome karyotyping is one of the important tasks considered in the field of cytogenetics. It is performed by cytogeneticists in which they segment and classify individual human chromosome images obtained during metaphase stage of cell division. A healthy human cell consists of 22 pairs of autosomes and a single pair of sex chromosomes (X and Y), thus giving a total of 23 pairs of chromosomes. Doctors examine the individual chromosomes and assign them to

© Springer Nature Switzerland AG 2019
L. Leal-Taixé and S. Roth (Eds.): ECCV 2018 Workshops, LNCS 11134, pp. 315–325, 2019.
https://doi.org/10.1007/978-3-030-11024-6_21

one of the 24 chromosome classes on the basis of various differentiating characteristics like banding pattern, centromere position, and length of chromosomes. An example of a karyotyped image obtained is shown in Fig. 1.

Fig. 1. An example chromosome karyotyped image.

In clinical labs, karyotypes provide doctors with the diagnostic information for specific birth defects, genetic disorders, and cancers mainly occurring due to structural changes, such as chromosomal deletions, duplications, translocations, or inversions. This process of manual segmentation and analysis of each and every chromosome for diagnosis purpose consumes a considerable amount of time and is highly dependent on expert knowledge. Thus, it motivates us to automate or semi-automate the karyotyping process in order to assist doctors and reduce their cognitive load by expediating the task of karyotyping. In this paper, we attempt to automate the classification stage of karyotyping with the assumption of availability of segmented and straightened individual chromosomes.

In recent past years, researchers have shown interest in automating the karyotyping process and proposed various machine learning and deep learning techniques [22,23,27,31] with encouraging results. The main problem with these existing methods is that the performance of classifier deteriorates when the resolution of chromosome images is very low. The non-availability of high resolution images and requirement to obtain very high classification accuracy persuaded us to explore existing super-resolution techniques [11,16,30,37] for low-resolution image classification tasks.

Although image analysis would be ideal with high quality images, but this is not always possible in practice because of non-availability of high resolution images. Considering the fact that higher the image resolution, the easier is the classification, we take cues from established literature on low resolution image classification and propose an end-to-end deep learning framework for automating chromosome classification of low-resolution images. The proposed network is an integration of deep super-resolution layers with a standard classification network (*e.g.* Xception network [8]) which is trained in an end-to-end manner and we named it as *Super-Xception* network. Before feeding the individual chromosome image as input to Super-Xception model, we perform a pre-processing step of length normalization to preserve the important distinguishing characteristic of chromosomes. During these explorations, we make the following main contributions in the paper:

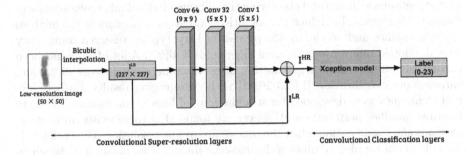

Fig. 2. Proposed architecture of Super-Xception network for chromosome classification. A low-resolution image of size 50×50 is given as an input to the network which is resized to image I^{LR} of size 227×227 via bicubic interpolation. Subsequently, I^{LR} is passed through convolutional super-resolution layers and a high-resolution image I^{HR} is produced. Further, I^{HR} is fed to convolutional classification network (Xception [8]) which outputs chromosome class labels in the range (0–23).

1. To the best of our knowledge, the proposed work is the first attempt to automate classification of low-resolution chromosomal images.
2. We propose an end-to-end trainable *Super-Xception* network for automatic chromosome classification of low-resolution images. The architecture of the network is shown in Fig. 2.
3. We experimentally verify that the proposed Super-Xception network achieves superior performance for automatic chromosome classification of low-resolution images than the state-of-the-art networks like Deep Convolutional Network (DCNN) [31], ResNet-50 [17] and Xception [8] on a publicly available Bioimage Chromosome Classification dataset [1, 29].

The remainder of the paper is organized as follows: Sect. 2 gives an overview of related work in the field of chromosome karyotyping and super-resolution of images. Section 3 describes the proposed methodology for automatic chromosome classification which is followed by a brief description of deep super-resolution layers and Xception network in Sects. 3.1 and 3.2, respectively. In Sect. 4, we explain the proposed architecture of Super-Xception network. Subsequently, Sect. 5 gives details about the dataset, the training setup utilized and a discussion on the obtained results. Finally, we conclude the paper and discuss future directions in Sect. 6.

2   Related Work

Cytogeneticists spend considerable amount of manual effort and time in the karyotyping process which involves segmenting individual chromosomes from cell spread metaphase image and classifying the obtained individual chromosome segments to 24 classes. To reduce the cognitive load and aid doctors in the analysis of chromosomes and accelerate the process of karyotyping, research community have developed many computational algorithms [5,6,27]. A lot of work has been carried out on automatic segmentation of overlapping chromosomes [3,28] and chromosome classification [13,23,26,31] with encouraging results. Earlier, several techniques were developed for straightening of bent chromosomes [21,22] to improve classifier performance. However, we found that there exists no work on chromosome classification when the images are of low resolution. Generally, it is difficult to obtain high resolution chromosome images from hospitals/labs which results in poor performance of the classifier. This motivated us to take up the task of automating chromosome classification in scenarios where the chromsome images are of inferior quality. Here, we make an assumption that we have been provided with segmented and straightened individual chromosomes.

There exists numerous super-resolution techniques for conversion of low-resolution (LR) to high-resolution (HR) images in vision field for better performance. Existing super-resolution (SR) algorithms are grouped into four groups: image statistical methods [19], example-based methods [10,11,15,16,18,30,35, 37], prediction models [20] and edge-based methods [14,34]. However, with the advancement in deep learning techniques, researchers have started employing Convolutional Neural Networks for SR tasks as well, which perform better than state-of-the-art traditional methods. Dong et al. [11] proposed first convolutional neural networks for image super-resolution which learns a deep mapping between low and high resolution patches. Subsequently, variants of deep super-resolution networks were proposed. To avoid general up-scaling of input patches, a deconvolutional layer is added based on super resolution CNN (SRCNN) [11] in [12] which results in acceleration of CNN training and testing. A convolutional deep network is proposed in [24] to learn the mapping between LR image and residue between LR and HR image to expedite CNN training for very deep network. Kim et al. [25] uses a deep recursive layer in order to circumvent adding weight layers which will prevent increasing network parameters. In this paper, we borrowed the idea from [7] for incorporating super-resolution layers into a convolutional network (i.e. Xception network [8]) for classification. The experiments have shown that the SR-specific convolutional layers help in improving classification performance by recovering texture details from the low resolution images.

While there is huge corpus of deep networks for image classification [17,32,33, 36], we chose to use state-of-the-art Xception network [8] for chromosome classification. Because in general, traditional convolutional layers of CNNs classify images by learning feature maps in 3D space. Each convolutional layer performs mapping of correlations spatially and across channels simultaneously. But, the depthwise separable convolutional layers used in Xception network explicitly divide this task of learning feature maps into series of sub-tasks that independently look at cross-channel and spatial cross-relations. This makes the network learn robust feature representations with lesser parameters.

3 Proposed Methodology

This section gives an overview of the proposed method for automatic classification of low resolution chromosome images. As we are aware of the fact that low resolution images hinder the performance of any image classifier, hence our proposed method works upon improving the resolution of the image before classification. Higher the resolution of images, easier is the classification and hence, better is the performance of the classifier. However, in case of chromosomes, it is not always possible to obtain high resolution chromosome images due to which it becomes difficult to automate the chromosome classification process. To alleviate this issue, we proposed a network which first converts a low-resolution image to its higher resolution version by employing convolutional super-resolution layers [7] and further, passes the obtained high-resolution image to convolutional classification network like Xception network [8] to produce chromosome class label. We named the proposed network as *Super-Xception* whose architecture is shown in the Fig. 2. In the following subsections, we discuss few details of the convolutional super-resolution layers and Xception network.

3.1 Convolutional Super-Resolution Network

The major difference between the proposed Super-Xception network and the conventional Xception network [8] lies in the addition of three convolutional super-resolution layers following [7]. As a result, Super-Xception network becomes more deeper and consequently, it will store more knowledge about the images in form of increased network parameters. The main purpose of introducing these super-resolution layers is to improve the resolution and recover the texture details of the low-resolution images. The last layer of these super-resolution block produces a residual image which is the difference of the high-resolution (HR) and low-resolution (LR) image. The better learning of these layers depends on the fact that the HR and LR images are largely similar, i.e. more similarities must be removed from the residual image [7]. The CNNs can learn the detailed information from the residual images more easily than LR-HR CNNs [11,12].

3.2 Xception Network

The Xception network [8] is made up of *depthwise separable convolutional layers*, which consists of a depthwise convolution (a spatial convolution performed independently for each channel) followed by a pointwise convolution (a 1×1 convolution across channels). It is based on the hypothesis that the mapping of cross-channel correlations and spatial correlations in the feature maps of convolutional neural networks can be entirely decoupled. We can think of this as looking for correlations across a 2D space first, followed by looking for correlations across a 1D space. Intuitively, this 2D + 1D mapping is easier to learn than a full 3D mapping. The architecture of Xception network [8] consists of 36 convolutional layers which acts as the feature-extractor. This is followed by a *softmax* layer for the image classification purpose. These 36 convolutional layers are structured into 14 modules having linear residual connections around them, except for the first and last modules. Precisely, the Xception architecture is a linear stack of depthwise separable convolution layers with residual connections.

4   Architecture of Super-Xception Network

The proposed architecture of Super-Xception network, as shown in Fig. 2, consists of two sub-networks: super-resolution and classification network. The convolutional super-resolution layers, shown on the left side of Fig. 2, recover the texture details of low-resolution images to feed into the following convolutional categorisation layers. Next, the classification model solves the task of label assigning to the image. Since our network is the augmentation of Xception network with the deep super-resolution layers, hence we named it as *Super-Xception* network.

The convolutional super-resolution layers take a bicubic-interpolated low-resolution image (of the desired size) I^{LR} and learn the mapping $g(I^{LR})$ from LR image I^{LR} to residual image $I^{HR} - I^{LR}$, where I^{HR} is the high-resolution version of the image. We used three typical stacked convolutional-ReLU layers as the super-resolution layers in Super-Xception network. The empirical basic setting of the layers is $f_1 = 9{\times}9$, $f_2 = 5{\times}5$, $f_3 = 5{\times}5$, $n_1 = 64$, $n_2 = 32$ and $n_3 = 1$ following from [7], where f_m and n_m represent the size and number of the filters of the mth layer, respectively. The output obtained from the last convolutional layer of super-resolution network is summed with the interpolated version of low-resolution image I^{LR} to construct the full super-resolution image I^{HR} which is further fed into the remaining classification layers of Super-Xception network.

We used layers of Xception network [8] as the underlying classification layers for our Super-Xception network. The high-resolution image I^{HR} is passed through the Xception network which learns the feature representation of the image. A *softmax* layer at the end is used for assigning labels in the range (0–23) to the learnt feature-representation.

5   Experiments

This section is divided into the following subsections: Sect. 5.1 provides details of the publicly available online Bioimage Chromosome Classification dataset [1,29]. In Sect. 5.2, we elaborate on the training details utilized to perform our experiments. Subsequently, Sect. 5.3 discusses the results obtained from the experiments we conducted and provides comparison with the baseline models.

5.1 Dataset

We have utilized publicly available online Bioimage Chromosome Classification dataset [1,29] to conduct our experiments. This dataset contains a total of 5256 chromosomes images of healthy patients, manually segmented and labeled by an expert cytogenecist. We have divided these 5256 images into three sets of 4176, 360 and 720 each for training, validation and testing purpose, respectively. While conducting our experiments, we have set the resolution of chromosome images to be 50×50 in grayscale which is interpolated to the desired size of 227×227. Furthermore, we have employed a pre-processing step of length normalization [31] to every chromosome image in the dataset.

5.2 Training Details

The performance of our model was compared with the baseline networks created using traditional deep CNN [31], AlexNet [7], ResNet-50 [17], and Xception [8] networks. The deep CNN network was trained using Adam optimizer with learning rate of 10^{-4} and rest of the parameters were set to default values. For ResNet-50 network, we used stochastic gradient descent with learning rate of 10^{-3}, momentum of 10^{-6}, decay parameter set as 0.9 and nestrov set to be true. The Xception and proposed Super-Xception networks were trained with Adam optimizer with learning rate of 10^{-4} and rest of the parameters were assigned default values. The number of epochs used to train deep CNN, ResNet-50, Super-AlexNet, Xception and Super-Xception models were set to 150, 30, 100, 50 and 80 respectively. For best trained model, we observed validation results at each epoch and tracked model parameters corresponding to the lowest validation loss. Deep CNN, AlexNet and ResNet-50 networks were implemented using Theano [4] and Keras [9] while Xception and Super-Xception models were implemented in Tensorflow [2] and Keras [9].

5.3 Results and Discussion

Table 1 shows the results of the experiments performed during evaluation of our proposed network and baseline networks. Row 1 of Table 1 shows the accuracy of a traditional deep CNN network comprised of 6 convolution layers having number of filters as 16, 16, 32, 64, 128 and 256 respectively. Each convolutional layer uses Rectified Linear Units (ReLU) and is followed by a Max-pool layer of size 2×2. The last convolutional layer is proceeded by two fully connected layers with 1024 and 512 hidden units and having *sigmoid* as their activation function. The last layer is the *softmax* activated fully connected layer having 24 units each representing one of the 24 chromosome classes.

Subsequently, row 2 of Table 1 represents the performance of ResNet-50 which is a minor improvement over traditional deep CNN network. Next, we perform the classification using Super-ResNet model which is the augmentation of ResNet-50 to the convolutional super-resolution layers. This network gives a

Table 1. Table showing comparison of classification accuracy of our proposed Super-Xception network with that of baseline deep networks for chromosome classification.

S.No.	Network architecture	Accuracy (%)
1	Traditional Deep CNN [31]	87.50
2	ResNet-50 [17]	87.64
3	Super-AlexNet [7]	89.30
4	Super-ResNet	90.55
5	Xception network [8]	91.80
6	Super-Xception (proposed)	**92.36**

boost of **2.91%** in accuracy over ResNet-50 (row 4 of Table 1). This improvement is the result of incorporation of convolutional super-resolution layers before feeding to the traditional classification network. This further explains that the poor performance of other baseline models is due to the low-resolution of chromosomal images. Thus, this motivates us to use convolutional super-resolution layers before any classification network for chromosome classification.

Similarly, we also implemented Super-AlexNet [7] using concatenation of convolutional super-resolution layers to the AlexNet model proposed by Cai et al. The performance of this model is shown in row 3 of Table 1.

Next, row 5 of Table 1 gives the classification accuracy of Xception network [8] which is a considerable improvement over traditional deep CNN network and ResNet-50 model. This encourages us to employ the Xception network in concatenation to convolutional super-resolution layers in our proposed Super-Xception network.

Finally, the row 6 of Table 1 represents the performance of our proposed method, i.e. Super-Xception network which achieves the highest classification accuracy of **92.36%**, outperforming various existing state-of-the-art algorithms for automatic chromosome classification.

6   Conclusion

The paper started by explaining the need to automate chromosome classification for assisting cytogeneticists in the analysis of chromosome images and saving their valuable time. Further, we consider the situations where there is non-availability of high resolution chromosome images which affect the accuracy of the classifier. Therefore, we explored the use of convolutional super-resolution layers before feeding low resolution chromosome images to a convolutional classifier. We demonstrated via experimentation that super-resolution helps in enhancing the resolution of images and thereby improving the performance of classifier. Next, we propose the use of Xception network for classification of chromosome images after the convolutional super-resolution layers. We evaluated our proposed architecture on a publicly available online Bioimage Chromosome

Classification dataset of healthy humans and compared its performance against several baseline classification networks. We observed that our network beats various state-of-the-art networks available for automatic chromosome classification. Going ahead, we would explore techniques to detect various structural abnormalities like deletions, inversions and translocations etc. present in chromosomes of unhealthy humans to diagnose various birth defects and genetic disorders.

References

1. Bioimage chromosome classification: Dataset online. http://bioimlab.dei.unipd.it/ChromosomeDataSet4Seg.htm
2. Abadi, M., et al.: Tensorflow: a system for large-scale machine learning. In: OSDI, vol. 16, pp. 265–283 (2016)
3. Agam, G., Dinstein, I.: Geometric separation of partially overlapping nonrigid objects applied to automatic chromosome classification. IEEE Trans. Pattern Anal. Mach. Intell. **19**, 1212–1222 (1997)
4. Al-Rfou, R., et al.: Theano: a python framework for fast computation of mathematical expressions. arXiv preprint arXiv:1605.02688 472, 473 (2016)
5. Balaji, V.S., Vidhya, S.: Separation of touching and overlapped human chromosome images. In: Gupta, S., Bag, S., Ganguly, K., Sarkar, I., Biswas, P. (eds.) Advancements of Medical Electronics. Lecture Notes in Bioengineering. Springer, New Delhi (2015). https://doi.org/10.1007/978-81-322-2256-9_6
6. Britto, A.P., Ravindran, G.: A review of cytogenetics and its automation. J. Med. Sci. **7**, 1–18 (2007)
7. Cai, D., Chen, K., Qian, Y., Kämäräinen, J.K.: Convolutional low-resolution fine-grained classification. Pattern Recognit. Lett. (2017)
8. Chollet, F.: Xception: deep learning with depthwise separable convolutions. arXiv preprint (2016)
9. Chollet, F., et al.: Keras (2015)
10. Dai, D., Timofte, R., Van Gool, L.: Jointly optimized regressors for image super-resolution. In: Computer Graphics Forum, vol. 34, pp. 95–104. Wiley Online Library (2015)
11. Dong, C., Loy, C.C., He, K., Tang, X.: Image super-resolution using deep convolutional networks. IEEE Trans. Pattern Anal. Mach. Intell. **38**(2), 295–307 (2016)
12. Dong, C., Loy, C.C., Tang, X.: Accelerating the super-resolution convolutional neural network. In: Leibe, B., Matas, J., Sebe, N., Welling, M. (eds.) ECCV 2016. LNCS, vol. 9906, pp. 391–407. Springer, Cham (2016). https://doi.org/10.1007/978-3-319-46475-6_25
13. Errington, P.A., Graham, J.: Application of artificial neural networks to chromosome classification. Cytom. Part A **14**(6), 627–639 (1993)
14. Fattal, R.: Image upsampling via imposed edge statistics. In: ACM Transactions on Graphics (TOG), vol. 26, p. 95. ACM (2007)
15. Freedman, G., Fattal, R.: Image and video upscaling from local self-examples. ACM Trans. Graph. (TOG) **30**(2), 12 (2011)
16. Glasner, D., Bagon, S., Irani, M.: Super-resolution from a single image. In: 2009 IEEE 12th International Conference on Computer Vision, pp. 349–356. IEEE (2009)
17. He, K., Zhang, X., Ren, S., Sun, J.: Deep residual learning for image recognition. In: Proceedings of the IEEE Conference on Computer Vision and Pattern Recognition, pp. 770–778 (2016)

18. Huang, J.B., Singh, A., Ahuja, N.: Single image super-resolution from transformed self-exemplars. In: Proceedings of the IEEE Conference on Computer Vision and Pattern Recognition, pp. 5197–5206 (2015)
19. Huang, J., Mumford, D.: Statistics of natural images and models. In: IEEE Computer Society Conference on Computer Vision and Pattern Recognition, vol. 1, pp. 541–547. IEEE (1999)
20. Irani, M., Peleg, S.: Improving resolution by image registration. CVGIP: Graph. Models Image Process. **53**, 231–239 (1991)
21. Jahani, S., Setarehdan, S.K.: An automatic algorithm for identification and straightening images of curved human chromosomes. Biomed. Eng. Appl. Basis Commun. **24**(06), 503–511 (2012)
22. Javan-Roshtkhari, M., Setarehdan, S.K.: A new approach to automatic classification of the curved chromosomes. In: 5th International Symposium on Image and Signal Processing and Analysis, ISPA 2007, pp. 19–24. IEEE (2007)
23. Jindal, S., Gupta, G., Yadav, M., Sharma, M., Vig, L.: Siamese networks for chromosome classification. In: The IEEE International Conference on Computer Vision (ICCV), October 2017
24. Kim, J., Kwon Lee, J., Mu Lee, K.: Accurate image super-resolution using very deep convolutional networks. In: Proceedings of the IEEE Conference on Computer Vision and Pattern Recognition, pp. 1646–1654 (2016)
25. Kim, J., Kwon Lee, J., Mu Lee, K.: Deeply-recursive convolutional network for image super-resolution. In: Proceedings of the IEEE Conference on Computer Vision and Pattern Recognition, pp. 1637–1645 (2016)
26. Lerner, B., Levinstein, M., Rosenberg, B., Guterman, H., Dinstein, L., Romem, Y.: Feature selection and chromosome classification using a multilayer perceptron neural network. In: IEEE International Conference on Neural Networks, vol. 6, pp. 3540–3545 (1994)
27. Lerner, B.: Toward a completely automatic neural-network-based human chromosome analysis. IEEE Trans. Syst. Man Cybern. Part B (Cybern.) **28**, 544–552 (1998)
28. Madian, N., Jayanthi, K.: Overlapped chromosome segmentation and separation of touching chromosome for automated chromosome classification. In: International Conference of the IEEE Engineering in Medicine and Biology Society (EMBC), pp. 5392–5395 (2012)
29. Poletti, E., Grisan, E., Ruggeri, A.: Automatic classification of chromosomes in Q-band images. In: 30th Annual International Conference of the IEEE Engineering in Medicine and Biology Society, EMBS 2008, pp. 1911–1914. IEEE (2008)
30. Schulter, S., Leistner, C., Bischof, H.: Fast and accurate image upscaling with super-resolution forests. In: Proceedings of the IEEE Conference on Computer Vision and Pattern Recognition, pp. 3791–3799 (2015)
31. Sharma, M., Saha, O., Sriraman, A., Vig, L., Hebbalaguppe, R., Karande, S.: Crowdsourcing for chromosome segmentation and deep classification. In: CVPR 2017. IEEE CVPR 2017 (2017)
32. Simonyan, K., Zisserman, A.: Very deep convolutional networks for large-scale image recognition. CoRR abs/1409.1556 (2014). http://arxiv.org/abs/1409.1556
33. Szegedy, C., et al.: Going deeper with convolutions. CoRR abs/1409.4842 (2014), http://arxiv.org/abs/1409.4842
34. Yang, C.-Y., Ma, C., Yang, M.-H.: Single-image super-resolution: a benchmark. In: Fleet, D., Pajdla, T., Schiele, B., Tuytelaars, T. (eds.) ECCV 2014. LNCS, vol. 8692, pp. 372–386. Springer, Cham (2014). https://doi.org/10.1007/978-3-319-10593-2_25

35. Yang, J., Lin, Z., Cohen, S.: Fast image super-resolution based on in-place example regression. In: 2013 IEEE Conference on Computer Vision and Pattern Recognition (CVPR), pp. 1059–1066. IEEE (2013)
36. Zeiler, M.D., Fergus, R.: Visualizing and understanding convolutional networks. CoRR abs/1311.2901 (2013). http://arxiv.org/abs/1311.2901
37. Zeyde, R., Elad, M., Protter, M.: On single image scale-up using sparse-representations. In: Boissonnat, J.-D., et al. (eds.) Curves and Surfaces 2010. LNCS, vol. 6920, pp. 711–730. Springer, Heidelberg (2012). https://doi.org/10.1007/978-3-642-27413-8_47

Feature2Mass: Visual Feature Processing in Latent Space for Realistic Labeled Mass Generation

Jae-Hyeok Lee, Seong Tae Kim, Hakmin Lee, and Yong Man Ro$^{(\boxtimes)}$

School of Electrical Engineering, KAIST, Daejeon, Republic of Korea
{heuyklee,stkim4978,zpqlam12,ymro}@kaist.ac.kr

Abstract. This paper deals with a method for generating realistic labeled masses. Recently, there have been many attempts to apply deep learning to various bio-image computing fields including computer-aided detection and diagnosis. In order to learn deep network model to be well-behaved in bio-image computing fields, a lot of labeled data is required. However, in many bioimaging fields, the large-size of labeled dataset is scarcely available. Although a few researches have been dedicated to solving this problem through generative model, there are some problems as follows: (1) The generated bio-image does not seem realistic; (2) the variation of generated bio-image is limited; and (3) additional label annotation task is needed. In this study, we propose a realistic labeled bio-image generation method through visual feature processing in latent space. Experimental results have shown that mass images generated by the proposed method were realistic and had wide expression range of targeted mass characteristics.

Keywords: Feature processing in latent space · Image synthesis
Bio-image generation · Medical mass generation

1 Introduction

Generating realistic labeled bio-images is a highly important task. Recently, there have been many attempts to apply deep learning to computer-aided detection or diagnosis in various bioimaging fields [2, 8, 11–13]. In order to learn high-performance deep network models, there is immense demand for large amounts of labeled data. However, in many bioimaging fields, the large-size of labeled dataset is scarcely available. Therefore, it is becoming increasingly important to generate realistic labeled data using small amounts of data in bioimaging fields where suffering from lack of labeled data.

Although there have been a few researches dedicated to solving this problem through generative model, there were some limitations as follows: (1) The generated bio-image does not seem realistic [3,9]; (2) the variation of generated bio-image is limited [1,4,7,10]; and (3) additional label annotation task is needed which requires expensive cost [6,7].

© Springer Nature Switzerland AG 2019
L. Leal-Taixé and S. Roth (Eds.): ECCV 2018 Workshops, LNCS 11134, pp. 326–334, 2019.
https://doi.org/10.1007/978-3-030-11024-6_22

In order to overcome aforementioned limitations, we propose a novel realistic labeled bio-image generation method through visual feature processing in latent space. The proposed method learns the generative model with adversarial learning to form manifold in latent feature space using few existing annotated images. After learning the generative model, the encoder of the generative model could map mass images onto the manifold of the latent feature space and we define it as visual feature. The processed visual features, the results of the proposed visual feature processing, could be decoded into pixel space through decoder of the generative model to generate wide expression range of realistic mass image which has targeted characteristics.

The main contribution of this paper is summarized as follows:

(1) We have proposed a novel method for generating realistic labeled masses that is not confined to the expression range of the limited real-world data.
(2) Through the proposed method, we have succeeded in forming an appropriate manifold for the characteristics of masses in latent space which is difficult due to the non-rigid nature of the masses.
(3) Comprehensive experiments have been conducted to validate the effectiveness of the proposed method. Experimental results show that masses generated by the proposed method are remarkably realistic. Moreover, the generated masses have a wide expression range of targeted mass characteristics.

2   Generating Realistic Labeled Masses by Visual Feature Processing in Latent Space

2.1   Overview of the Proposed Mass Generation

In this paper, we design the proposed method to generate breast masses according to the medical description. The BIRADS (Breast Imaging Reporting and Data System) [5] which is designed to characterize the masses on breast imaging is used as the medical description in this paper.

Overall architecture of the proposed method is shown in Fig. 1. As seen in Fig. 1, the proposed architecture is built upon Generative Adversarial Networks and it includes four main modules: a mass generator (autoencoder) module (G),

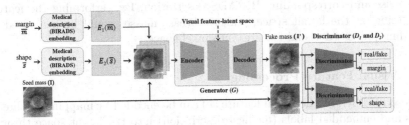

Fig. 1. Overall architecture of the proposed method for synthesizing masses through visual feature processing.

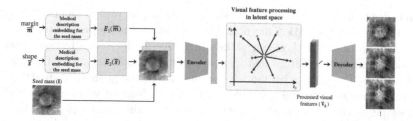

Fig. 2. Visual feature processing in the latent space for mass generation using the proposed method.

two discriminator modules (D_1 and D_2), and BIRADS description embedding modules (E_1 and E_2). The two discriminators scheme is adopted to effectively extract and backpropagate the BIRADS description characteristics of each generated mass.

The goal of learning phase is to let the G learns the manifold of the breast masses which will be used in generating phase. Overall explanation of the learning/generating phase procedure of the proposed architecture is as follows.

In the learning phase, as seen in Fig. 1, breast mass image and two of the major information in BIRADS, margin ($\bar{m}$) and shape ($\bar{s}$) labels are inputted to the network. The margin and shape labels are embedded into $E_1(\bar{m})$ and $E_2(\bar{s})$ through BIRADS description embedding modules before inputted to G. Then G generates the fake mass (I') using the inputted mass (I) and embedded labels as

$$I' = G(I, E_1(\bar{m}), E_2(\bar{s}))), \tag{1}$$

where $E_1(\bar{m})$ and $E_2(\bar{s})$ denotes the embedded margin ($\bar{m}$) and shape ($\bar{s}$) labels of BIRADS description.

In the generating phase, as seen in Fig. 2, we use the G and BIRADS description embedding modules which are trained to approximate breast mass manifold. G includes encoder and decoder which consist of convolution layer and transposed convolution layer, respectively. In front of G, a seed breast mass and corresponding margin or shape labels are embedded through BIRADS embedding modules similar to learning phase. When the breast mass with embedded labels come into the input of G, the encoder maps it on the latent space formed by the seed mass and corresponding BIRADS description. By performing the feature processing on the latent space, realistic breast masses could be generated by decoding processed visual features into pixel space.

2.2 Visual Feature Processing

As described before, the visual feature ($\bar{v}$) can be encoded by mapping the breast mass and embedded labels (medical description) into the latent space through encoder. If a visual feature in the latent space is fed to the decoder, a breast mass representing the visual feature is generated. The generated breast mass contains characteristics of seed breast mass and embedded medical description. To increase the non-linear diversity in mass generation, we devise visual feature processing to consider multitudinous possible visual features on the manifold where visual features of the breast masses exist. Note embedded labels (medical description) and seed mass fix the visual features within the latent space.

Visual Feature Processing by Interpolation. The various masses are generated from multitudinous possible visual features on the manifold. A visual feature can be obtained by interpolation processing with adjacent fixed visual features. Namely, a new visual feature is acquired through interpolated between adjacent visual features which are fixed by embedded labels (medical description) and seed mass. Interpolation between N different visual features allows considering possible visual features within the range of N visual features.

$$\bar{v}_{\text{interpolated}} = \sum_{k=1}^{N} \alpha_k \bar{v}_k,$$

$$\text{where } 0 \leq \alpha_k \leq 1 \text{ and } \sum_{k=1}^{N} \alpha_k = 1. \tag{2}$$

α_k denotes the weight multiplied by the visual feature $\bar{v}_k$ in the interpolation. If these N visual features are linearly independent, that is, if the only condition for making a linear combination of visual features 0 is that all α_k is zero, then these N visual features form $(N - 1)$-dimension hyperplane. In other words, when N is less than the dimension of the visual feature itself, if N visual features are linearly independent of each other, then all possible visual features in the hyperplane of $(N - 1)$-dimension can be considered.

2.3   Mass Generation Through Visual Feature Processing

In this section, we describe in detail deep learning procedure how the breast mass is generated through the visual feature processing. In the learning procedure, the G learns the manifold of the breast masses which could be used in generating phase. In the generating phase, G and BIRADS description embedding modules are used to generate realistic breast masses.

The behavior of BIRADS description embedding modules in learning and generating phase is as follows. In the learning and generating phases, the BIRADS description embedding modules map one-hot label form of BIRADS description label into the size of the breast mass image. Then the breast mass image and the embedded labels are concatenated and then inputted into the encoder.

The details of each generation step in the generating phase are as follows: (1) The encoder receives the concatenated input and maps it into the 1024-dimensional latent feature space. (2) The aforementioned processing to the visual feature is applied to generate a visual feature of the breast mass with appearance and characteristic that is not presented in the seed breast mass image. In feature processing in learned latent feature space, there is room for expansion since visual feature processing is able to include any operations applicable to visual features besides interpolation. (3) When a processed visual feature is inputted to the decoder, the decoder maps it into the pixel.

2.4 Learning Strategy of the Proposed Deep Network Framework

In this study, the proposed deep network framework utilizes two BIRADS description labels (*i.e.* margin and shape), and it has two discriminators (D_1 and D_2) to predict them. The loss function of D_1 is defined as

$$
\begin{aligned}
L_{D_1} = E_{I \sim P_{\text{data}}} [\log(D_1^{RF}(I)) + \log(1 - D_1^{RF}(I')) \\
+ \lambda_1 (\log(1 - (\bar{m} - D_1^m(I))) + \log(1 - (\bar{m} - D_1^m(I'))))],
\end{aligned}
\tag{3}
$$

where the $D_1^{RF}(\cdot)$ and $D_1^m(\cdot)$ denotes the prediction about real/fake and estimated margin label of D_1, respectively. λ_1 is the weight multiplied by each loss term to balance overall loss function. The first two terms of loss function represent the general GAN loss of adversarial learning that predicts the real/fake of the real breast mass image (I) and generated breast mass image (I'). The loss terms in $\lambda_1(\cdot)$ decrease when D_1 predicts the ground truth margin label ($\bar{m}$) more precisely from the inputted I and I'.

The loss function of D_2 is defined as

$$
\begin{aligned}
L_{D_2} = E_{I \sim P_{\text{data}}} [\log(D_2^{RF}(I)) + \log(1 - D_2^{RF}(I')) \\
+ \lambda_2 (\log(1 - (\bar{s} - D_2^s(I))) + \log(1 - (\bar{s} - D_2^s(I'))))],
\end{aligned}
\tag{4}
$$

where $D_2^s(\cdot)$ denotes the prediction about shape label of D_2. The first two terms of loss function represent the general GAN loss of adversarial learning that predicts the real/fake of the I and I' by G. The loss terms in $\lambda_2(\cdot)$ decrease when D_2 predict the ground truth shape label ($\bar{s}$) from the inputted I and I'.

The loss term that predicts the BIRADS description label by taking I' as an input serves as noise in the early learning phase when G does not generate a realistic breast mass. However, after G has been able to generate a breast masses that is similar to real breast masses, it pushes D to predict the BIRADS description label better for the generated masses which has non-linearly different aspect (but does not differ much enough to have different margins and shape labels). Therefore, it makes D_1 and D_2 have a data augmentation effect.

Next, the loss function of G is defined as

$$
\begin{aligned}
L_G = E_{I \sim P_{\text{data}}} [\log(D_1^{RF}(I')) + \log(D_2^{RF}(I')) \\
+ \lambda_3 (\log(1 - (\bar{m} - D_1^m(I'))) + \log(1 - (\bar{s} - D_2^s(I')))) + \lambda_4 \cdot L1(I, I')],
\end{aligned}
\tag{5}
$$

where λ_3 and λ_4 are the weights multiplied by each loss term to balance overall loss function. The loss term $L1(I, I')$ denotes reconstruction loss using L1-norm between real breast mass I and generated breast mass I'. The first two loss terms in loss function, like the loss functions of D_1 and D_2, mean the general GAN losses of adversarial learning for real/fake predictions of D_1 and D_2 for the I'. The loss terms in $\lambda_3(\cdot)$ decrease when G could generate I' that has more strong characteristics along BIRADS description $\bar{m}$, $\bar{s}$. Like the loss term in D, after D has been able to properly identify the BIRADS description label, it pushes G represents the characteristic of the BIRADS description label better which is used in I' generation. The last $L1$ loss term pushes G to form a manifold similar to the real data distribution.

3   Experimental Results

3.1   Dataset

For identifying the effectiveness of the proposed method, we utilized the publicly available DDSM dataset. The mammograms scanned by Howtek 960 were selected from DDSM dataset for the experiments. A total of 841 regions of interest (ROI) were used. The size of seed image I was resized to 64 by 64. For the BIRADS description, as aforementioned, shape and margin of masses were selected from BIRADS descriptions. Since these are representative characteristics of breast masses and widely used for recording in clinical reports.

3.2   Architecture and Training Details

Each BIRADS description embedding module consisted of two fully-connected layers which have 256 and 4096 neurons. The encoder and decoder of the proposed architecture composed of seven convolution and transposed convolution layers, respectively. The discriminator module composed of ten convolution layers and three fully-connected layers. Each module utilizes LeakyReLU-Conv (or Transposed Conv)-BatchNorm structure.

For training the generator and discriminator, the Adam optimization was used with learning rate 0.0002 and pytorch default Adam optimizer settings. The values of loss function balancing weights λ_1, λ_2, λ_3, and λ_4 were 10, 10, 10, and 300, respectively. We utilized a batch size of 512 and trained the network for 8000 epochs. For image data augmentation, horizontal flipping, vertical flipping, and cropping were performed in a random manner.

3.3   Visual Feature Processing in Latent Space with Interpolation

Visual Feature Interpolation Between Two Visual Features. The visual feature interpolation results between two visual features are shown in Fig. 3. The two visual features were selected from 841 visual features of 841 mass ROIs in the dataset. In experiments, two visual features were selected and equidistant visual features between the two features were interpolated. The interpolated visual features were decoded into pixel space. The leftmost and rightmost images in Fig. 3 are two seed breast mass images. Among the images in the middle, the leftmost and rightmost images represent decoded images from visual features fixed with seed image and embedded labels. The eight images that exist between them are generated images through the proposed visual features interpolation.

Visual Feature Interpolation from Three Visual Features. The visual feature interpolation results from three visual features are shown in Fig. 4. The three visual features were selected from 841 visual features of 841 mass ROIs in the dataset. As seen in Fig. 4, twelve interpolated visual features from the three visual features were visualized. By inputting twelve visual features into the decoder and mapping them to pixel space, we verified that the manifold from these three seed breast masses was formed suitably.

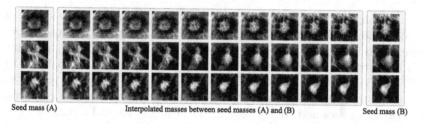

Seed mass (A)   Interpolated masses between seed masses (A) and (B)   Seed mass (B)

Fig. 3. Generated breast masses through the proposed visual feature interpolation between two visual features.

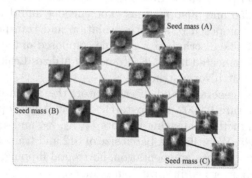

Fig. 4. Generated breast masses through the proposed visual feature interpolation from three visual features.

3.4   Visual Feature Processing Within a Specific BIRADS Category

This section demonstrates that generating masses with intended annotation information is achievable through the proposed method. Figure 5 shows the generated masses using visual features obtained from the seed masses with a specific BIRADS category (C) (*e.g.* ill-defined margins and round shape). The total number of seed masses used in the experiment was 161. Among them, 20 masses

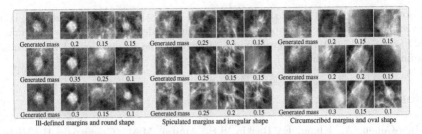

Fig. 5. Generated breast masses through the proposed visual feature processing with visual features belonging to a specific BIRADS category. The seed breast masses have ill-defined margins and round shape (left), speculated margins and irregular shape (middle), and circumscribed margins and oval shape (right).

had ill-defined margins and round shape, 104 masses had spiculate margins and irregular shape, and 37 masses had circumscribed margins and oval shape.

As seen in Fig. 5, the masses in the left side of corresponding three seed masses were generated from interpolated visual features. The interpolated visual feature was calculated as follows: (1) Twenty visual features in a specific BIRADS category ($\bar{v}_{sel}^{C}$) were randomly selected out of the number of candidate masses in a specific category; (2) The corresponding twenty weights (α_{sel}^{C}) were randomly initialized in the unit of 0.05.

In Fig. 5, the top three masses which have the largest weights α_{sel}^{C} and corresponding weights are represented in the right side of each generated mass. As seen in Fig. 5, the generated masses were realistic and had target characteristics (*e.g.* ill-defined margins and round shape). Therefore, the masses which are generated utilizing visual features in a specific BIRADS description category did not require additional labeling cost.

4 Conclusions

In this paper, we proposed the novel bio-image generation method through visual feature processing. The proposed method learned the generative model with adversarial learning to effectively form manifold in latent feature space using a limited number of annotated mass images. After learning the generative model, the encoder of the generative model could map mass images onto the manifold of the latent feature space (defined as visual feature). By decoding the processed visual features, the mass image was generated. Through extensive experiments, we verified that the masses generated by the proposed method were realistic and had a wide expression range. Moreover, it was possible to generate masses with the target characteristics. By generating the masses with the target characteristics, it could alleviate the labeling workload for utilizing generated masses in real-world. It is expected that the proposed method could be generalized to other bioimaging fields where suffering from lack of annotated data.

Acknowledgement. This work was supported by Institute for Information & communications Technology Promotion (IITP) grant funded by the Korea government (MSIT) (No. 2017-0-01778, Development of Explainable Human-level Deep Machine Learning Inference Framework).

References

1. Ben-Cohen, A., Klang, E., Raskin, S.P., Amitai, M.M., Greenspan, H.: Virtual PET images from CT data using deep convolutional networks: initial results. In: Tsaftaris, S.A., Gooya, A., Frangi, A.F., Prince, J.L. (eds.) SASHIMI 2017. LNCS, vol. 10557, pp. 49–57. Springer, Cham (2017). https://doi.org/10.1007/978-3-319-68127-6_6
2. Cheng, J.Z., et al.: Computer-aided diagnosis with deep learning architecture: applications to breast lesions in us images and pulmonary nodules in CT scans. Sci. Rep. **6**, 24454 (2016)
3. Chuquicusma, M.J., Hussein, S., Burt, J., Bagci, U.: How to fool radiologists with generative adversarial networks? A visual turing test for lung cancer diagnosis. In: 2018 IEEE 15th International Symposium on Biomedical Imaging (ISBI 2018), pp. 240–244. IEEE (2018)
4. Costa, P., et al.: Towards adversarial retinal image synthesis. arXiv preprint arXiv:1701.08974 (2017)
5. D'Orsi, C.J.: ACR BI-RADS atlas: breast imaging reporting and data system. American College of Radiology (2013)
6. Frid-Adar, M., Diamant, I., Klang, E., Amitai, M., Goldberger, J., Greenspan, H.: GAN-based synthetic medical image augmentation for increased CNN performance in liver lesion classification. arXiv preprint arXiv:1803.01229 (2018)
7. Frid-Adar, M., Klang, E., Amitai, M., Goldberger, J., Greenspan, H.: Synthetic data augmentation using GAN for improved liver lesion classification. In: 2018 IEEE 15th International Symposium on Biomedical Imaging (ISBI 2018), pp. 289–293. IEEE (2018)
8. Gordon, M., et al.: Segmentation of inner and outer bladder wall using deep-learning convolutional neural network in CT urography. In: Medical Imaging 2017: Computer-Aided Diagnosis, vol. 10134, p. 1013402. International Society for Optics and Photonics (2017)
9. Kitchen, A., Seah, J.: Deep generative adversarial neural networks for realistic prostate lesion MRI synthesis. arXiv preprint arXiv:1708.00129 (2017)
10. Nie, D., et al.: Medical image synthesis with context-aware generative adversarial networks. In: Descoteaux, M., Maier-Hein, L., Franz, A., Jannin, P., Collins, D.L., Duchesne, S. (eds.) MICCAI 2017. LNCS, vol. 10435, pp. 417–425. Springer, Cham (2017). https://doi.org/10.1007/978-3-319-66179-7_48
11. Roth, H.R., et al.: Improving computer-aided detection using convolutional neural networks and random view aggregation. IEEE Trans. Med. Imaging **35**(5), 1170–1181 (2016)
12. Tsehay, Y.K., et al.: Convolutional neural network based deep-learning architecture for prostate cancer detection on multiparametric magnetic resonance images. In: Medical Imaging 2017: Computer-Aided Diagnosis, vol. 10134, p. 1013405. International Society for Optics and Photonics (2017)
13. Zhang, W., et al.: Deep convolutional neural networks for multi-modality isointense infant brain image segmentation. NeuroImage **108**, 214–224 (2015)

Ordinal Regression with Neuron Stick-Breaking for Medical Diagnosis

Xiaofeng Liu[1,2]($\boxtimes$) (iD), Yang Zou[1] (iD), Yuhang Song[3] (iD), Chao Yang[3] (iD), Jane You[4] (iD), and B. V. K. Vijaya Kumar[1,5] (iD)

[1] Carnegie Mellon University, Pittsburgh, PA 15213, USA
liuxiaofeng@cmu.edu, yzou2@andrew.cmu.edu
[2] Fanhan Information Tech, Suzhou, China
[3] University of Southern California, Los Angeles, CA 90089, USA
yuhangso@usc.edu,chaoy@usc.edu
[4] The Hong Kong Polytechnic University, Kowloon, Hong Kong
csyjia@comp.polyu.edu.hk
[5] Carnegie Mellon University Africa, Kigali, Rwanda
kumar@ece.cmu.edu

Abstract. The classification for medical diagnosis usually involves inherently ordered labels corresponding to the level of health risk. Previous multi-task classifiers on ordinal data often use several binary classification branches to compute a series of cumulative probabilities. However, these cumulative probabilities are not guaranteed to be monotonically decreasing. It also introduces a large number of hyper-parameters to be fine-tuned manually. This paper aims to eliminate or at least largely reduce the effects of those problems. We propose a simple yet efficient way to rephrase the output layer of the conventional deep neural network. We show that our methods lead to the state-of-the-art accuracy on Diabetic Retinopathy dataset and Ultrasound Breast dataset with very little additional cost.

Keywords: Medical diagnosis · Ordinal regression
Deep neural network · Stick-breaking · Unimodal label smoothing

1 Introduction

Recent advances in deep neural networks (DNN) for natural image tasks have prompted a surge of interest in adapting similar models to medical images [1–3]. However, some of the special characteristics of medical diagnosis have, in our opinion, not been anfficiently explored.

The classes of a medical image usually represent the health risk levels, which are inherently ordered. For instance, the Diabetic Retinopathy Diagnosis (DR) involves five levels: no DR (1), mild DR (2), moderate DR (3), severe DR (4) and proliferative DR (5) [4,5]. The Breast Imaging-Reporting and Data System

---

X. Li and Y. Zou are equally contributed.

© Springer Nature Switzerland AG 2019
L. Leal-Taixé and S. Roth (Eds.): ECCV 2018 Workshops, LNCS 11134, pp. 335–344, 2019.
https://doi.org/10.1007/978-3-030-11024-6_23

(BIRADS) also includes five diagnostic labels: 1-healthy, 2-benign, 3-probably benign, 4-may contain malignant and 5-probably contains malignant [1,6]. Similar ordinal labeling systems for liver (LIRADS), gynecology (GIRADS), colonography (CRADS) have been established soon afterward [2].

Surely, the ordinal data is not unique to the medical image classification. Some other examples of ordinal labels include the age of a person [7], face expression intensity [8], aesthetic [9], star rating of a movie [10], etc., and are traditionally referred to ordinal regression tasks [11]. Two of the most straightforward approaches either cast it as a multi-class classification problem [12] and optimize the cross-entropy (CE) loss or treat it as a metric regression problem [13] and minimize the absolute/squared error loss (i.e., MAE/MSE). The former (Fig. 1(a)) assumes that the classes are independent of each other, which totally fails to explore the inherent ordering between the labels. The latter (Fig. 1(c)) treats the discrete labels as continuous numerical values, in which the adjacent classes are equally distant. This assumption violates the non-stationary property of many image related tasks, easily resulting in over-fitting [14].

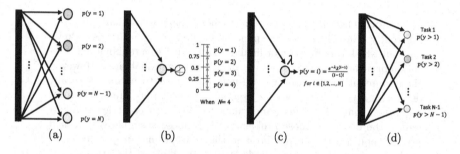

Fig. 1. The architecture of output layer used in previous ordinal regression methods: (a) multi-class classification, (b) regression, (c) poisson, and (d) multi-task classification. We learn a discriminative mapping from sample $\mathbf{x}$ to an ordinal variable y.

Recently, better results were achieved via a $N-1$ binary classification subtasks (Fig. 1(b)) using sigmoid output with MSE loss [11] or softmax output with CE loss [2,6,15,16], when we have N levels as the class label. We can transform N levels to a series of labels of length $N-1$. Then the first class is $[0,...,0]$, followed by the second class $[1,...,0]$, third class $[1,1,..,0]$ and so forth. The sub-branches in Fig. 1(b) calculate the cumulative probability $p(y > i|\mathbf{x})$, where i index the class[1]. With the cumulative probability, then it is trivial to define the corresponding discrete probabilities $p(y = i|\mathbf{x})$ via subtraction. These techniques are closely related to their non-deep counterparts [17,18]. However, the cumulative probabilities $p(y > 1|\mathbf{x}), ..., p(y > N-1|\mathbf{x})$ are calculated by several branches independently, therefore, can not guarantee they are monotonically decreasing. That leads to the $p(y = i|\mathbf{x})$ are not guaranteed to be strictly positive and results

---

[1] We will always index probabilities from zero for the remainder of this paper.

poor learning efficiency in the early stage of training. Moreover, $N - 1$ weights need to be manually fine-tuned to balance the CE loss of each branch.

Besides, under the one-hot target label encoding, the CE loss $-\log(p(y = l|\mathbf{x})))$ essentially only cares about the ground truth class l. [19] argues that misclassifying an adult as a baby is more severe than misclassifying as a teenager, even if the probabilities of the adult class are the same. [5,20,21] propose to use a single output neuron to calculate a parameter of a unimodal distribution, and strictly require that the $p(y = i|\mathbf{x})$ follows a Poisson or Binomial distribution, but suffers from lacking the ability to control the variance [21]. Since the peak (also the mean and variance) of a Poisson distribution is equal to a designated λ, we can not assign the peak to the first or last class, and its variance is very high when we need the peak in the very later classes.

Furthermore, the agreement rate of the radiologists for a malignancy is usually less than 80%, which results in a noisy labeled dataset [22,23]. Despite the distinction between adjacent labels is often unclear, it is more likely that a well-trained annotator will mislabel a Severe DR (4) sample to Moderate DR (3) rather than No DR (1).

In this paper, we propose to address the issues discussed above. Briefly, we rephrase the conventional softmax-based output layer to the neuron stick-breaking formulations to guarantee the cumulative probabilities are monotonically decreasing. We evaluated our approaches in the context of medical diagnosis on two datasets, and obtained promising results. We note that although the methods shown here were originally developed for medical images, they are essentially applicable to other ordinal regression problems (Fig. 3).

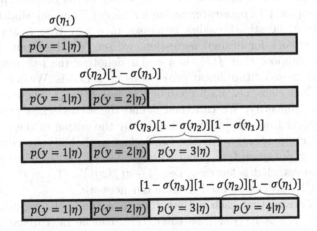

Fig. 2. The Stick-breaking process for 4 classes with 3 boundaries. In [24], η is the linear projection in LGMs.

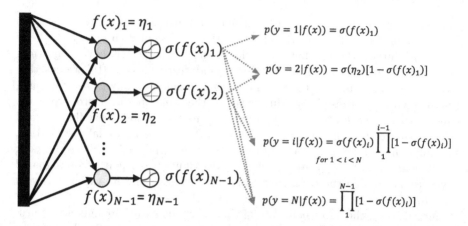

Fig. 3. Our neuron Stick-breaking architecture for N classes with $N-1$ output neurons, followed by sigmoid units and linear operations.

2   Neuron Stick-Breaking for Ordinal Regression

In the stick-breaking approach, we define a stick of unit length between $[0, 1]$, and sequentially break off parts of the stick which then become the discrete probabilities for that class (Fig. 2(a)) [25]. The stick-breaking process is a subset of the random allocation processes [26] and a generalization of continuation ratio models [27]. It is closely associated with the associated Bayesian non-parametric methods, e.g., [25] used it in constructive definitions of the Dirichlet process [28]. [24] further proposed its parameterization for Latent Gaussian Models (LGMs).

To introduce the stick-breaking processes in a way that is appropriate a deep neural network for ordinal regression, we set $N - 1$ output neurons for N levels, and suppose that $f(x)_i$ is a scalar denoting the i-th output of our neural network to substitute linear projections η_i in LGMs. We define the stick length of the first class, i.e., its probability, to be $\sigma(f(x)_1)$, where $\sigma(\cdot)$ denotes the sigmoid nonlinearity. We can then define the second class probability as what was left over from that stick multiplied by the output of the second class, i.e., $(1 - \sigma(f(x)_1))\sigma(f(x)_2)$. For the third class probability we compute $(1 - \sigma(f(x)_1))(1 - \sigma(f(x)_2))\sigma(f(x)_3)$ and so forth, where the last class probability for $p(N|\mathbf{x})$ receives what is left over, i.e., $(1 - \sigma(f(x)_1))...(1 - \sigma(f(x)_{N-1}))$. The conventional CE loss can be used to train our network.

It can be derived that each output $f(x)_i$ is actually the log-ratio $f(x)_i = \log(p(y = i|x)/p(y > i|x))$ [24], so these $f(x)_i$ can be interpreted as defining decision boundaries that try to separate the i-th class from all the classes that come after it. By doing so, the prediction is still a discrete probability (i.e., $\sum_i^{N=1} p(y = i) = 1$), and each $p(y = i) \geq 0$, then we do guarantee the relationship of $p(y > 1) \geq p(y > 2) \geq p(y > N - 1)$.

A nice property of our method is that unlike the approaches that only output a single distribution parameter [5,21,29], we obtain a slightly more expressive model since each boundary of two adjacent classes gets its own scalar output $f(x)_i$. The discrete probabilities can also be calculated via our predefined linear manipulations instead of having to estimate cumulative probabilities first [11, 17, 18]. Therefore, the weights of each branch in [11] are no longer necessary.

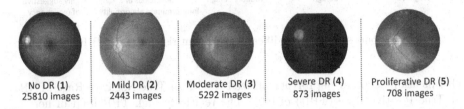

No DR (1)   Mild DR (2)   Moderate DR (3)   Severe DR (4)   Proliferative DR (5)
25810 images   2443 images   5292 images   873 images   708 images

Fig. 4. Some samples with different retinopathy level in the DR dataset.

3   Experiments

3.1   Datasets

We make use of two typical ordinal datasets in the medical area suitable for DNN implementations. The first dataset contains images of Diabetic Retinopathy (DR)[2]. In this dataset, a large amount of high-resolution fundus (i.e., interior surface at the back of the eye) images data have been labeled as five levels of DR, with levels 1 to 5 representing the No DR, Mild DR, Moderate DR, Severe DR, and Proliferative DR, respectively. The left and right fundus image from 17563 patients are publicly available. Following the setting in [21], we adopt the subject-independent ten-fold cross-validation, i.e., the validation set consisting of 10% of the patients is set aside. The images belonging to a patient will only appear in a single fold, in this way we can avoid contamination. The images are also preprocessed as in [5, 21] and subsequently resized as 256×256 size images. Some examples can be found in Fig. 4.

The second dataset is the Ultrasound BIRADS (US-BIRADS) [6]. It is comprised of 4904 breast images which are labeled with the BIRADS system. Considering the relatively limited number of samples in level 5, we usually regard the 4–5 as a single level [6]. That results 2700 healthy (1) images, 1113 benign (2) images, 359 probably benign (3), and 732 may contain/contain malignant images. We divide this dataset into 5 subsets for subject-independent five-fold cross validation. We show some samples at different levels in Fig. 5.

3.2   Evaluations

There are several possible evaluation metrics for ordinal data. As a classification problem, the performance of a system can be simply measured by the average

---

[2] https://www.kaggle.com/c/diabetic-retinopathy-detection.

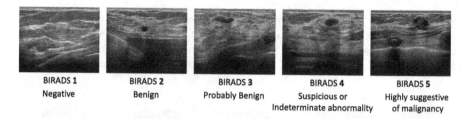

BIRADS 1　　　BIRADS 2　　　BIRADS 3　　　BIRADS 4　　　　　BIRADS 5
Negative　　　Benign　　　Probably Benign　　Suspicious or　　　Highly suggestive
　　　　　　　　　　　　　　　　　　Indeterminate abnormality　of malignancy

Fig. 5. Some samples with different malignant risk in the US-BIRADS.

classification accuracy. [6] further utilized the Mean True Negative Rate (TNR) at True Positive Rate (TPR) of 0.95. The relatively high TPR used in here is fitted for strict TPR requirement of medical applications to avoid misdiagnosing diseased case as healthy. However, they do not consider the severity of different misclassification. Following the previous metrics in the Kaggle competition of DR dataset, we choose the quadratic weighted kappa (QWK)[3] to implicitly punish the misclassification proportional to the distance between the ground-of-truth label and predicted label of the network [30]. The QWK is formulated as:

$$k = 1 - \frac{\sum_{i,j} \mathbf{W}_{i,j} \mathbf{O}_{i,j}}{\sum_{i,j} \mathbf{W}_{i,j} \mathbf{E}_{i,j}} \tag{1}$$

to measures the level of disagreement between two raters ($\mathcal{A}$ and $\mathcal{B}$). In here, the $\mathcal{A}$ is the *argmax* prediction of our classifier and $\mathcal{B}$ is the ground truth. The $\mathbf{W}$ is a $N \times N$ matrix where $\mathbf{W}_{i,j}$ denotes the cost associated with misclassifying label i as label j. In QWK, $\mathbf{W}_{i,j} = (i - j)^2$. $\mathbf{O}_{i,j}$ counts the number of images that received a rating i by $\mathcal{A}$ and a rating j by $\mathcal{B}$. The quadratic calculation is one possible choice and one can plug in other distance metrics into kappa calculation. The matrix of expected ratings $\mathbf{E}$, is calculated, assuming that there is no correlation between rating scores. As a result, k is a scalar in $[-1, 1]$, and $k = 1$ indicates the two raters are total agreement, whereas $k < 0$ means the classifier performs worse than random choice.

The Mean Absolute Error (MAE) metric is also popular in related ordinal datasets [11], which is computed using the average of the absolute errors between the ground truth and the estimated result. Here, we also propose its use in evaluating the proposed method on two medical ordinal benchmarks.

3.3　Networks and Training Details

For fair comparison, we choose similar backbones neural networks as in previous works on DP and US-BIRADS datasets. We adjust the last layer and softmax normalization to our neuron stick-breaking formulation. The ResNet [31] style model with 11 ResBlocks as in [21] has been adopted for DR dataset. We use four stick-breaking neurons as our output structure and calculate the $p(y = i|\mathbf{x})$

---

[3] https://www.kaggle.com/c/diabetic-retinopathy-detection#evaluation.

via the predefined linear operations. AlexNet style architecture [32] with six convolution layers and following two dense layers is used for US-BIRADS image dataset as in [6]. 3 stick-breaking neurons are employed as the last layer. All of networks in our training use the $\mathcal{L}_2$ norm of 10^{-4}, ADAM optimizer [33] with 128 training batch-size and initial learning rate of 10^{-3}. The learning rate will be divided by ten when either the validation loss or the valid set QWK plateaus. We set our hyper-parameters $\eta = 0.15$, $\tau = 1$.

Table 1. Performance on the DR dataset.

Evaluations	Mean TNR@TPR = 0.95			Valid Acc	Valid QWK	MAE
	1 vs 2–4	1–2 vs 3–4	1–3 vs 4			
MC	41.5%	30.9%	31.1%	82.4%	0.724	0.37
RG	40.3%	30.6%	30.8 %	76.2%	0.705	0.38
Poisson [21]	38.8%	30.0%	29.6 %	77.1%	0.713	0.38
MT [6]	42.7%	31.7%	31.3%	82.8%	0.726	0.36
NSB	44.0%	33.1%	32.6%	84.2%	0.743	0.32

Table 2. Performance on the US-BIRADS dataset. *Our implementations have slightly higher TNR using MC baseline than the results reported in [6]

Evaluations	Mean TNR@TPR = 0.95			Valid Acc	Valid QWK	MAE
	1 vs 2–5	1–2 vs 3–5	1–3 vs 4–5			
MC	33.2%*	28.7%*	29.8%*	73.3%	0.678	0.42
RG	31.6%	28.5%	29.5%	73.0%	0.677	0.44
Poisson [21]	29.6%	27.2%	29.5%	72.2%	0.665	0.45
MT [6]	38.5%	29.2%	31.3%	76.5%	0.685	0.41
NSB	39.1%	30.2%	32.0%	78.3%	0.694	0.39

3.4 Numerical Experiments

We conduct our experiments on both datasets with the evaluation metrics discussed earlier. The results in DR dataset are shown in Table 1. Several baseline methods are chosen for comparison, e.g., multi-class classification with CE loss (MC), regression with MSE loss (RG), Poisson distribution output with CE loss (Poisson), and multi-task network with a series of CE loss (MT). The RG is usually worse than MC, but appear to be competitive w.r.t. MAE, since RG optimizes similar metric MSE in its training stage. The Poisson gets the lowest results in the most of evaluations due to its uncontrollable variance. The and MT are more promising than MC as they consider ordinal information. By addressing their limitations, we achieve the state-of-the-art performance in all of the evaluation tasks using the neuron stick-breaking (NSB). The leading performance of our method is also observed on the US-BIRADS dataset (Table 2).

4   Conclusions

We have introduced the stick-breaking presses for DNN-based ordinal regression problem. By reformulating the neurons of the last layer and softmax function, we not only fully consider the ordinal property of the class labels, but also guarantee the cumulative probabilities are monotonically decreasing. We also show how these approaches offer improved performance in DR and US BIRADS datasets. In future work, we intend to leverage our methods for more general ordinal regression tasks.

Acknowledgement. This work was supported in part by the National Natural Science Foundation 61308099, 61304032 and 61675202, Hong Kong Government General Research Fund GRF 152202/14E, PolyU Central Research Grant G-YBJW, Youth Innovation Promotion Association, CAS (2017264), Innovative Foundation of CIOMP, CAS (Y586320150), 11ZDGG001,CXJJ-16S038,CXJJ-17S017.

References

1. Geras, K.J., Wolfson, S., Shen, Y., Kim, S., Moy, L., Cho, K.: High-resolution breast cancer screening with multi-view deep convolutional neural networks. arXiv preprint arXiv:1703.07047 (2017)
2. Li, X., Kao, Y., Shen, W., Li, X., Xie, G.: Lung nodule malignancy prediction using multi-task convolutional neural network. In: Medical Imaging 2017: Computer-Aided Diagnosis, vol. 10134. International Society for Optics and Photonics (2017)
3. Gentry, A.E., Jackson-Cook, C.K., Lyon, D.E., Archer, K.J.: Penalized ordinal regression methods for predicting stage of cancer in high-dimensional covariate spaces. Cancer Inform. **14**, 201–208 (2015)
4. Gulshan, V.: Development and validation of a deep learning algorithm for detection of diabetic retinopathy in retinal fundus photographs. JAMA **316**(22), 2402–2410 (2016)
5. Beckham, C., Pal, C.: A simple squared-error reformulation for ordinal classification. arXiv preprint arXiv:1612.00775 (2016)
6. Ratner, V., Shoshan, Y., Kachman, T.: Learning multiple non-mutually-exclusive tasks for improved classification of inherently ordered labels. arXiv preprint arXiv:1805.11837 (2018)
7. Eidinger, E., Enbar, R., Hassner, T.: Age and gender estimation of unfiltered faces. IEEE Trans. Inf. Forensics Secur. **9**(12), 2170–2179 (2014)
8. Zhao, R., Gan, Q., Wang, S., Ji, Q.: Facial expression intensity estimation using ordinal information. In: Proceedings of the IEEE Conference on Computer Vision and Pattern Recognition, pp. 3466–3474 (2016)
9. Cardoso, J.S., da Costa, J.F.P., Cardoso, M.J.: Modelling ordinal relations with SVMs: an application to objective aesthetic evaluation of breast cancer conservative treatment. Neural Netw. **18**(5–6), 808–817 (2005)
10. Koren, Y., Sill, J.: OrdRec: an ordinal model for predicting personalized item rating distributions. In: Proceedings of the Fifth ACM Conference on Recommender Systems, pp. 117–124. ACM (2011)
11. Niu, Z., Zhou, M., Wang, L., Gao, X., Hua, G.: Ordinal regression with multiple output CNN for age estimation. In: Proceedings of the IEEE Conference on Computer Vision and Pattern Recognition, pp. 4920–4928 (2016)

12. Geng, X., Zhou, Z.H., Smith-Miles, K.: Automatic age estimation based on facial aging patterns. IEEE Trans. Pattern Anal. Mach. Intell. **29**(12), 2234–2240 (2007)
13. Fu, Y., Huang, T.S.: Human age estimation with regression on discriminative aging manifold. IEEE Trans. Multimed. **10**(4), 578–584 (2008)
14. Chang, K.Y., Chen, C.S., Hung, Y.P.: Ordinal hyperplanes ranker with cost sensitivities for age estimation. In: 2011 IEEE Conference on Computer Vision and Pattern Recognition (CVPR), pp. 585–592 IEEE (2011)
15. Fu, H., Gong, M., Wang, C., Batmanghelich, K., Tao, D.: Deep ordinal regression network for monocular depth estimation. In: Proceedings of the IEEE Conference on Computer Vision and Pattern Recognition, pp. 2002–2011 (2018)
16. Chen, S., Zhang, C., Dong, M., Le, J., Rao, M.: Using ranking-CNN for age estimation. In: The IEEE Conference on Computer Vision and Pattern Recognition (CVPR) (2017)
17. Cheng, J., Wang, Z., Pollastri, G.: A neural network approach to ordinal regression. In: IEEE International Joint Conference on Neural Networks, IJCNN 2008 (IEEE World Congress on Computational Intelligence), pp. 1279–1284. IEEE (2008)
18. Frank, E., Hall, M.: A simple approach to ordinal classification. In: De Raedt, L., Flach, P. (eds.) ECML 2001. LNCS (LNAI), vol. 2167, pp. 145–156. Springer, Heidelberg (2001). https://doi.org/10.1007/3-540-44795-4_13
19. Hou, L., Yu, C.P., Samaras, D.: Squared earth mover's distance-based loss for training deep neural networks. arXiv preprint arXiv:1611.05916 (2016)
20. da Costa, J.F.P., Alonso, H., Cardoso, J.S.: The unimodal model for the classification of ordinal data. Neural Netw. **21**(1), 78–91 (2008)
21. Beckham, C., Pal, C.: Unimodal probability distributions for deep ordinal classification. arXiv preprint arXiv:1705.05278 (2017)
22. Nishikawa, R.M., Comstock, C.E., Linver, M.N., Newstead, G.M., Sandhir, V., Schmidt, R.A.: Agreement between radiologists' interpretations of screening mammograms. In: Tingberg, A., Lång, K., Timberg, P. (eds.) IWDM 2016. LNCS, vol. 9699, pp. 3–10. Springer, Cham (2016). https://doi.org/10.1007/978-3-319-41546-8_1
23. Salazar, A.J., Romero, J.A., Bernal, O.A., Moreno, A.P., Velasco, S.C.: Reliability of the BI-RADS final assessment categories and management recommendations in a telemammography context. J. Am. Coll. Radiol. **14**(5), 686–692 (2017)
24. Khan, M., Mohamed, S., Marlin, B., Murphy, K.: A stick-breaking likelihood for categorical data analysis with latent Gaussian models. In: Artificial Intelligence and Statistics, pp. 610–618 (2012)
25. Sethuraman, J.: A constructive definition of Dirichlet priors. Statistica Sinica **4**, 639–650 (1994)
26. Agresti, A.: An Introduction to Categorical Data Analysis, vol. 135. Wiley, New York (1996)
27. Wan Kai, P.: Continuation-ratio model for categorical data: a Gibbs sampling approach. In: Proceedings of the International Multiconference of Engineers and Computer Scientists, vol. 1 (2008)
28. Frigyik, B.A., Kapila, A., Gupta, M.R.: Introduction to the Dirichlet distribution and related processes. Department of Electrical Engineering, University of Washignton, UWEETR-2010-0006 (2010)
29. Gutiérrez, P.A., Tiňo, P., Hervás-Martínez, C.: Ordinal regression neural networks based on concentric hyperspheres. Neural Netw. **59**, 51–60 (2014)
30. Cohen, J.: Weighted kappa: nominal scale agreement provision for scaled disagreement or partial credit. Psychol. Bull. **70**(4), 213 (1968)

31. He, K., Zhang, X., Ren, S., Sun, J.: Deep residual learning for image recognition. In: Proceedings of the IEEE Conference on Computer Vision and Pattern Recognition, pp. 770–778 (2016)
32. Krizhevsky, A., Sutskever, I., Hinton, G.E.: Imagenet classification with deep convolutional neural networks. In: Advances in Neural Information Processing Systems, pp. 1097–1105 (2012)
33. Kingma, D.P., Ba, J.: Adam: a method for stochastic optimization. arXiv preprint arXiv:1412.6980 (2014)

Multi-level Activation for Segmentation of Hierarchically-Nested Classes

Marie Piraud[✉], Anjany Sekuboyina, and Björn H. Menze

Department of Computer Science,
Technische Universität München, Munich, Germany
marie.piraud@tum.de

Abstract. For many biological image segmentation tasks, including topological knowledge, such as the nesting of classes, can greatly improve results. However, most 'out-of-the-box' CNN models are still blind to such prior information. In this paper, we propose a novel approach to encode this information, through a multi-level activation layer and three compatible losses. We benchmark all of them on nuclei segmentation in bright-field microscopy cell images from the 2018 Data Science Bowl challenge, offering an exemplary segmentation task with cells and nested subcellular structures. Our scheme greatly speeds up learning, and outperforms standard multi-class classification with soft-max activation and a previously proposed method stemming from it, improving the Dice score significantly (p-values < 0.007). Our approach is conceptually simple, easy to implement and can be integrated in any CNN architecture. It can be generalized to a higher number of classes, with or without further relations of containment.

Keywords: Segmentation · Multiclass · Inclusion · Nested classes
Class hierarchy

1 Introduction

For certain multi-class segmentation tasks, the classes have a hierarchical topological relation: one class is nested into another one, meaning that the set of pixels of the second class is spatially surrounded by pixels from the first one, as illustrated in Fig. 1(a). This is in the case of several important biological and medical image analysis tasks: anatomical structures are organized along the anatomical tree, tumors are often contained in one particular organ or anatomical structure, or intracellular features follow a specific organization within the cell. Informing the network about this type of structural relations between classes as a prior can significantly improve segmentation results, enabling the algorithm to focus on the hidden and unforseen features [1,2]. Convolutional Neural Networks

Electronic supplementary material The online version of this chapter (https://doi.org/10.1007/978-3-030-11024-6_24) contains supplementary material, which is available to authorized users.

© Springer Nature Switzerland AG 2019
L. Leal-Taixé and S. Roth (Eds.): ECCV 2018 Workshops, LNCS 11134, pp. 345–353, 2019.
https://doi.org/10.1007/978-3-030-11024-6_24

(CNNs), which have become the state-of-the-art for most image segmentation applications, have proven to be able to learn and encode very complex structures and relations between objects. However, very few CNN models are able to encode topological information as a prior.

In the literature, most of it predating the widespread use of CNNs, we distinguish three main avenues that have been pursued with that objective: (i) The first option is to use cascaded geometries [3], by training independently successive segmentation networks, the first for the surrounding class, and the second for the nested one. (ii) A second option can be to modify the loss term to penalize predictions which do not respect the expected topology, either by modifying the cross-entropy loss taking into account label-relations [2] or by integrating class relations through a specifically designed Wasserstein distance matrix in the Dice score loss [4]; both methods relying on soft-max activation. (iii) A third option is integrating label context via Conditional [5,6] and Markov [7] Random Fields that, although used as postprocessing routines in most application, can be integrated with deep learning architectures. All aforementioned methods however handle the nesting of classes in a rather indirect way – either in separate stages or through the loss, that often needs to be parametrized – and are therefore not optimally using information on class relations. Moreover, soft-max activation and cross-entropy loss assume that the classes are mutually-exclusive, as a pixel cannot belong to several classes at the same time, which does not make a natural basis for classes with hierarchical topological constraints. Applying such a standard method to segment nested-classes can lead to unreasonable results, with e.g. tumors detected outside of the organ of interest [3], or nuclei at the border of the cell (see Fig. 3), thereby limiting the quality of the results.

As a paradigm shift, we propose to consider the segmentation of hierarchically-nested classes as a generalized logistic regression problem by using a multi-level activation layer. This naturally and directly enforces the nesting of the classes, trading off neighbourhood constraints with local observations automatically and permits to segment all nested classes with a single output channel. This novel activation requires to move away from traditional cross-entropy loss, such that we introduce three adapted loss functions, and show that they all greatly speed up the learning process, and perform better than standard multi-class classification and the method from Ref. [2], on nuclei segmentation in bright-field microscopy images. We provide a second benchmark of our method on liver lesion segmentation in Computer Tomography (CT) images in the Supplementary Material. On top of being conceptually simple, the multi-level activation method is easy to implement, does not need parametrization and can be integrated in any CNN architecture.

2   Method

We start by describing our methodological contributions. We first introduce the new activation layer, and a matching thresholding scheme to infer the output segmentation map. We then propose three loss functions adapted to this activation, in Sect. 2.2.

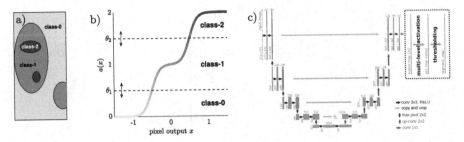

Fig. 1. *Illustration of the method.* (a) Sketch of 3 nested classes. (b) Corresponding multi-level activation [Eq. (1), with $h = 1$ and $\kappa = 10$]. (c) Multi-level activation block, which can be implemented on top of any segmentation architecture, here the U-Net [8].

2.1   Multi-level Activation Layer

Inspired by continuous regression, we propose a new multi-level activation layer, thereby generalizing logistic regression to hierarchically-nested classes [class-m $\subset$ class-$(m-1) \subset ... \subset$ class-1 $\subset$ class-0]. This activation function should have the same number of levels as the number of classes $m+1$, we therefore construct it from m equally-spaced sigmoids

$$a(x) = \sum_{n=1}^{m} \sigma\left(\kappa\left[x + h\left(n - \frac{m+1}{2}\right)\right]\right), \tag{1}$$

where σ is the sigmoid function, κ its steepness and h the spacing between consecutive sigmoids. A similar activation function has also been introduced for unsupervised RGB image segmentation [9]. In the case of $m+1 = 3$ classes, which is illustrated in Fig. 1(a), it becomes a two-level sigmoid $a(x) = \sigma\left[\kappa(x + h/2)\right] + \sigma\left[\kappa(x - h/2)\right]$. This is illustrated in Fig. 1(b) for $h = 1$ and $\kappa = 10$, that we use in the following. This pixel-wise activation layer is designed to replace the soft-max layer of any CNN architecture, see Fig. 1(c), enabling the segmentation of nested classes with one output channel, inherently respecting their hierarchy. Note that it does not enforce the topology as a strict constraint in the segmentation map, but the hierarchy holds as long as the output map of the network remains smooth, which is the case if the resolution of the image is high enough.

Further generalizing logistic regression, we infer the output segmentation map from the activation map $a(x_i) \in [0, m]$ by setting m thresholds. For $m = 2$, class-0 is assigned to pixel i if $a(x_i) < \theta_1$, class-1 if $\theta_1 \leq a(x_i) < \theta_2$, and class-2 if $\theta_2 \leq a(x_i)$, see Fig. 1(b). The optimal values for $\theta_{\{1,2\}}$ can either be determined through validation or preset, e.g. to 0.5 and 1.5.

2.2   Loss Functions

Standard cross-entropy takes probability maps as input, and therefore cannot be used directly after multi-level activation, as $a(x) \in [0, m]$. To this end, we introduce different loss functions to accommodate this new activation, that are inspired both from regression and standard multi-class classification.

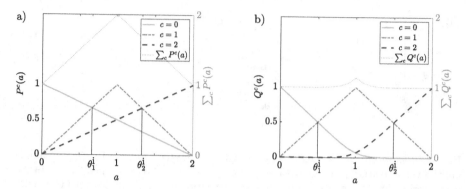

Fig. 2. *Class-'probabilities'*. Functions to map the output of the activation layer a to pseudo-probabilities. (a) $P^c(a)$ for the MCE loss, see Eq. (3), and (b) $Q^c(a)$ for the NCE loss, with $t = 10$, see Eq. (5).

Sum of Squared Error Loss. Considering the segmentation of nested classes as a regression problem, where the output map should be as close as possible to a layered-cake structure, we first propose the following Sum of Squared Error (SSE) loss

$$\mathcal{L}_{\text{SSE}} = -\frac{1}{N_{\text{tot}}} \sum_{\text{pixels } i} [a(x_i) - c_i]^2 \,, \tag{2}$$

where N_{tot} is the total number of pixels, x_i the CNN output for pixel i and $c_i \in \{0, 1, ..., m\}$ the corresponding target label, chosen consistently with Eq. (1).

Modified and Normalized Cross-Entropy Losses. Considering the problem from a multi-class classification perspective, we combine the multi-level activation with cross-entropy loss. We therefore need to map the activation $a(x) \in [0, m]$ to the interval $[0, 1]$ to mimic class-probabilities. For each class c, this mapping should peak at the target value c, which becomes the attractor during training. Focussing on the two-level case, we first propose the mapping

$$P^{c=0}(a) = 1 - a/2 \,,$$
$$P^{c=1}(a) = 1 - |1 - a| \,,$$
$$P^{c=2}(a) = a/2 \,. \tag{3}$$

Those pseudo-class-probabilities are illustrated in Fig. 2(a), but note that they are not strict probabilities, as they do not respect the addition rule ($\sum_c P^c(a) = 2 - |1 - a| \neq 1$). With this transformation, the activation map can be integrated into a Modified Cross-Entropy (MCE) loss

$$\mathcal{L}_{\text{MCE}} = -\frac{1}{N_{\text{tot}}} \sum_{\text{pixels } i} \sum_{\text{classes } c} \omega^c y_i^c \log\left(P^c[a(x_i)]\right) \,, \tag{4}$$

where $y_i^{c'} = 1$ for the ground-truth label c' of pixel i and $y_i^{c \neq c'} = 0$ otherwise. The $P^c(a)$ functions display different slopes, see Fig. 2(a), which biases the training process towards class-1, that has a higher slope and will be favored in backpropagation. To compensate, we add the class-weights w^c in Eq. (4), that are chosen to be proportional to the inverse of the number of pixels of each class in the training set, $w^c = N_{\text{tot}}/N_c$.

To make up for the drawbacks of MCE, we propose a second transformation

$$Q^{c=0}(a) = s(1-a),$$
$$Q^{c=2}(a) = s(a-1), \tag{5}$$

where $Q^{c=1}(a) = 1 - |1-a|$ is unchanged, and we use the softplus function $s(x) = \frac{1}{t}\log(1 + e^{tx})$, a smoothed version of the rectifier. Unlike in MCE, where the slopes were biased towards class-1, the $Q^c(a)$ functions, which are shown in Fig. 2(b) for $t = 10$, have the same slope around the maximum. Furthermore, they are asymptotically normalized, as we have $\sum_c Q^c(a) \to_{t\to\infty} 1$. From there we define the Normalized Cross-Entropy (NCE) loss

$$\mathcal{L}_{\text{NCE}} = -\frac{1}{N_{\text{tot}}} \sum_{\text{pixels } i} \sum_{\text{classes } c} y_i^c \log\left(Q^c[a(x_i)]\right), \tag{6}$$

which leads to a balanced training.

The generalization to a higher number of nested classes is possible, and is presented explicitly for four classes in the Supplementary Material. We also present how MCE and NCE can be combined with standard cross-entropy, by the introduction of more output channels. For this reason, the use of those cross-entropy based losses, albeit counter-intuitive in the absence of soft-max activation and seemingly more convoluted than SSE, is of great interest: it enables the encoding of any hierarchical tree of topologically-nested and mutually-exclusive classes in a CNN.

3 Detection of Nuclei in Cells

Dataset and Training Strategy. We benchmark our method on the 2018 Data Science Bowl competition from Kaggle, whose challenge is to detect nuclei in cell images from different microscopy modalities. The simultaneous segmentation of cells and nuclei is an application of nested classes, as we have nuclei (class-2) $\subset$ cells (class-1) $\subset$ background (class-0). We select all bright-field microscopy images, on which the cells are clearly visible, and complement the available nuclei segmentation by a manual segmentation of the cell bodies (see Fig. 3). Another challenge from this competition is to deal with the limited number of training images in this modality ($N_{\text{im}} = 16$). We therefore rely on online data augmentation, and perform random flips, warping, rotations, translations and rescaling of the images at each training epoch. The images, resized to 512×512 pixels, are then fed into a U-Net like architecture [8]. We perform 4-fold cross-validation and a rotating testing scheme: we split the dataset into 4 subsets to perform cross-validation and further split each validation set into 4, for testing,

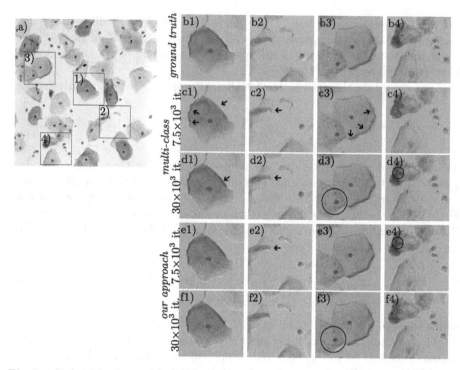

Fig. 3. *Examples of nuclei segmentation.* (a) Selected regions of a bright-field microscopy image are overlaid with (b) the ground truth segmentation, (c–d) results from standard multi-class segmentation after 7.5 and 30×10^3 iterations respectively, and (e–f) results from multi-level activation with MCE loss, our best performing method, after 7.5 and 30×10^3 iterations respectively. The cell- (respectively nuclei-) class is displayed in red (resp. green). Arrows indicate false positives and circles false negatives. (Color figure online)

such that we always train on 12 images, validate on 3 and test on one, in a 16-fold rotating fashion. For each fold, we select the threshold value θ_2 giving the best Dice score on the validation set and compute the scores of the test image after 30×10^3 iterations. Note that due to online data augmentation, the model does not tend to overfit.

Results. Qualitative results for standard multi-class segmentation and multi-level activation with MCE loss, after 7.5×10^3 iterations and after convergence, are presented in Fig. 3. Early on in the training process, multi-class segmentation outputs false positives for the nuclei class, in darker regions of the cells, even very close to the cell border, see Figs. 3(c1)–(c3). Those slowly disappear in the training process, as the CNN learns the relationship between classes, although some imperfections remain, see Figs. 3(d1)–(d2). This is strongly disfavored by multi-level activation, as the output map $\{x_i\}$ would have to oscillate on very short length scales, and we see that most such artefacts do not appear on Figs. 3(e)–(f).

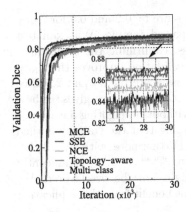

Fig. 4. *Scores for nuclei segmentation.* Mean validation Dice scores for the methods listed in the table (rows I, II and VI to VIII).

Table 1. *Scores for nuclei segmentation.* Mean test Dice scores for standard multi-class (row I), the 'topology-aware' loss [2] (row II) and multi-level activation (rows III-VIII). In rows III to V we use the threshold $\theta_2^{\natural}$. In rows VI to VIII, θ_2 is selected during validation and we report its mean value. Grey cells highlight significant improvement over multi-class, i.e. p-values < 0.05 using the paired samples Wilcoxon test.

Model	θ_2	Test Dice
I - Multi-class	–	0.839 (0.055)
II - Topology-aware [2]	–	0.842 (0.055)
III - NCE, Eq. (6)	$\theta_2^{\natural} = 1.5$	0.841 (0.058)
IV - SSE, Eq. (2)	$\theta_2^{\natural} = 1.5$	0.863 (0.051)
V - MCE, Eq. (4)	$\theta_2^{\natural} = 4/3$	0.844 (0.049)
VI - NCE, Eq. (6)	1.31 (0.09)	0.853 (0.056)
VII - SSE, Eq. (2)	1.39 (0.08)	0.863 (0.053)
VIII - MCE, Eq. (4)	1.74 (0.05)	0.868 (0.051)

On the contrary, the spatial regularisation provided by multi-level activation can lead to false negatives at the beginning of the training process, as on Fig. 3(e4), which are then detected by the converged model, see Fig. 3(f4). The circles on Figs. 3(d3) and (f3) outline difficult cases which are missed by both methods.

We now compare quantitatively two soft-max based methods – standard multi-class segmentation and the 'topology-aware' method from Ref. [2] – with our multi-level activation layer, combined with the three losses introduced in Sect. 2.2. The validation Dice scores for the nuclei class are shown in Fig. 4 for each method of this benchmark. The corresponding test scores are reported in Table 1, for (i) a pre-determined value $\theta_2^{\natural}$ and (ii) the value of θ_2 selected during validation. In (i), we choose the *a priori* inferred value $\theta_2^{\natural} = 1.5$ for NCE and SSE, and $\theta_2^{\natural} = 4/3$ for MCE, the values where P^1 and P^2, respectively Q^1 and Q^2, intersect (see Fig. 2). While all methods perform comparatively well for cell segmentation, with mean test Dice scores ranging from 0.977 (0.01) to 0.979 (0.01), there are quantitative discrepancies in the nuclei segmentation. The two soft-max based methods perform on par: we report a mean test Dice score of 0.839 (0.055) for standard multi-class, which we consider as our baseline in the following, and of 0.842 (0.055) for the 'topology-aware' loss [2]. Indeed, multi-class is not plagued by the detection of nuclei outside cells, but rather outputs false positives near the border of the cell, as we have seen above, a problem which is not addressed by the method of Ref. [2].

In Fig. 4, we see that our three proposed methods converge much faster, and outperform the soft-max based ones during validation. Our methods indeed cross the 0.8 validation Dice score after 1.3 to 3.2×10^3 iterations, whereas the soft-max-based methods need more than three times as much iterations to achieve this accuracy. Using θ_2^i, we improve the test Dice score by 0.2 and 0.5 for $\mathcal{L}_{\text{NCE}}$ and $\mathcal{L}_{\text{MCE}}$ and by 2.4 points with $\mathcal{L}_{\text{SSE}}$. The paired samples Wilcoxon test gives a p-value of 0.0008 for $\mathcal{L}_{\text{SSE}}$ vs multi-class, confirming the significance of this improvement. Threshold selection during validation improves the $\mathcal{L}_{\text{NCE}}$ and $\mathcal{L}_{\text{MCE}}$ results further, exceeding the multi-class score by 1.4 and 2.9 Dice points respectively (with p-values 0.007 and 0.001). $\mathcal{L}_{\text{MCE}}$ therefore gives the best model of this benchmark. Note that using $\mathcal{L}_{\text{MCE}}$ without reweighting [i.e. $\omega^c = 1$ in Eq. (4)] strongly undersegments nuclei, confirming that the training is then biased towards class-1, as anticipated in Sect. 2.2. Furthermore, with $\omega^c \propto 1/N_c$, the thresholds selected by validation, with mean $\theta_2^{\text{mean}} = 1.74$, significantly differ from $\theta_2^i = 4/3$, indicating that class-2 might now be overfavored. We retrospectively verified that all other models do not benefit from the application of the weighting scheme $\omega^c \propto 1/N_c$.

Discussion. Our proposed multi-level activation layer, greatly speeds up learning and outperforms the soft-max based methods. It indeed permits to significantly improve the nuclei test Dice scores in all cases (with p-values < 0.007). This novel activation layer introduces thresholds in the multi-class classification context, which can be adjusted at validation time, leading to a significant performance gain for $\mathcal{L}_{\text{NCE}}$ and $\mathcal{L}_{\text{MCE}}$. But this is not the only benefit of our method, as all proposed loss functions outperform multi-class without threshold adjustment, significantly for $\mathcal{L}_{\text{SSE}}$, proving that our regression-like method is better suited to the problem.

4   Conclusion

In this work, we have proposed a new paradigm for multi-class segmentation with topological constraints of inclusion. It consists in a novel multi-level activation layer and three matching loss functions, based on regression and cross-entropy loss. This scheme can be implemented in any network architecture, with minimal changes. We benchmarked our method on the segmentation of nuclei in bright-field microscopy images, giving significant improvement and speed-up over the soft-max based methods. In the Supplementary Material, we provide a second benchmark on liver lesions segmentation, in a larger and more imbalanced dataset, with the same conclusions. We expect those results to transfer to other tasks with nested classes, as nothing was handcrafted for the problems at stake. $\mathcal{L}_{\text{MCE}}$ turned out to be the best performing loss in this paper, but the other losses also perform well, and might be better suited for different applications.

Informing the network on the relations between classes with the multi-level activation thus permits to train on less data, which is often crucial in biomedical applications. Finally, as shown in the Supplementary Material, the multi-level activation layer and the associated losses can be straightforwardly generalized to a deeper nesting hierarchy. We also show how $\mathcal{L}_{\text{MCE}}$ and $\mathcal{L}_{\text{NCE}}$ can be used alongside normal cross-entropy to segment nested classes together with further classes without topological prior. This enables the encoding of any tree of prior relations of containment between classes.

References

1. Nosrati, M.S., Hamarneh, G.: Local optimization based segmentation of spatially-recurring, multi-region objects with part configuration constraints. IEEE Trans. Med. Imaging **33**(9), 1845–1859 (2014)
2. BenTaieb, A., Hamarneh, G.: Topology aware fully convolutional networks for histology gland segmentation. In: Ourselin, S., Joskowicz, L., Sabuncu, M.R., Unal, G., Wells, W. (eds.) MICCAI 2016. LNCS, vol. 9901, pp. 460–468. Springer, Cham (2016). https://doi.org/10.1007/978-3-319-46723-8_53
3. Christ, P.F., et al.: Automatic liver and lesion segmentation in CT using cascaded fully convolutional neural networks and 3D conditional random fields. In: Ourselin, S., Joskowicz, L., Sabuncu, M.R., Unal, G., Wells, W. (eds.) MICCAI 2016. LNCS, vol. 9901, pp. 415–423. Springer, Cham (2016). https://doi.org/10.1007/978-3-319-46723-8_48
4. Fidon, L., Li, W., Garcia-Peraza-Herrera, L.C., Ekanayake, J., Kitchen, N., Ourselin, S., Vercauteren, T.: Generalised wasserstein dice score for imbalanced multi-class segmentation using holistic convolutional networks. In: Crimi, A., Bakas, S., Kuijf, H., Menze, B., Reyes, M. (eds.) BrainLes 2017. LNCS, vol. 10670, pp. 64–76. Springer, Cham (2018). https://doi.org/10.1007/978-3-319-75238-9_6
5. Bauer, S., Tessier, J., Krieter, O., Nolte, L.-P., Reyes, M.: Integrated spatio-temporal segmentation of longitudinal brain tumor imaging studies. In: Menze, B., Langs, G., Montillo, A., Kelm, M., Müller, H., Tu, Z. (eds.) MCV 2013. LNCS, vol. 8331, pp. 74–83. Springer, Cham (2014). https://doi.org/10.1007/978-3-319-05530-5_8
6. Alberts, E., Charpiat, G., Tarabalka, Y., Huber, T., Weber, M.-A., Bauer, J., Zimmer, C., Menze, B.H.: A nonparametric growth model for brain tumor segmentation in longitudinal MR sequences. In: Crimi, A., Menze, B., Maier, O., Reyes, M., Handels, H. (eds.) BrainLes 2015. LNCS, vol. 9556, pp. 69–79. Springer, Cham (2016). https://doi.org/10.1007/978-3-319-30858-6_7
7. Liu, Z., Li, X., Luo, P., et al.: Deep learning Markov random field for semantic segmentation. IEEE Trans. Pattern Anal. Mach. Intell. **8828**(c), 1 (2017)
8. Ronneberger, O., Fischer, P., Brox, T.: U-Net: convolutional networks for biomedical image segmentation. In: Navab, N., Hornegger, J., Wells, W.M., Frangi, A.F. (eds.) MICCAI 2015. LNCS, vol. 9351, pp. 234–241. Springer, Cham (2015). https://doi.org/10.1007/978-3-319-24574-4_28
9. Bhattacharyya, S., Dutta, P., Nandi, P.K.: Multilevel activation functions for true color image segmentation using a self supervised parallel self organizing neural network (PSONN) architecture: a comparative study. Int. J. Comput. Sci. **1**(8), 2452–2464 (2007)

Detecting Synapse Location and Connectivity by Signed Proximity Estimation and Pruning with Deep Nets

Toufiq Parag[1(✉)], Daniel Berger[2], Lee Kamentsky[1], Benedikt Staffler[3], Donglai Wei[1], Moritz Helmstaedter[3], Jeff W. Lichtman[2], and Hanspeter Pfister[1]

[1] SEAS, Harvard University, Cambridge, MA, USA
toufiq.parag@gmail.com
[2] MCB, Harvard University, Cambridge, MA, USA
[3] Max Planck Institute for Brain Research, Frankfurt, Germany

Abstract. Synaptic connectivity detection is a critical task for neural reconstruction from Electron Microscopy (EM) data. Most of the existing algorithms for synapse detection do not identify the cleft location and direction of connectivity simultaneously. The few methods that computes direction along with contact location have only been demonstrated to work on either dyadic (most common in vertebrate brain) or polyadic (found in fruit fly brain) synapses, but not on both types. In this paper, we present an algorithm to automatically predict the location as well as the direction of both dyadic and polyadic synapses. The proposed algorithm first generates candidate synaptic connections from voxelwise predictions of signed proximity generated by a 3D U-net. A second 3D CNN then prunes the set of candidates to produce the final detection of cleft and connectivity orientation. Experimental results demonstrate that the proposed method outperforms the existing methods for determining synapses in both rodent and fruit fly brain. (Code at: https://github.com/paragt/EMSynConn).

1 Introduction

Connectomics has become a fervent field of study in neuroscience and computer vision recently. The goal of EM connectomics is to reconstruct the neural wiring diagram from Electron Microscopic (EM) images of animal brain. Neural reconstruction of EM images consists of two equally important tasks: (1) trace the anatomical structure of each neuron by labeling each voxel within a cell with a unique id; and (2) find the location and direction of synaptic connections among multiple cells.

The enormous amount of EM volume emerging from a tiny amount of tissue constrains any subsequent analysis to be performed (semi-) automatically to acquire a comprehensive knowledge within a practical time period [1,2]. Discovering the anatomical structure entails a 3D segmentation of EM volume. Numerous studies have addressed this task with many different approaches, we

© Springer Nature Switzerland AG 2019
L. Leal-Taixé and S. Roth (Eds.): ECCV 2018 Workshops, LNCS 11134, pp. 354–364, 2019.
https://doi.org/10.1007/978-3-030-11024-6_25

refer interested readers to [3–9] for further details. In order to unveil the connectivity, it is necessary to identify the locations *and* the direction of synaptic communications between two or more cells. Resolving the location of synaptic contact is crucial for neurobiological reasons, and, because the strength of connection between two cells is determined by the number of times they make a synaptic contact. The direction of the synaptic contact reveals the direction of information flow from presynaptic to postsynaptic cells. By defining the edges, the location and connectivity orientation of synapses complete the directed network of neural circuitry that a neural reconstruction seek to discover. In fact, discovering synaptic connectivity was one of the primary reasons to employ the immensely complex and expensive apparatus of electron microscopy for connectomics in the first place. Other imaging modalities (e.g., light microscopy) are either limited by their resolution or by a conclusive and exhaustive strategy (e.g., using reagents) to locate synapses [10–12].

In terms of complexity, identification of neural connectivity is as challenging as tracing the neurons [13]. With rapid and outstanding improvement in automated EM segmentation in recent years, detection of synaptic connectivity may soon become a bottleneck in the overall neural reconstruction process [14]. Although fewer in number when compared against those in neurite segmentation, there are past studies on synaptic connectivity detection; we mention some notable works in the relevant literature section below. Despite many discernible merits of previous works, very few of them aim to identify both the location and direction of synaptic junctions. Among these few methods, namely by [13–15], none of them have been shown to be generally applicable on different types of synapses typically found on different species of animals, e.g., dyadic connections in vertebrate (mouse, rat, zebra finch, etc.) and polyadic connections in non-vertebrate (fruit fly) brain[1]. Apart from a few, the past approaches do not benefit from the advantages deep (fully) convolutional networks offer. Use of hand crafted features could stifle the utility of a method on widely divergent EM volumes collected from different animals with different tissue processing and imaging techniques.

In this paper, we propose a general method to automatically detect both the 3D location and direction of both dyadic (vertebrate) and polyadic (fruit fly) synaptic contacts. The proposed algorithm is designed to predict the proximity (and polarity, as we will explain later) of every 3D voxel to a synaptic cleft using a deep fully convolutional network, namely a U-net [16]. A set of putative locations, along with their connection direction estimates, are computed given a segmentation of the volume and the voxelwise prediction from the U-net. A second stage of pruning, performed by a deep convolutional network, then trims the set of candidates to produce the final prediction of 3D synaptic cleft locations and the corresponding directions.

The use of CNNs makes the proposed approach generally applicable to new data without the need for feature selection. Estimation of the location and

---

[1] Although, there are examples of polyadic connections in mouse cerebellum between mossy fibers and granule cells.

connectivity at both voxel and segment level improves the accuracy but do not require any additional annotation effort (no need for labels for other classes such as vesicles). We show that our proposed algorithm outperforms the existing approaches for synaptic connectivity detection on both vertebrate and fruit fly datasets. Our evaluation measure (Sect. 3), which is critical to assess the actual performance of a synapse detection method, has also been confirmed by a prominent neurobiologist to correctly quantify actual mistakes on real dataset.

1.1 Relevant Literature

Initial studies on automatic synaptic detection focused on identifying the cleft location by classical machine learning/vision approaches using pre-defined features [17–22]. These algorithms assumed subsequent human intervention to determine the synaptic partners given the cleft predictions. Roncal et al. [23] combine the information provided by membrane and vesicle predictions with a CNN (not fully convolutional) and apply post-processing to locate synaptic clefts. To establish the pre- and post-synaptic partnership, [24] augmented the synaptic cleft detection with a multi-layer perceptron operating on hand designed features. On the other hand, Kreshuk et al. [15] seek to predict vesicles and clefts for each neuron boundary by a random forest classifier (RF) and then aggregate these predictions with a CRF to determine the connectivity for polyadic synapses in fruit fly. Dorkenwald et al. [13] utilize multiple CNNs, RFs to locate synaptic junctions as well as vesicles, mitochondria, and to decide the dyadic orientation in vertebrate EM data. SynEM [14] attempts to predict connectivity by classifying each neuron boundary (interfaces) to be synaptic or not using a RF classifier operating on a confined neighborhood and has been shown to perform better than [13] in terms of connectivity detection.

2 Method

The proposed method is designed to first predict both the location and direction of synaptic communication at the voxel level. Section 2.1 illustrates how this is performed by training a deep encoder-decoder type network, namely the U-net, to compute the proximity and direction of connection with respect to synapses at every voxel. The voxelwise predictions are clustered together after discretization and matched with a segmentation to establish synaptic relations between pairs of segment ids. Afterwards, a separate CNN is trained to discard the candidates that do not correspond to an actual synaptic contact, both in terms of location and direction, as described in Sect. 2.2.

2.1 Voxelwise Synaptic Cleft and Partner Detection

In order to learn both the position and connection orientation of a synapse, the training labels for voxels are modified slightly from the traditional annotation. It is the standard practice to demarcate only the synaptic cleft with a single strip of id, or color, as the overlaid color shows in Fig. 1(a). In contrast, the proposed method requires the neighborhood of the pre- and post-synaptic neurons at the junction of synaptic expression to be marked by two ids or colors as depicted in Fig. 1(b). To distinguish the partners unambiguously, these ids can follow a particular pattern, e.g., pre-synaptic partners are always marked with odd id and post-synaptic partners are annotated with even ids. Such annotations inform us about both the location and direction of a connection with practically no increase in annotation effort. Note that, although we explain and visualize the labels in 2D and in 1D for better understanding, our proposed method learns a function of the 3D annotations.

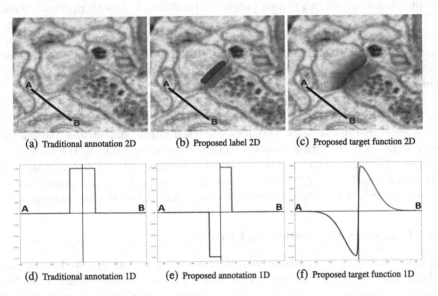

(a) Traditional annotation 2D   (b) Proposed label 2D   (c) Proposed target function 2D

(d) Traditional annotation 1D   (e) Proposed annotation 1D   (f) Proposed target function 1D

Fig. 1. The traditional and proposed annotation of synapses and the signed proximity function that the proposed method estimates are shown in 2D in (a), (b), (c) and in 1D in (d), (e), (f) respectively for illustration purposes. The U-net learns the signed proximity functions in 3D. (Color figure online)

For voxelwise prediction of position and direction, ids of all pre- and post-synaptic labels (red and blue in Fig. 1(b)) are converted to 1 and −1 respectively; all remaining voxels are labeled with 0. However, our approach *does not* directly learn from the discrete labels presented in Fig. 1(b). Instead, we attempt to learn a smoother version of the discrete labels, where the transition from 1 and −1 to 0 occurs gradually, as shown in Fig. 1(c). The dissimilarities among these three types of annotations can be better understood in 1D. The Figs. 1(d), (e), and (f) plot the labels perpendicular to the black line drawn underneath the labels in images in the top row of Fig. 1. The proposed approach attempts to learn a 3D version of the smooth function in Fig. 1(c) and (f). Effectively, this target function computes a signed proximity from the synaptic contact, where the sign indicates the connectivity orientation and the absolute function value determines the closeness or affinity of any voxel to the nearest cleft. Mathematically, this function can be formulated as

$$\text{proximity}_{\text{signed}}(x) = \left\{ \exp \frac{-d(x)^2}{2\sigma^2} \right\} \left\{ \frac{2}{1 + \exp(-\alpha\, d(x))} - 1 \right\}, \qquad (1)$$

where $d(x)$ is the signed distance between voxel at x and the synaptic cleft, and α and σ are parameters that control the smoothness of transition. We solve a regression problem using a 3D implementation of U-net with linear final layer activation function to approximate this function. There are multiple motivations to approximate a smooth signed proximity function. A smooth proximity function as a target also eliminates the necessity of estimating the abrupt change near the annotation boundary and therefore assists the gradient descent to approach a more meaningful local minimum. Furthermore, some recent studies have suggested that a smooth activation function is more useful than its discrete counterparts for learning regression [25, 26].

Our 3D U-net for learning signed proximity has an architecture similar to the original U-net model in [16]. The network has a depth of 3 where it applies two consecutive $3 \times 3 \times 3$ convolutions at each depth and utilizes parametric leaky ReLU [27] activation function. The activation function in the final layer is linear. The input and output of the 3D U-net are $316 \times 316 \times 32$ grayscale EM volumes and $228 \times 228 \times 4$ proximity values, respectively. A weighted mean squared error loss is utilized to learn the proximity values during training.

2.2   Candidate Generation and Pruning

For computing putative pairs of pre- and post-synaptic partners, we first threshold the signed proximity values at an absolute value of τ and compute connected components for pre and post-synaptic sites separately. Given a segmentation S for the EM volume, every pre-synaptic connected component e is paired with one or more segment $s_{i_e} \in S$, $i_e = 1, \ldots, m_e$ based on a minimum overlap size ω to form pre-synaptic site candidates T_{e,i_e}. Similarly, post-synaptic site candidates T_{o,j_o} are generated by associating each post-synaptic connected component o is with a set of segments $s_{j_o} \in S$, $j_o = 1, \ldots, n_o$. The set $\mathcal{C}$ of candidate pairs of synaptic partners are computed by pairing up pre-synaptic candidate T_{e,i_e} with post-synaptic T_{o,j_o} wherever segment s_{j_o} is a neighbor of s_{i_e}, i.e., s_{i_e} shares a boundary with segment s_{j_o}.

$$\mathcal{C} = \left\{ \{ T_{e,i_e}, T_{o,j_o} \} \mid s_{j_o} \in \text{Nbr}(s_{i_o}), \ \forall e, o, i_e, j_o \right\}. \qquad (2)$$

A 3D CNN is utilized to distinguish the correct synaptic partner pairs from the false positive candidates, i.e., to produce a binary decision for each candidate. The groundtruth labels for training this second convolutional network were computed by matching the segmentation S with the groundtruth segmentation of the volume G. The pruning network is constructed with 5 layer convolutions of size $3 \times 3 \times 3$ followed by two densely connected layers. The input to the 3D deep convolutional pruning (or trimming) network comprises $160 \times 160 \times 16$ subvolumes of the grayscale EM image, the predicted signed proximity values from 3D U-net and the segmentation masks of s_{i_e}, s_{j_o}, extracted from a 3D window centered at the closest point between the connected components e and o, as shown in Fig. 2.

It is worth mentioning here that we have contemplated the possibility of combining the voxelwise network and the candidate trimming network to facilitate end-to-end training, but did not pursue that direction due to the difficulty in formulating a differentiable operation to transform voxelwise signed proximities to region wise candidates. We have, however, attempted to employ a region proposal network based method, in particular the mask R-CNN [28], to our problem. The proposal generating network of mask R-CNN method resulted in a low recall rate for locating the synapses in our experiments (leading to low recall in the final result after trimming). We observed Mask R-CNNs to struggle with targets with widely varying size in our dataset. Furthermore, we had difficulty in merging many proposals [28] produced for one connection, leading to lower final precision rate as well.

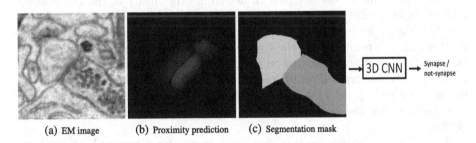

(a) EM image   (b) Proximity prediction   (c) Segmentation mask

Fig. 2. Candidate pruning by 3D CNN. The EM image, proximity prediction and segmentation mask on one section of input subvolume are shown in (a), (b), (c) respectively. The cyan and yellow segmentation masks are provided as separate binary masks, shown here in one image (c) to save space. (Color figure online)

3   Experiments and Results

The deep nets for this work were implemented in Theano with Keras interface[2]. For both the network training, we used rotation and flip in all dimensions for data augmentation. For the candidate trimming network, we also displaced the center of the window by a small amount to augment the training set. The parameters for the target signed proximity and the candidate overlap calculation remained the same as $\alpha = 5, \tau = 0.3$ (absolute value), $\omega = 100$. The parameter σ was set

---

[2] Code at: https://github.com/paragt/EMSynConn.

to 10 for the mouse and rat dataset but 14 for the TEM fly data to account for the difference in z-resolution.

Evaluation: It is critical to apply the most biologically meaningful evaluation formula in order to correctly assess the performance of any given method. Distance based methods [14,18], for example, are unrealistically tolerant to false positive detections nearby. On the other hand, pixelwise error computation [29] is more stringent than necessary for extracting the wiring diagram – two detections with 50% and 60% pixelwise overlap need not be penalized differently for connectomics purposes. Measures computed solely on overlap [23] becomes ambiguous when one prediction overlaps two junctions. We resolve this ambiguity by considering a detection be correct only if it overlaps with the span of synaptic expression (as delineated by an expert) *and* connects two cells with correct synaptic orientation, i.e., pre and post-synaptic partners. All the precision and recall values reported in the experiments on rat (Sect. 3.1) and mouse (Sect. 3.2) data are computed with this measure.

3.1   Rat Cortex

Our first experiment was designed to determine the utility of the two stages, i.e., voxelwise prediction and candidate set pruning, of the proposed algorithm. The EM images we used in this experiment were collected from rat cortex using SEM imaging at resolution of $4 \times 4 \times 30$ nm. We used a volume of 97 images to train the 3D U-net and validated on a different set of 120 images. The candidate pruning CNN was trained on 97 images and then fine tuned on the 120 image dataset. For testing we used a third volume of 145 sections. The segmentation used to compute the synaptic direction was generated either by the method of [30].

Figure 3(a) compares the precision recall curves for detecting both location and connectivity with two variants. (1) 3 Label + pruning - where the proximity approximation is replaced by 3-class classification among pre-, post-synaptic, and rest of the voxels (Fig. 1(b)). (2) Proximity + [Roncal, arXiv14] - where the proposed pruning network is replaced by VESICLE [23] style post-processing. For the proposed (blue o) and 3 Label + pruning (red x) technique, each point on the plot correspond to a threshold on the prediction of the 3D trimming CNN. For the Proximity + [Roncal, arXiv14] technique (black o), we varied several parameters of the VESICLE post-processing.

This experiment suggests that the pruning network is substantially more effective than morphological post-processing [23]. The proposed signed proximity approximation yields 3% more true positives in the initial candidate set than those generated by the multiclass prediction. As discussed earlier in Sect. 2.1, a smooth target function places the focus on learning difficult examples by removing the necessity to learn the sharp boundaries. Empirically, we have noticed the training procedure to spend a significant number of iterations to infer the sharp boundary of a discrete label like Figure 1(b) and (c). Furthermore, we observed that the wider basin of prediction can identify more true positives and offers

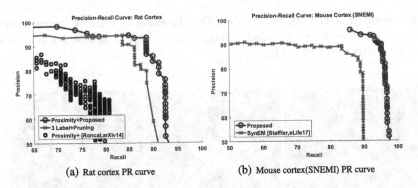

(a) Rat cortex PR curve   (b) Mouse cortex(SNEMI) PR curve

Fig. 3. Precision recall curves for *synapse location and connectivity* for rat cortex (a) and mouse cortex (SNEMI) (b) experiments. Plot (a) suggests combining voxelwise signed proximity prediction with pruning performs significantly better than the versions that replaces one of these components with alternative strategies. Plot (b) indicates significant improvement achieved over performance of [14] on the same dataset. (Color figure online)

more information for the following pruning stage to improve the F-score of our method to 91.03% as opposed 87.5% of the 3 Label + pruning method.

3.2 Mouse Cortex Data (SNEMI)

We experimented next on the SEM dataset from Kasthuri et al. [31] that was used for the SNEMI challenge [32] to compare our performance with that of SynEM [14] (which was shown to outperform [13]). The synaptic partnership information was collected from the authors of [31] to compute the signed proximities for training the 3D U-net. Similar to the rat cortex experiment, we used 100 sections for training the voxelwise U-net and candidate pruning CNN and used 150 sections for validation of the voxelwise proximity U-net. The test dataset consists of 150 sections of size 1024 × 1024 that is referred to as AC3 in [14]. The segmentation used to compute the synaptic direction was generated either by the method of [30].

The authors of [14] have kindly provided us with their results on this dataset. We read off the cleft detection and the connectivity estimation from their result and computed the error measures as explained in Sect. 3. The precision recall curve for detecting both cleft and connectivity is plotted in Fig. 3(b). In general, the SynEM method performs well overall, but produces significantly higher false negative rates than the proposed method. Among the synapses it detects, SynEM assigns the pre and post-synaptic partnership very accurately, although it used the actual segmentation groundtruth for such assignment whereas we used a segmentation output. Visual inspection of the detection performances also verifies the lower recall rate of [14] than ours. In Fig. 4 we show the groundtruth, the cleft estimation of SynEM (missed connection marked with red x) and the connected components corresponding to the predictions of the proposed method, both computed at the largest F-score. The direction of synaptic connection in image of Fig. 4(c) is color coded – purple and green indicates pre and post-synaptic partners respectively.

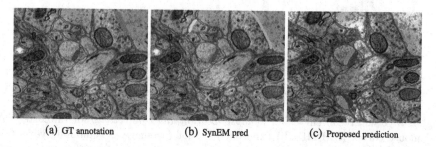

(a) GT annotation   (b) SynEM pred   (c) Proposed prediction

Fig. 4. Qualitative results on mouse cortex data [31]. Left to right, groundtruth annotation, output of SynEM [14] (red x marks missed location), and that of the proposed method. In (c), purple and green indicates pre and post-synaptic partner respectively. (Color figure online)

3.3 Fruit Fly Data (CREMI)

Our method was applied on the 3 TEM volumes (resolution $4 \times 4 \times 40$ nm) of the CREMI challenge [29]. We annotated the training labels for synaptic partners for all 3 volumes given the synaptic partner list provided on the website. All the experimental settings for this experiment remain the same as other except those mentioned in Sect. 3. Out of the 125 training images, we used the first 80 for training and the remaining images for validation. The segmentation used to compute the synaptic direction was generated either by the method of [3].

The performance is only measured in terms of synaptic partner identification task, as the pixelwise cleft error measure is not appropriate for our result (refer to the output provided in Fig. 4(c)). At the time of this submission the our method, which is identified as HCBS on CREMI leaderboard, holds the 2nd place overall (error difference with the first is 0.002) and performed better than both variants of [15] (Table 1).

Table 1. Result on CREMI data, lower is better

Method	Submission	CREMI score	FP	FN
HCBS (proposed)	Tr66_80K	0.449	223.000	286.667
IAL [15]	PSP_unar	0.461	266.667	281.000
IAL [15]	PSP_full	0.464	187.333	310.000

4   Conclusion

We propose a general purpose synaptic connectivity detector that locates the location and direction of a synapse at the same time. Our method was designed to work on both dyadic and polyadic synapses without any modification to its component techniques. The utilization of deep CNNs for learning location and direction of synaptic communication enables it to be directly applicable to any new dataset without the need for manual selection of features. Experiments on multiple datasets suggests the superiority of our method on existing algorithms for synaptic connectivity detection. One straightforward extension of the proposed two stage method is to enhance the candidate pruning CNN to distinguish between excitatory and inhibitory synaptic connections by adopting a 3-class classification scheme.

References

1. Jain, V., Seung, S., Turaga, S.: Machine that learn to segment images: a crucial technology for connectomics. Curr. Opinion Neurobiol. **20**, 653–666 (2010)
2. Helmstaedter, M.: The mutual inspirations of machine learning and neuroscience. Neuron **86**(1), 25–28 (2015)
3. Funke, J., Tschopp, F.D., Grisaitis, W., Singh, C., Saalfeld, S., Turaga, S.C.: A deep structured learning approach towards automating connectome reconstruction from 3D electron micrographs. arXiv:1709.02974 (2017)
4. Lee, K., Zung, J., Li, P., Jain, V., Seung, H.S.: Superhuman accuracy on the SNEMI3D connectomics challenge. arXiv:1706.00120 (2017)
5. Januszewski, M., Maitin-Shepard, J., Li, P., Kornfeld, J., Denk, W., Jain, V.: Flood-filling networks. arXiv:1611.00421 (2016)
6. Parag, T., Ciresan, D.C., Giusti, A.: Efficient classifier training to minimize false merges in electron microscopy segmentation. In: The IEEE International Conference on Computer Vision (ICCV), December 2015
7. Liu, T., Zhang, M., Javanmardi, M., Ramesh, N., Tasdizen, T.: SSHMT: semi-supervised hierarchical merge tree for electron microscopy image segmentation. In: Leibe, B., Matas, J., Sebe, N., Welling, M. (eds.) ECCV 2016. LNCS, vol. 9905, pp. 144–159. Springer, Cham (2016). https://doi.org/10.1007/978-3-319-46448-0_9
8. Parag, T., Plaza, S., Scheffer, L.: Small sample learning of superpixel classifiers for EM segmentation. In: Golland, P., Hata, N., Barillot, C., Hornegger, J., Howe, R. (eds.) MICCAI 2014. LNCS, vol. 8673, pp. 389–397. Springer, Cham (2014). https://doi.org/10.1007/978-3-319-10404-1_49
9. Beier, T., Pape, C., Rahaman, N., Prange, T., Berg, S.E., et al.: Multicut brings automated neurite segmentation closer to human performance. Nat. Methods **14**, 101–102 (2017)
10. Morgan, J.L., Lichtman, J.W.: Why not connectomics? Nat. Methods **10**(6), 494–500 (2013)
11. Denk, W., Briggman, K.L., Helmstaedter, M.: Structural neurobiology: missing link to a mechanistic understanding of neural computation. Nat. Rev. Neurosci. **13**(5), 351–358 (2011)
12. Lichtman, J.W., Pfister, H., Shavit, N.: The big data challenges of connectomics. Nat. Neurosci. **17**(11), 1448–1454 (2014)

13. Dorkenwald, S., et al.: Automated synaptic connectivity inference for volume electron microscopy. Nat. Methods **14**(4), 435–442 (2017)
14. Staffler, B., Berning, M., Boergens, K.M., Gour, A., Smagt, P.V.D., Helmstaedter, M.: SynEM, automated synapse detection for connectomics. eLife **6**, e26414 (2017)
15. Kreshuk, A., Funke, J., Cardona, A., Hamprecht, F.A.: Who Is talking to whom: synaptic partner detection in anisotropic volumes of insect brain. In: Navab, N., Hornegger, J., Wells, W.M., Frangi, A.F. (eds.) MICCAI 2015. LNCS, vol. 9349, pp. 661–668. Springer, Cham (2015). https://doi.org/10.1007/978-3-319-24553-9_81
16. Ronneberger, O., Fischer, P., Brox, T.: U-Net: convolutional networks for biomedical image segmentation. In: Navab, N., Hornegger, J., Wells, W.M., Frangi, A.F. (eds.) MICCAI 2015. LNCS, vol. 9351, pp. 234–241. Springer, Cham (2015). https://doi.org/10.1007/978-3-319-24574-4_28
17. Kreshuk, A., et al.: Automated detection and segmentation of synaptic contacts in nearly isotropic serial electron microscopy images. PLoS ONE **6**(10), e24899 (2011)
18. Becker, C., Ali, K., Knott, G., Fua, P.: Learning context cues for synapse segmentation. IEEE Trans. Med. Imaging **32**(10), 1864–1877 (2013)
19. Kreshuk, A., Koethe, U., Pax, E., Bock, D.D., Hamprecht, F.A.: Automated detection of synapses in serial section transmission electron microscopy image stacks. PLoS ONE **9**(2), e87351 (2014)
20. Plaza, S.M., Parag, T., Huang, G.B., Olbris, D.J., Saunders, M.A., Rivlin, P.K.: Annotating synapses in large EM datasets. arXiv:1409.1801 (2014)
21. Jagadeesh, V., Anderson, J., Jones, B., Marc, R., Fisher, S., Manjunath, B.: Synapse classification and localization in electron micrographs. Pattern Recognit. Lett. **43**, 17–24 (2014)
22. Huang, G.B., Plaza, S.: Identifying synapses using deep and wide multiscale recursive networks. arXiv: 1409.1789 (2014)
23. Roncal, W.G., et al.: VESICLE: volumetric evaluation of synaptic interfaces using computer vision at large scale. arXiv:1403.3724 (2014)
24. Huang, G.B., Scheffer, L.K., Plaza, S.M.: Fully-automatic synapse prediction and validation on a large data set. arXiv:1604.03075 (2016)
25. Hou, L., Samaras, D., Kurc, T., Gao, Y., Saltz, J.: ConvNets with smooth adaptive activation functions for regression. In: Proceedings of the 20th AISTATS (2017)
26. Mobahi, H.: Training recurrent neural networks by diffusion. arXiv:1601.04114 (2016)
27. He, K., Zhang, X., Ren, S., Sun, J.: Delving deep into rectifiers: surpassing human-level performance on ImageNet classification. In: ICCV (2015)
28. He, K., Gkioxari, G., Dollár, P., Girshick, R.: Mask R-CNN. In: ICCV (2017)
29. Funke, J., Saalfeld, S., Bock, D., Turaga, S., Perlman, E.: Cremi challenge. https://cremi.org
30. Parag, T., et al.: Anisotropic EM segmentation by 3D affinity learning and agglomeration. arXiv:1707.08935 (2017)
31. Kasthuri, N., Hayworth, K., Berger, D., Schalek, R., et al.: Saturated reconstruction of a volume of neocortex. Cell **162**(3), 648–661 (2015)
32. Arganda-Carreras, I., Seung, H.S., Vishwanathan, A., Berger, D.R.: Snemi challenge. http://brainiac2.mit.edu/SNEMI3D/

2D and 3D Vascular Structures Enhancement via Multiscale Fractional Anisotropy Tensor

Haifa F. Alhasson[1,2]ⓘ, Shuaa S. Alharbi[1,2]ⓘ, and Boguslaw Obara[1(✉)]

[1] School of Computer Sciences, Durham University, Durham, UK
boguslaw.obara@durham.ac.uk
[2] Computer College, Qassim University, Buraidah, Qassim, Kingdom of Saudi Arabia

Abstract. The detection of vascular structures from noisy images is a fundamental process for extracting meaningful information in many applications. Most well-known vascular enhancing techniques often rely on Hessian-based filters. This paper investigates the feasibility and deficiencies of detecting curve-like structures using a Hessian matrix. The main contribution is a novel enhancement function, which overcomes the deficiencies of established methods. Our approach has been evaluated quantitatively and qualitatively using synthetic examples and a wide range of real 2D and 3D biomedical images. Compared with other existing approaches, the experimental results prove that our proposed approach achieves high-quality curvilinear structure enhancement.

Keywords: Curvilinear structures · Image enhancement
Enhancement filter · Tensor representation · Hessian matrix
Diffusion tensor · Fractional diffusion tensor · FAT

1 Introduction

The enhancement of vessel-like structures in images plays an important role in various applications of computer vision, image processing, and medical analysis. The enhancement phase can be immediately improved upon by advancing the acquisition, interpretation and image analysis techniques. A wide range of curvilinear structures enhancement methods analyse image derivatives, most of them employ the analysis of Hessian matrix, such as [4,10,16]. The Hessian matrix is based on second-order Gaussian derivatives, calculated at different scales (controlled by standard deviation σ). This enables the differentiation between particular shapes, such as rounded, tubular, and planar structures. These approaches suffer from many deficiencies, which can be seen in different curve patterns and in the suppression of junctions and rounded structures [8].

Electronic supplementary material The online version of this chapter (https://doi.org/10.1007/978-3-030-11024-6_26) contains supplementary material, which is available to authorized users.

© Springer Nature Switzerland AG 2019
L. Leal-Taixé and S. Roth (Eds.): ECCV 2018 Workshops, LNCS 11134, pp. 365–374, 2019.
https://doi.org/10.1007/978-3-030-11024-6_26

Recently, the use of diffusion tensors (such as the Regularised Volume Ratio tensor (RVR) [8]) has improved the detection of vessel-like structures. The Fractional Anisotropic Tensor (FAT) is another well-known diffusion tensor measure, which has been reviewed in [14]. FAT measures the variance of eigenvalues across different structures, i.e., it measures the change of anisotropy along the vessels. In terms of ellipsoid glyphs, cigar-shaped (linear) and pancake-shaped ellipsoids (planar) can result in equal FAT measures though their shapes differ greatly [6]. This feature gives FAT less potential to fail in the junctions and has more chance of getting closer to uniformity in the final response. Thus, FAT plays a major role in many attempts towards diffusion tensor regularization [2]. An optimal enhancement function should achieve a high and uniform response to (i) variable vascular morphology, (ii) the intensity non-uniformities caused by blood contrast or in the background, (iii) unambiguity of the vessel boundary, and (iv) background noise.

Our contribution in this paper is a novel multiscale approach for either 2D or 3D images by preprocessing the eigenvalues and junctions reconstructing at each scale. Our proposed method has shown a surpassed performance when compared to the competing state-of-the-art approaches.

2   Related Work

One of the early attempts to use eigenvalue analysis for vessel enhancement was by Sato [16]. A later attempt that received wide acceptance was in the work of Frangi et al. [4]. In their work, they proposed a Hessian-based approach, known as Vesselness, to enhance curve-like features. The Vesselness measure is used to describe an image whenever a dark curvilinear structure appears with respect to the background. However, the main drawback of this approach are the very small curve-like feature responses at junctions, due to the large eigenvalues. The use of the Hessian matrix was further developed in the Neuriteness method, proposed by Meijering et al. [10]. It consists of a detection stage, which implies a feasible neurite with a value in every individual pixel of the image, and the actual tracing stage. This last stage determines which pixels are successive and which are most likely to reflect the centerline of the neurites. Furthermore, Obara et al. [12] used a Phase Congruency Tensor (PCT) by [9] in combination with Vesselness (PCT ves.) [4] and Neuriteness (PCT neu.) [10] in order to improve their results in detecting edges and to not rely on image intensities. The advantage of this approach is its insensitivity to intensity and noise variations in images.

Recently, motivated by the detection of spherical diffusion tensors, Jerman et al. [8] proposed a new measure based on the Volume Ratio, which overcomes the deficiencies of using a Hessian matrix such as: non-uniformity, variation of eigenvalues with image intensity, and non-uniformity of enhancement across scales. However, the problem of having lower intensities on junctions and crossings has not been completely solved by this approach. For more details, we provide further background of the enhancement approaches (please refer to the supplementary materials).

3 Methodology

In this section, we introduce a novel approach in order to enhance vessel-like structure in images. We hypothesize that an enhancement function should take the degree of anisotropy of the target structure into account, should be preserving the transactions between isotropic and anisotropic tissues and should be robust to sustain low-magnitude eigenvalues. Furthermore, an enhancement function should solve the fitting problem in the elliptical cross-section structures, which yield a uniform response across different vascular structures and more effective suppression of background noise without affecting the junctions or cross-sections.

Biological tissue samples are often anisotropic, because the cell and vessel membranes limit the motion of water molecules. Since the shape of the curvilinear structures is anisotropic, the junctions in these tissues have an isotropic shape, which explains why other established methods could not detect non-circular cross-sections [4, 10] or having less uniformity in the junctions and crossing [8]. In order to avoid the low filter response at junctions, we regularise eigenvalues, calculated from Hessian representation of an image $I(x)$ at each scale σ, to fulfill the following condition for 3D images:

$$\lambda_2 \geq \lambda_3 \wedge |\lambda_{2,3}| \gg |\lambda_1|. \tag{1}$$

This eigenvalues regularization process is combined with a junctions reconstruction step at each scale σ. This paper proposed a new Hessian-based enhancement approach called Multiscale-Fractional Anisotropic Tensor $\overline{MFAT}$.

3.1 Fractional Anisotropic Tensor-Based Vascular Structures Enhancement

Enhancement Function in 3D. The anisotropy on a voxel level is quantified in terms of FAT and is expressed as an invariant of the three independent diffusion tensor eigenvalues at each scale σ, and it is expressed in [6] as:

$$FAT_\lambda^\sigma = \sqrt{\tfrac{3}{2}}\sqrt{\tfrac{(\lambda_1 - \overline{D}_\lambda)^2 + (\lambda_2 - \overline{D}_\lambda)^2 + (\lambda_3 - \overline{D}_\lambda)^2}{\lambda_1{}^2 + \lambda_2{}^2 + \lambda_3{}^2}}. \tag{2}$$

The response of FAT_λ^σ ranges between 0 and 1. The mean diffusivity $\overline{D}_\lambda$ is defined as:

$$\overline{D}_\lambda = \frac{T_r}{3}, \tag{3}$$

where T_r refers to the trace of diffusion tensor, which represents the affected area much more accurately than images, representing the diffusion in only one direction, and defined as:

$$T_r = \sum_{i=1}^{3} \lambda_i. \tag{4}$$

Recently, Pardos et al. [15] proposed another representation of anisotropic diffusion tensors, in probabilistic form based on a ternary diagram, called *Finetti*

Diagram [1], analysed for each tensor, and proved its feasibility. They describe the main limitation of eigenvalue-based measures as its partial representation of the tensor information which is only related to image intensities. They proved that the probability-based FAT measure has better detection of curve-like structures. The Probabilistic Fractional Anisotropic Tensor FAT_p, at each scale σ, can be expressed as:

$$FAT_p^\sigma = \sqrt{\tfrac{3}{2}} \sqrt{\frac{(p_1 - \overline{D}_p)^2 + (p_2 - \overline{D}_p)^2 + (p_3 - \overline{D}_p)^2}{p_1{}^2 + p_2{}^2 + p_3{}^2}}. \tag{5}$$

The relative importance of each ellipsoid axis p_i is defined as:

$$p_i = \frac{\lambda_i}{T_r}, \tag{6}$$

where the mean of diffusivity is set to be $\overline{D}_p = \tfrac{1}{3}$ as in [15].

Both forms of fractional anisotropic have been modified in this work from the original version in Eqs. 2 and 5. Our enhancement function is based on the modifications that have been done in [8]. They add absolute values to account for differently signed eigenvalues, which results in a more uniform response. Also, they eliminate λ_1 to get more normalized results, and by regularizing the value of λ_3 at each scale σ using cut-off threshold τ. Our new enhancement function of $\overline{FAT}_\lambda^\sigma$ is defined as follows:

$$\overline{FAT}_\lambda^\sigma = \sqrt{\tfrac{3}{2}} \sqrt{\frac{(\lambda_2 - \overline{D}_\lambda)^2 + (\lambda_\rho) - \overline{D}_\lambda)^2 + (\lambda_\nu - \overline{D}_\lambda)^2}{\lambda_2{}^2 + \lambda_\rho{}^2 + \lambda_\nu{}^2}}, \tag{7}$$

where τ_ρ is corresponding to λ_ρ, which is adopted from the work has been done in [8]. We propose using another cut-off thresholding τ_ν to regulate λ_3 at each point $\boldsymbol{x}$ in each scale σ to fulfil the condition in Eq. 1. Both λ_ρ and λ_ν can be obtained from:

$$\lambda_{\rho,\nu} = \begin{cases} \lambda_3(\boldsymbol{x}, \sigma) & \text{if } \lambda_3(\boldsymbol{x}, \sigma) > \tau_{\rho,\nu} \max_{\boldsymbol{x}}\left(\lambda_3(\boldsymbol{x}, \sigma)\right), \\ \tau_{\rho,\nu} \max_{\boldsymbol{x}}\left(\lambda_3(\boldsymbol{x}, \sigma)\right) & \text{if } 0 < \lambda_3(\boldsymbol{x}, \sigma) \leqslant \tau_{\rho,\nu} \max_{\boldsymbol{x}}\left(\lambda_3(\boldsymbol{x}, \sigma)\right), \\ 0 & \text{otherwise}, \end{cases} \tag{8}$$

where τ_ρ and τ_ν are between $[0, 1]$. With the above eigenvalues regularization, both Eqs. 5 and 6 can be written as follows:

$$\overline{FAT}_p^\sigma = \sqrt{\tfrac{3}{2}} \sqrt{\frac{(p_2 - \overline{D}_p)^2 + (p_\rho - \overline{D}_p)^2 + (p_\nu - \overline{D}_p)^2}{p_2{}^2 + p_\rho{}^2 + p_\nu{}^2}}, \tag{9}$$

where

$$p_2 = \left| \frac{\lambda_2}{T_r} \right|, \quad p_\rho = \left| \frac{\lambda_\rho}{T_r} \right|, \quad p_\nu = \left| \frac{\lambda_\nu}{T_r} \right|.$$

The inverted response of either Eq. 7 or Eq. 9 assure a positive response at vessel and the junctions. Furthermore, in order to remove noise from the background, we add more restrictions. Therefore, the response $R_{\lambda,p}^\sigma$ can be written as follows:

$$R_{\lambda,p}^\sigma = \begin{cases} 0 & \text{if } \lambda_\rho > \lambda_\rho - \lambda_2 \vee \lambda_\rho \geq 0 \vee \lambda_2 \geq 0, \\ 1 & \text{if } \lambda_\rho - \lambda_2 = \max_{\boldsymbol{x}}(\lambda_\rho - \lambda_2), \\ 1 - \overline{FAT}_{\lambda,p}^\sigma & \text{otherwise}. \end{cases} \tag{10}$$

Using the similar concept of the magnitude regularization in [2], the junctions reconstruction is obtained by a maximized co-addition of response at each scale σ and the final enhancement function $\overline{MFAT}_{\lambda,p}$ using either Eqs. 7 or 9 as follows:

$$\overline{MFAT}_{\lambda,p}^{\sigma} = \overline{MFAT}_{\lambda,p}^{\sigma-1} + \delta \tanh\left(R_{\lambda,p}^{\sigma} - \delta\right), \tag{11}$$

$$\overline{MFAT}_{\lambda,p} = \max_{\sigma}\left(\overline{MFAT}_{\lambda,p}^{\sigma}, R_{\lambda,p}^{\sigma}\right), \tag{12}$$

where σ is the current scale and $\sigma - 1$ is a previous scale. δ is the step size during the calculation of the solution. Considered as possible improvements at the beginning of this section, our enhancement method produce a highly uniform response that is very close to the ground truth of typical curvilinear structures.

Enhancement in 2D. Our proposed function $\overline{MFAT}_{\lambda,p}$ can be also defined for 2D case. In such case, there are three eigenvalues λ_2, λ_ρ, and λ_ν that are defined in Eq. 8. The corresponding response $R_{\lambda,p}^{\sigma}$ for 2D images as follows:

$$R_{\lambda,p}^{\sigma} = \begin{cases} 0 & \text{if } \lambda_\rho > \lambda_\rho - \lambda_2 \vee \lambda_\rho \geq 0 \vee \lambda_2 \geq 0 \vee \lambda_\rho - \lambda_2 < \max_x(\lambda_\rho - \lambda_2), \\ 1 & \text{if } \lambda_\rho - \lambda_2 = \min_x(\lambda_\rho - \lambda_2), \\ 1 - \overline{FAT}_{\lambda,p}^{\sigma} & \text{otherwise.} \end{cases} \tag{13}$$

4   Results

In this section, we present quantitative and qualitative validations for our proposed approach against both synthetic and real-world 2D and 3D imaging data. We then compare the results with state-of-the-art approaches. The Receiver Operating Characteristic (ROC) curve [3] is widely adopted in similar analysis. We used the Area Under the Curve (AUC) of the ROC curve to compare the curvilinear structure enhancement approaches.

4.1   Profile Analysis

The profile of our proposed $\overline{MFAT}_{\lambda,p}$ methods and other state-of-the-art enhancement methods on a synthetic, vessel-like structure are shown in Fig. 1. We evaluate our approach using Eqs. 7 and 9, which refer them to $\overline{MFAT}_\lambda$ and $\overline{MFAT}_p$, respectively. Hessian-based methods, such as vesselness and neuritness, have an enhanced signal at the center of the vessel, i.e., a peak value of one at the centre-line of the vessel, and their respective value quickly drops off and decreases with the perceived thickness of the vessel. On the other hand, the most recent approach (RVR), despite producing a defined response, still shows a poor response to non-crossing junctions. The proposed approach matches all the features of previous methods and shows a more uniform response at non-crossing and crossing junctions.

370 H. F. Alhasson et al.

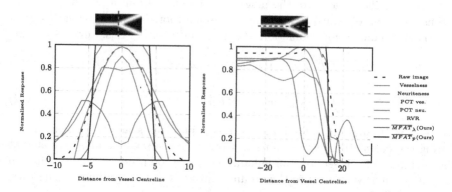

Fig. 1. Cross-sectional profile of a synthetic vessel image (black, dashed line), non-crossing junction in vessel-like structure enhanced by the proposed $\overline{MFAT}_{\lambda,p}$ methods (black and red solid line) and by the state-of-the-art methods (see legend for colours). All images were normalised such that the brightest pixel in the whole image has a value of 1 and the darkest a value of 0. (Color figure online)

4.2 Application to 2D Retinal Images

Although a visual inspection can provide some qualitative information, a more rigorous form of quantitative validation is required to measure the effectiveness of curvilinear structure enhancement approaches. The quality of the approach is measured by using the following publicly available retinal image datasets: DRIVE [11], STARE [7], and HRF [13]. In particular, we evaluate our approach alongside state-of-the-art approaches, calculating the mean ROC curve and the mean of AUC between the enhanced images and the ground truth. The results are shown in Figs. 2, 3, and Table 1 (results for DRIVE, STARE and unhealthy HRF datasets can be found in the supplementary material). A higher AUC value indicates a better enhancement of curvilinear structures, with a value of 1 indicating that the enhanced image is identical to the ground truth image. Our experimental results clearly show that the proposed approaches outperform state-of-the-art approaches, as illustrated as mean AUC in Table 1.

4.3 3D Vascular Network Complexity

In order to validate our approach in 3D, we used synthetic vascular networks produced by VascuSynth [5]. In order to make the images more realistic, a small amount of Gaussian noise ($\sigma^2 = 10$) is added and a Gaussian smoothing kernel with a standard deviation of 1 is applied. Samples of the results are shown in Fig. 4. The results, in terms of AUC and the mean ROC curve over the 9 enhanced images, can be found in the supplementary material (Table 1 and Fig. 4, respectively). Furthermore, our proposed approach is also applied across a wider range of different 2D/3D images and the results can be found in supplementary material.

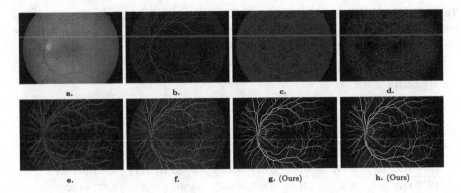

Fig. 2. A sample image from the healthy HRF retina dataset, alongside the enhanced images from the state-of-the-art approaches. (a) The original grayscale image, (b) Vesselness [4], (c) Neuriteness [10], (d) PCT ves. [12], (e) PCT neu. [12], (f) RVR [8], (g) $\overline{MFAT}_\lambda$ and (h) $\overline{MFAT}_p$ methods.

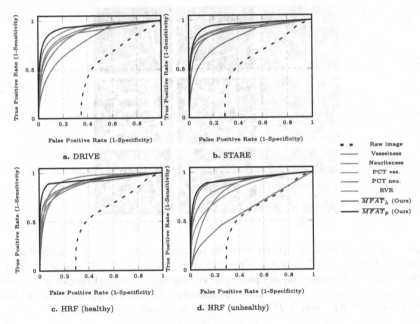

Fig. 3. Mean ROC curves are calculated for all the 2D retina images enhanced using the state-of-the-art approaches alongside our proposed method (see legend for colours). Correspondingly, the mean AUC values for all datasets can be found in Table 1.

5   Implementation

The software was implemented and written in MATLAB 2017a on Windows 8.1 Pro 64-bit PC with an Intel Core i7-4790 CPU (3.60 GHz) with 16 GB RAM. The software is made available at: https://github.com/Haifafh/MFAT.

372   H. F. Alhasson et al.

Table 1. Mean AUC values for the state-of-the-art approaches and our proposed methods across the DRIVE, STARE and HRF datasets. Samples of enhanced images are shown in Fig. 2 and the mean ROC curves can be seen in Fig. 3.

Enhancement approach	AUC (StDev)			
	DRIVE	STARE	HRF (healthy)	HRF (unhealthy)
Raw image	0.416 (0.064)	0.490 (0.076)	0.530 (0.075)	0.541 (0.073)
Vesselness [4]	0.888 (0.243)	0.898 (0.215)	0.913 (0.020)	0.904 **(0.020)**
Neuriteness [10]	0.909 (0.022)	0.927 (0.039)	0.896 (0.024)	0.879 (0.059)
PCT ves. [12]	0.890 (0.037)	0.899 (0.056)	0.888 **(0.011)**	0.837 (0.030)
PCT neu. [12]	0.817 (0.121)	0.827 (0.165)	0.901 (0.029)	0.777 (0.022)
RVR [8]	0.934 (0.024)	0.939 (0.024)	0.926 (0.022)	0.823 (0.026)
$\overline{MFAT}_\lambda$(Ours)	**0.940 (0.013)**	**0.950 (0.016)**	**0.935** (0.024)	**0.921 (0.020)**
$\overline{MFAT}_p$(Ours)	**0.940 (0.013)**	**0.950 (0.016)**	**0.935** (0.024)	**0.921 (0.020)**

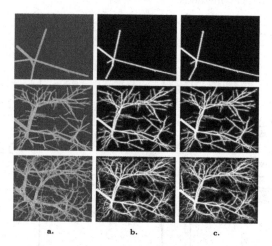

a.   b.   c.

Fig. 4. A selection of 3D synthetic vascular network images generated with the VascuSynth Software. Each image has a resolution of (167 × 167 × 167 voxels) and have different nodes to increase the complexity of structure. (a) original images with different number of nodes (5, 200 and 1000) respectively. (b-c) are the enhance images from the proposed $\overline{MFAT}_\lambda$ and $\overline{MFAT}_p$ methods respectively.

6   Conclusion

This paper proposed a novel method $\overline{MFAT}_{\lambda,p}$, which takes the advantages of Fractional Anisotropic Tensor to enhance curvilinear structures. Our approach adds an enhancement improvement using regularised eigenvalues and junction reconstruction in multiscale scheme. The proposed method is evaluated qualitatively and quantitatively using different 2D and 3D images. Furthermore, compared with established methods, the experimental work with of the proposed method yield excellent segmentation results. The use of this approach significantly improves upon previous image analysis methods, since the enhancement result of the proposed approach is very close to the expected ideal enhancement function.

References

1. Aitchison, J.: The Statistical Analysis of Compositional Data. Chapman and Hall, London (1986)
2. Coulon, O., Alexander, D.C., Arridge, S.: Diffusion tensor magnetic resonance image regularization. Med. Image Anal. **8**(1), 47–67 (2004)
3. Fawcett, T.: An introduction to ROC analysis. Pattern Recogn. Lett. **27**(8), 861–874 (2006)
4. Frangi, A.F., Niessen, W.J., Vincken, K.L., Viergever, M.A.: Multiscale vessel enhancement filtering. In: Wells, W.M., Colchester, A., Delp, S. (eds.) MICCAI 1998. LNCS, vol. 1496, pp. 130–137. Springer, Heidelberg (1998). https://doi.org/10.1007/BFb0056195
5. Hamarneh, G., Jassi, P.: VascuSynth: simulating vascular trees for generating volumetric image data with ground-truth segmentation and tree analysis. Comput. Med. Imaging Graph. **34**(8), 605–616 (2010)
6. Hansen, C.D., Johnson, C.R.: Visualization Handbook. Academic Press, Cambridge (2011)
7. Hoover, A., Kouznetsova, V., Goldbaum, M.: Locating blood vessels in retinal images by piecewise threshold probing of a matched filter response. IEEE Trans. Med. Imaging **19**(3), 203–210 (2000)
8. Jerman, T., Pernuš, F., Likar, B., Špiclin, Ž.: Enhancement of vascular structures in 3D and 2D angiographic images. IEEE Trans. Med. Imaging **35**(9), 2107–2118 (2016)
9. Kovesi, P.: Phase congruency detects corners and edges. In: The Australian Pattern Recognition Society Conference, Brisbane, Australia, pp. 309–318 (2003)
10. Meijering, E., Jacob, M., Sarria, J.C., Steiner, P., Hirling, H., Unser, M.: Design and validation of a tool for neurite tracing and analysis in fluorescence microscopy images. Cytometry Part A **58A**(2), 167–176 (2004)
11. Niemeijer, M., Staal, J., van Ginneken, B., Loog, M., Abramoff, M.D.: Comparative study of retinal vessel segmentation methods on a new publicly available database. In: Image Processing in Medical Imaging, San Diego, USA, pp. 648–657, May 2004
12. Obara, B., Fricker, M., Gavaghan, D., Grau, V.: Contrast-independent curvilinear structure detection in biomedical images. IEEE Trans. Image Process. **21**(5), 2572–2581 (2012)
13. Odstrcilik, J., et al.: Retinal vessel segmentation by improved matched filtering: evaluation on a new high-resolution fundus image database. IET Image Process. **7**(4), 373–383 (2013)
14. Peeters, T., Rodrigues, P., Vilanova, A., ter Haar Romeny, B.: Analysis of distance/similarity measures for diffusion tensor imaging. In: Laidlaw, D., Weickert, J. (eds.) Visualization and Processing of Tensor Fields. MATHVISUAL, pp. 113–136. Springer, Heidelberg (2009). https://doi.org/10.1007/978-3-540-88378-4_6

15. Prados, F., et al.: Analysis of new diffusion tensor imaging anisotropy measures in the three-phase plot. J. Magn. Reson. Imaging **31**(6), 1435–1444 (2010)
16. Sato, Y., et al.: Three-dimensional multi-scale line filter for segmentation and visualization of curvilinear structures in medical images. Med. Image Anal. **2**(2), 143–168 (1998)

Improved Dictionary Learning with Enriched Information for Biomedical Images

Shengda Luo and Alex Po Leung$^{(\boxtimes)}$

Macau University of Science and Technology, Taipa, Macau, China
pleung@must.edu.mo

Abstract. With dictionary learning using k-means or k-means++, the optimal value of k is traditionally determined empirically using a validation set. The optimal k, which should depend on the particular problem, is chosen with previously determined values from prior work. We argue that there is rich information from clustering with a number of values of k. We propose a novel method to extract information from clustering with all reasonable values of k at the same time. It is shown that our method improves the performance of dictionary learning for the popular bag-of-features model in image classification with simple patterns like cells such as biomedical images. Our experiments demonstrate that, our proposed dictionary learning method outperforms popular methods, on two well-known datasets by 12.5% and 8.5% compared to k-means/k-means++ dictionary learning and by 8.9% and 6.1% compared to sparse coding.

1 Introduction

Many methods for the popular bag-of-features model (BoF) have been proposed in recent years [4,7,8]. On images with simple patterns, there is not enough information to be extracted by dictionary learning. There are much fewer visual words to be learned from the simple patterns of visual objects which severely limit the descriptive power of the visual words. The lack of sufficient resolution or descriptive power of object patterns makes it very hard for the classifier to classify the input images very accurately. Recently, a dictionary learning method in [11] is proposed to deal with this problem by extracting more information dictionary learning. The extra information is generated by the clustering results with different values of k using the k-means++ algorithm. However, the high-dimensional feature vectors used in the method [11] makes the curse of dimensionality a much bigger problem with performance degradation.

In this work, it is shown that our dictionary learning method significantly improves the accuracy of the BoF model for classifying the low-resolution images with simple patterns. The improvement is achieved by bringing in the extra information obtained through dictionary learning. In this work, there are three

L. Leal-Taixé and S. Roth (Eds.): ECCV 2018 Workshops, LNCS 11134, pp. 375–384, 2019.
https://doi.org/10.1007/978-3-030-11024-6_27

variants of our proposed method using the multi-channel kernel for the SVM, concatenation of features, and random sampling for k with clustering.

The variant of the proposed method using the multi-channel kernel is called Enriched Dictionary Learning with the Multiple-Channel Kernel (ED-M). The variant using concatenation of features is called as Enriched Dictionary Learning by Concatenation (ED-C). The computational efficiency of the ED-M method can be improved using random sampling for different values of k for k-means++. We call this more efficient ED-M method Enriched Dictionary Learning with the Multiple-Channel Kernel and Random Sampling (ED-MRS). In the experiment section, the BoF model using our three proposed algorithms (ED-M, ED-C, and ED-MRS) are compared with the model using previous state-of-the-art dictionary learning methods (see Table 1). Experiments show that the best result can be obtained by the BoF model using our proposed dictionary learning method.

The differences between our three methods and the method [4] are as follows: (a) For concatenation, we combine the histograms of images in our ED-C method instead of combining clustering results in the method [4]. It has been shown in our experiments that this method for concatenation performs much better than the method in [4], and (b) In our methods ED-M and ED-MRS, extra information is added to the BoF model using the multi-channel kernel (again only concatenation is used in [4]).

Table 1. This table summarizes the dictionary learning methods that be compared in Sect. 4. The SVM kernels of the BoF model using them are shown in the rightmost column.

Dictionary learning method	SVM kernel
Proposed ED-M method	Multi-channel kernel
Proposed ED-C method	Chi-square kernel
Proposed ED-MRS method	Multi-channel kernel
K-means++	Chi-square kernel
K-means	Chi-square kernel
Method in [11]	Chi-square kernel
SIFT sparse coding [10]	Kernel in [10]

We divide the remainder of this paper into 4 sections. In Sect. 2, a brief introduction of the related work is given. Our dictionary learning methods are described in detail in Sect. 3. In Sect. 4, with the BoF model, our dictionary learning method and all its variants are evaluated on two datasets by comparing them with different dictionary learning methods. The last section concludes our work.

2   Related Work

The BoF model is one of the most popular methods for image classification. In this paper, we focus on the dictionary learning methods for this model.

The k-means algorithm became one of the most widely used dictionary learning methods after it was proposed to generate a dictionary in [2]. There are three main issues in the standard k-means algorithm. The efficiency of the k-means algorithm is lower when the value of k or the number of feature descriptors is very big. The result of the k-means algorithm is easily influenced by the positions of its initial centers. Finally, the noise in the image can affect the result of the k-means algorithm because the algorithm treats each descriptor equally.

Some algorithms are proposed to improve the standard k-means algorithm and the BoF model. The Simple Random Sampling K-means (SRS-K) Algorithm [1] is proposed to improve the efficiency of the k-means algorithm by reducing the number of descriptors. In order to generate the initial centers of the k-means algorithm more reasonably, the k-means++ algorithm with a proven statistical guarantee is used to instead of the k-means algorithm. In addition, the BISecting K-means (BIS-K) Algorithm [12] is proposed to address the same issue. The Spatial Pyramid Matching (SPM) [5] Method is one of the most commonly used variants of the BoF model. In order to improve the efficiency of the SPM Method, the ScSPM Method [10] is proposed. In the ScSPM Method, the sparse coding of the SIFT descriptors is instead of the k-means algorithm as the method for dictionary learning. Although these methods are meaningful, they neglect the information obtained from the clustering results of the k-means algorithms with different values of k. In [11], a dictionary learning method is proposed to improve the accuracy of the BoF model for image classification. It is a also method proposed to exploit extra information obtained from clustering. However, the method makes the curse of dimensionality a bigger problem when k for k-means++ is relatively large. We compare our proposed method with this previous method in our experiments.

3   The Proposed Dictionary Learning Method

3.1   The Motivation

What motivated us is the question: can a single empirically determined optimal k for k-means or k-means++ be improved for dictionary learning? The disadvantages to use an empirical k can be (1) rich information might be lost if the empirical k is not carefully chosen by extensive experiments and (2) sometimes, the optimal k, which should depend on the particular problem, is chosen with previously determined values from prior work or past experience. We, therefore, aim to extract rich information from various histograms using clustering with a large number of possible values of k.

In our experiments, it is demonstrated that our method significantly improves the performance of dictionary learning over state-of-the-art methods for the popular bag-of-features (BoF) model in image classification with biomedical images.

However, the method is a general method to improve dictionary learning for images with simple patterns.

With enriched information from dictionary learning, we focus on datasets with low-resolution images with simple patterns for classification using BoF model. Traditionally, the performance of the BoF model with these images may not be ideal because there is not enough information to be obtained from such images using dictionary learning with simple patterns. It is our goal that extra information can be extracted to obtain an enriched dictionary for the BoF model.

We propose a novel dictionary learning method to learn the dictionary using extra information. Using our method, the accuracy of the BoF model can be improved significantly. It is unnecessary for the new method to obtain a very high-dimensional feature vector in the large ($\sum_{n=2}^{k}$ n-word) dictionary which makes the curse of dimensionality a bigger problem. In our method, there are three variants of our dictionary learning method: the ED-M, the ED-C, and the ED-MRS (see Table 1).

3.2   Notations

To be more precise, notations used in the rest of this paper are defined in this subsection. N is defined as the number of the images used for training. S_j is the set of SIFT descriptors extracted from the j-th image, and $\mathbb{S} = \{S_1 \cup ... \cup S_N\}$ is the set of all SIFT descriptors from all N training images. To extract enriched information from various histograms with multiple k's using k-means++, we have the set of all k's used, $k \in \mathcal{K} = \{2, 3, ..., K\}$. For clustering, c_k is the set of k cluster centers obtained with $k \in \mathcal{K}$ using k-means++. We have the set of all histograms obtained with k-means++ $h_{k \in \mathcal{K}, n \in \{1,2,...,N\}} \in \mathcal{H}$ where $h_{k,n}$ indicates the histogram generated for the n-th image by using the k-th clustering result.

3.3   Feature Extraction for Enriched Information

Our proposed enriched information step is acheived using Algorithm 1. With k-means++ algorithm for clustering, it has been shown that the performance is better due to its statistical guarantee. In Algorithm 1, for each $k \in \mathcal{K}$, we have one iteration with clustering and the associated histograms. The k-means++ is, therefore, performed $|\mathcal{K}|$ times with k values in $\mathcal{K}$. $|\mathcal{K}|$ sets of clustering centers are then used to obtain $|\mathcal{K}|$ sets of histograms for every single image.

The curse-of-dimensionality which leads to poor performance is avoided in our dictionary learning method with the multi-channel kernel considering that we can have a very-high dimensional feature vector from the $\sum_{n=2}^{k}$ n-word dictionary. The kernel makes the feature vectors significantly shorter. To be more specific, in our Algorithm 1, for each image one histogram is generated using the cluster centers from k-means++ with one particular k, so the number of bins is exactly k in this histogram.

Algorithm 1. Feature Extraction for Enriched Information

Require: The SIFT descriptors of features in training images S; The set of values $k \in \mathcal{K}$ for clustering with k-means++

Ensure: The set of all histograms of all training images $\mathcal{H}$.

1: **for** each value $k \in \mathcal{K}$ **do**
2:     Cluster all features S using k-means++ with k to obtain the set of cluster centers c_k
3:     **for** each image $j \in 1, 2, ..., N$ in the training set **do**
4:         Bin S_j for the histogram: $h_{i,j}$ with centers c_k
5:     **end for**
6: **end for**

3.4 Enriched Dictionary Learning with the Multiple-Channel Kernel (ED-M)

For classification, we propose the ED-M algorithm after feature extraction (see Table 1) is shown in Algorithm 2. The ED-M utilizes the multi-channel kernel of the SVM to combine features obtained in Algorithm 1 for the classification in the BoF model.

With $\mathcal{H}$ from Algorithm 1, the multi-channel chi-square kernel is calculated using histograms $\mathcal{H}$. For each channel k, we have histogram $h_{k,j} \in \mathcal{H}$ where j can be any image in the training set, i.e. $1 < j < N$. The chi-square kernel between two histograms from two images j_1 and j_2 in channel k is obtained by

$$\chi^2(h_{k,j_1}, h_{k,j_2}) = 1 - \sum_{z=1}^{k} \frac{\left[(h_{k,j_1})_z - (h_{k,j_2})_z\right]^2}{\frac{1}{2}\left[(h_{k,j_1})_z + (h_{k,j_2})_z\right]} \tag{1}$$

where z is a particular bin in histogram $(h_{k,j})$ and $(h_{k,j})_z$ is the value of bin z in $h_{k,j}$.

After computing the multi-channel chi-square matrix, the SVM is trained with the matrix to obtain the support vectors. Each element in the matrix M_{j_1,j_2} of this matrix is computed using

$$M_{j_1,j_2} = \frac{1}{|\mathcal{K}|} \sum_{k \in \mathcal{K}} \chi^2(h_{k,j_1}, h_{k,j_2}) \tag{2}$$

where $\chi^2(.,.)$ is the chi-square kernel in Eq. 1.

3.5 Enriched Dictionary with the Multiple-Channel Kernel and Random Sampling (ED-MRS)

To improve computational efficiency, we propose a randomized version of the ED-M method using random sampling. The new algorithm is called Enriched Dictionary with the Multiple-Channel Kernel and Random Sampling (ED-MRS). Essentially, a random subset $\mathcal{K}_{MRS}$ from $\mathcal{K}$ is obtained before clustering. That means we have $\mathcal{K}_{MRS} \subset \mathcal{K}$. In our experiments, it is demonstrated that a significant speedup can be acheived with ED-MRS with some reasonable performance decrease.

In the ED-MRS algorithm, $\mathcal{K}_{MRS} \subset \mathcal{K}$ is obtained using random sampling. $\mathcal{K}_{MRS}$ is then used as the set of the k values for the k-means++ instead of $\mathcal{K}$.

Algorithm 2. Enriched Dictionary Learning with the Multiple-Channel Kernel (ED-M).

Require: The SIFT descriptors of features in training images S; The set of values $k \in \mathcal{K}$ for clustering with k-means++
Ensure: The Trained Model of the SVM, i.e. the support vectors.
1: Obtain all histograms for all training image $\mathcal{H}$ by invoking Algorithm 1
2: With $\mathcal{H}$ as input, the chi-square kernel matrix is computed for each channel (Eq. 1)

$$\chi^2(h_{k,j_1}, h_{k,j_2}) = 1 - \sum_{z=1}^{k} \frac{[(h_{k,j_1})_z - (h_{k,j_2})_z]^2}{\frac{1}{2}[(h_{k,j_1})_z + (h_{k,j_2})_z]}$$

3: The matrix of the multi-channel kernel is computed (Eq. 2)

$$M_{j_1,j_2} = \frac{1}{|\mathcal{K}|} \sum_{k \in \mathcal{K}} \chi^2(h_{k,j_1}, h_{k,j_2})$$

4: Train the SVM by using the matrix of the multi-channel kernel

---

It means that the only difference between the ED-MRS algorithm and the ED-M algorithm, i.e. Algorithm 2 is the use of randomly sampled values of $k \in \mathcal{K}_{MRS}$ for ED-MRS. More specifically, $|\mathcal{K}_{MRS}|$ is used in ED-MRS, instead of $|\mathcal{K}|$ in the Eq. 2.

3.6 Enriched Dictionary Learning with Concatenation (ED-C)

Instead of using the multi-channel kernel for different values of k, it is natural to also consider a simple concatenation for the proposed method with the chi-square kernel. Therefore, we have enriched dictionary learning with concatenation (ED-C) which combines enriched information from clustering to learn the dictionary (see Algorithm 3 and Table 1).

Like ED-M, in Algorithm 3, S, and $\mathcal{K}$ are needed as the input to Algorithm 1 which computes $\mathcal{H}$. With histograms $\mathcal{H}$, for the same image j, $\{h_{k,j} : k \in \mathcal{K}\}$ can be concatenated to form one feature vector. With only one feature vector for one image, the SVM is then trained using the chi-square kernel.

Algorithm 3. Enriched Dictionary Learning with Concatenation (ED-C)

Require: The SIFT descriptors of features in training images S; The set of values $k \in \mathcal{K}$ for clustering with k-means++
Ensure: The Trained Model of the SVM, i.e. the support vectors.
1: Obtain all histograms for all training image H by invoking Algorithm 1
2: Concatenate the histograms with different values of k to obtain one feature vector for image j, i.e. $H_j = [h_{2,j}, h_{3,j}, ..., h_{k,j}]$
3: Computing the chi-square kernel matrix (Eq.1)

$$\chi^2(H_{j_1}, H_{j_2}) = 1 - \sum_{z=1}^{i} \frac{[(H_{j_1})_z - (H_{j_2})_z]^2}{\frac{1}{2}[(H_{j_1})_z + (H_{j_2})_z]}$$

4: Training the SVM by using the chi-square kernel matrix

4 Experiments

4.1 Datasets and Performance Metrics

Our experiments[1] are conducted using two medical datasets: human epithelial type 2 cells dataset (SNPHEp-2 Cell Dataset)[2] [9] and pap-smear cells dataset[3] [3]. One motivation for us to use medical datasets is that medical image classification is a very important problem with challenging domain specific sub-problems to tackle. With fast-growing volumes of medical data/images collected by various systems or projects, medical data analysis has become a big data problem. One way to solve this problem is to use automated medical image classification. Cell image classification is an important type of medical image classification. Recognizing cells is a challenge in image classification because the resolutions of the cell images are usually very low. In addition, the image patterns on the cells are simple so not a lot of features can be extracted from these patterns. We show that our methods performs well in these medical images. The performance of our method in the experiment is evaluated by accuracy which is computed using true negative (tn), false negative (fn), true positive (tp), false positive (fp) and the number of classes (l): $accuracy = \left(\sum_{i=1}^{l} (tp_i + tn_i) / (tp_i + tn_i + fp_i + fn_i) \right) / l$.

4.2 The SNPHEp-2 Dataset

The anti-nuclear antibody test is a useful diagnostic method for autoimmune diseases and the Indirect Immunofluorescence protocol using human epithelial type 2 (HEp-2) cells is the important standard for the test [6]. The SNPHEp-2 Cell Dataset contains 1,884 cell images with the image size roughly 80-by-80 pixels and the images are divided into 5 classes: Homogeneous, Coarse speckled, Fine speckled, Nucleolar and Centromere. In the public SNPHEp-2 dataset, all the 1,884 cell images are extracted from 40 specimen images and these 40 specimens are equally split into 20 for training and 20 for testing. The numbers of the cell images extracted from different specimens are different. We use the cell images. Hence, the numbers of the cell images for training (905 cell images) or testing (979 cell images) are different. As shown in Table 2, when the value of the k is large, it takes almost 10 days to run a single experiment. For a fair comparison, for each k and each method, we run the program 20 times. However, it takes weeks to finish computation with a 5-fold cross validation. In the SNPHEp-2 dataset, a five-fold validation for training and testing were created by randomly selecting the training (905 cell images) and test (979 cell images) images. The "Split-50-1" means that the first fold of these five-fold validation. Because of limited computational resources, only the first split (Split-50-1) which contain 450 images for training and 493 images for testing, is used for our experiments.

---

[1] Our code is made available on the web at https://sites.google.com/site/apleung/.
[2] Available from: http://staff.itee.uq.edu.au/lovell/snphep2/.
[3] Available from: http://mde-lab.aegean.gr/downloads.

4.3   The PAP-Smear Dataset

The term pap-smear refers to human cell samples stained with the Papanicolau method for the ease of observation under a microscope [3]. The classification of pap-smear cells helps to detect cancer cells. The pap-smear cell dataset collected by Jan Jantzen et al. in 2005 [3]. The dataset consists of 917 cell images which are divided into 7 classes: superficial squamous epithelial, intermediate squamous epithelial, columnar epithelial, mild squamous non-keratinizing dysplasia, moderate squamous non-keratinizing dysplasia, severe squamous non-keratinizing dysplasia, and squamous cell carcinoma in situ intermediate. The whole pap-smear cell dataset [3] is used in our experiments. The dataset is randomly divided into the training set (50% images) and the test set (50% images) for the experiments. The results of the methods are compared with the reported accuracy of image classification and the computational efficiency.

4.4   Comparison with State-of-the-Art Algorithms

In the experiments, the BoF model using different dictionary learning methods (see Table 1) are compared using the two datasets. All experiments are conducted on an Intel Xeon E5-2690 CPU. We use MATLAB to implement six BoF model variants: three variants using our methods (see Table 1) and the three variants using the k-means, the kmeans++ and the dictionary method in [11]. The remaining one variant is from [10] which is a publicly available version of ScSPM based on sparse coding. To have a fair comparison, all the variants use the SIFT descriptor as the feature descriptor. In order to obtain reliable results, we repeat our experiments for each variant 20 times using the same datasets. The averages over 20 experiments are taken as our results for the accuracy.

To clearly show the comparison for the accuracy at different values of k, Fig. 1 is plotted to show the comparison among six variants (three variants using our methods and three variants based on k-means, k-means++ or the dictionary method in [11]). In Fig. 1, with the value of k increased between 20 and 350, the accuracy rate of the BoF model using our ED-M are larger than that of the model using other methods. On the SNPHEp-2 Cell Dataset and the pap-smear dataset, The BoF model using our ED-M method outperforms that using the k-means++ algorithm by nearly 12.4% and 8.6%.

In Table 2, the highest accuracies from the six BoF model variants in Fig. 1 are compared with the accuracy of ScSPM. With the use of our ED-M method for dictionary learning, the BoF model obtains a much higher accuracy in the comparison. The BoF Model using our ED-MRS method speeding up our ED-M method outperforms the BoF model using other methods except for the ED-M and the ED-C.

The improvements of the proposed ED-M and ED-C over sparse coding and k-means come at a computational cost which makes our methods slower than traditional k-means dictionary learning. However, the proposed methods can

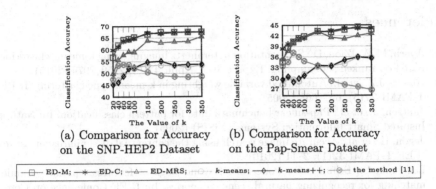

(a) Comparison for Accuracy on the SNP-HEP2 Dataset

(b) Comparison for Accuracy on the Pap-Smear Dataset

Fig. 1. This figure is plotted to show the comparison among six k-means based variants. The dictionary methods for the BoF model are used to denote the BoF model variants.

Table 2. This table shows the comparison on the two datasets. The highest accuracies for the six BoF model variants in Fig. 1 obtained with their respective optimal values of k are compared with the accuracy of ScSPM.

Dictionary learning method used in the BoF model	For the SNPHEp2 dataset			For the pap-smear dataset		
	Accuracy	optimal k	Execution time	Accuracy	optimal k	Execution time
Proposed our ED-M	**67.5**	200	44853 s	**44.5**	300	91755 s
Proposed ED-C	**67.5**	300	46569 s	44.1	300	96796 s
Proposed ED-MRS	65.5	350	1695 s	41.9	150	1921 s
Sparse coding	58.6	NA	452 s	38.4	NA	644 s
k-means++	55.1	200	416 s	35.9	300	813 s
k-means	53.4	200	353 s	35.9	300	1215 s
The method in [11]	53.8	60	28731 s	37.2	60	32022 s

be made more efficient using random sampling techniques like our proposed ED-MRS. With the speed up using ED-MRS to improve the performance of dictionary learning, the computational cost of our improved methods is lowered as can be seen in Table 2.

5 Conclusions

In this paper, a novel dictionary learning method is proposed to improve the accuracy of the BoF model for the image classification with simple patterns such as biomedical images. The improvement is achieved by the adding of the extra information from clustering with all reasonable values of k at the same time. Our experiments demonstrate that, with medical imaging datasets, the proposed dictionary learning method outperforms state-of-the-art methods, such as k-means/k-means++ clustering and sparse coding.

Acknowledgement. This work is supported by the Macau Science and Technology Development Fund (No. 112/2014/A3).

References

1. Ayech, M.W., Ziou, D.: Segmentation of terahertz imaging using k-means clustering based on ranked set sampling. Expert Syst. Appl. **42**(6), 2959–2974 (2015)
2. Huang, J.Z., et al.: Automated variable weighting in k-means type clustering. IEEE T-PAMI **27**(5), 657–668 (2005)
3. Jantzen, J., et al.: Pap-smear benchmark data for pattern classification. In: Nature Inspired Smart Information Systems (NiSIS) (2005)
4. Jegou, H., et al.: Accurate image search using the contextual dissimilarity measure. IEEE T-PAMI **32**(1), 2–11 (2010)
5. Lazebnik, S., Schmid, C., Ponce, J.: Beyond bags of features: spatial pyramid matching for recognizing natural scene categories. In: IEEE Conference on Computer Vision and Pattern Recognition (CVPR) (2006)
6. Meroni, P.L., Schur, P.H.: Ana screening: an old test with new recommendations. Ann. Rheum. Dis. **69**(8), 1420–1422 (2010)
7. Philbin, J., et al.: Object retrieval with large vocabularies and fast spatial matching. In: IEEE Conference on Computer Vision and Pattern Recognition (CVPR) (2007)
8. Philbin, J., et al.: Improving particular object retrieval in large scale image databases. In: IEEE Conference on Computer Vision and Pattern Recognition (CVPR) (2008)
9. Wiliem, A., et al.: Classification of human epithelial type 2 cell indirect immunofluoresence images via codebook based descriptors. In: IEEE Workshop on Applications of Computer Vision (WACV) (2013)
10. Yang, J., et al.: Linear spatial pyramid matching using sparse coding for image classification. In: IEEE Conference on Computer Vision and Pattern Recognition (CVPR) (2009)
11. Zhang, S., Leung, A.P.: A novel approach to dictionary learning for the bag-of-features model. In: Wavelet Analysis and Pattern Recognition (ICWAPR) (2017)
12. Zhao, C., Li, X., Cang, Y.: Bisecting k-means clustering based face recognition using block-based bag of words model. Optik-Int. J. Light Electron Opt. **126**(19), 1761–1766 (2015)

Visual and Quantitative Comparison of Real and Simulated Biomedical Image Data

Tereza Nečasová(⊠) and David Svoboda

Centre for Biomedical Image Analysis, Masaryk University, Brno, Czech Republic
necasovat@fi.muni.cz

Abstract. The simulations in biomedical image analysis provide a solution when the real image data are difficult to be annotated or if they are available only in small quantities. The progress in simulations rapidly grows in the recent years. Nevertheless, the comparative techniques for the assessment of the plausibility of generated data are still unsatisfactory or none. This paper aims to point out the problem of insufficient comparison of real and synthetic data, which is done in many cases only by visual inspection or based on subjective measurements. The selected texture features are first compared in a univariate manner by quantile-quantile plots and Kolmogorov-Smirnov test. The evaluation is then extended into multivariate assessment using the PCA for a visualization and furthermore for a quantitative measure of similarity by Jaccard index. Two different image datasets were used to show the results and the importance of the validation of simulated data in many aspects.

Keywords: Feature comparison · Validation of simulation
Statistical evaluation · Similarity visualisation

1 Introduction

The research in the last decades showed the power of technical progress besides other things in biomedical imaging, especially in the generation of artificial image data, which should resemble the real images. From the images of spots and particles, over nuclei and subcellular components, also the images of multiple-target, cell populations and tissues are possible to be synthesized as summarized in [16].

Despite the methods for simulations differ, the main objectives for generating artificial image data are the same: (1) to use the simulated data for validating the segmentation algorithms with unhidden ground truth; (2) to perceive the biological processes and understand the cell behavior; and last but not least: (3) to reduce the time and inconsistency among manual annotators, which is even higher in three-dimensional image data and time-lapse sequences.

© Springer Nature Switzerland AG 2019
L. Leal-Taixé and S. Roth (Eds.): ECCV 2018 Workshops, LNCS 11134, pp. 385–394, 2019.
https://doi.org/10.1007/978-3-030-11024-6_28

Nevertheless, one can legitimately ask for a plausibility of the artificial data. There are many characteristics that can be computed and subsequently used for the comparison of real and synthetic data, such as shape, number of cells in the image, number of various elements etc. The comparison made on these features could support the expectation that the simulated data are of sufficient quality. This paper is focused on methods for validating texture, as we found this feature to be variously interpreted and independent of the work of annotator. This feature is also given by every single image, which makes this feature applicable to all available images.

The first step of quality assessment is the visual inspection, which is mentioned almost every time. While some of the works ends with the visual evaluation of experts, other outspread with quantitative measurements. In [1], for example, the quality of generated images is assessed by measuring the largest magnification in which the image data look realistic. In [8], the authors suggested to compute the sensitivity and specificity over 6 differently experienced human test subjects, who had to classify, whether the image is synthetic or real. This decision was made in limited time, which should imitate the real conditions. In contrast to expert-based evaluation, there also exist the approaches based on quantitative evaluation. In particular, the Q-Q plots of texture descriptors were used in [8,12]. Furthermore, [13] showed the histograms of real and synthetic data accompanied by means, standard deviations and p-values of Kolmogorov-Smirnov tests. Note, that all of these validation techniques were assessed univariately. This paper extends these evaluations into multiple dimensions to compare the mutual information of the data points. The aim of this paper is also to visualize the data and their mutual comparison. We suggest this by a reduction of a multidimensional feature space using principal component analysis.

2   Datasets

For the demonstration of the proposed approach two different datasets of images are presented. The first dataset comes from Uppsala university [8]. In this paper, a simulation framework for generating images used for Pap smear analysis in cervix cancer screening was developed. The total number of 25 monochromatic 2D histology images of real data and 5 batches of synthetic image data (each consisting of 5 images, 25 images in total) were included in the reference dataset provided by the authors.

The images in the second dataset consisted of 180 images of lung cancer cells with filopodial protrusions from 3D time-lapse acquired by fluorescence microscope [11]. The two subtypes of lung cancer cells were analyzed in this paper – the cells with overexpressing phenotype (90 real images and 90 synthetic images) and the cells with phospho-defective phenotype (also 90 real images and 90 synthetic images).

The texture of histopathology images for Pap smear analysis was evaluated over the whole 2D image as it was described by the authors of [8]. Unlike this dataset, in case of lung cancer cells, only the texture of the central interior regions ($31 \times 31 \times 3$ voxels) was compared in real and synthetic data following the same procedure as proposed by the authors of [11].

These two image datasets have been separately used as the input samples for testing the proposed validation method.

3   Methods

Haralick texture features [3] belong to very popular and widespread [2,7,13,15] image descriptors. In this paper, we evaluated 14 Haralick descriptors. In the following text, methods of statistical comparison will be presented. Although these methods are well known and widely used, they have not been applied together in this context.

3.1   Univariate Comparison of Feature Distributions

After achieving 14 values for each image in both, real and synthetic data, a comparison of distributions in these groups was performed using the quantile-quantile plot (Q-Q plot) [17]. When comparing two samples, the empirical quantiles are plotted in the x-y figure against each other for every descriptor. This method reveals the identical distribution in both samples if the points of the quantiles lie along the straight line with the slope of 1, while diversion of the points from this line indicates differences in distribution. This method has no assumptions put on the input data, and furthermore, it is not necessary to identify the distributions that are compared. In case of image descriptors, the Q-Q plot can help to compare the distribution of both groups of data in each descriptor separately, i.e. univariately.

Since the Q-Q plot is only a visual technique for data comparison, this procedure can be accompanied by the statistical test of Kolmogorov-Smirnov [9]. The tested null hypothesis is that the cumulative distribution functions is the same for the both samples $A = \{a_i | i = 1, \ldots, n_A; a_i \in \mathbb{R}\}$ and $B = \{b_i | i = 1, \ldots, n_B; b_i \in \mathbb{R}\}$. The empirical cumulative distribution for sample A is defined as $F_A(x) = \frac{\#\{a \in A | a \leq x\}}{n_A}$ and in the same manner for sample B. In our case, A stands for a sample of real data and B for a sample of synthetic data. The test statistic for the two samples is based on the largest distances between the two empirical distribution functions, which is $KS(A, B) = \sup_{x \in \mathbb{R}} |F_A(x) - F_B(x)|$. The value of Kolmogorov-Smirnov statistic is then compared to the critical value and the null hypothesis is then rejected if $KS(A, B) > \sqrt{\frac{1}{n_A} + \frac{1}{n_B}} \kappa_\alpha$, where κ_α is chosen according to the α level of significance. Note that the Kolmogorov-Smirnov test is a non-parametric technique, which means it has no assumptions put on the given data. Therefore, it is easy to apply Kolmogorov-Smirnov test also to the Haralick descriptors with no limitation and with a clear decision if the data reveals the similarity in a particular descriptor.

3.2   Reduction of the Feature Space

As one could be interested in the assessment of all 14 Haralick features simultaneously, we suggest the multivariate assessment. This approach describes every image by a vector in a 14-dimensional space. It is not possible to see visually the positions of the real and synthetic data points in such a high-dimensional vector space. Therefore the reduction with the retention of most of the total variability in three features is convenient. Since some of the Haralick descriptors are correlated, the reduction of the feature space is possible to perform and was done by applying the Principal Component Analysis (PCA), originally proposed by [10] and then extended by [4]. PCA is a reduction procedure with transformation to another uncorrelated feature space. The aim of the technique is to preserve the most of the variability in the new first features (components) by extracting the principal pattern of the linear system of descriptors. Afterwards, only some of the components can be selected to represent the new reduced data with the particular proportion of the variability. Other redundant features can be discarded.

The original feature space given by d descriptors ($d = 14$) and n_A real images and n_B synthetic images ($n_A + n_B = n$) can be represented as a matrix

$$X_{n,d} = \begin{pmatrix} x_{11}^A & \cdots & x_{1d}^A \\ \vdots & \ddots & \vdots \\ x_{n_A 1}^A & \cdots & x_{n_A d}^A \\ x_{11}^B & \cdots & x_{1d}^B \\ \vdots & \ddots & \vdots \\ x_{n_B 1}^B & \cdots & x_{n_B d}^B \end{pmatrix} = \begin{pmatrix} x_{11} & \cdots & x_{1d} \\ \vdots & \ddots & \vdots \\ x_{n1} & \cdots & x_{nd} \end{pmatrix} \tag{1}$$

where x_{ij} is value of j-th descriptor measured in i-th image. The matrix X can be centered by subtracting the sample multivariate mean $\bar{x}$ and scaled/standardized before further operations. In case of centered PCA, the distances among objects are equal to the distances in the original space, but the central point of the axis is shifted to the centroid of objects. This is used especially, when the scales of the variables are similar. In case of standardized PCA the variables are transformed to the variables with unit variance. It can be used if the scales of the variables are measured in different units, such as the case of Haralick descriptors. The transformation of PCA is then given by

$$Y_{n,d} = (X_{n,d} - 1_n \bar{x}^T)\hat{\Gamma}, \tag{2}$$

where $\hat{\Gamma}$ contains the eigenvectors of the sample covariance or correlation matrix $\hat{\Sigma}$ of the input data so that, $\hat{\Gamma}^T \hat{\Sigma} \hat{\Gamma} = \hat{\Lambda} = diag(\hat{\lambda}_1, \hat{\lambda}_2, \ldots, \hat{\lambda}_d)$, where the eigenvalues are in the order from the highest to the lowest $\hat{\lambda}_1 \geq \hat{\lambda}_2 \geq \cdots \geq \hat{\lambda}_d \geq 0$. The new feature space is formed by principal components Y_i (the i-th column of the matrix $Y_{n,d}$).

PCA has an assumption of quantitative variables (but there exist some modifications), independence of objects and multivariate normality, which is sometimes difficult to achieve. However, some works [6] state that PCA is sufficiently robust to overcome this.

Showing only the first two or three principal components in an x-y plot or x-y-z plot, respectively, one can have an idea about mutual position and clusters of the real and synthetic data in the uncorrelated reduced feature space. Note that the PCA is independent of the group assignment in this case and it is used only for visualization.

3.3 Overlap of Samples

Now we have an analogue situation as we had in a univariate approach. The visual inspection gives us a subjective information about the similarity of the groups, but the objective assessment is missing. Let us compare the overlap of the data points of each sample in the reduced feature space. We will do that by comparing the ellipsoids that envelope these data points (see Fig. 2). The construction of ellipsoids is based on the sample covariance matrices and sample means to fit the data points on a level of 95% joint confidence interval. This enables to omit 5% of potential multidimensional outliers. Finally, the intersection volume and the volume of union are compared by the Jaccard similarity index [5]:

$$J(A, B) = \frac{V_A \cap V_B}{V_A \cup V_B}, \tag{3}$$

where the V_A and V_B stand for the volume of the ellipsoid constructed in reduced feature space over sample A or B, respectively. The index ranges values between $0 \leq J(A, B) \leq 1$, in case of total similarity it yields 1, in case of no intersection the index is equal to 0.

4 Results

First, the datasets were assessed univariately using the Q-Q plots for all of the 14 descriptors. To see the differences and similarities, the datasets were also compared in real image data only, divided randomly into two groups with an expectation of good results of homogeneous groups. The randomization into two groups was performed three times with similar results. In case of reference Pap smear real data divided into two groups (see Fig. 1), one can see the high level of similarity. Even if the points diverse from the straight line in some of the cases, the p-values of Kolmogorov-Smirnov test retain the null hypothesis stating to have the same distribution in both groups of real data.

To assess the mutual relationships in a multidimensional feature space, PCA was applied to all 14 Haralick features. The data were pre-processed by Tukey's ladder of powers in case of a violation of normality, centred and normalized, because the individual descriptors are measured in different scales. The three principal components with the largest contribution on the explained variability were used for a visualization. Analyzing the results of PCA, many input variables

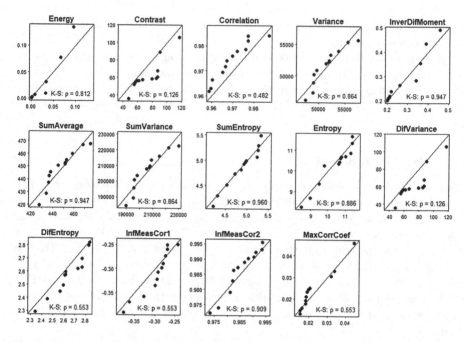

Fig. 1. Q-Q plots showing the similarity in distributions of 14 Haralick descriptors in comparison of two random samples of real image data from Pap smear test. The each plot is enriched by p-values of Kolmogorov-Smirnov test (K-S) supporting the difference between sample distributions when the value is ≤0.05 (in case of level of significance $\alpha = 0.05$).

(descriptors) entering the transform were found to be highly correlated. This supports the idea that reduced space for visualization is needed.

To see as much as possible of the variability and the mutual positions of the samples, the points were depicted in the transformed 3D feature space given by principal components as axes. Inspecting the reference phospho-defective lung cancer cells dataset (see Fig. 2), one can see only a partial overlap of the ellipsoids enveloping the synthetic data (blue) with those for real image data (yellow) (a–c). On the contrary, the visualisation of the two subsets of real data reveals a high overlap of the ellipsoids in all views (d–f). For a detailed description of all results, see the Table 1. The values of Jaccard similarity indices computed over volumes of ellipsoids correspond to the visualization done by PCA. When comparing the real and synthetic data of Pap smear images, the intersection volume covered only 16.1% of the volume of union of the two ellipsoids ($J = 0.161$). The best results were observed when comparing real *vs.* real image datasets ($J \geq 0.652$). The visual comparison of real overexpressing lung cancer cells with synthetic revealed visually a good overlap, however the Jaccard index was smaller according to the fact, that ellipsoid enveloping synthetic data was smaller than the ellipsoid enveloping real data.

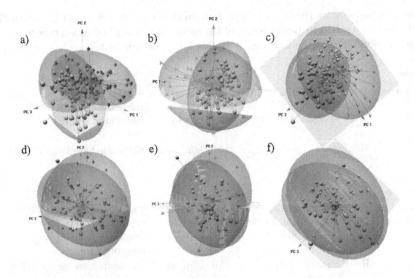

Fig. 2. Visual comparison of data in 3D feature space reduced by PCA into the three main components (axes PC1, PC2, PC3). Frontal (a, d), horizontal (b, e) and vertical (c, f) view on real (yellow) and synthetic (blue) data (a–c) and two groups of real data of lung cancer cells (d–f). The interactive tool of **pca3d** library in R software [14] enabled to rotate the set of points in all directions with the possibility of showing id of images, distances to the centroids and ellipsoids around each subset. The greater the intersection of each pair of ellipsoids, the higher the similarity of the corresponding evaluated samples can be expected. (Color figure online)

5   Discussion

The real and synthetic data were compared to each other, at first univariately in Q-Q plots, which gave us some information about distributions. However, it was not possible to conclude from Fig. 1 that the synthetic images covered only a limited part of the variability as it is shown in Fig. 2(a). The PCA helped to reduce the high-dimensional feature space and therefore to visualize the important part of the variability and the position of the groups of images in a feature space. It was possible to visually assess the overlap of the ellipsoids constructed over 95% joint confidence interval representing a given group. To express this overlap numerically, the Jaccard index was suggested.

Exploring the subset of real images, the Jaccard values was never higher than 0.8. This is according to the variability given by each subset of real data and it should be kept in mind also when comparing real and synthetic data. The value of Jaccard $J = 1$ is impossible to achieve and if so, this result would refer to the overfitted simulator to the particular real dataset.

The low performance of the comparison of cervix data could result from evaluation of the Haralick features over the whole image consisting of many cells,

Table 1. Results of methods for comparison on datasets ($R \times S$ – real vs. synthetic; $R \times R$ – real vs. real). The performance of the methods is described in a sentence ($+++$ suggest no difference in the samples, $+$ stands for a low similarity).

Dataset		Q-Q plots	K-S p-value	Visualization by PCA	Jaccard
Pap smear	R × S	Diverging a lot from the straight line in 4 descriptors (++)	Significant difference in 6 cases (+)	Synthetic data lie in the plane crossing the ellipsoid of real data (+)	0.161
	R × R	Good (++)	All right, no rejection (+++)	Ellipsoids have large overlap (+++)	0.652
Lung cells					
Over-expressing	R × S	Diverging a lot from the straight line in 1 descriptor (++)	Significant difference in 4 cases (++)	The ellipsoid of the synthetic data is smaller, but fitting a majority (++)	0.583
	R × R	Perfect (+++)	All right, no rejection (+++)	Ellipsoids have large overlap (+++)	0.796
Phospho-defective	R × S	Diverging a lot from the straight line in 5 descriptors (++)	Significant difference in 6 cases (+)	Ellipsoids overlap only in part of the data (++)	0.284
	R × R	Perfect (+++)	All right, no rejection (+++)	Ellipsoids have large overlap (+++)	0.659

in contrast to the lung cancer cells. The inner regions of single cells provide more homogeneous part of the image suitable for the evaluation.

Note that the similarity evaluation of cervix data was done only on 25+25 images. Despite the small sample size, the limitations of the synthesized variability were conspicuous.

In this paper, only the texture feature was assessed, however the PCA could be applied also to other characteristics of an image, such as shape. The descriptors are nevertheless based on some pre-processing and could be affected by the chosen method.

6   Conclusion

In the last years, the methods of cell image synthesis have been rapidly improving. However, the evaluation of the similarity of such generated data compared to real data, is still not sufficient.

This paper aimed to show new possibilities for texture comparison in (1) viewing data in context of multiple dimensions given by texture descriptors, (2) observe the mutual position of real and synthetic image data points in feature space reduced by PCA, and (3) quantitative measurement of similarity by comparing the volumes of ellipsoids enveloping given group of data in a feature space. The described methods were applied to two datasets showing differences between groups of images. In two randomly chosen subsets of real images there was observed only a small difference between the groups with Jaccard index ≥ 0.652. The experiments comparing real and synthetic data showed different levels of similarity. The Jaccard indices revealed corresponding results to the visual inspection in reduced feature space and univariate statistical comparisons.

In the future work we plan to extend our method for time-lapse image data, where the texture is time varying. The vision is also to give a constructive feedback to the designer of the synthesizing algorithm in identifying, why the images differ in a chosen descriptor.

Acknowledgement. This work was supported by Czech Science Foundation, grant No. GA17-05048S.

References

1. Apou, G., Feuerhake, F., Forestier, G., Naegel, B., Wemmert, C.: Synthesizing whole slide images. In: 2015 9th International Symposium on Image and Signal Processing and Analysis (ISPA), pp. 154–159, September 2015
2. Boland, M.V., Murphy, R.F.: A neural network classifier capable of recognizing the patterns of all major subcellular structures in fluorescence microscope images of HeLa cells. Bioinformatics **17**(12), 1213–1223 (2001)
3. Haralick, R.M., Shanmugam, K., Dinstein, I.: Textural features for image classification. IEEE Trans. Syst. Man Cybern. **SMC-3**(6), 610–621 (1973)
4. Hotelling, H.: Analysis of a complex of statistical variables into principal components. J. Educ. Psych. **24**, 417 (1933)
5. Jaccard, P.: Étude comparative de la distribution florale dans une portion des alpes et des jura. Bulletin del la Société Vaudoise des Sciences Naturelles **37**, 547–579 (1901)
6. Jolliffe, I.: Principal Component Analysis. Springer, New York (2002). https://doi.org/10.1007/b98835
7. Kovacheva, V.N., Snead, D., Rajpoot, N.M.: A model of the spatial tumour heterogeneity in colorectal adenocarcinoma tissue. BMC Bioinform. **17**(1), 255 (2016)
8. Malm, P., Brun, A., Bengtsson, E.: Simulation of bright-field microscopy images depicting pap-smear specimen. Cytometry Part A **87**, 212–226 (2015)
9. Massey, F.J.: The Kolmogorov-Smirnov test for goodness of fit. J. Am. Stat. Assoc. **46**(253), 68–78 (1951)
10. Pearson, K.: LIII. On lines and planes of closest fit to systems of points in space. Lond. Edinb. Dublin Philos. Mag. J. Sci. **2**(11), 559–572 (1901)
11. Sorokin, D.V., Peterlík, I., Ulman, V., Svoboda, D., Maška, M.: Model-based generation of synthetic 3D time-lapse sequences of motile cells with growing filopodia. In: IEEE Internationl Symposium on Biomedical Imaging, pp. 822–826 (2017)
12. Sorokin, D.V., et al.: FiloGen: a model-based generator of synthetic 3D time-lapse sequences of single motile cells with growing and branching filopodia. IEEE Trans. Med. Imaging **37**(12), 2630–2641 (2018). https://doi.org/10.1109/TMI.2018.2845884

13. Svoboda, D., Ulman, V.: MitoGen: a framework for generating 3D synthetic time-lapse sequences of cell populations in fluorescence microscopy. IEEE Trans. Med. Imaging **36**(1), 310–321 (2017)
14. R Development Core Team: R: a language and environment for statistical computing. R Foundation for Statistical Computing (2010). http://www.r-project.org
15. Tesar, L., Smutek, D., Shimizu, A., Kobatake, H.: 3D extension of Haralick texture features for medical image analysis. In: Proceedings of the Fourth IASTED International Conference on Signal Processing, Pattern Recognition, and Applications, SPPRA 2007, pp. 350–355. ACTA Press, Anaheim (2007)
16. Ulman, V., Svoboda, D., Nykter, M., Kozubek, M., Ruusuvuori, P.: Virtual cell imaging: a review on simulation methods employed in image cytometry. Cytometry Part A **89**(12), 1057–1072 (2016)
17. Wilk, M.B., Gnanadesikan, R.: Probability plotting methods for the analysis for the analysis of data. Biometrika **55**(1), 1–17 (1968)

Instance Segmentation of Neural Cells

Jingru Yi[1](✉)(iD), Pengxiang Wu[1](iD), Menglin Jiang[1](iD), Daniel J. Hoeppner[2],
and Dimitris N. Metaxas[1]

[1] Department of Computer Science, Rutgers University, Piscataway, NJ 08854, USA
{jy486,pw241,menglin.jiang,dnm}@cs.rutgers.edu
[2] Astellas Research Institute of America, San Diego, CA 92121, USA
daniel.hoeppner@astellas.com

Abstract. Instance segmentation of neural cells plays an important role
in brain study. However, this task is challenging due to the special shapes
and behaviors of neural cells. Existing methods are not precise enough
to capture their tiny structures, e.g., filopodia and lamellipodia, which
are critical to the understanding of cell interaction and behavior. To this
end, we propose a novel deep multi-task learning model to jointly detect
and segment neural cells instance-wise. Our method is built upon SSD,
with ResNet101 as the backbone to achieve both high detection accuracy
and fast speed. Furthermore, unlike existing works which tend to produce
wavy and inaccurate boundaries, we embed a deconvolution module into
SSD to better capture details. Experiments on a dataset of neural cell
microscopic images show that our method is able to achieve better performance in terms of accuracy and efficiency, comparing favorably with
current state-of-the-art methods.

Keywords: Neural cell · Instance segmentation · Cell detection
Cell segmentation

1 Introduction

The cellular mechanism involved in the lineage path from a single neural stem
cell remains mysterious in neural science. With the aid of real-time microscopy
imaging system [15], the specification of neurons, astrocytes, and oligodendro-
cytes from a single neural stem cell could be recorded as a time-lapse video.
As an important tool to explore the interactions between the cells, neural cell
instance segmentation algorithm is in great desire since it locates and segments
the cells at the same time. In particular, a fast and accurate instance segmentation tool is crucial when we analyze large video datasets. However, neural cell
instance segmentation is a challenging problem due to various factors, such as
cell mitosis, cell distortion, cell adhesion, unclear cell contours and background
impurities. Besides, the tiny and slender structures such as filopodia and lamellipodia involved in cell movement render the problem even more difficult.

Recent years have witnessed a significant improvement in object detection and segmentation due to deep neural network (DNN) techniques

© Springer Nature Switzerland AG 2019
L. Leal-Taixé and S. Roth (Eds.): ECCV 2018 Workshops, LNCS 11134, pp. 395–402, 2019.
https://doi.org/10.1007/978-3-030-11024-6_29

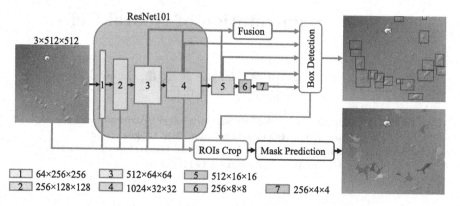

Fig. 1. Overview of our approach. The input image, which has the size of 640 × 512, is resized to 512 × 512 before being fed into the network. The feature maps are displayed as "number of channels × height × width". Block 1–4 are from Residual-101 [8], block 5–7 are the original convolutional blocks of SSD [13].

[9,10,14,19,21,22]. For example, region-based convolutional network (R-CNN) [5,6,18] was proposed to achieve accurate object detection and classification. To accelerate object detection, the one-stage detector YOLO [16], YOLO9000 [17], and SSD [13] were also proposed. These methods substantially outperform traditional methods [20] which are based on hand-crafted features and classifiers. In the semantic segmentation field, Long *et al.* [14] introduced a ground-breaking fully convolutional network (FCN) that achieves end-to-end, pixel-wise semantic segmentation. Ronneberger *et al.* [19] further extended FCN and proposed a U-Net architecture where successive deconvolutional layers with skip-connections are employed to produce more precise output. To combine both detection and segmentation, i.e., perform instance segmentation, Dai *et al.* [1] proposed a multi-task network cascades (MNC) model that predicts the object box, class, and mask simultaneously. As MNC is time-consuming in prediction, Li *et al.* [11] proposed fully convolutional instance-aware semantic segmentation (FCIS), which predicts the segmentation mask directly from a score map. He *et al.* [7] presented Mask R-CNN, which adds a mask prediction branch to FPN network [12]. However, these methods do not exploit the global context information, which has been proven to be very useful in visual classification tasks [14,19]. Consequently, they fail to accurately predict the fine details of neural cells, such as the filopodia and lamellipodia. Moreover, many of these methods suffer from slow prediction speed. Therefore, they are not suitable for analyzing large microscopic videos.

To overcome the above drawbacks, we propose a novel deep multi-task learning model for neural cell instance segmentation, which takes full advantage of global context information in both detection and segmentation. The overview of our approach is shown in Fig. 1. In particular, our model is based on SSD network [13]. Unlike original SSD, we employ ResNet101 [8] as the backbone instead of VGG network to increase the detection accuracy and speed. To further improve the detection accuracy for fine structures, we utilize a fusion strategy to propagate the context information from the high-level feature maps to the low-level ones. Thanks to the ability of our model to learn the global semantic context, our mask prediction is more precise than the state-of-the-art methods.

2   Methods

The framework of our neural cell instance segmentation approach is illustrated in Fig. 1. The input image is resized to 512×512 before being fed into the network. Note that the predicted boxes range from 0 to 1, and thus the shrinkage of the image does not affect the predictions. Our network jointly predicts the detection bounding box and the segmentation mask for each cell in the image. Below, we first introduce our cell detection module, and then present our cell segmentation module.

2.1   Neural Cell Detection

Our cell detection method builds upon SSD [4,13]. Unlike original SSD, we replace VGG [4,8] in SSD with ResNet101 network [8] to improve its cell detection accuracy, as ResNet101 is proved to have higher accuracy than VGG network [8]. Moreover, our experiments show that ResNet101-based SSD (0.1017 s) runs faster than VGG16-based SSD (0.1537 s). The network architecture is shown in Fig. 1. In order to detect cells of different sizes, our box detection module concatenates multi-scale feature maps, which are denoted by blocks 3–7 in Fig. 1. Each feature map is divided into a series of grids, and each grid has the size of 1×1. A grid works as an anchor box that centers in the grid and has a specific scale (i.e., width and height) and aspect ratio. These grids are referred to as default boxes in SSD [13]. As a shallow feature map has a smaller reception field than a deep feature map, the scale of a default box on a shallow feature map is smaller than that on a deep feature map. For example, the scale of a default box on a block 3 feature map is below 0.1, whereas the scale on a block 7 feature map could be as large as 0.75. Finally, following SSD [13], our cell detection module predicts the offsets between the default boxes and the cell bounding boxes with a 3×3 convolutional layer, and predicts the confidence score for each box with another 3×3 convolutional layer.

One drawback of SSD is that its shallow layers contain less semantic information than the deep layers. Consequently, although SSD predicts object locations using multi-scale feature maps, the shallow feature maps could not help detect small objects correctly. To solve this issue and improve our detection accuracy for small cells, we fuse the feature maps in blocks 3–5 and replace the original feature maps in block 3, so as to inject more semantic information to the shallow feature map (see Fig. 1). Specifically, we first use a single 1×1 convolutional layer to transform the feature maps from blocks 3–5 to have the same channel number 256. Then the transformed feature maps from blocks 4–5 are up-sampled to have the same size as the one from block 3 by bilinear interpolation. Finally,

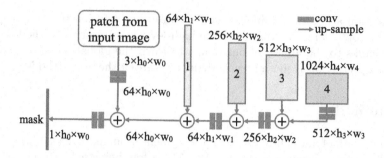

Fig. 2. Architecture of our mask prediction module. The feature maps are displayed as "number of channels × height × width". The convolutional layers are 3 × 3 with stride 1. Up-sample is bilinear interpolation.

the three transformed feature maps are concatenated together and expanded to have channel number 512 by a 1 × 1 convolutional layer.

The objective loss for cell detection is a weighted combination of localization loss and confidence loss:

$$L_{\text{det}} = \frac{1}{N_{\text{pos}}}(L_{\text{locs}} + \alpha L_{\text{conf}}), \tag{1}$$

where α is a weight factor, N_{pos} is the number of positive predicted boxes, L_{locs} is a smooth L_1 loss [6] of bounding-box regression offsets [5,13]:

$$L_{\text{locs}} = \sum_{i \in \text{pos}} \sum_{m \in \{cx,cy,w,h\}} \text{smooth}_{L_1}(l_i^m - g_i^m), \tag{2}$$

where $i \in \text{pos}$ denotes the set of positive predicted boxes, and l_i^m and g_i^m refer to the predicted and ground-truth offset boxes, respectively. $m \in \{cx, cy, w, h\}$ indicates the specific localization feature, such as center of the box (cx, cy), width of the box w, and height of the box h. L_{conf} is a binary cross entropy loss between the ground-truth confidence and the predicted box confidence:

$$L_{\text{conf}} = -\sum_i (x_i \log p_i + (1 - x_i) \log(1 - p_i)), \tag{3}$$

where x_i is the ground-truth confidence, and p_i is the predicted box confidence. Particularly, the ground-truth confidence of a default box will be set to 1 if the Jaccard index between this default box and the ground-truth box is greater than 0.5, otherwise the confidence will be set to 0.

2.2 Neural Cell Segmentation

As shown in Fig. 1, after obtaining the bounding box of a cell, we crop the cell box from the input image and feature maps in blocks 1–4, and pass them to our mask prediction module. The architecture of our mask prediction module is shown in

Fig. 2. Motivated by FCN [14] and U-Net [19], we combine the shallow layers with deep layers using a single addition operation. In this way, we propagate the context information from deep layers to shallow layers. To make sure two feature maps have the same size when applying the summation operation, we use bilinear interpolation to upsample the crops from deep layers. As the crops are tiny, we also utilize the patch from the input image to take advantage of its finer details. In this way, the details of the crops are reserved, which improves segmentation accuracy. The objective loss of our mask prediction module is a binary-cross entropy loss:

$$L_{\text{masks}} = -\frac{1}{N} \sum_{j}^{N} \sum_{i} (t_{ij} \log p_{ij} + (1 - t_{ij}) \log(1 - p_{ij})), \qquad (4)$$

where p_{ij} and t_{ij} are the predicted and ground-truth mask values at position i for the j-th positive predicted bounding box (whose overlap with the ground-truth box exceeds a certain threshold), respectively, and N is the total number of positive predicted bounding boxes.

3   Experiments

3.1   Experimental Settings

Our neural cell image dataset builds on a collection of time-lapse microscopic videos [15]. In particular, we sample 386 images from the videos for training, 129 for validation, and 129 for testing. The image size is 640×512. The ground-truth is labeled by experts. Our method is implemented with PyTorch. During the training process, the ResNet101 network is fine-tuned with the weights pre-trained on ImageNet [2], while other parts of the network are initialized with random weights sampled from a standard Gaussian distribution. To avoid overfitting, we employ data augmentation and early-stop strategy in training. To accelerate the training process, we first train the cell detector. Then we fix the weights of the detection network and train the segmentation network. Note that our model could also be trained in an end-to-end manner. We compare our method with the state-of-the-art instance segmentation algorithms, namely MNC [1], FCIS [11] and Mask R-CNN [7]. All the methods are tested on NVIDIA K40 GPUs.

Following conventions in existing works [1,11], we evaluate the instance segmentation accuracy using average precision (AP) [3] at intersection-over-union (IoU) thresholds of 0.5 and 0.7. In particular, we consider a cell instance segmentation result as a combination of a detection bounding box, a confidence score of the box, and a segmentation mask. During evaluation, all the bounding boxes are sorted by their confidence scores to make sure that boxes with high confidence scores are considered first. For each box, the IoU between its predicted mask and the ground-truth mask is calculated. The box will be considered as a true positive if the IoU score is greater than a threshold (e.g., 0.5 or 0.7), and

Table 1. Evaluation results of neural cell instance segmentation. Time is evaluated on a single NVIDIA K40 GPU.

Method	AP@0.5	AP@0.7	IoU@0.5	IoU@0.7	Time (sec)
MNC [1]	48.72	11.37	62.73	75.47	0.4750
FCIS [11]	66.02	7.13	64.85	75.07	0.2130
Mask R-CNN [7]	59.94	25.87	72.10	79.30	0.7486
Ours	**87.39**	**58.38**	**76.23**	**79.64**	**0.1920**

the corresponding cell is recorded as detected. On the contrary, any repetitive detection or its corresponding mask whose IoU is smaller than the threshold is considered as a false positive. Finally, the AP metric [3] summarizes the shape of the precision/recall curve and measures both instance detection and segmentation accuracy. In addition to AP at mask-IoU, we also measure the average mask IoU at thresholds of 0.5 and 0.7. The computational efficiency of all the methods is also measured according to their testing time.

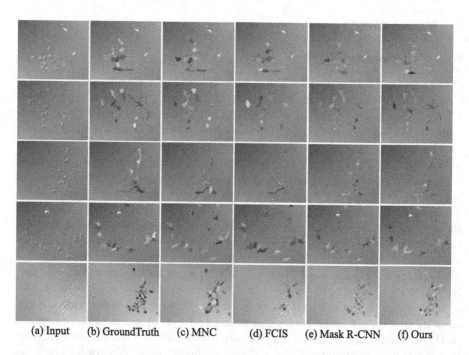

(a) Input   (b) GroundTruth   (c) MNC   (d) FCIS   (e) Mask R-CNN   (f) Ours

Fig. 3. Neural cell instance segmentation results of MNC [1], FCIS [11], Mask R-CNN [7] and our method. Compared to MNC, FCIS and Mask R-CNN, our method is more accurate and could capture the tiny and slender structures of neural cells, such as filopodia and lamellipodia.

3.2 Neural Cell Instance Segmentation Results

The evaluation results are summarized in Table 1, which indicates our model outperforms the state-of-the-art methods by a large margin. Several instance segmentation results are provided in Fig. 3 for qualitative evaluation. It can be observed from Fig. 3 that MNC and FCIS are not able to capture the slender and tiny filopodia and lamellipodia of cells. The mask boundaries predicted from FCIS are wavy. Moreover, for images that contain multiple small cells (e.g. the last row in Fig. 3), MNC could not distinguish the cells which are attached or very close to each other, and FCIS is weak in detecting these small cells. The coarse mask prediction and poor detection of smaller cells from MNC and FCIS explain their low AP at mask-IoU of 0.7 (see Table 1). Mask R-CNN is better at capturing tiny structures. However, it fails to capture the long and slender structures. Compared with the state-of-the-art methods, our model learns global semantic context information in both detection and segmentation, thereby exhibiting better performance in detecting small cells and capturing the tiny and slender structures of cells.

4 Conclusion

In this paper, we propose a novel method for neural cell instance segmentation. Compared with existing methods, our model could better detect small cells and capture their tiny and slender structures such as filopodia and lamellipodia. These properties indicate a great potential of our method in neural science research.

References

1. Dai, J., He, K., Sun, J.: Instance-aware semantic segmentation via multi-task network cascades. In: Proceedings of the IEEE CVPR, pp. 3150–3158 (2016)
2. Deng, J., Dong, W., Socher, R., Li, L.J., Li, K., Li, F.F.: ImageNet: a large-scale hierarchical image database. In: Proceedings of the IEEE CVPR, pp. 248–255 (2009)
3. Everingham, M., Van Gool, L., Williams, C.K.I., Winn, J., Zisserman, A.: The PASCAL visual object classes (VOC) challenge. IJCV 88(2), 303–338 (2010)
4. Fu, C.Y., Liu, W., Ranga, A., Tyagi, A., Berg, A.C.: DSSD: deconvolutional single shot detector. arXiv:1701.06659 (2017)
5. Girshick, R.B.: Fast R-CNN. In: Proceedings IEEE ICCV, pp. 1440–1448 (2015)
6. Girshick, R.B., Donahue, J., Darrell, T., Malik, J.: Rich feature hierarchies for accurate object detection and semantic segmentation. In: Proceedings IEEE CVPR, pp. 580–587 (2014)
7. He, K., Gkioxari, G., Dollár, P., Girshick, R.B.: Mask R-CNN. In: Proceedings IEEE ICCV, pp. 2980–2988 (2017)
8. He, K., Zhang, X., Ren, S., Sun, J.: Deep residual learning for image recognition. In: Proceedings IEEE CVPR, pp. 770–778 (2016)
9. Krizhevsky, A., Sutskever, I., Hinton, G.E.: ImageNet classification with deep convolutional neural networks. In: Proceedings NIPS, pp. 1097–1105 (2012)

10. LeCun, Y., Bottou, L., Bengio, Y., Haffner, P.: Gradient-based learning applied to document recognition. Proc. IEEE **86**(11), 2278–2324 (1998)
11. Li, Y., Qi, H., Dai, J., Ji, X., Wei, Y.: Fully convolutional instance-aware semantic segmentation. In: Proceedings IEEE CVPR, pp. 4438–4446 (2017)
12. Lin, T.Y., Dollár, P., Girshick, R.B., He, K., Hariharan, B., Belongie, S.J.: Feature pyramid networks for object detection. In: Proceedings IEEE CVPR, pp. 936–944 (2017)
13. Liu, W., et al.: SSD: single shot multibox detector. In: Leibe, B., Matas, J., Sebe, N., Welling, M. (eds.) ECCV 2016. LNCS, vol. 9905, pp. 21–37. Springer, Cham (2016). https://doi.org/10.1007/978-3-319-46448-0_2
14. Long, J., Shelhamer, E., Darrell, T.: Fully convolutional networks for semantic segmentation. In: Proceedings IEEE CVPR, pp. 3431–3440 (2015)
15. Ravin, R., et al.: Potency and fate specification in CNS stem cell populations in vitro. Cell Stem Cell **3**(6), 670–680 (2008)
16. Redmon, J., Divvala, S., Girshick, R.B., Farhadi, A.: You only look once: unified, real-time object detection. In: Proceedings IEEE CVPR, pp. 779–788 (2016)
17. Redmon, J., Farhadi, A.: YOLO9000: better, faster, stronger. In: Proceedings IEEE CVPR, pp. 6517–6525 (2017)
18. Ren, S., He, K., Girshick, R.B., Sun, J.: Faster R-CNN: towards real-time object detection with region proposal networks. In: Proceedings NIPS, pp. 91–99 (2015)
19. Ronneberger, O., Fischer, P., Brox, T.: U-Net: convolutional networks for biomedical image segmentation. In: Navab, N., Hornegger, J., Wells, W.M., Frangi, A.F. (eds.) MICCAI 2015. LNCS, vol. 9351, pp. 234–241. Springer, Cham (2015). https://doi.org/10.1007/978-3-319-24574-4_28
20. Wu, P., Yi, J., Zhao, G., Huang, Z., Qiu, B., Gao, D.: Active contour-based cell segmentation during freezing and its application in cryopreservation. IEEE TBME **62**(1), 284–295 (2015)
21. Yi, J., Wu, P., Hoeppner, D.J., Metaxas, D.N.: Fast neural cell detection using light-weight SSD neural network. In: Proceedings of the IEEE CVPR Workshop, pp. 860–864 (2017)
22. Yi, J., Wu, P., Hoeppner, D.J., Metaxas, D.N.: Pixel-wise neural cell instance segmentation. In: Proceedings IEEE ISBI, pp. 373–377 (2018)

Densely Connected Stacked U-network for Filament Segmentation in Microscopy Images

Yi Liu$^{(\boxtimes)}$, Wayne Treible, Abhishek Kolagunda, Alex Nedo, Philip Saponaro, Jeffrey Caplan, and Chandra Kambhamettu

University of Delaware, Newark, DE 19713, USA
{yliu,wtreible,abhi,aon,saponaro,jcaplan,chandrak}@udel.edu

Abstract. Segmenting filamentous structures in confocal microscopy images is important for analyzing and quantifying related biological processes. However, thin structures, especially in noisy imagery, are difficult to accurately segment. In this paper, we introduce a novel deep network architecture for filament segmentation in confocal microscopy images that improves upon the state-of-the-art U-net and SOAX methods. We also propose a strategy for data annotation, and create datasets for microtubule and actin filaments. Our experiments show that our proposed network outperforms state-of-the-art approaches and that our segmentation results are not only better in terms of accuracy, but also more suitable for biological analysis and understanding by reducing the number of falsely disconnected filaments in segmentation.

Keywords: Image segmentation · Filaments segmentation
Neural networks · Microscopy images

1 Introduction

Filamentous structures are ubiquitous among biological systems and can be imaged by confocal fluorescence microscopy. Segmentation of these filamentous structures is important for understanding the mechanism of their formations and behavior.

There have been several attempts at segmenting filament structures based on traditional image processing techniques [1,2,6,11,13,14]. Most of these traditional image processing approaches are based on photometric and geometric properties of filamentous structures. Because our aim is to study dynamic movements with high magnification microscopy, the images collected which contain higher levels of noise cause many traditional approaches to fail. Another common feature of these traditional methods is that appropriate parameter values need to be set accordingly to achieve a decent segmentation for different images [12,14]. Hence, these methods work well only for a small data set, as it is cumbersome to adjust parameters for every individual image.

© Springer Nature Switzerland AG 2019
L. Leal-Taixé and S. Roth (Eds.): ECCV 2018 Workshops, LNCS 11134, pp. 403–411, 2019.
https://doi.org/10.1007/978-3-030-11024-6_30

More recent approaches for general segmentation tasks are based on neural networks and have shown impressive performance for these types of tasks. Deep learning approaches have been applied to segment structures similar to filamentous structures [4,5,10]. Deep learning has been proven to work better than conventional image segmentation methods in the tasks mentioned above, but there is a limited number of works that segment filamentous structures in microscopy images. Though filamentous structures are similar to vesicular networks, retinal vessels, and cracks due to their piece-wise linear elements, the photometric and geometric properties of these structures vary significantly. Moreover, segmentation of filamentous structures in confocal microscopy images is complicated by optical blurring, noise, clutter, over exposure, and complex geometric properties such as overpass, convergence, and dense networks.

In this paper, we propose a new method utilizing a deep learning approach for automated segmentation of filamentous structures in microscopy images. Our work is built on U-net architecture [9], and we improve its performance for filament segmentation. Also, since there is no public data set for filament networks in microscopy images and it is time-consuming to annotate a large-scale data set for filamentous structures, we propose a semi-automatic annotation process based on a traditional segmentation method and a deep learning approach. By using this strategy, we create two data sets of microtubules and actin filaments.

The rest of this paper is organized as follows. Section 2 gives overview of work related to this paper. Section 3 details the process of data annotation, the architecture of network we proposed and training details. Section 4 describes our experiments, results and evaluations. Conclusions and future work will be given in Sect. 5.

2   Related Work

Filament Segmentation. There have been many works segmenting filamentous structures by using traditional methods like morphological approach [2], region-based approach [1,6] and curve fitting approaches [11,13,14]. To make segmentation more robust to noise, Yue *et al.* [15] applied morphological operation and diffusion filtering algorithm to make the segmentation more robust to excessive white noise. Xu *et al.* [13] proposed a method called regulated sequential evolution. Combined with Stretching Open Active Contours (SOACs), they achieved more robust segmentation results. Based on SOACs method, Xu *et al.* [14] developed a convenient software tool called SOAX to segment filamentous structures. SOAX provides an easy-to-use user interface and is popular among researchers to do quantification analysis of biopolymer networks. However, SOACs method is a time-consuming method due to iterations. Moreover, to increase accuracy, it is necessary to adjust parameters depending on the type of filament and quality of the image [14]. As parameters for different images are mainly chosen empirically, it is hard for researcher to perform large-scale quantitative analysis. With appropriate parameters, many false predictions can be caused by other cell structures, over exposure, artifacts of images and so on. To improve the efficiency and accuracy, we want to apply deep learning approaches to filament segmentation. Though SOAX is not efficient in dealing with huge volumes of data and lacking accuracy in segmentation, it can assist our data annotation process and we will present the details in Sect. 3.

Vessel-like Structure Segmentation. Applying deep learning approaches to filamentous structure segmentation is rare, but there have been works using deep learning methods to segment vessel-like structures. Saponaro et al. [10] adapted U-net architecture to segment vesicular networks of fungal hyphae in macroscopic microscopy images. Fu et al. [5] utilized fully convolutional neural networks and fully-connected Conditional Random Field (CRFs) for retinal vessel segmentation in fundus image. Fan et al. [4] proposed a method for pavement cracks detection based on a convolutional neural network. Since the U-net [9] works well on vessel-like structure segmentation in microscopy images [10], we adapted and improved U-net architecture to segment filamentous structures on our data sets.

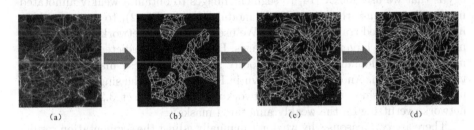

(a)   (b)   (c)   (d)

Fig. 1. An example of data annotation process. (a) Original image of mircrotubules. (b) SOAX Segmentation result (c) Segmentation result of U-net which is trained with SOAX segmentation result (d) Manually labeled ground truth based on U-net result

Neural Network Architecture. Ronneberger et al. [9] proposed U-net architecture which has achieved remarkable success in segmenting objects in biomedical microscopy images. This architecture is based on the idea of Fully-Convolutional Networks, and it contains contracting path to capture features and an expansion path to retrieve localization information. This architecture also applies overlap-tile strategy and allows the network training on relatively few training samples. Costa et al. [3] has applied this network to vessel segmentation in eye fundus images and it achieved a 0.9755 area under curve (AUC). This inspired us to apply this network on filamentous structures.

However, sometimes U-net creates small gaps where the hyphal networks are supposed to be continuous [10]. This can be caused by artifacts of the image or the U-net architecture itself. Newell et al. [8] introduce stacked hourglass networks for human pose estimation. This work has shown that repeatedly performing pooling and up-sampling with intermediate supervision can improve the performance of the network. To increase efficiency in a deep neural network, Huang et al. [7] introduces Dense Convolutional Network (DenseNet). In DenseNet, all layers with the same feature-map sizes are connected together in feed-forward fashion, which can encourage feature reuse, strengthen feature propagation and reduce the number of parameters [7]. Inspired by these works, our neural network architecture can take advantage from these networks to make our method more robust and avoid creating small gaps in filaments segmentation.

3   Method

Our goal is to create an efficient tool for filament segmentation in microscopy images. We utilize a semi-automatic scheme to annotate ground truth, and train our network on the data set.

3.1   Data Annotation

We propose a semi-automatic strategy to annotate filamentous structures in microscopy image to reduce the work of annotation. The main idea of this strategy is that we use SOAX [14] to segment images to obtain a weakly annotated mask. Then we use the single U-net module [9] (see Fig. 2), to train on these initially annotated training samples. We use this trained network to obtain segmentations for a larger amount of images. Based on the predicted segmentation masks, we ask domain experts to modify and correct these masks to finalize the ground truth. An example is shown in Fig. 1. We use the single U-net module instead of using our proposed network architecture (Sect. 3.2) to avoid the network overfitting on the weakly annotated masks.

There are two reasons why we don't manually adjust the segmentation results of SOAX directly. First, the average time to run SOAX on a whole image at an approximate resolution of 2k by 2k pixels takes approximately 6 hours on high-end workstations. More false positive segmentations will be created due to noisy areas in the microscopy images, which will increase the work of manual modification. Therefore, we crop one image to several sub-images and then run them through SOAX, as shown in Fig. 1 (b) and (e). Since U-net takes patches as input, we only create training patches where there are SOAX segmentations and use 128 by 128 patches for training. After training, we use U-net to obtain the initial segmentation results of the entire image. From our experiments, the predicted initial segmentation results from single U-net module are more accurate than results of SOAX. Many false positive segmentations made by SOAX are removed, as shown in Fig. 1 (b), (c), (f), and (g). The IoU of results from SOAX and the single U-net module are 0.6189 and 0.7919 respectively when compared to the manually labeled images.

In total, we took 24 microscopy images with size of $122.03 \times 132.84\,\mu m$ (1400×1524 pixels) and 17 slices in Z direction and obtained maximum intensity projection(MIP) on Z direction of these images. We cropped these 24 MIP images into 40 sub-images. By applying data augmentation strategy as in the work of Ronneberger et al. [9], we performed rigid transformation and γ correction on each valid patch and created 709800 training patches in total. We used these patches to train U-net and ran the trained network on 53 microscopy images including previous 24 images. In the end, domain experts manually checked and modified 53 full-resolution segmentation results, and each image took 10 to 25 min. We use 25 full-resolution images as the training set and 28 images as test set in all our experiments. We also create a data set for actin filaments with 10 microscopy images.

3.2   Network Description

In this paper, we build our network architecture based on U-net architecture [9], and we also adapted features of Stacked Hourglass Network [8]. Similar to U-net, we build up a module with contracting and expansion paths. Then we stack multiple modules end-to-end in a feed-forward fashion, which is similar to how Newell *et al.* [8] stack their hourglass network. The output of each module will be the input of next module. This allows the network repeatedly reevaluate previous prediction and features across all scales. The output of each U-net module will also go through a shared 1 × 1 convolutional layer to obtain a segmentation map. The loss function will take each intermediate output into consideration by assigning different weights to the loss values of the segmentation maps. This intermediate weighted supervision process can help each module optimize individually while attempting to improve upon the previous module's segmentation. To help the network maintain the residual information that exists at intermediary stages, we add cross-connections between layers with the same feature-map sizes.

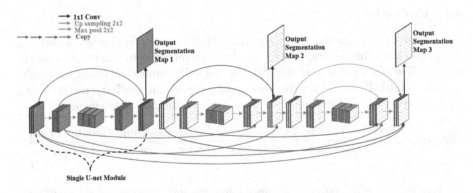

Fig. 2. An illustration of our proposed network.

The network architecture is shown in Fig. 2. It contains three modules, each module includes two max pooling steps and two up-sampling steps. At each step, it contains two 3 × 3 convolutional layers followed by a rectified linear unit and one drop out layer with rate 0.2 inserted between the two convolutional layers to facilitate network generalization. For the contracting paths, each step will be followed by a 2 × 2 max pooling operation, and the number of feature channels will be doubled. For expansion paths, 2×2 up-sampling operation will be applied after each step halving the number of feature channels, and a concatenation operation on feature-map with matching size from all previous contracting paths. To obtain a segmentation map for each module, their output is connected to a shared 1×1 convolutional layer.

3.3   Training and Testing

For the annotation process, we used a single module of our proposed network, and we train this model for 20 epochs with a batch size of 64. On the microtubule data set we created, we train our proposed network for 15 epochs with a batch size of 64. The size of input patches is 128×128, and the number of training patches is 5032407. For each module, the numbers of feature channels are 32, 64, 128 for corresponding stages. All networks are trained using Adam optimizer with a learning rate of 0.0001 and a dice coefficient loss. Dropout rates of all dropout layers are set to 0.2. Due to GPU memory constrains, we implemented a generator to generate data batch-by-batch and fit our model. For our proposed network, there are multiple outputs. We compile the model and assign a weight of 0.2, 0.3 and 0.5 for the loss of first, second, and third module output separately. All experiments are conducted on a laboratory server with two NVIDIA GeForce Titan X (Pascal) GPUs.

4   Experiments

4.1   Evaluation

For evaluation, the Intersection over Union (IoU) method is applied, which is a commonly used metric. IoU metric can be very sensitive to pixel wise segmentation. Considering that our test data is manually annotated based on results of U-net and IoU metric can be biased, we propose an auxiliary metric called Skeletonized IoU (SKIoU) modified from IoU and defined as following:

$$SKIoU = \frac{2 * Skeletonized\ Intersection\ of\ Prediction\ and\ Ground\ Truth}{Skeletonized\ Prediction + Skeletonized\ Ground\ Truth};$$
(1)

This metric will ignore small misalignments and thickness of microtubules, as curvatures and length is much more important for domain experts. SKIoU will be much less sensitive and can be a fair metric for different methods.

We used both metrics along with opinions from domain experts to compare segmentation results of different approaches.

4.2   Segmentation Results on Microtubules

We have run 6 experiments on microtubules and results are shown in Table 1, and examples of segmentations results are shown in Fig. 3.

Table 1. Segmentation results on microtubles with different approaches.

Model	Epochs	Loss weights	IoU	SKIoU
SOAX	15	–	0.6189	0.8833
U-net	15	–	0.9335	0.9746
U-net	30	–	0.9336	0.9747
Our network without cross-connection	5	0.20;0.30;0.50	0.9084	0.9650
Our network with cross-connection	5	0.20;0.30;0.50	0.9256	0.9723
Our network without cross-connection	15	0.20;0.30;0.50	0.9432	**0.9792**
Our network with cross-connection	15	0.20;0.30;0.50	**0.9439**	0.9775

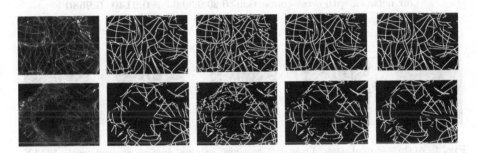

Fig. 3. Segmentation of microtubules. From left to right: original image, ground truth, SOAX, U-net module, proposed network with cross connection

All neural networks perform better than SOAX software with regards to IoU and SKIoU. Our proposed network achieves highest score in IoU, and the network without cross connections achieves highest score in SKIoU. In general, the SKIoUs of all networks are very close to each other and our proposed network is slightly higher than single U-net Module with respect to IoU metric.

As shown in Fig. 3, networks with multiple modules stacked together outperforms single U-net module. Segmented results of our proposed network contain less disconnected microtubules and fragments than U-net, which is crucial for future quantification analysis. For example, These fragments will be considered as single microtubules in the future analysis and influence the final quantification result.

We also train single U-net for 30 epochs. The result is almost the same with results of 15 training epochs, which indicates that U-net can be hardly improved by training more epochs. Cross connections can improve the efficiency of our network. Table 1 showed that after 5 epochs, network with cross connections learns better than the one without cross connections.

4.3 Segmentation Results on Actin Filament

The structure of actin filaments is more complicated and denser than that of microtubules. Instead of training our network with actin filaments data, we applied the network trained with microbules data on actin filaments dataset. From Table 2, though our network achieves the highest IoU and SKIoU score, difference of SKIoU is rather small. However, it can be seen in Fig. 4 that U-net creates more fragments and gaps.

Table 2. Segmentation results on actin filaments with different approaches.

Model	Loss weights	IoU	SKIoU
SOAX	–	0.6247	0.8946
U-net	–	0.8846	0.9469
Our network with cross-connection	0.20;0.30;0.50	**0.9140**	**0.9580**

Fig. 4. Actin segmentation. From left to right: original image, ground truth, SOAX, U-net, proposed network with cross connection

5   Conclusion and Perspectives

In this paper, we propose a new densely connected, stacked U-network architecture and also introduce a semi-automatic strategy to annotate filamentous structures. From our experiments, we show that the proposed deep network architecture not only achieves better accuracy but also produces segmentations that are more useful for biological analysis by reducing the number of falsely disconnected filaments and noise in segmentation than other state-of-the-art methods.

In the future, we will implement an application to quantify length, curvature and other information of filaments. Also, we will track the movement of filamentous structures over time, and by fusing the results of filaments and other structures like stromules, domain experts can better understand the formation and behavior of these structures.

Acknowledgements. The National Institute of Health R01 grant GM097587 supported this work. Microscopy access was supported by grants from the NIH (P20 GM103446 and S10 OD016361).

References

1. Almi'ani, M.M., Barkana, B.D.: A modified region growing based algorithm to vessel segmentation in magnetic resonance angiography (2015)
2. Chang, S., Kulikowski, C.A., Dunn, S.M., Levy, S.: Biomedical image skeletonization: a novel method applied to fibrin network structures (2001)
3. Costa, P., et al.: Towards adversarial retinal image synthesis. arXiv preprint arXiv:1701.08974 (2017)
4. Fan, Z., Wu, Y., Lu, J., Li, W.: Automatic pavement crack detection based on structured prediction with the convolutional neural network. arXiv preprint arXiv:1802.02208 (2018)
5. Fu, H., Xu, Y., Wong, D.W.K., Liu, J.: Retinal vessel segmentation via deep learning network and fully-connected conditional random fields. In: 2016 IEEE 13th International Symposium on Biomedical Imaging (ISBI), pp. 698–701. IEEE (2016)
6. Fuller, N., Aboudarham, J., Bentley, R.: Filament recognition and image cleaning on meudon hα spectroheliograms (2005)
7. Huang, G., Liu, Z., Weinberger, K.Q., van der Maaten, L.: Densely connected convolutional networks. In: Proceedings of the IEEE Conference on Computer Vision and Pattern Recognition, vol. 1, p. 3 (2017)
8. Newell, A., Yang, K., Deng, J.: Stacked hourglass networks for human pose estimation. In: Leibe, B., Matas, J., Sebe, N., Welling, M. (eds.) ECCV 2016. LNCS, vol. 9912, pp. 483–499. Springer, Cham (2016). https://doi.org/10.1007/978-3-319-46484-8_29
9. Ronneberger, O., Fischer, P., Brox, T.: U-Net: convolutional networks for biomedical image segmentation. In: Navab, N., Hornegger, J., Wells, W.M., Frangi, A.F. (eds.) MICCAI 2015. LNCS, vol. 9351, pp. 234–241. Springer, Cham (2015). https://doi.org/10.1007/978-3-319-24574-4_28
10. Saponaro, P., et al.: DeepXScope: segmenting microscopy images with a deep neural network. In: Proceedings of the IEEE Conference on Computer Vision and Pattern Recognition Workshops, pp. 91–98 (2017)
11. Smith, M.B., Li, H., Shen, T., Huang, X., Yusuf, E., Vavylonis, D.: Segmentation and tracking of cytoskeletal filaments using open active contours (2010)
12. Xiao, X., Geyer, V.F., Bowne-Anderson, H., Howard, J., Sbalzarini, I.F.: Automatic optimal filament segmentation with sub-pixel accuracy using generalized linear models and B-spline level-sets. Med. Image Anal. 32, 157–172 (2016)
13. Xu, T., Vavylonis, D., Huang, X.: 3D actin network centerline extraction with multiple active contours (2014)
14. Xu, T., et al.: SOAX: a software for quantification of 3D biopolymer networks. Sci. Rep. 5, 9081 (2015)
15. Yue, G., Jiang, L., Liu, C., Yang, G., Ai, J., Chen, X.: Automated segmentation of microtubules in Cryo-EM images with excessive white noise. In: Kim, K.J., Joukov, N. (eds.) Information Science and Applications (ICISA) 2016. LNEE, vol. 376, pp. 339–348. Springer, Singapore (2016). https://doi.org/10.1007/978-981-10-0557-2_34

Deep Convolutional Neural Networks Based Framework for Estimation of Stomata Density and Structure from Microscopic Images

Swati Bhugra[1](✉)(iD), Deepak Mishra[1](✉)(iD), Anupama Anupama[1](✉)(iD),
Santanu Chaudhury[1](✉)(iD), Brejesh Lall[1](✉)(iD), Archana Chugh[1](✉)(iD),
and Viswanathan Chinnusamy[2](✉)(iD)

[1] Indian Institute of Technology Delhi, New Delhi, India
{eez138301,eez138244,santanuc,brejesh}@ee.iitd.ac.in,
{blz138031,achugh}@bioschool.iitd.ac.in
[2] Indian Agricultural Research Institute, New Delhi, India
viswanathan@iari.res.in

Abstract. Analysis of stomata density and its configuration based on scanning electron microscopic (SEM) image of a leaf surface, is an effective way to characterize the plant's behaviour under various environmental stresses (drought, salinity etc.). Existing methods for phenotyping these stomatal traits are often based on manual or semi-automatic labeling and segmentation of SEM images. This is a low-throughput process when large number of SEM images is investigated for statistical analysis. To overcome this limitation, we propose a novel automated pipeline leveraging deep convolutional neural networks for stomata detection and its quantification. The proposed framework shows a superior performance in contrast to the existing stomata detection methods in terms of precision and recall, 0.91 and 0.89 respectively. Furthermore, the morphological traits (i.e. length & width) obtained at stomata quantification step shows a correlation of 0.95 and 0.91 with manually computed traits, resulting in an efficient and high-throughput solution for stomata phenotyping.

Keywords: High-throughput phenotyping
Deep convolutional neural networks · Stomata counting
Stomata quantification

1 Introduction

The study of cells, notably in shoots, based on scanning electron microscopic (SEM) images is important for understanding the plant functions [18]. This has

---

S. Bhugra and D. Mishra—Authors have contributed equally.

Electronic supplementary material The online version of this chapter (https://doi.org/10.1007/978-3-030-11024-6_31) contains supplementary material, which is available to authorized users.

© Springer Nature Switzerland AG 2019
L. Leal-Taixé and S. Roth (Eds.): ECCV 2018 Workshops, LNCS 11134, pp. 412–423, 2019.
https://doi.org/10.1007/978-3-030-11024-6_31

become a priority for the plant biology community, in order to increase the plants' yield and tolerance to various environmental stresses (drought, salinity etc.). In particular, the analysis of stomatal morphology and its density (termed as stomata phenotyping) is critical for breeding high yield cultivars [18], since it plays a key role in regulating the temperature of the plants through gas exchange between the atmosphere and leaf surface [30]. However, despite the advances in microscopy, the statistical data that is required for breeding a more significantly yielding plant cultivar is currently a bottleneck for biologists [15]. This is due to the fact, that they mainly rely on manual or semi-automatic approaches to compute the stomatal phenotypic traits. For example, authors in [18,30] manually counted the stomata and visually scored the degree of stomatal opening. On the other hand, ImageJ [22], an open source software with user interactive functionalities has been employed in [4,5]. However, these methods are susceptible to intra-rater or inter-rater repeatability resulting in low accuracy and reproducibility [16]. Thus, an automated tool is required for an efficient and high-throughput analysis of stomatal phenotypic traits.

Very few methods have been published to automate this process over the past decades. Authors in [11] proposed a framework using template matching to detect stomata, this is followed by binarization for extracting stomatal aperture. In [21], the authors employed maximum stable external regions (MSER) for simultaneous detection and quantification of grapevine stomata. In contrast to these image processing methods for estimating stomatal density, [26] adopted a machine learning approach utilizing a cascade object detector (COD) based on haar-like features in oak species. Similarly, Jayakody et al. [9] employed histogram of oriented gradients (HOG) features in contrast to haar-like features, so as to reduce the training time of the COD for detecting grapevine stomata and used binarization for segmenting the stomatal aperture. However, these approaches are proposed for detecting stomata in SEM images with homogeneous background. Thus, they are not suitable for the investigated images with feature rich background. Also, the stomata segmentation is limited by binarization [9,11] due to (a) low contrast between the background and stomatal aperture and (b) varying degree of aperture's occlusion in the presence of papillae (for sample image, see Fig. 1).

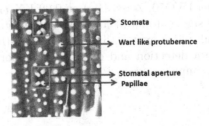

Fig. 1. A high resolution patch from sample SEM image.

In the past few years, deep convolutional neural networks (CNNs) have shown promising results on various computer vision tasks [7,10,13,19]. Thus, in order to overcome the aforementioned challenges, we propose a novel deep learning framework for automatic stomata detection and its quantification. In the first step, a single shot multibox detector (SSD) is employed to deal with (a) different stomata configurations, and (b) feature rich background with abundance of similar non-stomata objects in the SEM image. The second step involves the extraction of stomatal aperture (segmentation) from the detected stomata. However, this segmentation task is eclipsed by the small size of stomata in the investigated SEM data. Thus, super-resolution convolutional neural network (SRCNN) [3] scheme is applied with detected stomata as an input prior to the segmentation step. This is done to enhance the visualization of small stomatal structures. Although authors in [11,20] proposed watershed and threshold based segmentation for extracting the stomatal aperture, these algorithms are not suitable for the investigated images due to the (a) low contrast between background and stomatal aperture and (b) papillae occlusion. These problems are solved by utilizing a deep learning framework [2] based on fully convolutional neural network (FCNN) [14]. The authors in [2] presented a framework for high resolution SEM images containing only a single stomata. In contrast, our automated pipeline handles a more challenging image data-set containing multiple stomata, with no prior information about the stomata parameters (count, shape and size) thus facilitating high-throughput stomata analysis.

The rest of the paper is organized as follows: In Sect. 2 the experiment protocol for data acquisition is elucidated, the proposed methodology is explained in Sect. 3, results are discussed in Sects. 4 and 5 concludes the paper.

2   Dataset

Drought experiment is conducted on different rice cultivars during the kharif season at the phenomics facility (Indian Agricultural Research Institute). The investigated cultivars are divided into three groups of differing irrigation intensities i.e. well-watered, reduced watered and unwatered. The leaf samples of these cultivars are collected at different drought stages and immediately fixed by liquid nitrogen. Images (1024 × 768) of the leaf surface are taken with a scanning electron microscope (model EVO50, Zeiss, UK) at 9.00 KX magnification (termed as Data-1, containing single stomata) and 1.00 KX magnification (termed as Data-2, containing multiple stomata) to develop a high-throughput phenotyping pipeline for stomata detection and quantification (for sample image from Data-1 and Data-2, see supplementary Fig. 2).

3   Methodology

In this section, we introduce the proposed framework (workflow shown in Fig. 2). The method consists of a detection stage for computing the stomatal density and a segmentation stage for computing its morphological traits.

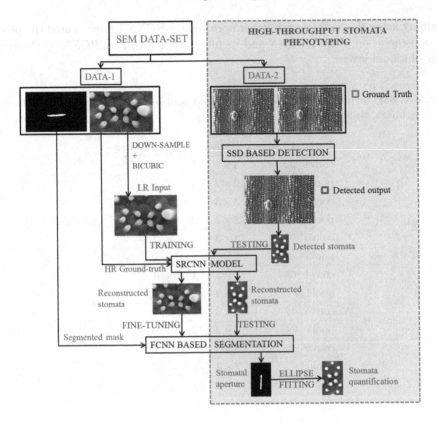

Fig. 2. Workflow of the proposed framework.

3.1 Stomata Counting

Stomata density is estimated by counting the stomata on a SEM image of a given leaf surface [26]. A number of methods have been proposed in literature [29] to predict the count of objects in an image based on regressors trained with its global features. A global regressor ignores the spatial information, thus a pixel-level object density map regression was proposed in [12]. However, these methods cannot easily provide locations of the objects which is essential for subsequent stomata quantification. Thus, the task of stomata counting is implemented based on detection and localization of individual stomata.

In recent years, counting object by detection benefits from the superior performance of CNN. Region-based convolutional neural networks (R-CNN) [7] is the first deep learning approach improving the detection accuracy based on object proposal algorithm [7] and learning the features for these proposal region using a CNN. Later, Spatial pyramid pooling in deep convolutional networks (SPPnet) [8] was introduced to speed up the detection of R-CNN by introducing a spatial pyramid pooling (SPP) layer, which shares features between proposals. This was further improved by Fast-RCNN [6] which proposed an end to end training using the SPP layer. Furthermore, Faster-RCNN [19] presented the proposal generation based on CNN and its integration with Fast-RCNN by sharing convolutional layers.

Table 1. SSD architecture. The names conv and pool represent the convolutional and pooling layers, respectively.

Layer	Channels	Kernel	Stride	Padding
conv1	32	5×5	1	2
pool1	-	2×2	2	0
conv2	48	3×3	1	1
pool2	-	2×2	2	0
conv3	64	3×3	1	1
pool3	-	2×2	2	0
conv4	64	3×3	1	1
pool4	-	2×2	2	0
conv5	48	3×3	1	1
pool5	-	2×2	2	0
conv6	48	3×3	1	1
pool6	-	2×2	2	0
conv7	32	3×3	1	1

In contrast to the previously mentioned proposal based methods, single shot multibox detector (SSD) [13] is a state-of-the-art detector which looks for objects in a set of default boxes over different feature levels and scales. It is free from proposal generation, subsequent feature sampling and classification. Thus, SSD is a suitable choice for the current objective of high-throughput stomata detection. However, unlike the complex images with multiple instances of different objects, which were considered in the original work [13], the leaf microscopic images (in this work) are utilized only for stomata detection. The remaining leaf region is considered as background, thus a shallow version of SSD (architecture shown in Table 1) is employed. Each convolutional (conv) layer is followed by batch normalization and exponential linear units. Boxes of aspect ratios 0.5, 1.0 and 2.0 are generated from the outputs of the conv4 to conv7 layers at different scales varying from 0.08 to 0.96. The model is trained to detect stomata in these boxes using Adam optimizer with initial learning rate of 0.0001 and a decay factor of 10^{-4}. SSD is trained for 100 epochs with batch size of 16 and L_2 regularization of weights with 0.0005 decay factor. Bounding box annotations of stomata corresponding to SEM images (Data-2) are manually generated with the help of two expert biologists to obtain the ground truth labels. Since, the investigated SEM images are high resolution (1024×768) comprising of small-scale stomata, downsampling will lead to loss of discriminative details. Thus, to overcome the limitation of computational cost associated with the CNNs, high resolution patches of size 256×256 with 75% overlap are sampled from these images. 2000 images with the corresponding bounding box annotations are utilized for training and 440 are used for validation. The weights corresponding to the minimum validation loss are used for testing. Detected stomata is then individually utilized for computation of its morphological features, explained in the next sub-section.

3.2 Stomata Segmentation

Stomata are pores on the leaf surface that controls the transpiration of plants through opening and closing of its aperture [18]. Thus, it is important to accurately compute the stomatal opening. However, the accuracy of its quantification depends on the aperture segmentation step. Threshold based segmentation employed in [9,11,17] and watershed segmentation in [20] are proposed for images containing stomata with contrast homogeneous background and no papillae occlusion. Thus, these proposed algorithms are not suitable for the investigated images. Authors in [2] presented a solution to overcome these challenges inspired from FCNN [14]. However, the direct application of this framework is not suitable, since the investigated images comprises of small size stomata. Thus, prior to the segmentation step, the detected stomata from the SSD model are super-resolved.

Although, nearest neighbor, bilinear, and bicubic interpolations are conventional methods to generate a high-resolution image, these methods produce oversmoothed images with artifacts such as aliasing and blur around the edges [24]. Example-based super-resolution methods proposed in [25,28] that learn the relationship between low-resolution and high-resolution image pairs, yield higher image quality over these linear interpolation methods. But the computation time of the example based methods is not suitable for this high-throughput stomata phenotyping task. In contrast, super-resolution convolutional neural network (SRCNN) [3] directly learn an end-to-end mapping between the low resolution image and the high-resolution image thus, SRCNN is utilized.

SRCNN [23] consists of three convolutional layer for patch extraction and representation, non-linear mapping and reconstruction. The first layer uses 9×9 kernel size with 64 feature maps to extract compact representation of the LR image. This is followed by a second layer consisting of 32 feature maps with 5×5 kernel size, that maps LR feature maps into HR feature maps. The last layer with 5×5 kernel size is used for HR image reconstruction. Since, the HR images corresponding to Data-2 are unavailable (acquired at 1.00 KX magnification), Data-1 employed by authors [2] in the segmentation network (termed here as HR images) is utilized for training the SRCNN. The HR images are downscaled to 64×102 and then upscaled to 160×256 using bicubic interpolation (termed LR) as input and the corresponding HR as output. Down-scale of 64×102 is chosen, since in the investigated images (Data-2), this patch size is found to be sufficient to contain individual stomata. A total of 90 and 39 images are used as training and validation dataset respectively and an Adam optimiser to minimise the mean square error loss with 10^{-4} learning rate.

The next step is the extraction of stomatal aperture using the framework presented in [2]. The authors trained the network on Data-1 (HR images), thus for its application on the investigated images, it is fine-tuned using the SRCNN output. In total, 117 HR images and the corresponding masks (available from [2]) are used for this purpose. Images are first down-sampled (64×102) and then super-resolved to 160×256 (using the trained SRCNN) to obtain the desired data. This dataset is divided into training and validation sets containing 78 and 39 images, respectively. Training set images are augmented using random translation, rotation, flipping and zooming which results in 960 samples. Network is initialized with the weights used in [2] which are fine tuned using an Adam optimizer. An initial learning rate of 10^{-6} with decay factor of 10^{-8} and weighted binary cross-entropy loss is used during training. The network is trained for 500 epochs with a batch-size of 20.

At the test time, the patches of size 64×102 extracted at each detected stomata location (Data-2) obtained from the SSD network is super-resolved using the aforementioned trained SRCNN model. The binary mask corresponding to the stomatal aperture using this resolved image is extracted by utilizing the fine-tuned segmentation network. Since stomata exhibit an approximate elliptical shape [20], ellipse fitting [27] is then used on this segmented mask to compute its primary morphological features: (1) major-axis (l), (2) minor-axis (w), (3) area and (4) the ratio of width and length (w/l).

4   Results

In this section, we evaluate the performance of the proposed framework in terms of stomata density and its quantification (Table 2).

Table 2. Stomata detection results.

Method	Precision	Recall
Interactive spatial density detection	0.70	0.85
MSER	0.18	0.10
Template Matching	0.19	0.15
HOG based COD	0.35	0.30
SSD model with NMS	**0.91**	**0.89**

The detection step of the proposed framework is compared with Liu's MSER, Laga's template matching approach and Jayakody's HOG based COD (shown in Table 1) in terms of precision (P) and recall (R) given by: $P = TP/(TP+FP)$ & $R = TP/(TP+FN)$ (where, TP is true positive, FP is false positive and FN is false negative, calculated using 0.80 Intersection over Union (IoU) between the predicted and ground truth bounding boxes) on 93 stomata test data. Figure 3 shows the results from the existing stomata detection approaches on a cropped section of the investigated image (due to limited space, the results on the original image is shown in supplementary Fig. 4). MSER algorithm assumes that the object of interest are brighter than their boundaries and there exists some optimal threshold at which individual object can be segmented. However, due to the presence of wart like protuberance and papillae with higher grayscale intensity than the stomatal aperture, this results in the detection of background objects (high FP and FN, shown in Fig. 3(a)). For the extraction of stomatal aperture, the detected regions obtained from MSER algorithm are further filtered based on eccentricity, since they exhibit elliptical shape (shown in supplementary Fig. 5(b)). The template matching approach requires manual selection of both the threshold and templates. We utilized 50 stomata templates, but due to the feature rich background, large number of false positives are generated (Fig. 3(b)). Recent work that utilizes HOG based COD [9], performs better than the previously mentioned image based algorithms. Although, HOG works well in representing the shape of an object, it is also limited by the occlusion of the stomata due to the presence of papillae and the varying level of deformation (closing) of stomata under the drought experiment (Fig. 3(c)). Figure 3(d) shows the stomata detection based on SSD model. Since, overlapping patch based detection approach is employed, multiple bounding boxes for each detected stomata is obtained. To eliminate this redundant counting, non-maximum suppression (NMS) is then utilised for an accurate computation of stomatal density (Fig. 3(e)).

We also compare the detection results with pixel level object density regression method, presented in [1]. Arteta et al. [1] proposed an interactive counting algorithm that predicts the spatial density map based on pixel level ridge-regression with dot annotation as user input and also provide candidate regions containing the objects of interest for iterative user annotation. Figure 4(a) shows the predicted density map and Fig. 4(b) shows the candidate regions containing stomata after the third iteration (the numbers mentioned along these detected regions denotes the total stomata count). Due to the presence of wart like protuberances in the SEM images that look similar to the papillae arrangement around the stomatal aperture, the total stomata count is overestimated in few detected regions. In contrast, to the existing methods, the proposed framework performs considerably better and achieves high recall and precision without any manual intervention (supplementary Fig. 4(d–e)).

The windows detected as stomata from the SSD model after NMS, is segmented to extract the stomata aperture for computing its morphological traits. Threshold based segmentation proposed by [9,11,17] for this purpose leads to the segmentation of papillae and wart like protuberance as they exhibit higher grayscale intensity w.r.t. background than stomata. In addition to this low contrast, the accuracy of the watershed segmentation is also limited by the aperture occlusion (results shown in supplementary Fig. 6). Thus, the deep learning framework presented by authors in [2] is employed. Since, the framework was trained

420   S. Bhugra et al.

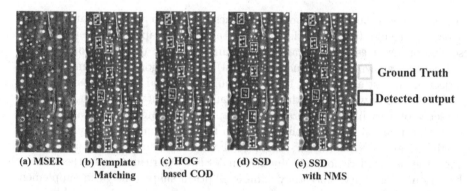

Ground Truth

Detected output

(a) MSER   (b) Template   (c) HOG   (d) SSD   (e) SSD
            Matching   based COD   with NMS

Fig. 3. Stomata detection based on (a) MSER (b) Template Matching (c) HOG based COD (d) SSD model and (e) SSD model with NMS.

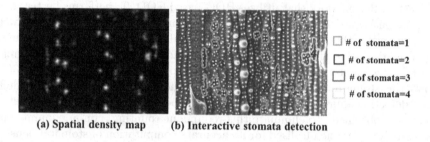

□ # of stomata=1
□ # of stomata=2
□ # of stomata=3
  # of stomata=4

(a) Spatial density map   (b) Interactive stomata detection

Fig. 4. Interactive stomata counting.

on HR dataset collected at 9.00 KX magnification, the detected stomata are super-resolved using SRCNN model (details mentioned in Sect. 3.2). The model is trained using Data-1 and MSE of .0072 is obtained after 2000 epochs (sample output shown in Fig. 5).

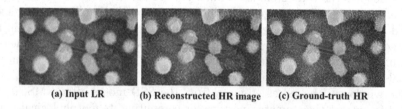

(a) Input LR   (b) Reconstructed HR image   (c) Ground-truth HR

Fig. 5. An example of the reconstructed high-resolution image (magnification of ×2.5): (a) Low-resolution image, (b) reconstructed output based on SRCNN scheme and (c) original test image.

We hypothesize that this model is qualitatively sufficient as a pre-processing step for subsequent stomatal aperture segmentation and quantitatively evaluate the accuracy of the segmented mask (results shown in supplementary Figs. 7 and 8) in terms of IoU. The mean IoU with the ground truth is computed to be 0.8602 on 50 test images. The primary morphological features (length and width) is computed by ellipse fitting on the generated segmented mask (supplementary Figs. 7(d) and 8(d)). These computed features are compared with the corresponding ground truth features, collected by an expert biologist using ImageJ. The major-axis (corresponding to the length of stomata) and minor-axis (corresponding to the width of stomata) of the ellipse shows a correlation of 0.95 (result shown in supplementary Fig. 9) and 0.91 respectively using 50 detected stomata.

The proposed approach is fully automatic and computationally efficient, that enabled high-throughput phenotyping (Fig. 6) in drought stress environment. This shows the potential of our framework to be employed in other biotic and abiotic stress experiments (salt, SO_2 etc.) based on stomatal responses.

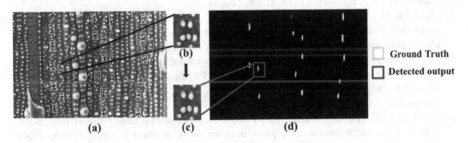

Fig. 6. High throughput stomata phenotyping (a) SSD with NMS (b) LR stomata (input to SRCNN) (c) HR stomata (SRCNN output) and (d) Ellipse fitting on segmented output.

5   Conclusion

In this paper, we presented a novel deep learning framework for automated stomata phenotyping. The framework comprises of SSD based detection, SRCNN for super-resolving small detected stomata followed by its segmentation, based on Fully Convolutional Neural Network. We have shown that our method performs better on a challenging data-set, that includes varying degrees of stomatal occlusion, dynamic feature rich background and small size of stomata, compared with existing approaches. This shows its potential application in various biotic and abiotic stress studies. We plan to apply this framework on SEM images from other cultivars.

Acknowledgments. This work is supported by National Agricultural Science Fund (NASF) under Indian Council of Agricultural Research (ICAR), Delhi, India [Phenomics of moisture deficit stress tolerance and nitrogen use efficiency in rice and wheat-Phase II]. The authors are thankful to the Department of Textile Technology, Indian Institute of Technology Delhi (IIT Delhi) for the SEM facility.

References

1. Arteta, C., Lempitsky, V., Noble, J.A., Zisserman, A.: Interactive object counting. In: Fleet, D., Pajdla, T., Schiele, B., Tuytelaars, T. (eds.) ECCV 2014. LNCS, vol. 8691, pp. 504–518. Springer, Cham (2014). https://doi.org/10.1007/978-3-319-10578-9_33

2. Bhugra, S., Mishra, D., Anupama, A., Chaudhury, S., Lall, B., Chugh, A.: Automatic quantification of stomata for high-throughput plant phenotyping (2018). (Accepted at ICPR18)

3. Dong, C., Loy, C.C., He, K., Tang, X.: Image super-resolution using deep convolutional networks. IEEE Trans. Pattern Anal. Mach. Intell. **38**(2), 295–307 (2016)

4. Dow, G.J., Bergmann, D.C., Berry, J.A.: An integrated model of stomatal development and leaf physiology. New Phytol. **201**(4), 1218–1226 (2014)

5. Eisele, J.F., Fäßler, F., Bürgel, P.F., Chaban, C.: A rapid and simple method for microscopy-based stomata analyses. PloS One **11**(10), e0164576 (2016)

6. Girshick, R.: Fast R-CNN. In: 2015 IEEE International Conference on Computer Vision (ICCV), pp. 1440–1448. IEEE (2015)

7. Girshick, R., Donahue, J., Darrell, T., Malik, J.: Rich feature hierarchies for accurate object detection and semantic segmentation. In: Proceedings of the IEEE Conference on Computer Vision and Pattern Recognition, pp. 580–587 (2014)

8. He, K., Zhang, X., Ren, S., Sun, J.: Spatial pyramid pooling in deep convolutional networks for visual recognition. In: Fleet, D., Pajdla, T., Schiele, B., Tuytelaars, T. (eds.) ECCV 2014. LNCS, vol. 8691, pp. 346–361. Springer, Cham (2014). https://doi.org/10.1007/978-3-319-10578-9_23

9. Jayakody, H., Liu, S., Whitty, M., Petrie, P.: Microscope image based fully automated stomata detection and pore measurement method for grapevines. Plant Methods **13**(1), 94 (2017)

10. Krizhevsky, A., Sutskever, I., Hinton, G.E.: Imagenet classification with deep convolutional neural networks. In: Advances in Neural Information Processing Systems, pp. 1097–1105 (2012)

11. Laga, H., Shahinnia, F., Fleury, D.: Image-based plant stomata phenotyping. In: 2014 13th International Conference on Control Automation Robotics & Vision (ICARCV), pp. 217–222. IEEE (2014)

12. Lempitsky, V., Zisserman, A.: Learning to count objects in images. In: Advances in Neural Information Processing Systems, pp. 1324–1332 (2010)

13. Liu, W., et al.: SSD: single shot multibox detector. In: Leibe, B., Matas, J., Sebe, N., Welling, M. (eds.) ECCV 2016. LNCS, vol. 9905, pp. 21–37. Springer, Cham (2016). https://doi.org/10.1007/978-3-319-46448-0_2

14. Long, J., Shelhamer, E., Darrell, T.: Fully convolutional networks for semantic segmentation. In: Proceedings of the IEEE Conference on Computer Vision and Pattern Recognition, pp. 3431–3440 (2015)

15. Minervini, M., Scharr, H., Tsaftaris, S.A.: Image analysis: the new bottleneck in plant phenotyping [applications corner]. IEEE Sig. Process. Mag. **32**(4), 126–131 (2015)

16. Nutter Jr., F., Gleason, M., Jenco, J., Christians, N.: Assessing the accuracy, intrarater repeatability, and inter-rater reliability of disease assessment systems. Phytopathology **83**(8), 806–812 (1993)

17. Omasa, K., Onoe, M.: Measurement of stomatal aperture by digital image processing. Plant Cell Physiol. **25**(8), 1379–1388 (1984)

18. Rao, Y., et al.: EARLY senescence 1 encodes a SCAR-LIKE PROTEIN2 that affects water loss in rice. Plant Physiol. 00991 (2015)
19. Ren, S., He, K., Girshick, R., Sun, J.: Faster R-CNN: towards real-time object detection with region proposal networks. In: Advances in Neural Information Processing Systems, pp. 91–99 (2015)
20. Sanyal, P., Bhattacharya, U., Bandyopadhyay, S.K.: Analysis of SEM images of stomata of different tomato cultivars based on morphological features. In: 2008 Second Asia International Conference on Modeling & Simulation, AICMS 08, pp. 890–894. IEEE (2008)
21. Scarlett, L., Tang, J., Petrie, P., Whitty, M.: A fast method to measure stomatal aperture by MSER on smart mobile phone. In: Applied Industrial Optics: Spectroscopy, Imaging and Metrology, pp. AIW2B-2. Optical Society of America (2016)
22. Schneider, C.A., Rasband, W.S., Eliceiri, K.W.: Nih image to imageJ: 25 years of image analysis. Nature Methods 9(7), 671 (2012)
23. Sharma, M., Chaudhury, S., Lall, B.: Deep learning based frameworks for image super-resolution and noise-resilient super-resolution. In: 2017 International Joint Conference on Neural Networks (IJCNN), pp. 744–751. IEEE (2017)
24. Siu, W.C., Hung, K.W.: Review of image interpolation and super-resolution. In: Signal & Information Processing Association Annual Summit and Conference (APSIPA ASC), 2012 Asia-Pacific, pp. 1–10. IEEE (2012)
25. Timofte, R., De Smet, V., Van Gool, L.: Anchored neighborhood regression for fast example-based super-resolution. In: Proceedings of the IEEE International Conference on Computer Vision, pp. 1920–1927 (2013)
26. Vialet-Chabrand, S., Brendel, O.: Automatic measurement of stomatal density from microphotographs. Trees 28(6), 1859–1865 (2014)
27. Xie, Y., Ji, Q.: A new efficient ellipse detection method. In: 2002 Proceedings of 16th International Conference on Pattern Recognition, vol. 2, pp. 957–960. IEEE (2002)
28. Yang, J., Wright, J., Huang, T.S., Ma, Y.: Image super-resolution via sparse representation. IEEE Trans. Image Process. 19(11), 2861–2873 (2010)
29. Zhang, C., Li, H., Wang, X., Yang, X.: Cross-scene crowd counting via deep convolutional neural networks. In: 2015 IEEE Conference on Computer Vision and Pattern Recognition (CVPR), pp. 833–841. IEEE (2015)
30. Zhang, H., Niu, X., Liu, J., Xiao, F., Cao, S., Liu, Y.: RNAi-directed downregulation of vacuolar h+-ATPase subunit a results in enhanced stomatal aperture and density in rice. PloS One 8(7), e69046 (2013)

A Fast and Scalable Pipeline for Stain Normalization of Whole-Slide Images in Histopathology

Milos Stanisavljevic[1]($\boxtimes$), Andreea Anghel[1], Nikolaos Papandreou[1],
Sonali Andani[1], Pushpak Pati[1], Jan Hendrik Rüschoff[2], Peter Wild[3],
Maria Gabrani[1], and Haralampos Pozidis[1]

[1] IBM Research – Zurich, 8803 Rüschlikon, Switzerland
{ysm,aan,npo,sop,pus,mga,hap}@zurich.ibm.com
[2] Senckenberg Institute of Pathology, Universitätsklinikum Frankfurt,
60590 Frankfurt am Main, Germany
JanHendrik.Rueschoff@usz.ch
[3] Institute of Pathology and Molecular Pathology,
UniversitätsSpital Zürich, 8091 Zürich, Switzerland
Peter.Wild@kgu.de

Abstract. Stain normalization is one of the main tasks in the processing pipeline of computer-aided diagnosis systems in modern digital pathology. Some of the challenges in this tasks are memory and runtime bottlenecks associated with large image datasets. In this work, we present a scalable and fast pipeline for stain normalization using a state-of-the-art unsupervised method based on stain-vector estimation. The proposed system supports single-node and distributed implementations. Based on a highly-optimized engine, our architecture enables high-speed and large-scale processing of high-magnification whole-slide images (WSI). We demonstrate the performance of the system using measurements from different datasets. Moreover, by using a novel pixel-sampling optimization we show lower processing time per image than the scanning time of ultrafast WSI scanners with the single-node implementation and additional 3.44 average speed-up with the 4-nodes distributed pipeline.

Keywords: Histopathological image processing · Whole-slide images
Stain normalization · Distributed computing · Color deconvolution

1 Introduction

In digital pathology, computer-aided diagnosis (CAD) has become an essential part of the clinical work with the advent of high-resolution whole-slide imaging technology. The fusion of machine learning (ML) based image analysis algorithms, and digitized histological slides are assisting the pathologists in terms of workload reduction, efficient decision support [10,23] and interpretability of the results [21]. Given the vast amount of gigapixel-sized whole-slide imaging data,

© Springer Nature Switzerland AG 2019
L. Leal-Taixé and S. Roth (Eds.): ECCV 2018 Workshops, LNCS 11134, pp. 424–436, 2019.
https://doi.org/10.1007/978-3-030-11024-6_32

and the need to accelerate the time-to-insight, there is an increasing demand to build automated and scalable pipelines for large-scale and fast image analysis.

Color normalization of stained tissue samples is one of the main preprocessing steps in whole-slide image (WSI) processing [24]. Despite the standardized staining protocols, variations in the staining results are very frequent due to differences in the staining parameters, e.g. antigen concentration and incubation time and temperature, different conditions between slide scanners, etc. [21]. Such color/intensity variations can adversely affect the performance and accuracy of the CAD systems. Therefore, stain normalization techniques have been proposed to generate images with a standardized appearance of the different stains [1,2,7–9,11,15,17].

In this work, we use the Macenko method [11] to implement a high-performance stain normalization system. The algorithm does not involve intermediate steps that require training of model parameters and is thus computationally less expensive. Our stain normalization system is based on an optimized multi-core implementation of the singular-value decomposition-based method (SVD) in [11]. In addition, to support the processing of high-magnification images, where the size of the image may not fit in the CPU memory (e.g., a 40X magnification WSI of 160 k × 80 k pixels corresponds to 37.5 GB of data in RGB), we devise an iterative multi-batch implementation. Furthermore, we design 2 system flavors: single-node and distributed multi-node versions. The latter offers a scalable solution that enables large-scale and high-speed processing of high-resolution WSIs using a cluster of nodes with multi-core CPUs. Finally, our implementation supports multiple image formats (e.g., .svs, .tiff, .ndpi) which enables the evaluation of stain normalization on datasets generated by different scanners.

Our contributions are the four-fold as follows:

(a) A high-performance implementation of the Macenko algorithm [11] that enables processing of gigapixel WSI (magnification 40X and beyond);
(b) A distributed architecture that uses computing power of a cluster to further accelerate the stain normalization workload;
(c) A pipeline that supports multiple execution modes, i.e., single- or multi-node execution, depending on the image size and the system resources, e.g., available RAM, cluster nodes (machines);
(d) An evaluation of the proposed system on WSI datasets generated by different scanning systems thus having different image formats and characteristics.

In the next sections, we present the architecture and implementation aspects of our novel stain normalization system. We discuss the optimization steps and the role of the various parameters in the runtime and accuracy of the algorithm.

2   Stain Normalization of Whole-Slide Images

The stain normalization method presented in [11] belongs to the class of unsupervised normalization methods. The algorithm estimates first the hematoxylin and eostin (H&E) stain vectors of the WSI of interest by using an SVD app-roach on the non-background pixels. Second, the algorithm applies a correction to account for the intensity variations due to noise. The algorithm is based on the principle that the color of each pixel (RGB channels) is a linear combination of the two stain vectors which are unknown and need to be estimated.

As a reference implementation of the Macenko algorithm [11] we use a pub-licly available MATLAB implementation [19]. We outline the algorithmic steps in Algorithm 1. Additional details are available in [22].

Algorithm 1. SVD method for obtaining the stain vectors

1: Convert RGB to optical density (OD)
2: Remove data with negligible optical density
3: Calculate SVD of the OD tuples and use the largest 2 values to create SVD plane
4: Project data onto the plane, normalize to unit length
5: Calculate the angle ϕ of each point with respect to the 1st (or 2nd) SVD direction
6: Find the robust extremes (α^{th} and $(100-\alpha)^{th}$ percentiles) of the angle ϕ
7: Find the projection of the extreme values back to OD space
8: Use this projection as optical density matrix (ODM, see [17])
9: Calculate the individual stain concentrations (C_h and C_e) using the inverse of ODM

10: Find the robust max. ($(100-\alpha)^{th}$ percentile) of the individual stain concentrations

11: Normalize and transform concentrations to OD space and then back to RGB

---

3 High-Performance Stain Normalization Architecture

3.1 Optimized Multi-core Architecture

We develop two optimized single-node implementations: (a) single-batch and (b) multi-batch. The single-batch implementation is intended to minimize the processing time on a single-node, while the multi-batch implementation enables processing of 40X WSI when their size is larger than RAM of a single node (Table in Fig. 4(c)). Both implementations follow the steps shown in Algorithm 1. Due to multiple optimizations, we reorganize the steps as in Fig. 1.

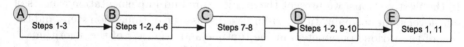

Fig. 1. Mapping of the Macenko Algorithm 1 steps to our optimized implementation

To enable single-batch processing of 40X images on state-of-the-art machines with 64 GB of RAM, only RGB pixel values are permanently stored in memory.

Steps 1–2 of Algorithm 1 are executed multiple times, in the processing blocks *A*, *B* and *D* in Fig. 1, because these blocks operate on non-background pixels in OD space. *Step* 1 is executed also in block *E*, because this block requires all pixels in OD space. *Step* 1 is performed using a 256-entry lookup-table that greatly speeds up the logarithm calculation. Moreover, *Step* 2 removes the background pixels which significantly reduces both the processing and the memory load. In the multi-batch implementation, batches of RGB pixel values are only temporarily stored in RAM and are read from the file system in the blocks *A*, *B*, *D*, and *E*.

To speed up the CPU processing we perform the following optimizations:

(a) In block *A*, during SVD calculation, the covariance matrix is calculated using the property that the element (i, j) of the matrix, $\Sigma_{ij} = \frac{1}{N^2}(\sum_p x_{p,i} x_{p,j} - \sum_p x_{p,i} \sum_p x_{p,j})$, requires only the sums of OD components.

(b) In blocks *B* and *D*, which are benchmarked as the most time-consuming steps, partial sorting is performed to find the percentiles from *Steps* 6 and 10. This partial sorting runs 2–3x faster compared to full sorting. In the multi-batch implementation, individual batches are partially sorted and then combined using an optimized merging function to calculate the global robust extremes.

(c) For the exponential function in the processing block *B*, we use the fast exponentiation library [4] since it performs 5–10x faster compared to the corresponding function in the standard C library.

(d) Since the processing blocks *A*, *B*, *D*, and *E* perform many independent operations on individual pixels, their execution is parallelized across all available CPU threads using the OpenMP library [13].

Given that the processing blocks *B* and *D* are the most time-consuming due to the difficulty of parallelizing the sorting operation, we propose another optimization that is using a Monte Carlo sampling technique [5]. In this method, a sample of non-background pixels is randomly chosen from the set of all non-background pixels in order to estimate the required robust extremes from *Steps* 6 and 10. Despite different methods for estimating the population percentiles [18], estimating the variance of the percentile estimates is unreliable, thus making the analytical estimation of the required sample size difficult [3]. Therefore, we derive the optimal sample size based on empirical results in Sect. 5.

3.2 Distributed Architecture

We present a novel distributed implementation of the Macenko algorithm. This implementation is useful when the WSI size is significantly larger than the RAM of a single node. The distributed solution uses all the optimizations presented in Sect. 3.1. We provide 2 multi-node implementations: (1) single-batch (the local image partition is fully read once) and (2) multi-batch (the local image is split into batches which temporarily reside in RAM and read multiple times when needed). For inter-node communication we use the MPI library [12].

Figure 2 shows an overview of the multi-node setup. The WSI typically resides in a file system shared across all nodes. We split the WSI into partitions WSI_i,

$i \in \{0,1,2,3\}$, and assign each partition to a separate node. Each node reads only its assigned partition. All nodes run the optimized Macenko algorithm on their partitions in parallel. Some processing steps need synchronization across nodes, e.g. *Steps* 6 and 10 in Algorithm 1. Thus one node needs to aggregate the relevant pixel data and compute, e.g. the global robust percentiles. We call this node *master*. Figure 2 shows a cluster of 4 nodes interconnected via a network, each node being assigned a part of the image. All nodes are slaves and node 0 is also master. We use this cluster setup for the experiments run in Sect. 5.

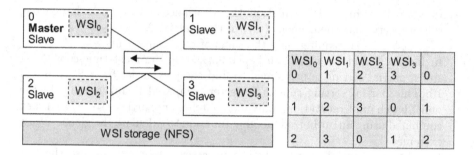

Fig. 2. Cluster setup and image partitioning scheme.

To describe the image partitioning, we define the partitioning element granularity as being a tile (stripe) for the single-batch implementation and a batch (e.g., a set of tiles/stripes) for the multi-batch implementation. The tile (stripe) is a rectangular contiguous part of the image, e.g., a tile is a 256×256-pixel image region. Let N be the number of nodes (indexed from 0). The image is composed of elements (tiles or batches) that form a grid with C columns and L rows. The total number of elements E is equal to CxL. Each element e can be uniquely described by 2 coordinates c and l, where $c \in \{0, ..., C-1\}$ and $l \in \{0, ..., L-1\}$. Given c and l, we compute the element index as $e(c,l) = l \cdot C + c$. The partitioning across nodes is performed by assigning element $e(c,l)$ to node $[e(c,l)$ mod $N]$. Figure 2 shows a partitioning example, where $N = 4$, $C = 5$ and $L = 3$. This partitioning scheme is preferred over assigning contiguous sets of elements to each node in order to reduce the node imbalance due to input content. For example for 2 nodes and an image in which the top half is background, the contiguous scheme would assign an empty image to node 0. In this case, there will be a large processing imbalance between the 2 nodes, impacting the scalability of the distributed system. For the multi-node single-batch implementation, given t_H the tile height, t_W the tile width, H the WSI height and W the WSI width, all variables expressed in pixels, $C = \lceil W/t_W \rceil$ and $L = \lceil H/t_H \rceil$. For the multi-node multi-batch implementation, the user defines a batch size B_{size} as being the maximum number of pixels that can reside in RAM at any given time. Assuming square batches, then a batch will have the width and height equal to $\lfloor \sqrt{B_{size}} \rfloor$, which implies that $C = \lceil W/\lfloor \sqrt{B_{size}} \rfloor \rceil$ and $L = \lceil H/\lfloor \sqrt{B_{size}} \rfloor \rceil$.

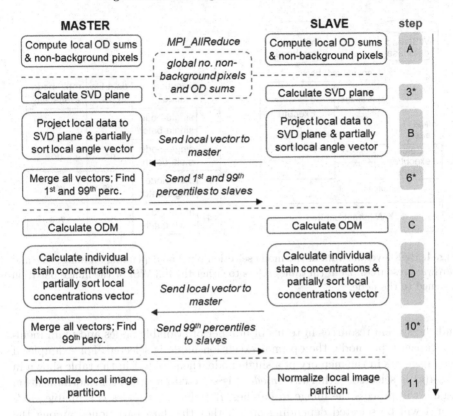

Fig. 3. Communication stages across nodes at different stages of the stain normalization algorithm.

Figure 3 shows the communication flow across nodes at different algorithm stages. First, each node reads its partition, runs *Steps* 1–2 of Algorithm 1 and computes the local OD sums and number of non-background pixels. Next, we run an MPI reduction phase to compute on all nodes the global number of non-background pixels and OD sums. Then, each node runs *Steps* 3–5 and sends its local vectors of angles to the master, where the global 1st and 99th percentiles of the projected angles are computed. The master then sends these percentiles to all slaves so that they can run *Steps* 7–9. The master computes the global 99th percentiles of the stain concentrations based on the local concentration vectors sent by the slaves. The global percentiles are sent to all slaves which are used for normalization. Finally each node writes its image partition to a file.

3.3   Mode Selection Pipeline

Figure 4 shows the pipeline architecture for implementing mode selection depending on the image size and the system resources. Given the input image size, which depends on the image format and the targeted magnification, e.g., 10X, 40X, etc.,

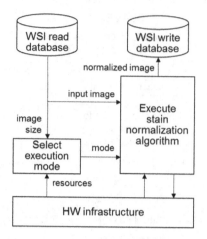

	execution mode	data fits in RAM	multi-node availability
1	single-node single-batch	yes	no
2	single-node multi-batch	no	no
3	multi-node single-batch	yes	yes
4	multi-node multi-batch	no	yes

Fig. 4. High-level diagram of the mode selection pipeline depending on image size and hardware resources. *Data* (in table) refers to either the full WSI or the image partition assigned to the node.

and the system resources in terms of number of available nodes and main memory capacity per node, the optimal execution mode is selected. For example, if the image fits in the memory of a single node, then *mode* 1 in the table shown in Fig. 4(c) is selected. Otherwise, *mode* 2 is selected and the stain normalization engine will process the image in batches. If a cluster of nodes is available, *mode* 3 or 4 will be selected depending on whether the data partitioned among the different nodes fits in RAM or not, respectively.

4   Whole-Slide Image Datasets

To analyze the performance and scalability of our pipeline, we used H&E-stained WSIs from 4 datasets. The first one is part of TUPAC MICCAI 2016 [20] and provides breast WSIs for prediction of tumor and proliferation scores. These WSIs are in Aperio format, single-file pyramidal tiled TIFF (.svs), with JPEG compression scheme. The CAMELYON16 dataset [6] is part of the ISBI challenge on cancer metastasis detection in lymph node. These slides are in Philips format, single-file pyramidal tiled TIFF or BigTIFF (.tif) with non-standard metadata and JPEG compression scheme. The remaining 2 datasets are proprietary but we used them to test the flexibility of our pipeline to different WSI formats. One dataset provides slides in Ventana format, single-file pyramidal tiled BigTIFF with non-standard metadata. The other dataset contains slides in Hamamatsu format, single-file TIFF-like format (.ndpi) with proprietary metadata. All the slides include 2.5X, 10X and 40X magnifications, except for the fourth dataset that includes 2.5X and 10X magnifications only. A de facto community standard for reading various WSI formats is OpenSlide C library that provides a simple interface to WSIs [14]. However, we wrote the proprietary functions that rely on the existing API from libTIFF and BigTIFF standard libraries for reading and writing of supported WSI formats that allow significantly faster read times as shown in Table 1 for various image formats and magnifications. In addition, our read functions have lower memory requirements compared to OpenSlide library functions.

Table 1. Image read speed-up of our implementation compared to OpenSlide

Scanner type	10X speed-up	40X speed-up
Aperio	4.7	4.7
Philips	4.9	22.2
Ventana	6.4	4.6
Hamamatsu	14.3	N.A

5   Experimental Results

40X WSI Processing. Figure 5 shows three images generated by different scanners, which we will further refer to as Scanner A, B and C, respectively. The top row shows the original images and the bottom row shows the normalized versions after running the normalization pipeline of Sect. 3. Each panel in Fig. 5 corresponds to a 1024×1024-pixel region of the image at 40X magnification. While the input images (top row) show significant color variation, the normalized ones show more uniform color contrast as a result of the normalization process.

Single-Node Results. Figures 6(a)–(d) present measurements of the processing time of the single-node system. Figures 6(a)–(b) show the total processing time, including the time to read the images, as a function of the image size for the single- and multi-batch implementations in double-logarithmic scale. The different colors correspond to images in 2.5X, 10X, and 40X magnification, while the different markers correspond to the different datasets. The multi-batch implementation exhibits a moderate time increase that is mainly attributed to the multiple image reading overhead. A number of 4 batches has been used in all single-node multi-batch measurements. Figures 6(c)–(d) show the corresponding processing time only as a function of the number of non-background pixels. For each magnification, the measurements scale almost linearly with the number of non-background pixels. The processing time shows an offset for higher magnifications due to the initial memory allocation and final image normalization steps that are performed on the whole image.

Single-Node vs. Reference Results. Table 2 reports the average execution time over all images for all datasets in 10X magnification using the single-node implementation described in Sect. 3.1, compared with the original MATLAB code in [19] and reference C++ implementation based on it using OpenSlide library for reading of the images. All measurements have been collected on a

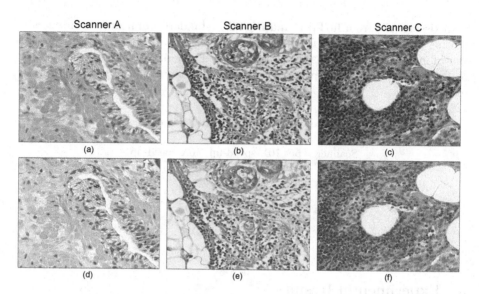

Fig. 5. Input images from different datasets and scanners (a)–(c) and normalized output images (d)–(f) after applying the stain normalization pipeline (Color figure online)

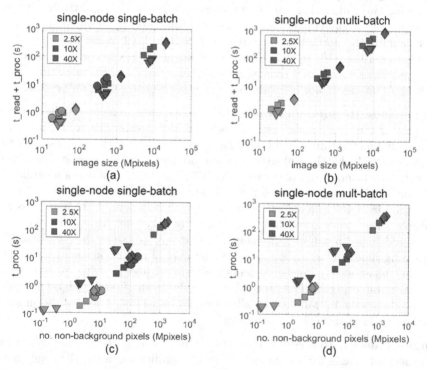

Fig. 6. Experimental results showing the performance of the proposed stain normalization pipeline on WSI from different datasets and magnification factors (Color figure online)

Table 2. MATLAB vs. single-node implementations (averaged for 10X images)

Implementation	t_proc + t_read(s)	Gain
MATLAB [13]	147	1
Reference w/OpenSlide	124	1.19
Single-batch	18	8.17
Multi-batch	37	3.97

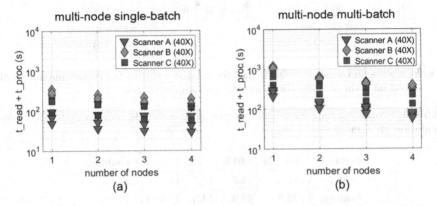

Fig. 7. Performance of distributed implementation based on the number of nodes for different image types and 40X magnification. (Color figure online)

single node with a 10-core Intel® i7-6950X CPU at 3 GHz and 64 GB of RAM. Our implementation achieves a speed-up factor larger than 8 for 10X images.

Multi-Node Results. Figures 7(a)–(b) show the scalability results of the multi-node single-batch and multi-batch implementations, respectively. Measurements have been collected on a cluster of nodes with an 8-core Intel® Xeon® E5-2630v3 CPU and 64 GB of RAM. We show aggregated processing and read time as a function of the number of nodes for 40X magnification images. Each point and color represent an image and a dataset, respectively. For the single-batch implementation the speed-ups when increasing the number of processing nodes compared to the single-node measurements are as follows: 1.70X (2 nodes), 2.29X (3 nodes) and 2.80X (4 nodes). For the multi-batch implementation we measure the following average speed-ups compared to the single-node multi-batch measurements: 1.87X (2 nodes), 2.60X (3 nodes) and 3.30X (4 nodes). The reasons for the sub-linear scaling are the communication overhead of *Blocks* B and D in Fig. 3, and aggregation of intermediate results (merging of the vectors) in *Blocks* 6* and 10* in Fig. 3.

Single-Node Pixel Sampling Results. Figures 8(a)–(b) show the Euclidean distance (E_d) of ODM and the relative error of the robust maximum of the individual stain concentrations ($maxC_h$ and $maxC_e$), respectively, between the sampling and no-sampling results. The measured E_d values of the individual

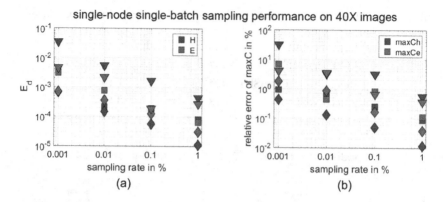

Fig. 8. Euclidean distance of ODM and the relative error of the robust maximum of the individual stain concentrations for various sampling rates.

Table 3. Processing time for different sampling rates, single-node single-batch implementation (40X images)

Dataset	0.001%	0.01%	0.1%	1%	No sampling
Scanner A	15.6	15.7	15.7	16.2	20.8
Scanner B	42.8	42.9	43.3	44.6	177.7
Scanner C	15.7	15.8	16.0	16.9	113.0

stains are almost negligible compared to typical values such as the ones reported in Table 1 of [1] with a sampling rate of non-background pixels as low as 0.01%. Similarly, the relative error of the robust maximum estimation drops below 1% for a sampling rate of 1%. The higher sampling rate value in case of robust maximum estimation is required to offset the error aggregation from ODM estimation. Nevertheless, the increase in total processing time with respect to the sampling rate is negligible even for rates as large as 1%, as shown in Table 3. The average processing time (without read time) for different sampling rates and for the single-node single-batch implementation (no-sampling) is shown in Table 3. Thanks to the sampling method, the overall processing time is reduced by a factor of 1.3–9x depending on the image type, for 40X magnification. This effectively reduces the processing time to normalization time yielding this implementation as fast as methods that apply a fixed reference normalization template regardless of the input image [16].

Best Single-Batch Results. Table 4 shows the average speed-ups across all 40X magnification datasets of the single-node single-batch (with 1% sampling), four-node single-batch (with and without sampling) when compared to the single-node single-batch implementation without sampling. By combining the sampling technique with the distributed pipeline we attain an average speed-up of 3.44 and 5.19 vs. the single-node with and without sampling, respectively.

Table 4. Single-batch implementations (averaged for 40X images)

Implementation	Gain
Single-node	1
Single-node w/ sampling	1.51
Four-node	2.8
Four-node w/sampling	5.19

6 Conclusions

We built a fast and scalable pipeline to enable large-scale stain normalization of high-resolution histopathological whole-slide images. Our pipeline uses a highly optimized low-level engine that performs the required image processing functions and is based on a distributed computing architecture that is scalable in both image size and number of computing nodes. The presented pipeline tackles the memory and runtime bottlenecks of high-magnification images and enables the preprocessing of large datasets, which is a critical prerequisite for any ML framework applied to biomedical images. Our next steps involve: (a) performance evaluation of ML frameworks applied to stain normalized images, (b) automation of the pipeline mode selection, and (c) automated batch distribution based on the number of non-background pixels for load balancing across nodes.

References

1. Alsubaie, N., Trahearn, N., Raza, S.E.A., Snead, D., Rajpoot, N.M.: Stain deconvolution using statistical analysis of multi-resolution stain colour representation. PloS One **12**(1), e0169875 (2017). https://doi.org/10.1371/journal.pone.0169875
2. Bejnordi, B.E., et al.: Stain specific standardization of whole-slide histopathological images. IEEE Trans. Med. Imaging **35**(2), 404–415 (2016)
3. Brown, M.B., Wolfe, R.A.: Estimation of the variance of percentile estimates. Comput. Stat. Data Anal. **1**, 167–174 (1983)
4. Fast approximate function of exponential function exp and log. https://github.com/herumi/fmath
5. Harrison, R.L.: Introduction to Monte Carlo simulation. In: Granja, C., Leroy, C. (eds.) American Institute of Physics Conference Series. American Institute of Physics Conference Series, vol. 1204, pp. 17–21 (2010). https://doi.org/10.1063/1.3295638
6. ISBI challenge on cancer metastasis detection in lymph node. https://camelyon16.grand-challenge.org/data/
7. Janowczyk, A., Basavanhally, A., Madabhushi, A.: Stain normalization using sparse autoencoders (StaNoSA): application to digital pathology. Comput. Med. Imaging Graph. **57**, 50–61 (2017)
8. Khan, A.M., Rajpoot, N., Treanor, D., Magee, D.: A nonlinear mapping approach to stain normalization in digital histopathology images using image-specific color deconvolution. IEEE Trans. Biomed. Eng. **61**(6), 1729738 (2014)

9. Li, X., Plataniotis, K.N.: A complete color normalization approach to histopathology images using color cues computed from saturation-weighted statistics. IEEE Trans. Biomed. Eng. **62**(7), 1862–1873 (2015)
10. Litjens, G., et al.: A survey on deep learning in medical image analysis. Med. Image Anal. **42**, 60–88 (2017)
11. Macenko, M., et al.: A method for normalizing histology slides for quantitative analysis. In: 2009 IEEE International Symposium on Biomedical Imaging, pp. 1107–1110 (2009)
12. Open MPI: Open Source High Performance Computing. https://www.open-mpi.org/software/ompi/v3.1/
13. OpenMP 4.0 Specifications. https://www.openmp.org/specifications/
14. OpenSlide is a C library that provides a simple interface to read whole-slide images. https://openslide.org/
15. Rabinovich, A., Agarwal, S., Laris, C., Price, J., Belongie, S.: Unsupervised color decomposition of histologically stained tissue samples. In: Advances in Neural Information Processing Systems, pp. 667–674 (2003)
16. Reinhard, E., Adhikhmin, M., Gooch, B., Shirley, P.: Color transfer between images. IEEE Comput. Graph. Appl. **21**(5), 34–41 (2001). https://doi.org/10.1109/38.946629
17. Ruifrok, A.C., Johnston, D.A.: Quantification of histochemical staining by color deconvolution. Anal. Quant. Cytol. Histol. **23**(4), 291–9 (2001)
18. Schoonjans, F., De Bacquer, D., Schmid, P.: Estimation of population percentiles (Cambridge, Mass.). Epidemiology **22**(5), 750 (2011)
19. Staining unmixing and normalization. https://github.com/mitkovetta/staining-normalization
20. Tumor Proliferation Assessment Challenge 2016, TUPAC16 - MICCAI Grand Challenge. http://tupac.tue-image.nl/node/3
21. Veta, M., Pluim, J.P.W., van Diest, P.J., Viergever, M.A.: Breast cancer histopathology image analysis: a review. IEEE Trans. Biomed. Eng. **61**(5), 1400–1411 (2014)
22. Vink, J.P., Leeuwen, M.B.V., Deurzen, C.H.M.V., Haan, G.D.: Efficient nucleus detector in histopathology images. J. Microsc. **249**(2), 124–135 (2013)
23. Wernick, M.N., Yang, Y., Brankov, J.G., Yourganov, G., Strother, S.C.: Machine learning in medical imaging. IEEE Sig. Process. Mag. **27**(4), 25–38 (2010)
24. Zerhouni, E., Lnyi, D., Viana, M., Gabrani, M.: Wide residual networks for mitosis detection. In: 2017 IEEE 14th International Symposium on Biomedical Imaging (ISBI 2017), pp. 924–928 (2017)

A Benchmark for Epithelial Cell Tracking

Jan Funke[1], Lisa Mais[2], Andrew Champion[1], Natalie Dye[3],
and Dagmar Kainmueller[2(✉)]

[1] HHMI Janelia Research Campus, Ashburn, USA
[2] BIH/MDC, Berlin, Germany
dagmar.kainmueller@mdc-berlin.de
[3] MPI-CBG, Dresden, Germany

Abstract. Segmentation and tracking of epithelial cells in light microscopy (LM) movies of developing tissue is an abundant task in cell- and developmental biology. Epithelial cells are densely packed cells that form a honeycomb-like grid. This dense packing distinguishes membrane-stained epithelial cells from the types of objects recent cell tracking benchmarks have focused on, like cell nuclei and freely moving individual cells. While semi-automated tools for segmentation and tracking of epithelial cells are available to biologists, common tools rely on classical watershed based segmentation and engineered tracking heuristics, and entail a tedious phase of manual curation. However, a different kind of densely packed cell imagery has become a focus of recent computer vision research, namely electron microscopy (EM) images of neurons. In this work we explore the benefits of two recent neuron EM segmentation methods for epithelial cell tracking in light microscopy. In particular we adapt two different deep learning approaches for neuron segmentation, namely Flood Filling Networks and MALA, to epithelial cell tracking. We benchmark these on a dataset of eight movies with up to 200 frames. We compare to Moral Lineage Tracing, a combinatorial optimization approach that recently claimed state of the art results for epithelial cell tracking. Furthermore, we compare to Tissue Analyzer, an off-the-shelf tool used by Biologists that serves as our baseline.

1 Introduction

Epithelia are thin tissues that cover body structures like organs and cavities. They are commonly composed of a single layer of cells tightly connected by junctions. In a developing organism, cells in epithelia are very dynamic. They move greatly, to the extent that they change neighbors over time despite the tight connections. They undergo cell divisions, cell death, and a large variety of shape changes.

Biologists are interested in a mechanistic understanding of the principles that govern epithelial development on the level of individual cells. A powerful approach towards this goal are high throughput studies, where membrane-stained

---

J. Funke and L. Mais—Shared first authors.

© Springer Nature Switzerland AG 2019
L. Leal-Taixé and S. Roth (Eds.): ECCV 2018 Workshops, LNCS 11134, pp. 437–445, 2019.
https://doi.org/10.1007/978-3-030-11024-6_33

developing epithelia are imaged over time with fluorescence light microscopy (LM), and cells are segmented and tracked in the resulting movies to allow for quantitative analysis.

Current computational tools that Biologists use to segment and track epithelial cells rely on non-learned methods watershed or thresholding for 2d segmentation, combined with heuristics for tracking cells over time [1–3]. So far the computer vision community has shown little interest in this problem despite its abundant importance for Cell Biologists. Recent cell tracking challenges [4,5] have excluded epithelial cells from their benchmarks, and to our knowledge, only one recent approach has tackled epithelial cell tracking with modern methodology, namely the Moral Lineage Tracing (MLT) approach and its fast variants [6–8].

However, the related image analysis problem of segmenting neurons in 3d electron microscpy (EM) images has recently become a subject of study for a number of computer vision groups. Neurons are tree-structured densely packed cells, and the membranes that separate them are so thin that they are prone to fall prey to partial volume effects. In essence, it cannot be assumed that even a single pixel of membrane separates two neurons in EM imagery. These properties hold analogously for 2d+t epithelial cell tracks in light microscopy data.

There are however two key structural difference between neurons in 3d EM data and epithelial cell tracks in 2d+t LM data: First, when a neuron branches, the two emerging branches diverge immediately, making it unlikely to share a boundary later on. Conversely, when an epithelial cell divides, the daughter cells may reside next to each other for a long time. Consequently, in general, methods for 3d neuron EM segmentation are not directly applicable to cell tracking. Second, the location of the root of a tree-shaped neuron is not known a priori, whereas the root of a cell lineage tree is known to lie in the first frame of a movie. This known direction of object branchings can be leveraged for cell tracking.

In this work, we propose extensions of two state of the art deep learning based 3d neuron segmentation methods to make them applicable to 2d+t tracking of densely packed objects, namely MALA [9] and Flood Filling Networks (FFN) [10]. The core contribution of our work is a benchmark on a dataset of eight epithelial cell movies. We benchmark against a current state of the art tool used by Biologists, namely the Tissue Analyzer [1] (formerly known as Packing Analyzer [11]). Furthermore we benchmark against the current state of the art for epithelia tracking in the computer vision literature, namely the MLT approach [6–8]. Here, to allow for a fair comparison of MLT to our deep learning based methods, we have "modernized" MLT to be based on a U-Net [12] as opposed to a Random Forests [13] as employed in the original MLT. In particular, we use cell candidates and tracking scores as predicted by the MALA approach. This allows us to investigate the difference between a combinatorial optimization method (MLT) compared to greedy agglomeration and matching (MALA).

Our comparative evaluation of the standard segmentation and tracking error metrics SEG and TRA [5] reveals that MALA, FFN and the U-Net based MLT significantly outperform Tissue Analyzer. Differences among the three deep learning based methods are more subtle, yet their run-times differ significantly. Our results suggest that MALA, which is the fastest approach, performs en par with MLT and slightly better than FFN in terms of accuracy. We therefore suggest MALA as our method of choice to be employed for epithelial cell tracking by biologists. Our code for both MALA and FFN is freely available on github.[1]

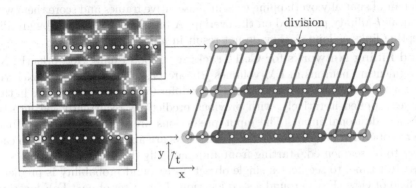

Fig. 1. The MALA method for cell tracking. A lineage (left, cell divisions are indicated by horizontally striped labels in the frame preceding the division) is represented by labelling affinity edges (right) as "cut" (red) or "connect" (green) between neighboring pixels within and across frames. Given that cells in subsequent frames overlap, this formulation allows to segment (in 2d) and track cells (over time). Shown on a coarsened pixel grid for illustration purposes. (Color figure online)

2   Methods

MALA for Cell Tracking. MALIS plus agglomeration (MALA [9]) is a method that has recently been proposed to address the problem of segmenting neurons in EM volumes: There, a 3d U-Net is trained to predict affinities on edges between voxels using a variant of the MALIS loss [14], such that edge affinities are high if the incident voxels are part of the same object and low otherwise. The prediction of affinities is followed by a simple hierarchical agglomeration, where initial fragments obtained by a watershed are iteratively merged according to the predicted affinities between them until a given threshold.

Acknowledging the similarity between the problem addressed here and the segmentation of neurons in (anisotropic) volumes, we modified the MALA method to segment and track cells in 2d+t videos. For that, we treat a movie sequence as a 3d volume, indexed by (x, y, t). The affinities between voxels are now spatial (in x and y) or temporal (in t). Affinities in space represent a segmentation of a single image into individual cells, whereas affinities across time encode the continuation of a lineage (see Fig. 1).

---

[1] github.com/anonymous/repository.

Since agglomeration on the resulting 2d+t affinity graph is not guaranteed to produce a *moral* lineage (i.e., cells can only split, not merge), we diverge from the MALA approach and create a segmentation and tracking in two steps: First, we perform a watershed segmentation and agglomeration for each frame independently to find cells (thus ignoring affinities in t). Second, we track the found cells with a simple forward heuristic: we enumerate potential links between each pair of spatially overlapping cells in consecutive frames and score them with the mean t-affinity predicted on the overlap. A lineage is then found by greedily accepting links as long as they do not result in a merge.

Flood Filling Networks for Cell Tracking. Flood Filling Networks (FFNs) for segmenting neurons in EM volumes [10] are based on a CNN for pixel-wise foreground-background segmentation. They differ from traditional CNNs in that they are applied iteratively, with previous predictions recurrently fed into the CNN as additional input. The input predictions are initialized to 0.5. To be able to cope with densely packed objects, FFNs are applied individually to each object to be segmented, starting from automatically determined seed points.

At test time, to segment a single object, foreground probability is predicted in a field of view (FoV) around a seed location. Then a set of next FoV locations is determined and stored in a queue to be processed until empty: If a prediction one step away from the seed exceeds a user-defined probability threshold, it forms the center of a subsequent FoV. Here, a step is an axis-aligned offset of user-defined length. A binary segmentation of a single object is derived by thresholding the final full foreground probability image. Figure 2 shows a few exemplary FoV steps at test time. At training time, input FoVs are first formed at seed locations. Once training yields predictions above a user-defined threshold, additional training data is formed one step, but never further, away from the seed, employing previous predictions as input.

Fig. 2. FFN at test time: From left to right, a few steps of FoV movement are shown, with resulting predictions. These steps cover a cell division, visible as a sudden wider diameter of the object. The FoV can only move backwards in time, and hence does not jump into the second daughter cell that stems from this division (not depicted). Very right: Resulting binary segmentation.

FFNs are designed for pixel-wise foreground-background segmentation of individual objects. This makes them not well-suited for objects that touch themselves: For the example of a dividing epithelia cell, the mother cell as well as the two daughter cells belong to the same foreground object, where the daughter cells often reside right next to each other, and partial volume effects often cause little to no boundary to be visible in the time dimension. Hence FFNs would not allow for distinguishing these daughter cells.

We overcome this limitation of FFNs for cell tracking applications by leveraging the knowledge that cells can divide over time but not merge. This leads us to propose the following modification: (1) We pick seeds reversely in time. (2) During training as well as testing, we allow for the FoV to only move backwards in time. This yields non-branching leaf-to-root tracks for all cells that form leafs in the lineage forest: When the FoV encounters a cell division site while filling a daughter cell, it is not allowed to move into the respective sibling cell. (3) Given the single-cell tracks resulting from (2), we detect cell divisions, i.e. pairs of single-cell tracks that stem from the same mother cell, by a simple Dice-score based overlap criterion. As with MALA, the resulting tracking graph is not guaranteed to be moral, as it may contain cell merges. Analogous to MALA, we greedily enforce morality by adding edges from our tracking graph to our final feasible solution one by one as long as morality is not violated, while rejecting edges that do lead to a violation.

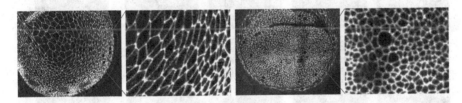

Fig. 3. Overview of the used datasets: Left: peripodial tissue with large cells in the center and thin elongated cells at the edge. Right: proper disc tissue with small roundish cells.

3   Results and Discussion

We evaluate MALA, FFN, MLT, and Tissue Analyzer (TA) on 2d+t movies of developing Drosophila wing epithelia. These epithelia consist of two layers, namely the proper disc layer that develops into the fly's wing, and the peripodial layer whose biological function is a current research topic. Each layer can be captured individually as a 2d+t movie as described in [15]. Our dataset contains 8 movies: 5 proper disc and 3 peripodial layers (see Fig. 3), containing between 160 and 200 frames. We perform leave-one-out cross-validation of MALA, FFN, and MLT on all 8 movies. For each fold, a validation movie is held out from the training set to check for early stopping during training. The validation movie is chosen to be of the same class (i.e. proper disc or peripodial) as the test movie.

For MALA, we trained a 3D U-Net with a receptive field of 88×88 pixels in xy, and 28 time frames. The U-Net follows the architecture proposed in [12], consisting of four layers with downsampling factors of 2. We trained the network

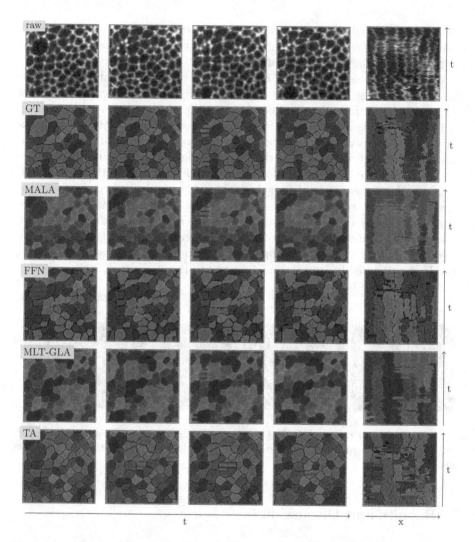

Fig. 4. Qualitative results of the investigated methods. Cell divisions are indicated by horizontally striped labels in the frame preceding the division. The red highlight in the first row indicates the same pixel line in the xy and xt views. (Color figure online)

for 150,000 iterations using the Adam optimizer [16] with an initial learning rate of $\alpha = 5 \cdot 10^{-5}$, $\beta_1 = 0.95$, $\beta_2 = 0.999$, and $\epsilon = 10^{-8}$.

We used the same network as for MALA to generate affinities for MLT. We employed the fast MLT solver GLA (see [7]) since neither other MLT solver terminated within 100 hours of runtime on a single movie.

For FFN, we trained a 3D Conv Net with 8 layers and 32 filters, FoV of $25 \times 25 \times 25$ pixels, step size of 6 pixels for moving the FoV, and probability threshold 0.9.

For Tissue Analyzer results on proper disc movies, we evaluate the automated tracking results that formed the basis for our ground truth data via manual curation by biologists. In this sense, our reported Tissue Analyzer results are biased towards an unfair advantage. On peripodial movies however, automated Tissue Analyzer results were deemed too inaccurate to form a suitable basis for manual curation. Instead, biologists used the interactive mode of Tissue Analyzer to generate ground truth, iteratively curating each frame individually and then using it to initialize segmentation of the next frame. For this reason we do not report automated Tissue Analyzer results for peripodial movies.

We evaluate the standard tracking error metrics SEG and TRA [4] to measure 2d segmentation and tracking accuracy, respectively (see Table 1). Both measures range from 0 to 1, where 1 indicates a perfect result. Figure 4 shows some exemplary results. The average run-times of our methods for processing a single movie are 35 min (MALA), 42 min (MLT) and 90 min (FFN).

Table 1. Quantitative results of the investigated methods. Shown are the mean and standard deviation of the SEG and TRA measure over each of the used datasets (peripodial: 3 movies, proper disc: 5 movies).

	PERIPODIAL		PROPER DISC	
	SEG	TRA	SEG	TRA
MALA	**0.907** ± 0.029	**0.997** ± 0.001	**0.817** ± 0.009	**0.995** ± 0.001
FFN	0.879 ± 0.035	0.985 ± 0.012	0.796 ± 0.013	0.987 ± 0.006
MLT-GLA	**0.904** ± 0.026	0.993 ± 0.004	**0.818** ± 0.010	**0.995** ± 0.001
TA	–	–	0.758 ± 0.009	0.865 ± 0.003

Discussion. Concerning TRA scores, MALA and MLT yield almost perfect tracking performance, with scores very close to 1 on all eight individual movies. FFN yields slightly lower TRA scores than MALA and MLT. We note two technicalities that put FFN at a disadvantage w.r.t. the TRA score: (1) The ground truth is a dense tesselation of the image. While MALA and MLT produce a dense tesselation without boundary, FFN often leaves a few background pixels between objects. In case of a cell death, an FFN track of a cell might stop a few slices earlier in time than the respective ground truth track, which is counted as "missing segmentations" that contribute ten-fold to TRA compared to a superfluous segment that would be counted if the space was filled. (2) FFN maintains a queue of seeds and iteratively picks them for filling a new object if they have not been covered by a previous object. Towards the end of the seed queue, seeds can lie on the aforementioned background regions. In this case, filling will produce an object that lies mostly within a pre-existing object, and only a few pixels will be added as a new segment. This "noise" counts as false split errors in the TRA measure. We hypothesize that some more steps of simple postprocessing, like morphological growing of labels and sorting out very small components, may alleviate these disadvantages.

However, in addition to the above technical disadvantages, in some videos we did find some "catastrophic merge errors" yielded by FFN, where two neighboring cells are merged over their entire tracks. This may happen if the iterative FFN filling "leaks" into a neighboring cell early on, which cannot be amended later. In contrast, MALA and MLT first perform pure 2d segmentations and link them over time in a second step, which makes the results less prone to such large merge errors.

Concerning SEG scores, MALA and MLT are en par again, whereas FFN yields slightly lower scores, potentially again caused by the fact that it may leave a few pixels between cells blank, whereas neither ground truth nor MALA nor MLT do. All methods yield smaller scores for proper disc as compared to peripodial movies, which is simply due to the smaller size of the respective cells and the nature of the Dice score.

4   Conclusion

We have shown that FFN can be extended successfully for tracking applications. However we were unable to get FFN to outperform the cheaper MALA and MLT. MALA is fastest and most accurate method in our study and should hence make for a useful tool for biologists to segment and track epithelial cells, once integrated into a manual correction framework as e.g. provided by Tissue Analyzer. The flourescence microscopy data analyzed in this work is of such quality that cheap greedy agglomeration of local deep learning based predictions is not outperformed by expensive combinatorial optimization as in MLT.

References

1. Aigouy, B., Umetsu, D., Eaton, S.: Segmentation and quantitative analysis of epithelial tissues. In: Dahmann, C. (ed.) Drosophila. MMB, vol. 1478, pp. 227–239. Springer, New York (2016). https://doi.org/10.1007/978-1-4939-6371-3_13
2. Stegmaier, J., et al.: Real-time three-dimensional cell segmentation in large-scale microscopy data of developing embryos. Dev. Cell **36**(2), 225–240 (2016)
3. Farrell, D.L., Weitz, O., Magnasco, M.O., Zallen, J.A.: SEGGA: a toolset for rapid automated analysis of epithelial cell polarity and dynamics. Development **144**(9), 1725–1734 (2017)
4. Maška, M., et al.: A benchmark for comparison of cell tracking algorithms. Bioinformatics **30**(11), 1609–1617 (2014)
5. Ulman, V., et al.: An objective comparison of cell-tracking algorithms. Nat. Methods **14**(12), 1141 (2017)
6. Jug, F., Levinkov, E., Blasse, C., Myers, E.W., Andres, B.: Moral lineage tracing. In: Proceedings of the IEEE Conference on Computer Vision and Pattern Recognition, pp. 5926–5935 (2016)
7. Rempfler, M., et al.: Efficient algorithms for moral lineage tracing. In: Proceedings of the IEEE Conference on Computer Vision and Pattern Recognition, pp. 4695–4704 (2017)

8. Rempfler, M., Kumar, S., Stierle, V., Paulitschke, P., Andres, B., Menze, B.H.: Cell lineage tracing in lens-free microscopy videos. In: Descoteaux, M., Maier-Hein, L., Franz, A., Jannin, P., Collins, D.L., Duchesne, S. (eds.) MICCAI 2017. LNCS, vol. 10434, pp. 3–11. Springer, Cham (2017). https://doi.org/10.1007/978-3-319-66185-8_1

9. Funke, J., et al.: A deep structured learning approach towards automating connectome reconstruction from 3D electron micrographs. CoRR abs/1709.02974 (2017)

10. Januszewski, M., et al.: High-precision automated reconstruction of neurons with flood-filling networks. bioRxiv, p. 200675 (2017)

11. Aigouy, B., et al.: Cell flow reorients the axis of planar polarity in the wing epithelium of drosophila. Cell **142**(5), 773–786 (2010)

12. Ronneberger, O., Fischer, P., Brox, T.: U-Net: convolutional networks for biomedical image segmentation. In: Navab, N., Hornegger, J., Wells, W.M., Frangi, A.F. (eds.) MICCAI 2015. LNCS, vol. 9351, pp. 234–241. Springer, Cham (2015). https://doi.org/10.1007/978-3-319-24574-4_28

13. Breiman, L.: Random forests. Mach. Learn. **45**(1), 5–32 (2001)

14. Briggman, K., Denk, W., Seung, S., Helmstaedter, M.N., Turaga, S.C.: Maximin affinity learning of image segmentation. In: Bengio, Y., Schuurmans, D., Lafferty, J.D., Williams, C.K.I., Culotta, A. (eds.) Advances in Neural Information Processing Systems 22, pp. 1865–1873. Curran Associates, Inc. (2009)

15. Dye, N.A., et al.: Cell dynamics underlying oriented growth of the drosophila wing imaginal disc. Development (2017). dev-155069

16. Kingma, D.P., Ba, J.: Adam: a method for stochastic optimization. arXiv preprint arXiv:1412.6980 (2014)

Automatic Fusion of Segmentation and Tracking Labels

Cem Emre Akbaş[1]($\boxtimes$), Vladimír Ulman[1,2], Martin Maška[1], Florian Jug[2], and Michal Kozubek[1]

[1] Center for Biomedical Image Analysis, Faculty of Informatics, Masaryk University, Brno, Czech Republic
{akbas,xulman,xmaska,kozubek}@fi.muni.cz
[2] Max Planck Institute of Molecular Cell Biology and Genetics, Dresden, Germany
jug@mpi-cbg.de
https://cbia.fi.muni.cz/

Abstract. Labeled training images of high quality are required for developing well-working analysis pipelines. This is, of course, also true for biological image data, where such labels are usually hard to get. We distinguish human labels (gold corpora) and labels generated by computer algorithms (silver corpora). A naturally arising problem is to merge multiple corpora into larger bodies of labeled training datasets. While fusion of labels in static images is already an established field, dealing with labels in time-lapse image data remains to be explored. Obtaining a gold corpus for segmentation is usually very time-consuming and hence expensive. For this reason, gold corpora for object tracking often use object detection markers instead of dense segmentations. If dense segmentations of tracked objects are desired later on, an automatic merge of the detection-based gold corpus with (silver) corpora of the individual time points for segmentation will be necessary. Here we present such an automatic merging system and demonstrate its utility on corpora from the Cell Tracking Challenge. We additionally release all label fusion algorithms as freely available and open plugins for Fiji (https://github.com/xulman/CTC-FijiPlugins).

Keywords: Label fusion · Image annotation · Segmentation labels
Tracking labels

1 Introduction

Reliably obtaining high quality segmentation results is, in general, difficult. On biological microscopy data it is common to have segmentation results from multiple sources – either human annotations or automatic segmentations. Multiple solutions have been proposed to merge labels from multiple sources into one consensus labeling [1–3].

© Springer Nature Switzerland AG 2019
L. Leal-Taixé and S. Roth (Eds.): ECCV 2018 Workshops, LNCS 11134, pp. 446–454, 2019.
https://doi.org/10.1007/978-3-030-11024-6_34

The widespread use of deep learning [4] across many bioimage analysis and computer vision tasks has impelled both communities to establish various publicly available repositories of annotated image data for training as well as objective benchmarking of the developed algorithms. Whereas fusion of labels in static images is by now common practice, dealing with labels in time-lapse image data is largely unexplored. This is particularly true in cell tracking applications for which typically no complete gold corpora exist for dense segmentation [5]. Additionally, the few existing gold corpora for cell tracking make use of simplified detection markers instead of complete dense segmentations [6–8]. In order to recover proper segmentation labels of all tracked cells, an automatic solution to merge a simplified gold tracking corpus with dense segmentation corpora for the individual time points is needed.

In this paper, we address the problem of obtaining dense segmentation and tracking results for multidimensional time-lapse light microscopy image data from partial segmentations and detection-based tracking annotations. For a given video, a simplified gold tracking corpus is obtained with a unique detection label for all occurrences of the same cell. Next, silver segmentation corpora are generated for each frame by a set of automatic segmentation methods. This results in the production of image sequences that contain ideally similar but still inconsistent segmentation masks. Finally, we merge those sequences to form a single silver segmentation corpus per frame and merge it with a detection based tracking corpus driven by gold tracking markers to generate a complete and dense tracking corpus. In summary, we present a fully automatic approach to establish a combined silver segmentation and tracking corpus from multiple automatic segmentation results and a detection based gold tracking corpus.

2   Proposed Method

The proposed method follows a majority or weighted majority voting scheme. A flowchart showcasing the proposed method can be found in Fig. 1. The required inputs are (i) expert annotated tracking detection markers (gold tracking corpus). Such markers can either be single pixels or simple objects, like small circles, and (ii) dense segmentations generated by automated segmentation routines (silver segmentation corpora). During merging of these resources, each simplified gold tracking marker at each time-point will consider all dense segmentation masks that cover more than 50% of it as in [9]. The dense segmentation masks that fail to cover more than 50% of any simplified gold tracking marker are discarded. Note that for each simplified gold tracking marker, there can exist at most one such segmentation mask. Consequently, a cumulative gray-scale mask with counts of how many times an image element was observed in the considered masks is computed. This fused mask is thresholded and labeled according to the corresponding gold marker label. Results are put into an output image that accumulates these relabeled dense segmentations. Note that these relabeled segmentation masks can overlap or consist of unconnected components. We are simply removing overlapping areas. Furthermore, if the relabeled segmentation mask size is reduced by more than 10%, it is removed entirely to prevent from spurious objects. Finally, if the relabeled segmentation masks consist of unconnected components (i.e. isolated islands), these components are also removed and only the largest component is kept. The flow of the proposed merging is illustrated in Fig. 2 and its pseudocode can be found in Algorithm 1.

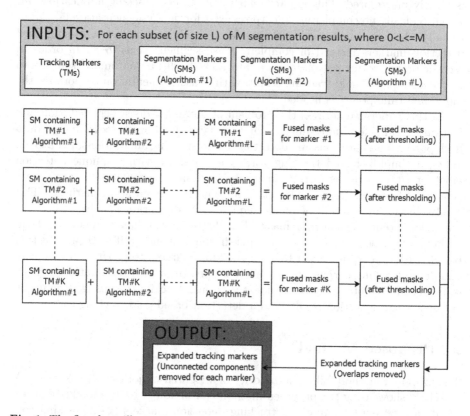

Fig. 1. The flowchart illustrating the proposed merging of a gold tracking corpus with dense silver segmentation corpora.

The silver dense segmentation corpus was created using a traditional majority voting scheme with a threshold value of 2/3 of the number of input segmentation results. The fused silver segmentation and gold tracking corpora allowed us to calculate various spatio-temporal characteristics (e.g., the average cell overlap due to its movement between consecutive images) of the real videos. The pseudocode of this algorithm is provided in Algorithm 1.

In order to obtain the best possible dense silver corpus, this method is applied to all possible combinations of available segmentation results. For N segmentation results, $2^N - 1$ different non-empty input sets for merging are processed. Each merging result is compared to the dense gold segmentation corpus in terms of SEG accuracy measure introduced in [7]. The input combination that produces

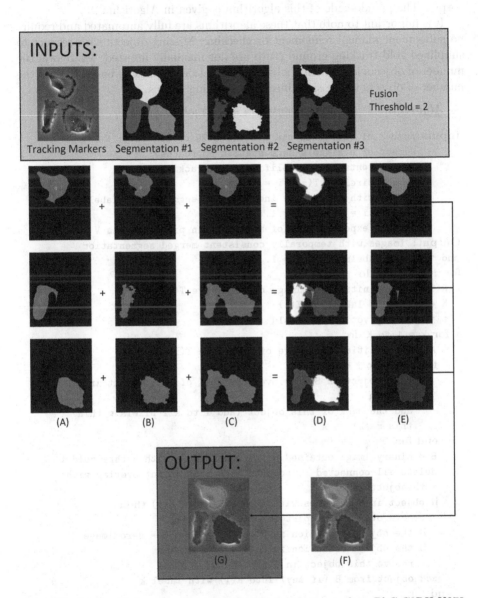

Fig. 2. Illustration of the proposed method with sample inputs from PhC-C2DH-U373 dataset. (A)-(C): Segmentation results from different sources, (D): Fused masks for each marker before thresholding, (E): Fused masks after thresholding, (F): Expanded tracking markers after removing overlaps and (G): Final expanded markers after removing unconnected components for each marker

the highest SEG score is taken as the input set of the dense silver segmentation corpus. The pseudo-code of this algorithm is given in Algorithm 2.

It is important to note that these algorithms are fully automated and require no subsequent manual refinement or checking. Missing objects with respect to simplified gold tracking ground truth are not manually inserted. Therefore, the number of objects in the dense silver segmentation corpus can be lower than the number of objects in the simplified gold tracking corpus.

Algorithm 1: *Merge_Segmentation_and_Tracking_Labels*

```
Inputs:Number of frames in the processed 2D or 3D video: N
       Number of available segmentation approaches: M
       Images containing simplified gold tracking labels
       (e.g., circles) T(i), i = 1...N
       Images with temporally inconsistent segmentation labels
       S(i,j), i = 1...N, j = 1...M
       Minimal expected size of an object in pixels/voxels V
Output: Images with temporally consistent merged segmentation
and tracking labels R(i), i = 1...N
for i = 1 to N do
  R(i) = zero-initialized image of size like T(i)
  K = number of labels in T(i)
  t = majority voting threshold
  for k = 1 to K do
    A = zero-initialized image of size like T(i)
    for j = 1 to M do
      if some object in S(i,j) overlaps >50% of k-th object in
      T(i) then
        add the mask of this object (add 1 to all pixels within
        this mask) to A
    end for
    B = binary image obtained by thresholding A with a threshold t
    delete all connected components in B that do not overlap with
    k-th object in T(i)
    if object in B overlaps with some object in R(i) then
      remove overlapping part in both B and R(i)
      if the object reduction in B was >10% then B = zero image
      if the object reduction in R(i) was >10% then
        remove this object in R(i)
    add object from B (if any) into R(i) with label k
  end for
  remove all unconnected object components in R(i) whose size is
  smaller than V
end for
return R
```

Algorithm 2: *Find_Optimal_Combination_of_Segmentation_Approaches*

Input: The same as in Algorithm 1 plus gold segmentation labels
for selected frames or selected objects only G(i), i = 1...N,
where G(i) can be empty or incomplete for some frames
Output: The same as in Algorithm 1 but for the optimal subset
of segmentation approaches
SEG_{best} = 0
for each non-empty subset Z of 1...M do
  R = result of Algorithm 1 run with input segmentation
  approaches restricted to set Z (the input parameter M will be
  equal to |Z|)
  SEG = average Jaccard index for all objects in G compared to
  corresponding objects in R
  if SEG > SEG_{best} then SEG_{best} = SEG, R_{best} = R
end for
return R_{best}

3 Experimental Results

In the experiments, simulated datasets are used due to the availability of complete and dense gold segmentation and tracking corpora. Experiments are carried out using two time-lapse videos of Fluo-N2DH-SIM+ training dataset from Cell Tracking Challenge [8], one of the few resources for which a large simplified gold tracking corpus is available. For both videos, segmentation results of 13 different algorithms from Cell Tracking Challenge are available. In the experiments, six segmentation results that perform above a certain threshold are used for merging. First video is a sequence of 65 images and the second video is a sequence of 150 images. Therefore, segmentation markers are merged using $2^6 - 1$ (empty set is excluded) different combinations of inputs to get the best possible dense silver segmentation corpus and compared to the gold segmentation corpus in this case of simulated datasets with complete and dense ground truth. The combination that gives the highest SEG score is selected as the input set of dense silver segmentation corpus. For the first video, merging outputs that produce the highest SEG score is obtained using four segmentation results; HD-Hau-GE, KTH-SE (1), FR-Ro-GE and LEID-NL. While on the second video, three segmentation results, KTH-SE (1), PAST-FR and FR-Ro-GE, produce the optimal merging outputs in terms of SEG score over reference objects. Experimental results obtained on the first video and the second video are presented in Table 1. Computation time was 12 h for the first video and 21 h for the second video for 63 different combinations of six available segmentation results. Experiments are carried out on a Linux SMP Debian 4.9.65 machine that runs on Intel(R) Core(TM) i7 CPU 920 with 12 GB RAM.

It is shown in Table 1 that on the first video, our merging tool outper-forms segmentation results of individual algorithms in terms of SEG score. This improvement can be observed in Fig. 3. On the second video (Table 1), merged segmentation result produces the same SEG score as KTH-SE (1) does. The SEG score is known to permit various sources of segmentation errors that, however, lead to the same coefficient value in the case of the second video (Table 1). The number of not expanded markers are more in KTH-SE (1) segmentation (203 markers due to not found, 96 markers due to unresolved collision; 299 markers in total) than in the merged segmentation (128 markers due to not found, 163 markers due to unresolved collision; 291 markers in total). Moreover, the merged segmentation contains more expanded markers (3072 markers) than KTH-SE (1) segmentation does (3064 markers). Therefore, the merged segmentation is not

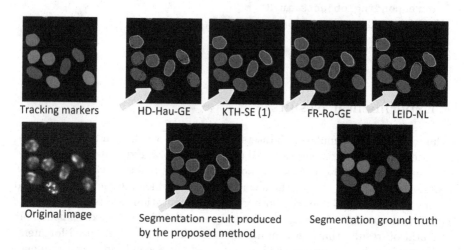

Fig. 3. A sample set of gold tracking markers, segmentation sources that achieve the best possible merging result, (visually enhanced) original image, segmentation result produced by the proposed method and the segmentation ground truth of the 41-st frame of the first video. The segmentation results are shown in blue and are overlaid with contours of the ground truth to facilitate the comparison. Yellow arrows point on the same nuclei that is under-/over-segmented in the results. (Color figure online)

Table 1. SEG scores for segmented objects in the first video (second row) and in the second video (third row). First column denotes the merging outputs that are obtained using results of HD-Hau-GE, KTH-SE (1), FR-Ro-GE and LEID-NL for the first video and using results of KTH-SE (1), PAST-FR and FR-Ro-GE for the second video. Rest of the columns present individual algorithm results.

Merged	HD-Hau-GE	KTH-SE (1)	UZH-CH	PAST-FR	FR-Ro-GE	LEID-NL
0.873	0.798	0.865	0.807	0.844	0.848	0.864
0.657	0.579	0.657	0.574	0.629	0.640	0.605

identical to the original KTH-SE (1) segmentation despite the SEG score values are the same. Since the other inputs scored lower SEG score values, they must be deviating from the segmentation ground truth in more regions than KTH-SE (1) does. We also observed a similar performance on real datasets. The proposed method is voting-based, suggesting that most of individual over-segmentations will be stripped away unless majority supports them. Similarly, most of individual under-segmentations will be recovered. This leads to a merged segmentation that is more compact in shape (compare, e.g., top row with column (E) in Fig. 2), and increases the SEG score. On the other hand, sometimes majority of input results misses a cell or nuclei largely or completely, leading to a decrease of the overall SEG score. Similarly, removing overlapping parts of colliding markers decreases the SEG score while removing unconnected components (i.e. isolated islands) increases it. Therefore, our tool provides an increase in the segmentation accuracy for the images, for which removed areas of unconnected components are larger than overlapping parts of colliding markers.

4   Discussion and Future Directions

We have presented a method for creating large, dense tracking labels by merging existing corpora of various partial dense segmentations and a detection based tracking corpus. This method has the potential to save impossible amounts of manual human data annotation time when creating dense training data for microscopy datasets. We demonstrated the proposed method on datasets from the Cell Tracking Challenge [8], showing that it generates high quality labels even on large bodies of data. The fused silver segmentation and simplified gold tracking corpora allowed us to calculate more precise and more complete spatio-temporal characteristics. Such characteristics cannot often be computed from pure tracking results due to simplified markers. Additionally, the merged labels can now be used to train various (end-to-end) processing routines.

In our experiments, simulated datasets are used due to the availability of full segmentation results for all frames. Additionally, this allowed us to evaluate the performance of the proposed method more accurately. Each possible combination of available segmentation sources is used as the input set in order to obtain the best possible merging result. Therefore, the proposed method is capable of producing more accurate segmentation results than individual segmentation sources. We also showed that the proposed method improves the quality of the final segmentation during merging in terms of SEG accuracy measure. While the proposed method may not always provide more accurate segmentation results than any individual segmentation source does, it ideally provides the most complete tracking result compared to any single silver segmentation corpus.

Future extensions can make use of more involved merging schemes such as STAPLE [1], SIMPLE [2], or image-based alternatives [10,11]. This could further improve the quality of merged segmentation labels. A comprehensive study using a large collection of CTC participant results and all CTC datasets will be performed.

Acknowledgements. This work has been supported by the German Federal Ministry of Research and Education (BMBF) under the code 031L0102 (de.NBI), and by the Czech Science Foundation (GACR), grant P302/12/G157.

References

1. Warfield, S.K., Zou, K.H., Wells, W.M.: Simultaneous truth and performance level estimation (STAPLE): an algorithm for the validation of image segmentation. IEEE Trans. Med. Imaging **23**(7), 903–921 (2004)
2. Langerak, T.R., van der Heide, U.A., Kotte, A.N.T.J., Viergever, M.A., van Vulpen, M., Pluim, J.P.W.: Label fusion in atlas-based segmentation using a selective and iterative method for performance level estimation (SIMPLE). IEEE Trans. Med. Imaging **29**(12), 2000–2008 (2010)
3. Lampert, T.A., Stumpf, A., Gançarski, P.: An empirical study into annotator agreement, ground truth estimation, and algorithm evaluation. IEEE Trans. Image Process. **25**(6), 2557–2572 (2016)
4. LeCun, Y., Bengio, Y., Hinton, G.: Deep learning. Nature **521**(6), 436–444 (2015)
5. Coutu, D.L., Schroeder, T.: Probing cellular processes by long-term live imaging-historic problems and current solutions. J. Cell Sci. **126**(17), 3805–3815 (2013)
6. Amat, F., et al.: Fast, accurate reconstruction of cell lineages from large-scale fluorescence microscopy data. Nat. Methods **11**(9), 951–958 (2014)
7. Maška, M., Ulman, V., Svoboda, D., et al.: A benchmark for comparison of cell tracking algorithms. Bioinformatics **30**(11), 1609–1617 (2014)
8. Ulman, V., Maška, M., Magnusson, K.E.G., et al.: An objective comparison of cell-tracking algorithms. Nat. Methods **14**(12), 1141–1152 (2017)
9. Matula, P., Maška, M., Sorokin, D.V., Matula, P., Ortiz-de Solórzano, C., Kozubek, M.: Cell tracking accuracy measurement based on comparison of acyclic oriented graphs. PLOS ONE **10**(12), 1–19 (2015)
10. Schlesinger, D., Jug, F., Myers, G., Rother, C., Kainmueller, D.: Crowd sourcing image segmentation with iaSTAPLE. In: IEEE International Symposium on Biomedical Imaging, pp. 401–405 (2017)
11. Liu, X., Montillo, A., Tan, E.T., Schenck, J.F.: iSTAPLE: improved label fusion for segmentation by combining STAPLE with image intensity. In: SPIE Medical Imaging, pp. 866–920 (2013)

Identification of *C. elegans* Strains Using a Fully Convolutional Neural Network on Behavioural Dynamics

Avelino Javer[1,2(✉)], André E. X. Brown[3,4], Iasonas Kokkinos[5], and Jens Rittscher[1,2]

[1] Institute of Biomedical Engineering, Department of Engineering Science, University of Oxford, Oxford, UK
{avelino.javer,jens.rittscher}@eng.ox.ac.uk
[2] Big Data Institute, University of Oxford, Oxford, UK
[3] MRC London Institute of Medical Sciences, London, UK
andre.brown@imperial.ac.uk
[4] Institute of Clinical Sciences, Imperial College London, London, UK
[5] Facebook AI Research, Paris, France
iasonask@fb.com

Abstract. The nematode *C. elegans* is a promising model organism to understand the genetic basis of behaviour due to its anatomical simplicity. In this work, we present a deep learning model capable of discerning genetically diverse strains based only on their recorded spontaneous activity, and explore how its performance changes as different embeddings are used as input. The model outperforms hand-crafted features on strain classification when trained directly on time series of worm postures.

Keywords: Behavioural phenotyping · Classification · Deep learning

1 Introduction

Animals interact with the world through their behaviour which involves the processing of sensory inputs and the generation of motor outputs by the neural system. Until recently most of the studies of animal behaviour relied on manual scoring certain expert defined actions by human reviewers. While time consuming, these approaches also lack objectivity and can result in poor reproducibility of experimental results. Advances in recording, storage and processing technology make it now possible to collect time-lapse recordings, and analyse large data collections in a controlled manner [1]. Inspired by the recent advancements in recognising human actions [3,14,15], computer vision methods are now being adopted to develop computer assisted approaches for the quantitative analysis of animal behaviour [6,8,9,17].

The nematode worm *C. elegans* is particularly appropriate for behaviour quantification. Due to its experimental amenability and its small nervous system,

© Springer Nature Switzerland AG 2019
L. Leal-Taixé and S. Roth (Eds.): ECCV 2018 Workshops, LNCS 11134, pp. 455–464, 2019.
https://doi.org/10.1007/978-3-030-11024-6_35

it is the perfect candidate to understand the genetic basis of behaviour [17] and to dissect the neural circuits responsible for complex behaviours such as foraging, navigating and mating [6]. Even more it has a simple morphology that can be abstracted as the coordinates of its midline (skeleton). This abstraction has been shown to be effective in characterising worm behaviour particularly in large sets of data [2,12,16,19–21].

Recently proposed convolutional networks for object recognition [10,18] and semantic segmentation [13] not only demonstrate that such approaches can outperform traditional methods, they also illustrate that it is possible to learn such models directly from raw image data. Here, we aim to investigate if biologically relevant motion signatures can be learned directly from video data. To achieve this goal we developed a framework for training a deep learning classifier that can predict the worm's strain type based on its recorded behaviour. We consider diverse sets of inputs for the model: some derived from the worm skeletons extracted using traditional computer vision methods, while others are learned using an autoencoder on the raw images.

The datasets used in our study are described in Sect. 2. The different approaches for extracting relevant signatures that capture the pose of the worm are detailed in Sect. 3. The deep learning based model for classification is presented in Sect. 4. Finally, we present our results in Sect. 5 and summarise our conclusions. Overall our results are very promising. When using inputs that are derived directly from the worm postures the classifier outperforms the accuracy obtained using hand-crafted features. However, although the image reconstruction results obtained by the autoencoder are very convincing, the classification performance degrades when the autoencoder embeddings are used as inputs. Potential approaches to improve the classification accuracy are discussed in Sect. 6.

2 Datasets

All the videos were segmented, tracked, and skeletonised using Tierpsy Tracker [7] (http://ver228.github.io/tierpsy-tracker/).

Single-Worm (SW) Dataset. The data was obtained from the Open Worm Movement Database [7] (http://movement.openworm.org/). Each of the videos in this dataset focuses on a single worm that is followed, with the help of a motorised stage, as it moves around the recording plate. We restricted our analysis to include only 15 min videos of young adults on food, and where at least 50% of the frames were successfully skeletonized by the tracking software. We include mostly videos that were used in published papers [2,16].

The dataset comprises 10476 videos of individual worms divided between 365 different classes. It includes mutants of the laboratory control strain (N2) affecting neurodevelopment, synaptic and extrasynaptic signalling, muscle function, and morphology as well as wild isolates representing some of the natural heterogeneity of *C. elegans*. All the videos for a given strain are given the same class label, except N2 where hermaphrodites and males are considered as separated classes. We only included classes that have at least six videos.

Multi-Worm (MW) Dataset. The dataset consists of recordings of a fixed 2×2 mm area taken with a high-resolution camera. There are either 5 or 10 worms in each of the recorded plates. The twelve strains used in this dataset are part of the divergent set from the Caenorhabditis elegans Natural Diversity Resource (CeNDR) [4]. This small subset of CeNDR collection is a representative sample of the genetic diversity found among the *C. elegans* wild isolates. A total of 308 videos were collected, with between 25 and 28 videos per strain.

One important difference with the SW dataset is that due to the overlap between worms trajectories the identity of individual worm is frequently lost. The results is that rather than having continuous data for each worm along the video, we have a series of fragments terminated every time two or more worms encounter.

3   Postural Embeddings

One key consideration in our study is how the pose of a given worm should be embedded to facilitate the classification task. The skeletonization summarises the worm posture and its head to tail orientation. Therefore embeddings extracted from skeletons have the advantage that they implicitly take the anatomy of the worm into account. Alternatively, it is possible to learn a representation directly from the image data using an autoencoder. In the following sections we provide the details for each of these approaches. The embeddings are then stacked over time to create the postural maps presented in Fig. 1 and fed to the classifier as explained in the next section.

3.1   Skeletons Angles and Eigenworms

As a preprocessing step the skeletons are interpolated in space to have a total of 49 evenly spaced points. The skeletons are interpolated also in time to achieve a constant temporal sampling separation of 0.04 s. Due to clutter, artefacts or the worm coiling over itself the skeletonisation can fail. If the time gap of unskeletonised frames is less than 0.25 s linear interpolation between the closest skeletonised frames is used to compensate for the missing data. Larger gaps coming mostly from coiling/turning worms are set to zero. Finally the skeletons are smoothed in both space and time using the Savitzky-Golay filter.

The dimensions of each skeleton is 49×2. To further reduce the dimensionality and focus on the posture, we follow the procedure introduced in ref [19]. As a first step we calculate the tangent angle between consecutive points as

$$\theta'_i = \arctan\left(\frac{x_{i+1} - x_i}{y_{i+1} - y_i}\right) \tag{1}$$

$$\theta_i = \theta'_i - \frac{1}{N_s - 1} \sum_{n=1}^{N_s - 1} \theta'_n, \tag{2}$$

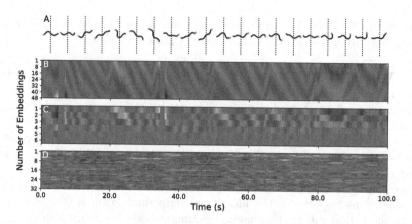

Fig. 1. Comparison between the different types of embeddings for the same worm movie. (A) Example of the worm postures at intervals of 128 frames. The blue lines represent the worm skeletons, the orange circles show the head side and the dash lines align to the corresponding column in the maps below. (B) Skeletons angles, the elements in the embeddings are ordered from head to tail. (C) Eigenworms, the elements are sorted from the most important PCA to the least important. (D) Embeddings from the autoencoder.

where $N_s = 49$ is the total number of segments, x_i and y_i are each segment coordinates, and θ_i is the corresponding segment angle. The resulting embedding has 48 elements as shown in Fig. 1B.

In a second step the angles are projected onto a set of eigenvectors u_μ previously calculated from the PCA of all the skeletons angles in the SW dataset, also called eigenworms. Stephen et al. [19] demonstrated that the first four eigenvectors are sufficient to capture 95% of the observed postural variance. Following Li et al. [12] we decided to use the first six eigenvectors that capture 98% of the total variance. An example of the resulting embeddings is shown in Fig. 1C.

3.2 Autoencoder

For the MW dataset we also extracted the embeddings directly from videos using the convolutional autoencoder described in Fig. 2A. Since most of the pixels in the video are background we only use regions of 128×128 pixels around each individual worms. We set the embedding dimension to have 32 elements. We used 95% of the videos for training and the rest was reserved as the test set. During training we used data augmentation by applying random shifts and flips to the images. We used the L_1-norm as loss function, and train with stochastic gradient descent (SGD) using a learning rate (lr) of 10^{-4} and momentum of 0.9. We stopped the training when the loss function in the test set did not show any improvement. Some examples of the encoded/decoded images are shown in Fig. 2B.

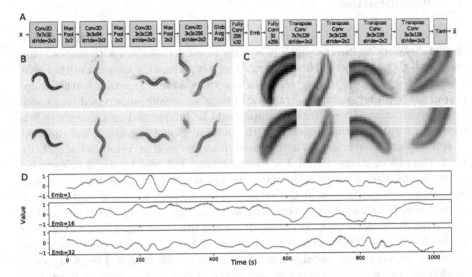

Fig. 2. The embeddings learned by the autoencoder can recover the worm shape with high accuracy. (A) Autoencoder architecture. The blue blocks show the encoder module, the grey block the embedding, and the red blocks the decoder module. (B) Comparison between the original image, on top, and the autoencoder reconstruction, bottom, of four randomly selected images. The reconstruction is highly similar to the original and it even suppresses objects surrounding the worm in the centre of the image. It is likely that this denoising behaviour arises from the model regression to the sample mean [11]. (C) Same as B but zoomed on the worm head. (D) Example of three elements of the embedding vector over time. The signals are continuous indicating a smooth temporal transition between the embeddings for different postures in the video. (Color figure online)

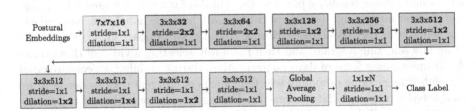

Fig. 3. Architecture of the fully convolutional classification model. The model starts with a simple 7 × 7 convolution and is followed by a series of strided convolution. Since the time dimension in the embedding maps is much larger than the embeddings dimension, we used asymmetric strides 1 × 2 after the second strided convolution. We then used a series of dilated convolutions in order to increase the explored space without reducing temporal resolution as in ref [23]. Note that the dilation only occurs in the time dimension. Finally, we condensed the learned features using a global average pooling and create a classification layer using a 1 × 1 convolution.

4   Classification

The classification model is shown in Fig. 3 and was inspired by the Dilated Resnet Network architecture [23]. Contrary to most classifiers with stacked convolutions, this architecture does not aggressively reduce the network output size. The result is that the output layers before the classifier generate feature maps rich in spatial information and capable of improve weakly-supervised tasks such as object location. These features maps could be interpreted as a timeseries feature transformation that together with the final global average is not different in spirit from the averages of user defined features used in Yemini *et al.* [22]. In brief, the model starts with a 7 × 7 convolution, followed by five 3 × 3 strided convolutions, then a series of dilated convolutions (2-4-2-1), and finally a classification layer consisting on global average pooling and a 1 × 1 convolution. Each convolution is followed by batch normalisation and a leaky ReLU activation. The strided convolutions modules condense the time dimension by a factor of 32 while the dilation layers add an extra factor of four. Therefore each row in the resulting features map contains the information of 128 frames. The statistics of the feature maps are then summarised by the global average pooling layer. One of the advantages of this model is that it can be applied to inputs of arbitrary size. We can use the same model with trajectories of different length or even combine several trajectories together in order to get predictions at the population level. This is particularly useful in the case of the MW dataset where the worm trajectories are fragmented and their individual identity is lost.

Training. We trained both datasets using SGD with a mini-batch size of eight. For the MW dataset model we used Adam as the optimiser with a lr of 10^{-4} for the angles and eigenworms, and a lr of 10^{-5} for the autoencoder embeddings. 75% of the data is used for training and 25% for testing. For the SW dataset we used a lr 10^{-3}, a momentum of 0.9 and weight decay of 10^{-4}. The lr is reduced to 10^{-4} when the loss reaches a plateau. Two thirds of the data are used for training and the rest for testing. In order to compensate for class imbalance, particularly problematic in the SW dataset, during training we sampled in two steps: first randomly selecting a strain, and then randomly selecting a video of that strain. Additionally, as a form of data augmentation, during training we concatenated the embeddings along randomly selected chunks of different trajectories until we completed a map with 22500 elements. During testing we evaluated the results concatenating all the embedding available for a given video.

Comparison with Manually-Defined Features. In order to have a baseline for comparison, we trained a simple classifier using the manually-defined features used in Yemini *et al.* [22]. This set of features is the best method reported in the literature to identify mutant strains from the control strain N2. The trained classifier consists in a fully connected layer followed by a softmax layer. Before training we z-transform data (subtracting the mean and dividing by the standard deviation) and set to zero any remaining undefined value. We trained using

SGD with a lr of 10^{-3}, a momentum of 0.9 and a mini-batch size of 64. We used the same data partition between training and test sets used for the fully convolutional classifier.

Table 1. Classifier results.

Training	Top-1 Acc.	Top-5 Acc.	F1-score
MW Manually-defined features	83.49	99.08	0.8323
MW eigenworms	98.17	99.08	0.9816
MW angles	**98.17**	**99.08**	**0.9803**
MW autoencoder	58.72	93.58	0.5944
SW Manually-defined features	43.20	66.47	0.3574
SW eigenworms	49.40	72.73	0.4204
SW angles	**58.44**	**81.99**	**0.5323**

5 Results

Classification Accuracy. The classification results are presented in Table 1. Overall, the best results are obtained when the skeleton angles are used as input. A similar result is obtained in the MW dataset when the input of the model are the eigenworms, however for the SW dataset the top1 accuracy is almost ten percentage points lower. This suggests that there is some relevant information that is lost in the eigenworm transform. Nevertheless the eigenworms have the advantage of requiring less operations due to the smaller embedding size (6 vs 48) and by consequence the models can be trained considerably faster. This, combined with the fact that the eigenworms still produce better results than the manually-defined features makes them a promising alternative for small datasets. By contrast, when the autoencoder embeddings (Sect. 3.2) are used as input, the performance degrades significantly. It is hard to pinpoint what causes the drop in accuracy. The autoencoder produces denoised reconstructions of the original images. Therefore, the lower accuracy is not likely to be caused by a limited model capacity. One possible explanation might be that the embedding representation entangles the worm postures with other information presented in the images such as the texture or the worm orientation. This extra information might cause the model to overfit since it might be learning to identify individual videos rather than the actual differences between strains. One possible solution could be to condition the autoencoder embeddings to the worm skeletons. We plan to explore this possibility in detail in a future work.

Learned Features. We visualise the features learned by the classifier using t-SNE (Fig. 4). For the MW dataset the features cluster nicely along the strain type as it is expected from the model high classification accuracy. The SW data shows a larger overlap, particularly the control strain N2. This is not particularly surprising since most of the strains present in the database are mutants of N2 and some might not even have a clear different behavioural phenotype with respect to their parent strain. More interesting is to observe a clear cluster formed by the wild type isolates, as well as a degree of separation among the Uncordinate (Unc) and Egg-laying defective (Egl) strains [5].

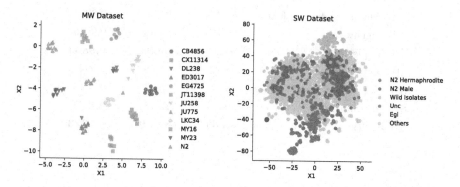

Fig. 4. The features learned by the classifier cluster according to the strain type. t-SNE visualization of the activations of classifier penultimate layer on the test set data. (A) The features from the MW Dataset cluster tightly according to the strain type. The only exception is a DL238 video that clusters with ED3017 and it is likely to be a mislabelled sample. (B) The features from the SW Dataset show a higher degree of overlapping. For visualization purposes we grouped some strains that share similar behaviour. N2 hermaprodites, the control strain with 483 videos, N2 male with 19 videos, the wild isolates with 208 videos among 20 different strains, Unc, Uncoodinate meaning animals with deviations in self-propelled movement with 519 videos among 58 strains, Egl, Egg-laying defective with 357 videos among 38 strains.

6   Conclusions

We have demonstrated that it is possible to train a classifier to distinguish between *C. elegans* strains using individual postural dynamics alone. More importantly, this classifier considerably improves the accuracy over the state of the art classification method given by the manual-crafted features defined in Yemeni *et al.* [22].

The main limitation of our current setup seems to be data overfitting rather than model capacity since all the trained models were able to fit almost perfectly their corresponding training data. More data should be available as the Open Worm Movement Database grows. Additionally, it might be possible to develop better sampling methods that could be used as data augmentation and help to reduce the early overfitting.

A logical next step will be to train an end-to-end model capable of classifying strains directly from the raw videos. However, to gather a dataset that contains the range of variability observed across laboratories remains a challenge. For example the SW dataset is probably the world largest worm behavioural dataset but all the data comes from a single laboratory using one type of setup. By contrast, there are several worm trackers available capable of extracting the skeletons from raw video. Those skeletons should not strongly depend on the imaging setup, and therefore a model trained on these inputs should be more easily deployed among the worm community.

Acknowledgments. This work was supported by grants EPSRC SeeBiByte Programme EP/M013774/1 to JR and Medical Research Council MC-A658-5TY30 to AEXB. AJ benefited from both grants.

References

1. Brown, A.E.X., de Bivort, B.: Ethology as a physical science. Nat. Phys. **14**(7), 653–657 (2018). https://doi.org/10.1038/s41567-018-0093-0
2. Brown, A.E., Yemini, E.I., Grundy, L.J., Jucikas, T., Schafer, W.R.: A dictionary of behavioral motifs reveals clusters of genes affecting caenorhabditis elegans locomotion. Proc. Natl. Acad. Sci. **110**(2), 791–796 (2013)
3. Carreira, J., Zisserman, A.: Quo vadis, action recognition? a new model and the kinetics dataset. In: 2017 IEEE Conference on Computer Vision and Pattern Recognition (CVPR), pp. 4724–4733. IEEE (2017)
4. Cook, D.E., Zdraljevic, S., Roberts, J.P., Andersen, E.C.: Cendr, the caenorhabditis elegans natural diversity resource. Nucleic Acids Res. **45**(D1), D650–D657 (2016)
5. Fay, D.S.: Classical genetic methods. WormBook: the online review of *C. elegans* biology, pp. 1–58 (2013)
6. Hall, S.S.: Neuroscience: as the worm turns. Nature **494**(7437), 296–299 (2013). https://doi.org/10.1038/494296a
7. Javer, A., et al.: An open source platform for analyzing and sharing worm behavior data. bioRxiv (2018). https://doi.org/10.1101/377960, https://www.biorxiv.org/content/early/2018/07/26/377960
8. Jhuang, H., et al.: Automated home-cage behavioural phenotyping of mice. Nat. Commun. **1**, 68 (2010)
9. Kabra, M., Robie, A.A., Rivera-Alba, M., Branson, S., Branson, K.: Jaaba: interactive machine learning for automatic annotation of animal behavior. Nat. Methods **10**(1), 64 (2013)
10. Krizhevsky, A., Sutskever, I., Hinton, G.E.: Imagenet classification with deep convolutional neural networks. In: Advances in Neural Information Processing Systems, pp. 1097–1105 (2012)
11. Lehtinen, J., et al.: Noise2Noise: learning image restoration without clean data. In: Dy, J., Krause, A. (eds.) Proceedings of the 35th International Conference on Machine Learning. Proceedings of Machine Learning Research, vol. 80, pp. 2965–2974. PMLR, Stockholmsmässan, Stockholm, Sweden, 10–15 July 2018. http://proceedings.mlr.press/v80/lehtinen18a.html
12. Li, K., Javer, A., Keaveny, E.E., Brown, A.E.: Recurrent neural networks with interpretable cells predict and classify worm behaviour. bioRxiv p. 222208 (2017)

13. Long, J., Shelhamer, E., Darrell, T.: Fully convolutional networks for semantic segmentation. In: Proceedings of the IEEE Conference on Computer Vision and Pattern Recognition, pp. 3431–3440 (2015)
14. Rahmani, H., Mian, A., Shah, M.: Learning a deep model for human action recognition from novel viewpoints. IEEE Trans. Pattern Anal. Mach. Intell. **99**(1), 1–1 (2017)
15. Schindler, K., Van Gool, L.: Action snippets: How many frames does human action recognition require? In: IEEE Conference on Computer Vision and Pattern Recognition, CVPR 2008, pp. 1–8. IEEE (2008)
16. Schwarz, R.F., Branicky, R., Grundy, L.J., Schafer, W.R., Brown, A.E.: Changes in postural syntax characterize sensory modulation and natural variation of *C. elegans* locomotion. PLoS Comput. Biol. **11**(8), e1004322 (2015)
17. Sengupta, P., Samuel, A.D.: Caenorhabditis elegans: a model system for systems neuroscience. Curr. Opin. Neurobiol. **19**(6), 637–643 (2009)
18. Simonyan, K., Zisserman, A.: Very deep convolutional networks for large-scale image recognition. arXiv preprint arXiv:1409.1556 (2014)
19. Stephens, G.J., Johnson-Kerner, B., Bialek, W., Ryu, W.S.: Dimensionality and dynamics in the behavior of *C. elegans*. PLoS Comput. Biol. **4**(4), e1000028 (2008)
20. Wählby, C., et al.: An image analysis toolbox for high-throughput *C. elegans* assays. Nat. Methods **9**(7), 714 (2012)
21. Yan, G., et al.: Network control principles predict neuron function in the caenorhabditis elegans connectome. Nature **550**(7677), 519 (2017)
22. Yemini, E., Jucikas, T., Grundy, L.J., Brown, A.E., Schafer, W.R.: A database of caenorhabditis elegans behavioral phenotypes. Nat. Methods **10**(9), 877 (2013)
23. Yu, F., Koltun, V., Funkhouser, T.: Dilated residual networks. In: Computer Vision and Pattern Recognition, vol. 1, p. 2 (2017)

Towards Automated Multiscale Imaging and Analysis in TEM: Glomerulus Detection by Fusion of CNN and LBP Maps

Elisabeth Wetzer[1]([⊠]) [ID], Joakim Lindblad[1,4] [ID], Ida-Maria Sintorn[1,3],
Kjell Hultenby[2], and Nataša Sladoje[1,4] [ID]

[1] Uppsala University, Uppsala, Sweden
{elisabeth.wetzer,joakim.lindblad,ida.sintorn}@it.uu.se
[2] Karolinska Institute, Solna, Sweden
kjell.hultenby@ki.se
[3] Vironova AB, Stockholm, Sweden
[4] Mathematical Institute of Serbian Academy of Sciences and Arts, Belgrade, Serbia

Abstract. Glomerulal structures in kidney tissue have to be analysed at a nanometer scale for several medical diagnoses. They are therefore commonly imaged using Transmission Electron Microscopy. The high resolution produces large amounts of data and requires long acquisition time, which makes automated imaging and glomerulus detection a desired option. This paper presents a deep learning approach for Glomerulus detection, using two architectures, VGG16 (with batch normalization) and ResNet50. To enhance the performance over training based only on intensity images, multiple approaches to fuse the input with texture information encoded in local binary patterns of different scales have been evaluated. The results show a consistent improvement in Glomerulus detection when fusing texture-based trained networks with intensity-based ones at a late classification stage.

Keywords: Glomerulus detection · Transmission Electron Microscopy · Convolutional Neural Networks · Local binary patterns Digital pathology

1 Introduction

The glomerulus is a structure in the kidney which acts as a filtration barrier for metabolic waste from the bloodstream. A number of diseases, such as minimal change disease, systemic lupus and many others, can affect the glomerulus and have serious impact on the kidneys and their function. Analysis of the thickness of the glomerular basement membrane (GBM), deposits of amyloid fibres, protein or virus-like deposits in the membrane, and foot process effacement, are some of the necessary nephropathological diagnostic procedures. Diagnostically relevant

L. Leal-Taixé and S. Roth (Eds.): ECCV 2018 Workshops, LNCS 11134, pp. 465–475, 2019.
https://doi.org/10.1007/978-3-030-11024-6_36

glomerular structures, such as protein fibres and deposits, are of nanometer-scale dimensions, which makes Transmission Electron Microscopy (TEM) the preferred imaging technique for glomerular analysis.

The first step in the analysis is detection of glomeruli in the sample. This is typically done at low magnification which allows a relatively large field of view (FOV) of the sample. A pathologist then continues the analysis of zoomed-in regions of interest, i.e., at higher magnification, focusing on the relevant structures of the glomerulus. This multi-scale analysis is currently performed manually, requiring that a pathologist spends a long time at the electron microscope. Figure 1 shows a typical sample mesh used in TEM, and a series of visualizations at increasing magnifications to the level at which the foot processes along the GBM are visible.

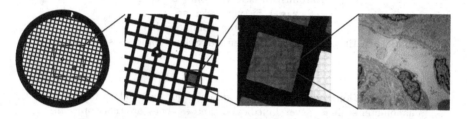

Fig. 1. A series of magnifications illustrating the vast search space for glomeruli on a mesh grid used for TEM with a diameter of 3 mm (left) to a single acquired image of size $16 \times 16\,\mu m$ (right). For ground truth annotation, to reliably identify a glomerulus, the foot processes along the GBM were used for recognition

Fully automated image acquisition of the relevant portions of the sample (glomeruli) in high magnification would significantly reduce the consumption of precious expert time and allow the expert to perform the diagnosis at his/her choice of time and place, rather than at the microscope.

We suggest a two-step approach to automate the imaging process: (1) Scanning is first performed at low magnification to identify regions of interest, followed by (2) imaging of only those detected regions of interest at high magnification. In this study, we focus on the first step: glomerulus detection in low magnification TEM images. The detection is based on classification of whole (low-mag) images as either part of a glomerulus or as other kidney tissue. An example of such a low-mag image is shown in Fig. 1 (right).

In bright-field microscopy images, glomeruli are recognized and detected by their characteristic texture; a variant of the LBP texture descriptor, named multi-radial color LBP (mcLBP) has recently shown to perform very well on the task [18]. In this study, we combine the ability of LBPs to describe the fine textural details with the classification power of Convolutional Neural Networks (CNNs). We are particularly inspired by the approach proposed in [1,8], where authors compute dense LBP feature maps which, in combination with raw image data, are classified using deep CNNs.

2 Background and Preliminaries

2.1 Previous Work

The descriptive power of recently suggested mcLBP for glomeruli detection in bright-field microscopy images [18], results from concatenated histograms of LBPs with different radii, computed for each RGB color channel separately. To further boost the performance and decrease the number of false positive detections, authors train a deep CNN, GoogleLeNet. They observed that the deep learning based approach solely performs worse than the one based on mcLBP. A number of other papers have demonstrated that it is often beneficial to combine hand crafted and learned features [12,13,16,17]. This can be seen as a variation of transfer learning, where the network is helped by additional views of the imaged data.

Approaches to combine the power of machine learning and LBPs in texture-based classification include extraction of histograms of LBP responses over sliding windows (in histopathological whole-slide images), followed by support vector machine (SVM) classification [18]. LBP histograms have also been used in combination with learned features of CNNs [12]. LBP-like features can also be learned, as in [11]. Instead of computing LBP histograms, LBPs can be used as a dense feature extractor, and combined with CNN [1,8]. Furthermore, LBPs can be interpreted as convolutional layers, with learned parameters [6,9].

We are following the very promising approach proposed in [1,8], where authors use dense LBP maps, in combination with the raw image data, as input for a CNN. The generation of LBP codes of an image results in an unordered set of binary codes where the distance between code values of two patterns does not reflect the distance between the patterns. This makes the direct usage of LBP codes unsuitable for CNNs; the discrete convolution operation computes a weighted sum of input values, similar to interpolation, but interpolation of the LBP codes does not have a meaningful interpretation. Therefore, a dissimilarity measure, defined in [8] for all possible codes, is used in multidimensional scaling (MDS), which is then applied to map the unordered set of codes into a metric space. This enables the (meaningful) use of convolutions on LBP maps.

2.2 Preliminaries

Local Binary Patterns (LBP) [14] are among the most successful texture descriptors in image analysis. Over time, a number of variants have been proposed [10], finding numerous applications [15].

In general, the LBP code $LBP_{r,p}(c)$, for a pixel c with intensity value g_c, is

$$LBP_{r,p}(c) = \sum_{i=0}^{p-1} s(g_i - g_c)\, 2^i \qquad s(x) = \begin{cases} 1 & x \geq 0, \\ 0 & x < 0 \end{cases} \qquad (1)$$

where $g_i \in \{0 \ldots p-1\}$ are pixels sampled equidistantly in a circle of radius r in the neighborhood of g_c (Fig. 2).

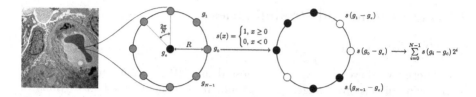

Fig. 2. LBP code sampling for intensity images

LBP codes are most often binned over the full image into a histogram, thereby providing a feature vector of size 2^p for the entire image. In [8] however, an LBP code is generated for every pixel without any following binning. Hence, a value in the range $[0, 2^{p-1}]$ is obtained for every pixel. This texture representation is, however, not well suited as an input to a deep convolutional network. CNNs are based on discrete convolutions which can be seen as a weighted average of their input. On the other hand, LBP codes are binary encoded such that codes with similar numeric values may represent not at all similar patterns. Performing numerical operations such as averaging is therefore not reasonable on a set of LBP codes; they need to be mapped into a metric space first. Such an approach, using multidimensional scaling to map LBP codes into Euclidean space, is proposed in [8].

Multidimensional Scaling (MDS) is a common technique in data science. Using (dis-)similarities of data points, MDS can be used to map the data from an unordered set $\mathbf{X} \subseteq \{2_2^8\}$ into a metric space by numerical optimization [2].

Non-metric multidimensional scaling is performed on the dissimilarity matrix $\Delta = (\delta_{ij}) \in \mathbb{R}_+^{n \times n}$. The so-called representation function $f(\delta_{ij})$ specifies the relation between the dissimilarities and their corresponding metric values $\mathbf{D} = (d_{ij}) \in \mathbb{R}_+^{n \times n}$ which lie in an Euclidean space and approximate a monotonic transformation of δ_{ij}. The resulting optimization problem aims to minimize an objective function referred to as stress. We follow [8] and use non-metric stress normalized by the sum of squares of the inter-point distances, also known as Kruskal's normalized stress-1 criterion [7]:

$$\text{Stress-1} = \sqrt{\frac{\sum [f(\delta_{ij}) - d_{ij}(\mathbf{X})]^2}{\sum d_{ij}^2(\mathbf{X})}} \tag{2}$$

Dissimilarity Measure. To apply MDS to the set of LBP codes, we use one of the dissimilarity measures between the codes suggested in [8]:

$$\delta_{ij} = \delta(P_i, P_j) = \min \left\{ \tilde{\delta}(P_i^0, P_j^0), \tilde{\delta}(\text{rev}(P_i^0), P_j^0), \tilde{\delta}(P_i^0, \text{rev}(P_j^0)) \right\}. \tag{3}$$

Here, $\tilde{\delta}(P_i, P_j) = \|CDF(P_i) - CDF(P_j)\|_1$, where $CDF(P)$ is the cumulative distribution function of bit values; this approximates the Earth Mover's Distance between the strings (more details about the efficient computation can be found in [8]). P^0 is the concatenation of the binary string P and an additional bit of 0 and rev(P) the rearrangement of a string P in reverse order.

LBP Maps are obtained by MDS (using Eq. (2)) applied to LBP codes computed for every image pixel. We follow recommendations from [1,8] and map the LBP codes into a 3-dimensional space. An example of a resulting LBP map is shown in Fig. 3, visualized as an RGB image.

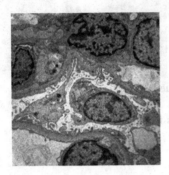

Fig. 3. Intensity image of Glomerulus and its corresponding LBP map in 3D metric space

3   Method

3.1   Dataset

16-bit intensity images of the size 2048×2048 pixels were acquired using MiniTEM[1], a desktop, low-voltage (25 keV) transmission electron microscope. The dataset consists of 494 images, grouped in two sets used for training and testing. The sets were independently acquired at different occasions using the built-in automatic imaging function in MiniTEM. The *training set* consists of 260 images, 70 of which have been marked as containing glomerulus specific structures, and 190 to contain other kidney tissue. The field of view (FOV) covered by one image is $16\,\mu m$, yielding a pixel size of $7.8\,nm$. The *test set* consists of 56 images containing glomerulus tissue, and 178 images of other kidney tissue (from two different samples). Example images of both classes, i.e., glomerulus and non-glomerulus, are shown in Fig. 4, illustrating the difficult task of distinguishing the two. Ground truth annotation was done on an image level based on the visual detection of foot processes.

---

[1] Vironova AB, Stockholm.

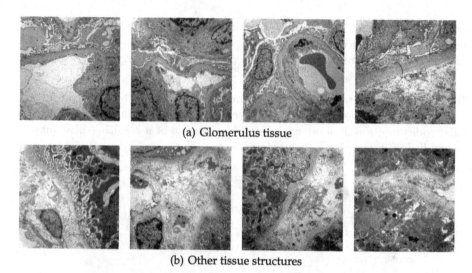

(a) Glomerulus tissue

(b) Other tissue structures

Fig. 4. Example images from the two classes

3.2 Architecture

We compare two architectures for the CNN models: VGG16 and ResNet50. They are trained from scratch on either the raw image data or the LBP maps. We evaluate fusion of raw and LBP data at three different depths of the networks.

Data augmentation, consisting of $0°, 90°, 180°, 270°$ rotations and mirroring, is performed for all training data, leading to $8\times$ data augmentation without interpolation. LBP codes are computed on the TEM intensity images. Following the LBP computation, the input data (intensity images as well as LBP maps) were resized to 224×224 pixels using nearest neighbor interpolation.

VGG16-like Architecture: The architecture used in the experiments is a modification of the VGG16 network [19], shown in Fig. 5(a). A batch normalization layer is introduced after each convolutional layer.

ResNet50: ResNet50 is a residual neural network with a total of 177 layers including batch normalizations and activation layers. The layers are learning residual functions with respect to the layer inputs [5].

We have investigated three different fusion strategies – early, mid and late fusion – to combine texture and intensity information. To enhance multi-scale descriptive power of LBPs, we observe $LBP_{1,8}$, $LBP_{2,8}$, and $LBP_{3,8}$, and create their corresponding maps.

Early Fusion: In the early fusion model, the raw image layer is stacked with the three layers of (3D) LBP maps and fed into the input layer of the CNN. The

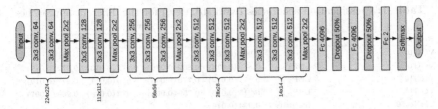

(a) VGG16 – a batch normalization layer was introduced after each convolutional layer

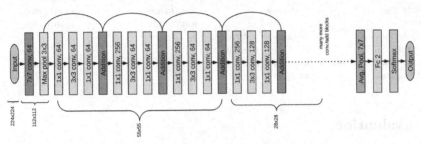

(b) ResNet50 architecture as introduced in [5]

Fig. 5. Used architectures. Early fusion takes place in the input layer, mid fusion in the second fully connected layer (VGG16 only), and late fusion after the softmax layer.

intensity image and LBP maps are subsequently jointly used in training using cross-entropy loss and stochastic gradient descent. In the multi-scale experimental setup, the raw image layer is stacked with the, in total, nine layers of LBP maps corresponding to the varying radii ($r \in \{1, 2, 3\}$) in LBP extraction.

Mid Fusion: The mid fusion model is only tested for the VGG16-like architecture. It uses a two-stream architecture; one CNNs is trained on the normalized intensity images, the other on the (single scale) 3-layer LBP maps. Once the two networks are trained, the outputs of the second fully connected layers of both architectures are concatenated, resulting in 2×4096 features. A linear SVM is then trained on the resulting 8192-feature vectors.

Late Fusion: Two CNNs are independently trained, one using the normalized intensity data as input, the other the 3-layer LBP maps. As in [1], the output probabilities of the softmax layers of the two networks are concatenated and a linear SVM is trained to classify the data based on such 4-feature vectors. For the multi-scale setup, the outputs of four networks are fused, thus resulting in 8-feature vectors for the SVM.

Table 1. Classification accuracies (with std. dev.) for the different approaches.

Architecture	Input	No fusion	Early fusion	Mid fusion	Late fusion
VGG16	Intensity	0.907 (0.061)			
VGG16	$LBP_{1,8}$	0.843 (0.014)	0.839 (0.076)	0.971 (0.013)	0.972 (0.017)
VGG16	$LBP_{2,8}$	0.941 (0.012)	0.770 (0.046)	0.970 (0.011)	0.977 (0.019)
VGG16	$LBP_{3,8}$	0.915 (0.013)	0.759 (0.068)	0.972 (0.009)	0.969 (0.007)
ResNet50	Intensity	0.964 (0.016)			
ResNet50	$LBP_{1,8}$	0.926 (0.018)	0.728 (0.004)		**0.984** (0.003)
ResNet50	$LBP_{2,8}$	0.929 (0.073)	0.724 (0.008)		0.979 (0.007)
ResNet50	$LBP_{3,8}$	0.946 (0.016)	0.731 (0.018)		**0.984** (0.006)
VGG16	Multiscale		0.863 (0.026)		0.983 (0.008)
ResNet	Multiscale		0.857 (0.021)		0.980 (0.004)
VGG16 Transfer	Intensity	0.877 (0.062)			
ResNet50 Transfer	Intensity	0.963 (0.005)			
VGG16 ResNet50 Ensemble	Intensity				0.970 (0.005)
SVM, baseline	$LBP_{2,8}$	0.752			

4   Evaluation

All models are trained from scratch for 20 epochs using stochastic gradient descent with momentum of 0.9, a learning rate of 0.001, an L_2 regularization of 10^{-4} and a mini-batch size of 16. Average accuracy (ratio of the correctly identified test samples and their total number) over seven runs of CNN experiments for two types of architectures, VGG16 and ResNet50, are reported in Table 1 and Fig. 6. We present results obtained by networks trained solely on one type of input (intensity images or LBP maps), as well as results obtained by different methods of fusion (early, mid, or late) of the intensity images and LBP maps, with different (indicated) parameters. *Multiscale* refers to the fusion of the LBP maps of three different radii with the intensity image data (4 networks fused).

For comparison, transfer learning on the intensity data is evaluated for the VGG16, as well as the ResNet50 architecture. Both networks were pretrained on ImageNet [3], whereafter the last fully connected layer (in each) was retrained on the glomerulus data. Results are included in Table 1. The transfer learning performance is slightly lower than the from-scratch performance; we assume this is due to TEM images differing significantly from ImageNet data.

The effect of architecture ensembles has been investigated for reference by training a linear SVM on the softmax layer output of the VGG16 like architecture and ResNet50 architecture which were trained from scratch on the intensity images. The approach is similar to the late fusion, but with two different architectures on the same input, instead of the same architecture with two different input sources. It improves the outcome slightly compared to a single architecture performance, but does not reach the performance of the multiple input ensembles (fusion) utilizing the LBP maps.

As a reference performance, classification based on (multiple versions of classic) LBP histograms, using a linear SVM classifier, is performed. We observe

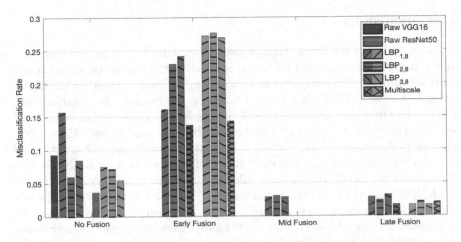

Fig. 6. Misclassification rate of different approaches, VGG16 in blue, ResNet50 in orange. Late fusion models, in particular based on ResNet50, give best results

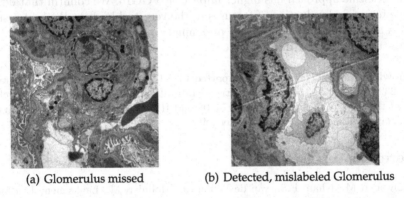

(a) Glomerulus missed   (b) Detected, mislabeled Glomerulus

Fig. 7. The only two misclassifications of the ResNet50 Late Fusion of intensity images and $LBP_{3,8}$: (a) False negative and (b) False positive detection (confirmed as mislabeled)

uniform $LBP_{1,8}$ and $LBP_{2,8}$, as well as two *rotation-invariant* versions of $LBP_{1,8}$ and $LBP_{2,8}$: by bit-wise shifting [14], and by using the discrete Fourier transform [4]. The best accuracy, reached by the DFT rotation-invariant $LBP_{2,8}$, is 0.752, which is considerably worse than the performance of the proposed method.

During manual post-validation of the results, one image, consistently classified as a false positive Glomerulus detection (and included in the quantitative evaluation as such), is found to have been incorrectly labelled during ground truth annotation. The only two misclassified images are shown in Fig. 7.

5   Conclusions

Our results show a consistent improvement in classification accuracy when texture information in form of LBP maps is fused with intensity information and classified using CNNs, compared to only relying on either classic SVM classification of LBPs, or CNN classification based on the intensity information only. Mid and late fusion exhibit similar performance for the VGG16 architecture, and both yield clearly better results than the early fusion strategy. ResNet50 exhibits superior performance to VGG16 when applied to a single type of input, in all cases but one (for $LBP_{2,8}$). The early fusion of input sources for ResNet50 performs the worst for all LBP maps, while the late fusion gives very good results, of which all exceed the accuracy achieved by VGG16. The multiscale approach of fusing LBP maps of varying LBP radii and intensity information gave the best results among all experiments for the early fusion setup, yet the late fusion yields overall best results. For the late fusion we cannot draw any clear conclusion about optimal LBP radius, the different radii perform roughly equally well. The multi-scale approach has higher impact on VGG16. We confirm that delaying the fusion and reduction of features to the very end leads to the best results for this application. Our promising preliminary results encourage continuation of the study on a larger dataset.

Acknowledgment. This work is supported by VINNOVA, MedTech4Health grants 2016-02329 and 2017-02447, the Ministry of Education, Science, and Techn. Development of the Rep. of Serbia (proj. ON174008 and III44006), and the Centre for Interdisciplinary Mathematics, Uppsala University.

References

1. Anwer, R.M., Khan, F.S., van de Weijer, J., Molinier, M., Laaksonen, J.: Binary patterns encoded convolutional neural networks for texture recognition and remote sensing scene classification. ISPRS J. Photogramm. Remote. Sens. **138**, 74–85 (2018)
2. Borg, I., Groenen, P.J.F.: Modern Multidimensional Scaling - Theory and Applications. Springer, New York (2005)
3. Deng, J., Dong, W., Socher, R., Li, L.J., Li, K., Fei-Fei, L.: ImageNet: a large-scale hierarchical image database. In: IEEE Conference on Computer Vision and Pattern Recognition, pp. 248–255 (2009)
4. Fernández, A., Ghita, O., González, E., Bianconi, F., Whelan, P.F.: Evaluation of robustness against rotation of LBP, CCR and ILBP features in granite texture classification. Mach. Vis. Appl. **22**(6), 913–926 (2011)
5. He, K., Zhang, X., Ren, S., Sun, J.: Deep residual learning for image recognition. In: IEEE Conference on Computer Vision and Pattern Recognition (CVPR), pp. 770–778 (2016)
6. Juefei-Xu, F., Boddeti, V.N., Savvides, M.: Local binary convolutional neural networks. In: IEEE Conference on Computer Vision and Pattern Recognition (CVPR), vol. 1, pp. 19–28. IEEE (2017)
7. Kruskal, J.B., Wish, M.: Multidimensional Scaling. Sage University Papers Series. Quantitative Applications in the Social Sciences, vol. 11, pp. 234–778 (1978)

8. Levi, G., Hassner, T.: Emotion recognition in the wild via convolutional neural networks and mapped binary patterns. In: Proceedings of ACM International Conference on Multimodal Interaction, pp. 503–510. ACM (2015)

9. Li, L., Feng, X., Xia, Z., Jiang, X., Hadid, A.: Face spoofing detection with local binary pattern network. J. Vis. Commun. Image Represent. **54**, 182–192 (2018)

10. Liu, L., Fieguth, P., Guo, Y., Wang, X., Pietikainen, M.: Local binary features for texture classification: taxonomy and experimental study. Patt. Rec. **62**, 135–160 (2017)

11. Lu, J., Liong, V.E., Zhou, X., Zhou, J.: Learning compact binary face descriptor for face recognition. IEEE Trans. PAMI **37**(10), 2041–2056 (2015)

12. Majtner, T., Yildirim-Yayilgan, S., Hardeberg, J.Y.: Combining deep learning and hand-crafted features for skin lesion classification. In: International Conference on Image Processing Theory Tools and Applications (IPTA), pp. 1–6. IEEE (2016)

13. Nahid, A.A., Kong, Y.: Histopathological breast-image classification using local and frequency domains by convolutional neural network. Information **9**(1), 19 (2018)

14. Ojala, T., Pietikainen, M., Maenpaa, T.: Multiresolution gray-scale and rotation invariant texture classification with local binary patterns. IEEE Trans. PAMI **24**(7), 971–987 (2002)

15. Pietikainen, M., Hadid, A., Zhao, G., Ahonen, T.: Computer Vision Using Local Binary Patterns. Springer, London (2011)

16. Rezaeilouyeh, H., Mollahosseini, A., Mahoor, M.H.: Microscopic medical image classification framework via deep learning and shearlet transform. J. Med. Imaging **3**(4), 044501 (2016)

17. Sadanandan, S.K., Ranefall, P., Wählby, C.: Feature augmented deep neural networks for segmentation of cells. In: Hua, G., Jégou, H. (eds.) ECCV 2016. LNCS, vol. 9913, pp. 231–243. Springer, Cham (2016). https://doi.org/10.1007/978-3-319-46604-0_17

18. Simon, O., Yacoub, R., Jain, S., Tomaszewski, J.E., Sarder, P.: Multi-radial LBP features as a tool for rapid glomerular detection and assessment in whole slide histopathology images. Sci. Rep. **8**(1), 2032 (2018)

19. Simonyan, K., Zisserman, A.: Very deep convolutional networks for large-scale image recognition. arXiv preprint arXiv:1409.1556 (2014)

Pre-training on Grayscale ImageNet Improves Medical Image Classification

Yiting Xie and David Richmond[✉]

IBM, Watson Health, Cambridge, MA 02142, USA
daverichmond@gmail.com

Abstract. Deep learning is quickly becoming the de facto standard approach for solving a range of medical image analysis tasks. However, large medical image datasets appropriate for training deep neural network models from scratch are difficult to assemble due to privacy restrictions and expert ground truth requirements, with typical open source datasets ranging from hundreds to thousands of images. A standard approach to counteract limited-size medical datasets is to pre-train models on large datasets in other domains, such as ImageNet for classification of natural images, before fine-tuning on the specific medical task of interest. However, ImageNet contains color images, which introduces artefacts and inefficiencies into models that are intended for single-channel medical images. To address this issue, we pre-trained an Inception-V3 model on ImageNet *after* converting the images to grayscale through a common transformation. Surprisingly, these models do not show a significant degradation in performance on the original ImageNet classification task, suggesting that color is not a critical feature of natural image classification. Furthermore, models pre-trained on grayscale ImageNet outperformed color ImageNet models in terms of both speed and accuracy when refined on disease classification from chest X-ray images.

Keywords: Domain adaptation · Transfer learning

1 Introduction

Deep learning algorithms, especially Convolutional Neural Networks (ConvNets), have gained great popularity in the field of medical image analysis in recent years [1]. ConvNet-based algorithms are rapidly replacing traditional machine learning algorithms, based on human-engineered features, for tasks such as image classification [2], object detection [3], and semantic segmentation [4].

There are two general strategies for training ConvNets: (1) training a model from randomly initialized weights, and (2) pre-training a model on a related task, and then refining the model on the target task. The former approach, referred to as "training from scratch", typically requires very large datasets to avoid overfitting and achieve state of the art results. Since, medical datasets are often very

---

Y. Xie and D. Richmond—Equal contribution.

© Springer Nature Switzerland AG 2019
L. Leal-Taixé and S. Roth (Eds.): ECCV 2018 Workshops, LNCS 11134, pp. 476–484, 2019.
https://doi.org/10.1007/978-3-030-11024-6_37

small, due to privacy restrictions and the expert knowledge required to generate ground truth, transfer learning from a pre-trained model is a popular approach for medical image analysis. There are numerous publicly available models that have been pre-trained on the ImageNet dataset [5], which consists of over 1.2 million labeled photographs. In a recent paper, Rajpurkar et al. [2] fine-tuned a DenseNet model, pre-trained on ImageNet, on a large-scale chest X-ray dataset [6] for a multi-disease classification problem and achieved state-of-the-art results.

However, the choice to start from a pre-trained model has implications for the final ConvNet design. In order to take a ConvNet that was pre-trained on natural images, and fine-tune it on medical images, the medical images need to be pre-processed to conform with the shape and structure of the original color images used to train the network. Since medical images often contain only a single channel, this usually involves stacking each grayscale image to a 3-channel pseudo-color image to mimic the RGB structure of natural images. However, the stacked 3-channel grayscale image does not contain any color information. Therefore, it is unclear whether the filters learned from color images are fully utilized in transfer learning, especially for filters in the first and second layers of the ConvNet, which represent lower level features such as colors and edges.

To address this issue, we trained a ConvNet using a grayscale version of the ImageNet data. A ConvNet was first trained from scratch on grayscale images converted from the ImageNet dataset using a standard transformation [7]. Then the pre-trained ConvNet was fine-tuned on two large-scale chest X-ray datasets for two different tasks: the NIH x-ray dataset [6] for multi-disease classification, and the Indiana University chest x-ray dataset [8] for normal image classification. We demonstrate that a network pre-trained on grayscale ImageNet is a better starting point for transfer learning on medical images, because it (1) leads to more accurate classification performance of the final model, (2) increases the speed of inference, due to the simplified kernel in the first model layer, and (3) removes the need for unnecessary pre-processing before inference.

2 Method

This study consists of two parts: training Inception-V3 models [9] from scratch on ImageNet and then fine-tuning the pre-trained models on the NIH and Indiana X-ray datasets.

Inception-V3 was first trained from scratch on the original color ImageNet dataset (LSVRC2012) to reproduce published state-of-the-art results (see Fig. 1(a)). The color ImageNet model was evaluated on the original test set of LSVRC2012. Then the same ConvNet architecture[1] was trained from scratch (using the same optimization parameters) on the same ImageNet dataset (LSVRC2012) after converting the images to grayscale, using the Luma transformation [7] (see Fig. 1(b)). The grayscale model was evaluated on the grayscale version of the same test set.

---

[1] The only difference was that the kernel on the input layer was reduced from 3-channel to 1-channel.

The pre-trained color Inception-V3 model was then fine-tuned on both the NIH and Indiana University X-ray datasets for the respective disease classification tasks (see Fig. 2(a)). The fine-tuned model was tested on a held-out test set to establish the benchmark performance. Next, the pre-trained grayscale Inception-V3 model was fine-tuned on the NIH and Indiana University X-ray datasets for the same disease classification tasks (see Fig. 2(b)). The fine-tuned model was tested on the same held-out test set to compare performance of the two approaches.

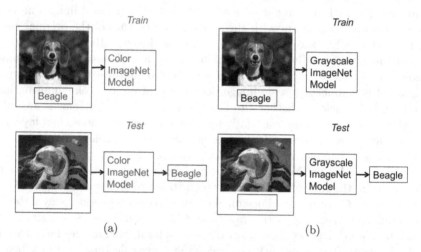

(a)   (b)

Fig. 1. Training a model from scratch on ImageNet. (a) A 3-channel model is trained and tested on color ImageNet data. (b) A 1-channel model is trained and tested on grayscale ImageNet data. (Color figure online)

3   Results

The ConvNet models described in this section were implemented in Tensorflow, and trained using asynchronous Stochastic Gradient Descent (SGD) on two NVIDIA GTX 1080 Ti GPUs.

3.1   Experiment 1: Training Color and Grayscale Models from Scratch for ImageNet-Based Classification

Training and validation images were from the ImageNet Large Scale Visual Recognition Challenge 2012 (LSVRC2012 [5,10]). In total, 1,281,167 images were used for training and 50,000 images for validation. For the classification challenge, there are 1000 image categories and each image belongs to one category.

For training on the color ImageNet data, standard augmentation methods [11] were used: cropping images based on a distorted version of the annotated bounding box, random horizontal flipping, and altering the intensities of the

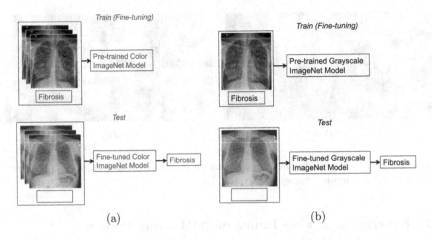

(a)   (b)

Fig. 2. Fine-tuning the ImageNet-trained models on X-ray data. (a) The color model is fine-tuned and tested on X-ray data after converting the X-ray images to 3-channel pseudo-color images. (b) The grayscale model is fine-tuned and tested on X-ray data without any image transformation. (Color figure online)

RGB channel. RMSProp optimizer was used with a decay factor of 0.9. The initial learning rate was set to 0.01 with a decay factor of 0.94 every 2 epochs [9]. The batch size was set to 64. The network was trained until the loss converged. The model converged after about 14 days and 1.67 million steps (around 84 epochs). The validation accuracy was 0.9169 for top-5 and 0.7372 for top-1. The state-of-the-art validation accuracy using Inception-V3 on the same dataset is 0.939 for top-5 and 0.780 for top-1 [12].

For training on the grayscale ImageNet data, the same hyper-parameters and augmentation methods were used. After augmentation, the color images were converted to grayscale, using the Luma transformation [7]. The batch size was set to 64 and the network was trained until the loss converged. The model converged after about 16 days and 1.92 million steps (around 100 epochs). The validation images were also converted to grayscale, and the validation accuracy was 0.9117 for top-5 and 0.7323 for top-1. Surprisingly, the performance of the model trained and tested on grayscale ImageNet was only 0.5% lower than the color model, suggesting that color is not a critical feature in image classification. The results are summarized in Table 1. Figure 3 shows the first-layer kernels learned from the color model and the grayscale model.

Table 1. Evaluation results on ImageNet classification

	Top-5 accuracy	Top-1 accuracy
Color	0.9169	0.7372
Grayscale	0.9117	0.7323

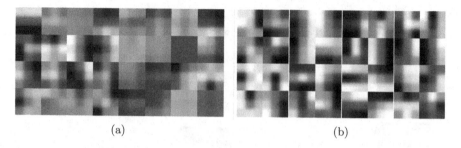

(a)   (b)

Fig. 3. First-layer kernels learned by training on (a) color ImageNet, and (b) grayscale ImageNet. (Color figure online)

3.2   Experiment 2: Fine-Tuning on NIH X-ray Dataset

The NIH X-ray dataset consists of 112,120 frontal chest X-ray images from more than 30,000 patients. There is a total of 14 lung diseases in this dataset: Atelectasis, Cardiomegaly, Emphysema, Effusion, Hernia, Infiltration, Mass, Nodule, Pneumonia, Pneumothorax, Consolidation, Edema, Fibrosis, and Pleural thickening. Each X-ray image could contain any number of the 14 diseases, or no finding. In total, 60,361 images have no findings. The image disease labels were mined from radiological reports using natural language processing and released together with the X-ray images.

The X-ray dataset was partitioned into 3 subsets for training, validation and testing following the same strategy used by Wang et al. [6]: 70% for training, 10% for validation, and 20% for testing. Since the same patient could have multiple X-ray images in this dataset, partition was performed to ensure that there were no overlapping patients among the 3 subsets. Each X-ray image was downsampled to a fixed size compatible with the network input, and in the case of the color model, stacked to form a 3-channel image. Random horizontal flipping was used for training data augmentation. The final fully-connected layer in the pre-trained model was replaced with a fully connected layer producing a 14-label output. A sigmoid nonlinearity was used and the final output was the disease probabilities for the 14 disease classes. The learning rate was set to 0.0001 and the batch size was set to 32. The network was trained end-to-end until the validation loss converged. For evaluation, the Area Under the ROC Curve (AUC) was calculated for the 14 diseases on the testing subset.

The color model converged after about 85 k steps. The grayscale model converged after about 250 k steps. The AUC values on the test dataset is summarized in Table 2. The p-values were also computed to assess the statistical significance of the differences between each pair of ROC curves [13]. When comparing the grayscale vs color model, all 14 categories had improved performance, and 8 out of 14 categories had performance improvements that were statistically significant. Furthermore, the grayscale model was approximately 20% faster for inference than the color model (see Table 4).

Table 2. Results (AUC) on NIH X-ray test data for 14 diseases after fine-tuning a pre-trained Inception-V3 model (c = color, g = grayscale). * p < 0.05, ** p < 0.01

Disease	Avg	Atelectasis	Cardiomegaly	Emphysema	Effusion	Hernia	Infiltration
AUC (c)	0.7498	0.7613	0.7785	0.7898	0.8320	0.6843	0.6835
AUC (g)	0.7706	0.7824**	0.8091*	0.8393**	0.8423*	0.7035	0.6895
Mass	Nodule	Pneumonia	Pneumothorax	Consolidation	Edema	Fibrosis	PT
0.7132	0.6807	0.6905	0.8145	0.7489	0.8689	0.7310	0.7204
0.7498**	0.7096**	0.7021	0.8326*	0.7606	0.8784	0.7454	0.7452*

3.3 Experiment 3: Fine-Tuning on Indiana University X-ray Dataset

The Indiana University X-ray dataset consists of around 8000 X-ray images from more than 3000 different patients. There are more than 100 types of disease labels in this dataset as well as the label indicating whether the image is normal or not. In our experiment, one frontal X-ray image was selected for each patient with associated medical report, resulting in a total of 3691 patients and images. A binary classification task of normal versus abnormal was performed on this dataset.

The Indiana University X-ray dataset was partitioned into 70%, 10%, and 20% for training, validation, and testing. Random horizontal flipping was used for training augmentation. The softmax loss was used and the final layer output was the probability indicating whether the image was normal or not. The learning rate was set to 0.0001 and the batch size was set to 32. The network was trained end-to-end until the validation loss converged. For evaluation, the accuracy and the Area Under the ROC Curve (AUC) was calculated on the testing subset.

The color model converged after about 11 k steps. The grayscale model converged after about 9 k steps. The accuracy and AUC values on the test dataset is summarized in Table 3. For the Indiana X-ray dataset, the grayscale model had improved performance; however, the difference in performance was not statistically significant. Inference with the grayscale model was approximately 5% faster (see Table 4).

Table 3. Results on the Indiana X-ray test data for normal vs abnormal classification using pre-trained Inception-V3 model.

	Accuracy	AUC
Color	0.7225	0.7124
Grayscale	0.7262	0.7285

Table 4. Inference time (ms/image)

	NIH	Indiana University
Color	8.0	7.5
Grayscale	6.4	7.1

4 Discussion and Conclusion

Due to the limited size of most medical imaging datasets, pre-training ConvNet models on large image repositories, such as ImageNet, is a common initialization strategy. However, due to the long training time required to train models from scratch on ImageNet, they are typically downloaded from publications focused on processing natural images. This leads to artefacts, whereby single-channel medical images must be pre-processed to 3-channel pseudo-color images before they can be analyzed by the network.

We show that transferring ImageNet data to a single-channel (i.e., grayscale) domain leads to better pre-trained models that (1) achieve higher classification accuracy after being fine-tuned on medical X-ray image data, (2) are faster during inference, and (3) avoid unnecessary pre-processing. We hypothesize that the network pre-trained on grayscale images has the potential to learn more features relevant to grayscale images, which serves to boost the transfer learning performance when applied to a grayscale medical dataset.

Surprisingly, after converting both training and testing sets of the ImageNet LSVRC2012 data to grayscale, the test set performance was only reduced by 0.5%, from a top-5 accuracy of 0.9169 for the color model to 0.9117 for the grayscale model. This result was counter to our expectation that color would be an important feature for accurate classification of natural images. However, it seems to be consistent with the success of colorization methods [14,15] which produce realistic-looking color images from grayscale image information.

We also compared class-specific performance between the two models. While for the majority of the classes, the two models had very similar performance, the color model outperformed grayscale model on classes such as ice-cream and mink. For example, the grayscale model classified some ice-cream images into the chocolate sauce class. The grayscale model performed better on classes including pier and printer (the color model classified a lot of pier images into suspension bridges). An intuitive explanation could be that color information is more important for discriminating between certain classes such as ice cream vs chocolate sauce (e.g., chocolate sauce is brown) but not for other classes such as pier vs suspension bridge. Figure 4 shows some example images from these two classes in color and in grayscale.

In conclusion, color does not seem to be a critical feature for accurate classification of natural images, and pre-training on grayscale images can give a boost in both speed and accuracy when fine-tuning on medical images. In future, it would be interesting to apply this approach to semantic segmentation and object detection in medical images, through the use of standard network architectures such as fully convolutional networks (FCN), and region-based convolutional neural networks (R-CNN). It would also be interesting to explore additional image transformations that may be more appropriate for different imaging modalities, such as Ultrasound and Magnetic Resonance Imaging.

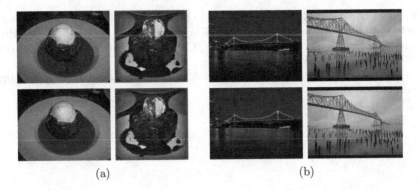

(a)   (b)

Fig. 4. Example images belonging to (a) the ice-cream class and (b) the pier class. Upper row shows the color images and lower row shows the corresponding grayscale images. (Color figure online)

References

1. Lijens, G., et al.: A survey on deep learning in medical image analysis. Med. Image Anal. **42**, 60–88 (2017)
2. Rajpurkar, P., et al.: CheXNet: radiologist-level pneumonia detection on chest X-Rays with deep learning. https://arxiv.org/pdf/1711.05225.pdf
3. van Ginneken, B., Setio, A.A., Jacobs, C., Ciompi, F.: Off-the-shelf convolutional neural network features for pulmonary nodule detection in computed tomography scans. In: IEEE ISBI, pp. 286–289 (2015)
4. Wang, J., MacKenzie, J.D., Ramachandran, R., Chen, D.Z.: A deep learning approach for semantic segmentation in histology tissue images. In: Ourselin, S., Joskowicz, L., Sabuncu, M.R., Unal, G., Wells, W. (eds.) MICCAI 2016. LNCS, vol. 9901, pp. 176–184. Springer, Cham (2016). https://doi.org/10.1007/978-3-319-46723-8_21
5. ImageNet. http://www.image-net.org/
6. Wang, X., Peng, Y., Lu, L., Lu, Z., Bagheri, M., Summers, R.M.: ChestX-ray8: hospital-scale Chest X-ray database and benchmarks on weakly-supervised classification and localization of common thorax diseases. In: IEEE CVPR, pp. 2097–2106 (2017)
7. Luma. https://en.wikipedia.org/wiki/Luma_%28video%29
8. Open-i Biomedical Image Search Engine. https://openi.nlm.nih.gov/faq.php
9. Szegedy, C., Vanhoucke, V., Ioffe, S., Shlens, J., Wojna, Z.: Rethinking the inception architecture for computer vision. In: CVPR, pp. 2818–2826 (2016)
10. Russakovsky, O., et al.: ImageNet large scale visual recognition challenge. IJCV **115**(3), 211–252 (2015)
11. Krizhevsky, A., Sutskever, I., Hinton, G.E.: ImageNet classification with deep convolutional neural networks. In: NIPS, pp. 1097–1105 (2012)
12. TensorFlow-Slim image classification model library. https://github.com/tensorflow/models/tree/master/research/slim
13. DeLong, E.R., DeLong, D.M., Clarke-Pearson, D.L.: Comparing the areas under two or more correlated receiver operating characteristic curves: a nonparametric approach. Biometrics **44**(3), 837–845 (1988)

14. Larsson, G., Maire, M., Shakhnarovich, G.: Learning representations for automatic colorization. In: Leibe, B., Matas, J., Sebe, N., Welling, M. (eds.) ECCV 2016. LNCS, vol. 9908, pp. 577–593. Springer, Cham (2016). https://doi.org/10.1007/978-3-319-46493-0_35

15. Zhang, R., Isola, P., Efros, A.A.: Colorful image colorization. https://arxiv.org/pdf/1603.08511.pdf

W34 – 1st Workshop on Interactive and Adaptive Learning in an Open World

W34 – 1st Workshop on Interactive and Adaptive Learning in an Open World

When applying learning algorithms to real-world problems, limitations are often related to the lack of representative, non-changing, annotated data rather than sophisticated models and algorithms. To overcome these barriers, the annotation and learning of models needs to be coupled strongly through human-machine interaction. Furthermore, models need to adapt as needed to handle either shifts or completely novel data. The goal of this workshop was to discuss and present the advances in technologies that support annotation, model learning through expert guidance, and continuous model adaptation.

The interactive and adaptive learning (IAL) workshop tried to bridge one of the gaps between results of basic AI research and their real-world applicability - availability of useful and easy-to-produce annotations and working solutions for efficient model adaptation. Hence, the workshop focused on exchange on the following topics: continuous and lifelong learning, interactive segmentation and detection to support annotation, active learning, and open set learning.

We had five invited speakers covering a broad spectrum of topics related to interactive and adaptive learning in an open world. In addition, we invited extended abstract submissions related to the workshop scope, from which we accepted ten abstracts for poster presentation.

The workshop successfully served as a venue for exchanging recent trends in the field of interactive and adaptive learning in an open world. The combination of invited speakers covering a broad technical spectrum as well as a short and informal poster session allowed for detailed discussions and for fostering connections. The audience raised the strong interest in continuing the workshop within the next years.

September 2018

Alexander Freytag
Vittorio Ferrari
Mario Fritz
Uwe Franke
Terrence Boult
Juergen Gall
Walter Scheirer
Angela Yao
Erik Rodner

Workshop on Interactive and Adaptive Learning in an Open World

Alexander Freytag[1](✉), Vittorio Ferrari[2,3], Mario Fritz[4], Uwe Franke[5],
Terrence Boult[6], Juergen Gall[7], Walter Scheirer[8], Angela Yao[7],
and Erik Rodner[1]

[1] Carl Zeiss AG, Jena, Germany
`alexander.freytag@zeiss.com`
[2] Google, Mountain View, USA
[3] University of Edinburgh, Edinburgh, UK
[4] CISPA Helmholtz Center i.G., Saarbrücken, Germany
[5] Daimler AG, Stuttgart, Germany
[6] University of Colorado, Colorado Springs, Colorado Springs, USA
[7] University of Bonn, Bonn, Germany
[8] University of Notre Dame, Notre Dame, USA

Abstract. Next generation machine learning requires stepping away from classical batch learning towards interactive and adaptive learning. This is essential to cope with demanding machine learning applications we have already today. Our workshop at ECCV 2018 in Munich therefore served as a discussion forum for experts in this field and in the following we give a brief overview. **Please note that this discussion paper has not been not peer-reviewed and only contains the subjective summary of the workshop organizers.**

Keywords: Interactive learning · Adaptive learning · Open set
Continuous learning

1 Scope of the Workshop

Learning algorithms are the backbone of computer vision research and still focused on training from large amounts of already annotated data. The limitations we are currently observing in many applications are mostly due to the lack of annotations or changing data distributions over time. To overcome these barriers, the annotation and learning of models needs to be coupled strongly through human-machine interaction. Furthermore, models need to adapt as needed to handle either shifts or completely novel data. The goal of this workshop was to discuss and present the advances in technologies that support annotation, model learning through expert guidance, and continuous model adaptation.

The interactive and adaptive learning (IAL) workshop tried to bridge one of the gaps between results of basic AI research and their real-world applicability: availability of useful and easy-to-produce annotations and working solutions for

© Springer Nature Switzerland AG 2019
L. Leal-Taixé and S. Roth (Eds.): ECCV 2018 Workshops, LNCS 11134, pp. 487–493, 2019.
https://doi.org/10.1007/978-3-030-11024-6_38

efficient model adaptation. In consequence, the following topics have been central to the workshop:

- Online and incremental learning
- Interactive segmentation and detection to support annotation
- Transfer learning
- Active or self-taught
- Continuous/lifelong learning
- Open set learning
- Open domain learning
- Efficient fine-tuning of generic models.

The topics are often seen as separated research fields, however, they should be considered jointly. While preparing this workshop, we once phrased this area as *Machine Didactics*, referring to the fact that we need to improve not only the training but also the teaching of models, which includes the way we collect and annotate data. For a lot of applications, it is simply unreasonable to assume that there is a clear division between annotation phase and the phase where a model is trained and tested with the data. In practice, this is always a continuous cycle of improvement and challenging the annotators with more data and further requirements. Currently, this process is still driven by manual work both from machine learning engineers as well as domain experts. The basic question for the future would be how this can be assisted by proper algorithms as well, such as active learning algorithms choosing the examples to annotate or bootstrapped feedback loops that allow experts to tune and check annotations rather than creating them from scratch with a lot of effort.

Another important aspect of the workshop stems from the fact that there are often unclear requirements of machine learning algorithms in the beginning. In reality, the number of classes that need to be differentiated in a classification task is simply often not defined or is likely to increase and change over time. This is referred to as an *open world* situation and is far more challenging than the standard ImageNet-like competition task most researchers focus on today. We were therefore very happy to have an associated challenge on open-set face recognition organized by Terry and Walter that was presented in detail during the workshop.

In addition to the aforementioned risks, a real-world machine learning application is likely to face changes of input conditions resulting from changing a sensor or the application field. Dealing with this problem requires training from only a few examples by transfer learning or learning of generic representations that allow for jump-starting learning for various tasks.

We invited extended abstract submissions related to the workshop scope and also compiled the list of invited speakers according to the fit of their main research interests to the workshop idea.

2   Invited Speakers

2.1   Incremental Learning: A Critical View on the Current State of Affairs (Tinne Tuytelaars)

In the first invited talk of the workshop, Tinne Tuytelaars (KU Leuven) gave an overview on recent developments in the field of incremental learning. She highlighted current scenarios of incremental learning and argued that the majority of existing approaches is hardly comparable due to not-matching assumptions on the availability of tasks and data over time. She presented several approaches from her recent work [1–4] which tackle this issue and address the problem of catastrophic forgetting, e.g., by encouraging sparse representations to leave model capacity for subsequent tasks that are added over time.

2.2   Results and Evaluation of the Open-Face Challenge (Manuel Günther)

Manuel Günther (UCCD) presented the UnConstrained College Students (UCCS) dataset which is an Open-Face Challenge [5]. Subjects are photographed using a long-range high-resolution surveillance camera. Faces inside these images are of various poses, and varied levels of blurriness and occlusion. The challenge comes with a closed set recognition problem as well as an open set recognition problem. In addition, different attack scenarios are evaluated. More information about the challenge, the data, terms of usage, and recent results can be found on the challenge's webpage at http://vast.uccs.edu/Opensetface/.

During the discussion, the spent effort and the availability of the dataset was positively acknowledged. All participants further agreed on the difficulty of the task of re-identifying individuals based on single sub-images. Nonetheless, issues have been raised why the re-identification task is posed on single images, whereas the ground truth to validate the ids required entire video clips (which would also likely be the final application scenario).

2.3   Recognition with Unseen Compositions and Novel Environments (Kristen Grauman)

Kristen Grauman (UT Austin) put emphasis on two aspects of open-ended learning: how to recognize unseen compositions of objects and operators as well as how to operate and navigate in unseen environments.

In her recent work [6], Kristen and her team show how operations such as slicing an apple, i.e., operations which transform objects, can be modeled as object-operator pairs and can be realized as operators applied to object representations. Appropriate embeddings are learned by optimizing a triplet-loss and additionally adding semantic regularizers, e.g., enforcing operators to be invertible which resembles undoing a transformation. In consequence, the notion of operators can also be generalized to new compositions of operator-object-pairs.

In the second part of her talk, Kristen focused on self-learning agents which are faced with environments that have been unseen at training time [7]. Based on a reinforcement learning approach, they proposed an additional reward for actions which reduce the estimated uncertainty about the agent's environment. An interesting future direction is to combine this unsupervised exploration with active look-ahead strategies [8].

2.4 Interactive Video Segmentation: The DAVIS Benchmark and First Approaches (Jordi Pont-Tuset)

Jordi Pont-Tuset (Google AI) gave an overview of his work on video segmentation. In particular, he presented the DAVIS benchmark [9] and the video segmentation approach published in [10]. The latter only requires the annotation of a few key frames and allows propagating the region segmentation to the whole video. This work is one example for the focus of the workshop on reducing annotation efforts by interactive segmentation and in general assisting the annotator by propagating annotations in an intelligent manner. Especially for pixel-wise video segmentation, fully manual annotation often renders intractable. One of the key ideas of the underlying algorithm is to perform metric learning to phrase the segmentation as a retrieval problem on the pixel level later on.

2.5 Towards Continual Learning and Interactive Annotation (Christoph Lampert)

Christoph Lampert (IST Austria) presented recent results in the area of lifelong learning and interactive annotation. In the first part of this talk, he reviewed iCARL, the Incremental Classifier and Representation Learning [11], which jointly learns appropriate embeddings and classification models upon the presence of newly added data. In continuous learning scenarios, it is further possible that unlabeled data is available and individuals tasks can be selected for annotation. How to select tasks such that information can be optimally transferred was shown in [12]. To assist in the annotation of new data, learnable bounding box dialogs for interactive annotation were presented in [13]. Finally, his work in [14] shows a simple yet powerful statistic test to detect if an incoming stream of data deviates from data a model has been trained on. By comparing distributions of model confidence scores, e.g., the maximum class score of deep convnets, the KS-test yields a probability if an entire batch of test samples stems from a different data distribution, e.g., induced by sensor drifts.

2.6 Elements of Continuous Learning for Wildlife Monitoring (Joachim Denzler)

Joachim Denzler (Univ. Jena) presented recent advances in continuous learning, especially focusing on active learning and anomaly detection. With the contributions of his group, he showed how application experts can be assisted in analyzing large-scale data using interactive machine learning tools, e.g., by spotting abnormal instances [15–17], interactively learning object classifiers [18,19], regression models for animal age [20], or object detectors [21], and classifying large data collections from camera traps in a semi-automated fashion [22–24]. In summary, the recent tools and techniques already add large value to the application scientist's work. Nonetheless, reliable and efficient interactive learning with deep neural networks remains an unsolved problem.

3   Extended Abstracts

Neal et al.	Open set learning with counterfactual images
Günther et al.	Open-set recognition challenge
Busto et al.	Open set domain adaptation for image and action recognition
Dwivedi and Roig	Evaluation of plug and play modules for multi-domain learning
Jin et al.	Unsupervised hard example mining from videos for improved object detection
Osep et al.	Towards large-scale video object mining
Wang and Sharma	Unsupervised representation learning on multispectral imagery by predicting held-out bands
Sharma and Wang	Human-in-the-loop segmentation for improved segmentation and annotations
Bauermeister et al.	Adaptive network architectures via linear splines
Rakelly et al.	Few-shot segmentation propagation with guided networks

4   Summary and Next Steps

The workshop successfully served as a venue for exchanging recent trends in the field of interactive and adaptive learning in an open world. The combination of invited speakers covering a broad technical spectrum as well as a short and informal poster session allowed for detailed discussions and for fostering connections.

The audience raised the strong interest in continuing the workshop within the next years. Of great benefit would be the continuation of a co-located challenge, especially in the area of open-set recognition.

References

1. Aljundi, R., Chakravarty, P., Tuytelaars, T.: Expert gate: lifelong learning with a network of experts. In: CVPR, pp. 7120–7129 (2017)

2. Aljundi, R., Babiloni, F., Elhoseiny, M., Rohrbach, M., Tuytelaars, T.: Memory aware synapses: learning what (not) to forget. In: Ferrari, V., Hebert, M., Sminchisescu, C., Weiss, Y. (eds.) ECCV 2018. LNCS, vol. 11207, pp. 144–161. Springer, Cham (2018). https://doi.org/10.1007/978-3-030-01219-9_9
3. Rannen, A., Aljundi, R., Blaschko, M.B., Tuytelaars, T.: Encoder based lifelong learning. In: IEEE Conference on Computer Vision and Pattern Recognition, CVPR (2017)
4. Aljundi, R., Rohrbach, M., Tuytelaars, T.: Selfless sequential learning. arXiv preprint arXiv:1806.05421 (2017)
5. Günther, M., Cruz, S., Rudd, E.M., Boult, T.E.: Toward open-set face recognition. In: IEEE Conference on Computer Vision and Pattern Recognition - Workshops, CVPRW, pp. 573–582. IEEE (2017)
6. Nagarajan, T., Grauman, K.: Attributes as operators: factorizing unseen attribute-object compositions. In: Ferrari, V., Hebert, M., Sminchisescu, C., Weiss, Y. (eds.) ECCV 2018. LNCS, vol. 11205, pp. 172–190. Springer, Cham (2018). https://doi.org/10.1007/978-3-030-01246-5_11
7. Jayaraman, D., Grauman, K.: Learning to look around: intelligently exploring unseen environments for unknown tasks. In: IEEE Conference on Computer Vision and Pattern Recognition, CVPR (2018)
8. Ramakrishnan, S.K., Grauman, K.: Sidekick policy learning for active visual exploration. In: Ferrari, V., Hebert, M., Sminchisescu, C., Weiss, Y. (eds.) ECCV 2018. LNCS, vol. 11216, pp. 424–442. Springer, Cham (2018). https://doi.org/10.1007/978-3-030-01258-8_26
9. Caelles, S., et al.: The 2018 DAVIS challenge on video object segmentation. arXiv preprint arXiv:1803.00557 (2018)
10. Chen, Y., Pont-Tuset, J., Montes, A., Van Gool, L.: Blazingly fast video object segmentation with pixel-wise metric learning. In: Proceedings of the IEEE Conference on Computer Vision and Pattern Recognition, pp. 1189–1198 (2018)
11. Rebuffi, S.A., Kolesnikov, A., Sperl, G., Lampert, C.H.: iCaRL: incremental classifier and representation learning. In: CVPR (2017)
12. Pentina, A., Lampert, C.H.: Multi-task learning with labeled and unlabeled tasks. In: International Conference on Machine Learning, ICML (2017)
13. Konyushkova, K., Uijlings, J., Lampert, C.H., Ferrari, V.: Learning intelligent dialogs for bounding box annotation. In: IEEE Conference on Computer Vision and Pattern Recognition, CVPR (2018)
14. Sun, R., Lampert, C.H.: KS(conf): a light-weight test if a ConvNet operates outside of its specifications. In: German Conference on Pattern Recognition, GCPR (2018)
15. Barz, B., Rodner, E., Garcia, Y.G., Denzler, J.: Detecting regions of maximal divergence for spatio-temporal anomaly detection. IEEE Trans. Pattern Anal. Mach. Intell. (2018)
16. Garcia, Y.G., Shadaydeh, M., Mahecha, M., Denzler, J.: Extreme anomaly event detection in biosphere using linear regression and a spatiotemporal MRF model. Nat. Hazards, 1–19 (2018)
17. Schultheiss, A., Käding, C., Freytag, A., Denzler, J.: Finding the unknown: novelty detection with extreme value signatures of deep neural activations. In: Roth, V., Vetter, T. (eds.) GCPR 2017. LNCS, vol. 10496, pp. 226–238. Springer, Cham (2017). https://doi.org/10.1007/978-3-319-66709-6_19
18. Käding, C., Freytag, A., Rodner, E., Bodesheim, P., Denzler, J.: Active learning and discovery of object categories in the presence of unnameable instances. In: IEEE Conference on Computer Vision and Pattern Recognition, CVPR, pp. 4343–4352 (2015)

19. Käding, C., Rodner, E., Freytag, A., Denzler, J.: Watch, ask, learn, and improve: a lifelong learning cycle for visual recognition. In: European Symposium on Artificial Neural Networks, ESANN, pp. 381–386 (2016)
20. Käding, C., Rodner, E., Freytag, A., Mothes, O., Barz, B., Denzler, J.: Active learning for regression tasks with expected model output changes. In: British Machine Vision Conference, BMVC (2018)
21. Brust, C.A., Käding, C., Denzler, J.: Active learning for deep object detection. In: arXiv preprint arXiv:1809.09875 (2018)
22. Körschens, M., Barz, B., Denzler, J.: Towards automatic identification of elephants in the wild. In: AI for Wildlife Conservation Workshop, AIWC (2018)
23. Brust, C.A., et al.: Towards automated visual monitoring of individual gorillas in the wild. In: ICCV Workshop on Visual Wildlife Monitoring, ICCV-WS, pp. 2820–2830 (2017)
24. Freytag, A., Rodner, E., Simon, M., Loos, A., Kühl, H.S., Denzler, J.: Chimpanzee faces in the wild: log-euclidean CNNs for predicting identities and attributes of primates. In: Rosenhahn, B., Andres, B. (eds.) GCPR 2016. LNCS, vol. 9796, pp. 51–63. Springer, Cham (2016). https://doi.org/10.1007/978-3-319-45886-1_5

W35 – 1st Multimodal Learning
and Applications Workshop

W35 – 1st Multimodal Learning and Applications Workshop

The exploitation of the power of big data in the last few years led to a big step forward in many applications of Computer Vision. However, most of the tasks tackled so far are involving mainly visual modality due to the unbalanced number of labeled samples available among modalities (e.g., there are many huge labeled datasets for images while not as many for audio or IMU based classification), resulting in a huge gap in performance when algorithms are trained separately. The workshop addressed various themes in the field of multimodal data fusion and representation (e.g. we had contribution proposing method to deal with modality fusion between Audio-Video, Video-Lidar, Text-Image, etc.). As expected we have attracted researcher from different environments, we had nearly equal contributions from academia and industry.

As part of the program we had the privilege to have two eminent invited speakers: Daniel Cremers from TU Munich and Raquel Urtasun from Uber ATG Toronto. In their talks they have shown how multimodal learning is a topic of tremendous importance, for industrial applications such as automotive and SLAM technologies. The workshop, despite its first edition, has been very successful. We received 28 valid submissions all reviewed by at least two reviewers resulting in 11 papers accepted (39% acceptance rate). Three paper have been presented as oral while the other 8 as poster plus a brief spotlight session. Given the quality of the papers we have decided to propose a best paper award which has been sponsored by Bosch.

We would like to express our gratitude to all the Authors, to the Invited Speakers and to the members of the Program Committee for the amazing contribution they have done to the workshop.

September 2018

Paolo Rota
Vittorio Murino
Michael Yang
Bodo Rosenhahn

Boosting LiDAR-Based Semantic Labeling by Cross-modal Training Data Generation

Florian Piewak[1,2]([✉])[ID], Peter Pinggera[1][ID], Manuel Schäfer[1][ID], David Peter[1][ID], Beate Schwarz[1][ID], Nick Schneider[1][ID], Markus Enzweiler[1][ID], David Pfeiffer[1][ID], and Marius Zöllner[2,3][ID]

[1] Daimler AG, R&D, Stuttgart, Germany
florian.piewak@daimler.com
[2] Karlsruhe Institute of Technology (KIT), Karlsruhe, Germany
[3] Forschungszentrum Informatik (FZI), Karlsruhe, Germany

Abstract. Mobile robots and autonomous vehicles rely on multi-modal sensor setups to perceive and understand their surroundings. Aside from cameras, LiDAR sensors represent a central component of state-of-the-art perception systems. In addition to accurate spatial perception, a comprehensive semantic understanding of the environment is essential for efficient and safe operation. In this paper we present a novel deep neural network architecture called *LiLaNet* for point-wise, multi-class semantic labeling of semi-dense LiDAR data. The network utilizes virtual image projections of the 3D point clouds for efficient inference. Further, we propose an automated process for large-scale cross-modal training data generation called *Autolabeling*, in order to boost semantic labeling performance while keeping the manual annotation effort low. The effectiveness of the proposed network architecture as well as the automated data generation process is demonstrated on a manually annotated ground truth dataset. *LiLaNet* is shown to significantly outperform current state-of-the-art CNN architectures for LiDAR data. Applying our automatically generated large-scale training data yields a boost of up to 14% points compared to networks trained on manually annotated data only.

Keywords: Semantic point cloud labeling · Semantic segmentation Semantic scene understanding · Automated training data generation Automated label trasfer

1 Introduction

Within the fields of mobile robotics and autonomous driving, vehicles are typically equipped with multiple sensors of complementary modalities such as cameras, LiDAR and RADAR in order to generate a comprehensive and robust

---

D. Pfeiffer—Contributed while with Daimler AG.

© Springer Nature Switzerland AG 2019
L. Leal-Taixé and S. Roth (Eds.): ECCV 2018 Workshops, LNCS 11134, pp. 497–513, 2019.
https://doi.org/10.1007/978-3-030-11024-6_39

- road
- sidewalk
- person
- rider
- small vehicle
- large vehicle
- two wheeler
- construction
- pole
- traffic sign
- vegetation
- terrain

Fig. 1. Example of a LiDAR point cloud labeled by *LiLaNet*. Point colors correspond to the Cityscapes semantic class color coding [5]. The test vehicle is headed to the top right, the corresponding camera image is shown on the top left for clarity. (Color figure online)

representation of the environment [17,30,33,35]. Each sensor modality leverages its specific strengths to extract as much information as possible from the observed scene. Based on the combined sensor data, a detailed environment model, for example in the form of a dynamic occupancy grid map [20], is created. This environment model provides the basis for high-level tasks such as object tracking [32], situation analysis and path planning [2]. In order to master these high-level tasks, it is essential for an autonomous vehicle to not only distinguish between generic obstacles and free-space, but to also obtain a deeper semantic understanding of its surroundings. Within the field of computer vision, the corresponding task of semantic image labeling has experienced a significant boost in recent years due to the resurgence of advanced deep learning techniques [9]. However, detailed semantic information of similar quality has to be extracted independently from each of the sensor modalities to maximize system performance, availability and safety. Therefore, in this paper we introduce *LiLaNet* (**LiDAR La**beling **Net**work), an efficient deep neural network architecture for point-wise, multi-class semantic labeling of semi-dense LiDAR data.

As has been well established within the camera domain, large-scale datasets are of paramount importance for training competitive deep neural networks. Consequently, large-scale generic datasets such as ImageNet [25] and COCO [19], as well as medium-scale datasets dedicated to road scenarios such as KITTI [10] and Cityscapes [5] have been made available for this purpose. In contrast, within the LiDAR domain only indoor datasets [1,7,26] or outdoor datasets [12] obtained from high-resolution stationary sensors have been published to date. For this reason some authors [3,8,34] have resorted to the indirect extraction of the desired LiDAR point semantics from the KITTI dataset, using annotated object bounding boxes or the camera road detection benchmark. While this type of indirect extraction eventually yields viable training datasets, it is relatively cumbersome and limited to only a small set of semantic classes. Hence, here we propose a so-called *Autolabeling* process, an effective approach for the automated generation of large amounts of semantically annotated mobile LiDAR data by the direct transfer of high-quality semantic information from a registered reference camera image. The semantic information in the reference image is obtained using an off-the-shelf neural network. We show that the datasets obtained with this approach significantly boost the LiDAR-based semantic labeling performance, in particular when augmented with a small manually annotated dataset for fine-tuning.

Our main contributions can be summarized as follows:

1. An efficient Convolutional Neural Network (CNN) architecture for high-quality semantic labeling of semi-dense point clouds, as provided by state-of-the-art mobile LiDAR sensors.
2. A large-scale automated cross-modal training data generation process for boosting the LiDAR-based semantic labeling performance.
3. A thorough quantitative evaluation of the semantic labeling performance, including an analysis of the proposed automated training data generation process.

2   Related Work

LiDAR-based semantic labeling has gained increased attention in recent years due to the availability of improved mobile sensor technology, providing higher resolution and longer range at reduced cost. The various proposed approaches of LiDAR-based semantic labeling can be discriminated by the way the point-wise 3D information is utilized.

The first approaches using depth information for semantic labeling were based on RGB-D data, which complements RGB image data with an additional depth channel [6,11], allowing to recycle 2D semantic image labeling algorithms. Often a stereo camera was used to create a dense depth image, which was then fused with the RGB image. Tosteberg [29] developed a technique to use depth information of a LiDAR sensor accumulated over time to project it into the camera space. The accumulation yields a depth image of increased density without requiring dedicated upsampling algorithms.

A different category of approaches considers the 3D LiDAR data as an unordered point cloud, including PointNet [22], PointNet++ [23] and PointCNN [18]. The PointNet architecture [22] combines local point features with globally extracted feature vectors, allowing for the inference of semantic information on a point-wise basis. Extending this idea, PointNet++ [23] introduces a hierarchical PointNet architecture to generate an additional mid-level feature representation for an improved handling of point neighborhood relations. Both approaches are evaluated successfully on indoor scenes but reach their limits in large scale outdoor scenarios. The PointCNN [18] approach is based on unordered point clouds as well, but introduces modified convolution layers extended by permutations and weighting of the input features. This allows to transfer the advantages of traditional CNNs to unordered point cloud processing. However, the approach is only used for object detection and has not yet been applied to semantic labeling of point clouds.

Yet another way of representing LiDAR input data is within cartesian 3D space, which is used in the SEGCloud [28] and OctNet [24] methods. Here a Voxel (SEGCloud) or an OctTree (OctNet) representation is created and the convolution layers are extended to 3D convolutions. These approaches retain the original 3D structure of the input points, making them more powerful in preserving spatial relations. However, the algorithms have to cope with the high sparsity of the data, and inference time as well as memory requirements increase drastically for large-scale outdoor scenes.

A possible solution to avoid the computational complexity of 3D convolutions is the rendering of 2D views of the input data. Based on such 2D views, state-of-the-art image-based deep learning algorithms can be applied. Depending on the use case, different viewpoints or virtual cameras may be used. Caltagirone et al. [3] use a top-view image of a LiDAR point cloud for labeling road points within a street environment. This top-view projection of the LiDAR points is a valid choice for road detection, but the resulting mutual point occlusions generate difficulties for more general semantic labeling task as in our case. An alternative is to place the virtual camera origin directly within the sensor itself. The resulting 2D view is often visualized via a cylindrical projection of the LiDAR points (see Fig. 2), which is particularly suitable for the regular measurement layout of common rotating LiDAR scanners. In this case, the sensor view provides a dense depth image, which is highly advantageous for subsequent processing steps. Wu et al. [34] uses this type of input image for the SqeezeSeg architecture, which performs a SqeezeNet-based [15] semantic labeling to segment cars, pedestrians and cyclist. The bounding boxes of the KITTI object detection dataset [10] are used to transfer the point-wise semantic information required for training and evaluation. The approach of Dewan et al. [8] uses the cylindrical projection of the LiDAR data as an input for a CNN based on the Fast-Net architecture [21] to distinguish between movable and non-movable points. Similar to Wu et al. [34], the KITTI object detection dataset is used for transferring the ground-truth bounding box labels to the enclosed points.

Varga et al. [31] propose an alternative method to generate a semantically labeled point cloud at runtime, based on a combined setup of fisheye cameras and LiDAR sensors. First, pixel-wise semantics are extracted from the camera images via a CNN model trained on Cityscapes [5]. Subsequently, the LiDAR points are projected into the images to transfer the semantic information from pixels to 3D points. However, no semantic information is inferred on the LiDAR point cloud itself, and spatial and temporal registration of the sensor modalities remains a challenge. In the present paper we take the idea of [31] one step further and utilize a joint camera/LiDAR sensor setup to generate large amounts of 3D semantic training data. The data is then used to train a deep neural network to infer point-wise semantic information directly on LiDAR data. We show that combining the large amounts of automatically generated data with a small manually annotated dataset boosts the overall semantic labeling performance significantly.

3   Method

We introduce a novel CNN architecture called *LiLaNet* for the point-wise, multi-class semantic labeling of LiDAR data. To obtain high output quality and retain efficiency at the same time, we aim to transfer lessons learned from image-based semantic labeling methods to the LiDAR domain. The cylindrical projection of a 360° point cloud captured with a state-of-the-art rotating LiDAR scanner is used as input to our networks. Training is boosted by an efficient automated cross-modal data generation process, which we refer to as *Autolabeling*.

3.1   LiDAR Images

LiDAR sensors measure the time of flight of emitted laser pulses in order to determine the distance of surrounding objects with high accuracy. In addition, modern sensors even provide coarse reflectivity estimates on a point-wise basis. For the following experiments we consider a Velodyne VLP32C LiDAR scanner, which features 32 vertically stacked send/receive modules rotating around a common vertical axis. While rotating, each module periodically measures the distance and reflectivity at its current orientation, i.e. at the respective azimuth and elevation angles. We combine the measurements of a full 360° scan to create cylindrical depth and reflectivity images, as illustrated in Fig. 2. This projection represents the view of a virtual 360° cylindrical camera placed at the sensor origin. At ten revolutions per second, images of size 1800×32 pixels are obtained.

The cylindrical point cloud projection provides dense depth and reflectivity images which are free from mutual point occlusions. This allows for the application of optimized 2D convolution layers, as used with great success in state-of-the-art image-based CNN architectures. In this way, inference time is reduced drastically compared to the use of full 3D input representations such as voxel grids or octtrees. Further, since measurement times and orientation angles are known with high accuracy, it is straightforward to transform the cylindrical image back into a full three-dimensional point cloud representation without any loss of information.

In cases where no laser reflection is received by the sensor, for example when pointed towards the sky, pixels corresponding to the respective measurement angles are marked as invalid in the resulting depth image.

3.2   Class Mapping

Based on initial experiments we conducted with regard to the discrimination of different semantic classes in LiDAR data, we first apply a mapping of the original Cityscapes labelset [5] to a reduced set of 13 semantic classes (see Table 1). This reduced label set is better tailored to the specific properties of the data provided

Fig. 2. Example of a depth image (center, blue = close, red = far) and reflectivity image (right, black = non-reflective, cyan = highly reflective) resulting from the cylindrical point cloud projection. The corresponding camera image is shown on the left. Note that here the 360° LiDAR scan has been cropped to the camera field of view for illustration. (Color figure online)

by current LiDAR sensors, where limited spatial resolution and coarse reflectivity estimates prohibit truly fine-grained semantic differentiation. For example, the original 'truck' and 'bus' classes are merged into a common 'large vehicle' class. Similarly, the original 'motorcycle' and 'bicycle' classes are combined into a single 'two wheeler' class. The 'fence' class is not retained in our mapping, as such thin and porous structures are hardly captured by LiDAR sensors. Note that the reduced label set still provides an abundance of valuable semantic information with adequate detail, which is highly beneficial for a large set of application scenarios.

3.3 LiLaNet Network Architecture

Using the LiDAR images described in Sect. 3.1 as input, we present a dedicated CNN architecture for high-quality LiDAR-based semantic labeling. To cope with the low resolution and extreme asymmetry in the aspect ratio of the used LiDAR images, we propose a dedicated network block called *LiLaBlock*, which is inspired by the GoogLeNet inception modules of [27]. The block structure is illustrated in Fig. 3. In order to successfully handle relevant objects of various aspect ratios, the *LiLaBlock* applies convolution kernels of sizes 7×3, 3×7 and 3×3 in parallel.

Table 1. Mapping of the Cityscapes label set [5] to the reduced LiDAR label set

Cityscapes	LiDAR Semantics	Cityscapes	LiDAR Semantics
road	road	building	construction
sidewalk	sidewalk	wall	construction
person	person	fence	unlabeled
rider	rider	pole	pole
car	small vehicle	traffic sign	traffic sign
truck	large vehicle	traffic light	construction
bus	large vehicle	vegetation	vegetation
on rails	large vehicle	terrain	terrain
motorcycle	two wheeler	sky	sky
bicycle	two wheeler		

The output is then concatenated and the dimension is decreased by a factor of three via a bottleneck. In this way the dimensionality of the feature space is reduced yielding a more compact representation. At the same time the inference complexity of the *LiLaNet* is lowered. Note that each convolution is followed by a rectified linear unit layer (ReLU layer).

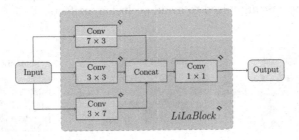

Fig. 3. The *LiLaBlock* structure allows to cope with the extreme asymmetry in the aspect ratio of the input LiDAR images.

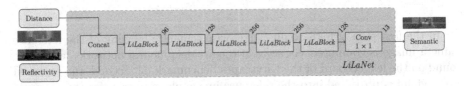

Fig. 4. The *LiLaNet* consists of a sequence of five consecutive *LiLaBlocks*. The final 1×1 convolution reduces the dimensionality to the desired label set.

The full *LiLaNet* consists of a sequence of five *LiLaBlocks* with a varying number of kernels, as shown in Fig. 4. The two input channels represent the concatenated depth and reflectivity images, while the output provides the corresponding point-wise semantic image labeling, according to the label set defined in Sect. 3.2.

The network training is performed via the Adam solver [16]. We use the suggested default values of $\beta_1 = 0.9$, $\beta_2 = 0.999$ and $\epsilon = 10^{-8}$. The learning rate is fixed at $\alpha = 10^{-3}$ ($\alpha = 10^{-4}$ for fine-tuning) and the batch size is set to $b = 5$, while the weights are initialized with MSRA [14].

3.4 Autolabeling

Generating manually annotated training data for LiDAR-based semantic labeling at scale presents a huge effort and entails even higher cost compared to manual image annotations in the 2D domain. This is due to both the additional spatial dimension and the sparsity of the data, which results in a representation that is non-intuitive and cumbersome for human annotators. For these reasons, we introduce an efficient automated process for large-scale training data generation called *Autolabeling*.

As illustrated in Fig. 5, the *Autolabeling* concept is based on the use of one or more reference cameras in conjunction with the LiDAR sensor capturing the point cloud data. The obtained reference camera images have to be registered to the LiDAR data in space and time. Preferably, the spatial displacement between the sensor origins is minimized to avoid occlusion artifacts.

Fig. 5. Overview of the *Autolabeling* process for large-scale automated training data generation. Each pixel of the reference camera image is classified via an image-based semantic labeling network. Subsequently, the point cloud is projected into the camera image and the reference labels are transfered to the corresponding LiDAR points.

In the first step, a high-quality pixel-wise semantic labeling of the reference camera image is computed via state-of-the-art deep neural networks, as can be found on the leaderboard of the Cityscapes benchmark [5]. Second, the captured point cloud is projected into the reference image plane to transfer the semantic information of the image pixels to the corresponding LiDAR points. While a single reference camera will in general only cover a fraction of the full point cloud, it is straightforward to extend the approach to multiple cameras for increased coverage.

The described fully automated procedure yields semantically labeled point clouds which can directly be used to train LiDAR-based semantic labeling networks such as *LiLaNet*. In the following subsections we describe the various stages of the data generation process in more detail.

Semantic Image Labeling. For the experiments in the present paper we use an efficient reference network as described in [4] to obtain the pixel-wise semantic labeling of the camera images. The network is trained on the Cityscapes dataset and achieves an Intersection-over-Union (IoU) test score of 72.6% with regard to the original Cityscapes label set. Since the Cityscapes dataset was designed with vehicle-mounted front-facing cameras in mind, we also use a single front-facing camera to evaluate the proposed automated training data generation process.

Note that the *Autolabeling* process can be applied using any image-based reference network providing sufficient output quality. Moreover, the process will in general directly benefit from the ongoing research and improvements in image-based semantic labeling networks.

Fig. 6. Example of the point projection with (right) and without (left) ego-motion correction. The colors of the semantically labeled images represent the Cityscapes label set, while the projected points are color-coded according to distance (dark green = far away, yellow = close). Note that invalid LiDAR points are not projected into these images. (Color figure online)

Point Projection. In order to project the 3D points captured by a scanning LiDAR into the reference camera image plane, several aspects have to be taken into account. Since the LiDAR scanner rotates around its own axis in order to obtain a 360° point cloud, each measurement is taken at a different point in time. In contrast, the camera image is taken at a single point in time, or at least with a comparatively fast shutter speed.

To minimize potential adverse effects introduced by the scanning motion of the LiDAR, we apply a point-wise ego-motion correction using vehicle odometry. First, the measured 3D points are transformed from the LiDAR coordinate system to the vehicle coordinate system via the extrinsic calibration parameters of the sensor. Given the points $p_v = (x_v, y_v, z_v)$ in the vehicle coordinate system, the wheel odometry data is used to compensate for the ego-motion of the vehicle. To this end, the time difference Δt between the point measurement timestamp t_p and the image acquisition timestamp t_c of the camera is computed for each point. In case of a rolling shutter camera, half of the shutter interval t_r is added to move the reference timestamp to the image center:

$$\Delta t = t_c - t_p + \frac{t_r}{2} \tag{1}$$

The time difference Δt is used to extract the corresponding ego-motion data of the vehicle from the odometry sensor. This yields a transformation matrix $T_{\Delta t}$ describing the motion that occurred between the two timestamps of interest. Using the transformation matrix $T_{\Delta t}$, each point p_v is ego-motion corrected with

$$\begin{bmatrix} p_{t_c} \\ 1 \end{bmatrix} = \begin{bmatrix} x_{t_c} \\ y_{t_c} \\ z_{t_c} \\ 1 \end{bmatrix} = T_{\Delta t}^{-1} * \begin{bmatrix} x_v \\ y_v \\ z_v \\ 1 \end{bmatrix} \tag{2}$$

This effectively transforms each point p_v in the vehicle coordinate system to its corresponding position $p_{t_c} = (x_{t_c}, y_{t_c}, z_{t_c})$ at camera timestamp t_c. Finally, the corrected points p_{t_c} are transformed to the camera coordinate system and projected to the image plane using a pinhole camera model [13]. An exemplary result of the point projection with and without ego-motion correction is shown in Fig. 6.

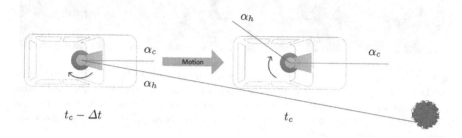

Fig. 7. Illustration of the timing problem (top view), where the camera (orange) is mounted on top of the LiDAR (blue). At a given timestamp, the rotating LiDAR measures points only at the angle α_h (blue line). The tree (green) is detected by the LiDAR at timestamp $t_c - \Delta t$, while the camera captures an image of the tree at t_c. This time difference Δt results in a spatial displacement of the sensor origins, which causes occlusion artifacts resembling a large mounting distance between the two sensors. (Color figure online)

4 Dataset

To train *LiLaNet*, a large dataset was created based on the *Autolabeling* process described Sect. 3. Approximately 555,000 frames of different road types (cities, rural roads, highways) were recorded and automatically labeled. Subsequently the recorded frames were split into subsets for training, validation and testing, with a split of approximately 62% - 13% - 25%. Details are listed in Table 2. The dataset split was performed on a sequence basis instead of via random selection in order to prevent correlations in between subsets. The training dataset was used to train *LiLaNet*, while the validation dataset was used to optimize the network architecture (not shown within this publication). The testing dataset is used to evelute the achieved LiDAR-based semantic labeling performance and the benefits of the proposed *Autolabeling* process.

Table 2. Split of the data into the different datasets for training, validation and testing.

	Training	Validation	Testing
Original frames	344,027	73,487	137,682
Optimized frames	57,315	12,259	22,964
Manually annotated keyframes	1,909	373	718

An essential factor for accurate *Autolabeling* results is a small spatial distance between the LiDAR sensor and the reference camera, as occlusion artifacts tend to introduce inconsistencies to the datasets. This can be accommodated by both a small mounting distance of the two sensors and explicitly taking time synchronization into account. In the used setup, the camera is not being triggered by the LiDAR sensor, which results in cases where the LiDAR sensor orientation is not well aligned with the front-facing camera during image acquisition time. This misalignment causes a significant timestamp difference between the projected point cloud and the image data. While this effect is compensated by the ego-motion correction described in Sect. 3.4, it usually results in a significant translatory motion between the two sensors while driving, which in turn leads to considerable occlusion artifacts. See Fig. 7 for an illustration of the problem. For this reason, we define a maximum heading deviation range $\gamma_h = 60°$ which is allowed between the camera principal axis orientation α_c and the current LiDAR azimuth angle α_h at the camera time stamp t_c. All captured frames which lie outside of this maximum deviation range are discarded, yielding an optimized subset of the originally recorded data (see Table 2).

Based on the optimized datasets, 3,000 keyframes were selected equally distributed across all frames for manual annotation. This manually annotated data forms the basis for the evaluation in Sect. 5. Note that invalid LiDAR points are not being annotated and hence the class 'sky' is not considered for the evaluation in the present paper.

5   Experiments

The *Autolabeling* process introduced in Sect. 3.4 was applied to automatically generate the large-scale dataset described in Sect. 4, which in turn was used to train the proposed *LiLaNet* architecture for LiDAR based semantic labeling. In this section we evaluate different training strategies for *LiLaNet* in detail. In particular, we analyze the impact of boosting the training via the large-scale datasets obtained from the *Autolabeling* process. Note that all evaluations are based on the testing subset of the manually annotated keyframes. Following the Cityscapes Benchmark Suite [5], we apply the Intersection-over-Union (IoU) metric for performance evaluation. We define the following evaluation schemes, which are also visualized in Fig. 8:

(1) **Autolabeling:**
This evaluation considers inaccuracies of the image CNN as well as projection errors. No LiDAR-based CNN is trained for this evaluation.
(2) *LiLaNet* **Manual Annotations:**
This evaluation assesses the performance of the LiDAR-based semantic labeling using a small set of cost-intensive manually annotated point clouds from the annotated keyframes for training (see Table 2).

(3) **LiLaNet Autolabeled Reduced:**
This evaluation measures the performance of the LiDAR-based semantic labeling using a small set of automatically generated training data, based on the annotated keyframes (same keyframes that constitute the training subset of the manually annotated dataset shown in Table 2).

(4) **LiLaNet Autolabeled Full:**
This evaluation assesses the performance of the LiDAR-based semantic labeling when using the *Autolabeling* process on the full training dataset of the original frames (see Table 2).

(5) **LiLaNet Finetuned:**
This evaluation measures the performance of the LiDAR-based semantic labeling by fine-tuning the network using a small set of manually annotated data (2) with a pre-training based on the full *Autolabeling* process (4).

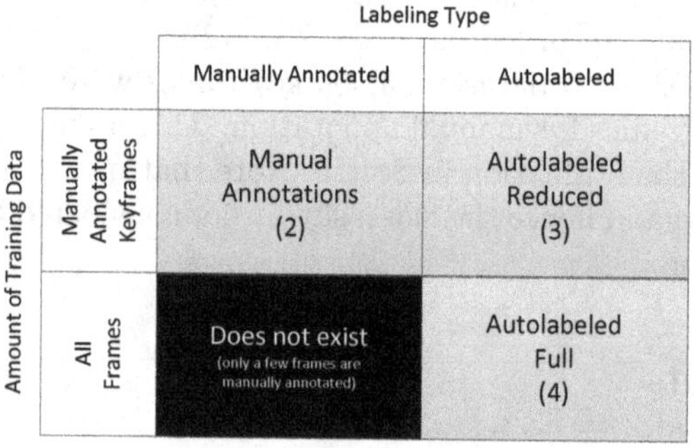

Fig. 8. Overview of the various training strategies, which differ in the amount of training data (see Table 2) as well as the labeling type of the ground truth.

Table 3. Class-wise and overall IoU scores of the different approaches. The highest IoU scores of each column (excluding the first row) are marked in bold.

	road	sidewalk	person	rider	small vehicle	large vehicle	two wheeler	construction	pole	traffic sign	vegetation	terrain	mean IoU
Image Labeling [4] based on Cityscapes	98.0%	81.5%	81.4%	61.3%	94.7%	80.8%	70.2%	91.8%	58.0%	71.8%	92.7%	69.0%	79.3%
(1) *Autolabeling* no CNN	89.2%	60.2%	**75.3%**	**51.3%**	79.3%	**57.3%**	45.0%	68.5%	28.9%	39.4%	78.0%	53.2%	60.5%
(2) *LiLaNet* Manual Annotations	90.8%	61.6%	48.8%	15.2%	79.7%	37.4%	22.4%	71.1%	35.9%	69.4%	75.1%	59.9%	55.6%
(3) *LiLaNet* Autolabeled Reduced	86.8%	51.3%	44.9%	13.2%	72.6%	32.7%	19.0%	60.2%	20.9%	45.7%	66.4%	44.2%	46.5%
(4) *LiLaNet* Autolabeled Full	89.7%	61.7%	72.2%	46.6%	79.6%	49.6%	38.3%	75.0%	31.5%	50.2%	78.0%	49.8%	60.2%
(5) *LiLaNet* Finetuned	**94.1%**	**73.9%**	73.8%	48.9%	**86.4%**	52.2%	**49.2%**	**83.4%**	**46.6%**	**75.7%**	**84.8%**	**67.4%**	**69.7%**
(4) SqueezeSeg [34] Autolabeled Full	89.0%	60.9%	56.7%	6.1%	76.4%	39.2%	25.9%	66.6%	18.6%	46.8%	73.0%	57.3%	51.4%
(5) SqueezeSeg [34] Finetuned	92.2%	68.2%	56.8%	12.9%	80.1%	38.5%	33.1%	72.0%	26.1%	67.1%	75.7%	63.0%	57.1%

The used image-based semantic labeling network (Sect. 3.4) was previously analyzed in detail in [4], achieving an IoU score of 72.6% on the Cityscapes Benchmark Suite. In addition, we re-evaluate the image-based approach on the Cityscapes test set when using the class mapping defined in Sect. 3.2. This yields an IoU score of 79.3%, detailed results are listed in Table 3. Compared to the pure image-based semantic labeling result, the *Autolabeling* (1) output used to generate our large-scale dataset shows worse performance scores. This may be attributed to various reasons. First of all, the semantic image labeling CNN is optimized towards the specific properties of high-resolution camera data, which may lead to a slight reduction in performance when transferring the labels into the LiDAR domain. Also, despite the ego-motion correction efforts described in Sect. 4, the remaining inaccuracies still result in a certain amount of occlusion artifacts. Finally, a multi-sensor setup is rarely free from small calibration offsets in practice, even if optimized manually. These imperfections cause projection misalignments of the points within the images, which results in inaccurate label assignments, in particular for points at a large distance to the sensors.

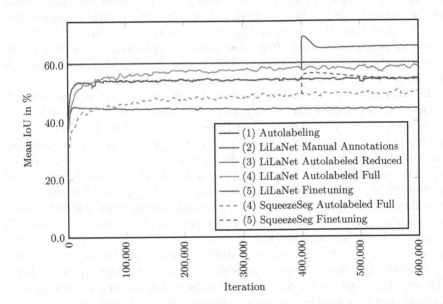

Fig. 9. Mean IoU of the different approaches and network architectures during training.

The detailed results of the various training strategies applied to *LiLaNet* are listed in Table 3 and illustrated in Fig. 9. It can be seen that the training on manually annotated data (2) yields a higher performance than the training on autolabeled data (3), but only as long as the same amount of data is being used. This is due to the imperfect results of the *Autolabeling* output itself. However, as stated previously, in practice the amount of available manually annotated data is severely limited by the high cost of point-wise manual annotation. In contrast, the *Autolabeling* process allows to automatically generate training data sets of arbitrary size at low cost. When using the large amount of automatically generated data for training (4), *LiLaNet* in fact outperforms its respective variant trained on manual annotations (2) by 4.6% points with regard to mean IoU. Moreover, the network seems to generalize well within the LiDAR domain and suppresses some errors introduced by the *Autolabeling* process, which is indicated by the improved performance for some classes when compared to the pure *Autolabeling* output (e.g. 'construction', 'pole', 'traffic sign'). Furthermore, Fig. 9 shows that the training on the small amount of data in (2) and (3) saturates after several thousand iterations, while the training on the large-scale dataset (4) continues to increase output performance. Finally, using the manual annotations to fine-tune *LiLaNet* after pre-training on the automatically generated dataset (5) boosts performance by another 9.5% points. This corresponds to a total gain of 14.1% points over the training on manually annotated data only. Note that after fine-tuning most classes achieve a significantly higher performance than obtained by the pure *Autolabeling* output itself. Hence, the LiDAR-based semantic labeling result provided by *LiLaNet* with a training supported by the *Autolabeling* process outperforms the image-based semantic labeling results projected into the LiDAR domain. It is worth noting that the network fine-tuning reaches its maximum performance only after a few thousand iterations and soon starts to overfit on the small manually annotated dataset, as can be seen in Fig. 9. A qualitative result of the fine-tuned network is shown in Fig. 1.

In order to compare the presented *LiLaNet* architecture to the state-of-the-art, we also analyze the performance of the SqueezeSeg architecture [34], recently proposed for LiDAR-based semantic labeling on a smaller set of semantic classes ('car', 'pedestrian', 'cyclist'). Note that we evaluate the SqueezeSeg approach without its Conditional Random Field (CRF) stage for a fair comparison. The results in Table 3 as well as Fig. 9 illustrate that *LiLaNet* outperforms the SqueezeNet architecture in each class. This may be due to the following reasons: First of all, SqueezeNet uses five horizontal pooling layers which increases the learnable feature size drastically. Consequently, the network may have difficulties in capturing small but relevant objects. Further, the SqueezeSeg architecture does not distinguish between different object shapes and sizes in the design of the convolution kernels, as is done in our *LiLaBlock* structure. However, note that SqueezeNet does indeed also benefit from our combined process of fine-tuning after pre-training on an automatically generated dataset.

6   Conclusion

Autonomous vehicles require a comprehensive and robust environment representation, including a detailed semantic understanding of their surroundings. This can be obtained by a combination of different sensor modalities, where each sensor independently contributes to the overall environmental model. In the present paper we consider the point-wise multi-class semantic labeling of 3D point clouds and transfer the concept of pixel-wise image-based semantic labeling to the LiDAR domain. We propose *LiLaNet*, a novel CNN architecture for efficient LiDAR-based semantic labeling. This architecture significantly outperforms current state-of-the-art CNNs for multi-class LiDAR-based semantic labeling when evaluated on a manually annotated ground truth dataset.

Furthermore, we present a fully automated process for large-scale cross-modal training data generation called *Autolabeling*. The approach is based on the use of reference cameras in order to transfer high-quality image-based semantic labeling results to LiDAR point clouds. Combining the automatically generated training dataset with a fine-tuning step based on small-scale manually annotated data yields a performance boost of up to 14% points while keeping manual annotation efforts low.

References

1. Armeni, I., Sax, S., Zamir, A.R., et al.: Joint 2D–3D-semantic data for indoor scene understanding. In: arXiv preprint: arXiv:1702.01105 (2017)
2. Bai, H., Cai, S., Ye, N., et al.: Intention-aware online POMDP planning for autonomous driving in a crowd. In: International Conference on Robotics and Automation (ICRA) (2015)
3. Caltagirone, L., Scheidegger, S., Svensson, L., et al.: Fast LIDAR-based road detection using fully convolutional neural networks. In: arXiv preprint: arXiv:1706.08355 (2017)
4. Cordts, M.: Understanding Cityscapes: Efficient Urban Semantic Scene Understanding. Ph.D. thesis, Technische Universität Darmstadt (2017)
5. Cordts, M., Omran, M., Ramos, S., et al.: The Cityscapes dataset for semantic urban scene understanding. In: Conference on Computer Vision and Pattern Recognition (CVPR) (2016)
6. Couprie, C., Farabet, C., Najman, L., et al.: Indoor semantic segmentation using depth information. In: arXiv preprint: arXiv:1301.3572 (2013)
7. Dai, A., Chang, A.X., Savva, M., et al.: ScanNet: richly-annotated 3D reconstructions of indoor scenes. In: Conference on Computer Vision and Pattern Recognition (CVPR) (2017)
8. Dewan, A., Oliveira, G.L., Burgard, W.: Deep semantic classification for 3D LiDAR Data. In: arXiv preprint: arXiv:1706.08355 (2017)
9. Garcia-Garcia, A., Orts-Escolano, S., Oprea, S., et al.: A review on deep learning techniques applied to semantic segmentation. In: arXiv preprint: arXiv:1704.06857 (2017)
10. Geiger, A., Lenz, P., Urtasun, R.: Are we ready for autonomous driving? the KITTI vision benchmark suite. In: Conference on Computer Vision and Pattern Recognition (CVPR) (2012)
11. Gupta, S., Girshick, R., Arbeláez, P., Malik, J.: Learning rich features from RGB-D images for object detection and segmentation. In: Fleet, D., Pajdla, T., Schiele, B., Tuytelaars, T. (eds.) ECCV 2014. LNCS, vol. 8695, pp. 345–360. Springer, Cham (2014). https://doi.org/10.1007/978-3-319-10584-0_23
12. Hackel, T., Savinov, N., Ladicky, L., et al.: SEMANTIC3D.NET: A new large-scale Point Cloud Classification Benchmark. Annals of Photogrammetry, Remote Sensing and Spatial Information Sciences (ISPRS) IV-1/W1, pp. 91–98 (2017)
13. Hartley, R., Zisserman, A.: Multiple View Geometry. Cambridge University Press (2003)

14. He, K., Zhang, X., Ren, S., et al.: Delving deep into rectifiers: surpassing human-level performance on ImageNet classification. In: International Conference on Computer Vision (ICCV) (2015)
15. Iandola, F.N., Han, S., Moskewicz, M.W., et al.: SqueezeNet: AlexNet-level accuracy with 50x fewer parameters and <0.5MB model size. In: arXiv preprint: arXiv:1602.07360 (2016)
16. Kingma, D.P., Ba, J.: Adam: a method for stochastic optimization. In: arXiv preprint: arXiv:1412.6980 (2014)
17. Levinson, J., Askeland, J., Becker, J., et al.: Towards fully autonomous driving: Systems and algorithms. In: Intelligent Vehicles Symposium (IV) (2011)
18. Li, Y., Bu, R., Sun, M., et al.: PointCNN. In: arXiv preprint: arXiv:1801.07791 (2018)
19. Lin, T.-Y., et al.: Microsoft COCO: common objects in context. In: Fleet, D., Pajdla, T., Schiele, B., Tuytelaars, T. (eds.) ECCV 2014. LNCS, vol. 8693, pp. 740–755. Springer, Cham (2014). https://doi.org/10.1007/978-3-319-10602-1_48
20. Nuss, D.: A Random Finite Set Approach for Dynamic Occupancy Grid Maps with Real-Time Application. Ph.D. thesis, University of Ulm (2016)
21. Oliveira, G.L., Burgard, W., Brox, T.: Efficient deep models for monocular road segmentation. In: International Conference on Intelligent Robots and Systems (IROS) (2016)
22. Qi, C.R., Su, H., Mo, K., et al.: PointNet: Deep learning on point sets for 3D classification and segmentation. In: Computer Vision and Pattern Recognition (CVPR) (2017)
23. Qi, C.R., Yi, L., Su, H., et al.: PointNet++: deep hierarchical feature learning on point sets in a metric space. In: Advances in Neural Information Processing Systems (NIPS) (2017)
24. Riegler, G., Ulusoy, A.O., Geiger, A.: OctNet: learning deep 3D representations at high resolutions. In: Computer Vision and Pattern Recognition (CVPR) (2017)
25. Russakovsky, O., Deng, J., Su, H., et al.: ImageNet large scale visual recognition challenge. Int. J. Comput. Vis. 115(3), 211–252 (2015)
26. Silberman, N., Hoiem, D., Kohli, P., Fergus, R.: Indoor segmentation and support inference from RGBD images. In: Fitzgibbon, A., Lazebnik, S., Perona, P., Sato, Y., Schmid, C. (eds.) ECCV 2012. LNCS, vol. 7576, pp. 746–760. Springer, Heidelberg (2012). https://doi.org/10.1007/978-3-642-33715-4_54
27. Szegedy, C., Vanhoucke, V., Ioffe, S., et al.: Rethinking the inception architecture for computer vision. In: Conference on Computer Vision and Pattern Recognition (CVPR) (2016)
28. Tchapmi, L.P., Choy, C.B., Armeni, I., et al.: SEGCloud: semantic segmentation of 3D point clouds. In: arXiv preprint: arXiv:1710.07563 (2017)
29. Tosteberg, P.: Semantic Segmentation of Point Clouds using Deep Learning. Master thesis, Linköping University (2017)
30. Urmson, C., Baker, C., Dolan, J., et al.: Autonomous driving in traffic: boss and the urban challenge. AI Mag. 30(2), 17–28 (2009)
31. Varga, R., Costea, A., Florea, H., et al.: Super-sensor for 360-degree environment perception: point cloud segmentation using image features. In: International Conference on Intelligent Transportation Systems (ITSC) (2017)
32. Vu, T.d., Burlet, J., Aycard, O., et al.: Grid-based localization and local mapping with moving object detection and tracking grid-based localization and local mapping with moving object detection and tracking. J. Inf. Fusion 12(1), 58–69 (2011)

33. Wei, J., Snider, J.M., Kim, J., et al.: Towards a viable autonomous driving research platform. In: Intelligent Vehicles Symposium (IV) (2013)
34. Wu, B., Wan, A., Yue, X., et al.: SqueezeSeg: convolutional neural nets with recurrent CRF for real-time road-object segmentation from 3D LiDAR point cloud. In: arXiv preprint: arXiv:1710.07368 (2017)
35. Ziegler, J., Bender, P., Schreiber, M., et al.: Making Bertha Drive - An Autonomous Journey on a Historic Route. Intell. Transp. Syst. Mag. **6**(2), 8–20 (2014)

Learning to Learn from Web Data Through Deep Semantic Embeddings

Raul Gomez[1,2]([⊠]) [iD], Lluis Gomez[2] [iD], Jaume Gibert[1] [iD],
and Dimosthenis Karatzas[2] [iD]

[1] Eurecat, Centre Tecnològic de Catalunya,
Unitat de Tecnologies Audiovisuals, Barcelona, Spain
{raul.gomez,jaume.gibert}@eurecat.org
[2] Computer Vision Center, Universitat Autònoma de Barcelona, Barcelona, Spain
{lgomez,dimos}@cvc.uab.es

Abstract. In this paper we propose to learn a multimodal image and
text embedding from Web and Social Media data, aiming to leverage the
semantic knowledge learnt in the text domain and transfer it to a visual
model for semantic image retrieval. We demonstrate that the pipeline can
learn from images with associated text without supervision and perform
a thorough analysis of five different text embeddings in three different
benchmarks. We show that the embeddings learnt with Web and Social
Media data have competitive performances over supervised methods in
the text based image retrieval task, and we clearly outperform state of the
art in the MIRFlickr dataset when training in the target data. Further
we demonstrate how semantic multimodal image retrieval can be performed using the learnt embeddings, going beyond classical instance-level
retrieval problems. Finally, we present a new dataset, InstaCities1M,
composed by Instagram images and their associated texts that can be
used for fair comparison of image-text embeddings.

Keywords: Self-supervised learning · Webly supervised learning
Text embeddings · Multimodal retrieval · Multimodal embeddings

1 Introduction

1.1 Why Should We Learn to Learn from Web Data?

Large annotated datasets, powerful hardware and deep learning techniques are
allowing to get outstanding machine learning results. Not only in traditional
classification problems but also in more challenging tasks such as image captioning or language translation. Deep neural networks allow building pipelines that
can learn patterns from any kind of data with impressive results. One of the
bottlenecks of training deep neural networks is, though, the availability of properly annotated data, since deep learning techniques are data hungry. Despite the
existence of large-scale annotated datasets such as ImageNet [11], COCO [16] or
Places [40] and tools for human annotation such as Amazon Mechanical Turk,

© Springer Nature Switzerland AG 2019
L. Leal-Taixé and S. Roth (Eds.): ECCV 2018 Workshops, LNCS 11134, pp. 514–529, 2019.
https://doi.org/10.1007/978-3-030-11024-6_40

the lack of data limits the application of deep learning to specific problems where it is difficult or economically non-viable to get proper annotations.

A common strategy to overcome this problem is to first train models in generic datasets as ImageNet and then fine-tune them to other areas using smaller, specific datasets [36]. But still we depend on the existence of annotated data to train our models. Another strategy to overcome the insufficiency of data is to use computer graphics techniques to generate artificial data inexpensively. However, while synthetic data has proven to be a valuable source of training data for many applications such as pedestrian detection [19], image semantic segmentation [28] and scene text detection and recognition [8,26], nowadays it is still not easy to generate realistic complex images for some tasks.

An alternative to these strategies is learning from free existing *weakly* annotated multimodal data. Web and Social Media offer an immense amount of images accompanied with other information such as the image title, description or date. This data is noisy and unstructured but it is free and nearly unlimited. Designing algorithms to learn from Web data is an interesting research area as it would disconnect the deep learning evolution from the scaling of human-annotated datasets, given the enormous amount of existing Web and Social Media data.

1.2 How to Learn from Web Data?

In some works, such as in the WebVision Challenge [14], Web data is used to build a classification dataset: queries are made to search engines using class names and the retrieved images are labeled with the querying class. In such a configuration the learning is limited to some pre-established classes, thus it could not generalize to new classes. While working with image labels is very convenient for training traditional visual models, the semantics in such a discrete space is very limited in comparison with the richness of human language expressiveness when describing an image. Instead we define here a scenario where, by exploiting distributional semantics in a given text corpus, we can learn from every word associated to an image. As illustrated in Fig. 1, by leveraging the richer semantics encoded in the learnt embedding space, we can infer previously unseen concepts even though they might not be explicitly present in the training set.

The noisy and unstructured text associated to Web images provides information about the image content that we can use to learn visual features. A strategy to do that is to embed the multimodal data (images and text) in the same vectorial space. In this work we represent text using five different state of the art methods and eventually embed images in the learn semantic space by means of a regression CNN. We compare the performance of the different text space configurations under a text based image retrieval task.

2   Related Work

Multimodal image and text embeddings have been lately a very active research area. The possibilities of learning together from different kinds of data have

Fig. 1. Top-ranked results of combined text queries by our semantic image retrieval model. The learnt joint image-text embedding permits to learn a rich semantic manifold even for previously unseen concepts even though they might not be explicitly present in the training set.

Fig. 2. First retrieved images for multimodal queries (concepts are added or removed to bias the results) with Word2Vec on WebVision.

motivated this field of study, where both general and applied research has been done. DeViSE [22] proposes a pipeline that, instead of learning to predict ImageNet classes, it learns to infer the Word2Vec [21] representations of their labels. The result is a model that makes semantically relevant predictions even when it makes errors, and generalizes to classes outside of its labeled training set. Gordo and Larlus [7] use captions associated to images to learn a common embedding space for images and text through which they perform semantic image retrieval. They use a *tf-idf* based BoW representation over the image captions as a semantic similarity measure between images and they train a CNN to minimize a margin loss based on the distances of triplets of query-similar-dissimilar images. Gomez *et al.* [5] use LDA [1] to extract topic probabilities from a bunch of Wikipedia articles and train a CNN to embed its associated images in the same topic space. Wang *et al.* [32] propose a method to learn a joint embedding of images and text for image-to-text and text-to-image retrieval, by training a neural net to embed in the same space Word2Vec [21] text representations and CNN extracted features.

Other than semantic retrieval, joint image-text embeddings have also been used in more specific applications. Patel *et al.* [23] use LDA [1] to learn a joint image-text embedding and generate contextualized lexicons for images using only visual information. Gordo *et al.* [6] embed word images in a semantic space relying in the graph taxonomy provided by WordNet [27] to perform text recognition. In a more specific application, Salvador *et al.* [29] propose a joint embedding of food images and its recipes to identify ingredients, using Word2Vec [21] and LSTM representations to encode ingredient names and cooking instructions and a CNN to extract visual features from the associated images.

The robustness against noisy data has also been addressed by the community, though usually in an implicit way. Patrini *et al.* [24] address the problem of training a deep neural network with label noise with a loss correction approach and Xiau *et al.* [33] propose a method to train a network with a limited number of clean labels and millions of noisy labels. Fu *et al.* [4] propose an image tagging method robust to noisy training data and Xu *et al.* [34] address social image tagging correction and completion. Zhang *et al.* [20] show how label noise affects the CNN training process and its generalization error.

2.1 Contributions

The work presented here brings in a performance comparison between five state of the art text embeddings in multimodal learning, showing results in three different datasets. Furthermore it proves that multimodal learning can be applied to Web and Social Media data achieving competitive results in text-based image retrieval compared to pipelines trained with human annotated data. Finally, a new dataset formed by Instagram images and its associated text is presented: InstaCities1M.

3 Multimodal Text-Image Embedding

One of the objectives of this work is to serve as a fair comparative of different text embeddings methods when learning from Web and Social Media data. Therefore we design a pipeline to test the different methods under the same conditions, where the text embedding is a module that can be replaced by any text representation.

The proposed pipeline is as follows: First, we train the text embedding model on a dataset composed by pairs of images and correlated texts (I, x). Second, we use the text embedding model to generate vectorial representations of those texts. Given a text instance x, we denote its embedding by $\phi(x) \in \mathbb{R}^d$. Third, we train a CNN to regress those text embeddings directly from the correlated images. Given an image I, its representation in the embedding space is denoted by $\psi(I) \in \mathbb{R}^d$. Thereby the CNN learns to embed images in the vectorial space defined by the text embedding model. The trained CNN model is used to generate visual embeddings for the test set images. Figure 3 shows a diagram of the visual embedding training pipeline and the retrieval procedure.

In the image retrieval stage the vectorial representation in the joint text-image space of the querying text is computed using the text embedding model. Image queries can also be handled by using the visual embedding model instead of the text embedding model to generate the query representation. Furthermore, we can generate complex queries combining different query representations applying algebra in the joint text-image space. To retrieve the most semantically similar image I_R to a query x_q, we compute the cosine similarity of its vectorial representation $\phi(x_q)$ with the visual embeddings of the test set images $\psi(I_T)$, and retrieve the nearest image in the joint text-image space:

$$\underset{I_T \in \text{Test}}{\arg\min} \frac{\langle \phi(x_q), \psi(I_T) \rangle}{||\phi(x_q)|| \cdot ||\psi(I_T)||}. \tag{1}$$

State of the art text embedding methods trained on large text corpus are very good generating representations of text in a vector space where semantically similar concepts fall close to each other. The proposed pipeline leverages the semantic structure of those text embedding spaces training a visual embedding model that generates vectorial representations of images in the same space, mapping semantically similar images close to each other, and also close to texts correlated to the image content. Note that the proposed joint text-image embedding can be extended to other tasks besides image retrieval, such as image annotation, tagging or captioning.

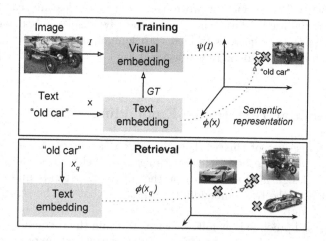

Fig. 3. Pipeline of the visual embedding model training and the image retrieval by text.

3.1 Visual Embedding

A CNN is trained to regress text embeddings from the correlated images minimizing a sigmoid cross-entropy loss. This loss is used to minimize distances between the text and image embeddings. Let $\{(I_n, x_n)\}_{n=1:N}$ be a batch of image-text pairs. If $\sigma(\cdot)$ is the component-wise sigmoid function, we denote $p_n = \sigma(\phi(x_n))$ and $\hat{p}_n = \sigma(\psi(I_n))$, and let the loss be:

$$L = -\frac{1}{N} \sum_{n=1}^{N} [p_n \log \hat{p}_n + (1 - p_n) \log(1 - \hat{p}_n)], \qquad (2)$$

where the sum's inner expression is averaged over all vector components. The GoogleNet architecture [30] is used, customizing the last layer to regress a vector of the same dimensionality as the text embedding. We train with a Stochastic Gradient Descent optimizer with a learning rate of 0.001, multiplied by 0.1 every 100,000 iterations, and a momentum of 0.9. The batch size is set to 120 and random cropping and mirroring are used as online data augmentation. With these settings the CNN trainings converge around 300K–500K iterations. We use the Caffe [10] framework and initialize with the ImageNet [11] trained model to make the training faster. Notice that, despite initializing with a model trained with human-annotated data, this does not denote a dependence on annotated data, since the resulting model can generalize to much more concepts than the ImageNet classes. We trained one model from scratch obtaining similar results, although more training iterations were needed.

3.2 Text Embeddings

Text vectorization methods are diverse in terms of architecture and the text structure they are designed to deal with. Some methods are oriented to vectorize individual words and others to vectorize full texts or paragraphs. In this work we consider the top-performing text embeddings and test them in our pipeline to evaluate their performance when learning from Web and Social Media data. Here we explain briefly the main characteristics of each text embedding method used.

LDA [1]: Latent Dirichlet Allocation learns latent topics from a collection of text documents and maps words to a vector of probabilities of those topics. It can describe a document by assigning topic distributions to them, which in turn have word distributions assigned. An advantage of this method is that it gives interpretable topics.

Word2Vec [21]: Using large amounts of unannotated plain text, Word2Vec learns relationships between words automatically using a feed-forward neural network. It builds distributed semantic representations of words using the context of them considering both words before and after the target word.

FastText [2]: It is an extension of Word2Vec which treats each word as composed of character ngrams, learning representations for ngrams instead of words. The vector for a word is made of the sum of its character n grams, so it can generate embeddings for out of vocabulary words.

Doc2Vec [12]: Extends the Word2Vec idea to documents. Instead of learning feature representations for words, it learns them for sentences or documents.

GloVe [25]: It is a count-based model. It learns the vectors by essentially doing dimensionality reduction on the co-occurrence counts matrix. Training is performed on aggregated global word-word co-occurrence statistics from a corpus.

To the best of our knowledge, this is the first time these text embeddings are trained from scratch on the same corpus and evaluated under the image retrieval by text task. We used Gensim[1] implementations of LDA, Word2Vec, FastText and Doc2Vec and the GloVe implementation by Maciej Kula[2]. While LDA and Doc2Vec can generate embeddings for documents, Word2Vec, GloVe and FastText only generate word embeddings. To get documents embeddings from these methods, we consider two standard strategies: First, computing the document embedding as the mean embedding of its words. Second, computing a *tf-idf* weighted mean of the words in the document. For all embeddings a dimensionality of 400 has been used. The value has been selected because is the one used in the Doc2Vec paper [12], which compares Doc2Vec with other text embedding methods, and it is enough to get optimum performances of Word2Vec, FastText and GloVe, as [2,21,25] show respectively. For LDA a dimensionality of 200 has also been considered.

4   Experiments

4.1   Benchmarks

InstaCities1M. A dataset formed by Instagram images associated with one of the 10 most populated English speaking cities all over the world (in the images captions one of this city names appears). It contains 100K images for each city, which makes a total of 1M images, split in 800K training images, 50K validation images and 150K test images. The interest of this dataset is that is formed by recent Social Media data. The text associated with the images is the description and the hashtags written by the photo up-loaders, so it is the kind of free available data that would be very interesting to be able to learn from. The InstaCities1M dataset is available on https://gombru.github.io/2018/08/01/InstaCities1M/.

WebVision [15]. It contains more than 2.4 million images crawled from the Flickr Website and Google Images search. The same 1,000 concepts as the ILSVRC 2012 dataset [11] are used for querying images. The textual information accompanying those images (caption, user tags and description) is provided. The validation set, which is used as test in this work, contains 50K images.

---

[1] http://radimrehurek.com/gensim.
[2] http://github.com/maciejkula/glove-python.

MIRFlickr [9]. It contains 25,000 images collected from Flickr, annotated using 24 predefined semantic concepts. 14 of those concepts are divided in two categories: (1) strong correlation concepts and (2) weak correlation concepts. The correlation between an image and a concept is strong if the concept appears in the image predominantly. For differentiation, we denote strong correlation concepts by a suffix "*". Finally, considering strong and weak concepts separately, we get 38 concepts in total. All images in the dataset are annotated by at least one of those concepts. Additionally, all images have associated tags collected from Flickr. Following the experimental protocol in [13,17,18,35] tags that appear less than 20 times are first removed and then instances without tags or annotations are removed.

4.2   Retrieval on InstaCities1M and WebVision Datasets

Experiment Setup. To evaluate the learnt joint embeddings, we define a set of textual queries and check visually if the TOP-5 retrieved images contain the querying concept. We define 24 different queries. Half of them are single word queries and the other half two word queries. They have been selected to cover a wide area of semantic concepts that are usually present in Web and Social Media data. Both simple and complex queries are divided in four different categories: Urban, weather, food and people. The simple queries are: Car, skyline, bike; sunrise, snow, rain; ice-cream, cake, pizza; woman, man, kid. The complex queries are: Yellow + car, skyline + night, bike + park; sunrise + beach; snow + ski; rain + umbrella; ice-cream + beach, chocolate + cake; pizza + wine; woman + bag, man + boat, kid + dog. For complex queries, only images containing both querying concepts are considered correct.

Table 1. Performance on InstaCities1M and WebVision. First column shows the mean P@5 for all the queries, second for the simple queries and third for complex queries.

Text embedding	InstaCities1M			WebVision		
Queries	All	S	C	All	S	C
LDA 200	0.40	0.73	0.07	0.11	0.18	0.03
LDA 400	0.37	0.68	0.05	0.14	0.18	0.10
Word2Vec mean	0.46	0.71	**0.20**	0.37	0.57	0.17
Word2Vec tf-idf	0.41	0.63	0.18	**0.41**	0.58	**0.23**
Doc2Vec	0.22	0.25	0.18	0.22	0.17	0.27
GloVe	0.41	0.72	0.10	0.36	**0.60**	0.12
GloVe tf-idf	**0.47**	**0.82**	0.12	0.39	0.57	0.22
FastText tf-idf	0.31	0.50	0.12	0.37	0.60	0.13

Table 2. Performance on transfer learning. First column shows the mean P@5 for all the queries, second for the simple queries and third for complex queries.

Text embedding	Train: WebVision Test: InstaCities			Train: InstaCities Test: WebVision		
Queries	All	S	C	All	S	C
LDA 200	0.14	0.25	0.03	0.33	0.55	0.12
LDA 400	0.17	0.25	0.08	0.24	0.39	0.10
Word2Vec mean	0.41	**0.63**	0.18	0.33	0.52	0.15
Word2Vec tf-idf	**0.42**	0.57	**0.27**	0.32	0.50	0.13
Doc2Vec	0.27	0.40	0.15	0.24	0.33	0.15
GloVe	0.36	0.58	0.15	0.29	0.53	0.05
GloVe tf-idf	0.39	0.57	0.22	**0.51**	**0.75**	**0.27**
FastText tf-idf	0.39	0.57	0.22	0.18	0.33	0.03

Results and Conclusions. Tables 1 and 2 show the mean Precision at 5 for InstaCities1M and WebVision datasets and transfer learning between those

Fig. 4. First retrieved images for city related complex queries with Word2Vec on InstaCites1M.

Fig. 5. First retrieved images for text non-object queries with Word2Vec on InstaCites1M.

datasets. To compute transfer learning results, we train the model with one dataset and test with the other. Figures 1 and 4 show the first retrieved images for some complex textual queries. Figure 5 shows results for non-object queries, proving that our pipeline works beyond traditional instance-level retrieval. Figure 2 shows that retrieval also works with multimodal queries combining an image and text.

For complex queries, where we demand two concepts to appear in the retrieved images, we obtain good results for those queries where the concepts tend to appear together. For instance, we generally retrieve correct images for "skyline + night" and for "bike + park", but we do not retrieve images for "dog + kid". When failing with this complex queries, usually images where only one of the two querying concepts appears are retrieved. Figure 6 shows that in some cases images corresponding to semantic concepts between the two querying concepts are retrieved. That proves that the common embedding space that has been learnt has a semantic structure. The performance is generally better in InstaCites1M than in WebVision. The reason is that the queries are closer to the kind of images people tend to post in Instagram than to the ImageNet classes. However, the results on transfer learning show that WebVision is a better dataset to train than InstaCites1M. Results show that all the tested text embeddings methods work quite well for simple queries. Though, LDA fails when is trained in WebVision. That is because LDA learns latent topics with semantic sense from the training data. Every WebVision image is associated to one of the 1,000 ImageNet classes, which influences a lot the topics learning. As a result, the embedding fails when the queries are not related to those classes. The top performing methods are GloVe when training with InstaCites1M and Word2Vec when training with WebVision, but the difference between their performance is small. FastText achieves a good performance on WebVision but a bad performance on InstaCites1M compared to the other methods. An explanation is that, while Social Media data contains more colloquial vocabulary, WebVision contains domain specific and diverse vocabulary, and since FastText learns representations for character ngrams, is more suitable to learn representations from corpus that are morphologically rich. Doc2Vec does not work well in any database. That is because it is oriented to deal with larger texts than the ones we find accompanying images in Web and Social Media. For word embedding methods Word2Vec and GloVe, the results computing the text representation as the mean or as the *tf-idf* weighted mean of the words embeddings are similar.

Error Analysis. Remarkable sources of errors are listed and explained in this section.

Visual Features Confusion: Errors due to the confusion between visually similar objects. For instance retrieving images of a quiche when querying "pizza". Those errors could be avoided using more data and a higher dimensional representations, since the problem is the lack of training data to learn visual features that generalize to unseen samples.

Errors from the Dataset Statistics: An important source of errors is due to dataset statistics. As an example, the WebVision dataset contains a class which is "snow leopard" and it has many images of that concept. The word "snow" appears frequently in the images correlated descriptions, so the net learns to embed together the word "snow" and the visual features of a "snow leopard". There are many more images of "snow leopard" than of "snow", therefore, when we query "snow" we get snow leopard images. Figure 7 shows this error and how we can use complex multimodal queries to bias the results.

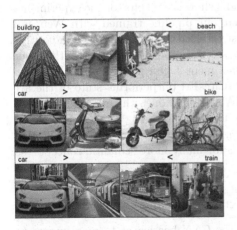

Fig. 6. First retrieved images for simple (left and right columns) and complex weighted queries with Word2Vec on InstaCites1M.

Fig. 7. First retrieved images for text queries using Word2Vec on WebVision. Concepts are removed to bias the results.

Words with Different Meanings or Uses: Words with different meanings or words that people use in different scenarios introduce unexpected behaviors. For instance when we query "woman + bag" in the InstaCities1M dataset we usually retrieve images of pink bags. The reason is that people tend to write "woman" in an image caption when pink stuff appears. Those are considered errors in our evaluation, but inferring which images people relate with certain words in Social Media can be a very interesting research.

4.3   Retrieval in the MIRFlickr Dataset

To compare the performance of our pipeline to other image retrieval by text systems we use the MIRFlickr dataset, which is typically used to train and evaluate image retrieval systems. The objective is to prove the quality of the multimodal embeddings learnt solely with Web data comparing them to supervised methods.

Experiment Setup. We consider three different experiments: (1) Using as queries the tags accompanying the query images and computing the MAP of all the queries. Here a retrieved image is considered correct if it shares at least one tag with the query image. For this experiment, the splits used are 5% queries set and 95% training and retrieval set, as defined in [18,35]. (2) Using as queries the class names. Here a retrieved image is considered correct if it is tagged with the query concept. For this experiment, the splits used are 50% training and 50% retrieval set, as defined in [31]. (3) Same as experiment 1 but using the MIRFlickr train-test split proposed in Zhang et al. [38].

Results and Conclusions. Tables 3 and 4 show the results for the experiments 1 and 3 respectively. We appreciate that our pipeline trained with Web and Social Media data in a multimodal self-supervised fashion achieves competitive results. When trained with the target dataset, our pipeline outperforms the other methods. Table 5 shows results for the experiment 2. Our pipeline with the GloVe *tf-idf* text embedding trained with InstaCites1M outperforms state of the art methods in most of the classes and in MAP. If we train with the target dataset, results are improved significantly. Notice that despite being applied here to the classes and tags existing in MIRFlickr, our pipeline is generic and has learnt to produce joint image and text embeddings for many more semantic concepts, as seen in the qualitative examples.

4.4   Comparing the Image and Text Embeddings

Experiment Setup. To evaluate how the CNN has learnt to map images to the text embedding space and the semantic quality of that space, we perform the following experiment: We build random image pairs from the MIRFlickr dataset and we compute the cosine similarity between both their image and their text embeddings. In Fig. 8 we plot the images embeddings distance vs the text embedding distance of 20,000 random image pairs. If the CNN has learnt

Table 3. MAP on the image by text retrieval task on MIRFlickr as defined in [18,35].

Method	Train	Map
LDA 200	InstaCites1M	0.736
LDA 400	WebVision	0.627
Word2Vec tf-idf	InstaCites1M	0.720
Word2Vec tf-idf	WebVision	0.738
GloVe tf-idf	InstaCites1M	**0.756**
GloVe tf-idf	WebVision	0.737
FastText tf-idf	InstaCities1M	0.677
FastText tf-idf	WebVision	0.734
Word2Vec tf-idf	MIRFlickr	0.867
GloVe tf-idf	MIRFlickr	**0.883**
DCH [35]	MIRFlickr	0.813
LSRH [13]	MIRFlickr	0.768
CSDH [18]	MIRFlickr	0.764
SePH [17]	MIRFlickr	0.735
SCM [37]	MIRFlickr	0.631
CMFH [3]	MIRFlickr	0.594
CRH [39]	MIRFlickr	0.581
KSH-CV [41]	MIRFlickr	0.571

Table 4. MAP on the image by text retrieval task on MIRFlickr as defined in [38].

Method	Train	Map
GloVe tf-idf	InstaCites1M	**0.57**
GloVe tf-idf	MIRFlickr	**0.73**
MML [38]	MIRFlickr	0.63
InfR [38]	MIRFlickr	0.60
SBOW [38]	MIRFlickr	0.59
SLKL [38]	MIRFlickr	0.55
MLKL [38]	MIRFlickr	0.56

Table 5. AP scores for 38 semantic concepts and MAP on MIRFlickr. Blue numbers compare our method trained with InstaCities and other methods trained with the target dataset.

Method	GloVe tf-idf	MMSHL [31]	SCM [37]	GloVe tf-idf
Train	MIRFlickr			InstaCities
animals	**0.775**	0.382	0.353	0.707
baby	**0.337**	0.126	0.127	0.264
baby*	**0.627**	0.086	0.086	0.492
bird	**0.556**	0.169	0.163	0.483
bird*	**0.603**	0.178	0.163	0.680
car	**0.603**	0.297	0.256	0.450
car*	**0.908**	0.420	0.315	0.858
female	**0.693**	0.537	0.514	0.481
female*	**0.770**	0.494	0.466	0.527
lake	**0.403**	0.194	0.182	0.230
sea	**0.720**	0.469	0.498	0.565
sea*	**0.859**	0.242	0.166	0.731
tree	**0.727**	0.423	0.339	0.398
tree*	**0.894**	0.423	0.339	0.506
clouds	**0.792**	0.739	0.698	0.613
clouds*	**0.884**	0.658	0.598	0.710
dog	**0.800**	0.195	0.167	0.760
dog*	**0.901**	0.238	0.228	0.865
sky	**0.900**	0.817	0.797	0.809
structures	**0.850**	0.741	0.708	0.703
sunset	**0.601**	0.596	0.563	0.590
transport	**0.650**	0.394	0.368	0.287
water	**0.759**	0.545	0.508	0.555
flower	**0.715**	0.433	0.386	0.645
flower*	**0.870**	0.504	0.411	0.818
food	**0.712**	0.419	0.355	0.683
indoor	**0.806**	0.677	0.659	0.304
plant _life	**0.846**	0.734	0.703	0.564
portrait	**0.825**	0.616	0.524	0.474
portrait*	**0.841**	0.613	0.520	0.483
river	**0.436**	0.163	0.156	0.304
river*	**0.497**	0.134	0.142	0.326
male	**0.666**	0.475	0.469	0.330
male*	**0.743**	0.376	0.341	0.338
night	**0.589**	0.564	0.538	0.542
night*	**0.804**	0.414	0.420	0.720
people	**0.910**	0.738	0.715	0.640
people*	**0.945**	0.677	0.648	0.658
MAP	**0.738**	0.451	0.415	0.555

correctly to map images to the text embedding space, the distances between the embeddings of the images and the texts of a pair should be similar, and points in the plot should fall around the identity line $y = x$. Also, if the learnt space has a semantic structure, both the distance between images embeddings and the distance between texts embeddings should be smaller for those pairs sharing more tags: The plot points' color reflects the number of common tags of the image pair, so pairs sharing more tags should be closer to the axis origin.

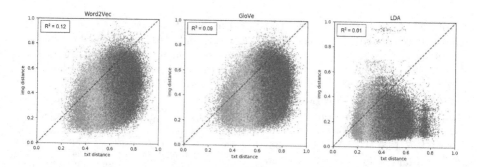

Fig. 8. Text embeddings distance (X) vs the images embedding distance (Y) of different random image pairs for LDA, Word2Vec and GloVe embeddings trained with InstaCities1M. Distances have been normalized between [0,1]. Points are red if the pair does not share any tag, orange if it shares 1, light orange if it shares 2, yellow if it shares 3 and green if it shares more. R^2 is the coefficient of determination of images and texts distances. (Color figure online)

As an example, take a dog image with the tag "dog", a cat image with the tag "cat" and one of a scarab with the tag "scarab". If the text embedding has been learnt correctly, the distance between the projections of dog and scarab tags in the text embedding space should be bigger than the one between dog and cat tags, but smaller than the one between other pairs not related at all. If the CNN has correctly learnt to embed the images of those animals in the text embedding space, the distance between the dog and the cat image embeddings should be similar than the one between their tags embeddings (and the same for any pair). So the point given by the pair should fall in the identity line. Furthermore, that distance should be nearer to the coordinates origin than the point given by the dog and scarab pair, which should also fall in the identity line and nearer to the coordinates origin that another pair that has no relation at all.

Results and Conclusions. The plots for both the Word2Vec and the GloVe embeddings show a similar shape. The resulting blob is elongated along the $y = x$ direction, which proves that both image and text embeddings tend to provide similar distances for an image pair. The blob is thinner and closer to the identity line when the distances are smaller (so when the image pairs are related), which means that the embeddings can provide a valid distance for semantic concepts that are close enough (dog, cat), but fails inferring distances between weak related concepts (car, skateboard). The colors of the points in the plots show that the space learnt has a semantic structure. Points corresponding to pairs having more tags in common are closer to the coordinates origin and have smaller distances between the image and the text embedding. From the colors it can also be deducted that the CNN is good inferring distances for related images pairs: there are just a few images having more than 3 tags in common with image embedding distance bigger than 0.6, while there are many images with bigger distances that do not have tags in common. However, the visual embedding sometimes fails and infers small distances for image pairs that are not related, as those images pairs having no tags in common and an image embedding distance below 0.2.

The plot of the LDA embedding shows that the learnt joint embedding is not so good in terms of the CNN images mapping to the text embedding space nor in terms of the space semantic structure. The blob does not follow the identity line direction that much which means that the CNN and the LDA are not inferring similar distances for images and texts of pairs. The points colors show that the CNN is inferring smaller distances for more similar image pairs only when the pairs are very related.

The coefficient of determination R^2 measures the proportion of the variance in a dependent variable that is predicted by linear regression and a predictor variable. In this case, it can be interpreted as a measure of how much image distances can be predicted from text distances and, therefore, of how well the visual embedding has learnt to map images to the joint image-text space. It ratifies our plots' visual inspection proving that visual embeddings trained with Word2Vec and GloVe representations have learnt a much more accurate mapping than LDA, and shows that Word2Vec is better in terms of that mapping.

5 Conclusions

In this work we learn a joint visual and textual embedding using Web and Social Media data and we benchmark state of the art text embeddings in the image retrieval by text task, concluding that GloVe and Word2Vec are the best ones for this data, having a similar performance and competitive performances over supervised methods in the image retrieval by text task. We show that our models go beyond instance-level image retrieval to semantic retrieval and that can handle multiple concepts queries and also multimodal queries, composed by a visual query and a text modifier to bias the results. We clearly outperform state of the art in the MIRFlick dataset when training in the target data. The code used in the project is available on https://github.com/gombru/LearnFromWebData.

Acknowledgments. This work was supported by the Doctorats Industrials program from the Generalitat de Catalunya, the Spanish project TIN2017-89779-P, the H2020 Marie Skłodowska-Curie actions of the European Union, grant agreement No 712949 (TECNIOspring PLUS), and the Agency for Business Competitiveness of the Government of Catalonia (ACCIO).

References

1. Blei, D.M., Ng, A.Y., Jordan, M.I.: Latent dirichlet allocation. J. Mach. Learn. Res. (2003)
2. Bojanowski, P., Grave, E., Joulin, A., Mikolov, T.: Enriching Word Vectors with Subword Information (2016)

3. Ding, G., Guo, Y., Zhou, J.: Collective matrix factorization hashing for multimodal data. In: Proceedings IEEE Computer Society Conference Computer Vision and Pattern Recognition (2014)
4. Fu, J., Wu, Y., Mei, T., Wang, J., Lu, H., Rui, Y.: Relaxing from vocabulary: robust weakly-supervised deep learning for vocabulary-free image tagging. In: Proceedings IEEE International Conference Computer Vision and Pattern Recognition (2015)
5. Gomez, L., Patel, Y., Rusiñol, M., Karatzas, D., Jawahar, C.V.: Self-supervised learning of visual features through embedding images into text topic spaces. In: CVPR (2017)
6. Gordo, A., Almazan, J., Murray, N., Perronin, F.: LEWIS: latent embeddings for word images and their semantics. In: Proceedings IEEE International Conference Computer Vision and Pattern Recognition (2015)
7. Gordo, A., Larlus, D.: Beyond instance-level image retrieval: leveraging captions to learn a global visual representation for semantic retrieval. In: CVPR (2017)
8. Gupta, A., Vedaldi, A., Zisserman, A.: Synthetic data for text localisation in natural images. In: CVPR (2016)
9. Huiskes, M.J., Lew, M.S.: The MIR flickr retrieval evaluation. In: Proceeding 1st ACM International Conference Multimedia Information Retrieval - MIR 2008 (2008)
10. Jia, Y., et al.: Caffe: Convolutional Architecture for Fast Feature Embedding. arXiv (2014)
11. Deng, J., Dong, W., Socher, R., Li, L.-J., Li, K., Li, F.-F.: ImageNet: a large-scale hierarchical image database. In: CVPR (2009)
12. Le, Q.V., Mikolov, T.: Distributed representations of sentences and documents. In: NIPS (2014)
13. Li, K., Qi, G.J., Ye, J., Hua, K.A.: Linear subspace ranking hashing for cross-modal retrieval. IEEE Trans. Pattern Anal. Mach. Intell. (2017)
14. Li, W., et al.: WebVision Challenge: Visual Learning and Understanding With Web Data (2017)
15. Li, W., Wang, L., Li, W., Agustsson, E., Van Gool, L.: WebVision Database: Visual Learning and Understanding from Web Data (2017)
16. Lin, T.-Y., et al.: Microsoft COCO: common objects in context. In: Fleet, D., Pajdla, T., Schiele, B., Tuytelaars, T. (eds.) ECCV 2014. LNCS, vol. 8693, pp. 740–755. Springer, Cham (2014). https://doi.org/10.1007/978-3-319-10602-1_48
17. Lin, Z., Ding, G., Hu, M., Wang, J.: Semantics-preserving hashing for cross-view retrieval. In: Proceedings IEEE Computer Society Conference on Computer Vision and Pattern Recognition (2015)
18. Liu, L., Lin, Z., Shao, L., Shen, F., Ding, G., Han, J.: Sequential discrete hashing for scalable cross-modality similarity retrieval. IEEE Trans. Image Process. (2017)
19. Mar, J., David, V., Ger, D., Antonio, M.L.: Learning appearance in virtual scenarios for pedestrian detection. In: CVPR (2010)
20. Melucci, M.: Relevance feedback algorithms inspired by quantum detection. IEEE Trans. Knowl. Data Eng. (2016)
21. Mikolov, T., Corrado, G., Chen, K., Dean, J.: Efficient estimation of word representations in vector space. In: ICLR (2013)
22. Norouzi, M., et al.: Zero-shot learning by convex combination of semantic embeddings. In: NIPS (2013)
23. Patel, Y., Gomez, L., Rusiñol, M., Karatzas, D.: Dynamic lexicon generation for natural scene images. In: Hua, G., Jégou, H. (eds.) ECCV 2016. LNCS, vol. 9913, pp. 395–410. Springer, Cham (2016). https://doi.org/10.1007/978-3-319-46604-0_29

24. Patrini, G., Rozza, A., Menon, A., Nock, R., Qu, L.: Making deep neural networks robust to label noise: a loss correction approach. In: CVPR (2016)
25. Pennington, J., Socher, R., Manning, C.: GloVe: global vectors for word representation. In: EMNLP (2014)
26. Phan, T.Q., Shivakumara, P., Tian, S., Tan, C.L.: Recognizing text with perspective distortion in natural scenes. In: Proceedings IEEE Computer Society Conference on Computer Vision and Pattern Recognition (2013)
27. Princeton University: WordNet (2010). http://wordnet.princeton.edu/
28. Ros, G., Sellart, L., Materzynska, J., Vazquez, D., Lopez, A.M.: The SYNTHIA dataset: a large collection of synthetic images for semantic segmentation of urban scenes. In: 2016 IEEE Computer Society Conference on Computer Vision and Pattern Recognition (2016)
29. Salvador, A., et al.: Learning cross-modal embeddings for cooking recipes and food images. In: CVPR (2017)
30. Szegedy, C., et al.: Going deeper with convolutions. In: Proceedings IEEE Computer Society Conference on Computer Vision and Pattern Recognition (2015)
31. Wang, J., Li, G.: A multi-modal hashing learning framework for automatic image annotation. In: 2017 IEEE Second International Conference on Data Science in Cyberspace (2017)
32. Wang, L., Li, Y., Lazebnik, S.: Learning deep structure-preserving image-text embeddings. In: CVPR (2016)
33. Xiao, T., Xia, T., Yang, Y., Huang, C., Wang, X.: Learning from massive noisy labeled data for image classification. In: Proceedings IEEE Computer Society Conference on Computer Vision and Pattern Recognition (2015)
34. Xu, X., He, L., Lu, H., Shimada, A., Taniguchi, R.I.: Non-linear matrix completion for social image tagging. IEEE Access (2017)
35. Xu, X., Shen, F., Yang, Y., Shen, H.T., Li, X.: Learning discriminative binary codes for large-scale cross-modal retrieval. IEEE Trans. Image Process. (2017)
36. Yosinski, J., Clune, J., Bengio, Y., Lipson, H.: How transferable are features in deep neural networks? In: NIPS (2014)
37. Zhang, D., Li, W.J.: Large-scale supervised multimodal hashing with semantic correlation maximization. In: AAAI, pp. 2177–2183 (2014)
38. Zhang, X., Zhang, X., Li, X., Li, Z., Wang, S.: Classify social image by integrating multi-modal content. Multimed. Tools Appl. (2018)
39. Zhen, Y., Yeung, D.Y.: Co-regularized hashing for multimodal data. In: Advances in Neural Information Processing Systems, pp. 1385–1393 (2012)
40. Zhou, B., Lapedriza, A., Khosla, A., Oliva, A., Torralba, A.: Places: a 10 million image database for scene recognition. IEEE Trans. Pattern Anal. Mach. Intell. (2017)
41. Zhou, B., Liu, L., Oliva, A., Torralba, A.: Recognizing city identity via attribute analysis of geo-tagged images. In: Fleet, D., Pajdla, T., Schiele, B., Tuytelaars, T. (eds.) ECCV 2014. LNCS, vol. 8691, pp. 519–534. Springer, Cham (2014). https://doi.org/10.1007/978-3-319-10578-9_34

Learning from #Barcelona Instagram Data What Locals and Tourists Post About Its Neighbourhoods

Raul Gomez[1,2]([✉]) [iD], Lluis Gomez[2] [iD], Jaume Gibert[1] [iD],
and Dimosthenis Karatzas[2] [iD]

[1] Eurecat, Centre Tecnòlogic de Catalunya, Unitat de Tecnologies Audiovisuals,
Barcelona, Spain
{raul.gomez,jaume.gibert}@eurecat.org
[2] Computer Vision Center, Universitat Autònoma de Barcelona, Barcelona, Spain
{lgomez,dimos}@cvc.uab.es

Abstract. Massive tourism is becoming a big problem for some cities, such as Barcelona, due to its concentration in some neighborhoods. In this work we gather Instagram data related to Barcelona consisting on images-captions pairs and, using the text as a supervisory signal, we learn relations between images, words and neighborhoods. Our goal is to learn which visual elements appear in photos when people is posting about each neighborhood. We perform a language separate treatment of the data and show that it can be extrapolated to a tourists and locals separate analysis, and that tourism is reflected in Social Media at a neighborhood level. The presented pipeline allows analyzing the differences between the images that tourists and locals associate to the different neighborhoods.

The proposed method, which can be extended to other cities or subjects, proves that Instagram data can be used to train multi-modal (image and text) machine learning models that are useful to analyze publications about a city at a neighborhood level. We publish the collected dataset, *InstaBarcelona* and the code used in the analysis.

Keywords: Self-supervised learning · Webly supervised learning
Social media analysis · City tourism analysis

1 Introduction

Instagram is an image based social network where people tend to post high quality personal pictures accompanied by a caption. Captions are diverse, but they usually describe the photo content, the place where the photo was taken or the feelings the photo brings in. The objective of adding this text, which usually contains hashtags, is that other Instagram users can find the photo using one of the words and follow the author if they like what they post. The number of

L. Leal-Taixé and S. Roth (Eds.): ECCV 2018 Workshops, LNCS 11134, pp. 530–544, 2019.
https://doi.org/10.1007/978-3-030-11024-6_41

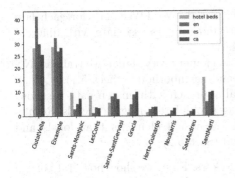

Fig. 1. % of mentions per district respect to the total districts mentions in each language. In yellow, the % of hotel beds per district. (Color figure online)

Fig. 2. Img2NeighCtx image by neighborhood retrieval results for *La Barceloneta* in English (top), Spanish (middle) and Catalan (bottom).

images updated to Instagram is huge: If we search for images accompanied by the word "Barcelona" we find more than 1 million.

This work shows how Instagram data can be exploited to obtain information about a city that has very interesting social and commercial applications. Specifically, we analyze images and captions related to Barcelona. Barcelona is a very touristic city which revives around 10 million tourists every year. That causes conflicts between tourists and locals and between the tourism industry and other local organizations, conflicts that are highly concentrated on neighborhoods with requested tourist attractions. Measuring the tourism overcrowding per neighborhood is not easy, since some areas receive high touristic interest but they don't have hotels or tourism installations. This work proposes a method to do that by exploiting Instagram data.

We perform a multi-modal, language separate analysis using the text of the captions and its associated images, designing a pipeline that learns relations between words, images and neighborhoods in a self-supervised way. We focus on a per-neighborhood analysis, and analyze how the differences of tourism activity between Barcelona districts and neighborhoods are reflected on Instagram. Notice that, despite in this work we apply the proposed pipeline to Barcelona, it is extensible to any other city with enough Social Media activity to collect the required data. The proposed method works as follows:

1. We split the data depending on whether it contains captions in a local language, Spanish and Catalan, or English, which we consider to be locals vs tourists publications (Sect. 3).
2. We count the mentions of the different districts and neighborhoods and the most used words in each data split. The results confirm that the language-separate treatment can be extrapolated to a locals vs tourists analysis (Sects. 4.1 and 4.2).

3. We train a semantic word embedding model, Word2Vec [11], for each language and show the words that locals and tourists associate with different neighborhood names (Sects. 4.3 and 4.4).
4. Using the semantic word embeddings as a supervisory signal, we train a CNN than learns relations between images and neighborhoods (Sect. 5.1).
5. Using the trained models in a retrieval approach with unseen data we show, for each language, the most related images to different neighborhoods. Results show interesting differences between the visual elements that locals and tourists associate to each neighborhood (Sect. 5.2).

The contributions of this work are as follows: First, we show how state of the art multi-modal text and images techniques can be applied to learn from Instagram data. Second, we show how Instagram data related to a city can be used to do a per-neighborhood analysis obtaining very useful social and commercial information. Specifically, we propose a method to analyze tourism activity at a neighborhood level using only images and text. Third, we provide a new dataset, *InstaBarcelona*, formed by Instagram images related to Barcelona and its captions, and the code and models used to perform the subsequent experiments.

2   Related Work

Deep learning advances and the availability of "free" Web and Social Media data have motivated the research of pipelines that can learn from images and associated text in a self-supervised way. In order to do that, state of the art algorithms vectorize text using word embedding methods, such as Word2Vec [11] and GloVe [13], topic models [2] or LSTM encodings. Then features are extracted from images using a CNN, and a model is trained to learn relations from those representations. This pipeline was originally proposed by Frome et al. with DeVISE [12] which, instead of learning to predict ImageNet classes, it learns to infer the Word2Vec [11] representations of their labels. Later, Gordo and Larlus [6] used captions associated to images to learn a common embedding space for images and text through which they perform semantic image retrieval. Learning from Web data, Gomez et al. [5] use LDA [2] to extract topic probabilities from a bunch of Wikipedia articles and train a CNN to embed its associated images in the same topic space. In a more specific application, Salvador et al. [14] collected data from cooking websites and proposed a joint embedding of food images and its recipes to identify ingredients, using Word2Vec [11] and LSTM representations to encode ingredient names and cooking instructions and a CNN to extract visual features from the associated images.

Social Media data has already been exploited in city analysis. In [8], Instagram uses publications texts and geolocations to find neighborhoods with similar activity across different United States cities. To do that they look for words shared between cities but not between neighborhoods of a city, train a topic model [2] and find neighborhoods that share topics. Chang [7] exploits similar data to analyze popular hashtags in different locations and show cultural differences between different cities and neighborhoods. Boy et al. [3] analyze Instagram

Amsterdam activity to study how the different neighborhoods, events and cultures of the city are represented in Instagram. Kuo *et al.* [10] mine data from different sources (Instagram, Twitter, TripAdvisor, etc.) and modalities (images, text and geolocations) related to New York City to analyze citizens behavior in differents aspects such as trends, food or transportation. Singh *et al.* [15] detect raze, age and gender of people in New York City Instagram images to analyze social diversity of different neighborhoods and compare it to census-based metrics. With a more similar objective as ours, Garcia-Palomares *et al.* [4] use geolocated Social Media photographs on Panoramio to identify the main tourist attractions in eight major European cities. They compare tourist and locals activity and study the distribution of it over the city. However, our work differs in the data, since they use geolocations in their analysis instead of images and text.

To our knowledge, this is the first work exploiting multi-modal image-text Social Media data to do a per neighborhood analysis of a city comparing tourism vs local activity.

3   Dataset: InstaBarcelona

To perform the presented analysis we gathered a dataset of Instagram images related to Barcelona uploaded between September and December of 2017. That means images with a caption where the word "Barcelona" appears. We collected around 1.3 million images. In order to discard spam and other undesirable images, we performed several dataset cleanings: *Users with many publications* tend to be spam or commercial accounts. We found 335,880 different users, where the user with more publications has 4,357. Figure 3 shows the number of publications of the top 5,000 users. We blacklisted the users having more than 50 publications and discarded all their content. The number of blacklisted accounts was 2,123. *Images with short captions* are not desirable since they usually do not provide enough information of the image to learn from. We discarded all the images accompanied with captions shorter than 3 words. *Repeated images* tend to be spam and should be discarded. *Images containing other city names in their captions* were also discarded, since they tend to be spam and to not provide information related to Barcelona. *Images with captions in other languages* than English, Spanish or Catalan were discarded since in this work we analyze publications related to those languages. To infer the language of the captions Google's language detection API[1] was used.

The resulting dataset, *InstaBarcelona*, contains 597,766 image-captions pairs and is made publicly available for download. From those pairs 331,037 are English publications, 171,825 Spanish publications and 94,311 Catalan publications (Fig. 4). The dataset is available on https://gombru.github.io/2018/08/02/InstaBarcelona/.

---

[1] https://code.google.com/archive/p/language-detection/.

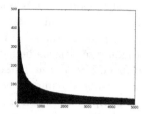

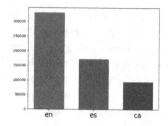

Fig. 3. Number of publications of top 5000 users.

Fig. 4. Number of images per language.

4 Textual Analysis

Barcelona is divided in 10 districts, which are divided in several neighborhoods[2], as shown in Fig. 5. In this section we use districts and neighborhoods names to perform a textual analysis and show how tourism is reflected in Instagram activity related to Barcelona.

Fig. 5. Barcelona map showing its districts and neighborhoods.

4.1 Most Frequent Words

Figure 6 shows the most used words in each language. Words without a semantic meaning (connectors, etc.), "barcelona", "bcn" and words related to Nueva Barcelona del Cerro Santo city, in Venezuela, have been removed. While in

---

[2] http://www.barcelona.cat/en/living-in-bcn/living-neighbourhood.

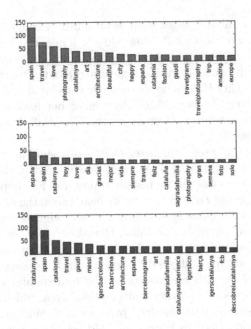

Fig. 6. $^{0}/_{000}$ of most frequent words instances respect to the total words on each of the languages. Red shows English dataset results, green Spanish and blue Catalan. (Color figure online)

English most of the top words are related to tourism ("travel", "photography", "art", "architecture", "trip") in the local languages other kind of terms appear in the top words ("hoy", "día", "gracias", "vida", "messi", "igersbarcelona", "fcbarcelona"), which supports our assumption of considering English publications as tourists publications, and Spanish and Catalan as locals publications.

4.2 Most Mentioned Districts

To compute the number of mentions per district for each language, we take into account district names, its neighborhoods names, and other abbreviations and names that are often used. Figure 1 shows, for each language, the % of mentions per district respect to the total districts mentions in that language. It also shows the number of hotel beds in each district given by the city hall of Barcelona [1]. *Ciutat Vella* and *Eixample* are the most mentioned districts in the three languages. This makes sense since those districts concentrate the most representative and touristic Barcelona attractions, and people tend to post more on Instagram when they are traveling and to use the word Barcelona when they are uploading a Barcelona representative image. The % of images that this most touristic districts concentrate is much bigger for English than for local languages, specially for *Ciutat Vella*, Barcelona's old town, known as the most touristic district. In all the other Barcelona districts, the % of publications is always higher for local languages than for English. The number of hotel beds is also markedly higher in *Ciutat Vella* and *Eixample*, which is consistent with our results. However, obtaining tourism measures for city areas is difficult. The number of hotel beds, which is the most meaningful of the tourism measures provided by Barcelona City Hall, is not necessarily correlated with tourism activity, since one district could be very visited by tourist but have few hotel beds due to, for instance, its urbanism. Over more, the City Hall does not provide this data per neighborhood.

Figure 7 shows, for each language, the % of mentions per neighborhood respect to the total neighborhood mentions of a district in that language. The *Ciutat Vella* plot shows that all its neighborhoods are highly popular among all tourists and locals, being *La Barceloneta*, its beach area, the most mentioned one in all languages. *La Barceloneta* is a former fisher neighborhood which receives now a lot of tourism attention. *El Gòtic*, Barcelona's old town, concentrates a markedly higher % of publications in English than in other languages, and is in fact the neighborhood most affected by tourism in Barcelona. *Sant Pere*, commonly known as *El Born*, is also mentioned by tourists and locals in a similar %. *El Raval* neighborhood is a very multi-cultural area, which has traditionally been considered dangerous due to drug presence and delinquency. However, its geographical situation close to Barcelona's old town has transformed it lately into a more touristic area. The plot shows that *El Raval* is still an area more popular among locals.

The *Eixample* plot shows clearly that the only reason why this district is one of the most mentioned, specially by tourists, is the *Sagrada Família*, which names both a temple and an *Eixample* neighbourhood. The Sagrada Família temple is the top tourism attraction in Barcelona, and all the touristic activity in *Eixample* big district is concentrated around the temple. *Sant Antoni*, which is a neighborhood of increasing popularity with high probability of becoming a touristic area, is still mentioned more in local languages. The other neighborhoods are not very mentioned because they are residential areas without neighborhood identities.

The *Sant Martí* district plot, shows that *El Poblenou* is the most popular neighbourhood in it, specially among english speakers. *El Poblenou* is a former industrial neighbourhood which lately is getting popular due to the 22@ plan, which aims to concentrate in that area technological firms headquarters and design studies. Due to its modernization and geographical situation in the seaside, *El Poblenou* is in danger to become a neighborhood with overcrowded tourism, as well as happened with *La Barceloneta*. This analysis strengthens that hypothesis, showing that *El Poblenou* and *Diagonal Mar* are the only neighborhoods among *Sant Martí* where the English % of posts is superior to the ones of local languages.

The *Sants-Montjuic* district plot shows that the most mentioned neighborhood among all languages is *Sants*, which is justifiable because it's also the district name. In this district, the only neighborhood where the % of English posts dominate over the local languages is *Poble Sec*. *Poble Sec* is an area besides the *Ciutat Vella* district which is also overcrowded by tourism, as the plot indicates. Tourism influence is getting expanded across *El Raval* to *Poble Sec*, which is getting popular as a bar and eating area across young people and, lately, across tourists. The *Sarrià* plot shows that its only neighborhood where the % of English publications respect to the total is superior to the other languages is *Vallvidrera*. That is because in *Vallvidrera* there is the Tibidabo mountain, which attracts tourist that tend to post photos from its panoramic views.

The *Gràcia* district, and specially its neighborhood *Vila de Gràcia* it's a popular area, specially for young people, which is attracting many tourists lately. The plot clearly shows how *Vila de Gràcia* concentrates most of the posts from the three languages. It also shows that *Vallcarca* and *La Salut* neighborhoods are the ones where the % of English posts are superior. That is because in this area the Park Güell, a big touristic claim, is located.

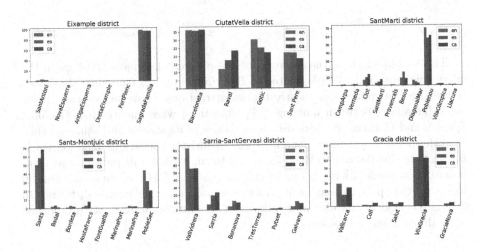

Fig. 7. % of mentions per neighborhood respect to the total district neighborhoods mentions in each language.

4.3 Word2Vec

Word2Vec [11] learns vector representations from non annotated text, where words having similar semantics have similar representations. In this work we use Gensim Word2Vec implementation[3] and train a different model for each one of the analyzed languages: English, Spanish and Catalan. The objective is to learn the different contexts where the authors use words depending on their language. The models are trained using the CBOW mode with a dimensionality of 300, a window of 8 and 25 epochs over the text corpus.

---

[3] https://radimrehurek.com/gensim/models/word2vec.html.

4.4   Words Associated to Districts

Using the Word2Vec learned models for each language, we can infer the words that users writing in English, Spanish or Catalan (tourist or locals) relate with each one of the Barcelona's neighborhoods. Next, we show the closest words in the Word2Vec space to the four *Ciutat Vella* neighborhoods using the three Word2Vec models learned. Closest words of the English trained Word2Vec are shown in red, of the Spanish one in green, and of the Catalan one in blue. Spelling variants and synonyms have been removed from the results.

Barceloneta
hotelw, seaside, beachlife, beachview, port, bcnbeach
ramblademar, torremapfre, hotelvela, paseomaritimo
portolimpic, hotelwela, vilaolimpica, torremapfre, bogatell

Born
barcelonaspots, gothicdistrict, oldtown, catedraldelmar
passeigdelborn, portalnou, callejuelas, rinconesmagicos
mercatdelborn, ccm, banysorientals, cafedelborn, laribera

Gotic
cathedral, history, gargoyles, churches, architecture
edadmedia, laribera, carrerdelbisbe, mercadodelborn
carrerdelbisbe, plaçadelrei, catedraldelmar, carrercomtal

Raval
cccb, macba, zeligbar, poblesec, elborn, grafity, gotico
rambladelraval, ravalcultural, fueradrogas, narcopisos
ravalcultural, somdebarri, ravalescultura, botigadecomics

This examples show the interests of the different language speakers in the query neighborhoods, Words related to *Barceloneta* and *El Gòtic* neighborhoods in the three languages are mostly tourist attractions. However, we can appreciate differences between languages. For instance, when mentioning *El Gòtic*, Spanish and Catalan speakers use along names of its streets and squares, while English speakers use more general words. Tourist publications mentioning *El Born* relate this district to Barcelona's old town, while locals publications mention its promenade, its market or its culture center (CCM). When mentioning *El Raval*, tourists publications mention its museums and other nearby districts. On the contrary, locals publications talk about its cultural activity, its promenade or its drug presence problem.

4.5   Beyond Districts

The trained Word2Vec models provide information that can be used beyond a district analysis. They can infer the words that Instagram users relate to Barcelona and any other word in the training vocabulary. For the following queries, the translation of the English query word to the corresponding language has been used, and the translation of the local languages results to English are shown.

Beach
summer, seaside, sand, sunset, sunny, whotel, seaview
seaview, passeigmaritim, mediterráneo, novaicaria
bogatell, novaicaria, mediterrani, lamarbella, voley

Tourism
landscape, architecture, bluesky, spain, aroundtheworld
catalanfood, adventure, crossing, eatanddrink, fair
route, beatifullplaces, mycity, heritage, walking

Food
tapas, fastfood, breakfast, sangria, seafood, blackrice
sushi, ham, soup, chicken, hamburguer, fruit
cannelloni, omelette, bread, soup, fruit, fries

Neighborhood
quaint, hidden, restaurants, lively, locals, gracia, corners
gotico, turists, citizens, park, streets, shops, people
ribera, citizen, ravalnotforsale, citizenfight, street, walking

This experiments also show clear differences between the models trained with the different languages. For instance, when mentioning *Food* English speakers write along Spanish most characteristic dishes, while locals write about more daily meals. When mentioning *Neighborhood*, tourists talk about its restaurants or appearance, while locals talk more about its people.

5   Visual Analysis

An image worths a thousand words. Word2Vec allows us to find the words that authors relate neighborhoods when using different languages. That is possible because Word2Vec learns word embeddings to a vectorial space where semantic similar words (words appearing in similar contexts), are mapped nearby. Img2NeighCtx (Image to Neighborhood Context) is a Convolutional Neural Network that, learning from images and associated captions, allows us to find the images that authors relate to the different neighborhoods when using different languages.

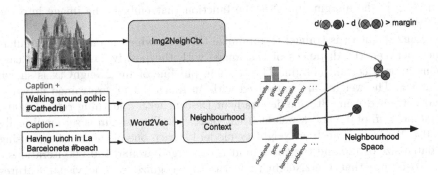

Fig. 8. Training procedure of Img2NeighCtx. The CNN is trained to maximize the difference of distances between the image and the positive caption and the image and the negative caption in the *Neighborhood Space* space until a certain margin.

5.1   Img2NeighCtx

Word2Vec allows us to compute a similarity between two words. To compute a vector encoding the similarities of a caption with each of the 82 Barcelona's districts and neighborhoods, we sum up the cosine similarities of all the caption words with each neighborhood name in the Word2Vec space and L2 normalize the vector. We call the resulting vector *Neighborhood Context* (NC). Let W be the Word2Vec representations of all the words in a caption c and $N = \{n_j\}_{j=1:J}$ be all the neighborhoods names Word2Vec representations ($J = 82$). The neighborhood context of each word w in the caption is represented by

$$NC(w) = \left(\frac{\langle w, n_1 \rangle}{||w|| \cdot ||n_1||}, \frac{\langle w, n_2 \rangle}{||w|| \cdot ||n_2||}, \ldots, \frac{\langle w, n_J \rangle}{||w|| \cdot ||n_J||} \right) \quad (1)$$

We eventually compute the *Neighborhood Context* of the caption c as:

$$NC(c) = \sum_{w \in W} NC(w) \tag{2}$$

which is L2 normalized.

Img2NeighCtx is a GoogleNet based CNN that learns to infer NC from images. The last classification layer is replaced by a fully connected layer with 82 outputs, which is the dimensionality of the *Neighborhood Space*, and uses a ranking loss to learn to embed images with similar captions *Neighborhood Contexts* nearby. Img2NeighCtx receives three inputs: the image (i), its caption embedding (NC^+), and a negative caption embedding (NC^-). The negative caption embedding is selected randomly from the 50% most distant batch caption embeddings. We define the loss by

$$L(i, NC^+, NC^-) = \tfrac{1}{2}max\left(0, m - \Phi_i^T NC^+ + \Phi_i^T NC^-\right) \tag{3}$$

where m is the margin and Φ is the function that embeds the image into the *Neighborhood Space*.

Img2NeighCtx is trained to minimize this loss, which maximizes the difference between the distances of the image with the positive and negative captions upon a certain margin. The training pipeline of Img2NeighCtx is shown in Fig. 8. The weights are initialized with an ImageNet [9] pretrained network, and is trained using Stochastic Gradient Descent with a learning rate of 0.001, a momentum of 0.9 and a weight decay of $2e - 4$. The margin is set empirically to 0.4. We trained an Img2NeighCtx model for each one of the languages using a batch size of 120 and the three models converged around $100,000$ iterations.

To ensure that Img2NeighCtx learns to recognize generic visual features instead of overfitting to the training data, we randomly split each language dataset in three subsets: 80% training set, 5% validation set and 15% retrieval set. The validation set is used to monitor overfitting when training the model. The retrieval set is not used to train, but to test the model in the following experiments. This configurations ensures that the trained models can generalize beyond the data used in this work.

5.2   Images Associated to Districts

Once Img2NeighCtx has been trained to embed images in the *Neighborhood Space*, it can be used in a straightforward manner in an image by neighbourhood retrieval task. The CNN has learned from the images and the associated captions to extract visual features useful to relate images to the different neighborhoods. Using as a query a neighborhood represented as a one hot vector in the *Neighborhood Space*, we can infer the kind of images that Instagram users writing in English, Spanish or Catalan relate to that neighborhood. To do that we retrieve the nearest images in the *Neighborhood Space*. Figures 2 and 9 show the first retrieved images for some of the neighborhoods. Images in the top row (red) correspond to the English trained model, in the second (green) to the

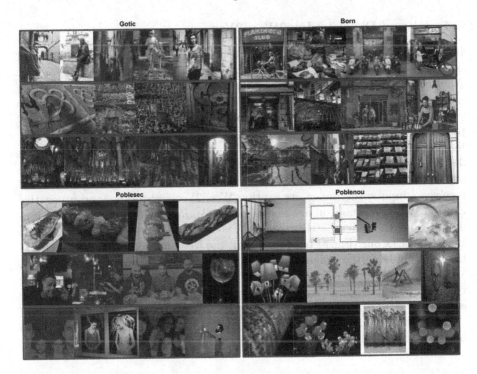

Fig. 9. Img2NeighCtx image by neighborhood retrieval results for different neighborhoods in each of the languages. (Color figure online)

Spanish one, and in the third (blue) to the Catalan one. When posting about *La Barceloneta* (Fig. 2), tourists tend to post photos of the drinks they have at the beach, while locals tend to post photos of themselves posing. When talking about *El Born* (*Sant Pere*) (Fig. 9), tourist tend to post photos of bikes, since there are many tourist oriented stores offering bike renting services there, while locals tend to post photos of its bars and streets. When posting about *El Poblesec* Fig. 9, tourist tend to post photos of the food they have in its popularity increasing restaurants, while locals tend to post photos of themselves, its bars or its art galleries. When posting about *El Poblenou* Fig. 9, the kind of images people post using the three languages are similar and related to design and art. This is because *El Poblenou* neighbourhood has been promoted as a technology and design hub in Barcelona, following the 22@ plan. This plan has attracted many foreign workers to live in the area. Therefore, and in contrast to other neighborhoods, the majority of English publications related to *El Poblenou* are not from tourists but from people that have settled here, and appear to have the same interests in *El Poblenou* as the Catalan and Spanish speakers.

5.3 Beyond Districts: Img2Word2Vec

Img2NeighCtx is very useful to retrieve images associated to each neighborhood in each one of the languages. In a similar way we trained Img2NeighCtx to predict *Neighborhood Contexts* from images, we can train a net to directly embed images in the Word2Vec space. We call that net Img2Word2Vec.

First, the embeddings of all the captions in the Word2Vec space are computed as the mean of its word embeddings and L2 normalized. Img2Word2Vec has the same structure as Img2NeighCtx, but the last fully connected layer has 300 outputs, which is the dimensionality of the Word2Vec space. It uses a ranking loss to learn to embed semantically similar images nearby. Img2Word2Vec receives 3 inputs: the image, its caption Word2Vec embedding, and a negative caption Word2Vec embedding. The negative caption embedding is selected randomly from the other batch captions. The training pipeline is similar to the Img2NeighCtx one (Fig. 8) but leaving out the Neighborhood Context computation and applying the ranking loss directly to captions Word2Vec embeddings. We trained one Img2Word2Vec model for each language. The splits and the training parameters used were the same as for Img2NeighCtx. All the models converged around 150, 000 iterations.

The trained Img2Word2Vec models can be used to relate text and images beyond districts and neighborhoods names, retrieving images related to any text

Fig. 10. Img2Word2Vec image by text retrieval results for different queries in each of the languages.

concept present in the vocabulary. Figure 10 shows retrieval results for different query words. When using the word *food*, tourist tend to post photos of themselves in front of "healthy" and well presented dishes or seafood. As a contrast, locals tend to post photos where only the food appears, and it tends to be international and more diverse. For *friends* tourist tend to post photos of a group of friends in the beach, while locals tend to appear around a table, though they are more diverse. Associated with the word *views*, tourists post photos of Barcelona's views taken from popular places (Montjuic and Park Güell). As a contrast, locals photos are more diverse and include photos taken from houses and of other Barcelona areas, such as the port. When using the word *market*, tourist photos are mainly from Mercat de la Boqueria, an old market in Barcelona's old town that has turned into a very touristic place. Meanwhile, locals photos are more divers and include markets where people do their daily shopping. In general, English speakers images are much less variant than local languages speakers images, and more concentrated in popular spots. That proves that the assumption that English speakers images correspond mainly to tourists is true, and also that tourism is strongly concentrated in certain Barcelona areas, as [4] also concluded.

6 Conclusions

Extensive experiments have demonstrated that Instagram data can be used to learn relations between words, images and neighborhoods that allow us to do a per neighborhood analysis of a city. Results have shown that the assumption that English publications represent tourists activity and local languages publications correspond to locals activity is true. Both the textual and the visual analysis have demonstrated to reflect the actual tourists and locals behavior in Barcelona.

The retrieval results for both Img2NeighCtx and Img2Word2Vec nets have been obtained in blind and image only test sets, which proves that similar results can be obtained with external images. Moreover, Img2Word2Vec can be used to obtain results for any term in the vocabulary. In this work the *InstaBarcelona* dataset has been used. However, models can be scaled to larger datasets, since both Word2Vec and CNNs scale well with big data. The experiments can also be extended straightforward to other cities or subjects. The code used in the project is available on https://github.com/gombru/insbcn.

Acknowledgments. This work was supported by the Doctorats Industrials program from the Generalitat de Catalunya, the Spanish project TIN2017-89779-P, the H2020 Marie Skłodowska-Curie actions of the European Union, grant agreement No 712949 (TECNIOspring PLUS), and the Agency for Business Competitiveness of the Government of Catalonia (ACCIO).

References

1. Ayuntament de Barcelona: Barcelona stadistics. Observatory districts (2017). http://www.bcn.cat/estadistica/angles/documents/districtes/index.htm
2. Blei, D.M., Ng, A.Y., Jordan, M.I.: Latent Dirichlet allocation. J. Mach. Learn. Res. **3**, 993–1022 (2003)
3. Boy, J.D., Uitermark, J.: Reassembling the city through Instagram. Trans. Inst. Br. Geogr. **42**, 612–624 (2017)
4. García-Palomares, J.C., Gutiérrez, J., Mínguez, C.: Identification of tourist hot spots based on social networks: a comparative analysis of European metropolises using photo-sharing services and GIS. Appl. Geogr. **63**, 408–417 (2015)
5. Gomez, L., Patel, Y., Rusiñol, M., Karatzas, D., Jawahar, C.V.: Self-supervised learning of visual features through embedding images into text topic spaces. In: CVPR (2017)
6. Gordo, A., Larlus, D.: Beyond instance-level image retrieval: leveraging captions to learn a global visual representation for semantic retrieval. In: CVPR (2017)
7. He, Y., Yang, X., Zhang, X.: Instagram post data analysis. arXiv (2015)
8. Instagram: Instagram's Neighborhood Flavors - Instagram Engineering. Medium (2017)
9. Deng, J., Dong, W., Socher, R., Li, L.-J., Li, K., Fei-Fei, L.: ImageNet: a large-scale hierarchical image database. In: CVPR (2009)
10. Kuo, Y.H., et al.: Discovering the city by mining diverse and multimodal data streams. In: ACM International Conference on Multimedia (2014)
11. Mikolov, T., Corrado, G., Chen, K., Dean, J.: Efficient estimation of word representations in vector space. In: ICLR (2013)
12. Norouzi, M., et al.: Zero-shot learning by convex combination of semantic embeddings. In: NIPS (2013)
13. Pennington, J., Socher, R., Manning, C.: Glove: global vectors for word representation. In: EMNLP (2014)
14. Salvador, A., et al.: Learning cross-modal embeddings for cooking recipes and food images. In: CVPR (2017)
15. Singh, V.K., Hegde, S., Atrey, A.: Towards measuring fine-grained diversity using social media photographs. In: ICWSM (2017)

A Structured Listwise Approach to Learning to Rank for Image Tagging

Jorge Sánchez[1,2]([✉]), Franco Luque[1,2], and Leandro Lichtensztein[3]

[1] CONICET, Córdoba, Argentina
{jorge.sanchez,franco.luque}@unc.edu.ar
[2] Universidad Nacional de Córdoba, Córdoba, Argentina
[3] Deep Vision AI Inc., Córdoba, Argentina
leandro.lich@deepvisionai.com

Abstract. With the growing quantity and diversity of publicly available image data, computer vision plays a crucial role in understanding and organizing visual information today. Image tagging models are very often used to make this data accessible and useful. Generating image labels and ranking them by their relevance to the visual content is still an open problem. In this work, we use a bilinear compatibility function inspired from zero-shot learning that allows us to rank tags according to their relevance to the image content. We propose a novel listwise structured loss formulation to learn it from data. We leverage captioned image data and propose different "tags from captions" schemes meant to capture user attention and intra-user agreement in a simple and effective manner. We evaluate our method on the COCO-Captions, PASCAL-sentences and MIRFlickr-25k datasets showing promising results.

Keywords: Learning to rank · Zero-shot learning · Image tagging Visual-semantic compatibility · Multimodal embedding

1 Introduction

In the past decade, we have witnessed a tremendous growth in the quantity and diversity of media resources, especially images and videos. With all this information being stored and shared across social and media platforms, the ability to search and to organize such data efficiently is a problem of great practical importance.

One of the main characteristics of social media data is its multimodal nature: images and videos are frequently associated with user generated textual descriptions (brief captions, tags, hashtags, etc.), providing complementary information not necessarily present or apparent in the visual domain. Besides enriching and complementing the visual information, the textual information can be used to index the data, facilitating their access and analysis.

For computer agents trying to organize the data in an autonomous manner, being able to automatically generate and rank tags and labels is an important task. An alternative is to rely on a large pool of image classifiers and/or

© Springer Nature Switzerland AG 2019
L. Leal-Taixé and S. Roth (Eds.): ECCV 2018 Workshops, LNCS 11134, pp. 545–559, 2019.
https://doi.org/10.1007/978-3-030-11024-6_42

object detectors. However, using off-the-shelf classifiers for image tagging leads to results that does not resemble tags that a human user would choose to describe the content of an image. For instance, predictions cast by models trained on ImageNet [1] correspond to leaf nodes in the WordNet [2] lexical ontology and tend to be overly specific. Moreover, image datasets annotated with object categories usually consist of a restricted set of labels that reflects the presence or absence of objects in images, disregarding other objects or visual properties that sometimes are more relevant from the perceptual point of view. For instance, if we look at some of the examples in Table 1 we see that annotations based on a fixed set of object categories often miss important visual information (e.g. the mirror in the first image) or give the same "relevance" to all objects, irrespective of their role in explaining the semantic content of the scene (e.g. apple vs. refrigerator in the third image).

Using annotations from tagging datasets, e.g. NUS-WIDE [3] or MIRFlickr [4], where annotations correspond to actual tags generated by users on the Flickr website, has also some difficulties. First, tags might be unrelated to the actual visual content of the images, e.g. pictures tagged with the camera brand/model they were captured with. Second, the set of possible tags, although richer, is still restricted to a closed set of possible words.

In this work, we aim at learning a visual-semantic compatibility function that allow us to rank textual descriptions (tags) according to their relevance to the image content, without restricting ourselves to a fixed vocabulary at test time. We propose a novel structured listwise ranking loss that encodes explicitly the relevance of the tags to the actual content on the visual domain. Our approach assumes the availability of a training set of image and ranked tags pairs. We build such a training set by leveraging captioned image data like the COCO Captions dataset [5]. Using multiple caption annotations, we propose a simple and yet effective method for the extraction of image tags and to rank them according to their relevance on explaining the visual scene. Our approach is based on the following observations: (i) common words chosen by different users are good candidates for image tags (intra-user agreement), and (ii) terms named earlier in a sentence are visually more relevant than those named at the end (user attention). We run extensive experimental evaluations on three different datasets.

The rest of the paper is organized as follows. First, we present an overview of related work. Then, we describe our model and propose different methods to infer ranked tags from image captions. Last, experiments, results and discussion are presented to conclude the paper.

2   Related Work

We now review related work on research areas that we believe are closely related to our work, namely: image tagging, zero-shot learning (ZSL) and embeddings for multi-modal data.

Tag Assignment and Refinement. We focus on tagging methods that use information provided by images and tags. A common intuition in such methods is that visually similar images should share a similar set of tags. In the TagProp model [6], tags for a test image are predicted based on a weighted sum of the annotations of the most visually similar images on the training set. In [7], a distance metric learning scheme is proposed, exploiting both image and tag information in a transductive way. The learning formulation involves a triplet-based max-margin objective, solved by stochastic gradient descent (SGD). TagCoocur+ [8] combines visual and tag information into a relevance score based on the co-occurrence frequencies both on the visual and textual domain. RobustPCA [9] factorizes the image-tag association matrix using a low rank decomposition with an ℓ_1 sparsity constraint. [10] proposes an approach based on Markov random walks on a graph built from image similarities and image-tag associations. The method proved to scale to very large datasets. [11] uses both images and tags to build a graph. Learning takes place on the structure of this graph based on samples and a pseudo-relevance measure. Different from other graph-based approaches, edge weights are also learned, allowing to minimize the effect of uninformative tags and visual words. We refer the reader to [12] for an extensive review of the problems and different approaches proposed in the literature.

Zero-Shot Learning and Recognition. Zero-shot learning aims at recognizing object categories that might not have been seen during training [13–16]. In the literature, there exists two formulations of this problem. In the original formulation, it is assumed that train an test classes are disjoint. In the generalized version of the zero-shot learning problem (GZSL) this assumption is relaxed and the sets are allowed to overlap. This problem has shown to be more difficult than ZSL. We refer the reader to [17] and [18] for recent surveys on the topic.

Most approaches dealing with either ZSL or GZSL assume that images and class labels can be encoded as points in some vector spaces, e.g. feature vectors extracted based on a pre-trained network [19,20] and word/attribute embeddings derived from side information [13,21–23]. A compatibility function between (the representations of) images and class labels is then learned from training data. In this case, the most common approach is based on the use of bilinear forms [16] and which we also follow in this work.

Multi-modal Embeddings. In the fields of computer vision (CV) and natural language processing (NLP), the use of convolutional neural networks (CNN) and distributional semantic models has lead to major advances. The combination of both modalities [24–26] has shown great potential on several linguistic tasks. For instance, [26] extends the skip-gram model of [22,23] by taking into account the visual information associated with a restricted set of words. The model showed good performance on a variety of semantic benchmarks. [27] uses autoencoders to learn grounded meaning representations from images and textual data. Experimental results on word similarity and word categorization showed that multimodal information improves over unimodal counterparts. Even though our approach does not learn a multimodal representation explicitly, we do constraint the visual and textual spaces to be aligned in terms of their semantics.

3 Our Model

Given an image $x \in \mathcal{X}$ and a tag $y \in \mathcal{Y}$, our goal is to learn a function $s :$ $\mathcal{X} \times \mathcal{Y} \to \mathbb{R}$ that provides us with a score regarding the compatibility between the semantics of y and the visual content in x. Following [16], we model s as a simple bilinear map:

$$s_{(\psi,\phi)}(x, y; W) = \psi(x)^T W \phi(y), \tag{1}$$

where $\psi : \mathcal{X} \to \mathbb{R}^D$ and $\phi : \mathcal{Y} \to \mathbb{R}^E$ denote image and word embeddings, respectively. For a given choice of (ψ, ϕ), our goal is to learn $W \in \mathbb{R}^{D \times E}$ from a suitable set of training samples.

In our work, we assume the availability of a training set $\mathcal{D} = \{(x_n, Y_n)\}_{n=1}^N$ consisting of images x_n and ordered tag-sets $Y_n = \{y_1^n, \cdots, y_{|Y_n|}^n\}$, with $r(y_1^n; x_n) \geq \cdots \geq r(y_{|Y_n|}^n; x_n)$ for a given relevance measure r, i.e. $(Y_n, \geq_{r(\cdot; x_n)})$ is a partially ordered set. In what follows, we assume r is given, and thus the preference order of the tags in Y_n is known, for all n. Later, in Sect. 3.2 we will discuss different formulations for r based on some consistencies observed in human-generated captions, when different annotators are asked to describe the content of an image.

3.1 Learning Formulation

We consider loss functions of the form:

$$L(W; r) = \sum_{n=1}^N \ell(\hat{Y}(x_n), Y_n), \tag{2}$$

with $Y_n = \{y_1^n, \ldots, y_{|Y_n|}^n\}$ the tags for x_n as ranked by $\geq_{r(\cdot; x_n)}$ and $\hat{Y}(x_n)$ the same set of tags but ranked according to $\geq_{s_{(\psi,\phi)}(\cdot, x_n; W)}$, i.e. the loss function ℓ encodes the cost of predicting an order for the tags in Y_n different from that induced by the ground-truth measure r.

Structured Joint Embedding (SJE). First, we follow [16] and consider loss functions of the form:

$$\ell_{SJE}(x, Y) = \max_{1 \leq i \leq |Y|} \left[\Delta(1, i) + s_{(\psi,\phi)}(x, y_i) - s_{(\psi,\phi)}(x, y_1) \right]_+, \tag{3}$$

with $[z]_+ \equiv \max(0, z)$. We explore two different formulations for the structured term $\Delta : \mathbb{N} \times \mathbb{N} \to \mathbb{R}$ over relative orders, namely:

$$\Delta^{(I)}(k, k') = 1 - \delta_{k,k'} \tag{4}$$

$$\Delta^{(II)}(k, k') = 1 - (k' - k + 1)^{-1}, \quad k' \geq k \tag{5}$$

Equation (4) corresponds to the structured loss of [16] when we assume the top-ranked tag to be the only relevant tag for the image under consideration. Equation (5) considers the relative order of the tags. Its effect on Eq. (3) is to ensure that the ground truth tag (top-1 in Y) receives a higher score than the other tags in the list.

Listwise Structured Joint Embedding (ListSJE). One of the shortcomings of the previous formulation is that it penalizes wrong associations only w.r.t to the most relevant tag in the list. Inspired by the likelihood loss formulation of Xia *et al.* [28], we propose the following cost function:

$$\ell_{ListSJE}^{K_{top}}(x, Y) = \sum_{k=1}^{K_{top}} \sum_{k < i \leq |Y|} \left[\Delta(k, i) + s_{(\psi, \phi)}(x, y_i) - s_{(\psi, \phi)}(x, y_k) \right]_+ \quad (6)$$

where we assume $K_{top} \leq |Y|$ and $\Delta(k, k') \equiv \Delta^{(II)}(k, k')$. Compared to Eq. (3), the loss given by Eq. (6) does also considers the relative ordering of the tags within the set of relevant annotations.

3.2   From Image Captions to Ranked Tags

Our formulation assumes the availability of a dataset $\mathcal{D} = \{(x_n, Y_n)\}_{n=1}^N$ of images, each of which is annotated with a list of tags sorted by decreasing relevance according to a given measure r. Note that, given a set of possible tags for an image, different definitions of r will lead to different preference relations for the tags in the set. Defining r is also challenging, since the notion of "visual relevance" for a tag might be influenced by external factors which are rather subjective and difficult to grasp, e.g. user intentions, pre-existing knowledge, social context, etc. Our approach is to build $\mathcal{D}$ from data by leveraging existing datasets like COCO [5] where, besides object categories, each image is annotated with a set of 5 different captions describing its visual content. Some example annotations are shown in Table 1. Next, we describe different approaches to extract a list of ranked tags from the captions available for each image.

Let $\mathcal{C}(x) = \{c_1, \ldots, c_Q\}$ be the set of captions corresponding to image x. We denote as $t(c_i) \equiv t_i = \{w : w \in c_i \text{ and } w \text{ is a noun}\}$ the set of nouns extracted from $c_i \in \mathcal{C}(x)$. Also, let $loc(w; c)$ denote the relative location of word w within c, e.g. $loc(w = \text{"dog"}; c = \text{"The dog bites."}) = 2/3$ as "dog" is the second word on a three-word sentence, and $count(w; c)$ the number of times word w appears in c. We define the following scores:

$$r_{loc}(w) = \max_{c \in \mathcal{C}(x)} \{1 - loc(w; c) : w \in c\} \quad (7)$$

$$r_{freq}(w) = \frac{count(w; c_1) + \cdots + count(w; c_Q)}{|t_1| + \cdots + |t_Q|} \quad (8)$$

The first is a proxy for visual attention (under the hypothesis that objects that are mentioned earlier in a sentence are those which are more relevant to the

Table 1. COCO example annotations (best viewed with magnification) and ranked tags obtained by the relevance score of Eq. (9) on nouns and $\alpha = 0.5$.

Categories	Captions	Tag / $r_{0.5}^{nn}$	
clock	1. A brown mirror hanging on the wall. 2. there is a mirror where u can see the reflection of a clock 3. a clock in the reflection of a mirror 4. A mirror on a wall reflecting a wooden clock. 5. A mirror with a reflection of a clock in it.	mirror clock reflection wall	0.633 0.580 0.425 0.371
backpack dog person surfboard	1. Two people walking with surf boards and two dogs. 2. People with surf boards walking from the shoreline accompanied by dogs on a sunny day. 3. A group of people and dogs carry their surfboards in hand. 4. Two boys with dogs carry surfboards down the beach. 5. Two people standing next to a river holding surfboards.	people surf group boy board dog surfboard shoreline river beach hand day	0.591 0.483 0.481 0.473 0.452 0.441 0.318 0.304 0.223 0.123 0.106 0.085
apple bottle bowl orange oven refrigerator sink wine glass	1. A bright red retro refrigerator in a mostly white kitchen 2. Cooking utensils and bowls hanging on a rack above an oven sitting in a kitchen with a refrigerator, sink and a window 3. a kitchen with a fridge and a sink below a window 4. a kitchen with a sink a refrigerator and a window 5. This kitchen has a red refrigerator and a black stove.	kitchen cooking utensil refrigerator rack retro sink fridge oven window stove	0.568 0.523 0.502 0.391 0.377 0.373 0.368 0.341 0.314 0.118 0.114

visual scene) while the second acts as a proxy for the agreement between different users and the terms they choose when asked to describe the content of a scene. We consider a simple combination of these scores and define a parameterized measure as follows:

$$r_\alpha(w) = \alpha\, r_{freq}(w) + (1 - \alpha)\, r_{loc}(w), \quad 0 \le \alpha \le 1 \qquad (9)$$

Here, the hyper-parameter α controls the strength of the frequency score w.r.t the location score.

We also consider two variations of the above based on the parse tree of each caption, namely:

1. Use compound nouns instead of only nouns, e.g. { "soccer field" } instead of { "soccer", "field" }.
2. Use a syntactic version of the relative location score: the relative distance of the word to the root in the syntactic dependency tree of the caption. Relevant nouns do not necessarily appear first in a sentence, but they always appear at the top of dependency trees. In particular, main nouns are at the root of nominal phrases, the most common caption type, and subject/object nouns

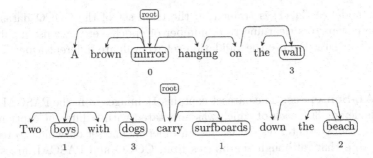

Fig. 1. Syntactic dependency trees for two COCO captions. Edges point from parents to children. Nouns are highlighted and annotated with their (absolute) distances to the root word. The first caption is a nominal phrase with root noun "mirror". The second caption is a declarative sentence with nouns "boys" and "surfboards" as subject and object respectively. Here, "dogs" occurs before "surfboards" but is less relevant according to the tree.

are directly attached to the root verb of declarative sentences. Examples of these are shown in Fig. 1. As a drawback, a natural language parser must be used, so errors made by the parser propagate to the score.

We denote the different combinations as r_α^{nn}, r_α^{cn}, $r_\alpha^{nn-syntactic}$ and $r_\alpha^{cn-syntactic}$, where the superscripts nn and cn denote nouns and compound-nouns, respectively.

We note that, choosing a particular form of relevance completely defines the training set $\mathcal{D}$ on which future models will be trained on. In what follows, when we refer to "a model" we refer not only to the loss function used to train the W matrix in Eq. (1) but also to the dataset (set of image and ranked tags pairs) used to train it.

4   Experiments

In this section we present experimental results regarding the models described above. We first present the datasets used in our experiments and the experimental setup we followed. Next, we discuss the benefits and limitations of the proposed approach and how it compares to other approaches in the literature.

4.1   Datasets

In our experiments, we use three different datasets: COCO Captions [5], PASCAL-sentences [29] and MIRFlickr-25k [4] that we describe next.

COCO. We use the training and validation sets of the 2014 release of the dataset, consisting of 123k images ($\sim$83k for training and $\sim$40k for validation) annotated with 5 different human descriptions each. In all our experiments, the bilinear model of Eq. (1) is trained on the train set of the COCO dataset. To tune the parameters (learning rate, number of epochs, etc.) we use a subset of the training data. We use the validation set to evaluate different aspects of the model.

PASCAL-Sentences. The dataset contains 1k images from the PASCAL VOC 2008 Challenge [30], each of which was annotated with 5 different captions. We use the PASCAL-sentences dataset as an independent set on which to test our model. Note that, although the images from COCO and PASCAL are similar in the sense that both datasets focus on generic object recognition in natural scenes (no iconic views), the number of objects per image differs considerably. For instance, around 10% for COCO images contain a single object while this number increases to 60% for the images in PASCAL VOC [5].

MIRFlickr-25k. The dataset contains 25k images collected from Flickr together with the tags that users assigned to them. There are 1386 different tags, with an average of 8.94 tags per image. Besides providing generic user tags, the images were also manually annotated for a set of 24 different concepts. A second round of annotations was performed for 14 of the original concepts, where the images were deemed relevant for a given concept only if a significant part of the concept appeared in the image.

4.2 Experimental Setup

Textual Features. In our experiments, we use pretrained word2vec[1] [22,23], GloVe[2] [31] and fastText[3] [32] word embeddings. Nouns are lemmatized before computing the vectors. For compound nouns, we compute the average vector of the lemmatized constituent words. We use spaCy[4] [33] to process caption sentences and extract nouns, compound nouns, their lemmatized versions and syntactic dependency trees.

Visual Features. We use VGG [19] and ResNet [20] convolutional architectures to extract visual features from the images. Additionally, we also implemented a simplified version of the multiscale R-MAC feature extractor [34] from the retrieval literature, where we do not include the PCA whitening step after the region-level feature pooling operation. Visual features are extracted from the penultimate fully connected layer of a pre-trained VGG-19 or ResNet-152 architecture. For R-MAC we consider three different scales (1, 2 and 4) and pool features from activations of the last convolutional layer of a VGG-16 network. We L2-normalize the max pooled features, average them and re-normalize the resulting vector.

---

[1] https://code.google.com/archive/p/word2vec/.
[2] https://spacy.io/models/en#en_core_web_md.
[3] https://fasttext.cc/docs/en/english-vectors.
[4] https://spacy.io/.

Model Training. To train our model we use mini-batch gradient descent with a batch size of 16 over 10 epochs. We use the Adam optimizer with an initial learning rate of 0.0001. All models were implemented in PyTorch v0.4.0 [35]. To train our models we used 3 NVIDIA GTX 1080Ti cards on an Intel Xeon machine @ 2.6 GHz with 64 GB of RAM. Training a single bilinear model took approximately 2 h.

4.3 Experimental Results

In this section, we evaluate and discuss different aspects of our model. These evaluations are carried out on the COCO and PASCAL-Sentences datasets. Next, we compare the performance of our approach with other methods proposed in the literature on the challenging MIRFlickr-25k dataset.

Tags from Captions. In Sect. 3.2 we presented a simple approach to extract a set of tags from the captions describing a given visual scene. These tags correspond to the nouns (or compound nouns) extracted from each image caption. As such, they can all be considered as "relevant" to the actual visual content. In our approach, however, what matters is not the relevance score of any particular tag but the order in which they appear in the annotation list. Instead of trying to predict a ground truth order, we rank the different approaches according to their ability to lead to predictable tags. That is, we train a bilinear model as in Eq. (1) for each of the losses in Sect. 3.1. We chose the best tag generation scheme based on the performance on the validation set of the COCO dataset. For these experiments, we rely on VGG-19 and word2vec as image and tag features, respectively. We use precision@1 and precision@5 as performance metrics. Tables 2, 3 and 4 show results for the different formulations and parameter α, for each of the losses presented in Sect. 3.1. Best results are highlighted in bold. For $\ell_{ListSJE}$ we set $K_{top} = 5$.

From the tables we see that, when considering p@1, the models based on simple nouns and $\alpha = 0.75$, $r_{0.75}^{nn}$, perform best for all loss functions. Among them, the ℓ_{SJE} formulation with the $\Delta^{(II)}$ structured loss leads to the best p@1 score on the COCO validation set. This behavior changes when we consider p@5 as the evaluation metric. In this case, the model based on compound nouns leads to the best performance for all losses. We also note that, for p@5, setting $\alpha = 0$ gives the best results. Interestingly, in these models the word frequencies play no role. Only relative location scores are considered.

Also interesting is that the best performance is observed for the listwise formulation of Eq. (6).[5] For the SJE loss of Eq. (3), $\Delta^{(II)}$ is preferred over $\Delta^{(I)}$. In what follows, we focus on the $r_{0.75}^{nn}$ and $r_{0.0}^{cn}$ relevance measures.

---

[5] In preliminary experiments, we explored the use of the tag scores, as given by the relevance measure r, directly into the structured loss term in Eqs. (3) and (6). However, we did not observe any improvement w.r.t to the simpler formulations given by Eqs. (4) and (5).

Table 2. Tag predictability measured on the COCO validation set, using VGG-19 and wor2vec features and the loss function of Eq. (3) with $\Delta = \Delta^{(I)}$.

Method		α				
		0.0	0.25	0.5	0.75	1.0
p@1	Nouns	0.4621	0.5752	0.6332	**0.6457**	0.5744
	Nouns (syntactic)	0.4108	0.6203	0.6257	0.6350	0.5730
	Compound-nouns	0.4435	0.5561	0.6095	**0.6155**	0.5018
	Compound-nouns (syntactic)	0.4540	0.6019	0.6086	0.6140	0.5035
p@5	Nouns	**0.6876**	0.6814	0.6788	0.6786	0.6634
	Nouns (syntactic)	0.6812	0.6791	0.6808	0.6782	0.6628
	Compound-nouns	0.6952	0.6915	0.6920	0.6868	0.6438
	Compound-nouns (syntactic)	**0.7015**	0.6977	0.6973	0.6880	0.6438

Table 3. Tag predictability measured on the COCO validation set, using VGG-19 and wor2vec features and the loss function of Eq. (3) with $\Delta = \Delta^{(II)}$.

Method		α				
		0.0	0.25	0.5	0.75	1.0
p@1	Nouns	0.4810	0.5848	0.6395	**0.6527**	0.5865
	Nouns (syntactic)	0.4391	0.6257	0.6309	0.6389	0.5859
	Compound-nouns	0.4638	0.5664	0.6161	**0.6243**	0.5205
	Compound-nouns (syntactic)	0.4755	0.6069	0.6137	0.6195	0.5191
p@5	Nouns	**0.7162**	0.7118	0.7031	0.7003	0.6747
	Nouns (syntactic)	0.7064	0.7024	0.7029	0.6981	0.6752
	Compound-nouns	**0.7230**	0.7169	0.7124	0.7055	0.6537
	Compound-nouns (syntactic)	0.7200	0.7119	0.7109	0.7037	0.6537

Influence of the Parameter K_{top}. Next, we focus on the listwise ranking loss of Eq. (6). In particular, we evaluate the influence of the parameter K_{top} and different word embeddings on tag predictability. Results are shown in Fig. 2 for $r^{nn}_{0.75}$ and $r^{cn}_{0.0}$. Considering the choice of word embedding, fastText and word2vec exhibit a similar performance, outperforming GloVe vectors for all values of K_{top}. When comparing different image features, VGG-19 shows better performance than ResNet-152 and R-MAC features for both $r^{nn}_{0.75}$ and $r^{cn}_{0.0}$ measures for all values of the parameter. In what follows, we choose VGG-19 and word2vec features as the best configuration.

Results on PASCAL-Sentences. We now turn to the evaluation of our model on the PASCAL-sentences dataset. Figure 3 shows precision@k for different values of k for $(\psi, \phi) = $ (VGG-19, word2vec) and the ranking loss of Eq. (6). We also consider a varying number of *distractors*, i.e. tags sampled at random from

Table 4. Tag predictability measured on the COCO validation set, using VGG-19 and wor2vec features and the loss function of Eq. (6) with $K_{top} = 5$.

	Method	α				
		0.0	0.25	0.5	0.75	1.0
p@1	Nouns	0.4660	0.5619	0.6250	**0.6424**	0.5791
	Nouns (syntactic)	0.4284	0.6085	0.6166	0.6274	0.5797
	Compound-nouns	0.4488	0.5391	0.5972	**0.6123**	0.5092
	Compound-nouns (syntactic)	0.4722	0.5897	0.5979	0.6027	0.5098
p@5	Nouns	0.7415	0.7411	**0.7417**	0.7385	0.6899
	Nouns (syntactic)	0.7302	0.7322	0.7329	0.7322	0.6897
	Compound-nouns	**0.7472**	0.7468	0.7461	0.7405	0.6646
	Compound-nouns (syntactic)	0.7392	0.7391	0.7382	0.7335	0.6639

the set of all tags extracted from all the images in the dataset which are different from those of the query. Distractors are only sampled at test time. Additionally, we show the performance of a random ranker (dashed lines).

From the figure we observe that precision increases with k. This is to be expected since we rank a fixed pool of potential tags per image. However, the relative gain w.r.t to the random ranker is greater for a larger number of distractors. For instance, for the model trained on the $r_{0.75}^{nn}$ setting and $k = 5$ the gain in performance is $+25\%$, $+68\%$, $+110\%$ and $+176\%$ for 0, 5, 10 and 20 distractors per image, respectively. It is also interesting to note that for $k = 1$,

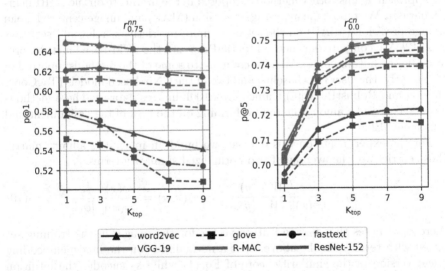

Fig. 2. Precision@$\{1,5\}$ for $r_{0.75}^{nn}$ (left) and $r_{0.0}^{cn}$ (right) as a function of K_{top} in Eq. (6), measured on the validation set of the COCO dataset (best viewed in color). (Color figure online)

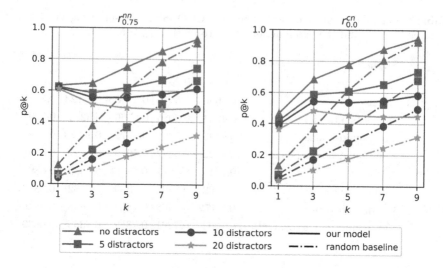

Fig. 3. Precision@k on the PASCAL-sentences dataset using VGG-19 and word2vec features (best viewed in color). (Color figure online)

there is a large gap between the noun and compound-noun based systems, with the former giving +0.2 absolute improvement w.r.t the latter. For larger values of k, the difference decreases significantly.

Results on MIRFlickr-25k. In this section we compare the performance of our approach against other methods proposed in the literature on the MIRFlickr-25k dataset. We report mean average precision (MAP) and image-centered mean average precision (MiAP) on the set of 14 more restrictive ("relevant" set) tags as in [12]. We compare our method to TagProp and the SVM-based method proposed by the authors in [6]. We also compare to some of the methods reported in [12], namely: the UserTags baseline and two of the CNN-based models (TagCooccur+ [8] and RobustPCA [9]) trained on a 100k images dataset. These methods where shown to be among the top performing on the task of tag assignment and refinement [12].

For the experiments on this dataset, we build an image-tag affinity matrix whose entries are the average of two normalized similarity terms:

$$s_1(x,y) = \frac{\phi(x)^T W \psi(y)}{\|\phi(x)\| \, \|W\psi(y)\|}, \qquad s_2(x,y) = \frac{\phi(x)^T \phi_y}{\|\phi(x)\| \, \|\phi_y\|} \qquad (10)$$

where ϕ_y denotes the average feature vector for the images in the training set tagged with term y. In the above, s_1 is a normalized (on the image embedding space) version of the similarity score of Eq. (1) while s_2 encodes the intuition similar images should share similar tags. To compute ϕ_y, we generated train and test splits as in [6] and divided the dataset by taking every second image for training and the rest for testing. The matrix W was trained as before using the ranked tags derived from the train set of the COCO dataset. Results are shown in Table 5.

Compared to the handcrafted feature-based methods of [6] (SVM and Tag-Prop) our approach compares favorably. Although this is to be expected (we rely on more robust visual features), we opted to present the original results of [6] for reference. Note, however, that both TagProp and SVM achieve a better MAP score than CNN+TagCooccur+ [8] which is based on VGG-16 convolutional features. Compared to CNN+RobustPCA [9], our models are behind in terms of MAP but compare favorably in terms of MiAP.

Table 5. Results on the MIRFlickr-25k set.

Method	MAP	MiAP
TagProp (Rank) [6]	0.404	-
SVM [6]	0.466	-
UserTags [12]	0.263	0.204
CNN+TagCooccur+ [8,12]	0.381	0.277
CNN+RobustPCA [9,12]	0.627	0.376
Our ($r_{0.75}^{nn}$, $K_{top} = 1$)	0.521	0.389
Our ($r_{0.0}^{cn}$, $K_{top} = 7$)	0.514	0.370

5   Conclusions

In this paper, we proposed a new method to learn a visual-semantic compatibility based on a structured listwise ranking loss formulation. Since there is no dataset containing per-image ranked tags in the literature – which is required to train our model – we take advantage of images captions from publicly available datasets and proposed several methods to automatically extract a list of tags from image captions, sorted according to its relevance to the visual content of the scene. Based on the this, we were able to train models that compare favorably to some other methods proposed in the literature, showing promising results. In future work, we want to explore different tag inference mechanisms as well as to include explicit models of visual attention, integrating the visual and semantic feature generation into an end-to-end architecture.

Acknowledgments. This work was supported in part by grants PICT 2014-1651 and 2016-0118 from ANPCyT, Argentinean Ministry of Education, Culture, Science and Technology. This work used Nabucodonosor Cluster from CCAD-UNC, which is part of SNCAD, Argentina.

References

1. Deng, J., Dong, W., Socher, R., Li, L.J., Li, K., Fei-Fei, L.: ImageNet: a large-scale hierarchical image database. In: IEEE Conference on Computer Vision and Pattern Recognition, CVPR 2009, pp. 248–255. IEEE (2009)
2. Miller, G.A.: WordNet: a lexical database for English. Commun. ACM **38**(11), 39–41 (1995)
3. Chua, T.S., Tang, J., Hong, R., Li, H., Luo, Z., Zheng, Y.: NUS-WIDE: a real-world web image database from National University of Singapore. In: Proceedings of the ACM International Conference on Image and Video Retrieval, p. 48. ACM (2009)
4. Huiskes, M.J., Lew, M.S.: The MIR Flickr retrieval evaluation. In: Proceedings of the 1st ACM International Conference on Multimedia Information Retrieval, pp. 39–43. ACM (2008)
5. Lin, T.-Y., et al.: Microsoft COCO: common objects in context. In: Fleet, D., Pajdla, T., Schiele, B., Tuytelaars, T. (eds.) ECCV 2014. LNCS, vol. 8693, pp. 740–755. Springer, Cham (2014). https://doi.org/10.1007/978-3-319-10602-1_48
6. Verbeek, J., Guillaumin, M., Mensink, T., Schmid, C.: Image annotation with TagProp on the MIRFlickr set. In: Proceedings of the International Conference on Multimedia Information Retrieval, pp. 537–546. ACM (2010)
7. Wu, P., Hoi, S.C.H., Zhao, P., He, Y.: Mining social images with distance metric learning for automated image tagging. In: Proceedings of the Fourth ACM International Conference on Web Search and Data Mining, pp. 197–206. ACM (2011)
8. Li, X., Snoek, C.G., Worring, M.: Learning social tag relevance by neighbor voting. IEEE Trans. Multimedia **11**(7), 1310–1322 (2009)
9. Zhu, G., Yan, S., Ma, Y.: Image tag refinement towards low-rank, content-tag prior and error sparsity. In: Proceedings of the 18th ACM International Conference on Multimedia, pp. 461–470. ACM (2010)
10. Ma, H., Zhu, J., Lyu, M.R.T., King, I.: Bridging the semantic gap between image contents and tags. IEEE Trans. Multimedia **12**(5), 462–473 (2010)
11. Gao, Y., Wang, M., Zha, Z.J., Shen, J., Li, X., Wu, X.: Visual-textual joint relevance learning for tag-based social image search. IEEE Trans. Image Process. **22**(1), 363–376 (2013)
12. Li, X., Uricchio, T., Ballan, L., Bertini, M., Snoek, C.G., Bimbo, A.D.: Socializing the semantic gap: a comparative survey on image tag assignment, refinement, and retrieval. ACM Comput. Surv. (CSUR) **49**(1), 14 (2016)
13. Lampert, C.H., Nickisch, H., Harmeling, S.: Attribute-based classification for zero-shot visual object categorization. IEEE Trans. Pattern Anal. Mach. Intell. **36**(3), 453–465 (2014)
14. Rohrbach, M., Stark, M., Schiele, B.: Evaluating knowledge transfer and zero-shot learning in a large-scale setting. In: 2011 IEEE Conference on Computer Vision and Pattern Recognition (CVPR), pp. 1641–1648. IEEE (2011)
15. Chao, W.-L., Changpinyo, S., Gong, B., Sha, F.: An empirical study and analysis of generalized zero-shot learning for object recognition in the wild. In: Leibe, B., Matas, J., Sebe, N., Welling, M. (eds.) ECCV 2016. LNCS, vol. 9906, pp. 52–68. Springer, Cham (2016). https://doi.org/10.1007/978-3-319-46475-6_4
16. Akata, Z., Reed, S., Walter, D., Lee, H., Schiele, B.: Evaluation of output embeddings for fine-grained image classification. In: Proceedings of the IEEE Conference on Computer Vision and Pattern Recognition, pp. 2927–2936 (2015)

17. Xian, Y., Lampert, C.H., Schiele, B., Akata, Z.: Zero-shot learning-a comprehensive evaluation of the good, the bad and the ugly. arXiv preprint arXiv:1707.00600 (2017)
18. Fu, Y., Xiang, T., Jiang, Y.G., Xue, X., Sigal, L., Gong, S.: Recent advances in zero-shot recognition: toward data-efficient understanding of visual content. IEEE Signal Process. Mag. **35**(1), 112–125 (2018)
19. Simonyan, K., Zisserman, A.: Very deep convolutional networks for large-scale image recognition. arXiv preprint arXiv:1409.1556 (2014)
20. He, K., Zhang, X., Ren, S., Sun, J.: Deep residual learning for image recognition. In: Proceedings of the IEEE Conference on Computer Vision and Pattern Recognition, pp. 770–778 (2016)
21. Akata, Z., Perronnin, F., Harchaoui, Z., Schmid, C.: Label-embedding for image classification. IEEE Trans. Pattern Anal. Mach. Intell. **38**(7), 1425–1438 (2016)
22. Mikolov, T., Chen, K., Corrado, G., Dean, J.: Efficient estimation of word representations in vector space. arXiv preprint arXiv:1301.3781 (2013)
23. Mikolov, T., Sutskever, I., Chen, K., Corrado, G.S., Dean, J.: Distributed representations of words and phrases and their compositionality. In: Advances in Neural Information Processing Systems, pp. 3111–3119 (2013)
24. Loeff, N., Alm, C.O., Forsyth, D.A.: Discriminating image senses by clustering with multimodal features. In: Proceedings of the COLING/ACL on Main Conference Poster Sessions, pp. 547–554. Association for Computational Linguistics (2006)
25. Lazaridou, A., Bruni, E., Baroni, M.: Is this a wampimuk? Cross-modal mapping between distributional semantics and the visual world. In: Proceedings of the 52nd Annual Meeting of the Association for Computational Linguistics (Volume 1: Long Papers), vol. 1, pp. 1403–1414 (2014)
26. Lazaridou, A., Pham, N.T., Baroni, M.: Combining language and vision with a multimodal skip-gram model. arXiv preprint arXiv:1501.02598 (2015)
27. Silberer, C., Ferrari, V., Lapata, M.: Visually grounded meaning representations. IEEE Trans. Pattern Anal. Mach. Intell. **39**(11), 2284–2297 (2017)
28. Xia, F., Liu, T.Y., Wang, J., Zhang, W., Li, H.: Listwise approach to learning to rank: theory and algorithm. In: Proceedings of the 25th International Conference on Machine Learning, pp. 1192–1199. ACM (2008)
29. Rashtchian, C., Young, P., Hodosh, M., Hockenmaier, J.: Collecting image annotations using Amazon's Mechanical Turk. In: Proceedings of the NAACL HLT 2010 Workshop on Creating Speech and Language Data with Amazon's Mechanical Turk, pp. 139–147. Association for Computational Linguistics (2010)
30. Everingham, M., Van Gool, L., Williams, C.K., Winn, J., Zisserman, A.: The pascal visual object classes (VOC) challenge. Int. J. Comput. Vis. **88**(2), 303–338 (2010)
31. Pennington, J., Socher, R., Manning, C.: Glove: global vectors for word representation. In: Proceedings of the 2014 Conference on Empirical Methods in Natural Language Processing (EMNLP), pp. 1532–1543 (2014)
32. Bojanowski, P., Grave, E., Joulin, A., Mikolov, T.: Enriching word vectors with subword information. arXiv preprint arXiv:1607.04606 (2016)
33. Honnibal, M., Montani, I.: spaCy 2: natural language understanding with Bloom embeddings, convolutional neural networks and incremental parsing (2017, to appear)
34. Tolias, G., Sicre, R., Jégou, H.: Particular object retrieval with integral max-pooling of CNN activations. arXiv preprint arXiv:1511.05879 (2015)
35. Paszke, A., et al.: Automatic differentiation in PyTorch. In: NIPS-W (2017)

Visually Indicated Sound Generation by Perceptually Optimized Classification

Kan Chen[1], Chuanxi Zhang[1(✉)], Chen Fang[2], Zhaowen Wang[2], Trung Bui[2], and Ram Nevatia[1]

[1] University of Southern California, Los Angeles, USA
{kanchen,chuanxiz,nevatia}@usc.edu
[2] Adobe Research, San Jose, USA
{cfang,zhawang,bui}@adobe.com

Abstract. Visually indicated sound generation aims to predict visually consistent sound from the video content. Previous methods addressed this problem by creating a single generative model that ignores the distinctive characteristics of various sound categories. Nowadays, state-of-the-art sound classification networks are available to capture semantic-level information in audio modality, which can also serve for the purpose of visually indicated sound generation. In this paper, we explore generating fine-grained sound from a variety of sound classes, and leverage pre-trained sound classification networks to improve the audio generation quality. We propose a novel Perceptually Optimized Classification based Audio generation Network (POCAN), which generates sound conditioned on the sound class predicted from visual information. Additionally, a perceptual loss is calculated via a pre-trained sound classification network to align the semantic information between the generated sound and its ground truth during training. Experiments show that POCAN achieves significantly better results in visually indicated sound generation task on two datasets.

Keywords: Visually indicated sound generation · Perceptual loss

1 Introduction

When we observe visual events in the world, such as a stick hitting a metal object, or a car racing or a helicopter flying, we can immediately imagine and associate some sounds with these events. The objective of our paper is to synthesize realistic sound that correspond to the visual content in a silent video

---

K. Chen and C. Zhang—Equal contribution. Project page: www.github.com/kanchen-usc/VIG.

Electronic supplementary material The online version of this chapter (https://doi.org/10.1007/978-3-030-11024-6_43) contains supplementary material, which is available to authorized users.

© Springer Nature Switzerland AG 2019
L. Leal-Taixé and S. Roth (Eds.): ECCV 2018 Workshops, LNCS 11134, pp. 560–574, 2019.
https://doi.org/10.1007/978-3-030-11024-6_43

(*i.e.*, visually indicated sound generation). This ability is useful for many real applications, such as sound/video editing automation, enhanced experience of immersion in virtual reality and assistance for people with visual impairments.

Visually indicated sound generation is a challenging problem that involves parsing visual information and converting it into sound in audio modality. A number of methods have been suggested in recent work such as [1–3], which adopt a Convolutional Neural Network (CNN) to encode visual features and a Long Short Term Memory Network (LSTM) [4] or a Generative Adversarial Network (GAN) to generate sound. One common characteristic in these approaches is that they consider visually indicated sounds to belong to variations of a single class even though the sounds for different activities can be quite different. For example, in Fig. 1, the sound of hitting "iron cabinet" lasts longer than hitting "water"; besides, spectrograms of these two sounds show different distributions: the sound of hitting "iron cabinet" contains more high-frequency components than the sound of hitting "water".

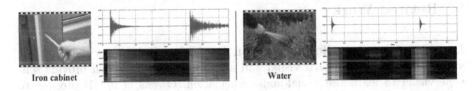

Fig. 1. Difference between sound of hitting "iron cabinet" and "water" in sound wave and spectrogram. It is hard for a generic model to handle all kinds of sound generation.

To address the significant variations, we introduce the concept of sound classes where each type of action generates sounds belonging to a specific class and then use class predictions to generate more finely tuned sounds. We average sound clips of same class to create a base sample. Given visual features, our audio generation model predicts sound class and transforms the predicted sound class's base sample to visually consistent sound. Furthermore, we leverage a state-of-the-art sound classification network to compute a *perceptual loss* [5] during training; this loss aims to align the predicted sound's semantic characteristics with ground truth in the feature space of the pre-trained sound classification network.

In implementation, we propose a novel Perceptually Optimized Classification based Audio generation Network (POCAN). POCAN adopts a CNN+LSTM structure to encode visual features, predict sound class and regress sound spectrograms. The generated sound wave is calculated as the Inverse Short Time Fourier Transform (ISTFT) [6] of the predicted spectrogram, which is the sum of predicted regression parameters and a base sample corresponding to the predicted sound class. During training, a pre-trained SoundNet [7] is deployed to compute the perceptual loss as the feature difference between the predicted sound and its ground truth. Analogous perceptual loss has been used for image generation [5] but is novel to audio generation, to the best of our knowledge.

We evaluate POCAN on the popular Greatest Hits Dataset [1]. Besides, we collected visual frames and evaluate POCAN on a subset of AudioSet [8]. Quantitative evaluations are conducted on sound classification and retrieval tasks which have also been used in [1,3] and have shown to have a high correlation with subjective evaluations. In both of these tests, POCAN outperforms state-of-the-art methods by a large margin. Besides, we provide some generated sound samples in the supplementary material for qualitative evaluation.

Our contributions are three-fold: (1) We propose to generate visually indicated sound considering different sound classes; (2) We leverage pre-trained SoundNet and apply a perceptual loss to refine POCAN during training; (3) We collect a visually indicated sound generation dataset and plan to release it upon publication.

In the following paper, we first discuss related work in Sect. 2. More details of POCAN and collected dataset are provided in Sects. 3 and 4 respectively. Finally we compare POCAN with other approaches in Sect. 5.

2   Related Work

Learning Visual-Audio Correlation by Video Self-supervision. Most videos contain synchronized visual and audio information, which provide self-supervision to learn the visual-audio correlation. Owens et al. [1] propose to learn visual features supervised by audio information, and achieve good performance in object detection task. On the other hand, Aytar et al. [7] deploy a deep convolutional network to learn efficient sound representations under visual supervision. Harwath et al. [9] apply visual supervision to predict similarity scores for input images and spoken audio spectrum. Arandjelovic et al. [10] propose a deep neural network to learn the visual-audio correlation, and achieve state-of-the-art performances on both visual and sound recognition tasks. POCAN also learns the audio-visual correlation and generates sound from visual frames under video self-supervision.

Mapping from visual signals to sound requires generating/retrieving reasonable sound clips based on visual information. Owens et al. [1] adopt a CNN+LSTM structure to regress cochleagram [11] of visually indicated sound based on video frames. Chen et al. [2] propose a GAN structure to generate sound of musical instruments conditioned on visual modality. Recently, Zhou et al. [3] adopt a SampleRNN [12] structure to generate visually indicated sound raw wave from visual features for each single sound class. Inspired by these models, POCAN adopts a CNN+LSTM structure to generate sound spectrograms.

Perceptual optimization has been successfully applied in image generation task [13–15]. Mahendran et al. [16] invert CNN features by minimizing a feature reconstruction loss to understand the visual information captured by different network layers. Based on this, Dosovitskiy et al. [17] propose to invert CNN features to image via a per-pixel reconstruction loss. Johnson et al. [5] apply a feature reconstruction loss to generate images, which achieves better performance. Inspired by this success, we adopt a perceptual loss in audio modality to further boost sound generation.

Multimodal learning aims to learn the relationship between different modalities. Significant progress has been observed in visual and language modality learning, which includes Image Retrieval [18] and Visual Question Answering (VQA) [19,20]. Recently, Chen et al. [21,22] introduce regression and attention mechanisms in the grounding task. Based on recent progress in video detection and classification [23–25], Hendricks et al. [26] address the problem of temporal localization using natural language. In this paper, we focus on the learning of audio and visual modalities.

3 Method

POCAN is composed of two parts: classification based audio generation and perceptual optimization, which is shown in Fig. 2. In this work, we focus on generating visually indicated sound with fixed time length. We first present the framework of POCAN in Sect. 3.1, followed by the details of classification based audio generation and perceptual optimization in Sects. 3.2 and 3.3 respectively. Finally, we illustrate how to train POCAN and generate sound wave in Sect. 3.4.

3.1 Framework

The goal of POCAN is to generate a sound wave y given the corresponding video clip's frame sequence $\{x\}$. We do not generate raw sound wave directly from visual information; instead, we predict the spectrogram $\mathbf{s}$ of sound clip y, which can be converted back to a wave form via an Inverse Short Term Fourier Transform (ISTFT) [6]. To achieve this, fine-grained audio generation part predicts sound class probability distribution p as well as spectrogram regression parameters $\mathbf{d}$ based on visual features. According to the predicted distribution p, the most probable sound class's base sample is selected, and the synthesized sound spectrogram $\mathbf{s}'$ is the addition of base sample and the predicted regression parameters. To capture semantic characteristics of real sound y, synthesized spectrogram $\mathbf{s}'$ is converted to wave form $\hat{y}$ via ISTFT. A perceptual loss $\mathcal{L}_p$ is then calculated by comparing the difference between SoundNet features of y and $\hat{y}$. The objective for POCAN is:

$$\arg\min_{\theta} \sum_{x} \mathcal{L}_{cls}(\boldsymbol{p}, c) + \lambda \mathcal{L}_{reg}(\mathbf{s}', \mathbf{s}) + \mu \mathcal{L}_p(\hat{y}, y) \tag{1}$$

where θ denotes the POCAN's parameters to be optimized. λ, μ are hyperparameters. c is the class label of sound clip y. $\mathcal{L}_{cls}$ is the loss for sound class prediction. $\mathcal{L}_{reg}$ is a regression loss for synthesizing sound spectrogram $\mathbf{s}'$. $\mathcal{L}_p$ is a perceptual loss for capturing semantic characteristics from real sound clip y.

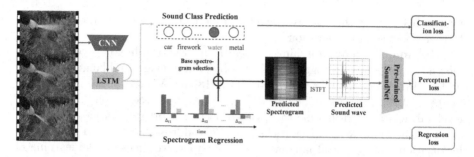

Fig. 2. Framework of Perceptually Optimized Classification based Audio generation Network (POCAN). Video frames are first processed by a CNN and then fed into a LSTM. To generate sound clips, POCAN predicts sound classes and regresses LSTM's hidden states into spectrograms and then transform the predicted spectrograms into sound waveforms. To increase the quality of generated sound, a pre-trained Sound-Net [7] is applied to calculate perceptual loss during the training stage.

3.2 Classification Based Audio Generation Network

For visual input, each video frame x_i is encoded as a visual feature vector $\mathbf{x}_i \in \mathbb{R}^{d_v}$ by a pre-trained CNN [27]. d_v represents the dimension of visual feature vectors. To encode the temporal information in video frames, we feed these video features $\{\mathbf{x}_t\}$ into a LSTM [4], where the encoding procedure can be written as

$$
\begin{aligned}
i_t &= \sigma(\mathbf{W}_{vi}\mathbf{x}_t + \mathbf{W}_{hi}h_{t-1} + b_i) \\
f_t &= \sigma(\mathbf{W}_{vf}\mathbf{x}_t + \mathbf{W}_{hf}h_{t-1} + b_f) \\
o_t &= \sigma(\mathbf{W}_{vo}\mathbf{x}_t + \mathbf{W}_{ho}h_{t-1} + b_o) \\
g_t &= \phi(\mathbf{W}_{vg}\mathbf{x}_t + \mathbf{W}_{hg}h_{t-1} + b_g) \\
c_t &= f_t \odot c_{t-1} + i_t \odot g_t \\
h_t &= o_t \odot \phi(c_t)
\end{aligned}
\tag{2}
$$

where ϕ is the hyperbolic tangent function and $\odot$ represents the element-wise production between two vectors. The encoded features are represented as LSTM hidden states $\{\mathbf{h}_i\} \in \mathbb{R}^{d_h}$. d_h is the dimension of hidden space.

To predict sound class and regression parameters, we project the hidden states $\{\mathbf{h}_i\}$ into an audio space:

$$
f_i = \mathbf{W}\mathbf{h}_i + \mathbf{b}
\tag{3}
$$

where $\mathbf{W} \in \mathbb{R}^{(d_c+d_s)\times d_h}$, $\mathbf{b} \in \mathbb{R}^{(d_c+d_s)}$ are training parameters to be optimized. d_c denotes the number of sound classes, d_s is the feature dimension of sound spectrogram. The first d_c elements in f_i represent logits of sound class probability prediction for frame x_i, while the rest elements record regression parameters of spectrogram. The classification loss $\mathcal{L}_{cls}$ is:

$$\mathcal{L}_{cls}(\boldsymbol{p}, c) = -\log \boldsymbol{p}[c], \quad \boldsymbol{p} = \frac{1}{t_s} \sum_{i=1}^{t_s} \sigma(\boldsymbol{f}_i[0 : d_c - 1]) \tag{4}$$

where σ is a softmax function. t_s is the length of sequence $\{\boldsymbol{f}_i\}$, which is the same as the time length of spectrogram to be generated.

To synthesize spectrogram, we average different sound spectrograms according to their classes in the training set. Each class j then has an averaged spectrogram $\mathbf{A}_j \in \mathbb{R}^{d_s \times t_s}$ as a base sample. The synthesized sound spectrogram is calculated as:

$$\mathbf{s}' = \mathbf{d} + \mathbf{A}_{j^*}, \quad \text{s.t.} \quad j^* = \arg\max_i \{\boldsymbol{p}[i]\} \tag{5}$$

where regression parameters $\mathbf{d} \in \mathbb{R}^{d_s \times t_s}$ are generated by stacking vectors $\{\boldsymbol{f}_i[d_c : d_c + d_s - 1]\}$. After obtaining fine-grained sound spectrogram, the regression loss $\mathcal{L}_{reg}$ is calculated by a smooth L1 regression loss function $g(.)$:

$$\mathcal{L}_{reg} = \|g(\mathbf{s}' - \mathbf{s})\|_1, \quad g(x) = \begin{cases} 0.5x^2, & |x| < 1 \\ |x| - 0.5, & |x| \geq 1 \end{cases} \tag{6}$$

3.3 Perceptual Optimization

To further improve the realism of the generated sound, we leverage state-of-the-art sound classification networks to capture different sound's semantic characteristics. Specifically, we adopt a pre-trained SoundNet [7], freeze its parameters and apply it to encode sound features for both real sound y and synthesized sound $\hat{y}$ during training. The synthesized sound wave $\hat{y}$ is generated from an ISTFT operation from predicted spectrogram $\mathbf{s}'$. The perceptual loss is then calculated by comparing features from real sound and synthesized sound:

$$\mathcal{L}_p = \|g(\phi(\hat{y}) - \phi(y))\|_1 \tag{7}$$

where $\phi(.)$ denotes the feed-forward feature extraction process of SoundNet [7]. Other notations are the same as Eq. 6.

3.4 Training and Sound Wave Generation

Due to different sampling rates in visual and audio modalities (audio signal sample rate is much higher than the video frame rate), the length of visual feature sequence is shorter than the time length of audio's spectrogram. We uniformly replicate visual features in each time step so that visual sequence's length is the same as audio's spectrogram. The parameters to be optimized include parameters in LSTM and projection parameters in Eq. 3. POCAN is trained end-to-end using the Adam [28] algorithm.

Following [1] and [3], we generate and evaluate sound wave in two ways. First is directly converting synthesized sound spectrogram into sound wave via ISTFT;

we denote this generated sound as *raw sound*, which is useful for evaluating what information is captured by the audio features. Second, for the task of generating plausible visually indicated sound to human ears, we use the generated *raw sound* as a query and retrieve the nearest neighbor in the training set according to the similarities between spectrogram features, and set the retrieved real sound wave as our generation result. The similarity between two spectrogram features $\mathbf{s}_1$ and $\mathbf{s}_2$ is calculated as:

$$\text{sim}(\mathbf{s}_1, \mathbf{s}_2) = \left\langle \frac{1}{t_s} \sum_{i=1}^{t_s} \mathbf{s}_1[i], \frac{1}{t_s} \sum_{i=1}^{t_s} \mathbf{s}_2[i] \right\rangle \quad (8)$$

where $\langle .,. \rangle$ represents cosine distance. We denote this second type of sound as *exemplar sound*, which is used for retrieval and human evaluation.

Table 1. Number training and testing samples in visually indicated sound generation (VIG) dataset

Class	Dog bark	Cattle	Sheep bleat	Chicken	Church bell
# Train	1124	739	1117	1085	1095
# Test	59	60	60	86	61
Class	Helicopter	Fire alarm	Hammer	Gunshot	Fireworks
# Train	1111	854	435	1001	1109
# Test	58	60	60	171	60
Class	Thunder-storm	Car racing	Rail transport	Splash water	Spray
# Train	1109	1098	1012	862	1119
# Test	62	72	167	58	60

4   Datasets

We evaluate POCAN on two datasets: Greatest Hits Dataset [1] and a manually annotated subset from AudioSet [8].

Greatest Hits Dataset (GHD) [1] contains 977 videos from indoor (64%) and outdoor (36%) scenes. There are 733 videos (21436 clips) and 244 videos (7008 clips) in this dataset for training and testing respectively. There are 17 sound classes in GHD ($d_c = 17$). Each labeled video lasts 0.5s with a single class label.

Visually Indicated sound Generation dataset (VIG) is a subset from AudioSet [8]. AudioSet [8] is a large-scale dataset of manually annotated audio events. There are 2,084,320 human labeled 10-s sound clips in 632 audio event classes from Youtube videos. Among them, we manually select 16,024 high quality sound clips in 15 classes which have strong correlation with visual frames ($d_c = 15$). Each sound clip belongs to one video. The number of training and test clips for each class is shown in Table 1. Some examples of video clips and corresponding sound clips are visualized in Fig. 3.

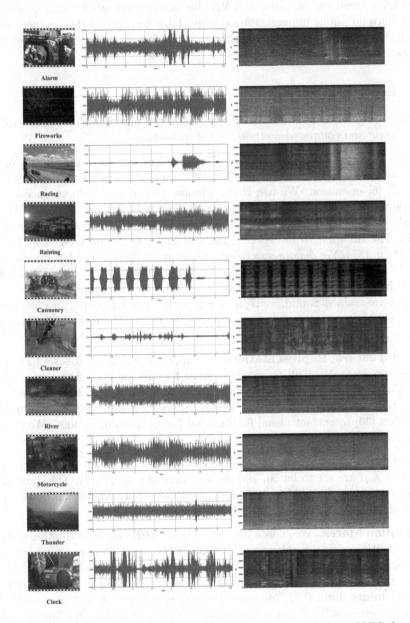

Fig. 3. Some examples of video clips and corresponding sound clips of VIG dataset

5 Experiments

POCAN is evaluated on GHD and VIG for visually indicated sound generation task. Since no public implementation is available for state-of-the-art method on GHD[1], we re-implemented the method in [1], but there may be differences from the authors' implementation.

5.1 Experiment Setup

We introduce the details of feature representation, model initialization, evaluation metric and compared method in this subsection.

Audio Feature Representation. To calculate regression loss in Eq. 6, we compute spectrogram of each sound wave via a Short Time Fourier Transform (STFT) [6] operation. We use Hann window [29] of size 2048 to encode and decode sound spectrograms. The feature dimension is 1025 ($d_s = 1025$). We use sample rate of 22.05 kHz and 8 kHz for sound wave on GHD and VIG respectively. The time length for spectrograms is 22 ($t_s = 22$) on GHD and 157 on VIG ($t_s = 157$). We denote spectrogram feature as "spec". For fair comparison with [1], we also extract cochleagram [11] for each sound clip, which is denoted as "coch", the feature dimension is 42 ($d_s = 42$). For perceptual loss in Eq. 7, we apply a pre-trained SoundNet [7] and extract its conv7 features for each sound clip's real and predicted sound wave during training. The feature dimension is 1024.

Visual Feature Representation. We apply a 200-layer ResNet [27] pre-trained on ImageNet [30] to extract visual feature for each frame in a video clip. The feature dimension is 2048 ($d_v = 2048$). We denote these features as "res". For fair comparison with [1], we also apply an AlexNet [31] pre-trained on ImageNet [30] to extract visual features, with dimension $d_v = 4096$. We denote these features as "alex".

Model Initialization. During training, we set the batch size as 40. Hyperparameters λ, μ are set to be 50, 100 during training respectively. The dimension of hidden states of LSTM is 128 ($d_h = 128$). We apply Xavier method [32] to initialize training parameters in POCAN.

Evaluation Metric. We choose Recall at top K (R@K) as the evaluation metric. For generating each *exemplar sound*, we check the top K retrieved samples from the training set in the ranking list of each test sample. If there exists a retrieved training sample having the same sound class as the test sample, we consider it as a successful retrieval. R@K measures the success ratio of all test samples in the top K retrieval results. Besides, to compare with [1], we also train a 5-layer sound neural network classifier from real sound in the training set, and feed generated *raw sound* to check the classification results.

---

[1] Project page of Greatest Hits Dataset (GHD): http://vis.csail.mit.edu.

Compared Approach. We choose [1] as the compared method, which achieves state-of-the-art performance on GHD. We also re-implemented and evaluated [1] on VIG. We are unable to compare with [3] as the code and dataset is not publicly available at this time.

5.2 Performance on GHD

We evaluate different models' *exemplar sound* for R@K and *raw sound* for classification task on GHD respectively.

Comparison in R@K. Following the settings of [1], we adopt AlexNet features for visual modality and cochleagram for audio modality. The performance of [1] (alex + coch) is shown in Table 2. By replacing audio features with spectrogram, we observe a slight improvement in R@K (0.44% in R@1). Fixing spectrogram features, we then replace AlexNet features with ResNet features (Owens *et al.* [1] (res + spec)), and observe a further improvement of 2.19%, 2.72%, 7.55% in R@1, R@5, R@10 respectively.

Based on this feature combination (res + spec), we evaluate the Classification based Audio generation Network (CAN) in POCAN. In Table 2, we observe a significant improvement of 12.79%, 10.15%, 6.38% in R@1, R@5, R@10 respectively. This indicates CAN generates better sound so that the most similar retrieved samples contain more characteristics of the test sample's sound class. We further evaluate the full POCAN model on GHD and observe that POCAN achieves new state-of-the-art performance in similar sound retrieval task, with 15.68%, 13.70% and 7.15% increase over the method of [1] (res + spec) on R@1, R@5, R@10 respectively.

Table 2. Different models' performances of R@K on GHD (K = 1, 5, 10)

Model	K = 1	K = 5	K = 10
Owens *et al.* [1] (alex + coch)	0.1471	0.3982	0.4896
Owens *et al.* [1] (alex + spec)	0.1515	0.4077	0.5083
Owens *et al.* [1] (res + spec)	0.1734	0.4349	0.5838
CAN (res + spec)	0.3013	0.5364	0.6476
POCAN (res + spec)	**0.3302**	**0.5719**	**0.6553**

Sound Classification. Similar to [1], we evaluate whether generated sound contains semantic information of the sound class. We train a 5-layer neural network to classify different sounds. Each layer is a 1D convolution layer followed by a rectified linear unit (ReLU) non-linear activation function. This network is trained by real sound clips from the training set of GHD. In test stage, we generate the *raw sounds* from different models, and feed them into the pre-trained classifier. We calculate average classification accuracy for test set of GHD as the

Table 3. Classification accuracy of different model's generated sound by a pre-trained 5-layer neural network classifier.

Model	Accuracy (%)
Owens *et al.* [1] (res + spec)	20.11
CAN (res + spec)	35.46
POCAN (res + spec)	**36.32**
Real sound clips	51.34

metric. The classifier's performance as well as different models' sound classification accuracies are provided in Table 3. It is worth noticing that our neural network classifier achieves 51.34% classification accuracy, while a pre-trained SVM mentioned in [1] achieves 45.8%, which indicates that our classifier is better at classifying sound.

We observe that fine-grained generation part achieves better performance than [1] in sound classification task, This indicates that *raw sound* generated by fine-grained generation part provides more sound class information than that of [1], which is easier for classifier to recognize. We further apply the perceptual loss and evaluate sound generated by POCAN. Our classifier reports the highest classification accuracy of 36.32%, which is 16.11% higher than that of [1]. Besides, we draw the confusion matrix for sound classification results of [1] and POCAN in Fig. 4. From confusion matrices, we find POCAN's sound achieves consistently better performance over [1] in all sound categories. The sound classes with obvious improvement include tile, water and cloth.

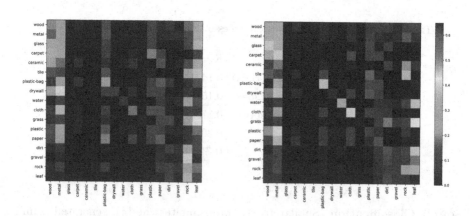

Fig. 4. Comparison of confusion matrices of sound classification results by a pre-trained 5-layer neural network classifier. Each row is the confusion made for a single sound class. Left and right figure is confusion matrix of sound generated by [1] and POCAN respectively.

Table 4. Different models' performances of R@K on VIG (K = 1, 5, 10)

Model	K = 1	K = 5	K = 10
Owens *et al.* [1] (res + spec)	0.0997	0.2888	0.4640
CAN (res + spec)	0.1180	0.3469	0.4709
POCAN (res + spec)	**0.1223**	**0.3625**	**0.4802**

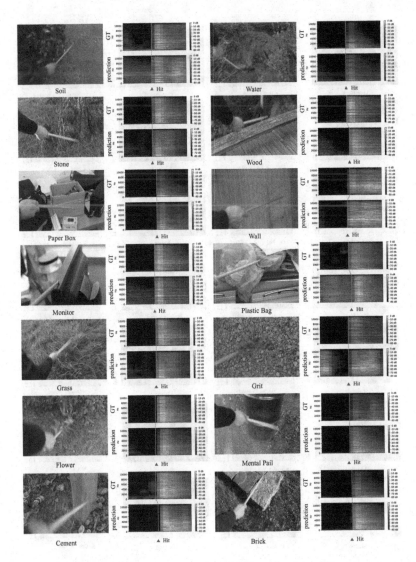

Fig. 5. Spectrograms of ground truth sound (GT) and retrieved *exemplar sound* by POCAN on GHD dataset. For each sample, we label some moments when actions happen in GT and *exemplar sound*.

5.3   Performance on VIG

Comparison in R@K. Based on the feature combination of ResNet as visual features ("res") and spectrogram as audio features ("spec"), we evaluate different models' R@K on VIG. In Table 4, by adopting CAN, we observe an improvement of 1.83%, 5.81% and 0.69% in R@1, R@5 and R@10 respectively. After applying the perceptual loss, POCAN achieves the state-of-the-art performance,

Fig. 6. Spectrograms of ground truth sound (GT) and retrieved *exemplar sound* by POCAN on VIG dataset. For each sample, we label some moments when actions happen in GT and *exemplar sound*.

with 2.26%, 7.37% and 1.62% increase in R@1, R@5 and R@10 over [1] respectively. We notice that the room for improvement on VIG is still big. This may be because the time length of sound clips in VIG is 10 s, while it is only 0.5 s on GHD. In this case, the sequences of both audio and visual features become 20 times longer, which brings extra difficulty for a system to generate reasonable sound.

5.4 Qualitative Evaluation

For qualitative evaluation, we visualize some spectrograms of *exemplar sound* generated by POCAN as well as its corresponding ground truth in Figs. 5 and 6. For each sample, we label its sound class and some time points when action happens in that clip. We observe the pattern of *exemplar sound* is similar to ground truth sound, and the occurrence of sound events are temporally close. However, POCAN also retrieves less similar samples which contain more actions or noise (*e.g.*, first result in row 2 of Fig. 6). The project page is in http://www.github.com/kanchen-usc/VIG, with demo video available online.

6   Conclusion

We proposed a novel Perceptually Optimized Classification based Audio generation Network (POCAN) which aims to produce visually indicated sound conditioned on video frames. Compared to previous methods, we consider sound class information and adopt a perceptual loss during training stage. To evaluate POCAN, we collect a visually indicated sound generation dataset from AudioSet [8]. Experiments show that POCAN provides significant improvement in visually indicated sound generation task on two datasets.

References

1. Owens, A., Isola, P., McDermott, J., Torralba, A., Adelson, E.H., Freeman, W.T.: Visually indicated sounds. In: CVPR (2016)
2. Chen, L., Srivastava, S., Duan, Z., Xu, C.: Deep cross-modal audio-visual generation. In: ACM MM Workshop (2017)
3. Zhou, Y., Wang, Z., Fang, C., Bui, T., Berg, T.L.: Visual to sound: generating natural sound for videos in the wild. CoRR (2017)
4. Hochreiter, S., Schmidhuber, J.: Long short-term memory. Neural Comput. **9**, 1735–1780 (1997)
5. Johnson, J., Alahi, A., Fei-Fei, L.: Perceptual losses for real-time style transfer and super-resolution. In: Leibe, B., Matas, J., Sebe, N., Welling, M. (eds.) ECCV 2016. LNCS, vol. 9906, pp. 694–711. Springer, Cham (2016). https://doi.org/10.1007/978-3-319-46475-6_43
6. Welch, P.: The use of fast Fourier transform for the estimation of power spectra: a method based on time averaging over short, modified periodograms. IEEE Trans. Audio Electroacoust. **15**, 70–73 (1967)

7. Aytar, Y., Vondrick, C., Torralba, A.: SoundNet: learning sound representations from unlabeled video. In: NIPS (2016)
8. Gemmeke, J.F., et al.: Audio set: an ontology and human-labeled dataset for audio events. In: ICASSP (2017)
9. Harwath, D., Torralba, A., Glass, J.: Unsupervised learning of spoken language with visual context. In: NIPS (2016)
10. Arandjelovic, R., Zisserman, A.: Look, listen and learn. In: ICCV (2017)
11. Muthusamy, Y.K., Cole, R.A., Slaney, M.: Speaker-independent vowel recognition: spectrograms versus cochleagrams. In: ICASSP (1990)
12. Mehri, S., et al.: SampleRNN: an unconditional end-to-end neural audio generation model. In: ICLR (2016)
13. Simonyan, K., Vedaldi, A., Zisserman, A.: Deep inside convolutional networks: visualising image classification models and saliency maps. In: CVPR (2014)
14. Szegedy, C., et al.: Intriguing properties of neural networks. In: ICLR (2014)
15. Yosinski, J., Clune, J., Nguyen, A., Fuchs, T., Lipson, H.: Understanding neural networks through deep visualization. In: CVPR (2015)
16. Mahendran, A., Vedaldi, A.: Understanding deep image representations by inverting them. In: CVPR (2015)
17. Dosovitskiy, A., Brox, T.: Inverting visual representations with convolutional networks. In: CVPR (2016)
18. Chen, K., Bui, T., Fang, C., Wang, Z., Nevatia, R.: AMC: attention guided multimodal correlation learning for image search. In: CVPR (2017)
19. Antol, S., et al.: VQA: visual question answering. In: ICCV (2015)
20. Chen, K., Wang, J., Chen, L.C., Gao, H., Xu, W., Nevatia, R.: ABC-CNN: an attention based convolutional neural network for visual question answering. In: CVPRW (2016)
21. Chen, K., Kovvuri, R., Gao, J., Nevatia, R.: MSRC: multimodal spatial regression with semantic context for phrase grounding. IJMIR **7**, 17–28 (2018)
22. Chen, K., Kovvuri, R., Nevatia, R.: Query-guided regression network with context policy for phrase grounding. In: ICCV (2017)
23. Gao, J., Chen, K., Nevatia, R.: CTAP: complementary temporal action proposal generation. In: Ferrari, V., Hebert, M., Sminchisescu, C., Weiss, Y. (eds.) ECCV 2018. LNCS, vol. 11206, pp. 70–85. Springer, Cham (2018). https://doi.org/10.1007/978-3-030-01216-8_5
24. Myers, G.K., et al.: The 2014 SESAME multimedia event detection and recounting system. In: Proceedings of TRECVID (2014)
25. Gao, J., Yang, Z., Sun, C., Chen, K., Nevatia, R.: TURN TAP: temporal unit regression network for temporal action proposals (2017)
26. Hendricks, L.A., Wang, O., Shechtman, E., Sivic, J., Darrell, T., Russell, B.: Localizing moments in video with natural language. In: ICCV (2017)
27. He, K., Zhang, X., Ren, S., Sun, J.: Deep residual learning for image recognition. In: CVPR (2016)
28. Kingma, D.P., Ba, J.: Adam: a method for stochastic optimization. In: ICLR (2015)
29. Harris, F.J.: On the use of windows for harmonic analysis with the discrete Fourier transform. Proc. IEEE **66**, 51–83 (1978)
30. Deng, J., Dong, W., Socher, R., Li, L.J., Li, K., Fei-Fei, L.: ImageNet: a large-scale hierarchical image database. In: CVPR (2009)
31. Krizhevsky, A., Sutskever, I., Hinton, G.E.: ImageNet classification with deep convolutional neural networks. In: NIPS (2012)
32. Glorot, X., Bengio, Y.: Understanding the difficulty of training deep feedforward neural networks. In: AISTATS (2010)

CentralNet: A Multilayer Approach for Multimodal Fusion

Valentin Vielzeuf[1,2]([✉]), Alexis Lechervy[2], Stéphane Pateux[1],
and Frédéric Jurie[2]

[1] Orange Labs, Rennes, France
{valentin.vielzeuf,stephane.pateux}@orange.com
[2] Normandie Univ., UNICAEN, ENSICAEN, CNRS, Caen, France
{alexis.lechervy,frederic.jurie}@unicaen.fr

Abstract. This paper proposes a novel multimodal fusion approach, aiming to produce best possible decisions by integrating information coming from multiple media. While most of the past multimodal approaches either work by projecting the features of different modalities into the same space, or by coordinating the representations of each modality through the use of constraints, our approach borrows from both visions. More specifically, assuming each modality can be processed by a separated deep convolutional network, allowing to take decisions independently from each modality, we introduce a central network linking the modality specific networks. This central network not only provides a common feature embedding but also regularizes the modality specific networks through the use of multi-task learning. The proposed approach is validated on 4 different computer vision tasks on which it consistently improves the accuracy of existing multimodal fusion approaches.

Keywords: Multimodal fusion · Neural networks
Representation learning · Multi-task learning

1 Introduction and Related Work

Multimodal approaches are key elements for many computer vision applications, from video analysis to medical imaging, through natural language processing and image analysis. The main motivation for such approaches is to extract and combine relevant information from the different modalities and hence take better decisions than using only one. The recent literature abounds with examples in different domains such as video classification [1,2], emotion recognition [3–5], human activity recognition [6], or more recently food classification from pictures and recipes [7].

The literature on multimodal fusion [8–10] usually distinguishes the methods accordingly with the level at which the fusion is done (typically early vs late fusion). There is no consensus on which level is the best, as it is task dependent. For instance, Simonyan *et al.* [6] propose a two stream convolutional neural network for human activity recognition, fusing the modalities at prediction level.

© Springer Nature Switzerland AG 2019
L. Leal-Taixé and S. Roth (Eds.): ECCV 2018 Workshops, LNCS 11134, pp. 575–589, 2019.
https://doi.org/10.1007/978-3-030-11024-6_44

Similarly, for audiovisual emotion recognition, several authors report better performance with late fusion approaches [11,12]. In contrast, Arevalo et al. [13] propose an original Gated Multimodal Unit to weight the modalities depending on the input and achieve state of the art results on a textual-visual dataset, while Chen et al. [14] follow an early fusion hard-gated approach for textual-visual sentiment analysis.

Opposing early and late fusion is certainly too limited a view on the problem. As an illustration, Neverova et al. [15] applies a heuristic consisting in fusing similar modalities earlier than the others. Several hybrid or multilayer approaches have also been proposed, such as the approach of Yang et al. [16] doing fusion by boosting across all layers on human activity videos. Catalina Cangea et al. [17] propose a multilayer cross connection from 2D to 1D to share information between modalities of different dimensions. A multilayer method is also applied on text and image multimodal datasets in the paper of Gu et al. [18]. Kang et al. [19] use a multilayer approach, aggregating several layers of representation into a contextual representation. These hybrid methods can be viewed as learning a *joint representation*, following the classification made by Baltruvsaitis et al. [20]. With this type of approach the different modalities are projected into the same multimodal space, e.g. using concatenation, element-wise products, etc.

Baltruvsaitis et al. [20] oppose *joint representations* with *coordinated representations* where some constraints between the modalities force the representations to be more complementary. These constraints can aim at maximizing the correlation between the multimodal representations, as in Andrew et al. [9] who propose a deep Canonical Correlation Analysis method. On their side, Chandar et al. [21] propose CorrNet using autoencoders. Neverova et al. [22,23] propose modDrop and modout regularization, consisting in dropping modalities during the training phase. Finally, Hu et al. [5] applies an ensemble-like method to solve the problem of multimodal fusion for emotion classification.

This paper borrows from both visions, namely the joint representations and the coordinated representations. Our fusion method builds on existing deep convolutional neural networks designed to process each modality independently. We suggest to connect these networks using an additional central network dedicated to the projection of the features coming from different modalities into the same common space. In addition, the global loss allows to back propagate some global constraints on each modality, coordinating their representations. As an interesting property, the proposed approach automatically identifies which are the best levels for fusing the information and how these levels should be combined. The approach is multitask in the sense that it simultaneously tries to satisfy per modality losses as well as the global loss defined on the joint space.

The rest of the paper is organized as follows: the next section presents our contribution while Sect. 3 gives an experimental validation of the approach.

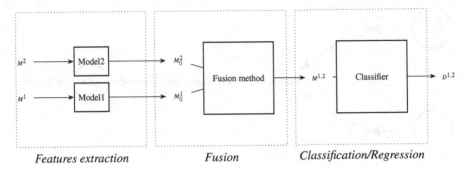

Features extraction   *Fusion*   *Classification/Regression*

Fig. 1. Generic representation of a multimodal fusion model. M^1 and M^2 respectively denote modality 1 and modality 2, M_0^1 and M_0^2 are the modality features fed to the fusion method, $M^{1,2}$ is the joint representation produced by the fusion method, and $D^{1,2}$ the decision obtained from the joint representation.

2   CentralNet

We refer to *multimodal fusion* as the combination of information provided by different media, under the form of their associated features or the intermediate decisions. More formally, if M^1 and M^2 denote the two media and D^1 and D^2 the decisions inferred respectively by M^1 and M^2, the goal is to make a better prediction $D^{1,2}$ using both M^1 and M^2. More than 2 modalities can be used. This paper addresses the case of classification tasks, but any other task, *e.g.* regression, can be addressed in the same way.

This paper focuses on the case of neural nets, for which the data are sequentially processed by a succession of layers. We assume having one neural net per modality, capable of inferring a decision from each modality taken in isolation, and want to combine them. One recurrent question with multimodal fusion is where the fusion has to be done: close to the data (early fusion), at the decision level (late fusion) or in between. In case of neural networks, the fusion can be done at any level between the input and the output of the different unimodal networks. For the sake of presentation, let us consider that the neural networks are split into 3 parts: the layers before the fusion (considered as being the feature generation part of the networks), the layers used for the fusion and finally the classification parts of the networks. This is illustrated by Fig. 1.

For simplicity, we assume that the extracted features (at the input of the fusion layers) have the same dimensionality. If it is not the case, the features can be projected, *e.g.* with 1×1 convolutional layers or zero padded to give them the same size. In practice, the last convolution layers or the first dense layers of separately trained unimodal networks can be used as features.

2.1   CentralNet Architecture

The CentralNet architecture is a neural network which combines the features issued from different modalities, by taking, as input of each one of its layers, a

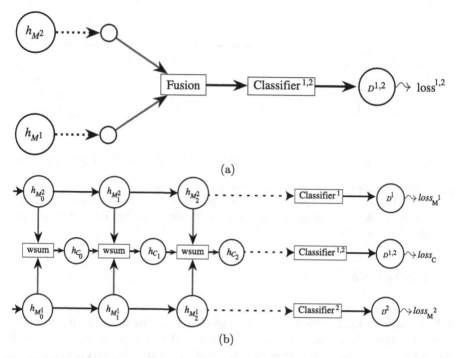

Fig. 2. (a) **Basic fusion method**, fusing the hidden representations of the modalities at a given layer and then using only joint representation. Fusing at a low-level layer is called early fusion while fusing at the last layer is called late fusion. (b) **Our CentralNet fusion model**, using both unimodal hidden representations and a central joint representation at each layer. The fusion of the unimodal representations is done here using a learned weighted sum. For the sake of simplicity, only the overall synoptic views of the architectures are represented. More details are provided in Sect. 2.

weighted sum of the layers of the corresponding unimodal networks and of its own previous layers. This is illustrated in Fig. 2(b). Such fusion layers can be defined by the following equation:

$$h_{C_{i+1}} = \alpha_{C_i} h_{C_i} + \sum_{k=1}^{n} \alpha_{M_i^k} h_{M_i^k} \qquad (1)$$

where n is the number of modalities, α are scalar trainable weights, $h_{M_i^k}$ is the hidden representation of each modality at layer i, and h_{C_i} is the central hidden representation. The resulting representation $h_{C_{i+1}}$ is then fed to an operating layer cell (which can be a convolutional or a dense layer followed by an activation function).

Regarding the first layer of the central network ($i = 0$), as we do not have any previous central hidden representation, we only weight and sum the representations of M^1 and M^2, issued from unimodal networks. At the output level, the last weighted sum is done between the unimodal predictions and the central prediction. Then, the output of the central net (classification layer) is used as the final prediction.

2.2 Learning the CentralNet Model

All trainable weights of the unimodal networks, the ones of the CentralNet and the fusion parameters $\alpha_{M_i^k}$, are optimized together by applying a stochastic gradient descent using the Adam approach. The global loss is defined as:

$$loss = loss_C + \sum_k \beta_k loss_{M^k} \tag{2}$$

where $loss_C$ is the (classification) loss computed from the output of the central model and $loss_{M^k}$ the (classification) loss when using only modality k. The weights β_k are cross validated (in practice, $\beta_k = 1$ in all of our experiments).

As already observed by Neverova *et al.* [22], when dealing with multimodal fusion it is crucial to maintain the performance of the unimodal neural networks. It is the reason why the global loss includes the unimodal losses. It helps generalizations by acting as a multitask regularization. We name this method "Multi-Task" in the rest of the paper.

2.3 Implementation Details

The α_{C_i} weights are initialized following a uniform probability distribution. Before training, the weighted sum is therefore equivalent to a simple average.

During our experiments, we also found out that rewriting Eq. (1) as:

$$h_{C_{i+1}} = \alpha_{C_i} h_{C_i} + \alpha_{modalities} \sum_{k=1}^{n} \alpha_{M_i^k} h_{M_i^k} \tag{3}$$

leads to better and stable performance.

On overall, CentralNet is easy to implement and can build on the top of existing architectures already known to be efficient for each modality. The number of trainable parameters dedicated to the fusion is less important than in other previous multilayer attempts such as [18], which may help to prevent overfitting. And even if the weighted sum is a simple linear operation, the network has the ability to learn complex joint representation, because of the non-linearity introduced by the central network.

Finally, the resulting values of the α allow some interesting interpretations on where the modalities are combined. For instance, getting α_{M^k} values close to 0 for $k > 0$ is equivalent to early fusion, while having all the α_{C_i} close to 0 up to the last weighted sum would be equivalent to late fusion.

3   Experiments

The proposed method is experimentally validated on 4 different multimodal datasets, namely Multimodal MNIST (a toy dataset), Audiovisual MNIST, Montalbano [24] and MM-IMDb [13], receiving each a separate section in the following. Each dataset is processed with a dedicated features extractor on which we plug our fusion method. Regarding the fusion networks, they are made of convolution+pooling or dense layers, with ReLU and batch normalization. The kernel size of the convolution is always 5×5 and the pooling stride is 2.

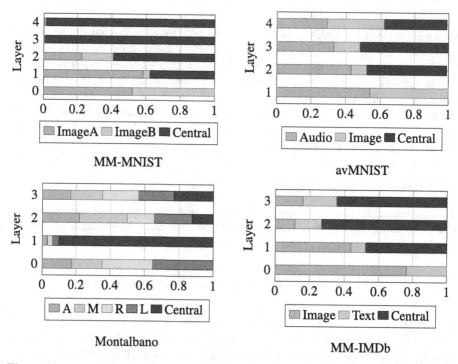

Fig. 3. Visualization of the α_i weights after training. They are displayed as the percentage given to each modality and to the central hidden representations across layers and datasets. We observe that the learned fusion strategy is different for each dataset.

The performance of the proposed method is compared to 5 different fusion approaches, ranging from the simplest baseline to recent state-of-the-art approaches. (a) 'Weighted mean' is the weighted average of single modality scores. The weights are considered as some parameters of the model, learnt with the rest of the model. (b) 'Concat' consists in concatenating the unimodal scores and inferring the final score with a single-layer linear perceptron. (c) 'Concat+Multi-Task' is the same as 'Concat' but uses the same Multi-Task loss as with the CentralNet. (d) 'Moddrop' is implemented following Neverova *et al.* [22]. (e) The 'Gated Multimodal Unit' (GMU) is implemented following Arevalo *et al.* [13].

In the following, to assess the statistical significance of our results, the performance is averaged over 64 runs. The confidence interval at 99% is computed using the estimate of the standard deviation and the Student's law.

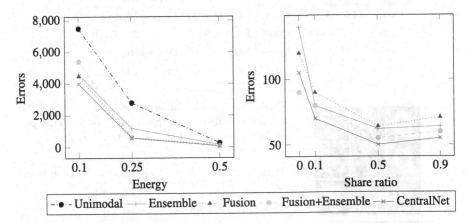

Fig. 4. Errors as a function of the energy per modality (left-hand side, share ratio $= 0.5$) and of the share ratio (right-hand side, energy $= 0.5$), for different fusion methods. Better viewed in color. (Color figure online)

3.1 Multimodal MNIST

The 'Multimodal MNIST' dataset is a toy dataset made of pairs of images (A, B), computed from the MNIST dataset. A and B are supposed to be 2 views of the same MNIST image but from different (artificially generated) modalities. We produce them by computing a Principal Component Analysis of the original MNIST dataset. Each one of the 2 (artificial) modalities is created by associating with it a set of singular vectors. This allows to control the amount of energy provided to each modality, which is the sum of the *energy* contained in the chosen vectors, and the *share ratio*, defined here as the percentage of the singular vectors shared between modalities. Figure 5 shows some of these generated image pairs. The original MNIST contains 55000 training samples and 10000 test samples. We transformed all of these images into pairs of 28×28 images, following the process explained above.

Several authors, *e.g.*, [9,21–23], generate a multimodal version of MNIST by dividing MNIST images into several smaller images (typically quarter of images) which are each considered as modalities. In contrast, our approach has the advantage of allowing to control two important factors: the amount of information per modality and the dependence between modalities.

The unimodal neural network architecture used with this dataset is the LeNet5 neural network [25]. It achieves 95 errors on the MNIST test set [25].

Table 1. The architecture of the CentralNet for the mMNIST dataset. "Dense" layers are fully-connected layers followed by a ReLU activation, while "Pred" layers are fully-connected layers followed by softmax activation.

Image A		Central		Image B	
Type	Size	Type	Size	Type	Size
Conv	14 × 14 × 32	Conv	14 × 14 × 32	Conv	14 × 14 × 32
Conv	7 × 7 × 64	Conv	7 × 7 × 64	Conv	7 × 7 × 64
Dense	1024	Dense	1024	Dense	1024
Pred	10	Pred	10	Pred	10

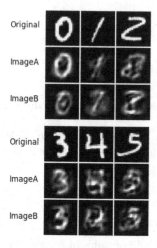

Fig. 5. MM-MNIST: some examples generated with half of the energy per modality and no sharing.

Table 2. Number of errors on the MM-MNIST test set for different methods, using 50% energy per modality and 50% of shared vectors.

Method	Errors	Fusion layer
Baseline	66 ± 1.5	_
Ensemble 2 classifiers	64 ± 1.3	_
Ensemble 3 classifiers	60 ± 1.0	_
Fusion Subtract	**64 ± 1.8**	**2**
Fusion Sum	68 ± 2.1	2
Fusion Prod	71 ± 2.1	2
Fusion+Ensemble Subtract	63 ± 1.5	1
Fusion+Ensemble Sum	**56 ± 2.1**	**0**
Fusion+Ensemble Prod	63 ± 1.5	2
Baseline on one modality	230 ± 2.7	_
Concat + Multi-Task	62 ± 1.2	_
Moddrop[22]	60 ± 1.5	_
Gated Multimodal Unit[13]	68 ± 1.8	_
CentralNet	**53 ± 1.2**	_

The architecture is composed of two convolutional layers, followed by two fully connected layers. In our version, batch normalization and dropout are added to further improve its performance. We measure the performance by counting how many of the 10000 images of the MNIST test set are misclassified. The Central-Net architecture in this case is therefore composed of three LeNet5, as described in Table 1. The "Ensemble 3 classifiers" method also uses three LeNet5, while other methods are using two LeNet5, one for each modality. We use dropout (50% dropping) on the fully connected layers and batch normalization. The learning rate is 0.01, the batch size is 128 and the model is trained on 100 epochs for all experiments, except for Moddrop and Gated Multimodal Units, where hyper-parameters are found by a random grid search. Thus for Moddrop, the learning rate is changed into 0.05 and the modality drop probability is of 0.2. For Gated Multimodal Units, the dropout is changed into 25% dropping.

First, we evaluate different alternatives for fusion (see Fig. 2(b)) using element-wise sum, subtract and product, for several configurations of our toy dataset. The energy is in {0.1, 0.25, 0.5} and share ratio in {0, 0.1, 0.5, 0.9}, allowing to assess the improvement given by fusion on each configuration. We also evaluate the Fusion+Ensemble method, *i.e.*, an ensemble of classifiers build on the top of the outputs of the fusion method (each modality make a prediction, as well as the fusion method, giving an ensemble of 3 classifiers). Finally, we also report the results of our CentralNet approach.

Table 3. The architecture of the CentralNet model on the avMNIST dataset.

Part	Image		Central		Audio	
	Type	Output size	Type	Output size	Type	Output size
Features extraction					Conv1	$56 \times 56 \times 8$
					Conv2	$28 \times 28 \times 16$
	Conv1	$14 \times 14 \times 32$			Conv3	$14 \times 14 \times 32$
Fusion	Conv	$7 \times 7 \times 64$	Conv	$7 \times 7 \times 64$	Conv	$7 \times 7 \times 64$
	Dense	1024	Dense	1024	Dense	1024
	Pred	10	Pred	10	Pred	10

We numbered the layers of LeNet5 from 0 (input level) to 4 (prediction level) and evaluate the methods for the 5 different fusion depth, in order to find out which one yields is the best. Figure 4 reports the performance of the different methods. The performance of the Fusion and Fusion+Ensemble methods are given in the case of their best fusion depth.

These results first underline the proportionality relation between the energy per modality and the error rate. It is also worth noting that not sharing enough or too much information between the modalities lowers the accuracy and the interest of a fusion approach. This observation is in line with [8,20].

As shown in Table 2 the optimal fusion layer obtained for each method differs but is early. Other properties are highlighted: A complementarity between Fusion and Ensemble exists, as shown by the improvement brought by the Fusion+Ensemble method. Nevertheless, as soon as the modalities share a large amount of information, the Ensemble method outperforms the Fusion method. It implies that the benefit of the fusion depends on the nature of the dataset and can be null.

Independently to the chosen configuration, our CentralNet approach achieves the best results, except in the case of a null share ratio (first point of the right-hand side of the Fig. 4). In this case, the modalities are not sharing information, so the better performance of the Fusion+Ensemble (fusing at layer 0) compared

584   V. Vielzeuf et al.

to CentralNet might be explained by the difficulty to find relation between independent modalities and thus constructing a stable joint representation from the learned weighted sum. A comparison with an Ensemble of 3 models applied on original images suggests that this performance does not come only from a larger number of parameters.

Table 3 shows that in the lowest layers of CentralNet, the modalities are taken into account, while on last layers the weight of central previous hidden layer dominates. This is in line with our observations on the Fusion+Ensemble results.

3.2 Audiovisual MNIST

Audiovisual MNIST is a novel dataset we created by assembling visual and audio features. The first modality, disturbed image, is made of the 28×28 PCA-projected MNIST images, generated as explained in the previous section, with only 25% of the energy, to better assess the benefits of the fusion method. The second modality, audio, is made of audio samples on which we have computed 112×112 spectrograms. The audio samples are the pronounced digits of the Free Spoken Digits Database [26] augmented by adding randomly chosen 'noise' samples from the ESC-50 dataset [27], to reach the same number of examples as in MNIST (55000 training examples, 10000 testing examples).

For processing the image modality, we use the LeNet5 architecture [25], as in the previous section. For the audio modality, we use a 6-layer CNN, adding two convolution-pooling blocks. The whole architecture is detailed on Table 3.

We use dropout (50% dropping) on the fully connected layers and batch normalization. The learning rate is 0.001, the batch size is 128 and the model is trained on 100 epochs for all experiments, except Moddrop and Gated Multimodal Units, where hyper-parameters are found by a random grid search. Thus for Moddrop, the learning rate is changed into 0.005 and the modality drop probability is of 0.32. For Gated Multimodal Units, the dropout is changed into 35% dropping.

Table 4. Accuracy on the audiovisual MNIST dataset.

Method	Accuracy
Disturbed image	72.8 ± 0.3
Audio	86.1 ± 0.15
Weighted mean	94.7 ± 0.12
Concat	93.7 ± 0.17
Concat + Multi-Task	94.8 ± 0.11
Moddrop [22]	94.8 ± 0.10
Gated Multimodal Unit [13]	94.1 ± 0.14
CentralNet	$\mathbf{95.0 \pm 0.12}$

The performance is measured as the per sample accuracy on the 10000 test samples. We observe from Table 4, that the fusion methods are all performing better than unimodal ones. Both ensembles, Moddrop and simple weighted mean yield good performance but CentralNet performs best. Figure 3 shows that all the modalities are used at each layer, meaning that they all bring information.

3.3 Montalbano

The Montalbano dataset [24] gathers more than 14000 samples of 20 Italian sign gesture categories. These videos were recorded with a Kinect, capturing audio, skeleton joints, RGB and depth. The task is to recognize the gestures from the video data. The performance is measured as the macro accuracy, which is the average of the per class accuracy.

Fig. 6. The different raw visual modalities provided by the organizers of the ChaLearn challenge on Montalbano dataset. Neverova *et al.* [15] propose to focus on right and left hands, skeleton and audio.

The features used in these experiments are those provided by Neverova *et al.* [22]: audio features (size 350), motion capture of the skeleton (size 350), RGB+depth left/right hands features (size 400). Features are zero-padded (if needed) to give vectors of size 400. The fusion architecture includes one multi-layer perceptron per modality, each having 3 layers of size: 400×128, 128×42, 42×21. CentralNet architecture connects the 3 layers of the different modalities into a central network (Fig. 6).

We use dropout (50% dropping) and batch normalization. The learning rate is 0.05 (we multiply the learning rate by 0.96 at each epoch), the batch size is 42 containing two samples of each class and the model is trained on 100 epochs for all experiments. For Moddrop, the modality drop probability is of 0.5.

Table 5 shows that the performance obtained with each modality varies from 46% (left hand) to 88% (mocap). Basic late fusion gives significant improvement, suggesting complementarity between modalities. CentralNet outperforms all other approaches. Figure 3 shows the weights of the different modalities at each level. At the first layer (layer 0), the weights reflect the dimensionality of the layers. At the next layer, almost no information is taken from the modalities, while at layers 2 and 3, the weight given to each modality and to the central representation are relatively similar. This may be interpreted as an hybrid fusion strategy, mixing "early" and "late" fusions.

Table 5. Accuracy on the Montalbano validation set (same protocol as [22]).

Method	Accuracy
Left	46.0 ± 0.7
Audio	59.3 ± 0.3
Right	79.0 ± 0.3
Mocap	88.0 ± 0.3
Weighted mean	97.54 ± 0.02
Concat	97.76 ± 0.05
Concat + Multi-Task	98.02 ± 0.04
Moddrop	98.19 ± 0.03
Gated Multimodal Unit	97.98 ± 0.04
CentralNet	**98.27 ± 0.03**

Fantasy, Drama   **Horror, Mystery**

Fig. 7. Two movie samples extracted from the mm-IMDB dataset. For each, we can see the poster and the associated plot. The genres to predict are displayed on the top of the figure.

3.4 MM-IMDb

The MM-IMDb dataset [13] comprises respectively 15552, 2608 and 7799 training, validation and test movies, along with their plot, poster, genres and other 50 additional metadata fields such as year, language, writer, director, aspect ratio, *etc.*. The task is to predict a movie genre based on its plot and on its poster (*cf.* Fig. 7). One movie can belong to more than one of the 23 possible genres. The task hence has to be evaluated as a multilabel classification task. As in [7,13], we measure the performance with the micro, macro, weighted and per sample F1 scores. For these experiments, we use the features kindly provided by the authors [13]. The visual feature of size 4096 is extracted from the posters using the VGG-16 [28] network pretrained on Imagenet. The 300-d textual one are computed with a fine-tuned word2vec [29] encoder.

We build a multilayer perceptron on the top of the features of each modality. For both modalities, the network has 3 layers of size $input\_size \times 4096$, 4096×512 and 512×23. The CentralNet architecture (see Table 6 is the same, taking 4096-d vectors as inputs, zero-padding the textual features to reach the visual features size.

Table 6. Architecture of the CentralNet on the MM-IMDb dataset.

Text		Central		Visual	
Type	Size	Type	Size	Type	Size
Dense	2048	Dense	2048	Dense	2048
Dense	512	Dense	512	Dense	512
Pred	23	Pred	23	Pred	23

We use dropout (50% dropping) and batch normalization. The learning rate is 0.01 and the batch size is 128. For Moddrop, the modality drop probability is of 0.25. The loss of the models is a cross entropy, but we put a weight of 2.0 on the positives terms to balance precision and recall. More formally, the loss is:

$$loss = -\log(2\sigma(pred))y - (1-y)log(1 - \sigma(pred)) \qquad (4)$$

with $\sigma(pred)$ the sigmoid activation of the last output of the network and y the multiclass label. As recommended by Arevalo *et al.* [13], we also use early stopping on the validation set.

Table 7 reports the performance measured during the different experiments. First of all, the worst confidence interval we observe is very small, of the order of ± 0.001. For making the table more readable, we do not include it.

Table 7. F1 scores of the different methods on the MM-IMDb test set.

Method	Micro	Macro	Weighted	Samples
Text (alone)	0.602	0.489	0.585	0.606
Image (alone)	0.478	0.256	0.421	0.484
Weighted mean	0.635	0.550	0.626	0.634
Concat	0.611	0.506	0.599	0.614
Concat + Multi-Task	0.623	0.528	0.613	0.622
Moddrop [22]	0.624	0.526	0.614	0.625
Gated Multimodal Unit [13]	0.630	0.541	0.617	0.630
CentralNet	**0.639**	**0.561**	**0.631**	**0.639**

Second, one can observe that the textual modality clearly outperforms the visual one. Third, we note that even the basic fusion methods, such as the concatenation of the features, improve the score. Finally, the Concat+Multi-Task and Concat+ModDrop methods are outperformed by a significant margin by Gated Multimodal Unit and CentralNet, which is giving the best performance. Figure 3 shows that CentralNet gives more weight to the first layers, indicating that an "early fusion" strategy is privileged in this case, even if the two modalities contribute significantly at all levels.

4   Conclusions

This paper introduced a novel approach for the fusion of multimedia information. It consists in a joint representation having the form of a central network connecting the different layers of modality specific neural networks. The loss of this central network not only allows to learn how to combine the different modalities but also adds some constraints on the modality specific networks, enforcing their complementary aspects. This novel model achieves state-of-the-art results on several different multimodal problems. It also addresses elegantly the *late versus early* fusion paradigm.

References

1. Abu-El-Haija, S., et al.: YouTube-8M: a large-scale video classification benchmark. CoRR abs/1609.08675 (2016)
2. Wang, Z., et al.: Truly multi-modal YouTube-8M video classification with video, audio, and text. CoRR abs/1706.05461 (2017)
3. Dhall, A., et al.: Collecting large, richly annotated facial-expression databases from movies. IEEE MultiMedia 19, 34–41 (2012)
4. Ringeval, F., Schuller, B., Valstar, M., Gratch, J., Cowie, R., Pantic, M.: Summary for avec 2017: real-life depression and affect challenge and workshop. In: Proceedings of the 2017 ACM on Multimedia Conference, pp. 1963–1964. ACM (2017)
5. Hu, P., Cai, D., Wang, S., Yao, A., Chen, Y.: Learning supervised scoring ensemble for emotion recognition in the wild. In: Proceedings of the 19th ACM International Conference on Multimodal Interaction, pp. 553–560. ACM (2017)
6. Simonyan, K., Zisserman, A.: Two-stream convolutional networks for action recognition in videos. In: Advances in Neural Information Processing Systems, pp. 568–576 (2014)
7. Kiela, D., Grave, E., Joulin, A., Mikolov, T.: Efficient large-scale multi-modal classification. CoRR abs/1802.02892 (2018)
8. Atrey, P.K., Hossain, M.A., El Saddik, A., Kankanhalli, M.S.: Multimodal fusion for multimedia analysis: a survey. Multimedia Syst. 16(6), 345–379 (2010)
9. Andrew, G., Arora, R., Bilmes, J., Livescu, K.: Deep canonical correlation analysis. In: International Conference on Machine Learning, pp. 1247–1255 (2013)
10. Lahat, D., Adali, T., Jutten, C.: Multimodal data fusion: an overview of methods, challenges, and prospects. Proc. IEEE 103(9), 1449–1477 (2015)
11. Kim, D.H., Lee, M.K., Choi, D.Y., Song, B.C.: Multi-modal emotion recognition using semi-supervised learning and multiple neural networks in the wild. In: Proceedings of the 19th ACM International Conference on Multimodal Interaction, pp. 529–535. ACM (2017)

12. Vielzeuf, V., Pateux, S., Jurie, F.: Temporal multimodal fusion for video emotion classification in the wild. In: Proceedings of the 19th ACM International Conference on Multimodal Interaction, pp. 569–576. ACM (2017)
13. Arevalo, J., Solorio, T., Montes-y Gómez, M., González, F.A.: Gated multimodal units for information fusion. In: ICLR Worshop (2017)
14. Chen, M., Wang, S., Liang, P.P., Baltrušaitis, T., Zadeh, A., Morency, L.P.: Multimodal sentiment analysis with word-level fusion and reinforcement learning. In: Proceedings of the 19th ACM International Conference on Multimodal Interaction, pp. 163–171. ACM (2017)
15. Neverova, N., Wolf, C., Taylor, G.W., Nebout, F.: Multi-scale deep learning for gesture detection and localization. In: Agapito, L., Bronstein, M.M., Rother, C. (eds.) ECCV 2014. LNCS, vol. 8925, pp. 474–490. Springer, Cham (2015). https://doi.org/10.1007/978-3-319-16178-5_33
16. Yang, X., Molchanov, P., Kautz, J.: Multilayer and multimodal fusion of deep neural networks for video classification. In: Proceedings of the 2016 ACM on Multimedia Conference, pp. 978–987. ACM (2016)
17. Cangea, C., Velickovic, P., Liò, P.: XFlow: 1D-2D cross-modal deep neural networks for audiovisual classification. CoRR abs/1709.00572 (2017)
18. Gu, Z., Lang, B., Yue, T., Huang, L.: Learning joint multimodal representation based on multi-fusion deep neural networks. In: Liu, D., Xie, S., Li, Y., Zhao, D., El-Alfy, E.S. (eds.) ICONIP 2017. LNCS, vol. 10635, pp. 276–285. Springer, Cham (2017). https://doi.org/10.1007/978-3-319-70096-0_29
19. Kang, M., Ji, K., Leng, X., Lin, Z.: Contextual region-based convolutional neural network with multilayer fusion for sar ship detection. Remote Sens. 9(8), 860 (2017)
20. Baltrušaitis, T., Ahuja, C., Morency, L.P.: Multimodal machine learning: a survey and taxonomy. IEEE Trans. Pattern Anal. Mach. Intell. (2018)
21. Chandar, S., Khapra, M.M., Larochelle, H., Ravindran, B.: Correlational neural networks. Neural Comput. 28(2), 257–285 (2016)
22. Neverova, N., Wolf, C., Taylor, G., Nebout, F.: Moddrop: adaptive multi-modal gesture recognition. IEEE Trans. Pattern Anal. Mach. Intell. 38(8), 1692–1706 (2016)
23. Li, F., Neverova, N., Wolf, C., Taylor, G.: Modout: learning to fuse modalities via stochastic regularization. J. Comput. Vis. Imaging Syst. 2(1) (2016)
24. Escalera, S., et al.: ChaLearn looking at people challenge 2014: dataset and results. In: Agapito, L., Bronstein, M.M., Rother, C. (eds.) ECCV 2014. LNCS, vol. 8925, pp. 459–473. Springer, Cham (2015). https://doi.org/10.1007/978-3-319-16178-5_32
25. LeCun, Y., Bottou, L., Bengio, Y., Haffner, P.: Gradient-based learning applied to document recognition. Proc. IEEE 86(11), 2278–2324 (1998)
26. Jackson, Z.: Free-spoken-digit-dataset (2017). https://github.com/Jakobovski/decoupled-multimodal-learning
27. Piczak, K.J.: ESC: dataset for environmental sound classification. In: Proceedings of the 23rd ACM International Conference on Multimedia, pp. 1015–1018. ACM (2015)
28. Simonyan, K., Zisserman, A.: Very deep convolutional networks for large-scale image recognition. CoRR abs/1409.1556 (2014)
29. Mikolov, T., Sutskever, I., Chen, K., Corrado, G.S., Dean, J.: Distributed representations of words and phrases and their compositionality. In: Advances in Neural Information Processing Systems, pp. 3111–3119 (2013)

Where and What Am I Eating?
Image-Based Food Menu Recognition

Marc Bolaños[1,2]([✉]) [ID], Marc Valdivia[1], and Petia Radeva[1,2] [ID]

[1] Universitat de Barcelona, Barcelona, Spain
marc.bolanos@ub.edu
[2] Computer Vision Center, Bellaterra, Spain

Abstract. Food has become a very important aspect of our social activities. Since social networks and websites like Yelp appeared, their users have started uploading photos of their meals to the Internet. This phenomenon opens a whole world of possibilities for developing models for applying food analysis and recognition on huge amounts of real-world data. A clear application could consist in applying image food recognition by using the menu of the restaurants. Our model, based on Convolutional Neural Networks and Recurrent Neural Networks, is able to learn a language model that generalizes on never seen dish names without the need of re-training it. According to the Ranking Loss metric, the results obtained by the model improve the baseline by a 15%.

Keywords: Multimodal learning · Computer vision · Food recognition

1 Introduction

Food and nutrition is one of the main activities in people's lives. Nowadays, food does not only cover a basic need, but it has become a really important aspect of our social life. Since social networks appeared and, with them, food-focused applications (like TripAdvisor, Yelp, etc.), their users have started uploading photos of their meals to the Internet. It seems to be a strong and visible tendency in today's society to share pictures of absolutely every piece of food that we taste; exotic or local, fancy-looking or ordinary. Moreover, people post, on many different social media channels, plenty of videos of special restaurants where they eat. Every single day, thousands of people use social media to make recommendations, promote a particular place or give their friends a warning about a nearby restaurant. That is why, tags and location opportunities were introduced for all social media users to make their posts easier and faster to create. The creation of automatic tools for food recognition based on images could enable an easier generation of content, create food diaries for improving nutrition habits or even create personal food profiles for offering personalized recommendations.

The purpose of this work is to explore a problem that we call image-based food menu recognition, which consists in, given an image, determine its correct

© Springer Nature Switzerland AG 2019
L. Leal-Taixé and S. Roth (Eds.): ECCV 2018 Workshops, LNCS 11134, pp. 590–605, 2019.
https://doi.org/10.1007/978-3-030-11024-6_45

Restaurant Menu

tacos
chicken karaage
rice
red curry
falafel
salad
falafel
red snapper
spicy tuna
seafod ramen
fries
mochi

Fig. 1. Example of the Food Menu Recognition problem, where we have to retrieve the correct food name from a list of menu items.

menu item corresponding to the restaurant where it was taken (see Fig. 1). By being able to match the picture to an item of the menu it would be easier to retrieve the exact nutritional information of the food or any other data stored by the restaurant owners. Some of the main applications for this model would be creating a personalised profile with food preferences or a personal food diary for improving the eating habits.

The proposed methodology does not need to train a new model for each restaurant [32], instead it will learn to understand meal names in relation to a set of examples by learning a language model. We should point out the difficulty of the problem because of the context where we are working in. Restaurants usually use fancy names to refer to the dishes just to get the attention of their customers. Additionally, food presentation is different in every restaurant, having a high intra-class variability. Chefs try to surprise the customers by using unusual combinations of ingredients, colorful plates and/or sauces.

1.1 Health and Leisure

The work in [22] introduces the relationship that exists between food consumption and people's health. In Europe, despite being a first-world region, more than 4 million people die each year due to chronic diseases linked to unhealthy lifestyles. In many of these cases, the lack of basic knowledge or awareness is a crucial factor in all problems, most people simply do not pay much attention to their eating habits. Furthermore, as it is mentioned in [24], a great number of deaths related to coronary heart diseases are caused by a group of major risk factors among which bad eating habits are at the top.

On the other hand, for a lot of people being and feeling healthy is considered a must. Thanks to social networks, people share their healthy lifestyle on social media on a daily basis. Nowadays, going out for dinner and enjoying a cosy atmosphere in a restaurant is not enough. The healthier (and better looking) your food is, the better. Because of this important fact, today's restaurants are really visible online and they tend to use many different Internet channels to remain in the center of their customers' attention. Food-based applications like Yelp, help their users find opinions on the quality of the service in the place they plan to visit, and all the data introduced is generated by the users with their smartphones.

1.2   Food Analysis and Deep Learning

Considering the huge number of pictures of meals that people upload on the Internet, food analysis has become popular in the Deep Learning field. That is the reason why several public datasets have appeared. Some examples of public well-known datasets are Food-101 [8], UEC Food256 [16], or Vireo-Food 172 [9]. The most basic problem related to food explored in the literature is food detection [1], which consists in determining if any kind of food appears in an image. Food recognition is one of the most popular problems nowadays [2]. It consists in recognizing the food present on a picture given a pre-defined set of classes (dishes). Other applications of food analysis are food localization, which consists in detecting multiple dishes in a picture [7], calories estimation [13], ingredients detection [5], or multi-dishes recognition for self-service restaurants [3], which combines several of the aforementioned problems.

1.3   Restaurant Food Recognition

Several applications are focused on understanding customers' experiences in restaurants. Some sites like Yelp have plenty of information, but they are not able to classify a picture in the restaurant's menu automatically. It is the user who must do this manually. For this reason, we propose a model to solve this specific problem: locate the restaurant where customers are eating and recognize the meal that they chose from the menu [32]. Solving this problem would allow to create automatic personalized food diaries or personal food preferences, among other applications. The novelties of our work are the following:

- We propose a model that determines the similarity between a picture of food and the dish name provided in the restaurant's menu. Thanks to the language model learned, the system is able to detect the most probable food item in the menu using semantic information from LogMeal's API.
- We propose the first model for food menu recognition applicable to any restaurant. The system does not need previous information of a specific restaurant or a set of examples for a specific class to perform the prediction.
- We make public a dataset collected from Yelp[1]. Our dataset contains 53,877 images, from 313 restaurants and 3,498 different dishes.
- The results obtained over the collected data improve the baseline by a 15%.

---

[1] http://www.yelp.com.

In the context of the dataset, although ours is equivalent to the one proposed in [32], which is in Chinese, we were not able to perform tests on their dataset due to language issues. A critical component of our methodology is the language model, which allows to generalize for any restaurant, but considering the lack of embedding models pre-trained on Chinese, it is not possible to directly apply it.

This paper is organized as follows. In the related work (see Sect. 2), we explain previous papers published in relation with the problem that we want to solve. Our proposed model is introduced in the methodology (see Sect. 3). The dataset section (see Sect. 4) introduces the data used to train our model and how it was collected. In results (see Sect. 5), we explain and discuss the set of experiments done to choose the best parameters of the proposed model and their performance. Finally, we draw some conclusions and future work (see Sect. 6).

2   Related Work

Deep learning and Convolutional Neural Networks (CNNs) [17] have played a major role in the development of food-related methods in the last years. The huge amount of images related to food available on the internet in websites like Google Images, Instagram or Pinterest have allowed to collect large-scale datasets useful for training deep learning architectures. Even though, challenges inherent to the culinary world like intra-class variability (e.g. apple pie) and inter-class similarity (e.g. different types of pasta), demand the use of complex and smart algorithms. In this section we review the literature on works related to food analysis problems, some important works on multi-modal learning and food, and the application of these techniques in the restaurants context.

2.1   Food Analysis

In the literature there exist several problems and topics related to the analysis of food images. One of the most notable topics is food detection [1,23], where the goal is to detect whether a given image contains any food-related information/element. In a similar way, food recognition [2,20,25] is a widely explored topic, being the goal in this case to classify the image into a set of pre-defined list of classes related to food (usually prepared meals).

Other problems explored in the literature that are related to food analysis are calorie counting and monitoring or volume estimation, like in [19,31], where the authors present a mobile phone-based calories monitoring system to track the calories consumption for the users. Or focused on diabetes, Li et al. [18] estimate the amount of carbohydrate present in a meal from an image.

Other works have treated problems like food localization. In [7] the authors introduce the use of egocentric images to perform food detection and recognition. Food ingredients recognition [5,9] uses a state of the art CNN to predict a list of ingredients appearing in the meal. Food localization and recognition on self-service restaurants is presented in [3].

2.2   Multi-modal Food Analysis

Some times, food analysis uses context or additional information to improve the accuracy of the predictions. This complementary data can be of several types (e.g. images or text). Multi-modal Deep Learning [21] solves this particular problem, learning features over multiple modalities. The paper in [26] introduces a new large-scale dataset with more than 800.000 images and 1.000 recipes. The predictive model presented in the paper tries to join images and recipes through a retrieval task. The proposed solution generates two vectors. One of the vectors represents the image and the other one represents the recipe (text). For optimizing the model, they use the cosine similarity loss, which determines if a given recipe-image pair represents the same food.

The problem that we face also has two different inputs: we need to compare an image and a text sequence, so it could also be formulated as an image retrieval problem. The main differences of our proposal is that, instead of using a general purpose CNN to generate the features vector of the image, we use a semantic-based system for generating food categories that will be structured as a feature vector. Additionally, we use the dish name (text) instead of the recipe and intend to classify the input image into a set of menu items, being a problem more related to restaurant food recognition.

2.3   Restaurant Food Recognition

Seeing food analysis from a different perspective, in [4] the authors propose an automatic food logging system using smartphones. They use state of the art computer vision techniques and add context information of the restaurant to predict the food being consumed by the costumer. The system in [31] creates a calorie estimation from web video cameras in fast food restaurants across the United States. They focused on a reduced group of restaurants to understand the obesity problem. Similarly to our proposal, Xu et al. [32] introduces the context of the pictures to recognize the dish appearing in the image. Using the GPS information provided by the smart-phones they can determine a set of possible restaurants where the picture has been taken. This reduces the search space, which is really important when you try to determine the restaurant and menu item that appear in the picture taken by the user.

The system in [32] needs to train a discriminative model for each pair of restaurants in the dataset comparing their menus and images. Another common problem present in food recognition (or object recognition in general) is that it is limited to a predefined set of classes. This means that if the model was not trained to recognize a specific type of food, it will never provide it as a possible output. Furthermore, the complexity in the restaurants' food recognition resides in the need of training a different model for each restaurant. These models could be very accurate, but the number of outputs is also limited to the restaurant's menu. In this paper, we propose a model that solves these problems. It learns a language model considering a great amount of possible names and associates them to their corresponding pictures. Thus, our algorithm should be able to take a completely new restaurant's menu (never seen before) and a totally new picture associated to one of the menu's items and find out the correct menu item given the list. Thus, implying that the proposed model does not need to specifically learn every meal.

3   Image-Based Food Menu Recognition: Our Model

Figure 2 shows a scheme of our proposed model, which is based on image retrieval. Given two inputs: an image, and a dish name, it gives an output value based on their similarity. By using this, the prediction process consists in running the predictive model for each menu item and a single meal picture. The generated results produce a ranked list based on the most-similar-first criterion.

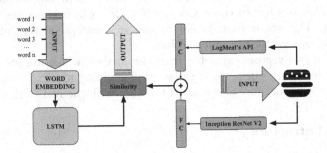

Fig. 2. Image-based food menu recognition model. On the one hand, the system gets an image and applies two different CNNs to generate the feature vectors. Each one is connected to a different fully connected layer to generate comparable structures and are combined performing an addition operation. On the other hand, the text sequence is processed by a word embedding and a Long Short Term Memory. Finally, we compute the similarity between the two inputs using the Euclidean similarity.

3.1   Image and Dish Name Embedding

Our method takes two different inputs, one in the form of an image, that will be transformed in two vectors of different modalities: a low-level vector and a high-level semantic vector, and the other in the form of text. Which means that they must be treated differently before embedding them into the system.

First, the image is converted in two vectors in parallel. One of them provides a low-level description of the food image by using the penultimate layer of the InceptionResNetV2 [29] CNN, composed by a vector of 1,536 values. This CNN is pre-built in the Keras [10] framework and trained using the ImageNet [12] dataset. The other vector provides a high-level semantic description of the food appearing in the image by using LogMeal's API[2]. This API provides three different CNNs that predict the dish [2], food group (or family) [2] and the ingredients

---

[2] http://www.logmeal.ml.

detected in the image [5]. More precisely, LogMeal's API provides (during the development of this paper) as output the probabilities of the image of belonging to 11 food groups (e.g. meat, vegetables, fish, soup, etc.), 200 dishes (e.g. pizza, spaghetti alla carbonara, etc.) and 1.092 ingredients (e.g. tomato, cheese, salt, garlic, etc.). In the implementation of our model, we are not using the ingredients output because, as we observed, the large dimensionality of the output and the noise that this group introduces to the system does not help obtaining better results. This, in order to build the semantic high-level vector, we concatenate the probabilities vector of the food groups together with the probabilities vector of the dishes.

Second, the text sequence input representing the meal's name is encoded using a word embedding. The inputs of our dataset are, in most of the cases, in English or Spanish. For this reason, and in order to make our model converge quicker, we need a word2vector pre-trained system supporting multiple languages. This is why we chose ConceptNet [28], which generates vectors of 300 features. The words that do not appear in ConceptNet's vocabulary are initialized using a vector of random values.

Unlike the two vectors extracted from the images, which are pre-computed and used as inputs to our system, the word embedding matrix is considered in the optimization procedure and trained together with the rest of the model.

3.2 Model Structure

More details about the image feature vectors generation and embedding can be seen in Fig. 3. One of them comes from LogMeal's API response and the other from the InceptionResNetV2. Later, each of them is inputted to the system and linked to a fully connected (FC) layer of 300 neurons. This layer transforms the feature vectors to the same size, so we can combine them applying an addition operation, which has been proven to be a simple yet effective way of multi-modal information merging [6].

Considering the text sequence that encodes the meal's name, it is generated using a Long Short Term Memory (LSTM) [15] network (Fig. 4) that encodes and joins the sequence of word embedding vectors generated in the first step. In order to match the dimensions of the image vector, the output size of the LSTM is also set to 300 neurons.

3.3 Similarity and Ranking

The last part of the model consists in processing the vectors provided from the image side and the text side in order to calculate their similarity, which will be a value between 0 and 1. Nevertheless, given a certain image and all the list of items in a restaurant's menu, we use the generated similarity values in order to build a sorted ranked list. It means that we need to run the model for each item in the menu on the same picture. The similarity function used to build the algorithm is an adaptation of the Euclidean distance $\frac{1}{1+\|q-p\|}$.

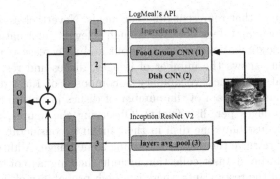

Fig. 3. Image processing part of our model. The system uses the food group and dish recognition outputs of LogMeal's API to create a semantic vector and connect it to a FC layer. The penultimate layer of the InceptionResNetV2 CNN is also used in parallel as a low-level feature vector which is connected to another FC layer. Finally, both partial results are combined performing an addition.

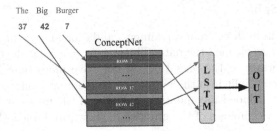

Fig. 4. The text sequence is encoded using a Word Embedding matrix, which is initialized using ConceptNet [28]. The generated vectors are connected to an LSTM.

4   Dataset

The dataset presented in this work was built using Yelp as the source of the information. We scraped the available public information of each restaurant, which consists in a list of menus for each restaurant, a list of dishes for each menu, and a list of images for each dish.

4.1   Dataset Characteristics

The dataset was built from restaurants located in California. We chose this location because of the amount of active Yelp users in this area. We make the dataset publicly available[3].

Analyzing the response of LogMeal's API, we decided to remove the ingredients information. Analyzing the outputs for images of the same dish name, we observe that they have similar activation points, and at the same time they are

---

[3] Available after paper publication due to blind review process.

different for images that represent different meals. Nevertheless, the ingredients recognition is noisy and does not give enough relevant information. Leading to an increase in the dimensionality of the input and a decrease of performance.

Table 1 (right) shows the number of images, dishes and restaurants in the dataset. The dataset dishes' vocabulary is composed of 1,584 different words. Figure 5 shows an histogram of the number of dishes per restaurant (left), and the number of images per dish (right). Observing the figures, the number of restaurants with just only one dish in their menu is considerably high, that is because we only retrieve the dishes containing some image. Additional problems that we found during dataset collection include the language of the dishes. Due to the location of the restaurants, there is a high probability of finding dishes in both English and Spanish, which introduces a problem: special characters. We encoded the text using the UTF-8 format, but there are some cases where the characters were represented by an empty symbol (_). We decided to remove these samples from the dataset in order to avoid errors during the word embedding.

4.2 Dataset Split

The dataset is split in three groups: training, validation and testing. Previously to the split process, we cleaned the data. This means removing the dishes encoded in a not valid format or the ones that do not have more than 5 images. The dishes are randomly split into three groups: the training group contains 80% of the dishes, 8% is included in validation and 12% of the meals are in the testing split. The number of images of the groups are shown in Table 1 (left).

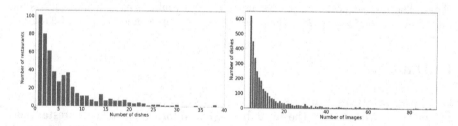

Fig. 5. Histogram of the number of dishes (with images) per restaurant in the dataset (left). Histogram of the number of images per dish in the dataset (right).

Table 1. Number of images in each split of the dataset (left). Number of images, dishes and restaurants of the dataset (right).

Split	# of images
Training	37,956
Validation	7,721
Test	10,794

Split	# of samples
# of images	53,877
# of dishes	3,498
# of restaurants	313

Considering that our model encodes the similarity of the image and text inputs, we need to provide both positive and negative samples in order to train it. The information downloaded from Yelp only contains positive examples, for this reason a set of negative samples has been generated for training (becoming a 50% of the total training samples). The negative examples have been generated assigning a wrong dish name to every image of the dataset. The validation and test splits are built randomizing the set of selected dishes in the menu together with the correct one. The groups of dishes where formed by randomly selecting between 10 and 20 dishes per menu. We generate a random list instead of using the menus of the restaurants to avoid restaurants that have few dishes in their menus.

5   Results

In this chapter we present the results obtained in our work, introduce the metrics used to evaluate the system and show the set of experiments created to find the best combination configuration of our model.

5.1   Ranking Loss and Accuracy Top-1 Distance

In order to compare the performance of the different methods, we use the Ranking Loss [30]. The lower the ranking loss is, the closer is the right value to the top of the list.

To complement the ranking loss error metric, we introduce our own accuracy metric in Eq. 1, which we call accuracy top-1 distance. This measure evaluates how close the ranked result is to the top. The difference with the ranking loss is that our metric only takes in consideration the distance from the position of the predicted class to the top of the ranking. We normalize the output between 0 and 1 using the number of labels in our ranking.

$$\text{accuracy top-1 distance} = \frac{n_{labels} - 1 - ranking_{position}}{n_{labels} - 1} \tag{1}$$

5.2   Experimental Setup

There are several components of our methodology that need to be tuned for finding the best configuration. The selection of the best combination of components was done using a forward propagation-grid search, and the policy we follow to choose the best parameter uses the ranking loss error over the test. The configurations to test where grouped in *similarity measures, losses, CNN features* and *sample weight*. For each step in the grid search, we select the configuration that obtains the best performance for each of the groups. Each configuration was calculated training the model 5 times. The representative model for each configuration was chosen considering the median value of the 5 runs. The results of the best configuration were obtained at the first epoch with a batch size of

64 samples and without applying any data augmentation or normalization process. Following, we detail the different model variants that we compare in the experimental section.

Similarity Measures: We tested two similarity function candidates. (a) the *Euclidean* similarity, which consists on a normalized version of the euclidean distance; and (b) the *Pearson similarity* (see Eq. 2), which is the absolute value of the Pearson correlation. Using the absolute value we get values between 0 and 1.

$$\rho = \left| \frac{\mathrm{cov}(X, Y)}{\sigma_x \sigma_y} \right| \tag{2}$$

Losses: We tested: (a) the binary cross-entropy (BCE) [27], which is a commonly used loss function for binary classification problems; and (b) the contrastive loss (CL) [14], which is usually used for Siamese networks [11]. The contrastive loss is a distance-based system and tries to minimize the separation between examples of the same semantic topic.

CNN Features: We also tested different CNN feature extraction configurations in our model: (a) using only the features from LogMeal's API (*LM*); (b) combination of the vectors from LogMeal and the InceptionResNetV2 CNN (*LM+Inc*); and (c) InceptionResNetV2 only (*Inc*).

Sample Weight: The last configuration to test is the sample weight. It indicates whether we want to assign a weight value to each dish in relation with the amount of images that it contains with respect to the total number of images in the dataset. This kind of weighing is usually useful when the dataset is unbalanced, giving more importance to the samples that are less frequent.

5.3   Experimental Results

Table 2 shows the results of the grid search. The last row of the table displays the baseline error (based on a random selection of an item in the menu) and accuracy value over validation and test. We have to consider that the values of the ranking loss follow the rule, the lower the better. Meanwhile, the accuracy has the opposite behavior, we want to achieve the higher possible value. The first two rows of the table compare the two similarity measures. Both similarity measures are tested with the same loss optimizer, CNN and sample weight values to be comparable. The error of the Euclidean similarity is 0.033 points better than the one using the Pearson function. Comparing the loss functions, we can see that even though the contrastive loss is usually used for similarity-based CNN models, in this case the binary one works better. If we compare the different CNN feature extraction methods, LM and Inc, the fist one works better. It is because LogMeal's models are trained using food images. Despite this considerations, the best results are obtained by the model using the combination of the two CNNs, meaning that both networks complement each other. Finally, we see that we obtain better results if we deactivate the sample weights. The cause for this

Table 2. Comparison of results for the different model configurations. CNN feat. indicates the combination of CNNs used in the model (LogMeal's API and InceptionResNetV2). The weight column indicates if the systems is using sample weight or not. The ranking loss is indicated with *r.loss* (the lower the better), and the accuracy top-1 distance is *acc.* (the higher the better). For each vertical section, a different configuration is tested. When a certain configuration is fixed it is shown in boldface.

				val		test	
similarities	losses	CNN feat.	weight	r. loss	acc.	r. loss	acc.
euclidean	binary	LM	NO	0.384	0.623	**0.362**	0.671
pearson	binary	LM	NO	0.416	0.602	0.395	0.639
euclidean	binary	LM	NO	0.384	0.623	**0.362**	0.671
euclidean	contrastive	LM	NO	0.405	0.398	0.375	0.664
euclidean	**binary**	LM	NO	0.384	0.623	0.362	0.671
euclidean	**binary**	LM+Inc	NO	0.372	0.641	**0.351**	0.678
euclidean	**binary**	Inc	NO	0.443	0.572	0.413	0.598
euclidean	**binary**	**LM+Inc**	NO	0.372	0.641	**0.351**	0.678
euclidean	**binary**	**LM+Inc**	YES	0.396	0.612	0.378	0.668
euclidean	**binary**	**LM+Inc**	**NO**	**0.372**	**0.641**	**0.351**	**0.678**
random selection (baseline)				0.5	0.5	0.5	0.5

might be that we do not have a set of pre-stablished classes, but instead we have a language model that links them semantically. This component of our architecture is able to better learn the importance of each sample without the need of forcing a specific weight during optimization. Concluding the table analysis, the best combination of parameters for our model improves the baseline by a 15%. The best ranking loss for the test group is 0.351 and the accuracy top-1 distance is 0.678. It means an improvement of 0.149 and 0.178 points respectively over the baseline.

5.4 Visual Results Analysis

In Figs. 6 and 7 we show some visualizations of the results obtained by our model. The visualization contains a picture of the meal, the ranked results of our system and the true prediction for the image. Figure 6 shows that the cases where the system works better is when the picture presents a single piece of food and the image is clear and centered as well as contains a common dish (with enough samples in the training set). Figure 7 shows examples of failure cases, where the images contain multiple meals on them, making the recognition harder. Additionally, it is appreciable that the dishes with long names are usually at the bottom of the ranking. It is because these meals do not contain a lot of images and are not very popular in the restaurants. So, the model is not able to learn them and retrieve good predictions.

Another problem that we encountered was that, even being uncommon, the data tagged by Yelp's users is misclassified because the pictures uploaded to the site are not verified. Sometimes, the users take photos of their dishes including

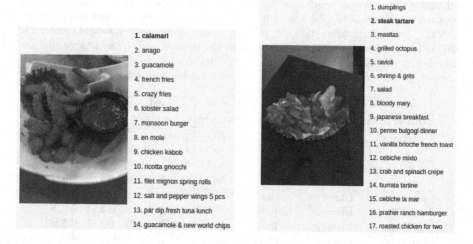

Fig. 6. Examples of ranked lists produced by our algorithm for images of the dishes 'calamari' (left) and 'steak tartare' (right). We observe the good results obtained when the names of the dishes are common enough.

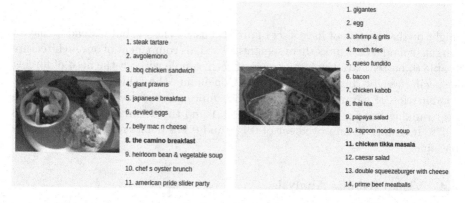

Fig. 7. Examples of ranked lists produced by our algorithm for images of the dishes 'the camino breakfast' (left) and 'chicken tikka masala' (right). Worse results are obtained when the names of the dishes are rare.

context information, and it is a possibility that this information includes other people's meals, which makes more difficult to classify the sample. The main difficulty for the algorithm is dealing with a high variety of names. The restaurants have some speciality dishes that they name at their own. These meals are really difficult to classify, even for a human. Visualizing the results and analyzing the responses of a random selection of the predictions, we have found some properties that usually work better in our system. The meals that contain common food names tend to get better results than the ones with exotic names. This fact is due to two main reasons: the first one is that the dataset has a lot of examples with common names and can learn them better, and the second one is that the exotic names do not tend to appear at the word embedding matrix, so the system has no initial information of them. Moreover, these names are present in just a few restaurants, so the system does not have enough examples to learn from.

6 Conclusions and Future Work

We can conclude that it is possible to build a model for food restaurant menu recognition that generalizes for any restaurant available, without the need of learning a different model per restaurant or restaurant pairs. This result is achieved thanks to learning a language model that jointly embeds the information from all the dishes available together with low and high-level (semantic) information coming from the images. The contributions that we have done to the scientific community are the following:

- We introduce the use of a language model for dishes and semantic image information by means of LogMeal's API to perform menu items recognition from restaurants.
- We propose a new model that determines the similarity between a food image and a menu item of a restaurant without the need of re-training for each restaurant, which improves the baseline by a 15%.
- We present a new dataset composed by the dishes and images of the restaurant's menu collected from Yelp. The dataset contains 53,877 images, 3,498 dishes and 313 restaurants.

One of the main issues to take into consideration in the future is the treatment of dishes with exotic names, which can not be easily learned by our language model. Furthermore, in the future we plan to introduce the GPS information of the images. The location of the user gives us a list of two or three candidate restaurants where they are eating. Combining the menus of these restaurants and applying the proposed system we would be able to determine where and what a person is eating.

References

1. Aguilar, E., Bolanos, M., Radeva, P.: Exploring food detection using CNNs. arXiv preprint arXiv:1709.04800 (2017)
2. Aguilar, E., Bolaños, M., Radeva, P.: Food recognition using fusion of classifiers based on CNNs. In: Battiato, S., Gallo, G., Schettini, R., Stanco, F. (eds.) ICIAP 2017. LNCS, vol. 10485, pp. 213–224. Springer, Cham (2017). https://doi.org/10.1007/978-3-319-68548-9_20
3. Aguilar, E., Remeseiro, B., Bolaños, M., Radeva, P.: Grab, pay and eat: semantic food detection for smart restaurants. arXiv preprint arXiv:1711.05128 (2017)
4. Bettadapura, V., Thomaz, E., Parnami, A., Abowd, G.D., Essa, I.: Leveraging context to support automated food recognition in restaurants. In: 2015 IEEE Winter Conference on Applications of Computer Vision (WACV), pp. 580–587. IEEE (2015)

5. Bolaños, M., Ferrà, A., Radeva, P.: Food ingredients recognition through multi-label learning. In: Battiato, S., Farinella, G.M., Leo, M., Gallo, G. (eds.) ICIAP 2017. LNCS, vol. 10590, pp. 394–402. Springer, Cham (2017). https://doi.org/10.1007/978-3-319-70742-6_37

6. Bolaños, M., Peris, Á., Casacuberta, F., Radeva, P.: VIBIKNet: visual bidirectional kernelized network for visual question answering. In: Alexandre, L.A., Salvador Sánchez, J., Rodrigues, J.M.F. (eds.) IbPRIA 2017. LNCS, vol. 10255, pp. 372–380. Springer, Cham (2017). https://doi.org/10.1007/978-3-319-58838-4_41

7. Bolanos, M., Radeva, P.: Simultaneous food localization and recognition. In: 2016 23rd International Conference on Pattern Recognition (ICPR), pp. 3140–3145. IEEE (2016)

8. Bossard, L., Guillaumin, M., Van Gool, L.: Food-101 – mining discriminative components with random forests. In: Fleet, D., Pajdla, T., Schiele, B., Tuytelaars, T. (eds.) ECCV 2014. LNCS, vol. 8694, pp. 446–461. Springer, Cham (2014). https://doi.org/10.1007/978-3-319-10599-4_29

9. Chen, J., Ngo, C.W.: Deep-based ingredient recognition for cooking recipe retrieval. In: Proceedings of the 2016 ACM on Multimedia Conference, pp. 32–41. ACM (2016)

10. Chollet, F., et al.: Keras (2015). https://keras.io

11. Chopra, S., Hadsell, R., LeCun, Y.: Learning a similarity metric discriminatively, with application to face verification. In: IEEE Computer Society Conference on Computer Vision and Pattern Recognition, CVPR 2005, vol. 1, pp. 539–546. IEEE (2005)

12. Deng, J., Dong, W., Socher, R., Li, L.J., Li, K., Fei-Fei, L.: ImageNet: a large-scale hierarchical image database. In: CVPR 2009 (2009)

13. Ege, T., Yanai, K.: Simultaneous estimation of food categories and calories with multi-task CNN. In: 2017 Fifteenth IAPR International Conference on Machine Vision Applications (MVA), pp. 198–201. IEEE (2017)

14. Hadsell, R., Chopra, S., LeCun, Y.: Dimensionality reduction by learning an invariant mapping. In: 2006 IEEE Computer Society Conference on Computer Vision and Pattern Recognition, vol. 2, pp. 1735–1742. IEEE (2006)

15. Hochreiter, S., Schmidhuber, J.: Long short-term memory. Neural Comput. 9(8), 1735–1780 (1997)

16. Kawano, Y., Yanai, K.: Automatic expansion of a food image dataset leveraging existing categories with domain adaptation. In: Agapito, L., Bronstein, M.M., Rother, C. (eds.) ECCV 2014. LNCS, vol. 8927, pp. 3–17. Springer, Cham (2015). https://doi.org/10.1007/978-3-319-16199-0_1

17. Krizhevsky, A., Sutskever, I., Hinton, G.E.: Imagenet classification with deep convolutional neural networks. In: Advances in Neural Information Processing Systems, pp. 1097–1105 (2012)

18. Li, H.C., Ko, W.M.: Automated food ontology construction mechanism for diabetes diet care. In: 2007 International Conference on Machine Learning and Cybernetics, vol. 5, pp. 2953–2958. IEEE (2007)

19. Liu, C., Cao, Y., Luo, Y., Chen, G., Vokkarane, V., Ma, Y.: DeepFood: deep learning-based food image recognition for computer-aided dietary assessment. In: Chang, C.K., Chiari, L., Cao, Y., Jin, H., Mokhtari, M., Aloulou, H. (eds.) ICOST 2016. LNCS, vol. 9677, pp. 37–48. Springer, Cham (2016). https://doi.org/10.1007/978-3-319-39601-9_4

20. Martinel, N., Foresti, G.L., Micheloni, C.: Wide-slice residual networks for food recognition. arXiv preprint arXiv:1612.06543 (2016)

21. Ngiam, J., Khosla, A., Kim, M., Nam, J., Lee, H., Ng, A.Y.: Multimodal deep learning. In: Proceedings of the 28th International Conference on Machine Learning (ICML 2011), pp. 689–696 (2011)
22. Organization, W.H., et al.: Food and health in Europe: a new basis for action. World Health Organization, Regional Office for Europe (2004)
23. Ragusa, F., Tomaselli, V., Furnari, A., Battiato, S., Farinella, G.M.: Food vs non-food classification. In: Proceedings of the 2nd International Workshop on Multimedia Assisted Dietary Management, pp. 77–81. ACM (2016)
24. Rozin, P., Fischler, C., Imada, S., Sarubin, A., Wrzesniewski, A.: Attitudes to food and the role of food in life in the usa, japan, flemish belgium and france: possible implications for the diet-health debate. Appetite **33**(2), 163–180 (1999)
25. Salvador, A., et al.: Learning cross-modal embeddings for cooking recipes and food images. In: The IEEE Conference on Computer Vision and Pattern Recognition (CVPR), July 2017 (2017)
26. Salvador, A., Hynes, N., Aytar, Y., Marin, J., Ofli, F., Weber, I., Torralba, A.: Learning cross-modal embeddings for cooking recipes and food images. Training **720**, 619–508 (2017)
27. Shore, J., Johnson, R.: Axiomatic derivation of the principle of maximum entropy and the principle of minimum cross-entropy. IEEE Trans. Inform. Theor. **26**(1), 26–37 (1980)
28. Speer, R., Lowry-Duda, J.: Conceptnet at semeval-2017 task 2: extending word embeddings with multilingual relational knowledge. arXiv preprint arXiv:1704.03560 (2017)
29. Szegedy, C., Ioffe, S., Vanhoucke, V., Alemi, A.A.: Inception-v4, inception-resnet and the impact of residual connections on learning. In: AAAI, vol. 4, p. 12 (2017)
30. Tsoumakas, G., Katakis, I., Vlahavas, I.: Mining multi-label data. In: Maimon, O., Rokach, L. (eds.) Data Mining and Knowledge Discovery Handbook, pp. 667–685. Springer, Boston (2009). https://doi.org/10.1007/978-0-387-09823-4_34
31. Wu, W., Yang, J.: Fast food recognition from videos of eating for calorie estimation. In: IEEE International Conference on Multimedia and Expo, ICME 2009, pp. 1210–1213. IEEE (2009)
32. Xu, R., Herranz, L., Jiang, S., Wang, S., Song, X., Jain, R.: Geolocalized modeling for dish recognition. IEEE Trans. Multimed. **17**(8), 1187–1199 (2015)

ThermalGAN: Multimodal Color-to-Thermal Image Translation for Person Re-identification in Multispectral Dataset

Vladimir V. Kniaz[1,2]($\boxtimes$)(iD), Vladimir A. Knyaz[1,2](iD), Jiří Hladůvka[3](iD), Walter G. Kropatsch[3](iD), and Vladimir Mizginov[1](iD)

[1] State Research Institute of Aviation Systems (GosNIIAS), Moscow, Russia
{vl.kniaz,knyaz,vl.mizginov}@gosniias.ru
[2] Moscow Institute of Physics and Technology (MIPT), Dolgoprudny, Russia
[3] PRIP, Institute of Visual Computing and Human-Centered Technology,
Vienna, Austria
{jiri,krw}@prip.tuwien.ac.at

Abstract. We propose a ThermalGAN framework for cross-modality color-thermal person re-identification (ReID). We use a stack of generative adversarial networks (GAN) to translate a single color probe image to a multimodal thermal probe set. We use thermal histograms and feature descriptors as a thermal signature. We collected a large-scale multispectral ThermalWorld dataset for extensive training of our GAN model. In total the dataset includes 20216 color-thermal image pairs, 516 person ID, and ground truth pixel-level object annotations. We made the dataset freely available (http://www.zefirus.org/ThermalGAN/). We evaluate our framework on the ThermalWorld dataset to show that it delivers robust matching that competes and surpasses the state-of-the-art in cross-modality color-thermal ReID.

Keywords: Person re-identification · Conditional GAN Thermal images

1 Introduction

Person re-identification (ReID) is of primary importance for tasks such as video surveillance and photo-tagging. It has been the focus of intense research in recent years. While modern methods provide excellent results during in a well-lit environment, their performance is not robust without a suitable light source.

Infrared cameras perceive thermal emission that is invariant to the lighting conditions. However, challenges of cross-modality color-infrared matching

Electronic supplementary material The online version of this chapter (https://doi.org/10.1007/978-3-030-11024-6_46) contains supplementary material, which is available to authorized users.

L. Leal-Taixé and S. Roth (Eds.): ECCV 2018 Workshops, LNCS 11134, pp. 606–624, 2019.
https://doi.org/10.1007/978-3-030-11024-6_46

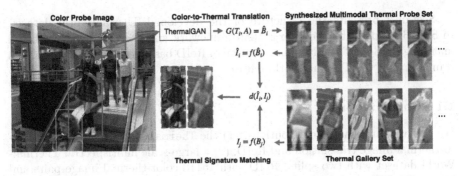

Fig. 1. Overview of color-thermal ReID using our `ThermalGAN` framework. We transform a single color probe image A to multimodal thermal probe set $\{B_1, \ldots, B_i\}$. We use thermal signatures I to perform matching with real thermal gallery set. (Color figure online)

reduce benefits of night mode infrared cameras. Recently cross-modality color-to-thermal matching received a lot of scholar attention [35,37,51,52]. Multiple datasets with infrared images [33,35,37,47] were developed for cross-modality infrared-to-color person ReID. Thermal cameras operate in longwave infrared (LWIR, 8–14 μ) and provide real temperatures of a person body which are more stable to viewpoint changes than near-infrared images [45,54,58].

This paper is focused on the development of a `ThermalGAN` framework for color-thermal cross-modality person ReID. We use assumptions of Bhuiyan [4] and Zhu [62] as a starting point for our research to develop a color-to-thermal transfer framework for cross-modality person ReID. We perform matching using calibrated thermal images to benefit from the stability of surface temperatures to changes in light intensity and viewpoint. Matching is performed in two steps. Firstly, we model a person appearance in a thermal image conditioned by a color image. We generate a multimodal thermal probe set from a single color probe image using a generative adversarial network (GAN). Secondly, we perform matching in thermal images using the synthesized thermal probe set and a real thermal gallery set (Fig. 1).

We collected a new ThermalWorld dataset to train our GAN framework and to test the ReID performance. The dataset contains two parts: ReID and Visual Objects in Context (VOC). The ReID split includes 15118 pairs of color and thermal images and 516 person ID. The VOC part is designed for training color-to-thermal translation using a GAN framework. It consists of 5098 pairs of color and thermal images and pixel-level annotations for ten classes: person, car, truck, van, bus, building, cat, dog, tram, boat.

We perform an evaluation of baselines and our framework on the Thermal-World dataset. The results of the evaluation are encouraging and show that our `ThermalGAN` framework achieves and surpasses the state-of-the-art in the cross-modality color-thermal ReID. The new `ThermalGAN` framework will be able to perform matching of color probe image with thermal gallery set in video surveillance applications.

Section 2 presents the structure of the developed ThermalWorld dataset. In Sect. 3 we describe the `ThermalGAN` framework and thermal signature-based matching. In Sect. 4 we give an evaluation of ReID baselines and the `ThermalGAN` framework on the ThermalWorld dataset.

1.1   Contributions

We present three main contributions: (1) the `ThermalGAN` framework for color-to-thermal image translation and ReID, (2) a large-scale multispectral Thermal-World dataset with two splits: ReID with 15118 color-thermal image pairs and 516 person ID, and VOC with 5098 pairs color-thermal image pairs with ground truth pixel-level object annotations of ten object classes, (3) an evaluation of the modern cross-modality ReID methods on ThermalWorld ReID dataset.

2   Related Work

2.1   Person Re-identification

Person re-identification has been intensively studied by computer vision society recently [3,4,9,12,40,47]. While new methods improve the matching performance steadily, video surveillance applications still pose challenges for ReID systems. Recent methods regarding person ReID can be divided into three kinds of approaches [4]: direct methods, metric learning methods and transform learning methods.

In [4] an overview of modern ReID methods was performed, and a new transform learning-based method was proposed. The method models an appearance of a person in a new camera using cumulative weight brightness transfer function (CWBTF). The method leverages a robust segmentation technique to segment the human image into meaningful parts. Matching of features extracted only from the body area provides an increased ReID performance. The method also exploits multiple pedestrian detections to improve the matching rate.

While the method provides the state-of-the-art performance on color images, night-time application requires additional modalities to perform robust matching in low-light conditions. Cross-modality color-infrared matching is gaining increasing attention. Multiple multispectral datasets were collected in recent years [33,35,37,47,51]. SYSU-MM01 dataset [47] includes unpaired color and near-infrared images. RegDB dataset [51] presents color and infrared images for evaluation of cross-modality ReID methods. Evaluation of modern methods on these datasets has shown that color-infrared matching is challenging. Nevertheless, it provides an increase in ReID robustness during the night-time.

Thermal camera has received a lot of scholar attention in the field of video surveillance [8,53]. While thermal cameras provide a significant boost in pedestrian detection [42,50] and ReID with paired color and thermal images [33], cross-modality person ReID is challenging [33–37] due to severe changes in a person appearance in color and thermal images.

Recently, generative adversarial networks (GAN) [13] have demonstrated encouraging results in arbitrary image-to-image translation applications. We hypothesize that color-to-thermal image translation using a dedicated GAN framework can increase color-thermal ReID performance.

2.2 Color-to-Thermal Translation

Transformation of the spectral range of an image has been intensively studied in such fields as transfer learning [39,46] domain adaptation [23–25,32] and cross-domain recognition [1,17,19,21,47,49,54,55]. In [30] a deep convolutional neural network (CNN) was proposed for translation of a near-infrared image to a color image. The approach was similar to image colorization [15,56] and style transfer [27,44] problems that were actively studied in recent years. The proposed architecture succeeded in a translation of near-infrared images to color images. Transformation of LWIR images is more challenging due to the low correlation between the red channel of a color image and a thermal image.

2.3 Generative Adversarial Networks

GANs increased the quality of image-to-image translation significantly [20,54,58] using an antagonistic game approach [13]. Isola et al. [20] proposed a pix2pix GAN framework for arbitrary image transformations using geometrically aligned image pairs sampled from source and target domains. The framework succeeded in performing arbitrary image-to-image translations such as season change and object transfiguration. Zhang et al. [54,58] trained the pix2pix network to transform a thermal image of a human face to the color image. The translation improved the quality of a face recognition performance in a cross-modality thermal to visible range setting. While human face has a relatively stable temperature, color-thermal image translation for the whole human body with an arbitrary background is more ambiguous and conditioned by the sequence of events that have occurred with a person.

We hypothesize that multimodal image generation methods can model multiple possible thermal outputs for a single color probe image. Such modeling can improve the ReID performance. Zhu et al. proposed a BicycleGAN framework [63] for modeling a distribution of possible outputs in a conditional generative modeling setting. To resolve the ambiguity of the mapping Zhu et al. used a randomly sampled low-dimension latent vector. The latent vector is produced by an encoder network from the generated image and compared to the original latent vector to provide an additional consistency loss. We propose a conditional color-to-thermal translation framework for modeling of a set of possible person appearances in a thermal image conditioned by a single color image.

3   ThermalWorld Dataset

We collected a new ThermalWorld dataset to train and evaluate our cross-modality ReID framework. The dataset was collected with multiple FLIR ONE

PRO cameras and divided into two splits: ReID and Visual Objects in Context (VOC). The ReID split includes 15118 aligned color and thermal image pairs of 516 IDs. The VOC split was created for effective color-to-thermal translation GAN training. It contains 5098 color and thermal image pairs and pixel-level annotations of ten object classes: person, car, truck, van, bus, building, cat, dog, tram, boat.

Initially, we have tried to train a color-to-thermal translation GAN model using only the ReID split. However, the trained network has poor generalization ability due to a limited number of object classes and backgrounds. This stimulated us to collect a large-scale dataset with aligned pairs of color and thermal images. The rest of this section presents a brief dataset overview. For more details on the dataset, please refer to the supplementary material.

3.1   ThermalWorld ReID Split

The ReID split includes pairs of color and thermal images captured by sixteen FLIR ONE PRO cameras. Sample images from the dataset are presented in Fig. 2. All cameras were located in a shopping mall area. Cameras #2, 9, 13 are located in underground passages with low-light conditions. Cameras #1, 3, 7, 8, 10, 12, 14 are located at the entrances and present both day-time and night-time images. Cameras #15,16 are placed in the garden. The rest of the cameras are located inside the mall.

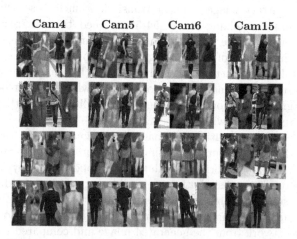

Fig. 2. Examples of person images from ThermalWorld ReID dataset.

We have developed a dedicated application for a smartphone to record sequences of thermal images using FLIR ONE PRO. Comparison to previous ReID datasets is presented in Table 1.

Table 1. Comparison to previous ReID datasets. #/# represents the number of color/infrared images or cameras.

Dataset	#ID	#images	#cam	Color	NIR	Thermal
iLDS [61]	119	476	2	✓	✗	✗
CAVIAR [6]	72	610	2	✓	✗	✗
PRID2011 [18]	200	971	2	✓	✗	✗
VIPER [14]	632	1264	2	✓	✗	✗
CUHK01 [28]	972	1942	2	✓	✗	✗
CUHK03 [29]	1467	13164	6	✓	✗	✗
SYSU [16]	502	24448	2	✓	✗	✗
Market [60]	1501	32668	6	✓	✗	✗
MARS [59]	1261	1191003	6	✓	✗	✗
RegDB [37]	412	4120/4120	1/1	✓	✗	✓
SYSU-MM01 [47]	491	287628/15792	4/2	✓	✓	✗
ThermalWorld	516	15818/15818	16/16	✓	✗	✓

3.2   ThermalWorld VOC Split

The VOC split of the dataset was collected using two FLIR ONE PRO cameras. We use insights of developers of previous multispectral datasets [2,8,11,19,43,55] and provide new object classes with pixel-level annotations. The images were collected in different cities (Paris, Strasbourg, Riva del Garda, Venice) during all seasons and in different weather conditions (sunny, rain, snow). Captured object temperatures range from $-20\,°C$ to $+40\,°C$.

We hypothesized that training a GAN to predict the relative temperature contrasts of an object (e.g., clothes/skin) instead of its absolute temperature can improve the translation quality. We were inspired by the previous work on the explicit encoding of multiple modes in the output [63], and we assumed that the thermal segmentation that provides average temperatures of the emitting objects in the scene could resolve the ambiguity of the generated thermal images. Examples from ThermalWorld VOC dataset are presented in Fig. 3.

We manually annotated the dataset, to automatically extract an object's temperature from the thermal images. Comparison to previous multispectral datasets and examples of all classes are presented in the supplementary material.

4   Method

Color-to-thermal image translation is challenging because there are multiple possible thermal outputs for a single color input. For example, a person in a cold autumn day and a hot summer afternoon may have a similar appearance in the visible range, but the skin temperature will be different.

Fig. 3. Examples of annotated images in ThermalWorld VOC dataset.

We have experimented with multiple state-of-the-art GAN frameworks [5,20, 26,63] for multi-modal image translation on the color-to-thermal task. We have found that GANs can predict object temperature with accuracy of approximately 5 °C.

However, thermal images must have accuracy of 1 °C to make local body temperature contrasts (e.g., skin/cloth) distinguishable. To improve the translation quality we developed two-step approach inspired by [48]. We have observed that relative thermal contrasts (e.g., eyes/brow) are nearly invariant to changes in the average body temperature due to different weather conditions.

We hypothesize that a prediction of relative thermal contrasts can be conditioned by an input color image and average temperatures for each object. Thus, we predict an absolute object temperature in two steps (Fig. 4). Firstly, we predict average object temperatures from an input color image. We term the resulting image as a "thermal segmentation" image $\hat{S}$.

Secondly, we predict the relative local temperature contrasts $\hat{R}$, conditioned by a color image A and a thermal segmentation $\hat{S}$. The sum of a thermal segmentation and temperature contrasts provides the thermal image: $\hat{B} = \hat{S} + \hat{R}$.

The sequential thermal image synthesis has two advantages. Firstly, the problem remains multimodal only in the first step (generation of thermal segmentation). Secondly, the quality of thermal contrasts prediction is increased due to lower standard deviation and reduced range of temperatures.

To address the multimodality in color-to-thermal translation, we use a modified `BicyleGAN` framework [63] to synthesize multiple color segmentation images for a single color image. Instead of a random noise sample, we use a temperature vector T_i, which contains the desired background and object temperatures.

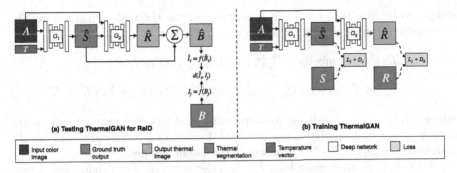

Fig. 4. Overview of our `ThermalGAN` framework.

The rest of this section presents a brief introduction to conditional adversarial networks, details on the developed `ThermalGAN` framework and features used for thermal signature matching.

4.1 Conditional Adversarial Networks

Generative adversarial networks produce an image $\hat{B}$ for a given random noise vector z, $G : z \rightarrow \hat{B}$ [13,20]. Conditional GAN receives extra bits of information A in addition to the vector z, $G : \{A, z\} \rightarrow \hat{B}$. Usually, A is an image that is transformed by the generator network G. The discriminator network D is trained to distinguish "real" images from target domain B from the "fakes" $\hat{B}$ produced by the generator. Both networks are trained simultaneously. Discriminator provides the adversarial loss that enforces the generator to produce "fakes" $\hat{B}$ that cannot be distinguished from "real" images B.

We train two GAN models. The first generator $G_1 : \{T_i, A\} \rightarrow \hat{S}_i$ synthesizes multiple thermal segmentation images $\hat{S}_i \in \mathbb{R}^{W \times H}$ conditioned by a temperature vector T_i and a color image $A \in \mathbb{R}^{W \times H \times 3}$. The second generator $G_2 : \{\hat{S}_i, A\} \rightarrow \hat{R}_i$ synthesizes thermal contrasts $\hat{R}_i \in \mathbb{R}^{W \times H}$ conditioned by a thermal segmentation $\hat{S}_i$ and the input color image A. We can produce multiple realistic thermal outputs for a single color image by changing only the temperature vector T_i.

4.2 Thermal Segmentation Generator

We use the modified `BicycleGAN` framework for thermal segmentation generator G_1. Our contribution to the original U-Net generator [41] is an addition of one convolutional layer and one deconvolutional layer to increase the output resolution. We use average background temperatures instead of the random noise sample to be able to control the appearance of the thermal segmentation. The loss function for the generator G_1 is given by [63]:

$$G_1^*(G_1, D_1) = \arg \min_{G_1} \max_{D_1} \mathcal{L}_{GAN}^{VAE}(G_1, D_1, E) + \lambda \mathcal{L}_1(G_1, E)$$

$$+ \mathcal{L}_{GAN}(G_1, D_1) + \lambda_{\text{thermal}} \mathcal{L}_1^{\text{thermal}}(G_1, E) + \lambda_{KL} \mathcal{L}_{KL}(E), \quad (1)$$

where $\mathcal{L}_{GAN}^{VAE}$ – is Variational Autoencoder-based loss [63] that stimulates the output to be multimodal, $\mathcal{L}_1$ – is an L^1 loss, $\mathcal{L}_{GAN}$ – loss provided by the discriminator D_1, $\mathcal{L}_1^{\text{thermal}}$ – is a loss of the latent temperature domain, $\mathcal{L}_{KL}$ – Kullback–Leibler-divergence loss, E – encoder network, λ – weight parameters. We train both generators independently.

4.3 Relative Thermal Contrast Generator

We hypothesize that the distribution of relative thermal contrasts conditioned by a thermal segmentation and a color image is unimodal (compare images B and R for various background temperatures in Fig. 5). Hence, we use a unimodal pix2pix framework [20] as a starting point for our relative contrast generator G_2. Our contribution to the original framework is two-fold. Firstly, we made the same modifications to the generator G_2 as for the generator G_1. Secondly, we use four channel input tensor. First three channels are RGB channels of an image A, the fourth channel is thermal segmentation $\hat{S}_i$ produced by generator G_1. We sum the outputs from the generators to obtain an absolute temperature image.

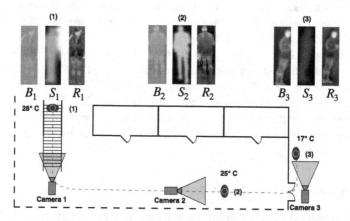

Fig. 5. Comparison of relative contrast R and absolute temperature B images for various camera locations. The relative contrast image R is equal to the difference of an absolute temperature B and a thermal segmentation S. Note that the person appearance is invariant to background temperature in relative contrast images.

4.4   Thermal Signature Matching

We use an approach similar to [4] to extract discriminative features from thermal images. The original feature signature is extracted in three steps [4]: (1) a person appearance is transferred from camera C_k to camera C_l, (2) the body region is separated from the background using stel component analysis (SCA) [22], (3) feature signature is extracted using color histograms [9] and maximally stable color regions (MSCR) [10].

However, thermal images contain only a single channel. We modify color features for absolute temperature domain. We use the monochrome ancestor of MSCR – maximally stable extremal regions (MSER) [31]. We use temperature histograms instead of color histograms. The resulting matching method includes four steps. Firstly, we transform the person appearance from a single color probe image A to multiple thermal images $\hat{B}_i$ using the ThermalGAN framework. Various images model possible variations of temperature from camera to camera. Unlike the original approach [4], we do not train the method to transfer person a appearance from camera to camera. Secondly, we extract body regions using SCA from real thermal images B_j in the gallery set and synthesized images $\hat{B}_i$. After that, we extract thermal signatures I from body regions

$$I = f(B) = \left[H_t(B), f_{\text{MSER}}(B) \right], \qquad (2)$$

where H_t is a histogram of body temperatures, f_{MSER} is MSER blobs for an image B.

Finally, we compute a distance between two signatures using Bhattacharyya distance for temperature histograms and MSER distance [6,31].

$$\begin{aligned} d(\hat{I}_i, I_j) = {} & \beta_H \cdot d_H(H_t(\hat{B}_i), H_t(B_j)) \\ & + (1 - \beta_H) \cdot d_{\text{MSER}}(f_{\text{MSER}}(\hat{B}_i), f_{\text{MSER}}(B_j)), \end{aligned} \qquad (3)$$

where d_H is a Bhattacharyya distance, d_{MSER} is a MSER distance [31], and β_H is a calibration weight parameter.

5   Evaluation

5.1   Network Training

The ThermalGAN framework was trained on the VOC split of the ThermalWorld dataset using the PyTorch library [38]. The VOC split includes indoor and outdoor scenes to avoid domain shift. The training was performed using the NVIDIA 1080 Ti GPU and took 76 h for G_1, D_1 and 68 h for G_2, D_2. For network optimization, we use minibatch SGD with an Adam solver. We set learning rate to 0.0002 with momentum parameters $\beta_1 = 0.5$, $\beta_2 = 0.999$ similar to [20].

616   V. V. Kniaz et al.

5.2   Color-to-Thermal Translation

Qualitative Comparison. For a qualitative comparison of the `ThermalGAN`
model on the color-to-thermal translation, we generate multiple thermal images
from the independent ReID split of ThermalWorld dataset. Our goal is to keep
the resulting images both realistic and diverse in terms of person relative thermal
contrasts. We compare our framework with five baselines: `pix2pix`+noise [20],
`cLR-GAN` [5,63], `cVAE-GAN` [26,63], `cVAE-GAN++` [26,63], `BicycleGAN` [63]. All
baselines were trained to convert color image to grayscale image representing
perceptual thermal contrasts (8-bit, grayscale). Our `ThermalGAN` framework was
trained to produce thermal images in degree Celsius. For comparison, they were
converted to perceptual thermal intensities. Results of multimodal thermal image
generation are presented in Fig. 6.

The results of `pix2pix`+noise are unrealistic and do not provide a changes
of thermal contrast. `cLR-GAN` and `cVAE-GAN` produce a slight variation of thermal contrasts but do not translate meaningful features for ReID. `cVAE-GAN++`
and `BicycleGAN` produce a diverse output, which fails to model thermal features present in real images. Our `ThermalGAN` framework combines the power of
`BicycleGAN` method with two-step sequential translation to produce the output
that is both realistic and diverse.

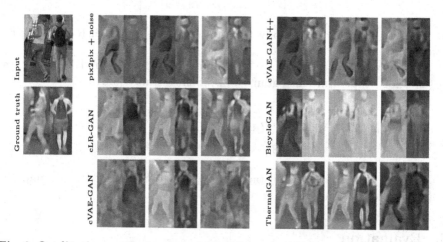

Fig. 6. Qualitative method comparison. We compare performance of various multimodal image translation frameworks on ThermalWorld ReID dataset. For each model,
we present three random output. The output of `ThermalGAN` framework is realistic,
diverse, and shows the small temperatures contrasts that are important for robust
ReID. Please note that only `ThermalGAN` framework produces output as calibrated
temperatures that can be used for thermal signature matching.

Quantitate Evaluation. We use the generated images to perform a quantitative analysis of our `ThermalGAN` framework and the baselines. We measure
two characteristics: diversity and perceptual realism. To measure multimodal

reconstruction diversity, we use the averaged Learned Perceptual Image Patch Similarity (LPIPS [57]) distance as proposed in [57,63]. For each baseline and our method, we calculate the average distance between 1600 pairs of random output thermal images, conditioned by 100 input color images. We measure perceptual realism of the synthesized thermal images using the human experts utilizing an approach similar to [56]. Real and synthesized thermal images are presented to human experts in a random order for one second. Each expert must indicate if the image is real or not. We perform the test on Amazon Mechanical Turk (AMT). We summarize the results of the quantitative evaluation in Fig. 7 and Table 2. Results of cLR-GAN, BicycleGAN and our ThermalGAN framework were most realistic. Our ThermalGAN model outperforms baselines in terms of both diversity and perceptual realism.

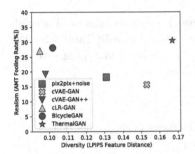

Fig. 7. Realism vs diversity for synthesized thermal images.

Table 2. Comparison with state-of-the-art multimodal image-to-image translation methods.

Method	Realism	Diversity
	AMT fooling rate [%]	LPIPS distance
Random real images	50.0%	
pix2pix+noise [20]	18.17	0.131
cVAE-GAN [26,63]	15.61	0.153
cVAE-GAN++ [26,63]	19.21	0.098
cLR-GAN [5,63]	27.10	0.095
BicycleGAN [63]	28.12	0.102
ThermalGAN	30.41	0.167

5.3 ReID Evaluation Protocol

We use 516 ID from the ReID split for testing the ReID performance. Please note, that we use independent VOC split for training color-to-thermal translation. We use cumulative matching characteristic (CMC) curves and normalized area-under-curve (nAUC) as a performance measure. The CMC curve presents a recognition performance versus re-identification ranking score. nAUC is an integral score of a ReID performance of a given method. To keep our evaluation protocol consistent with related work [4], we use 5 pedestrians in the validation set. We also keep independent the gallery set and the probe set according to the common practice.

We use images from color cameras for a probe set and images from thermal cameras for a gallery set. We exclude images from cameras #2, 9, 13 from the probe set, because they do not provide meaningful data in the visible range. We use a single color image in the single-shot setting. ThermalGAN ReID framework uses this single color image to generate 16 various thermal images. Baseline methods use the single input color image according to the common practice.

For the multi-shot setting, we use ten color images for the probe set. Therefore ThermalGAN framework generates 16 thermal images for each color probe image and generates 160 thermal images for the probe set.

5.4 Cross-Modality ReID Baselines

We compare our framework with six baseline models including hand-crafted features HOG [7] and modern deep-learning based cross-modality matching methods: One Stream Network (OSN) [47], Two Stream Network (TSN) [47], Deep Zero-Padding (DZP) [47], Two-stream CNN network (TONE_1) [52], and Modified two-stream CNN network (TONE_2) [51].

5.5 Comparison and Analysis

We show results of a comparison of our framework and baselines on Thermal-World ReID datasets in Table 3 for a single-shot setting and in Table 4 for the multi-shot setting. Results are given in terms of top-ranked matching rate and nAUC. We present the results in terms of CMC curves in Fig. 8.

Table 3. Experiments on ThermalWorld ReID dataset in single-shot setting.

Methods	ThermalWorld ReID single-shot					
	$r = 1$	$r = 5$	$r = 10$	$r = 15$	$r = 20$	nAUC
TONE_2 [51]	15.10	29.26	38.95	42.40	44.48	37.98
TONE_1 [52]	8.87	13.71	21.27	27.48	31.86	23.64
HOG [7]	14.29	23.56	33.45	40.21	43.92	34.86
TSN [47]	3.59	5.13	8.85	13.97	18.56	12.25
OSN [47]	13.29	23.11	33.05	40.06	42.76	34.27
DZP [47]	15.37	22.53	30.81	36.80	39.99	32.28
ThermalGAN	**19.48**	**33.76**	**42.69**	**46.29**	**48.19**	**41.84**

We make the following observations from the single-shot evaluation. Firstly, the two-stream network [47] performs the worst among other baselines. We assume that the reason is that fine-tuning of the network from near-infrared data to thermal range is not sufficient for effective matching. Secondly, hand-crafted HOG [7] descriptor provided discriminative features that present both in color and thermal images and can compete with some of modern methods. Finally, our ThermalGAN ReID framework succeeds in the realistic translation of meaningful features from color to thermal images and provides discriminative features for effective color-to-thermal matching.

Results in the multi-shot setting are encouraging and prove that multiple person detection improves the matching rate with a cross-modality setup. We

Table 4. Experiments on ThermalWorld ReID dataset in multi-shot setting.

Methods	ThermalWorld ReID multi-shot					
	r = 1	r = 5	r = 10	r = 15	r = 20	nAUC
TONE_2 [51]	20.11	38.19	51.62	56.73	59.38	50.30
TONE_1 [52]	11.10	17.79	24.18	31.58	36.66	27.46
HOG [7]	16.08	27.10	40.10	48.64	51.41	40.82
TSN [47]	8.71	14.97	21.10	26.30	29.87	23.21
OSN [47]	15.36	25.17	39.14	47.65	50.04	39.85
DZP [47]	14.62	24.14	33.09	39.57	44.08	34.78
ThermalGAN	**22.59**	**48.24**	**59.40**	**62.85**	**66.12**	**57.35**

conclude the following observations from the results presented in Table 4 and Fig. 8. Firstly, the performance of deep-learning-based baselines is improved in average in 5%. Secondly, multi-shot setting improves rank-5 and rank-10 recognition rates. Finally, our `ThermalGAN` method benefits from the multi-shot setting and can be used effectively with multiple person images provided by robust pedestrian detectors for thermal images [50].

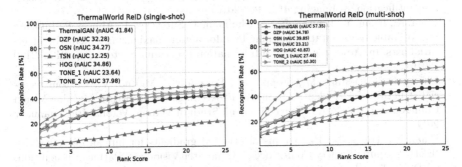

Fig. 8. CMC plot and nAUC for evaluation of baselines and `ThermalGAN` method in single-shot setting (left) and multi-shot setting (right).

6   Conclusion

We showed that conditional generative adversarial networks are effective for cross-modality prediction of a person appearance in thermal image conditioned by a probe color image. Furthermore, discriminative features can be extracted from real and synthesized thermal images for effective matching of thermal signatures. Our main observation is that thermal cameras coupled with a GAN ReID framework can significantly improve the ReID performance in low-light conditions.

We developed a `ThermalGAN` framework for cross-modality person ReID in the visible range and LWIR images. We have collected a large-scale multispectral ThermalWorld dataset to train our framework and compare it to baselines. We made the dataset publicly available. Evaluation of modern cross-modality ReID methods and our framework proved that our `ThermalGAN` method achieves the state-of-the-art and outperforms it in the cross-modality color-thermal ReID.

Acknowledgements. The reported study was funded by the Russian Science Foundation (RSF) according to the research project N° 16-11-00082.

References

1. Berg, A., Ahlberg, J., Felsberg, M.: A thermal infrared dataset for evaluation of short-term tracking methods. In: Swedish Symposium on Image Analysis (2015)
2. Berg, A., Ahlberg, J., Felsberg, M.: A thermal object tracking benchmark. In: 2015 12th IEEE International Conference on Advanced Video and Signal Based Surveillance (AVSS), pp. 1–6 (2015). http://ieeexplore.ieee.org/document/7301772/
3. Bhuiyan, A., Perina, A., Murino, V.: Person re-identification by discriminatively selecting parts and features. In: Agapito, L., Bronstein, M.M., Rother, C. (eds.) ECCV 2014. LNCS, vol. 8927, pp. 147–161. Springer, Cham (2015). https://doi.org/10.1007/978-3-319-16199-0_11
4. Bhuiyan, A., Perina, A., Murino, V.: Exploiting multiple detections for person re-identification. J. Imaging 4(2), 28 (2018)
5. Chen, X., Duan, Y., Houthooft, R., Schulman, J., Sutskever, I., Abbeel, P.: Infogan: interpretable representation learning by information maximizing generative adversarial nets. In: Advances in Neural Information Processing Systems, pp. 2172–2180 (2016)
6. Cheng, D.S., Cristani, M., Stoppa, M., Bazzani, L., Murino, V.: Custom pictorial structures for re-identification. In: Proceedings of the British Machine Vision Conference, BMVC 2011. Universita degli Studi di Verona, Verona, Italy, January 2011
7. Dalal, N., Triggs, B.: Histograms of oriented gradients for human detection. In: IEEE Computer Society Conference on Computer Vision and Pattern Recognition, CVPR 2005, vol. 1, pp. 886–893. IEEE (2005)
8. Davis, J.W., Keck, M.A.: A two-stage template approach to person detection in thermal imagery. In: Seventh IEEE Workshops on Application of Computer Vision, WACV/MOTIONS 2005, vol. 1, pp. 364–369. IEEE (2005)
9. Farenzena, M., Bazzani, L., Perina, A., Murino, V., Cristani, M.: Person re-identification by symmetry-driven accumulation of local features. In: 2010 IEEE Conference on Computer Vision and Pattern Recognition (CVPR), pp. 2360–2367. IEEE, March 2010
10. Forssén, P.E.: Maximally stable colour regions for recognition and matching. In: IEEE Conference on Computer Vision and Pattern Recognition, CVPR 2007, pp. 1–8. IEEE (2007)
11. Généreux, F., et al.: On the figure of merit of uncooled bolometers fabricated at INO. In: Infrared Technology and Applications XLII, vol. 9819, p. 98191U. International Society for Optics and Photonics (2016)

12. Gong, S., Cristani, M., Yan, S.: Person Re-Identification (Advances in Computer Vision and Pattern Recognition). Springer, London (2014). https://doi.org/10.1007/978-1-4471-6296-4
13. Goodfellow, I., et al.: Generative adversarial nets. In: Advances in Neural Information Processing Systems, pp. 2672–2680 (2014)
14. Gray, D., Brennan, S., Tao, H.: Evaluating appearance models for recognition, reacquisition, and tracking. In: IEEE International Workshop on Performance Evaluation for Tracking and Surveillance, Rio de Janeiro (2007)
15. Guadarrama, S., Dahl, R., Bieber, D., Norouzi, M., Shlens, J., Murphy, K.: Pixcolor: Pixel recursive colorization. arXiv preprint arXiv:1705.07208 (2017)
16. Guo, C.C., Chen, S.Z., Lai, J.H., Hu, X.J., Shi, S.C.: Multi-shot person re-identification with automatic ambiguity inference and removal. In: 2014 22nd International Conference on Pattern Recognition, pp. 3540–3545 (2014)
17. Herrmann, C., Müller, T., Willersinn, D., Beyerer, J.: Real-time person detection in low-resolution thermal infrared imagery with MSER and CNNs. In: Huckridge, D.A., Ebert, R., Lee, S.T. (eds.) SPIE Security + Defence, p. 99870I-8. SPIE, October 2016
18. Hirzer, M., Beleznai, C., Roth, P.M., Bischof, H.: Person re-identification by descriptive and discriminative classification. In: Heyden, A., Kahl, F. (eds.) SCIA 2011. LNCS, vol. 6688, pp. 91–102. Springer, Heidelberg (2011). https://doi.org/10.1007/978-3-642-21227-7_9
19. Hwang, S., Park, J., Kim, N., Choi, Y., So Kweon, I.: Multispectral pedestrian detection: benchmark dataset and baseline. In: The IEEE Conference on Computer Vision and Pattern Recognition (CVPR), June 2015
20. Isola, P., Zhu, J.Y., Zhou, T., Efros, A.A.: Image-to-image translation with conditional adversarial networks. In: 2017 IEEE Conference on Computer Vision and Pattern Recognition (CVPR), pp. 5967–5976. IEEE (2017)
21. John, V., Tsuchizawa, S., Liu, Z., Mita, S.: Fusion of thermal and visible cameras for the application of pedestrian detection. Sig. Image Video Process. 11(3), 517–524 (2016)
22. Jojic, N., Perina, A., Cristani, M., Murino, V., Frey, B.: Stel component analysis: modeling spatial correlations in image class structure. In: IEEE Conference on Computer Vision and Pattern Recognition, CVPR 2009, pp. 2044–2051. IEEE (2009)
23. Kniaz, V.V., Gorbatsevich, V.S., Mizginov, V.A.: Thermalnet: a deep convolutional network for synthetic thermal image generation. In: ISPRS - International Archives of the Photogrammetry, Remote Sensing and Spatial Information Sciences, vol. XLII-2/W4, pp. 41–45 (2017). https://doi.org/10.5194/isprs-archives-XLII-2-W4-41-2017
24. Kniaz, V.V., Mizginov, V.A.: Thermal texture generation and 3D model reconstruction using SFM and GAN. In: ISPRS - International Archives of the Photogrammetry, Remote Sensing and Spatial Information Sciences, vol. XLII-2, pp. 519–524 (2018). https://doi.org/10.5194/isprs-archives-XLII-2-519-2018
25. Knyaz, V.A., et al.: Deep learning of convolutional auto-encoder for image matching and 3D object reconstruction in the infrared range. In: The IEEE International Conference on Computer Vision (ICCV) Workshops, October 2017
26. Larsen, A.B.L., Sønderby, S.K., Larochelle, H., Winther, O.: Autoencoding beyond pixels using a learned similarity metric. In: Balcan, M.F., Weinberger, K.Q. (eds.) Proceedings of the 33rd International Conference on Machine Learning. Proceedings of Machine Learning Research, PMLR, New York, vol. 48, pp. 1558–1566, 20–22 June 2016. http://proceedings.mlr.press/v48/larsen16.html

27. Li, C., Wand, M.: Precomputed Real-Time Texture Synthesis with Markovian Generative Adversarial Networks. arXiv.org, April 2016
28. Li, W., Zhao, R., Wang, X.: Human reidentification with transferred metric learning. In: Lee, K.M., Matsushita, Y., Rehg, J.M., Hu, Z. (eds.) ACCV 2012. LNCS, vol. 7724, pp. 31–44. Springer, Heidelberg (2013). https://doi.org/10.1007/978-3-642-37331-2_3
29. Li, W., Zhao, R., Xiao, T., Wang, X.: DeepReID: deep filter pairing neural network for person re-identification. In: 2013 IEEE Conference on Computer Vision and Pattern Recognition, pp. 152–159. Chinese University of Hong Kong, Hong Kong. IEEE, January 2014
30. Limmer, M., Lensch, H.P.: Infrared colorization using deep convolutional neural networks. In: 2016 15th IEEE International Conference on Machine Learning and Applications (ICMLA), pp. 61–68. IEEE (2016)
31. Matas, J., Chum, O., Urban, M., Pajdla, T.: Robust wide baseline stereo from maximally stable extremal regions. In: Proceedings of the British Machine Vision Conference, pp. 36.1–36.10. British Machine Vision Association (2002)
32. Morerio, P., Cavazza, J., Murino, V.: Minimal-entropy correlation alignment for unsupervised deep domain adaptation. arXiv preprint arXiv:1711.10288 (2017)
33. Nguyen, D., Hong, H., Kim, K., Park, K.: Person recognition system based on a combination of body images from visible light and thermal cameras. Sensors **17**(3), 605–29 (2017)
34. Nguyen, D., Kim, K., Hong, H., Koo, J., Kim, M., Park, K.: Gender recognition from human-body images using visible-light and thermal camera videos based on a convolutional neural network for image feature extraction. Sensors **17**(3), 637–22 (2017)
35. Nguyen, D., Park, K.: Body-based gender recognition using images from visible and thermal cameras. Sensors **16**(2), 156–21 (2016)
36. Nguyen, D., Park, K.: Enhanced gender recognition system using an improved histogram of oriented gradient (HOG) feature from quality assessment of visible light and thermal images of the human body. Sensors **16**(7), 1134–25 (2016)
37. Nguyen, D.T., Hong, H.G., Kim, K.W., Park, K.R.: Person recognition system based on a combination of body images from visible light and thermal cameras. Sensors **17**(3), 605 (2017)
38. Paszke, A., et al.: Automatic differentiation in pytorch (2017)
39. Paul, A., Vogt, K., Rottensteiner, F., Ostermann, J., Heipke, C.: A comparison of two strategies for avoiding negative transfer in domain adaptation based on logistic regression. In: International Archives of the Photogrammetry, Remote Sensing and Spatial Information Sciences - ISPRS Archives, pp. 845–852. Gottfried Wilhelm Leibniz Universitat, Hannover, Germany, May 2018
40. Prosser, B., Gong, S., Xiang, T.: Multi-camera matching using bi-directional cumulative brightness transfer functions. In: Proceedings of the British Machine Vision Conference, BMVC 2008, pp. 64.1–64.10. Queen Mary, University of London, London, United Kingdom, British Machine Vision Association, January 2008
41. Ronneberger, O., Fischer, P., Brox, T.: U-Net: convolutional networks for biomedical image segmentation. In: Navab, N., Hornegger, J., Wells, W.M., Frangi, A.F. (eds.) MICCAI 2015. LNCS, vol. 9351, pp. 234–241. Springer, Cham (2015). https://doi.org/10.1007/978-3-319-24574-4_28
42. San-Biagio, M., Ulas, A., Crocco, M., Cristani, M., Castellani, U., Murino, V.: A multiple kernel learning approach to multi-modal pedestrian classification. In: 2012 21st International Conference on Pattern Recognition (ICPR), pp. 2412–2415. IEEE (2012)

43. St-Laurent, L., Maldague, X., Prévost, D.: Combination of colour and thermal sensors for enhanced object detection. In: 2007 10th International Conference on Information Fusion, pp. 1–8. IEEE (2007)

44. Ulyanov, D., Lebedev, V., Vedaldi, A., Lempitsky, V.S.: Texture networks - feed-forward synthesis of textures and stylized images. CoRR abs/1501.02565 1603, arXiv:1603.03417 (2016)

45. Méndez, H., Martín, C.S., Kittler, J., Plasencia, Y., García-Reyes, E.: Face recognition with LWIR imagery using local binary patterns. In: Tistarelli, M., Nixon, M.S. (eds.) ICB 2009. LNCS, vol. 5558, pp. 327–336. Springer, Heidelberg (2009). https://doi.org/10.1007/978-3-642-01793-3_34

46. Vogt, K., Paul, A., Ostermann, J., Rottensteiner, F., Heipke, C.: Unsupervised source selection for domain adaptation. Photogrammetric Eng. Remote Sens. **84**, 249–261 (2018)

47. Wu, A., Zheng, W.S., Yu, H.X., Gong, S., Lai, J.: RGB-infrared cross-modality person re-identification. In: The IEEE International Conference on Computer Vision (ICCV), October 2017

48. Wu, J., Wang, Y., Xue, T., Sun, X., Freeman, W.T., Tenenbaum, J.B.: MarrNet: 3D Shape Reconstruction via 2.5D Sketches. arXiv.org, November 2017

49. Xie, Z., Jiang, P., Zhang, S.: Fusion of LBP and HOG using multiple kernel learning for infrared face recognition. In: ICIS (2017)

50. Xu, D., Ouyang, W., Ricci, E., Wang, X., Sebe, N.: Learning cross-modal deep representations for robust pedestrian detection. In: 2017 IEEE Conference on Computer Vision and Pattern Recognition (CVPR), pp. 4236–4244. IEEE, April 2017

51. Ye, M., Lan, X., Li, J., Yuen, P.C.: Hierarchical discriminative learning for visible thermal person re-identification. In: AAAI (2018)

52. Ye, M., Wang, Z., Lan, X., Yuen, P.C.: Visible thermal person re-identification via dual-constrained top-ranking. In: Proceedings of the Twenty-Seventh International Joint Conference on Artificial Intelligence, pp. 1092–1099. International Joint Conferences on Artificial Intelligence Organization, California (2018)

53. Yilmaz, A., Shafique, K., Shah, M.: Tracking in airborne forward looking infrared imagery. Image Vis. Comput. **21**, 623–635 (2002)

54. Zhang, H., Patel, V.M., Riggan, B.S., Hu, S.: Generative adversarial network-based synthesis of visible faces from polarimetrie thermal faces. In: 2017 IEEE International Joint Conference on Biometrics (IJCB), pp. 100–107. IEEE (2017)

55. Zhang, M.M., Choi, J., Daniilidis, K., Wolf, M.T., Kanan, C.: VAIS - a dataset for recognizing maritime imagery in the visible and infrared spectrums. In: CVPR Workshops, pp. 10–16 (2015)

56. Zhang, R., Isola, P., Efros, A.A.: Colorful image colorization. In: Leibe, B., Matas, J., Sebe, N., Welling, M. (eds.) ECCV 2016. LNCS, vol. 9907, pp. 649–666. Springer, Cham (2016). https://doi.org/10.1007/978-3-319-46487-9_40

57. Zhang, R., Isola, P., Efros, A.A., Shechtman, E., Wang, O.: The unreasonable effectiveness of deep features as a perceptual metric. In: The IEEE Conference on Computer Vision and Pattern Recognition (CVPR), June 2018

58. Zhang, T., Wiliem, A., Yang, S., Lovell, B.C.: TV-GAN: Generative Adversarial Network Based Thermal to Visible Face Recognition, December 2017

59. Zheng, L., et al.: MARS: a video benchmark for large-scale person re-identification. In: Leibe, B., Matas, J., Sebe, N., Welling, M. (eds.) ECCV 2016. LNCS, vol. 9910, pp. 868–884. Springer, Cham (2016). https://doi.org/10.1007/978-3-319-46466-4_52

60. Zheng, L., Shen, L., Tian, L., Wang, S., Wang, J., Tian, Q.: Scalable person re-identification: a benchmark. In: Proceedings of the IEEE International Conference on Computer Vision, pp. 1116–1124. Tsinghua University, Beijing, China. IEEE, February 2015
61. Zheng, W.S., Gong, S., Xiang, T.: Associating groups of people. In: British Machine Vision Conference (2009)
62. Zhu, J.Y., et al.: Toward multimodal image-to-image translation. In: Advances in Neural Information Processing Systems, pp. 466–477. University of California, Berkeley, United States, January 2017
63. Zhu, J.Y., et al.: Toward multimodal image-to-image translation. In: Guyon, I., et al. (eds.) Advances in Neural Information Processing Systems, vol. 30, pp. 465–476. Curran Associates, Inc. (2017). http://papers.nips.cc/paper/6650-toward-multimodal-image-to-image-translation.pdf

Visual-Semantic Alignment Across Domains Using a Semi-Supervised Approach

Angelo Carraggi, Marcella Cornia$^{(\boxtimes)}$, Lorenzo Baraldi, and Rita Cucchiara

University of Modena and Reggio Emilia, Modena, Italy
angelo.carraggi@gmail.com,
{marcella.cornia,lorenzo.baraldi,rita.cucchiara}@unimore.it

Abstract. Visual-semantic embeddings have been extensively used as a powerful model for cross-modal retrieval of images and sentences. In this setting, data coming from different modalities can be projected in a common embedding space, in which distances can be used to infer the similarity between pairs of images and sentences. While this approach has shown impressive performances on fully supervised settings, its application to semi-supervised scenarios has been rarely investigated. In this paper we propose a domain adaptation model for cross-modal retrieval, in which the knowledge learned from a supervised dataset can be transferred on a target dataset in which the pairing between images and sentences is not known, or not useful for training due to the limited size of the set. Experiments are performed on two target unsupervised scenarios, respectively related to the fashion and cultural heritage domain. Results show that our model is able to effectively transfer the knowledge learned on ordinary visual-semantic datasets, achieving promising results. As an additional contribution, we collect and release the dataset used for the cultural heritage domain.

Keywords: Multi-modal retrieval · Visual-semantic embeddings
Semi-supervised learning

1 Introduction

Computer Vision and Natural Language Processing communities are converging toward unified approaches for pattern recognition problems, like providing descriptive feature vectors and finding cross-modality embedding spaces. As a matter of fact, architectures such as VGG [24] and ResNet [9] have been exploited for extracting representations from images, and word embeddings [2,19,22] are now a popular strategy for doing the same with text. The construction of common embeddings, on the other hand, has been proposed for solving tasks in which a connection between language and vision is needed, like automatic captioning [4,5,13] and retrieval of images and textual descriptions [1,8,11,20,27]: in this case, data from both modalities can be projected in the common space,

L. Leal-Taixé and S. Roth (Eds.): ECCV 2018 Workshops, LNCS 11134, pp. 625–640, 2019.
https://doi.org/10.1007/978-3-030-11024-6_47

and retrieved according to distances in the embedding. While the supervised training of a common visual-semantic embedding is feasible when using sufficiently large datasets, those techniques are unlikely applicable in the case of small scale datasets, or when the pairing between visual and textual elements is not provided. In both cases, it is beneficial to transfer the knowledge learned on large-scale datasets by using domain adaptation techniques.

Following this line of research, in this paper we propose a semi-supervised model for learning visual-semantic embeddings. Given a source dataset, in which the pairing between images and captions is known, our model is able to transfer its knowledge to a target domain, in which the pairing between the modalities is either not known in advance, or not useful for learning due to the restricted size of the set. The proposed model is based on a novel combination of visual and textual auto-encoders, embedding space learning strategies and domain alignment techniques. Specifically, two auto-encoders are trained, respectively for visual and textual data, and their intermediate representations are employed as features for training the visual-semantic embedding. The alignment between the distributions of the two modalities in the common embedding space ensures that the learned representations are general enough to be applied to the target domain.

We conduct experiments by using different source and target datasets. In particular, we test our model by transferring the knowledge learned on ordinary visual-semantic datasets to the case of fashion images and to the case of cultural heritage images. Preliminary analyses will showcase the distance between the source and target distributions, while experimental results will demonstrate the capabilities of the proposed approach, in comparison with two baselines which are built by ablating the core components of the method. As a complementary contribution, we collected and annotated the visual-semantic dataset used for the domain of cultural heritage.

To sum up, the contributions of this paper are threefold: (i) we propose a semi-supervised visual-semantic model which can transfer the knowledge learned on a source domain to a target, unsupervised, domain. To the best of our knowledge, we are the first to tackle this setting in the case of a visual-semantic embedding model. (ii) Secondly, we extensively evaluate our model under different settings and by using two different target domains, namely the fashion and cultural heritage domains. Experimental results will show that the proposed approach is able to outperform carefully designed baselines, and that the contributions provided by each of the components of the model are essential for gaining the final performance. (iii) Finally, we collect and release the visual-semantic dataset for cultural heritage used in this work.

2   Related Work

Matching visual data and natural language is a core challenge in computer vision and multimedia. Since visual and textual data belong to two distinct modalities, the problem is typically addressed by constructing a common visual-semantic embedding space in which images and corresponding sentences can be projected and compared. The retrieval, in this case, is then carried out by measuring distances inside the joint space, which should be low for matching text-image pairs and higher for non-matching pairs.

Following this line of work, Kiros et al. [14] introduced an encoder-decoder model capable of learning a common representation for images and text from which cross-modal retrieval can be effectively performed. Several other image and text matching methods have been proposed [7,8,11,20,27]. In particular, Faghri et al. [8] extended the method in [14] by exploiting the use of hard negatives and proposed a simple modification of standard loss functions obtaining a significant improvement in cross-modal retrieval performance. Wang et al. [27], instead, tackled the image-text matching problem using a two branch network. The network architecture consists of an embedding branch and a similarity network: while the embedding branch translates image and text into a feature representation, the similarity network decides how well the feature representations match, using logistic loss. On a different note, Dong et al. [6] proposed to search the visual space directly, instead of seeking a joint subspace for image and video caption retrieval. To this end, they introduced a deep neural model that encodes input captions into a multi-scale sentence embedding and transfers them into a visual feature space.

All of these methods have been proved to be effective to solve the cross-modal retrieval task, when trained with the supervision of a large dataset. None of them, however, addressed the problem in an unsupervised or semi-supervised setting. In this paper, instead, we are interested in adapting the knowledge learned on a given set of data (i.e. the source domain) to align images and text belonging to a different domain (i.e. the target domain), without directly training the network on the target domain. This solution, which is well known as domain adaptation, has been adopted in a wide variety of settings such as image classification [17], image-to-image translation [10], object detection [12], image captioning [3] and semantic segmentation [29]. Typically, it is addressed by minimizing the distance between feature space statistics of the source and target, or by using domain adversarial objectives where a domain classifier is trained to distinguish between the source and target representations.

Even though domain adaptation has been demonstrated to be effective for different computer vision and multimedia tasks, it has yet to be explored in the context of aligning images and corresponding sentences. Probably, the most important related method is that introduced in [26] which presents a semi-supervised approach to classify input images with the corresponding textual attributes. On the contrary, we aim at encoding entire sentences instead of textual attributes and at directly aligning them with the corresponding input image by addressing the cross-modal retrieval problem in a semi-supervised way.

3   Proposed Method

We propose a semi-supervised visual-semantic model which is capable of aligning images and text. In contrast to supervised cross-modal models, our proposal does not need a paired training set, in which the associations between images and captions are known in advance, but rather transfers the knowledge learned on a source annotated dataset to a target dataset in which the pairing between images and captions is unknown at training time.

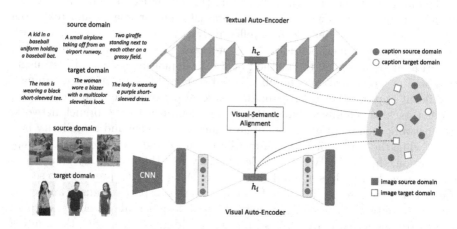

Fig. 1. Overview of our model. Two auto-encoders process visual and textual data and produce an intermediate representation for both modalities. These representations can be used to create a common embedding space in which images and corresponding sentences can be projected and compared. A semi-supervised visual-semantic alignment is exploited to match images and captions coming from a target domain, different from that used to train the model. (Color figure online)

The key element of our proposal is a network which can extract informative, discriminant and domain-invariant representations for both visual and textual data. Given a textual or visual input, this is processed by an auto-encoder which, through its reconstruction loss, naturally enforces the informativeness of its intermediate representation. Additional soft-constraints are then applied to the representation given by the auto-encoder, to ensure that the remaining desirable properties are met. Features extracted from the auto-encoder are employed to project the inputs in a joint visual-semantic embedding space, which can be trained on the source domain, so to ensure that the representation is also discriminant for cross-modal retrieval. Finally, the domain invariance of the features is enforced by applying alignment cost function between images and captions in the source and target domain. For the ease of the reader, we depict the overall architecture of the model in Fig. 1.

3.1   Textual Auto-Encoder

Recently, convolutional-based approaches for text representation have achieved competitive results in comparison to models based on recurrent neural networks [23,30]. This approach also features the additional benefit of being computationally friendly, as recurrent dependencies are removed and convolutions can be easily parallelized. Following this line of research, we develop an encoder-decoder model based on a purely convolutional network. The auto-encoder converts variable-length captions to fixed-length representations from which input sentences can be reconstructed. In particular, our model exploits 2-d convolutional layers for encoding an input sentence and deconvolutional layers (*i.e.* transpose convolutions) to decode from a hidden representation, without relying on a recurrent architecture.

For sentence encoding, we take inspiration from the architecture proposed in [23], in which the reduction in length carried out by convolutions is exploited to project the input into a representation with lower dimensionality. Furthermore, padding is exploited to process captions with variable length, without affecting the final performance. Given a caption c, each word $\mathbf{w}^t$ is embedded into a k-dimensional word vector $\mathbf{x}^t = \mathbf{W}_e[\mathbf{w}^t]$, where $\mathbf{W}_e$ is a learned word embedding matrix, normalized so that each word embedding has unit ℓ_2-norm. A sentence of length $T^{(0)}$ is obtained by stacking word embeddings $\mathbf{x}^t$ and padding the resulting matrix when necessary, thus obtaining a structure on which 2-d convolutions can be applied.

The input sequence is then fed to a network with N convolutional layers, where each of them reduces the length $T^{(n)}$ of its input to

$$T^{(n+1)} = \left\lfloor \frac{T^{(n)} - z}{r^{(n)}} + 1 \right\rfloor, \tag{1}$$

where $r^{(n)}$ is the stride of the n-th convolutional layer along the time dimension and z is the filter size. The output of the last convolutional layer is the intermediate representation vector $\mathbf{h}_c$ of the textual auto-encoder. This is obtained by using a convolutional layer with filter size equal to $T^{(n-1)}$ thus obtaining a vector that encapsulates the input sentence sub-structures.

For the decoding phase, we exploit strided deconvolutional layers to reconstruct the original sentence starting from $\mathbf{h}_c$. The decoder is composed of N layers that symmetrically increase the spatial size of the output by mirroring the corresponding convolutional layer of the encoder model. The output of the last layer of the decoder aims at reproducing the word embedding vector of each word of the original caption.

Denoting with $\hat{\mathbf{w}}^t$ the t-th word in the reconstructed caption $\hat{c}$, the probability of $\hat{\mathbf{w}}^t$ to be word v is defined as

$$p(\hat{\mathbf{w}}^t = v) = \frac{\exp[\tau^{-1} D_{\cos}(\hat{\mathbf{x}}^t, \mathbf{W}_e[v])]}{\sum_{v' \in V} \exp[\tau^{-1} D_{\cos}(\hat{\mathbf{x}}^t, \mathbf{W}_e[v'])]}, \tag{2}$$

where $D_{\cos}$ is the cosine similarity function, τ is a positive value representing the temperature parameter [30], $\hat{\mathbf{x}}^t$ is the reconstructed word embedding vector of the t-th word, and V is the vocabulary. Note that the cosine similarity can be obtained as the inner product between $\hat{\mathbf{X}} = \{\hat{\mathbf{x}}^0, \hat{\mathbf{x}}^1, ..., \hat{\mathbf{x}}^T\}$ and $\mathbf{W}_e$, since both matrices are ℓ_2-normed.

The overall loss function of the convolutional auto-encoder can be defined, for an input caption c, as the negative word-wise log-likelihood

$$\mathcal{L}_{\text{AE}}^{\text{c}}(c) = -\sum_t \log p(\hat{\mathbf{w}}^t = \mathbf{w}^t). \tag{3}$$

3.2 Visual Auto-Encoder

Given the auto-encoder for the textual part, we want to represent visual data in a similar way. In particular, we build an encoder-decoder model that can take an image feature vector as input and reconstruct it starting from an intermediate and more compact representation.

In detail, given an input image, we extract a feature vector from a pre-trained CNN and we feed it to an encoder model composed of a single fully connected layer. We indeed notice that a single layer leads to have a fairly informative representation of the image feature vector. Formally, let i be the input image and $\Phi(i)$ be the corresponding feature vector coming from the pre-trained convolutional network. We define the output of the encoder model $\mathbf{h}_i$ (*i.e.* the intermediate representation of the input image) as

$$\mathbf{h}_i = \tanh(W_e \Phi(i) + b_e), \tag{4}$$

where W_e and b_e are, respectively, the weight matrix and the bias vector of the encoder. Note that the output of the encoder layer is fed through a tanh non-linearity activation function.

The decoder model has a symmetric structure with respect to the encoder model. Therefore, starting from the intermediate vector $\mathbf{h}_i$, the decoder is composed by a single fully connected layer that transforms $\mathbf{h}_i$ to the size of the input image feature vector. Formally, the reconstructed image feature vector $\hat{i}$ is defined according to

$$\hat{i} = W_d \mathbf{h}_i + b_d, \tag{5}$$

where W_d and b_d are the weight matrix and the bias vector of the decoder fully connected layer. Overall, our image auto-encoder is trained to minimize the reconstruction error for each input image. Therefore, we define the decoder loss function as the mean square error between the original image feature vector $\Phi(i)$ and the corresponding reconstruction $\hat{i}$, as follows

$$\mathcal{L}_{\text{AE}}^{\text{i}}(i) = \|\hat{i} - \Phi(i)\|^2. \tag{6}$$

3.3 Visual-Semantic Embedding Space

The task of aligning images and corresponding sentences requires the ability to compare visual and textual data and to have a common representation of both domains. Therefore, we adopt the strategy of creating a joint visual-semantic embedding space in which visual and textual data can be projected and compared using a distance function.

Let $\mathbf{h}_i$ be the image representation coming from the encoder of the visual auto-encoder and $\mathbf{h}_c$ the corresponding textual representation coming from the convolutional auto-encoder for text. These representations can be compared in a joint embedding space by computing the cosine similarity between $\mathbf{h}_i$ and $\mathbf{h}_c$, so that the similarity between an image i and a caption c becomes

$$s(i,c) = \frac{\langle \mathbf{h}_i, \mathbf{h}_c \rangle}{\|\mathbf{h}_i\|\|\mathbf{h}_c\|}, \tag{7}$$

where, in the above formula, $\mathbf{h}_i$ and $\mathbf{h}_c$ are ℓ_2-normed to have the embedding space lying on the ℓ_2 ball.

In order to learn an embedding space with suitable cross-modal properties, we train this space according to a hinge triplet ranking loss with margin α, commonly used in image-text retrieval [8,14]:

$$\mathcal{L}_{\mathrm{SH}}(i,c) = \sum_{\bar{c}} [\alpha - s(i,c) + s(i,\bar{c})]_+$$
$$+ \sum_{\bar{i}} [\alpha - s(\bar{i},c) + s(i,c)]_+ \tag{8}$$

where $[x]_+ = \max(0,x)$. The loss defined above comprises two symmetric terms: the first sum is taken over all negative captions $\bar{c}$ given the query image i (*i.e.* all captions that do not describe the content of i), while the other is taken over all negative images $\bar{i}$ given the query c (*i.e.* all images that do not correspond to the description reported in c). In practice, given the size of the dataset and the number of possible negative samples, the sums of Eq. 8 are taken only inside the single mini-batch.

3.4   Aligning Distributions

In order to learn relationships between visual and textual features which can be exploited in a target unsupervised domain, we use domain alignment techniques. In particular, the distributions of text and images are aligned in the common embedding space through the Maximum Mean Discrepancy (MMD) criterion. The same alignment is applied to data coming from both the source and target domain, so that the MMD criterion, together with the triplet ranking loss, implicitly enforces an alignment between text and data coming from the target unsupervised domain.

MMD, in our case, can be viewed as a two-sample test between the distributions of text and images in the embedding space, and its loss can be defined as:

$$\mathcal{L}_{\mathrm{MMD}} = \|E_p[\xi(\mathbf{h}_i)] - E_q[\xi(\mathbf{h}_c)]\|_{\mathcal{H}_k}^2 \tag{9}$$

where p and q are, respectively, the distributions of the visual and textual embeddings (*i.e.*, $\mathbf{h}_i \sim p$ and $\mathbf{h}_c \sim q$) coming from both the source and target domain, ξ is a feature map defined through a kernel k, $\xi(\mathbf{x}) = k(\mathbf{x}, \cdot)$, and $\mathcal{H}_k$ is the reproducing kernel Hilbert space of k. The kernel is empirically chosen to be a Gaussian kernel, defined as follows:

$$k(\mathbf{x}, \mathbf{x}') = \exp\left(-\frac{1}{2\sigma^2}||\mathbf{x} - \mathbf{x}'||^2\right) \tag{10}$$

The MMD loss is minimized to shrink the gap between visual and textual features for the supervised and unsupervised datasets. Experimental results, which will be presented in the remainder of the paper, will show that the MMD loss helps to improve the model performance on the target domain.

3.5 Training

Our training protocol aims at learning the feature representations, the alignment and the visual semantic embedding jointly from scratch. Therefore, we minimize all the objective functions defined above at the same time. Recalling that $\mathcal{L}_{AE}^i$ is the loss function for the auto-encoder on the visual domain and $\mathcal{L}_{AE}^c$ is the loss function for the auto-encoder on the textual domain, we define a joint loss function for feature learning which is applied to both the source and target domain:

$$\mathcal{J}(i,c) = \mathcal{L}_{AE}^i(i) + \mathcal{L}_{AE}^c(c)$$
$$\mathcal{L}_{AE} = \sum_{i,c \in \mathcal{S}} \mathcal{J}(i,c) + \sum_{i,c \in \mathcal{T}} \mathcal{J}(i,c), \tag{11}$$

where $\mathcal{S}$ and $\mathcal{T}$ are respectively the source and target datasets. Finally, we obtain the loss function $\mathcal{L}$ for our model as:

$$\mathcal{L} = \mathcal{L}_{AE} + \mathcal{L}_{MMD} + \mathcal{L}_{SH}, \tag{12}$$

where $\mathcal{L}_{MMD}$ is the Maximum Mean Discrepancy function and $\mathcal{L}_{SH}$ is the ranking loss (applied only on the source domain). The loss is then minimized by backpropagation through Stochastic Gradient Descent.

4 Experimental Evaluation

In this section, in addition to describing employed datasets and implementation details, we provide extensive analyses and experiments to validate the proposed visual-semantic alignment model.

4.1 Datasets

For evaluating the effectiveness of our proposal, we perform experiments on different datasets. In particular, we employ two common visual-semantic datasets as source sets, and select two different target domains: fashion and artworks images.

A young man with shoulder length hair, who is wearing a dark jacket with a white collar.

A man who is wearing a golden armour is sitting on a throne and is surrounded by a large group of people.

A woman wearing a blue dress and a red cloak is sitting on a throne holding a naked baby and a book in her hands with two angels at the sides and a city in background.

A man with a light-blue cloak and a dog are looking to an angel over them.

A man with a white beard and a brown tunic is holding a crucifix.

A woman who is pointing the decapitated head of a man held by another man. On the right there are two men.

Fig. 2. Sample image-caption pairs from the EsteArtworks dataset. (Color figure online)

As source datasets, we use Flickr30K [28] and Microsoft COCO [15], which contain natural images and corresponding textual descriptions. Flickr30K is composed by 31,000 images, while COCO contains more than 120,000 images. Each image is annotated with 5 sentences describing the image content. Following the splits defined in [13], for Flickr30K we use 1,000 images for validation, 1,000 images for testing and the rest for training. For Microsoft COCO, instead, we use 5,000 images for both validation and test set.

To evaluate the generalization capabilities of our model, we employ two different target datasets containing image-sentence pairs respectively belonging to the fashion and cultural heritage domain. For the fashion domain, we employ Deep-Fashion [16], a large-scale publicly available dataset composed by over 800,000 fashion images ranging from well-posed shop images to unconstrained consumer photos. Only 78,979 images of this dataset are annotated with the corresponding sentences [31] which describe only the visual facts such as the color and the texture of the clothes or the length of the sleeves. These images are divided in train and test set, respectively composed by 70,000 and 8,979 images. In our experiments, we use 1,000 randomly selected training images as validation set. Following a common practice used for ordinary datasets [8], retrieval results on this dataset are reported by averaging over 8 folds of 1,000 test images each.

For the cultural heritage domain, instead, we collect 553 artworks from the Estense Gallery of Modena, which comprises Italian paintings and sculptures from the fourteenth to the eighteenth centuries. For each artwork, we collect at least one sentence describing the visual content of the artwork itself, without leveraging on personal cultural background regarding the opera or the depicted characters. Overall, we collect $1,278$ textual descriptions. Some image-sentence artwork pairs of our new EsteArtworks dataset are shown in Fig. 2. In our experiments, we split image samples in training, validation and test split according to a 60-20-20 ratio.

4.2 Implementation Details

In our experiments, we set the dimensionality of the intermediate representations for both auto-encoders to 500. For the textual auto-encoder, we set the number of convolutional and deconvolutional layers N to 3 and the word embedding dimensionality to 300. The filter size is set to $z = 4$, while the strides for each layer are set to $r = \{2, 2, 1\}$. For encoding input images, we exploit two popular CNNs: the ResNet-152 [9] and the VGG-19 [24]. In particular, we extract image features from the $fc7$ layer of VGG-19 and from the average pooling layer of ResNet-152, thus obtaining an input image feature vector dimensionality of 4096 and 2048, respectively. Since we use a single encoding layer in the visual auto-encoder, its output size is set to 500.

All experiments are performed with mini-batches of size 32 and using the Adam optimizer with an initial learning rate of 2×10^{-4} for 20 epochs, which is then decreased by a factor of 10 for the rest of the training. We set the margin α to 0.2 and the σ parameter of the Gaussian kernel to 1.0.

4.3 Analysis of Dataset Distributions

To get an insight of characteristics of the DeepFashion and EsteArtworks datasets, we analyze the distribution of image and textual features obtained, respectively, from CNNs and word embeddings, and compare them with those extracted from classical visual-semantic datasets.

For the visual part, we extract the activation coming from the $fc7$ layer of VGG-19 and the average pooling layer of ResNet-152. For textual counterpart, we embed each word of a caption with a word embedding strategy (*i.e.* GloVe [22] and FastText [2]). To get a feature vector for a sentence, we then sum the ℓ_2 normalized embeddings of the words, and ℓ_2 normalize again the result. This strategy has been largely used in image and video retrieval, and it is known for preserving the information of the original vectors into a compact representation with fixed dimensionality [25].

Figure 3 shows the distributions of visual and textual features of the Deep-Fashion and EsteArtworks datasets, compared with three ordinary visual-semantic datasets (*i.e.* Flickr8K, Flickr30K and COCO). In order to obtain a suitable two-dimensional representation of a K-dimensional space (with $K = 4096$ for the VGG-19, $K = 2048$ for the ResNet-152 and $K = 300$ for both

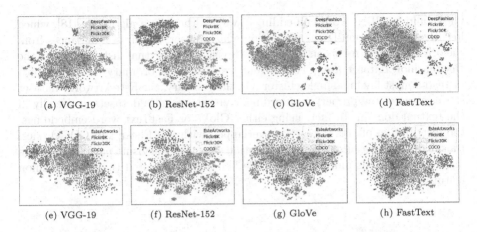

(a) VGG-19   (b) ResNet-152   (c) GloVe   (d) FastText

(e) VGG-19   (f) ResNet-152   (g) GloVe   (h) FastText

Fig. 3. Comparison between the visual and textual features of ordinary visual-semantic datasets (Flickr8K, Flickr30k, COCO) and those of the DeepFashion (plots a–d) and EsteArtworks (plots e–h) datasets. Visualization is obtained by running the t-SNE algorithm on top of the features. Best seen in color.

Table 1. Cross-domain caption and image retrieval results.

Target	Source	Model	Caption retrieval			Image retrieval		
			R@1	R@5	R@10	R@1	R@5	R@10
DeepFashion	Flickr30K	VSA-AE (*VGG-19*)	0.3	1.2	2.1	0.6	2.8	4.7
		VSA-AE (*ResNet-152*)	1.1	3.3	5.2	1.1	4.8	8.0
		VSA-E-MMD (*VGG-19*)	6.1	6.5	6.7	0.6	2.3	4.5
		VSA-E-MMD (*ResNet-152*)	2.0	5.3	6.6	1.0	4.0	6.6
		VSA-AE-MMD (*VGG-19*)	10.7	18.8	25.0	9.5	24.3	33.9
		VSA-AE-MMD (*ResNet-152*)	**13.5**	**23.3**	**30.3**	**10.6**	**27.2**	**38.2**
	COCO	VSA-AE (*VGG-19*)	0.4	1.4	2.3	0.3	1.9	3.9
		VSA-AE (*ResNet-152*)	0.4	1.5	2.7	0.3	2.6	5.3
		VSA-E-MMD (*VGG-19*)	4.6	6.0	6.4	0.4	2.0	3.7
		VSA-E-MMD (*ResNet-152*)	4.6	5.7	6.3	0.3	2.1	3.6
		VSA-AE-MMD (*VGG-19*)	12.9	21.5	27.7	10.7	28.2	37.8
		VSA-AE-MMD (*ResNet-152*)	**18.9**	**25.3**	**30.9**	**11.4**	**28.3**	**38.0**
EsteArtworks	Flickr30K	VSA-AE (*VGG-19*)	3.6	12.7	24.5	4.5	9.1	11.7
		VSA-AE (*ResNet-152*)	10.0	23.6	**39.1**	4.2	11.4	19.3
		VSA-E-MMD (*VGG-19*)	4.5	25.5	32.7	3.8	9.5	17.8
		VSA-E-MMD (*ResNet-152*)	8.2	**28.2**	37.3	6.8	15.5	24.2
		VSA-AE-MMD (*VGG-19*)	8.2	24.5	33.6	7.2	13.3	24.2
		VSA-AE-MMD (*ResNet-152*)	**10.9**	22.7	34.5	**8.0**	**17.8**	**25.0**
	COCO	VSA-AE (*VGG-19*)	2.7	17.3	22.7	3.4	7.6	12.1
		VSA-AE (*ResNet-152*)	9.1	18.2	23.6	3.0	14.0	17.0
		VSA-E-MMD (*VGG-19*)	7.3	19.1	30.0	5.7	11.0	16.3
		VSA-E-MMD (*ResNet-152*)	6.4	21.8	30.0	6.8	14.4	22.0
		VSA-AE-MMD (*VGG-19*)	10.9	26.4	37.3	**7.6**	16.3	24.2
		VSA-AE-MMD (*ResNet-152*)	10.9	**30.0**	**42.7**	**7.6**	**17.0**	**29.2**

GloVe and FastText word embeddings), we run the t-SNE algorithm [18], which iteratively finds a non-linear projection which preserves pairwise distances from the original space. As it can be seen, both visual and textual distributions of the DeepFashion dataset are very different from those of ordinary datasets which instead almost lay in a single cluster. On the contrary, the EsteArtworks dataset shares some of the properties of ordinary visual-semantic datasets, especially in the textual domain. In fact, using either GloVe or FastText word embeddings, the distribution of this dataset is overlapped with the Flickr and COCO ones, thus highlighting a similarity in the caption style. For the visual part, instead, the distribution shift is more evident while being less separated than DeepFashion features.

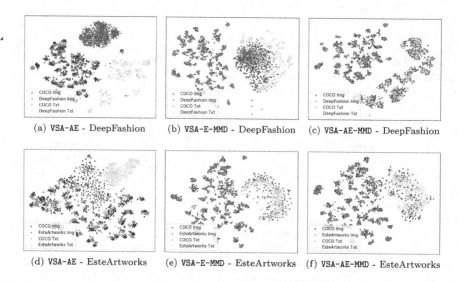

(a) VSA-AE - DeepFashion   (b) VSA-E-MMD - DeepFashion   (c) VSA-AE-MMD - DeepFashion

(d) VSA-AE - EsteArtworks   (e) VSA-E-MMD - EsteArtworks   (f) VSA-AE-MMD - EsteArtworks

Fig. 4. Visualization of the embedding spaces obtained by two considered baselines (VSA-AE and VSA-E-MMD) and that of our entire model (VSA-AE-MMD). Visualization is obtained by running the t-SNE algorithm on top of the visual and textual embedding vectors by comparing the COCO embedding space with the DeepFashion (plots a–c) and EsteArtworks (plots d–f) ones. Best seen in color.

4.4 Cross-Domain Retrieval Results

To evaluate the results of our model, we report rank-based performance metrics $R@K$ ($K = 1, 5, 10$) for image and caption retrieval. In particular, $R@K$ computes the percentage of test images or test sentences for which at least one correct result is found among the top-K retrieved sentences, in the case of caption retrieval, or the top-K retrieved images, in the case of image retrieval.

In our experiments, we compare the results obtained by our model with two different baselines. The first one is based on the two auto-encoders without the alignment of distributions given by the maximum-mean discrepancy function defined in Eq. 9. The second one is instead our model without the reconstruction losses for images and corresponding sentences defined in Eqs. 3 and 6 (*i.e.* our model without decoders). In the following, we refer to our complete visual-semantic alignment model as VSA-AE-MMD, to the first baseline without the distribution alignment as VSA-AE and to the second baseline without reconstruction losses as VSA-E-MMD.

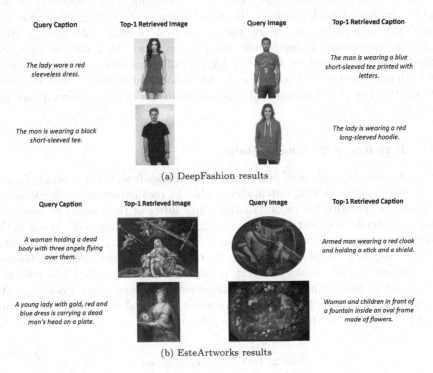

(a) DeepFashion results

(b) EsteArtworks results

Fig. 5. Examples of top-1 retrieved images and captions on the DeepFashion and EsteArtworks dataset. (Color figure online)

Table 1 shows the caption and image retrieval results on the two considered target domains when the model is trained on two different ordinary visual-semantic datasets. In particular, we report the results of our model and the two baselines by using both VGG-19 and ResNet-152 networks. As it can be observed, the overall performances of our visual-semantic alignment model are almost always better than those achieved by the two baselines. In particular, on the DeepFashion dataset both reconstruction losses and distribution alignment give a significant contribution to the final performances which overcome by a big margin the baselines. On the EsteArtworks dataset, instead, the gain of the alignment strategy is less evident even though the entire model still obtains a better performance than the two considered baselines. The difference in performance gain on the two datasets can be easily explained by the distribution analysis reported in Sect. 4.3. In fact, the visual and textual distributions of the EsteArtworks dataset are to some extent similar to those of Flickr30K and COCO, thus justifying the acceptable results even without using the distribution alignment or the reconstruction losses. On the contrary, the low baseline performances on the DeepFashion dataset is explained by the distance between this dataset and ordinary ones, on both visual and textual modalities.

As a further analysis, Fig. 4 shows the embedding spaces obtained by our model, compared with those of the two baselines. To obtain them, we run the t-SNE algorithm on top of the visual and textual embedding vectors (*i.e.* the outputs of the image and caption encoders). As it can be seen, our VSA-AE-MMD model leads to a better alignment of visual and textual embeddings on both target datasets. Finally, Fig. 5 reports some qualitative results by showing the top-1 retrieved images and captions on the fashion and cultural heritage domains.

4.5 Text Reconstruction Results

In addition to aligning visual and textual embeddings from two different domains in a semi-supervised way, our model is able to reconstruct the original input caption. To quantify the reconstruction capabilities of the model, we compute machine translation metrics between original and reconstructed sentences. In particular, we employ the BLEU [21] score, which is a modified form of precision between n-grams, to compare a candidate translation against multiple reference translations. Table 2 shows the text reconstruction results on Flickr30K and COCO when forcing the distribution alignment on the two target domains. As it can be seen, our model is able to reconstruct high quality sentences, achieving a BLUE score higher than 0.9 in all considered cases.

Table 2. Text reconstruction results.

Evaluation dataset	Unsupervised domain	BLEU@2	BLEU@3	BLEU@4
Flickr30K	DeepFashion	0.969	0.961	0.952
	EsteArtworks	0.955	0.942	0.928
COCO	DeepFashion	0.991	0.988	0.985
	EsteArtworks	0.988	0.984	0.980

5   Conclusions

In this paper, we addressed the problem of learning visual-semantic embeddings to perform cross-modal retrieval across different domains. In particular, we proposed a semi-supervised model that is able to transfer the knowledge learned on a source dataset to a target domain, where the pairing between images and corresponding sentences is either not known or not useful due to its limited size.

We applied the proposed strategy to two different target domains (*i.e.* fashion and cultural heritage) and we showed through extensive analyses and experiments the effectiveness of the proposed model. As a side contribution, given the lack of visual-semantic datasets for the cultural heritage domain, we collected artworks images and annotated them with the corresponding sentences.

Acknowledgements. This work was supported by the CultMedia project (CTN02_00015_9852246), co-founded by the Italian MIUR. We also acknowledge the support of Facebook AI Research with the donation of the GPUs used for this research.

References

1. Baraldi, L., Cornia, M., Grana, C., Cucchiara, R.: Aligning text and document illustrations: towards visually explainable digital humanities. In: International Conference on Pattern Recognition (2018)
2. Bojanowski, P., Grave, E., Joulin, A., Mikolov, T.: Enriching word vectors with subword information. arXiv preprint arXiv:1607.04606 (2016)
3. Chen, T.H., Liao, Y.H., Chuang, C.Y., Hsu, W.T., Fu, J., Sun, M.: Show, adapt and tell: adversarial training of cross-domain image captioner. In: IEEE International Conference on Computer Vision (2017)
4. Cornia, M., Baraldi, L., Serra, G., Cucchiara, R.: Visual saliency for image captioning in new multimedia services. In: IEEE International Conference on Multimedia and Expo Workshops (2017)
5. Cornia, M., Baraldi, L., Serra, G., Cucchiara, R.: Paying more attention to saliency: image captioning with saliency and context attention. ACM Trans. Multimedia Comput. Commun. Appl. **14**(2), 48 (2018)
6. Dong, J., Li, X., Snoek, C.G.: Predicting visual features from text for image and video caption retrieval. IEEE Trans. Multimedia **20**, 3377–3388 (2018)
7. Eisenschtat, A., Wolf, L.: Linking image and text with 2-way nets. In: IEEE International Conference on Computer Vision and Pattern Recognition (2017)
8. Faghri, F., Fleet, D.J., Kiros, J.R., Fidler, S.: Vse++: improving visual-semantic embeddings with hard negatives. arXiv preprint arXiv:1707.05612 (2017)
9. He, K., Zhang, X., Ren, S., Sun, J.: Deep residual learning for image recognition. In: IEEE International Conference on Computer Vision and Pattern Recognition (2016)
10. Hoffman, J., et al.: CyCADA: cycle-consistent adversarial domain adaptation. arXiv preprint arXiv:1711.03213 (2017)
11. Huang, Y., Wang, W., Wang, L.: Instance-aware image and sentence matching with selective multimodal LSTM. In: IEEE International Conference on Computer Vision and Pattern Recognition (2017)
12. Inoue, N., Furuta, R., Yamasaki, T., Aizawa, K.: Cross-domain weakly-supervised object detection through progressive domain adaptation. In: IEEE International Conference on Computer Vision and Pattern Recognition (2018)
13. Karpathy, A., Fei-Fei, L.: Deep visual-semantic alignments for generating image descriptions. In: IEEE International Conference on Computer Vision and Pattern Recognition (2015)
14. Kiros, R., Salakhutdinov, R., Zemel, R.S.: Unifying visual-semantic embeddings with multimodal neural language models. arXiv preprint arXiv:1411.2539 (2014)

15. Lin, T.-Y., et al.: Microsoft COCO: common objects in context. In: Fleet, D., Pajdla, T., Schiele, B., Tuytelaars, T. (eds.) ECCV 2014. LNCS, vol. 8693, pp. 740–755. Springer, Cham (2014). https://doi.org/10.1007/978-3-319-10602-1_48
16. Liu, Z., Luo, P., Qiu, S., Wang, X., Tang, X.: Deepfashion: powering robust clothes recognition and retrieval with rich annotations. In: IEEE International Conference on Computer Vision and Pattern Recognition (2016)
17. Long, M., Zhu, H., Wang, J., Jordan, M.I.: Deep transfer learning with joint adaptation networks. In: International Conference on Machine Learning (2017)
18. van der Maaten, L., Hinton, G.: Visualizing data using t-SNE. J. Mach. Learn. Res. **9**, 2579–2605 (2008)
19. Mikolov, T., Sutskever, I., Chen, K., Corrado, G.S., Dean, J.: Distributed representations of words and phrases and their compositionality. In: Advances in Neural Information Processing Systems (2013)
20. Nam, H., Ha, J.W., Kim, J.: Dual attention networks for multimodal reasoning and matching. In: IEEE International Conference on Computer Vision and Pattern Recognition (2017)
21. Papineni, K., Roukos, S., Ward, T., Zhu, W.J.: BLEU: a method for automatic evaluation of machine translation. In: 40th Annual Meeting on Association for Computational Linguistics (2002)
22. Pennington, J., Socher, R., Manning, C.D.: GloVe: global vectors for word representation. In: Conference on Empirical Methods in Natural Language Processing (2014)
23. Radford, A., Metz, L., Chintala, S.: Unsupervised representation learning with deep convolutional generative adversarial networks. In: International Conference on Learning Representations (2016)
24. Simonyan, K., Zisserman, A.: Very deep convolutional networks for large-scale image recognition. arXiv preprint arXiv:1409.1556 (2014)
25. Tolias, G., Sicre, R., Jégou, H.: Particular object retrieval with integral max-pooling of CNN activations. In: International Conference on Learning Representations (2016)
26. Tsai, Y.H.H., Huang, L.K., Salakhutdinov, R.: Learning robust visual-semantic embeddings. In: IEEE International Conference on Computer Vision (2017)
27. Wang, L., Li, Y., Lazebnik, S.: Learning two-branch neural networks for image-text matching tasks. IEEE Trans. Pattern Anal. Mach. Intell. (2018)
28. Young, P., Lai, A., Hodosh, M., Hockenmaier, J.: From image descriptions to visual denotations: new similarity metrics for semantic inference over event descriptions. Trans. Assoc. Computat. Linguist. **2**, 67–78 (2014)
29. Zhang, Y., David, P., Gong, B.: Curriculum domain adaptation for semantic segmentation of urban scenes. In: IEEE International Conference on Computer Vision (2017)
30. Zhang, Y., Shen, D., Wang, G., Gan, Z., Henao, R., Carin, L.: Deconvolutional paragraph representation learning. In: Advances in Neural Information Processing Systems (2017)
31. Zhu, S., Fidler, S., Urtasun, R., Lin, D., Loy, C.C.: Be your own prada: fashion synthesis with structural coherence. In: IEEE International Conference on Computer Vision (2017)

Generalized Bayesian Canonical Correlation Analysis with Missing Modalities

Toshihiko Matsuura[1]($\boxtimes$)(iD), Kuniaki Saito[1](iD), Yoshitaka Ushiku[1],
and Tatsuya Harada[1,2]

[1] The University of Tokyo, Tokyo, Japan
{matsuura,k-saito,ushiku,harada}@mi.t.u-tokyo.ac.jp
[2] RIKEN, Tokyo, Japan

Abstract. Multi-modal learning aims to build models that can relate information from multiple modalities. One challenge of multi-modal learning is the prediction of a target modality based on a set of multiple modalities. However, there are two challenges associated with the goal: Firstly, collecting a large, complete dataset containing all required modalities is difficult; some of the modalities can be missing. Secondly, the features of modalities are likely to be high dimensional and noisy. To deal with these challenges, we propose a method called Generalized Bayesian Canonical Correlation Analysis with Missing Modalities. This method can utilize the incomplete sets of modalities. By including them in the likelihood function during training, it can estimate the relationships among the non-missing modalities and the feature space in the non-missing modality accurately. In addition, this method can work well on high dimensional and noisy features of modalities. This is because, by a probabilistic model based on the prior knowledge, it is strong against outliers and can reduce the amount of data necessary for the model learning even if features of modalities are high dimensional. Experiments with artificial and real data demonstrate our method outperforms conventional methods.

Keywords: Multi-modal learning · Missing modalities
Bayesian inference · Canonical Correlation Analysis

1 Introduction

In the field of machine learning, multi-modal learning, which models relationships among multiple modalities, has been studied actively. One challenge of multi-modal learning is to construct a predictive model from a set of multiple modalities to a certain modality. We call the modality to be predicted *target modality* and the modality to be used to predict a target modality *source modality*. As a model for estimating the relationship between different modalities,

---

T. Matsuura and K. Saito—Contributed equally.

L. Leal-Taixé and S. Roth (Eds.): ECCV 2018 Workshops, LNCS 11134, pp. 641–656, 2019.
https://doi.org/10.1007/978-3-030-11024-6_48

	Source modalities		Target modality
	Modality 1	Modality 2	Modality 3
Element 1	✓	✗	✓
Element 2	✓	✗	✗
Element 3	✓	✓	✓
Element 4	✗	✓	✓
⋮	⋮	⋮	⋮

Fig. 1. An example of a real sample missing modalities. ✓ means that the modality is provided and ✗ means that it is not provided. In this figure, only Element 3 provides all modalities and the others have missing modalities in various patterns. GBCCA-M2 can utilize all elements in learning and predict a target modality from source modalities.

canonical correlation analysis (CCA) [9] is representative, and there are prior studies that actually use CCA for prediction [7]. Also, note that we will call the set of modalities collected from an object an *element*, and we will refer to a group of elements as a *sample* respectively.

There are two challenges in building such a model: some modalities are missing for any reason. For example, in purchaser behavior prediction, some people often refuse to provide some modalities because of their privacy. As Fig. 1 shows, there are various patterns of missing modalities, which makes the problem more difficult. Further, the features of modalities likely to be high dimensional and noisy. The situation occurs when we collect a large amount of information. To deal with these challenges, we propose a method called Generalized Bayesian Canonical Correlation Analysis with Missing Modalities (GBCCA-M2). This method can learn relationships among different modalities utilizing the incomplete sets of modalities by including them in the likelihood function. This study is motivated by the previous works [13, 26] which utilized incomplete sets of modalities. These previous works were proposed to learn the relationships between two different modalities, whereas our method can deal with more than two different modalities. In addition, this method works well on high dimensional and noisy modalities thanks to the prior knowledge incorporated on the parameters of a model. The prior knowledge is introduced to control the sparsity of the weight parameters linking each latent variable to modalities, which makes the model robust to high dimensional and noisy features of modalities. The main contributions of this paper are as follows:

- We propose Generalized Bayesian Canonical Correlation Analysis with Missing Modalities (GBCCA-M2) which is a learning model that can account for elements with missing modalities in the likelihood function.
- Through an experiment using artificial data, we demonstrate that GBCCA-M2 improves prediction performance when using elements with missing modalities, and it is effective for high dimensional and noisy modalities.
- Through an experiment using real data, we demonstrate that GBCCA-M2 is more effective for predicting purchaser behavior and retrieving images from English and Japanese sentences than existing methods.

2 Related Work

Through much research on multi-modal learning, it has been determined in various tasks that performance can be improved by using multiple source modalities rather than using only one [10, 25]. CCA [9] is a method that learns relationships between two modalities. Given pairs of modalities, the model learns to project them into the latent space where they are maximally correlated. CCA has many variants, such as Generalized CCA [5], kernel extensions [1, 15], probabilistic CCA (PCCA) [3] and Bayesian CCA (BCCA) [14, 23]. Generalized CCA extends to CCA in order to capture relationships among more than two modalities. The probabilistic models such as PCCA or BCCA incorporate prior knowledge into their parameters and can learn relationships between high dimensional and noisy features of modalities. We explain the details of BCCA in Sect. 3. The difficulty in learning relationships between paired modalities is that it is often expensive to collect a large number of paired modalities. In reality, there are a limited number of paired modalities; however, unpaired modalities may be accessible. To overcome this problem, extensions of CCA for semi-supervised learning have been proposed (e.g., Semi CCA [13], Semi PCCA [11, 26]). Semi PCCA can deal with elements that are missing modalities by describing likelihood for use with them. However, this method can only deal with the case where only one of the two modalities is missing. Therefore, we will introduce the methods that are used for general missing data analysis below.

Statistical analysis of missing data is roughly classified as one of the following three types [17]: (1) complete case analysis (CC) [12, 20], (2) imputation of missing values, and (3) describing likelihood for use with missing data. CC is simple, but elements with missing values are not utilized. As for imputation of missing values, this includes mean imputation, regression imputation, or multiple imputation. Methods for complementing missing values by autoencoder [8] have also been developed, and the extensions, such as Cascaded Residual Autoencoder [22] attacks the cases where the modalities are missing. Since imputations of missing values mainly assume that the missing values occur randomly, they are not suitable for the case of missing modalities. As for the studies on describing likelihood for use with missing data [6, 18, 26], it is known that these methods hold looser assumptions than CC and imputation of missing values. However, these methods merely estimate the distribution of data or regress missing values. Although a regression can be performed using parameters learned by Semi PCCA, this is not suitable for the case of multi-modal learning with missing modalities. In our experiments, we use CC and mean imputation to make spuriously complete data for comparison of methods.

3 Generalized Bayesian Canonical Correlation Analysis with Missing Modalities

Since our proposed method is motivated by Bayesian CCA (BCCA) [14, 23] and Semi CCA [13], we will first review these two methods separately.

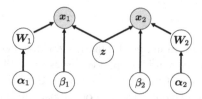

Fig. 2. Graphical illustration of the BCCA model as a plate diagram. The shaded nodes indicate the two observed variables, and the other nodes indicate the model parameters to be estimated. The latent variable z captures the correlation between x_1 and x_2.

3.1 Bayesian Canonical Correlation Analysis

BCCA [14,23] is a method that adapts the hierarchical Bayesian model to CCA [9]. Fujiwara et al. [7] proposed a new BCCA model to reconstruct images from human brain information. As shown in Fig. 2, the new model captures the relationships between the two modalities. In the model, modalities $x_i \in \mathbb{R}^{d_i}$ ($i = 1, 2$) are generated by common latent variables $z \in \mathbb{R}^{d_z}, d_z \leq \min(d_i)$ and weight matrices $W_i \in \mathbb{R}^{d_i \times d_z}$, where d_i and d_z represent the dimension of modalities and latent variables, respectively. In addition, weight matrices are controlled by parameters $\alpha_i \in \mathbb{R}^{d_i \times d_z}$. The likelihood of the modalities is

$$P(x_i|W_i, z) \propto \exp\left(-\frac{1}{2} \sum_{n=1}^{N} (x_i(n) - W_i z(n))^{\mathrm{T}} \beta_i (x_i(n) - W_i z(n)) \right), \quad (1)$$

where $\beta_i I_{d_z} (\beta_i \in \mathbb{R}^1)$ represents covariance of the Gaussian distribution, I_d represents a $d \times d$ identity matrix, and, N represents the sample size. The prior distribution of latent variables is

$$P_0(z) \propto \exp\left(-\frac{1}{2} \sum_{n=1}^{N} \|z(n)\|^2 \right). \quad (2)$$

Latent variables are generated from the Gaussian distribution whose mean is $\mathbf{0}$ and whose covariance is I. The prior distribution of weight matrices is

$$P_0(W_i|\alpha_i) \propto \exp\left(-\frac{1}{2} \sum_{s=1}^{d_i} \sum_{t=1}^{d_z} \alpha_{i(s,t)} W_{i(s,t)}^2 \right). \quad (3)$$

The (s, t) element of weight matrices is generated from the Gaussian distribution whose mean is $W_{i(s,t)}$ and whose covariance is $\alpha_{i(s,t)}$. Weight matrices are controlled by hyper-parameters α_i, whose hyper-prior distribution is

$$P_0(\alpha_i) = \prod_{s=1}^{d_i} \prod_{t=1}^{d_z} \mathcal{G}(\alpha_{i(s,t)}|\overline{\alpha}_{i(s,t)}, \gamma_{i(s,t)}), \quad (4)$$

where $\mathcal{G}(\alpha|\overline{\alpha}, \gamma)$ is the Gamma distribution whose mean is $\overline{\alpha}$ and whose confidence parameter is γ. This probability model (Eqs. (1) and (4)) is known as

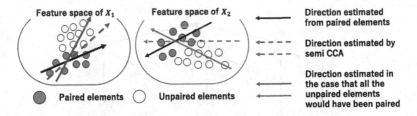

Fig. 3. An example of spatial estimation by Semi CCA. By using unpaired elements, we can estimate a direction closer to that estimated in the case that all the unpaired elements would have been paired, than by using only paired elements.

automatic relevance determination (ARD) [19], which drives unnecessary components to zero. The prior distribution of observation noise β_i is

$$P_0(\beta_i) = \frac{1}{\beta_i}, \tag{5}$$

which is called non-informative priors. Parameters are estimated by variational Bayesian inference [2], and the predictive distribution of the target modality is driven using these estimated parameters (Fig. 3).

3.2 Semi Canonical Correlation Analysis

Semi CCA [13] is a method that extends CCA to a semi-supervised one by combining CCA and principal component analysis (PCA). We denote the group of elements whose modalities are paired as P, the ones whose are not paired as U, and the sample covariance matrices as Σs. The solution of Semi CCA can be obtained by solving the following general eigenvalue problem.

$$B \begin{pmatrix} w_1 \\ w_2 \end{pmatrix} = \lambda C \begin{pmatrix} w_1 \\ w_2 \end{pmatrix}, \tag{6}$$

$$B = \beta \begin{pmatrix} 0 & \Sigma_{12}^{(P)} \\ \Sigma_{21}^{(P)} & 0 \end{pmatrix} + (1-\beta) \begin{pmatrix} \Sigma_{11}^{(P+U)} & 0 \\ 0 & \Sigma_{22}^{(P+U)} \end{pmatrix}, \tag{7}$$

$$C = \beta \begin{pmatrix} \Sigma_{12}^{(P)} & 0 \\ 0 & \Sigma_{21}^{(P)} \end{pmatrix} + (1-\beta) \begin{pmatrix} I_{D_1} & 0 \\ 0 & I_{D_2} \end{pmatrix}. \tag{8}$$

β represents the contribution ratio of CCA to PCA. Similar to this, we introduce contribution rates of elements missing modalities to GBCCA-M2. Semi CCA has an application in probabilistic models, such as Probabilistic Semi CCA [11, 26]. However, they are not suitable for high dimensional and noisy features of modalities because the premise that weight matrices become sparse in learning is not assumed, which causes overfitting.

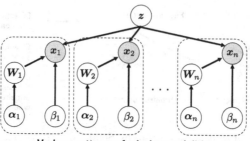

Various patterns of missing modalities

Fig. 4. Graphical illustration of the GBCCA-M2 model as a plate diagram. Each element used in learning has two or more modalities and various missing patterns. The shaded nodes x_i indicate the observed variables. The latent variable z captures the correlations among the x_is.

3.3 Generalized Bayesian Canonical Correlation Analysis with Missing Modalities

As mentioned in Sect. 1, some of the modalities are missing and the features of them are high dimensional and noisy. Considering these characteristics, the following functions are necessary for our method: (F1) dealing with various patterns of missing modalities, (F2) dealing with more than two different modalities, (F3) highly accurate prediction for high dimensional and noisy features of modalities. BCCA meets F3, so we extend it so as to meet F1 and F2 through the proposed GBCCA-M2. We construct the model of GBCCA-M2 while considering the following: (1) the number of modalities should be increased more than two, and all modalities are generated from common latent variables and (2) the contribution rates to the likelihood are changed according to how many modalities are missing. The graphical model of GBCCA-M2 is shown in Fig. 4. Now, we introduce the likelihood and prior distribution of GBCCA-M2, parameter estimation by a variational Bayesian inference, and the prediction of target modality using source modalities and estimated parameters.

The Likelihood and Prior Distribution: The likelihood of modalities is

$$P\left(x_i | W_i, z\right) = \prod_{m=1}^{M} P\left(x_i^{(m)} | W_i, z^{(m)}\right)^{\eta_m} \tag{9}$$

$$P\left(x_i^{(m)} | W_i, z^{(m)}\right) \propto \exp\left(-\frac{1}{2} \sum_{n=1}^{N_i^{(m)}} \left(x_i^{(m)}(n) - W_i z^{(m)}(n)\right)^{\mathrm{T}} \beta_i \left(x_i^{(m)}(n) - W_i z^{(m)}(n)\right)\right), \tag{10}$$

where $x_i^{(m)}$ represents the i-th modality of an element that has m sets of modalities, M represents the number of modalities, and $N_i^{(m)}$ represents the number of elements which have m sets of modalities and the i-th modality of them is not missing. Moreover, we introduce contribution rates η_m of elements missing modalities to the likelihood function and change them according to the degree of missing modalities. Especially, the more modalities are missing, the smaller the contribution rates should be ($\eta_1 < \eta_2 < \eta_3 < \cdots$), and the more elements missing modalities are, the smaller contribution rates should be, which is reflected in Fig. 5. Owing to them, we can properly utilize elements missing modalities. As with BCCA, prior distributions and the hyper-prior distribution of each parameter are as follows:

$$P_0\left(z^{(m)}\right) \propto \exp\left(-\frac{1}{2}\sum_{n=1}^{N^{(m)}} \|z^{(m)}(n)\|^2\right), \tag{11}$$

$$P_0\left(W_i|\alpha_i\right) \propto \exp\left(-\frac{1}{2}\sum_{s=1}^{d_i}\sum_{t=1}^{d_z} \alpha_{i_{(s,t)}} W_{i_{(s,t)}}^2\right), \tag{12}$$

$$P_0(\alpha_i) = \prod_{s=1}^{d_i}\prod_{t=1}^{d_z} \mathcal{G}\left(\alpha_{i_{(s,t)}}|\overline{\alpha}_{i_{(s,t)}}, \gamma_{i_{(s,t)}}\right), \tag{13}$$

$$P_0\left(\beta_i\right) = \frac{1}{\beta_i}. \tag{14}$$

Parameter Estimation by Variational Bayesian Inference: Given the likelihood (Eqs. (9) and (10)); the prior distribution (Eqs. (11), (12) and (14)); and the hyper-prior distribution (Eq. (13)), weight matrices are estimated as the posterior distribution $P(W_1, \cdots, W_M | x_1, \cdots, x_M)$. This posterior distribution is obtained by marginalizing the joint posterior distributions with respect to latent variables and variance parameters α_i, β_i as follows:

$$P\left(W_1, \cdots, W_M | x_1, \cdots, x_M\right) = \int dz d\alpha_1 \cdots d\alpha_M d\beta_1 \cdots d\beta_M$$
$$P(W_1, \cdots, W_M, z, \alpha_1, \cdots, \alpha_M, \beta_1, \cdots, \beta_M | x_1, \cdots, x_M). \tag{15}$$

This joint posterior distribution cannot be calculated analytically, so it is approximated by using a trial distribution with the following factorization based on variational Bayes inference.

$$Q\left(W_1, \cdots, W_M, z, \alpha_1, \cdots, \alpha_M, \beta_1, \cdots, \beta_M\right)$$
$$= Q_W(W_1) \cdots Q_W(W_M) Q_z(z) Q_\alpha(\alpha_1, \cdots, \alpha_M, \beta_1, \cdots, \beta_M). \tag{16}$$

The trial distribution of weight matrices $Q_W(W_i)$ is

$$Q_W\left(W_i\right) = \prod_{s=1}^{d_i}\prod_{t=1}^{d_z} \mathcal{N}\left(W_{i_{(s,t)}}|\overline{W}_{i_{(s,t)}}, \sigma_{i_{(s,t)}}^{-1}\right), \tag{17}$$

$$\overline{W}_{i_{(s,t)}} = \overline{\beta}_i \sigma_{i_{(s,t)}}^{-1} \sum_{m=1}^{M}\left(\eta_m \cdot \sum_{n=1}^{N_i^{(m)}} x_{i_s}^{(m)}(n) z_t^{(m)}(n)\right), \tag{18}$$

$$\sigma_{i_{(s,t)}}^{-1} = \overline{\beta}_i \sum_{m=1}^{M}\left(\eta_m \cdot \sum_{n=1}^{N_i^{(m)}} z_t^{(m)2}(n) + N_i^{(m)} \Sigma_{z^{(m)}(t,t)}^{-1}\right) + \overline{\alpha}_{i_{(s,t)}}. \tag{19}$$

The trial distribution of latent variable $Q_z\left(z^{(m)}\right)$ is

$$Q_z\left(z^{(m)}\right) = \prod_{n=1}^{N^{(m)}} \mathcal{N}\left(z^{(m)}(n)|\overline{z}^{(m)}(n), \Sigma_{z^{(m)}}^{-1}\right), \tag{20}$$

$$\overline{z}^{(m)}(n) = \Sigma_{z^{(m)}}^{-1} \sum_{i=1}^{M} \eta_m \overline{\beta}_i \overline{W}_i^{\mathrm{T}} x_i^{(m)}(n), \tag{21}$$

$$\Sigma_{z^{(m)}} = \sum_{i=1}^{M} \left[\eta_m \overline{\beta}_i \left(\overline{W}_i^{\mathrm{T}} \overline{W}_i + \Sigma_{W_i}^{-1}\right)\right] + \mathrm{I}, \tag{22}$$

$$\Sigma_{W_i} = \mathrm{diag}\left(\left[\sum_{s=1}^{d_i} \sigma_{i_{(s,1)}}, \cdots, \sum_{s=1}^{d_i} \sigma_{i_{(s,d_z)}}\right]\right). \tag{23}$$

Finally, the trial distribution of the inverse variances $Q_\alpha(\alpha_1, \cdots, \alpha_M, \beta_1, \cdots, \beta_M)$ is further factorized to $Q_\alpha(\alpha_1) \cdots Q_\alpha(\alpha_M) Q_\alpha(\beta_1) \cdots Q_\alpha(\beta_M)$. The expected values of α_i and β_i are

$$\overline{\alpha}_{i_{(s,t)}} = \left(\frac{1}{2} + \gamma_{i0_{(s,t)}}\right)\left(\frac{1}{2}\overline{W}_{i_{(s,t)}}^2 + \frac{1}{2}\sigma_{i_{(s,t)}}^{-1} + \gamma_{i0_{(s,t)}}\alpha_{i0_{(s,t)}}^{-1}\right)^{-1}, \tag{24}$$

$$\overline{\beta}_i = d_i N_i^{(M)} \left\{ \sum_{n=1}^{N_i^{(M)}} \|x_i(n) - \overline{W}_i \overline{z}(n)\|^2 \right. \tag{25}$$

$$\left. + \mathrm{Tr}\left[\Sigma_{W_i}^{-1}\left(\sum_{n=1}^{N_i^{(M)}} z(n)z^{\mathrm{T}}(n) + N_i^{(M)}\Sigma_z^{-1}\right) + N_i^{(M)}\Sigma_z^{-1}\overline{W}_i^{\mathrm{T}}\overline{W}_i\right] \right\}^{-1},$$

where $\gamma_{i0_{(s,t)}}, \alpha_{i0_{(s,t)}}$ are constant values (zero in our study). For estimating β_i, only elements having all modalities are used. By calculating $Q_W(W_i)$, $Q_z(z)$, and $Q_\alpha(\alpha_1, \cdots, \alpha_M, \beta_1, \cdots, \beta_M)$ successively, the parameter are estimated.

Predictive Distribution: When the new set of source modalities $X_{\mathrm{new}} \in \mathfrak{P}(\{x_1, \cdots, x_{M-1}\})$, where $\mathfrak{P}$ represents a power set (a set of all subsets), is obtained, the predictive distribution of the target modality $x_{M_{\mathrm{new}}}$ is

$$P(x_{M\mathrm{new}}|X_{\mathrm{new}}) = \int \mathrm{d}W_M \mathrm{d}z_{\mathrm{new}} P(x_{M\mathrm{new}}|W_M, z_{\mathrm{new}}) Q(W_M) P(z_{\mathrm{new}}|X_{\mathrm{new}}). \tag{26}$$

When the random variable W_M is replaced with the estimated $\overline{W}_M$, the predictive distribution is

$$P(x_{M\mathrm{new}}|X_{\mathrm{new}}) \simeq \int \mathrm{d}z_{\mathrm{new}} P(x_{M\mathrm{new}}|z_{\mathrm{new}}) P(z_{\mathrm{new}}|X_{\mathrm{new}}), \tag{27}$$

$$P(x_{M\mathrm{new}}|z_{\mathrm{new}}) \propto \exp\left[-\frac{1}{2}\overline{\beta}_M\|x_{M\mathrm{new}} - \overline{W}_M z_{\mathrm{new}}\|^2\right]. \tag{28}$$

Since the distribution $P(z_{\mathrm{new}}|X_{\mathrm{new}})$ is an unknown distribution, it is approximated based on the test distribution $Q_z(z)$ (Eq. (20)). The approximate distribution is obtained by using only the term related to $x_{i\text{new}}$ included in $\boldsymbol{X}_{\text{new}}$.

$$\tilde{Q}_z(\boldsymbol{z}_{\text{new}}) = \mathcal{N}\left(\boldsymbol{z}|\overline{\boldsymbol{z}}_{\text{new}}, \boldsymbol{\Sigma}_{z\text{new}}^{-1}\right), \tag{29}$$

$$\overline{\boldsymbol{z}}_{\text{new}} = \sum_{i=1}^{M-1} \overline{\beta}_i \boldsymbol{\Sigma}_{z\text{new}}^{-1} \overline{\boldsymbol{W}}_i^{\text{T}} \boldsymbol{x}_{i\text{new}}, \tag{30}$$

$$\boldsymbol{\Sigma}_{z\text{new}} = \sum_{i=1}^{M-1} \left(\overline{\beta}_i \left(\overline{\boldsymbol{W}}_i^{\text{T}} \overline{\boldsymbol{W}}_i + \boldsymbol{\Sigma}_{W_i}^{-1}\right)\right) + \text{I}. \tag{31}$$

Finally, the prediction distribution $P(\boldsymbol{x}_{M\text{new}}|\boldsymbol{X}_{\text{new}})$ is

$$\begin{aligned} P(\boldsymbol{x}_{M\text{new}}|\boldsymbol{X}_{\text{new}}) &\simeq \int \mathrm{d}\boldsymbol{z}_{\text{new}} P\left(\boldsymbol{x}_{M\text{new}}|\boldsymbol{z}_{\text{new}}\right) \tilde{Q}_z\left(\boldsymbol{z}_{\text{new}}\right) \\ &= \mathcal{N}\left(\boldsymbol{x}_{M\text{new}}|\overline{\boldsymbol{x}}_{M\text{new}}, \boldsymbol{\Sigma}_{M\text{new}}^{-1}\right), \end{aligned} \tag{32}$$

$$\overline{\boldsymbol{x}}_{M\text{new}} = \overline{\boldsymbol{W}}_M \boldsymbol{\Sigma}_{z\text{new}}^{-1} \sum_{i=1}^{M-1} \overline{\beta}_i \overline{\boldsymbol{W}}_i^{\text{T}} \boldsymbol{x}_{i\text{new}}, \tag{33}$$

$$\boldsymbol{\Sigma}_{M\text{new}} = \overline{\boldsymbol{W}}_M \boldsymbol{\Sigma}_{z\text{new}}^{-1} \overline{\boldsymbol{W}}_M^{\text{T}} + \overline{\beta}_M^{-1} \text{I}. \tag{34}$$

4   Preliminary Investigation

We conducted three experiments to investigate the basic characteristics of GBCCA-M2 using artificially generated data. In this section, we firstly describe the common experimental setup and then explain each experiment.

4.1   Common Experimental Setup

As a method for generating artificial data, we used a simple Gaussian latent model. The latent variables are denoted by $\boldsymbol{Z}_{\text{gen}} = \left\{\boldsymbol{z}_{\text{gen}}(n)\right\}_{n=1}^{N} \in \mathbb{R}^{d_{z_{\text{gen}}}}$ and observed modalities are denoted by $\boldsymbol{X}_i = \left\{\boldsymbol{x}_i(n)\right\}_{n=1}^{N} \in \mathbb{R}^{d_i}$. In this section, we considered the case of three observed modalities. $d_{z_{\text{gen}}}$ and d_i represent the dimension of the latent variables and modalities respectively, and N represents the sample size. Latent variables were extracted independently from $\mathcal{N}(\boldsymbol{0}, \text{I}_{d_z})$. $\boldsymbol{x}_i(n)$ were generated as follows: $\boldsymbol{x}_i(n) = \boldsymbol{W}_i \boldsymbol{z}_{\text{gen}}(n) + \boldsymbol{\mu}_i + \boldsymbol{\delta}_i(n)$, where each row of $\boldsymbol{W}_i$ was extracted from $\mathcal{N}(\boldsymbol{0}, \text{I}_{d_{z_{\text{gen}}}})$, mean $\boldsymbol{\mu}_i$ was extracted from $\mathcal{N}(\boldsymbol{0}, \text{I}_{d_i})$, and covariance of noise $\boldsymbol{\delta}_i(n)$ was determined as follows:

$$\boldsymbol{\delta}_i(n) = \alpha \left(\text{I}_{d_i} + \sum_{j=1}^{\frac{d_{z_{\text{gen}}}}{2}} \boldsymbol{u}_j(n)\boldsymbol{u}_j(n)^{\text{T}}\right). \tag{35}$$

$\boldsymbol{u}_j(n)$ were extracted independently from $\mathcal{N}\left(\boldsymbol{0}, \text{I}_{d_i}\right)$. The magnitude of the noise is controlled by α, which was changed in the experiment evaluating robustness

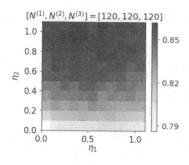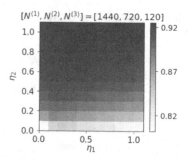

Fig. 5. Prediction performance when the contribution rates were changed.

against noise, and fixed in the other experiments. The number of elements in the test data was set to 500. X_1 and X_2 were set to the source modalities, and X_3 the target modality. The evaluation was performed by calculating the cosine similarities between the predicted modality and that of the test data.

4.2 Contribution Rates of Elements Missing Modalities

In GBCCA-M2, in order to utilize elements with various missing patterns efficiently, we introduced the contribution rates of elements missing modalities to the likelihood as shown in Eq. (9). In this experiment, we investigated the change in prediction performance when contribution rates were changed.

The dimension of each modality was set as $[d_1, d_2, d_3, d_{z_{\mathrm{gen}}}] = [250, 250, 250, 50]$. When the number of modalities was three, the patterns of missing modalities were divided into three categories of elements with one, two, and three modalities, respectively. We defined the number of elements with m sets of modalities $N^{(j)}$ and set them as $[N^{(1)}, N^{(2)}, N^{(3)}] = [120, 120, 120]$ and $[N^{(1)}, N^{(2)}, N^{(3)}] = [1440, 720, 120]$ (refer to Fig. 5). Moreover, the modality an element was missing was made uniform in each pattern. This was the same in all experiments. In Eq. (9), we fixed η_3 at 1.0 and varied η_1 and η_2 by increments of 0.1 in the range 0 to 1.0. Also, the dimension of latent variable z used in the proposed method was set to 150. Experiments were repeated ten times for each set of (η_1, η_2), and the average of cosine similarity was calculated.

The experimental results are shown in Fig. 5. Since the cosine similarity became maximal when η_2 was in the range 0.9 to 1.0, η_2 should be set to a value close to 1.0. This is because even if one modality is missing, it is possible to estimate parameters with the remaining two modalities. On the other hand, since the cosine similarity became maximal when η_1 was in the range 0.4 to 0.6, η_1 should be set to be smaller than η_2. This is because the element with one modality seems to be useful for estimating the distribution in the feature space of each modality, but it seems to deteriorate the estimation of the relationships between modalities. Moreover, since η_1 and η_2, which maximized cosine similarity when $[N^{(1)}, N^{(2)}, N^{(3)}] = [1440, 720, 120]$, were lower than when

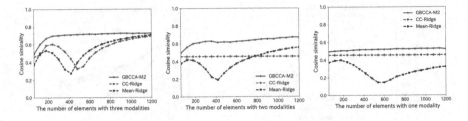

Fig. 6. Predict performance when the number of elements was changed.

$[N^{(1)}, N^{(2)}, N^{(3)}] = [120, 120, 120]$, the contribution rates should be decreased as the number of elements missing modalities increases.

4.3   The Number of Elements in Training

GBCCA-M2 utilizes elements missing modalities by including them in the likelihood function. In this experiment, we changed the number of elements in training according to the degree of missing modalities and investigated whether GBCCA-M2 can utilize elements missing modalities effectively.

Among the three kinds of missing patterns, the number of elements of any two patterns was fixed, and the number of elements of the remaining one pattern was changed. The number of elements to be fixed was set to 60 and the number of elements to be changed was set to $60, 120, \cdots, 1200$. The dimension of each modality and the contribution rates were set as follows: $[d_1, d_2, d_3, d_{z_{\mathrm{gen}}}] = [250, 250, 250, 50]$, $[\eta_1, \eta_2, \eta_3] = [0.4, 0.9, 1.0]$. Also, the dimension of latent variable z used in the GBCCA-M2 was set to 150. We used the following two methods for comparison: (1) CC and ridge regression (CC-Ridge) and (2) mean imputation and ridge regression (Mean-Ridge). CC-Ridge removes elements with missing modalities and performs ridge regression using the remaining elements. Ridge regression is a learning method that adds a square of the weight to the loss function in the linear least squares method and obtains a weight that minimizes it. Mean-Ridge substitutes the mean value of elements in the missing modalities and performs ridge regression.

Figure 6 shows the experimental results. When the number of elements with two modalities was increased in GBCCA-M2, the prediction performance approximately monotonically increased. This may be because elements with two modalities have a positive effect on the relationship estimation between the non-missing modalities and the estimation of the feature amount space in the non-missing modality. On the other hand, when the number of elements with one modality was increased, the prediction performance improved only in the range where the number of elements was small. This may be because when contribution rates are fixed, as the number of elements with one modality is increased, the negative effect on relationship estimation between the non-missing modality and the missing modality increases. Therefore, if η_1 is set appropriately, it should be possible to use elements with one modality effectively for learning.

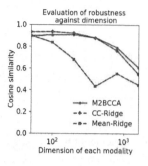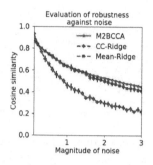

Fig. 7. Prediction performances when the dimension of modalities was changed (left) and when the noise of modalities was changed (right).

4.4 Evaluating Robustness Against Dimension and Noise

We described that the features of modalities are likely to be high dimensional and noisy. In order to show the effectiveness of GBCCA-M2 for such modalities, we conducted experiments to evaluate robustness against dimension and noise.

In the experiments evaluating robustness against dimension, we changed the parameter β, which represents the size of the dimension. The dimension of each modality was set to $[d_1, d_2, d_3, d_{z_{gen}}] = [50\beta, 50\beta, 50\beta, 10\beta]$, and the dimension of the latent variable z used in GBCCA-M2 was set to $30\,\beta$. We set β to 1, 2, 4, 8, 16, or 32. In the experiment evaluating robustness against noise, we changed α, which controlled the magnitude of the noise (Eq. (35)), by increments of 0.1 in the range 0.1 to 3.0. The dimension of each modality was set to $[d_1, d_2, d_3, d_{z_{gen}}] = [250, 250, 250, 50]$ and the dimension of latent variable z used in GBCCA-M2 was set to 150. In both experiments, the numbers of elements in training were set to 120 for all missing patterns. Also, the contribution rates were set as follows: $[\eta_1, \eta_2, \eta_3] = [0.4, 0.9, 1.0]$. As the comparison method, we used the same two methods as in the Experiment in Sect. 4.3.

Figure 7 shows the experimental results. When the dimension or noise of modality increased, GBCCA-M2 achieved higher prediction performance than the comparison methods. This may be because GBCCA-M2 is based on BCCA, which is effective for high dimensional and noisy features of modalities. Experimental results show that GBCCA-M2 is also effective for such cases.

5   Experiment with Real Data

5.1   Purchaser Behavior Prediction

We conducted an experiment to show the effectiveness of GBCCA-M2 using real purchaser dataset, in which modalities are actually missing. For the purchaser dataset, we used the INTAGE Single Source Panel (i-SSP) dataset from INTAGE Inc. This dataset includes attributes, purchase histories, and television program viewing information for the half year from January 1st, 2016 to June 30th, 2016.

Table 1. The number of elements by missing patterns in purchaser's data.

Attribute	Purchase	TV	The number of elements
✓	✗	✗	2683
✓	✓	✗	893
✓	✗	✓	2297
✓	✓	✓	809

Table 2. Comparison of each method in the actual purchaser's data.

Method	Cosine similarity	MAE	RMSE
GBCCA-M2	**0.408**	**104.8**	**383.2**
CC-Ridge	0.278	153.6	564.4
Mean-Ridge	0.397	109.3	397.7
CC-BCCA	0.404	113.5	390.2
Mean-BCCA	0.407	105.6	390.9
Semi CCA	0.402	105.6	389.4

In the attribute data, we converted the nominal scales such as occupation and residence to one-hot expression and used the proportional scales as they were. Purchasing information includes purchase data of beer, chocolate, and shampoo. We used the total number of purchases for each manufacturer as one modality. For the television program viewing information, we used the average television viewing time for each television program only if it was 20 hours or more. As a result of the above operation, the dimension of attribute information was 89, that of purchase situation was 67, and that of TV program viewing information was 226. Table 1 indicates the number of elements for each missing pattern. We extracted 100 elements with three modalities randomly as test data and used the remaining elements as learning data. We set the contribution rates and the dimension of the latent variable in GBCCA-M2 as follows: $[\eta_1, \eta_2, \eta_3, d_z] = [0.3, 0.8, 1.0, 30]$. In addition to CC-Ridge and Mean-Ridge, we used CC and BCCA (CC-BCCA), mean imputation and BCCA (Mean-BCCA), and Semi CCA for comparison. Television program viewing information was predicted from source modalities (i.e., attribute and purchase history). As the evaluation index, we calculated the following indexes using the predicted vector and the actual vector: (1) cosine similarity, (2) mean absolute error (MAE), and (3) root mean square error (RMSE). We did this 30 times and calculated the average.

Table 2 shows the experimental results. As for all evaluation index, GBCCA-M2 achieved best. This may be because GBCCA-M2 is effective for purchaser data in which features of modalities are high dimensional and noisy and there are many elements missing modalities. From the above findings, the effectiveness of GBCCA-M2 for a real purchaser dataset can be seen clearly.

5.2   Image Retrieval from English and Japanese Sentences

In this section, we report results on image retrieval from English and Japanese sentences learned with the dataset in which we made some modalities missing intentionally. In addition to MSCOCO [16] dataset, we used STAIR Captions [24], which is a Japanese image caption dataset based on images from MSCOCO. As the feature of images, we extracted the 4096-dimensional activations from 19-layer VGG model [21], and as the feature of sentences, we used

Table 3. Comparison of each method in the sentence-to-image retrieval.

Method	R@1	R@5	R@10
GBCCA-M2	**0.092**	**0.292**	**0.439**
CC-Ridge	0.074	0.263	0.411
Mean-Ridge	0.080	0.265	0.412
CC-BCCA	0.084	0.268	0.409
Mean-BCCA	0.082	0.262	0.382
Semi CCA	0.071	0.244	0.371

tf-idf-weighted bag-of-words vectors. For English, we pre-processed all the sentences with WordNet's lemmatizer [4] and removed stop words. For Japanese, we removed stop words and all parts of speech other than nouns, verbs, adjectives, and adjectival verbs. The final dimensions of English and Japanese sentences were 6245 and 7278, respectively. In training, we used 9000 elements (i.e, images and their corresponding English and Japanese sentences), made 50 % modalities missing randomly, and reduced the dimension of each modality to 1000 by PCA. For the evaluation, we used 1000 elements. We retrieved images form English and Japanese sentences and calculated Recall@K ($K = 1, 5, 10$). We set the contribution rates and the dimension of the latent variable as follows: $[\eta_1, \eta_2, \eta_3, d_z] = [0.3, 0.8, 1.0, 750]$ and used same methods in Sect. 5.1 as comparison methods. Table 3 shows the experimental results. We can see that GBCCA-M2 gives best results in all methods. By using GBCCA-M2, we can retrieve images more accurately by utilizing elements missing modalities.

6 Conclusion

In this study, we considered the two challenges associated with multi-modal learning and proposed GBCCA-M2, which utilizes elements missing modalities and can work well on high dimensional and noisy features of modalities. Moreover, we conducted experiments using artificially generated data as well as real data. The findings obtained in this study are as follows: (1) in order to utilize the elements missing modalities, it is effective to change the contribution rates to likelihood according to the degree of missing modalities, (2) GBCCA-M2, which uses a hierarchical Bayesian model, is effective for high dimensional and noisy features of modalities, and (3) because GBCCA-M2 is suited to the case that there are many elements missing modalities, and the features of modalities are high dimensional and noisy, it is effectively used for such multi-modal applications.

Acknowledgments. This work was partially funded by ImPACT Program of Council for Science, Technology and Innovation (Cabinet Office, Government of Japan) and INTAGE HOLDINGS Inc.

References

1. Akaho, S.: A kernel method for canonical correlation analysis. In: Proceedings of the International Meeting of the Psychometric Society. Springer-Verlag (2001)
2. Attial, H.: Inferring parameters and structure of latent variable models by variational bayes. In: Proceedings of the Fifteenth Conference on Uncertainty in Artificial Intelligence, pp. 21–30 (1999)
3. Bach, F.R., Jordan, M.I.: A probabilistic interpretation of canonical correlation analysis (2005). tR 688
4. Bird, S., Loper, E.: Nltk: the natural language toolkit. In: Proceedings of the ACL 2004 on Interactive Poster and Demonstration Sessions (2014)
5. Carroll, J.: Generalization of canonical correlation analysis to three or more sets of variables. In: Proceedings of the American Psychological Association, vol. 3, pp. 227–228 (1968)
6. Enders, C.K., Bandalos, D.L.: The relative performance of full information maximum likelihood estimation for missing data in structural equation models. Struct. Eqn. Model. Multidiscip. J. 8(3), 430–457 (2001)
7. Fujiwara, Y., Miyawaki, Y., Kamitani, Y.: Estimating image bases for visual image reconstruction from human brain activity. In: Advances in Neural Information Processing Systems 22, pp. 576–584. Curran Associates, Inc. (2009)
8. Hinton, G.E., Salakhutdinov, R.R.: Reducing the dimensionality of data with neural networks. Science 313, 504–507 (2006)
9. Hotelling, H.: Relations between two sets of variates. Biometrika 28(3), 321–377 (1936)
10. Huiskes, M.J., Thomee, B., Lew, M.S.: New trends and ideas in visual concept detection: the MIR flickr retrieval evaluation initiative. In: Proceedings of the International Conference on Multimedia Information Retrieval, pp. 527–536 (2010)
11. Kamada, C., Kanezaki, A., Harada, T.: Probabilistic semi-canonical correlation analysis. In: Proceedings of the 23rd ACM International Conference on Multimedia, pp. 1131–1134 (2015)
12. Kim, J.O., Curry, J.: The treatment of missing data in multivariate analysis. Sociol. Methods Res. 6(2), 215–240 (1977)
13. Kimura, A., et al.: Semicca: efficient semi-supervised learning of canonical correlations. Inf. Media Technol. 8(2), 311–318 (2013)
14. Klami, A., Kaski, S.: Local dependent components. In: Proceedings of the 24th International Conference on Machine Learning, pp. 425–432 (2007)
15. Lai, P.L., Fyfe, C.: Kernel and nonlinear canonical correlation analysis. Int. J. Neural Syst. 10, 365–377 (2000)
16. Lin, T.-Y., et al.: Microsoft COCO: common objects in context. In: Fleet, D., Pajdla, T., Schiele, B., Tuytelaars, T. (eds.) ECCV 2014. LNCS, vol. 8693, pp. 740–755. Springer, Cham (2014). https://doi.org/10.1007/978-3-319-10602-1_48
17. Little, R.J.A., Rubin, D.B.: Statistical Analysis with Missing Data. John Wiley & Sons, New York (2002)
18. Loh, P.L., Wainwright, M.J.: High-dimensional regression with noisy and missing data: provable guarantees with non-convexity. In: Advances in Neural Information Processing Systems, pp. 2726–2734. Curran Associates, Inc. (2011)
19. Neal, R.M.: Bayesian Learning for Neural Networks. Springer-Verlag, New York (1996). https://doi.org/10.1007/978-1-4612-0745-0
20. Roth, P.L.: Missing data: a concdptual review for applied psychologists. Pers. Psychol. 47(3), 537–560 (1994)

21. Simonyan, K., Zisserman, A.: Very deep convolutional networks for large-scale image recognition. arXiv:1409.1556 (2014)
22. Tran, L., Liu, X., Zhou, J., Jin, R.: Missing modalities imputation via cascaded residual autoencoder. In: IEEE Conference on Computer Vision and Pattern Recognition, pp. 4971–4980 (2017)
23. Wang, C.: Variational bayesian approach to canonical correlation analysis. IEEE Trans. Neural Netw. **18**(3), 905–910 (2007)
24. Yoshikawa, Y., Shigeto, Y., Takeuchi, A.: Stair captions: Constructing a large-scale japanese image caption dataset. In: Proceedings of the 55th Annual Meeting of the Association for Computational Linguistics, vol. 2, Short Papers, pp. 417–421 (2017)
25. You, Q., Luo, J., Jin, H., Yang, J.: Cross-modality consistent regression for joint visual-textual sentiment analysis of social multimedia. In: Proceedings of the Ninth ACM International Conference on Web Search and Data Mining, pp. 13–22 (2016)
26. Zhang, B., Hao, J., Ma, G., Yue, J., Shi, Z.: Semi-paired probabilistic canonical correlation analysis. In: Shi, Z., Wu, Z., Leake, D., Sattler, U. (eds.) IIP 2014. IAICT, vol. 432, pp. 1–10. Springer, Heidelberg (2014). https://doi.org/10.1007/978-3-662-44980-6_1

Unpaired Thermal to Visible Spectrum Transfer Using Adversarial Training

Adam Nyberg[1]([⊠])(iD), Abdelrahman Eldesokey[1]([⊠])(iD), David Bergström[2]([⊠])(iD), and David Gustafsson[2]([⊠])(iD)

[1] Computer Vision Laboratory, Linköping University, 581 83 Linköping, Sweden
{adany869,abdelrahman.eldesokey}@student.liu.se
[2] Swedish Defence Research Agency (FOI), 583 30 Linköping, Sweden
{david.bergstrom,david.gustafsson}@foi.se

Abstract. Thermal Infrared (TIR) cameras are gaining popularity in many computer vision applications due to their ability to operate under low-light conditions. Images produced by TIR cameras are usually difficult for humans to perceive visually, which limits their usability. Several methods in the literature were proposed to address this problem by transforming TIR images into realistic visible spectrum (VIS) images. However, existing TIR-VIS datasets suffer from imperfect alignment between TIR-VIS image pairs which degrades the performance of supervised methods. We tackle this problem by learning this transformation using an unsupervised Generative Adversarial Network (GAN) which trains on unpaired TIR and VIS images. When trained and evaluated on KAIST-MS dataset, our proposed methods was shown to produce significantly more realistic and sharp VIS images than the existing state-of-the-art supervised methods. In addition, our proposed method was shown to generalize very well when evaluated on a new dataset of new environments.

Keywords: Thermal imaging · Generative Adversarial Networks Unsupervised learning · Colorization

1 Introduction

Recently, thermal infrared (TIR) cameras have become increasingly popular due to their long wavelength which allows them to work under low-light conditions. TIR cameras require no active illumination as they sense emitted heat from objects and map it to a visual heat map. This opens up for many applications such as object detection for driving in complete darkness and event detection in surveillance. In addition, the cost of TIR cameras have gone significantly down while their resolution have improved significantly, resulting in a boost of interest. However, one limitation of TIR cameras is their limited visual interpretability for humans which hinders some applications such as visual-aided driving.

© Springer Nature Switzerland AG 2019
L. Leal-Taixé and S. Roth (Eds.): ECCV 2018 Workshops, LNCS 11134, pp. 657–669, 2019.
https://doi.org/10.1007/978-3-030-11024-6_49

| (a) TIR image | (b) Target VIS | (c) Generated VIS |

Fig. 1. An example of a TIR image (a), its corresponding VIS image (b) from the KAIST-MS dataset [4] and the VIS image (c) generated by our proposed method using only the TIR image (a) as an input.

To address this problem, TIR images can be transformed to visible spectrum (VIS) images which are easily interpreted by humans. Figure 1 shows an example of a TIR image, the corresponding VIS image and the VIS image generated directly from the TIR image. This is similar to colorization problems, where grayscale VIS images are mapped to color VIS images. However, transforming TIR images to VIS images is inherently challenging as they are not correlated in the electromagnetic spectrum. For instance, two objects of the same material and temperature, but with different colors in the VIS image, could correspond to the same value in the TIR image. Consequently, utilizing all the available information, i.e. spectrum, shape and context, is very crucial when solving this task. This also requires the availability of enormous amount of data to learn the latent relations between the two spectrums.

In colorization problems, only the chrominance needs to be estimated as the luminance is already available from the input grayscale images. Contrarily, TIR to VIS transformation requires the estimation of both the luminance and the chrominance based on the semantics of the input TIR images. Besides, generating data for learning colorization models is easy as color images could be computationally transformed to grayscale images to create image pairs with perfect pixel-to-pixel correspondences. In contrast, datasets containing registered TIR/VIS image pairs are very few and requires a sophisticated acquisition systems for good pixel-to-pixel correspondence.

The KAIST Multispectral Pedestrian Detection Benchmark (KAIST-MS) [4] introduced the first large-scale dataset with TIR-VIS image pairs. However, it was shown by [1] that the TIR-VIS image pairs in KAIST-MS does not have a perfect pixel-to-pixel correspondence, with a pixel error of up to 16 pixels (5%) in the horizontal direction. This would degrade the performance of supervised learning methods which tries to learn the pixel-to-pixel correspondences between image pairs and leads to corrupted output. To our knowledge there exist no large-scale public dataset of TIR-VIS image pairs with perfect pixel to pixel correspondence. Therefore, the method used for TIR to VIS image transformation need to control for this imperfection.

In this paper, we propose an unsupervised method for transforming TIR images, specifically long-wavelength infrared (LWIR), to visible spectrum (VIS) images. Our method is trained on unpaired images from the KAIST-MS dataset [4] which allows it to handle the imperfect registration between the TIR-VIS image pairs. Qualitative analysis shows that our proposed unsupervised method produces sharp and perceptually realistic VIS images compared to the existing state-of-the-art supervised methods. In addition, our proposed method achieves comparable results to state-of-the-art supervised method in terms of L1 error despite being trained on unpaired images. Finally, our proposed method generalizes very well when evaluated on our new FOI dataset, which demonstrates the generalization capabilities of our method contrarily to the existing state-of-the-art methods.

2 Related Work

Colorizing grayscale images has been extensively investigated in the literature. Scribbles [9] requires the user to manually apply strokes of color to different regions of a grayscale image and neighboring pixels with the same luminance should get the same color. Transfer techniques [16] use the color palette from a reference image and apply it to a grayscale image by matching luminance and texture. Both scribbles and transfer techniques require manual input from the user. Recently, colorization methods based on automatic transformation, i.e., the only input to the method is the grayscale image, have become popular. Promising results have been demonstrated in the area of automatic transformation using Convolutional Neural Networks (CNNs) [3,5,8,17] and Generative Adversarial Networks (GANs) [2,6,13] due to their abilities to model semantic representation in images.

In the infrared spectrum, less research has been done on transforming thermal images to VIS images. In [10], a CNN-based method was proposed to transform near-infrared (NIR) images to VIS images. Their method was shown to perform well as the NIR and VIS images are highly correlated in the electromagnetic spectrum. Kniaz et al. [7] proposed VIS to TIR transformation using a CNN model as a way to generate synthetic TIR images. The KAIST-MS [11] dataset introduced the first realistic large-scale dataset of TIR-VIS image pairs which opened up for developing TIR-VIS transformation models. Berg et al. [1] proposed a CNN-based model to transform TIR images to VIS images trained on the KAIST-MS dataset. However, the imperfect registration of the dataset caused the output from their method to be blurry and corrupted in some cases.

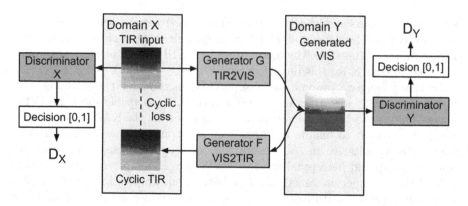

Fig. 2. The unpaired model is mapping between two different domains, X (TIR) and Y (VIS), using $G : X \rightarrow Y$ and $F : Y \rightarrow X$. This model produces three different losses; two adversarial losses based on D_Y and D_X, and one cycle consistency loss.

Generative Adversarial Networks (GANs) have shown promising results in unsupervised domain transfer [6,12,18,19]. An unsupervised method does not require a paired dataset, hence, eliminating the need for pixel to pixel correspondence. In [14,15], GANs have demonstrated a very good performance on transferring NIR images to VIS images. Isola *et al.* [6] has shown some qualitative results from the KAIST-MS dataset as and example for domain transfer. Inspired by [18], we employ an unsupervised GAN to transform TIR images to VIS images which eliminates the deficiencies caused by the imperfect registration in the KAIST-MS dataset as the training set does not need to be paired. Different from [1], our proposed method produces a very realistic and sharp VIS images. In addition, our proposed method is able to generalize very well on unseen data from different environments.

3 Method

Here we describe our proposed approach for transforming TIR images to VIS image while handling data miss-alignment in the KAIST-MS dataset.

3.1 Unpaired TIR-VIS Transfer

Inspired by [18], we perform unsupervised domain transfer between TIR and VIS images. Given TIR domain X with images $\{x_i : x_i \in X\}_{i=1}^{N}$ and VIS domain Y with images $\{y_j : y_j \in Y\}_{j=1}^{M}$, we aim to learn two transformations G and F between the two domains as shown in Fig. 2. TIR input images are transformed from the thermal domain X to the visible spectrum domain Y using the generator G, while the generator F performs in the opposite direction.

An adversarial discriminator D_X aims to discriminate between images x and the transformed images $F(y)$, while another discriminator D_Y discriminates between images y and $G(x)$.

3.2   Adversarial Training

The main objective of a GAN with a cyclic loss is to learn the two transformations $G : X \to Y$, $F : Y \to X$ and their corresponding discriminators D_X, D_Y [18]. During training, the generator G_G transforms an image $x \in X$ into a synthetic image $\hat{y}$. The synthetic image is then evaluated by the discriminator D_Y. The adversarial loss for the G_G is defined as:

$$\mathcal{L}_{G_G}(G_G, D_Y, x) = \mathbb{E}_{x \sim p_{data(x)}}[(D_Y(G_G(x)) - 1)^2] \tag{1}$$

where $p_{data(x)}$ is data distribution in X. The loss value becomes large if the synthetic image $\hat{y}$ was able to fool the discriminator into outputting a value close or equal to one. On the other hand, the discriminator tries to maximize the probability for real images while also minimizing the output on synthetic images, achieved by minimizing the following formula:

$$\mathcal{L}_{D_Y}(D_Y, x, y) = \mathbb{E}_{x \sim p_{data(x)}}[(D_Y(G_G(x)))^2] + \mathbb{E}_{y \sim p_{data(y)}}[(D_Y(y) - 1)^2]. \tag{2}$$

The total adversarial loss for the G transformation is then defined as:

$$\mathcal{L}_{GAN}(G_G, D_Y, x, y) = \mathcal{L}_{D_Y}(D_Y, y) + \min_{G_G} \max_{D_Y} \mathcal{L}_{G_G}(G_G, D_Y, x) \tag{3}$$

A similar loss is utilized to learn the transformation F. To reduce the space of possible transformations, a cycle-consistency loss [18] is employed which ensures that the learned transformation can map only a single input to the desired output. The cycle-consistency loss is defined as:

$$\mathcal{L}_{cyc}(G_G, G_F) = \mathbb{E}_{x \sim p_{data}(x)}[||G_F(G_G(x)) - x||_1] + \\ \mathbb{E}_{y \sim p_{data}(y)}[||G_G(G_F(y)) - y||_1] \tag{4}$$

Combining the above losses gives our total loss which is defined as:

$$\mathcal{L}(G_G, G_F, D_X, D_Y) = \mathcal{L}_{GAN}(G_G, D_Y, x, y) + \\ \mathcal{L}_{GAN}(G_F, D_X, y, x) + \\ \lambda \mathcal{L}_{cyc}(G_G, G_F) \tag{5}$$

where λ is a factor used to control the impact of the cyclic loss.

4 Experiments

For evaluation, we compare our proposed method with the existing state-of-the-art method on TIR to VIS transfer TIR2Lab [1]. The evaluation is performed on the KAIST-MS, the FOI dataset and the generalization capabilities of the evaluated methods are tested by training on the former and evaluating on the latter.

4.1 Datasets

The KIAST-MS dataset [4] contains paired TIR and VIS images which were collected by mounting a TIR and a VIS cameras on a vehicle in city and suburban environments. The KAIST-MS dataset consists of $33,399$ training image pairs and $29,179$ test image pairs captured during daylight with a spatial resolution of (640×512). Because the TIR camera used, FLIR A35, is only capable of capturing images with a resolution of (320×256) we resized all images to (320×256). The images were collected continuously during driving, resulting in multiple image pairs being very similar. To remove redundant images, only every fourth image pair was included in the training set, resulting in $8,349$ image pairs. For the evaluation, all image pairs from the test set were used.

The FOI dataset was captured using a co-axial imaging system capable of, theoretically, capturing TIR and VIS images with the same optical axis. Two cameras were used for all data collection, a TIR camera FLIR A65[1] and VIS camera XIMEA MC023CG-SY[2]. All images were cropped and re-sized to 320×256 pixels. This system was used to capture TIR-VIS image pairs in natural environments with fields and forests with a training set of $5,736$ image pairs and $1,913$ image pairs for the test set. The average registration error for all image pairs were between 0.8 and 2.2 pixels.

4.2 Experimental Setup

Since we use the architecture from [18], we crop all training and test images from the center to the size (256×256). TIR2Lab [1] was trained and evaluated on the full resolution of the images. All experiments were performed on GeForce GTX 1080 Ti graphics card[3].

KAIST-MS Dataset Experiments. A pretrained model for TIR2Lab [1] trained on the KAIST-MS dataset was provided by the authors. Our proposed model (TIRcGAN) was trained from scratch for 44 epochs using the same hyperparameters as [18]. Those parameters were batch size $= 1$, $\lambda = 10$ and for the ADAM

---

[1] http://www.flir.co.uk/automation/display/?id=56345.

[2] https://www.ximea.com/en/products/usb-31-gen-1-with-sony-cmos-xic/mc023cg-sy.

[3] https://www.nvidia.com/en-us/geforce/products/10series/geforce-gtx-1080-ti.

optimizer we used learning rate= $2e - 4$, $\beta_1 = 0.5$, $\beta_2 = 0.999$ and $\epsilon = 1e - 8$. Some examples from pix2pix model [6] on the KAIST-MS dataset were provided by the authors and are discussed in the qualitative analysis.

FOI Dataset Experiments. When training the TIR2Lab model, we used the same hyperparameters as mentioned in [1], except that we had to train for 750 epochs before it converged. For our TIRcGAN model, we trained for 38 epochs, using the same parameters as in the *KAIST-MS dataset experiments.*

Evaluation Metrics. For the quantitative evaluation we use L_1, root-mean-square error (RMSE), peak signal-to-noise ratio (PSNR) and Structural Similarity (SSIM) calculated between the transformed TIR image and the target VIS image. All metrics were calculated in the RGB color space normalized between 0 and 1 with standard deviation denoted as $\pm$.

Table 1. This table shows the qualitative results for the experiments calculated on RGB values normalized between 0 and 1. The standard deviation is denoted as $\pm$.

Model	Trained on	Evaluated on	L_1	RMSE	PSNR	SSIM
TIR2Lab	KAIST-MS	KAIST-MS	**0.13±0.04**	0.46±0.09	**14.7±2.20**	0.64±0.08
TIRcGAN (Ours)	KAIST-MS	KAIST-MS	0.15±0.05	**0.21±0.06**	13.92±2.48	0.55±0.10
TIR2Lab	FOI dataset	FOI dataset	0.12±0.04	0.15±0.05	17.05±2.52	0.81±0.07
TIRcGAN (Ours)	FOI dataset	FOI dataset	**0.11±0.05**	**0.14±0.05**	**17.63±2.83**	0.77±0.10
TIR2Lab	KAIST-MS	FOI dataset	0.32±0.11	0.39±0.11	8.48±2.68	0.54±0.06
TIRcGAN (Ours)	KAIST-MS	FOI dataset	**0.20±0.07**	**0.23±0.08**	**13.10±2.82**	0.60±0.10

4.3 Quantitative Results

Table 1 shows the quantitative results for the state-of-the-art method TIR2Lab [1] on the task of TIR to VIS domain transfer and our proposed method. Our method achieves comparable results to TIR2Lab in terms of L_1 despite the fact that our proposed method is unsupervised. On the other hand, our proposed method has a significantly lower RMSE than TIR2Lab which indicates its robustness against outliers. On the FOI dataset, our proposed method marginally outperforms TIR2Lab with respect to all evaluation metrics.

Model Generalization. To evaluate generalization capabilities of methods in comparison, we train them on the KASIT-MS dataset and evaluate on the FOI dataset. The former was captured in city and urban environment, while the latter was captured in natural environments and forests. As shown in Table 1, our proposed method maintains its performance to a big extent when evaluated on a different dataset. On the other hand, TIR2Lab model failed to generalize to unseen data.

(a) TIR input   (b) pix2pix [6]   (c) TIR2Lab [1]   (d) TIRcGAN   (e) Target VIS

Fig. 3. Example images from the KAIST-MS dataset experiment. It is possible to note that the pix2pix and TIRcGAN produce sharper images than the TIR2Lab model. TIRcGAN model is able to distinguish between yellow and white lanes as seen in the third row. *Note:* in the third row, the corresponding frame for the pix2pix model was not available, so the closest frame was used.

4.4   Qualitative Analysis

The KAIST-MS Dataset. As shown in Fig. 3, our proposed TIRcGAN produces much sharper and saturated images than the TIR2Lab model on the KAIST-MS dataset. In addition, TIRcGAN is more inclined to generate smooth lines and other objects as an attempt to make the transformed TIR image look more realistic. On the other hand, images from TIR2Lab are quite blurry and lacks details in some occasions. Pix2pix performs reasonably and produces sharp images, however, objects and lines are smeared out in some cases.

The FOI Dataset. Figure 4 show the results for the TIR2Lab and our proposed TIRcGAN models on the FOI dataset. TIRcGAN consistently outperform the TIR2Lab model when it comes to producing perceptually realistic VIS images. TIR2Lab produces blurry images that lacks a proper amount of details, while

(a) TIR input   (b) TIR2Lab [1]   (c) TIRcGAN   (d) Target VIS

Fig. 4. Example images from the FOI dataset experiment. We can see that the unpaired model produce much sharper and more realistic images.

TIRcGAN produces a significant amount of details that are very similar to the target VIS image.

Model Generalization. Figure 5 show the TIR2Lab and our TIRcGAN ability to generalize from one dataset collected on one environment to a new dataset from a different environment. Both models struggle at generating accurate colors or perceptually realistic images since the two datasets have different colors distribution. However, TIRcGAN was able to predict objects in the image with a reasonable amount of details contrarily to TIR2Lab which completely failed.

666   A. Nyberg et al.

(a) TIR input   (b) TIR2Lab [1]   (c) TIRcGAN   (d) Target VIS

Fig. 5. Examples for methods output when trained on the KAIST-MS dataset [4] and evaluated on the FOI dataset. Both models struggle with predicting the colors since the two datasets were captured in different environments. However, TIRcGAN can still predict the objects in the scene.

4.5 Failure Cases

Figure 6 shows examples where different models fail on the KAIST-MS dataset. For all methods, predicting humans is quite troublesome. Road crossing lines are also challenging as they are not always visible in the TIR images. Figure 7 shows some failure case on the FOI dataset. Both models fails in predicting dense forests, side-roads and houses since they are not very common in the dataset.

(a) TIR input   (b) pix2pix [6]   (c) TIR2Lab [1]   (d) TIRcGAN   (e) Target VIS

Fig. 6. Example images where different models fail on the KAIST-MS dataset. In the first row, we see that the model produces an inverse shadow, i.e., painting shadow only where there should not be shadow. In the second row we show that all the models struggle with producing perceptually realistic VIS images of humans.

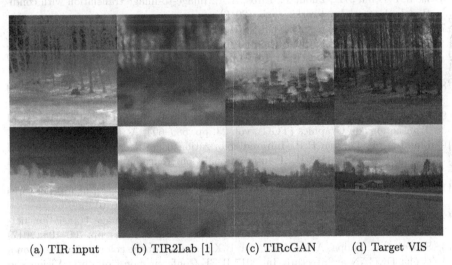

(a) TIR input   (b) TIR2Lab [1]   (c) TIRcGAN   (d) Target VIS

Fig. 7. Example images where models fail on the FOI dataset experiment. Here we see that the models are not able to accurately colorize houses and some roads.

5   Conclusions

In this paper, we addressed the problem of TIR to VIS spectrum transfer by employing unsupervised GAN model that train on unpaired data. Our method was able to handle misalginments in the KAIST-MS dataset and produced perceptually realistic and sharp VIS images compared to the supervised state-of-the-art methods. When our method was trained on the KAIST-MS dataset and evaluated on the new FOI dataset, it maintained its performance to a big extent. This demonstrated the generalization capabilities of our proposed method.

References

1. Berg, A., Ahlberg, J., Felsberg, M.: Generating visible spectrum images from thermal infrared. In: The IEEE Conference on Computer Vision and Pattern Recognition (CVPR) Workshops, June 2018

2. Cao, Y., Zhou, Z., Zhang, W., Yu, Y.: Unsupervised diverse colorization via generative adversarial networks. In: Ceci, M., Hollmén, J., Todorovski, L., Vens, C., Džeroski, S. (eds.) ECML PKDD 2017. LNCS (LNAI), vol. 10534, pp. 151–166. Springer, Cham (2017). https://doi.org/10.1007/978-3-319-71249-9_10

3. Cheng, Z., Yang, Q., Sheng, B.: Deep colorization. In: Proceedings of the IEEE International Conference on Computer Vision, pp. 415–423 (2015)

4. Hwang, S., Park, J., Kim, N., Choi, Y., So Kweon, I.: Multispectral pedestrian detection: benchmark dataset and baseline. In: Proceedings of the IEEE Conference on Computer Vision and Pattern Recognition, pp. 1037–1045 (2015)

5. Iizuka, S., Simo-Serra, E., Ishikawa, H.: Let there be color!: joint end-to-end learning of global and local image priors for automatic image colorization with simultaneous classification. ACM Trans. Graph. **35**(4), 110 (2016). (Proc. of SIGGRAPH 2016)

6. Isola, P., Zhu, J.Y., Zhou, T., Efros, A.A.: Image-to-image translation with conditional adversarial networks. arxiv (2016)

7. Kniaz, V.V., Gorbatsevich, V.S., Mizginov, V.A.: Thermalnet: a deep convolutional network for synthetic thermal image generation. ISPRS - Int. Arch. Photogramme. Remote Sens. Spat. Inf. Sci. 41–45, May 2017. https://doi.org/10.5194/isprs-archives-XLII-2-W4-41-2017

8. Larsson, G., Maire, M., Shakhnarovich, G.: Colorization as a proxy task for visual understanding. In: CVPR, vol. 2, p. 8 (2017)

9. Levin, A., Lischinski, D., Weiss, Y.: Colorization using optimization. In: ACM Transactions on Graphics (TOG), vol. 23, pp. 689–694. ACM (2004)

10. Limmer, M., Lensch, H.P.: Infrared colorization using deep convolutional neural networks. In: 2016 15th IEEE International Conference on Machine Learning and Applications (ICMLA), pp. 61–68. IEEE (2016)

11. Liu, J., Zhang, S., Wang, S., Metaxas, D.N.: Multispectral deep neural networks for pedestrian detection. arXiv preprint arXiv:1611.02644 (2016)

12. Liu, M.Y., Breuel, T., Kautz, J.: Unsupervised image-to-image translation networks. In: Advances in Neural Information Processing Systems, pp. 700–708 (2017)

13. Suárez, P.L., Sappa, A.D., Vintimilla, B.X.: Infrared image colorization based on a triplet DCGAN architecture. In: 2017 IEEE Conference on Computer Vision and Pattern Recognition Workshops (CVPRW), pp. 212–217. IEEE (2017)

14. Suárez, P.L., Sappa, A.D., Vintimilla, B.X.: Learning to colorize infrared images. In: De la Prieta, F., et al. (eds.) PAAMS 2017. AISC, vol. 619, pp. 164–172. Springer, Cham (2018). https://doi.org/10.1007/978-3-319-61578-3_16

15. Suárez, P.L., Sappa, A.D., Vintimilla, B.X.: Infrared image colorization based on a triplet dcgan architecture. In: 2017 IEEE Conference on Computer Vision and Pattern Recognition Workshops (CVPRW), pp. 212–217, July 2017. https://doi.org/10.1109/CVPRW.2017.32

16. Welsh, T., Ashikhmin, M., Mueller, K.: Transferring color to greyscale images. In: ACM Transactions on Graphics (TOG), vol. 21, pp. 277–280. ACM (2002)

17. Zhang, R., Isola, P., Efros, A.A.: Colorful image colorization. In: Leibe, B., Matas, J., Sebe, N., Welling, M. (eds.) ECCV 2016. LNCS, vol. 9907, pp. 649–666. Springer, Cham (2016). https://doi.org/10.1007/978-3-319-46487-9_40
18. Zhu, J.Y., Park, T., Isola, P., Efros, A.A.: Unpaired image-to-image translation using cycle-consistent adversarial networks. arXiv preprint (2017)
19. Zhu, J.Y., et al.: Toward multimodal image-to-image translation. In: Advances in Neural Information Processing Systems, pp. 465–476 (2017)

W36 – What Is Optical Flow for?

W36 – What Is Optical Flow for?

Traditionally, computer vision problems have been classified into three levels: low (image to image), middle (image to features), and high (features to analysis). Some typical low-level vision problems include optical flow, stereo and intrinsic image decomposition. The solution to these problems would then be combined to solve higher level problems, such as action recognition and visual question answering. For example, optical flow has been used as an input to structure from motion, action recognition, and visual effects.

Two recent developments in optical flow affect this general paradigm for solving computer vision.

First, highly accurate optical flow can finally be learned. In most high-level computer vision problems the state-of-the-art methods have been based on deep learning for a few years. However, in optical flow it is only within the last year that the top performing methods are end-to-end trainable networks. This opens a new research question of how should we integrate these learnable optical flow modules into large systems to solve the computer vision problem.

Second, top performing methods are now very accurate in optical flow benchmarks. This leads to a series of questions about the evaluation of flow. For example, are current methods accurate enough for higher level applications? In other words, is optical flow solved? If not, how should we design new benchmarks in the future to ensure they are most useful for higher level applications?

The goal of this workshop was to revisit the original plans of when and how to use optical flow for computer vision applications in light of these recent developments. We invited members of both researchers and practitioners of optical flow, to learn about recent progress, and to address these questions under the general topic of "What is optical flow for?".

There were in total nine valid submissions and each was reviewed by two experts. Based on the reviews, six paper were accepted. One paper was awarded the best paper and the authors received an NVIDIA GPU card. Beyond the accepted papers, we include a summary of the workshop and its results and takeaway in this collection (this paper has not been peer-reviewed).

We would like to thank all contributors, authors, reviewers, and invited speakers for helping us making this workshop a success.

September 2018

Fatma Güney
Laura Sevilla-Lara
Deqing Sun
Jonas Wulff

Devon: Deformable Volume Network for Learning Optical Flow

Yao Lu[1,2]([✉]), Jack Valmadre[3], Heng Wang[4], Juho Kannala[5],
Mehrtash Harandi[6], and Philip H. S. Torr[3]

[1] Australian National University, Canberra, Australia
yaolubrain@gmail.com
[2] Data61, CSIRO, Sydney, Australia
[3] University of Oxford, Oxford, UK
[4] Facebook, Cambridge, USA
[5] Aalto University, Helsinki, Finland
[6] Monash University, Melbourne, Australia

Abstract. We propose a new neural network module, Deformable Cost Volume, for learning large displacement optical flow. The module does not distort the original images or their feature maps and therefore avoids the artifacts associated with warping. Based on this module, a new neural network model is proposed. The full version of this paper can be found online (https://arxiv.org/abs/1802.07351).

1   Introduction

Warping has been used in variational methods [1,6] and neural network models [4,7,8] for iteratively refining optical flow estimations in a multi-stage framework. The first stage covers large displacements and outputs a rough estimation. Then the second image (or its feature maps) is warped by the roughly estimated optical flow such that pixels of large displacements in the second image are moved closer to their correspondences in the first image. As a result, the next stage, which receives the original first image and the warped second image as inputs, only needs to handle smaller displacements and refines the estimation.

Let $I : \mathbb{R}^2 \to \mathbb{R}^3$ denote the first image, $J : \mathbb{R}^2 \to \mathbb{R}^3$ denote the second image and $F : \mathbb{R}^2 \to \mathbb{R}^2$ denote the optical flow field of the first image. The warped second image is defined as

$$\tilde{J}(\mathbf{p}) = J(\mathbf{p} + F(\mathbf{p})) \tag{1}$$

for image location $\mathbf{p} \in \mathbb{R}^2$ [4].

The warping operation creates a transformed image reasonably well if the new pixel locations $\mathbf{p} + F(\mathbf{p})$ do not occlude or collide with each other. For example, affine transform $F(\mathbf{p}) = \mathbf{A}\mathbf{p} + \mathbf{t}$ where $\mathbf{A}$ and $\mathbf{t}$ are the transformation parameters. However, for real-world images, occlusions are common (e.g. when an object moves and the background is still). If an image is warped with the optical flow which induces occlusions, duplicates will be created.

© Springer Nature Switzerland AG 2019
L. Leal-Taixé and S. Roth (Eds.): ECCV 2018 Workshops, LNCS 11134, pp. 673–677, 2019.
https://doi.org/10.1007/978-3-030-11024-6_50

(a) First image   (b) Second image   (c) Ground truth opti-(d) Warped second
                                        cal flow   image

Fig. 1. Artifacts of using image warping. From (d), we can see the duplicates of the dragon head and wings. The images and the ground truth optical flow are from the Sintel dataset [2]. Warping is done with function `image.warp()` in the Torch-image toolbox.

The effect is demonstrated in Fig. 1. The artifacts cannot be cleaned simply by subtracting the first or the second image from the warped image, as shown in Fig. 1(e) and (f). Intuitively, imagine a pixel which is moved by warping to a new location. If no other pixel are moved to fill in its old location, the pixel will appear twice in the warped image. Mathematically, consider the following example. Assume the value of $J(\mathbf{p}_1)$ is unique in J, that is, $J(\mathbf{p}) \neq J(\mathbf{p}_1)$ for all $\mathbf{p} \neq \mathbf{p}_1$. Then for an optical flow field in which

$$F(\mathbf{p}_1) = 0, \quad F(\mathbf{p}_2) = \mathbf{p}_1 - \mathbf{p}_2, \tag{2}$$

we have

$$\tilde{J}(\mathbf{p}_1) = J(\mathbf{p}_1 + F(\mathbf{p}_1)) \tag{3}$$
$$= J(\mathbf{p}_1 + 0) = J(\mathbf{p}_1), \tag{4}$$
$$\tilde{J}(\mathbf{p}_2) = J(\mathbf{p}_2 + F(\mathbf{p}_2)) \tag{5}$$
$$= J(\mathbf{p}_2 + \mathbf{p}_1 - \mathbf{p}_2) = J(\mathbf{p}_1). \tag{6}$$

Therefore $\tilde{J}(\mathbf{p}_1) = \tilde{J}(\mathbf{p}_2) = J(\mathbf{p}_1)$. Since the value of $J(\mathbf{p}_1)$ is unique in image J but not unique in $\tilde{J}$, a duplicate is created on the warped second image $\tilde{J}$.

2   Deformable Cost Volume

Let I denote the first image, J denote the second image and $f_I : \mathbb{R}^2 \to \mathbb{R}^d$ and $f_J : \mathbb{R}^2 \to \mathbb{R}^d$ denote their feature maps of dimensionality d, respectively. The standard cost volume is defined as

$$C(\mathbf{p}, \mathbf{v}) = \|f_I(\mathbf{p}) - f_J(\mathbf{p} + \mathbf{v})\|, \tag{7}$$

for image location $\mathbf{p} \in \mathbb{R}^2$, neighbor $\mathbf{v} \in [-\frac{k-1}{2}, \frac{k-1}{2}]^2$ of neighborhood size k and a given vector norm $\| \cdot \|$.

The cost volume gives an explicit representation of displacements. To reduce the computational burden of constructing fully connected cost volumes, one

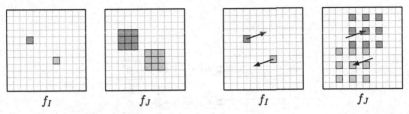

(a) Standard cost volume. For each location on the feature maps of the first image, the matching costs of a neighborhood of the same location on the feature maps of the second image are computed.

(b) Deformable cost volume. For each location on the feature maps of the first image, the matching costs of a **dilated** neighborhood of the same location, **offset by a flow vector**, on the feature maps of the second image are computed.

Fig. 2. Cost volumes

can embed the cost volume in a multi-scale representation and use warping to propagate the flow between two stages. However, as discussed in Sect. 1, warping induces artifacts and distortion. To avoid the drawbacks of warping, we propose a new neural network module, the deformable cost volume. The key idea is: instead of deforming images or their feature maps, as done with warping, we deform the cost volume and leave the images and the feature maps unchanged.

The proposed deformable cost volume is defined as

$$C(\mathbf{p}, \mathbf{v}, r, F) = \|f_I(\mathbf{p}) - f_J(\mathbf{p} + r \cdot \mathbf{v} + F(\mathbf{p}))\| \tag{8}$$

where r is the dilation factor and $F(\cdot)$ is an external flow field. The dilation factor r is introduced to enlarge the size of the neighborhood to handle large displacements without increasing computation significantly. This is inspired by the dilated convolution [3,9] which enlarges its receptive field in a similar way. $F(\cdot)$ can be obtained from the optical flow estimated from a previous stage or an external algorithm. If $F(\mathbf{p}) = 0$ for all $\mathbf{p}$ and $r = 1$, then the deformable cost volume is reduced to the standard cost volume. For non-integer $F(\mathbf{p})$, bilinear interpolation is used. The deformable cost volume is illustrated in Fig. 2.

Since the deformable cost volume does not distort f_I or f_J, the artifacts associated with warping will not be created. Optical flow can be inferred from the deformable cost volume solely without resorting to the feature maps of the first image to counter the duplicates.

The deformable cost volume is differentiable with respect to $f_I(\mathbf{p})$ and $f_J(\mathbf{p} + r \cdot \mathbf{v} + F(\mathbf{p}))$ for each image location $\mathbf{p}$. Due to bilinear interpolation, the deformable cost volume is also differentiable with respect to $F(\mathbf{p})$, using the same technique as in [4,5]. Therefore, the deformable cost volume can be inserted in a neural network for end-to-end learning optical flow.

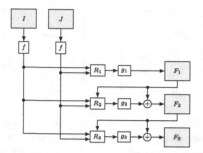

Fig. 3. Deformable Volume Network (Devon) with three stages. I denotes the first image, J denotes the second image, f denotes the shared feature extraction module (a fully convolutional network), R_t denotes the relation module (concatenation of several deformable cost volumes), g_t denotes the decoding module (a fully convolutional network) and F_t denotes the estimated optical flow for stage t.

3   Deformable Volume Network

Our proposed model is the deformable volume network (Devon), as illustrated in Fig. 3. Compared to previous neural network models, Devon has several major differences: (1) All feature maps in Devon have the same resolution. (2) Each stage computes on the undistorted images. No warping is used. (3) The decoding module only receives inputs from the relation module. (4) All stages share the feature extraction module.

References

1. Brox, T., Bruhn, A., Papenberg, N., Weickert, J.: High accuracy optical flow estimation based on a theory for warping. In: Pajdla, T., Matas, J. (eds.) ECCV 2004. LNCS, vol. 3024, pp. 25–36. Springer, Heidelberg (2004). https://doi.org/10.1007/978-3-540-24673-2_3
2. Butler, D.J., Wulff, J., Stanley, G.B., Black, M.J.: A naturalistic open source movie for optical flow evaluation. In: Fitzgibbon, A., Lazebnik, S., Perona, P., Sato, Y., Schmid, C. (eds.) ECCV 2012. LNCS, vol. 7577, pp. 611–625. Springer, Heidelberg (2012). https://doi.org/10.1007/978-3-642-33783-3_44
3. Chen, L.-C., Papandreou, G., Kokkinos, I., Murphy, K., Yuille, A.L.: Deeplab: semantic image segmentation with deep convolutional nets, atrous convolution, and fully connected crfs. arXiv (2016)
4. Ilg, E., Mayer, N., Saikia, T., Keuper, M., Dosovitskiy, A., Brox, T.: Flownet 2.0: evolution of optical flow estimation with deep networks. In: CVPR 2017 (2017)
5. Jaderberg, M., Simonyan, K., Zisserman, A., et al.: Spatial transformer networks. In: NIPS 2015 (2015)
6. Lucas, B.D., Kanade, T.: An iterative image registration technique with an application to stereo vision. In: IJCAI 1981 (1981)
7. Ranjan, A., Black, M.J.: Optical flow estimation using a spatial pyramid network. In: CVPR 2017 (2017)

8. Sun, D., Yang, X., Liu, M.-Y., Kautz, J.: PWC-Net: CNNs for optical flow using pyramid, warping, and cost volume. arXiv 2017 (2017)
9. Yu, F., Koltun, V.: Multi-scale context aggregation by dilated convolutions. In: ICLR 2015 (2015)

Using Phase Instead of Optical Flow
for Action Recognition

Omar Hommos[1], Silvia L. Pintea[1(✉)], Pascal S. M. Mettes[2],
and Jan C. van Gemert[1]

[1] Computer Vision Lab, Delft University of Technology, Delft, Netherlands
Silvia.Laura.Pintea@gmail.com
[2] Intelligent Sensory Interactive Systems, University of Amsterdam,
Amsterdam, Netherlands

Abstract. Currently, the most common motion representation for action recognition is optical flow. Optical flow is based on particle tracking which adheres to a Lagrangian perspective on dynamics. In contrast to the Lagrangian perspective, the Eulerian model of dynamics does not track, but describes local changes. For video, an Eulerian phase-based motion representation, using complex steerable filters, has been successfully employed recently for motion magnification and video frame interpolation. Inspired by these previous works, here, we proposes learning Eulerian motion representations in a deep architecture for action recognition. We learn filters in the complex domain in an end-to-end manner. We design these complex filters to resemble complex Gabor filters, typically employed for phase-information extraction. We propose a phase-information extraction module, based on these complex filters, that can be used in any network architecture for extracting Eulerian representations. We experimentally analyze the added value of Eulerian motion representations, as extracted by our proposed phase extraction module, and compare with existing motion representations based on optical flow, on the UCF101 dataset.

Keywords: Motion representation · Phase derivatives
Eulerian motion representation · Action recognition

1 Introduction

Recent advances in action classification rely on training Convolutional Neural Networks (ConvNets) on large video datasets [2,12,20,24]. Such ConvNets need to learn a suitable representation for motion, as it is important for discriminating similar actions that occur in a visually similar context: *e.g. Basketball Throw* and *Basketball Dunk* [11]. Motion information is typically modeled by using optical flow as input to a separate network stream [20], or by using $3D$ convolutions [24], on stacks of input RGB frames and optical flow field stacks [2,5,15,19,20,28]. In this paper, inspired from the suggestions in [18], we zoom in on an alternative

© Springer Nature Switzerland AG 2019
L. Leal-Taixé and S. Roth (Eds.): ECCV 2018 Workshops, LNCS 11134, pp. 678–691, 2019.
https://doi.org/10.1007/978-3-030-11024-6_51

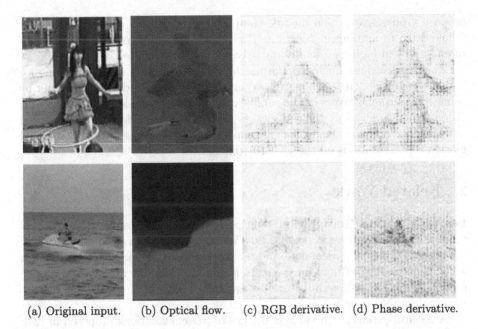

(a) Original input.   (b) Optical flow.   (c) RGB derivative.   (d) Phase derivative.

Fig. 1. Motion representations: (a) Original input. (b) Optical flow visualized in HSV space, where hue indicates the direction, and the saturation is the motion magnitude. (c) Difference of RGB (dRGB), over time. (d) Difference of phase (dPhase), over time (as described in Sect. 3). For *dRGB* and *dPhase*, red indicates a positive value, while blue indicates a negative value. The optical flow fails to capture the motion of the waves around the boat. The Eulerian representations better describe the motion at the boundaries of the objects. (Color figure online)

to using optical flow as a motion representation for deep action recognition in video: we investigate using phase in the complex domain instead of optical flow.

Optical flow follows the Lagrangian perspective on motion representations: tracking a pixel over time using its appearance, and the appearance information of neighboring pixels. Dissimilarly, an Eulerian motion representation focuses on the change in image information at a fixed spatial location, over time. Lagrangian methods require explicit point matching to obtain tracks, which is difficult on untextured surfaces, *e.g.* water, hula hoops, or in the presence of occlusion. Eulerian motion representations, instead, do not need to compute explicit correspondences, yet they are sensitive to sudden large motions. Figure 1 depicts this difference between optical flow and Eulerian representations, defined as RGB and phase derivatives over time, on a few video examples.

Previously, Eulerian representations based on RGB differences, have been considered in [27]. However, they were only used as an input to the same network architecture employed for RGB inputs. The performance is highly dependent on the choice of network architecture [2]. Hence, architecture-level changes are necessary to make full use of the Eulerian motion information. In this work, we propose a phase-extraction module composed of a complex convolutional layer followed by an arctangent function. The proposed module can be trained end-to-end and can be integrated in any existing network architecture.

This work brings forth: (i) the use of Eulerian motion representations for action recognition; (ii) learning phased information in an end-to-end manner by using convolutional layers in the complex domain and complex activations; (iii) an empirical analysis of the advantages and failure cases for the phase-based motion representations, as well as a comparison with existing optical flow-based motion representations on the UCF101 dataset.

2 Related Work

Learning Action Recognition. Top performing action recognition architectures use two-stream networks [4,5,20]. When using a separate motion stream, the input is typically optical flow, and the stream uses popular architectures such as VGG-16 or ResNet, and inter-stream fusion [4,5]. In this work, we adapt the motion stream of [20] architecture for our final network. However, our motion stream describes Eulerian motion.

A natural extension to video is the use of $3D$ convolutions proposed in [24]. In [2], the Inception architecture [22] enhanced with $3D$ convolutions proved effective. This architecture, coined *I3D*, coupled with a new large action recognition dataset, Kinetics [12], delivered state-of-the-art performance. In [28] $3D$ convolutions using $k_t \times k \times k$ filters, are replaced with the more effective $1 \times k \times k$ followed by $k_t \times 1 \times 1$ filters, to reduce computational costs. In this work, we do not consider $3D$ convolutions, but rather focus on learning Eulerian motion descriptions.

In [25] long term convolutions based on optical flow are proposed for action recognition. Recurrent Neural Networks (RNN) are also successfully used for modelling temporal information [3,16]. Our proposed model can be used in combination with such architectures. Where our proposed complex layer plays the feature extraction role.

Motion Representations for Action Recognition. To increase inference speed, in [27] RGB differences are used instead of optical flow. It does not outperform optical flow, yet it obtains comparable performance while being ×25 faster at inference-time. The use of motion vectors, that are similar to optical flow but capture only coarse-motion, is proposed in [29]. The motion vectors obtain a ×27 speed improvement over two-stream networks [20], while having comparable performance. Unlike these methods, we propose learning Eulerian motion representation in an end-to-end framework for tackling action recognition where optical flow fails.

A cascade of networks that learn to generate optical flow for the task of action recognition is used in [15,19]. A similar motion representation is used in [31] before the classification network. Explicit use of optical flow as an input remains superior over other methods for action recognition. However, our aim here is to research if we can find a complementary motion representation to the optical flow.

Phase-Based Methods. Video phase information has been successfully used before for tasks such as motion magnification and video frame interpolation. Work such as [6,9] reconstruct optical flow by extracting phase changes from image sequences and optimizing for velocity. Measuring phase difference of a stereo image pair helps in estimating disparity at each pixel location for depth estimation [7]. In [13,26,30] motion magnification of small movements was possible by measuring phase variations using a complex steerable pyramids over a sequence of images, and then magnifying motion in a reconstructed video. In [17], a ConvNet architecture was proposed to encode, manipulate, and then decode two subsequent input frames, to obtain an output frame with magnified motion. PhaseNet was proposed in [14], which is a decoder network that receives the decomposition of two input frames, the result of applying steerable pyramid filters, and tries to predict the decomposition of the target frame. Similar to these works, and inspired by [18] we adapt the idea of phase-based motion measurement, however dissimilar to previous works we propose to learn this end-to-end, through complex convolutions.

3   Phase-Based Motion Description

Fourier's shift theorem states that a shift in time domain corresponds to a related linear phase shift in the frequency domain. Since phase variations directly correspond to change [8,17,26], they can serve as a viable representation of motion. This does not only apply to the phase of the Fourier basis functions (sine waves), but also to the phase of other representations in the complex domain such as complex-steerable pyramids [26]. Here, we build on the idea of representing local motion through the phase responses obtained by using a complete set of complex filters.

3.1   Complex Filters for Motion Description

Fleet and Jepson [6] showed that the temporal evolution of contours of constant phase provides a good approximation to the motion field. In [6,9] complex quadrature filters are used to extract the contours of constant phase. The temporal derivative of these responses is then employed to estimate object velocity in videos. Specifically, a set of complex Gabor quadrature filters are used for extracting phase information. A complex quadrature Gabor filter, $H(x, y; \lambda, \theta, \psi, \sigma, \gamma)$, is defined as:

$$H(x, y; \lambda, \theta, \psi, \sigma, \gamma) = G(x, y; \lambda, \theta, \psi, \sigma, \gamma) + iG(x, y; \lambda, \theta, \frac{\pi}{2} - \psi, \sigma, \gamma) \quad (1)$$

$$= \exp\left(-\frac{x'^2 + \gamma^2 y'^2}{2\sigma^2}\right) \times \exp\left(i\left(2\pi\frac{x'}{\lambda} + \psi\right)\right), \quad (2)$$

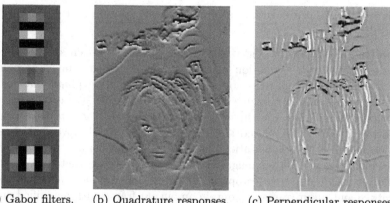

(a) Gabor filters.   (b) Quadrature responses.   (c) Perpendicular responses.

Fig. 2. Quadrauture versus perpendicular filters. (a) From top to bottom: the real and imaginary parts of a complex Gabor, followed by rotated real Gabor. Top and middle form the complex quadrature pair, while top and bottom form a complex perpendicular pair. (b) Phase responses to a complex quadrature Gabor. (c) Phase response to a complex perpendicular filter. In (b) only vertical orientations are highlighted, while both horizontal and vertical orientations are highlighted in (c), providing a more detailed description of the phase contours.

where $G(\cdot)$ is a standard Gabor filter, $i = \sqrt{-1}$, $x' = x\cos(\theta) + y\sin(\theta)$, and $y' = -x\sin(\theta) + y\cos(\theta)$, λ is the wavelength of the wave, θ represents its orientation, ψ is its phase offset, σ is the standard deviation of the Gaussian envelope, and γ is the spatial aspect ratio of the Gaussian, used to control its ellipticity.

In our case, we to not wish to precisely estimate the velocity of objects over time in the video, but rather describe the motion. Therefore, we relax the need of using quadrature filters for finding contours of constant phase and instead, we opt for the more simple perpendicular complex filters.

Perpendicular Filters. Learning complex quadrature filters using convolutional networks is difficult as it requires regularizing to ensure that the phase shift between the real and imaginary filters is $\pi/2$. Here we opt for using perpendicular filters. Combining information from two perpendicular orientations gives a more complete, but less-orientation sensitive, response.

To ensure that the learned filters are perpendicular, we fix the real filters, so they do not receive gradients during the training. We only update the imaginary filters during training and reinitialize the real filters as a $\pi/2$ rotated version of the imaginary filters. This choice avoids numeric problems when extracting the phase information as $\operatorname{atan}(\frac{x_i}{x_r})$, where x_r and x_i are the real and imaginary responses, respectively.

We find the perpendicular filters to be sufficient for describing motion contours in phase domain, and we validate this in our experiments. Figure 2 depicts the difference between the responses of quadrature complex filters and perpendicular complex filters.

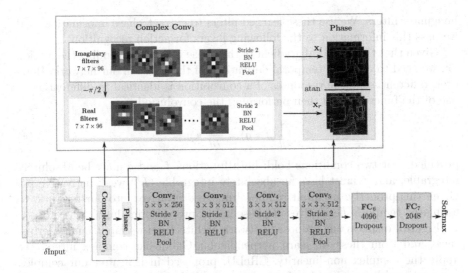

Fig. 3. Network Architecture. We input to our network temporal image derivatives. From the input information, we learn perpendicular complex Gabor-like filters, in our proposed complex layer. We use the responses of these filters to compute the phase. This information is subsequently send to the following layers in the network.

Sinusoidal Gabor Regularization. To encourage the learned filters to resemble Gabor filters, we propose a regularization. We only train the imaginary part of our complex filters. Since the imaginary Gabor filter is a sine multiplied by a Gaussian, we define the imaginary part of our complex filters as a multiplication between a filter initialized randomly and a non-trainable Gaussian kernel. We subsequently, regularize the trainable part of the filter to correspond to a sine.

In the Fourier domain a sine corresponds a single point, ignoring the domain symmetry. Thus, we minimize the L_2 distance from each point of the filter in the Fourier domain to the center of mass of the filter in the Fourier domain:

$$R(\mathbf{w}) = \sum_{i=1}^{n} \|\mathbf{w}_i - \mathrm{CoM}(\mathbf{w})\|_2, \qquad (3)$$

where n is the dimensionality of $\mathbf{w}$, $\mathbf{w}$ are the responses of the imaginary filters passed through a Real-FFT (Real Fast Fourier Transform), and $\mathrm{CoM}(\cdot)$ computes the center of mass.

3.2   Learning Phase-Based Descriptions

We adapt a standard ConvNet to learn phase, by learning complex Gabor-like filters. The trainable part of the filters is first initialized randomly. Only the imaginary part of the filters is trained, and regularized with the proposed Gabor regularization. The real part of the complex filter is a $\pi/2$ rotated version of the imaginary filters. We use these learned filters to extract phase information, and we pass this information to the following layers for action recognition.

Given that the temporal gradient of the phase is the one encoding the motion [6], we need to estimate temporal derivatives of the phase in our network. However, differentiating the responses of a convolution is identical to differentiating one of the functions and then performing the convolution:

$$\frac{\partial}{\partial t}(f * g) = \frac{\partial f}{\partial t} * g, \tag{4}$$

provided that two conditions hold: both functions f and g must be absolutely integrable, and f must have an absolutely integrable (L^1) weak derivative [1]. Given this property, we input temporal image derivatives into our network, to estimated temporal derivatives of phase in our proposed module.

Figure 3 displays our proposed network architecture: we input image derivatives, and from these we learn perpendicular Gabor-like complex filters. We apply the complex non-linearity, $\mathbb{C}$ReLU, proposed in [23] after our complex convolutional layer. $\mathbb{C}$ReLU effectively applies ReLU separately on the real and imaginary feature maps. We also use standard BN (Batch Normalization). We subsequently, estimate the phase as the arctangent of the responses of these filters, and we send this information to the following layers.

4   Experiments

4.1   Experimental Setup

We use the network architecture displayed in Fig. 3. This is a replica of VGG-M, corresponding to one stream in [20], but in which the first layer is replaced with our complex layer. For clarity we will refer to it as: *PhaseStream*. All experiments are performed on UCF101 [21], containing 101 action classes, with an average of 180 frames/video. We follow the standard training/testing data splitting. For the **Exp 1**, where we analyze design choices, we evaluate using only one standard data split. While, for **Exp 2**, we evaluate using the three standard data splits on UCF101. For all experiments, we use momentum SGD as an optimizer with momentum of 0.9. Videos are uniformly sampled from all classes to create a batch of 256. The dropout ratio is set to 0.9 and the learning rate is set to 0.01 and reduced by a factor of 10 at iterations 45000 and 75000. We train for 100,000 iterations. Data is augmented with random crops and flips.

4.2   Exp 1: Importance of Eulerian Information

Exp 1(a): The Use of Perpendicular Versus Quadrature Filters. To quantify the quality of learned perpendicular filters, we initialize our proposed complex layer with rotated Gabor filters. These filters are fixed throughout training. The results serve as a benchmark for the learning process. To compare quadrature filters with the perpendicular ones, our complex layer is initialized with quadrature Gabor filters, also fixed throughout training.

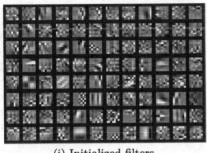

(i) Initialized filters.   (ii) Regularized complex filters.

Fig. 4. Exp 1(a): The effect of the sinusoidal Gabor regularization: (i) randomly initialized filters; (ii) trained filters with the sinusoidal Gabor regularization. The Gabor regularization compels the learned filters to be more similar to Gabor filters.

Table 1. Exp 1(a): Accuracy on UCF101 when using the proposed perpendicular complex filters when compared to quadrature Gabor filters. The network receives as input grayscale image derivatives over time, *dGray*. The perpendicular filters tend to generalize better than the quadrature filters.

Filter type	No. of filters	Training acc	Testing acc
Quadrature Gabor	24	~90 %	60.5 %
Perpendicular Gabor	24	~70 %	64.8 %
Perpendicular Gabor	96	~80 %	71.6 %

Table 1 shows the results of the experiment. We consider two settings for the filter banks: one consisting of 24 filters, similar to the one in [6]; and the other consisting of 96 filters, covering 12 logarithmically spaced frequencies between 0.2 and 5 Hz, over the same 8 directions $\theta = \pi/8 \times \{0, 1, .., 7\}$. From the experimental analysis we conclude that the perpendicular filters help the network generalize better to unseen data.

Figure 4(i) shows the initial set of complex filters, with random initialization. While Fig. 4(ii) shows the learned filters in our complex layer with the incorporated sinusoidal Gabor regularization described in Sect. 3.2. The regularization is effective in encouraging the learned complex filters to resemble Gabor filters.

Exp 1(b): The Importance of the Input. Table 2 shows the performance of different inputs on two network architectures: the VGG-M [20] and our variant of VGG-M in which we replace the first convolution with a complex convolution. We refer to it as *PhaseStream*. In Table 2(i) we consider Eulerian inputs: *dRGB* – derivative of RGB frames obtained by temporally subtracting 2 consecutive frames, *dPhase* – derivative of phase frames, *dGray* – derivative of grayscale frames; and non-Eulerian inputs: *RGB* and OF (Optical Flow). In Table 2(ii) we consider stacked variants of the inputs: *5 × OF* where we stack 5 consecutive OF inputs, *5 × dGray* and *5 × dPhase*. The Eulerian inputs perform better than

686   O. Hommos et al.

Table 2. Exp 1(b): Accuracy (%) on UCF101 for different network inputs for our proposed *PhaseStream* compared to the VGG-M [20]. (i) We compare Eulerian representation: *dGray* – derivative of grayscale inputs over time, *dRGB* – derivative of RGB frames, *dPhase* – derivative of phase images, with *OF* – optical flow, and RGB. The *dPhase* and *dGray* are stronger than using OF as input. (ii) We consider also stacked inputs: *5 × OF* – OF stacked over 5 frames, *5 × dGray* – 5 grayscale derivatives stacked, and *5 × dPhase* – 5 phase derivatives stacked. When stacking OF, *5 × OF*, there is a substantial gain over stacked Eulerian inputs. Overall, using the proposed *PhaseStream* is beneficial for all inputs except for stacked *dPhase, 5 × dPhase*. We highlight in bold the network architecture with the highest accuracy.

Input	VGG-M [20]	PhaseStream (our)
RGB	**52.3** %	51.3 %
OF	67.7 %	N/A
dRGB	45.5 %	**48.8** %
dGray	74.3 %	**74.4** %
dPhase	65.4 %	**70.1** %

(i) Different inputs.

Input	VGG-M [20]	PhaseStream (our)
5×OF	80.4 %	N/A
5×dGray	68.7 %	**75.3** %
5×dPhase	**70.8** %	68.2 %

(ii) Stacked inputs.

the non-Eulerian ones on the VGG-M. However, when stacking the inputs, OF outperforms the rest. Our *PhaseStream* obtains improved performance for all inputs except for *5 × dPhase*. We do not evaluate our *PhaseStream* network on OF inputs, as computing complex responses over OF does not seem theoretically informative. The stacked Eulerian representations do not perform well due to the large or fast motion, which may result in combining different motion patterns of different object or adding noise into the motion representation.

Table 3 shows the relative improvements in accuracy on the UCF101 dataset for VGG-M [20] and our *PhaseStream* with grayscale frame derivatives, *dGray*, as input. We show the top 10 classes with the largest improvements in accuracy. VGG-M performs better on action categories involving subtle motion, but which are more visual – containing a specific visual object such as: *Archery, ApplyLipstick*, or *PlayingFlute*. The *PhaseStream* obtains larger improvements over VGG-M from repetitive activities such as: *BoxingPunchingBag, Walking-WithDog, MoppingFloor, ShavingBeard*. Examples of video frames from these categories are displayed in Fig. 5. We show the network inputs, *dGray* inputs, on the second row. On the last row we show the associated temporal derivatives of phase information, which is the type of information we would expect the network to rely on.

Exp 1(c): Robustness of Motion Information. To quantify the robustness of motion information, we shuffle the input frames before calculating the temporal frame derivatives and OF, to be input to the network. This step effectively removes the temporal structure of the original video [19,28]. We analyze how our proposed *PhaseStream* performs when compared with the VGG-M [20] and

Table 3. Exp 1(b): The relative improvements in accuracy on UCF101 between VGG-M [20] and our *PhaseStream* with *dGray* as input. We show the top 10 classes for each one of the architectures. The networks learn complementary information.

VGG-M [20]	$\Delta\%$	PhaseStream (our)	$\Delta\%$
Archery	19.5 %	FloorGymnastics	19.4%
JumpingJack	15.8 %	TennisSwing	16.3 %
Rowing	13.9 %	BoxingPunchingBag	14.3 %
CricketShot	12.2 %	WalkingWithDog	13.9 %
Skijet	10.7 %	GolfSwing	12.8 %
BlowDryHair	10.5 %	MoppingFloor	11.8 %
PlayingFlute	10.4 %	HighJump	10.8 %
ApplyLipstick	9.4 %	UnevenBars	10.7 %
PlayingCello	9.1 %	ShavingBeard	9.3 %
HulaHoop	8.8 %	HandstandWalking	8.8 %

Table 4. Exp 1(c): Test accuracies on UCF101 when training our *PhaseStream*, VGG-M [20] and TSN [27] on standard inputs, as well as on temporally shuffled inputs. We also show the relative drop in performance, in percentages. The VGG-M suffers a slightly larger relative drop in performance, while TSN and our proposed *PhaseStream* suffer a comparable drop in performance, when the temporal ordering is lost.

Architecture input	VGG-M [20] dGray	TSN [27] $5 \times$ OF	PhaseStream (our) dGray
Standard accuracy	74.3 %	86.9 %	74.4 %
Shuffled accuracy	49.4 %	59.6 %	51.4 %
Relative change (%)	33.5 %	31.4 %	30.1 %

TSN [27]. For our *PhaseStream* as well as for VGG-M, we use as input grayscale temporal image derivatives, *dGray*.

Table 4 shows the test accuracies on UCF101, when feeding the networks standard inputs as well as temporally shuffled inputs. Optical flow numbers are taken from [19] for the TSN architecture [27]. We also show the relative drop in performance, in percentages, caused by the loss of temporal ordering. The TSN performs the best in terms of absolute accuracy scores. When looking at the relative scores, the VGG-M has a slightly larger relative loss of performance, while TSN and our proposed *PhaseStream* suffer a similar relative loss in accuracy.

4.3   Exp 2: Comparison with Existing Work

Table 5 shows the action recognition accuracy on the UCF101 dataset for a number of popular action recognition models: Two-Stream [20], Two-Stream ResNets [4], TSN [27], Motion Vectors [29], ActionFlow [15] and our *PhaseStream*. We

689 O. Hommos et al.

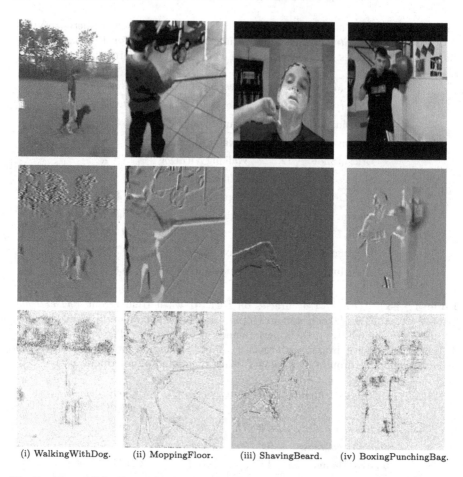

(i) WalkingWithDog.   (ii) MoppingFloor.   (iii) ShavingBeard.   (iv) BoxingPunchingBag.

Fig. 5. Exp 1(b): Examples of video frames from the classes *BoxingPunchingBag*, *WalkingWithDog*, *MopppingFloor*, *ShavingBeard*, where the *PhaseStream* performs better than the VGG-M [20]. We also display the temporal derivatives of grayscale inputs on the second row, and the temporal derivative of phase for these video frames, on the last row. These classes are characterized by repetitive motion patterns.

train our *PhaseStream* on a stack of five differences of grayscale inputs, $5 \times dGray$. Given that we focus on motion representations, we show the performance on the motion (temporal) stream only, for all the considered architectures.

TSN [27] achieves the best performance as it relies on an ensemble of 3 two-stream networks, and provides several architecture-level improvements over them. When it comes to Two-stream network [20], Two-stream ResNets [4], and Motion Vectors [29], the temporal input is a stack of 10 temporal representations. We use only a stack of 5 motion representations, as we did not see a great improvement from temporally stacking the Eulerian representations. Our proposed method on the temporal stream, obtains superior performance to

Table 5. Exp 2: Accuracy (%) on UCF101 comparing our proposed *PhaseStream* trained on 5 × *dGray*, with the Two-stream [20], Two-stream ResNet [4], TSN [27], Motion Vectors [29], and ActionFlow [15]. We show only the accuracy on the motion (temporal) stream for these methods, as we focus only on learning motion representations. The TSN method performs the best. Our proposed approach obtains superior performance to ActionFlow [15], while having slightly lower performance than Motion Vectors [29], and Two-stream ResNets [4], on the temporal stream.

Network	Motion (Temporal) stream
TSN [27]	83.8 %
Two-Stream [20]	81.2 %
Two-Stream ResNets [4]	79.1 %
Motion Vectors [29]	79.3 %
ActionFlow [15]	70.0 %
PhaseStream (our) on 5 × *dGray*	76.4 %

ActionFlow [15], while having slightly lower performance than Motion Vectors [29], and Two-stream ResNets [4]. These results validate that there is gain to be obtained from using Eulerian motion representations for action recognition.

4.4   Limitations and Possible Improvements

Our proposed phase-based motion description shares similar limitations to the classic phase-based approaches, namely dealing with noisy inputs and high-velocity actions. Learning an Eulerian transformation from two consecutive frames independently, could potentially solve the former problem, while increasing the number of proposed complex layers in the network architecture could help the performance.

Another limitation to keep in mind is the number of distinct overlapping motions patterns per spatial neighborhood. Having three or more motion patterns per neighborhood in a video, increases the likelihood of errors in the Eulerian motion representation. This can happen if the effective size of the receptive field of our perpendicular complex filters in the proposed complex layer is too high. A possible improvement to this proposed Eulerian method of learning motion representations for action recognition, is the use of 3D convolutional filters. This may alleviate the problem of achieving limited improvement when stacking Eulerian inputs.

The project was implemented using TensorFlow. The source code for our complex layer can be found at https://github.com/11maxed11/phase-based-action-recognition. More details can be found in [10].

5   Conclusions

We present a new architecture for learning phase-based descriptions from Eulerian inputs, in the context of action recognition. The proposed method relies on learning perpendicular complex filters in a ConvNet. To help the network learn Gabor-like complex filters we propose a regularization scheme based of frequency analysis, for our learned complex filters.

Empirical evaluation shows that this architecture delivers an improvement for several Eulerian inputs, while also exceeding the baseline for recognition using a single optical flow input. Further improvements of the proposed method are possible, by considering different alternative to boost the performance of the temporal representation by using LSTM layers [3,16], and 3D convolutional layers [24].

References

1. Bracewell, R.: "Convolution" and "two-dimensional convolution". In: The Fourier Transform and Its Applications (1965)
2. Carreira, J., Zisserman, A.: Quo vadis, action recognition? A new model and the kinetics dataset. In: CVPR, pp. 4724–4733. IEEE (2017)
3. Donahue, J., et al.: Long-term recurrent convolutional networks for visual recognition and description. In: CVPR, pp. 2625–2634 (2015)
4. Feichtenhofer, C., Pinz, A., Wildes, R.: Spatiotemporal residual networks for video action recognition. In: NIPS, pp. 3468–3476 (2016)
5. Feichtenhofer, C., Pinz, A., Zisserman, A.: Convolutional two-stream network fusion for video action recognition. In: CVPR, pp. 1933–1941 (2016)
6. Fleet, D.J., Jepson, A.D.: Computation of component image velocity from local phase information. IJCV 5(1), 77–104 (1990)
7. Fleet, D.J., Jepson, A.D., Jenkin, M.R.: Phase-based disparity measurement. CVGIP Image Underst. 53(2), 198–210 (1991)
8. Freeman, W.T., Adelson, E.H., et al.: The design and use of steerable filters. TPAMI 13(9), 891–906 (1991)
9. Gautama, T., Van Hulle, M.M., et al.: A phase-based approach to the estimation of the optical flow field using spatial filtering. TNN 13(5), 1127–1136 (2002)
10. Hommos, O.: Learning phase-based descriptions for action recognition. Master's thesis, Delft University of Technology, May 2018
11. Jain, M., van Gemert, J.C., Snoek, C.G.: What do 15,000 object categories tell us about classifying and localizing actions? In: CVPR, pp. 46–55 (2015)
12. Kay, W., et al.: The kinetics human action video dataset. CoRR (2017)
13. Kooij, J.F.P., van Gemert, J.C.: Depth-aware motion magnification. In: Leibe, B., Matas, J., Sebe, N., Welling, M. (eds.) ECCV 2016. LNCS, vol. 9912, pp. 467–482. Springer, Cham (2016). https://doi.org/10.1007/978-3-319-46484-8_28
14. Meyer, S., Djelouah, A., McWilliams, B., Sorkine-Hornung, A., Gross, M., Schroers, C.: PhaseNet for video frame interpolation. In: CVPR, pp. 498–507 (2018)
15. Ng, J.Y.H., Choi, J., Neumann, J., Davis, L.S.: ActionFlowNet: learning motion representation for action recognition. CoRR (2016)
16. Ng, J.Y.H., Hausknecht, M., Vijayanarasimhan, S., Vinyals, O., Monga, R., Toderici, G.: Beyond short snippets: deep networks for video classification. In: CVPR, pp. 4694–4702. IEEE (2015)

17. Oh, T.H., et al.: Learning-based video motion magnification. CoRR (2018)
18. Pintea, S.L., van Gemert, J.C.: Making a case for learning motion representations with phase. In: Hua, G., Jégou, H. (eds.) ECCV 2016. LNCS, vol. 9915, pp. 55–64. Springer, Cham (2016). https://doi.org/10.1007/978-3-319-49409-8_8
19. Sevilla-Lara, L., Liao, Y., Guney, F., Jampani, V., Geiger, A., Black, M.J.: On the integration of optical flow and action recognition. CoRR (2017)
20. Simonyan, K., Zisserman, A.: Two-stream convolutional networks for action recognition in videos. In: NIPS, pp. 568–576 (2014)
21. Soomro, K., Zamir, A.R., Shah, M.: UCF101: a dataset of 101 human actions classes from videos in the wild. CoRR (2012)
22. Szegedy, C., et al.: Going deeper with convolutions. In: CVPR, June 2015
23. Trabelsi, C., et al.: Deep complex networks. CoRR (2017)
24. Tran, D., Bourdev, L.D., Fergus, R., Torresani, L., Paluri, M.: C3D: generic features for video analysis. CoRR, abs/1412.0767, vol. 2. no. 7, p. 8 (2014)
25. Varol, G., Laptev, I., Schmid, C.: Long-term temporal convolutions for action recognition. TPAMI 40(6), 1510–1517 (2018)
26. Wadhwa, N., Rubinstein, M., Durand, F., Freeman, W.T.: Phase-based video motion processing. TOG 32(4), 80 (2013)
27. Wang, L., Xiong, Y., Wang, Z., Qiao, Y., Lin, D., Tang, X., Van Gool, L.: Temporal segment networks: towards good practices for deep action recognition. In: Leibe, B., Matas, J., Sebe, N., Welling, M. (eds.) ECCV 2016. LNCS, vol. 9912, pp. 20–36. Springer, Cham (2016). https://doi.org/10.1007/978-3-319-46484-8_2
28. Xie, S., Sun, C., Huang, J., Tu, Z., Murphy, K.: Rethinking spatiotemporal feature learning for video understanding. CoRR (2017)
29. Zhang, B., Wang, L., Wang, Z., Qiao, Y., Wang, H.: Real-time action recognition with enhanced motion vector CNNs. In: CVPR, pp. 2718–2726. IEEE (2016)
30. Zhang, Y., Pintea, S., van Gemert, J.: Video acceleration magnification. In: CVPR. IEEE (2017)
31. Zhu, Y., Lan, Z., Newsam, S., Hauptmann, A.G.: Hidden two-stream convolutional networks for action recognition. CoRR (2017)

Event Extraction Using Transportation of Temporal Optical Flow Fields

Itaru Gotoh[1], Hiroki Hiraoka[1], and Atsushi Imiya[2(✉)]

[1] School of Science and Engineering, Chiba University,
Yayoi-cho 1-33, Inage-ku, Chiba 263-8522, Japan
[2] Institute of Management and Information Technologies, Chiba University,
Yayoi-cho 1-33, Inage-ku, Chiba 263-8522, Japan
imiya@faculty.chiba-u.jp

Abstract. In this paper, we develop a method to transform a sequence of images to a sequence of events. Optical flow, which is the vector fields of pointwise motion computed from monocular image sequences, describes pointwise motion in an environment. The method extracts the global smoothness and continuity of motion fields and detects collapses of the smoothness of the motion fields in long-time image sequences using transportation of the temporal optical flow field.

1 Introduction

Optical flow is fundamentally pointwise local motion on an imaging plane (retina) [1–4]. This pointwise motion is low-level information for perception of global motion [5–8,34,35]. In this paper, we introduce a model for the extraction of queues for perception of global motion from the optical flow fields using temporal transportation [9,10] of optical flow fields along times.

Flow vectors locally extract point correspondences between a pair of successive images on the retina [1]. These local correspondences are applied to motion tracking because temporal evolution of a correspondence describes the temporal trajectory of a point in a video stream of images.

In Field VI of the human brain for motion perception, independent components of optical flow field on the retina [11,36] are transmitted from the medial superior temporal area (MST) to the middle temporal area (MT) [11–16]. Then, pointwise local motion is transformed to intermediate-level information for motion cognition. Flying insects also control motion using optical flow. Honey bees navigate using optical flow [17–21]. The compound eyes [18,19,38,39] of insects perceive spherical optical flow fields [38,39]. The divergence on the spherical optical flow filed indicates the direction of flying in the global environment [19]. Disparities of optical flow fields between the fields on the left and right hemi-spheres control the direction of fling in the local environment. Therefore, temporal optical flow fields generated on the spherical retina of an omnidirectional camera system provide queue for navigation [39]. These geometric properties of optical flow fields on the spherical retina are the basis of insect-inspired

© Springer Nature Switzerland AG 2019
L. Leal-Taixé and S. Roth (Eds.): ECCV 2018 Workshops, LNCS 11134, pp. 692–705, 2019.
https://doi.org/10.1007/978-3-030-11024-6_52

visual navigation. Geometrical processing of optical flow fields on the spherical retina yields syntactical information for robot navigation [37–39].

Autonomous vehicles navigate using images captured by a planar retina [40, 41]. We have develop an algorithm for the generation of motion semantics from optical flow fields generated on a planar retina, which is a common imaging process for non-compound eye systems.

In the previous paper, we introduced a model for the extraction of queue for recognising global spatial motion from scene flow fields using the temporal transportation of the vector field [40]. As a comparative study with our previous results, we apply the same idea to the optical flow field on a planar retina. This comparative study implies that for global motion perception, the optical flow fields, which is computed from monocular image sequence, possess the similar properties with those of the scene flow fields.

2 Metric for Optical Flow Fields

Setting $u(x) = (u(x), v(x))^\top$ for $x = (x, y)^\top \in \mathbf{R}^2$ to be the optical flow field on two-dimensional Euclidean space, the directional histogram [22] of $u(x)$ is obtained by integration of the magnitude of $u(x)$ in the region of interest (ROI), that is,

$$h_x(\theta; u) = \frac{1}{|\Omega(x)|} \int_{\Omega(x) \frac{u(y)}{|u(y)|} = (\cos\theta, \sin\theta)^\top} |u(y)| dy, \tag{1}$$

where $\Omega(x)$, $|\Omega(x)|$ and $x \in \mathbf{R}^2$ are the ROI, the area measure of the ROI and the reference point of the ROI, respectively.

The distance between two optical flow fields $u(x)$ and $v(x)$ in the region Λ is defined as

$$D(u, v)$$
$$= \left(\int_\Lambda \left(\min_\phi \min_{c(\theta, \theta')} \int_0^{2\pi} \int_0^{2\pi} |h_x(\theta - \phi; u) - h_x(\theta'; v)|^2 c_x(\theta, \theta') d\theta d\theta' \right) dx \right)^{\frac{1}{2}}, \tag{2}$$

where

$$\int_0^{2\pi} c_x(\theta, \theta') d\theta \le h_x(\theta'; u), \quad \int_0^{2\pi} c_x(\theta, \theta') d\theta' \le h_x(\theta; v), \tag{3}$$

for $c_x(\theta, \theta') \ge 0$, using the transportation [9] of the directional histograms [22] of the fields.

For the discrete optical flow field $u_{mn} = (u_{mn}, v_{mn})^\top$ at the point $(m, n)^\top$ on discrete plane $\mathbf{Z}^2$, let $\{f_{mn}(p)\}_{p=0}^{N-1}$ be the cyclic directional histogram for the directions $\omega_N = (\cos 2\pi \frac{p}{N} \sin 2\pi \frac{p}{N})^\top$. For the discrete cyclic histograms $F_{mn} = \{f_{mn}(i)\}_{i=0}^{N-1}$ and $G_{mn} = \{g_{mn}(i)\}_{i=0}^{N-1}$, such that $f_{mn}(i + N) = f_{mn}(i)$

and $g_{mn}(i + N) = g_{mn}(i)$, we define the transportation between the histograms as

$$d_{mn}(F_{mn}, G_{mn}) = \left(\min_{k} \min_{c_{ij}^{mn}} \sum_{i=0}^{N-1} \sum_{j=0}^{N-1} |f_{mn}(i) - g_{mn}(j - k)|^2 c(k)_{ij}^{mn} \right)^{\frac{1}{2}} , \quad (4)$$

$$\sum_{i=0}^{N-1} c_{ij}(k)^{mn} \le g_{mn}(j - k), \quad \sum_{j=0}^{N-1} c_{ij}(k)^{mn} \le f_{mn}(i), \quad c_{ij}^{mn} \ge 0. \quad (5)$$

Setting $A_{ij}^{mn}(k) = |f_{mn}(i) - g_{mn}(j - k)|^2$, the minimisation of $J_{mn}(k)$

$$J_{mn}(k) = \min_{c(k)_{ij}^{mn}} \sum_{i=0}^{N-1} \sum_{j=0}^{N-1} A_{ij}^{mn}(k) c(k)_{ij}^{mn}, \quad (6)$$

with the constraints of Eq. (5) is solved by linear programming for each $k = 0, 1, \cdots, N - 1$. Then, we define the metric between discrete vector fields $\boldsymbol{u}_{mn}$ and $\boldsymbol{v}_{mn}$ in the ROI Λ on the two-dimensional discrete plane $\mathbf{Z}^2$ as

$$d(\boldsymbol{u}, \boldsymbol{v}) = \sqrt{\sum_{(m,n)^\top \in \Lambda} d_{mn}(F_{mn}, G_{mn})^2}, \quad d_{mn}(F_{mn}, G_{mn}) = \min_{k} \sqrt{J_{mn}(k)}. \quad (7)$$

Figure 1 shows the process of transportation of a pair of circular histograms f and g. (a) and (b) show two probabilistic distribution on a circle. and their samples on the circle. The top row in (c) shows the residual values after the maximum flows moved from each bin of P to bins of Q. The bottom row in (c) shows the flows that moved from P to Q as the maximum flow between histograms.

3   Symbolisation of Global Motion

The temporal trajectory of the distance between a successive pair of optical flow fields $\boldsymbol{u}(\boldsymbol{x}, t + 1)$ and $\boldsymbol{u}(\boldsymbol{x}, t)$ of the spatiotemporal image $f(\boldsymbol{x}, t)$ is

$$H(t; f) = d(\boldsymbol{u}(\boldsymbol{x}, t + 1), \boldsymbol{u}(\boldsymbol{x}, t)). \quad (8)$$

Setting $H_t(t; f)$ and $H_{tt}(t; f)$ to be the first and second derivatives, respectively, of the histogram $H(t : f)$, we define the interval $I_i = [t_i, t_{i+1}]$ along the time axis t using a pair of successive points for extremals $H_{tt}(t; f) = 0$. Using the l_1 linear approximation of $H(t; f)$ such that

$$\bar{H}(t; f) = a_i t + b_i, \quad (9)$$

which minimises the criterion

$$J(a_i, b_i) = \sum_{i=1}^{n} \sum_{j=1}^{n(i)} |H(t_{i(j)}; f) - (a_i t_{i(j)} + b_i)|, \quad (10)$$

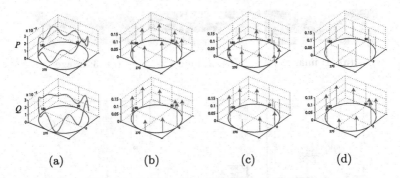

(a)   (b)   (c)   (d)

Fig. 1. Examples of the computation of the transportation distances. (a) and (b) show two probabilistic distributions on a circles and their samples on the circles. The top row in (c) shows the residual values after the maximum flows move from each bin of P to the bins of Q. The bottom row in (c) shows the flows that move from P to Q as the maximum flow between samples. (d) The state at the end of the computation. All sampled values of P are moved to bins of Q.

where $t_{i(j)} \in I_i$, we allocate signs for spatial motion.

From the sign of a_i, we define the symbols of motion of $f(\boldsymbol{x}, t)$ in the interval $I_i = [t_i, t_{i+1}]$ as $\{\nearrow, \rightarrow, \searrow\}$, where

$$
S(H(t; f)) = \begin{cases} \nearrow \text{ if } a_i > 0 \text{ if } t \in I_i, \\ \rightarrow \text{ if } a_i = 0 \text{ if } t \in I_i, \\ \searrow \text{ if } a_i < 0 \text{ if } t \in I_i, \end{cases} \quad S(\log H(t; f)) = \begin{cases} \nearrow \text{ if } a_i > 0 \text{ if } t \in I_i, \\ \rightarrow \text{ if } a_i = 0 \text{ if } t \in I_i, \\ \searrow \text{ if } a_i < 0 \text{ if } t \in I_i. \end{cases}
$$
(11)

4 Numerical Examples

Table 1. Statuses of three sequences from KITTI sceneflowDataset2015[44].

No.	Motion of car	Front car	Inter-vehicle dist.	Oncoming car	Additional conditions
1	accelerating	with	increasing	without	
2	turning right	with	outside of screen	with in the first frame	
3	stopping after braking	with		without	approaching to road crossing

For numerical experiments, three image sequences from left images of KITTI-Scene Flow Dataset2015 [44] are selected.

For event extraction using Eq. (11), we employ $S(H(t; f))$ and $S(\log H(t; f))$, since $S(\log H(t; f))$ allows us to detect symbols from small perturbations of $H(t; f)$.

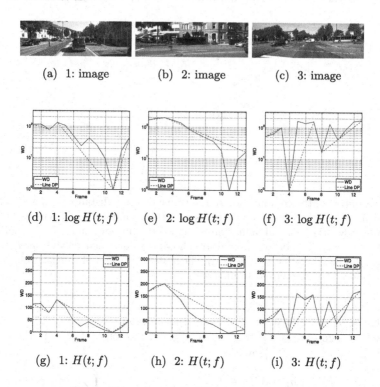

(a) 1: image   (b) 2: image   (c) 3: image

(d) 1: $\log H(t; f)$ (e) 2: $\log H(t; f)$ (f) 3: $\log H(t; f)$

(g) 1: $H(t; f)$ (h) 2: $H(t; f)$ (i) 3: $H(t; f)$

Fig. 2. Examples of the Wasserstein distances

Table 2. Extracted events

No.	Status	Car in front	Oncoming car	WD graph	
				$S(\log H(t; f))$	$S(H(t; f))$
1	acceleration	exists	no	→\\\↗	\↗\\↗
2	turn right	out of the view	exists	→\\\↗	↗↗\\\
3	deceleration and stop	exists	no	↗\↗\↗↗	↗\↗\↗↗

Table 1 lists statuses of the images. Figure 2 shows the temporal trajectories of the transportation of the vector fields. Table 2 shows the event strings extracted by linear approximation by using Eq. (10) and symbolisation by using Eq. (11). These experiments show that the algorithm extracts symbol strings, which describe the states in front of driving cars in various environments.

5 Dictionary Generation

Tables 4 and 3 show status and speed of objects in synthetic video sequences. Figure 3 shows top views of geometric configurations of objects in synthetic video sequences. Table 5 shows combinations of events as symbol strings captured by vehicle mounted camera in a synthetic world. In Figs. 4, 5 and 6, (a) and (b) show a frame view of the image sequence and its optical flow field, respectively.

In Fig. Figures 4, 5 and 6, (c), $\log H(t; f)$ and $\bar{H}(t; f)$ are the blue curve and red polygonal curve, respectively.

Tables 6 and 7 show the strings $S(\log H(t; f))$ and $S(H(t; f))$ detected by the algorithm using $\log H(t; f)$ and $H(t; f)$, respectively. Since both $\log H(t; f)$ and $H(t; f)$ are approximated by polygonal curves for the extraction of symbol strings, events are described by using $\vee$, $\wedge$ and M based on the semi-local shapes of the curves.

Table 3. Speed of objects in synthetic image sequences.

Object	ac-/de-celeration	The first frame spd. [km/h]	The last frame spd. [km/h]
ego-vehicle	no	30	30
oncoming vehicle	no	40	40
ego-vehicle	acceleration	5	30
ego-vehicle	deceleration	30	5
vehicle	no	30	30
vehicle in front	no	45	45
vehicle in front	no	15	15

Table 4. Geometry in synthetic image sequences.

Objects	Position [m]	Width [m]	Length [m]
camera	1.5	base line width 0.3	
white line	0.05	0.4	
lane		2.8	
pavement		1.0–1.5	
oncoming vehicle			$2.0 \times 4.5 \times 1.75$

Five pairs 1 and 2, 5 and 7, 6 and 8, 13 and 14, and 15 and 16 provide same environments with and without oncoming vehicles. These examples show that pairs 1 and 2, 5 and 7, 6 and 8, 13 and 14, possess same properties for symbol string. Pairs 1 and 2, and 13 and 14 imply that the temporal transportation of optical flow vector fields achieves recognition of oncoming vehicles. The algorithm detects acceleration and deceleration of the ego-vehicle.

The results observed in a pair 7 and 8 show that for the detection of the directions of turning additional information is required, since the optical flow fields for left and right turning possess the same statistical properties.

The difference of the results observed in a pair 15 and 16 depends on the background properties caused by trees, since the correspondences between a pair of natural scene contains ambiguities. Moreover, for the detection of oncoming vehicle, the pointwise optical flow vectors are required.

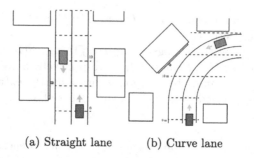

(a) Straight lane   (b) Curve lane

Fig. 3. Top views of geometric configurations of objects in synthetic video sequences simulating city environments. The blue car is the ego-vehicle for experiments. The green car is the object-vehicle for experiments. The lane width is 2.8 m. The pavement width is 1 m–1.5 m.

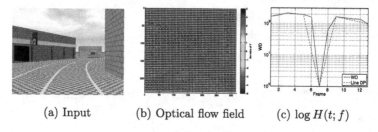

(a) Input   (b) Optical flow field   (c) $\log H(t; f)$

Fig. 4. Motion of synthetic image No. 7. (a) A frame view of the image seqence. (b) Optical flow field. (c) $\log H(t; f)$ and $\log \bar{H}(t; f)$ are drawn in the blue curve and red polygonal curve, respectively. (Color figure online)

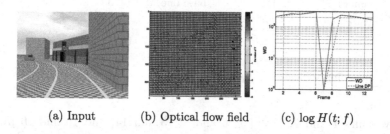

(a) Input   (b) Optical flow field   (c) $\log H(t; f)$

Fig. 5. Motion of synthetic image No. 8. (a) A frame view of the image sequence. (b) Optical flow field. (c) $\log H(t; f)$ and $\log \bar{H}(t; f)$ are drawn in the blue curve and red polygonal curve, respectively. (Color figure online)

The algorithm does not distinguish left and right turns, since the time trajectory of the distance between to field possess the shape profiles. However, it is possible to detect the stating frame of the turns, since the symbol $\wedge$ is detected on the frame. For detection of the straight motion from real sequences, symbol strings both $S(H(t; f))$ and $S(\log H(t; f))$ are necessary, since in real sequences of the straight motion temporal local-perturbation of the optical flow vectors are detected. This local-perturbation derives perturbations on $H(t; f)$ and $\log H(t; f)$.

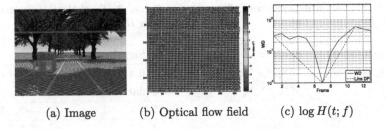

(a) Image   (b) Optical flow field   (c) $\log H(t; f)$

Fig. 6. Motion of synthetic image No. 16. (a) A frame view of the image sequence. (b) Optical flow field. (c) $\log H(t; f)$ and $\log \bar{H}(t; f)$ are drawn in the blue curve and red polygonal curve, respectively. (Color figure online)

Table 5. Events in synthetic data

No.	Motion	Car in front	Oncoming car	Event	Event label
1	straight	no	no	straight	const. spd
2			exist	straight	const. spd+obstacle
3			no	accelerate → straight	accelerate
4			no	straight → deceleration	deceleration
5	turn		no	straight → right curve	turn
6			no	straight → left curve	turn
7			exist	straight → right curve	turn +obstacle
8			exist	straight → left curve	turn +obstacle
9	straight	exist	no	inter-vehicle dist.	car in front
10			no	inter-vehicle dist. increase	car in front
11			no	inter-vehicle dist. decrease	car in front
12			no	passing in passing lane	car in front
13			no	passing in the opposite lane	car in front
14			exist	passing in the opposite lane	with obstacle
15		no	no	straight	const. spd
16			exist	straight	with obstacle

6 Discussions

For the function $f(\boldsymbol{x}, t)$ defined in $\mathbf{R}^n$, the total derivative with respect to the variable t is

$$\frac{df}{dt} = \nabla f^\top \frac{d\boldsymbol{x}}{dt} + f_t. \tag{12}$$

Mathematically, optical flow is the solution of the linear equation $\frac{df}{dt} = 0$. This inconsistent linear equation is solved by regularisation [3,23] and using local geometric constraints [1,33].

In the medical volumetric-image analysis, for instance, the motion analysis of the moving organs, we are required to deal with volumetric images defined in three-dimensional Euclidean space $\mathbf{R}^3$. In computer vision, optical flow is usually computed from planar images.

Table 6. Symbol strings extracted from $\log H(t; f)$

No	Signal shape	Symbols
1	M	↗↘↗↗↘↘
2	M	↗↘↗↘↘
3	V∧	→→→↘↗↘
4	∧	↗↗↘↘→→
5	∧V	↗↗↘↗↘↘
6	∧V	↗↗↘↗↘↘
7	∧V	↗↗↘↗↘↘
8	∧V	↗↗↘↗↘↘
9	$(V∧)^n$	↘↗↗↘↘↘↗
10	$(V∧)^n$	↘↗↗↘↘↘↗
11	$(V∧)^n$	↘↗↘↗↘↗↘
12	polygonal curve	→→→→→→↘
13	$M2$	↗↘↗↗↗↗↘
14	$M2$	↗↘↗↗↗↗↘
15	$(∧V)^n$	↗↘↗↘↗
16	V 2	→→↘↗↗→

Table 7. Symbol strings extracted from $H(t; f)$

No	Signal shape	Symbols
1	flat	→→→→→→→
2	flat	→→→→→→→
3	V∧	→→→↘↗↘
4	∧	↗↗↘↘→→
5	∧V	↗↗↘↗↘↘
6	∧V	↗↗↘↗↘↘
7	∧V	↗↗↘↗↘↘
8	∧V	↗↗↘↗↘↘
9	Flat	→→→→→→→
10	flat	→→→→→→→
11	flat	→→→→→→→
12	polygonal curve	→→→→→→↘
13	$M2$	↗↘↗↗↗↗↘
14	$M2$	↗↘↗↗↗↗↘
15	flat	→→→→→→→
16	flat	→→→→→→→

For motion analysis with range data, setting $f(x, y, t)$ to be a grey-label image, we deal with the following system of equations

$$\frac{df}{dt} = f_x \frac{dx}{dt} + f_y \frac{dy}{dt} + f_t = 0,$$

$$\frac{dg}{dt} = h_x \frac{dx}{dt} + h_y \frac{dy}{dt} - \frac{dz}{dt} + h_t = 0, \tag{13}$$

where $g(x, y) = h(x, y, t) - z$ for depth z of the temporal range image $h(x, y, t)$ [24].

For colour and multi-channel images, the system of equations

$$\frac{df^\alpha}{dt} = f_x^\alpha \frac{dx}{dt} + f_y^\alpha \frac{dy}{dt} + f_t^\alpha = 0, \quad \alpha = 1, 2, \cdots, k \tag{14}$$

is derived from the k-channel images [25, 26].

For the left image $f(x_l, y_l, t)$ and the right image $g(x_r, y_r, t)$ of temporal stereo-pair images, the system of equations

$$\frac{df}{dt} = f_x u_l + f_y v_l + f_t = 0 \tag{15}$$

$$\frac{dg}{dt} = g_x u_r + g_y v_r + g_t = 0 \tag{16}$$

derive the optical flow vectors $\boldsymbol{u}_l = (u_l, v_l)^\top$ and $\boldsymbol{u}_r = (u_r, v_r)^\top$ on the left and right images, respectively. After establishing correspondences between $\boldsymbol{x}_l$ and $\boldsymbol{x}_r$ and between $\boldsymbol{x}_l + \boldsymbol{u}_l$ and $\boldsymbol{x}_r + \boldsymbol{u}_r$, the stereo reconstruction algorithm computes scene flow $\dot{\boldsymbol{X}}$ in the space using disparities between temporal stereo-pair images. Estimation of correspondences is established by solving system of equations

$$f(x + d, y, t) = g(x, y, t), \quad f(x + u_l + d_1', y + v_l + d_2', t) = g(x + u_r, y + v_r, t) \quad (17)$$

for the displacement $\boldsymbol{d} = (d, 0)^\top$ and $\boldsymbol{d}' = (d_1', d_2')^\top$.

For images on a manifold $\mathcal{M}$, the optical flow vector filed is the solution of the equation

$$\frac{df}{dt} = \nabla_\mathcal{M} f^\top \frac{d\boldsymbol{\nu}}{dt} + f_t = 0 \quad (18)$$

where $\nabla_\mathcal{M}$ is the gradient operation on the manifold. For example, if $\mathcal{M}$ is the unit sphere S^2 in three-dimensional Euclidean space $\mathbf{R}^3$, the gradient operation is

$$\nabla_\mathcal{M} f = \left(\frac{\partial}{\partial \theta} f, \frac{1}{\cos \theta} \frac{\partial}{\partial \phi} f \right)^\top. \quad (19)$$

Equation (18) allows us to compute the optical flow vectors on a spherical retina, which is the mathematical model of compound eyes.

In this paper, we have shown a method to extract intermediate queues for motion perception from optical flow on flow fields on the plane [34–36,41]. It is possible to apply the event extraction method based on the transportation of optical flow fields for scene flow [40] and the optical flow field on non-planar retina [38]. In reference [38], we have shown a method to extract intermediate queue for motion perception from optical flow fields on a sphere.

Moreover, we have developed a method to decompose the optical flow fields [27,28] on the surface of the moving organs [42] employing three-dimensional optical flow computation.

The optical flow fields between a pair of successive images in a sequence provide queues for image alignment. Aligning images along the time axis achieves the tracking of images in a video sequence [2]. Therefore, tracking is a sequential alignment. Multiple alignment in a space by deformation fields derives the deformation-based average of images.

For a collection of images $\{f_i(\boldsymbol{x})\}_{i=1}^m$, setting $\boldsymbol{u}_i(\boldsymbol{x})$ to be the deformation fields, the minimiser f of the energy functional

$$J = \sum_{i=1}^m \int_{\mathbf{R}^n} (f(\boldsymbol{x} + \boldsymbol{u}_i(\boldsymbol{x})) - f_i(\boldsymbol{x}))^2 d\boldsymbol{x} \quad (20)$$

with appropriate constraints derives the deformation-based average of the collection of images $\{f_i(\boldsymbol{x})\}_{i=1}^m$ [29,43]. The deformation-based average was applied for motion analysis of a volumetric beating-heart sequence.

The directional gradient of an image $f(\boldsymbol{x})$ at the point $\boldsymbol{x} = (x, y)^\top$ in the direction of $\boldsymbol{\omega} = (\cos \theta, \sin \theta)^\top$ is computed as $\boldsymbol{\omega}^\top \nabla f$. The directional gradient evaluates the steepness, smoothness and flatness of $f(\boldsymbol{x})$ along the direction of vector $\boldsymbol{\omega}$. Setting F to be a injective mapping for gradient, the gradient-based feature constructed by F satisfies the relations $F(\nabla f) = 0$ and $F(\nabla f) = F(\nabla g)$ if $f = 0$ and $f = g + a$ for constant a, respectively.

The census transform is computed by

$$s(\boldsymbol{x}) = \frac{1}{2\pi} \int_0^{2\pi} u(\boldsymbol{\omega}^\top \nabla f) d\theta \qquad (21)$$

where u is the Heaviside function. The directional histogram (DH) is computed by

$$h_{\boldsymbol{x}}(\theta) = \frac{G_f(\theta, \boldsymbol{x})}{\int_0^{2\pi} G_f(\theta, \boldsymbol{x}) d\theta}, \quad G_f(\theta, \boldsymbol{x}) = \int_{\Omega(\boldsymbol{x})} \boldsymbol{\omega}^\top \nabla f(\boldsymbol{y}) d\boldsymbol{y}, \qquad (22)$$

such that $h_{\boldsymbol{x}}(\theta + 2\pi) = h_{\boldsymbol{x}}(\theta)$, where $\boldsymbol{x} \in \mathbf{R}^2$ is the centre of the region $\Omega(\boldsymbol{x})$. The vector $\boldsymbol{x}$ is used as the index of the DH. We call $h_{\boldsymbol{x}}(\theta)$ the HoG signature of f.

The census transform encodes local geometric property of the gradient vector fields as scalar function. The HoG signature encodes semi-global geometric properties of the gradient vector field as a scalar function. These encoded features are used for matching of images and motion detection [30]. Our transform in Eq. (1) encodes the global geometric properties of motions on the retina as a scalar function using optical flow vector fields. Then, using this encoded motion vector field, we define a metric between a pair of motion fields for the extraction of events on video streams.

Since $\boldsymbol{v} = \frac{-f_t}{|\nabla f|^2} \nabla f$ is a solution of $\frac{df}{dt} = 0$, the optical flow vector is expressed as $\boldsymbol{u} = \frac{-f_t}{|\nabla f|^2} \nabla f + \alpha \nabla f^\perp$ for an appropriate scalar α, where $\nabla f^\top(\nabla f^\perp) = 0$. If the motion perpendicular to the gradient of the edges of the segments is small, that is, α is small, $\boldsymbol{u} \sim \mu \nabla f$ for an appropriate real number μ. This relation between the optical flow filed and the gradient field implies that events in the image stream detected by the features encoded by Eq. (1) are those caused by the temporal fluctuations of the gradient of the foreground.

In ref. [32] the on-line algorithm for detection of a polygonal curve from a time signal of a string of conversation dialogs. was proposed based on the randomized Hough transform. This algorithm is pre-processing for the construction of the syntactic trees of conversation dialogs. The event detection from video sequence is an extension of syntactic analysis of dialog signals to image sequences.

In pedestrian detection, annotated data for designing classifier is generated using artificially generated virtual world [31]. It is possible to extend the idea for event detection from image observed by vehicle mounted camera system. We generated symbol sequences from events in virtual world. Events detected from generated symbol strings coincide with the events detected from real world test data sequences.

7   Conclusions

We proposed a method for the symbolisation of the temporal transition of environments using statistical analysis of the flow field. The algorithm allows us to interpret a sequence of images as a string of events.

A machine can control a car to avoid incidents by detecting abnormalities using event strings stored in a dictionary. The symbolisation of temporal optical fields is suitable for the generation of entries in such a dictionary.

We have introduced a framework for syntactical interpretation of dynamic scenes using the temporal transportation of the optical flow fields. The future work for us is to derive semantics of the motion fields from strings of symbols. Multiscale image analysis of the dynamic scenes provides hierarchies of the motions [32] in the scenes from temporal local deformation to global fluctuations. Therefore, these hierarchies of motions would define the syntactic structure and semantic meaning of dynamic scene. The optical flow fields are the important queries for linguistic analysis of the dynamic scene.

References

1. Lucas, B.D., Kanade, T.: An iterative image registration technique with an application to stereo vision. In: Proceedings of IJCAI 1981, pp. 674–679 (1981)
2. Tomasi, C., Kanade, T.: Detection and tracking of point features. Int. J. Comput. Vis. **9**, 137–154 (1991)
3. Horn, B.K.P., Schunck, B.G.: Determining optical flow. Artif. Intell. **17**, 185–203 (1981)
4. Hwang, S.-H., Lee, U.-K.: A hierarchical optical flow estimation algorithm based on the interlevel motion smoothness constraint. Pattern Recogn. **26**, 939–952 (1993)
5. Vaina, L.M., Beardsley, S.A., Rushton, S.K. (eds.): Optic Flow and Beyond. SL, vol. 324. Springer, Dordrecht (2004). https://doi.org/10.1007/978-1-4020-2092-6
6. Duffy, C.J.: Optic flow analysis for self-movement prerception. Int. Rev. Neurobiol. **44**, 199–218 (2000)
7. Lappe, M., Bremmer, F., van den Berg, A.V.: Perception of self-motion from visual flow. Trends Cogn. Sci. **3**, 329–336 (1999)
8. Calow, D., Krüger, N., Wörgötter, F., Lappe, M.: Statistics of optic flow for self-motion through natural scenes. In: Ilg, U., Bülthoff, H.H., Mallot, A.H., et al. (eds.) Dynamic Perception, pp. 133–138. IOS Press (2004)
9. Villani, C.: Optimal Transport. Old and New. Springer, Heidelberg (2009). https://doi.org/10.1007/978-3-540-71050-9
10. Rabin, J., Delon, J., Gousseau, Y.: Transportation distances on the circle. JMIV **41**, 147–167 (2011)
11. Sabatini, S.P.: A physicalist approach to first-order analysis of optic flow fields in extrastriate cortical areas. In: ICANN 1999 (1999)
12. Park, K.-Y., Jabri, M, Lee, S.-Y., Sejnowski, T.J.: Independent components of optical flows have MSTd-like receptive fields. In: Proceedings of the 2nd International Workshop on ICA and Blind Signal Separation, pp. 597–601 (2000)
13. Wurtz, R.: Optic flow: a brain region devoted to optic flow analysis? Curr. Biol. **8**, R554–R556 (1998)

14. Greenlee, M.: Human cortical areas underlying the perception of optic flow: brain imaging studies. Int. Rev. Neurobiol. **44**, 269–292 (2000)
15. Andersen, R.A.: Neural mechanisms of visual motion perception in primates. Neuron **18**, 865–872 (1997)
16. Newsome, W.T., Baré, E.B.: A selective impariment of motion perception following lesions of the middle temporal visual area (MT). J. Neurosci. **8**, 2201–2211 (1988)
17. Pan, C., Deng, H., Yin, X.-F., Liu, J.-G.: An optical flow-based integrated navigation system inspired by insect vision. Biol. Cybern. **105**, 239–252 (2011)
18. Franceschini, N.: Visual guidance based on optic flow: a biorobotic approach. J. Physiol. Paris **98**, 281–292 (2004)
19. Srinivasan, M.V.: Honeybees as a model for the study of visually guided flight, navigation, and biologically inspired robotics. Physiol. Rev. **91**, 413–460 (2011)
20. Serres, J.R., Ruffier, F.: Optic flow-based collision-free strategies: from insects to robots. Arthropod Struct. Dev. **46**, 703–717 (2017)
21. Sobey, P.J.: Active navigation with a monocular robot. Biol. Cybern. **71**, 433–440 (1994)
22. Fisher, N.I.: Statistical Analysis of Circular Data. Cambridge University Press, Cambridge (1993)
23. Weickert, J., Schnörr, C.: Variational optic flow computation with a spatio-temporal smoothness constraint. J. Math. Imaging Vis. **14**, 245–255 (2001)
24. Spies, H., Jähne, B., Barron, J.L.: Range flow estimation. Comput. Vis. Image Underst. **85**, 209–231 (2002)
25. Barron, J.L., Klette, R.: Quantitative color optical flow. In: Proceedings of ICPR 2002, vol. 4, pp. 251–255 (2002)
26. Golland, P., Bruckstein, A.M.: Motion from color. Comput. Vis. Image Underst. **68**, 346–362 (1997)
27. Kirisits, C., Lang, L.F., Scherzer, O.: Decomposition of optical flow on the sphere. GEM Int. J. Geomathematics **5**, 17–141 (2014)
28. Lukas, F., Lang, L.K., Scherzer, O.: Optical flow on evolving sphere-like surfaces. Inverse Probl. Imaging **11**, 305–338 (2017)
29. Rumpf, M., Wirth, B.: Variational methods in shape analysis. In: Scherzer, O. (ed.) Handbook of Mathematical Methods in Imaging, pp. 1819–1858. Springer, New York (2015). https://doi.org/10.1007/978-1-4939-0790-8_56
30. Hafner, D., Demetz, O., Weickert, J.: Why is the census transform good for robust optic flow computation? In: Kuijper, A., Bredies, K., Pock, T., Bischof, H. (eds.) SSVM 2013. LNCS, vol. 7893, pp. 210–221. Springer, Heidelberg (2013). https://doi.org/10.1007/978-3-642-38267-3_18
31. Vázquez, D., López, A.M., Marín, J., Ponsa, D., Gómez, D.: Virtual and real world Adaptation for pedestrian detection. IEEE PAMI **36**, 797–809 (2014)
32. Imiya, A.: Detection of piecewise-linear signals by the randomized Hough transform. Pattern Recogn. Lett. **17**, 771–776 (1996)
33. Imiya, A., Iwawaki, K.: Voting method for the detection of subpixel flow field. Pattern Recognit. Lett. **24**, 197–214 (2003)
34. Ohnishi, N., Imiya, A.: Featureless robot navigation using optical flow. Connect. Sci. **17**, 23–46 (2005)
35. Ohnishi, N., Imiya, A.: Appearance-based navigation and homing for autonomous mobile robot. Image Vis. Comput. **31**, 511–532 (2013)
36. Ohnishi, N., Imiya, A.: Independent component analysis of optical flow for robot navigation. Neurocomputing **71**, 2140–2163 (2008)

37. Alibouch, B., Radgui, A., Rziza, M., Aboutajdine, D.: Optical flow estimation on omnidirectional images: an adapted phase based method. In: Elmoataz, A., Mammass, D., Lezoray, O., Nouboud, F., Aboutajdine, D. (eds.) ICISP 2012. LNCS, vol. 7340, pp. 468–475. Springer, Heidelberg (2012). https://doi.org/10.1007/978-3-642-31254-0_53

38. Torii, A., Imiya, A., Sugaya, H., Mochizuki, Y.: Optical flow computation for compound eyes: variational analysis of omni-directional views. In: De Gregorio, M., Di Maio, V., Frucci, M., Musio, C. (eds.) BVAI 2005. LNCS, vol. 3704, pp. 527–536. Springer, Heidelberg (2005). https://doi.org/10.1007/11565123_51

39. Mochizuki, Y., Imiya, A.: Pyramid transform and scale-space analysis in image analysis. In: Dellaert, F., Frahm, J.-M., Pollefeys, M., Leal-Taixé, L., Rosenhahn, B. (eds.) Outdoor and Large-Scale Real-World Scene Analysis. LNCS, vol. 7474, pp. 78–109. Springer, Heidelberg (2012). https://doi.org/10.1007/978-3-642-34091-8_4

40. Kato, T., Itoh, H., Imiya, A.: Motion language of stereo image sequence. In: CVPR Workshops, pp. 1211–1218 (2017)

41. Ohnishi, N., Mochizuki, Y., Imiya, A., Sakai, T.: On-line planar area segmentation from sequence of monocular monochrome images for visual navigation of autonomous robot. In: VISAPP 2010, pp. 435–442 (2010)

42. Kameda, Y., Imiya, A.: The William Harvey code: mathematical analysis of optical flow computation for cardiac motion. In: Rosenhahn, B., Klette, R., Metaxas, D.N. (eds.) Human Motion, Understanding, Modelling, Capture, and Animation, Computational Imaging and Vision, vol. 36, pp. 81–104. Springer, Dordrecht (2006). https://doi.org/10.1007/978-1-4020-6693-1_4

43. Inagaki, S., Itoh, H., Imiya, A.: Multiple alignment of spatiotemporal deformable objects for the average-organ computation. In: Agapito, L., Bronstein, M.M., Rother, C. (eds.) ECCV 2014. LNCS, vol. 8928, pp. 353–366. Springer, Cham (2015). https://doi.org/10.1007/978-3-319-16220-1_25

44. http://www.cvlibs.net/datasets/kitti/eval_scene_flow.php

A Simple and Effective Fusion Approach for Multi-frame Optical Flow Estimation

Zhile Ren[1], Orazio Gallo[2], Deqing Sun[2], Ming-Hsuan Yang[3],
Erik B. Sudderth[4], and Jan Kautz[2(✉)]

[1] Brown University, Providence, USA
[2] NVIDIA, Santa Clara, USA
jkautz@nvidia.com
[3] UC Merced, Merced, USA
[4] UC Irvine, Irvine, USA

Abstract. To date, top-performing optical flow estimation methods only take pairs of consecutive frames into account. While elegant and appealing, the idea of using more than two frames has not yet produced state-of-the-art results. We present a simple, yet effective fusion approach for multi-frame optical flow that benefits from longer-term temporal cues. Our method first warps the optical flow from previous frames to the current, thereby yielding multiple plausible estimates. It then fuses the complementary information carried by these estimates into a new optical flow field. At the time of writing, our method ranks first among published results in the MPI Sintel and KITTI 2015 benchmarks.

Keywords: Multi-frame optical flow · Temporal optical flow fusion

1 Introduction

Despite recent advances in optical flow estimation, it is still challenging to account for complicated motion patterns. At video rates, even such complicated motion patterns are smooth for longer than just two consecutive frames. This suggests that information from frames that are adjacent in time could be used to improve optical flow estimates. Indeed, numerous methods have been developed [2,3,9,10]. However, none of the top three optical flow algorithms on the major benchmark datasets uses more than two frames [4,6].

We observe that, for some types of motion and in certain regions, past frames may carry more valuable information than recent ones, even if the optical flow changes abruptly—as is the case of occlusion regions and out-of-boundary pixels. Kennedy and Taylor [8] also leverage this observation, and select which *one* of multiple flow estimates from adjacent frames is the best for a given pixel. We propose a method to *fuse* the available information. Specifically, we first estimate per-frame optical flow using a two-frame network module, and then warp multiple optical flow estimates from the past to the current frame, which we can fuse with a second neural network module.

L. Leal-Taixé and S. Roth (Eds.): ECCV 2018 Workshops, LNCS 11134, pp. 706–710, 2019.
https://doi.org/10.1007/978-3-030-11024-6_53

Our approach offers several advantages. First, it allows to fully capitalize on motion information from past frames. Second, our fusion network is agnostic to the algorithm that generates the two-frame optical flow estimates; any standard method can be used as an input, making our framework flexible and straightforward to upgrade when improved two-frame algorithms become available. Finally, if the underlying optical flow algorithm is differentiable, our approach can be trained end-to-end. Extensive experiments show that the proposed algorithm outperforms published state-of-the-art, two-frame optical flow methods by significant margins on the KITTI [6] and Sintel [4] benchmarks. To further validate our results, we present alternative baseline approaches incorporating recurrent neural networks with the state-of-the-art deep-learning optical flow estimation methods, and show that the fusion approach achieves significant performance gains.

2 Proposed Model: Temporal FlowFusion

For clarity reasons, we focus on three-frame optical flow estimation. Given three input frames I_{t-1}, I_t, and I_{t+1}, our aim is to estimate the optical flow from frame t to frame $t+1$, $w^f_{t \to t+1}$. The superscript 'f' indicates that it fuses information from all the frames. We use two-frame methods, such as PWC-Net [11], to estimate three motion fields, $w_{t \to t+1}$, $w_{t-1 \to t}$, and $w_{t \to t-1}$. We backward warp $w_{t-1 \to t}$ using $w_{t \to t-1}$: $\widehat{w}_{t \to t+1} = \mathcal{W}(w_{t-1 \to t}; w_{t \to t-1})$, where $\mathcal{W}(x; w)$ denotes warping the input x using the flow w.

Now we have two candidates for the same frame: $\widehat{w}_{t \to t+1}$ and $w_{t \to t+1}$, we take inspiration from the work of Ilg $et\ al.$ who perform optical flow fusion in the spatial domain for two-frame flow estimation [7]. We extend this approach to the temporal domain. Our fusion network takes two flow estimates $\widehat{w}_{t \to t+1}$ and $w_{t \to t+1}$, the corresponding brightness constancy errors $E_{\widehat{w}} = |I_t - \mathcal{W}(I_{t+1}; \widehat{w}_{t \to t+1})|$ and $E_w = |I_t - \mathcal{W}(I_{t+1}; w_{t \to t+1})|$ as well as the current frame I_t. A visualization of the network structure is shown at Fig. 1. The dotted lines indicate that two sub-networks share the same weights, while the double vertical lines denote the feature concatenation.

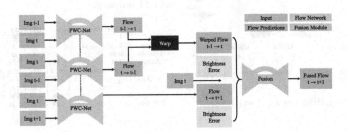

Fig. 1. Architecture of the proposed fusion approach.

We also propose two deep-learning baseline methods, shown at Fig. 2. **FlowNetS++**: FlowNetS [5] is a standard U-Net structure. We copy the encoded features from the previous pair of images to the current frame. **FlowNetS + GRU**: We use GRU-RCN [1] to extract abstract representations from videos and propagate encoded features in previous frames through time in a GRU-RCN unit and introduce a network structure, which we dub FlowNetS + GRU. We preserve the overall U-Net structure and apply GRU-RCN units at different levels of the encoder with different spatial resolutions. Encoded features at the sixth level are the smallest in resolution.

3 Experimental Results

We test two architectures as building blocks: FlowNetS [5] for its wide adoption, and PWC-Net [11] for its efficiency and performance on standard benchmarks. We follow Sun *et al.* [11] to design our training procedure and loss function. For consistency among different multi-frame algorithms, we use three frames as inputs.

For fusion networks, the network structure is similar to FlowNet2 [7] except for the first convolution layer, because our input to the fusion network has different channels. For the single optical flow prediction output by our fusion network, we set $\alpha = 0.005$ in the loss function [11] and use learning rate 0.0001 for fine-tuning.

We perform an ablation study of the two-frame and multi-frame methods using the virtual KITTI and Monkaa datasets, as summarized in Table 1. The Fusion approach consistently outperforms all other methods, including those using the GRU units. On the MPI Sintel [4] and KITTI benchmark [6], PWC-Fusion outperforms all two-frame optical flow methods including the state-of-the-art PWC-Net. This is also the first time a multi-frame optical flow algorithm consistently outperforms two-frame approaches across different datasets. We provide some visual results in Fig. 3 (Tables 2 and 3).

Table 1. Ablation study on the virtual KITTI dataset.

	FlowNetS	FlowNetS++	GRU 3	GRU 4	GRU 5	GRU 6	Fusion
EPE All	6.12	5.90	5.26	5.40	5.15	5.32	5.00
EPE Inside	4.03	3.87	3.61	3.64	3.58	3.59	3.14
EPE Outside	28.97	27.57	23.26	24.60	22.28	24.25	25.15
EPE Occlusion	7.44	7.11	5.93	6.27	5.82	6.18	6.14

	PWC-Net	GRU 3	GRU 4	GRU 5	GRU 6	Fusion
EPE All	2.34	2.17	2.13	2.12	2.16	2.07
EPE Inside	1.60	1.44	1.41	1.40	1.42	1.37
EPE Outside	10.43	10.01	9.94	10.02	9.86	9.71
EPE Occlusion	2.41	2.29	2.24	2.24	2.26	2.27

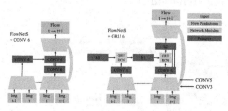

Fig. 2. Baseline network structures.

Table 2. Results of the MPI Sintel [4].

	EPE	Match	Unmatch	d0-10	d10-60	d60-140	s0-10	s10-40	s40+
PWC-Fusion	**4.566**	**2.216**	23.732	**4.664**	2.017	**1.222**	0.893	2.902	26.810
PWC-Net	4.596	2.254	**23.696**	4.781	2.045	1.234	0.945	2.978	**26.620**
ProFlow	5.015	2.659	24.192	4.985	2.185	1.771	0.964	2.989	29.987
DCFlow	5.119	2.283	28.228	4.665	2.108	1.440	1.052	3.434	29.351
FlowFieldsCNN	5.363	2.303	30.313	4.718	2.020	1.399	1.032	3.065	32.422
MR-Flow	5.376	2.818	26.235	5.109	2.395	1.755	0.908	3.443	32.221
LiteFlowNet	5.381	2.419	29.535	4.090	2.097	1.729	**0.754**	**2.747**	34.722
S2F-IF	5.417	2.549	28.795	4.745	2.198	1.712	1.157	3.468	31.262

Table 3. Results of the KITTI [6].

	Fl-all-Occ	Fl-fg-Occ	Fl-bg-Occ	Fl-all-Ncc	Fl-fg-Ncc	Fl-bg-Ncc
PWC-Fusion	**7.17**	**7.25**	**7.15**	**4.47**	**4.25**	**4.52**
PWC-Net	7.90	8.03	7.87	5.07	5.04	5.08
LiteFlowNet	9.38	7.99	9.66	5.49	5.09	5.58
MirrorFlow	10.29	17.07	8.93	7.46	12.95	6.24
SDF	11.01	23.01	8.61	8.04	18.38	5.75
UnFlow	11.11	15.93	10.15	7.46	12.36	6.38
MRFlow	12.19	22.51	10.13	8.86	17.91	6.86
ProFlow	15.04	20.91	13.86	10.15	17.9	8.44

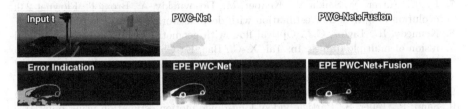

Fig. 3. Visual results of our fusion method. Green in the indication map means that PWC-Net+Fusion is more accurate than PWC-Net, and red means the opposite. (Color figure online)

4 Conclusions

We have presented a simple and effective fusion approach for multi-frame optical flow estimation. Multiple frames provide new information beyond what is available from two adjacent frames, in particular for occluded and out-of-boundary pixels. Thus we propose fusing the warped previous flow with the current flow estimate. Extensive experiments demonstrate the benefit of our approach: it outperforms both two-frame baselines and sensible multi-frame baselines based on GRUs. Moreover, it is top-ranked among all published flow methods on the MPI Sintel and KITTI 2015 benchmark.

Acknowledgement. We thank Fitsum Reda and Jinwei Gu for help with implementations, Xiaodong Yang for helpful discussions about RNN models, and Simon Baker for insightful discussions about multi-frame flow estimation.

References

1. Ballas, N., Yao, L., Pal, C., Courville, A.: Delving deeper into convolutional networks for learning video representations. arXiv preprint arXiv:1511.06432 (2015)
2. Black, M.J., Anandan, P.: Robust dynamic motion estimation over time. In: CVPR (1991)
3. Brox, T., Bruhn, A., Papenberg, N., Weickert, J.: High accuracy optical flow estimation based on a theory for warping. In: Pajdla, T., Matas, J. (eds.) ECCV 2004. LNCS, vol. 3024, pp. 25–36. Springer, Heidelberg (2004). https://doi.org/10.1007/978-3-540-24673-2_3

4. Butler, D.J., Wulff, J., Stanley, G.B., Black, M.J.: A naturalistic open source movie for optical flow evaluation. In: Fitzgibbon, A., Lazebnik, S., Perona, P., Sato, Y., Schmid, C. (eds.) ECCV 2012. LNCS, vol. 7577, pp. 611–625. Springer, Heidelberg (2012). https://doi.org/10.1007/978-3-642-33783-3_44
5. Dosovitskiy, A., et al.: Flownet: learning optical flow with convolutional networks. In: ICCV (2015)
6. Geiger, A., Lenz, P., Urtasun, R.: Are we ready for autonomous driving? The KITTI vision benchmark suite. In: CVPR (2012)
7. Ilg, E., Mayer, N., Saikia, T., Keuper, M., Dosovitskiy, A., Brox, T.: Flownet 2.0: evolution of optical flow estimation with deep networks. In: CVPR (2017)
8. Kennedy, R., Taylor, C.J.: Optical flow with geometric occlusion estimation and fusion of multiple frames. In: Tai, X.-C., Bae, E., Chan, T.F., Lysaker, M. (eds.) EMMCVPR 2015. LNCS, vol. 8932, pp. 364–377. Springer, Cham (2015). https://doi.org/10.1007/978-3-319-14612-6_27
9. Maurer, D., Bruhn, A.: Proflow: learning to predict optical flow. In: BMVC (2018)
10. Sand, P., Teller, S.: Particle video: long-range motion estimation using point trajectories. IJCV 80(1), 72–91 (2008)
11. Sun, D., Yang, X., Liu, M.Y., Kautz, J.: PWC-Net: CNNs for optical flow using pyramid, warping, and cost volume. In: CVPR (2018)

Unsupervised Event-Based Optical Flow Using Motion Compensation

Alex Zihao Zhu$^{(\boxtimes)}$ (iD), Liangzhe Yuan (iD), Kenneth Chaney (iD),
and Kostas Daniilidis (iD)

University of Pennsylvania, Philadelphia, PA 19104, USA
alexzhu@seas.upenn.edu

Abstract. In this work, we propose a novel framework for unsupervised learning for event cameras that learns to predict optical flow from only the event stream. In particular, we propose an input representation of the events in the form of a discretized 3D volume, which we pass through a neural network to predict the optical flow for each event. This optical flow is used to attempt to remove any motion blur in the event image. We then propose a loss function applied to the motion compensated event image that measures the motion blur in this image. We evaluate this network on the Multi Vehicle Stereo Event Camera dataset (MVSEC), along with qualitative results from a variety of different scenes.

Keywords: Event cameras · Unsupervised learning · Optical flow

1 Introduction

Event cameras, such as in Lichtsteiner et al. [3], are a neuromorphically inspired, asynchronous sensing modality, which detect changes in log light intensity. The changes are encoded as events, $e = \{x, y, t, p\}$, consisting of the pixel position, x, y, timestamp, t, accurate to microseconds, and the polarity, p. The cameras provide numerous benefits, such as extremely low latency for tracking very fast motions, high dynamic range, and significantly lower power consumption.

Recently, several methods have shown that flow and other motion information can be estimated by 'deblurring' the event image [1,5,7]. For frame data, unsupervised optical flow methods such as [2,4] have shown that neural networks can learn to predict optical flow from geometric constraints, without any ground truth labels.

In this work, we propose a novel input representation that captures the full spatiotemporal distribution of the events, and a novel unsupervised loss function that allows for efficient learning of motion information from only the event stream. Our input representation, a discretized event volume, discretizes the time domain, and then accumulates events in a linearly weighted fashion similar to interpolation. We train a neural network to predict a per-pixel optical flow from this input, which we use to attempt to deblur the events through motion compensation. During training, we then apply a loss that measures the motion blur in the motion compensated image, which the network is trained to minimize.

© Springer Nature Switzerland AG 2019
L. Leal-Taixé and S. Roth (Eds.): ECCV 2018 Workshops, LNCS 11134, pp. 711–714, 2019.
https://doi.org/10.1007/978-3-030-11024-6_54

2 Method

We propose a novel input representation generated by discretizing the time domain. In order to improve the resolution along the temporal domain beyond the number of bins, we insert events into this volume using a linearly weighted accumulation similar to bilinear interpolation.

Given a set of N input events $\{(x_i, y_i, t_i, p_i)\}_{i=0,...,N-1}$, we divide the range of the timestamps, $t_{N-1} - t_0$, which varies depending on the input events, into B bins. We then scale the timestamps to the range $[0, B-1]$, and generate the event volume as follows:

$$t_i^* = (B-1)(t_i - t_0)/(t_{N-1} - t_0) \tag{1}$$

$$V(x, y, t) = \sum_i p_i \max(0, 1 - |x - x_i|) \max(0, 1 - |y - y_i|) \max(0, 1 - |t - t_i^*|) \tag{2}$$

We treat the time domain as channels in a traditional 2D image, and perform 2D convolution across the x, y spatial dimensions.

Given optical flow for each pixel, $u(x, y), v(x, y)$, we propagate the events, with scaled timestamps, $\{(x_i, y_i, t_i^*, p_i)\}_{i=1,...,N}$, to a single time t':

$$\begin{pmatrix} x_i' \\ y_i' \end{pmatrix} = \begin{pmatrix} x_i \\ y_i \end{pmatrix} + (t' - t_i^*) \begin{pmatrix} u(x_i, y_i) \\ v(x_i, y_i) \end{pmatrix} \tag{3}$$

We then separate these propagated events by polarity, and generate a pair of images, T_+, T_-, consisting of the average timestamp at that pixel, similar to Mitrokhin et al. [5]. However, by generating these images using interpolation on the pixel coordinates rather than rounding them, this operation is fully differentiable.

$$T_{\{+,-\}}(x, y, t') = \frac{\sum_i \max(0, 1 - |x - x_i'|) \max(0, 1 - |y - y_i'|) t_i}{N(x, y)} \tag{4}$$

where $N(x, y)$ is the number of events contributing to each pixel. The loss is, then, the sum of the two images squared, as in Mitrokhin et al. [5].

$$\mathcal{L}_{\text{time}}(t') = \sum_x \sum_y T_+(x, y)^2 + T_-(x, y)^2 \tag{5}$$

As we scale the flow by $(t' - t_i*)$ in (3), the gradient through events with timestamps closer to t' will be weighted lower. To resolve this unequal weighting, we compute the loss both backwards and forwards:

$$\mathcal{L}_{\text{time}} = \mathcal{L}_{\text{time}}(t_0) + \mathcal{L}_{\text{time}}(t_{N-1}) \tag{6}$$

We combine this loss with a spatial smoothness loss, $\mathcal{L}_{\text{smoothness}}$, applied to the output flow, with our final loss being a weighted sum of the timestamp loss and the smoothness loss:

$$\mathcal{L}_{\text{total}} = \mathcal{L}_{\text{time}} + \lambda \mathcal{L}_{\text{smoothness}} \tag{7}$$

Our network consists of an encoder-decoder architecture, as defined in Zhu et al. [6].

Table 1. Quantitative evaluation of our optical flow network against EV-FlowNet and UnFlow. Average Endpoint Error (AEE) is computed in pixels, % Outlier is computed as the percent of points with AEE < 3 pix.

	Outdoor day1		Indoor flying1		Indoor flying2		Indoor flying3	
	AEE	%Outlier	AEE	%Outlier	AEE	%Outlier	AEE	%Outlier
dt = 1 frame								
Ours	**0.37**	**0.0**	0.59	**0.0**	1.02	3.2	0.89	2.5
EV-FlowNet	0.49	0.2	1.03	2.2	1.72	15.1	1.53	11.9
UnFlow	0.97	1.6	**0.50**	0.1	**0.70**	**1.0**	**0.55**	**0.0**
dt = 4 frames								
Ours	**1.23**	7.4	2.26	25.8	**3.92**	52.1	3.27	41.6
EV-FlowNet	**1.23**	**7.3**	**2.25**	**24.7**	4.05	**45.3**	3.45	39.7
UnFlow	2.95	40.0	3.81	56.1	6.22	79.5	**1.96**	**18.2**

3   Experiments

For all experiments, we train our network on the outdoor_day2 sequence from MVSEC [8], consisting of 11 min of stereo event driving data. Each input to the network consists of 30000 events, with volumes with resolution 256×256 and $B = 9$ bins. The model is trained for 300,000 iterations, and takes around 15 hours to train on a NVIDIA Tesla V100.

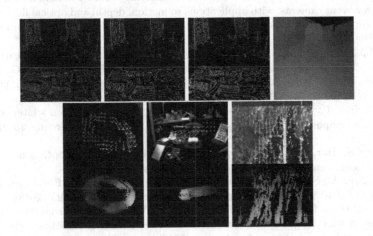

Fig. 1. Top: Result from MVSEC, left to right: blurred event image, deblurred image, predicted flow, ground truth flow. Bottom: Challenging scenes. Top images: sparse flow vectors on the grayscale image, bottom: dense flow output, colored by direction. Left to right: Fidget spinner spinning at 40 rad/s in the dark. Ball thrown quickly (the grayscale image does not pick up the ball). Water flowing outdoors. (Color figure online)

For evaluation, we tested on the same sequences as in EV-FlowNet [6], and present a comparison against their results as well as UnFlow [4]. We convert the output of our network, (u, v), into units of pixel displacement by the following scale factor: $(\hat{u}, \hat{v}) = (u, v) \times (B - 1) \times dt/(t_N - t_0)$, where dt is the test time window. From the quantitative results in Table 1, we can see that our method outperforms EV-FlowNet in almost all experiments, and nears the performance of UnFlow on the 1 frame sequences. As our event volume maintains the distribution of all of the events, we do not suffer from losing information as EV-FlowNet when there is a large motion. Our network also generalizes to a number of challenging scenes, as can be seen in Fig. 1.

4   Conclusions

In this work, we demonstrate a novel input representation for event cameras, which, when combined with our motion compensation based loss function, allows a deep neural network to learn to predict optical flow from the event stream only.

Acknowledgements. Thanks to Tobi Delbruck and the team at iniLabs for providing and supporting the DAVIS-346b cameras. We also gratefully appreciate support through the following grants: NSF-IIS-1703319, NSF-IIP-1439681 (I/UCRC), ARL RCTA W911NF-10-2-0016, and the DARPA FLA program. This work was supported in part by the Semiconductor Research Corporation (SRC) and DARPA.

References

1. Gallego, G., Rebecq, H., Scaramuzza, D.: A unifying contrast maximization framework for event cameras, with applications to motion, depth, and optical flow estimation. In: IEEE International Conference on Computer Vision Pattern Recognition (CVPR), vol. 1 (2018)
2. Yu, J.J., Harley, A.W., Derpanis, K.G.: Back to basics: unsupervised learning of optical flow via brightness constancy and motion smoothness. In: Hua, G., Jégou, H. (eds.) ECCV 2016. LNCS, vol. 9915, pp. 3–10. Springer, Cham (2016). https://doi.org/10.1007/978-3-319-49409-8_1
3. Lichtsteiner, P., Posch, C., Delbruck, T.: A 128 × 128 120 db 15 μ s latency asynchronous temporal contrast vision sensor. IEEE J. Solid-State Circuits **43**(2), 566–576 (2008)
4. Meister, S., Hur, J., Roth, S.: UnFlow: unsupervised learning of optical flow with a bidirectional census loss. In: AAAI, New Orleans, February 2018
5. Mitrokhin, A., Fermuller, C., Parameshwara, C., Aloimonos, Y.: Event-based moving object detection and tracking. arXiv preprint arXiv:1803.04523 (2018)
6. Zhu, A., Yuan, L., Chaney, K., Daniilidis, K.: EV-FlowNet: self-supervised optical flow estimation for event-based cameras. In: Proceedings of Robotics: Science and Systems, Pittsburgh, Pennsylvania, June 2018. https://doi.org/10.15607/RSS.2018.XIV.062
7. Zhu, A.Z., Chen, Y., Daniilidis, K.: Realtime time synchronized event-based stereo. In: The European Conference on Computer Vision (ECCV), September 2018
8. Zhu, A.Z., Thakur, D., Ozaslan, T., Pfrommer, B., Kumar, V., Daniilidis, K.: The multi vehicle stereo event camera dataset: an event camera dataset for 3D perception. IEEE Robot. Autom. Lett. **3**(3), 2032–2039 (2018)

MoA-Net: Self-supervised Motion Segmentation

Pia Bideau[✉], Rakesh R. Menon[✉], and Erik Learned-Miller[✉]

College of Information and Computer Sciences, University of Massachusetts Amherst, Amherst, USA
{pbideau,rrmenon,elm}@cs.umass.edu

Abstract. Most recent approaches to motion segmentation use optical flow to segment an image into the static environment and independently moving objects. Neural network based approaches usually require large amounts of labeled training data to achieve state-of-the-art performance. In this work we propose a new approach to train a motion segmentation network in a self-supervised manner. Inspired by visual ecology, the human visual system, and by prior approaches to motion modeling, we break down the problem of motion segmentation into two smaller subproblems: (1) modifying the flow field to remove the observer's rotation and (2) segmenting the rotation-compensated flow into static environment and independently moving objects. Compensating for rotation leads to essential simplifications that allow us to describe an independently moving object with just a few criteria which can be learned by our new motion segmentation network - the *Motion Angle Network* (MoA-Net). We compare our network with two other motion segmentation networks and show state-of-the-art performance on Sintel.

Keywords: Optical flow · Motion segmentation
Video segmentation · Camera motion · Visual ecology

1 Introduction

The human visual system has an incredible ability to detect motion, regardless of its complexity. While we are moving through the world our eye captures an enormous number of images over time. Images are projected onto our retina and the perceived motion (image change over time) is processed by the brain. In computer vision, optical flow is used to describe the motion between two consecutive images. Low level optical flow methods are based on two images alone [4,6,15,22,26,27]; other methods attempt to incorporate object knowledge and the knowledge about object motions [7,25,36]. In this work we propose a new approach to learning motion segmentation given an optical flow field as input.

The task of motion segmentation attempts to analyze the perceived motion and to segment a video sequence into the static environment (if any) and independently moving objects. Interpreting the motion field accurately and then

© Springer Nature Switzerland AG 2019
L. Leal-Taixé and S. Roth (Eds.): ECCV 2018 Workshops, LNCS 11134, pp. 715–730, 2019.
https://doi.org/10.1007/978-3-030-11024-6_55

drawing the right conclusions about what is moving in the world and what is static is a complex process. To get a sense for the complexity of the task of motion processing in the brain, we consider three different situations that produce very different optical flow fields.

The first situation pictures a stationary scene (with no camera motion) in which one object is moving. This might be a person walking in the world, which is pictured as a person moving across the observer's retina. This case is simple to interpret. The perceived motion on the retina exactly corresponds to the motion in the world.

The second situation pictures a stationary scene in which the observer is turning his head (rotating), walking through the world (translating), or rotating and translating at the same time. If the observer is only rotating, the entire image moves across the retina according to the observer's motion. If the observer is translating, the pictured motion on the retina is far more complex. The perceived motion depends on the scene geometry. Objects that are close lead to a "faster" motion than farther objects. Objects at the horizon create no change on the retina. Observing these different types of motion on the retina can be interpreted in several ways: (1) the entire world is moving while the observer stands still, (2) different "speeds" of motion might lead to the conclusion that some objects are moving faster than their environment or alternatively, that objects might be located at different depths, (3) the observer moves while the world is standing still. In many cases the last option may appear to be the most reasonable interpretation of the observed motion on the retina.

The third and last situation to consider is scene with both a moving observer and moving objects. Both the observer's motion and the object motions result in motion of the scene pictured on the retina as described in the previous two cases. However, if we track a moving object with our eyes, the object will not create any motion on the retina. The object will appear to be stationary while the world appears to be moving.

These three situations show that just because something is moving across the retina does not mean that it is actually moving in the world. *How do humans know what is moving in the world and what is not?* This question is the subject of current research in many different areas such as neuroscience, psychology, and computer science.

Eye movements play a key role in simplifying optical flow on the eye's retina and making it easier to interpret for our brain [33]. Optical flow produced by eye motions (rotations) contains no information about the scene's geometry and thus can be used for motion compensation without adding or reducing critical information. The two major reasons for eye movements are (1) to stabilize vision and (2) to change direction of gaze.

In this work we aim to develop an approach that accurately interprets the perceived optical flow on the retina. Inspired by visual ecology, we start with vision stabilization before processing the optical flow to segment independently moving objects. Of course we are not able to receive an image directly from our

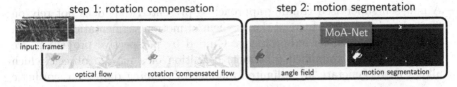

Fig. 1. Self-supervised Motion Segmentation. Given an optical flow our goal is to segment a frame into independently moving objects and static environment. Due to the complexity of optical flow fields, previous neural network models have had difficulty segmenting motion directly from optical flow. As in previous work [1], we use a two step approach, which first involves adjusting the optical flow for camera rotation (left) and then segments the angle of the compensated flow into static environment and moving objects (right). By training a network to segment from the angle field rather than raw optical flow, we significantly improve performance.

eye. Instead we use video sequences taken by a camera and methods to estimate the optical flow between two consecutive frames.

Unlike most CNN-based approaches, we are not relying on labeled training data, which is limited. Instead we carefully analyse the underlying geometry of optical flow and break down the problem of motion segmentation into two subproblems: compensating the optical flow for rotation (similar to vision stabilization of our eye movements) and segmenting the remaining optical flow into static background and moving objects. The step of compensating the flow for camera rotation is a challenging step especially since flow field is a noisy estimate of the motion field [1,2]. Estimating the camera rotation given the optical flow as input is not further explored in this work; approaches to estimate the camera rotation are presented in [1,2].

As stated already in several previous literature [1,2,8,17] the remaining optical flow (after compensating for rotation) has a simple geometrical pattern. We use this simple geometrical pattern of rotation compensated flow to synthesize training data in large amounts following rules of perspective projection. In this way we do not rely on any training dataset for motion segmentation, which are limited in size, the variety of shown scene structures, or quality.

Our contributions are as follows:

- Inspired by visual ecology, we present a two step approach for motion segmentation, which first involves compensation of the optical flow for camera rotation and then segments the compensated flow into static environment and independently moving objects. While this two step approach is a well established approach for motion segmentation [1,2,8], we present in this paper its great potential for *learning based* video segmentation methods. We aim to leverage the strength of classical geometrical approaches (based on perspective projection) and learning based approaches for motion segmentation.
- For evaluation purposes, motion segmentation ground truth for Sintel is generated and will be made publicly available.

- A new self-supervised training approach is presented that does not rely on limited training data. Instead the problem of motion segmentation is broken down into two smaller subproblems. Guided by perspective projection, we provide a highly simplified (abstract) definition of a moving object, which allows us to generate an unlimited amount of training data in a synthetic way.
- We show state-of-the-art performance on ground truth optical flow of Sintel.

Our paper is organized as follows. In Sect. 3 we review the flow field and how scene geometry, object motion and observer motion contribute to the formation process of optical flow. This geometrical background information leads us to a new approach of training a neural network, which is described in Sect. 4. Rather than relying on labeled training data, synthetic training data is automatically generated considering the geometry of optical flow. In Sect. 5 we evaluate our motion segmentation network and compare its performance to two other recently published networks for motion segmentation.

2   Related Work

Motion segmentation is studied for many years in the area of computer science [24,31,34] as well as neuroscience and psychology [11,12,33]. It is a highly complex task since it connects multiple different areas of computer vision. Three of them are motion or optical flow estimation, object understanding and understanding the 3D geometry of a scene. To show the large variety of existing motion segmentation approaches, we provide a brief overview presenting some fundamentally very different approaches tackling the same problem - approaches considering scene geometry, approaches focusing on general object segmentation (and thus rely more on appearance rather than scene geometry) and approaches that attempt to solve the problem of motion segmentation jointly, considering appearance as well as the geometrical structure. Most motion segmentation approaches rely on optical flow, except [32], which learn scene structure and motion coherently based on consecutive video frames rather than relying on point to point correspondences.

Geometrical based approaches relying on optical flow seek to find coherent motion patterns, while considering the scene geometry. These methods can be grouped into those that use projective geometry approximations [31,37] and those that use perspective projection [1,8,17,19]. [1,2,8] first attempt to simplify the observed motion field by compensating the flow field for camera rotation and then interpret the remaining flow using probabilistic models to segment the video into static environment and independently moving objects. This way they achieve highly accurate motion segmentations even videos that show complex scenes with high variation in depth.

Recently published approaches aim to learn motion patterns using neural networks. Those approaches directly take the optical flow as input, and motion segmentation patterns are learned without considering the scene geometry or the physical background behind the process of flow formation. Tokmakov et al.

learn motion patterns given optical flow [29,30]. A network segments a frame into static environment and moving objects given a flow represented as angle and magnitude separately. Besides their motion segmentation network, they benefit from the great ability of CNNs to learn object appearance. Jain et al. [9] learn motion patterns given the rgb-flow image as input. Despite the fact that both approaches do not take any geometrical information into account that can be extracted from optical flow, they achieve great performance on several standard video segmentation benchmarks [3,10,13,18,20,21,28].

In this work we present a new approach which, similar to [1,2,17], analyses the geometrical information provided by an optical flow image and reduces available information to its necessary minimum (the *flow angle* after compensation the optical flow for camera rotation) for the purpose of motion segmentation. Different from [1,2,17] a neural network is used for the final step of motion segmentation. Considering the geometrical background behind the process of flow formation allows us to generate an unlimited amount of synthetic training data, and thus the network can be trained in a self-supervised manner.

3   A Geometrical Analysis of the Flow Field

Optical flow describes where a pixel in the current frame will be in the next frame. These pixel displacements arise either due to the observer's motion or an object's motion. Object motion is very hard to predict, since objects move in many different ways. Their motion can be purely translational, rotational or both. Often their motion is articulated and thus can be described with neither rotation nor translation. In the following Section we review the formation process of optical flow due to observer's motion. The observer's motion or the camera motion can be translational as well as rotational in 3D. In this case the optical flow is determined by the camera motion itself (and speed), the camera's focal length and the scene depth. We first address the geometry of optical flow due to camera rotation only, which contains no information about independently moving objects or the scene depth. We continue with flow due to camera translation, which is informative in many regards, and thus is very valuable for the motion segmentation task.

3.1   Flow Due to Camera Rotation

Let f be the camera's focal length. A camera rotation is defined by its three rotational parameters (A, B, C). Given the three rotational parameters (A, B, C), we can compute the rotational optical flow vector at each pixel position (x, y) as follows [14]:[1]

$$v_r = \begin{pmatrix} u_r \\ v_r \end{pmatrix} = \begin{pmatrix} \frac{A}{f}xy - Bf - \frac{B}{f}x^2 + Cy \\ Af + \frac{A}{f}y^2 - \frac{B}{f}xy - Cx \end{pmatrix} \tag{1}$$

---

[1] This equation only holds if rotation angles are small. However camera rotation is always independent of the scene depth regardless their amount.

The rotational flow vector $\boldsymbol{v}_r$ is independent of the scene depth, thus it can be simply subtracted from the optical flow $\boldsymbol{v}$ to "stabilize" the image.

3.2 Flow Due to Camera Translation

Let (U, V, W) be the translational motion of the camera relative to an object. Let (X, Y, Z) be the real world coordinates in 3D of a point that projects to (x, y) in the image. The motion field vector (u, v) at the image location (x, y) due to a translational motion is given by

$$\boldsymbol{v}_t = \begin{pmatrix} u_t \\ v_t \end{pmatrix} = \frac{1}{Z} \begin{pmatrix} -fU + xW \\ -fV + yW \end{pmatrix}. \tag{2}$$

The translational flow vector $\boldsymbol{v}_t$ is inversely proportional to the scene depth Z, thus a large flow magnitude might be due to high motion speed, or the pictured object is just very close to the camera. Just based on the flow magnitude, we are not able to distinguish between the two possible sources - speed and depth. The 2D translational motion direction at each point in the image is then given by the angle of the motion field vector (u, v) at image location (x, y):

$$\theta = \texttt{atan}(-fV + yW, -fU + xW) = \texttt{atan}(-V' + yW, -U' + xW). \tag{3}$$

The translational flow direction at a particular pixel (x, y) however is purely determined by the parameters (U', V', W). The focal length does not need to be known explicitly.

3.3 Flow Due to Camera Translation and Object Motion

Above we discussed how optical flow is formed due to camera translation. Now if we consider a moving object in the scene like a walking person, this will change the optical flow. In areas of the moving object this adds the object's motion to the optical flow. So we obtain

$$\boldsymbol{v} = \boldsymbol{v}_t + \boldsymbol{v}_o. \tag{4}$$

Objects might move at different speeds and in different directions. This changes the observed optical flow field. The optical flow's magnitude is now determined by three pixel-motion sources - the scene depth, the camera motion and the object motion. This makes drawing a conclusion based on the magnitude alone very hard. One can not distinguish what is actually moving in the world based on the flow's magnitude.

The flow's direction however is easy to interpret, since it is only determined by the observer's motion direction and the object's motion direction. Any deviation from the optical flow that is caused by the observer's translation $\boldsymbol{v}_t$ indicates some independent object motion in the scene. We use this information to generate a dataset to train a network for motion segmentation.

4   Learning Motion Patterns

Motion patterns in optical flow are often quite difficult to interpret directly. Camera rotation and translation couple the scene depth, which makes it impossible to judge whether an object is moving or not. Motion magnitude as well as direction are dependent on camera motion, object motion and depth, when the camera is rotating and translating simultaneously. Inspired by visual ecology and the purpose of human eye movements, we use a two step approach for motion segmentation (see Fig. 1). The two steps are as follows:

1. Compensate optical flow for rotation
   - Compensate the optical flow for the rotational component of the observer's motion, similar to the way that image stabilization is done on the human retina, which is done via small eye rotations. The rotation compensated flow is v.
2. Segment optical flow v into static environment and moving objects
   - Given the flow v compute its direction θ at each pixel location.
   - A neural network MoA-Net (*Motion Angle - Net*work) takes an angle image as input and generates per-pixel motion labels.

Rather than having the network learn complex geometrical dependencies, the fundamental idea is to break down the observed optical flow into a pattern that is easier to interpret. The input to the network - the *angle image* - is simpler and contains all of the motion information that can be obtained from optical flow.

In this work we assume the rotation to be known and present an approach that automatically segments the optical flow v into static environment and moving objects. We leave the step of estimating the camera's rotation and compensating the flow for rotation for future work.

4.1   Network Architecture

Our basic network architecture is adopted from [29,30]. Originally this network took as input the optical flow angle and flow magnitude - leading to a three dimensional input of size $[height \times width \times 2]$. Instead our network takes the angle image, which just has two dimensions $[height \times width]$, as input. The angles are in the range of $[-\pi, \dots, \pi]$.

4.2   Training: Incorporating the Basics of Perspective Projection

Training a neural network for the task of motion segmentation usually requires large amounts of optical flow and its corresponding motion segmentations. The problem of using those datasets for training is that those datasets are often limited in size and the variety in scene geometry and motion is often restricted.

FlyingThings3D [16] is a relatively large synthetic flow dataset comprising 2700 videos, containing 10 stereo frames each. Along with these videos, ground truth optical flow, disparity, intrinsic, extrinsic camera parameters and object instance segmentation masks are provided. However this dataset doesn't picture realistic scenarios - random objects like tables, chairs and cars are flying in the 3D world.

Sintel [5,35] is a well-known optical flow dataset, containing 23 video sequences with 20 to 50 frames each. These short video sequences are taken from the computer animated movie by Blender. Thus the scenes are relatively realistic simulated. Videos come with ground truth optical flow, depth, intrinsic and extrinsic camera parameters and material segmentation.

Rather than relying on restricted datasets, the problem of motion segmentation is broken down into two small subproblems that can be each tackled separately. If a rotation compensated optical flow field is given, its geometry is easy to capture and motion information can be extracted. The optical flow's angle in areas of the static environment is completely determined by a translational motion direction of the camera that is projected onto the image plane. Moving objects move independently of the camera motion and thus are visible in the angle image due to its different motion direction. With this knowledge we can synthesize training data incorporating the physics of perspective projection for a motion segmentation network in an artificial manner.

Generating Training Data. For the purpose of motion segmentation we define a moving object as a *connected image region* that undergoes some *independent motion*. The connected image region can be of any size and shape - there are no limitations. True object motion can be quite complex, since objects can be deformable and articulated. If an object is articulated, each part might move independently of the other parts, e.g. a walking person. In case of a walking person, one arm might move forward while the other is standing still - here, although the body parts are physically connected, each part can move relatively independently of each other. The static environment undergoes a single pure translational motion due to the observers motion. Training data should contain these key criteria reflecting object motion and observer motion.

We generate training data for motion segmentation in 5 steps:

1. Generating connected object regions: To cover a large variety of different object shapes and sizes, we use the binary segmentations masks of FlyingThings3D [16,29] (Fig. 2a).
2. Modeling articulated object motion: To model object motion, each object region is split into n subregions using superpixels. n is a random number between one and ten. Splitting objects into subregions as shown in Fig. 2b leads to multiple different motion regions. In Fig. 2b we have eight motion regions including the region of static environment.
3. We assign to each motion region a translational 3D direction (Fig. 2c). A 3D translational direction is represented as a 3D unit vector. We generate a set of equally distributed translational motion direction on a sphere using the vertices of an icosahedron as approximation. Each vertex of an icosahedron represents a translational motion direction. To generate a large set of possible translational motion direction, we generate an icosahedron of frequency 50

which has 25002 vertices representing the set of translational motion directions.

4. Smoothing motion boundaries: To smooth motion boundaries within an object, we use a Gaussian filter with standard deviation $\sigma = 50$ (Fig. 2d). Object boundaries remain sharp.

5. We add random Gaussian noise with zero mean and standard deviation $\sigma = 0.1$ (Fig. 2e).

This procedure to generate training data is entirely independent of any color images or other labeled training data. It incorporates all geometrical information required to segment independently moving objects. This abstraction - reducing objects to *connected image regions* that undergo *independent motion* - allows us to train a network with unlimited training data in a fully unsupervised manner.

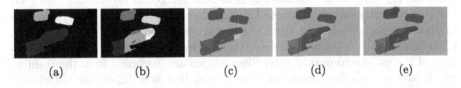

(a)　　　　(b)　　　　(c)　　　　(d)　　　　(e)

Fig. 2. Generating Training Data. The abstract object definition reduces an object to *connected image regions* that undergo *independent motion*. (a)–(e) show the process of generating abstract objects for the motion segmentation task.

5 Experiments and Results

We evaluate our work on Sintel [5,35] and FlyingThings3D [16]. We generated additional motion segmentation ground truth for Sintel to use this dataset for evaluation. Both datasets provide camera motion information, which allows us to evaluate the performance of MoA-Net, which requires flow angles of the rotation compensated flow field as input. We compare our work to two recently published motion segmentations approaches [9,30]. Both approaches are learning based approaches that attempt to learn motion patterns given the optical flow as input. In combination with a neural network that produces object segmentations based on appearance, both approaches have shown great results on a variety of different datasets [3,10,13,18,20,21,28]. For comparison purposes, we extract the motion segmentation network of both works and compare their performance on ground truth optical flow with our proposed method. The very modular motion segmentation pipeline of Tokmakov et al. [30] as well as of Jain et al. [9] allows us to analyze their "motion-stream" exclusively.

Compensating for Camera Rotation. Besides ground truth optical flow, Sintel and FlyingThings3D provide ground truth extrinsic and intrinsic camera matrices. This allows us to compensate the flow for camera rotation. We move image coordinates x_t along the optical flow and obtain new image coordinates x_{t+1}. The new image coordinates x_{t+1} are transformed into 3D camera coordinates X_{t+1}. We compute the camera motion (rotation and translation) between two consecutive frames and undo the camera rotation in 3D. The new camera coordinates X_{trans} (after undoing the camera's rotation) are projected back onto the 2D image plane. The rotation compensated flow can be obtained from the pixel displacement between image coordinates x_t and x_{trans}.

Evaluation. We use the evaluation scheme of [20]. We show results on two different motion segmentation networks and compare their performance with our motion network on Sintel and the test set of FlyingThings3D (Figs. 3 and 4).

Jain et al. train a motion segmentation network given rgb-flow images as input. For training, they used estimated optical flow images in rgb-format. Since no motion segmentation are available for ImageNet [23], they propose a procedure to produce (pseudo)-ground truth segmentations based on the provided object bounding boxes, the segmentations of their appearance network and the appearance of the estimated optical flow. Flow images are discarded from the training set, if average rgb-flow inside an object bounding box differs not sufficiently from the background's optical flow. Their segmentations are rather conservative - they often segment just a small portion of the moving object or nothing, which leads to an overall low performance of their motion segmentation network. On both datasets - Sintel and FlyingThings3D - their performance is rather low. One might argue that moving objects in Sintel and FlyingThings3D are quite different from objects that the network trained on ImageNet has seen before. Also, their automatic procedure to generate (pseudo)-ground truth significantly limits the variability of motion fields.

Tokmakov et al. trained their network on ground truth optical flow provided by the FlyingThings3D dataset. Each flow vector is represented using polar coordinates (flow magnitude and angle) during training. On Sintel as well as FlyingThings3D they show overall a good performance. If a video scene shows high variance in depth as in the bamboo video sequences of Sintel (Figs. 5 and 6), their segmentation is highly depth dependent, which leads to erroneous motion segmentations. Especially in those cases, MoA-Net outperforms both other motion segmentation networks by a large margin.

MoA-Net (ours) is trained purely on translational angle fields. This allows for producing motion segmentations that are completely independent upon the scene depth.

Results. On Sintel we outperform Tokmakov et al. by 4% points using the J-Mean metric and by more than 7% points regarding the F-Mean (see Table 1). On FlyingThings3D, the motion segmentation network of Tokmakov et al. produces high quality motion segmentation masks. Their accuracy in terms of IoU differs from their performance on Sintel by a large margin (39% points). This significant difference is very likely due to the similar nature of training and test data.

Table 1. Comparison to state-of-the-art. We compare our motion segmentation network with two recent motion segmentation networks that segment optical flow into static background and independently moving objects. The top results are highlighted in **blue**.

Motion Segmentation: Sintel						
Motion						
	J Mean	J Recall	J Decay	F Mean	F Recall	F Decay
	↑	↑	↓	↑	↑	↓
Tokmakov et al. [29,30]	50.38	**55.43**	45.32	52.43	54.95	45.58
Jain et al. [9]	30.27	24.78	32.72	28.07	14.02	31.89
Ours	**55.13**	55.24	**26.62**	**59.94**	**61.67**	**16.76**

When our MoA-Net is trained on the same ground truth flow as Tokmakov et al., but using only the optical flow's angle after compensating for camera rotation, we outperform their method (91.12% versus 89.13% - see Table 2)). Our proposed motion segmentation network, however, is trained in a self-supervised manner. We show significantly better performance than Jain et al. on Sintel as well as FlyingThings3D. We achieve state-of-the-art results on Sintel, whereas on FlyingThings3D we rank second best after Tokmakov et al.

Tokmakov et al. and Jain et al. do not need any preprocessing of the optical flow, however, here we show that a more analytical approach, which includes a step of preprocessing the optical flow - compensating for camera rotation, has a high potential for further improvements and solving the task of motion segmentation without the need of large training datasets.

Table 2. Comparison of motion networks trained on different training data and tested on FlyingThings3D-Test. Tokmakov et al. and ours-FT3D are trained using the provided ground truth optical flow of FlyingThings3D, Jain et al. relies on estimated optical flow of a subset of videos from ImageNet, and ours is trained on fully automatically generated training data as described in Sect. 4.2.

Motion Segmentation: FlyingThings3D-Test						
Motion						
	J Mean	J Recall	J Decay	F Mean	F Recall	F Decay
	↑	↑	↓	↑	↑	↓
Tokmakov et al. [29,30]	89.13	98.40	−2.11	93.55	98.54	−2.29
Jain et al. [9]	21.57	6.47	2.51	30.04	8.77	1.85
Ours (flow angle FT3D)	**91.12**	**99.78**	−0.02	**94.33**	**99.63**	−0.41
Ours (self-supervised)	75.53	95.76	3.55	82.25	97.65	1.68

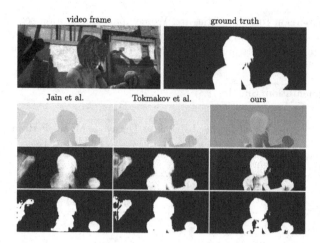

Fig. 3. Sintel - alley1: *first row*: input frame and ground truth motion segmentation. *Second row*: input to the motion segmentation network of the two different methods used for comparison an our input - optical flow as rgb image, optical flow in its angle and magnitude representation, angle of the rotation compensated flow. *Third row*: raw motion network output for each method. *Fourth row*: motion segmentation of each method (Color figure online)

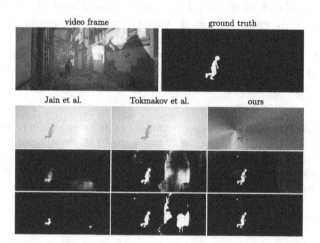

Fig. 4. Sintel - alley2: *first row*: input frame and ground truth motion segmentation. *Second row*: input to the motion segmentation network of the two different methods used for comparison an our input - optical flow as rgb image, optical flow in its angle and magnitude representation, angle of the rotation compensated flow. *Third row*: raw motion network output for each method. *Fourth row*: motion segmentation of each method (Color figure online)

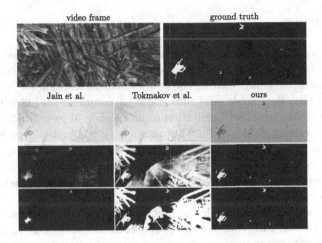

Fig. 5. Sintel - bamboo1: *first row*: input frame and ground truth motion segmentation. *Second row*: input to the motion segmentation network of the two different methods used for comparison an our input - optical flow as rgb image, optical flow in its angle and magnitude representation, angle of the rotation compensated flow. *Third row*: raw motion network output for each method. *Fourth row*: motion segmentation of each method (Color figure online)

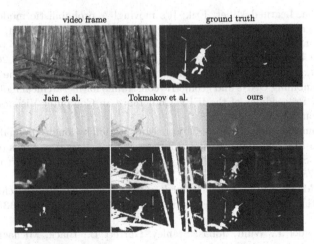

Fig. 6. Sintel - bamboo2: *first row*: input frame and ground truth motion segmentation. *Second row*: input to the motion segmentation network of the two different methods used for comparison an our input - optical flow as rgb image, optical flow in its angle and magnitude representation, angle of the rotation compensated flow. *Third row*: raw motion network output for each method. *Fourth row*: motion segmentation of each method (Color figure online)

6 Conclusion

We present a new approach for learning of motion segmentation in a self-supervised way. We break the problem of motion segmentation down into two smaller subtasks: (1) compensating the flow for camera rotation and (2) segmenting the remaining flow angle field into static environment and moving objects. This has led to an "abstract" definition of an moving object, which allowed us to synthesise training data in a fully automatic way and makes it possible to use a CNN for for the task of motion segmentation while simultaneously ensuring a correct interpretation of the scenes geometry. We show significant improvement in performance for motion segmentation among other motion segmentation networks, as shown in our experiments.

However, one has to note that the first step, which is compensating the flow for camera rotation, still remains subject of current research [1,2]. In future work we will investigate more the task of compensating the flow for camera rotation, which is comparable to motion compensation on our retina that is done by small eye rotations.

References

1. Bideau, Pia, Learned-Miller, Erik: It's moving! A probabilistic model for causal motion segmentation in moving camera videos. In: Leibe, Bastian, Matas, Jiri, Sebe, Nicu, Welling, Max (eds.) ECCV 2016. LNCS, vol. 9912, pp. 433–449. Springer, Cham (2016). https://doi.org/10.1007/978-3-319-46484-8_26
2. Bideau, P., RoyChowdhury, A., Menon, R.R., Learned-Miller, E.: The best of both worlds: combining CNNs and geometric constraints for hierarchical motion segmentation. In: Proceedings of the IEEE Conference on Computer Vision and Pattern Recognition, pp. 508–517 (2018)
3. Brox, Thomas, Malik, Jitendra: Object segmentation by long term analysis of point trajectories. In: Daniilidis, Kostas, Maragos, Petros, Paragios, Nikos (eds.) ECCV 2010. LNCS, vol. 6315, pp. 282–295. Springer, Heidelberg (2010). https://doi.org/10.1007/978-3-642-15555-0_21
4. Brox, T., Malik, J.: Large displacement optical flow: descriptor matching in variational motion estimation. IEEE Trans. Pattern Anal. Mach. Intell. $33(3)$, 500–513 (2011)
5. Butler, Daniel J., Wulff, Jonas, Stanley, Garrett B., Black, Michael J.: A naturalistic open source movie for optical flow evaluation. In: Fitzgibbon, Andrew, Lazebnik, Svetlana, Perona, Pietro, Sato, Yoichi, Schmid, Cordelia (eds.) ECCV 2012. LNCS, vol. 7577, pp. 611–625. Springer, Heidelberg (2012). https://doi.org/10.1007/978-3-642-33783-3_44
6. Horn, B.K., Schunck, B.G.: Determining optical flow. Artif. Intell. $17(1–3)$, 185–203 (1981)
7. Hur, Junhwa, Roth, Stefan: Joint optical flow and temporally consistent semantic segmentation. In: Hua, Gang, Jégou, Hervé (eds.) ECCV 2016. LNCS, vol. 9913, pp. 163–177. Springer, Cham (2016). https://doi.org/10.1007/978-3-319-46604-0_12
8. Irani, M., Anandan, P.: A unified approach to moving object detection in 2D and 3D scenes. $20(6)$, 577–589 (1998)

9. Jain, S., Xiong, B., Grauman, K.: Fusionseg: learning to combine motion and appearance for fully automatic segmention of generic objects in videos. In: CVPR (2017)
10. Jain, Suyog Dutt, Grauman, Kristen: Supervoxel-consistent foreground propagation in video. In: Fleet, David, Pajdla, Tomas, Schiele, Bernt, Tuytelaars, Tinne (eds.) ECCV 2014. LNCS, vol. 8692, pp. 656–671. Springer, Cham (2014). https://doi.org/10.1007/978-3-319-10593-2_43
11. Land, M.F.: Motion and vision: why animals move their eyes. J. Comp. Physiol. A 185(4), 341–352 (1999)
12. Lappe, M., Hoffmann, K.P., et al.: Optic flow and eye movements. Int. Rev. Neurobiol. 29–50 (2000)
13. Li, F., Kim, T., Humayun, A., Tsai, D., Rehg, J.M.: Video segmentation by tracking many figure-ground segments. In: Proceedings of the IEEE International Conference on Computer Vision, pp. 2192–2199 (2013)
14. Longuet-Higgins, H.C., Prazdny, K., et al.: The interpretation of a moving retinal image. Proc. R. Soc. Lond. B 208(1173), 385–397 (1980)
15. Lucas, B.D., Kanade, T., et al.: An iterative image registration technique with an application to stereo vision (1981)
16. Mayer, N., et al.: A large dataset to train convolutional networks for disparity, optical flow, and scene flow estimation. In: Proceedings of the IEEE Conference on Computer Vision and Pattern Recognition, pp. 4040–4048 (2016)
17. Narayana, M., Hanson, A., Learned-Miller, E.: Coherent motion segmentation in moving camera videos using optical flow orientations, pp. 1577–1584 (2013)
18. Ochs, P., Malik, J., Brox, T.: Segmentation of moving objects by long term video analysis. IEEE Trans. Pattern Anal. Mach. Intell. 36(6), 1187–1200 (2014)
19. Ogale, A.S., Fermüller, C., Aloimonos, Y.: Motion segmentation using occlusions 27(6), 988–992 (2005)
20. Perazzi, F., Pont-Tuset, J., McWilliams, B., Van Gool, L., Gross, M., Sorkine-Hornung, A.: A benchmark dataset and evaluation methodology for video object segmentation. In: Computer Vision and Pattern Recognition (2016)
21. Prest, A., Leistner, C., Civera, J., Schmid, C., Ferrari, V.: Learning object class detectors from weakly annotated video. In: 2012 IEEE Conference on Computer Vision and Pattern Recognition (CVPR), pp. 3282–3289. IEEE (2012)
22. Revaud, J., Weinzaepfel, P., Harchaoui, Z., Schmid, C.: EpicFlow: edge-preserving interpolation of correspondences for optical flow. In: Proceedings of the IEEE Conference on Computer Vision and Pattern Recognition, pp. 1164–1172 (2015)
23. Russakovsky, O., Deng, J., Su, H., Krause, J., Satheesh, S., Ma, S., Huang, Z., Karpathy, A., Khosla, A., Bernstein, M., et al.: Imagenet large scale visual recognition challenge. Int. J. Comput. Vis. 115(3), 211–252 (2015)
24. Sawhney, H.S., Guo, Y., Kumar, R.: Independent motion detection in 3d scenes. IEEE Trans. Pattern Anal. Mach. Intell. 22(10), 1191–1199 (2000)
25. Sevilla-Lara, L., Sun, D., Jampani, V., Black, M.J.: Optical flow with semantic segmentation and localized layers. In: Proceedings of the IEEE Conference on Computer Vision and Pattern Recognition, pp. 3889–3898 (2016)
26. Sun, D., Roth, S., Black, M.J.: Secrets of optical flow estimation and their principles. In: 2010 IEEE Conference on Computer Vision and Pattern Recognition (CVPR), pp. 2432–2439. IEEE (2010)
27. Sun, D., Yang, X., Liu, M.Y., Kautz, J.: PWC-Net: CNNs for optical flow using pyramid, warping, and cost volume. In: Proceedings of the IEEE Conference on Computer Vision and Pattern Recognition, pp. 8934–8943 (2018)

28. Tang, K., Sukthankar, R., Yagnik, J., Fei-Fei, L.: Discriminative segment annotation in weakly labeled video. In: Proceedings of the IEEE conference on computer vision and pattern recognition, pp. 2483–2490 (2013)
29. Tokmakov, P., Alahari, K., Schmid, C.: Learning motion patterns in videos. In: CVPR (2017)
30. Tokmakov, P., Alahari, K., Schmid, C.: Learning video object segmentation with visual memory. In: ICCV (2017)
31. Torr, P.H.: Geometric motion segmentation and model selection. Philos. Trans. R. Soc. Lond. A: Math. Phys. Eng. Sci. **356**(1740), 1321–1340 (1998)
32. Vijayanarasimhan, S., Ricco, S., Schmid, C., Sukthankar, R., Fragkiadaki, K.: SfM-Net: learning of structure and motion from video. arXiv preprint arXiv:1704.07804 (2017)
33. Walls, G.: The evolutionary history of eye movements. Vis. Res. **2**(1–4), 69–80 (1962)
34. Wang, J.Y., Adelson, E.H.: Representing moving images with layers. IEEE Trans. Image Process. **3**(5), 625–638 (1994)
35. Wulff, Jonas, Butler, Daniel J., Stanley, Garrett B., Black, Michael J.: Lessons and insights from creating a synthetic optical flow benchmark. In: Fusiello, Andrea, Murino, Vittorio, Cucchiara, Rita (eds.) ECCV 2012. LNCS, vol. 7584, pp. 168–177. Springer, Heidelberg (2012). https://doi.org/10.1007/978-3-642-33868-7_17
36. Wulff, J., Sevilla-Lara, L., Black, M.J.: Optical flow in mostly rigid scenes. In: IEEE Conference on Computer Vision and Pattern Recognition (CVPR), July 2017
37. Zamalieva, D., Yilmaz, A.: Background subtraction for the moving camera: a geometric approach **127**, 73–85 (2014)

"What Is Optical Flow For?": Workshop Results and Summary

Fatma Güney[1], Laura Sevilla-Lara[2], Deqing Sun[3], and Jonas Wulff[4(✉)]

[1] Oxford University, Oxford, UK
[2] Facebook Research, Menlo Park, USA
[3] NVIDIA, Santa Clara, USA
[4] Massachusetts Institute of Technology, Cambridge, USA
wulff@mit.edu

1 Introduction

Traditionally, computer vision problems have been classified into three levels: low (image to image), middle (image to features), and high (features to analysis) [11]. Some typical low-level vision problems include optical flow [7], stereo [10] and intrinsic image decomposition [1]. The solution to these problems would then be combined to solve higher level problems, such as action recognition and visual question answering. For example, optical flow has been used as an input to structure from motion, action recognition, and visual effects.

Two recent developments in optical flow affect this general paradigm for solving computer vision.

First, highly accurate optical flow can finally be learned [3,8,14,19]. In most high-level computer vision problems the state-of-the-art methods have been based on deep learning for a few years. However, in optical flow it is only within the last year that the top performing methods [8,19] are end-to-end trainable networks. This opens a new research question of how should we integrate these learnable optical flow modules into large systems to solve the computer vision problem.

Second, top performing methods are now very accurate in optical flow benchmarks. For example in KITTI, the state-of-the-art method achieves 92% accuracy, and in Sintel the average end-point-error is below 5 pixels, in images that are 1024 pixels wide (or 0.4%). This leads to a series of questions about the evaluation of flow. For example, are current methods accurate enough for higher level applications? In other words, is optical flow solved? If not, how should we design new benchmarks in the future to ensure they are most useful for higher level applications?

The goal of this workshop is to revisit the original plans of when and how to use optical flow for computer vision applications in light of these recent developments. We invite members of both researchers and practitioners of optical flow, to learn about recent progress, and to address these questions under the general topic of "What is optical flow for?".

F. Güney et al.—Equal contribution and alphabetical order.

L. Leal-Taixé and S. Roth (Eds.): ECCV 2018 Workshops, LNCS 11134, pp. 731–739, 2019.
https://doi.org/10.1007/978-3-030-11024-6_56

2   Survey and Speaker Results

To collect input on the leading question, "What is optical flow for?", we followed a two-stage approach. First, we solicited feedback from the community through a survey, sent out to researchers in the field of optical flow and general video analysis in advance to the workshop. Second, we invited 9 speakers, selected for their long experience in research on optical flow as well as applications, to answer the same question in short talks during the workshop. This section briefly summarizes the result of both.

2.1   Survey

In this section, we present the questions and the outcome of our survey on optical flow. In the survey, we grouped our questions in three main categories: the participant background, the current status and the future of optical flow. We follow the same organization here, by first explaining our goal in each subsection and then sharing our findings. While preparing the survey, our goal was to maximize the amount of information we collect while minimizing the amount of time the participant spends on answering the questions. With this purpose in mind, for almost all questions, we provided a set of options by asking the participant to select all that apply and also including the option "other" for the participant to write down their own answer if none of the options fit.

Participant Background. In the first part of the questionnaire, we asked participants about their background and their relation to optical flow. Our goal was to find out how informed the participants are about optical flow. The main questions included their current position, their rating of their knowledge on optical flow, and what computer vision problems they have worked on. We also asked more specific questions related to optical flow algorithms they use and optical flow benchmarks they check.

In total, 45 people took the survey, more than half of the participants are graduate students (63.6%) followed by postdoctoral research assistants or researchers (20.5%), professors (9.1%), and researchers in industry. More than half of the participants (55.6%) said that they have used and implemented optical flow, the remaining participants said that they have used optical flow (33.3%) or they at least know optical flow (11.1%). In summary, we can conclude that all of our participants had a research background and they were knowledgeable about optical flow.

We identified a set of computer vision tasks related to optical flow and shaped our questions around them throughout the survey. The experiences of our participants were roughly equally distributed over these tasks: action localization or recognition (37.8%), object tracking (31.1%), video object detection (22.2%), next-frame prediction (26.7%), video semantic segmentation (22.2%), and other video related tasks (35.6%).

Current Status of Optical Flow. The goal of our questions in this part is two-fold. First, we wanted to find out what participants think about the usefulness of optical flow for other computer vision tasks. We asked at which level these tasks benefit from optical flow and if participants know any examples of specific optical flow algorithms being used for any of these tasks. Our second goal was to find out about the problems related to optical flow, in particular in evaluation. We asked which property of an optical flow algorithm they consider more important, speed or efficiency or both. Lastly, we included questions related to their experiences with optical flow algorithms, what kind of strategies they follow to choose the optical flow algorithm they use and then the most common problems they encounter while using an optical flow algorithm.

In terms of usefulness of optical flow algorithms for the computer vision tasks we identified, most of our participants think that these tasks either definitely benefit from optical flow or it could potentially benefit. An interesting finding is the relative ordering of these tasks in benefiting from optical flow. Next-frame prediction sticks out as the task which benefit the most from optical flow followed by action recognition or localization, object tracking, video semantic segmentation, and video object detection. As expected, most of the participants (79.1%) said that both speed and accuracy are important for optical flow. This finding is supported by the outcome of another related question: how to choose the optical flow algorithm to use. The most effective factors were identified as the state-of-the-art on optical flow benchmarks (78.6%) and speed or being able to run on a GPU (76.2%). Following the importance of accuracy and speed for optical flow, 66.7% of the participants stated that they need a more accurate flow algorithm and 61.9% a faster flow algorithm. The more specific problems have been identified as errors at large displacements (52.4%), bad results in occluded regions (42.9%), not enough structure in the flow field (33.3%), problems in motion boundaries (28.6%), and artifacts, spurious objects in the flow field (26.2%). A considerable amount of participants (23.8%) have identified optical flow as their main bottleneck.

The Future of Optical Flow. In the last part, we asked our participants to speculate about the future of optical flow, starting with whether we need perfectly accurate optical flow. Next, we asked what we need to include in evaluation of optical flow that we currently do not consider, possibly more concerned about other tasks and the 3D world. Lastly, we asked what would eventually solve optical flow: better models, different learning strategies, or more data. We finished the survey by asking the participants to describe how they would use a *perfect* optical flow algorithm.

Almost half of the participants (48.8%) think that we need perfectly accurate optical flow only for certain applications such as computational photography or medical imaging. Only 17.1% of the participants think that current metrics are enough while the majority agrees that we need better means of evaluating optical flow. For this purpose, we suggested a set of options including performance on specific regions in the image (61%), robustness against noise (53.7%), performance at different levels of motion blur (41.5%), performance as input to another task (36.6%), different types of camera motion (36.6%), performance on mostly motion oriented tasks (26.8%), the 3D structure of the world (26.8%), and performance with respect to adverse conditions (26.8%). The last question was about choosing more likely directions that could eventually solve optical flow. The highest percentage belongs to unsupervised or self-supervised learning with 62.8%, followed by better models and better representations for optical flow with 48.8% for each.

To summarize, our participants come from research background with experience in computer vision problems related to optical flow. Most of the participants agree that video-related computer vision tasks benefit or could potentially benefit from optical flow. The accuracy and the speed are identified as the two most important factors in choosing which optical flow algorithm to use as well as regarding the problems when using optical flow algorithms. Following that, recent deep learning methods e.g. FlowNet variants which are both fast and fairly accurate are frequently employed for various tasks, despite being new. Most of the participants think that we need better, more specific ways of evaluating optical flow.

2.2   Speakers

Both Michael Black and Jitendra Malik pointed out that our leading question, "What is optical flow for?", has been addressed in the past [2,12]. In biology, research on motion perception and its purpose goes back at least as far as Gibson [5]; a list of what optical flow might be useful for in a biological system was given by Nakayama [12]. He identified 7 areas:

– Reasoning about the 3D structure of the environment
– Computing time to collision
– Image segmentation
– Computing ego-motion
– Computing saliency; control attention and eye movements
– Increasing contrast sensitivity
– Detect the motion of objects

As Jitendra Malik pointed out, this list, despite being over 30 years old, still applies today. Beyond this broad list, the speakers identified three large areas with close connection to optical flow: reasoning about the three-dimensional world, action understanding, and visualization and visual effects.

The Persistency of the Three-Dimensional World. As pointed out by Michael Black, an important distinction needs to be made between *optical flow* and the *motion field*. The first describes the motion of visual signals on the image plane, while the second models the motion of the three-dimensional scene relative to the observer, as projected into the two-dimensional image plane. With this distinction, a highlight moving across the surface of a static object would have induced non-zero optical flow, although the motion field is zero. In practice, however, both terms are often used interchangeably, and optical flow often refers to the motion field. The motion field establishes persistence in the world and models which parts of the scene correspond across time. Thus, it can be used to extract multiple views of the same object, or to reason about foreground/background assignment at object boundaries.

Thomas Brox echoed this use of the motion field to obtain a 3D representation of the scene and presented a learned approach to 3D reconstruction, DeMoN [20]. An important input to DeMoN is the optical flow itself, which is computed before feeding it to the main reconstruction pipeline; this two-stage approach is advantageous since it allows separate pre-training of the optical flow computation network, which in itself is non-trivial. Another use for optical flow is as an auxiliary learning task [25]. In this setting, predicting optical flow in addition to the actual target task (in this case, a camera pose update) provides additional gradients to the network and hence makes the training more effective.

Going beyond the reconstruction of a static three-dimensional environment, Lourdes Agapito described how flow can help to distinguish moving objects from a static scene and reconstruct both. In this application, three-dimensional, deformable shapes are modelled using a low-dimensional set of deformation bases; the deformation and camera pose can then be fitted to the optical flow field, yielding a reconstruction of the full, non-rigid scene, and thus pointing towards a full semantic understanding of the scene using optical flow as input.

Action Understanding. One of the classical applications of optical flow is to classify and understand actions of people in videos. Actions and activities are inherently temporal processes, and the underlying assumption is that optical flow can be used to compute a motion signature specific to a particular action.

Cordelia Schmidt pointed out that using optical flow as an additional input indeed helps. Interestingly, however, the accuracy of the flow itself (in terms of EPE) does not have a large impact on the accuracy of the classification. It is therefore questionable whether heavy computation should be invested in computing even better optical flow in order to improve the results of action recognition. Consequently, she presented recent work on action recognition [17] that does not require pre-computation of optical flow, but uses only a stream of frames as input. This sentiment was echoed by Laura Sevilla-Lara, who presented results that show that, while optical flow helps action recognition, randomly shuffling a sequence of frames containing an action does not, in fact, degrade performance to chance. This indicates that long-term motion signatures might not be as important as assumed. Instead, she suggested that what is important about optical flow in the context of action recognition is localization as object boundaries, as well as overall motion of the human body [15].

Kristen Grauman pointed to a different benefit of using optical flow in action recognition, in that it can serve as a coarse measure of saliency. Flow can therefore direct attention of an algorithm towards even fine details in the frame, which would otherwise get lost in the image. This mechanism works even when predicting optical flow from a single image; while just hallucinated, this flow can nevertheless improve action recognition by steering a network towards important image regions [4].

Overall, Jitendra Malik estimated action classification to lag about 10 years behind object detection, judging from the classification rates alone [6], and identified as the two main problems the long tail distribution of actions as well as current algorithms' inability to process long-range motion.

Visualization. Going back to the distinction between the motion field (the projected motion of the 3D environment) and optical flow (the motion of the 2D visual stimulus on the image plane), Michael Black pointed out that the later is important for artistic and visual applications. As an example, if optical flow is used for temporal resampling in order adjust frame rates between different playback and recording devices, it is important to take the motion of the image into account: The motion of a highlight on a static sphere should be properly interpolated, too. Similarly, applying optical flow to warp and deform images opens up interesting creative possibilities in the temporal domain, such as creating the flowing color-like effect in the movie *What dreams may come* [23], or to synthesize and transfer facial deformation in *The Matrix Reloaded* [21].

However, as pointed out by Richard Szeliski, for many such applications in artistic domains optical flow is currently not good enough, both in terms of accuracy as well as in terms of representation. For example, since most current optical flow methods use only two input frames, temporal consistency of flow-based visual effects that would satisfy the human visual system is often hard to achieve, and requires painstaking manual labor. Another example is the treatment of non-lambertian surfaces containing effects such as highlights, reflections, or subsurface scattering. All these effects are not well modelled using current optical flow energy terms, and algorithms therefore fail in the presence of such surface properties. Lastly, it is critical to be able to model more than one motion at each location, both for transparent motions such as reflections as well as for partially occupied pixels at motion boundaries. Especially the appearance at object boundaries is critical for sufficient visual quality for professional applications; Richard Szeliski hence called for novel optical flow benchmarks including these challenging scenarios.

Bill Freeman described a system that deals with the particular case of transparent motion, which uses a two-layer model of the scene to allow the user to take photos through obstacles such as fences [24]. Furthermore, he pointed out that tiny motions contain a lot of information about the physical properties of the world, such as oscillations of large structures and subtle change in appearance due to blood flow in a face. Properly magnified [13,22], these subtle motions can be made visible, and hence open up new applications in structural analysis and healthcare. Interestingly, while motion is crucial for this task, it is never represented directly as optical flow, but instead encoded using hand-crafted [22] or learned [13] spatio-temporal filters. This squares with the suggestion from the survey (see above) to explore different, novel representations of the motion beyond optical flow.

Other Remarks. Beyond these three main areas, several speakers mentioned other applications for optical flow. Jitendra Malik hypothesized that, to "solve vision", his bet is on unsupervised learning of motion and subsequently using motion as a supervisory signal for to learn other tasks. Kristen Grauman echoed this, and showed how motion can be used to improve training a per-pixel objectness classifier [9]. She also described 360° video compression as an additional application for flow; here, the video is stored as if projected onto the six sides of a cube, and optical flow is useful to determine the orientation of the cube to ensure best compressibility [16]. Lourdes Agapito talked about her working experiences with robotics companies and remarked that robotics is a sober exercise because the algorithms have to work in real scenarios. Robustness to real-life distortion is critical for the deployment of optical flow, yet is currently missing from the datasets.

Sun talked about an empirical study of CNN for optical flow, which shows that models matter, so does training [18]. The FlowNetC model, re-trained using the procedure of PWC-Net, outperforms the published FlowNet2 on Sintel final pass, although FlowNetC is a sub-network of the much larger FlowNet2 model. He also discussed about recent changes to the training procedures of PWC-Net, which brings about 10 to 20% improvement on Sintel and KITTI.

3   Panel Discussion

One audience asked about Unit-tests for optical flow. The discussion was leaning toward task-oriented metrics for specific applications. During the panel discussion, Bill Freeman posed an interesting challenge: "take a 15-second video, re-render it under different lighting conditions/viewpoints." A successful solution would require accurate reconstruction of the scene geometry, lighting, material properties, and motion. Richard Szeliski commented that, while standard frame-rate videos have become standard, extremely high-frame rate cameras may significant benefit specific applications, such as autonomous driving. The high frame rate would make many vision problems less challenging, such as motion and tracking.

4   Conclusion

In summary, the workshop was a reminder of wide variety of applications of optical flow: segmentation, action classification, visualization, medical imaging, depth estimation, just to name a few - and all of these applications have different requirements regarding accuracy and fidelity of the representation of motion.

Optical flow is not solved, not only in terms of the error in current benchmarks but in terms of impact for applications. Some applications like action recognition may not benefit directly from better optical flow, but it is not clear if this is intrinsic to the problem, or a consequence of the choice of categories or current recognition networks. At the same time, other applications of flow do benefit from better flow, like visual effects, or non-rigid structure from motion.

Improving these applications may require new benchmarks and evaluation metrics that are application specific, and that give insight into the impact of optical flow progress for different applications. In addition to new benchmarks, it will be interesting to explore better representations of motion, beyond simple optical flow, that may be more fit to applications.

References

1. Barrow, H., Tenenbaum, J., Hanson, A., Riseman, E.: Recovering intrinsic scene characteristics. Comput. Vis. Syst. **2**, 3–26 (1978)
2. Black, M.J.: Robust incremental optical flow. Ph.D. thesis. Yale university (1992)
3. Dosovitskiy, A., et al.: FlowNet: learning optical flow with convolutional networks (2015)
4. Gao, R., Xiong, B., Grauman, K.: Im2Flow: motion hallucination from static images for action recognition. In: CVPR (2018)
5. Gibson, J.J.: The Perception of the Visual World. Houghton Mifflin, Boston (1950)
6. Gu, C., et al.: AVA: a video dataset of spatio-temporally localized atomic visual actions. In: IEEE Conference on Computer Vision and Pattern Recognition, CVPR (2018)
7. Horn, B., Schunck, B.: Determining optical flow. Artif. Intell. **17**, 185–203 (1981)
8. Ilg, E., Mayer, N., Saikia, T., Keuper, M., Dosovitskiy, A., Brox, T.: FlowNet 2.0: evolution of optical flow estimation with deep networks (2017)
9. Jain, S., Xiong, B., Grauman, K.: Pixel objectness. arXiv preprint arXiv:1701.05349 (2017)
10. Lucas, B., Kanade, T.: An iterative image registration technique with an application to stereo vision, pp. 674–679 (1981)
11. Marr, D.: Vision: A Computational Investigation into the Human Representation and Processing of Visual Information. W.H. Freeman, New York (1982)
12. Nakayama, K.: Biological image motion processing: a review. Vis. Res. **25**(5), 625–660 (1985)
13. Oh, T.-H., et al.: Learning-based video motion magnification. In: Ferrari, V., Hebert, M., Sminchisescu, C., Weiss, Y. (eds.) ECCV 2018. LNCS, vol. 11208, pp. 663–679. Springer, Cham (2018). https://doi.org/10.1007/978-3-030-01225-0_39
14. Ranjan, A., Black, M.J.: Optical flow estimation using a spatial pyramid network (2017)
15. Sevilla-Lara, L., Liao, Y., Guney, F., Jampani, V., Geiger, A., Black, M.J.: On the integration of optical flow and action recognition. arXiv preprint arXiv:1712.08416 (2017)
16. Su, Y.C., Grauman, K.: Learning compressible 360° video isomers. In: The IEEE Conference on Computer Vision and Pattern Recognition (CVPR) Workshops, June 2018
17. Sun, C., Shrivastava, A., Vondrick, C., Murphy, K., Sukthankar, R., Schmid, C.: Actor-centric relation network. In: Ferrari, V., Hebert, M., Sminchisescu, C., Weiss, Y. (eds.) ECCV 2018. LNCS, vol. 11215, pp. 335–351. Springer, Cham (2018). https://doi.org/10.1007/978-3-030-01252-6_20

18. Sun, D., Yang, X., Liu, M.Y., Kautz, J.: Models matter, so does training: an empirical study of CNNs for optical flow estimation. arXiv preprint arXiv:1809.05571 (2018)
19. Sun, D., Yang, X., Liu, M.Y., Kautz, J.: PWC-Net: CNNs for optical flow using pyramid, warping, and cost volume (2018)
20. Ummenhofer, B., et al.: DeMoN: depth and motion network for learning monocular stereo. In: IEEE Conference on Computer Vision and Pattern Recognition, CVPR (2017). http://lmb.informatik.uni-freiburg.de//Publications/2017/UZUMIDB17
21. Wachowski, L., Wachowski, L.: The Matrix Reloaded (2003)
22. Wadhwa, N., Rubinstein, M., Durand, F., Freeman, W.T.: Phase-based video motion processing. ACM Trans. Graph. **32**(4), 80 (2013). (Proceedings SIGGRAPH 2013)
23. Ward, V.: What Dreams May Come (1998)
24. Xue, T., Rubinstein, M., Liu, C., Freeman, W.T.: A computational approach for obstruction-free photography. ACM Trans. Graph. **34**(4), 79 (2015). (Proc. SIGGRAPH)
25. Zhou, H., Ummenhofer, B., Brox, T.: DeepTAM: deep tracking and mapping. In: Ferrari, V., Hebert, M., Sminchisescu, C., Weiss, Y. (eds.) ECCV 2018. LNCS, vol. 11220, pp. 851–868. Springer, Cham (2018). https://doi.org/10.1007/978-3-030-01270-0_50. http://lmb.informatik.uni-freiburg.de/Publications/2018/ZUB18

Author Index

Printed in the United States
By Bookmasters